CompTIA® A+®
Complete Study Guide
Core 1 Exam 220-1101 and Core 2 Exam 220-1102
Fifth Edition

Quentin Docter

Jon Buhagiar

For my girls.
—Quentin Docter

For my wife and son.
—Jon Buhagiar

Acknowledgments

As we were putting together this book, I was reminded of the proverb that begins "It takes a village...." That beginning definitely holds true for creating a book of this scope and size. From beginning to end, scores of dedicated professionals have focused on delivering the best book possible to you, the readers.

First, I need to thank my coauthor, Jon Buhagiar. I appreciate him diving in and dedicating himself to helping to produce an excellent book. I also need to give special thanks to our technical editor, Chris Crayton. He was meticulous and thorough, and challenged me to always find new and better ways to communicate complex concepts. His entire focus was on providing the best training material possible, and I doubt there's better in the business. Now, on to the rest of the team.

Kenyon Brown and Kim Wimpsett kept us on track and moving forward, which was a challenge at times. Saravanan Dakshinamurthy had the fun job of keeping us organized, which is akin to herding cats. Copyeditor Elizabeth Welch reminded me yet again that I am no master of the English language and saved me from butchering it (too badly). Many thanks also go out to our proofreader, Arielle Guy, and our indexer, Tom Dinse. Without their great contributions, this book would not have made it into your hands.

On a personal note, I need to thank my family. My girls are all incredibly supportive. Unfortunately, book writing as a side hustle while holding down a full-time job takes up a lot of time. I end up hiding in my office a lot, but they're always there for me, and I couldn't do it without them. Another huge thanks goes to my late grandpa, Joe, who got me into computers and taught me so many lessons I will never be able to repay. Finally, thanks to my friends who keep me relatively sane—Sean, Kurtis, Tim, John, Cory, and others—and laugh at me when I tell them I spent my weekend writing about the laser printer imaging process.

—Quentin Docter

I would like to first thank my coauthor, Quentin Docter. Throughout the writing of this book, he helped me with his insight and his expertise in writing technical books. Without his words of wisdom and guidance, this book would not be the product it stands to be. I would also like to give special thanks to our technical editor, Chris Crayton. His thorough review of the material helped to identify many areas for us to elaborate on and polish.

I would also like to thank the many people who made this book possible: Kenyon Brown at Wiley Publishing, for giving me the opportunity to write this book and work with this wonderful team; Kim Wimpsett, for keeping us on track during the writing process; Christine O'Connor, who also kept us on track and organized during the publishing process; and our copyeditor, Liz Welch, for helping me use proper English. I'd also like to thank the many other people I've never met but who worked behind the scenes to make this book a success.

During the writing of this book, many others in my life supported me, and I'd like to take this opportunity to thank them as well. First and foremost, thanks to my wife and son for their support during the many evenings and weekends spent in my office at the computer. Finally, thanks to my friend and coworker, Bill, for encouraging me daily with his insight and jokes, as well as to all my other coworkers and friends. Thank you.

—Jon Buhagiar

About the Authors

Quentin Docter (A+, Network+, IT Fundamentals+, Cloud Essentials +, MCSE, CCNA, SCSA) is an IT consultant who started in the industry in 1994. Since then, he's worked as a tech and network support specialist, trainer, consultant, and webmaster. He has written more than a dozen books for Sybex, including books on A+, IT Fundamentals+, Cloud Essentials+, Server+, Windows, and Solaris 9 certifications, as well as PC hardware and maintenance.

Jon Buhagiar (Network+, A+, CCNA, MCSA, MCSE, BS/ITM) is an information technology professional with two decades of experience in higher education. During the past 22 years he has been responsible for network operations at Pittsburgh Technical College and has led several projects, such as virtualization (server and desktop), VoIP, Microsoft 365, and many other projects supporting the quality of education at the college. He has achieved several certifications from Cisco, CompTIA, and Microsoft, and has taught many of the certification paths. He is the author of several books, including Sybex's *CompTIA Network+ Review Guide: Exam N10-008* (2021) and *CCNA Certification Practice Tests: Exam 200-301* (2020).

About the Technical Editor

Chris Crayton is a technical consultant, trainer, author, and industry leading technical editor. He has worked as a computer technology and networking instructor, information security director, network administrator, network engineer, and PC specialist. Chris has authored several print and online books on PC repair, CompTIA A+, CompTIA Security+, and Microsoft Windows. He has also served as technical editor and content contributor on numerous technical titles for several of the leading publishing companies. He holds numerous industry certifications, has been recognized with many professional and teaching awards, and has served as a state-level SkillsUSA final competition judge.

Contents at a Glance

Contents

Chapter 22   Documentation and Professionalism   1453

Appendix A   Answers to the Review Questions   1515

Appendix   B   Answers to Performance-Based Questions   1561

Table of Exercises

Introduction

Welcome to the *CompTIA A+ Complete Study Guide*. This is the fifth edition of our best-selling study guide for the A+ certification sponsored by CompTIA (Computing Technology Industry Association). Thank you for choosing us to help you on your journey toward certification!

This book is written at an intermediate technical level; we assume that you already know how to *use* a personal computer and its basic peripherals, such as USB devices and printers, but we also recognize that you may be learning how to *service* some of that computer equipment for the first time. The exams cover basic computer service topics as well as more advanced issues, and they cover topics that anyone already working as a technician should be familiar with. The exams are designed to test you on these topics in order to certify that you have enough knowledge to fix and upgrade some of the most widely used types of personal computers and operating systems.

In addition to the prose in the chapters, we've included a lot of extra material to help your study prep. At the end of each chapter is a list of exam essentials to know as well as 20 review questions to give you a taste of what it's like to take the exams. In addition, there are eight bonus exams of at least 50 questions each. Finally, there are flashcards designed to help your recall. Before you dive into those, though, we recommend you take the assessment test at the end of this introduction to gauge your current knowledge level.

Don't just study the questions and answers—the questions on the actual exams will be different from the practice ones included with this book. The exams are designed to test your knowledge of a concept or objective, so use this book to learn the objective behind the question. That said, we're confident that if you can do well on our quizzes, you will be well equipped to take the real exam.

This book covers more than just the exams, however. We believe in providing our students with a foundation of IT knowledge that will prepare them for real jobs, not just to pass a test. After all, life is not a multiple-choice test with the answers clearly laid out in front of you!

For experienced IT professionals, you can use the book to fill in the gaps in your current computer service knowledge. You may find, as many PC technicians have, that being well versed in all the technical aspects of hardware and operating systems is not enough to provide a satisfactory level of support—you must also have customer-relations skills, understand safety concepts, and be familiar with change management and environmental impacts and controls. We include helpful hints in all of these areas.

What Is A+ Certification?

The A+ certification program was developed by CompTIA to provide an industry-wide means of certifying the competency of computer service technicians. The A+ certification is granted to those who have attained the level of knowledge and troubleshooting skills that are needed to provide capable support in the field of personal computers. It is similar to other certifications in the computer industry, such as the Cisco Certified Technician (CCT) program and the Microsoft Technology Associate (MTA) certification program. The theory behind these certifications is that if you need to have service performed on any of their products, you would sooner call a technician who has been certified in one of the appropriate certification programs than just call the first "expert" in the phone book.

The A+ certification program was created to offer a wide-ranging certification, in the sense that it is intended to certify competence with personal computers and mobile devices from many different makers/vendors. You must pass two tests to become A+ certified:

- The Core 1 220-1101 exam, which covers basic computer concepts, PC hardware, basic networking, mobile devices, and hardware troubleshooting
- The Core 2 220-1102 exam, which covers operating systems, security, software troubleshooting, and operational procedures

You don't have to take the 220-1101 and the 220-1102 exams at the same time. However, the A+ certification is not awarded until you've passed both tests.

Why Become A+ Certified?

There are several good reasons to get your A+ certification. The CompTIA Candidate's Information packet lists five major benefits:

- It demonstrates proof of professional achievement.
- It increases your marketability.
- It provides greater opportunity for advancement in your field.
- It is increasingly a requirement for some types of advanced training.
- It raises customer confidence in you and your company's services.

Provides Proof of Professional Achievement

The A+ certification is a status symbol in the computer service industry. Organizations that include members of the computer service industry recognize the benefits of A+ certification and push for their members to become certified. And more people every day are putting the "A+ Certified Technician" emblem on their business cards.

Increases Your Marketability

A+ certification makes individuals more marketable to potential employers. A+ certified employees also may receive a higher base salary because employers won't have to spend as much money on vendor-specific training.

Provides Opportunity for Advancement

Most raises and advancements are based on performance. A+ certified employees work faster and more efficiently and are thus more productive. The more productive employees are, the more money they make for their company. And, of course, the more money they make for the company, the more valuable they are to the company. So, if an employee is A+ certified, their chances of being promoted are greater.

Fulfills Training Requirements

Most major computer hardware vendors recognize A+ certification. Some of these vendors apply A+ certification toward prerequisites in their own respective certification programs, which has the side benefit of reducing training costs for employers.

Raises Customer Confidence

As the A+ Certified Technician moniker becomes better known among computer owners, more of them will realize that the A+ technician is more qualified to work on their computer equipment than a noncertified technician.

How to Become A+ Certified

A+ certification is available to anyone who passes the tests. You don't have to work for any particular company. It's not a secret society. It is, however, an elite group. To become A+ certified, you must do two things:

- Pass the Core 1 220-1101 exam
- Pass the Core 2 220-1102 exam

The exams can be taken at any Pearson VUE testing center. If you pass both exams, you will get a certificate in the mail from CompTIA saying that you have passed, and you will also receive a lapel pin and business card.

To register for the tests, go to www.pearsonvue.com/comptia. You'll be asked for your name, Social Security number (an optional number may be assigned if you don't wish to provide your Social Security number), mailing address, phone number, employer, when and where you want to take the test, and your credit card number. (Payment arrangements must be made at the time of registration.)

 Although you can save money by arranging to take more than one test at the same seating, there are no other discounts. If you have to repeat a test to get a passing grade, you must pay for each retake.

Tips for Taking the A+ Exam

Here are some general tips for taking your exam successfully:

- Bring two forms of ID with you. One must be a photo ID, such as a driver's license. The other can be a major credit card or a passport. Both forms must include a signature.
- Arrive early at the exam center so that you can relax and review your study materials, particularly tables and lists of exam-related information. When you enter the testing

room, you will need to leave everything outside; you won't be able to bring any materials into the testing area.

- Read the questions carefully. Don't be tempted to jump to an early conclusion. Make sure that you know exactly what each question is asking.

- Don't leave any unanswered questions. Unanswered questions are scored against you. Some questions will have multiple correct responses. When a question has more than one correct answer, a message at the bottom of the screen will prompt you to, for example, choose two. Be sure to read the messages displayed to know how many correct answers you must choose.

- When answering multiple-choice questions that you're not sure about, use a process of elimination to get rid of the obviously incorrect answers first. Doing so will improve your odds if you need to make an educated guess.

- For the hands-on questions where you need to complete a task, double-check that you have finished all parts of it, including checking all tabs available to you if they give you an interface to click on. Also, understand that these questions will take longer than multiple-choice ones. Spend the time needed on them; you will be able to make up time on the shorter multiple choice questions.

- On form-based tests (nonadaptive), because the hard questions will take the most time, save them for last. You can move forward and backward through the exam.

- For the latest pricing on the exams and updates to the registration procedures, visit CompTIA's website at www.comptia.org.

Who Should Read This Book?

If you are one of the many people who want to pass the A+ exams, and pass them confidently, then you should buy this book and use it to study for the exams.

This book was written to prepare you for the challenges of the real IT world, not just to pass the A+ exams. This study guide will do that by describing in detail the concepts on which you'll be tested.

What Does This Book Cover?

This book covers everything you need to know to pass the CompTIA A+ exams.

Part I of the book starts at Chapter 1 and concludes after Chapter 12. It covers all the topics on which you will be tested for Exam 220-1101:

Chapter 1: Motherboards, Processors, and Memory   Chapter 1 details the characteristics of motherboards and their built-in components. The CPU, RAM, and BIOS, which are attached to the motherboard, are also presented in Chapter 1.

Chapter 2: Expansion Cards, Storage Devices, and Power Supplies   Chapter 2 presents internal expansion options and popular forms of storage devices in use today, including traditional hard drives, solid-state drives, flash drives, and memory cards. Capacities, form factors, and the makeup of these components are also discussed. Finally, this chapter looks at providing power to computer components.

Chapter 3: Peripherals, Cables, and Connectors   Chapter 3 covers installation and characteristics of external peripheral devices, the ports they use, cables required, and the connectors used to attach them.

Chapter 4: Printers and Multifunction Devices   Chapter 4 starts by discussing different printing technologies, such as impact, inkjet, laser, virtual, and 3D printers. It then moves on to cover installing printers and performing printer maintenance.

Chapter 5: Networking Fundamentals   Chapter 5 covers characteristics of networking cable types and connectors, network devices, networking tools, and network topologies.

Chapter 6: Introduction to TCP/IP   Chapter 6 details the most common network protocol in use today. It covers TCP/IP structure, addressing (including IPv6), and common protocols in the suite.

Chapter 7: Wireless and SOHO Networks   Chapter 7 contains two main sections. The first is on wireless networking standards and security, and the second discusses setting up a small office, home office (SOHO) network and choosing an Internet connection type.

Chapter 8: Network Services, Virtualization, and Cloud Computing   Chapter 8 focuses on the types of functionality that servers provide on a network, with an emphasis on virtualization and cloud computing.

Chapter 9: Laptop and Mobile Device Hardware   Chapter 9 covers topics such as mobile device–specific hardware, components within a laptop display, and mobile device features.

Chapter 10: Mobile Connectivity and Application Support   Chapter 10 details the specific features of mobile devices that are unique to their formats. This chapter provides extensive hands-on steps for configuring a variety of connectivity options and application support on these devices.

Chapter 11: Troubleshooting Methodology and Resolving Core Hardware Problems   Chapter 11 introduces the best practice framework for resolving computer problems, which every technician should know. It also covers troubleshooting core hardware issues related to the motherboard, CPU, RAM, and power.

Chapter 12: Hardware and Network Troubleshooting   Chapter 12 finishes the troubleshooting side of hardware, including storage devices, video issues, mobile device issues, printers, and networking, including network troubleshooting tools.

Part II of the book, Chapters 13–22, covers all the topics on which you will be tested for Exam 220-1102:

Chapter 13: Operating System Basics   Chapter 13 begins by covering the fundamentals of understanding various operating systems. The chapter then shifts to focus on supporting applications installations. The chapter then concludes by introducing Windows 10 editions, features, the Windows interface, and file management.

Chapter 14: Windows Configuration   Chapter 14 explores Control Panel applets, Microsoft Management Console snap-ins, and Windows settings used to configure and customize the Windows operating system. The chapter also covers the Windows Registry and disk management.

Chapter 15: Windows Administration   Chapter 15 guides you through the installation and upgrade of the Windows operating system. The chapter then explores the various command-line tools used to administer Windows. Finally, the chapter covers the administration and support of networking that is common with Windows.

Chapter 16: Working with macOS and Linux   Chapter 16 covers common features and tools found in both the macOS and Linux operating systems. The chapter concludes by covering command-line tools used on Linux operating systems.

Chapter 17: Security Concepts   Just when you think this book couldn't get any better, we toss in a chapter devoted to security. This chapter introduces key security concepts you need to know for the exam, including information on physical security, social engineering, wireless networks, best practices, and data destruction methods.

Chapter 18: Securing Operating Systems   This chapter follows up on Chapter 17, which introduced security concepts, by providing specifics on how to secure Microsoft and mobile operating systems, prevent and remove malware, and configure network security on wired and wireless networks.

Chapter 19: Troubleshooting Operating Systems and Security   Troubleshooting is a major part of almost every technician's job. In Chapter 19, we talk about troubleshooting common operating system issues as well as security challenges you may encounter.

Chapter 20: Scripting and Remote Access   Network administrators and technicians need to know how to access systems remotely in order to use or troubleshoot them. The chapter shows you technologies used to do just that. Scripting is also included.

Chapter 21: Safety and Environmental Concerns   This chapter discusses the impacts computers can have on people as well as the environment. You learn how to avoid damaging a computer as well as avoid having it damage you, how to perform backups and disaster recovery, and how to properly dispose of computer components that are no longer needed.

Chapter 22: Documentation and Professionalism   This chapter covers the "softer" side of working with computers. Specifically, you learn to practice proper communication, show professionalism, and implement best practices associated with documentation and change management.

What's Included in the Book

We've included several learning tools throughout the book:

Assessment Tests   At the end of this introduction are two assessment tests—one for each exam—that you can use to check your readiness for the exams. Take these tests before you start reading the book; they will help you determine the areas on which you might need to brush up. The answers to the assessment test questions appear on a separate page after the last question of the test. Each answer includes an explanation and the chapter the material appears in.

Objective Map and Opening List of Objectives   At the beginning of the book, we have included a detailed exam objective map that shows you where each exam objective is covered. In addition, each chapter opens with a list of the exam objectives it covers. Use these resources to see exactly where each exam topic is covered.

Exam Essentials   Each chapter, just before the summary, includes a number of "exam essentials." These are the key topics that you should focus on when preparing for the exam.

Chapter Review Questions   To test your knowledge as you progress through the book, each chapter ends with review questions. As you finish each chapter, answer the review questions and then check your answers—the correct answers and explanations are in Appendix A. You can go back to reread the section that deals with each question you got wrong to ensure that you answer correctly the next time that you're tested on the material.

Performance-Based Questions   The A+ exams may ask you to perform tasks to correctly answer a question. This may mean dragging and dropping items into the correct order or clicking the correct area of an image or screenshot. While it's hard to simulate those in a paper book, the end of each chapter features a performance-based question. These questions will have you think through a topic presented in the chapter, and then perform a task.

Interactive Online Learning Environment and Test Bank

The interactive online learning environment that accompanies *CompTIA A+ Complete Study Guide: Exam 220-1101 and Exam 220-1102* provides a test bank with study tools to help you prepare for the certification exams and increase your chances of passing them the first time! The test bank includes the following elements:

Sample Tests   All the questions and answers in this book are provided, including the assessment tests, which you'll find at the end of this introduction, and the review questions at the end of each chapter. In addition, there are eight practice exams. Use these questions to test your knowledge of the study guide material. The online test bank runs on multiple devices.

Flashcards   Four sets of questions are provided in digital flashcard format (a question followed by a single correct answer). You can use the flashcards to reinforce your learning and provide last-minute test prep before the exam.

Glossary   The key terms from this book and their definitions are available as a fully searchable PDF.

eBooks   Read eBook versions of this Study Guide in multiple formats on your favorite device.

Audio Instruction   Over 2 hours of recorded instruction from the authors to help you study for the certification exam with confidence.

 Go to wiley.com/go/sybextestprep to register and gain access to this interactive online learning environment and test bank with study tools.

How to Use This Book

If you want a solid foundation for preparing for the A+ exams, this is the book for you. We've spent countless hours putting together this book with the intention of helping you prepare for the exams.

This book is loaded with valuable information, and you will get the most out of your study time if you understand how we put the book together. Here's a list that describes how to approach studying:

1. Take the assessment tests immediately following this introduction. It's okay if you don't know any of the answers—that's what this book is for. Carefully read over the explanations for any questions you get wrong, and make note of the chapters where that material is covered.

2. Study each chapter carefully, making sure you fully understand the information and the exam objectives listed at the beginning of the chapter. Again, pay extra-close attention to any chapter that includes material covered in questions you missed on the assessment test.

3. Read over the Summary and Exam Essentials. These will highlight the sections from the chapter you need to be familiar with before sitting for the exam.

4. Answer all the review questions at the end of each chapter. Specifically note any questions that confuse you, and study the corresponding sections of the book again. Don't just skim these questions. Make sure that you understand each answer completely.

5. Go over the electronic flashcards. These help you to prepare for the latest A+ exams, and they're really great study tools.

6. Take the practice exams.

Performance-Based Questions

CompTIA includes performance-based questions on the A+ exams. These are not the traditional multiple-choice questions with which you're probably familiar. These questions require the candidate to know how to perform a specific task or series of tasks. The candidate will be presented with a scenario and will be asked to complete a task. They will be taken to a simulated environment where they will have to perform a series of steps and will be graded on how well they complete the task.

The Sybex test engine does not include performance-based questions. However, at the end of each chapter, we have included a section called "Performance-Based Question," which is designed to measure how well you understood the chapter's topics. Some simply ask you to complete a task for which there is only one correct response. Others are more subjective, with multiple ways to complete the task. We provide the most logical or practical solution in Appendix B. Note that these questions may cover topic areas not covered in the actual A+ performance-based questions. However, we feel that being able to think logically is a great way to learn.

The CompTIA A+ Exam Objectives

The A+ exams consist of the Core 1 220-1101 exam and the Core 2 220-1102 exam. Following are the detailed exam objectives for each test.

Exam objectives are subject to change at any time without prior notice and at CompTIA's sole discretion. Please visit the A+ Certification page of CompTIA's website (comptia.org/certifications/a) for the most current listing of exam objectives.

A+ Certification Exam Objectives: 220-1101

The following table lists the domains measured by this examination and the extent to which they are represented on the exam:

Domain	Percentage of exam
1.0 Mobile Devices	15%
2.0 Networking	20%
3.0 Hardware	25%
4.0 Virtualization and Cloud Computing	11%
5.0 Hardware and Network Troubleshooting	29%
Total	100%

Objective Map

The following table lists where you can find the objectives covered in this book.

Objective	Chapter(s)
1.0 Mobile Devices	
1.1 Given a scenario, install and configure laptop hardware and components.	9

- Hardware/device replacement
    - Battery
    - Keyboard/keys
    - Random-access memory (RAM)
    - Hard disk drive (HDD)/solid-state drive (SSD) migration
    - HDD/SSD replacement
    - Wireless cards
- Physical privacy and security components
    - Biometrics
    - Near-field scanner features

Objective	Chapter(s)
1.4 Given a scenario, configure basic mobile-device network connectivity and application support.	10

- Wireless/cellular data network (enable/disable)

  - 2G/3G/4G/5G
  - Hotspot
  - Global System for Mobile Communications (GSM) vs. code-division multiple access (CDMA)
  - Preferred Roaming List (PRL) updates

- Bluetooth

  - Enable Bluetooth
  - Enable pairing
  - Find a device for pairing
  - Enter the appropriate PIN code
  - Test connectivity

- Location services

  - Global Positioning System (GPS) services
  - Cellular location services

- Mobile device management (MDM)/mobile application management (MAM)

  - Corporate email configuration
  - Two-factor authentication
  - Corporate applications

- Mobile device synchronization

  Account setup

  – Microsoft 365

  – Google Workspace

  – iCloud

Objective	Chapter(s)

- Bluetooth
- 802.11

  - a
  - b
  - g
  - n
  - ac (WiFi 5)
  - ax (WiFi 6)

- Long-range fixed wireless

  - Licensed
  - Unlicensed
  - Power
  - Regulatory requirements for wireless power

- NFC
- Radio-frequency identification (RFID)

2.4 Summarize services provided by networked hosts.   8

- Server roles

  - DNS
  - DHCP
  - Fileshare
  - Print servers
  - Mail servers
  - Syslog
  - Web servers
  - Authentication, authorization, and accounting (AAA)

- Internet appliances

  - Spam gateways
  - Unified threat management (UTM)

Objective	Chapter(s)

- ▪ Load balancers
- ▪ Proxy servers
- Legacy/embedded systems
  - ▪ Supervisory control and data acquisition (SCADA)
- Internet of Things (IoT) devices

**2.5 Given a scenario, install and configure basic wired/wireless small office/   7
home office (SOHO) networks.**

- Internet Protocol (IP) addressing
  - ▪ IPv4
    - – Private addresses
    - – Public addresses
  - ▪ IPv6
  - ▪ Automatic Private IP Addressing (APIPA)
  - ▪ Static
  - ▪ Dynamic
  - ▪ Gateway

2.6 Compare and contrast common network configuration concepts.   6

- ▪ DNS
  - ▪ Address
    - – A
    - – AAAA
  - ▪ Mail exchanger (MX)
  - ▪ Text (TXT)
    - – Spam management
      - ▪ DomainKeys Identified Mail (DKIM)
      - ▪ Sender Policy Framework (SPF)
      - ▪ Domain-based Message Authentication, Reporting, and Conformance (DMARC)

Objective	Chapter(s)

- DHCP
    - Leases
    - Reservations
    - Scope
- Virtual LAN (VLAN)
- Virtual private network (VPN)

2.7 Compare and contrast Internet connection types, network types, and their features.   5, 7

- Internet connection types
    - Satellite
    - Fiber
    - Cable
    - DSL
    - Cellular
    - Wireless Internet service provider (WISP)
- Network types
    - Local area network (LAN)
    - Wide area network (WAN)
    - Personal area network (PAN)
    - Metropolitan area network (MAN)
    - Storage area network (SAN)
    - Wireless local area network (WLAN)

2.8 Given a scenario, use networking tools.   12

- Crimper
- Cable stripper
- WiFi analyzer
- Toner probe
- Punchdown tool

Objective	Chapter(s)
• Cable tester	
• Loopback plug	
• Network tap	

3.0 Hardware

3.1 Explain basic cable types and their connectors, features, and purposes.	3, 5

- Network cables
  - Copper
    - Cat 5
    - Cat 5e
    - Cat 6
    - Cat 6a
    - Coaxial
    - Shielded twisted pair
      Direct burial
    - Unshielded twisted pair
    - Plenum
    - Optical
    - Fiber
    - T568A/T568B
- Peripheral cables
  - USB 2.0
  - USB 3.0
  - Serial
  - Thunderbolt
- Video cables
  - High-Definition Multimedia Interface (HDMI)
  - DisplayPort
  - Digital Visual Interface (DVI)
  - Video Graphics Array (VGA)

Objective	Chapter(s)
3.4 Given a scenario, install and configure motherboards, central processing units (CPUs), and add-on cards.	2

- Motherboard form factor

    - Advanced Technology eXtended (ATX)

    - Information Technology eXtended (ITX)

- Motherboard connector types

    - Peripheral Component Interconnect (PCI)

    - PCI Express (PCIe)

    - Power connectors

    - SATA

    - eSATA

    - Headers

    - M.2

- Motherboard compatibility

    - CPU sockets
      – Advanced Micro Devices, Inc. (AMD)

      – Intel

    - Server

    - Multisocket

    - Desktop

    - Mobile

- Basic Input/Output System (BIOS)/Unified Extensible Firmware Interface (UEFI) settings

    - Boot options

    - USB permissions

    - Trusted Platform Module (TPM) security features

    - Fan considerations

    - Secure Boot

    - Boot password

Objective	Chapter(s)

- Encryption
  - TPM
  - Hardware security module (HSM)
- CPU architecture
  - x64/x86
  - Advanced RISC Machine (ARM)
  - Single-core
  - Multicore
  - Multithreading
  - Virtualization support
- Expansion cards
  - Sound card
  - Video card
  - Capture card
  - NIC
- Cooling
  - Fans
  - Heat sink
  - Thermal paste/pads
  - Liquid

3.5 Given a scenario, install or replace the appropriate power supply.   2

- Input 110-120 VAC vs. 220-240 VAC
- Output 3.3V vs. 5V vs. 12V
- 20-pin to 24-pin motherboard adapter
- Redundant power supply
- Modular power supply
- Wattage rating

Objective	Chapter(s)
3.6 Given a scenario, deploy and configure multifunction devices/printers and settings.	4

- Properly unboxing a device—setup location considerations
- Use appropriate drivers for a given OS
    - Printer Control Language (PCL) vs. PostScript
- Device connectivity
    - USB
    - Ethernet
    - Wireless
- Public/shared devices
    - Printer share
    - Print server
- Configuration settings
    - Duplex
    - Orientation
    - Tray settings
    - Quality
- Security
    - User authentication
    - Badging
    - Audit logs
    - Secured prints
- Network scan services
    - Email
    - SMB
    - Cloud services
- Automatic document feeder (ADF)/flatbed scanner

Objective	Chapter(s)
3.7 Given a scenario, install and replace printer consumables.	4

- Laser
    - Imaging drum, fuser assembly, transfer belt, transfer roller, pickup rollers, separation pads, duplexing assembly
    - Imaging process: processing, charging, exposing, developing, transferring, fusing, and cleaning
    - Maintenance: Replace toner, apply maintenance kit, calibrate, clean
- Inkjet
    - Ink cartridge, print head, roller, feeder, duplexing assembly, carriage belt
    - Calibration
    - Maintenance: Clean heads, replace cartridges, calibrate, clear jams
- Thermal
    - Feed assembly, heating element
    - Special thermal paper
    - Maintenance: Replace paper, clean heating element, remove debris
    - Heat sensitivity of paper
- Impact
    - Print head, ribbon, tractor feed
    - Impact paper
    - Maintenance: Replace ribbon, replace print head, replace paper
- 3-D printer
    - Filament
    - Resin
    - Print bed

Objective	Chapter(s)

4.0 Virtualization and Cloud Computing

4.1 Summarize cloud-computing concepts.   8

- Common cloud models
  - Private cloud
  - Public cloud
  - Hybrid cloud
  - Community cloud
  - Infrastructure as a service (IaaS)
  - Software as a service (SaaS)
  - Platform as a service (PaaS)
- Cloud characteristics
  - Shared resources
  - Metered utilization
  - Rapid elasticity
  - High availability
  - File synchronization
- Desktop virtualization
  - Virtual desktop infrastructure (VDI) on premises
  - VDI in the cloud

4.2 Summarize aspects of client-side virtualization.   8

- Purpose of virtual machines
  - Sandbox
  - Test development
  - Application virtualization
    – Legacy software/OS
    – Cross-platform virtualization
  - Resource requirements
  - Security requirements

Objective	Chapter(s)

5.0 Hardware and Network Troubleshooting

5.1 Given a scenario, apply the best practice methodology to resolve problems. 11

- Always consider corporate policies, procedures, and impacts before implementing changes

1. Identify the problem

   Gather information from the user, identify user changes, and, if applicable, perform backups before making changes

   Inquire regarding environmental or infrastructure changes

2. Establish a theory of probable cause (question the obvious)

   If necessary, conduct external or internal research based on symptoms

3. Test the theory to determine the cause

   Once the theory is confirmed, determine the next steps to resolve the problem

   If the theory is not confirmed, re-establish a new theory or escalate

4. Establish a plan of action to resolve the problem and implement the solution

   Refer to the vendor's instructions for guidance

5. Verify full system functionality and, if applicable, implement preventive measures

6. Document the findings, actions, and outcomes

5.2 Given a scenario, troubleshoot problems related to motherboards, RAM, 11
CPU, and power.

- Common symptoms
    - Power-on self-test (POST) beeps
    - Proprietary crash screens (blue screen of death [BSOD]/pinwheel)
    - Black screen
    - No power
    - Sluggish performance
    - Overheating

Objective	Chapter(s)

- Burning smell
- Intermittent shutdown
- Application crashes
- Grinding noise
- Capacitor swelling
- Inaccurate system date/time

5.3 Given a scenario, troubleshoot and diagnose problems with storage drives and RAID arrays.   12

- Common symptoms
  - Light-emitting diode (LED) status indicators
  - Grinding noises
  - Clicking sounds
  - Bootable device not found
  - Data loss/corruption
  - RAID failure
  - Self-monitoring, Analysis, and Reporting Technology
  - (S.M.A.R.T.) failure
  - Extended read/write times
  - Input/output operations per second (IOPS)
  - Missing drives in OS

5.4 Given a scenario, troubleshoot video, projector, and display issues.   12

- Common symptoms
  - Incorrect data source
  - Physical cabling issues
  - Burned-out bulb
  - Fuzzy image
  - Display burn-in

Objective	Chapter(s)

- Dead pixels
- Flashing screen
- Incorrect color display
- Audio issues
- Dim image
- Intermittent projector shutdown

5.5 Given a scenario, troubleshoot common issues with mobile devices.   12

- Common symptoms
    - Poor battery health
    - Swollen battery
    - Broken screen
    - Improper charging
    - Poor/no connectivity
    - Liquid damage
    - Overheating
    - Digitizer issues
    - Physically damaged ports
    - Malware
    - Cursor drift/touch calibration

5.6 Given a scenario, troubleshoot and resolve printer issues.   12

- Common symptoms
    - Lines down the printed pages
    - Garbled print
    - Toner not fusing to paper
    - Paper jams
    - Faded print
    - Incorrect paper size

Objective	Chapter(s)

- Paper not feeding
- Multipage misfeed
- Multiple prints pending in queue
- Speckling on printed pages
- Double/echo images on the print
- Incorrect chroma display
- Grinding noise
- Finishing issues
    - Staple jams
    - Hole punch
- Incorrect page orientation

5.7 Given a scenario, troubleshoot problems with wired and wireless networks.	12

- Common symptoms
    - Intermittent wireless connectivity
    - Slow network speeds
    - Limited connectivity
    - Jitter
    - Poor Voice over Internet Protocol (VoIP) quality
    - Port flapping
    - High latency
    - External interference

A+ Certification Exam Objectives: 220-1102

The following table lists the domains measured by this examination and the extent to which they are represented on the exam.

Domain	Percentage of exam
1.0 Operating Systems	31%
2.0 Security	25%
3.0 Software Troubleshooting	22%
4.0 Operational Procedures	22%
Total	100%

Objective Map

The following table lists where you can find the objectives covered in the book.

Objective	Chapter(s)
1.0 Operating Systems	
1.1 Identify basic features of Microsoft Windows editions.	13

- Windows 10 editions
  - Home
  - Pro
  - Pro for Workstations
  - Enterprise
- Feature differences
  - Domain access vs. workgroup
  - Desktop styles/user interface
  - Availability of Remote Desktop Protocol (RDP)
  - Random-access memory (RAM) support limitations
  - BitLocker
  - gpedit.msc
- Upgrade paths
  - In-place upgrade

Objective	Chapter(s)
1.2 Given a scenario, use the appropriate Microsoft command-line tool.	15

- Navigation

    - cd
    - dir
    - md
    - rmdir
    - Drive navigation inputs:
    - M C: or D: or x:

- Command-line tools

    - ipconfig
    - ping
    - hostname
    - netstat
    - nslookup
    - chkdsk
    - net user
    - net use
    - tracert
    - format
    - xcopy
    - copy
    - robocopy
    - gpupdate
    - gpresult
    - shutdown
    - sfc
    - [command name] /?
    - diskpart
    - pathping
    - winver

Objective	Chapter(s)
1.3 Given a scenario, use features and tools of the Microsoft Windows 10 operating system (OS).	14

- Task Manager

  - Services
  - Startup
  - Performance
  - Processes
  - Users

- Microsoft Management Console (MMC) snap-in

  - Event Viewer (eventvwr.msc)
  - Disk Management (diskmgmt.msc)
  - Task Scheduler (taskschd.msc)
  - Device Manager (devmgmt.msc)
  - Certificate Manager (certmgr.msc)
  - Local Users and Groups (lusrmgr.msc)
  - Performance Monitor (perfmon.msc)
  - Group Policy Editor (gpedit.msc)

- Additional tools

  - System Information (msinfo32. exe)
  - Resource Monitor (resmon.exe)
  - System Configuration (msconfig. exe)
  - Disk Cleanup (cleanmgr.exe)
  - Disk Defragment (dfrgui.exe)
  - Registry Editor (regedit.exe)

Objective	Chapter(s)
1.5 Given a scenario, use the appropriate Windows settings.	14

- Time and Language
- Update and Security
- Personalization
- Apps
- Privacy
- System
- Devices
- Network and Internet
- Gaming
- Accounts

1.6 Given a scenario, configure Microsoft Windows networking features on a client/desktop.	15

- Workgroup vs. domain setup
  - Shared resources
  - Printers
  - File servers
  - Mapped drives
- Local OS firewall settings
  - Application restrictions and exceptions
  - Configuration
- Client network configuration
  - Internet Protocol (IP) addressing scheme
  - Domain Name System (DNS) settings
  - Subnet mask
  - Gateway
  - Static vs. dynamic

Objective	Chapter(s)

Objective	Chapter(s)
1.8 Explain common OS types and their purposes.	13, 14

- Workstation OSs

  - Windows
  - Linux
  - macOS
  - Chrome OS

- Cell phone/tablet OSs

  - iPadOS
  - iOS
  - Android

- Various filesystem types

  - New Technology File System (NTFS)
  - File Allocation Table 32 (FAT32)
  - Third extended filesystem (ext3)
  - Fourth extended filesystem (ext4)
  - Apple File System (APFS)
  - Extensible File Allocation Table (exFAT)

- Vendor life-cycle limitations
  - End-of-life (EOL)
  - Update limitations
- Compatibility concerns between OSs

| 1.9 Given a scenario, perform OS installations and upgrades in a diverse OS environment. | 14, 15 |

- Boot methods

  - USB
  - Optical media
  - Network
  - Solid-state/flash drives
  - Internet-based
  - External/hot-swappable drive
  - Internal hard drive (partition)

Objective	Chapter(s)

- Apple ID and corporate restrictions
- Best practices
  - Backups
  - Antivirus
  - Updates/patches
- System Preferences
  - Displays
  - Networks
  - Printers
  - Scanners
  - Privacy
  - Accessibility
  - Time Machine
- Features
  - Multiple desktops
  - Mission Control
  - Keychain
  - Spotlight
  - iCloud
  - Gestures
  - Finder
  - Remote Disc
  - Dock
- Disk Utility
- FileVault
- Terminal
- Force Quit

Objective	Chapter(s)
2.0 Security	
2.1 Summarize various security measures and their purposes.	17

- Physical security
    - Access control vestibule
    - Badge reader
    - Video surveillance
    - Alarm systems
    - Motion sensors
    - Door locks
    - Equipment locks
    - Guards
    - Bollards
    - Fences
- Physical security for staff
    - Key fobs
    - Smart cards
    - Keys
    - Biometrics
    - Retina scanner
    - Fingerprint scanner
    - Palmprint scanner
    - Lighting
    - Magnetometers
- Logical security
    - Principle of least privilege
    - Access control lists (ACLs)
    - Multifactor authentication (MFA)
    - Email
    - Hard token
    - Soft token
    - Short message service (SMS)
    - Voice call
    - Authenticator application

Objective	Chapter(s)

- Dictionary attack
- Insider threat
- Structured Query Language (SQL) injection
- Cross-site scripting (XSS)

- Vulnerabilities

  - Non-compliant systems
  - Unpatched systems
  - Unprotected systems (missing antivirus/missing firewall)
  - EOL OSs
  - Bring your own device (BYOD)

2.5 Given a scenario, manage and configure basic security settings in the Microsoft Windows OS.	18

- Defender Antivirus

  - Activate/deactivate
  - Updated definitions

- Firewall

  - Activate/deactivate
  - Port security
  - Application security

- Users and groups

  - Local vs. Microsoft account
  - Standard account
  - Administrator
  - Guest user
  - Power user

- Login OS options

  - Username and password
  - Personal identification number (PIN)
  - Fingerprint
  - Facial recognition
  - Single sign-on (SSO)

Objective	Chapter(s)
2.7 Explain common methods for securing mobile and embedded devices.	18

- Screen locks
    - Facial recognition
    - PIN codes
    - Fingerprint
    - Pattern
    - Swipe
- Remote wipes
- Locator applications
- OS updates
- Device encryption
- Remote backup applications
- Failed login attempts restrictions
- Antivirus/anti-malware
- Firewalls
- Policies and procedures

BYOD vs. corporate owned

Profile security requirements

- Internet of Things (IoT)

Objective	Chapter(s)
2.8 Given a scenario, use common data destruction and disposal methods.	17

- Physical destruction
    - Drilling
    - Shredding
    - Degaussing
    - Incinerating
- Recycling or repurposing best practices
    - Erasing/wiping
    - Low-level formatting
    - Standard formatting
- Outsourcing concepts
    - Third-party vendor
    - Certification of destruction/ recycling

Objective	Chapter(s)
2.9 Given a scenario, configure appropriate security settings on small office/home office (SOHO) wireless and wired networks.	18

- Home router settings
    - Change default passwords
    - IP filtering
    - Firmware updates
    - Content filtering
    - Physical placement/secure locations
    - Dynamic Host Configuration Protocol (DHCP) reservations
    - Static wide-area network (WAN) IP
    - Universal Plug and Play (UPnP)
    - Screened subnet
- Wireless specific
    - Changing the service set identifier (SSID)
    - Disabling SSID broadcast
    - Encryption settings
    - Disabling guest access
    - Changing channels
- Firewall settings
    - Disabling unused ports
    - Port forwarding/mapping

Objective	Chapter(s)
2.10 Given a scenario, install and configure browsers and relevant security settings.	18

- Browser download/installation
    - Trusted sources
    - Hashing
    - Untrusted sources
- Extensions and plug-ins
    - Trusted sources
    - Untrusted sources

Objective	Chapter(s)

Objective	Chapter(s)
3.4 Given a scenario, troubleshoot common mobile OS and application issues.	19

- Common symptoms

  - Application fails to launch
  - Application fails to close/crashes
  - Application fails to update
  - Slow to respond
  - OS fails to update
  - Battery life issues
  - Randomly reboots
  - Connectivity issues

    – Bluetooth

    – WiFi

    – Near-field communication (NFC)

    – AirDrop

    – Screen does not autorotate

Objective	Chapter(s)
3.5 Given a scenario, troubleshoot common mobile OS and application security issues.	19

- Security concerns

  - Android package (APK) source
  - Developer mode
  - Root access/jailbreak
  - Bootleg/malicious application
  - Application spoofing
- Common symptoms

  - High network traffic
  - Sluggish response time
  - Data-usage limit notification
  - Limited Internet connectivity
  - No Internet connectivity
  - High number of ads
  - Fake security warnings
  - Unexpected application behavior
  - Leaked personal files/data

Objective	Chapter(s)
4.0 Operational Procedures	
4.1 Given a scenario, implement best practices associated with documentation and support systems information management.	22

- Ticketing systems

    - User information

    - Device information

    - Description of problems

    - Categories

    - Severity

    - Escalation levels

    - Clear, concise written communication

        – Problem description

        – Progress notes

        – Problem resolution

- Asset management

    - Inventory lists

    - Database system

    - Asset tags and IDs

    - Procurement life cycle

    - Warranty and licensing

    - Assigned users

- Types of documents

    - Acceptable use policy (AUP)

    - Network topology diagram

    - Regulatory compliance requirements

    - Splash screens

    - Incident reports

    - Standard operating procedures

    - Procedures for custom installation of software package

    - New-user setup checklist

    - End-user termination checklist

- Knowledge base/articles

Objective	Chapter(s)
4.2 Explain basic change-management best practices.	22

- Documented business processes
  - Rollback plan
  - Sandbox testing
  - Responsible staff member
- Change management
  - Request forms
  - Purpose of the change
  - Scope of the change
  - Date and time of the change
  - Affected systems/impact
  - Risk analysis
  - Risk level
  - Change board approvals
  - End-user acceptance

4.3 Given a scenario, implement workstation backup and recovery methods.   22

- Backup and recovery
  - Full
  - Incremental
  - Differential
  - Synthetic
- Backup testing
  - Frequency
- Backup rotation schemes
  - On site vs. off site
  - Grandfather-father-son (GFS)
  - 3-2-1 backup rule

Objective	Chapter(s)
4.9 Given a scenario, use remote access technologies.	20

- Methods/tools

    - RDP
    - VPN
    - Virtual network computer (VNC)
    - Secure Shell (SSH)
    - Remote monitoring and management (RMM)
    - Microsoft Remote Assistance (MSRA)
    - Third-party tools

        – Screen-sharing software

        – Video-conferencing software

        – File transfer software

        – Desktop management software

        Security considerations of each access method

Exam objectives are subject to change at any time without prior notice at CompTIA's sole discretion. Please visit CompTIA's website (www.comptia.org) for the most current listing of exam objectives.

Assessment Test for Exam 220-1101

1. Which of the following is *not* considered a system component that can be found inside a computer?

   A. CPU

   B. RAM

   C. PCIe graphics adapter

   D. Motherboard

2. Which of the following is a physical memory format installed directly in today's desktop computer systems?

   A. DIMM

   B. HDD

   C. SSD

   D. eMMC

3. Which of the following are components that can commonly be found on a motherboard? (Choose all that apply.)

   A. Headers

   B. Fan connectors

   C. Gyroscope

   D. Scanner

   E. HDD

4. You are buying optical discs and need to ensure they have large capacity. What suffix indicates that the capacity of an optical disc is roughly twice that of its standard counterpart?

   A. DL

   B. R

   C. RW

   D. RE

5. You are replacing a power supply with a new one. What is the primary characteristic you should look for to ensure all internal components can be supported?

   A. Amperage rating

   B. 20-pin to 24-pin motherboard adapter

   C. Wattage rating

   D. Voltage rating

6. A user has asked you to install a RAID array. Except in the case of RAID 0, which do all types of RAID offer? (Choose two.)

   A. Faster read speeds

   B. Faster write speeds

   C. Redundancy

   D. Fault tolerance

   E. Ability to restore automatically from tape after a drive failure

7. Which of the following types of connectors would you expect to see on the end of a serial cable?

   A. DB-9

   B. RS-232

   C. Molex

   D. VGA

8. Which of the following video connectors has an analog variety and a digital variety?

   A. VGA

   B. HDMI

   C. DisplayPort

   D. DVI

9. Which of the following connectors will you not find on the end of a USB cable? (Choose two.)

   A. Lightning

   B. USB-C

   C. Molex

   D. DB-9

   E. eSATA

10. A technician is preparing to perform inkjet printer maintenance. Which of the following should they consider?

   A. Replace toner, apply maintenance kit, calibrate, clean.

   B. Replace paper, clean heating element, remove debris.

   C. Replace ribbon, replace print head, replace paper.

   D. Clean heads, replace cartridges, calibrate, clear jams.

11. What is the function of the laser in a laser printer?

   A. It heats up the toner so that it adheres to the page.

   B. It charges the paper so that it will attract toner.

   C. It creates an image of the page on the drum.

   D. It cleans the drum before a page is printed.

12. What is the component called that stores the material that ends up printed to the page in a laser printer?

   A. Toner cartridge

   B. Ink cartridge

   C. Laser module

   D. Laser cartridge

13. When used with network scanning services, what does SMB allow for?

   A. Scan to the cloud

   B. Scan to email

   C. Scan to a network folder

   D. Scan to secured print

14. Which network connectivity device stops broadcasts from being sent to computers on a different network segment?

   A. Hub

   B. Switch

   C. Router

   D. Firewall

15. Which of the following cable types is made with a plastic coating that does not produce toxic fumes when it burns?

   A. Plenum

   B. Fiber

   C. Coaxial

   D. UTP

16. Which of the following are standards used by coaxial cable? (Choose two.)

   A. RG-6

   B. RG-59

   C. RJ-11

   D. RJ-45

17. On which port does FTP run by default?

   A. 21

   B. 25

   C. 53

   D. 80

18. Which of the following protocols can be used by a client to access email on a server?

   A. DNS

   B. FTP

   C. SMTP

   D. IMAP

19. Which of the following protocols provide secure network transmissions? (Choose two.)

   A. SMTP

   B. SNMP

   C. SSH

   D. HTTPS

20. Which of the following is a company that provides direct access to the Internet for home and business computer users?

   A. ASP

   B. ISP

   C. DNS

   D. DNP

21. What is maximum range for a Bluetooth Class 2 device?

   A. 100 meters

   B. 10 meters

   C. 1 meter

   D. 0.5 meters

22. Which of the following 802.11 technologies can communicate in the 2.4 GHz and 5 GHz frequencies? (Choose two.)

   A. 802.11ax

   B. 802.11ac

   C. 802.11n

   D. 802.11g

23. One of your network users was recently caught at work browsing pornographic websites. Which of the following servers could be installed to prohibit this activity?

   A. Web

   B. Security

   C. Proxy

   D. DNS

24. Google Docs is an example of what type of cloud service?

   A. SaaS

   B. IaaS

   C. PaaS

   D. GaaS

25. Which type of software is required to run client-side virtualization on your home network?

   A. Terminal emulation

   B. Process replication

   C. Hyperthreading

   D. Hypervisor

26. You are installing a new display for a laptop. Which LCD component is responsible for providing brightness?

   A. Backlight

   B. Inverter

   C. Screen

   D. Digitizer

27. Your laptop has 4 GB of installed memory and uses shared video memory. If the video card is using 512 MB, how much is left for the rest of the system?

   A. 4 GB

   B. 3.5 GB

   C. 512 MB

   D. Cannot determine

28. On a typical laptop, which of the following components runs through the hinge from the base of the laptop up into the display unit?

   A. Webcam connector

   B. Speaker wires

   C. Microphone connector

   D. Wi-Fi antenna

29. Which of the following is used to remotely manage and delete corporate applications and associated data on mobile devices?

   A. Location services

   B. Synchronization

   C. MAM

   D. MDM

30. What term refers to copying data between a mobile device and a computer system to mirror such things as contacts, programs, pictures, and music?

    A. Calibration

    B. Remote wipe

    C. Pairing

    D. Synchronization

31. You want to send emails from your smartphone using a secure connection. Which port will enable that?

    A. 25

    B. 110

    C. 143

    D. 587

32. A user calls to report that their laptop is not booting up. What is the first step you should take?

    A. Quarantine the system.

    B. Identify the problem.

    C. Establish a theory of probable cause.

    D. Establish a plan of action to resolve the problem.

33. You are troubleshooting a network issue. What feature do switches most likely have to help troubleshoot connectivity issues?

    A. Port toggles

    B. Beep codes

    C. Indicator lights

    D. Log entries

34. Your laser printer has recently starting printing vertical white lines on documents it prints. What is the most likely cause of the problem?

    A. The print driver is faulty.

    B. The fuser is not heating properly.

    C. There is toner on the transfer corona wire.

    D. There is a scratch on the EP drum.

35. A desktop computer has recently started exhibiting slow performance, particularly when opening and saving files to the hard drive. What should you try first?

    A. Replace the hard drive.

    B. Remove old files and applications to free up disk space.

    C. Delete and reinstall the OS.

    D. Defragment the hard drive.

36. A network cable has not been working properly. Another technician suggests testing the cable. Which tool should be used that may be capable of doing this? (Choose two.)

    A. Loopback plug

    B. Network tap

    C. Cable tester

    D. Toner probe

Answers to Assessment Test 220-1101

1. C. System components are essential for the basic functionality of a computer system. Many of the landmarks found on the motherboard can be considered system components, even expansion slots to a degree. What you plug into those slots, however, must be considered peripheral to the basic operation of the system. See Chapter 1 for more information.

2. A. Except for DIMMs, all options represent some form of secondary storage, all of which are covered in Chapter 2. See Chapter 1 for more information.

3. A, B. Motherboards commonly have headers for lights and buttons and for powering cooling fans. Gyroscopes are most commonly found in mobile devices. Scanners are external devices. Although there might be one or more types of HDD interfaces built into the motherboard, the HDD itself is not. See Chapter 1 for more information.

4. A. DL stands for double or dual layer. With DVDs, the capacity almost doubles, but with Blu-ray discs, it actually does. R means recordable, and RW and RE are used to designate rewritable or re-recordable. See Chapter 2 for more information.

5. C. Wattage is the unit of output for power supplies. Make sure that the power supply has enough wattage to support all components. See Chapter 2 for more information.

6. C, D. Except for RAID 0, all implementations of RAID offer a way to recover from the failure of at least one drive, which is an example of fault tolerance, through the implementation of some mechanism that stores redundant information for that purpose. Some RAID types offer faster read and/or write performance. RAID 1, for instance, does not guarantee either. See Chapter 2 for more information.

7. A. Serial cables use a DB-9 connector. Some people will call them an RS-232 connector, but RS-232 is the transmission standard used by serial cables. Molex are power connectors. VGA is a video connector. See Chapter 3 for more information.

8. D. DVI comes in both analog (DVI-A) and digital (DVI-D) varieties. VGA is always analog; HDMI and DisplayPort are always digital. See Chapter 3 for more information.

9. C, D. USB cables are multipurpose cables that connect many types of peripherals. Connectors include USB-C, Lightning, and eSATA. Molex connectors provide power to PATA hard drives and optical drives. A DB-9 connector is found on the end of a serial cable. See Chapter 3 for more information.

10. D. Inkjet printer maintenance includes: clean heads, replace cartridges, calibrate, clear jams. Laser printer maintenance includes: replace toner, apply maintenance kit, calibrate, clean. Thermal printer maintenance includes: replace paper, clean heating element, remove debris. Impact printer maintenance includes: replace ribbon, replace print head, replace paper. See Chapter 4 for more information.

11. C. The laser creates an image on the photosensitive drum that is then transferred to the paper by the transfer corona. The fuser heats up the toner so that it adheres to the page. The transfer corona charges the page, and the eraser lamp cleans the drum before a page is printed. A rubber blade is also used to remove toner physically from the drum. See Chapter 4 for more information.

12. A. Laser printers use toner, which they melt to the page in the image of the text and graphics being printed. A toner cartridge holds the fine toner dust until it is used in the printing process. See Chapter 4 for more information.

13. C. The Server Message Block (SMB) protocol allows for the saving of scanned documents to a network folder. See Chapter 4 for more information.

14. C. A router does not pass along broadcasts to computers on other segments. Hubs and switches send broadcasts along because they do not segment traffic at the logical network address level. See Chapter 5 for more information.

15. A. The plenum is an air space within buildings used to circulate breathable air for occupants of a building. Fiber, coaxial, and UTP cables are normally enclosed with a PVC plastic coating, which produces toxic fumes if burned. For air ventilation spaces, plenum grade cable is required. All cable types have plenum-rated versions. See Chapter 5 for more information.

16. A, B. RG-6 and RG-59 are coaxial cable standards. RJ-11 and RJ-45 are connectors used with twisted pair cabling. See Chapter 5 for more information.

17. A. FTP operates on ports 20 and 21. Port 25 is used by SMTP, port 53 is DNS, and port 80 is HTTP. See Chapter 6 for more information.

18. D. The IMAP and POP3 protocols can be used to retrieve email from mail servers. DNS is used to resolve hostnames to IP addresses. FTP is for file transfers, and SMTP is used to send email. See Chapter 6 for more information.

19. C, D. Secure Shell (SSH) and Hypertext Transfer Protocol Secure (HTTPS) are both secure transport protocols. Simple Network Management Protocol (SNMP) and Simple Mail Transfer Protocol (SMTP) are not inherently secure. See Chapter 6 for more information.

20. B. An Internet service provider (ISP) provides direct access to the Internet. ASP is a programming language. DNS resolves host names to IP addresses. DNP is not a computer networking acronym. See Chapter 7 for more information.

21. B. A Bluetooth class 2 device (which includes headsets, keyboards, and mice) is 10 meters. Class 1 devices can transmit up to 100 meters, Class 3 one meter, and Class 4 half a meter. See Chapter 7 for more information.

22. A, C. 802.11ax (Wi-Fi 6) and 802.11n were designed to communicate at 2.4 GHz and 5 GHz. 802.11ac runs at 5 GHz, and 802.11g runs at 2.4 GHz. See Chapter 7 for more information.

23. C. A proxy server can be configured to block access to websites containing potentially objectionable material. Web servers host websites. There is no specific security server, although there are authentication servers that provide security. A DNS server resolves hostnames to IP addresses. See Chapter 8 for more information.

24. A. Google Docs is software, so it is an example of software as a service (SaaS). IaaS is infrastructure as a service. PaaS is platform as a service. GaaS is not a test objective and is not currently a cloud service type. See Chapter 8 for more information.

25. D. The hypervisor is the key piece of software needed for virtualization. Terminal emulation, process replication, and hyperthreading are not related to client-side virtualization. See Chapter 8 for more information.

26. A. The backlight provides light to the LCD screen. The inverter provides power to the backlight, and the screen displays the picture. Digitizers take physical input (such as touch) and turn it into electronic data. See Chapter 9 for more information.

27. B. If the laptop is using shared video memory, then the system memory is shared with the video card. If the video card is using 512 MB (half a gigabyte), then there is 3.5 GB left for the system. See Chapter 9 for more information.

28. D. In most laptops, the Wi-Fi antenna runs from the base of the unit through the hinge and into the display. The webcam and microphone are generally part of the display unit only. Speakers are most often in the base of the laptop, not the display. See Chapter 9 for more information.

29. C. Mobile application management (MAM) is a service that allows administrators to control corporate software on mobile devices, including updating and wiping apps. Mobile device management (MDM) controls which devices are on the network and can wipe entire devices. Location services does not manage software. Synchronization can back up apps and data but does not help with updates or deleting apps. For more information, see Chapter 10.

30. D. Synchronizing a mobile device with a computer system allows you to mirror personal data between the devices, regardless of which one contains the most current data. Calibration refers to matching the device's and user's perceptions of where the user is touching the screen. Remote wipes allow you to remove personal data from a lost or stolen device. Pairing is what must be done in Bluetooth for two Bluetooth devices to connect and communicate. For more information, see Chapter 10.

31. D. Port 587 is used by SMTP (an email sending protocol) secured with TLS. Ports 25 (SMTP), 110 (POP), and 143 (IMAP) are not secure. See Chapter 10 for more information.

32. B. In the best practice methodology to resolve problems, the first step is to identify the problem. Quarantining the system is not necessary. Establishing a theory of probable cause is the second step, and establishing a plan of action is the fourth step. See Chapter 11 for more information.

33. C. Switches and other connectivity devices have indicator lights to help indicate when things are working normally and when something isn't working right. There are no port toggles and switches don't use beep codes. A switch might make a log entry into an event logger, but this is less likely than it having indicator lights. See Chapter 11 for more information.

34. C. White streaks on printouts are most likely caused by toner on the transfer corona wire. Vertical black lines are caused by a scratch or a groove in the EP drum. If the fuser was not heating properly, toner would not bond to the paper and you would have smearing. Faulty print drivers will cause garbage to print or there will be no printing at all. See Chapter 12 for more information.

35. B. Hard drive performance can slow down if the drive gets short on space, particularly under 10 percent free space. Try removing old files and applications to free up disk space first. If that doesn't resolve it, then defragment. If neither of those work, it could indicate a failing hard drive. See Chapter 12 for more information.

36. C. Cable testers are for verifying that a cable works properly. Network taps create copies of network traffic for analysis. A loopback plug is for testing the ability of a network adapter to send and receive. A toner probe is used to trace a cable from one location to another. See Chapter 12 for more information.

Assessment Test for Exam 220-1102

1. Which will accomplish a specific task for the user?

   A. Driver

   B. Application

   C. Operating system

   D. Filesystem

2. Which operating system is a cloud-based operating system?

   A. Linux

   B. Android

   C. Windows 10

   D. Chrome OS

3. Which term defines the precompiled instructions that are programmed and allows an operating system and its applications to operate?

   A. Shell

   B. Source

   C. GUI

   D. Multithreading

4. Which term best describes the Android operating system?

   A. Server

   B. Workstation

   C. Mobile

   D. Cloud-based

5. You need to change a computer's name and join it to a domain. Which tool will allow you to perform these actions?

   A. Device Manager

   B. User Accounts

   C. System Properties

   D. Credential Manager

6. Which tab in Task Manager allows you to see processes separated by each user on the system?

   A. Processes

   B. Performance

   C. App History

   D. Users

7. Which RAID system requires three or more disks to provide fault tolerance?

    A. Mirroring

    B. Striping

    C. RAID-1

    D. Striping with parity

8. Which Windows Update branch allows you to install preview releases of updates for Windows 10?

    A. Semi-Annual Channel

    B. Semi-Annual Channel (Targeted)

    C. Long-Term Servicing Channel

    D. Insider Program

9. Which tool allows you to ready the operating system for imaging?

    A. Microsoft Deployment Toolkit

    B. Windows Assessment and Deployment Kit

    C. `sysprep.exe`

    D. Windows Imaging

10. Which element of the boot process holds the information that instructs the operating system to load from a specific partition?

    A. `winload.exe`

    B. `BOOTMGR`

    C. `winresume.exe`

    D. BCD

11. You need to configure a static IP address for Windows 10. Which of the following allows you to perform this task?

    A. The Network & Sharing Center

    B. Windows Defender Firewall

    C. The Network & Internet settings screen

    D. The VPN settings screen

12. Which filesystem performs on-the-fly defragmentation?

    A. FAT

    B. NTFS

    C. ext4

    D. FAT32

13. Which place can you find updates for Apple operating systems?

   A. iTunes

   B. App Store

   C. Keychain

   D. Mission Control

14. Which macOS feature is similar to Windows File Explorer?

   A. Keychain

   B. iCloud

   C. Spotlight

   D. Finder

15. Your system log files report an ongoing attempt to gain access to a single account. This attempt has been unsuccessful to this point. What type of attack are you most likely experiencing?

   A. Password-guessing attack

   B. Rootkit attack

   C. Worm attack

   D. TCP/IP hijacking

16. One of the vice presidents of the company calls a meeting with the information technology department after a recent trip to competitors' sites. They report that many of the companies they visited granted access to their buildings only after fingerprint scans, and the VP wants similar technology employed at this company. Of the following, which technology relies on a physical attribute of the user for authentication?

   A. Smartcard

   B. Biometrics

   C. Geofencing

   D. Tokens

17. What type of malware is able to conceal itself from many parts of the operating system and will obtain/retain elevated privileges?

   A. Worm

   B. Trojan

   C. Rootkit

   D. Botnet

18. A user wants to ensure that all contacts from their mobile device are copied onto their computer before migrating to a new device. Which of the following processes can accomplish this?

   A. Mirroring

   B. Synchronization

   C. Calling each contact

   D. Attaching the contacts to an email

19. With which mobile filesystem are files with `.ipa` file extensions typically associated?

    A. Android

    B. iOS

    C. Windows 10

    D. Blackberry OS

20. A technician is configuring a new Windows computer for a home office. Which of the following steps should the technician take to secure the workstation?

    A. Rename default accounts.

    B. Configure single sign-on.

    C. Disable Windows Update.

    D. Disable Action Center pop-ups.

21. You need to protect files on the desktop operating system with encryption but find out you do not have a TPM. What can you use to protect the files?

    A. BitLocker

    B. Encrypted File System

    C. BitLocker to Go

    D. Full-drive encryption

22. Which is a benefit of setup of a device with a Microsoft account?

    A. Access to the online store

    B. Automatic synchronization of OneDrive

    C. Active Directory authentication

    D. Offline authentication

23. Which critical system generally requires third-party tools to troubleshoot performance problems?

    A. RAM

    B. CPU

    C. Graphics

    D. Network

24. What is the last step that should be performed when removing malware?

    A. Investigate and verify symptoms.

    B. Enable System Protection.

    C. Educate the end user.

    D. Schedule scans and run updates.

25. Your mobile device is suffering from an intermittent wireless connection. What is recommended to alleviate signal drops?

    A. Shortening the SSID

    B. Using the 5 GHz band

    C. Reducing power on the WAP

    D. Using the 2.4 GHz band

26. You are receiving USB controller resource warning messages. What should you try to resolve the issue?

    A. Move USB devices around on the USB ports.

    B. Manually allot more endpoints.

    C. Upgrade drivers for the USB devices.

    D. Manually increase the output amperage.

27. Why is time drift a big problem on virtual machines?

    A. Lack of configuration for the NTP server

    B. Availability of the NTP server

    C. Shared physical RTC

    D. Emulated RTC

28. Which tool can be used to restart a failed service?

    A. `msconfig.exe`

    B. WinRE

    C. Computer Management MMC

    D. Resource Monitor

29. Which is a safety risk from overheating a lithium-ion battery?

    A. Reduced voltage

    B. Shock

    C. Explosion

    D. Shutdown

30. Which of these are not generally attributed to an intermittent wireless issue?

    A. Bluetooth devices

    B. Microwaves ovens

    C. WAPs

    D. Radar

31. You are trying to troubleshoot a problem with AirDrop. You have verified that both participants are within range and both Bluetooth and Wi-Fi are turned on. What could the problem be?

    A. AirDrop is configured for direct connection.

    B. The sender is not in the recipient's contacts list.

    C. The sender is in the blocked AirDrop list on the recipient's phone.

    D. The phones are connected to the same SSID.

32. Which network protocol and port does RDP operate on?

    A. TCP port 3389

    B. TCP port 22

    C. TCP port 23

    D. TCP port 443

33. Which line would be used to comment Windows batch script code?

    A. `//comment`

    B. `'comment`

    C. `REM comment`

    D. `# comment`

34. Which command will launch the Remote Desktop Connection utility?

    A. `msra.exe`

    B. `mstsc.exe`

    C. `quickassist.exe`

    D. `ssh.exe`

35. A client computer connects to the main office and is configured with an IP address from the main office, on the client computer. What is being described?

    A. Site-to-site VPN

    B. Remote Desktop connection

    C. SSH connection

    D. Host-to-site VPN

36. Zoom and Teams are classic examples of which of the following?

    A. Screen-sharing software

    B. Video-conferencing software

    C. File transfer software

    D. Desktop management software

37. Which remote access technology is used for encrypted console-based access?

    A. MSRA

    B. RDP

    C. Telnet

    D. SSH

38. Which of the following are good measures to take to help prevent ESD? (Choose two.)

    A. Decrease the humidity.

    B. Tie long hair back.

    C. Take your shoes off.

    D. Perform self-grounding.

39. Which of the following screwdrivers has a splined head?

    A. Flat-tipped

    B. Phillips

    C. Axial

    D. Torx

40. What type of software licensing agreement usually provides free trial software, with the expectation that you will pay for it if you decide to keep it?

    A. Freeware

    B. Shareware

    C. Open source

    D. Single user

41. How do antistatic mats and wrist straps drain the potential ESD?

    A. The use of magnets

    B. Through a resistor

    C. High-voltage probe

    D. Direct ground

42. When cleaning dust out of computer equipment, what should you always use?

    A. Multimeter

    B. Flashlight

    C. Air filter mask

    D. Mirror

43. Which is the most likely source of interference to wireless communications?

   A. Magnets

   B. ESD

   C. Surges

   D. Microwave ovens

44. While working on a user's system, you discover a sticky note attached to the bottom of the keyboard that has their username and password written on it. The user is not around, and you need to verify that the network connection is working. What should you do?

   A. Log in, verify access, and log out.

   B. Log in and stay logged in when you are finished.

   C. Text the user.

   D. Log in and change the user's password.

45. While installing a new network card, you accidentally broke a component off the card. What should you do?

   A. Explain that the card was broken out of the box.

   B. Install the card anyway.

   C. Inform the customer of the situation.

   D. Leave everything as is until you can locate a new card.

46. Which regulation is enforced by the Health & Human Services (HHS) that regulates the privacy of patient information related to health services?

   A. SOX

   B. FERPA

   C. HIPAA

   D. GLBA

47. Which ticket entry method is the easiest for end users to submit their own tickets?

   A. Email entry

   B. Portal entry

   C. Manual entry

   D. Application entry

48. What is typically used for protecting data center equipment during a power outage?

   A. Line interactive UPS

   B. Surge protector

   C. Standby UPS

   D. Online UPS

49. Which method is used to test a change in an isolated environment?

   A. Primary plan

   B. Backout plan

   C. Sandbox testing

   D. Technical evaluation

50. Which backup method can create a new current full backup from the files already contained on the backup media?

   A. Synthetic

   B. Copy

   C. Incremental

   D. Differential

Answers to Assessment Test 220-1102

1. B. An application is written to perform a specific task for the user of the operating system, such as word processing or data analysis. Drivers allow the operating system to communicate with the hardware. The operating system and the filesystem assist in running applications. See Chapter 13 for more information.

2. D. The Google Chrome OS is a true cloud-based operating system because all the data is stored in the cloud. Cloud-based operating systems require an Internet connection to access information. Android and Windows 10 use cloud storage, but are not considered cloud-based operating systems. Linux is strictly a workstation operating system. See Chapter 13 for more information.

3. B. The source, also known as the source code, is the code to be compiled, and this allows the operating system and applications to execute. The shell is a component of the operating system that allows execution of applications. The GUI is a graphical extension of the shell to allow the execution of applications. Multithreading is a term used to describe how an application can create multiple simultaneous requests to the processor. See Chapter 13 for more information.

4. C. The Android operating system is a mobile operating system often used with tablets and phones. A server is an operating system that is optimized to serve information. A workstation is an operating system that is optimized to execute and display the information retrieved from a server operating system. A cloud-based operating system is an operating system that requires network connectivity to access applications. See Chapter 13 for more information.

5. C. The System Properties applet (SYSDM.CPL) allows you to change the computer name and join the system to a domain. Device Manager is used to manage hardware resources. The User Accounts applet is used to manage user accounts. Credential Manager is used to manage stored credentials. See Chapter 14 for more information.

6. D. The Users tab in Task Manager allows you to see processes sorted by each user. The Processes tab shows you processes sorted by foreground and background applications. The Performance tab shows you the overall performance of the system with graphical charts. The App History tab displays historical information about processes, such as CPU time. See Chapter 14 for more information.

7. D. Striping with parity, also known as RAID-5, requires three or more disks and provides fault tolerance. Mirroring, also known as RAID-1, only requires two disks. Striping, also known as RAID-0, provides no fault tolerance. See Chapter 14 for more information.

8. D. The Insider Program allows for the installation of brand-new features before they are publicly released. The Semi-Annual Channel is normally delayed by three to four months. The Semi-Annual Channel (Targeted) branch will install updates as they are released to the general public. The Long-Term Servicing Channel never installs new features during the life of the version of Windows. See Chapter 15 for more information.

9. C. The `sysprep.exe` utility allows you to ready the operating system for imaging by resetting specific information, such as the computer name. The Microsoft Deployment Toolkit can assist in creating the steps, but it calls on the `sysprep` tool. The Windows Assessment and Deployment Kit allows you to customize the Windows operating system for imaging, but it does not ready the operating system for imaging. Windows Imaging (WIM) is a file format to contain the image. See Chapter 15 for more information.

10. D. The Boot Configuration Data (BCD) holds the information that instructs the Windows Boot Manager (BOOTMGR) to load the operating system from a specific partition. `winload .exe` loads the operating system kernel. BOOTMGR is the initial bootstrap program that reads the BCD. `winresume.exe` is used when resuming a previous session that has been suspended. See Chapter 15 for more information.

11. C. By clicking Start, then the Settings gear, and choosing Network & Internet, you can configure the properties of the network adapter to set up a static IP address. The Network & Sharing Center is used to view the network connection firewall profile and connection status. The Windows Defender Firewall is used to protect the operating system from malicious network connectivity. The VPN settings screen allows you to configure a virtual private network (VPN) connection. See Chapter 15 for more information.

12. C. The ext4 filesystem does not suffer from fragmentation, because it performs on-the-fly defragmentation. FAT is a 16-bit filesystem that suffers from fragmentation. NTFS is a journaled filesystem that suffers from fragmentation. FAT32 is a 32-bit filesystem that suffers from fragmentation. See Chapter 16 for more information.

13. B. The App Store is where you can find updates for the Apple operating system. iTunes is used to purchase and download music, videos, and other content. The Keychain is used to store credentials on behalf of the user. Mission Control is used to view all the currently running applications. See Chapter 16 for more information.

14. D. The macOS Finder is the equivalent to the Windows File Explorer. The Keychain is a password management system for the operating system. iCloud is a cloud-based storage and backup service. Spotlight helps you find applications, documents, and other files. See Chapter 16 for more information.

15. A. A password-guessing attack occurs when a user account is repeatedly attacked using a variety of passwords. A rootkit attack would not be immediately seen and would not show as an ongoing effort. A worm attack would not be visible as an ongoing attempt to gain access. TCP/IP hijacking is a form of on-path attack. See Chapter 17 for more information.

16. B. Biometrics relies on a physical characteristic of the user to verify identity. Biometric devices typically use either a hand pattern or a retinal scan to accomplish this. Smartcards contain a private certificate key and are protected with a passphrase. Geofencing, which uses GPS coordinates to require authentication, only happens within those parameters. Tokens are rotating numerical keys that you must physically have with you. See Chapter 17 for more information.

17. C. Rootkits are software programs that have the ability to hide certain things from the operating system. A worm is malware that replicates itself and infects other system. Trojans are programs that enter a system or network under the guise of another program. A botnet is a group of infected computers that can be remotely controlled via a command and control server. See Chapter 17 for more information.

18. B. Synchronization can copy all contacts, programs, email messages, pictures, music, and videos between a mobile device and a computer. Mirroring is a term reserved for when devices replicate themselves to similar devices. Calling the contacts won't achieve the desired result, and emailing contacts is inefficient and does not immediately result in placing the contacts on the computer. See Chapter 18 for more information.

19. B. The .ipa file extension is for iOS app store package files, and it is therefore associated with iOS. Android apps have an extension of .apk. Windows 10 uses .exe. Blackberry OS uses an extension of .jad. The latter two phone types were not discussed in detail in this book. See Chapter 18 for more information.

20. A. Renaming the default accounts on the new Windows computer is the easiest way to secure the operating system. Configuring single sign-on should only be performed if a resource is required that only uses SSO as authentication. Disabling Windows Update will do the opposite of securing the operating system. Disabling Action Center pop-ups will also do the opposite of securing the operating system. See Chapter 18 for more information.

21. B. Encrypted File System (EFS) will encrypt and protect files on an NTFS filesystem without a TPM. BitLocker requires a TPM and therefore will not work. BitLocker to Go is used with removable media. Full-drive encryption is used with mobile devices. See Chapter 18 for more information.

22. B. When you set up a device with a Microsoft account, you automatically synchronize files in OneDrive, along with other known folders. Access to the online store can be achieved by launching the Microsoft Store and logging in; it does not require the user to log into the operating system with the Microsoft account. Active Directory authentication is applicable if the workstation is joined to an Active Directory domain. Offline authentication is the default method if you are not signing in with a Microsoft account. See Chapter 18 for more information.

23. C. Graphics cards usually require third-party tools to diagnose performance problems. RAM problems can be diagnosed inside the operating system from Task Manager. CPU and network problems can be diagnosed inside the operating system from Task Manager. See Chapter 19 for more information.

24. C. The last step in the malware removal process is the education of the end user to prevent future occurrences of infection. Investigate and verify malware symptoms is the first step in the malware removal process. Enabling System Protection is one of the last steps, but it is not the last step. Scheduling scans and running updates should be performed after you have remediated the malware. See Chapter 19 for more information.

25. B. By using the 5 GHz wireless band, you can limit the amount of interference from external devices such as microwave ovens and Bluetooth devices. Shortening the SSID and reducing power on the WAP will have no effect on intermittent signal drops. Using the 2.4 GHz band will probably make signal drops worse. See Chapter 19 for more information.

26. A. Moving USB devices around on the USB ports is the first step in remediating USB issues related to resources. USB 2.0 devices should be consolidated to USB 2.0 ports and the same should be done for USB 3.0 devices. You cannot manually allot endpoints for USB devices. Upgrading the drivers for the USB devices will not solve power issues or endpoint issues; drivers for the USB controller should be updated. You cannot manually increase the output amperage for USB devices. See Chapter 19 for more information.

27. D. Normally a dedicated chip called the real-time clock (RTC) keeps time for physical machines. However, with virtual machines their RTC is emulated and susceptible to time drift. By default, Windows 10/11 are configured for `time.windows.com` as an NTP. The availability of the NTP server of `time.windows.com` is not any different than physical machines. When deploying virtual machines, the physical RTC is not shared; each VM gets an emulated RTC. See Chapter 19 for more information.

28. C. The Computer Management MMC under Services can be used to restart and configure failed services. Although services can be viewed with the `msconfig.exe` tool, they cannot be restarted with the tool; they can only be enabled or disabled on startup. The Windows Recovery Environment (WinRE) is used to troubleshoot and repair problems offline. Resource Monitor cannot be used to restart services. See Chapter 19 for more information.

29. C. The risk of thermal runaway is attributed to overheating a lithium-ion battery. When thermal runaway happens, you run the risk of explosion of the battery. Overheating a li-ion battery can cause reduced voltage, but that is not a safety risk. Overheating a li-ion battery will not cause a shock. Overheating of the li-ion battery will cause a shutdown, but that is not a safety risk. See Chapter 19 for more information.

30. C. Wireless access points (WAPs) are not generally subject to intermittent wireless issues. Adding more WAPs generally reduces connectivity problems. Microwave ovens and Bluetooth devices operate in the 2.4 GHz band and can affect 2.4 GHz wireless. Radar operates in the 5 GHz band and can affect 5 GHz wireless devices. See Chapter 19 for more information.

31. B. If the phones are within Bluetooth range of each other and Bluetooth and Wi-Fi are turned on, then security is most likely the cause. The sender must be in the recipient's contact list. AirDrop is not configurable for direct connection, so this is an invalid answer. You cannot block a sender from AirDrop. The phones being on the same SSID is not a concern as long as they are not configured as personal hotspots. See Chapter 19 for more information.

32. A. The Remote Desktop Protocol operates on TCP port 3389. The SSH protocol operates on TCP port 22. The Telnet service operates on TCP port 23, and HTTPS operates on TCP port 443. See Chapter 20 for more information.

33. C. The line of REM comment is used to comment Windows batch script code. The line //comment is used to comment JavaScript code. The line 'comment is used to comment VBScript code. The line # comment is used to comment Bash script code and PowerShell code. See Chapter 20 for more information.

34. B. The command mstsc.exe will launch the Remote Desktop Connection utility. From this utility you can remotely connect to a server or other workstation. The command msra.exe launches the Microsoft Remote Assistance utility to allow a trusted helper to remote in to help. The command quickassist.exe will launch the Quick Assist remote assistance utility to allow an assistant to remote in to help. The command ssh.exe launches the Secure Shell client that allows you to connect to a Linux/UNIX server or networking equipment. See Chapter 20 for more information.

35. D. The scenario being described is a host-to-site connection. A site-to-site VPN connection is built between two sites, such as the main site and a branch site. A Remote Desktop connection or SSH connection will not configure a site IP address on the client computer. See Chapter 20 for more information.

36. B. Zoom and Teams are classic examples of video-conferencing software, because they allow multiple attendees and have a form of attendee management. MSRA is an example of screen-sharing software. Dropbox is an example of file transfer software. Splashtop and Team-Viewer are examples of desktop management software. See Chapter 20 for more information.

37. D. The Secure Shell utility is used for secure console-based remote access. Microsoft Remote Assistance (MSRA) is used for screen sharing. The Remote Desktop Protocol is a protocol used for Remote Desktop connections. Telnet is a console-based remote access technology, but it is not encrypted. See Chapter 20 for more information.

38. B, D. Long hair or neckties can very easily hold a static charge and damage computer parts. In addition, if you don't have an ESD strap or mat, you should perform self-grounding before you touch sensitive computer equipment. Lower humidity actually increases the risk of ESD. Taking your shoes off will not limit ESD. See Chapter 21 for more information.

39. D. A Torx screwdriver has a splined head used for greater gripping of the screw. A flat-tipped screwdriver, as the name suggests, has a flat tip. A Phillips screwdriver has a cross used for better gripping over a normal flat-tip screwdriver. An axial screwdriver is not a type of screwdriver. See Chapter 21 for more information.

40. B. Shareware often provides a free trial of a program, with the expectation that you will pay for it if you keep it. Freeware and open source applications are generally totally free, although the developers may ask for donations. Single-user software is licensed for one user. See Chapter 21 for more information.

41. B. Typically, a 1 mega-ohm resistor is used to slowly drain or discharge the potential electrostatic discharge (ESD). Magnets are used to hold screws onto screwdrivers. High-voltage probes are used to drain high voltage stored up in electrical circuits and not ESD. Direct grounds are never used because they have potential for discard and possible electrocution. See Chapter 21 for more information.

42. C. An air filter mask will protect you from inhaling dust particles. A multimeter is used to measure voltage. Although useful, a flashlight and a mirror are not needed for cleaning dust out of computer equipment. See Chapter 21 for more information.

43. D. Microwave ovens operate in the 2.45 GHz range and can directly affect wireless communications. Magnets can generate a magnetic field, but they will not disrupt wireless communications. Electrostatic discharge (ESD) can kill components, but a discard from ESD in the same space as wireless will not cause interruptions. Electrical surges can affect the equipment running wireless, but it will not affect wireless communications. See Chapter 21 for more information.

44. C. You should text the user and let them know that you need to verify their network connection. You should not log in as another person, with their username and password. You should not log in and stay logged in when you are finished. You should definitely not log in and change the user's password. See Chapter 22 for more information.

45. C. You should be honest and inform the customer of the situation. Explaining that the card was broken out of the box is untruthful and deceptive. Installing the card anyway will cause new problems. Leaving everything as is until you can locate a new card does not help the customer, since you've created a new dilemma. See Chapter 22 for more information.

46. C. The Health Insurance Portability and Accountability Act (HIPAA) affects health-care providers and providers that process health records. The Sarbanes–Oxley Act (SOX) is enforced by the Securities and Exchange Commission (SEC) and regulates sensitive financial information and financial records. The Family Educational Rights and Privacy Act (FERPA) affects education providers and organizations that process student records. The Gramm–Leach–Bliley Act (GLBA) affects providers of financial services and safeguards customer information. See Chapter 22 for more information.

47. A. Email entry is the easiest for end users because it allows them to email the ticketing system and use a method of communication they are familiar with. Portal entry requires the end user to log in to the portal, then enter fields in a form to submit a ticket. Manual ticket entry is not done by the end user; it is completed by helpdesk staff. Application entry is an automated ticket that submits when an application has an issue; this is independent from what the user needs solved. See Chapter 22 for more information.

48. D. An online uninterruptable power supply (UPS) is commonly found in data centers, because power is continuously supplied from the batteries and no switchover is required. When power is out, the batteries just stop charging. A line interactive uninterruptable power supply (UPS) is common in server racks to protect network equipment. A surge protector protects against power surges and voltage spikes. A standby uninterruptable power supply (UPS) is the most common type of power protection used for personal computers. See Chapter 22 for more information.

49. C. Sandbox testing is used to test a change before placing it into production. The process from the sandbox testing will become the primary plan used when the change in production is green-lighted. The backout, also known as the rollback plan, is created in the event the primary plan fails in production. The technical evaluation is a technical evaluation of the change, along with a draft of the primary plan. See Chapter 22 for more information.

50. A. A synthetic backup uses the latest full backup and applies each of the daily backups to create a new full backup. The backup software performs this function by using the backup media already obtained. A copy backup is similar to a full backup, except that it does not reset the archive bits and requires backup from the servers. An incremental backup copies only those files that have changed since the last backup and leaves the archive bits unchanged. A differential backup backs up only the files that have changed since the last backup. See Chapter 22 for more information.

220-1101

Chapter

1

Motherboards, Processors, and Memory

THE FOLLOWING COMPTIA A+ 220-1101 EXAM OBJECTIVES ARE COVERED IN THIS CHAPTER:

✓ **3.2 Given a scenario, install the appropriate RAM.**

- **RAM types**
  - **Virtual RAM**
  - **Small outline dual inline memory module (SODIMM)**
  - **Double Data Rate 3 (DDR3)**
  - **Double Data Rate 4 (DDR4)**
  - **Double Data Rate 5 (DDR5)**
  - **Error correction code (ECC) RAM**
- **Single-channel**
- **Dual-channel**
- **Triple-channel**
- **Quad-channel**

✓ **3.4 Given a scenario, install and configure motherboards, central processing units (CPUs), and add-on cards.**

- **Motherboard form factor**
  - **Advanced Technology eXtended (ATX)**
  - **Information Technology eXtended (ITX)**
- **Motherboard connector types**
  - **Peripheral Component Interconnect (PCI)**
  - **PCI Express (PCIe)**

- Multicore
- Multithreading
- Virtualization support
- Cooling
  - Fans
  - Heat sink
  - Thermal paste/pads
  - Liquid

The computers we use daily, from the largest servers to the smallest smart watches and everything in between, are collections of different electronic components and software working together in a system. Digital computers have been around since the late 1930s, so they aren't new news. As you would imagine though, their looks and functionality have evolved considerably since then.

As technology improved over the years, computers got smaller and faster, and inventors added features that required new hardware devices. Inspired by typewriters, keyboards were added for ease of input. Visual displays required a monitor and a video card and a standard interface between them. Sound was provided by a different expansion card and speakers. Because of the newly added features, PCs were modular by necessity. That is, if a new feature or functionality were needed, a new component could be added. Or if a part failed, it could be replaced by a new one. Along the way in the late 1960s, the term *personal computer (PC)* was coined to differentiate between computers designed to be used by one person versus other options, such as a mainframe or one where multiple users share a processor. This book, and the CompTIA A+ exams, focus on PC hardware and software.

 Unless specifically mentioned otherwise, the terms *PC* and *computer* are used interchangeably throughout this book.

Much of the computing industry today is focused on smaller devices, such as laptops, tablets, and smartphones. Laptops have outsold desktop computers since 2005, and it seems that everyone has a smartphone glued to their hand today. Smaller devices require the same components as do their bigger desktop-sized cousins. Of course, the components are smaller and many times integrated into the same circuit board. The functionality of the individual parts is still critical, though, so what you learn here will serve you well regardless of the type of device you're working on.

Even though all parts inside a computer case are important, some are more important than others. You'll sometimes hear people refer to the "big three" computer parts, which are the motherboard, processor, and memory. Without these, a computer won't work, whereas if a sound card fails, it's probably not going to make the entire system inoperable. In this chapter, you will learn how to identify, install, and configure the big three, which are critical to computer functionality. You'll also learn about cooling systems, because too much heat will cause components to melt, which could make for a very bad day for the computer user.

With small computing devices being far more prevalent, you might wonder why we are starting the book talking about components that are primarily in desktop and larger systems. We intentionally cover this material first because it's important to understand what each component does individually. It helps you isolate the functionality of each piece of the system, which is critical for troubleshooting and fixing problems. Besides, if you are working (or want to be working) as a computer technician, you will likely see plenty of desktop-sized PCs in your travels!

Understanding Motherboards

The spine of the computer is the *motherboard*, otherwise known as the *system board* or *mainboard*. This is the *printed circuit board (PCB)*, which is a conductive series of pathways laminated to a nonconductive substrate that lines the bottom of the computer and is often of a uniform color, such as green, brown, blue, black, or red. It is the most important component in the computer because it connects all the other components together. Figure 1.1 shows a typical PC system board, as seen from above. All other components are attached to this circuit board. On the system board, you will find the central processing unit (CPU) slot or integrated CPU, underlying circuitry, expansion slots, video components, random access memory (RAM) slots, and a variety of other chips. We will be discussing each of these components throughout this book.

Motherboard Form Factors

There are hundreds, if not thousands, of different motherboards in the market today. It can be overwhelming trying to figure out which one is needed. To help, think of motherboards in terms of which type they are, based on a standard classification. System boards are classified by their *form factor* (design), such as ATX and ITX. Exercise care and vigilance when acquiring a motherboard and components separately. Motherboards will have different expansion slots, support certain processors and memory, and fit into some cases but not others. Be sure that the other parts are physically compatible with the motherboard you choose.

Advanced Technology Extended

Intel developed the *Advanced Technology eXtended (ATX)* motherboard in the mid-1990s to improve upon the classic AT-style motherboard architecture that had ruled the PC world for many years. The ATX motherboard has the processor and memory slots at right angles to the expansion cards, like the one in Figure 1.1. This arrangement puts the processor and memory in line with the fan output of the power supply, allowing the processor to run cooler. And because those components are not in line with the expansion cards, you can install full-length expansion cards—adapters that extend the full length of the inside of a standard computer case—in an ATX motherboard machine. ATX (and its derivatives, such as micro-ATX) is the primary PC motherboard form factor in use today. Standard ATX motherboards measure 12″ × 9.6″ (305 mm × 244 mm).

FIGURE 1.1   A typical motherboard

We will discuss expansion cards in more depth (and cover that part of Exam Objective 3.4) in Chapter 2, "Expansion Cards, Storage Devices, and Power Supplies."

Information Technology eXtended

The *Information Technology eXtended (ITX)* line of motherboard form factors was developed by VIA Technologies in the early 2000s as a low-power, small form factor (SFF) board for specialty uses, including home-theater systems, compact desktop systems, gaming systems, and embedded components. ITX itself is not an actual form factor but a family of form factors. The family consists of the following form factors:

- **Mini-ITX**—6.7″ × 6.7″ (170 mm × 170 mm)
- **Nano-ITX**—4.7″ × 4.7″ (120 mm × 120 mm)
- **Pico-ITX**—3.9″ × 2.8″ (100 mm × 72 mm)
- **Mobile-ITX**—2.4″ × 2.4″ (60 mm × 60 mm)

The mini-ITX motherboard has four mounting holes that line up with three or four of the holes in the ATX and micro-ATX form factors. In mini-ITX boards, the rear interfaces are placed in the same location as those on the ATX motherboards. These features make mini-ITX boards compatible with ATX cases. This is where the mounting compatibility ends, because despite the PC compatibility of the other ITX form factors, they are used in embedded systems, such as set-top boxes, home entertainment systems, and smartphones, and lack the requisite mounting and interface specifications. Figure 1.2 shows the three larger forms of ITX motherboards, next to two ATX motherboards for comparison.

FIGURE 1.2   ITX motherboards

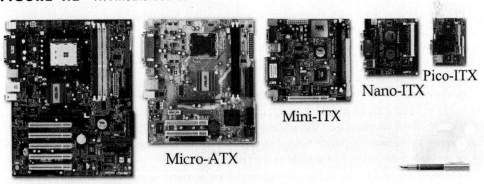

Pico-ITX

Nano-ITX

Mini-ITX

Micro-ATX

Standard-ATX

System Board Components

Now that you understand the basic types of motherboards and their form factors, it's time to look at the key characteristics and components of the motherboard and, where applicable, their locations relative to each other. The following list summarizes key concepts you need to know about motherboards:

- Bus architecture
- Chipsets
- Expansion slots
- Memory slots and cache
- Central processing units and processor sockets
- Power connectors
- Onboard non-volatile storage connectors (such as for hard drives)
- Motherboard headers
- BIOS/UEFI/firmware
- CMOS and CMOS battery
- Front-panel connectors and headers

In the following sections, you will learn about some of the most common components of a motherboard, what they do, and where they are located on the motherboard. We'll show what each component looks like so that you can identify it on most any motherboard that you run across. In the case of some components, this chapter provides only a brief introduction, with more detail to come in later chapters.

Bus Architecture

In a PC, data is sent from one component to another via a *bus*, which is a common collection of signal pathways. In the very early days, PCs used serial buses, which sent one bit at a time and were painfully slow. Brilliant engineers realized that they could redesign the bus and send 8 bits at a time (over synchronized separate lines), which resulted in a big speed increase. This was known as a *parallel bus*.

The downside of parallel communications is the loss of circuit length (how long the circuit could be) and throughput (how much data could move at one time). The signal could travel only a short distance, and the amount of data was limited due to the careful synchronization needed between separate lines, the speed of which must be controlled to limit skewing the arrival of the individual signals at the receiving end.

What was once old is new again, as engineers have discovered methods to make serial transmissions work at data rates that are many times faster than parallel signals. Therefore, nearly everything you see today uses a serial bus. The only limitation of serial circuits is in the capability of the transceivers, which tends to grow over time at a refreshing rate due to technical advancements. Examples of specifications that have heralded the dominance of serial communications are Serial Advanced Technology Attachment (Serial ATA, or SATA), Universal Serial Bus (USB), IEEE 1394/FireWire, and Peripheral Component Interconnect Express (PCIe).

> The term *bus* is also used in any parallel or bit-serial wiring implementation where multiple devices can be attached at the same time in parallel or in series (daisy-chained). Examples include Small Computer System Interface (SCSI), USB, and Ethernet.

On a motherboard, several different buses are used. Expansion slots of various architectures, such as PCIe, are included to allow for the insertion of external devices or adapters. Other types of buses exist within the system to allow communication between the CPU, RAM, and other components with which data must be exchanged. Except for CPU slots and sockets and memory slots, there are no insertion points for devices in many closed bus systems because no adapters exist for such an environment.

The various buses throughout a given computer system can be rated by their bus speeds. The higher the bus speed, the higher its performance. In some cases, various buses must be synchronized for proper performance, such as the system bus and any expansion buses that run at the front-side bus speed. Other times, one bus will reference another for its own speed. The internal bus speed of a CPU is derived from the front-side bus clock, for instance. The buses presented throughout this chapter are accompanied by their speeds, where appropriate.

Chipsets

A *chipset* is a collection of chips or circuits that perform interface and peripheral functions for the processor. This collection of chips is usually the circuitry that provides interfaces for memory, expansion cards, and onboard peripherals, and it generally dictates how a motherboard will communicate with the installed peripherals.

Chipsets are usually given a name and model number by the original manufacturer. For example, B550 and X570 are chipsets that support Advanced Micro Devices, Inc. (AMD) processors, and Z490 and H410 are Intel motherboard chipsets. Typically, the manufacturer and model tell you that your particular chipset has a certain set of features (for example, type of CPU and RAM supported, type and brand of onboard video, and so on). Don't worry about memorizing any chipset names—you can look them up online to understand their features.

Chipsets can be made up of one or several integrated circuit chips. Intel-based motherboards, for example, typically use two chips. To know for sure, you must check the manufacturer's documentation, especially because cooling mechanisms frequently obscure today's chipset chips, sometimes hindering visual brand and model identification.

Chipsets can be divided into two major functional groups, called Northbridge and Southbridge. Let's take a brief look at these groups and the functions they perform.

AMD and Intel have integrated the features of Northbridge and South-bridge into most of their CPUs. Therefore, the CPU provides Northbridge and Southbridge functionality as opposed to separate chipsets.

Northbridge

The *Northbridge* subset of a motherboard's chipset is the set of circuitry or chips that performs one very important function: management of high-speed peripheral communications. The Northbridge is responsible primarily for communications with integrated video using PCIe, for instance, and processor-to-memory communications. Therefore, it can be said that much of the true performance of a PC relies on the specifications of the Northbridge component and its communications capability with the peripherals it controls.

When we use the term *Northbridge,* we are referring to a functional subset of a motherboard's chipset. There isn't actually a Northbridge brand of chipset.

The communications between the CPU and memory occur over what is known as the *front-side bus (FSB),* which is just a set of signal pathways connecting the CPU and main memory, for instance. The clock signal that drives the FSB is used to drive communications by certain other devices, such as PCIe slots, making them local-bus technologies. The *back-side bus (BSB),* if present, is a set of signal pathways between the CPU and external cache memory. The BSB uses the same clock signal that drives the FSB. If no back-side bus exists, cache is placed on the front-side bus with the CPU and main memory.

The Northbridge is directly connected to the Southbridge (discussed next). It controls the Southbridge and helps to manage the communications between the Southbridge and the rest of the computer.

Southbridge

The *Southbridge* subset of the chipset is responsible for providing support to the slower onboard peripherals (USB, Serial and Parallel ATA, parallel ports, serial ports, and so on), managing their communications with the rest of the computer and the resources given to them. These components do not need to keep up with the external clock of the CPU and do not represent a bottleneck in the overall performance of the system. Any component that would impose such a restriction on the system should eventually be developed for FSB attachment.

In other words, if you're considering any component other than the CPU, memory and cache, or PCIe slots, the Southbridge is in charge. Most motherboards today have integrated USB, network, and analog and digital audio ports for the Southbridge to manage, for example, all of which are discussed in more detail later in this chapter or in Chapter 3, "Peripherals, Cables, and Connectors." The Southbridge is also responsible for managing communications with the slower expansion buses, such as PCI, and legacy buses.

Figure 1.3 is a photo of the chipset of a motherboard, with the heat sink of the Northbridge at the top left, connected to the heat-spreading cover of the Southbridge at the bottom right.

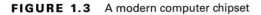

FIGURE 1.3   A modern computer chipset

Figure 1.4 shows a schematic of a typical motherboard chipset (both Northbridge and Southbridge) and the components with which they interface. Notice which components interface with which parts of the chipset.

FIGURE 1.4   A schematic of a typical motherboard chipset

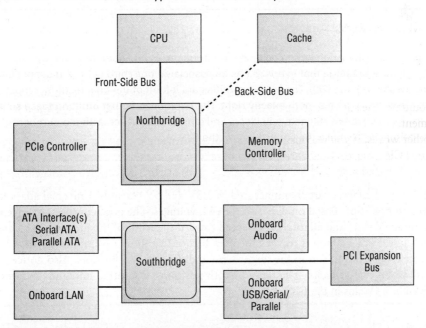

Expansion Slots

The most visible parts of any motherboard are the *expansion slots*. These are small plastic slots, usually from 1 to 6 inches long and approximately ½ inch wide. As their name suggests, these slots are used to install various devices in the computer to expand its capabilities. Some expansion devices that might be installed in these slots include video, network, sound, and disk interface cards.

If you look at the motherboard in your computer, you will more than likely see one of the main types of expansion slots used in computers today, which are PCI and PCIe. In the following sections, we will cover how to visually identify the different expansion slots on the motherboard.

PCI Expansion Slots

It's now considered an old technology, but many motherboards in use today still contain 32-bit *Peripheral Component Interconnect (PCI)* slots. They are easily recognizable because they are only around 3 inches long and classically white, although modern boards take liberties with the color. PCI slots became extremely popular with the advent of Pentium-class processors in the mid-1990s. Although popularity has shifted from PCI to PCIe, the PCI slot's service to the industry cannot be ignored; it has been an incredibly prolific architecture for many years.

PCI expansion buses operate at 33 MHz or 66 MHz (version 2.1) over a 32-bit (4-byte) channel, resulting in data rates of 133 MBps and 266 MBps, respectively, with 133 MBps being the most common, server architectures excluded. PCI is a shared-bus topology, however, so mixing 33 MHz and 66 MHz adapters in a 66 MHz system will slow all adapters to 33 MHz. Older servers might have featured 64-bit PCI slots as well, since version 1.0, which double the 32-bit data rates. See the sidebar "Arriving at the Exact Answer" for help with understanding the math involved in frequencies and bit rates.

Arriving at the Exact Answer

To get the math exactly right when dealing with frequencies and data rates ending in 33 and 66, you have to realize that every 33 has an associated one-third (1/3), and every 66 has an associated two-thirds (2/3). The extra quantities are left off of the final result but must be added back on to get the math exactly right. The good news is that omitting these small values from the equation still gets you close, and a bit of experience with the numbers leads to being able to make the connection on the fly.

PCI slots and adapters are manufactured in 3.3V and 5V versions. Universal adapters are keyed to fit in slots based on either of the two voltages. The notch in the card edge of the common 5V slots and adapters is oriented toward the front of the motherboard, and the notch in the 3.3V adapters toward the rear. Figure 1.5 shows several PCI expansion slots. Note the 5V 32-bit slot in the foreground and the 3.3V 64-bit slots. Also notice that a universal 32-bit card, which has notches in both positions, is inserted into and operates fine in the 64-bit 3.3V slot in the background.

FIGURE 1.5 PCI expansion slots

PCIe Expansion Slots

The most common expansion slot architecture that is being used by motherboards is *PCI Express (PCIe)*. It was designed to be a replacement for PCI, as well as an older video card standard called accelerated graphics port (AGP). PCIe has the advantage of being faster than AGP while maintaining the flexibility of PCI. PCIe has no plug compatibility with either AGP or PCI. Some modern PCIe motherboards can be found with regular PCI slots for backward compatibility, but AGP slots have not been included for many years.

PCIe is casually referred to as a bus architecture to simplify its comparison with other bus technologies. True expansion buses share total bandwidth among all slots, each of which taps into different points along the common bus lines. In contrast, PCIe uses a switching component with point-to-point connections to slots, giving each component full use of the corresponding bandwidth and producing more of a star topology versus a bus. Furthermore, unlike other expansion buses, which have parallel architectures, PCIe is a serial technology, striping data packets across multiple serial paths to achieve higher data rates.

PCIe uses the concept of *lanes*, which are the switched point-to-point signal paths between any two PCIe components. Each lane that the switch interconnects between any two intercommunicating devices comprises a separate pair of wires for both directions of traffic. Each PCIe pairing between cards requires a negotiation for the highest mutually supported number of lanes. The single lane or combined collection of lanes that the switch interconnects between devices is referred to as a *link*.

There are seven different link widths supported by PCIe, designated x1 (pronounced "by 1"), x2, x4, x8, x12, x16, and x32, with x1, x4, and x16 being the most common. The x8 link width is less common than these but more common than the others. A slot that supports a particular link width is of a physical size related to that width because the width is based on the number of lanes supported, requiring a related number of wires. As a result, an x8 slot is longer than an x1 slot but shorter than an x16 slot. Every PCIe slot has a 22-pin portion in common toward the rear of the motherboard, which you can see in Figure 1.7, in which the rear of the motherboard is to the left. These 22 pins comprise mostly voltage and ground leads. (The PCIe slots are the longer and lighter ones in Figure 1.6.)

FIGURE 1.6   PCIe expansion slots

Four major versions of PCIe are currently available in the market: 1.x, 2.x, 3.0, and 4.0. For the four versions, a single lane, and therefore an x1 slot, operates in each direction (or transmits and receives from either communicating device's perspective), at a data rate of 250 MBps (almost twice the rate of the most common PCI slot), 500 MBps, approximately 1 GBps, and roughly 2 GBps, respectively.

 PCIe 5.0 was formally ratified by the PCI Special Interest Group (PCI-SIG) in 2019, and motherboards supporting the architecture started hitting the market in late 2021. Much like its predecessors, it doubles the speed of the previous version. Therefore, a PCIe 5.0 x1 adapter operates at about 4 MBps in each direction. The slots are forward and backward compatible. For example, you can put a PCIe 4.0 video card into a motherboard with a PCIe 5.0 slot, but you won't get the full performance that PCIe 5.0 is capable of. The inverse is true as well—a PCIe 5.0 card will work in a 4.0 slot but at the 4.0 standard's speed. PCIe 6.0 is expected around 2023.

An associated bidirectional link has a nominal throughput of double these rates. Use the doubled rate when comparing PCIe to other expansion buses because those other rates are for bidirectional communication. This means that the 500 MBps bidirectional link of an x1 slot in the first version of PCIe was comparable to PCI's best, a 64-bit slot running at 66 MHz and producing a throughput of 533 MBps.

Bidirectional means that data flows in both directions, often simultaneously. *Unidirectional* means data flows in only one direction.

Combining lanes simply results in a linear multiplication of these rates. For example, a PCIe 1.1 x16 slot is capable of 4 GBps of throughput in each direction, 16 times the 250 MBps x1 rate. Bidirectionally, this fairly common slot produces a throughput of 8 GBps. Each subsequent PCIe specification doubles this throughput. The aforementioned PCIe 5.0 will produce bidirectional throughput of approximately 128 GBps, which is faster than some DDR4 standards (which is to say, it's really, really fast).

Using Shorter Cards in Longer Slots

Up-plugging is defined in the PCIe specification as the ability to use a higher-capability slot for a lesser adapter. In other words, you can use a shorter (fewer-lane) card in a longer slot. For example, you can insert an x8 card into an x16 slot. The x8 card won't completely fill the slot, but it will work at x8 speeds if up-plugging is supported by the motherboard. Otherwise, the specification requires up-plugged devices to operate at only the x1 rate. This is something you should be aware of and investigate in advance. Down-plugging is possible only on open-ended slots, although not specifically allowed in the official specification. Even if you find or make (by cutting a groove in the end) an open-ended slot that accepts a longer card edge, the inserted adapter cannot operate faster than the slot's maximum rated capability because the required physical wiring to the PCIe switch in the Northbridge is not present.

Because of its high data rate, PCIe is the current choice of gaming aficionados. Additionally, technologies similar to NVIDIA's Scalable Link Interface (SLI) allow such users to combine preferably identical graphics adapters in appropriately spaced PCIe x16 slots with a hardware bridge to form a single virtual graphics adapter. The job of the bridge is to provide non-chipset communication among the adapters. The bridge is not a requirement for SLI to work, but performance suffers without it. SLI-ready motherboards allow two, three, or four PCIe graphics adapters to pool their graphics processing units (GPUs) and memory to feed graphics output to a single monitor attached to the adapter acting as the primary SLI device. SLI implementation results in increased graphics performance over single-PCIe and non-PCIe implementations.

Refer back to Figure 1.6, which is a photo of an SLI-ready motherboard with three PCIe x16 slots (every other slot, starting with the top one), one PCIe x1 slot (second slot from the top), and two PCI slots (first and third slots from the bottom). Notice the latch and tab that secures the x16 adapters in place by their hooks. Any movement of these high-performance devices can result in temporary failure or poor performance.

Using Riser Cards

Most PC expansion cards plug directly into the motherboard. A special type of expansion card, called a *riser card*, provides additional slots that other expansion cards plug into. The other expansion cards are then parallel to the motherboard, as opposed to perpendicular. Figure 1.7 shows an example of a riser card. It's an older example, but it illustrates the concept well.

FIGURE 1.7   Riser card in a motherboard

By Dale Mahalko, Gilman, WI, USA CC BY-SA 3.0 from Wikimedia Commons

Riser cards aren't often found in desktop PCs today but do still find some use in rack-mounted servers with low-profile cases. The motherboard must be designed to accept a riser card, and the case needs to be built for it as well, for the external portion of the expansion card to be accessible.

Memory Slots and Cache

Memory, or *random access memory (RAM)*, slots are the next most notable slots on a motherboard. These slots are designed for the modules that hold memory chips that make up primary memory, which is used to store currently used data and instructions for the CPU. Many types of memory are available for PCs today. In this chapter, you will become familiar with the appearance and specifications of the slots on the motherboard so that you can identify them and appropriately install or replace RAM.

For the most part, PCs today use memory chips arranged on a small circuit board. A *dual in-line memory module (DIMM)* is one type of circuit board. Today's DIMMs differ in the number of conductors, or pins, that each particular physical form factor uses. Some common examples include 168-, 184-, 240-, and 288-pin configurations. In addition, laptop memory comes in smaller form factors known as small outline DIMMs (SODIMMs) and Micro-DIMMs. More detail on memory packaging and the technologies that use them can be found later in this chapter in the section "Understanding Memory."

Memory slots are easy to identify on a motherboard. Classic DIMM slots were usually black and, like all memory slots, were placed very close together. DIMM slots with color-coding are more common these days, however. The color-coding of the slots acts as a guide to the installer of the memory. See the section "Single-, Dual-, Triple-, and Quad-Channel Memory" later in this chapter for more on the purpose of this color-coding. Consult the motherboard's documentation to determine the specific modules allowed as well as their required orientation. The number of memory slots varies from motherboard to motherboard, but the structure of the different slots is similar. Metal pins in the bottom make contact with the metallic pins on each memory module. Small metal or plastic tabs on each side of the slot keep the memory module securely in its slot. Figure 1.8 shows four memory slots, with the CPU socket included for reference.

FIGURE 1.8 Double Data Rate (DDR) memory slots

Sometimes, the amount of primary memory installed is inadequate to service additional requests for memory resources from newly launched applications. When this condition occurs, the user may receive an "out of memory" error message and an application may fail to launch. One solution for this is to use the hard drive as additional RAM. This space on the hard drive is known as a *swap file* or a *paging file*. The technology in general is known as *virtual memory* or *virtual RAM*. The paging file is called PAGEFILE.SYS in modern Microsoft operating systems. It is an optimized space that can deliver information to RAM at the request of the memory controller faster than if it came from the general storage pool of the drive. It's located at c:\pagefile.sys by default. Note that virtual memory cannot be used directly from the hard drive; it must be paged into RAM as the oldest contents of RAM are paged out to the hard drive to make room. The memory controller, by the way, is the chip that manages access to RAM as well as adapters that have had a few hardware memory addresses reserved for their communication with the processor.

Nevertheless, relying too much on virtual memory (check your page fault statistics in the Reliability and Performance Monitor) results in the entire system slowing down noticeably. An inexpensive and highly effective solution is to add physical memory to the system, thus reducing its reliance on virtual memory. More information on virtual memory and its configuration can be found in Chapter 13, "Operating System Basics."

Another type of memory common in PCs is *cache memory*, which is small and fast and logically sits between the CPU and RAM. Cache is a very fast form of memory forged from static RAM, which is discussed in detail in the section "Understanding Memory" later in this chapter. Cache improves system performance by predicting what the CPU will ask for next and prefetching this information before being asked. This paradigm allows the cache to be smaller in size than the RAM itself. Only the most recently used data and code or that which is expected to be used next is stored in cache.

You'll see three different cache designations:

Level 1 Cache   *L1 cache* is the smallest and fastest, and it's on the processor die itself. In other words, it's an integrated part of the manufacturing pattern that's used to stamp the processor pathways into the silicon chip. You can't get any closer to the processor than that.

Though the definition of L1 cache has not changed much over the years, the same is not true for other cache levels. L2 and L3 cache used to be on the motherboard but now have moved on-die in most processors as well. The biggest differences are the speed and whether they are shared.

Level 2 Cache   *L2 cache* is larger but a little slower than L1 cache. For processors with multiple cores, each core will generally have its own dedicated L1 and L2 caches. A few processors share a common L2 cache among the cores.

Level 3 Cache   *L3 cache* is larger and slower than L1 or L2, and is usually shared among all processor cores.

The typical increasing order of capacity and distance from the processor die is L1 cache, L2 cache, L3 cache, RAM, and HDD/SSD (hard disk drive and solid-state drive—more on these in Chapter 2). This is also the typical decreasing order of speed. The following list includes representative capacities of these memory types. The cache capacities are for each core of the 10th generation Intel Core i7 processor. The other capacities are simply modern examples.

- L1 cache—80 KB (32 KB for instructions and 48 KB for data)
- L2 cache—512 KB
- L3 cache—8–16 MB
- RAM—16–256 GB
- HDD/SSD—100s of GB to several TB

One way to find out how much cache your system has is to use a utility such as CPU-Z, as shown in Figure 1.9. CPU-Z is freeware that can show you the amount of cache, processor name and number, motherboard and chipset, and memory specifications. It can be found at www.cpuid.com.

FIGURE 1.9   Cache in a system

Figure 1.9 shows L1D and L1I caches. Many CPUs will split L1 cache into cache for data (L1D) or instructions (L1I). It's highly unlikely you'll be tested on this, but it's interesting to know.

Central Processing Unit and Processor Socket

The "brain" of any computer is the *central processing unit (CPU)*. There's no computer without a CPU. There are many different types of processors for computers—so many, in fact, that you will learn about them later in this chapter in the section "Understanding Processors."

Typically, in today's computers, the processor is the easiest component to identify on the motherboard. It is usually the component that has either a fan or a heat sink (usually both) attached to it (as shown in Figure 1.10). These devices are used to draw away and disperse the heat that a processor generates. This is done because heat is the enemy of microelectronics. Today's processors generate enough heat that, without heat dispersal, they would permanently damage themselves and the motherboard in a matter of minutes, if not seconds.

FIGURE 1.10   Two heat sinks, one with a fan

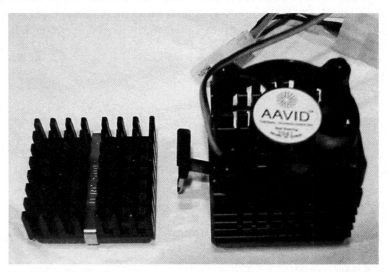

CPU sockets are almost as varied as the processors that they hold. Sockets are basically flat and have several columns and rows of holes or pins arranged in a square, as shown in Figure 1.11. The left socket is known as Socket AM4, made for AMD processors such as the Ryzen, and has holes to receive the pins on the CPU. This is known as a *pin grid array (PGA)* arrangement for a CPU socket. The holes and pins are in a row/column orientation, an array of pins. The right socket is known as LGA 1200, and there are spring-loaded pins in the socket and a grid of lands on the CPU. The *land grid array (LGA)* is a newer technology that places the delicate pins (yet more sturdy than those on chips) on the cheaper motherboard instead of on the more expensive CPU, opposite to the way that the aging PGA does. The device with the pins has to be replaced if the pins become too damaged to function. The PGA and LGA are mentioned again later in this chapter in the section "Understanding Processors."

FIGURE 1.11   CPU socket examples

Modern CPU sockets have a mechanism in place that reduces the need to apply considerable force to the CPU to install a processor, which was necessary in the early days of personal computing. Given the extra surface area on today's processors, excessive pressure applied in the wrong manner could damage the CPU packaging, its pins, or the motherboard itself. For CPUs based on the PGA concept, *zero insertion force (ZIF)* sockets are exceedingly popular. ZIF sockets use a plastic or metal lever on one of the two lateral edges to lock or release the mechanism that secures the CPU's pins in the socket. The CPU rides on the mobile top portion of the socket, and the socket's contacts that mate with the CPU's pins are in the fixed bottom portion of the socket. The image of Socket AM4 shown on the left in Figure 1.11 illustrates the ZIF locking mechanism at the right edge of the socket.

For processors based on the LGA concept, a socket with a different locking mechanism is used. Because there are no receptacles in either the motherboard or the CPU, there is no opportunity for a locking mechanism that holds the component with the pins in place. LGA-compatible sockets, as they're called despite the misnomer, have a lid that closes over the CPU and is locked in place by an L-shaped arm that borders two of the socket's edges. The nonlocking leg of the arm has a bend in the middle that latches the lid closed when the other leg of the arm is secured. The right image in Figure 1.11 shows an LGA socket with no CPU installed and the locking arm secured over the lid's tab, along the bottom edge.

Listing out all the desktop PC socket types you might encounter would take a long time. Instead, we'll give you a sampling of some that you might see. The first thing you might notice is that sockets are made for Intel or AMD processors, but not both. Keep that compatibility in mind when replacing a motherboard or a processor. Make sure that the processor and motherboard were designed for each other (even within the Intel or AMD families); otherwise, they won't fit each other and won't work. Table 1.1 lists some common desktop socket/CPU relationships. Servers and laptops/tablets generally have different sockets altogether, although some CPU sockets will support processors designed for desktops or servers.

TABLE 1.1 Desktop PC socket types and the processors they support

Socket	Released	Type	Processors
LGA 1200	2020	LGA	Intel Comet Lake and Rocket Lake
Socket AM4	2017	PGA	AMD Ryzen 3, Ryzen 5, Ryzen 7, Ryzen 9, Athlon 200GE
Socket TR4	2017	LGA	AMD Ryzen Threadripper
LGA 2066 (Socket R4)	2017	LGA	Intel Skylake-X and Kaby Lake-X
LGA 1151 (Socket H4)	2015	LGA	Intel Skylake, Kaby Lake, and Coffee Lake
Socket FM2+	2014	PGA	AMD Kaveri and Godavari
Socket AM1	2014	PGA	AMD Athlon and Sempron
LGA 1150 (Socket H3)	2013	LGA	Intel Haswell, Haswell Refresh, and Broadwell
Socket FM2	2012	PGA	AMD Trinity

Some legacy sockets, such as Socket 5 and Socket 7, supported both AMD and Intel platforms, but it's unlikely that you will see one in the wild, as they are over 25 years old now.

Playing the Name Game

Back in simpler times, Intel marketed only one or two processors at a time. For example, when the 80486DX was in the market, they didn't have much else. Then the Pentium came along, followed by the Celeron (which everyone knew was a stripped-down Pentium), and the Pentium M, which was the mobile version of the Pentium. The active roster of processors started to expand.

Now, there are a lot of active chips, including the Xeon and the Core series (i9, i7, i5, i3, and m3), and even the Pentium and Celeron are still kicking around. And with new innovation coming nearly every year, it's difficult to keep track of what's current.

In about 2013, Intel began to publicize its project code names a bit more to make it easier to keep track of the new technology bundles. No longer were techs able to remember that an i7 required a specific type of socket, but they needed to know *which* i7 they were dealing with. For example, a Broadwell-based (2014) i7 requires an LGA 1150 socket, whereas most Kaby Lake (2016) i7s use an LGA 1151. One pin makes a huge difference!

Odds are you aren't going to need to memorize all possible Intel chip and motherboard socket combinations for the exam or the real world. In the real world, the Internet's always there to remind you of which socket you need for a specific processor. To give you a flavor, though, Table 1.2 covers a few of Intel's recent CPU architecture codenames and the associated processor model numbers.

To make things even more interesting, you might hear references to the *n*th generation of the i5, i7, or i9 processor. For example, Rocket Lake is considered 11th generation. Intel codenames over the past several years have had some variation of a "Lake" name, such as Coffee Lake (2017), Comet Lake (2019), and Rocket Lake (2020). Perhaps the names keep it interesting for the engineers.

When you go to the parts store, though, you're probably not going to ask for a Rocket Lake i7. You'll ask for an i7, see what they have in stock—usually they will have the current generation and possibly the previous one, and then figure out what motherboard you need. (Or alternatively, based on your motherboard, you'll figure out which i7 you can use.)

What does all of this mean you need to do? First, get comfortable knowing that a new architecture may require a different motherboard. Second, feel free to memorize some of the more common combinations of motherboards and processors if you find it helpful, although you won't be tested on it. It may be handy in the real world to know that if you have an 11th gen Intel chip, you need a board with an LGA 1200 socket. (Or you can always Google it!)

TABLE 1.2   Select Intel desktop processors

Name (Year)	Gen	Socket	Core i9	Core i7	Core i5	Core i3
Alder Lake (2021)	12th	LGA 1700	129xx	127xx	126xx	n/a
Rocket Lake (2020)	11th	LGA 1200	119xx	117xx	116xx	n/a
					115xx	
					114xx	
Comet Lake (2019)	10th	LGA 1200	109xx	107xx	106xx	103xx
					105xx	101xx
					104xx	

Multisocket and Server Motherboards

When it comes to motherboard compatibility, the two biggest things to keep in mind are the processor type and the case. If either of those are misaligned with what the motherboard supports, you're going to have problems.

Thus far, as we've talked about desktop motherboards and their CPU sockets, we have shown examples of boards that have just one socket. There are motherboards that have more than one CPU socket and conveniently, they are called *multisocket* (typically written as two words) motherboards. Figure 1.12 shows a two-socket motherboard made by GIGABYTE. The two CPU sockets are easily identifiable and note that each CPU socket has eight dedicated memory slots.

FIGURE 1.12   GIGABYTE multisocket motherboard

Trying to categorize server motherboards can be a bit challenging. Servers are expected to do a lot more work than the average PC, so it makes sense that servers need more powerful hardware. Servers can, and quite often do, make do with a single processor on a "normal" PC motherboard. At the same time, there are motherboards designed specifically for servers that support multiple processors (two and four sockets are common) and have expanded memory and networking capabilities as well. Further, while server motherboards are often ATX-sized, many server manufacturers create custom boards to fit inside their chassis. Regardless, multisocket and server motherboards will generally use the same CPU sockets that other motherboards use.

Mobile Motherboards

In small mobile devices, space is at a premium. Some manufacturers will use standard small-factor motherboards, but most create their own boards to fit inside specific cases. An example of an oddly shaped Dell laptop motherboard is shown in Figure 1.13. When replacing a laptop motherboard, you almost always need to use one from the exact same model, otherwise it won't fit inside the case.

FIGURE 1.13   Dell laptop motherboard

Nearly all laptop processors are soldered onto the motherboard, so you don't have to worry about CPU socket compatibility. If the CPU dies, you replace the entire motherboard. We will cover laptop components more extensively in Chapter 9, "Laptop and Mobile Device Hardware."

Power Connectors

In addition to these sockets and slots on the motherboard, a special connector (the 24-pin white block connector shown in Figure 1.14) allows the motherboard to be connected to the power supply to receive power. This connector is where the ATX power connector (mentioned in Chapter 2 in the section "Understanding Power Supplies") plugs in.

FIGURE 1.14   An ATX power connector on a motherboard

Onboard Nonvolatile Storage Connectors

Nearly all users store data, and the most widely used data storage device is a hard drive. Hard drives are great because they store data even when the device is powered off, which explains why they are sometimes referred to as nonvolatile storage. There are multiple types of hard drives, and we'll get into them in more detail in Chapter 2. Of course, those drives need to connect to the motherboard, and that's what we'll cover here.

Integrated Drive Electronics/Parallel ATA

At one time, *integrated drive electronics (IDE)* drives were the most common type of hard drive found in computers. Though often thought of in relation to hard drives, IDE was much more than a hard drive interface; it was also a popular interface for many other drive types, including optical drives and tape drives. Today, we call it IDE Parallel ATA (PATA) and consider it to be a legacy technology. Figure 1.15 shows two PATA interfaces; you can see that one pin in the center is missing (as a key) to ensure that the cable gets attached properly. The industry now favors Serial ATA instead.

FIGURE 1.15   Two PATA hard drive connectors

Serial ATA

Serial ATA (SATA) began as an enhancement to the original ATA specifications, also known as *IDE* and, today, *PATA*. Technology is proving that the orderly progression of data in a single-file path is superior to placing multiple bits of data in parallel and trying to synchronize their transmission to the point that all of the bits arrive simultaneously. In other words, if you can build faster transceivers, serial transmissions are simpler to adapt to the faster rates than are parallel transmissions.

The first version of SATA, known as SATA 1.5 Gbps (and also by the less-preferred terms SATA I and SATA 150), used an 8b/10b-encoding scheme that requires 2 non-data overhead bits for every 8 data bits. The result is a loss of 20 percent of the rated bandwidth. The silver lining, however, is that the math becomes quite easy. Normally, you have to divide by 8 to convert bits to bytes. With 8b/10b encoding, you divide by 10. Therefore, the 150 MBps throughput for which this version of SATA was nicknamed is easily derived as 1/10 of the 1.5 Gbps transfer rate. The original SATA specification also provided for hot swapping at the discretion of the motherboard and drive manufacturers.

Similar math works for SATA 3 Gbps, tagged as SATA II and SATA 300, and SATA 6 Gbps, which you might hear called SATA III or SATA 600. Note that each subsequent version doubles the throughput of the previous version. Figure 1.16 shows four SATA headers on a motherboard that will receive the data cable. Note that identifiers silkscreened onto motherboards often enumerate such headers. The resulting numbers are not related to the SATA version that the header supports. Instead, such numbers serve to differentiate headers from one another and to map to firmware identifiers, often visible within the BIOS configuration utility.

Another version of SATA that you will see is *external SATA (eSATA)*. As you might expect based upon the name, this technology was developed for devices that reside outside of the case, not inside it. Many motherboards have an eSATA connector built in. If not, you can buy an expansion card that has eSATA ports and plugs into internal SATA connectors. Figure 1.17 shows an example of how the two ports are different. Finally, SATA and eSATA standards are compatible. In other words, SATA 6 Gbps equals eSATA 6 Gbps.

FIGURE 1.16   Four SATA headers

FIGURE 1.17   SATA (left) and eSATA (right) cables and ports

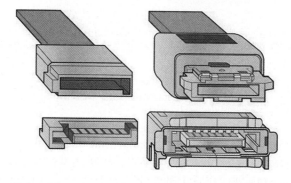

SATA and eSATA ports do not provide power, like USB does. Therefore, when connecting SATA and eSATA drives, a separate power connection is required in addition to the data cable.

M.2

The most recent development in expansion connections is *M.2* (pronounced "M dot 2"). So far it's primarily used for hard drives, but other types of devices, such as Wi-Fi, Bluetooth, Global Positioning System (GPS), and near-field communication (NFC) adapters are built for M.2 as well. We will cover M.2 in more depth in Chapter 2, thanks to how important it is to storage solutions.

It's important to call out that M.2 is a form factor, not a bus standard. The form factor supports existing SATA, USB, and PCIe buses. This means that if you hook up a SATA device to an M.2 slot (with the appropriate connector), the device speed will be regulated by SATA standards. Figure 1.18 shows two M.2 connectors on a motherboard.

FIGURE 1.18   Two M.2 slots

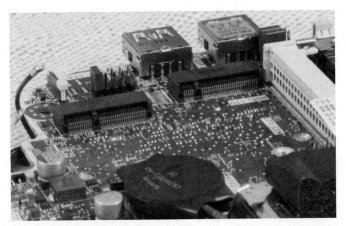

Photo credit: Andrew Cunningham/Ars Technica

 M.2 is closely associated with hard drives, and the M.2 form factor is also in CompTIA A+ exam objective 3.3, "Given a scenario, select and install storage devices." Because of that, we will go into more depth about M.2 and hard drive data transfer speeds in Chapter 2 when we discuss solid-state drives (SSDs).

Motherboard Headers

From the time of the very first personal computer, there has been a minimum expectation as to the buttons and LEDs that should be easily accessible to the user. At first, they generally appeared on the front of the case. In today's cases, buttons and LEDs have been added and placed on the top of the case or on a beveled edge between the top and the front. They have also been left on the front or have been used in a combination of these locations. These buttons and lights, as well as other external connectors, plug into the motherboard through a series of pins known as *headers*. Examples of items that are connected using a header include:

- Power button
- Power light
- Reset button
- Drive activity lights
- Audio jacks
- USB ports

Headers for different connections are often spread throughout different locations on the motherboard—finding the right one can sometimes be a frustrating treasure hunt. Other headers are grouped together. For example, most of the headers for the items on the front or top panel of the case are often co-located. The purpose for the header will be printed on the motherboard, and while that may tell you what should connect there, it often lacks detail in how it should be connected. The motherboard manufacturer's website is a good place to go if you need a detailed diagram or instructions. Figure 1.19 shows several headers on a motherboard. On the left is a USB header, then a system fan header in the center, and a block of front panel headers on the right, including the hard drive light, reset button, chassis intrusion detector, and power light.

FIGURE 1.19 Motherboard headers

Power Button and Light

Users expect a *power button* to use to turn the computer on. (These were on the side or back of very early PCs.) The soft power feature available through the front power button, which is no more than a relay, allows access to multiple effects through the contact on the motherboard, based on how long the button is pressed. These effects can be changed through the BIOS or operating system. Users also expect a *power light*, often a green LED, to assure them that the button did its job.

Reset Button

The *reset button* appeared as a way to reboot the computer from a cold startup point without removing power from the components. Keeping the machine powered tends to prolong the life of the electronics affected by power cycling. Pressing the reset button also gets around software lockups because the connection to the motherboard allows the system to restart from the hardware level. One disadvantage to power cycling is that certain circuits, such as memory chips, might need time to drain their charge for the reboot to be completely successful. This is why there is always a way to turn the computer off as well.

Drive Activity Light

In the early days of personal computing, the hard disk drive's LED had to be driven by the drive itself. Before long, the motherboard was equipped with drive headers, so adding pins to drive the *drive activity light* was no issue. These days, all motherboards supply this connectivity. The benefit of having one LED for all internal drives is that all the drives are represented on the front panel when only one LED is provided. The disadvantage might be that you cannot tell which drive is currently active. This tends to be a minor concern because you often know which drive you've accessed. If you haven't intentionally accessed any drive, it's likely the drive that holds the operating system or virtual-memory swap file is being accessed by the system itself. In contrast, external drives with removable media, such as optical drives, supply their own activity light on their faceplate.

Audio Jacks

Early generations of optical drives had to have a special cable attached to the rear of the drive, which was then attached to the sound card if audio CDs were to be heard through the speakers attached to the sound card. Sound emanating from a CD-ROM running an application, such as a game, did not have to take the same route and could travel through the same path from the drive as general data. The first enhancement to this arrangement came in the form of a front 3.5 mm jack on the drive's faceplate that was intended for headphones but could also have speakers connected to it. The audio that normally ran across the special cable was rerouted to the front jack when something was plugged into it.

Many of today's motherboards have 10-position pin headers designed to connect to standardized front-panel audio modules. Some of these modules have legacy AC'97 analog ports on them, whereas others have high-definition (HD) audio connections. Motherboards that accommodate both have a BIOS setting that enables you to choose which header you want to activate, with the HD setting most often being the default.

USB Ports

So many temporarily attached devices feature USB connectivity, such as USB keys (flash drives) and cameras, that front-panel connectivity is a must. Finding your way to the back of the system unit for a brief connection is hardly worth the effort in some cases. For many years, motherboards have supplied one or more 10-position headers for internal connectivity of front-panel USB ports. Because this header size is popular for many connectors, only 9 positions tend to have pins protruding, while the 10th position acts as a key, showing up in different spots for each connector type to discourage the connection of the wrong cable. Figure 1.20 shows USB headers on a motherboard. The labels "USB56" and "USB78" indicate that one block serves ports 5 and 6, while the other serves ports 7 and 8, all of which are arbitrary, based on the manufacturer's numbering convention. In each, the upper left pin is "missing," which is the key.

FIGURE 1.20   Two motherboard USB headers

BIOS/UEFI and the POST Routine

Firmware is the name given to any software that is encoded in hardware, usually a read-only memory (ROM) chip, and it can be run without extra instructions from the operating system. Most computers, large printers, and devices with no operating system use firmware in some sense. The best example of firmware is a computer's *Basic Input/Output System (BIOS)*, which is burned into a chip. Also, some expansion cards, such as SCSI cards and graphics adapters, use their own firmware utilities for setting up peripherals.

The BIOS chip, also referred to as the ROM BIOS chip, is one of the most important chips on the motherboard. This special memory chip contains the BIOS system software that boots the system and allows the operating system to interact with certain hardware in the computer in lieu of requiring a more complex device driver to do so. The BIOS chip is easily identified: If you have a brand-name computer, this chip might have on it the name of the manufacturer and usually the word *BIOS*. For clones, the chip usually has a sticker or printing on it from one of the major BIOS manufacturers (AMI, Phoenix, Award, Winbond, and others). On later motherboards, the BIOS might be difficult to identify or it might even be integrated into the Southbridge, but the functionality remains regardless of how it's implemented.

The successor to the BIOS is the *Unified Extensible Firmware Interface (UEFI)*. The extensible features of the UEFI allow for the support of a vast array of systems and platforms by allowing the UEFI access to system resources for storage of additional modules that can be added at any time. In the following section, you'll see how a security feature known as Secure Boot would not be possible with the classic BIOS. It is the extensibility of the UEFI that makes such technology feasible.

Figure 1.21 gives you an idea of what a modern BIOS/UEFI chip might look like on a motherboard. Despite the 1998 copyright on the label, which refers only to the oldest code present on the chip, this particular chip can be found on motherboards produced as late as 2009. Notice also the Reset CMOS jumper at the lower left and its configuration silkscreen at the upper left. You might use this jumper to clear the CMOS memory, discussed shortly, when an unknown password, for example, is keeping you out of the BIOS/UEFI configuration utility. The jumper in the photo is in the clear position, not the normal operating position. System bootup is typically not possible in this state.

FIGURE 1.21   A BIOS chip on a motherboard

At a basic level, the BIOS/UEFI controls system boot options such as the sequence of drives from which it will look for operating system boot files. The boot sequence menu from a BIOS/UEFI is shown in Figure 1.22. Other interface configuration options will be available too, such as enabling or disabling integrated ports or an integrated video card. A popular option on corporate computers is to disable the USB ports, which can increase security and decrease the risk of contracting a virus.

FIGURE 1.22   BIOS boot sequence

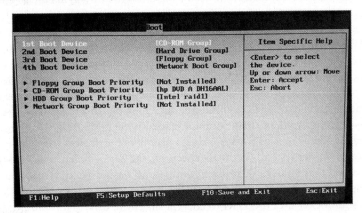

Most BIOS/UEFI setup utilities have more to offer than a simple interface for making selections and saving the results. For example, these utilities often offer diagnostic routines that you can use to have the BIOS/UEFI analyze the state and quality of the same components that it inspects during bootup, but at a much deeper level.

Consider the scenario where a computer is making noise and overheating. You can use the BIOS/UEFI configuration utility to access built-in diagnostics to check the rotational speed of the motherboard fans. If the fans are running slower than expected, the noise could be related to the bearings of one or more fans, causing them to lose speed and, thus, cooling capacity.

There is often also a page within the utility that gives you access to such bits of information as current live readings of the temperature of the CPU and the ambient temperature of the interior of the system unit. On such a page, you can set the temperature at which the BIOS/UEFI sounds a warning tone and the temperature at which the BIOS/UEFI shuts down the system to protect it. You can also monitor the instantaneous fan speeds, bus speeds, and voltage levels of the CPU and other vital landmarks to make sure that they are all within acceptable ranges. You might also be able to set a lower fan speed threshold at which the system warns you. In many cases, some of these levels can be altered to achieve such phenomena as overclocking, which is using the BIOS/UEFI to set the system clock higher than what the CPU is rated for, or undervolting, which is lowering the voltage of the CPU and RAM, which reduces power consumption and heat production.

BIOS/UEFI Security and Encryption

The BIOS/UEFI has always played a role in system security. Since the early days of the personal computer, the BIOS allowed the setting of two passwords—the user (or boot) password and the supervisor/administrator, or access, password. The boot password is required to leave the initial power-on screens and begin the process of booting an operating system. The administrator password is required before entering the BIOS/UEFI configuration utility. It is always a good idea to set the administrator password, but the boot password should not be set on public systems that need to boot on their own, in case of an unforeseen power cycle.

In more recent years, the role of the BIOS/UEFI in system security has grown substantially. BIOS/UEFI security has been extended to a point where the operating system is ready to take it over. The BIOS/UEFI was a perfect candidate to supervise security and integrity in a platform-independent way. Coupled with the *Trusted Platform Module (TPM)*, a dedicated security coprocessor, or cryptoprocessor, the BIOS can be configured to boot the system only after authenticating the boot device. This authentication confirms that the hardware being booted to has been tied to the system containing the BIOS/UEFI and TPM, a process known as *sealing*. Sealing the devices to the system also prohibits the devices from being used after removing them from the system. For further security, the keys created can be combined with a PIN or password that unlocks their use or with a USB flash drive that must be inserted before booting.

Microsoft's BitLocker uses the TPM to encrypt the entire drive. Normally, only user data can be encrypted, but BitLocker encrypts operating-system files, the Registry, the hibernation file, and so on, in addition to those files and folders that file-level encryption secures. If any changes have occurred to the Windows installation, the TPM does not release the keys required to decrypt and boot to the secured volume. TPM is configured in Windows under Start ➤ Settings ➤ Update & Security ➤ Windows Security ➤ Device security, as shown in Figure 1.23.

Most motherboards come with a TPM chip installed, but if they don't, it's not possible to add one. In those situations, you can enable the same functionality by using a *hardware security module (HSM)*. An HSM is a security device that can manage, create, and securely store encryption keys—it enables users to safely encrypt and decrypt data. An HSM can take a few different forms. The simplest is a USB or PCIe device that plugs into a system. It could be set up for file encryption and decryption, required for the computer to boot, or both. For large-scale solutions, HSM-enabled servers can provide crypto services to an entire network.

When a certain level of UEFI is used, the system firmware can also check digital signatures for each boot file it uses to confirm that it is the approved version and has not been tampered with. This technology is known as *Secure Boot*. An example of a BIOS/UEFI's boot security screen is shown in Figure 1.24. The boot files checked include option ROMs (defined in the following section), the boot loader, and other operating-system boot files. Only if the signatures are valid will the firmware load and execute the associated software.

FIGURE 1.23 Windows TPM configuration screen

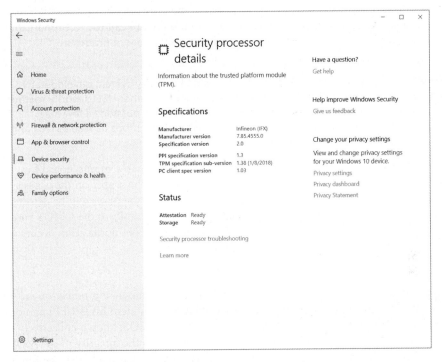

FIGURE 1.24 Secure boot in UEFI

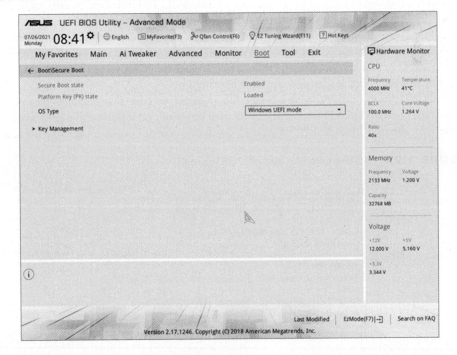

The problem can now arise that a particular operating system might not be supported by the database of known-good signatures stored in the firmware. In such a situation, the system manufacturer can supply an extension that the UEFI can use to support that operating system—a task not possible with traditional BIOS-based firmware.

 LoJack for Laptops is a UEFI-enabled security system developed by Absolute Software. It performs similarly to other UEFI security methods already discussed, such as drive encryption, but adds a few features. For example, LoJack can remotely track stolen laptops as well as lock and delete certain files.

Some BIOS firmware can monitor the status of a contact on the motherboard for intrusion detection. If the feature in the BIOS is enabled and the sensor on the chassis is connected to the contact on the motherboard, the removal of the cover will be detected and logged by the BIOS. This can occur even if the system is off, thanks to the CMOS battery. At the next bootup, the BIOS will notify you of the intrusion. No notification occurs over subsequent boots unless additional intrusion is detected.

POST

A major function of the BIOS/UEFI is to perform a process known as a *power-on self-test (POST)*. POST is a series of system checks performed by the system BIOS/UEFI and other high-end components, such as the SCSI BIOS and the video BIOS, known collectively as *option ROMs*. Among other things, the POST routine verifies the integrity of the BIOS/UEFI itself. It also verifies and confirms the size of primary memory. During POST, the BIOS also analyzes and catalogs other forms of hardware, such as buses and boot devices, as well as manages the passing of control to the specialized BIOS/UEFI routines mentioned earlier. The BIOS/UEFI is responsible for offering the user a key sequence to enter the configuration routine as POST is beginning. Finally, once POST has completed successfully, the BIOS/UEFI selects the boot device highest in the configured boot order and executes the master boot record (MBR) or similar construct on that device so that the MBR can call its associated operating system's boot loader and continue booting up.

The POST process can end with a beep code or displayed code that indicates the issue discovered. Each BIOS/UEFI publisher has its own series of codes that can be generated. Figure 1.25 shows a simplified POST display during the initial boot sequence of a computer.

FIGURE 1.25   An example of a system POST screen

```
AMIBIOS(C)2001 American Megatrends, Inc.
BIOS Date: 02/22/06 20:54:49  Ver: 08.00.02

Press DEL to run Setup
Checking NVRAM..

128MB OK
Auto-Detecting Pri Channel (0)...IDE Hard Disk
Auto-Detecting Pri Channel (1)...IDE Hard Disk
Auto-Detecting Sec Channel (0)...CDROM
Auto-Detecting Sec Channel (1)...
```

Flashing the System BIOS/UEFI

If ever you find that a hardware upgrade to your system is not recognized, even after the latest and correct drivers have been installed, perhaps a BIOS/UEFI upgrade, also known as *flashing the BIOS*, is in order. Only certain hardware benefits from a BIOS/UEFI upgrade, such as drives and a change of CPU or RAM types. Very often, this hardware is recognized immediately by the BIOS/UEFI and has no associated driver that you must install. So, if your system doesn't recognize the new device, and there's no driver to install, the BIOS/UEFI is a logical target.

Let's be clear about the fact that we are not talking about entering the BIOS/UEFI setup utility and making changes to settings and subsequently saving your changes before exiting and rebooting. What we are referring to here is a replacement of the burned-in code within the BIOS itself. You might even notice after the upgrade that the BIOS setup utility looks different or has different pages and entries than before.

On older systems and certain newer ones, a loss of power during the upgrade results in catastrophe. The system becomes inoperable until you replace the BIOS/UEFI chip, if possible, or the motherboard itself. Most new systems, however, have a fail-safe or two. This could be a portion of the BIOS/UEFI that does not get flashed and has just enough code to boot the system and access the upgrade image. It could be a passive section to which the upgrade is installed and switched to only if the upgrade is successful. Sometimes this is controlled on screen. At other times, there may be a mechanism, such as a jumper, involved in the recovery of the BIOS/UEFI after a power event occurs. The safest bet is to make sure that your laptop has plenty of battery power and is connected to AC power or your desktop is connected to an uninterruptible power supply (UPS).

In all cases, if you think you need a BIOS/UEFI upgrade, do not consult the BIOS/UEFI manufacturer. Instead, go to the motherboard or system manufacturer and check its website. The motherboard or system manufacturer vendors have personalized their BIOS/UEFI code after licensing it from the BIOS/UEFI publisher. The vendor will give you access to the latest code as well as the appropriate flashing utility for its implementation.

CMOS and CMOS Battery

Your PC has to keep certain settings when it's turned off and its power cord is unplugged:

- Date
- Time
- Hard drive/optical drive configuration
- Memory
- CPU settings, such as overclocking
- Integrated ports (settings as well as enable/disable)

- Boot sequence
- Power management
- Virtualization support
- Security (passwords, Trusted Platform Module settings, LoJack)

Consider a situation where you added a new graphics adapter to your desktop computer, but the built-in display port continues to remain active, prohibiting the new interface from working. The solution might be to alter your BIOS/UEFI configuration to disable the internal graphics adapter, so that the new one will take over. Similar reconfiguration of your BIOS/UEFI settings might be necessary when overclocking—or changing the system clock speed—is desired, or when you want to set BIOS/UEFI-based passwords or establish TPM-based whole-drive encryption, as with Microsoft's BitLocker. While not so much utilized today, the system date and time can be altered in the BIOS/UEFI configuration utility of your system; once, in the early days of personal computing, the date and time actually might have needed to be changed this way.

Your PC keeps these settings in a special memory chip called the *complementary metal oxide semiconductor (CMOS)* memory chip. Actually, CMOS (usually pronounced *see-moss*) is a manufacturing technology for integrated circuits. The first commonly used chip made from CMOS technology was a type of memory chip, the memory for the BIOS/UEFI. As a result, the term *CMOS* stuck and is the accepted name for this memory chip.

The BIOS/UEFI starts with its own default information and then reads information from the CMOS, such as which hard drive types are configured for this computer to use, which drive(s) it should search for boot sectors, and so on. Any overlapping information read from the CMOS overrides the default information from the BIOS/UEFI. A lack of corresponding information in the CMOS does not delete information that the BIOS knows natively. This process is a merge, not a write-over. CMOS memory is usually *not* upgradable in terms of its capacity and might be integrated into the BIOS/UEFI chip or the Southbridge.

Although there are technical differences, in the real world the terms BIOS/UEFI and CMOS (and BIOS/UEFI chip and CMOS chip) are used interchangeably. You will hear someone say, "Did you check the BIOS/UEFI?" or, "Did you check CMOS settings?" and they're referring to the same thing. Even though it's an oversimplification, most people feel comfortable with thinking about the BIOS/UEFI as the firmware that controls the boot process, whereas CMOS is the chip itself. It's incredibly unlikely that the A+ exam or any person is going to ask you to differentiate between the two, unless you get a job focusing specifically on those technologies.

To keep its settings, integrated circuit-based memory must have power constantly. When you shut off a computer, anything that is left in this type of memory is lost forever. The CMOS manufacturing technology produces chips with very low power requirements. As a result, today's electronic circuitry is more susceptible to damage from electrostatic discharge (ESD). Another ramification is that it doesn't take much of a power source to keep CMOS chips from losing their contents.

To prevent CMOS from losing its rather important information, motherboard manufacturers include a small battery called the *CMOS battery* to power the CMOS memory, shown in the bottom-left corner of Figure 1.26. The batteries come in different shapes and sizes, but they all perform the same function. Most CMOS batteries look like large watch batteries or small cylindrical batteries. Today's CMOS batteries are most often of a long-life, non-rechargeable lithium chemistry.

FIGURE 1.26   CMOS battery

 There's a lot to know about motherboards—they are complex devices that connect everything together inside the computer! For the A+ exam, remember that you will need to be familiar with the following concepts:

- Form factors, such as ATX and ITX
- Connector types including PCI, PCIe, power, SATA, eSATA, M.2, and headers
- Compatibility concerns such as AMD and Intel CPU sockets and different board types such as server, multisocket, desktop, and mobile
- BIOS/UEFI boot options, USB permissions, TPM, fan configurations, secure boot, boot passwords
- Security and encryption using TPM and HSM

Understanding Processors

Now that you've learned the basics of the motherboard, you need to learn about the most important component on the motherboard: the CPU. The role of the CPU, or central processing unit, is to control and direct all the activities of the computer using both external and internal buses. From a technical perspective, the job of the CPU is to process, or do math, on large strings of binary numbers—0s and 1s. It is a processor chip consisting of an array of *millions* of transistors. Intel and Advanced Micro Devices, Inc. (AMD) are the two largest PC-compatible CPU manufacturers. Their chips were featured in Table 1.1 during the discussion of the sockets into which they fit.

Today's AMD and Intel CPUs should be compatible with every PC-based operating system and application in the market. It's possible that you could run into an app that doesn't work quite right on an AMD chip, but those cases are exceedingly rare. From a compatibility standpoint, the most important thing to remember is that the motherboard and processor need to be made for each other. The rest of the hardware plugs into the motherboard and will be CPU brand agnostic.

> The term *chip* has grown to describe the entire package that a technician might install in a socket. However, the word originally denoted the silicon wafer that is generally hidden within the carrier that you actually see. The external pins that you see are structures that can withstand insertion into a socket and are carefully threaded from the wafer's minuscule contacts. Just imagine how fragile the structures must be that you *don't* see.

Older CPUs are generally square, with contacts arranged in a pin grid array (PGA). Prior to 1981, chips were found in a rectangle with two rows of 20 pins known as a *dual in-line package (DIP)*—see Figure 1.27. There are still integrated circuits that use the DIP form factor; however, the DIP form factor is no longer used for PC CPUs. Most modern CPUs use the LGA form factor. Figure 1.11, earlier in this chapter, shows an LGA socket next to a PGA socket. Additionally, the ATX motherboard in Figure 1.2 has a PGA socket, whereas the micro ATX motherboard has an LGA.

FIGURE 1.27   DIP and PGA

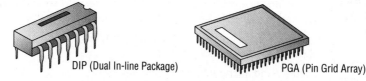

DIP (Dual In-line Package)   PGA (Pin Grid Array)

Intel and AMD both make extensive use of an inverted socket/processor combination of sorts. As mentioned earlier, the LGA packaging calls for the pins to be placed on the motherboard, while the mates for these pins are on the processor packaging. As with PGA, LGA is named for the landmarks on the processor, not the ones on the motherboard. As a result, the grid of metallic contact points, called *lands*, on the bottom of the CPU gives this format its name.

You can easily identify which component inside the computer is the CPU because it is a large square lying flat on the motherboard with a very large heat sink and fan (refer to Figure 1.10). The CPU is almost always located very close to the RAM to improve system speed, as shown in Figure 1.1, Figure 1.2, and Figure 1.8.

CPU Architecture

As noted in the previous section, the functional job of the processor is to do math on very large strings of 0s and 1s. How the CPU goes about doing that depends upon its architecture. For commonly used processors, there are two major categories—those based on Complex Instruction Set Computing (CISC) and those based on Reduced Instruction Set Computer (RISC).

x64/x86

CISC (pronounced like *disk*, but with a "c") and RISC (pronounced *risk*) are examples of an instruction set architecture (ISA). Essentially, it's the set of commands that the processor can execute. Both types of chips, when combined with software, can ultimately perform all the same tasks. They just go about it differently. When programmers develop code, they develop it for a CISC or a RISC platform.

As the CISC name implies, instructions sent to the computer are relatively complex (as compared to RISC), and as such they can do multiple mathematical tasks with one instruction, and each instruction can take several clock cycles to complete. We'll talk more about CPU speeds in the "CPU Characteristics" section later, but for now, know that if a CPU is advertised as having 3.8 GHz speed, that means it can complete roughly 3.8 billion cycles in one second. The core of a processor can only do one thing at a time—it just does them very, very quickly so it looks like it's multitasking.

CISC was the original ISA for microprocessors, and the most well-known example of CISC technology is the x64/x86 platform popularized by Intel. AMD processors are CISC chips as well. So where did the terms x64 and x86 come from? First, just a bit more theory.

There is a set of data lines between the CPU and the primary memory of the system—remember the *bus*? The most common bus today is 64 bits wide, although there are still some 32-bit buses kicking around out there. In older days, buses could theoretically be as narrow as 2 bits, and 8-bit and 16-bit buses were popular for CPUs for several years. The wider the bus, the more data that can be processed per unit of time, and hence, more work can be performed. Internal registers in the CPU might be only 32 bits wide, but with a 64-bit system bus, two separate pipelines can receive information simultaneously. For true 64-bit CPUs, which have 64-bit internal registers and can run x64 versions of Microsoft operating systems, the external system data bus will always be 64 bits wide or some larger multiple thereof.

In the last paragraph we snuck in the term *x64*, and by doing that we also defined it. It refers to processors that are designed to work with 64 bits of data at a time. To go along with it, the operating system must also be designed to work with x64 chips.

Contrast that with processors that can handle only 32 bits of information at once. Those are referred to as *x86* processors. You might look at that last sentence and be certain that we made a typo, but we didn't. For a long time when 32-bit processors were the fastest on the PC market, Intel was the dominant player. Their CPUs had names like 80386 (aka i386) and 80486 (i486) and were based on the older 16-bit 80286 and 8086. Since the i386 and i486 were the most popular standards, the term x86 sprung up to mean a 32-bit architecture. So even though it may seem counterintuitive due to the numbers, x64 is newer and faster than x86.

Advanced RISC Machine

Moving into the RISC architecture, the primary type of processor used today is known as an *Advanced RISC Machine (ARM)* CPU. Depending on who you talk to and which sources you prefer, there are conflicting stories on if that's actually the right acronym, as ARM is also known as an Acorn RISC Machine. Regardless of what it stands for, ARM is a competing technology to Intel and AMD x64-based CPUs.

Based on the RISC acronym, one might think that the reduced set of instructions the processor can perform makes it inferior somehow, but that's not the case. Tasks just need to get executed in different ways. To use a human example, let's say that we tell you to add the number 7 to itself seven times. One way to do that is to use one step of multiplication: 7 × 7 equals 49. But what if we said you can't use multiplication? You can still get to the answer by using addition. It will just take you seven steps instead of one. Same answer, different process. That's kind of how RISC compares to CISC.

RISC processors have some advantages over their CISC counterparts. They can be made smaller than CISC chips and they produce less heat, making them ideal for mobile devices. In fact, nearly all smartphones use RISC-based chips, such as Apple's A15 and Samsung's Exynos series processors. On the downside, RISC processors use more memory than CISC ones do because it takes more code to complete a task with a RISC chip.

Like x64/x86, ARM processors have evolved over time—64-bit implementations are the most current, and they are designated ARM64; 32-bit versions are known simply as ARM.

CPU Cores

Older processors were *single-core*, meaning that there was one set of instruction pathways through the processor. Therefore, they could process one set of tasks at a time. Designers then figured out how to speed up the computer by creating multiple cores within one processor package. Each core effectively operates as its own independent processor, provided that the operating system and applications are able to support *multicore* technology. (Nearly all do.)

Today, almost all desktop CPUs in the market are multicore. The number of cores you want may determine the processor to get. For example, the 10th-generation Intel Core i7 has eight cores whereas the i5 has six.

As an interesting aside, throughout the 1980s and 1990s, processor clock speeds grew at very fast rates. But they haven't gotten much faster over the last 10–15 years as designers ran into technical limitations for increasing speeds. Instead, computers have gotten faster because of the introduction of multicore processors, which is basically like having four (or six or eight) separate processors in one computer.

CPU Characteristics

When looking for a processor, you might have several decisions to make. Do you want an Intel or AMD CPU? Which model? How fast should it be? What features does it need to support? In this section, we will take a look at some characteristics of processor performance.

Speed

The speed of the processor is generally described in clock frequency. Older chips were rated in megahertz (MHz) and new chips in gigahertz (GHz). Since the dawn of the personal computer industry, motherboards have included oscillators, quartz crystals shaved down to a specific geometry so that engineers know exactly how they will react when a current is run through them. The phenomenon of a quartz crystal vibrating when exposed to a current is known as the *piezoelectric effect*. The crystal (XTL) known as the *system clock* keeps the time for the flow of data on the motherboard. How the front-side bus uses the clock leads to an *effective* clock rate known as the *FSB speed*. As discussed in the section "Types of Memory" later in this chapter, the FSB speed is computed differently for different types of RAM (DDR3, DDR4, DDR5, and so forth). From here, the CPU multiplies the FSB speed to produce its own internal clock rate, producing the third *speed* mentioned thus far.

As a result of the foregoing tricks of physics and mathematics, there can be a discrepancy between the front-side bus frequency and the internal frequency that the CPU uses to latch data and instructions through its pipelines. This disagreement between the numbers comes from the fact that the CPU is capable of splitting the clock signal it receives from the external oscillator that drives the front-side bus into multiple regular signals for its own internal use. In fact, you might be able to purchase a number of processors rated for different (internal) speeds that are all compatible with a single motherboard that has a front-side bus rated, for instance, at 1,333 MHz. Furthermore, you might be able to adjust the internal clock rate of the CPU that you purchased through settings in the BIOS.

The speed of a processor can also be tweaked by *overclocking*, or running the processor at a higher speed than the one at which the manufacturer rated it. Running at a higher speed requires more voltage and also generates more heat, which can shorten the life of the CPU. Manufacturers often discourage the practice (of course, they want you to just buy a faster and more expensive CPU), and it usually voids any warranty. However, some chips are sold today that specifically give you the ability to overclock them. Our official recommendation is to not do it unless the manufacturer says it's okay. If you're curious, plenty of information on how to overclock is available online.

Multithreading and Hyper-Threading

The string of instructions that a CPU runs is known as a *thread*. Old processors were capable of running only one thread at a time, whereas newer ones can run multiple threads at once. This is called *multithreading*.

Intel markets their multithreading technology as *Hyper-Threading Technology (HTT)*. HTT is a form of simultaneous multithreading (SMT). SMT takes advantage of a modern CPU's superscalar architecture. Superscalar processors can have multiple instructions operating on separate data in parallel.

HTT-capable processors appear to the operating system to be two processors. As a result, the operating system can schedule two processes at the same time, as in the case of symmetric multiprocessing (SMP), where two or more processors use the same system resources. In fact, the operating system must support SMP in order to take advantage of HTT. If the current process stalls because of missing data caused by, say, cache or branch prediction issues, the execution resources of the processor can be reallocated for a different process that is ready to go, reducing processor downtime.

HTT manifests itself in the Windows 10 Task Manager by, for example, showing graphs for twice as many CPUs as the system has cores. These virtual CPUs are listed as logical processors (see Figure 1.28).

FIGURE 1.28 Logical processors in Windows

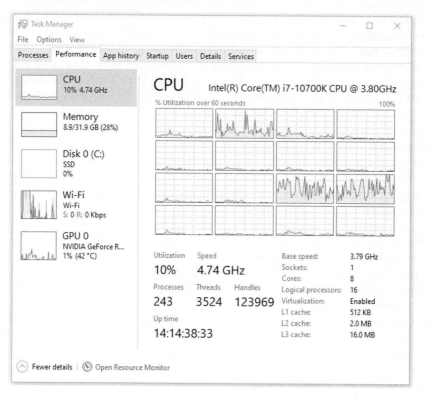

For an in-market example, compare the Intel i5 with the Intel i7. Similar models will have the same number of cores (say, four), but the i7 supports HTT, whereas the i5 does not. This gives the i7 a performance edge over its cousin. The i9 will be even one further step up from the i7. For everyday email and Internet use, the differences won't amount to much. But for someone who is using resource-intensive apps such as online gaming or virtual reality, the differences, especially between i5 and i9 processors, can be important.

Real World Scenario

Which CPU Do You Have?

The surest way to determine which CPU your computer is using is to open the case and view the numbers stamped on the CPU, a process that today requires removal of the active heat sink. However, you may be able to get an idea without opening the case and removing the heat sink and fan because many manufacturers place a very obvious sticker somewhere on the case indicating the processor type. Failing this, you can always go to the manufacturer's website and look up the information on the model of computer you have.

An easier way may be to look in Control Panel ➤ System, to get the About screen as shown in Figure 1.29. Even more detailed information can be found by running the System Information by clicking Start and entering **msinfo32.exe**. Click System Information when it appears as the Best Match. Of course, third-party utilities such as CPU-Z that we showed you earlier will work too. A final way to determine a computer's CPU is to save your work, exit any open programs, and restart the computer. Watch closely as the computer boots back up. You should see a notation during the POST routine that tells you what chip you are using.

FIGURE 1.29   System information in the About screen

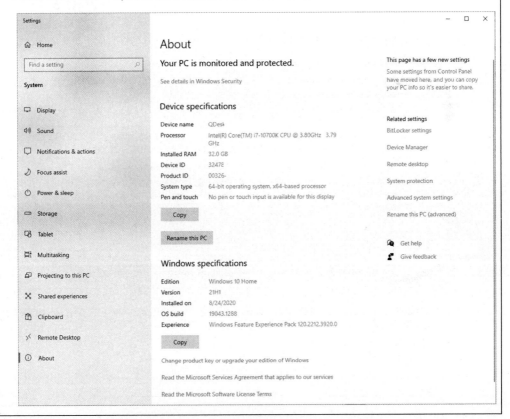

Virtualization Support

Many of today's CPUs support virtualization in hardware, which eases the burden on the system that software-based virtualization imposes. For more information on virtualization, see Chapter 8, "Virtualization and Cloud Computing." AMD calls its virtualization technology *AMD-V* (V for virtualization), whereas Intel calls theirs *Virtualization Technology (VT)*. Most processors made today support virtual technology, but not all. Keep in mind that the BIOS/UEFI and operating system must support it as well for virtualization to work. You may need to manually enable the virtualization support in the BIOS/UEFI before it can be used. If you have an Intel processor and would like to check its support of VT, visit the following site to download the Intel Processor Identification Utility:

```
https://downloadcenter.intel.com/download/7838
```

As shown in Figure 1.30, the CPU Technologies tab of this utility tells you if your CPU supports Intel VT.

FIGURE 1.30   Intel Processor Identification Utility

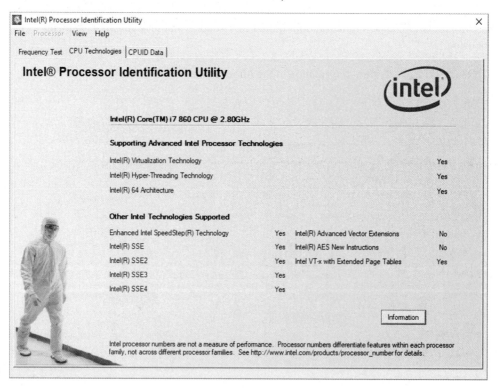

The CompTIA A+ objectives for CPUs aren't quite as long as they were for motherboards. For CPUs, be sure to understand the differences between x64/x86/ARM, single-core and multicore, multithreading, and virtualization support.

Understanding Memory

"More memory, more memory, I don't have enough memory!" Adding memory is one of the most popular, easy, and inexpensive ways to upgrade a computer. As the computer's CPU works, it stores data and instructions in the computer's memory. Contrary to what you might expect from an inexpensive solution, memory upgrades tend to afford the greatest performance increase as well, up to a point. Motherboards have memory limits; operating systems have memory limits; CPUs have memory limits.

To identify memory visually within a computer, look for several thin rows of small circuit boards sitting vertically, potentially packed tightly together near the processor. In situations where only one memory stick is installed, it will be that stick and a few empty slots that are tightly packed together. Figure 1.31 shows where memory is located in a system—in this case, all four banks are full.

FIGURE 1.31   Location of memory within a system

Important Memory Terms

There are a few technical terms and phrases that you need to understand with regard to memory and its function:

- Parity checking

- Error-correction code (ECC)

- Single- and double-sided memory

- Single-, dual-, triple-, and quad-channel memory

 ECC will sometimes be referred to as error correcting code as well. As with other acronyms in computing that might have multiple ways to spell it out, focus less on what it stands for and more on what it does.

These terms are discussed in detail in the following sections.

Parity Checking and Memory Banks

Parity checking is a rudimentary error-checking scheme that offers no error correction. Parity checking works most often on a byte, or 8 bits, of data. A ninth bit is added at the transmitting end and removed at the receiving end so that it does not affect the actual data transmitted. If the receiving end does not agree with the parity that is set in a particular byte, a parity error results. The four most common parity schemes affecting this extra bit are known as *even*, *odd*, *mark*, and *space*. Even and odd parity are used in systems that actually compute parity. Mark (a term for a digital pulse, or 1 bit) and space (a term for the lack of a pulse, or a 0 bit) parity are used in systems that do not compute parity but expect to see a fixed bit value stored in the parity location. Systems that do not support or reserve the location required for the parity bit are said to implement *non-parity memory*.

The most basic model for implementing memory in a computer system uses eight memory chips to form a set. Each memory chip holds millions or billions of bits of information, each in its own *cell*. For every byte in memory, one bit is stored in each of the eight chips. A ninth chip is added to the set to support the parity bit in systems that require it. One or more of these sets, implemented as individual chips or as chips mounted on a memory module, form a *memory bank*.

A bank of memory is required for the computer system to recognize electrically that the minimum number of memory components or the proper number of additional memory components has been installed. The width of the system data bus, the external bus of the processor, dictates how many memory chips or modules are required to satisfy a bank. For example, one 32-bit, 72-pin SIMM (single in-line memory module) satisfies a bank for an old 32-bit CPU, such as a i386 or i486 processor. Two such modules are required to satisfy a bank for a 64-bit processor—a Pentium, for instance. However, only a single 64-bit, 168-pin DIMM is required to satisfy the same Pentium processor. For those modules that have fewer than eight or nine chips mounted on them, more than 1 bit for every byte is being handled by some of the chips. For example, if you see three chips mounted, the two larger chips customarily handle 4 bits, a nibble, from each byte stored, and the third, smaller chip handles the single parity bit for each byte.

Even and odd parity schemes operate on each byte in the set of memory chips. In each case, the number of bits set to a value of 1 is counted up. If there is an even number of 1 bits in the byte (0, 2, 4, 6, or 8), even parity stores a 0 in the ninth bit, the parity bit; otherwise, it stores a 1 to even up the count. Odd parity does just the opposite, storing a 1 in the parity bit to make an even number of 1s odd and a 0 to keep an odd number of 1s odd. You can see that this is effective only for determining if there was a blatant error in the set of bits received, but there is no indication as to where the error is and how to fix it. Furthermore, the total 1-bit count is not important, only whether it's even or odd. Therefore, in either the even or odd scheme, if an even number of bits is altered in the same byte during transmission, the error goes undetected because flipping 2, 4, 6, or all 8 bits results in an even number of 1s remaining even and an odd number of 1s remaining odd.

Mark and space parity are used in systems that want to see 9 bits for every byte transmitted but don't compute the parity bit's value based on the bits in the byte. Mark parity always uses a 1 in the parity bit, and space parity always uses a 0. These schemes offer less error detection capability than the even and odd schemes because only changes in the parity bit can be detected. Again, parity checking is *not* error correction; it's error detection only, and not the best form of error detection at that. Nevertheless, an error can lock up the entire system and display a memory parity error. Enough of these errors and you need to replace the memory. Therefore, parity checking remains from the early days of computing as an effective indicator of large-scale memory and data-transmission failure, such as with serial interfaces attached to analog modems or networking console interfaces, but not so much for detecting random errors.

In the early days of personal computing, almost all memory was parity-based. As quality has increased over the years, parity checking in the RAM subsystem has become more uncommon. As noted earlier, if parity checking is not supported, there will generally be fewer chips per module, usually one less per column of RAM.

Error Checking and Correction

The next step in the evolution of memory error detection is known as *error-correction code (ECC)*. If memory supports ECC, check bits are generated and stored with the data. An algorithm is performed on the data and its check bits whenever the memory is accessed. If the result of the algorithm is all zeros, then the data is deemed valid and processing continues. ECC can detect single- and double-bit errors and actually correct single-bit errors. In other words, if a particular byte—group of 8 bits—contains errors in 2 of the 8 bits, ECC can recognize the error. If only 1 of the 8 bits is in error, ECC can correct the error.

Single- and Double-Sided Memory

Commonly speaking, the terms *single-sided memory* and *double-sided memory* refer to how some memory modules have chips on one side and others have chips on both sides. Double-sided memory is essentially treated by the system as two separate memory modules. Motherboards that support such memory have memory controllers that must switch between the two "sides" of the modules and, at any particular moment, can access only the side to which they have switched. Double-sided memory allows more memory to be inserted into a computer, using half the physical space of single-sided memory, which requires no switching by the memory controller.

Single-, Dual-, Triple-, and Quad-Channel Memory

Standard memory controllers manage access to memory in chunks of the same size as the system bus's data width. This is considered communicating over a single channel. Most modern processors have a 64-bit system data bus. This means that a standard memory controller can transfer exactly 64 bits of information at a time. Communicating over a single channel is a bottleneck in an environment where the CPU and memory can both operate faster than the conduit between them. Up to a point, every channel added in parallel between the CPU and RAM serves to ease this constriction.

Memory controllers that support dual-channel and greater memory implementation were developed in an effort to alleviate the bottleneck between the CPU and RAM. *Dual-channel memory* is the memory controller's coordination of two memory banks to work as a synchronized set during communication with the CPU, doubling the specified system bus width from the memory's perspective. *Triple-channel memory*, then, demands the coordination of three memory modules at a time. *Quad-channel memory* is the coordination of four memory modules at once. Collectively, they are known as *multichannel memory* implementations.

Because today's processors largely have 64-bit external data buses, and because one stick of memory satisfies this bus width, there is a 1:1 ratio between banks and modules. This means that implementing multichannel memory in today's most popular computer systems requires that two, three, or four memory modules be installed at a time. Note, however, that it's the motherboard, not the memory, that implements multichannel memory (more on this in a moment). *Single-channel memory*, in contrast, is the classic memory model that dictates only that a complete bank be satisfied whenever memory is initially installed or added. One bank supplies only half the width of the effective bus created by dual-channel support, for instance, which by definition pairs two banks at a time.

In almost all cases, multichannel implementations support single-channel installation, but poorer performance should be expected. Multichannel motherboards often include slots of different colors, usually one of each color per set of slots. To use only a single channel, you populate slots of the same color, skipping neighboring slots to do so. Filling neighboring slots in a dual-channel motherboard takes advantage of its dual-channel capability.

Because of the special tricks that are played with memory subsystems to improve overall system performance, care must be taken during the installation of disparate memory modules. In the worst case, the computer will cease to function when modules of different speeds, different capacities, or different numbers of sides are placed together in slots of the same channel. If all of these parameters are identical, there should be no problem with pairing modules. Nevertheless, problems could still occur when modules from two different manufacturers or certain unsupported manufacturers are installed, all other parameters being the same. Technical support or documentation from the manufacturer of your motherboard should be able to help with such issues.

Although it's not the make-up of the memory that leads to multichannel support but instead the technology on which the motherboard is based, some memory manufacturers still package and sell pairs and triplets of memory modules in an effort to give you peace of mind when you're buying memory for a system that implements multichannel memory architecture. Keep in mind, the motherboard memory slots have the distinctive color-coding, not the memory modules.

I Can't Fill All My Memory Slots

As a reminder, most motherboard manufacturers document the quantity and types of modules that their equipment supports. Consult your documentation when you have questions about supported memory. Most manufacturers require that slower memory be inserted in lower-numbered memory slots. This is because such a system adapts to the first module it sees, looking at the lower-numbered slots first. Counterintuitively, however, it might be required that you install modules of larger capacity rather than smaller modules in lower-numbered slots.

Additionally, memory technology continues to advance after each generation of motherboard chipsets is announced. Don't be surprised when you attempt to install a single module of the highest available capacity in your motherboard and the system doesn't recognize the module, either by itself or with others. That capacity of module might not have been in existence when the motherboard's chipset was released. Sometimes, flashing the BIOS is all that is required. Other times it just won't work. Consult the motherboard's documentation.

One common point of confusion, not related to capacity, when memory is installed is the lack of recognition of four modules when two or three modules work fine, for example. In such a case, let's say your motherboard's memory controller supports a total of four modules. Recall that a double-sided module acts like two separate modules. If you are using double-sided memory, your motherboard might limit you to two such modules comprising four sides (essentially four virtual modules), even though you have four slots on the board. If instead you start with three single-sided modules, when you attempt to install a double-sided module in the fourth slot, you are essentially asking the motherboard to accept five modules, which it cannot.

Finally, know that dual- and quad-channel memory support is common today, but triple-channel is less so. As with anything else, check the motherboard's documentation to see what it supports.

Types of Memory

Memory comes in many formats. Each one has a particular set of features and characteristics, making it best suited for a particular application. Some decisions about the application of the memory type are based on suitability; others are based on affordability to consumers or marketability to computer manufacturers. The following list gives you an idea of the vast array of memory types and subtypes:

- DRAM (dynamic random access memory)

  ADRAM (asynchronous DRAM)

  FPM DRAM (fast page mode DRAM)

  EDO DRAM (extended data out DRAM)

  BEDO DRAM (burst EDO DRAM)

  SDRAM (synchronous DRAM)

  SDR SDRAM (single data rate SDRAM)

  DDR SDRAM (double data rate SDRAM)

  DDR2 SDRAM (double data rate, version two, SDRAM)

  DDR3 SDRAM (double data rate, version three, SDRAM)

  DDR4 SDRAM (double data rate, version four, SDRAM)

  DDR5 SDRAM (double data rate, version five, SDRAM)

- SRAM (static random access memory)
- ROM (read-only memory)

Pay particular attention to all synchronous DRAM types as that's the most common type in use. Note that the type of memory does not dictate the packaging of the memory. Conversely, however, you might notice one particular memory packaging holding the same type of memory every time you come across it. Nevertheless, there is no requirement to this end. Let's detail the intricacies of some of these memory types.

DRAM

DRAM is dynamic random access memory. This is what most people are talking about when they mention RAM. When you expand the memory in a computer, you are adding DRAM chips. You use DRAM to expand the memory in the computer because it's a cheaper type of memory. Dynamic RAM chips are cheaper to manufacture than most other types because they are less complex. *Dynamic* refers to the memory chips' need for a constant update signal (also called a *refresh signal*) in order to keep the information that is written there. If this signal is not received every so often, the information will bleed off and cease to exist. Currently, the most popular implementations of DRAM are based on synchronous DRAM and include DDR3 and DDR4. Occasionally you will see some DDR2, and DDR5 is new so it hasn't been widely adopted yet. Before discussing these technologies, let's take a quick look at the legacy asynchronous memory types, none of which should appear on modern exams.

Asynchronous DRAM

Asynchronous DRAM (ADRAM) is characterized by its independence from the CPU's external clock. Asynchronous DRAM chips have codes on them that end in a numerical value that is related to (often 1/10 of the actual value of) the access time of the memory. Access time is essentially the difference between the time when the information is requested from memory and the time when the data is returned. Common access times attributed to asynchronous DRAM were in the 40- to 120-nanosecond (ns) vicinity. A lower access time is obviously better for overall performance.

Because ADRAM is not synchronized to the front-side bus, you would often have to insert wait states through the BIOS setup for a faster CPU to be able to use the same memory as a slower CPU. These wait states represented intervals in which the CPU had to mark time and do nothing while waiting for the memory subsystem to become ready again for subsequent access.

Common asynchronous DRAM technologies included fast page mode (FPM), extended data out (EDO), and burst EDO (BEDO). Feel free to investigate the details of these particular technologies, but a thorough discussion of these memory types is not necessary here. The A+ technician should be concerned with synchronous forms of RAM, which are the only types of memory being installed in mainstream computer systems today.

Synchronous DRAM

Synchronous DRAM (SDRAM) shares a common clock signal with the computer's system-bus clock, which provides the common signal that all local-bus components use for each step that they perform. This characteristic ties SDRAM to the speed of the FSB and hence the processor, eliminating the need to configure the CPU to wait for the memory to catch up.

Originally, *SDRAM* was the term used to refer to the only form of synchronous DRAM on the market. As the technology progressed, and more was being done with each clock signal on the FSB, various forms of SDRAM were developed. What was once called simply SDRAM needed a new name retroactively. Today, we use the term *single data rate SDRAM (SDR SDRAM)* to refer to this original type of SDRAM.

> **SDR SDRAM** *SDR SDRAM* is a legacy RAM technology, and it is presented here only to provide a basis for the upcoming discussion of DDR and other more advanced RAM. With SDR SDRAM, every time the system clock ticks, 1 bit of data can be transmitted per data pin, limiting the bit rate per pin of SDRAM to the corresponding numerical value of the clock's frequency. With today's processors interfacing with memory using a parallel data-bus width of 8 bytes (hence the term *64-bit processor*), a 100 MHz clock signal produces 800 MBps. That's mega *bytes* per second, not mega *bits*. Such memory modules are referred to as PC100, named for the true FSB clock rate upon which they rely. PC100 was preceded by PC66 and succeeded by PC133, which used a 133 MHz clock to produce 1,066 MBps of throughput.

Note that throughput in megabytes per second is easily computed as eight times the rating in the name. This trick works for the more advanced forms of SDRAM as well. The common thread is the 8-byte system data bus. Incidentally, you can double throughput results when implementing dual-channel memory.

DDR SDRAM *Double data rate (DDR) SDRAM* earns its name by doubling the transfer rate of ordinary SDRAM; it does so by double-pumping the data, which means transferring a bit per pin on both the rising and falling edges of the clock signal. This obtains twice the transfer rate at the same FSB clock frequency. It's the increasing clock frequency that generates heating issues with newer components, so keeping the clock the same is an advantage. The same 100 MHz clock gives a DDR SDRAM system the impression of a 200 MHz clock compared to an SDR SDRAM system. For marketing purposes, and to aid in the comparison of disparate products (DDR vs. SDR, for example), the industry has settled on the practice of using this effective clock rate as the speed of the FSB.

Module Throughput Related to FSB Speed

There is always an 8:1 module-to-chip (or module-to-FSB speed) numbering ratio because of the 8 bytes that are transferred at a time with 64-bit processors (*not* because of the ratio of 8 bits per byte). The formula in Figure 1.32 explains how this relationship works.

FIGURE 1.32   The 64-bit memory throughput formula

$$
\begin{array}{ll}
\text{FSB in MHz} & \text{(cycles/second)} \\
\underline{\text{X 8 bytes}} & \text{(bytes/cycle)} \\
\text{throughput} & \text{(bytes/second)}
\end{array}
$$

Because the actual system clock speed is rarely mentioned in marketing literature, on packaging, or on store shelves for DDR and higher, you can use this advertised FSB frequency in your computations for DDR throughput. For example, with a 100 MHz clock and two operations per cycle, motherboard makers will market their boards as having an FSB of 200 MHz. Multiplying this effective rate by 8 bytes transferred per cycle, the data rate is 1,600 MBps. Because DDR made throughput a bit trickier to compute, the industry began using this final throughput figure to name the memory modules instead of the actual frequency, which was used when naming SDR modules. This makes the result seem many times better (and much more marketable), while it's really only twice (or so) as good, or close to it.

In this example, the module is referred to as PC1600, based on a throughput of 1,600 MBps. The chips that go into making PC1600 modules are named DDR200 for the effective FSB frequency of 200 MHz. Stated differently, the industry uses DDR200 memory chips to manufacture PC1600 memory modules.

Let's make sure that you grasp the relationship between the speed of the FSB and the name for the related chips as well as the relationship between the name of the chips (or the speed of the FSB) and the name of the modules. Consider an FSB of 400 MHz, meaning an actual clock signal of 200 MHz, by the way—the FSB is double the actual clock for DDR, remember. It should be clear that this motherboard requires modules populated with DDR400 chips and that you'll find such modules marketed and sold as PC3200.

Let's try another. What do you need for a motherboard that features a 333 MHz FSB (actual clock is 166 MHz)? Well, just using the 8:1 rule mentioned earlier, you might be on the lookout for a PC2667 module. Note, however, that sometimes the numbers have to be played with a bit to come up with the industry's marketing terms. You'll have an easier time finding PC2700 modules that are designed specifically for a mother-board like yours, with an FSB of 333 MHz. The label isn't always technically accurate, but round numbers sell better, perhaps. The important concept here is that if you find PC2700 modules and PC2667 modules, there's absolutely no difference; they both have a 2667 MBps throughput rate. Go for the best deal; just make sure that the memory manufacturer is reputable.

DDR2 SDRAM   Think of the 2 in *DDR2* as yet another multiplier of 2 in the SDRAM technology, using a lower peak voltage to keep power consumption down (1.8V vs. the 2.5V of DDR). Still double-pumping, DDR2, like DDR, uses both sweeps of the clock signal for data transfer. Internally, DDR2 further splits each clock pulse in two, dou-bling the number of operations it can perform per FSB clock cycle. Through enhance-ments in the electrical interface and buffers, as well as through adding off-chip drivers, DDR2 nominally produces four times the throughput that SDR is capable of producing.

Continuing the DDR example, DDR2, using a 100 MHz actual clock, transfers data in four operations per cycle (effective 400 MHz FSB) and still 8 bytes per operation, for a total of 3,200 MBps. Just as with DDR, chips for DDR2 are named based on the per-ceived frequency. In this case, you would be using DDR2-400 chips. DDR2 carries on the effective FSB frequency method for naming modules but cannot simply call them PC3200 modules because those already exist in the DDR world. DDR2 calls these mod-ules PC2-3200. (Note the dash to keep the numeric components separate.)

As another example, it should make sense that PC2-5300 modules are populated with DDR2-667 chips. Recall that you might have to play with the numbers a bit. If you mul-tiply the well-known FSB speed of 667 MHz by 8 to figure out what modules you need, you might go searching for PC2-5333 modules. You might find someone advertising such modules, but most compatible modules will be labeled PC2-5300 for the same marketability mentioned earlier. They both support 5,333 MBps of throughput.

DDR3 SDRAM   The next generation of memory devices was designed to roughly double the performance of DDR2 products. Based on the functionality and characteristics of DDR2's proposed successor, most informed consumers and some members of the industry surely assumed the forthcoming name would be DDR4. This was not to be, however, and DDR3 was born. This naming convention proved that the 2 in DDR2 was not meant to be a multiplier but instead a revision mark of sorts. Well, if DDR2 was the second version of DDR, then DDR3 is the third. *DDR3* is a memory type, designed to be twice as fast as the DDR2 memory, that operates with the same system clock speed. Just as DDR2 was required to lower power consumption to make up for higher frequencies, DDR3 must do the same. In fact, the peak voltage for DDR3 is only 1.5V.

The most commonly found range of actual clock speeds for DDR3 tends to be from 133 MHz at the low end to less than 300 MHz. Because double-pumping continues with DDR3, and because four operations occur at each wave crest (eight operations per cycle), this frequency range translates to common FSB implementations from 1,066 MHz to more than 2,000 MHz in DDR3 systems. These memory devices are named following the conventions established earlier. Therefore, if you buy a motherboard with a 1,600 MHz FSB, you know immediately that you need a memory module populated with DDR3-1600 chips, because the chips are always named for the FSB speed. Using the 8:1 module-to-chip/FSB naming rule, the modules that you need would be called PC3-12800, supporting a 12,800 MBps throughput.

The earliest DDR3 chips, however, were based on a 100 MHz actual clock signal, so we can build on our earlier example, which was also based on an actual clock rate of 100 MHz. With eight operations per cycle, the FSB on DDR3 motherboards is rated at 800 MHz, quite a lot of efficiency while still not needing to change the original clock with which our examples began. Applying the 8:1 rule again, the resulting RAM modules for this motherboard are called PC3-6400 and support a throughput of 6,400 MBps, carrying chips called DDR3-800, again named for the FSB speed.

DDR4 SDRAM   Continuing the inevitable march of technology, *DDR4* is the next iteration of SDRAM on the market. As you would expect, the speed of DDR4 is roughly double that of DDR3. DDR3 provided data rates of approximately 800 Mbps to 2,133 Mbps, whereas DDR4 ranges between 1,600 Mbps and 3,200 Mbps. DDR also runs at a lower voltage—1.2 volts. Finally, DDR4 can support more memory per module, up to 512 GB per chip. Realistically, though, no one produces motherboards (or RAM) that support that quantity. The largest you will see are 64 GB sticks.

DDR5 SDRAM   After a long wait, *DDR5* finally hit the market at the end of 2021. Intel's Alder Lake platform was the first to support it; AMD chips could support DDR5 in early 2022 with the Zen 4 release.

DDR5 doubles the speed of DDR4 to 6.4 Gbps, as is expected for a new memory standard. Improved power efficiency means it runs at 1.1 volts. DDR5 is also the first memory module to be available in up to 128 GB modules.

SRAM

Static random access memory (SRAM) doesn't require a refresh signal like DRAM does. The chips are more complex and are thus more expensive. However, they are considerably faster. DRAM access times come in at 40 nanoseconds (ns) or more; SRAM has access times faster than 10ns. SRAM is classically used for cache memory.

ROM

ROM stands for read-only memory. It is called read-only because you could not write to the original form of this memory. Once information had been etched on a silicon chip and manufactured into the ROM package, the information couldn't be changed. Some form of ROM is normally used to store the computer's BIOS because this information normally does not change often.

The system ROM in the original IBM PC contained the power-on self-test (POST), BIOS, and cassette BASIC. Later, IBM computers and compatibles included everything but the cassette BASIC. The system ROM enables the computer to "pull itself up by its bootstraps," or *boot* (find and start the operating system).

Through the years, different forms of ROM were developed that could be altered, later ones more easily than earlier ones. The first generation was the *programmable ROM (PROM)*, which could be written to for the first time in the field using a special programming device, but then no more. You may liken this to the burning of a DVD-R.

The *erasable PROM (EPROM)* followed the PROM, and it could be erased using ultraviolet light and subsequently reprogrammed using the original programming device. These days, flash memory is a form of *electronically erasable PROM (EEPROM)*. Of course, it does not require UV light to erase its contents, but rather a slightly higher than normal electrical pulse.

Although the names of these memory devices are different, they all contain ROM. Therefore, regardless which of these technologies is used to manufacture a BIOS chip, it's never incorrect to say that the result is a ROM chip.

Memory Packaging

The memory slots on a motherboard are designed for particular module form factors or styles. RAM historically evolved from form factors no longer seen for such applications, such as dual in-line package (DIP), single in-line memory module (SIMM), and single in-line pin package (SIPP). The most popular form factors for primary memory modules today are as follows:

- DIMM (dual in-line memory module)
- SODIMM (small outline dual in-line memory module)

Desktop computers will use DIMMs. Laptops and smaller devices require SODIMMs or smaller memory packaging. So, in addition to coordinating the speed of the components, their form factor is an issue that must be addressed.

DIMM

One type of memory package is known as a DIMM, which stands for dual in-line memory module. DIMMs are 64-bit memory modules that are used as a package for the SDRAM family: SDR, DDR, DDR2, DDR3, DDR4, and DDR5. The term *dual* refers to the fact that, unlike their SIMM predecessors, DIMMs differentiate the functionality of the pins on one side of the module from the corresponding pins on the other side. With 84 pins per side, this makes 168 independent pins on each standard SDR module, as shown with its two keying notches as well as the last pin labeled 84 on the right side in Figure 1.33. SDR SDRAM modules are no longer part of the CompTIA A+ objectives, and they are mentioned here as a foundation only.

FIGURE 1.33   An SDR dual in-line memory module (DIMM)

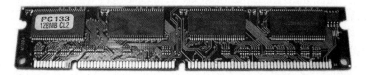

The DIMM used for DDR memory has a total of 184 pins and a single keying notch, whereas the DIMM used for DDR2 has a total of 240 pins, one keying notch, and possibly an aluminum cover for both sides, called a *heat spreader* and designed like a heat sink to dissipate heat away from the memory chips and prevent overheating. The DDR3 DIMM is similar to that of DDR2. It has 240 pins and a single keying notch, but the notch is in a different location to avoid cross-insertion. Not only is the DDR3 DIMM physically incompatible with DDR2 DIMM slots, it's also electrically incompatible. A DDR4 DIMM is the same length as a DDR3 DIMM, but is about 0.9mm taller and has 288 pins. The key is in a different spot, so you can't put DDR4 memory into a DDR2 or DDR3 slot. Finally, DDR5 has 288 pins as DDR4 does but is keyed differently so that DDR4 modules won't fit into DDR5 slots, and vice versa. Table 1.3 summarizes some key differences between the types of DDR we've introduced in this chapter.

TABLE 1.3 DDR characteristics

Characteristic	DDR	DDR2	DDR3	DDR4	DDR5
Pins	184	240	240	288	288
Max memory	1 GB	8 GB	32 GB	64 GB	128 GB
Channels	1	1	1	1	2
Voltage	2.5 v	1.8 v	1.5 v	1.2 v	1.1 v

Figure 1.34 shows, from top to bottom, DDR4, DDR3, and DDR2 DIMMs.

FIGURE 1.34 DDR4, DDR3, and DDR2 DIMMs

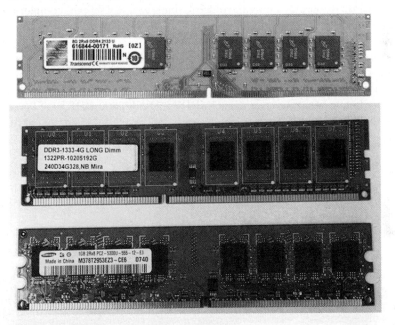

Inserting and Removing Memory Modules

The original single in-line memory modules had to be inserted into their slots at a 45° angle. The installer then had to apply slight pressure as the module was maneuvered upright at a 90° angle to the motherboard, where a locking mechanism would grip the module and prevent it from returning to its 45° position. This procedure created a pressure that reinforced the contact of the module with its slot. Releasing the clips on either end of the module unlocked it and allowed it to return to 45°, where it could be removed.

DIMM slots, by comparison, have no spring action. DIMMs are inserted straight into the slot with the locking tabs pulled away from the module. The locking tabs are at either end of the module, and they automatically snap into place, securing the module. Pulling the tabs away from the module releases the module from the slot, allowing it to be effortlessly removed.

SODIMM

Laptop computers and other computers that require much smaller components don't use standard RAM packages, such as DIMMs. Instead, they call for a much smaller memory form factor, such as a *small outline DIMM (SODIMM)*. SODIMMs are available in many physical implementations, including the older 32-bit (72- and 100-pin) configuration and newer 64-bit (144-pin SDR SDRAM, 200-pin DDR/DDR2, 204-pin DDR3, 260-pin DDR4, and 262-pin DDR5) configurations.

All 64-bit modules have a single keying notch. The 144-pin module's notch is slightly off center. Note that although the 200-pin SODIMMs for DDR and DDR2 have slightly different keying, it's not so different that you don't need to pay close attention to differentiate the two. They are not, however, interchangeable. DDR3, DDR4, and DDR5 are keyed differently from the others as well. Figure 1.34 shows a DDR3 SODIMM compared to DDR3 and DDR2 DIMMs.

FIGURE 1.35   DDR3 SODIMM vs. DDR3 and DDR2 DIMMs

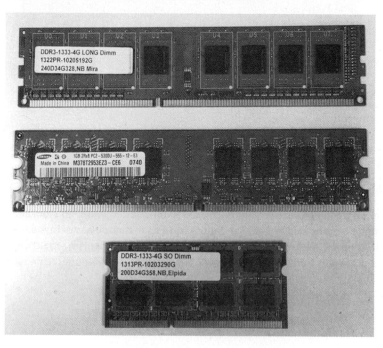

For the A+ exam, be sure to know the differences between SODIMMs and DIMMs, DDR3, DDR4, and DDR5, ECC RAM, and single-, dual-, triple-, and quad-channel RAM. Also understand what virtual RAM is.

Understanding Cooling Systems

It's a basic concept of physics: electronic components turn electricity into work and heat. The excess heat must be dissipated or it will shorten the life of the components. In some cases (like with the CPU), the component will produce so much heat that it can destroy itself in a matter of seconds if there is not some way to remove this extra heat.

Air-cooling methods are used to cool the internal components of most PCs. With air cooling, the movement of air removes the heat from the component. Sometimes, large blocks of metal called *heat sinks* are attached to a heat-producing component in order to dissipate the heat more rapidly.

Fans

When you turn on a computer, you will often hear lots of whirring. Contrary to popular opinion, the majority of the noise isn't coming from the hard disk (unless it's about to go bad). Most of this noise is coming from the various fans inside the computer. Fans provide airflow within the computer.

Most PCs have a combination of the following seven fans:

Front Intake Fan   This fan is used to bring fresh, cool air into the computer for cooling purposes.

Rear Exhaust Fan   This fan is used to take hot air out of the case.

Power Supply Exhaust Fan   This fan is usually found at the back of the power supply, and it is used to cool the power supply. In addition, this fan draws air from inside the case into vents in the power supply. This pulls hot air through the power supply so that it can be blown out of the case. The front intake fan assists with this airflow. The rear exhaust fan supplements the power supply fan to achieve the same result outside of the power supply.

CPU Fan   This fan is used to cool the processor. Typically, this fan is attached to a large heat sink, which is in turn attached directly to the processor.

Chipset Fan   Some motherboard manufacturers replaced the heat sink on their onboard chipset with a heat sink and fan combination as the chipset became more advanced. This fan aids in the cooling of the onboard chipset (especially useful when overclocking—setting the system clock frequency higher than the default).

Video Card Chipset Fan As video cards get more complex and have higher performance, more video cards have cooling fans directly attached. Despite their name, these fans don't attach to a chipset in the same sense as to a chipset on a motherboard. The chipset here is the set of chips mounted on the adapter, including the GPU and graphics memory. On many late-model graphics adapters, the equivalent of a second slot is dedicated to cooling the adapter. The cooling half of the adapter has vents in the back-plane bracket to exhaust the heated air.

Memory Module Fan The more capable memory becomes of keeping up with the CPU, the hotter the memory runs. As an extra measure of safety, regardless of the presence of heat spreaders on the modules, an optional fan setup for your memory might be in order. See the upcoming section "Memory Cooling" for more information.

Motherboard Fan Power Connectors

It's important to be aware of the two main types of fan connections found on today's moth-erboards. One of these connectors has only three connections, while the other has four. The fan connectors and motherboard headers are interchangeable between the two pinouts, but if a chassis fan has four conductors, it's a sign that it's calling for connectivity to an extra +5VDC (volts direct current) connection that the most common 3-pin header doesn't offer. A more rare 3-pin chassis-fan connector features a +12VDC power connection for heavier-duty fans and a rotation pin used as an input to the motherboard for sensing the speed of the fan.

4-pin CPU connections place the ground and power connections in pins 1 and 2, respec-tively, so that 2-pin connectors can be used to power older fans. The 4-pin header also offers a tachometer input signal from the fan on pin 3 so that the speed of the fan can be monitored by the BIOS and other utilities. Look for markings such as *CPU FAN IN* to identify this function. Pin 4 might be labeled *CPU FAN PWM* to denote the pulse-width modulation that can be used to send a signal to the fan to control its speed. This is the function lost when a 3-pin connector is placed in the correct position on a 4-pin header. Four-pin chassis-fan connectors can share the tachometer function but replace the speed control function with the extra 5V mentioned earlier.

Other power connections and types will be covered in Chapter 2, including the Molex con-nector, which can be used to power chassis and CPU fans using an adapter or the built-in connector on mostly older fans manufactured before the motherboard connectors were standardized. Figure 1.36 shows two 3-pin chassis-fan headers on a motherboard.

FIGURE 1.36   3-pin chassis-fan headers

Figure 1.37 shows a 4-pin CPU fan header with an approaching 3-pin connector from the fan. Note that the keying tab is lined up with the same three pins it's lined up with in the 3-pin connectors.

FIGURE 1.37   A 4-pin CPU fan header

This physical aspect and the similar pin functions are what make these connectors interchangeable, provided that the header's function matches the role of the fan being connected. Figure 1.38 shows the resulting unused pin on the 4-pin header. Again, controlling the fan's speed is not supported in this configuration.

FIGURE 1.38   Position of a 3-pin connector on a 4-pin header

Ideally, the airflow inside a computer should resemble what is shown in Figure 1.39, where the back of the chassis is shown on the left in the image.

FIGURE 1.39 System unit airflow

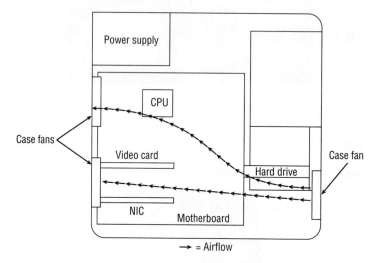

Note that you must pay attention to the orientation of the power supply's airflow. If the power supply fan is an exhaust fan, as assumed in this discussion, the front and rear fans will match their earlier descriptions: front, intake; rear, exhaust. If you run across a power supply that has an intake fan, the orientation of the supplemental chassis fans should be reversed as well. The rear chassis fan(s) should always be installed in the same orientation the power supply fan runs to avoid creating a small airflow circuit that circumvents the cross-flow of air throughout the case. The front chassis fan and the rear fans should always be installed in reverse orientation to avoid having them fight against each other and thereby reduce the internal airflow. Reversing supplemental chassis fans is usually no harder than removing four screws and flipping the fan. Sometimes, the fan might just snap out, flip, and then snap back in, depending on the way it is rigged up.

Memory Cooling

If you are going to start overclocking your computer, you will want to do everything in your power to cool all of its components, and that includes the memory.

There are two methods of cooling memory: passive and active. The passive memory cooling method just uses the ambient case airflow to cool the memory through the use of enhanced heat dissipation. For this, you can buy either heat sinks or, as mentioned earlier, special "for memory chips only" devices known as *heat spreaders*. Recall that these are special aluminum or copper housings that wrap around memory chips and conduct the heat away from them.

Active cooling, on the other hand, usually involves forcing some kind of cooling medium (air or water) around the RAM chips themselves or around their heat sinks. Most often, active cooling methods are just high-speed fans directing air right over a set of heat spreaders.

Hard Drive Cooling

You might be thinking, "Hey, my hard drive is doing work all the time. Is there anything I can do to cool it off?" There are both active and passive cooling devices for hard drives. Most common, however, is the active cooling bay. You install a hard drive in a special device that fits into a 5¼″ expansion bay. This device contains fans that draw in cool air over the hard drive, thus cooling it. Figure 1.40 shows an example of one of these active hard drive coolers. As you might suspect, you can also get heat sinks for hard drives.

FIGURE 1.40   An active hard disk cooler

Chipset Cooling

Every motherboard has a chip or chipset that controls how the computer operates. Like other chips in the computer, the chipset is normally cooled by the ambient air movement in the case. However, when you overclock a computer, the chipset may need to be cooled more because it is working harder than it normally would be. Therefore, it is often desirable to replace the onboard chipset cooler with a more efficient one. Refer back to Figure 1.4 for a look at a modern chipset cooling solution.

CPU Cooling

Probably the greatest challenge in cooling is the computer's CPU. It is the component that generates the most heat in a computer (aside from some pretty insane GPUs out there). As a matter of fact, if a modern processor isn't actively cooled all of the time, it will generate enough heat to burn itself up in seconds. That's why most motherboards have an internal CPU heat sensor and a CPU_FAN sensor. If no cooling fan is active, these devices will shut down the computer before damage occurs.

There are multiple CPU cooling methods, but the two most common are air cooling and liquid cooling.

Air Cooling

The parts inside most computers are cooled by air moving through the case. The CPU is no exception. However, because of the large amount of heat produced, the CPU must have (proportionately) the largest surface area exposed to the moving air in the case. Therefore, the heat sinks on the CPU are the largest of any inside the computer.

The CPU fan often blows air down through the body of the heat sink to force the heat into the ambient internal air where it can join the airflow circuit for removal from the case. However, in some cases, you might find that the heat sink extends up farther, using radiator-type fins, and the fan is placed at a right angle and to the side of the heat sink. This design moves the heat away from the heat sink immediately instead of pushing the air down through the heat sink. CPU fans can be purchased that have an adjustable rheostat to allow you to dial in as little airflow as you need, aiding in noise reduction but potentially leading to accidental overheating.

It should be noted that the highest-performing CPU coolers use copper plates in direct contact with the CPU. They also use high-speed and high-CFM cooling fans to dissipate the heat produced by the processor. CFM is short for cubic feet per minute, an airflow measurement of the volume of air that passes by a stationary object per minute. Figure 1.41 shows a newer, large heat sink with a fan in the center. In the picture it can be tough to gauge size—this unit is about six inches across! (And to be fair, this heat sink should have a second fan on one of the sides, but with the second fan the heatsink wouldn't fit into the author's case—the RAM was in the way.)

FIGURE 1.41 Large heat sink and fan

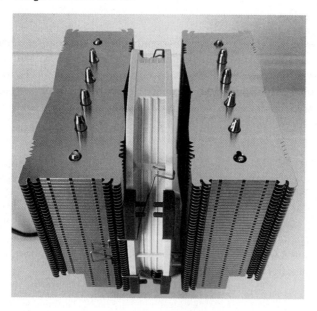

Most new CPU heat sinks use tubing to transfer heat away from the CPU. With any cooling system, the more surface area exposed to the cooling method, the better the cooling. Plus, the heat pipes can be used to transfer heat to a location away from the heat source before cooling. This is especially useful in cases where the form factor is small and with laptops, where open space is limited.

With advanced heat sinks and CPU cooling methods like this, it is important to improve the thermal transfer efficiency as much as possible. To that end, cooling engineers came up with a glue-like compound that helps to bridge the extremely small gaps between the CPU and the heat sink, which avoids superheated pockets of air that can lead to focal damage of the CPU. This product is known as *thermal transfer compound*, or simply *thermal compound* (alternatively, *thermal grease* or *thermal paste*), and it can be bought in small tubes. Single-use tubes are also available and alleviate the guesswork involved with how much you should apply. Watch out, though; this stuff makes quite a mess and doesn't want to come off your fingers very easily. An alternative to the paste is a small *thermal pad*, which provides heat conductivity between the processor and the heat sink.

Apply the compound by placing a bead in the center of the heat sink, not on the CPU, because some heat sinks don't cover the entire CPU package. That might sound like a problem, but some CPUs don't have heat-producing components all the way out to the edges. Some CPUs even have a raised area directly over the silicon die within the packaging, resulting in a smaller contact area between the components. You should apply less than you think you need because the pressure of attaching the heat sink to the CPU will spread the compound across the entire surface in a very thin layer. It's advisable to use a clean, lint-free applicator of your choosing to spread the compound around a bit as well, just to get the spreading started. You don't need to concern yourself with spreading it too thoroughly or too neatly because the pressure applied during attachment will equalize the compound quite well. During attachment, watch for oozing compound around the edges, clean it off immediately, and use less next time.

Improving and Maintaining CPU Cooling

In addition to using thermal compound, you can enhance the cooling efficiency of a CPU heat sink by lapping the heat sink, which smoothens the mating surface using a very fine sanding element, about 1000 grit in the finishing stage. Some vendors of the more expensive heat sinks will offer this service as an add-on.

If your CPU has been in service for an extended period of time, perhaps three years or more, it is a smart idea to remove the heat sink and old thermal compound and then apply fresh thermal compound and reattach the heat sink. Be careful, though; if your thermal paste has already turned into thermal "glue," you can wrench the processor right out of the socket, even with the release mechanism locked in place. Invariably, this damages the pins on the chip. Try running the computer for a couple of minutes to warm the paste and then try removing the heat sink again.

Counterintuitively perhaps, you can remove a sealed heat sink from the processor by gently rotating the heat sink to break the paste's seal. Again, this can be made easier with heat.

If the CPU has risen in the socket already, however, rotating the heat sink would be an extremely bad idea. Sometimes, after you realize that the CPU has risen a bit and that you need to release the mechanism holding it in to reseat it, you find that the release arm is not accessible with the heat sink in place. This is an unfortunate predicament that will present plenty of opportunity to learn.

If you've ever installed a brand-new heat sink onto a CPU, you've most likely used thermal compound or the thermal compound patch that was already applied to the heat sink for you. If your new heat sink has a patch of thermal compound pre-applied, don't add more. If you ever remove the heat sink, don't try to reuse the patch or any other form of thermal compound. Clean it all off and start fresh.

Liquid Cooling

Liquid cooling is a technology whereby a special water block is used to conduct heat away from the processor (as well as from the chipset). Water is circulated through this block to a radiator, where it is cooled.

The theory is that you could achieve better cooling performance through the use of liquid cooling. For the most part, this is true. However, with traditional cooling methods (which use air and water), the lowest temperature you can achieve is room temperature. Plus, with liquid cooling, the pump is submerged in the coolant (generally speaking), so as it works, it produces heat, which adds to the overall liquid temperature.

The main benefit to liquid cooling is silence. Only one fan is needed: the fan on the radiator to cool the water. So, a liquid-cooled system can run extremely quietly.

There are two major classifications of liquid cooling systems in use with PCs today: all-in-one (AIO) coolers and custom loop systems. AIO systems are relatively easy to install—they require about as much effort as a heat sink and fan—and comparably priced to similarly effective air systems. Figure 1.42 shows an example from Corsair, with the pump in front and the fans behind it, attached to the radiator.

FIGURE 1.42 AIO liquid cooling system

AIO systems come in three common sizes: 120 mm (with one fan, and the most common), 240 mm (two fans, for overclocked components), and 360 mm (three fans, for high-end multicore overclocked components). Options with RGB lighting are readily available if that's the style you want. Custom loop systems can quickly become complex and expensive, but many hardcore gamers swear by their performance. The components are essentially the same as those in an AIO system—there's a radiator, pump, fans, some tubes, and liquid. However, each part is purchased separately, and some assembly is required.

Water cooling systems often require more room inside the case than heat sinks, as well as special headers on the motherboard (or in the case) to support the fans. As always, check your documentation to be sure that your other hardware is compatible!

Cooling objectives you need to know for the exam include fans, heat sinks, thermal paste and pads, and liquid cooling.

Summary

In this chapter, we took a tour of the key internal system components of a PC. You learned primarily about the "big three," which are the motherboard, processor, and memory. Included in the motherboard discussion were form factors, connector types, such as PCIe, SATA, M.2, and headers, BIOS/UEFI settings, encryption, and the CMOS battery. CPU topics included features such as compatibility, architecture, multithreading, and virtualization. With RAM you learned about different types (SODIMMs, DDR2, DDR3, DDR4, and DDR5) and concepts such as single-, dual-, triple-, and quad-channel, error correction, and parity.

Finally, the chapter ended with cooling systems, which keep the components from damaging themselves with excess heat. This chapter laid the foundation for the rest of the book, including the next few chapters on additional hardware components.

Exam Essentials

Know three form factors of system boards.   Know the characteristics of and differences between ATX and ITX motherboards.

Know the components of a motherboard.   Be able to describe, identify, and replace (where applicable) motherboard components, such as chipsets, expansion slots, memory slots, processor sockets, BIOS/UEFI (firmware), and CMOS batteries.

Be able to identify and differentiate motherboard connector types.   Understand the differences between PCI, PCIe, SATA, eSATA, and M.2 connectors, as well as power connectors and headers.

Understand core concepts of motherboard compatibility.   Know that Intel and AMD chips use different sockets and therefore are incompatible with each other. Also know differences between server, multisocket, desktop, and laptop motherboards.

Understand CPU architecture.   Know the differences between x64, x86, and ARM processors, implications of single-core versus multicore CPUs, and multithreading and virtualization support.

Know what the BIOS/UEFI is responsible for.   The BIOS/UEFI controls boot options, fan speeds, USB permissions, and security options such as the boot password, TPM, HSM, and Secure Boot.

Understand the purposes and characteristics of memory.   Know about the characteristics that set the various types of memory apart from one another. This includes the actual types of memory, such as DRAM (which includes several varieties), SRAM, ROM, and CMOS, as well as memory packaging, such as DIMMs and SODIMMs. Also have a firm understanding of the different levels of cache memory as well as its purpose in general.

Know how to replace RAM, given a scenario.   RAM must match the motherboard in form factor and in speed. For example, some motherboards will only accept DDR4 or DDR5 memory. The speed should be compatible with the motherboard, as indicated in the documentation.

Understand the purposes and characteristics of cooling systems.   Know the different ways internal components can be cooled and how overheating can be prevented.

Review Questions

The answers to the chapter review questions can be found in Appendix A.

1. Which computer component contains all the circuitry necessary for other components or devices to communicate with one another?

   A. Motherboard

   B. CPU

   C. RAM

   D. Expansion bus

2. You are told by a technician over the phone that you need to bring replacement DDR4 SDRAM memory. What type of packaging is used for DDR4 SDRAM memory?

   A. 224-pin DIMM

   B. 240-pin DIMM

   C. 288-pin DIMM

   D. 296-pin DIMM

3. You need to replace memory in a desktop PC and go to purchase RAM. When you are at the store, you need to find the appropriate type of memory. What memory chips would you find on a stick of PC3-16000?

   A. DDR-2000

   B. DDR3-2000

   C. DDR3-1600

   D. PC3-2000

4. A client wants you to build a new PC for her, with a smaller case and lower power requirements. When selecting a motherboard, which form factor should you choose for a smaller size and lower power consumption?

   A. ATX

   B. AT

   C. DTX

   D. ITX

5. A motherboard failed on a desktop PC with an Intel Core i5-10600K processor. When you are looking for a replacement motherboard, which CPU socket does it need to have?

   A. LGA 1366

   B. LGA 1150

   C. LGA 1200

   D. LGA 1700

6. You have just replaced a processor in a computer and now need to add a cooling mechanism. What should you use to attach the cooling system to the processor?

   A. Heat sink

   B. Thermal paste

   C. Fan

   D. Superglue

7. A technician asks you how to get a computer's processor to run faster than it currently does. What are they trying to achieve?

   A. Hyper-Threading

   B. Overclocking

   C. Virtualization

   D. Multicore support

8. You are assembling a new computer and are looking at new cooling systems. Which of the following cooling systems requires the use of a pump?

   A. Liquid

   B. Thermal paste

   C. Heat sink

   D. Heat sink plus fan

9. Which of the following types of processors will likely generally be preferred for mobile devices?

   A. x64

   B. x86

   C. ARM

   D. LGA

10. You press the front power button on a computer and the system boots. Later, you press it briefly and the system hibernates. When you press it again, the system resumes. You press and hold the button and the system shuts down. What is this feature called?

    A. Programmable power

    B. Soft power

    C. Relay power

    D. Hot power

11. You are training new technicians to install RAM and pointing out differences between packages. Which of the following are the numbers of pins that can be found on DIMM modules used in desktop motherboards? (Choose two.)

    A. 180

    B. 184

    C. 200

D. 204

E. 232

F. 240

12. You are installing a new computer, and the user wants to use virtualization. Which hardware components need to support virtual technology for this to work properly? (Choose two.)

A. RAM

B. Motherboard

C. CPU

D. BIOS

13. You find out that a disgruntled ex-employee's computer has a boot password that must be entered before the operating system is ever loaded. There is also a password preventing your access to the BIOS utility. Which of the following motherboard components can most likely be used to return the computer to a state that will allow you to boot the system without knowing the password?

A. Cable header

B. Power reset connector

C. Toggle switch

D. Jumper

14. Your Core i5 fan has a 4-pin connector, but your motherboard only has a single 3-pin header with the CPU_FAN label. Which of the following will be the easiest solution to get the necessary cooling for your CPU?

A. Plug the 4-pin connector into the 3-pin header.

B. Buy a 4-pin to 3-pin adapter.

C. Leave the plug disconnected and use only the heat sink.

D. Add an extra chassis fan.

15. You are installing a new video card into a PCIe slot. What is the combined total throughput of a PCIe 2.0 x16 slot?

A. 500 MBps

B. 1 GBps

C. 16 GBps

D. 32 GBps

16. Which of the following allows you to perform the most complete restart of the computer without removing power?

A. Start ➤ Restart

B. Start ➤ Hibernate

C. Reset button

D. Power button

17. You have just found out that a new UEFI upgrade exists for your computer, and you obtain a copy on a flash drive to install it. Which of the following is most helpful when flashing the UEFI on a desktop computer system?

A. DVD-ROM

B. Uninterruptable power supply

C. Internet connection

D. Windows administrator password

18. The 32 GB of DDR4 memory has failed in a client's desktop computer. The client requests that you upgrade the system for better performance when replacing the RAM. Which of the following is the best option?

A. Install two new 32 GB DDR4 RAM modules.

B. Install two new 128 GB DDR4 RAM modules.

C. Install two new 32 GB DDR5 RAM modules.

D. Install two new 128 GB DDR5 RAM modules.

19. You are replacing an HP laptop's motherboard. Which type of motherboard should you use?

A. ATX

B. AT

C. One for the specific model

D. mini-ITX

20. You need to install a new video card into a desktop computer. What type of expansion slot is preferred today for high-performance graphics adapters?

A. AGP

B. PCIe

C. PCI

D. SATA

Performance-Based Question 1

You will encounter performance-based questions on the A+ exams. The questions on the exam require you to perform a specific task, and you will be graded on whether or not you were able to complete the task. The following requires you to think creatively in order to measure how well you understand this chapter's topics. You may or may not see similar questions on the actual A+ exams. To see how your answer compares to the authors', refer to Appendix B.

You have been asked to remove a dual in-line memory module and insert one with a larger capacity in its place. Describe the process for doing so.

Performance-Based Question 2

Identify the component each arrow points to in the following image of an ATX motherboard.

Chapter

2

Expansion Cards, Storage Devices, and Power Supplies

THE FOLLOWING COMPTIA A+ 220-1101 EXAM OBJECTIVES ARE COVERED IN THIS CHAPTER:

✓ **3.3 Given a scenario, select and install storage devices.**

- ▪ **Hard drives**
    - ▪ **Speeds**
        - ▪ **5,400rpm**
        - ▪ **7,200rpm**
        - ▪ **10,000rpm**
        - ▪ **15,000rpm**
    - ▪ **Form factor**
        - ▪ **2.5**
        - ▪ **3.5**
- ▪ **SSDs**
    - ▪ **Communications interfaces**
        - ▪ **Non-volatile Memory Express (NVMe)**
        - ▪ **SATA**
        - ▪ **Peripheral Component Interconnect Express (PCIe)**
    - ▪ **Form factors**
        - ▪ **M.2**
        - ▪ **mSATA**
- ▪ **Drive configurations**
    - ▪ **Redundant Array of Independent (or Inexpensive) Disks (RAID) 0, 1, 5, 10**

- Removable storage
    - Flash drives
    - Memory cards
    - Optical drives

✓ **3.4 Given a scenario, install and configure motherboards, central processing units (CPUs), and add-on cards.**

- Expansion cards
    - Sound card
    - Video card
    - Capture card
    - NIC

✓ **3.5 Given a scenario, install or replace the appropriate power supply.**

- Input 115V vs. 220V
- Output 3.3V vs. 5.5V vs. 12V
- 20-pin to 24-pin motherboard adapter
- Redundant power supply
- Modular power supply
- Wattage rating

As a PC technician, you need to know quite a bit about hardware. Given the importance and magnitude of this knowledge, the best way to approach learning about it is in sections. The first chapter introduced the topic via the primary core components, and this chapter follows up where it left off. First, we will look at adding functionality by plugging expansion cards into the motherboard. Then, we will focus on storage devices that hold data persistently—that is, they don't require power to maintain data like RAM does. Finally, we will end the chapter by looking at the simple-looking but potentially dangerous box that gives the components the energy they need—the power supply.

Installing and Configuring Expansion Cards

An *expansion card* (also known as an *adapter card*) is simply a circuit board that you install into a computer to increase the capabilities of that computer. Expansion cards come in varying formats for different uses, but the important thing to note is that no matter what function a card has, the card being installed must match the bus type of the motherboard into which it is being installed. For example, you can install a PCIe network card into a PCIe expansion slot only.

For today's integrated components (those built into the motherboard), you might not need an adapter to achieve the related services, but you will still need to install a driver— a software program that lets the operating system talk to the hardware—to make the integrated devices function with the operating system. Most motherboard manufacturers supply drivers with their motherboards, typically on a flash drive, that contain all the device drivers needed to get the built-in electronics recognized by the operating system. Execution of the driver's setup program generally results in all components working properly.

The following are the four most common categories of expansion cards installed today:

- Video
- Multimedia
- Network Interface
- Input/Output

Let's take a quick look at each of these card types, their functions, and what some of them look like.

Video

A *video card* (sometimes called a *graphics card*) is the expansion card that you put into a computer to allow the computer to present information on some kind of display, typically a monitor or a projector. A video card is also responsible for converting the data sent to it by the CPU into the pixels, addresses, and other items required for display. Sometimes, video cards can include dedicated chips to perform some of these functions, thus accelerating the speed of display.

You will encounter two classes of video cards: onboard cards and add-on cards. Onboard (or integrated) cards are built into the motherboard. As mentioned earlier, you need to install a device driver to get them to work properly, but those often come packaged with the motherboard itself. The upside to an integrated card is that it frees up an expansion slot. The manufacturer can either leave the slot open or design the motherboard and/or case to be smaller. One downside is that if the video card fails, you need a new motherboard, or you can install an add-on card. A second downside is that the onboard video cards aren't typically high-end. Onboard cards generally share system memory with the processor, which limits the quality of graphics one can produce. If the user wants great graphics from a powerful video card, then an add-on card is almost always the way to go. For example, serious gamers will always insist on a separate video card.

As for add-on cards, PCIe is the preferred expansion slot type. You might be able to find the rare, outdated motherboard that still offers a legacy AGP slot, and you might see some cheap PCI video cards, but they are uncommon. The technology on which PCIe was designed performs better for video than those on which AGP and PCI are based. Figure 2.1 shows an example of a PCIe x16 video card. The video card pictured is 10.6" (270 mm) long and takes up quite a bit of space inside the case. Most cards today have built-in fans like this one does to reduce the chance of overheating.

FIGURE 2.1   A PCIe video expansion card

There is an extensive range of video cards available today on the market. For everyday usage, cards with 1–2 GB of video memory are inexpensive and will do the trick. For gamers, high-end cards with a minimum of 8 GB GDDR5 are recommended. Of course, over the lifespan of this book, that number is sure to increase. (As of this writing, cards with 24 GB GDDR6 are available.) High-end video cards can easily cost several thousand dollars.

The main two standards for video cards are the NVIDIA GeForce series and the AMD Radeon (formerly ATI Radeon) line. Gamers will debate the pros and cons of each platform but know that you can get a range of performance, from good to phenomenal, from either one. When looking for a card, know how much memory is wanted or needed and how many and which types of video ports (such as HDMI or DisplayPort) are available. We will talk more about the pros and cons of several video connectors in Chapter 3, "Peripherals, Cables, and Connectors."

Multimedia

The most basic and prolific multimedia adapter is the sound card. Video capture cards also offer multimedia experiences but are less common than sound cards.

Sound Cards

Just as there are devices to convert computer signals into printouts and video information, there are devices to convert those signals into sound. These devices are known as *sound cards*. Although sound cards started out as pluggable adapters, this functionality is one of the most common integrated technologies found on motherboards today. A sound card typically has small, round ⅛ jacks on the back of it for connecting microphones, headphones, and speakers as well as other sound equipment. Older sound cards used a DA15 game port, which could be used for either joysticks or Musical Instrument Digital Interface (MIDI) controllers. Figure 2.2 shows an example of a sound card with a DA15 game port.

FIGURE 2.2   A classic sound card

In our section on video cards, we noted that integrated cards have inferior performance to add-on ones, and though the same holds true for sound cards, the difference isn't quite as drastic. Many of today's motherboards come equipped with 5.1 or 7.1 analog or digital audio and support other surround sound formats as well. For everyday users and even many gamers, integrated audio is fine.

For users who need extra juice, such as those who produce movies or videos or do other audio/video (A/V) editing, a specialized add-on sound card is a must. Very good quality sound cards can be found for under $100, compared with cheaper models around $20— there isn't a huge difference in price as there is with CPUs and video cards. Look for a card with a higher sampling rate (measured in kilohertz [kHz]) and higher signal-to-noise ratio (measured in decibels [dB]). The de facto standard for sound cards is the Sound Blaster brand. Although other brands exist, they will often tout "Sound Blaster compatibility" in their advertising to show that they are legit.

Integrated motherboard audio will typically have about a 90 kHz sampling rate and 85–90 dB signal-to-noise ratio (SNR or S/N). A good add-on sound card can provide sampling of 190 kHz or more and an SNR of 115 dB or higher. The difference is noticeable, especially in professional productions that may be played at loud volumes.

In addition to audio output, many A/V editors will require the ability to input custom music from an electronic musical keyboard or other device. A term you will hear in relation to this is the MIDI standard. As noted earlier, old sound cards would sometimes have a round 5-pin MIDI port, which was used to connect the musical keyboard or other instrument to the computer. Today, digital musical instrument connections are often made via USB. Nonetheless, you will still see the term *MIDI compatible* used with a lot of digital musical devices.

Video Capture Cards

A *video capture card* is a stand-alone add-on card often used to save a video stream to the computer for later manipulation or sharing. This can be video from an Internet site, or video from an external device such as a digital camera or smartphone. Video-sharing sites on the Internet make video capture cards quite popular with enterprises and Internet users alike. Video capture cards need and often come with software to aid in the processing of multimedia input. While video and sound cards are internal expansion devices, capture cards can be internal (PCIe) or external (USB).

Not all video capture cards record audio signals while processing video signals. If this feature is important to you or the end user, be sure to confirm that the card supports it. Also know that capture cards work with standard video resolutions, and specific cards might be limited on the resolutions they support. Double-check the specifications to make sure the card will meet the need, and also make sure to get reviews of the software used with the device.

Network Interface Card

A *network interface card (NIC)* is an expansion card that connects a computer to a network so that it can communicate with other computers on that network. It translates the data from the parallel data stream used inside the computer into the serial data stream that makes up the frames used on the network. Internal cards have a connector for the type of expansion bus on the motherboard (PCIe or PCI) and external cards typically use USB. In addition to physically installing the NIC, you need to install drivers for the NIC in order for the computer to use the adapter to access the network. Figure 2.3 shows a PCIe x1 Ethernet NIC with an RJ-45 port. (Network connectors are covered in more detail in Chapter 3.)

FIGURE 2.3   A network interface card

Many computers, especially mobile devices, have NIC circuitry integrated into their motherboards. Therefore, a computer with an integrated NIC wouldn't need to have a NIC expansion card installed unless it was faster or you were using the second NIC for load balancing (splitting the traffic between two cards to increase speed), security, or fault-tolerance (having a backup in case one fails) applications.

You will see two different types of network cards: wired and wireless. A wired card has an interface for the type of network it is connecting to (such as fiber connectors, Registered Jack 45 [RJ-45] for unshielded twisted pair [UTP], antenna for wireless, or BNC for legacy coax). Wireless cards of course don't need to use wires, so they won't necessarily have one of these ports. Some do, just for compatibility or desperate necessity.

Wireless NICs have the unique characteristic of requiring that you configure their connecting device before configuring the NIC. Wired NICs can generally create a link and begin operation just by being physically connected to a hub or switch. The wireless access point or ad hoc partner computer must also be configured before secure communication, at a minimum, can occur by using a wireless NIC. These terms are explained in greater detail in Chapter 7, "Wireless and SOHO Networks." Figure 2.4 shows a PCI wireless NIC for a desktop computer. On the back of it (the left side of the picture) is the wireless antenna.

FIGURE 2.4 A wireless NIC

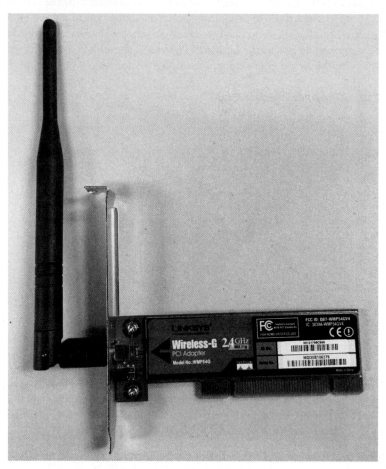

 **Real World Scenario**

The Way of the Dinosaur. . .

Before high-speed, wireless Internet was available pretty much everywhere you went, wannabe web users needed to connect to the Internet using the plain old telephone system (POTS). Doing so required a device called a modem.

Old telephone lines were analog, and of course computers are digital. The modem got its name because it *mo*dulated and *dem*odulated analog and digital signals to enable computers to connect to each other over analog telephone lines. Modems look a bit like network cards, but the connector is smaller. Instead of the 8-pin RJ-45 connector, phone lines use the 4-pin RJ-11 connector. For those of you interested in history, a modem is shown in Figure 2.5. Notice it has two connectors. It's probably too hard to see in Figure 2.5, but modems with two connectors have a small telephone icon etched into the faceplate. This tells you which connector to use to plug into the wall, and which one to plug a telephone into. If the modem was in use, the telephone could not be used. Only one connection at a time!

FIGURE 2.5   An internal analog modem

Input/Output

An *input/output card* is often used as a catchall phrase for any expansion card that enhances the system, allowing it to interface with devices that offer input to the system, output from the system, or both. The following are common examples of modern I/O cards:

- USB cards
- Storage cards, such as eSATA
- Thunderbolt cards

Figure 2.6 shows a 7-port PCIe x1 USB expansion card (left) next to an eSATA card (right). USB cards commonly come in 2-, 4-, and 7-port configurations, whereas eSATA cards often have one or two external ports. This eSATA card also has two internal SATA connectors on the top (left, in the picture) of the card. You'll also find cards that have multiple port types, such as eSATA and USB.

FIGURE 2.6   USB and eSATA expansion cards

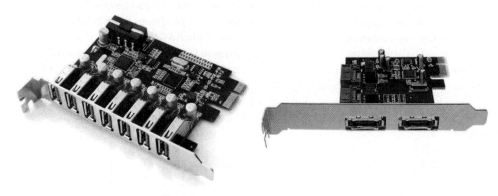

These cards are to be installed in a compatible slot on the motherboard. Their configuration is minimal, and it is usually completed through the operating system's Plug and Play (PnP) process. Nevertheless, check the BIOS settings after installation for new entries in the menu structure. It's the job of the BIOS to track all the hardware in the system and supply resources as needed. For example, a new Thunderbolt expansion card might allow you to configure whether attached Thunderbolt devices should be allowed to wake the system, how long a delay should be observed before waking the system, and various settings for how to use memory and other resources.

Adapter Configuration

Expansion cards might require configuration. However, most can be recognized automatically by a PnP operating system. In other words, resources are handed out automatically without jumper settings, or the installation of device drivers is handled or requested automatically. Supplying the drivers might be the only form of configuration required.

Some adapters, however, require more specific configuration steps during installation. For example:

- Two or more PCIe graphics adapters that support SLI (see Chapter 1, "Motherboards, Processors, and Memory,") must be bridged together with special hardware that comes with the adapters.

- Most sound cards tend to work with no specific configuration, but advanced features will need to be implemented through the operating system or through utilities that came with the adapter.

- The functions of video capture cards are sometimes not native to the operating system and therefore come with advanced utilities that must be learned and configured before the adapters will work as expected.

- Wireless network adapters often require the installation of a screw-on antenna, which should be postponed until after the card is fully inserted and physically secured in the system. Software configuration that allows these cards to communicate with a wireless access point can be challenging for the novice.

- Wired network adapters tend to be easier to configure than wireless ones. Nevertheless, even wired NICs might require manual configuration of certain protocol settings, such as IP addressing, duplex, and speed, in order for them to be productive.

In general, installation and configuration steps for expansion cards can be summarized as follows:

1. Ensure that the computer is powered off.

2. Install the adapter into an open slot.

3. Connect power, if needed.

   This most often applies to video cards.

4. After booting up the computer, install the driver.

   Again, Plug and Play may take care of this automatically for you.

5. If the card isn't recognized or providing the expected functionality, check the BIOS for configuration settings.

6. For other configuration options, use the utility provided by the manufacturer, if applicable.

In any event, consult the documentation provided with your adapter or the manufacturer's website for additional configuration requirements or options. The more specialized the adapter, the more likely it will come with specialty-configuration utilities.

For the exam, you will be expected to know how to install and configure add-on cards. The types of expansion cards in the exam objectives are sound, video, capture, and network interface.

Understanding Storage Devices

What good is a computer without a place to put everything? Storage media hold the files that the operating system needs to operate and the data that users need to save. What about saving to the cloud? The computers that make up the cloud, rather than the local computer, hold the storage media. The many different types of storage media differ in terms of their capacity (how much they can store), access time (how fast the computer can access the information), and the physical type of media used.

Hard Disk Drive Systems

Hard disk drive (HDD) systems (or *hard drives* for short) are used for permanent storage and quick access. Hard drives typically reside inside the computer, where they are semi-permanently mounted with no external access (although there are external and removable hard drives) and can hold more information than other forms of storage. Hard drives use a *magnetic storage* medium, and they are known as *conventional drives* to differentiate them from newer solid-state storage media.

The hard disk drive system contains the following three critical components:

Controller   This component controls the drive. The controller chip controls how the drive operates and how the data is encoded onto the platters. It controls how the data sends signals to the various motors in the drive and receives signals from the sensors inside the drive. Nearly all hard disk drive technologies incorporate the controller and drive into one assembly. Today, the most common and well known of these technologies is Serial Advanced Technology Attachment (SATA).

Hard Disk   This is the physical storage medium. Hard disk drive systems store information on small discs (from under 1 inch to 5 inches in diameter), also called platters, stacked together and placed in an enclosure.

Host Bus Adapter   The host bus adapter (HBA) is the translator, converting signals from the controller to signals that the computer can understand. Most motherboards today incorporate the host adapter into the motherboard's circuitry, offering headers for drive-cable connections. Legacy host adapters and certain modern adapters house the hard drive controller circuitry.

Figure 2.7 shows a hard disk drive and host adapter. The hard drive controller is integrated into the drive in this case, but it could reside on the host adapter in other hard drive technologies. This particular example shows a hard drive plugging into an expansion card. Today's drives almost always connect straight to the motherboard, again with the HBA being integrated with the drive itself.

FIGURE 2.7   A hard disk drive system

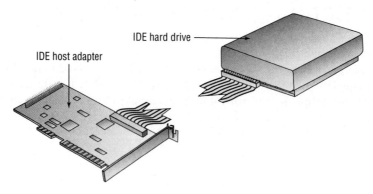

IDE hard drive

IDE host adapter

Hard drives, regardless of whether they are magnetic or solid-state, most often connect to the motherboard's SATA or Parallel Advanced Technology Attachment (PATA) interfaces. You learned about SATA and PATA in Chapter 1, but Figure 2.8 provides a reminder of what the interfaces look like; SATA is on the top.

The back of the hard drive will have data and power connectors. Figure 2.9 shows the data and power connectors for a PATA drive and a SATA drive.

FIGURE 2.8   Four SATA and two PATA ports

Today, IDE (PATA) hard drives are essentially obsolete. Most of that is due to the limitations in transfer speeds. Most PATA hard drives follow the ATA/100 standard, which has a maximum transfer speed of 100 MBps. There are faster ATA standards, such as ATA/133 and ATA/167, but drives using those standards are rare. SATA III (also known as SATA 6 Gb/s), on the other hand, has a maximum transfer speed of 600 MBps.

There's another hard drive connector type called SAS, or Serial Attached SCSI. (SCSI is pronounced "scuzzy" and stands for Small Computer System Interface—aren't acronyms within acronyms great?) SAS tends to be a bit faster than SATA, and it's used mostly in enterprise computing applications. You won't see many SAS ports on conventional desktop or laptop motherboards. SAS is not on the A+ exam objectives, but it is on the A+ acronym list.

FIGURE 2.9   PATA (top) and SATA (bottom) hard drive data and power connectors

Power   Data

Anatomy of a Hard Drive

A hard drive is constructed in a cleanroom to avoid the introduction of contaminants into the hermetically sealed drive casing. Once the casing is sealed, most manufacturers seal one or more of the screws with a sticker warning that removal of or damage to the seal will result in voiding the drive's warranty. Even some of the smallest contaminants can damage the precision components if allowed inside the hard drive's external shell. The following is a list of the terms used to describe these components in the following paragraphs:

- Platters
- Read/write heads
- Tracks
- Sectors
- Cylinders
- Clusters (allocation units)

Inside the sealed case of the hard drive lie one or more platters, where the actual data is stored by the read/write heads. The heads are mounted on a mechanism that moves them in tandem across both surfaces of all platters. Older drives used a stepper motor to position the heads at discrete points along the surface of the platters, which spin at thousands of revolutions per minute on a spindle mounted to a hub. Newer drives use voice coils for a more analog movement, resulting in reduced data loss because the circuitry can sense where the data is located through a servo scheme, even if the data shifts due to changes in physical disc geometry. Figure 2.10 shows the internal components of a conventional hard drive.

FIGURE 2.10   Anatomy of a hard drive

By Eric Gaba, Wikimedia Commons user Sting, CC BY-SA 3.0, `https://commons.wikimedia.org/w/index.php?curid=11278668`

Before a hard drive can store data, it must be prepared. Factory preparation for newer drives, or low-level formatting in the field for legacy drives, maps the inherent flaws of the platters so that the drive controllers know not to place data in these compromised locations. Additionally, this phase in drive preparation creates concentric rings, or *tracks*, which are drawn magnetically around the surface of the platters. Sectors are then delineated within each of the tracks. *Sectors* are the magnetic domains that represent the smallest units of storage on the disk's platters. This is illustrated in Figure 2.11. Magnetic-drive sectors commonly store only 512 bytes (½ KB) of data each.

FIGURE 2.11   Cylinders, tracks, and sectors

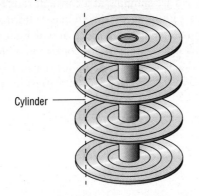
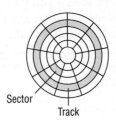

The capacity of a hard drive is a function of the number of sectors it contains. The controller for the hard drive knows exactly how the sectors are laid out within the disk assembly. It takes direction from the BIOS when writing information to and reading information from the drive. The BIOS, however, does not always understand the actual geometry of the drive. For example, the BIOS does not support more than 63 sectors per track. Nevertheless, almost all hard drives today have tracks that contain many more than 63 sectors per track. As a result, a translation must occur from where the BIOS believes it is directing information to be written to where the information is actually written by the controller. When the BIOS detects the geometry of the drive, it is because the controller reports dimensions that the BIOS can understand. The same sort of trickery occurs when the BIOS reports to the operating system a linear address space for the operating system to use when requesting that data be written to or read from the drive through the BIOS.

After initial drive preparation, the drive is formatted with a file system, by the operating system, and then it's ready to store data. Filesystems laid down on the tracks and their sectors routinely group a configurable number of sectors into equal or larger sets called *clusters* or *allocation units*. This concept exists because operating system designers have to settle on a finite number of addressable units of storage and a fixed number of bits to address them uniquely.

We will talk more about filesystems such as FAT32, NTFS, and others in Chapter 13, "Operating System Basics."

No two files are allowed to occupy the same sector, so the opportunity exists for a waste of space if small files occupy only part of a sector. Clusters exacerbate the problem by having a similar foible: the operating system does not allow any two files to occupy the same cluster. Thus, the larger the cluster size, the larger the potential waste. So although you can increase the cluster size (generally to as large as 64 KB, which corresponds to 128 sectors), you should keep in mind that unless you are storing a notable number of very large files, the waste will escalate astoundingly, perhaps negating or reversing your perceived storage-capacity increase.

HDD Speeds

As the electronics within the HBA and controller get faster, they are capable of requesting data at higher and higher rates. If the platters are spinning at a constant rate, however, the information can be accessed only as fast as a given fixed rate. To make information available to the electronics more quickly, manufacturers increase the speed at which the platters spin from one generation of drives to the next, with multiple speeds coexisting in the marketplace for an unpredictable period, at least until the demand dies down for one or more speeds.

The following spin rates have been used in the industry for the platters in conventional magnetic hard disk drives:

- 5,400 rpm
- 7,200 rpm
- 10,000 rpm

- 12,000 rpm
- 15,000 rpm

While it is true that a higher revolutions per minute (rpm) rating results in the ability to move data more quickly, there are many applications that do not benefit from increased disk-access speeds. As a result, you should choose only faster drives, which are also usually more expensive per byte of capacity, when you have an application for this type of performance, such as for housing the partition where the operating system resides or for very disk-intensive programs. For comparison, a 7,200 rpm SATA hard drive can sustain data read speeds of about 100 MBps, which is about the same as a PATA ATA/100 7,200 rpm drive. A 10,000 rpm (also known as 10k) SATA drive can top out around 200 MBps.

 All 15,000 rpm drives are SAS drives, not SATA or PATA drives.

Higher speeds also consume more energy and produce more heat. The lower speeds can be ideal in laptops, where heat production and battery usage can be issues with higher-speed drives. Even the fastest conventional hard drives are slower than solid-state drives are at transferring data.

HDD Form Factors

Physically, the most common hard drive *form factors* (sizes) are 3.5" and 2.5". Desktops traditionally use 3.5" drives, whereas the 2.5" drives are made for laptops—although most laptops today avoid using conventional HDDs. Converter kits are available to mount a 2.5" drive into a 3.5" desktop hard drive bay. Figure 2.12 shows the two drives together. As you can see, the 2.5" drive is significantly smaller in all three dimensions, but it does have the same connectors as its bigger cousin.

FIGURE 2.12   A 3.5" and 2.5" hard drive

Solid-State Drives

Unlike conventional hard drives, *solid-state drives (SSDs)* have no moving parts—they use the same solid-state memory technology found in the other forms of flash memory. You can think of them as big versions of the flash drives that are so common.

Because they have no moving parts, SSDs are capable of transferring data much more quickly than HDDs could ever dream of doing. Recall from the "HDD Speeds" section that a 10k SATA HDD tops out at about 200 MBps. Even the slowest SSDs will run circles around that. The true speed of an SSD will be determined, of course, by the drive itself, but also the interface to which it's attached.

And because there's no need for spinning platters and read/write heads, SSDs can be made much smaller than HDDs, making them better for laptops and portable devices. SSDs have several other advantages over their mechanical counterparts as well, including the following:

- Faster start-up and read times
- Less power consumption and heat produced
- Silent operation
- Generally more reliable because of a lack of moving parts
- Less susceptible to damage from physical shock and heat production
- Higher data density per square centimeter

The disadvantages of SSDs are as follows:

- The technology to build an SSD is more expensive per byte.
- All solid-state memory is limited to a finite number of write (including erase) operations. Lack of longevity could be an issue. As the technology matures, this is becoming less and less of a problem.

You will find that SSDs in the market generally have lower overall capacity than HDDs. For example, it's not uncommon to find HDDs over 8 TB in size, with 18 TB drives pacing the market. Conversely, the biggest commercially available SSD (as of this writing) is 8 TB. As for cost, HDDs run about 3 cents per GB and low-end SATA SSDs are about three times as expensive. Faster SSDs such as NVMe drives (which we'll get to in a minute) can be from four to ten times as expensive. Of course, prices are subject to (and it's guaranteed they will) change!

When used as a replacement for traditional HDDs, SSDs are expected to behave in a similar fashion, mainly by retaining contents across a power cycle. With SSD, you can also expect to maintain or exceed the speed of the HDD. SSDs can be made faster still by including a small amount of DRAM as a cache.

SSDs come in various shapes and sizes and have a few different interfaces and form factors. We will cover those in the upcoming "SSD Communication Interfaces" and "SSD Form Factors" sections.

Hybrid Drives

A cost-saving alternative to a standard SSD that can still provide a significant increase in performance over conventional HDDs is the *hybrid drive*. Hybrid drives can be implemented in two ways: a solid-state hybrid drive and a dual-drive storage solution. Both forms of hybrid drives can take advantage of solutions such as Intel's Smart Response Technology (SRT), which informs the drive system of the most used and highest-value data. The drive can then load a copy of such data into the SSD portion of the hybrid drive for faster read access.

It should be noted that systems on which data is accessed randomly do not benefit from hybrid drive technology. Any data that is accessed for the first time will also not be accessed from flash memory, and it will take as long to access it as if it were accessed from a traditional hard drive. Repeated use, however, will result in the monitoring software's flagging of the data for caching in the SSD.

Solid-State Hybrid Drive

The *solid-state hybrid drive (SSHD)* is a conventional HDD manufactured with a substantial amount of flash memory–like solid-state storage aboard. The SSHD is known to the operating system as a single drive, and individual access to the separate components is unavailable to the user.

Dual-Drive Solutions

Dual-drive storage solutions can also benefit from technologies such as Intel's SRT. However, because they are implemented as two separate drives (one conventional HDD and one SSD), each with its own separate file system and drive letter, the user can also manually choose the data to move to the SSD for faster read access. Users can choose to implement dual-drive systems with SSDs of the same size as the HDD, resulting in a fuller caching scenario.

SSD Communication Interfaces

It's been said that the advent of the SSD was a major advancement for the computer industry. Solid-state drives are basically made from the same circuitry that RAM is, and they are really, really fast. When they were first on the market, the limitation in the system was the SATA controller that most hard drives were plugged into. So as enterprising computer engineers are known to do, some started looking into ways to overcome this barrier. The result is that there have been more interfaces designed for storage devices, with much faster speeds.

The CompTIA A+ exam objectives list three technologies as SSD communications interfaces: SATA, PCIe, and NVMe. We will cover them now.

SATA

At this point, SATA is a technology you should be somewhat familiar with. We covered it in Chapter 1, and the interface is shown earlier in this chapter in Figure 2.8. SATA is a bit unique among the other subjects in this SSD section because it can support mechanical hard drives as well as SSDs.

SSDs came onto the market in the mid-1990s before SATA was even a thing, but they were limited in popularity because of the major bottleneck—the PATA communications interface. Once SATA came along in the early 2000s, the two technologies felt like glorious companions. SATA 1.x could transfer data at 150 MBps, which was a lot faster than the conventional hard drives at the time. (The most common conventional standard was ATA/100, which maxed out at 100 MBps.) Then, of course, came SATA 2.x (300 MBps) and eventually SATA 3.x (600 MBps). Comparatively, conventional hard drives appear to be painfully slow. And they are.

Keep in mind that of all the SSD technologies we discuss in this chapter, the SATA interface is the slowest of them. So while SATA SSDs are about 6x faster than conventional HDDs, there is a lot of performance upside. SATA SSDs are still popular today because they are plentiful and cheap (compared to other SSDs), and motherboards usually have more SATA connectors than any other type of hard drive connector.

PCIe

Peripheral Component Interconnect Express (PCIe) is another technology that was covered in Chapter 1 and is used for SSDs. PCIe was first introduced in 2002, technically a year before SATA, and both technologies took a little while to get widely adopted. Like SATA, PCIe has gone through several revisions, with each version being faster than the previous one. Table 2.1 shows the throughput of PCIe versions.

TABLE 2.1   PCIe standards and transfer rates

Version	Transfer rate	Throughput per lane (one direction)	Total x16 throughput (bidirectional)
1.0	2.5 GTps	250 MBps	8 GBps
2.0	5.0 GTps	500 MBps	16 GBps
3.0	8.0 GTps	1 GBps	32 GBps
4.0	16.0 GTps	2 GBps	64 GBps
5.0	32.0 GTps	4 GBps	128 GBps

PCIe 6.0 is under development and is either coming soon or already released, depending on when you read this book. It doubles the transfer rate to 64.0 GT/s and improves encoding and error correction, helping total throughput. It is backward compatible with older PCIe standards.

Looking at Table 2.1, something might immediately jump out at you. The transfer rate is specified in gigatransfers per second (GTps). This unit of measure isn't very commonly used, and most people talk about PCIe in terms of its data throughput. Before moving on, though, let's take a quick look at what GTps means. (It's highly unlikely you will be tested on this, but you might be curious.)

PCIe is a serial bus that embeds clock data into the data stream to help the sender and receiver keep track of the order of transmissions. Two clock bits are used for every eight bits of data. Therefore, PCIe uses what's called "8b/10b" encoding—8 bits of data are sent in a 10-bit bundle, which is decoded at the receiving end. Gigatransfers per second refers to the total number of bits sent, whereas the throughput data you might be more used to seeing refers to data only and not the clock.

A little math using PCIe 1.0 might help illustrate the transfer rate versus data throughput. PCIe 1.0 has a transfer rate of 2.5 billion (giga) bits per second. Because it uses 8b/10b encoding, you then multiply by 0.8 (8/10) to get to bits of data, which is 2 trillion. But that's bits. Divide that by 8 to turn it into bytes, and you are left with 250 million bytes, or 250 MBps. Again, don't expect to see this on the test, but we know that some of you like these technical details!

Also remember that PCIe cards can have different numbers of channels—x1, x2, x4, x8, and x16. So, for example, a PCIe 3.0 x4 card will have total data throughput of 8 GBps (1 GBps for one lane in one direction, times two for bidirectional, times four for the four channels).

What does all of this mean for SSDs? First, take a look at a picture of a PCIe SSD in Figure 2.13. This is a PCIe 2.0 x4 Kingston HyperX Predator. These drives came in capacities up to 960 GB and supported data reads of up to 2.64 GBps and maximum write speeds of 1.56 GBps. The drive is a little dated by today's standards, but it still serves as a great example. First, it's the most common PCIe SSD size, which is x4. PCIe x2 drives are also common, with x8 and x16 drives being relatively rare. Second, notice the transfer speeds. Based on Table 2.1, PCIe 2.0 x4 has a maximum throughput of 4 GBps. This drive doesn't get to that level, especially on write speeds. This is the difference between theoretical maximums of standards versus practical realities of creating hardware. Even so, you can see that this PCIe SSD is significantly faster than a SATA SSD.

FIGURE 2.13 Kingston PCIe x4 SSD

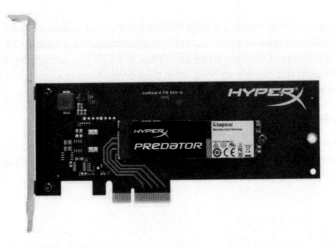

> Remember that, unlike SATA, which is designed for storage devices such as hard drives and optical drives, PCIe is more of a universal connector. Video cards, sound cards, network cards, and many other devices use PCIe slots as well. Before attempting to install a PCIe hard drive into a computer, make sure that there's an open PCIe slot of the appropriate type first!

NVMe

Created by a consortium of manufacturers, including Intel, Samsung, Dell, SanDisk, and Seagate, and released in 2011, *Non-Volatile Memory Express (NVMe)* is an open standard designed to optimize the speed of data transfers. Unlike SATA and PCIe, NVMe isn't related to a specific type of connector. Said another way, there is no NVMe connector—think of it as a nonvolatile memory chip that can be used in SATA, PCIe, or M.2 (which we will cover in the next section) slots. Figure 2.14 shows a 1 TB Western Digital NVMe SSD.

FIGURE 2.14   M.2 NVMe SSD

NVMe drives are frighteningly fast—current NVMe SSDs can support data reads of up to 3.5 GBps, provided that the interface they are plugged into supports it as well, of course. An NVMe SATA 3 SSD will still be limited to 600 MBps; older PCIe versions in theory might have limitations, but you're not going to find any PCIe 1.0 or 2.0 NVMe SSDs, so it's not a problem.

One potential issue you might see with NVMe hard drives is that in order to be a boot drive, the motherboard must support it. If the motherboard has a built-in M.2 slot, odds are that the BIOS will support booting from an NVMe drive. If you are adding it using a PCIe port, the BIOS might not be able to boot from that drive. Always check the motherboard documentation to ensure it supports what you're trying to do.

SSD Form Factors

Whereas a *communications interface* is the method the device uses to communicate with other components, a *form factor* describes the shape and size of a device. The two SSD form factors you need to know for the A+ exam are mSATA and M.2.

mSATA

The Serial ATA International Organization has developed several specifications—you've already been introduced to SATA and eSATA. Next on the list is a form factor specifically designed for portable devices such as laptops and smaller—*mini-Serial ATA (mSATA)*. mSATA was announced in 2009 as part of SATA version 3.1 and hit the market in 2010.

mSATA uses the same physical layout as the Mini PCI Express (mPCIe) standard, and both have a 30 mm-wide 52-pin connector. The wiring and communications interfaces between the two standards are different though. mSATA uses SATA technology, whereas mPCIe uses PCIe. In addition, mPCIe card types are as varied as their larger PCIe cousins are, including video, network, cellular, and other devices. mSATA, on the other hand, is dedicated to storage devices based on SATA bus standards. mSATA cards come in 30 mm × 50.95 mm full-size and 30mm × 26.8 mm half-size cards. Figure 2.15 shows a full-sized mSATA SSD on top of a 2.5" SATA SSD.

FIGURE 2.15   mSATA SSD and a 2.5" SATA SSD

By Vladsinger - Own work, CC BY-SA 3.0, https://commons.wikimedia.org/w/index .php?curid=30037926

The wiring differences between mSATA and mPCIe can pose some interesting challenges. Both types of cards will fit into the same slot, but it depends on the motherboard as to which is supported. You might have heard us say this before, but as always, check the motherboard's documentation to be sure.

M.2

Originally developed under the name Next Generation Form Factor (NGFF), *M.2* (pronounced "M dot 2") was born from the desire to standardize small form factor SSD hard drives. We touched briefly on M.2 in Chapter 1, and we mentioned that although M.2 is primarily used for hard drives, it supports other types of cards such as Wi-Fi, Bluetooth, Global Positioning System (GPS), and near-field communication (NFC) connectivity, as well as PCIe and SATA connections. It's a form factor designed to replace the mSATA standard for ultrasmall expansion components in laptops and smaller devices. Whereas mSATA uses a 30mm 52-pin connector, M.2 uses a narrower 22 mm 66-pin connector.

One interesting connectivity feature of M.2 is that the slots and cards are keyed such that only a specific type of card can fit into a certain slot. The keys are given letter names to distinguish them from each other, starting with the letter *A* and moving up the alphabet as the location of the key moves across the expansion card. Table 2.2 explains the slot names, some interface types supported, and common uses.

TABLE 2.2 M.2 keying characteristics

Key	Common interfaces	Uses
A	PCIe x2, USB 2.0	Wi-Fi, Bluetooth, and cellular cards
B	PCIe x2, SATA, USB 2.0, USB 3.0, audio	SATA and PCIe x2 SSDs
E	PCIe x2, USB 2.0	Wi-Fi, Bluetooth, and cellular cards
M	PCIe x4, SATA	PCIe x4 SSDs

Let's look at some examples. Figure 2.16 shows four different M.2 cards. From left to right, they are an A- and E-keyed Wi-Fi card, two B- and M-keyed SSDs, and an M-keyed SSD. Of the four, only the M-keyed SSD can get the fastest speeds (up to 1.8 GBps), because it supports PCIe x4. SSDs on the market are keyed B, M, or B+M. A B-keyed or M-keyed SSD won't fit in a B+M socket. A B+M keyed drive will fit into a B socket or an M socket, however.

Another interesting feature of the cards is that they are also named based on their size. For example, you will see card designations such as 1630, 2242, 2280, 22110, or 3042. The first two numbers refer to the width, and the rest to the length (in millimeters) of the card. In Figure 2.16, you see a 1630, a 2242, and two 2280 cards.

Figure 2.17 shows a motherboard with two M.2 slots. The one on the left is E-keyed, and the one on the right is B-keyed. The left slot is designed for an E-keyed Wi-Fi NIC, and the right one for a B-keyed SSD.

FIGURE 2.16   Four M.2 cards

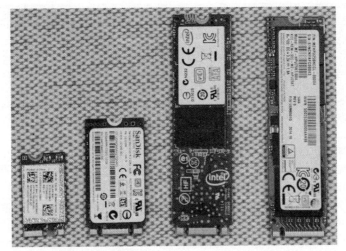

Photo credit: Andrew Cunningham/Ars Technica

FIGURE 2.17   M.2 E-keyed and B-keyed slots

Photo credit: Andrew Cunningham/Ars Technica

Many motherboards today come with protective covers over the M.2 slots. Adding these covers to provide a bit of safety within the case is a welcome feature. An example is shown in Figure 2.18. The bottom M.2 slot is covered, and the top slot (just above the PCIe x4 connector) has the cover removed. Notice the screw holes to support 42 mm, 60 mm, 80 mm, and 110 mm length devices.

FIGURE 2.18   M.2 connectors covered and uncovered

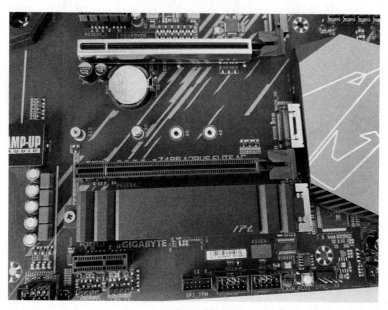

As mentioned earlier, M.2 is a form factor, not a bus standard. M.2 supports SATA, USB, and PCIe buses. What does that mean for M.2 hard drives? It means that if you purchase an M.2 SATA hard drive, it will have the same speed limitation as SATA III, or about 600 MBps. That's not terrible, but it means that the primary advantage of an M.2 SATA drive versus a conventional SATA SSD is size. An M.2 PCIe hard drive is an entirely different story. PCIe, you will recall, is much faster than SATA. A PCIe 2.0 x1 bus supports one-way data transfers of 500 MBps. That is close to SATA III speed, and it's only a single lane for an older standard. NVMe M.2 drives kick up the speed even further. If you want the gold standard for hard drive speed, NVMe M.2 is the way to go.

To wrap up this section on SSDs, let's look at one more picture showing the difference in sizes between a few options, all from the manufacturer Micron. Figure 2.19 has a 2.5" SSD on top, with (from left to right) a full-sized mSATA drive, an M.2 22110 drive, and an M.2 2280 drive. All are SSDs that can offer the same capacity, but the form factors differ quite a bit from each other.

RAID

Multiple hard drives can work together as one system, often providing increased performance (faster disk reads and writes) or fault tolerance (protection against one disk failing). Such systems are called *Redundant Array of Independent (or Inexpensive) Disks (RAID)*. RAID can be implemented in software, such as through the operating system, or in hardware, such as through the motherboard BIOS or a RAID hardware enclosure. Hardware RAID is more efficient and offers higher performance but at an increased cost.

FIGURE 2.19   Four different SSDs

Photo courtesy of TweakTown.com

There are several types of RAID. The following are the most commonly used RAID levels:

RAID 0   *RAID 0* is also known as *disk striping*, where a striped set of equal space from at least two drives creates a larger volume. This is in contrast to unequal space on multiple disks being used to create a simple *volume set*, which is not RAID 0. RAID 0 doesn't provide the fault tolerance implied by the *redundant* component of the name. Data is written across multiple drives, so one drive can be reading or writing while another drive's read-write head is moving. This makes for faster data access. If any one of the drives fails, however, all content is lost. Some form of redundancy or fault tolerance should be used in concert with RAID 0.

RAID 1   Also known as *disk mirroring*, *RAID 1* is a method of producing fault tolerance by writing all data simultaneously to two separate drives. If one drive fails, the other contains all of the data, and it will become the primary drive. Disk mirroring doesn't help access speed, however, and the cost is double that of a single drive. If a separate host adapter is used for the second drive, the term *duplexing* is attributed to RAID 1. Only two drives can be used in a RAID 1 array.

RAID 5   *RAID 5* combines the benefits of both RAID 0 and RAID 1, creating a redundant striped volume set. Sometimes you will hear it called a *stripe set with parity*. Unlike RAID 1, however, RAID 5 does not employ mirroring for redundancy. Each stripe places data on n-1 disks, and parity computed from the data is placed on the remaining disk. The parity is interleaved across all the drives in the array so that neighboring stripes have parity on different disks. If one drive fails, the parity information for the stripes that lost data can be used with the remaining data from the working drives to derive what was on the failed drive and to rebuild the set once the drive is replaced.

The same process is used to continue to serve client requests until the drive can be replaced. This process can result in a noticeable performance decrease, one that is predictable because all drives contain the same amount of data and parity. Furthermore, the loss of an additional drive results in a catastrophic loss of all data in the array. Note that while live requests are served before the array is rebuilt, nothing needs to be computed for stripes that lost their parity. Recomputing parity for these stripes is required only when rebuilding the array. A minimum of three drives is required for RAID 5. The equivalent space of one drive is lost for redundancy. The more drives in the array, the less of a percentage this single disk represents.

Figure 2.20 illustrates RAID 1 and RAID 5.

FIGURE 2.20   RAID 1 and RAID 5

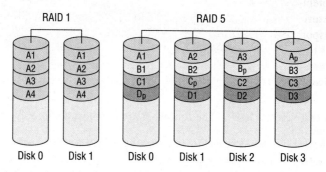

RAID 10   Also known as *RAID 1+0, RAID 10* adds fault tolerance to RAID 0 through the RAID 1 mirroring of each disk in the RAID 0 striped set. Its inverse, known as *RAID 0+1*, mirrors a complete striped set to another striped set just like it. Both of these implementations require a minimum of four drives and, because of the RAID 1 component, use half of your purchased storage space for mirroring.

There are other implementations of RAID that are not included in the CompTIA A+ exam objectives. Examples include RAID 3 and RAID 4, which place all parity on a single drive, resulting in varying performance changes upon drive loss. RAID 6 is essentially RAID 5 with the ability to lose two disks and still function. RAID 6 uses the equivalent of two parity disks as it stripes its data and distributed parity blocks across all disks in a fashion similar to that of RAID 5. A minimum of four disks is required to make a RAID 6 array.

Removable Storage and Media

Thus far we've focused on storage media that is internal to a PC, but external and removable storage options exist as well. Among the other types of storage available are flash drives, memory cards, optical drives, and external hard drives. The following sections present the details about removable storage solutions.

Flash Memory

Once used only for primary memory, the same components that sit on your motherboard as RAM can be found in various physical sizes and quantities among today's solid-state storage solutions. These include older removable and nonremovable flash memory mechanisms, Secure Digital (SD) and other memory cards, and USB flash drives. Each of these technologies has the potential to store reliably a staggering amount of information in a minute form factor. Manufacturers are using innovative packaging for some of these products to provide convenient transport options (such as keychain attachments) to users. Additionally, recall the SSD alternatives to magnetic hard drives mentioned earlier in this chapter.

For many years, modules known as flash memory have offered low- to mid-capacity storage for devices. The name comes from the concept of easily being able to use electricity to alter the contents of the memory instantly. The original flash memory is still used in devices that require a nonvolatile means of storing critical data and code often used in booting the device, such as routers and switches.

For example, Cisco Systems uses flash memory in various forms to store its Internetwork Operating System (IOS), which is accessed from flash during bootup and, in certain cases, throughout operation uptime and therefore during an administrator's configuration sessions. Lesser models store the IOS in compressed form in the flash memory device and then decompress the IOS into RAM, where it is used during configuration and operation. In this case, the flash memory is not accessed again after the boot-up process is complete, unless its contents are being changed, as in an IOS upgrade. Certain devices use externally removable PC Card technology as flash memory for similar purposes.

The following sections explain a bit more about today's most popular forms of flash memory: USB flash drives and memory cards.

USB Flash Drives

USB flash drives are incredibly versatile and convenient devices that enable you to store large quantities of information in a very small form factor. Many such devices are merely extensions of the host's USB connector, extending out from the interface but adding little to its width, making them easy to transport, whether in a pocket or a laptop bag. Figure 2.21 illustrates an example of one of these components and its relative size.

FIGURE 2.21   A USB flash drive

USB flash drives capitalize on the versatility of the USB interface, taking advantage of Windows' Plug and Play, AutoPlay, and Safely Remove Hardware features and the physical connector strength. Upon insertion, these devices announce themselves to Windows File Explorer as removable drives, and they show up in the Explorer window with a drive letter. This software interface allows for drag-and-drop copying and most of the other Explorer functions performed on standard drives. Note that you might have to use the Disk Management utility (discussed in Chapter 13) to assign a drive letter manually to a USB flash drive if it fails to acquire one itself. This can happen in certain cases, such as when the previous letter assigned to the drive has been taken by another device in the USB flash drive's absence.

SD and Other Memory Cards

Today's smaller devices require some form of removable solid-state memory that can be used for temporary and permanent storage of digital information. Modern electronics, as well as most contemporary digital still cameras, use some form of removable memory card to store still images permanently or until they can be copied off or printed out. Of these, the *Secure Digital (SD)* format has emerged as the preeminent leader of the pack, which includes the older MultiMediaCard (MMC) format on which SD is based. Both of these cards measure 32 mm × 24 mm, and slots that receive them are often marked for both. The SD card is slightly thicker than the MMC and has a write-protect notch (and often a switch to open and close the notch), unlike MMC.

Even smaller devices, such as mobile phones, have an SD solution for them. One of these products, known as *miniSD*, is slightly thinner than SD and measures 21.5 mm × 20 mm. The other, *microSD*, is thinner yet and only 15 mm × 11 mm. Both of these reduced formats have adapters that allow them to be used in standard SD slots. Figure 2.22 shows an SD card and a microSD card next to a ruler based on inches.

FIGURE 2.22   Typical SD cards

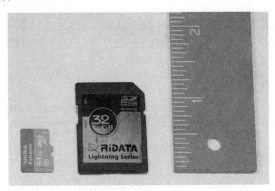

Table 2.3 lists additional memory card formats, the slots for some of which can be seen in the images that follow the table.

TABLE 2.3   Additional memory card formats

Format	Dimensions	Details	Year introduced
CompactFlash (CF)	36 mm × 43 mm	Type I and Type II variants; Type II used by IBM for Microdrive	1994
xD-Picture Card	20 mm × 25 mm	Used primarily in digital cameras	2002

Figure 2.23 shows the memory-card slots of an HP PhotoSmart printer, which is capable of reading these devices and printing from them directly or creating a drive letter for access to the contents over its USB connection to the computer. Clockwise from the upper left, these slots accommodate CF/Microdrive, SmartMedia, Memory Stick (bottom right), and MMC/SD. The industry provides almost any adapter or converter to allow the various formats to work together.

FIGURE 2.23   Card slots in a printer

Nearly all of today's laptops have built-in memory card slots and many desktops will have readers built into the front or top panel of the case as well. If a computer doesn't have memory card slots built into the case, it's easy to add external card readers. Most are connected via USB, such as the one shown in Figure 2.24 (front first, then back), and are widely available in many different configurations.

FIGURE 2.24   A USB-attached card reader

Hot-Swappable Devices

Many of the removable storage devices mentioned are hot-swappable. This means that you can insert and remove the device with the system powered on. Most USB-attached devices without a filesystem fall into this category. Non–hot-swappable devices, in contrast, either cannot have the system's power applied when they are inserted or removed or have some sort of additional conditions for their insertion or removal. One subset is occasionally referred to as cold-swappable, the other as warm-swappable. The system power must be off before you can insert or remove cold-swappable devices. An example of a cold-swappable device is anything connected to a SATA connector on the motherboard.

Warm-swappable devices include USB flash drives and external drives that have a filesystem. Windows and other operating systems tend to leave files open while accessing them and write cached changes to them at a later time, based on the algorithm in use by the software. Removing such a device without using the Safely Remove Hardware and Eject Media utility can result in data loss. However, after stopping the device with the utility, you can remove it without powering down the system—hence, the *warm* component of the category's name. These are officially hot-swappable devices.

Hardware-based RAID systems benefit from devices and bays with a single connector that contains both power and data connections instead of two separate connectors. This is known as Single Connector Attachment (SCA). SCA interfaces have ground leads that are longer than the power leads so that they make contact first and lose contact last. SATA power connectors are designed in a similar fashion for the same purpose. This arrangement ensures that no power leads make contact without their singular ground leads, which would often result in damage to the drive. Drives based on SCA are hot-swappable. RAID systems that have to be taken offline before drives are changed out, but the system power can remain on, are examples of warm-swappable systems.

Optical Drives

The final category of storage devices we will look at is optical drives. They get their name because instead of storing data using magnetic fields like conventional HDDs, they read and write data with the use of a laser. The laser scans the surface of a spinning plastic disc, with data encoded as small bits and bumps in the track of the disc.

With the popularity of high-speed Internet access and streaming services, optical drives have lost much of their popularity. For about 20 years they were practically required components, but today they are far less common. The most advanced optical storage technology used is the *Blu-ray Disc (BD)* drive. It replaced the *digital versatile disc (DVD)*, also called *digital video disc drive*, which in turn replaced the *compact disc (CD)* drive. Each type of optical drive can also be expected to support the technology that came before it. Such optical storage devices began earnestly replacing floppy diskette drives in the late 1990s. Although, like HDDs, these discs have greater data capacity and increased performance over floppies, they are not intended to replace hard disk drives. HDDs greatly exceed the capacity and read/write performance of optical drives.

The CDs, DVDs, and BDs used for data storage, which may require multiple data reads and writes, are virtually the same as those used for permanent recorded audio and video. The way that data, audio, and video information is written to consumer-recordable versions makes them virtually indistinguishable from such professionally manufactured discs. Any differences that arise are due to the format used to encode the digital information on the disc. Despite the differences among the professional and consumer formats, newer players have no issue with any type of disc used. Figure 2.25 shows an example of an internal 5¼" DVD-ROM drive, which also accepts CD-ROM discs. Modern optical drives are indistinguishable from older ones, aside from obvious markings concerning their capabilities. External drives that connect via USB are more popular (and portable!) than their internal cousins.

FIGURE 2.25   A DVD-ROM drive

Optical Disc Capacities

The amount of data that can be stored on the three primary formats of optical disc varies greatly, with each generation of disc exceeding the capacity of all previous generations. We'll start with the oldest first to show the progression of technologies.

When CDs first were used with computers, they were a huge change from floppy disks. Instead of installing the program of the day using 100 floppy disks, you could use a single CD-ROM, which can hold approximately 650 MB in its original, least-capable format. Although CDs capable of storing 700 MB eventually became and continue to be the most common, discs with 800 MB and 900 MB capacities have been standardized as well.

CDs were rather limited in technology, though. For example, data could only be written to one side, and only one layer of data was permitted on that side. DVDs came along with much higher base capacity, but also the ability to store on both sides and have two layers of data on each side.

The basic DVD disc is still a single-sided disc that has a single layer of encoded information. These discs have a capacity of 4.7 GB, over five times the highest CD capacity. Simple multiplication can sometimes be used to arrive at the capacities of other DVD varieties. For example, when another media surface is added on the side of the disc where the label is often applied, a double-sided disc is created. Such double-sided discs (DVD DS, for double-sided) have a capacity of 9.4 GB, exactly twice that of a single-sided disc.

Practically speaking, the expected 9.4 GB capacity from two independent layers isn't realized when those layers are placed on the same side of a DVD, resulting in only 8.5 GB of usable space. This technology is known as DVD DL (*DL* for dual-layer), attained by placing two media surfaces on the same side of the disc, one on top of the other, and using a more sophisticated mechanism for reading and writing. The loss of capacity is due to the space between tracks on both layers being 10 percent wider than normal to facilitate burning one layer without affecting the other. This results in about 90 percent remaining capacity per layer. Add the DL technology to a double-sided disc, and you have a disc capable of holding 17.1 GB of information—again, twice the capacity of the single-sided version.

The current generation of optical storage technology, Blu-ray, was designed for modern high-definition video sources. The equipment used to read the resulting discs employs a violet laser, in contrast to the red laser used with standard DVD and CD technologies. Taking a bit of creative license with the color of the laser, the Blu-ray Disc Association named itself and the technology Blu-ray Disc (BD), after this visibly different characteristic. Blu-ray technology further increases the storage capacity of optical media without changing the form factor. On a 12 cm disc, similar to those used for CDs and DVDs, BD derives a 25 GB storage capacity from the basic disc. When you add a second layer to the same or opposite side of the disc, you attain 50 GB of storage. The Blu-ray laser is of a shorter wavelength (405nm) than that of DVD (650nm) and CD (780nm) technologies. As a result, and through the use of refined optics, the laser can be focused on a much smaller area of the disc. This leads to a higher density of information being stored in the same area.

Optical Drive Data Rates

Optical drives are rated in terms of their data transfer speed. The first CD-ROM drives transferred data at the same speed as home audio CD players, 150 KBps, referred to as 1X. Soon after, CD drives rated as 2X drives that would transfer data at 300 KBps appeared. They increased the spin speed in order to increase the data transfer rate. This system of ratings continued up until the 8X speed was reached. At that point, the CDs were spinning so fast that there was a danger of them flying apart inside the drive. So, although future CD drives used the same rating (as in 16X, 32X, and so on), their rating was expressed in terms of theoretical maximum transfer rate; 52X is widely regarded as the highest multiplier for data CDs. Therefore, the drive isn't necessarily spinning faster, but through electronics and buffering advances, the transfer rates continued to increase.

The standard DVD-ROM 1X transfer rate is 1.4 MBps, already nine times that of the comparably labeled CD-ROM. As a result, to surpass the transfer rate of a 52X CD-ROM drive, a DVD-ROM drive need only be rated 6X. DVD transfer rates of 24X at the upper end of the scale are common.

The 1X transfer rate for Blu-ray is 4.5 MBps, roughly 3¼ times that of the comparable DVD multiplier and close to 30 times that of the 1X CD transfer rate. It takes 2X speeds to play commercial Blu-ray videos properly, and 16X drives are common today.

Recordable Discs and Burners

Years after the original factory-made CD-ROM discs and the drives that could read them were developed, the industry, strongly persuaded by consumer demand, developed discs that, through the use of associated drives, could be written to once and then used in the same fashion as the original CD-ROM discs. The firmware with which the drives were equipped could vary the power of the laser to achieve the desired result. At standard power, the laser allowed discs inserted in these drives to be read. Increasing the power of the laser allowed the crystalline media surface to be melted and changed in such a way that light would reflect or refract from the surface in microscopic increments. This characteristic enabled mimicking the way in which the original CD-ROM discs stored data.

Eventually, discs that could be written to, erased, and rewritten were developed. Drives that contained the firmware to recognize these discs and control the laser varied the laser's power in three levels. The original two levels closely matched those of the writable discs and drives. The third level, somewhere in between, could neutralize the crystalline material without writing new information to the disc. This medium level of power left the disc surface in a state similar to its original, unwritten state. Subsequent high-power laser usage could write new information to the neutralized locations. Drives capable of writing to optical discs are known as *burners*, because they essentially burn a new image into the disc.

Two different types of writable CD are available. The first type is one that is recordable (-R), and the second is rewritable (-RW). For the first (CD-R), data is written once and then the disc is finalized. With rewritable CDs (CD-RW), data can be rewritten multiple times. Note that over time and with several rewrites, these types of discs can become unstable.

Burnable DVDs use similar nomenclature to CDs, with a notable twist. In addition to DVD-R and DVD-RW, there are "plus" standards of DVD+R and DVD+RW. This is thanks to there being two competing DVD consortiums, each with their own preferred format. The "plus" standards come from the DVD+RW Alliance, whereas the "dash" counterparts are specifications of the DVD Forum. The number of sectors per disc varies between the "plus" and "dash" variants, so older drives might not support both types. The firmware in today's drives knows to check for all possible variations in encoding and capability. You shouldn't run into problems today, but it is possible.

Finally, the Blu-ray Disc Association duplicated the use of the -R suffix to denote a disc capable of being recorded only once by the consumer. Instead of the familiar -RW, however, the association settled on -RE, short for re-recordable. As a result, watch for discs labeled BD-R and BD-RE. Dual-layer versions of these discs can be found as well. Table 2.4 draws together the most popular optical-disc formats and lists their respective capacities. Figures in bold in the table are the most common industry-quoted capacities.

TABLE 2.4   Optical discs and their capacities

Disc format	Capacity
CD SS (includes recordable versions)	650 MB, **700 MB**, 800 MB, 900 MB
DVD-R/RW SS, SL	4.71 GB (**4.7 GB**)
DVD+R/RW SS, SL	4.70 GB (**4.7 GB**)
DVD-R, DVD+R DS, SL	**9.4 GB**
DVD-R SS, DL	8.54 GB (**8.5 GB**)
DVD+R SS, DL	8.55 GB (**8.5 GB**)
DVD+R DS, DL	17.1 GB
BD-R/RE SS, SL	25 GB
BD-R/RE SS, DL	50 GB
BD-R/RE DS, DL	100 GB

SS = single-sided; DS = double-sided; SL = single-layer; DL = dual-layer

Installing, Removing, and Configuring Storage Devices

The removal and installation of storage devices, such as hard drives and optical drives, is pretty straightforward. There really isn't any deviation in the process of installing or exchanging the hardware. Fortunately, with today's operating systems, little to no configuration is required for such devices. The Plug and Play BIOS and operating system work together to recognize the devices. However, you still have to partition and format out-of-the-box hard drives before they will allow the installation of the operating system. Nevertheless, today's operating systems allow for a pain-free partition/format/setup experience by handling the entire process, if you let them.

Removing Storage Devices

Removing any component is frequently easier than installing the same part. Consider the fact that most people could destroy a house, perhaps not safely enough to ensure their well-being, but they don't have to know the intricacies of construction to start smashing away. On the other hand, very few people are capable of building a house. Similarly, many could figure out how to remove a storage device, as long as they can get into the case to begin with, but only a few could start from scratch and successfully install one without tutelage.

This section details the removal of internal storage devices, and the section "Installing Storage Devices" details their installation. The focus here is on internal devices as opposed to external ones. Today's external storage devices are eSATA-, USB-, and perhaps FireWire-attached devices, making them completely Plug and Play. Only the software preparation of external hard drives is a consideration, but the same procedure for the software preparation of internal devices works for external devices as well.

In Exercise 2.1, you'll remove an internal storage device.

EXERCISE 2.1

Removing an Internal Storage Device

1. With the power source removed from the system, ground yourself and the computer to the same source of ground.

2. Remove the cover from the system, exposing the internal components.

3. Unplug all connections from the storage device you wish to remove. These include data and power connections as well as any others, such as audio connections to the sound card or motherboard (for an optical drive). Always be sure to grip the connector, not the wires.

4. Gather the appropriate antistatic packaging for all static-sensitive components that will be reused in the future, including any adapter cards that the storage device plugs into.

5. Remove any obstructions that might hinder device removal, such as component cables attached to adapter cards or the adapter cards themselves, storing them in antistatic packaging so that they can be reused.

6.   Remove related adapter cards from the motherboard, storing them in antistatic pack-
     aging so that they can be reused.

7.   Remove the machine screws holding the storage device to the chassis. These could be
     on the side of the device or on the bottom.

8.   Some devices, especially hard drives because they have no front access from the case,
     pull out of the chassis toward the rear of the case, whereas others, such as optical
     drives, generally pull out from the front. A gentle nudge from the rear of the device
     starts it on its way out the front. Go ahead and remove the device from the case. If you
     discover other components that obstruct the storage device's removal, repeat step 5.

Installing Storage Devices

An obvious difference among storage devices is their *form factor*. This is the term used to
describe the physical dimensions of a storage device. Form factors commonly have the following characteristics:

▪   3¼" wide vs. 5¼" wide

▪   Half height vs. full height vs. 1" high and more

▪   Any of the laptop specialty form factors

You will need to determine whether you have an open bay in the chassis to accommodate
the form factor of the storage device that you want to install. Adapters exist that allow a
device of small size to fit into a larger bay. For obvious reasons, the converse is not also true.

In Exercise 2.2, you'll install an internal storage device.

Installing an Internal Storage Device

1.   With the power source removed from the system, ground yourself and the computer to
     the same source of ground.

2.   Remove the cover from the system, exposing the internal components.

3.   Locate an available bay for your component, paying attention to your device's need for
     front access. If you do not see one, look around; some cases provide fastening points
     near the power supply or other open areas of the case. If you still do not see one,
     investigate the possibility of sacrificing a rarely or never used device to make room.

4.   Remove any obstructions that might hinder device installation, such as component
     cables attached to adapter cards or the adapter cards themselves, storing them in anti-
     static packaging to be reused.

5. Find the proper screws for the storage device, and set any jumpers on the drive while it is in hand. Then insert the device into the bay. Keep in mind that some insert from the rear of the bay and some from the front.

6. Line up the screw holes in the device with the holes in the bay. Note that many devices rarely insert as far as they can before lining up with the chassis's holes, so don't be surprised when pushing the device all the way into the bay results in misalignment. Other devices that require front access stop themselves flush with the front of the case, and still others require you to secure them while holding them flush.

7. Use at least two screws on one side of the device. This keeps the device from sliding in the bay as well as from rotating, which happens when you use only one screw or one screw on each side. If the opposite side is accessible, go ahead and put at least one screw in the other side. Most devices allow for as many as four screws per side, but eight screws are not necessary in the vast majority of situations.

8. Connect the data cable from the device to the adapter card or motherboard header.

9. Attach a power connector from the power supply to the device. Be sure to insert the connector completely.

10. Once the drive is attached, unground yourself, and turn the computer on to verify that the drive is functional.

11. If the drive is working properly, replace the computer cover.

There's quite a lot to know about storage devices, and there are several objectives to keep in mind as you prepare for the A+ exam. You will need to know the following:

- Hard drive speeds
  - 5,400 rpm, 7,200 rpm, 10,000 rpm, and 15,000 rpm

- Hard drive form factors
  - 2.5 and 3.5

- SSD communication interfaces
  - NVMe, SATA, and PCIe

- SSD form factors
  - M.2 and mSATA

- Drive configurations such as RAID 0, RAID 1, RAID 5, and RAID 10
- Removable storage
  - Flash drives

  - Memory cards

  - Optical drives

Understanding Power Supplies

The computer's components would not be able to operate without power. The device in the computer that provides this power is the *power supply* (see Figure 2.26). A power supply converts 110V or 220V AC current into the DC voltages that a computer needs to operate. These are +3.3VDC, +5VDC, −5VDC (on older systems), +12VDC, and −12VDC. The jacket on the leads carrying each type of voltage has a different industry-standard color-coding for faster recognition. Black ground leads offer the reference that gives the voltage leads their respective magnitudes. The +3.3VDC voltage was first offered on ATX motherboards.

FIGURE 2.26   A desktop power supply

 You will see the term PSU in reference to a *power supply unit*.

Throughout this section, you will see us use the terms *watts*, *volts*, and *amps*. If you're working with electricity a lot, you might also see the term *ohms*. To help understand what these terms mean, let's use an analogy of water flowing through a pipe. Amps would be the amount of water flowing through the pipe; voltage would be the water pressure; and watts would be the power that the water could provide. (Watts mathematically are volts × amps.) If there were a filter or other barrier in the pipe, that would provide resistance, which is measured in ohms. In non-analogous terms, amps are the unit of current flow; volts are the unit of force; watts are the unit for power (watts = volts × amps); and ohms are resistance.

 The abbreviation *VDC* stands for *volts DC. DC* is short for *direct current*. Unlike alternating current (AC), DC does not alter the direction in which the electrons flow. AC for standard power distribution does so 50 or 60 times per second (50 or 60 Hz, respectively). Sometimes you will see people abbreviate a current such as positive 5 volts as +5V, and other times as +5VDC. It's really a matter of preference.

Be aware that DC voltage is not safer than AC voltage, despite its common use in batteries and lower-power components. Direct current is more likely to cause a prolonged clamping of the muscles than AC, which is more likely to fibrillate the heart, which results in a deadly loss of coordination of the various cardiac muscles. Furthermore, power supplies contain transformers and capacitors that can discharge *lethal* amounts of current even when disconnected from the wall outlet for long periods. They are not meant to be serviced, especially by untrained personnel. Do *not* attempt to open them or do any work on them. Simply replace and recycle them when they go bad.

Power Supply Input

Computer power supplies need to get their power from somewhere, and that is typically a wall outlet. There may be an intermediary battery backup device in-between called an uninterruptible power supply (UPS), which we will talk about later in the "Battery Backup Systems" section, but the point is that the power supply doesn't just generate its own power. It converts AC power from the wall into DC power that components use.

Countries have differing standards on the voltage provided by wall outlets. In the United States, it's typically 110V and 220V. The 110V outlets are the "normal" outlets that most electronics, including computers, are plugged into. The 220V outlets are for high-energy devices such as electric ranges and clothes dryers. Fortunately, the two plugs are completely different (as shown in Figure 2.27) to help us avoid plugging the wrong thing into the wrong place and frying the component. As noted, though, other countries have different standards, and power supply manufacturers want to ensure their devices work in different countries.

FIGURE 2.27   110V (left) and 220V (right) wall outlets

Therefore, some power supplies have a recessed, two-position slider switch, often a red one, on the rear that is exposed through the case. You can see the one for the power supply shown in Figure 2.26. *Dual-voltage options* on such power supplies read 110 and 220, 115 and 230, or 120 and 240. This selector switch is used to adjust for the voltage level used in the country where the computer is in service. As noted earlier, in the United States, the power grid supplies anywhere from 110V to 120V. However, in Europe, for instance, the voltage supplied is double, ranging from 220V to 240V.

Although the voltage is the same as what is used in the United States to power high-voltage appliances, the amperage is much lower. The point is, the switch is not there to allow multiple types of outlets to be used in the same country. If the wrong voltage is chosen in the United States, the power supply will expect more voltage than it receives and might not power up at all. If the wrong voltage is selected in Europe, however, the power supply will receive more voltage than it is set for. The result could be disastrous for the entire computer and could result in sparking or starting a fire. Always check the switch before powering up a new or recently relocated computer. In the United States and other countries that use the same voltage, check the setting of this switch if the computer fails to power up.

Power Supply Output and Ratings

Power supplies all provide the same voltages to a system, such as +3.3V, +5V, and +12V. Each of these can be referred to as a *rail*, because each one comes from a specific tap (or rail) within the power supply. Some power supplies provide multiple 12V rails in an effort to supply more power overall to components that require 12V. For instance, in dual-rail power supplies, one rail might be dedicated to the CPU, while the other is used to supply power to all of the other components that need 12V.

The problem that can arise in high-powered systems is that although the collective power supplied by all rails is greater than that supplied by power supplies with a single rail, each rail provides less power on its own. As a result, it is easier to overdraw one of the multiple rails in such a system, causing a protective shutdown of the power supply. Care must be taken to balance the load on each of the rails if a total amperage greater than any one rail is to be supplied to attached components. Otherwise, if the total power required is less than any single rail can provide, there is no danger in overloading any one rail.

Power supplies are rated in watts. A watt is a unit of power. The higher the number, the more power your computer can draw from the power supply. Think of this rating as the "capacity" of the device to supply power. Most computers require power supplies in the 350- to 500-watt range. Higher wattage power supplies, say 750- to 900-watt, might be required for more advanced systems that employ power-hungry graphics cards or multiple disk drives, for instance. As of this writing, power supplies of up to 2,000 watts were available for desktop machines. It is important to consider the draw that the various components and subcomponents of your computer place on the power supply before choosing one or its replacement.

Real World Scenario

How much power do you really need?

Having a power supply that doesn't provide sufficient wattage to system components will result in brownouts, intermittent reboots, or even the system failing to power up. Having too much power is a little inefficient, but you won't have to worry about failures such as those. The question is, how much do you really need?

Most power-hungry devices (and we're looking at you, video cards) will give you a minimum power supply requirement. Generally speaking, the video card is the biggest power user, so if you meet these requirements, you should be fine. The manufacturer assumes you have otherwise standard gear in the system and adds a bit of a buffer.

Another option, if you are building a system, is to use the System Builder feature on a website we love called `PCPartPicker.com`. As you add components to the system, the site automatically calculates the estimated wattage drawn and displays it on the page. Pick a PSU that supplies more than that amount of power and you should be in the clear.

Power Connectors

The connectors coming from the power supply are quite varied these days. Some PSUs will have connectors permanently attached, where other PSUs give you the ability to attach and detach power connectors as needed, based on the devices installed in the system. The following sections detail and illustrate the most common power connectors in use today.

ATX, ATX12V, and EPS12V Connectors

ATX motherboards use a single block connector from the power supply. When ATX boards were first introduced, this connector was enough to power all the motherboard, CPU, memory, and all expansion slots. The original ATX system connector provides the six voltages required, plus it delivers them all through one connector: an easy-to-use single 20-pin connector. Figure 2.28 shows an example of an ATX system connector.

FIGURE 2.28   20-pin ATX power connector

When the Pentium 4 processor was introduced, it required much more power than previous CPU models. Power measured in watts is a multiplicative function of voltage and current. To keep the voltage low meant that amperage would have to increase, but it wasn't feasible to supply such current from the power supply itself. Instead, it was decided to deliver 12V at lower amperage to a voltage regulator module (VRM) near the CPU. The higher current at a lower voltage was possible at that shorter distance from the CPU.

As a result of this shift, motherboard and power supply manufacturers needed to get this more varied power to the system board. The solution was the ATX12V 1.0 standard, which added two supplemental connectors. One was a single 6-pin auxiliary connector that supplied additional +3.3V and +5V leads and their grounds. The other was a 4-pin square mini-version of the ATX connector, referred to as a P4 (for the processor that first required them) connector, which supplied two +12V leads and their grounds. EPS12V uses an 8-pin version, called the processor power connector, which doubles the P4's function with four +12V leads and four grounds. Figure 2.29 illustrates the P4 connector. The 8-pin processor power connector is similar but has two rows of 4 and, despite its uncanny resemblance, is keyed differently from the 8-pin PCIe power connector to be discussed shortly.

FIGURE 2.29   ATX12V P4 power connector

PCIe devices require more power than PCI ones did. So, for ATX motherboards with PCIe slots, the 20-pin system connector proved inadequate. This led to the ATX12V 2.0 standard and the even higher-end EPS12V standard for servers. These specifications call for a 24-pin connector that adds further positive voltage leads directly to the system connector. The 24-pin connector looks like a larger version of the 20-pin connector. The corresponding pins of the 24-pin motherboard header are actually keyed to accept the 20-pin connector. Adapters are available if you find yourself with the wrong combination of motherboard and power supply. Some power supplies feature a 20-pin connector that snaps together with a separate 4-pin portion for flexibility, called a 20+4 connector, which can be seen in Figure 2.30. Otherwise, it will just have a 24-pin connector. The 6-pin auxiliary connector disappeared with the ATX12V 2.0 specification and was never part of the EPS12V standard.

FIGURE 2.30   A 24-pin ATX12V 2.x connector, in two parts

 The adapter mentioned in the previous paragraph is called a *20-pin to 24-pin motherboard adapter*, which is a specific subobjective of A+ exam 220-1101 objective 3.5: Given a scenario, install or replace the appropriate power supply.

ATX12V 2.1 introduced a different 6-pin connector, which was shaped a lot like the P4 connector (see Figure 2.31). This 6-pin connector was specifically designed to give additional dedicated power to the PCIe adapters that required it. It provided a 75W power source to such devices.

FIGURE 2.31   A 6-pin ATX12V 2.1 PCIe connector

ATX12V 2.2 replaced the 75W 6-pin connector with a 150W 8-pin connector, as shown in Figure 2.32. The plastic bridge between the top two pins on the left side in the photo keeps installers from inserting the connector into the EPS12V processor power header but clears the notched connector of a PCIe adapter. The individual pin keying should avoid this issue, but a heavy-handed installer could defeat that. The bridge also keeps the connector from being inserted into a 6-pin PCIe header, which has identically keyed corresponding pins.

FIGURE 2.32 An 8-pin ATX12V 2.2 PCIe connector

Proprietary Power Connectors

Although the internal peripheral devices have standard power connectors, manufacturers of computer systems sometimes take liberties with the power interface between the motherboard and power supply of their systems. It's uncommon but not unheard of. In some cases, the same voltages required by a standard ATX power connector are supplied using one or more proprietary connectors. This makes it virtually impossible to replace power supplies and motherboards with other units "off the shelf." Manufacturers might do this to solve a design issue or simply to ensure repeat business.

SATA Power Connectors

SATA drives arrived on the market with their own power requirements in addition to their new data interfaces. (Refer back to Figure 2.9 to see the SATA data and power connectors.) You get the 15-pin SATA power connector, a variant of which is shown in Figure 2.33. The fully pinned connector is made up of three +3.3V, three +5V, and three +12V leads interleaved with two sets of three ground leads. Each of the five sets of three common pins is supplied by one of five single conductors coming from the power supply. When the optional 3.3V lead is supplied, it is standard to see it delivered on an orange conductor.

FIGURE 2.33 SATA power connector

Note that in Figure 2.33, the first three pins are missing. These correspond to the 3.3V pins, which are not supplied by this connector. This configuration works fine and alludes to the SATA drives' ability to accept Molex connectors or adapters attached to Molex connectors, thus working without the optional 3.3V lead.

Older PATA hard drives and optical drives used a thicker 4-pin power connector called a Molex connector. An example is shown in Figure 2.34. The connector is keyed with two beveled corners, making it nearly impossible to install incorrectly.

FIGURE 2.34   Molex power connector

Modular Power Supplies

On older PSUs, all power connectors were hardwired into the power supply itself. This had a number of interesting side effects. One was that no matter how many or how few internal devices were present, there were a fixed number of connectors. Power supply manufacturers generally provided enough so most users wouldn't run short of connectors. The flip side of this was that there were often four to six unused connectors, but the cables were still taking up space inside the case. Zip ties and thick rubber bands helped maintain the chaos.

As the variety of internal components became more complex, the need arose to have more flexibility in terms of the connectors provided. Out of this need rose an elegant solution—the *modular power supply*. From a functional standpoint, it works just as a non-modular power supply does. The difference is that none of the power cables are permanently attached. Only the ones that are needed are connected. Figure 2.35 shows the side of a fully modular power supply. The top row has connectors for the motherboard (left and center) and CPU or PCIe device. On the bottom row, you can see four 6-pin peripheral connectors and three 8-pin ones to power the CPU or PCIe devices.

FIGURE 2.35   Modular power supply

You will also see semi-modular PSUs on the market. Generally, the motherboard and CPU connectors will be hardwired, whereas the peripheral connectors can be added as needed. There are two potential disadvantages to using a fully modular or semi-modular power supply. First, some PSU manufacturers use proprietary connectors. Always be sure to keep the extra power connectors around (many come with a bag to store unused cables) just in case they are needed. Second, modular PSUs can take up a little more room in the case. Plugging the power connectors into the PSU can take up an extra ¼ or ½ inch. Usually this isn't an issue, but it can be in smaller cases.

Redundant Power Supplies

Nearly every computer you will work with has one and only one power supply—is that enough? If the PSU supplies the right amount of wattage to safely power all components, then the answer is nearly always yes. There are some instances, though, where power redundancy is helpful or even critical. Within the realm of power redundancy, there are two paths you can take: redundant power supplies within a system or battery backups. Let's look at both.

Multiple PSUs

It's almost unheard of to see two power supplies installed in a desktop computer. There's generally no need for such a setup and it would just be a waste of money. And for laptops and mobile devices, it's simply not an option. For servers, though, having a *redundant power supply (RPS)*, meaning a second PSU installed in the system, might make sense. The sole reason to have two power supplies is in case one fails, the other can take over. The transition between the two is designed to be seamless and service will not be disrupted.

Based on its name and our description so far, it might seem as though this means installing two full-sized PSUs into a computer case. Given the limited amount inside a case, you can imagine how problematic this could be. Fortunately, though, PSU manufacturers make devices that have two identical PSUs in one enclosure. One such example is shown in Figure 2.36. The total device is designed to fit into ATX cases and is compliant with ATX12V and EPS12V standards. If one fails, the other automatically takes over. They are hot-swappable, so the failed unit can be replaced without powering the system down.

FIGURE 2.36   Hot-swappable redundant PSUs

Photo: Rainer Knäpper, Free Art License, `http://artlibre.org/licence/lal/en/`, `https://commons.wikimedia.org/wiki/File:PC-Netzteil_(redundant).jpg`

Although an RPS can help in the event of a PSU failure, it can't keep the system up and running if there is a power outage.

Battery Backup Systems

The second type of power redundancy is a battery backup system that the computer plugs into. This is commonly referred to as an *uninterruptible power supply (UPS)*.

These devices can be as small as a brick, like the one shown in Figure 2.37, or as large as an entire server rack. Some just have a few indicator lights, whereas others have LCD displays that show status and menus and come with their own management software. The back of the UPS will have several power plugs. It might divide the plugs such that a few of them provide surge protection only, whereas others provide surge protection as well as backup power, as shown in Figure 2.38.

FIGURE 2.37 An uninterruptible power supply

FIGURE 2.38 The back of an uninterruptible power supply

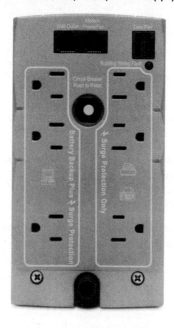

Inside the UPS are one or more batteries and fuses. Much like a surge suppressor, a UPS is designed to protect everything that's plugged into it from power surges. UPSs are also designed to protect against power sags and even power outages. Energy is stored in the batteries, and if the power fails, the batteries can power the computer for a period of time so that the administrator can then safely power it down. Many UPSs and operating systems will also work together to safely power down automatically a system that gets switched to UPS power. These types of devices may be overkill for Uncle Bob's machine at home, but they're critically important fixtures in server rooms.

The UPS should be checked periodically to make sure that its battery is operational. Most UPSs have a test button that you can press to simulate a power outage. You will find that batteries wear out over time, and you should replace the battery in the UPS every couple of years to keep the UPS dependable.

UPSs all have a limit as to how many devices they can handle at once. These power limitations should be strictly observed. If overloaded, it can cause a short, which could potentially result in fire.

Replacing Power Supplies

Sometimes power supplies fail. Sometimes you grow out of your power supply and require more wattage than it can provide. Often, it is just as cost effective to buy a whole new case with the power supply included rather than dealing with the power supply alone. However, when you consider the fact that you must move everything from the old case to the new one, replacing the power supply becomes an attractive proposition. Doing so is not a difficult task.

Regardless of which path you choose, you must make sure the power connection of the power supply matches that of the motherboard to be used. Additionally, the physical size of the power supply should factor into your purchasing decision. If you buy a standard ATX-compatible power supply, it might not fit in the petite case you matched up to your micro ATX motherboard. In that scenario, you should be on the lookout for a smaller form factor power supply to fit the smaller case. Odds are that the offerings you find will tend to be a little lighter in the wattage department as well.

Exercise 2.3 details the process to remove an existing power supply. Use the reverse of this process to install the new power supply. Just keep in mind that you might need to procure the appropriate adapter if a power supply that matches your motherboard can no longer be found. There is no post-installation configuration for the power supply, so there is nothing to cover along those lines. Many power supply manufacturers have utilities on their websites that allow you to perform a presale configuration so that you are assured of obtaining the most appropriate power supply for your power requirements.

EXERCISE 2.3

Removing a Power Supply

1.   With the power source removed from the system, ground yourself and the computer to the same source of ground.

2.   Remove the cover from the system, exposing the internal components.

3.   After locating the power supply, which can come in a variety of formats and appear on the left or right side of the case, follow all wiring harnesses from the power supply to their termini, disconnecting each one.

4.   Remove any obstructions that appear as if they might hinder the removal of the power supply.

5.   Using the dimensions of the power supply, detectable from the inside of the case, note which machine screws on the outside of the case correspond to the power supply. There are often four such screws in a non-square pattern. If your case has two side panels, and you removed only one, there will likely be one or more screws holding the other panel on that appear to be for the power supply. These do not need to be removed. If all case screws have been removed, pay attention to their location and do not use these holes when securing the new power supply.

6.   Remove the screws that you identified as those that hold the power supply in place. Be aware that the power supply is not lightweight, so you should support it as you remove the final couple of screws.

7.   Maneuver the power supply past any obstructions that did not have to be removed, and pull the power supply out of the case.

AC Adapters as Power Supplies

Just as the power supply in a desktop computer converts AC voltages to DC for the internal components to run on, the AC adapter of a laptop computer converts AC voltages to DC for the laptop's internal components. And AC adapters are rated in watts and selected for use with a specific voltage just as power supplies are rated. One difference is that AC adapters are also rated in terms of DC volts out to the laptop or other device, such as certain brands and models of printer.

Because both power supplies and AC adapters go bad on occasion, you should replace them both and not attempt to repair them yourself. When replacing an AC adapter, be sure to match the size, shape, and polarity of the tip with the adapter you are replacing. However, because the output DC voltage is specified for the AC adapter, be sure to replace it with one of equal output voltage, an issue not seen when replacing AT or ATX power supplies, which have standard outputs. Additionally, and as with power supplies, you can replace an AC adapter with a model that supplies more watts to the component because the component uses only what it needs.

You can read more on this subject later in Chapter 9, "Laptop and Mobile Device Hardware."

For the exam, you need to know the characteristics of power supplies as well as how to install and replace them. Topics you should be familiar with include:

- Input 115V vs. 220V
- Output 3.3V vs. 5V vs. 12V
- 20-pin to 24-pin motherboard adapter
- Redundant power supply
- Modular power supply
- Wattage rating

Summary

In this chapter, you learned about three classes of personal computer components that finish our tour of the inside of the case—expansion cards, storage devices, and power supplies.

Expansion cards add helpful capabilities, such as video, audio, network connections, and additional ports for devices and peripherals. Storage devices provide long-term data capacity. Examples include conventional spinning hard drives and SSDs. RAID arrays can help provide performance increases and additional data protection. Other removable storage devices include flash drives, memory cards, and optical drives.

Finally, we discussed power supply safety as well as the various connectors, and we compared and contrasted power supplies and AC adapters. You also learned how to remove, install, and configure storage devices and how to replace power supplies.

Exam Essentials

Know how to install and configure expansion cards to provide needed functionality. Understand the functionality that video cards, sound cards, network cards, and capture cards provide. Know where to install them and broadly how to configure them.

Be familiar with the components of a conventional hard drive system and the anatomy of a hard drive. Most of today's hard drive systems consist of an integrated controller and disc assembly that communicates to the rest of the system through an external host adapter. The hard disk drives consist of many components that work together, some in a physical sense and others in a magnetic sense, to store data on the disc surfaces for later retrieval. Be familiar with magnetic hard drive speeds, including 5,400, 7,200, 10,000, and 15,000 rpm. Form factors are 2.5" and 3.5".

Understand the advantages that solid-state drives have over conventional drives.   SSDs are much faster than magnetic hard drives, produce less heat, and can be made much smaller physically. They are also less susceptible to shock from drops.

Know the differences between three SSD communications interfaces and two form factors.   The SSD communications interfaces are NVMe, SATA, and PCIe. The two form factors to know are M.2 and mSATA.

Understand the details surrounding optical storage.   From capacities to speeds, you should know what the varieties of optical storage offer as well as the specifics of the technologies this storage category comprises.

Understand the different flash drive and memory card options available.   Know the differences between SD cards, CompactFlash, microSD, miniSD, and xD. Be able to identify which cards can fit into specific types of slots natively or with an adapter.

Understand the characteristics of four types of RAID configurations.   You need to know RAID 0, RAID 1, RAID 5, and RAID 10. RAID 0 is disk striping, which can improve speed but does not provide fault tolerance. RAID 1 is disk mirroring, which gives fault tolerance but no performance increase. RAID 5 is striping with parity, which can give some performance boost along with fault tolerance. RAID 10, also known as RAID 1+0, adds mirroring to a striped set. Understand what hot-swappable means.

Know about power supplies and their connectors.   Power supplies are commonly made in ATX and other, smaller form factors. Regardless of their type, power supplies must offer connectors for motherboards and internal devices. Know the differences among the connectors and why you might need a 20-pin to 24-pin motherboard adapter. Also understand why AC adapters are related to power supplies.

Understand power supply characteristics that determine performance.   Power supplies can take input from 115V to 220V and often have a switch on the back to determine which source to expect. Output to internal components will be 2.4V, 5V, and 12V. Capacity is measured in watts. There are also redundant and modular power supplies.

Know how to remove, install, and configure storage devices.   Know the difference between the data and power connectors used on storage devices. Know what it means to partition and format a hard drive. Be aware of the physical differences in storage device form factors.

Know how to remove, install, and configure power supplies.   Know the difference between the modern motherboard power headers and know when an adapter might be required. Be familiar with how to fasten power supplies to the chassis as well as how to unfasten them.

Review Questions

The answers to the chapter review questions can be found in Appendix A.

1. You are installing a new graphics adapter in a Windows 10 system. Which of the following expansion slots is designed for high-speed, 3D graphics adapters?

   A. USB

   B. NVMe

   C. PCI

   D. PCIe

2. You need to install a new hard drive into a desktop computer. Which of the following is not one of the three major components of a hard disk drive system?

   A. Drive interface

   B. Disk controller

   C. Hard disk

   D. Host adapter

3. You install a new NIC for a user, and he asks what it does. Which of the following best characterizes the functions of this device?

   A. Multimedia

   B. Communications

   C. Input/Output

   D. Storage

4. A client wants to ensure that their server does not lose power if their power supply fails. Which of the following best describes the type of power supply needed in this situation?

   A. A power supply that provides twice as much wattage than what is needed to power system components

   B. A power supply that provides a voltage output selector

   C. A modular power supply

   D. A redundant power supply

5. A client is looking for a desktop storage technology that provides the fastest possible data transfers. Which technology should you recommend?

   A. SATA

   B. NVMe

   C. 10,000 rpm

   D. 15,000 rpm

6. You are choosing an optical drive format for a client. Which optical disc format supports a data capacity of 25 GB?

    A. Double-sided, double-layer DVD+R

    B. Single-sided, single-layer Blu-ray Disc

    C. Double-sided, single-layer DVD-R

    D. Double-sided, single-layer DVD+R

7. Which of the following best describes the concept of hot-swappable devices?

    A. Power does not need to be turned off before the device is inserted or removed.

    B. The device can be removed with power applied after it is properly stopped in the operating system.

    C. Care must be taken when swapping the device because it can be hot to the touch.

    D. The device can be swapped while still hot, immediately after powering down the system.

8. Of the following voltage pairings, which one accurately represents the input and output, respectively, of power supplies and AC adapters?

    A. AC in, AC out

    B. DC in, DC out

    C. AC in, DC out

    D. DC in, AC out

9. What are the output voltages that have been commonly produced by PC power supplies over the years? (Choose five.)

    A. +3.3VDC

    B. −3.3VDC

    C. +5VDC

    D. −5VDC

    E. +12VDC

    F. −12VDC

    G. +110VDC

    H. −110VDC

10. You are installing a new power supply in a desktop computer. Which of the following statements about power supplies is true?

    A. You must make sure that the voltage selector switch on the back of the power supply is switched to the lower setting if the computer is going to be used in Europe.

    B. SATA hard drives most often use the same type of power connector that PATA hard drives use.

    C. Power supplies require a 20-pin to 24-pin motherboard adapter to supply power to ATX-based motherboards.

    D. Power supplies convert AC input to DC output.

11. You have been asked to install a new hard drive for a client. Which of the following is not a consideration when installing an internal storage device?

   A. You should match the form factor of the drive or adapt it to an available drive bay or slot.

   B. You should secure the drive with at least two screws on one side and preferably two on each side.

   C. Due to the high revolutions at which modern hard drives spin, you must secure an external power source because the internal power supplies do not have the capacity.

   D. You need to be sure that the routing of the drive's data cable, if applicable, does not obstruct the engineered flow of air across internal components.

12. A client just bought a new digital camera for his photography business. Which of the following is specifically designed as an internal storage device for cameras?

   A. Memory cards

   B. Optical discs

   C. Flash drives

   D. mSATA

13. When installing multiple add-on cards of the same type, which type of cards might you need to bridge together to function as a single unit?

   A. Video

   B. Sound

   C. USB

   D. eSATA

14. You are purchasing a new video card for a desktop computer. For the best performance, which type of video card should you purchase?

   A. PCI x16

   B. PCI x128

   C. AGP

   D. PCIe x128

   E. PCIe x16

15. Which of the following is not a consideration when upgrading power supplies?

   A. You might find that you do not have a matching motherboard connector on your new power supply.

   B. You might find that your case has a nonremovable power supply.

   C. You might find that your power rating is not adequate on the new power supply.

   D. You might find that you do not have enough of the appropriate connectors coming from the power supply for the devices that you have installed.

16. You are choosing a flash standard for a client. They want the smallest flash cards possible. Which standard should you recommend?

   A. SD

   B. CompactFlash

   C. microSD

   D. miniSD

   E. xD

17. Your goal is to build the fastest computer possible. Which of the following hard drive technologies should you choose for the fastest read performance?

   A. M.2 PCIe

   B. M.2 SATA

   C. NVMe PCIe

   D. NVMe SATA

18. You have been asked to configure a RAID 5 system for a client. Which of the following statements about RAID 5 is true?

   A. It provides fault tolerance but no performance improvement.

   B. It provides performance improvement but no fault tolerance.

   C. If multiple drives in the array fail, the data can be saved provided that one drive is still operational.

   D. It requires at least three drives to implement.

19. You have a motherboard with integrated video, and the video fails. You install a video add-on card. Which of the following statements are the most accurate? (Choose two.)

   A. The add-on card will not function properly because of the integrated video.

   B. The add-on card will function if it is bridged to the integrated video chipset.

   C. The add-on card will be detected automatically and function properly if it's PCIe.

   D. For the card to work properly, you might need to disable the integrated video in the BIOS.

   E. The add-on card will work properly by using the integrated card's video driver.

20. When replacing a power supply, which of the following tends to vary among power supplies and must be chosen properly to support all connected devices?

   A. Wattage

   B. Voltage

   C. Amperage

   D. Resistance

Performance-Based Question

You will encounter performance-based questions on the A+ exams. The questions on the exam require you to perform a specific task, and you will be graded on whether or not you were able to complete the task. The following requires you to think creatively in order to measure how well you understand this chapter's topics. You may or may not see similar questions on the actual A+ exams. To see how your answer compares to the authors', refer to Appendix B.

Detail the process for removing a power supply from a computer chassis.

Chapter

3

Peripherals, Cables, and Connectors

THE FOLLOWING COMPTIA A+ 220-1101 EXAM OBJECTIVES ARE COVERED IN THIS CHAPTER:

✓ **3.1 Explain basic cable types and their connectors, features, and purposes.**

- Peripheral cables
    - USB 2.0
    - USB 3.0
    - Serial
    - Thunderbolt
- Video cables
    - High-Definition Multimedia Interface (HDMI)
    - DisplayPort
    - Digital Visual Interface (DVI)
    - Video Graphics Array (VGA)
- Hard drive cables
    - Serial Advanced Technology Attachment (SATA)
    - Small Computer System Interface (SCSI)
    - External SATA (eSATA)
    - Integrated Drive Electronics (IDE)
- Adapters
- Connector types
    - microUSB
    - miniUSB
    - USB-C
    - Molex
    - Lightning port

Thus far, our discussion of computer components has focused primarily on those inside the case. With knowledge of the key internal components under your belt, it is time to turn our attention to the outside of the computer. Dozens of external devices are available to enhance a computer's functionality. We'll cover a variety of them that add video, audio, input, output, and storage capabilities.

Of course, to connect external peripherals, we need some sort of cable and connector. Not everything is wireless yet! Consequently, we will also discuss the interfaces and cables associated with common peripherals. With that, it's now time to think outside the box.

Understanding Cables and Connectors

Peripheral devices add much-needed functionality to computers, beyond the core components. Having a fast processor and terabytes of hard drive space is great, but it doesn't complete the picture. Users need the ability to input data and easily see and use the output that the processor generates. Of course, the types of devices that can input or receive output are quite varied. In the following sections, we are going to break peripheral devices into four categories:

- Video
- Audio
- Input and output
- Storage

We realize that video and audio are indeed input or output devices, but because they are more specialized, we will cover them separately. After this section, you will have a good understanding of purposes of and uses for several common peripheral devices, as well as how they connect to a PC.

 Knowledge of peripheral devices was previously tested on A+ exams. With the 220-1101 version, the objectives covering peripherals were removed. Even though you might not see these items on the exam, we feel it's important to cover them, as having this knowledge will make you a more complete technician. Besides, it will help you understand what all the cables and connectors are for!

Video Devices

The primary method of getting information out of a computer is to use a computer video display. Display systems convert computer signals into text and pictures and display them on a TV-like screen. As a matter of fact, early personal computers used television screens because it was simpler to use an existing display technology than to develop a new one. The most common video device used is a monitor.

Monitors

Most display systems work the same way. First, the computer sends a signal to a device called the *video adapter*—an expansion board installed in an expansion bus slot or the equivalent circuitry integrated into the motherboard—telling it to display a particular graphic or character. The adapter then renders the character for the display—that is, it converts the single instruction into several instructions that tell the display device how to draw the graphic and sends the instructions to the display device based on the connection technology between the two. The primary differences after that are in the type of video adapter you are using (digital or analog) and the type of display (LCD, LED, IPS, and so forth).

Many monitors sold today are touch screens. *Touch screen* technology converts stimuli of some sort, which are generated by actually touching the screen, to electrical impulses that travel over serial connections to the computer system. These input signals allow for the replacement of the mouse, both in terms of movement and in clicking. With onscreen keyboards, the external keyboard can be retired as well. This technology is used extensively with smartphones, tablets, and Internet of Things (IoT) devices, such as automobile information systems, security systems, and smart thermostats. Many laptops today have touch screens as well. The technology has invaded the PC market, too, but has yet to totally dominate it. It's probably just a matter of time, though.

Types of Monitors

PC monitors today are generally based on some form of *liquid crystal display (LCD)* technology. First used with portable computers and then adapted to desktop monitors, LCDs are based on the concept that when an electrical current is passed through a semi-crystalline liquid, the crystals align themselves with the current. When transistors are combined with these liquid crystals, patterns can be formed. Patterns can then be combined to represent numbers or letters. LCDs are relatively lightweight and don't consume much power.

Liquid crystals produce no light, so LCD monitors need a lighting source to display an image. Traditional LCDs use a fluorescent bulb called a *backlight* to produce light. Most LCDs today use a panel of *light-emitting diodes (LEDs)* instead, which consume less energy, run cooler, and live longer than fluorescent bulbs. Therefore, when you see a monitor advertised as an LED monitor, it's really an LCD monitor with LED backlighting.

Another type of LED monitor is an *organic light-emitting diode (OLED)* display. Unlike LED displays, OLEDs are the image-producing parts of the display *and* the light source. Because of this there is no need for a backlight with its additional power and space requirements, unlike in the case of LCD panels. Additionally, the contrast ratio of OLED displays exceeds that of LCD panels, regardless of backlight source. This means that in darker surroundings, OLED displays produce better images than do LCD panels. In addition, if thin-film electrodes and a flexible compound are used to produce the OLEDs, an OLED display can be made flexible, allowing it to function in novel applications where other display technologies could never work. OLED monitors are usually high-quality displays.

 Nearly all monitors in use today are flat screen monitors based on LCD technology. Occasionally, though, you will run into a monitor that's not flat and can be over a foot deep. These relics are based on old television technology called the cathode ray tube (CRT). CRT monitors are bulky and heavy, and almost certainly use an analog signal (and VGA connector) instead of digital.

Other acronyms you will see when looking at LCD monitors include twisted nematic (TN), vertical alignment (VA), and in-plane switching (IPS). The short explanation of the differences is that each technology aligns the liquid crystals in a different manner, resulting in performance differences. Generally speaking, TN monitors are the fastest but have the worst color performance and contrast ratios (the difference between black and lit pixels), whereas VA are the slowest but have the most vivid color contrasts. IPS is somewhere in between the two. The speed aspect often makes TN the choice for gamers.

Adjusting Display Settings

Although most monitors are automatically detected by the operating system and configured for the best quality that they and the graphics adapter support, sometimes manually changing display settings, such as for a new monitor or when adding a new adapter, becomes necessary. Let's start by defining a few important terms:

- Refresh rate
- Resolution
- Multiple displays

Each of these terms relates to settings available through the operating system by way of display-option settings.

Refresh Rate   The *refresh rate*—technically, the vertical scan frequency—specifies how many times in one second the image on the screen can be completely redrawn, if necessary. Measured in screen draws per second, or hertz (Hz), the refresh rate indicates how much effort is being put into checking for updates to the displayed image.

For LCD screens, the refresh rate may or may not be adjustable. The lowest standard refresh rate is 60 Hz, but higher-end monitors will be in the 240 Hz to 360 Hz range.

Higher refresh rates translate to more fluid video motion. Think of the refresh rate as how often a check is made to see if each pixel has been altered by the source. If a pixel should change before the next refresh, the monitor is unable to display the change in that pixel. Therefore, for gaming and home-theater systems, higher refresh rates are an advantage.

While the refresh rate is selected for the monitor, the refresh rate you select must be supported by both your graphics adapter and your monitor because the adapter drives the monitor. If a monitor supports only one refresh rate, it does not matter how many different rates your adapter supports—without overriding the defaults, you will be able to choose only the one common refresh rate. It is important to note that as the resolution you select increases, the higher supported refresh rates begin to disappear from the selection menu. If you want a higher refresh rate, you might have to compromise by choosing a lower resolution. Exercise 3.1 shows you where to change the refresh rate in Windows 10.

EXERCISE 3.1

Changing the Refresh Rate in Windows 10

1. Right-click a blank portion of the desktop.

2. Click Display Settings, as shown in Figure 3.1.

FIGURE 3.1 Display Settings

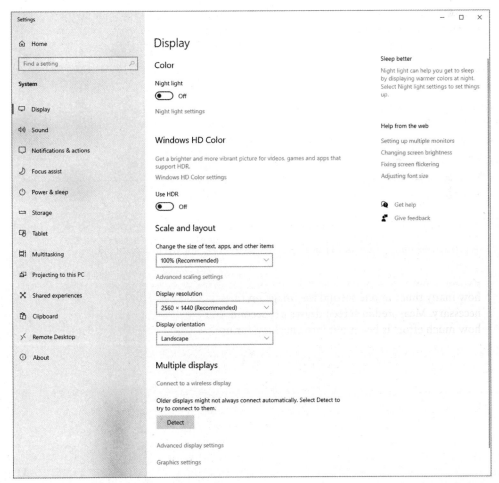

(continues)

3. At the bottom of the window, click the Advanced Display Settings link, as shown in Figure 3.2.

   You will see the resolution, refresh rate, and other display information.

FIGURE 3.2 Advanced Display Settings

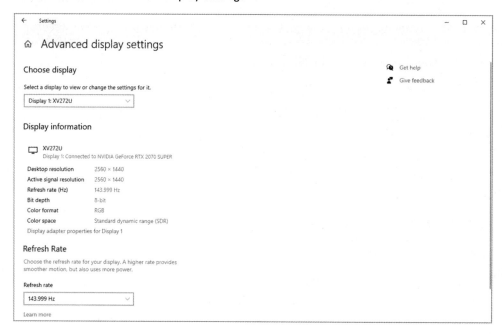

4. Click the Display Adapter Properties for Display 1.

   A properties dialog box will appear, similar to the one shown in Figure 3.3.

FIGURE 3.3   Monitor and video adapter properties

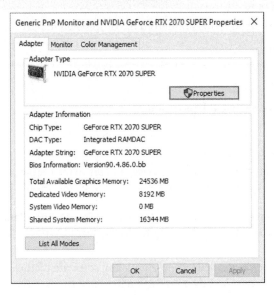

5.   Click the Monitor tab, as shown in Figure 3.4.

Any available refresh rates will be shown in the Screen Refresh Rate drop-down box.

FIGURE 3.4   Monitor tab

(continues)

EXERCISE 3.1 *(continued)*

6. Select the desired screen refresh rate from the drop-down menu.

7. Click OK to accept the changes.

There are two things to note:

- Your monitor may only support one refresh rate. This is pretty common for LCD monitors.

- Just because a refresh rate appears in the properties dialog box, it does not mean that the associated monitor will be able to handle that rate.

Consider keeping the Hide Modes That This Monitor Cannot Display check box selected, to avoid choosing a refresh rate not supported by your hardware.

Resolution   *Resolution* is defined by how many software picture elements (pixels) are used to draw the screen. An advantage of higher resolutions is that more information can be displayed in the same screen area. A disadvantage is that the same objects and text displayed at a higher resolution appear smaller and might be harder to see. Up to a point, the added crispness of higher resolutions displayed on high-quality monitors compensates for the negative aspects.

The resolution is described in terms of the visible image's dimensions, which indicate how many rows and columns of pixels are used to draw the screen. For example, a resolution of 2560 × 1440 means 2560 pixels across (columns) and 1440 pixels down (rows) were used to draw the pixel matrix. The video technology in this example would use 2560 × 1440 = 3,686,400 pixels to draw the screen. Resolution is a software setting that is common among CRTs, LCDs, and projection systems, as well as other display devices.

Setting the resolution for your monitor is fairly straightforward. If you are using an LCD, for best results you should use the monitor's *native resolution*, which comes from the placement of the transistors in the hardware display matrix of the monitor. For a native resolution of 1680 × 1050, for example, there are 1,764,000 transistors (LCDs) or cells (OLED) arranged in a grid of 1680 columns and 1050 rows. Trying to display a resolution other than 1680 × 1050 through the operating system tends to result in the monitor interpolating the resolution to fit the differing number of software pixels to the 1,764,000 transistors, often resulting in a distortion of the image on the screen.

Some systems will scale the image to avoid distortion, but others will try to fill the screen with the image, resulting in distortion. On occasion, you might find that increasing the resolution beyond the native resolution results in the need to scroll the desktop in order to view other portions of it. In such instances, you cannot see the entire desktop all at the same time. The monitor has the last word in how the signal it receives from the adapter is displayed. Adjusting your display settings to those that are recommended for your monitor can alleviate this scrolling effect.

To change the resolution in Windows 10, right-click the desktop and choose Display Settings (as in Exercise 3.1). There is a pull-down menu for resolution. Click it and choose the resolution you want, as shown in Figure 3.5.

FIGURE 3.5 Adjusting the resolution in Windows 10

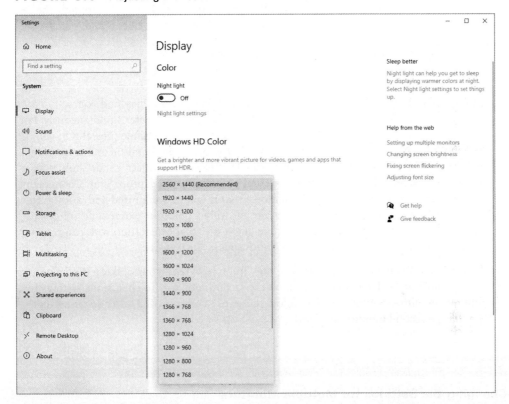

Understanding Aspect Ratios

The term *aspect ratio* refers to the relationship between the horizontal and vertical pixel counts that a monitor can display. For example, old square-ish CRTs were shaped to support a display that conformed to 4:3 ratios, such as 800 × 600 or 1024 × 768. If you divide the first number by 4 and multiply the result by 3, the product is equal to the second number. Additionally, if you divide the first number by the second number, the result is approximately 1.3, the same as 4 ÷ 3. Displays with a 16:10 aspect ratio have measurements that result in a dividend of 16 ÷ 10 = 1.6.

When LCD monitors first became popular, they had wider screens and most supported a 16:10 ratio. Because the ATSC (Advanced Television Systems Committee) standard for wide-screen television aspect ratios is 16:9 (1.778), computer monitors are trending more toward this same aspect ratio. As a result, the once popular 1920 × 1200, 16:10 resolution is now less common than the 1920 × 1080, 16:9 resolution. If you have a monitor that supports one and you try to set it to the other, the image may look squished or stretched, or the monitor may not display at all.

Multiple Displays   Whether regularly or just on occasion, you may find yourself in a position where you need to use two monitors on the same computer simultaneously. For example, you may need to work in multiple spreadsheets at the same time and having two monitors makes it much easier. Or, if you are giving a presentation and would like to have a presenter's view on your laptop's LCD but need to project a slide show onto a screen, you might need to connect an external projector to the laptop. Simply connecting an external display device does not guarantee that it will be recognized and work automatically. You might need to change the settings to recognize the external device or adjust options such as the resolution or the device's virtual orientation with respect to the built-in display. Exercise 3.2 guides you through this process.

When you have dual displays, you have the option to extend your desktop onto a second monitor or to clone your desktop on the second monitor. To change the settings for multiple monitors in Windows 10, follow the steps in Exercise 3.2, after ensuring that you have a second monitor attached.

EXERCISE 3.2

Changing the Settings for Multiple Monitors

1. Right-click a blank portion of the desktop.

2. Click Display Settings to open the Display Settings window.

If a second monitor has been detected, you will see a screen similar to the one shown in Figure 3.6. Otherwise, you will need to scroll down and click the Detect button in the Multiple Displays section.

Notice that the second monitor is highlighted. If you were to change settings such as scale, resolution, or orientation, it would affect the monitor that's highlighted.

FIGURE 3.6   Multiple displays detected

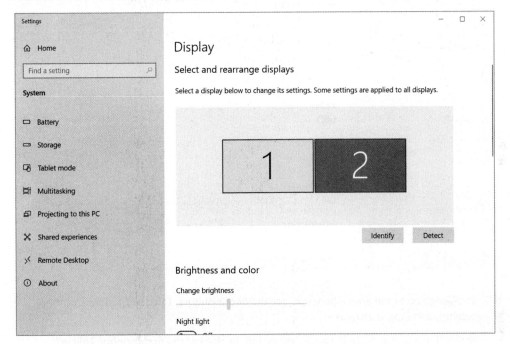

3.   Scroll down in Display Settings.

Under the Multiple Display settings, you will have options to show an image on only one of the monitors, duplicate the displays, or extend the displays.

4.   Choose Extend These Displays, as shown in Figure 3.7.

(continues)

EXERCISE 3.2 *(continued)*

FIGURE 3.7 Extending the displays

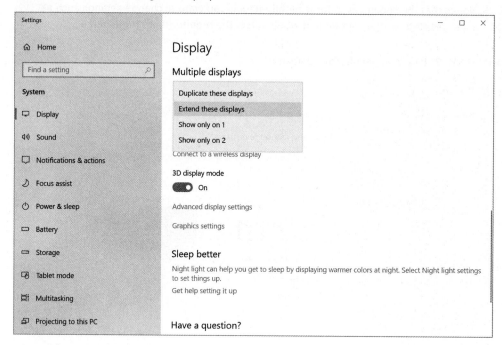

5. Scroll back up to the area where you see the two monitors. Click and hold the second monitor, and drag it around.

   Notice that you can place it above, below, left, or right of the first monitor. This will affect some display features, including where you need to move the mouse cursor to get it to appear on the second monitor.

6. Move the second monitor to be above the first monitor, and close Display Settings.

7. Move your mouse until you get the cursor to appear on the second screen.

8. (Optional) Open Display Settings and configure the second monitor to be in the position you want it to be relative to the first monitor.

Selecting a Monitor

If you go to your favorite online retailer and search for monitors, the number of choices can be overwhelming. Here are a few tips to help narrow the field to a manageable number of options.

Determine what the monitor will be used for.   If it's a general-purpose monitor, it doesn't need to be the newest and fanciest technology. If it will be for a gamer, though, the minimum performance specifications just went up.

Choose a size.   This depends on how far the user will be sitting from the screen. For a regular office or home office setup, somewhere between 24" and 27" is the most popular today, with some people preferring the slightly larger 32". Anything bigger than that could be too large or not fit on the desk. If it will be viewed from across the room, then go as large as makes sense.

Pick a resolution.   The resolutions available may be somewhat dependent on the size of monitor you choose. Remember that higher resolutions result in sharper images. Three common options today are:

> **1080p/Full High Definition (FHD) (1920 × 1080)**   This is the basic resolution used today. It's tenable for monitors up to 24", but for larger monitors a higher resolution is needed; otherwise, icons and images appear oversized.

> **1440p/Quad High Definition (QHD) (2560 × 1440)**   For 27" and larger displays, this is the base performance you want to look for. Sometimes you will hear this referred to as 2k resolution.

> **2160p/Ultra High Definition (UHD) (3840 × 2160)**   Commonly referred to as 4k, it's the resolution of choice for serious gamers and others who want ultra-sharp and crisp pictures. It's also great for those wanting to watch 4k movies on a monitor.

Choose a refresh rate.   Basic, run-of-the-mill LCD screens will have a 60 Hz refresh rate; slightly nicer models will boast a 75 Hz rate. You probably won't notice too much of a difference between them. Gamers or those using their computer monitor to watch live-action sports or movies will want at least 144 Hz as a minimum. Hard-core gamers and ultimate performance seekers will want to go to at least 240 Hz. That kind of refresh rate is overkill for people staring at office applications and email all day.

Consider the price.   Last but not least is price. The higher the specs, the more it will cost. Balance the user's needs with their budget to determine the right monitor to select.

Projection Systems

Another major category of display device is the video projection system, or *projector*. A portable projector can be thought of as a condensed video display with a lighting system that projects the image onto a screen or other flat surface for group viewing. Interactive whiteboards have become popular over the past decade to allow presenters to project an image onto the board as they use virtual markers to draw electronically on the displayed image. Remote participants can see the slide on their system as well as the markups made by the presenter. The presenter can see the same markups because the board transmits them to the computer to which the projector is attached, causing them to be displayed by the projector in real time.

To accommodate using portable units at variable distances from the projection surface, a focusing mechanism is included on the lens. Other adjustments, such as keystone, trapezoid, and pincushion, are provided through a menu system on many models as well as a way to rotate the image 180 degrees for ceiling-mount applications.

The key characteristics of projectors are resolution and brightness. Resolutions are similar to those of computer monitors. Brightness is measured in lumens. A *lumen (lm)* is a unit of measure for the total amount of visible light that the projector gives off, based solely on what the human eye can perceive and not on invisible wavelengths. Sometimes the brightness is even more of a selling point than the maximum resolution that the system supports because of the chosen environment in which it operates. For example, it takes a lot more to display a visible image in a well-lit office than it does in a darkened theater.

If you are able to completely control the lighting in the room where the projection system is used, producing little to no ambient light, a projector producing as little as 1,300 lumens is adequate in a home theater environment, while you would need one producing around 2,500 lumens in the office. However, if you can only get rid of most of the ambient light, such as by closing blinds and dimming overhead lights, the system should be able to produce 1,500 to 3,500 lumens in the home theater and 3,000 to 4,500 lumens in the office. If you have no control over a very well-lit area, you'll need 4,000 to 4,500 lumens in the home theater and 5,000 to 6,000 lumens in the business setting.

By way of comparison, a 60W standard light bulb produces about 800 lumens. Output is not linear, however, because a 100W light bulb produces over double, at 1,700 lm. Nevertheless, you couldn't get away with using a standard 100W incandescent bulb in a projector. The color production is not pure enough and constantly changes throughout its operation due to deposits of soot from the burning of its tungsten filament during the production of light. High-intensity discharge (HID) lamps, like the ones found in projection systems, do more with less by using a smaller electrical discharge to produce far more visible light. Expect to pay considerably more for projector bulbs than for standard bulbs of a comparable wattage.

 Real World Scenario

Burning Up

Although it doesn't take long for the fan to stop running and the projector to cool down, this phase should never be skipped to save time. With projector bulbs being one of the priciest consumables in the world of technology, doing so may cost you more than a change in your travel arrangements.

A fellow instructor relayed the story of carrying his own portable projector with him on the road. At the end of a week's class, he would power down the projector and get his laptop and other goodies packed away. Just before running out of the door, he would unplug the projector and pack it up. As with many instructors, this gentleman's presentations increased in density and length as he became more and more comfortable with the material.

Over time, his presentation had been running later and later each Friday afternoon, edging him ever closer to his airline departure time. He admitted that he had gotten into the habit of yanking the power plug for his projector from the wall and quickly stuffing the unit into the carrying case before darting out the door. It's no wonder then that a few months after he started this behavior, his projector failed catastrophically. Replacing the bulb was not the solution.

One caveat with projectors is that you must never pull the electrical plug from the outlet until you hear the internal fan cut off. There is enough residual heat generated by the projector bulb that damage to the electronics or the bulb itself (discoloration or outright failure) can occur if the fan is not allowed to remove enough heat before it stops running. Without a connection to an electrical outlet, the fan stops immediately. The electronics have the appropriate level of heat shielding so that the fan removes enough heat during normal operation to avoid damage to the shielded components.

Webcams

Years ago, owing to the continued growth of the Internet, video camera–only devices known as *webcams* started their climb in popularity. Today, with the prevalence of working from home and services like Zoom and Google Meet, it seems that everyone has been introduced to webcams.

Webcams make great security devices as well. Users can keep an eye on loved ones or property from anywhere that Internet access is available. Care must be taken, however, because the security that the webcam is intended to provide can backfire on the user if the webcam is not set up properly. Anyone who happens upon the web interface for the device can control its actions if there is no authentication enabled. Some webcams provide a light that illuminates when someone activates the camera. Nevertheless, it is possible to decouple the camera's operation and that of its light.

Nearly every laptop produced today has a webcam built into its bezel. An example is shown in Figure 3.8—this one has a light and two microphones built in next to it. If a system doesn't have a built-in camera, a webcam connects directly to the computer through an I/O interface, typically USB. Webcams that have built-in wired and wireless NIC interfaces for direct network attachment are prevalent as well. A webcam does not have any self-contained recording mechanism. Its sole purpose is to transfer its captured video directly to the host computer, usually for further transfer over the Internet—hence, the term *web*.

FIGURE 3.8 An integrated webcam

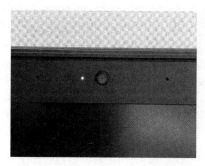

Audio Devices

Audio devices, true to their name, produce sound by plugging into a sound card. Many sound cards today are integrated into a device's motherboard, but some computers still have separate audio expansion cards. Audio devices can provide output, such as through speakers or headphones, or input with a microphone.

Speakers and headphones generally connect with a 1/8" (3.5 mm) audio connector, as shown in Figure 3.9. Most audio connectors have two thin black bands engraved on them, which separates the connector into three parts: the tip, ring, and sleeve. Because of this, sometimes you will see these connectors referred to as *TRS connectors*. The tip provides left audio, the first band above the black groove (the ring) provides right audio, and the sleeve is the ground. You'll notice that the connector in Figure 3.9 has three black bands, providing four connections and making it a TRRS connector. The fourth one is for the microphone.

FIGURE 3.9 1/8" audio connector

Headsets that provide audio and a microphone are popular for audio conferencing calls and video gaming. A sample headset is shown in Figure 3.10. This model connects via USB, as do most headsets. Volume controls and a microphone mute are located on the right earpiece.

FIGURE 3.10   A USB headset

Although discussed throughout this chapter, the *microphone* has yet to be formally defined, a definition that is at once technical and simple. Microphones convert sound waves into varying electrical signals. The result can be recorded, transmitted, or altered in a variety of ways, including amplification.

When installing a microphone, you must match its connector with an available one on the computer. Modern choices include the classic analog pink TRS connector and USB. Wireless versions also exist, but their receiver might still be connected to a standard I/O port. Alternatively, the microphone could be paired with a built-in Bluetooth transceiver, headphones, or headset.

Configuring a microphone on a PC is most often performed through the Recording tab of the Sound applet in Control Panel. Options include setting the levels and choosing enhancements, such as noise suppression and echo cancellation. Specialized applications may also have internal configuration for the microphone, passing most details of the configuration back to the operating system.

Input and Output Devices

An *input device* is one that transfers information from outside the computer system to an internal storage location, such as system RAM, video RAM, flash memory, or disk storage. Without input devices, computers would be unable to change from their default boot-up state. An *output device* does the opposite of an input device—it takes information that's stored in RAM or another location and spits it back out somewhere for the user to do something with it. We've already covered monitors, which are the most common output device. The other major type of output device is a printer. Chapter 4, "Printers and Multifunction Devices," is dedicated to them. Further, some devices are capable of managing both input and output.

Frequently, when discussed together, input and output are abbreviated as I/O.

Keyboard

The *keyboard* is easily the most popular input device, so much so that it's more of a necessity. Very few users would even think of beginning a computing session without a working keyboard. Fewer still would even know how. The U.S. English keyboard places keys in the same orientation as the QWERTY typewriter keyboards, which were developed in the 1860s. Wired keyboards are almost always attached via USB. Wireless keyboards will often have a USB dongle that is attached to the computer, but they can also use Bluetooth.

Keyboards have also added separate number pads to the side and function keys (not to be confused with the common laptop key labeled *Fn*), placed in a row across the top of the keyboard above the numerical row. Key functionality can be modified by using one or more combinations of the Ctrl, Alt, Shift, and laptop Fn keys along with the normal QWERTY keys.

Technically speaking, the keys on a keyboard complete individual circuits when each one is pressed. The completion of each circuit leads to a unique scan code that is sent to the keyboard connector on the computer system. The computer uses a keyboard controller chip or function to interpret the code as the corresponding key sequence. The computer then decides what action to take based on the key sequence and what it means to the computer and the active application, including simply displaying the character printed on the key.

In addition to the layout for a standard keyboard, other keyboard layouts exist—some not nearly as popular. For example, without changing the order of the keys, an ergonomic keyboard is designed to feel more comfortable to users as they type. The typical human's hands do not rest with the fingers straight down. Ergonomic keyboards, therefore, should not place keys flat and along the same plane. To accomplish that goal, manufacturers split the keyboard down the middle, angling keys on each side downward from the center. Doing so fits the keys to the fingers of the hands when they are in a relaxed state. Figure 3.11 shows an example of an ergonomic keyboard. Even more exotic-looking ergonomic keyboards exist and may provide better relief for users who suffer from repetitive-use problems such as carpal tunnel.

FIGURE 3.11   An ergonomic keyboard

Mouse

Although the computer *mouse* was born in the 1970s at Xerox's Palo Alto Research Center (PARC), it was in 1984 that Apple made the mouse an integral part of the personal computer with the introduction of the Macintosh. In its most basic form, the mouse is a hand-fitting device that uses some form of motion-detection mechanism to translate its own physical two-dimensional movement into onscreen cursor motion. Many variations of the mouse exist, including trackballs, tablets, touch pads, and pointing sticks. Figure 3.12 illustrates the most recognizable form of the mouse.

FIGURE 3.12   A computer mouse

The motion-detection mechanism of the original Apple mouse was a simple ball that protruded from the bottom of the device so that when the bottom was placed against a flat surface that offered a slight amount of friction, the mouse would glide over the surface but the ball would roll, actuating two rollers that mapped the linear movement to a Cartesian plane and transmitted the results to the software interface. This method of motion detection has been replaced by optical receptors to catch LED light reflected from the surface the mouse is used on. Note that most optical mice will have problems working on a transparent glass surface because of the lack of reflectivity.

The mouse today can be wired to the computer system or connected wirelessly. A wired mouse typically uses a USB port, which also provides power. Wireless versions will have a USB dongle or connect via Bluetooth. They are powered with batteries, and the optical varieties deplete these batteries more quickly than their mechanical counterparts.

The final topic is one that is relevant for any mouse: buttons. The number of buttons that you need your mouse to have depends on the software interfaces you use. For the Macintosh, one button has always been sufficient, but for a Windows-based computer, at least two are recommended—hence, the term *right-click*. Today, the mouse is commonly found to have a wheel on top to aid in scrolling and other specialty movement. The wheel has even developed a click in many models, sort of an additional button underneath the wheel. Buttons on the side of the mouse that can be programmed for whatever the user desires are common today as well.

There are several variants on pointer devices, such as *trackballs*. A trackball is like an inverted mouse. Both devices place the buttons on the top, which is where your fingers will be. A mouse places its tracking mechanism on the bottom, requiring that you move the entire assembly as an analogue for how you want the cursor on the screen to move. In contrast, a trackball places the tracking mechanism, usually a ball that is about one inch in diameter, on the top with the buttons. You then have a device that need not be moved around on the desktop and can work in tight spaces and on surfaces that would be incompatible with the use of a mouse. The better trackballs place the ball and buttons in such a configuration that your hand rests ergonomically on the device, allowing effortless control of the onscreen cursor.

Other input devices you may encounter are touch pads (especially on laptops), signature pads, game controllers, barcode and QR code scanners, magnetic or chip readers, and near-field communication (NFC) devices such as tap-to-pay devices. They almost always connect to the computer using a USB port.

KVM Switches

Some users will need multiple computers in the same location, but they don't want to hassle with multiple sets of input and output devices. For them, a KVM switch may be a good solution.

A KVM switch isn't an input or output device per se, but it allows you to switch between sets of input and output devices. The *KVM switch* is named after the devices among which it allows you to switch. The initials stand for *keyboard, video,* and *mouse.* KVM switches come in a variety of models, with different connector types available.

The purpose of the switch is to allow you to have multiple computers attached to the same keyboard, monitor, and mouse. You can use these three devices with only one system at a time. Some switches have a dial that you turn to select which system attaches to the components, while others feature buttons for each system connected. Common uses of KVM switches include using the same components alternately for a desktop computer and a laptop docking station or having a server room with multiple servers but no need to interface with them simultaneously.

Storage Devices

We spent quite a lot of time in Chapter 2, "Expansion Cards, Storage Devices, and Power Supplies," discussing storage options, such as hard drives and optical drives. These devices are frequently internal to the case, but external options are available as well.

Take optical drives, for instance. In order to save space on laptops, manufacturers usually don't include internal optical drives. If users want to play a Blu-ray or DVD movie, they will need to attach an external optical drive. External optical drives can be used for data backups as well. These external drives will most likely connect via USB or eSATA.

External storage drives can greatly enhance the storage capacity of a computer, or they can provide networked storage for several users. A plethora of options is available, from single drives to multi-drive systems with several terabytes of capacity. Figure 3.13 shows an external network-attached storage (NAS) device.

FIGURE 3.13   A network-attached storage device

Looking at Figure 3.13, you can see that this is a self-enclosed unit that can hold up to four hard drives. Some hold more; some hold fewer. Nicer NAS systems enable you to hot-swap hard drives and have built-in fault tolerance as well.

In addition to the hardware, the NAS device contains its own operating system, meaning that it acts like its own file server. In most cases, you can plug it in, do some very minor configuration, and have instant storage space on your network. As far as connectivity goes, NAS systems will connect to a PC through a USB or eSATA port, but that is primarily so you can use that PC to run the configuration software for the NAS. The NAS also connects to the network, and that is how all network users access the storage space.

Understanding Cables and Connectors

Peripheral devices used with a computer need to attach to the motherboard somehow. They do so through the use of ports and cables. A *port* is a generic name for any connector on a computer or peripheral into which a cable can be plugged. A *cable* is simply a way of connecting a peripheral or other device to a computer using multiple copper or fiber-optic conductors inside a common wrapping or sheath. Typically, cables connect two ports: one on the computer and one on some other device.

The A+ exam objectives break cables and connectors into two different subobjectives, but really they need to be discussed together. After all, a cable without a connector doesn't do much good, and neither does a connector without a cable. In the following sections, we'll look at three different classifications of cables and the connectors that go with them: peripheral, video, and hard drive.

 For the A+ exam, you will also need to be familiar with network cables and connectors. We will cover those in depth in Chapter 5, "Networking Fundamentals."

Peripheral Cables and Connectors

Some cables are for specific types of devices only. For example, HDMI can transmit audio as well as video, and SCSI supports more than just hard drives. For the most part, though, we associate HDMI with video and SCSI with storage devices.

Unlike HDMI and SCSI, the cables and connectors in this section are specifically designed to connect a variety of devices. For example, someone may have a USB hub with a wireless mouse, network card, Lightning cable (to charge an iPhone), and flash drive all attached at the same time. Those four devices serve very different purposes, but they all share the USB connection in common. We'll start with the highly popular USB and then discuss Lightning ports, Thunderbolt cables, and serial cables.

Universal Serial Bus

Universal Serial Bus (USB) cables are used to connect a wide variety of peripherals, such as keyboards, mice, digital cameras, printers, scanners, hard drives, and network cards, to computers. USB was designed by several companies, including Intel, Microsoft, and IBM, and is currently maintained by the USB Implementers Forum (USB-IF).

USB technology is fairly straightforward. Essentially, it is designed to be Plug and Play—just plug in the peripheral and it should work, provided that the software is installed to support it. Many standard devices have drivers that are built into the common operating systems or automatically downloaded during installation. More complex devices come with drivers to be installed before the component is connected.

USB host controllers can support up to 127 devices, which is accomplished through the use of a 7-bit identifier. The 128th identifier, the highest address, is used for broadcasting to all endpoints. Realistically speaking, you'll probably never get close to this maximum. Even if you wanted to try, you won't find any computers with 127 ports. Instead, you would plug in a device known as a *USB hub* (shown in Figure 3.14) into one of your computer's USB ports, which will give you several more USB ports from one original port. Understand that a hub counts as a device for addressing purposes. Hubs can be connected to each other, but interconnection of host controllers is not allowed; each one and its connected devices are isolated from other host controllers and their devices. As a result, USB ports are not considered networkable ports. Consult your system's documentation to find out if your USB ports operate on the same host controller.

FIGURE 3.14   A 4-port USB hub

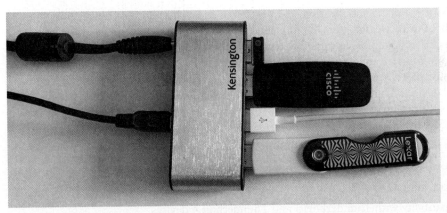

Another nice feature of USB is that devices can draw their power from the USB cable, so you may not need to plug in a separate power cord. This isn't universally true, though, as some peripherals still require external power.

USB Standards

Even though USB was released in 1996, the first widely used standard was USB 1.1, which was released in 1998. It was pretty slow—only 12 Mbps at full speed and 1.5 Mbps at low speed—so it was only used for keyboards, mice, and printers. When USB 2.0 came out in 2000 with a faster transfer rate of 480 MBps (called *Hi-Speed*), video devices were possible. The newer USB 3.x and USB4 standards have increased throughput even further. Table 3.1 lays out the specifications and speeds for you.

TABLE 3.1   USB specifications

Specification	Release year	Maximum speed	Trade name	Color
USB 1.1	1998	12 Mbps	Full-Speed	White
USB 2.0	2000	480 Mbps	Hi-Speed	Black
USB 3.0	2008	5 Gbps	SuperSpeed	Blue
USB 3.1	2013	10 Gbps	SuperSpeed+	Teal
USB 3.2	2017	20 Gbps	SuperSpeed+	Red
USB4	2019	40 Gbps	USB4 40 Gbps	n/a

The USB 1.x and 2.x specifications didn't recommend a specific color for the ports, but when USB 3.0 was released, the USB Implementers Forum suggested that the ports and cable connectors be colored blue, to signify that they were capable of handling higher speeds. Device manufacturers are not required to follow the color-coding scheme, so you may see some inconsistency. A yellow USB port is "always on," meaning it's capable of charging a connected device even if the PC is sleeping or shut down.

USB4 is the newest standard, and it's based on Thunderbolt 3 specifications. Other features of USB4 include:

- Up to 40 Gbps data transfers (there is a 20 Gbps standard and a 40 Gbps one)
- Support for DisplayPort and PCIe tunnelling
- Support for dual 4k video displays or one 8k display
- Compatibility with Thunderbolt 3 and Thunderbolt 4 devices
- Backward compatibility with USB down to USB 2.0
- Required use of USB-C connectors

USB Power

As mentioned previously, USB ports provide power to devices plugged into them. Typical power for attached USB devices is 5V. The maximum current (amps) and wattage will depend on the connected device and USB standard being used.

All USB ports are also capable of functioning as charging ports for devices such as tablets, smartphones, and smart watches. The charging standard, called *USB Battery Charging*, was released in 2007. USB Power Delivery (PD) was developed in 2012. Technically, they are different standards, but in practice, USB ports are capable of supporting both standards at the same time. Table 3.2 outlines some of the versions and the maximum power that they provide. The newest version, USB PD 3.1, requires the use of a USB-C cable.

TABLE 3.2   USB power standards

Standard	Year	Maximum power
USB Battery Charging 1.0	2007	5V, 1.5A (7.5W)
USB Battery Charging 1.2	2010	5V, 5A (20W)
USB Power Delivery 1.0	2012	20V, 5A (100W)
USB Power Delivery 2.0 (specified use of Type-C connectors but only up to 15W)	2014	5V, 3A (15W)
USB Power Delivery 3.0	2015	20V, 5A (100W)
USB Power Delivery 3.1	2021	48V, 5A (240W)

A smartphone or tablet typically needs a minimum of about 7.5 watts to charge properly. The Battery Charging 1.0 standard was good enough, but not for larger devices. For example, about 20 watts is required to power a small laptop computer, and standard 15-inch laptops can require 60 watts or more. With USB PD, one USB port can now provide enough power for a laptop as well as a small printer.

Because of the capabilities of USB PD, it's becoming common to see devices up to laptop size lose their standard AC power ports and adapters—they may just have a USB-C port instead. To get the full capabilities of USB PD, you need to use a USB-C port and cable.

USB Cables and Connectors

In order to achieve the full speed of the specification that a device supports, the USB cable needs to meet that specification as well. In other words, USB 1.x cables cannot provide USB 2.0 and 3.x performance, and USB 2.0 cables cannot provide USB 3.x performance.

Otherwise, the connected device will have to fall back to the maximum version supported by the cable. This is usually not an issue, except for the lost performance, but some high-performance devices will refuse to operate at reduced levels. Note that all specifications are capable of Low Speed, which is a 1.5 Mbps performance standard that has existed since the beginning of USB time.

Throughout most of its history, USB has relied on a small suite of standard connectors. The two broad classifications of connectors are designated Type-A and Type-B connectors, and there are micro and mini versions of each. A standard USB cable has some form of Type-A connector on the end that plugs into the computer or hub, and some form of Type-B or proprietary connector on the device end. Figure 3.15 shows five classic USB 1.x/2.0 cable connectors. From left to right, they are as follows:

- Micro-USB

- Mini-USB

- Type-B

- Type-A female

- Type-A male

FIGURE 3.15   Standard USB connectors

By Techtonic (edited from USB types.jpg) [Public domain], via Wikimedia Commons

Small form factor devices, including many smartphones and smaller digital cameras, use a *micro-USB* or *mini-USB* connector, unless the manufacturer has developed its own proprietary connector. Micro-USB connectors (and modified ones) are popular with many Android phone manufacturers.

In 2014, a new connector named *USB Type-C* (or simply *USB-C*) was developed. USB-C is designed to replace Type-A and Type-B, and, unlike its predecessors, it's reversible. That means no more flipping the connector over several times to figure out which way it connects. Type-C cables will also be able to provide more power to devices than classic cables were. Figure 3.16 shows a Type-C connector and a Type-A connector. You can see that while the Type-A connector is rectangular-shaped, the Type-C connector has rounded corners and looks more like an elongated oval.

FIGURE 3.16   USB Type-C (top) and Type-A (bottom)

 One point of confusion for many is dissociating the connector type from the standard. Because USB 3.1 and USB-C were both released around the same time, people often think that they are one and the same—but they're not. USB 3.1 can be implemented using classic A and B connectors, and USB 2.0 can work over a Type-C connector.

USB was designed to be a short-distance technology. Because of this, USB cables are limited in length. USB 1.x and 2.0 can use cables up to 5 meters long, whereas USB 3.x can use cables up to 3 meters long. The maximum length of a USB4 cable is even shorter yet at 80 centimeters (0.8 meters). In addition, if you use hubs, you should never use more than five hubs between the system and any component.

Despite the seemingly locked-up logic of USB connectivity, it is occasionally necessary to alter the interface type at one end of a USB cable. For that reason, there are a variety of simple, passive converters on the market with a USB interface on one side and a USB or different interface on the other. Along with adapters that convert USB Type-A to USB Type-B, there are adapters that will convert a male connector to a female one. In addition, you can convert USB to a lot of other connector types, such as USB to Ethernet (shown in Figure 3.17), USB to SATA, USB to eSATA, USB to PS/2, USB to serial, and a variety of others.

FIGURE 3.17   Kensington USB to Ethernet adapter

For more information on USB, check out www.usb.org.

Lightning

Introduced in 2012 with the iPhone 5, the *Lightning connector* is Apple's proprietary connector for iPhones and iPads. It's an 8-pin connector that replaced Apple's previous 30-pin dock connector. A standard Lightning cable has a USB Type-A connector on one end and the Lightning connector on the other, as shown in Figure 3.18. It's not keyed, meaning that you can put it in with either edge up.

FIGURE 3.18 Lightning cable

Lightning cables support USB 2.0. You will find cables that are USB-C to Lightning, as well as various Lightning adapters, such as those to HDMI, DisplayPort, audio, and Lightning to female USB Type-A (so you can plug a USB device into an iPad or iPhone).

There are rumors that Apple may do away with the Lightning connector in a future iPhone release and instead use USB-C. After all, Apple has added USB-C ports to laptops and iPads, and USB-C is the port of the future. The same rumors have persisted since the iPhone 8 was released in 2017, and it seems that Apple has little reason to move away from its proprietary connector.

Thunderbolt

Where there's lightning, there's thunder, right? Bad joke attempts aside, in computer circles Lightning connectors don't have anything to do with Thunder(bolt). *Thunderbolt*, created in collaboration between Intel and Apple and released in 2011, combines PCI Express 2.0 x4 with the DisplayPort 1.x technology. While it's primarily used for video (to replace DisplayPort), the connection itself can support multiple types of peripherals, much like USB does.

Thunderbolt Standards

For most of their histories, Thunderbolt and USB have been competing standards. Thunderbolt was designed more for video applications and USB was the slower "jack of all trades" port, but in reality, they could be used for almost the exact same list of peripherals. It just depended on what your computer supported. But as we pointed out in the USB section, the new USB4 version is based on Thunderbolt 3, providing the same speed and using the same connectors. Table 3.3 shows the four Thunderbolt versions and some key characteristics.

TABLE 3.3   Thunderbolt standards

Version	Year	Maximum throughput	Connector	Other new features
Thunderbolt 1	2011	10 gbps	Mini DisplayPort	
Thunderbolt 2	2013	20 gbps	Mini DisplayPort	DisplayPort 1.2 (can send video to a 4k display)
Thunderbolt 3	2015	40 gbps	USB-C	10 gbps Ethernet support
Thunderbolt 4	2020	40 gbps	USB-C	Can support two 4k displays or one 8k display; 32 gbps PCIe

Thunderbolt 3 was released in 2015 and doubled the bandwidth to 40 Gbps. It supports PCIe 3.0 and DisplayPort 1.2, meaning that it can support dual 4K displays at 60 Hz or a single 4K display at 120 Hz. It also provides up to 100 watts of power to a device.

Thunderbolt 4 is the current standard, released in 2020. Perhaps the most interesting thing about the new release is what it *doesn't* do, which is increase data transfer rates versus Thunderbolt 3. It still has a maximum bandwidth of 40 Gbps. And the maximum of 100 watts of power to attached devices didn't change either. The big advantages Thunderbolt 4 has include support for two 4k displays or one 8k display and the requirement to support 32 Gbps data transfers via PCIe, up from 16 Gbps in version 3.

Thunderbolt Cables and Connectors

The most common Thunderbolt cable is a copper, powered active cable extending as far as 3 meters, which was designed to be less expensive than an active version of a DisplayPort cable of the same length. There are also optical cables in the specification that can reach as far as 60 meters. Copper cables can provide power to attached devices, but optical cables can't.

Additionally, and as is the case with USB, Thunderbolt devices can be daisy-chained and connected via hubs. Daisy chains can extend six levels deep for each controller interface, and each interface can optionally drive a separate monitor, which should be placed alone on the controller's interface or at the end of a chain of components attached to the interface.

As noted in Table 3.3, Thunderbolt changed connectors between versions 2 and 3. Figure 3.19 shows two Thunderbolt 2 interfaces next to a USB port on an Apple MacBook Pro. Note the standard lightning-bolt insignia by the port. Despite its diminutive size, the Thunderbolt port has 20 pins around its connector bar, like its larger DisplayPort cousin. Of course, the functions of all the pins do not directly correspond between the two interface types, because Thunderbolt adds PCIe functionality.

FIGURE 3.19   Two Thunderbolt 2 interfaces

Starting with Thunderbolt 3, the connector was changed to standard USB-C connectors, as shown in Figure 3.20. Notice that the lightning bolt icon remained the same.

FIGURE 3.20   Two Thunderbolt 3 interfaces

By Amin - Own work, CC BY-SA 4.0, `https://commons.wikimedia.org/w/index.php?curid=67330543`

Converters are available that connect Thunderbolt connectors to VGA, HDMI, and DVI monitors. Active converters that contain chips to perform the conversion are necessary in situations such as when the technology is not directly pin-compatible with Thunderbolt—as with VGA and DVI-A analog monitor inputs, for example. Active converters are only slightly more expensive than their passive counterparts but still only a fraction of the cost of Thunderbolt hubs. One other advantage of active connectors is that they can support resolutions of 4k (3840 × 2160) and higher.

Serial Ports

Before USB came along in 1998, *serial ports* were considered slow and inferior to parallel ports. Still, serial enjoyed use among peripherals that didn't need to transfer information at high speeds, such as mice, modems, network management devices, and even printers. Figure 3.21 shows a 9-pin serial port. It's the one marked "Serial," and it's also the only male connector on the back of the PC.

FIGURE 3.21 Several peripheral ports

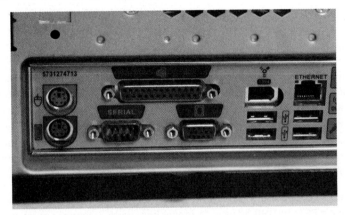

As you might expect, a serial cable attaches to the serial port. Figure 3.22 shows a female *DB-9* serial connector. To make things more confusing, sometimes you will hear people refer to the image in Figure 3.22 as an RS-232 cable or connector. Even though the terms are often used interchangeably, there is a technical difference.

FIGURE 3.22 DB-9 serial connector

DB-9 refers to a specific type of D-sub connector that has 9 pins. *RS-232*, on the other hand, is a communications standard for serial transmission. In other words, systems may communicate with each other using RS-232 over a DB-9 connection. But RS-232 can be used on other types of serial cables as well, such as DB-15 or DB-25. Generally speaking, if someone asks for an RS-232 serial cable, they *mean* a DB-9 cable with female connectors. But it's always best to confirm.

RS-232 did have a few advantages over USB—namely, longer cable length (15 meters vs. 3–5 meters) and a better resistance to electromagnetic interference (EMI). Still, USB has made old-school serial ports nearly obsolete. About the only time they are used today is for management devices that connect to servers or network routers with no keyboard and monitor installed.

Other Keyboard and Mouse Connectors

At one time, the most popular connectors for keyboards and mice were round connectors called *Personal System/2 (PS/2)* connectors. The PS/2 connector (there are two on the left in Figure 3.21) is a smaller 6-pin mini-DIN connector. Many PCs included a PS/2 keyboard connector as well as a PS/2 mouse connector right above it on the motherboard. The keyboard connector was colored purple, and the mouse one green. The ends of the keyboard and mouse cables would be purple and green as well. Today, the PS/2-style connector has been replaced by the USB port.

If you do run into a keyboard or mouse with a PS/2 connector, or a motherboard with a PS/2 port, you can buy a PS/2-to-USB adapter to make them work with more current hardware.

Video Cables and Connectors

Computer displays are ubiquitous—they're easily the most widely used peripheral. Different standards exist to connect displays to the computer, and you need to be familiar with five of them for the exam: VGA, DVI (and variants), HDMI, and DisplayPort. We will start with the older technologies and work toward the present.

Video Graphics Array Connector

The *Video Graphics Array (VGA) connector* was the de facto video standard for computers for years and is still in use today. First introduced in 1987 by IBM, it was quickly adopted by other PC manufacturers. The term *VGA* is often used interchangeably to refer to generic analog video, the 15-pin video connector, or a 640 × 480 screen resolution (even though the VGA standard can support much higher resolutions). Figure 3.23 shows a VGA port, as well as the male connector that plugs into the port. Nearly all VGA connectors are blue.

FIGURE 3.23   VGA connector and port

Understanding D-Sub Ports and Connectors

The VGA connector is an example of a *D-subminiature connector*, also known as a *D-sub connector*. For a number of years, D-sub was the most common style of connector found on computers. Their names are typically designated with DX-n, where the letter X is replaced by a letter from *A* to *E*, which refers to the size of the connector, and the letter n is replaced by the number of pins or sockets in the connector.

D-sub connectors are usually shaped like a trapezoid and have at least two rows of pins with no other keying structure or landmark. Several were shown in Figure 3.21. At the bottom center in Figure 3.21 is a DE-15F 15-pin display-connector port, which may also be referred to as an HD-15 or DB-15 port. The top one is a classic DB-25 parallel port, and the bottom left is a *DB-9* serial port. The IEEE 1394 (FireWire) and two dusty USB ports are shown for a size comparison.

The "D" shape ensures that only one orientation is possible. If you try to connect them upside down or try to connect a male connector to another male connector, they just won't go together and the connection can't be made. By the way, male interfaces have pins, while female interfaces have sockets. Be on the lookout for the casual use of *DB* to represent any D-sub connector. This is very common and is accepted as an unwritten de facto standard, even if some are technically DE- or DA- connectors. Also note that you will see them written without the hyphen or with a space, such as DB15 or DB 15.

VGA technology is the only one on the objectives list that is purely analog. It has been superseded by newer digital standards, such as DVI, HDMI, and DisplayPort, and it was supposed to be phased out starting in 2013. A technology this widely used will be around for quite a while, though, and you'll still see it occasionally in the wild (or still in use).

 All the video connector types introduced from here on are digital standards.

Digital Visual Interface

The analog VGA standard ruled the roost for well over a decade but it had a lot of short-comings. Digital video can be transmitted farther and at higher quality than analog, so development of digital video standards kicked off in earnest. The first commercially available one was a series of connectors known collectively as *Digital Visual Interface (DVI)* and was released in 1999.

At first glance, the DVI connector might look like a standard D-sub connector. On closer inspection, however, it begins to look somewhat different. For one thing, it has quite a few pins, and for another, the pins it has are asymmetrical in their placement on the connector. The DVI connector is usually white and about an inch long. Figure 3.24 shows what the connector looks like coming from the monitor.

FIGURE 3.24 DVI connector

There are three main categories of DVI connectors:

DVI-A *DVI-A* is an analog-only connector. The source must produce analog output, and the monitor must understand analog input.

DVI-D *DVI-D* is a digital-only connector. The source must produce digital output, and the monitor must understand digital input.

DVI-I *DVI-I* is a combination analog/digital connector. The source and monitor must both support the same technology, but this cable works with either a digital or an analog signal.

The DVI-D and DVI-I connectors come in two varieties: single-link and dual-link. The dual-link options have more conductors—taking into account the six center conductors—than their single-link counterparts; therefore, the dual-link connectors accommodate higher speed and signal quality. The additional link can be used to increase screen resolution for devices that support it. Figure 3.25 illustrates the five types of connectors that the DVI standard specifies.

FIGURE 3.25 Types of DVI connectors

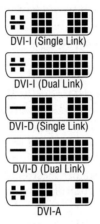

DVI-A and DVI-I analog quality is superior to that of VGA, but it's still analog, meaning that it is more susceptible to noise. However, the DVI analog signal will travel farther than the VGA signal before degrading beyond usability. Nevertheless, the DVI-A and VGA interfaces are pin-compatible, meaning that a simple passive *DVI-to-VGA adapter*, as shown in Figure 3.26, is all that is necessary to convert between the two. As you can see, the analog portion of the connector, if it exists, comprises the four separate color and sync pins and the horizontal blade that they surround, which happens to be the analog ground lead that acts as a ground and physical support mechanism even for DVI-D connectors.

FIGURE 3.26 DVI-to-VGA adapter

It's important to note that DVI-I cables and interfaces are designed to interconnect two analog or two digital devices; they cannot convert between analog and digital. DVI cables must support a signal of at least 4.5 meters, but better cable assemblies, stronger transmitters, and active boosters result in signals extending over longer distances.

One thing to note about analog versus digital display technologies is that all graphics adapters and all monitors deal with digital information. It is only the connectors and cabling that can be made to support analog transmission. Before DVI and HDMI encoding technologies were developed, consumer digital video display connectors could not afford the space to accommodate the number of pins that would have been required to transmit 16 or more bits of color information per pixel. For this reason, the relatively few conductors of the inferior analog signaling in VGA were appealing.

High-Definition Multimedia Interface

High-Definition Multimedia Interface (HDMI) is an all-digital technology that advances the work of DVI to include the same dual-link resolutions using a standard HDMI cable but with higher motion-picture frame rates and digital audio right on the same connector. HDMI was introduced in 2002, which makes it seem kind of old in technology years, but it's a great, fast, reliable connector that will probably be around for several years to come. HDMI cabling also supports an optional Consumer Electronics Control (CEC) feature that allows transmission of signals from a remote-control unit to control multiple devices without separate cabling to carry infrared signals.

HDMI cables, known as Standard and High Speed, exist today in the consumer space. Standard cables are rated for 720p resolution as well as 1080i, but not 1080p. High Speed cables are capable of supporting not only 1080p, but also the newer 4k and 8k technologies. Figure 3.27 shows an HDMI cable and port.

FIGURE 3.27   HDMI cable and port

In June 2006, revision 1.3 of the HDMI specification was released to support the bit rates necessary for HD DVD and Blu-ray Disc. This version also introduced support for "deep color," or color depths of at least one billion colors, including 30-, 36-, and 48-bit color. However, not until version 1.4, which was released in May 2009, was the High Speed HDMI cable initially required.

With version 1.4 came HDMI capability for the controlling system—the television, for instance—to relay Ethernet frames between its connected components and the Internet, alleviating the need for each and every component to find its own access to the LAN for Internet access. Both Standard and High Speed cables are available with this Ethernet channel. Each device connected by such a cable must also support the HDMI Ethernet Channel specification, however.

Additional advances that were first seen in version 1.4 were 3D support, 4K resolution (but only at a 30 Hz refresh rate), an increased 120 Hz refresh rate for the 1080 resolutions, and an Audio Return Channel (ARC) for televisions with built-in tuners to send audio back to an A/V receiver without using a separate output cable. Version 1.4 also introduced the anti-vibration Type-E locking connector for the automotive-video industry and cables that can also withstand vibration as well as the hot/cold extremes that are common in the automotive world.

Version 2.0 of HDMI (2013) introduced no new cable requirements. In other words, the existing High Speed HDMI cable is fully capable of supporting all new version 2 enhancements. These enhancements include increasing the 4K refresh rate to 60 Hz, a 21:9 theatrical widescreen aspect ratio, and 32-channel audio. Note that 7.1 surround sound comprises only eight channels, supporting the more lifelike Rec. 2020 color space and multiple video and audio streams to the same output device for multiple users. Version 2.0a, released in 2015, primarily added high dynamic range (HDR) video, but it does not require any new cables or connectors.

The most recent version (as of this writing) is HDMI 2.1, released in November 2017. Version 2.1 specifies a new cable type called 48G, which provides for 48 Gbps bandwidth. 48G cables are backward compatible with older HDMI versions. You can also use older cables with 48G-capable devices, but you just won't get the full 48 Gbps bandwidth. HDMI 2.1 also provides for 120 Hz refresh rates for 4k, 8k, and 10k video, and it supports enhanced Audio Return Channel (eARC), which is needed for object-based audio formats, such as DTS:X and Dolby Atmos.

Even though the HDMI connector is not the same as the one used for DVI, the two technologies are electrically compatible. HDMI is compatible with DVI-D and DVI-I interfaces through proper adapters, but HDMI's audio and remote-control pass-through features are lost. Additionally, 3D video sources work only with HDMI. Figure 3.28 shows a *DVI-to-HDMI adapter* between DVI-D and the Type-A 19-pin HDMI interface. Compare the DVI-D interface in Figure 3.28 to the DVI-I interface in Figure 3.26, and note that the ground blade on the DVI-D connector is narrower than that of the DVI-A and DVI-I connectors. The DVI-D receptacle does not accept the other two plugs for this reason, as well as because the four analog pins around the blade have no sockets in the DVI-D receptacle.

FIGURE 3.28 DVI-to-HDMI adapter

Unlike DVI-D—and, by extension DVI-I—DVI-A and VGA devices cannot be driven passively by HDMI ports directly. An *HDMI-to-VGA adapter* must be active in nature, powered either externally or through the HDMI interface itself.

HDMI cables should meet the signal requirements of the latest specification. As a result, and as with DVI, the maximum cable length is somewhat variable. For HDMI, cable length depends heavily on the materials used to construct the cable. Passive cables tend to extend no farther than 15 meters, while adding electronics within the cable to create an active version results in lengths as long as 30 meters.

Smaller HDMI connectors

Multiple versions of HDMI connectors are available in the marketplace. The standard connector that you're probably used to seeing, and the one shown in Figure 3.27 and Figure 3.28, is the 19-pin Type-A connector. The Type-A connector and the 29-pin Type-B connector were specified in HDMI version 1.0 and haven't changed much since then. Type-B connectors were intended for higher-resolution products but are not used in the market today.

HDMI version 1.3 specified a smaller 19-pin Type-C connector for portable devices. The Type-C connector, also referred to as a *mini-HDMI connector*, is compatible with the Type-A connector, but it still requires an adapter due to its smaller size. HDMI version 1.4 specified two more interfaces: Type-D and Type-E. If Type-C is a mini-HDMI interface, then you might refer to the Type-D connector as micro-HDMI. Figure 3.29 shows all five HDMI connectors. Also compatible with Type-A interfaces because they have the same 19 pins, Type-D interfaces require just a simple adapter for conversion.

FIGURE 3.29   HDMI connector types

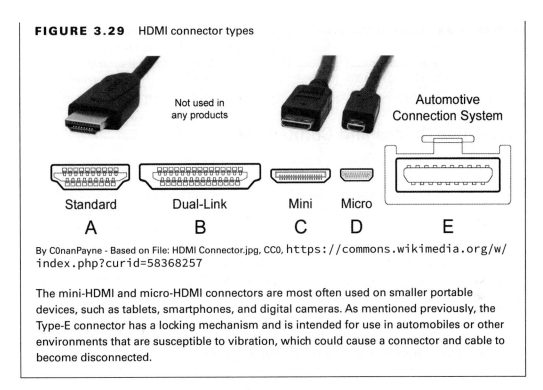

By C0nanPayne - Based on File: HDMI Connector.jpg, CC0, `https://commons.wikimedia.org/w/index.php?curid=58368257`

The mini-HDMI and micro-HDMI connectors are most often used on smaller portable devices, such as tablets, smartphones, and digital cameras. As mentioned previously, the Type-E connector has a locking mechanism and is intended for use in automobiles or other environments that are susceptible to vibration, which could cause a connector and cable to become disconnected.

DisplayPort

DisplayPort is a royalty-free digital display interface from the Video Electronics Standards Association (VESA) that uses less power than other digital interfaces and VGA. Introduced in 2008, it's designed to replace VGA and DVI. To help ease the transition, it's backward compatible with both standards, using an adapter. In addition, an adapter allows HDMI and DVI voltages to be lowered to those required by DisplayPort because it is functionally similar to HDMI and DVI. DisplayPort cables can extend 3 meters, unless an active cable powers the run, in which case the cable can extend to 33 meters. DisplayPort is intended primarily for video, but, like HDMI, it can transmit audio and video simultaneously.

Figure 3.30 shows a DisplayPort port on a laptop as well as a connector. The Display-Port connector latches itself to the receptacle with two tiny hooks. A push-button mechanism serves to release the hooks for removal of the connector from the receptacle. Note the beveled keying at the bottom-left corner of the port.

FIGURE 3.30   A DisplayPort port and cable

The DisplayPort standard also specifies a smaller connector, known as the *Mini Display-Port (MDP) connector*. The MDP is electrically equivalent to the full-size DP connector and features a beveled keying structure, but it lacks the latching mechanism present in the DP connector. The MDP connector looks identical to a Thunderbolt 2 connector, which we covered in the "Peripheral Cables and Connectors" section earlier in this chapter.

Hard Drive Cables and Connectors

At the beginning of this chapter, we said that we were going to move outside the box and talk about external peripherals, cables, and connectors. For the most part that's true, but here we need to take a small digression to talk about connecting hard drives, most of which are internal. Some of this you already learned in Chapter 2, so this could feel like a review. Of course, there are SATA and PATA connectors, but we'll also throw in two new ones—SCSI and eSATA.

 NOTE   Optical drives use the same connectors as hard drives.

Remember that all drives need some form of connection to the motherboard so that the computer can "talk" to the disk drive. Regardless of whether the connection is built into the motherboard (*onboard*) or on an adapter card (*off-board*), internal or external, the standard for the attachment is based on the drive's requirements. These connections are known as *drive interfaces*. The interfaces consist of circuitry and a port, or *header*.

Serial Advanced Technology Attachment

The most common hard drive connector used today is *Serial Advanced Technology Attachment (SATA)*. Figure 3.31 shows SATA headers, which you have seen before, and a SATA cable. Note that the SATA cable is flat, and the connector is keyed to fit into the motherboard header in only one way. SATA data cables have a 7-pin connector. SATA power cables have 15 pins and are wider than the data connector.

FIGURE 3.31   SATA connectors and cable

The SATA we've discussed so far is internal, but there's an external version as well, appropriately named *external SATA (eSATA)*. It uses the same technology, only in an external connection. The port at the bottom center of Figure 3.32 is eSATA. It entered the market in 2003, is mostly intended for hard drive use, and can support up to 15 devices on a single bus.

FIGURE 3.32   eSATA

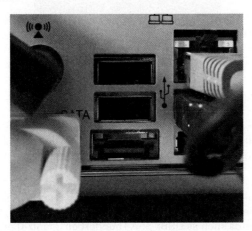

Table 3.4 shows some of the eSATA specifications.

TABLE 3.4   eSATA specifications

Version	Year	Speed	Names
Revision 1.0	2003	1.5 Gbps	SATA I, SATA 1.5 Gb/s
Revision 2.0	2005	3.0 Gbps	SATA II, SATA 3Gb/s
Revision 3.0	2009	6.0 Gbps	SATA III, SATA 6Gb/s

You will commonly see the third generation of eSATA (and SATA) referred to as SATA 6 or SATA 6 Gb/s. This is because if they called it SATA 3, there would be confusion with the second generation, which had transfer speeds of 3.0 Gbps.

An interesting fact about eSATA is that the interface does not provide power, which is a big negative compared to its contemporary high-speed serial counterparts. To overcome this limitation, there is another eSATA port that you might see, called *Power over eSATA*, eSATA+, eSATAp, or eSATA/USB. It's essentially a combination eSATA and USB port. Since the port is a combination of two others, neither sanctioning body officially recognizes it (which is probably why there are so many names—other companies call it what they want to). Figure 3.33 shows this port.

FIGURE 3.33   USB over eSATA

You can see that this port is slightly different from the one in Figure 3.32, and it's also marked with a USB icon next to the eSATA one. On the market, you can purchase cables that go from this port to an eSATA device and provide it with power via the eSATAp port.

> You might have noticed that the most recent eSATA specification was released over a decade ago. eSATA is basically dead, because newer standards such as USB4 and Thunderbolt 3 (and 4) provide not only power but faster data transmission speeds as well.

Parallel Advanced Technology Attachment

Prior to SATA, the most popular hard drive connector was *Integrated Drive Electronics (IDE)*, which has now been renamed *Parallel Advanced Technology Attachment (PATA)*. There is no difference between PATA and IDE, other than the name. Figure 3.34 shows PATA connectors on a motherboard next to a PATA cable. Refer back to Chapter 2, Figure 2.9, to see a direct comparison of SATA and PATA connectors on a hard drive.

FIGURE 3.34   PATA connectors and cable

PATA drives use a 40-pin flat data cable, and there are a few things to note about it. First, there is an off-colored stripe (often red, pink, or blue) along one edge of the cable to designate where pin 1 is. On a PATA drive, pin 1 is always on the edge nearest the power connector. The second thing to note is that there are three connectors—one for the motherboard and two for drives. PATA technology specifies that there can be two drives per cable, in a primary and secondary configuration. The primary drive will be attached to the other end of the cable, and the secondary, if connected, will use the middle connector. In addition, the drive itself may need to be configured for primary or secondary by using the jumper block on the drive. Most PATA drives will auto-configure their status based on their position on the cable, but if there is a conflict, they can be manually configured.

Power is supplied by a 4-pin power connector known as a *Molex connector*, shown in Figure 3.35. If you have a PATA drive and a SATA-supporting power supply (or vice versa), you can buy an adapter to convert the power to what you need. The same holds true for data connectors as well.

FIGURE 3.35   Molex power connector

Small Computer System Interface

A fourth type of hard drive connector is called *Small Computer System Interface (SCSI)*. The acronym is pronounced "scuzzy," even though the original designer intended for it to be called "sexy." The most common usage is for storage devices, but the SCSI standard can be used for other peripherals as well. You won't see many SCSI interfaces in home computers—it's more often found in servers, dedicated storage solutions, and high-end workstations.

Early versions of SCSI used a parallel bus interface called *SCSI Parallel Interface (SPI)*. Starting in 2005, SPI was replaced by Serial Attached SCSI (SAS), which, as you may guess, is a serial bus. If you compare SCSI to other popular drive interfaces at the time, SCSI was generally faster but more expensive than its counterparts, such as IDE.

SCSI Parallel Interface

Although it's essentially obsolete now, you might find some details of SPI interesting. The first standard, ratified in 1986, was an 8-bit bus that provided for data transfers of 5 Mbps.

Because it was an 8-bit bus, it could support up to seven devices. (The motherboard or expansion card header was the eighth.) Each device needed a unique ID from 0 to 7, and devices were attached in a daisy-chain fashion. A terminator (essentially a big resistor) needed to be attached to the end of the chain; otherwise, the devices wouldn't function.

In 1994, the 8-bit version was replaced by a 16-bit version that supported up to 15 devices and had a transfer speed of 320 Mbps. Compared to the 100 Mbps supported by IDE at the time, you can see why people wanted SCSI!

SPI had different connectors, depending on the standard; 50-pin, 68-pin, and 80-pin connectors were commonly used. Figure 3.36 shows two 50-pin Centronics connectors, which were common for many years. Figure 3.37 shows a terminator, with the top cover removed so that you can see the electronics.

FIGURE 3.36   Two 50-pin SCSI connectors

By Smial at German Wikipedia - Own work, CC BY-SA 2.0 de, `https://commons.wikimedia.org/w/index.php?curid=1009512`

FIGURE 3.37   A SCSI terminator

By Adamantios - Own work, CC BY-SA 3.0, `https://commons.wikimedia.org/w/index.php?curid=6116837`

Serial Attached SCSI

Of the newer SCSI implementations, the one you will most likely encounter is SAS. For example, as we mentioned in Chapter 2, most 15,000 rpm hard drives are SAS drives. From an architectural standpoint, SAS differs greatly from SPI, starting with the fact that it's serial, not parallel. What they do share is the use of the SCSI command architecture, which is a group of commands that can be sent from the controller to the device to make it do something, such as write or retrieve data.

A SAS system of hard drives works much like the SATA and PATA systems you've already learned about. There's the controller, the drive, and the cable that connects it. SAS uses its own terminology, though, and adds a component called an *expander*. Here are the four components of a SAS system:

Initiator   Think of this as the controller. It sends commands to target devices and receives data back from them. These can be integrated or an add-on card. Each initiator can have a direct connection to 128 devices.

Target   This is the device, typically a hard drive. It can also be multiple hard drives functioning in a RAID array.

Service Delivery Subsystem   The service delivery subsystem transmits information between an initiator and a target. Often this is a cable, but it can also be a server backplane (where multiple devices connect).

Expander   An expander is a device that allows for multiple initiators to be combined into one service delivery subsystem. Through the use of expanders, one initiator can support up to 16,256 devices.

Figure 3.38 shows a SAS cable and connector. It's slightly wider than a SATA power and data connector together. The other end of a cable such as this might have an identical SAS connector or a mini-SAS connector, or it might pigtail into four SATA or mini-SAS connectors.

FIGURE 3.38   A SAS connector

By Adamantios - Own work, CC BY-SA 3.0, https://commons.wikimedia.org/w/index.php?curid=6117374

Table 3.5 lists SAS standards and maximum throughput.

TABLE 3.5 SAS standards and speeds

Standard	Year	Throughput
SAS-1	2005	3 Gbps
SAS-2	2009	6 Gbps
SAS-3	2013	12 Gbps
SAS-4	2017	22.5 Gbps

SAS offers the following advantages over SPI:

- No terminator is required.
- Up to 16,256 devices can be connected to a single system.
- Each SAS device has its own link to the controller, so there are no issues with contention (when multiple devices try to use the same link at the same time, causing interference).
- SAS provides faster data transfer speeds than SPI.
- SAS devices are compatible with SATA 2.0 and higher—SATA drives can be connected to SAS controllers.

With the invention of super-fast M.2 and NVMe hard drives, which you learned about in Chapter 2, it's hard to say what the future of SAS is. For example, SAS-5 (45 Gbps) has been under development since around 2018, but there is no official release date and there seems to be no impetus to get it to market. Most likely, SAS will continue to have a place in corporate environments with large-scale storage solutions, while the others will provide leading-edge speed for the workstation environment, particularly among laptops and smaller devices.

Summary

In this chapter, you first learned about peripheral types. We broke them into four categories: video, audio, input/output, and storage. Video peripherals include monitors, projectors, and webcams. There aren't many audio connectors, but most use the TRS connector you learned about. Input and output devices are plentiful, and we concentrated on keyboards and mice. Storage devices and optical drives can be external, and an example is an external network-attached storage (NAS) device.

In the second section of the chapter, you learned about various cable and connection types, and the purposes and uses of peripheral types. First, you learned about peripheral cables and connectors, such as USB, Lightning, Thunderbolt, and serial. Then we moved on to video cables. Topics included the analog VGA standard, as well as the digital standards DVI, HDMI, and DisplayPort. Then, we covered hard drive connections and cables related to SATA, eSATA, IDE (PATA), and SCSI.

Exam Essentials

Recognize and understand different peripheral connectors and adapters. Expansion cards and motherboards have external connectivity interfaces. The interfaces have connectors that adhere to some sort of standard for interconnecting with a cable or external device. Knowing these specific characteristics can help you differentiate among the capabilities of the interfaces available to you. Understanding when to use an adapter to convert one connector to another is crucial to achieving connectivity among differing interfaces. Adapters you should know are DVI-to-HDMI, USB-to-Ethernet, and DVI-to-VGA.

Recognize and be able to describe display connectors specifically. Although a type of peripheral connector, display connectors are in a class all their own. Types include VGA, HDMI, mini-HDMI, DisplayPort, and the various versions of DVI.

Recognize and understand the purpose of hard drive cables and connectors. The connectors you should recognize are SATA, eSATA, IDE (PATA), and SCSI. Molex connectors are used to power PATA devices. They each connect hard drives or optical drives.

Know the various peripheral cables and their connectors. Multipurpose cables include USB, Lightning, Thunderbolt, and serial. USB has the largest variety of connectors, including USB-A and USB-B and their mini- and micro- versions, as well as the newer USB-C. USB cables also can have proprietary connectors, such as Apple's Lightning connector. Thunderbolt can use a proprietary connector or USB-C. Serial cables have a DB-9 connector.

Review Questions

The answers to the chapter review questions can be found in Appendix A.

1. Which of the following could be used with an analog monitor? (Choose two.)
   A. HDMI
   B. DVI-A
   C. DVI-D
   D. DisplayPort
   E. VGA

2. You are attaching an external hard drive to a computer with USB 2.0 ports. The user is concerned about data transfer speed. What is the maximum speed of USB 2.0?
   A. 480 Mbps
   B. 5 Gbps
   C. 10 Gbps
   D. 20 Gbps

3. You got a new desktop computer for a designer at your company. On the front panel is a rectangular yellow USB port. What does that mean?
   A. It's USB 2.0.
   B. It's USB 3.0.
   C. It's a port capable of charging devices even with the system powered off.
   D. It's a port to be used with USB-C compatible devices.

4. You are installing a replacement monitor on a desktop computer. Which of the following is true regarding a monitor's refresh rate?
   A. As long as the graphics adapter can refresh the image at a particular rate, the attached monitor can accommodate that refresh rate.
   B. The refresh rate is normally expressed in MHz.
   C. The refresh rate is normally selected by using the controls on the front panel of the monitor.
   D. As you lower the resolution, the maximum refresh rate allowed tends to increase.

5. Which of the following connector types is typically not associated with hard drive use?
   A. USB-C
   B. eSATA
   C. DB-9
   D. SCSI

6. The company photographer is interested in buying a new digital camera. He wants to be able to plug it directly into his laptop to transfer pictures for editing. What type of connector will most likely be on his camera?

   A. Mini-USB

   B. Thunderbolt

   C. Molex

   D. Lightning

7. You are installing a new video card that has an HDMI port. Which of the following is true about HDMI cables? (Choose all that apply.)

   A. They can transmit analog or digital signals.

   B. They can transmit audio as well as video.

   C. They are not used to connect to projectors.

   D. They can use HDMI or mini-HDMI connectors.

8. Which of the following display interfaces is equivalent to DisplayPort with PCIe added in?

   A. Thunderbolt

   B. HDMI

   C. DVI

   D. VGA

9. Which two of the following standards use the same connector? (Choose two.)

   A. eSATA

   B. Thunderbolt 3

   C. USB4

   D. USB 2.0

   E. Mini-USB

10. How do you connect a DVI-A interface on a peripheral to a DVI-D interface on the computer?

    A. With a DVI-I cable.

    B. With a cable that is terminated on one end with a DVI-A connector and on the other end with a DVD-D connector.

    C. You wouldn't interconnect those two interfaces.

    D. With a standard DVI cable.

11. A technician says he needs to provide power to an older IDE hard drive and a DVD-ROM in a desktop. The computer now has a new fully modular power supply, and the technician wants to know what type of power connectors he should use. What do you tell him?

  A. SATA

  B. SCSI

  C. Serial

  D. Molex

12. Which of the following connectors is oval shaped?

  A. Micro-USB

  B. Mini-USB

  C. Thunderbolt 2

  D. Thunderbolt 3

13. Which of the following connector types are capable of conducting power and transmitting data? (Choose all that apply.)

  A. Lightning

  B. Molex

  C. USB-C

  D. DB-9

  E. Micro-USB

14. Which of the following statements is true about eSATA cables and connectors?

  A. eSATA cables provide power and data to devices.

  B. eSATA connectors are smaller than USB-C connectors.

  C. eSATA is faster than USB4 and Thunderbolt 3.

  D. eSATA maximum throughput is 6 Gbps.

15. Which of the following is not an example of a connector for a standard peripheral input device?

  A. 1/8" jack

  B. Molex

  C. D-sub

  D. USB

16. You are asked to hook up a projector in a classroom. What type of cable are you most likely to need?

  A. USB Type A

  B. eSATA

  C. HDMI

  D. DB-9

17. A user with an iPhone 12 needs to charge her device and asks you to bring a cable. Which of the following connector types should you ensure that the cable has?

A. Thunderbolt

B. Lightning

C. Mini-USB

D. Micro-USB

18. Which of the following types of cables will transfer data at the slowest rate?

A. USB4

B. Serial

C. Thunderbolt 3

D. HDMI

19. What is the maximum data transfer rate of USB High Speed?

A. 10 Gbps

B. 5 Gbps

C. 480 Mbps

D. 12 Mbps

20. VGA cables use what type of signal between the adapter and monitor?

A. Digital

B. Analog

C. Composite

D. Compressed

Performance-Based Question

You will encounter performance-based questions on the A+ exams. The questions on the exam require you to perform a specific task, and you will be graded on whether you were able to complete the task. The following requires you to think creatively in order to measure how well you understand this chapter's topics. You may or may not see similar questions on the actual A+ exams. To see how your answers compare to the authors', refer to Appendix B.

Looking at the back of a computer, you see the interfaces shown in the following graphic. Which type of cables do you need to plug into each one?

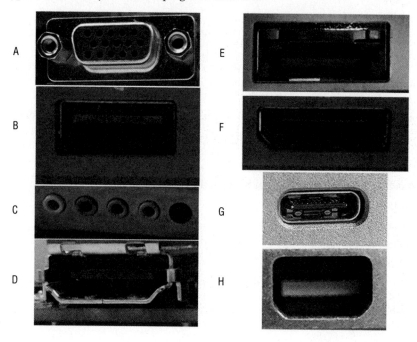

Chapter

4

Printers and Multifunction Devices

THE FOLLOWING COMPTIA A+ 220-1101 EXAM OBJECTIVES ARE COVERED IN THIS CHAPTER:

✓ **3.6 Given a scenario, deploy and configure multifunction devices/printers and settings.**

- Properly unboxing a device – setup location considerations
- Use appropriate drivers for a given OS
  - Printer Control Language (PCL) vs. PostScript
- Device connectivity
  - USB
  - Ethernet
  - Wireless
- Public/shared devices
  - Printer share
  - Print server
- Configuration settings
  - Duplex
  - Orientation
  - Tray settings
  - Quality
- Security
  - User authentication
  - Badging
  - Audit logs
  - Secured prints
- Network scan services
  - Email

- SMB
- Cloud services
- Automatic document feeder (ADF)/flatbed scanner

✓ 3.7 Given a scenario, install and replace printer consumables.

- Laser
  - Imaging drum, fuser assembly, transfer belt, transfer roller, pickup rollers, separation pads, duplexing assembly
  - Imaging process: processing, charging, exposing, developing, transferring, fusing, and cleaning
  - Maintenance: Replace toner, apply maintenance kit, calibrate, clean
- Inkjet
  - Ink cartridge, print head, roller, feeder, duplexing assembly, carriage belt
  - Calibration
  - Maintenance: Clean heads, replace cartridges, calibrate, clear jams
- Thermal
  - Feed assembly, heating element
  - Special thermal paper
  - Maintenance: Replace paper, clean heating element, remove debris
  - Heat sensitivity of paper
- Impact
  - Print head, ribbon, tractor feed
  - Impact paper
  - Maintenance: Replace ribbon, replace print head, replace paper
- 3-D printer
  - Filament
  - Resin
  - Print bed

Even as technology processes and almost all of our lives seem digitized, our society is still reliant on paper. When we conduct business, we use different types of paper documents, such as contracts, letters, and, of course, money. And because most of those documents are created on computers, printers are inherently important. Even with electronic business being the norm in many situations, you will likely still have daily situations that require an old-fashioned hard copy of something.

Printers are electromechanical output devices that are used to put information from the computer onto paper. They have been around since the introduction of the computer. Other than the display monitor, the printer is the most popular output device purchased for a computer because a lot of people want and sometimes need to have paper copies of the documents they create.

In this chapter, we will discuss the details of each major type of printing technology, including impact printers, inkjet printers, laser printers, and thermal printers. We'll also get into three-dimensional (3D) printers, which are an entirely different output animal and have nothing to do with putting ink on paper. They are so different that it's almost a misnomer to call them printers. *Unless we specifically talk about 3D printing, assume we mean the classic two-dimensional kind.* Once we cover the different types, we'll talk about installing and configuring printers and finish up with a section on printer maintenance.

Take special note of the section on laser printers. The A+ 220-1101 exam tests these subjects in detail, so we'll cover them in depth.

Printer troubleshooting is covered in Chapter 12, "Hardware and Network Troubleshooting."

Understanding Print Technologies and Imaging Processes

Several types of printers are available on the market today. As with all other computer components, there have been significant advancements in printer technology over the years. Most of the time, when faced with the decision of purchasing a printer, you're going to be weighing performance versus cost. Some of the higher-quality technologies, such as color laser printing, are relatively expensive for the home user. Other technologies are less expensive but don't provide the same level of quality.

In the following sections, you will learn about the various types of print technologies that you will see as a technician as well as their basic components and how they function. Specifically, we are going to look at four classifications of classic printing—impact, inkjet, laser, and thermal—and then finish up with a primer on 3D printing.

Impact Printers

The most basic type of printer is in the category known as an *impact printer*. Impact printers, as their name suggests, use some form of impact and an inked *printer ribbon* to make an imprint on the paper. Impact printers also use a paper feed mechanism called a *tractor feed* that requires special paper. Perhaps you've seen it before—it's continuous-feed paper with holes running down both edges.

There are two major types of impact printers: daisy-wheel and dot-matrix. Each type has its own service and maintenance issues.

Daisy-Wheel Printers

The first type of impact printer to know about is the *daisy-wheel printer*. This is one of the oldest printing technologies in use. These impact printers contain a wheel (called the daisy wheel because it looks like a daisy) with raised letters and symbols on each "petal" (see Figure 4.1). When the printer needs to print a character, it sends a signal to the mechanism that contains the wheel. This mechanism is called the *print head*. The print head rotates the daisy wheel until the required character is in place. An electromechanical hammer (called a *solenoid)* then strikes the back of the petal containing the character. The character pushes up against an inked ribbon that ultimately strikes the paper, making the impression of the requested character.

FIGURE 4.1   A daisy-wheel printer mechanism

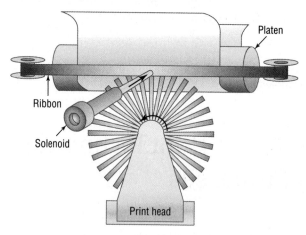

Daisy-wheel printers were among the first types of impact printer developed. Their speed is rated by the number of *characters per second (cps)* they can print. The earliest printers could print only two to four characters per second. Aside from their poor speed, the main disadvantage of this type of printer is that it makes a lot of noise when printing—so much so, in fact, that special enclosures were developed to contain the noise. There is also no concept of using multiple fonts; the font is whatever the character on the wheel looks like.

The daisy-wheel printer has a few advantages, of course. First, because it is an impact printer, you can print on multipart forms (like carbonless receipts), assuming that they can be fed into the printer properly. Sometimes, you will hear this type of paper referred to as *impact paper*. Second, it is relatively inexpensive compared to the price of a laser printer of the same vintage. Finally, the print quality is easily readable; the level of quality was given a name: *letter quality (LQ)*. Today, LQ might refer to quality that's better than an old-school typewriter (if you're familiar with them) but not up to inkjet standards.

Dot-Matrix Printers

The other type of impact printer to understand is the *dot-matrix printer*. These printers work in a manner similar to daisy-wheel printers, but instead of a spinning, character-imprinted wheel, the print head contains a row of pins (short, sturdy stalks of hard wire). These pins are triggered in patterns that form letters and numbers as the print head moves across the paper (see Figure 4.2).

FIGURE 4.2   Formation of images in a dot-matrix printer

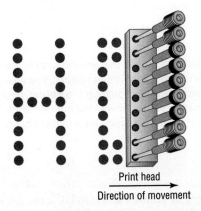

Print head
Direction of movement

The pins in the print head are wrapped with coils of wire to create a solenoid and are held in the rest position by a combination of a small magnet and a spring. To trigger a particular pin, the printer controller sends a signal to the print head, which energizes the wires around the appropriate print wire. This turns the print wire into an electromagnet, which repels the print pin, forcing it against the ink ribbon and making a dot on the paper. The arrangement of the dots in columns and rows creates the letters and numbers that you see on the page. Figure 4.2 illustrates this process.

The main disadvantage of dot-matrix printers is their image quality, which can be quite poor compared to the quality produced with a daisy wheel. Dot-matrix printers use patterns of dots to make letters and images, and the early dot-matrix printers used only nine pins to make those patterns. The output quality of such printers is referred to as *draft quality*— good mainly for providing your initial text to a correspondent or reviser. Each letter looked fuzzy because the dots were spaced as far as they could be and still be perceived as a letter or image. As more pins were crammed into the print head (17-pin and 24-pin models were eventually developed), the quality increased because the dots were closer together. Dot-matrix technology ultimately improved to the point that a letter printed on a dot-matrix printer was *almost* indistinguishable from daisy-wheel output. This level of quality is known as *near letter quality (NLQ)*.

Most impact printers have an option to adjust how close the print head rests from the ribbon. So if your printing is too light, you may be able to adjust the print head closer to the ribbon. If it's too dark or you get smeared printing, you may be able to move the print head back.

Dot-matrix printers are noisy, but the print wires and print head are covered by a plastic dust cover, making them quieter than daisy-wheel printers. They also use a more efficient printing technology, so the print speed is faster (typically starting around 72 cps). Some dot-matrix printers (like the Epson DFX series, which can run up to 1550 cps) can print close to a page per second! Finally, because dot-matrix printers are also impact printers, they can use multipart forms. Because of these advantages, dot-matrix printers quickly made daisy-wheel printers obsolete.

For the exam, remember that you need to know about the print head, ribbon, tractor feed, and impact paper. You will also need to know maintenance items such as replacing the ribbon, replacing the print head, and replacing paper. We will cover the maintenance items in the "Performing Printer Maintenance" section later in this chapter.

Inkjet Printers

One of the most popular types of printers in use today is the *inkjet printer*. As opposed to impact printers, which strike the page, these printers spray ink on the page to form the image. Inkjet printers typically use a reservoir of ink, a pump, and a nozzle to accomplish this. Older inkjet printers were messy, noisy, and inefficient, but the technology is good enough now that you see plenty of photo printers using inkjet technology. You might also hear these types of printers referred to as bubble-jet printers, but that term is copyrighted by Canon. You can think of inkjets as spraying droplets of ink in a very high-definition dot-matrix pattern, although printer manufacturers would likely scoff at the comparison to an older technology.

In the following sections, you will learn the parts of an inkjet printer as well as how inkjet printers work.

Parts of a Typical Inkjet Printer

Inkjet printers are simple devices. They contain very few parts (even fewer than dot-matrix printers) and, as such, are inexpensive to manufacture. It's common today to have a $40 to $50 inkjet printer with print quality that rivals that of basic laser printers.

The printer parts can be divided into the following categories:

- Print head/ink cartridge
- Head carriage, belt, and stepper motor
- Paper feed mechanism
- Control, interface, and power circuitry

Why So Cheap?

The cost of inkjet printers is pretty low—one would think that the printer companies make very little money on them (which is true). So why do they price them so low?

The answer is that printer companies make the vast majority of their profits from ink cartridge sales. They figure that if they can get you into their printer, you will buy their ink refills—which is true—so you are then a captive consumer. Ink cartridges are very cheap to produce and have a high profit margin.

Print Head/Ink Cartridge

The first part of an inkjet printer is the one that people see the most: the *print head*. This part of a printer contains many small nozzles (usually 100 to 200) that spray the ink in small droplets onto the page. Many times, the print head is part of the *ink cartridge*, which contains a reservoir of ink and the print head in a removable package. Most color inkjet printers include multiple print heads. Either there will be one for the black cartridge and one for the color one, or there will be one for each of the *CMYK* (cyan, magenta, yellow, and black) print inks. The print cartridge must be replaced as the ink supply runs out.

Inside the ink cartridge are several small chambers. At the top of each chamber are a metal plate and a tube leading to the ink supply. At the bottom of each chamber is a small pinhole. These pinholes are used to spray ink on the page to form characters and images as patterns of dots, similar to the way a dot-matrix printer works but with much higher resolution.

There are two methods of spraying the ink out of the cartridge. Hewlett-Packard (HP) popularized the first method: when a particular chamber needs to spray ink, an electric signal is sent to the heating element, energizing it. The elements heat up quickly, causing the ink to vaporize. Because of the expanding ink vapor, the ink is pushed out of the pinhole and forms a bubble. As the vapor expands, the bubble eventually gets large enough to break off into a droplet. The rest of the ink is pulled back into the chamber by the surface tension of the ink. When another drop needs to be sprayed, the process begins again. The second method, developed by Epson, uses a piezoelectric element (either a small rod or a unit that looks like a miniature drum head) that flexes when energized. The outward flex pushes the ink from the nozzle; on the return, it sucks more ink from the reservoir.

When the printer is done printing, the print head moves back to its maintenance station. The *maintenance station* contains a small suction pump and ink-absorbing pad. To keep the ink flowing freely, before each print cycle the maintenance station pulls ink through the ink nozzles using vacuum suction. The pad absorbs this expelled ink. The station serves two functions: to provide a place for the print head to rest when the printer isn't printing and to keep the print head in working order.

Head Carriage, Belt, and Stepper Motor

Another major component of the inkjet printer is the head carriage and the associated parts that make it move. The *print head carriage* is the component of an inkjet printer that moves back and forth during printing. It contains the physical as well as electronic connections for the print head and (in some cases) the ink reservoir. Figure 4.3 shows an example of a head carriage. Note the clips that keep the ink cartridge in place and the electronic connections for the ink cartridge. These connections cause the nozzles to fire, and if they aren't kept clean, you may have printing problems.

FIGURE 4.3   A print head carriage (holding two ink cartridges) in an inkjet printer

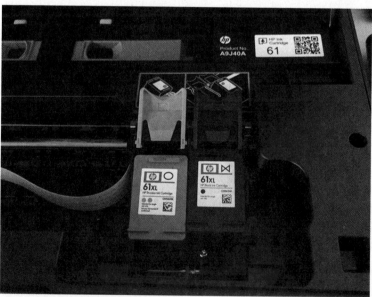

The stepper motor and belt make the print head carriage move. A *stepper motor* is a precisely made electric motor that can move in the same very small increments each time

it is activated. That way, it can move to the same position(s) time after time. The motor that makes the print head carriage move is also often called the *carriage motor* or *carriage stepper motor*. Figure 4.4 shows an example of a stepper motor.

FIGURE 4.4   A carriage stepper motor

In addition to the motor, a belt is placed around two small wheels or pulleys and attached to the print head carriage. This belt, called the *carriage belt*, is driven by the carriage motor and moves the print head back and forth across the page while it prints. To keep the print head carriage aligned and stable while it traverses the page, the carriage rests on a small metal *stabilizer bar*. Figure 4.5 shows the entire system—the stepper motor, carriage belt, stabilizer bar, and print head carriage.

We will cover inkjet printer maintenance in the "Performing Printer Maintenance" section later in this chapter. For now, though, know that if any part of the print carriage assembly breaks in an inkjet printer, it will likely be faster and less expensive to just go buy a new printer rather than trying to fix it. The only maintenance you should need to do is clean the print heads, replace ink cartridges, and clear paper jams.

Paper Feed Mechanism

In addition to getting the ink onto the paper, the printer must have a way to get the paper into the printer. That's where the *paper feed mechanism* comes in. The paper feed mechanism picks up paper from the paper drawer and feeds it into the printer. This component consists of several smaller assemblies. First are the *pickup rollers* (see Figure 4.6), which are one or more rubber rollers with a slightly grippy texture; they rub against the paper as they rotate and feed the paper into the printer. They work against small cork or rubber patches known as *separation pads* (see Figure 4.7), which help keep the rest of the paper in place so that only one sheet goes into the printer. The pickup rollers are turned on a shaft by the *pickup stepper motor*.

FIGURE 4.5   Carriage stepper motor, carriage belt, stabilizer bar, and print head carriage in an inkjet printer

Stepper motor

Carriage belt

Stabilizer bar

Print head carriage

FIGURE 4.6   Inkjet pickup roller (center darker roller)

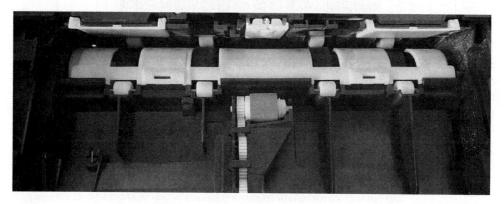

    Clean pickup rollers (and other rubber rollers) with mild soap and water, not with alcohol. Alcohol can dry out the rollers, making them brittle and ineffective.

FIGURE 4.7   Inkjet separation pads

Sometimes the paper that is fed into an inkjet printer is placed into a *paper tray*, which is simply a small plastic tray in the front of the printer that holds the paper until it is fed into the printer by the paper feed mechanism. On smaller printers, the paper is placed vertically into a *paper feeder* at the back of the printer; it uses gravity, in combination with feed rollers and separation pads, to get the paper into the printer. No real rhyme or reason dictates which manufacturers use these different parts; some models use them, and some don't. Generally, more expensive printers use paper trays because they hold more paper. Figure 4.8 shows an example of a paper tray on an inkjet printer.

FIGURE 4.8   A paper tray on an inkjet printer

Next are the *paper feed sensors*. These components tell the printer when it is out of paper as well as when a paper jam has occurred during the paper feed process. Figure 4.9 shows an example of a paper feed sensor. Finally, there is the *duplexing assembly*, which allows for printing on both sides of a page. After the first side is printed and has a few seconds to dry, the duplexing assembly will pull the paper back in and flip it over to print the second side. Not all inkjet printers have one, but those that do will usually have them near the back bottom of the printer. Figure 4.10 shows the duplexing assembly rollers. This area is the most likely one to incur a paper jam, so there's usually a removable panel inside the printer for easy access to clear the problem.

FIGURE 4.9   A paper feed sensor on an inkjet printer

FIGURE 4.10   Duplexing assembly rollers

Being able to identify the parts of an inkjet printer is an important skill for an A+ candidate. In Exercise 4.1, you will identify the parts of an inkjet printer. For this exercise, you'll need an inkjet printer.

Many of the exercises in this chapter require printer hardware. If you don't have the proper hardware on which to practice, you can find many helpful videos online showing how to identify parts and install and perform maintenance on printers. Sites such as IFixit.com and YouTube .com are good places to start.

EXERCISE 4.1

Identifying the Parts of an Inkjet Printer

1. Unplug the inkjet printer from the power source and the computer.

2. Open the top cover to expose the inner print mechanism.

3. Locate and identify the paper tray.

4. Locate and identify the paper feed sensor.

5. Locate and identify the pickup roller(s).

6. Locate and identify the separation pad(s).

7. Locate and identify the print head, carriage assembly, and belt.

8. Locate and identify the ink cartridge(s).

Control, Interface, and Power Circuitry

The final component group is the electronic circuitry for printer control, printer interfaces, and printer power. The *printer control circuits* are usually on a small circuit board that contains all the circuitry to run the stepper motors the way the printer needs them to work (back and forth, load paper and then stop, and so on). These circuits are also responsible for monitoring the health of the printer and for reporting that information back to the PC.

The second power component, the *interface circuitry* (commonly called a *port*), makes the physical connection to whatever signal is coming from the computer (USB, serial, network, infrared, etc.) and also connects the physical interface to the control circuitry. The interface circuitry converts the signals from the interface into the data stream that the printer uses.

The last set of circuits the printer uses is the *power circuits*. Essentially, these conductive pathways convert 110V (in the United States) or 220V (in most of the rest of the world) from a standard wall outlet into the voltages that the inkjet printer uses, usually 12V and 5V, and distribute those voltages to the other printer circuits and devices that need it. This is accomplished through the use of a *transformer*. A transformer, in this case, takes the 110V AC current and changes it to 12V DC (among others). This transformer can be either internal (incorporated into the body of the printer) or external. Either design can be used in today's inkjets, although the integrated design is preferred because it is simpler and doesn't show the bulky transformer.

The Inkjet Printing Process

Before you print to an inkjet printer, you must ensure that the device is calibrated. *Calibration* is the process by which a device is brought within functional specifications. For example, inkjet printers need their print heads aligned so that they print evenly and don't print funny-looking letters and unevenly spaced lines. The process is part of the installation for all inkjet printers. Printers will typically run a calibration routine every time you install new ink cartridges. You will only need to manually initiate a calibration if the printing alignment appears off.

Just as with other types of printing, the inkjet printing process consists of a set of steps that the printer must follow in order to put the data onto the page being printed. The following steps take place whenever you click the Print button in your favorite software (like Microsoft Word or Google Chrome):

1. You click the Print button (or similar) that initiates the printing process.

2. The software from which you are printing sends the data to be printed to the printer driver that you have selected.

> The function and use of the printer driver are discussed later in this chapter.

3. The printer driver uses a page-description language to convert the data being printed into the format that the printer can understand. The driver also ensures that the printer is ready to print.

4. The printer driver sends the information to the printer via whatever connection method is being used (USB, network, serial, and so on).

5. The printer stores the received data in its onboard print buffer memory.

   A *print buffer* is a small amount of memory (typically 512 KB to 16 MB) used to store print jobs as they are received from the printing computer. This buffer allows several jobs to be printed at once and helps printing to be completed quickly.

6. If the printer has not printed in a while, the printer's control circuits activate a cleaning cycle.

   A *cleaning cycle* is a set of steps the inkjet printer goes through to purge the print heads of any dried ink. It uses a special suction cup and sucking action to pull ink through the print head, dislodging any dried ink or clearing stuck passageways.

7. Once the printer is ready to print, the control circuitry activates the paper feed motor.

   This causes a sheet of paper to be fed into the printer until the paper activates the paper feed sensor, which stops the feed until the print head is in the right position and the leading edge of the paper is under the print head. If the paper doesn't reach the paper feed sensor in a specified amount of time after the stepper motor has been activated, the Out Of Paper light is turned on and a message is sent to the computer.

8. Once the paper is positioned properly, the print head stepper motor uses the print head belt and carriage to move the print head across the page, little by little.

9. The motor is moved one small step, and the print head sprays the dots of ink on the paper in the pattern dictated by the control circuitry.

   Typically, this is either a pattern of black dots or a pattern of CMYK inks that are mixed to make colors.

10. Then the stepper motor moves the print head another small step; the process repeats all the way across the page.

    This process is so quick, however, that the entire series of starts and stops across the page looks like one smooth motion.

11. At the end of a pass across the page, the paper feed stepper motor advances the page a small amount. Then the print head repeats step 8.

12. Depending on the model, either the print head returns to the beginning of the line and prints again in the same direction or it moves backward across the page so that printing occurs in both directions. This process continues until the page is finished.

13. Once the page is finished, the feed stepper motor is actuated and ejects the page from the printer into the output tray. (On printers with a duplexing assembly, the paper is only partially ejected so the duplexing assembly can grab it, pull it back in, and flip it over for printing on the second side.)

    If more pages need to print, the process for printing the next page begins again at step 7.

14. Once printing is complete and the final page is ejected from the printer, the print head is *parked* (locked into rest position) and the print process is finished.

The exam objectives list several things you need to know for the exam. They include parts such as the ink cartridge, print head, roller, feeder, duplexing assembly, and carriage belt. Calibration is an exam objective as well. Finally, you'll need to know maintenance concepts such as cleaning print heads, replacing cartridges, calibration, and clearing jams. We'll cover the maintenance topics in the "Performing Printer Maintenance" section later in this chapter.

Laser Printers

Laser printers and inkjet printers are referred to as *page printers* because they receive their print job instructions one page at a time rather than receiving instructions one line at a time. There are two major types of page printers that use the electrophotographic (EP) imaging process. The first uses a laser to scan the image onto a photosensitive drum, and the second uses an array of light-emitting diodes (LEDs) to create the image on the drum. Even though they write the image in different ways, both types still follow the laser printer imaging process. Since the A+ exam focuses on the laser printer imaging process and not on differences between laser and LED, we'll focus on the same here.

Xerox, Hewlett-Packard, and Canon were pioneers in developing the laser printer technology we use today. Scientists at Xerox developed the electrophotographic (EP) imaging process in 1971. HP introduced the first successful desktop laser printer in 1984, using Canon hardware that used the EP process. This technology uses a combination of static electric charges, laser light, and a black powdery ink-like substance called *toner*. Printers that use this technology are called EP process laser printers, or just *laser printers*. Every laser printer technology has its foundations in the EP printer imaging process.

Let's discuss the basic components of the EP laser printer and how they operate so that you can understand the way an EP laser printer works.

Basic Components

Most printers that use the EP imaging process contain nine standard assemblies: the toner cartridge, laser scanner, high-voltage power supply, DC power supply, paper transport assembly (including paper-pickup rollers and paper-registration rollers), transfer corona, fusing assembly, printer controller circuitry, and ozone filter. Let's discuss each of the components individually, along with a duplexing assembly, before we examine how they all work together to make the printer function.

The Toner Cartridge

The EP toner cartridge (see Figure 4.11), as its name suggests, holds the toner. Toner is a black carbon substance mixed with polyester resins to make it flow better and iron oxide particles to make it sensitive to electrical charges. These two components make the toner capable of being attracted to the photosensitive drum and of melting into the paper. In addition to these components, toner contains a medium called the *developer* (also called the *carrier*), which carries the toner until it is used by the EP process.

FIGURE 4.11   An EP toner cartridge

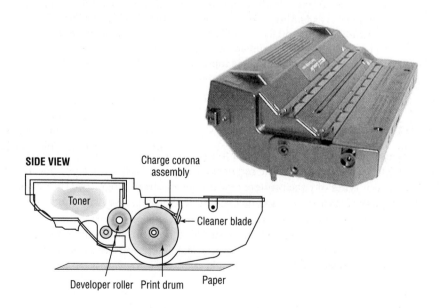

The toner cartridge also contains the EP print drum. This drum is coated with a photosensitive material that can hold a static charge when not exposed to light but *cannot* hold a charge when it *is* exposed to light—a curious phenomenon and one that EP printers exploit for the purpose of making images. Finally, the drum assembly contains a cleaning blade that continuously scrapes the used toner off the photosensitive drum to keep it clean.

Exposing a photosensitive drum to dust or light can damage it, but touching it will most likely render the drum inoperable! It's best to just not mess around with them.

In most laser printers, *toner cartridge* means an EP toner cartridge that contains toner and a photosensitive drum in one plastic case. In some laser printers, however, the toner and photosensitive drum can be replaced separately instead of as a single unit. If you ask for a toner cartridge for one of these printers, all you will receive is a cylinder full of toner. Consult the printer's manual to find out which kind of toner cartridge your laser printer uses.

Never ship a printer anywhere with a toner cartridge installed! The jostling that happens during shipping could cause toner to spill out of the cartridge and all over the inside of the printer. This will be a huge mess to clean up! If the printer is a laser printer, remove the toner cartridge first. You can put it in a sealed, airtight bag to ship, if needed. If it's an LED page printer, there is a method to remove the photosensitive drum and toner cartridge. Also be careful to avoid too much jostling or turning the printer on its side or upside down when unboxing it. (And remember that A+ exam objective 3.6 calls out properly unboxing a printer!) Check your manual for details.

The Laser Scanning Assembly

As we mentioned earlier, the EP photosensitive drum can hold a charge if it's not exposed to light. It is dark inside an EP printer, except when the laser scanning assembly shines on particular areas of the photosensitive drum. When it does that, the drum discharges, but only in the area that has been exposed. As the drum rotates, the laser scanning assembly scans the laser across the photosensitive drum, exposing the image onto it. Figure 4.12 shows the laser scanning assembly.

Laser light is damaging to human eyes. Therefore, the laser is kept in an enclosure and will operate only when the laser printer's cover is closed.

FIGURE 4.12 The EP laser scanning assembly (side view and simplified top view)

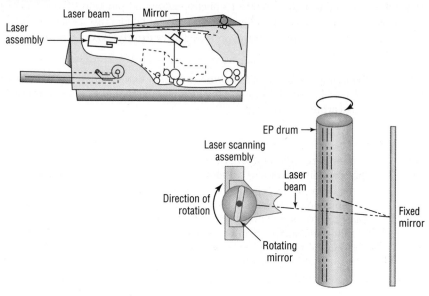

High-Voltage Power Supply

The EP process requires high-voltage electricity. The high-voltage power supply (HVPS) provides the high voltages used during the EP process. This component converts AC current from a standard wall outlet (120V and 60 Hz) into higher voltages that the printer can use. This high voltage is used to energize both the charging corona and the transfer corona.

 Anything with the words *high voltage* in it should make you pause before opening a device and getting your hands into it. The HVPS can hurt or kill you if you're working inside a laser printer and don't know what you're doing.

DC Power Supply

The high voltages used in the EP process can't power the other components in the printer (the logic circuitry and motors). These components require low voltages, between +5VDC and +24VDC. The DC power supply (DCPS) converts house current into three voltages: +5VDC and −5VDC for the logic circuitry and +24VDC for the paper transport motors. This component also runs the fan that cools the internal components of the printer.

Paper Transport Assembly

The paper transport assembly is responsible for moving the paper through the printer. It consists of a motor and several rubberized rollers that each performs a different function.

The first type of roller found in most laser printers is the *feed roller*, or *paper pickup roller* (see Figure 4.13). This D-shaped roller, when activated, rotates against the paper and pushes one sheet into the printer. This roller works in conjunction with a special rubber separation pad to prevent more than one sheet from being fed into the printer at a time.

FIGURE 4.13 Paper transport rollers

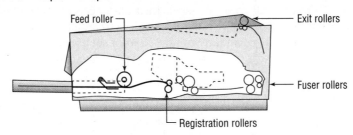

Another type of roller that is used in the printer is the *registration roller* (also shown in Figure 4.13). There are actually two registration rollers, which work together. These rollers synchronize the paper movement with the image-formation process in the EP cartridge. The rollers don't feed the paper past the EP cartridge until the cartridge is ready for it.

Both of these rollers are operated with a special electric motor known as an *electronic stepper motor*. This type of motor can accurately move in very small increments. It powers all the paper transport rollers as well as the fuser rollers.

The Transfer Corona Assembly

When the laser writes (exposes) the images on the photosensitive drum, the toner then sticks to the exposed areas. (We'll cover this later in the "Electrophotographic Imaging Process" section.) How does the toner get from the photosensitive drum onto the paper? The *transfer corona assembly* (see Figure 4.14) is given a high-voltage charge, which is transferred to the paper, which, in turn, pulls the toner from the photosensitive drum.

FIGURE 4.14 The transfer corona assembly

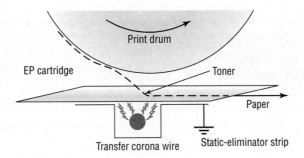

Included in the transfer corona assembly is a *static-charge eliminator strip* that drains away the charge imparted to the paper by the corona. If you didn't drain away the charge, the paper would stick to the EP cartridge and jam the printer.

There are two types of transfer corona assemblies: those that contain a transfer *corona wire* and those that contain a transfer *corona roller*. The transfer corona wire is a small-diameter wire that is charged by the HVPS. The wire is located in a special notch in the floor of the laser printer (under the EP print cartridge). The transfer corona roller performs the same function as the transfer corona wire, but it's a roller rather than a wire. Because the transfer corona roller is directly in contact with the paper, it supports higher speeds. For this reason, the transfer corona wire is used infrequently in laser printers today.

Fusing Assembly

The toner in the EP toner cartridge will stick to just about anything, including paper. This is true because the toner has a negative static charge and most objects have a net positive charge. However, these toner particles can be removed by brushing any object across the page. This could be a problem if you want the images and letters to stay on the paper permanently.

To solve this problem, EP laser printers incorporate a device known as a *fuser* (see Figure 4.15), which uses two rollers that apply pressure and heat to fuse the plastic toner particles to the paper. You may have noticed that pages from either a laser printer or a copier (which uses a similar device) come out warm. This is because of the fuser.

FIGURE 4.15   The fuser

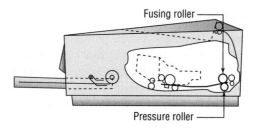

The fuser is made up of three main parts: a halogen heating lamp, a Teflon-coated aluminum-fusing roller, and a rubberized pressure roller. The fuser uses the halogen lamp to heat the fusing roller to between 329° F (165° C) and 392° F (200° C). As the paper passes between the two rollers, the pressure roller pushes the paper against the fusing roller, which melts the toner into the paper.

  The fuser can cause severe burns! Be careful when working with it.

Printer Controller Circuitry

Another component in the laser printer that we need to discuss is the *printer controller assembly*. This large circuit board converts signals from the computer into signals for the various assemblies in the laser printer using a process known as *rasterizing*. This circuit board is usually mounted under the printer. The board has connectors for each type of interface and cables to each assembly.

When a computer prints to a laser printer, it sends a signal through a cable to the printer controller assembly. The controller assembly formats the information into a page's worth of line-by-line commands for the laser scanner. The controller sends commands to each of the components, telling them to wake up and begin the EP imaging process.

Ozone Filter

Your laser printer uses various high-voltage biases inside the case. As anyone who has been outside during a lightning storm can tell you, high voltages create ozone. Ozone is a chemically reactive gas that is created by the high-voltage coronas (charging and transfer) inside the printer. Because ozone is chemically reactive and can severely reduce the life of laser printer components, many older laser printers contain a filter to remove ozone gas from inside the printer as it is produced. This filter must be removed and cleaned with compressed air periodically. (Cleaning it whenever the toner cartridge is replaced is usually sufficient.) Most newer laser printers don't have ozone filters. This is because these printers don't use transfer corona wires but instead use transfer corona rollers, which dramatically reduce ozone emissions.

Duplexing Assembly

Any laser printer worth its money today can print on both sides of the paper (as can some nicer models of inkjet printers, mentioned earlier). This is accomplished through the use of a *duplexing assembly*. Usually located inside or on the back of the printer, the assembly is responsible for taking the paper, turning it over, and feeding back into the printer so the second side can be printed.

Electrophotographic Imaging Process

The *electrophotographic (EP) imaging process* is the process by which an EP laser printer forms images on paper. It consists of seven major steps, each designed for a specific goal. Although many different manufacturers word these steps differently or place them in a different order, the basic process is still the same. Here are the steps in the order in which you will see them on the exam:

1. Processing
2. Charging
3. Exposing
4. Developing
5. Transferring

6. Fusing

7. Cleaning

Before any of these steps can begin, however, the controller must sense that the printer is ready to start printing (toner cartridge installed, fuser warmed to temperature, and all covers in place). Printing cannot take place until the printer is in its ready state, usually indicated by an illuminated Ready LED light or a display that says something like 00 READY (on HP printers). The computer sends the print job to the printer, which begins processing the data as the first step to creating output.

Step 1: Processing

The *processing step* consists of two parts: receiving the image and creating the image. The computer sends the print job to the printer, which receives it via its print interface (USB, wireless, etc.). Then, the printer needs to create the print job in such a way that it can accurately produce the output.

If you think back to our discussion of impact printing earlier in this chapter, you might recall that impact printers produce images by creating one strip of dots at a time across the page. Laser printers use the same concept of rendering one horizontal strip at a time to create the image. Each strip across the page is called a *scan line* or a *raster line*.

A component of the laser printer called the *Raster Image Processor* (RIP) manages raster creation. Its responsibility is to generate an image of the final page in memory. How the raster gets created depends on the page-description language that your system is using, such as PostScript (PS) or Printer Control Language (PCL). (We will get into the details of PS and PCL in the "Page-Description Languages" section later in the chapter.) Ultimately, this collection of lines is what gets written to the photosensitive drum and onto the paper.

Step 2: Charging

The next step in the EP process is the *charging step* (see Figure 4.16). In this step, a special wire or roller (called a *charging corona*) within the EP toner cartridge (above the photosensitive drum) gets high voltage from the HVPS. It uses this high voltage to apply a strong, uniform negative charge (around –600VDC) to the surface of the photosensitive drum.

FIGURE 4.16   The charging step of the EP process

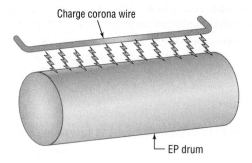

Charge corona wire

EP drum

Step 3: Exposing

Next is exposing the drum to the image, often referred to as the *exposing step*. In this step, the laser is turned on and scans the drum from side to side, flashing on and off according to the bits of information that the printer controller sends it as it communicates the individual bits of the image. Wherever the laser beam touches, the photosensitive drum's charge is severely reduced from –600VDC to a slight negative charge (around –100VDC). As the drum rotates, a pattern of exposed areas is formed, representing the image to be printed. Figure 4.17 shows this process.

FIGURE 4.17   The exposing step of the EP process

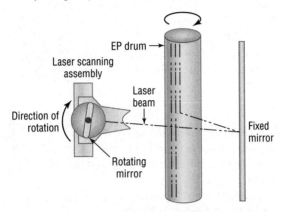

At this point, the controller sends a signal to the pickup roller to feed a piece of paper into the printer, where it stops at the registration rollers.

Step 4: Developing

Now that the surface of the drum holds an electrical representation of the image being printed, its discrete electrical charges need to be converted into something that can be transferred to a piece of paper. The EP process step that accomplishes this is the *developing step* (see Figure 4.18). In this step, toner is transferred to the areas that were exposed in the exposing step.

FIGURE 4.18   The developing step of the EP process

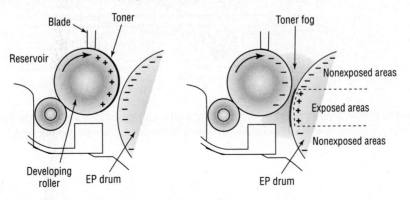

A metallic roller called the *developing roller* inside an EP cartridge acquires a –600VDC charge (called a *bias voltage*) from the HVPS. The toner sticks to this roller because there is a magnet located inside the roller and because of the electrostatic charges between the toner and the developing roller. While the developing roller rotates toward the photosensitive drum, the toner acquires the charge of the roller (–600VDC). When the toner comes between the developing roller and the photosensitive drum, the toner is attracted to the areas that have been exposed by the laser (because these areas have a lesser charge, –100VDC). The toner also is repelled from the unexposed areas (because they are at the same –600VDC charge and like charges repel). This toner transfer creates a fog of toner between the EP drum and the developing roller.

The photosensitive drum now has toner stuck to it where the laser has written. The photosensitive drum continues to rotate until the developed image is ready to be transferred to paper in the next step.

Step 5: Transferring

At this point in the EP process, the developed image is rotating into position. The controller notifies the registration rollers that the paper should be fed through. The registration rollers move the paper underneath the photosensitive drum, and the process of transferring the image can begin; this is the *transferring step*.

The controller sends a signal to the charging corona wire or roller (depending on which one the printer has) and tells it to turn on. The corona wire/roller then acquires a strong *positive* charge (+600VDC) and applies that charge to the paper. Thus charged, the paper pulls the toner from the photosensitive drum at the line of contact between the roller and the paper because the paper and toner have opposite charges. Once the registration rollers move the paper past the corona wire, the static-eliminator strip removes all charge from that line of the paper. Figure 4.19 details this step. If the strip didn't bleed this charge away, the paper would be attracted to the toner cartridge and cause a paper jam.

FIGURE 4.19   The transferring step of the EP process

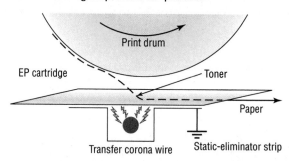

The toner is now held in place by weak electrostatic charges and gravity. It will not stay there, however, unless it is made permanent, which is the reason for the fusing step.

Step 6: Fusing

The penultimate step before the printer produces the finished product is called the *fusing step*. Here the toner image is made permanent. The registration rollers push the paper toward the fuser rollers. Once the fuser grabs the paper, the registration rollers push for only a short time longer. The fuser is now in control of moving the paper.

As the paper passes through the fuser, the 350° F fuser roller melts the polyester resin of the toner, and the rubberized pressure roller presses it permanently into the paper (see Figure 4.20). The paper continues through the fuser and eventually exits the printer.

FIGURE 4.20 The fusing step of the EP process

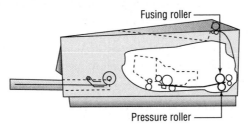

Once the paper completely exits the fuser, it trips a sensor that tells the printer to finish the EP process with the cleaning step.

Step 7: Cleaning

In the last part of the laser imaging process, a rubber blade inside the EP cartridge scrapes any toner left on the drum into a used toner receptacle inside the EP cartridge, and a fluorescent lamp discharges any remaining charge on the photosensitive drum. (Remember that the drum, being photosensitive, loses its charge when exposed to light.) This step is called the *cleaning step* (see Figure 4.21).

FIGURE 4.21 The cleaning step of the EP process

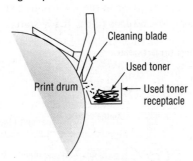

The EP cartridge is constantly cleaning the drum. It may take more than one rotation of the photosensitive drum to make an image on the paper. The cleaning step keeps the drum fresh for each use. If you didn't clean the drum, you would see ghosts of previous pages printed along with your image.

> **NOTE**   The amount of toner removed in the cleaning process is quite small, and the cartridge will run out of toner before the used toner receptacle fills up. The toner that's in the receptacle is useless because the imaging process has already chemically altered it. In addition, it's considered a hazardous substance. Recycle the print cartridge and don't pay attention to the leftover toner.

At this point, the printer can print another page, and the EP process can begin again.

Summary of the EP Imaging Process

Figure 4.22 provides a diagram of all the parts involved in the EP printing process. Here's a summary of the process, which you should commit to memory:

1. The printer receives and processes the image and stores a page in memory.

2. The printer places a uniform –600VDC charge on the photosensitive drum by means of a charging corona.

3. The laser "paints" an image onto the photosensitive drum, discharging the image areas to a much lower voltage (–100VDC).

4. The developing roller in the toner cartridge has charged (–600VDC) toner stuck to it. As it rolls the toner toward the photosensitive drum, the toner is attracted to (and sticks to) the areas of the photosensitive drum that the laser has discharged.

5. The image is then transferred from the drum to the paper at its line of contact by means of the transfer corona wire (or corona roller) with a +600VDC charge. The static-eliminator strip removes the high positive charge from the paper, and the paper, now holding the image, moves on.

6. The paper then enters the fuser, where a fuser roller and the pressure roller make the image permanent. The paper exits the printer.

7. The printer uses a rubber scraper to clean the photosensitive drum. At that point, it is ready to print the next page or it returns to the ready state.

FIGURE 4.22   The EP imaging process

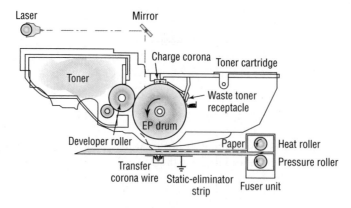

There have been a lot of concepts covered in the laser printing section. For the A+ certification exam, be sure you are familiar with laser printer parts, including the imaging drum, fuser assembly, transfer belt, transfer roller, pickup rollers, separation pads, and duplexing assembly. Also know the steps of the imaging process in order. They are processing, charging, exposing, developing, transferring, fusing, and cleaning.

Thermal Printers

The types of printers that you have learned about so far in this chapter account for 90 percent of all paper printers that are used with home or office computers and that you will see as a repair technician. The remaining 10 percent consist of other types of printers that primarily differ by the method they use to put colored material on the paper to represent what is being printed. Examples of these include solid ink, dye sublimation, and thermal printers. Keep in mind that, for the most part, these printers operate like other paper printers in many ways: they all have a paper feed mechanism (sheet-fed or roll); they all require consumables such as ink or toner and paper; they all use the same interfaces, for the most part, as other types of printers; and they are usually about the same size.

Thermal printing technology is primarily used in point-of-sale (POS) terminals. They print on special *thermal paper*, which is a kind of waxy paper that comes on a roll; it's heat-sensitive paper that turns black when heat passes over it. *Thermal printers* work by using a print head that is the width of the paper. When it needs to print, a heating element heats certain spots on the print head. The paper below the heated print head turns black in those spots. As the paper moves through the printer, the pattern of blackened spots forms an image on the page of what is being printed. Another type of thermal printer uses a heat-sensitive ribbon instead of heat-sensitive paper. A thermal print head melts wax-based ink from the ribbon onto the paper. These are called *thermal transfer printers* or *thermal wax-transfer printers*.

Thermal direct printers typically have long lives because they have few moving parts. The only unique part that you might not be as familiar with is the paper feed assembly, which often needs to accommodate a roll of paper instead of sheets. The paper is somewhat expensive, doesn't last long (especially if it is left in a very warm place, like a closed car in summer), and produces poorer-quality images than the paper used by most of the other printing technologies.

Thermal printer concepts you need to know for the A+ exam include components and materials such as the feed assembly, heating element, and the special heat-sensitive thermal paper. Store it in a cool location! For maintenance, know how to replace paper, clean the heating element, and remove debris. We'll cover the maintenance topics in the "Performing Printer Maintenance" section later in this chapter.

3D Printers

In 2011, the first commercially available 3D printer hit the market. Although the word "printing" is used, the technology and process are completely different from putting ink to paper. *3D printing* is really a fabrication process, also called *additive manufacturing*. In it, a three-dimensional product is produced by "printing" thin layers of a material and stacking those layers on top of each other.

The first 3D printers were used in manufacturing environments. Over time, smaller, more economical models have been made for home use as well, although the technology still remains fairly expensive. There are two primary categories of 3D printers intended for the home and small business use. The first uses rolls of plastic *filament* to create objects, and the second uses a reservoir of liquid *resin* and UV light. We won't cover them here, but 3D printers in industrial applications can use a variety of materials, including aluminum, copper, and other metals. Some enterprising soul also created a 3D printer that prints using melted chocolate. They very likely deserve a Nobel Prize.

Parts of a 3D Filament Printer

They can produce complex creations, but 3D filament (FDM) printers are relatively simple devices with few parts. For the examples here, we will use smaller 3D printers designed for home or small business use. Therefore, we'll focus on printers that use plastic filament as opposed to other materials. The primary components are as follows:

- Frame
- Printing plate or print bed
- Extruder
- Cooling fan
- PCB circuit board
- Filament

The frame holds the printer together. On the bottom of the printer will be the printing plate (or *print bed*), where the object is created. The extruder heats up and melts the filament, which is used to create the object. A cooling fan keeps the extruder from overheating. A PCB circuit board will be installed somewhere, to control the movement of the extruder assembly. Some printers will also have electronic displays and a clear protective case. Figure 4.23 shows a simple MakerBot 3D printer 24. It's relatively easy to see the frame, printing plate, display, and filament tube. 3D printers are connected to a computer using a USB cable.

On most 3D printers, the extruder is attached to metal rods that control the position of the extruder on x-, y-, and z-axes. As mentioned earlier, the extruder heats up and melts plastic filament. The extruder then moves around to create the object, adding one thin layer of material to the printing plate at a time. Figure 4.24 shows an extruder from a different 3D printer—it's the small black block at the bottom of the image. In this image, the filament tube is seen coming from the top of the extruder assembly.

FIGURE 4.23   A 3D filament printer

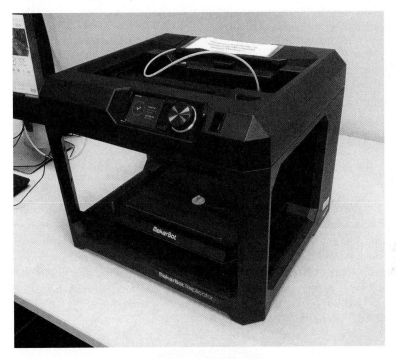

FIGURE 4.24   3D printer extruder

Filament comes on a spool, much like wire, and is shown in Figure 4.25. Be sure that the filament is compatible with the printer you intend to use it with. Here are the things to consider when purchasing replacement filament:

Type More than a dozen different types of plastic filament are available. The most popular are polylactic acid (PLA) and acrylonitrile butadiene styrene (ABS). Each has different characteristics—for example, ABS shrinks as it cools, so a heated printing plate is recommended.

Size The most common size is 1.75 mm, but 3.0 mm filament (which is actually 2.85 mm thick) was the original size and is still used today.

Color The printer doesn't really care what color you use, but a variety of colors are available.

Replacing filament is a straightforward process. The 3D printer's app (or interface panel) will have a Replace Filament button or option. Once you start the process, the extruder will heat up and start to expel the current filament. At some point, it will tell you to replace the roll. You remove the old roll and feed the new filament through the filament tube into the extruder. After a short time, you will see the new color come through as melted filament (if you changed colors), and you can use the app or interface panel to stop the replacement.

FIGURE 4.25 3D printer PLA filament

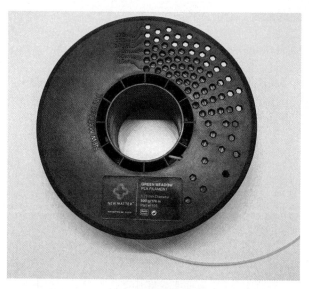

Parts of a 3D Resin Printer

3D resin printers, also called *stereolithography/digital light processing printers (SLA/DLP)*, look and act markedly different from filament printers. SLA/DLP printers use a reservoir of liquid resin combined with UV light that hardens the resin to create objects. The print bed is often at the top, and the printed object appears to rise out of the liquid reservoir. SLA/DLP printers can print objects in much finer detail than FDM can, but they're also slower and require a bit more effort at the end of printing. Figure 4.26 shows a Formlabs resin printer, with a finished 3D print inside.

FIGURE 4.26   Formlabs Form 3 resin printer

Photo courtesy `formlabs.com`

Explaining how resin printing works is much easier with the use of a visual aid, so take a look at Figure 4.27. Most resin printers appear to be upside down. The print bed is on top and moves up as the image is printed. In the middle is the resin tank with a transparent bottom, filled with liquid resin. A light source at the bottom (an LCD in cheaper models and a laser in nicer ones) shines ultraviolet (UV) light on the resin to cure it. As the first layer of the object is "printed," the print bed moves up slightly and the laser writes the next layer.

When the 3D object is finished printing, uncured resin is removed with a rinse of isopropyl alcohol. Some objects will be put into post-curing to strengthen them even more.

FIGURE 4.27   Resin printing in action

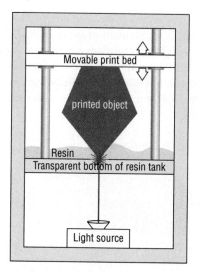

The 3D Printing Process

Every 3D printer comes with its own software that helps manage the printing process; therefore, you will see some nuances in the process from printer to printer. From a big-picture standpoint, though, the printing process is similar for all 3D printers. The following are general steps taken to get from idea to 3D printed object:

1. Design the object using a computer-aided design (CAD) program.

    The most well-known commercial software for this is probably AutoCAD by Autodesk. Another option is the free Tinkercad.

2. Export the file from the CAD software. Doing so will cause the CAD program to "slice" the object into layers, preparing it for printing. The exported file will be an STL file.

    This step will vary somewhat, depending on the 3D printer's software. In many cases, the STL file can be imported into the printer's app, and the app will slice the file yet again, formatting the model specifically for the printer. Some apps can't slice, though, so third-party slicing software is needed. Examples include Cura, SliceCrafter, and Slic3r. Most slicers are free, although commercial versions are available.

3. Send the job to the printer. This is basically just pushing the Print button.

4. The printer will perform a calibration and self-test. On FDM printers, the extruder will heat up and calibrate its position on the x-, y-, and z-axes.

5. Printing begins.

    Small print jobs may take over an hour, depending on the printer and the size of the object. Larger jobs may take days to complete. The maximum object size will be determined by the model of printer. After the job is done, a little sanding or filing may be required to remove excess filament. A completed 3D print job (actually several jobs) is shown in Figure 4.28. In total, the objects are about 1.5" long. Higher-end 3D printers can create components that move, such as hinges and latches.

FIGURE 4.28   3D printed objects

The list of 3D printer exam objectives is rather short, but don't let its brevity deceive you. The objectives include filament, resin, and print bed. Each of those objectives are rather broad, so they could imply needing some depth of knowledge about the subject!

Installing and Maintaining Printers

Odds are that everyone either owns a printer or has easy access to a printer at a library, work, or some other place. Many retailers and computer manufacturers make it incredibly easy to buy a printer because they often bundle a printer with a computer system as an incentive to get you to buy.

The CompTIA A+ 220-1101 exam will test your knowledge of the procedures to install and maintain printers. In the following sections, we will discuss connecting printers through various interfaces, installing and sharing local and networked printers, implementing network printer security and scan services, performing printer maintenance, and installing printer upgrades.

Many inkjet and laser printers today provide several functions, including copying, scanning, and faxing. These devices go by several names, including multifunctional printer, multifunction device (MFD), multifunction product (MFP), or all-in-one printer.

Printer Interface Components

A printer's *interface* is the collection of hardware and software that allows the printer to communicate with a computer. The hardware interface is commonly called a *port*. Each printer has at least one interface, but some printers have several interfaces, to make them more flexible in a multiplatform environment. If a printer has several interfaces, it can usually switch between them on the fly so that several computers can print at the same time.

An interface incorporates several components, including its interface type and the *interface software*. Each aspect must be matched on both the printer and the computer. For example, an HP LaserJet M480F has only a USB port. Therefore, you must use a USB cable (or wireless networking) as well as the correct software for the platform being used (for example, a Mac HP LaserJet M480F driver if you connect it to an iMac computer).

Interface Types

When we say *interface types*, we're talking about the ports used in getting the printed information from the computer to the printer. There are two major classifications here: wired and wireless. Wired examples are serial, parallel, USB, and Ethernet. Wireless options include 802.11 and Bluetooth. You've learned about the wired connections in Chapter 3, "Peripherals, Cables, and Connectors," and you will learn more about the wireless connections in Chapter 5, "Networking Fundamentals." Here you will learn how they apply to printers.

Serial

When computers send data serially, they send it 1 bit at a time, one after another. The bits stand in line like people at a movie theater, waiting to get in. Old-time serial (DB-9) connections were painfully slow, but new serial technology (Thunderbolt, eSATA, and others) makes it a more viable option than parallel. While it's quite common to see USB (another type of serial connection) printers on the market, it's rare to find any other types of serial printers out there.

Parallel

When a printer uses parallel communication, it is receiving data 8 bits at a time over eight separate wires (one for each bit). Parallel communication was the most popular way of communicating from computer to printer for many years, mainly because it was faster than serial. In fact, the *parallel port* became so synonymous with printing that a lot of companies simply started referring to parallel ports as printer ports. Today, though, parallel printers are rare. The vast majority of wired printers that you see will be USB or Ethernet.

A parallel cable consists of a male DB-25 connector that connects to the computer and a male 36-pin Centronics connector that connects to the printer. Most of the cables are shorter than 10 feet. The industry standard that defines parallel communications is IEEE 1284; parallel cables should be IEEE 1284–compliant.

WARNING Keep printer cable lengths shorter than 10′. Some people try to run printer cables more than 50′. If the length is greater than 10′, communications can become unreliable due to crosstalk, which is the degrading of a signal due to electromagnetic interference (EMI).

Universal Serial Bus

The most popular type of wired printer interface is the Universal Serial Bus (USB). In fact, it is the most popular interface for just about every peripheral. The convenience for printers is that it has a higher transfer rate than older serial or parallel connections, and it automatically recognizes new devices. And, of course, USB is physically very easy to connect.

Ethernet

Many printers sold today have a wired Ethernet interface that allows them to be hooked directly to an Ethernet cable. These printers have an internal network interface card (NIC) and ROM-based software that allow them to communicate on the network with servers and workstations.

As with any other networking device, the type of network interface used on the printer depends on the type of network to which the printer is being attached. It's likely that the only connection type that you will run into is RJ-45 for an Ethernet connection.

Wireless

The latest trend in printer interface technology is to use wireless. Clearly, people love their Wi-Fi because it enables them to roam around their home or office and still remain connected to one another and to their network. It logically follows that someone came up with the brilliant idea that it would be nice if printers could be that mobile as well—after all, many are on carts with wheels. Some printers have built-in Wi-Fi interfaces, while others can accept wireless network cards. Wi-Fi–enabled printers support nearly all 802.11 standards (a, b, g, n, ac, ax), and the availability of devices will mirror the current popularity of each standard.

The wireless technology that is especially popular among peripheral manufacturers is *Bluetooth*. Bluetooth is a short-range wireless technology; most devices are specified to work within 10 meters (33 feet). Printers such as the HP Sprocket series and OfficeJet 150 mobile printers have Bluetooth capability.

When printing with a Bluetooth-enabled device (like a smartphone or tablet) and a Bluetooth-enabled printer, all you need to do is get within range of the device (that is, move closer), select the printer driver from the device, and choose Print. The information is transmitted wirelessly through the air using radio waves and is received by the device.

NOTE When Wi-Fi is used to connect printers to a network on a more permanent basis, it is known as *infrastructure mode*. Wi-Fi and Bluetooth can be used to connect a printer temporarily to a single computer (or mobile device), and the connection does not have permanent status. This type of configuration is known as an *ad hoc* network connection.

Interface Software

Now that we've looked at the ways that you can connect your printer, it's time to face a grim reality: computers and printers don't know how to talk to each other. They need help. That help comes in the form of interface software used to translate software commands into commands that the printer can understand.

There are two major components of interface software: the page-description language and the driver software. The page-description language (PDL) determines how efficient the printer is at converting the information to be printed into signals that the printer can understand. The driver software understands and controls the printer and must be written to communicate between a specific operating system and a specific printer. It is very important that you use the correct interface software for your printer. If you use either the wrong page-description language or the wrong driver software, the printer will print garbage—or possibly nothing at all.

Page-Description Languages

A *page-description language* works just as its name implies: it describes the whole page being printed by sending commands that describe the text as well as the margins and other settings. The controller in the printer interprets these commands and turns them into laser pulses (or pin strikes). Several printer communication languages exist, but the three most common are PostScript (PS), *Printer Control Language (PCL)*, and Graphics Device Interface (GDI).

Hewlett-Packard (HP) developed PCL in 1984, and HP's name for the acronym is Printer Command Language. The CompTIA A+ exam objectives say Printer Control Language (yet the acronyms list at the end of the objectives uses "Command"). They're not going to ask you to define the acronym on the exam. Be familiar with the basics of what it does, where it's used, and the problems caused by using the wrong page description language.

The first page-description language was PostScript. Developed by Adobe, it was first used in the Apple LaserWriter printer. It made printing graphics fast and simple. Here's how PostScript works. The PostScript printer driver describes the page in terms of "draw" and "position" commands. The page is divided into a very fine grid (as fine as the resolution of the printer). When you want to print a square, a communication like the following takes place:
POSITION 1,42%DRAW 10%POSITION 1,64%DRAW10D% . . .

These commands tell the printer to draw a line on the page from line 42 to line 64 (vertically). In other words, a page-description language tells the printer to draw a line on the page and gives it the starting and ending points—and that's that. Rather than send the printer the location of each and every dot in the line and an instruction at each and every location to print that location's individual dot, PostScript can get the line drawn with fewer than five instructions. As you can see, PostScript uses commands that are more or less in English. The commands are interpreted by the processor on the printer's controller and converted into the print-control signals.

When HP developed PCL, it was originally intended for use with inkjet printers as a competitor to PostScript. Since then, its role has been expanded to virtually every printer type, and it's a de facto industry standard.

 In general, PCL is more used for standard office-type printing where most things are text-based, whereas PS is more for graphics-intensive printing.

GDI is actually a Windows component and is not specific to printers. Instead, it's a series of components that govern how images are presented to both monitors and printers. GDI printers work by using computer processing power instead of their own. The printed image is rendered to a bitmap on the computer and then sent to the printer. This means that the printer hardware doesn't need to be as powerful, which results in a less expensive printer. Generally speaking, the least expensive laser printers on the market are GDI printers.

 Most newer printers can handle both PS and PCL (and GDI) and will automatically translate for you. Therefore, it's less likely that you'll install the wrong printer driver than it was several years ago.

The main advantage of page-description languages is that they move some of the processing from the computer to the printer. With text-only documents, they offer little benefit. However, with documents that have large amounts of graphics or that use numerous fonts, page-description languages make the processing of those print jobs happen much faster. This makes them an ideal choice for laser printers, although nearly every type of printer uses them.

 Real World Scenario

Life without a Page-Description Language

Page-description languages make printing an efficient process. But what about when they are not used? In situations like this, the computer sends all the instructions the printer needs in a serial stream, like so: Position 1, print nothing; Position 2, strike pins 1 and 3; Position 3, print nothing. This type of description language works well for dot-matrix printers, but it can be inefficient for laser printers. For example, if you wanted to print a page using a standard page-description language and only one character was on the page, there would be a lot of signal wasted on the "print nothing" commands.

With graphics, the commands to draw a shape on the page are relatively complex. For example, to draw a square, the computer (or printer) has to calculate the size of the square and convert that into a lot of "strike pin *x*" (or "turn on laser") and "print nothing" commands. This is where the other types of page-description languages come into the picture.

If you're working with an older laser printer and it's printing garbage, check the driver. It might have the letters *PS* or *PCL* at the end of the name. If a PS driver is installed for a printer that wants PCL (or vice versa), garbage output could be the result.

Driver Software

The *driver* software controls how the printer processes the print job. When you install a printer driver for the printer you are using, it allows the computer to print to that printer correctly (assuming that you have the correct interface configured between the computer and printer). The driver must be written specifically for the operating system the computer is using and for the printer being used. In other words, Mac clients need a different driver than Windows clients need, even to print to the same printer.

If you're working with a Windows-based operating system, Microsoft refers to the software that is installed on the computer and lets you print as the "printer." The physical device where the paper comes out is referred to as the "print device." Here, when we say "printer," we mean the physical device.

When you need to print, you select the printer driver for your printer from a pre-configured list. The driver that you select has been configured for the type, brand, and model of printer, as well as the computer port to which it is connected. You can also select which paper tray the printer should use as well as any other features the printer has (if applicable). Also, each printer driver is configured to use a particular page-description language.

If the wrong printer driver is selected, the computer will send commands in the wrong language. If that occurs, the printer will print several pages full of garbage (even if only one page of information was sent). This "garbage" isn't garbage at all but the printer page-description language commands printed literally as text instead of being interpreted as control commands.

For the A+ exam, be familiar with three device connectivity interfaces: USB, Ethernet, and wireless. Also know how to use proper drivers, and understand the basic differences between PCL and PostScript.

Installing and Sharing Local Printers

Although every device is different, there are certain accepted methods used for installing almost all of them. The following procedure works for installing many kinds of devices:

1. Choose the proper setup location for the device.

2. Attach the device using a local port (generally USB, but may be something else) and connect the power.

3. Install and update the device driver and calibrate the device.

4. Configure options and settings.

5. Print a test page.

6. Verify compatibility with the operating system and applications.

7. Educate users about basic functionality.

Before installing any device, read your device's installation instructions. There are exceptions to every rule.

Step 1: Choose the Proper Setup Location for the Device

Before installing the printer, scout out the best location for it. If it's a home-based printer, you may want to choose a convenient but inconspicuous location. In an office setting, having the printer centrally located may save a lot of headaches. Consider the users and how easy or difficult it will be for them to get to the printer. Also consider connectivity. For a wireless printer, how close is it to an access point? (It should be close.) If it's a wired printer, it will need to be near an RJ-45 wall jack. Finally, always choose a flat, stable surface. After you determine the location, be sure to carefully unbox the device. You may need a box cutter, scissors, or other types of tools to get the box open without destroying it. Avoid dropping or banging the printer. Some printers are very heavy, so they may be easy to drop—employ team lifting if needed. If it's a laser printer with toner cartridges installed, don't turn it on its side or upside down. Most printers will come with a quick setup guide—often a glossy poster-sized printout—that will show you how to properly unbox and connect the device. When you are done with the box, save it if you think you might need to move the printer later, or recycle it and the packing materials.

Step 2: Attach the Device Using a Local Port and Connect the Power

After you have unboxed the printer, with the device powered off, connect it to the host computer. Today, the vast majority of local printers are USB, but you will occasionally find ones that use different ports as well.

Once you have connected the device, connect power to it using whatever supplied power adapter comes with it. Some devices have their own built-in power supply and just need an AC power cord connecting the device to the wall outlet, while others rely on an external transformer and power supply. Finally, turn on the device.

Step 3: Install and Update the Device Driver and Calibrate the Device

Once you have connected and powered up the device, Windows should automatically recognize it. When it does, a screen will pop up saying that Windows is installing the driver. If a driver is not found, you will be given the option to specify the location of the driver. You can insert the driver media (flash drive, DVD, etc.) that came with the device, and the wizard will guide you through the device driver installation.

If Windows fails to recognize the device, you can start the process manually by initiating the Add Printer Wizard to troubleshoot the installation and to install the device drivers. To start the wizard in Windows 10, click Start, type **printer**, and then click Printers & Scanners when it appears under Best Match. Click Add A Printer Or Scanner, as shown in Figure 4.29. If a printer is not detected, a link will appear with the words "The printer that I want isn't listed." Click that link, and it will start the wizard shown in Figure 4.30.

FIGURE 4.29 Printers & scanners

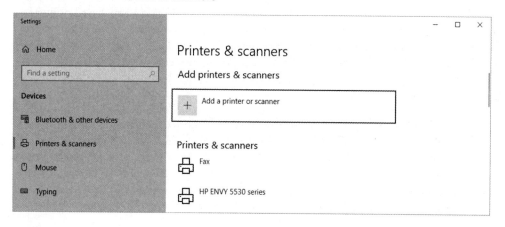

  This might go without saying at this point, but it bears repeating: you need the right driver—one that matches both your printer and your operating system—in order for everything to work right.

Once the driver is installed, the device will function. But some devices, such as inkjet printers, must be calibrated. If the printer requires this step, it will tell you. You'll need to walk through a few steps before the printer will print, but instructions will be provided either on your computer screen or on the printer's display.

FIGURE 4.30   Add Printer Wizard

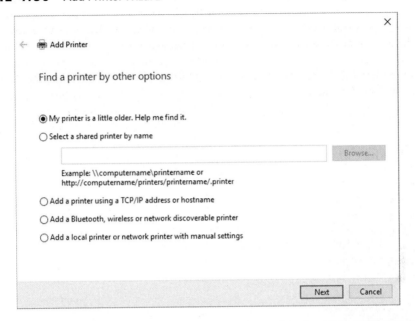

When you are working with print media, it is especially important to calibrate all your hardware, including your monitor, scanner, printer, and digital camera, to ensure color matching.

Each manufacturer's process is different, but a typical alignment/calibration works like this:

1. During software installation, the installation wizard asks you if you would like to calibrate now, to which you will respond Yes or OK.

2. The printer prints out a sheet with multiple sets of numbered lines. Each set of lines represents an alignment instance.

3. The software will ask you which set(s) looks the best. Enter the number and click OK or Continue.

4. Some alignment routines end at this point. Others will reprint the alignment page and see if the alignment "took." If not, you can reenter the number of the one that looks the best.

5. Click Finish to end the alignment routine.

Step 4: Configure Options and Settings

Once you have installed the software and calibrated the device, you can configure any options that you would like for the printer. All the settings and how to change them can be found online or in your user manual.

Where you configure specific printer properties depends a lot on the printer itself. As a rule of thumb, you're looking for the Printer Properties or Printing Preferences applet. In Windows 10, if you open Printers & Scanners, you will see the list of printers that are installed. Clicking an installed printer will show three buttons: Open Queue, Manage, and Remove Device, as shown in Figure 4.31. The Open Queue button lets you manage print jobs, and the Remove Device button is self-explanatory. Click Manage to get the screen like the one shown in Figure 4.32. Here you have options to print a test page, as well as the Printer properties and Printing preferences link. Figure 4.33 shows the General tab of the Printer Properties window, and Figure 4.34 shows the Printing Preferences window.

FIGURE 4.31   Three printer management buttons

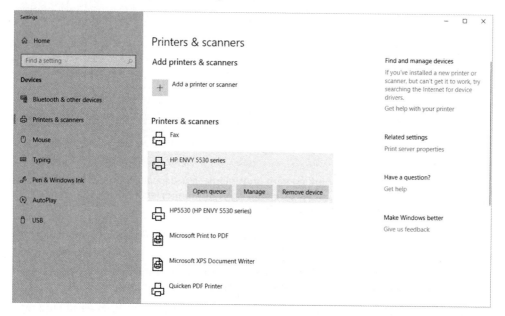

From the printer's Properties dialog box (Figure 4.33), you can configure nearly any option that you want to for your printer. The Properties dialog box will be pretty much the same for any printer that you install, and we'll cover a few options here in a minute. First, though, notice the Preferences button on the General tab. Clicking the Preferences button is another way to get to Printing Preferences (Figure 4.34). That window will have configuration options based on your specific model of printer. Usually, though, this is where you can find *orientation* (portrait or landscape), duplexing, quality, color, and paper tray settings (if applicable) for the printer.

FIGURE 4.32   Manage your device options

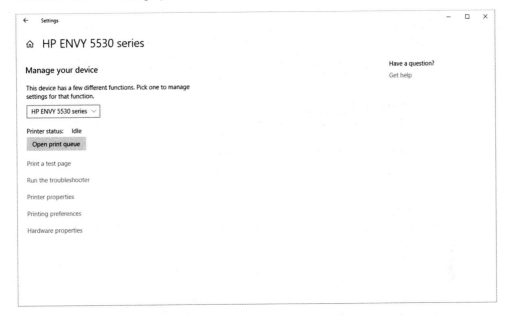

FIGURE 4.33   Printer Properties

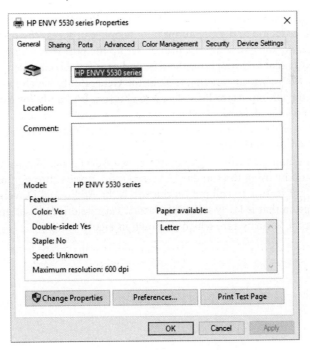

FIGURE 4.34   Printing Preferences

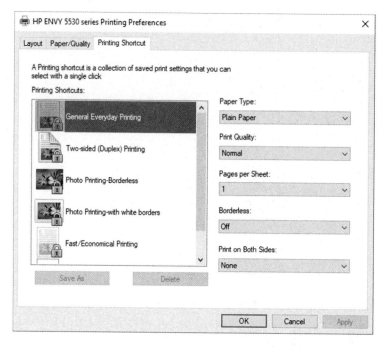

Now back to the Properties dialog box. The printer's Properties dialog box is less about how the printer does its job and more about how people can access the printer. From the Properties dialog box, you can share the printer, set up the port that it's on, configure when the printer will be available throughout the day, and specify who can use it. Let's take a look at a few key tabs. We've already taken a look at the General tab, which has the Preferences button as well as the all-important Print Test Page button. It's handy for troubleshooting!

Figure 4.35 shows the Sharing tab. If you want other users to be able to print to this printer, you need to share it. Notice the warnings above the Share This Printer check box. Those are important to remember. When you share the printer, you give it a share name. Network users can map the printer through their own Add Printer Wizard (choosing a networked printer) and by using the standard \\computer_name\share_name convention. One other important feature to call out on this tab is the Additional Drivers button. This one provides a description that is fairly self-explanatory. Permissions for user authentication are managed through the Security tab, which is shown in Figure 4.36.

FIGURE 4.35   Printer Properties Sharing tab

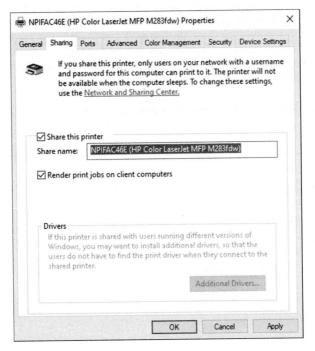

FIGURE 4.36   Printer Properties Security tab

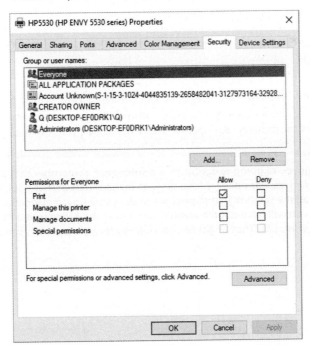

If you are on a public network and want others to be able to find and print to your shared printer, you first need to enable file and printer sharing for public networks. Open the Network and Sharing Center, and then click Change Advanced Sharing Settings on the left side. In Advanced Sharing Settings, open the Guest or Public network and click Turn On File And Printer Sharing, as shown in Figure 4.37.

FIGURE 4.37   Turning on file and printer sharing

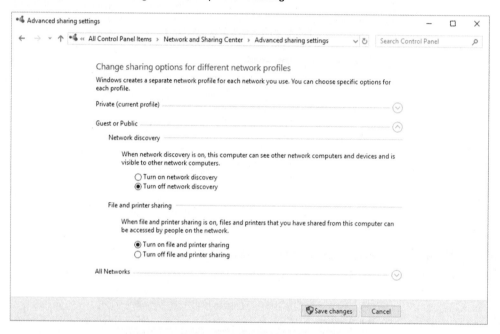

Figure 4.38 shows the Ports tab. Here you can configure your printer port and add and delete ports. There's also a check box to enable printer pooling. This would be used if you have multiple physical printers that operate under the same printer name.

If you're going to configure a printer pool, remember that all of the output can appear on any of the devices that are part of that pool. Make sure that all the printers in that pool are in the same physical location. Otherwise, you will have people wandering all over the office trying to find their printouts. That might be entertaining for you, but not so much for them.

FIGURE 4.38   Printer Properties Ports tab

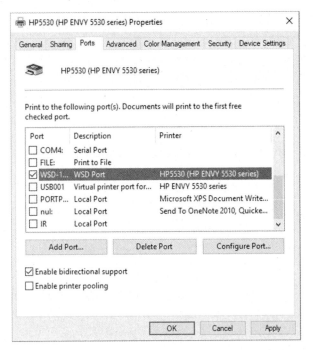

Figure 4.39 shows the important Advanced tab of the printer's Properties dialog box. On this tab, you can configure the printer to be available during only certain hours of the day. This might be useful if you're trying to curtail after-hours printing of non–work-related documents, for example. You can also configure the spool settings. For faster printing, you should always spool the jobs instead of printing directly to the printer. However, if the printer is printing garbage, you can try printing directly to it to see if the spooler is causing the problem.

Regarding the check boxes at the bottom, you will always want to print spooled documents first because that speeds up the printing process. If you need to maintain an electronic copy of all printed files, select the Keep Printed Documents check box. Keep in mind that doing so will eat up a lot of hard disk space and could potentially create a security risk.

Finally, the Printing Defaults button takes you to the Printing Preferences window (shown earlier in Figure 4.34). The Print Processor button lets you select alternate methods of processing print jobs (not usually needed), and the Separator Page button lets you specify a file to use as a separator page (a document that prints out at the beginning of each separate print job, usually with the user's name on it), which can be useful if you have several (or several dozen) users sharing one printer.

FIGURE 4.39 Printer Properties Advanced tab

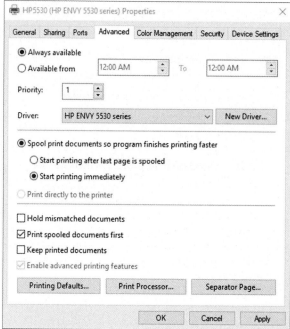

Step 5: Print a Test Page

Once you have configured your printer, you are finished and can print a test page to test its output. Windows has a built-in function for doing just that—you saw links to do so in Figure 4.32 and Figure 4.33. Click the link or button, and Windows will send a test page to the printer. If the page prints, your printer is working. If not, double-check all your connections. If they appear to be in order, then skip ahead to Chapter 12 for troubleshooting tips.

Step 6: Verify Compatibility with Operating System and Applications

Once your printer is installed and you have printed a test page, everything else should work well, right? That's usually true, but it's good practice to verify compatibility with applications before you consider the device fully installed.

With printers, this process is rather straightforward. Open the application you're wondering about and print something. For example, open Microsoft Word, type in some gibberish (or open a real document, if you want), and print it. If you are running non-Microsoft applications (such as a computer-aided drafting program or accounting software) and have questions about their compatibility with the printer, try printing from those programs as well.

Step 7: Educate Users about Basic Functionality

Most users today know how to print, but not everyone knows how to install the right printer or how to print efficiently. This can be a significant issue in work environments.

Say your workplace has 10 different printers, and you just installed number 11. First, your company should use a naming process to identify the printers in a way that makes sense. Calling a printer HPLJ4 on a network does little to help users understand where that printer is in the building. Naming it after its physical location might make more sense.

After installing the printer, offer installation assistance to those who might want to use the device. Show users how to install the printer in Windows (or if printer installation is automated, let them know that they have a new printer and where it is). Also, let users know the various options available on that printer. Can it print double-sided? If so, you can save a lot of paper. Show users how to configure that. Is it a color printer? Do users really need color for rough drafts of documents or presentations? Show users how to print in black and white on a color printer to save the expensive color ink or toner cartridges.

On the printer we've used as an example in this chapter, most of the options involving print output are located in Preferences (refer to Figure 4.34). Two of them are on the Printing Shortcut tab: Duplex (or Print On Both Sides) and Print Quality (Best, Normal, Draft). Orientation (Portrait or Landscape) is set on the Layout tab. This printer does not have a collate feature, which is used if you are printing several copies of a longer document. Collation enables you to select whether you want it to print pages in order (1, 2, 3. . . 1, 2, 3. . . and so on) or multiple copies of the same page at once (1, 1, 1. . . 2, 2, 2. . . and so forth).

In Exercise 4.2, we'll step through the process of installing a USB printer in Windows 10.

EXERCISE 4.2

Installing a USB Printer in Windows 10

For this exercise, you will need the following items:

- A USB printer

- A USB printer cable

- The software driver that came with the printer (flash drive, DVD, or downloaded)

- A computer with a free USB port and the ability to access the driver

  1. Turn on the computer.

  2. Plug the printer into the wall outlet and turn it on.

(continues)

EXERCISE 4.2 *(continued)*

3. Access the driver file to begin the installation process. You can do this in one of two ways, as follows:

   a. Insert the DVD (or CD) into the computer's optical drive. The driver disc's autorun feature should automatically start the installation program. If not, click Start and type **computer**. Click the Computer Desktop App under Best Match. Find the optical drive, and double-click the `setup.exe` or `install.exe` file on the disc.

   b. Double-click the `setup.exe` or `install.exe` program on the thumb drive or from the location to which you downloaded it.

4. Follow the prompts in the installation program to install the driver.

5. Once the software has been installed, plug one end of the USB cable into the printer and the other end into the free USB port. Some installation programs will prompt you for this step.

6. Windows will automatically detect the new printer, install the driver, and configure it.

   Windows will display a balloon in the lower-right corner of the screen that says, "Your hardware is now installed and is ready to use." If Windows doesn't properly detect the printer, open the Add Printer Wizard to begin the installation process again, and manually specify the location of the printer driver (such as the disc or thumb drive).

7. Print a test page to see if the printer can communicate and print properly.

 Real World Scenario

Which Printer Did That Go To?

One of the authors used to work at a satellite office in Salt Lake City for a company whose headquarters were in Houston. Because of printer problems, a new network printer had been installed, which had a different network name from the previous printer.

At the end of the month, one of the accountants printed her monthly reconciliation report, which typically ran about 400 pages. (A hard copy was required for regulatory reasons.) Puzzled when it didn't come out of the printer, she printed it again. And again. And again. After the fourth failed attempt, and several hours later, she decided to ask someone in IT what the problem was.

It turns out that she had mapped (installed) the new network printer but had gotten a few letters wrong in the printer name. Instead of being at her office, all her print jobs were sent to a printer in the Houston office. And, of course, there were people in Houston trying to print similar reports and who just kept refilling the printer with paper because they didn't want to cut someone else's report off in the middle.

While this wasn't a catastrophic failure, it was annoying. She had unintentionally wasted three reams of paper, the associated toner, and hours of printer life. It wasn't a malicious act, and she was a literate computer user, but it's illustrative of the need to educate and help users with installing and configuring devices. Had the printer been mapped correctly the first time, the waste could have been avoided.

For the A+ exam, know how to properly unbox a device and consider location when setting it up. Also be familiar with configuration settings such as duplex, orientation, tray settings, and print quality.

Installing and Sharing Networked Printers

The previous section was about installing a printer attached to your local computer. There are advantages to that approach, such as being able to manage and control your own printer, not to mention having a printer at your own desk. That doesn't happen often in the business world these days!

There are some big disadvantages as well. First, it means that all users who need to print to your device may need local accounts on your computer, unless you are on a network domain. If so, you will need to manage security for these accounts and the printer. Second, your computer is the print server. The *print server* is the device that hosts the printer and processes the necessary printer commands. This can slow your system down. Third, because your computer is the print server, if for any reason it's turned off, no one will be able to print to that device.

There is another option, though. Instead of needing a specific computer to be the print server, why not make the print server part of the printer itself, or make it a separate network device that hosts the printers? That is exactly the principle behind network printing. Next, we will cover two types of network printing—local network printing and cloud printing—as well as talk about data privacy concerns with printing to public or shared printers.

Local Network Printing

The key to local network printing is that you are moving the print server from your computer to another location, accessible to other users on the network. Therefore, the print server needs a direct attachment to the network, via either a wired (RJ-45) or wireless connection. You will find two major varieties of print servers. The first, called an *integrated print server*, is incorporated into the printer itself, and the second is a separate hardware print server. If you are using a stand-alone print server, the printers attach to the print server, either physically or logically. In most cases, if a printer is capable of connecting directly to a network, it has the capability to be its own print server.

Installing and using a networked printer is very similar to installing and using a local printer. You need to ensure that both devices are plugged in, turned on, and attached to the network (either with an RJ-45 Ethernet connection or by using wireless). Probably the biggest difference is that when you install it, you need to tell your computer that you are adding a networked printer instead of a local printer. For example, in Windows 10, when you open the Add Printer utility (shown in Figure 4.30), you choose Add A Bluetooth, Wireless Or Other Network Discoverable Printer instead of Add A Local Printer. From there, you will be asked to install the printer driver, just as if the printer were directly attached to your computer. Once it's installed, you use it just as you would use a local printer, including setting the configuration options that we looked at in earlier sections. Every computer on the local network should be able to see and add the printer in the same way.

The print server needs to have drivers available (installed) for all the types of clients that will connect to its printers. For example, if the network has Mac, Linux, and Windows 10 clients, the server will need to have all three drivers. If not, users may not be able to install the printer properly and may not be able to print.

There are a few other ways that you can add shared networked printers: by using TCP, Bonjour, or AirPrint.

TCP Printing

Printers that are network-aware need IP addresses, so it makes sense that you can add a networked printer by using TCP/IP, also known as *TCP printing*. Exercise 4.3 walks you through the general process of installing a TCP printer, using Windows 10 as an example.

EXERCISE 4.3

Installing a TCP/IP Printer in Windows 10

1. Connect the printer to the network and power it on.

2. Configure the printer with an IP address, if it does not already have one.

    Most network-aware printers will have their own display panel where you can configure or verify network settings. The IP address needs to be on the same subnet as the computer trying to add the printer.

3. From your Windows 10 computer, start the Add Printer wizard.

4. Choose Add A Printer Using A TCP/IP Address Or Hostname, and then click Next.

5. On the next screen, shown in Figure 4.40, you have a few options. One is to let the system automatically detect the device. If so, leave Device Type as Autodetect and click Next. Otherwise, set Device Type to TCP/IP Device and move to the next step. For this exercise, let's do the latter.

FIGURE 4.40   Adding an IP printer

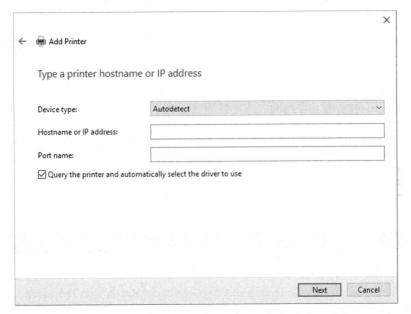

6. Enter the IP address (or hostname) of the printer that you want to add, add a port name (it's just for identification), and then click Next.

7. Select the make and model of your printer from the list.

8. You will be prompted to install the driver; continue installing the printer as you would any other local or networked printer.

Some installations will ask you which TCP printing protocol you want to use, RAW or LPR. RAW (also called the Standard TCP/IP Port Monitor) is the default, and it uses TCP port 9100. It also uses the Simple Network Management Protocol (SNMP) for bidirectional communication between the computer and the printer. LPR is older, and the protocol is included for use with legacy systems. It's limited to source ports 721–731 and the destination port 515.

We will discuss ports and port numbers in Chapter 6, "Introduction to TCP/IP."

After the printer is installed, it will appear in your Printers & Scanners window, just as any other printer would.

There are a few advantages to using TCP printing. First, it sends the print jobs directly to the printer, so your system does not need to act as the print server or spend processing time dealing with formatting the print job. Second, it allows clients with different OSs, such as Linux or macOS, to add printers without worrying about intra-OS conflicts.

Bonjour

Apple introduced *Bonjour* in 2002 (then under the name Rendezvous) as an implementation of zero configuration networking. It's designed to enable automatic discovery of devices and services on local networks using TCP/IP as well as to provide hostname resolution. Currently, it comes installed by default on Apple's macOS and iOS operating systems. Bonjour makes it easy to discover and install printers that have been shared by other Bonjour-enabled clients on the network.

Even though Apple developed Bonjour, it does work on other operating systems. For example, it comes with iTunes and the Safari browser, so if you have either of those installed on a Windows computer, odds are that you have Bonjour as well. Once installed, the Bonjour service starts automatically and scans the network looking for shared devices. Exercise 4.4 shows you how to see if Bonjour is installed in Windows.

EXERCISE 4.4

Determining if Bonjour Is Installed in Windows

1. Click Start, type **services**, and then click Services under Best Match. The Services window will open.

2. Sort the list by name and look for the Bonjour service, as shown in Figure 4.41.

FIGURE 4.41   Bonjour service is running and set to start automatically.

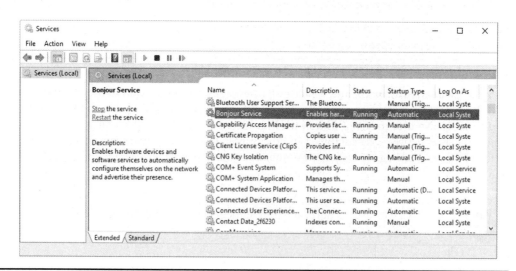

Bonjour works only on a single broadcast domain, meaning that it will not find a printer or other device if it's on the other side of a router from your computer. All major printer manufacturers support Bonjour technology.

If you are using a Mac, adding a Bonjour printer is easy. You open System Preferences ➤ Print And Scan, click the plus sign under Printers to open the Add Printer window, and look for the printer on the list. If the Mac doesn't have the driver available, you will be asked to provide it. Otherwise, you're done.

In order to add or share a Bonjour printer from Windows, you need to download Bonjour Print Services for Windows. It's found on Apple's support site at `https://support.apple.com/kb/dl999`.

AirPrint

The one big complaint that Apple aficionados had about Bonjour was that it didn't support printing from iPhones or iPads. In 2010, Apple introduced *AirPrint* to meet that need.

The idea behind AirPrint is quite simple. Mobile devices can automatically detect AirPrint-enabled printers on their local network and print to them without requiring the installation of a driver. To be fair, what Apple really did was eliminate the need for a specific printer driver to be installed on the client and replaced it with the AirPrint concept. Then it was up to the printer manufacturers to develop their own drivers that talked to AirPrint. HP was happy to oblige with its Photosmart Plus series, and other manufacturers soon followed. The list of AirPrint-enabled printers is available at `https://support.apple.com/en-us/HT201311`. From the end-user standpoint, though, no driver is required.

There really is no installation process, and printing is easy. Just be sure that your mobile device is on the same local network as an AirPrint printer. When you attempt to print from your device, select the printer to which you want to print, and it should work.

> You can also purchase AirPrint servers, which are small print servers that enable you to connect almost any printer to the network and make them AirPrint compatible.

Network Printer Security

When printing to a public printer, or one that is shared in a common workspace, there may be data privacy concerns. For example, employees in Human Resources (HR) might need to print confidential personnel files, or someone in the Mergers group might have a highly restricted contract to print. Let's take a look at some security options for networked printers.

User Authentication

Requiring users to authenticate (log in) to the printer is one step that can improve printer security. Not all printers have this capability, but most newer laser printers and MFDs designed for office use will. Figure 4.42 shows the front of a Xerox AltaLink MFD. In the center of the picture is a touchscreen display where a user can copy, scan to email, look at printer jobs, configure the device, and use a secure print feature called SafeQ. If a user taps the LogIn button in the upper-left corner, they will be presented with a keyboard so that they can enter their username and password. While functional, this is a bit old-school. An easier way for many users is to scan their work badge (this is called *badging*) on the badge reader at the left of the unit. Doing so will automatically log them in and provide access to secure printing features.

FIGURE 4.42   Xerox AltaLink badge scanner and touchscreen

Secured Prints

Printing a document is usually pretty straightforward. On the computer, the user hits some sort of Print button, chooses the printer to send it to, and presses Print again (or OK, or something similar). Then they get up and walk to the printer to retrieve the hard copy. Most office denizens have been well trained in this process.

Some print jobs might contain sensitive information, though, so the user wants to ensure that they are physically at the printer before it starts printing. Or, perhaps the user has printed to a device in a different building and wants the printer to wait to start printing until they can get there. In cases like these, a *secured prints* feature can be used to hold the print job until the user is ready for it.

Looking back at Figure 4.42, you can see a feature on the bottom center of the touchscreen called SAFEQ Print. YSoft SAFEQ is an industry-standard enterprise print management suite adopted by many organizations, and it works seamlessly with many printers. The administrator sets it up on the printer (and we mean logical printer here, not necessarily the physical device), and when the user prints to that printer, the job waits for them until they authenticate on the physical printer and tell it to start. Figure 4.43 shows the SAFEQ user authentication screen. Once logged in, the user will be presented with the job(s) to print, as shown in Figure 4.44.

FIGURE 4.43   SAFEQ authentication screen

FIGURE 4.44   Secured print job

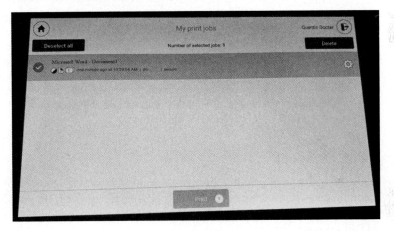

Audit Logs

Being able to see who used (or perhaps abused) a printer after the fact can come in handy. Some printers have the ability to save a list of documents that have been printed as an *audit log*. The Xerox printer we've used as an example in this section does just that, and the log is shown in Figure 4.45.

Other printers will integrate logging software into the operating system's standard logging utilities. For example, some HP printers will install an audit log into Windows Event Viewer. (We will cover Event Viewer in Chapter 14, "Windows 10 Configuration.") Third-party audit software is also available for use.

FIGURE 4.45   Xerox print log

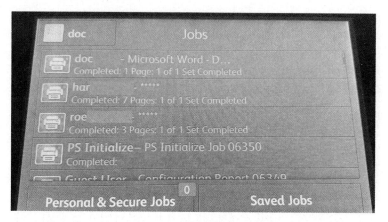

    Another security issue is storing print jobs on print servers. Print jobs are cached on the print server (it's called *hard drive caching*), and they can be saved indefinitely. We looked at the check box to keep printed documents in Figure 4.39. If you are configuring a printer for a public area, do not select this option. If you're printing to a public printer (such as at a hotel), and you can see the printer properties, check to make sure that this option is not selected. That will help ensure that your files will not be cached on the hotel computer's hard drive.

Network Scan Services

Scanning is really the opposite of printing. Instead of printing to get electronic information onto paper, scanning takes printed information and stores it electronically. In the office environment, the two most popular types of scanners are flatbed scanners and automatic document feeder (ADF) scanners.

To use a *flatbed scanner*, simply open the lid and lay the document to be scanned on the scanner glass, aligning it to the proper corner as shown in Figure 4.46. There will be an icon on the scanning bed that shows where the document should go. Close the lid and press Scan on the touchscreen, and scanning will begin.

If you have more than one document to scan, using a flatbed scanner can be a real pain. Fortunately, some scanners have an attachment called an *automatic document feeder (ADF)* that lets you scan multiple pieces of paper in one job. Figure 4.47 shows an example with paper loaded in it. It's common to have ADFs that allow for up to 50 pages to be scanned at once.

FIGURE 4.46   A flatbed scanner

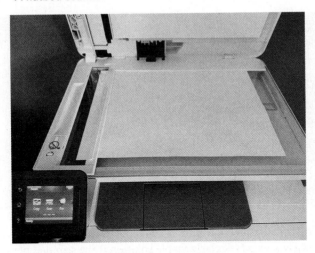

FIGURE 4.47   Automatic document feeder (ADF) on an MFD

Whenever you scan a document, you need to figure out where to send it. MFDs don't usually have the memory to save images of scans—besides, the point of scanning a document is usually to email it to someone or save it on a hard drive for later retrieval. Let's take a look at three different ways to send or save scanned materials. For all three of these options, it's assumed that the scanner is connected to the network.

Scan to Email   Using a *scan to email* option, the scanner will simply email the file, usually in PDF format, to an email recipient. This is probably the most common method that people use when scanning files. Figure 4.48 shows an example of setting up scan to email.

FIGURE 4.48   Scan to email

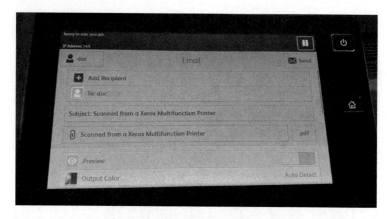

Scan to Folder   An alternative option to emailing a scanned file is to save it in a network folder. This is a particularly viable solution if the scanned file is too large to be emailed.

The protocol the printer uses to transport the file from itself to the network folder is called *Server Message Block (SMB)*. In addition, the administrator must set up the MFD to support SMB scanning, and the recipient folder needs to be properly shared and secured too. Performing the scan from the MFD is done via a screen similar to the one shown in Figure 4.48, except instead of selecting an email recipient, you would navigate to the folder where you want to save the file.

Scan to Cloud   The final option is to use cloud services to save the scan. Various file saving and sharing services support scanning to the cloud, such as Google Drive, OneDrive, Box, and Dropbox, among others. In addition, some printer manufacturers such as HP and Epson offer scan to cloud services. The exact process to follow depends on which cloud service you use to save the file. Exercise 4.5 has you "scan" a document to Google Drive—and it doesn't require you to have an actual scanner! Of course, you do need an Android device to make it work.

EXERCISE 4.5

Scanning a Document to Google Drive

This exercise requires the use of an Android phone or tablet.

1. On the Android device, open the Google Drive app.

2. In the bottom-right corner, tap Add. It should have a plus sign next to it.

3. Tap Scan. It should have a camera icon next to it.

4. Take a photo of the object you want to scan.

5. Tap Done to save the scanned document to Google Drive.

To make the process even shorter, you can install the Drive scan widget on your Home screen.

Networked printers are great, and there are several concepts that could appear on the A+ exam related to them. They include:

- Printer share and print server
- Security concepts such as user authentication, badging, secured prints, and audit logs
- Network scan services including email, SMB, and cloud services
- Understanding the differences between an automatic document feeder (ADF) and a flatbed scanner

Performing Printer Maintenance

Considering the amount of work they do, printers last a pretty long time. Some printers handle over 100,000 pages per month, yet they're usually pretty reliable devices. You can help your printers live long and fulfilling lives by performing the right maintenance, and smoothly running printers always make your officemates happy. After all, going to get your print job from the printer and discovering that the printer is in the shop is a very frustrating experience!

Regardless of the type of printer you use, giving it a regular checkup is a good idea. You're probably familiar with some of the activities that fall under maintenance, such as replacing paper, ink, or toner cartridges. We'll look at those as well as some additional, more involved maintenance procedures.

Replacing Consumables

To maintain a printer properly, you need to replace consumables such as toner or ink cartridges, assemblies, filters, and rollers on occasion. Trying to cut costs by buying cheaper supplies rarely pays off.

Whenever purchasing supplies for your printer, always get supplies from the manufacturer or from an authorized reseller. This way, you'll be sure that the parts are of high quality. Using unauthorized parts can damage your printer and possibly void your warranty.

Printer Paper

Most people don't give much thought to the kind of paper they use in their printers. It's a factor that can have a tremendous effect on the quality of the hard-copy printout, however, and the topic is more complex than people think. For example, the wrong paper can cause frequent paper jams and possibly even damage components.

Several aspects of paper can be measured; each gives an indication as to the paper's quality. The first factor is *composition*. Paper is made from a variety of substances. Paper used to be made from cotton and was called rag stock. It can also be made from wood pulp, which is cheaper. Most paper today is made from the latter or a combination of the two.

Another aspect of paper is the property known as *basis weight* (or simply *weight*). The weight of a particular type of paper is the actual weight, in pounds, of a ream (500 sheets) of the standard size of that paper made of that material. For regular bond paper, that size is 17 × 22.

The final paper property we'll discuss is the *caliper* (or thickness) of an individual sheet of paper. If the paper is too thick, it may jam in feed mechanisms that have several curves in the paper path. On the other hand, a paper that's too thin may not feed at all.

These are just three of the categories we use to judge the quality of paper. Because there are so many different types and brands of printers as well as paper, it would be impossible to give the specifications for the "perfect" paper. However, the documentation for any printer will give specifications for the paper that should be used in that printer.

Many impact printers need to use special paper that has tractor feed perforations on the side, or they will not work properly. When replacing tractor feed paper, it's very easy to get it misaligned, and it will feed crookedly and ultimately jam the printer. Similarly, thermal printers also require special paper that needs to be loaded properly. In many cases, if you load it upside down, the unit will not produce images. By comparison, adding paper to a laser or inkjet printer is usually very easy.

For best results, store paper in an area where it will not get wet or be exposed to excessive humidity.

Ink and Toner

The area in which using recommended supplies is the biggest concern is ink and toner cartridges. Using the wrong ink or toner supplies is the easiest way to ruin a perfectly good printer.

Dot-matrix printers use a cloth or polyester ribbon soaked in ink and coiled up inside a plastic case. This assembly is called a *printer ribbon* (or *ribbon cartridge*). Once the ribbon has run out of ink, it must be discarded and replaced. Ribbon cartridges are developed closely with their respective printers. For this reason, ribbons should be purchased from the same manufacturer as the printer. The wrong ribbon could jam in the printer as well as cause quality problems.

It is possible to re-ink a ribbon. Some vendors sell a bottle of ink solution that can be poured into the plastic casing, where the cloth ribbon will soak up the solution. This can be a messy process, and you should do this only if the manufacturer recommends it.

Inkjet cartridges have a liquid ink reservoir. The ink in these cartridges is sealed inside. Once the ink runs out, the cartridge must be removed and discarded. A new, full cartridge is installed in its place. Because the ink cartridge contains the printing mechanism as well as ink, it's like getting a new printer every time you replace the ink cartridge.

In some inkjet printers, the ink cartridge and the print head are in separate assemblies. This way, the ink can be replaced when it runs out, and the print head can be used several times. This approach works fine if the printer is designed to work this way. However, some people think that they can do this on their integrated cartridge/print head system, using special ink cartridge refill kits. These kits consist of a syringe filled with ink and a long needle. The needle is used to puncture the top of an empty ink cartridge, and the syringe is then used to refill the reservoir.

Do not use ink cartridge refill kits! There are several problems with these kits (the ones you see advertised with a syringe and a needle). First, the kits don't use the same kind of ink that was originally in the ink cartridges. The new ink may be thinner, causing it to run out or not print properly. Also, the print head is often supposed to be replaced around this same time. Refilling the cartridge doesn't replace the print head, so you'll have print-quality problems. Finally, the hole the syringe leaves cannot be plugged and may allow ink to leak out. These problems can happen with do-it-yourself kits as well as with cartridges refilled by office supply stores or private printer supply sellers. Here's the bottom line: *buy new ink cartridges from the printer manufacturer*. Yes, they are a bit more expensive, but in the long run you will save money because you won't have any of the problems described here.

The final type of consumable is toner. Each model of laser printer uses a specific toner cartridge. You should check the printer's manual to see which toner cartridge your printer needs. Many businesses will recycle your toner or ink cartridges for you, refill them, and sell them back to you at a discount. Don't buy them. While some businesses that perform this "service" are more legitimate than others, using recycled parts is more dangerous to your hardware than using new parts. The reason for this is that refilled cartridges are more likely to break or leak than new parts, and this leakage could cause extensive damage to the inside of your printer. And again, using secondhand parts can void your warranty, so you're left with a broken printer that you have to pay for. Avoid problems like this by buying new parts.

 Real World Scenario

Think Before You Refill

Just as with ink cartridges, you should always buy the exact model of toner cartridge recommended by the manufacturer. The toner cartridges have been designed specifically for a particular model. Additionally, *never* refill toner cartridges, for most of the same reasons we don't recommend refilling ink cartridges. The printout quality will be poor, and the fact that you're just refilling the toner means that you might *not* be replacing the photosensitive drum (which is usually inside the cartridge), and the drum might *need* to be replaced.

Simply replacing refilled toner cartridges with proper, name-brand toner cartridges has solved most laser printer quality problems that we have run across. We keep recommending the right ones, but clients keep coming back with the refilled ones. The result is that we take our clients' money to solve their print-quality problems when all it involves is a toner cartridge, our (usually repeat) advice to buy the proper cartridge next time, and the obligatory minimum charge for a half hour of labor (even though the job of replacing the cartridge takes all of 5 minutes).

Always properly recycle your used ink and toner cartridges. Just don't buy recycled cartridges!

Performing Scheduled Maintenance

When shopping for a printer, one of the characteristics you should look for is the printer's capacity, which is often quoted in monthly volume. This is particularly important if the printer will be serving in a high-load capacity. Every printer needs periodic maintenance, but printers that can handle a lot of traffic typically need it less frequently. Check the printer specifications to see how often scheduled maintenance is suggested. Never, ever fall behind on performing scheduled maintenance on a printer.

Many laser printers have LCD displays that provide useful information, such as error messages or notices that you need to replace a toner cartridge. The LCD display will also tell you when the printer needs scheduled maintenance. How does it know? Printers keep track of the number of pages they print, and when the page limit is reached, they display a message, usually something simple like *Perform user maintenance*. The printer will still print, but you should perform the maintenance.

Being the astute technician that you are, you clean the printer with the recommended cleaning kit or install the maintenance kit that you purchased from the manufacturer. Now, how do you get the maintenance message to go away? Reset the page count using a menu option. For example, on many HP laser printers, you press the Menu button until you get to the Configuration menu. Once there, you press the Item key until the display shows *Service Message = ON*. Then press the plus key (+) to change the message to *Service Message = OFF*. Bring the printer back online, and you're ready to go.

When performing maintenance on an impact printer, always carefully inspect the print head for damage. Replace damaged print heads with authorized parts from the manufacturer.

Performing routine maintenance will keep the printer clean, make it last longer, and help prevent annoying paper jams.

Using Cleaning Solutions

With all of the ink or toner they use, printers get dirty. If printers get too dirty or if the print heads get dirty, you'll notice print problems. No one wants this to happen.

Most printers have a self-cleaning utility that is activated through a menu option or by pressing a combination of buttons on the printer itself. It's recommended that you run the cleaning sequence every time you replace the toner or ink cartridges. If you experience print-quality problems, such as lines in the output, run the cleaning routine.

Sometimes, the self-cleaning routines aren't enough to clear up the problem. If you are having print-quality issues, you might want to consider purchasing a cleaning or maintenance kit, which frequently comes with a cleaning solution.

 Cleaning kits are often designed for one specific type of printer and should be used only on that type of printer. For example, don't apply an inkjet cleaning solution to a laser printer.

Each cleaning kit comes with its own instructions for use. Exercise 4.6 walks you through the steps of using an inkjet cleaning solution. Note that the steps for your printer might differ slightly; please consult your manual for specific instructions. After using a cleaning kit on a laser or inkjet printer, it's best to perform a calibration per the printer's instructions.

EXERCISE 4.6

Using an Inkjet Cleaning Solution

1. Power on the printer, and open the top cover to expose the area containing the print cartridges.

2. Initiate a self-cleaning cycle. When the print head moves from its resting place, pull the AC power plug. This lets you freely move the print heads without damaging them.

3. Locate the sponge pads on which to apply the cleaning solution.

   They'll be in the area where the print heads normally park.

4. Use a cotton swab or paper towel to gently soak up any excess ink in the pads.

5. Using the supplied syringe, apply the cleaning solution to the sponge pads until they are saturated.

6. Plug the printer back into the wall outlet, and turn it on. The print heads will park themselves.

7. Turn the printer back off. Let the solution sit for at least 3 hours.

(continues)

8. Power the printer back on, and run three printer cleaning cycles.

9. Print a nozzle check pattern (or a test page) after each cleaning cycle to monitor the cleaning progress.

That should take care of it. If not, refer to your printer's manual for more instructions.

Thermal printers require special attention because they contain a heating element. Always unplug the device and ensure that it's cooled off before trying to clean it. Thermal printer cleaning cards, cleaning pens, and kits are widely available in the marketplace. If you need to remove any debris (from any printer), use compressed air or a specialized computer vacuum.

Ensuring a Suitable Environment

Printers won't complain if the weather outside is too hot or too cold, but they are susceptible to environmental issues. Here are some things to watch out for in your printer's environment:

Heat   Laser printers can generate a lot of heat. Because of this, ensure that your laser printer is in a well-ventilated area. Resist the temptation to put the laser printer in the little cubbyhole in your desk. Overheating will reduce the shelf life of your printer.

Humidity   High humidity can cause printer paper to stick together. Sticky paper leads to paper jams. Humidity over 80 or 90 percent can cause issues.

Light   The laser printer's toner cartridge contains a photosensitive drum. Exposing that drum to light could ruin the drum. While the drum is encased in plastic, it's best to avoid exposing the printer or toner cartridges to extreme light sources. Under no circumstance should you open the toner cartridge, unless you're ready to get rid of it as well as clean up a big mess.

Ozone   Laser printers that use corona wires produce ozone as a by-product of the printing process. In offices, ozone can cause respiratory problems in small concentrations, and it can be seriously dangerous to people in large amounts. Ozone is also a very effective oxidizer and can cause damage to printer components.

Fortunately, laser printers don't produce large amounts of ozone, and most laser printers have an ozone filter. Ozone is another reason to ensure that your printer area has good ventilation. Also, replace the ozone filter periodically; check your printer's manual for recommendations on when to do this.

Ammonia   A printer doesn't produce ammonia, but it is contained in many cleaning products. Ammonia can greatly reduce the printer's ability to neutralize ozone and can cause permanent damage to toner cartridges. It's best to avoid using ammonia-based cleaners near laser printers.

Printer maintenance is an exam objective for laser, inkjet, thermal, and impact printers. Be familiar with replacing toner, ink cartridges, and print ribbons, replacing ribbons and print heads, cleaning heads, heating elements, and other components and applying maintenance kits, calibrating, removing debris, clearing jams, and replacing paper.

Installing Printer Upgrades

The printer market encompasses a dizzying array of products. You can find portable printers, photo printers, cheap black-and-white printers for under $30, high-end color laser printers for over $5,000, and everything in between. Most of the cheaper printers do not have upgrade options, but higher-end printers will have upgrade options, including memory, network cards, and firmware. Let's examine some ways that you can upgrade a slower printer or add functionality without breaking the bank.

Most of the upgrades discussed here are for laser printers only. Inkjets are less expensive and usually not upgradeable. In addition, note that installing printer upgrades is not currently listed in the A+ exam objectives. This section is good for your general knowledge, but there's no need to memorize every detail.

Installing Printer Memory

When purchasing a memory upgrade for your printer, you need to make sure of two things. First, buy only memory that is compatible with your printer model. Most printers today use standard computer dual in-line memory modules (DIMMs), but check your manual or the manufacturer's website to be sure. If you're not sure, purchasing the memory through the manufacturer's website (or an authorized reseller) is a good way to go. Second, be sure that your printer is capable of a memory upgrade. It's possible that the amount of memory in your printer is at the maximum that it can handle.

Once you have obtained the memory, it's time to perform the upgrade. The specific steps required to install the memory will depend on your printer. Check the manual or the manufacturer's website for instructions tailored to your model.

Exercise 4.7 walks you through the general steps for installing memory into a laser printer.

EXERCISE 4.7

Installing Memory into a Laser Printer

1. Turn off the printer.

2. Disconnect all cables from the printer (power and interface cables).

3. Find the area in which you need to install the memory.

   On most HP LaserJet printers, this is in the back, on a piece of hardware called the *formatter board*. Tabs near the top and bottom of the board hold the formatter board in. Remove the formatter board from the printer. Other brands have different configurations. For example, on many Xerox laser printers, you remove a panel on the top of the unit (underneath the paper output tray) to get to the memory.

   If your printer requires you to remove a component (such as the formatter board) to upgrade the memory, place that component on a grounded surface, such as an anti-static work mat.

4. If you are replacing an existing memory module, remove the old module, being careful not to break off the latches at the end of the module that hold it in.

5. Insert the new memory module, making sure that any alignment notches on the memory module are lined up with the device before inserting it.

6. Replace the removable component (if necessary).

7. Reconnect the power and interface cables.

8. Power on the printer.

9. Follow the printer manual's instructions for running a self-test to ensure that the memory is recognized.

Some printers require that you manually enable the added memory. Here are the steps to do that in Windows:

1. Open the Printers & Scanners app.

2. Click the printer and choose Manage.

3. On the Device Settings tab, click Printer Memory in the Installable Options section, as shown in Figure 4.49.

4. Select the amount of memory that is now installed.

   Click OK.

FIGURE 4.49   Printer installable options

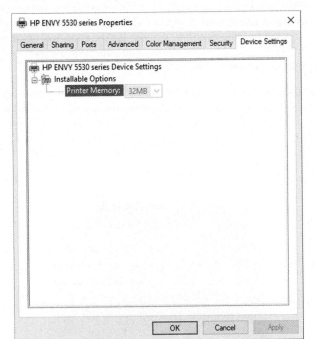

Installing a Network Interface Card

Many printers today have network capabilities, but not all do. Installing a NIC directly into a printer is an option on some devices. The NIC in a printer is similar to the NIC in a computer, with a couple of important differences. First, the NIC in a printer has a small processor on it to perform the management of the NIC interface (functions that the software on a host computer would do). This software is usually referred to as a print server, but be careful because that term can also refer to a physical computer that hosts many printers. Second, the NIC in a printer is proprietary, for the most part—that is, the same manufacturer makes the printer and the NIC.

When a person on the network prints to a printer with a NIC, they are printing right to the printer and not going through any third-party device (although in some situations, that is desirable and possible with NICs). Because of its dedicated nature, the NIC option installed in a printer makes printing to that printer faster and more efficient—that NIC is dedicated to receiving print jobs and sending printer status to clients.

> Most printer NICs come with management software installed that allows clients to check their print jobs' status as well as toner levels from any computer on the network. You access the configuration options by typing the IP address of the printer into your web browser and generally entering an authorized username and password.

Your manual is the best place to check to see if you can install a print server—internal ones look like regular expansion cards. Specific steps for installing the print server will also be in the manual or on the manufacturer's website. Generally speaking, it's very similar to installing a NIC into a computer. Figure 4.50 shows an internal HP print server.

FIGURE 4.50   HP print server expansion card

Upgrading Printer Firmware

As with upgrading memory, methods to upgrade a printer's firmware depend on the model of printer. Most of the time, upgrading a printer's firmware is a matter of downloading and/or installing a free file from the manufacturer's website. Printer firmware upgrades are generally done from the machine hosting the printer (again, usually called the print server).

Firmware is usually upgraded for one of two reasons. One, if you are having compatibility issues, a firmware upgrade might solve them. Two, firmware upgrades can offer newer features that are not available on previous versions.

Installing Other Upgrades

While we've covered some of the most important upgrades, most printers (especially laser printers) can be upgraded with additional capabilities as well. Each manufacturer, with the documentation for each printer, includes a list of all of the accessories, options, and upgrades available. The following options can be included on that list:

- Hard drives
- Trays and feeders
- Finishers

Hard Drives

For a printer to print properly, the type style, or *font*, being printed must be downloaded to the printer along with the job being printed. Desktop publishing and graphic design businesses that print color pages on slower color printers are always looking for ways to speed up their print jobs, so they install multiple fonts into the onboard memory of the printer to make them *printer-resident fonts*. There's a problem, however: most printers have a limited amount of storage space for these fonts. To solve this problem, printer manufacturers made it possible for hard drives to be added to many printers. The hard drives can be used to store many fonts used during the printing process and are also used to store a large document file while it is being processed for printing.

Trays and Feeders

One option that is popular in office environments is the addition of paper trays. Most laser and inkjet printers come with at least one paper tray (usually 500 sheets or fewer). The addition of a paper tray allows a printer to print more sheets between paper refills, thus reducing its operating cost. Also, some printers can accommodate multiple paper trays, which can be loaded with different types of paper, stationery, and envelopes. The benefit is that you can print a letter and an envelope from the same printer without having to leave your desk or change the paper in the printer.

Related to trays is the option of *feeders*. Some types of paper products need to be watched as they are printed to make sure that the printing happens properly. One example is envelopes: you usually can't put a stack of envelopes in a printer because they won't line up straight or they may get jammed. An accessory that you might add for this purpose is the *envelope feeder*. An envelope feeder typically attaches to the front of a laser printer and feeds in envelopes, one at a time. It can hold usually between 100 and 200 envelopes.

Finishers

A printer's *finisher* does just what its name implies: it finishes the document being printed. It does this by folding, stapling, hole punching, sorting, or collating the sets of documents being printed into their final form. So rather than printing out a bunch of paper sheets and then having to collate and staple them, you can have the finisher do it. This particular option, while not cheap, is becoming more popular on laser printers to turn them into multifunction copiers. As a matter of fact, many copiers are now digital and can do all the same things that a laser printer can do but much faster and for a much cheaper cost per page.

Summary

In this chapter, we discussed how different types of printers work as well as the most common methods of connecting them to computers. You learned how computers use page-description languages to format data before they send it to printers and drivers to talk to them. You also learned about the various types of consumable supplies and how they relate to each type of printer.

The most basic category of printer currently in use is the impact printer. Impact printers form images by striking something against a ribbon, which in turn makes a mark on the paper. You learned how these printers work and the service concepts associated with them.

One of the most popular types of printer today is the inkjet printer, so named because of the mechanism used to put ink on the paper.

The most complex type of printer is the laser printer. The A+ 220-1101 exam covers this type of printer more than any other. You learned about the steps in the electrophotographic (EP) imaging process, the process that explains how laser printers print. We also explained the various components that make up this printer and how they work together.

3D printers are relatively new to the market. They're not printers in the sense that they put ink to paper. They're actually fabricators, which make 3D objects out of filament or resin.

You then learned about the interfaces used to connect printers to PCs and how to install and share a printer. Proper steps include connecting the device, installing the driver, configuring options, validating application and operating system compatibility, and educating users on how to use the device. Installing the device is the first step, but you're not done until you ensure that it works properly and that users know how to access it.

Installing network printers usually involves a few more steps than are needed to install local printers, and the device is connected to the network instead of to a host. Networked printers are often used for scan services, such as scanning to email, SMB, and the cloud. Security becomes critical here as well, so you should be familiar with user authentication, badging, secured prints, and audit logs.

Finally, we looked at how to perform printer maintenance, including the importance of using recommended supplies and various types of upgrades you can install in printers.

Exam Essentials

Know the differences between types of printer technologies (for example, laser, inkjet, thermal, impact).   Laser printers use a laser and toner to create the page. Inkjet printers spray ink onto the page. Thermal printers use heat to form the characters on the page. Impact printers use a mechanical device to strike a ribbon, thus forming an image on the page.

Know the three most common ways to connect a printer.   The methods are USB, Ethernet, and wireless.

Be familiar with printer configuration settings.   Know how duplex, orientation, tray settings, and print quality are configured.

For networked printers, understand security and scan services options.   Security can include user authentication and badging, audit logs, and secured prints. Network scan services include scan to email, scan to a folder (using the SMB protocol), and scan to cloud.

Understand the basics of how 3D printers create objects.   3D printers use filament or resin. It's most often a plastic composite but filament can be made of other material, such as aluminum or copper. 3D printers create objects by stacking thin layers of filament on top of each other.

Know how to install and configure printers.   The basic procedure is as follows:

1. Find a suitable location for the printer and properly unbox the device.

2. Attach the device using a local or network port and connect the power.

3. Install and update the device driver and calibrate the device.

4. Configure options and default settings.

5. Print a test page.

6. Verify compatibility with the operating system and applications.

7. Educate users about basic functionality.

Know the seven steps in the laser imaging process.   The seven steps are processing, charging, exposing, developing, transferring, fusing, and cleaning.

Know the key parts in a laser printer and appropriate maintenance procedures.   Key parts are the imaging drum, fuser assembly, transfer belt, transfer roller, pickup rollers, separation pads, and duplexing assembly. Maintenance includes replacing toner, applying a maintenance kit, calibrating, and cleaning.

Know the key parts in an inkjet printer and appropriate maintenance procedures.   Inkjet parts include the ink cartridge, print head, roller, feeder, duplexing assembly, and carriage belt. Maintenance items include cleaning heads, replacing cartridges, calibrating, and clearing paper jams.

Know the key components in a thermal printer and appropriate maintenance procedures.   The feed assembly and heating element are important thermal printer parts. The paper is also important here because it's special heat-sensitive paper. Maintenance includes replacing paper, cleaning the heating element, and removing debris.

Know the key parts in an impact printer and appropriate maintenance procedures.   Impact printer parts to know include the print head, ribbon, tractor feed (and special tractor feed paper), and impact paper. Maintenance includes replacing the ribbon, print head, and paper.

Understand the importance of using recommended supplies.   Using consumables (paper, ink, toner) that are recommended for your printer is important. Using bad supplies could ruin your printer and void your warranty.

Review Questions

The answers to the chapter review questions can be found in Appendix A.

1. Which voltage is applied to the paper to transfer the toner to the paper in an EP process laser printer?

   A. +600VDC

   B. −600VDC

   C. +6000VDC

   D. −6000VDC

2. Which types of printers are referred to as page printers because they receive their print job instructions one page at a time? (Choose two.)

   A. Daisy-wheel

   B. Dot-matrix

   C. Inkjet

   D. Laser

   E. Thermal

3. Which of the following is not an advantage of a Universal Serial Bus (USB) printer interface?

   A. It has a higher transfer rate than a serial connection.

   B. It has a higher transfer rate than a parallel connection.

   C. It automatically recognizes new devices.

   D. It allows the printer to communicate with networks, servers, and workstations.

4. You have a finance manager who needs to print contracts in triplicate. Which type of printers are best for printing on multipart forms?

   A. Inkjet printers

   B. Laser printers

   C. Thermal printers

   D. Dot-matrix printers

5. Which step in the EP imaging process uses a laser to discharge selected areas of the photosensitive drum, thus forming an image on the drum?

   A. Exposing

   B. Transferring

   C. Developing

   D. Cleaning

6. Which of the following is fed through an extruder on a 3D printer to create objects?

   A. Resin

   B. Dye

   C. Filament

   D. Extrusion powder

7. Recently, employees have been printing off unauthorized materials that may contain hate speech. Which of the following can be used to see which users printed specific jobs?

   A. Audit logs

   B. Badging

   C. User authentication

   D. Secured prints

8. Which device in an inkjet printer contains the print head?

   A. Toner cartridge

   B. Ink cartridge

   C. Daisy wheel

   D. Paper tray

9. What is the correct order of the steps in the EP imaging process?

   A. Developing, exposing, transferring, fusing, charging, cleaning, processing

   B. Charging, processing, exposing, developing, transferring, fusing, cleaning

   C. Processing, transferring, exposing, developing, charging, cleaning, fusing

   D. Processing, charging, exposing, developing, transferring, fusing, cleaning

10. The network administrator has set up security on office MFDs that requires users to authenticate before printing. Which of the following are valid methods for users to authenticate to the MFD? (Choose two.)

   A. Use an authentication log.

   B. Enable secured print.

   C. Type their username and password on the MFD's touchscreen.

   D. Use SMB.

   E. Use their company ID for badging.

11. What is typically included in the EP laser printer toner cartridge? (Choose three.)

   A. Toner

   B. Print drum

   C. Laser

   D. Cleaning blade

12. What happens during the developing stage of laser printing?

    A. An electrostatic charge is applied to the drum to attract toner particles.

    B. Heat is applied to the paper to melt the toner.

    C. The laser creates an image of the page on the drum.

    D. An electrostatic charge is applied to the paper to attract toner particles.

13. Which of the following are possible interfaces for printers? (Choose three.)

    A. Parallel

    B. SATA

    C. USB

    D. Network

14. You have just installed a new printer, but it prints only garbled text. Which of the following is likely the problem?

    A. Wrong IP address

    B. Worn print head

    C. Incorrect printer drivers

    D. Unsupported printer

15. Which printer contains a wheel that looks like a flower with raised letters and symbols on each "petal"?

    A. Inkjet printer

    B. Daisy-wheel printer

    C. Dot-matrix printer

    D. Laser printer

16. What part of a laser printer supplies the voltages for charging and transferring corona assemblies?

    A. High-voltage power supply (HVPS)

    B. DC power supply (DCPS)

    C. Controller circuitry

    D. Transfer corona

17. Which printer part gets the toner from the photosensitive drum onto the paper?

    A. Laser-scanning assembly

    B. Fusing assembly

    C. Corona assembly

    D. Drum

18. Which step in the laser printer printing process occurs immediately after the exposing phase?

   A. Charging

   B. Fusing

   C. Transferring

   D. Developing

19. Which laser printer component permanently presses the toner into the paper?

   A. Transfer corona

   B. Fuser assembly

   C. Printer controller circuitry

   D. Paper transport assembly

20. Which of the following most accurately describes how to obtain a firmware upgrade for your laser printer?

   A. Download the firmware upgrade for free from the manufacturer's website.

   B. Pay to download the firmware upgrade from the manufacturer's website.

   C. Have a certified laser printer technician come to your site and install a new firmware chip.

   D. Contact the manufacturer of the printer, and they will send you the firmware upgrade on a DVD.

Performance-Based Question

You will encounter performance-based questions on the A+ exams. The questions on the exam require you to perform a specific task, and you will be graded on whether or not you were able to complete the task. The following requires you to think creatively in order to measure how well you understand this chapter's topics. You may or may not see similar questions on the actual A+ exams. To see how your answer compares to the authors', refer to Appendix B.

Your network has several inkjet printers in use. A user is complaining that their documents are consistently printing with extra smudges along the lines of print on one of them. What steps would you take to clean the printer?

Chapter

5

Networking Fundamentals

THE FOLLOWING COMPTIA A+ 220-1101 EXAM OBJECTIVES ARE COVERED IN THIS CHAPTER:

✓ **2.2 Compare and contrast common networking hardware.**

- **Routers**
- **Switches**
    - **Managed**
    - **Unmanaged**
- **Access points**
- **Patch panel**
- **Firewall**
- **Power over Ethernet (PoE)**
    - **Injectors**
    - **Switch**
    - **PoE standards**
- **Hub**
- **Cable modem**
- **Digital subscriber line (DSL)**
- **Optical networking terminal (ONT)**
- **Network interface card (NIC)**
- **Software-defined networking (SDN)**

✓ **2.7 Compare and contrast Internet connection types, network types, and their features.**

- **Network types**
    - **Local area network (LAN)**
    - **Wide area network (WAN)**

- Personal area network (PAN)
- Metropolitan area network (MAN)
- Storage area network (SAN)
- Wireless local area network (WLAN)

✓ **3.1 Explain basic cable types and their connectors, features, and purposes.**

- Network cables
  - Copper
    - Cat 5
    - Cat 5e
    - Cat 6
    - Cat 6a
    - Coaxial
    - Plenum
    - Shielded twisted pair
      - Direct burial
    - Unshielded twisted pair
  - Plenum
  - Optical
    - Fiber
  - T568A/T568B
- Connector types
  - RJ11
  - RJ45
  - F type
  - Straight tip (ST)
  - Subscriber connector (SC)
  - Lucent connector (LC)
  - Punchdown block

Looking around most homes or offices today, it's hard to imagine a world without networks. Nearly every place of business has some sort of network. Wireless home networks have exploded in popularity in the last decade, and it seems that everywhere you go, you can see a dozen wireless networks from your smartphone, tablet, or laptop.

It didn't used to be that way. Even when not thinking about networks, we're still likely connected to one via the ubiquitous Internet-enabled smartphones in our pockets and purses. We take for granted a lot of what we have gained in technology over the past few years, much less the past several decades.

Thirty years ago, if you wanted to send a memo to everyone in your company, you had to use a photocopier and interoffice mail. Delivery to a remote office could take days. Today, one mistaken click of the Reply All button can result in instantaneous embarrassment. Email is an example of one form of communication that became available with the introduction and growth of networks.

This chapter focuses on the basic concepts of how a network works, including the way it sends information, the hardware used, and the common types of networks you might encounter. It used to be that in order to be a PC technician, you needed to focus on only one individual (but large) computer at a time. In today's environment, though, you will in all likelihood need to understand combinations of hardware, software, and network infrastructure in order to be successful.

If the material in this chapter interests you, you might consider studying for, and eventually taking, CompTIA's Network+ exam. It is a non–company-specific networking certification similar to A+ but for network-related topics. You can study for it using Sybex's *CompTIA Network+ Study Guide*, by Todd Lammle, available at your favorite online bookseller.

Understanding Networking Principles

Stand-alone personal computers, first introduced in the late 1970s, gave users the ability to create documents, spreadsheets, and other types of data and save them for future use. For the small-business user or home-computer enthusiast, this was great. For larger companies, however, it was not enough. Larger companies had greater needs to share information between offices and sometimes over great distances. Stand-alone computers were insufficient for the following reasons:

- Their small hard drive capacities were insufficient.

- To print, each computer required a printer attached locally.

- Sharing documents was cumbersome. People grew tired of having to save to a floppy and then take that disk to the recipient. (This procedure was called *sneakernet*.)

- There was no email. Instead, there was interoffice mail, which was slow and sometimes unreliable. Imagine snail mail without post office efficiency.

To address these problems, networks were born. A *network* links two or more computers together to communicate and share resources. Their success was a revelation to the computer industry as well as to businesses. Now departments could be linked internally to offer better performance and increase efficiency.

You have probably heard the term *networking* in a social or business context, where people come together and exchange names for future contact and access to more resources. The same is true with a computer network. A computer network enables computers to link to each other's resources. For example, in a network, every computer does not need a printer connected locally in order to print. Instead, you can connect a printer to one computer, or you can connect it directly to the network and allow all the other computers to access it. Because they allow users to share resources, networks can increase productivity as well as decrease cash outlay for new hardware and software.

In many cases, networking today has become a relatively simple plug-and-play process. Wireless network cards can automatically detect and join networks, and then you're seconds away from surfing the web or sending email. Of course, not all networks are that simple. Getting your network running may require a lot of configuration, and one messed-up setting can cause the whole thing to fail.

To best configure your network, there is a lot of information you should understand about *how* networks work. The following sections cover the fundamentals, and armed with this information, you can then move on to how to make it work *right*.

Network Types

One of the ways to think about how networks are structured is to categorize them by network type. Some networks are small in scale whereas others span the globe. Some are designed to be wireless only, whereas others are designed specifically for storage. Understanding the basic structure of the network can often help you solve a problem. There are six different types of networks you need to be familiar with, and we'll cover them here:

- Local area network (LAN)

- Wide area network (WAN)

- Personal area network (PAN)

- Metropolitan area network (MAN)

- Storage area network (SAN)
- Wireless local area network (WLAN)

The *local area network (LAN)* was created to connect computers in a single office or building. Expanding on that, a *wide area network (WAN)* includes networks outside the local environment and can also distribute resources across great distances. Generally, it's safe to think of a WAN as multiple dispersed LANs connected together. Today, LANs exist in many homes (wireless networks) and nearly all businesses. WANs are fairly common too, as businesses embrace mobility and more of them span greater distances. Historically, only larger corporations used WANs, but many smaller companies with remote locations now use them as well.

Having two types of network categories just didn't encompass everything that was out there, so the industry introduced several more terms: the personal area network, the metropolitan area network, the storage area network, and the wireless local area network. The *personal area network (PAN)* is a very small-scale network designed around one person within a very limited boundary area. The term generally refers to networks that use Bluetooth technology. On a larger scale is the *metropolitan area network (MAN)*, which is bigger than a LAN but not quite as big as a WAN. A *storage area network (SAN)* is designed for optimized large-scale, long-term data storage. And the *wireless local area network (WLAN)* is like a LAN, only wireless. We'll cover all of these concepts in more detail in the following sections.

Local Area Networks (LANs)

The 1970s brought us the minicomputer, which was a smaller version of large mainframe computers. Whereas the mainframe used *centralized processing* (all programs ran on the same computer), the minicomputer used *distributed processing* to access programs across other computers. As depicted in Figure 5.1, distributed processing allows a user at one computer to use a program on another computer as a *backend* to process and store information. The user's computer is the *frontend*, where data entry and minor processing functions are performed. This arrangement allowed programs to be distributed across computers rather than be centralized. This was also the first time network cables rather than phone lines were used to connect computers.

FIGURE 5.1 Distributed processing

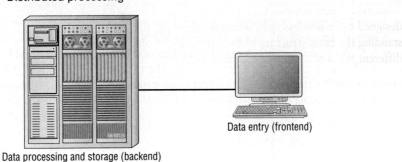

Data entry (frontend)

Data processing and storage (backend)

By the 1980s, offices were beginning to buy PCs in large numbers. Portables were also introduced, allowing computing to become mobile. Neither PCs nor portables, however, were efficient in sharing information. As timeliness and security became more important, floppy disks were just not cutting it. Offices needed to find a way to implement a better means to share and access resources. This led to the introduction of the first type of PC *local area network (LAN)*: ShareNet by Novell, which had both hardware and software components. LANs simply link computers in order to share resources within a closed environment. The first simple LANs were constructed a lot like the LAN shown in Figure 5.2.

FIGURE 5.2   A simple LAN

After the introduction of ShareNet, more LANs sprouted. The earliest LANs could not cover large distances. Most of them could only stretch across a single floor of the office and could support no more than 30 computers. Furthermore, they were still very rudimentary and only a few software programs supported them. The first software programs that ran on a LAN were not capable of being used by more than one user at a time. (This constraint was known as *file locking*.) Nowadays, multiple users often concurrently access a program or file. Most of the time, the only limitations will be restrictions at the record level if two users are trying to modify a database record at the same time.

Wide Area Networks (WANs)

By the late 1980s, networks were expanding to cover large geographical areas and were supporting thousands of users. The concept of a *wide area network (WAN)* was born. WANs were first implemented with mainframes at massive government expense, but started attracting PC users as networks went to this new level. Employees of businesses with offices across the country communicated as though they were only desks apart. Soon the whole world saw a change in the way of doing business, across not only a few miles but across countries. Whereas LANs are limited to single buildings, WANs can span buildings, states, countries, and even continental boundaries. Figure 5.3 shows an example of a simple WAN.

Generally speaking, it's safe to think of a WAN as multiple dispersed LANs connected together. Historically, only larger corporations used WANs, but many smaller companies with remote locations now use them as well. The networks of today and tomorrow are no longer limited by the inability of LANs to cover distance and handle mobility. WANs play an important role in the future development of corporate networks worldwide.

FIGURE 5.3   A simple WAN

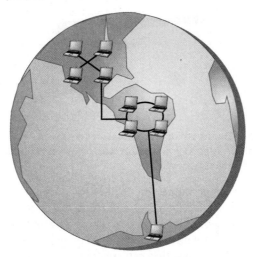

Personal Area Networks (PANs)

In moving from LANs to WANs, we increased the scope. Going the other way, a *personal area network (PAN)* is going to be much smaller in scale. The term PAN is most commonly used in reference to Bluetooth networks. In 1998, a consortium of companies formed the Bluetooth Special Interest Group (SIG) and formally adopted the name *Bluetooth* for its technology. The name comes from a tenth-century Danish king named Harald Blåtand, known as Harold Bluetooth in English. (One can only imagine how he got that name.) King Blåtand had successfully unified warring factions in the areas of Norway, Sweden, and Denmark. The makers of Bluetooth were trying to unite disparate technology industries, namely computing, mobile communications, and the auto industry.

Although the most common use of a PAN is in association with Bluetooth, a PAN can also be created with other technologies, such as infrared.

Current membership in the Bluetooth SIG includes Microsoft, Intel, Apple, IBM, Toshiba, and several cell phone manufacturers. The technical specification IEEE 802.15.1 describes a *wireless personal area network (WPAN)* based on Bluetooth version 1.1.

The first Bluetooth device on the market was an Ericsson headset and cell phone adapter, which arrived on the scene in 2000. While mobile phones and accessories are still the most common type of Bluetooth device, you will find many more, including wireless keyboards, mice, and printers. Figure 5.4 shows a Bluetooth USB adapter.

FIGURE 5.4 Bluetooth USB adapter

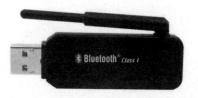

 We cover Bluetooth in more detail in Chapter 7, "Wireless and SOHO Networks." Also, if you want to learn more about Bluetooth, you can visit www.bluetooth.com.

One of the defining features of a Bluetooth WPAN is its temporary nature. With traditional Wi-Fi, you need a central communication point, such as a wireless router or access point, to connect more than two devices together. (This is referred to as *infrastructure*.) Bluetooth networks are formed on an *ad hoc* basis, meaning that whenever two Bluetooth devices get close enough to each other, they can communicate directly with each other—no central communication point is required. This dynamically created network is called a *piconet*. A Bluetooth-enabled device can communicate with up to seven other devices in one piconet. Two or more piconets can be linked together in a *scatternet*. In a scatternet, one or more devices would serve as a bridge between the piconets.

Metropolitan Area Networks (MANs)

For those networks that are larger than a LAN but confined to a relatively small geographical area, there is the term *metropolitan area network (MAN)*. A MAN is generally defined as a network that spans a city or a large campus. For example, if a city decides to install wireless hotspots in various places, that network could be considered a MAN.

One of the questions a lot of people ask is, "Is there really a difference between a MAN and a WAN?" There is definitely some gray area here; in many cases they are virtually identical. Perhaps the biggest difference is who has responsibility for managing the connectivity. In a MAN, a central IT organization, such as the campus or city IT staff, is responsible. In a WAN, it's implied that you will be using publicly available communication lines, and there will be a phone company or other service provider involved.

Storage Area Networks (SANs)

A *storage area network (SAN)* is designed to do exactly what it says, which is to store information. Although a SAN can be implemented a few different ways, imagine a network (or network segment) that holds nothing but networked storage devices, whether they be network-attached storage (NAS) hard drives or servers with lots of disk space dedicated solely to storage. This network won't have client computers or other types of servers on it. It's for storage only. Figure 5.5 shows what a SAN could look like.

FIGURE 5.5   Storage area network (SAN)

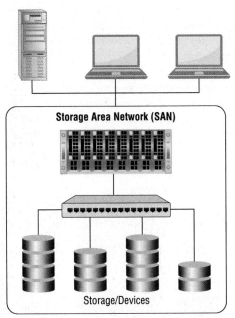

Perhaps you're thinking, why would someone create a network solely for storage? It's a great question, and there are several benefits to having a SAN.

Dedicated SANs relieve network loads.   With a SAN, all storage traffic, which may include huge data files or videos, is sent to a specific network or network segment, relieving traffic on other network segments.

SANs offer fast data access.   Most SANs use high-speed Fibre Channel connections, which allow for very fast access even for huge files.

SANs are easily expandable.   In most cases, it's a matter of connecting a new storage unit, which might even be hot-swappable (removed and replaced without powering down the system), and a few clicks to configure it. Then it's ready to go.

Block-level storage is more efficient.   This is getting into the weeds a bit, but most SANs are configured to store and retrieve data in a system called *block storage*. This contrasts with the file-based access systems you're probably used to, such as the ones in Windows and macOS. For anyone who has used a Windows-based or Mac computer, file storage is instantly recognizable. It's based on the concept of a filing cabinet. Inside the filing cabinet are folders, and files are stored within the folders. Each file has a unique name when you include the folders and subfolders it's stored in. For example, `c:\files\doc1.txt` is different from `c:\papers\doc1.txt`. The hierarchical folder structure and the naming scheme of file storage make it relatively easy for humans to navigate. Larger data sets and multiple embedded folders can make it trickier—who here hasn't spent 10 minutes trying to figure out which folder they put that file in?—but it's still pretty straightforward.

With file storage, each file is treated as its own singular entity, regardless of how small or large it is. With *block storage*, files are split into chunks of data of equal size, assigned a unique identifier, and then stored on the hard drive. Because each piece of data has a unique address, a file structure is not needed. Figure 5.6 illustrates what this looks like.

FIGURE 5.6   Block storage

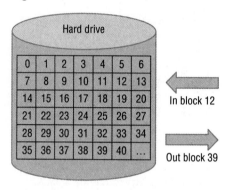

Block storage allows a file to be broken into more manageable chunks rather than being stored as one entity. This allows the operating system to modify one portion of a file without needing to open the entire file. In addition, since data reads and writes are always of the same block size, data transfers are more efficient and therefore faster. Latency with block storage is lower than with other types of storage.

One of the first common use cases for block storage was for databases, and it remains the best choice for large, structured databases today. Block storage is also used for storage area networks (SANs).

The downsides to SANs are that they are a bit complicated to set up and can be more expensive to run than non-SAN storage solutions. For huge networks that need to get data to large numbers of users, though, they're a good choice.

Wireless Local Area Networks (WLANs)

Wireless networks are everywhere today. If you use your smartphone, tablet, or laptop to look for wireless networks, chances are you will find several. A *wireless local area network (WLAN)* is simply a LAN, but one in which clients connect wirelessly rather than through network cables.

Wireless clients on a network typically access the network through a *wireless access point (WAP)*. The WAP may connect wirelessly to another connectivity device, such as a wireless router, but more likely uses a wired connection to a router or switch. (We'll talk about all of these devices later in the chapter.)

In addition to LANs, WANs, and others, the A+ exam 220-1101 objective 2.7 covers Internet connection types such as satellite, fiber, cable, and so on. We cover these in Chapter 7. There, we show you the details of each type of connection and factors to consider when choosing one for yourself or a client.

Primary Network Components

Technically speaking, two or more computers connected together constitute a network. But networks are rarely that simple. When you're looking at the devices or resources available on a network, there are three types of components of which you should be aware:

- Servers
- Clients or workstations
- Resources

Every network requires two more items to tie these three components together: a network operating system (NOS) and some kind of shared medium (wired or wireless connectivity). These components are covered later in their own sections.

Servers

Servers come in many shapes and sizes. They are a core component of the network, providing a link to the resources necessary to perform any task. The link that the *server* provides could be to a resource existing on the server itself or to a resource on a client computer. The server is the critical enabler, offering directions to the client computers regarding where to go to get what they need.

Servers offer networks the capability of centralizing the control of resources and security, thereby reducing administrative difficulties. They can be used to distribute processes for balancing the load on computers and can thus increase speed and performance. They can also compartmentalize files for improved reliability. That way, if one server goes down, not all of the files are lost.

Servers can perform several different critical roles on a network. For example, a server that provides files to the users on the network is called a *file server*. Likewise, one that hosts printing services for users is called a *print server*. Servers can be used for other tasks as well, such as authentication, remote access services, administration, email, and so on.

Networks can include multipurpose and single-purpose servers. A multipurpose server can be, for example, both a file server and a print server at the same time. If the server is a single-purpose server, it is a file server only or a print server only. Another distinction we use in categorizing servers is whether they are dedicated or nondedicated:

Dedicated Servers A *dedicated server* is assigned to provide specific applications or services for the network and nothing else. Because a dedicated server specializes in only a few tasks, it requires fewer resources than a nondedicated server might require from the computer that is hosting it. This savings may translate to efficiency and can thus be considered as having a beneficial impact on network performance. A web server is an example of a dedicated server; it is dedicated to the task of serving up web pages and nothing else.

Nondedicated Servers Nondedicated servers are assigned to provide one or more network services *and* local access. A *nondedicated server* is expected to be slightly more flexible in its day-to-day use than a dedicated server. Nondedicated servers can be used to direct network traffic and perform administrative actions, but they also are often used to serve as a frontend for the administrator to work with other applications or services or to perform services for more than one network. For example, a dedicated web server might serve out one or more websites, whereas a nondedicated web server serves out websites but might also function as a print server on the local network or as the administrator's workstation.

The nondedicated server is not what some would consider a true server, because it can act as a workstation as well as a server. The workgroup server at your office is an example of a nondedicated server. It might be a combination file, print, and email server. Plus, because of its nature, a nondedicated server could also function well in a peer-to-peer environment. It could be used as a workstation in addition to being a file, print, and email server.

We will talk in more depth about server roles in Chapter 8, "Network Services, Virtualization, and Cloud Computing."

Many networks use both dedicated and nondedicated servers to incorporate the best of both worlds, offering improved network performance with the dedicated servers and flexibility with the nondedicated servers.

Workstations

Workstations are the computers on which the network users do their work, performing activities such as word processing, database design, graphic design, email, and other office or personal tasks. A *workstation* is basically an everyday computer, except for the fact that it is connected to a network that offers additional resources. Workstations can range from diskless computer systems to desktops or laptops. In network terms, workstations are also known as *client computers*. As clients, they are allowed to communicate with the servers in the network to use the network's resources.

It takes several items to make a workstation into a network client. You must install a *network interface card (NIC)*, a special expansion card that allows the PC to talk on a network. You must connect it to a cabling system that connects to other computers (unless your NIC supports wireless networking). And you must install special software, called *client software*, which allows the computer to talk to the servers and request resources from them. Once all this has been accomplished, the computer is "on the network." We'll cover more details on how NICs work and how to configure them in the "Network Interface Cards" section later in this chapter.

 Network client software comes with all operating systems today. When you configure your computer to participate in the network, the operating system utilizes this software.

To the client, the server may be nothing more than just another drive letter. However, because it is in a network environment, the client can use the server as a doorway to more storage or more applications or to communicate with other computers or other networks. To users, being on a network changes a few things:

- They can store more information because they can store data on other computers on the network.

- They can share and receive information from other users, perhaps even collaborating on the same document.

- They can use programs that would be too large or complex for their computer to use by itself.

- They can use hardware not attached directly to their computer, such as a printer.

 Real World Scenario

Is That a Server or a Workstation?

This is one of the things that author Quentin Docter does when teaching novice technicians. In the room, there will be a standard-looking mini-tower desktop computer. He points to it and asks, "Is that a server or a workstation?" A lot of techs will look at it and say it's a workstation because it is a desktop computer. The real answer is, "It depends."

Although many people have a perception that servers are ultra-fancy, rack-mounted devices, that isn't necessarily true. It's true that servers typically need more powerful hardware than do workstations because of their role on the network, but that doesn't have to be the case. (Granted, having servers that are less powerful than your workstations doesn't make logical sense.) What really differentiates a workstation from a server is what operating system it has installed and what role it plays on the network.

For example, if that system has Windows Server 2022 installed on it, you can be pretty sure that it's a server. If it has Windows 10, it's more than likely going to be a client, but not always. Computers with operating systems such as Windows 10 can be both clients on the network and nondedicated servers, as would be the case if you share your local printer with others on the network.

The moral of the story? Don't assume a computer's role simply by looking at it. You need to understand what is on it and its role on the network to make that determination.

Network Resources

We now have the server to share the resources and the workstation to use them, but what about the resources themselves? A *resource* (as far as the network is concerned) is any item that can be used on a network. Resources can include a broad range of items, but the following items are among the most important:

- Printers and other peripherals
- Disk storage and file access
- Applications

When only a few printers (and all the associated consumables) have to be purchased for the entire office, the costs are dramatically lower than the costs for supplying printers at every workstation.

Networks also give users more storage space to store their files. Client computers can't always handle the overhead involved in storing large files (for example, database files) because they are already heavily involved in users' day-to-day work activities. Because servers in a network can be dedicated to only certain functions, a server can be allocated to store all of the larger files that are used every day, freeing up disk space on client computers. In addition, if users store their files on a server, the administrator can back up the server periodically to ensure that if something happens to a user's files, those files can be recovered.

Files that all users need to access (such as emergency contact lists and company policies) can also be stored on a server. Having one copy of these files in a central location saves disk space, as opposed to storing the files locally on everyone's system.

Applications (programs) no longer need to be on every computer in the office. If the server is capable of handling the overhead that an application requires, the application can reside on the server and be used by workstations through a network connection. Apps can also be cloud based, which basically means they will reside on a computer somewhere on the Internet. We cover cloud computing in Chapter 8.

The sharing of applications over a network requires a special arrangement with the application vendor, who may wish to set the price of the application according to the number of users who will be using it. The arrangement allowing multiple users to use a single installation of an application is called a *site license*.

Being on a Network Brings Responsibilities

You are part of a community when you are on a network, which means that you need to take responsibility for your actions. First, a network is only as secure as the users who use it. You cannot randomly delete files or move documents from server to server. You do not own your email, so anyone in your company's management team can choose to read it. In addition, sending something to the printer does not necessarily mean that it will print immediately—your document may not be the first in line to be printed at the shared printer. Plus, if your workstation has also been set up as a nondedicated server, you cannot turn it off.

Network Operating Systems

PCs use a disk operating system that controls the filesystem and how the applications communicate with the hard disk. Networks use a *network operating system (NOS)* to control the communication with resources and the flow of data across the network. The NOS runs on the server. Some of the more popular NOSs are Linux, Microsoft's Windows Server series (Server 2022, Server 2019, and so on), and macOS Server. Several other companies offer network operating systems as well.

Network Resource Access

We have discussed two major components of a typical network—servers and workstations—and we've also talked briefly about network resources. Let's dive a bit deeper into how those resources are accessed on a network.

There are generally two resource access models: peer-to-peer and client-server. It is important to choose the appropriate model. How do you decide which type of resource model is needed? You must first think about the following questions:

- What is the size of the organization?
- How much security does the company require?

- What software or hardware does the resource require?
- How much administration does it need?
- How much will it cost?
- Will this resource meet the needs of the organization today and in the future?
- Will additional training be needed?

Networks cannot just be put together at the drop of a hat. A lot of planning is required before implementation of a network to ensure that whatever design is chosen will be effective and efficient, and not just for today but for the future as well. The forethought of the designer will lead to the best network with the least amount of administrative overhead. In each network, it is important that a plan be developed to answer the previous questions. The answers will help the designer choose the type of resource model to use.

Peer-to-Peer Networks

In a peer-to-peer network, the computers act as both service providers and service requestors. An example of a peer-to-peer resource model is shown in Figure 5.7.

FIGURE 5.7   The peer-to-peer resource model

The peer-to-peer model is great for small, simple, inexpensive networks. This model can be set up almost instantly, with little extra hardware required. Many versions of Windows (Windows 11, Windows 10, and others) as well as Linux and macOS are popular operating system environments that support the peer-to-peer resource model. Peer-to-peer networks are also referred to as *workgroups*.

Generally speaking, there is no centralized administration or control in the peer-to-peer resource model. Every workstation has unique control over the resources that the computer owns, and each workstation must be administered separately. However, this very lack of centralized control can make administering the network difficult; for the same reason, the network isn't very secure. Each user needs to manage separate passwords for each computer on which they wish to access resources, as well as set up and manage the shared resources on their own computer. Moreover, because each computer is acting as both a workstation and a server, it may not be easy to locate resources. The person who is in charge of a file may have moved it without anyone's knowledge. Also, the users who work under this arrangement need more training because they are not only users but also administrators.

Will this type of network meet the needs of the organization today and in the future? Peer-to-peer resource models are generally considered the right choice for small companies that don't expect future growth. Small companies that expect growth, on the other hand, should not choose this type of model.

A rule of thumb is that if you have no more than 10 computers and centralized security is not a key priority, a workgroup may be a good choice for you.

Client-Server Resource Model

The client-server model (also known as *server-based model*) is better than the peer-to-peer model for large networks (say, more than 10 computers) that need a more secure environment and centralized control. Server-based networks use one or more dedicated, centralized servers. All administrative functions and resource sharing are performed from this point. This makes it easier to share resources, perform backups, and support an almost unlimited number of users.

This model also offers better security than the peer-to-peer model. However, the server needs more hardware than a typical workstation/server computer in a peer-to-peer resource model. In addition, it requires specialized software (the NOS) to manage the server's role in the environment. With the addition of a server and the NOS, server-based networks can easily cost more than peer-to-peer resource models. However, for large networks, it's the only choice. An example of a client-server resource model is shown in Figure 5.8.

FIGURE 5.8   The client-server resource model

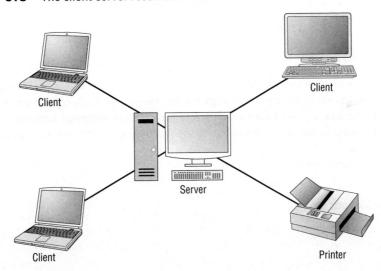

Server-based networks are often known as *domains*. The key characteristic of a server-based network is that security is centrally administered. When you log into the network, the login request is passed to the server responsible for security, sometimes known as a *domain controller*. (Microsoft uses the term *domain controller*, whereas other vendors of server products do not.) This is different from the peer-to-peer model, where each individual workstation validates users. In a peer-to-peer model, if the user jsmith wants to be able to log into different workstations, they need to have a user account set up on each machine. This can quickly become an administrative nightmare! In a domain, all user accounts are stored on the server. User jsmith needs only one account and can log into any of the workstations in the domain.

Client-server resource models are the desired models for companies that are continually growing, that need to support a large environment, or that need centralized security. Server-based networks offer the flexibility to add more resources and clients almost indefinitely into the future. Hardware costs may be higher, but with the centralized administration, managing resources becomes less time consuming. Also, only a few administrators need to be trained, and users are responsible for only their own work environment.

> If you are looking for an inexpensive, simple network with little setup required, and there is no need for the company to grow in the future, then the peer-to-peer network is the way to go. If you are looking for a network to support many users (more than 10 computers), strong security, and centralized administration, consider the server-based network your only choice.

Whatever you decide, always take the time to plan your network before installing it. A network is not something you can just throw together. You don't want to find out a few months down the road that the type of network you chose does not meet the needs of the company—this could be a time-consuming and costly mistake.

Network Topologies

A *topology* is a way of physically laying out the network. When you plan and install a network, you need to choose the right topology for your situation. Each type differs from the others by its cost, ease of installation, fault tolerance (how the topology handles problems such as cable breaks), and ease of reconfiguration (such as adding a new workstation to the existing network).

There are five primary topologies:

- Bus
- Star (or hub-and-spoke)
- Ring
- Mesh
- Hybrid

Each topology has advantages and disadvantages. Table 5.1 summarizes the advantages and disadvantages of each topology, and then we will go into more detail about each one.

TABLE 5.1   Topologies—advantages and disadvantages

Topology	Advantages	Disadvantages
Bus	Cheap. Easy to install.	Difficult to reconfigure. A break in the bus disables the entire network.
Star	Cheap. Very easy to install and reconfigure. More resilient to a single cable failure.	More expensive than bus.
Ring	Efficient. Easy to install.	Reconfiguration is difficult. Very expensive.
Mesh	Best fault tolerance.	Reconfiguration is extremely difficult, extremely expensive, and very complex.
Hybrid	Gives a combination of the best features of each topology used.	Complex (less so than mesh, however).

Bus Topology

A *bus topology* is the simplest. It consists of a single cable that runs to every workstation, as shown in Figure 5.9. This topology uses the least amount of cabling. Each computer shares the same data and address path. With a bus topology, messages pass through the trunk, and each workstation checks to see if a message is addressed to it. If the address of the message matches the workstation's address, the network adapter retrieves it. If not, the message is ignored.

FIGURE 5.9   The bus topology

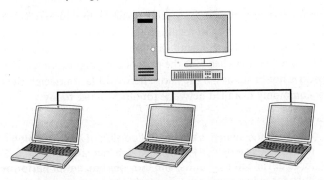

Cable systems that use the bus topology are easy to install. You run a cable from the first computer to the last computer. All of the remaining computers attach to the cable somewhere in between. Because of the simplicity of installation, and because of the low cost of the cable, bus topology cabling systems are the cheapest to install.

Although the bus topology uses the least amount of cabling, it is difficult to add a workstation. If you want to add another workstation, you have to reroute the cable completely and possibly run two additional lengths of it. Also, if any one of the cables breaks, the entire network is disrupted. Therefore, such a system is expensive to maintain and can be difficult to troubleshoot. You will rarely run across physical bus networks in use today.

Star Topology

A *star topology* (also called a *hub-and-spoke topology*) branches each network device off a central device called a *hub* or a *switch*, making it easy to add a new workstation. If a workstation goes down, it does not affect the entire network; if the central device goes down, the entire network goes with it. Because of this, the hub (or switch) is called a *single point of failure*. Figure 5.10 shows a simple star network.

FIGURE 5.10 The star topology

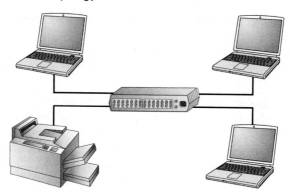

Star topologies are very easy to install. A cable is run from each workstation to the switch. The switch is placed in a central location in the office (for example, a utility closet). Star topologies are more expensive to install than bus networks because several more cables need to be installed, plus the switches. But the ease of reconfiguration and fault tolerance (one cable failing does not bring down the entire network) far outweigh the drawbacks. This is by far the most commonly installed network topology in use today.

Although the switch is the central portion of a star topology, some older networks use a device known as a hub instead of a switch. Switches are more advanced than hubs, and they provide better performance than hubs for only a small price increase. Colloquially, though, many administrators use the terms *hub* and *switch* interchangeably.

Ring Topology

In a *ring topology*, each computer connects to two other computers, joining them in a circle and creating a unidirectional path where messages move from workstation to workstation. Each entity participating in the ring reads a message and then regenerates it and hands it to its neighbor on a different network cable. See Figure 5.11 for an example of a ring topology.

FIGURE 5.11   The ring topology

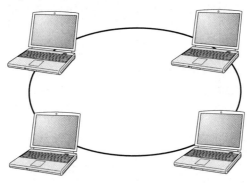

The ring makes it difficult to add new computers. Unlike a star topology network, a ring topology network will go down if one entity is removed from the ring. Physical ring topology systems rarely exist anymore, mainly because the hardware involved was fairly expensive and the fault tolerance was very low.

   You might have heard of an older network architecture called Token Ring. Contrary to its name, it does *not* use a physical ring. It actually uses a physical star topology, but the traffic flows in a logical ring from one computer to the next.

Mesh Topology

The *mesh topology* is the most complex in terms of physical design. In this topology, each device is connected to every other device (see Figure 5.12). This topology is rarely found in wired LANs, mainly because of the complexity of the cabling. If there are x computers, there will be $(x \times (x - 1)) \div 2$ cables in the network. For example, if you have five computers in a mesh network, it will use $(5 \times (5 - 1)) \div 2 = 10$ cables. This complexity is compounded when you add another workstation. For example, your 5-computer, 10-cable network will jump to 15 cables if you add just one more computer. Imagine how the person doing the cabling would feel if you told them they had to cable 50 computers in a mesh network—they'd have to come up with $(50 \times (50 - 1)) \div 2 = 1,225$ cables! (Not to mention figuring out how to connect them all.)

FIGURE 5.12   The mesh topology

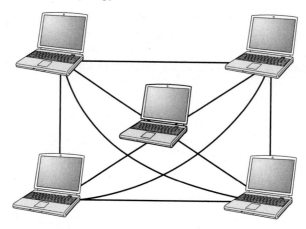

Because of its design, the physical mesh topology is expensive to install and maintain. Cables must be run from each device to every other device. The advantage you gain is high fault tolerance. With a mesh topology, there will always be a way to get the data from source to destination. The data may not be able to take the direct route, but it can take an alternate, indirect route. For this reason, the mesh topology is often used to connect multiple sites across WAN links. It uses devices called *routers* to search multiple routes through the mesh and determine the best path. However, the mesh topology does become inefficient with five or more entities because of the number of connections that need to be maintained.

Hybrid Topology

The *hybrid topology* is simply a mix of the other topologies. It would be impossible to illustrate it because there are many combinations. In fact, most networks today are not only hybrid but heterogeneous. (They include a mix of components of different types and brands.) The hybrid network may be more expensive than some types of network topologies, but it takes the best features of all the other topologies and exploits them.

Table 5.1, earlier in this chapter, summarizes the advantages and disadvantages of each type of network topology.

Rules of Communication

Regardless of the type of network you choose to implement, the computers on that network need to know how to talk to each other. To facilitate communication across a network, computers use a common language called a *protocol*. We'll cover protocols more in Chapter 6, "Introduction to TCP/IP," but essentially they are languages much like English is a language. Within each language, there are rules that need to be followed so that all computers understand the right communication behavior.

To use a human example, within English there are grammar rules. If you put a bunch of English words together in a way that doesn't make sense, no one will understand you. If you just decide to omit verbs from your language, you're going to be challenged to get your point across. And if everyone talks at the same time, the conversation can be hard to follow.

Computers need standards to follow to keep their communication clear. Different standards are used to describe the rules that computers need to follow to communicate with each other. The most important communication framework, and the backbone of all networking, is the OSI model.

The OSI model is not specifically listed in the CompTIA A+ exam objectives. However, it's a critical piece of networking knowledge and a framework with which all technicians should be familiar. For example, you might hear (on the exam or in real life) someone talking about a "Layer 3" device, and you need to understand the implications of that!

OSI Model

The International Organization for Standardization (ISO) published the *Open Systems Interconnection (OSI)* model in 1984 to provide a common way of describing network protocols. The ISO put together a seven-layer model providing a relationship between the stages of communication, with each layer adding to the layer above or below it.

This OSI model is a theoretical model governing computer communication. Even though at one point an "OSI protocol" was developed, it never gained wide acceptance. You will never find a network that is running the "OSI protocol."

Here's how the theory behind the OSI model works. As a transmission takes place, the higher layers pass data through the lower layers. As the data passes through a layer, that layer tacks its information (also called a *header*) onto the beginning of the information being transmitted until it reaches the bottom layer. A layer may also add a trailer to the end of the data. The bottom layer sends the information out on the wire (or in the air, in the case of wireless).

At the receiving end, the bottom layer receives and reads the information in the header, removes the header and any associated trailer related to its layer, and then passes the remainder to the next highest layer. This procedure continues until the topmost layer receives the data that the sending computer sent.

The OSI model layers are listed here from top to bottom, with descriptions of what each of the layers is responsible for:

7—Application Layer   The Application layer allows access to network services. This is the layer at which file services, print services, and other applications operate.

6—Presentation Layer   This layer determines the "look," or format, of the data. The Presentation layer performs protocol conversion and manages data compression, data translation, and encryption. The character set information also is determined at this level. (The *character set* determines which numbers represent which alphanumeric characters.)

5—Session Layer   This layer allows applications on different computers to establish, maintain, and end a session. A *session* is one virtual conversation. For example, all the procedures needed to transfer a single file make up one session. Once the session is over, a new process begins. This layer enables network procedures, such as identifying passwords, logins, and network monitoring.

4—Transport Layer   The Transport layer controls the data flow and troubleshoots any problems with transmitting or receiving datagrams. It also takes large messages and segments them into smaller ones and takes smaller segments and combines them into a single, larger message, depending on which way the traffic is flowing. Finally, the TCP protocol (one of the two options at this layer) has the important job of verifying that the destination host has received all packets, providing error checking and reliable end-to-end communications.

3—Network Layer   The Network layer is responsible for logical addressing of messages. At this layer, the data is organized into chunks called *packets*. The Network layer is something like the traffic cop. It is able to judge the best network path for the data based on network conditions, priority, and other variables. This layer manages traffic through packet switching, routing, and controlling congestion of data.

2—Data Link Layer   This layer arranges data into chunks called *frames*. Included in these chunks is control information indicating the beginning and end of the datastream. The Data Link layer is very important because it makes transmission easier and more manageable, and it allows for error checking within the data frames. The Data Link layer also describes the unique physical address (also known as the *MAC address*) for each NIC. The Data Link layer is subdivided into two sections: Media Access Control (MAC) and Logical Link Control (LLC).

1—Physical Layer   The Physical layer describes how the data gets transmitted over a communication medium. This layer defines how long each piece of data is and the translation of each into the electrical pulses or light impulses that are sent over the wires, or the radio waves that are sent through the air. It decides whether data travels unidirectionally or bidirectionally across the hardware. It also relates electrical, optical, mechanical, and functional interfaces to the cable.

Figure 5.13 shows the complete OSI model. Note the relationship of each layer to the others and the function of each layer.

A helpful mnemonic device to remember the OSI layers in order is "All People Seem To Need Data Processing."

FIGURE 5.13   The OSI model

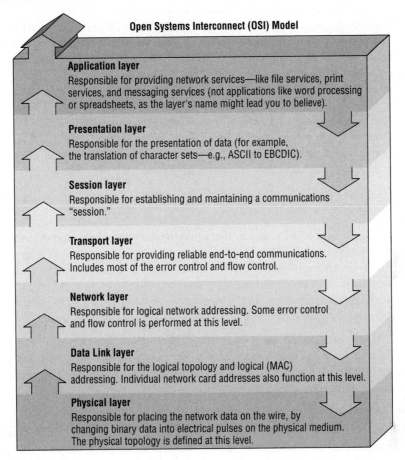

Open Systems Interconnect (OSI) Model

Application layer
Responsible for providing network services—like file services, print services, and messaging services (not applications like word processing or spreadsheets, as the layer's name might lead you to believe).

Presentation layer
Responsible for the presentation of data (for example, the translation of character sets—e.g., ASCII to EBCDIC).

Session layer
Responsible for establishing and maintaining a communications "session."

Transport layer
Responsible for providing reliable end-to-end communications. Includes most of the error control and flow control.

Network layer
Responsible for logical network addressing. Some error control and flow control is performed at this level.

Data Link layer
Responsible for the logical topology and logical (MAC) addressing. Individual network card addresses also function at this level.

Physical layer
Responsible for placing the network data on the wire, by changing binary data into electrical pulses on the physical medium. The physical topology is defined at this level.

IEEE 802 Standards

Continuing with our theme of communication, it's time to introduce one final group of standards. You've already learned that a protocol is like a language; think of the IEEE 802 standards as syntax, or the rules that govern who communicates, when they do it, and how they do it.

The Institute of Electrical and Electronics Engineers (IEEE) formed a subcommittee to create standards for network types. These standards specify certain types of networks, although not every network protocol is covered by the IEEE 802 committee specifications. This model contains several standards. The ones commonly in use today are 802.3 CSMA/CD (Ethernet) LAN and 802.11 Wireless networks. The IEEE 802 standards were designed primarily for enhancements to the bottom three layers of the OSI model. The IEEE 802 standard breaks the Data Link layer into two sublayers: a Logical Link Control (LLC) sublayer and a Media Access Control (MAC) sublayer. The Logical Link Control sublayer manages data link communications. The Media Access Control sublayer watches out for data collisions and manages physical addresses, also referred to as MAC addresses.

You've most likely heard of 802.11ax (Wi-Fi 6), 802.11ac (Wi-Fi 5), or 802.11n wireless networking. The rules for communicating with all versions of 802.11 are defined by the IEEE standard. Another very well-known standard is 802.3 CSMA/CD. You might know it by its more popular name, Ethernet.

The original 802.3 CSMA/CD standard defines a bus topology network that uses a 50-ohm coaxial baseband cable and carries transmissions at 10 Mbps. This standard groups data bits into frames and uses the *Carrier Sense Multiple Access with Collision Detection (CSMA/CD)* cable access method to put data on the cable. Currently, the 802.3 standard has been amended to include speeds up to 400 Gbps over multimode fiber-optic cable.

Breaking the CSMA/CD acronym apart may help illustrate how it works:

CS First, there is the Carrier Sense (CS) part, which means that computers on the network are listening to the wire at all times.

MA Multiple Access (MA) means that multiple computers have access to the line at the same time. This is analogous to having five people on a conference call. Everyone is listening, and everyone in theory can try to talk at the same time. Of course, when more than one person talks at once, there is a communication error. In CSMA/CD, when two machines transmit at the same time, a data *collision* takes place and the intended recipients receive none of the data.

CD This is where the Collision Detection (CD) portion of the acronym comes in; the collision is detected and each sender knows they need to send again. Each sender then waits for a short, random period of time and tries to transmit again. This process repeats until transmission takes place successfully.

The CSMA/CD technology is considered a *contention-based* access method.

The only major downside to 802.3 is that with large networks (more than 100 computers on the same segment), the number of collisions increases to the point where more collisions than transmissions are taking place.

Other examples of contention methods exist, such as Carrier Sense Multiple Access with Collision Avoidance (CSMA/CA). Whereas CSMA/CD tries to fix collisions after they happen, CSMA/CA tries to avoid them in the first place by actively listening and only transmitting when the channel is clear. Wireless Ethernet uses CSMA/CA.

For the A+ exam, remember that you will need to differentiate between network types: LAN, WAN, PAN, MAN, SAN, and WLAN. The rest of the previous sections aren't specifically exam objectives, but the knowledge you gained will be invaluable in your career and could also help you figure out the answer to tricky exam questions!

Identifying Common Network Hardware

We have looked at the types of networks, network topologies, and the way communications are handled. That's all of the logical stuff. To really get computers to talk to each other requires hardware. Every computer on the network needs to have a network adapter of some type. In many cases, you also need some sort of cable to hook them together. (Wireless networking is the exception, but at the backend of a wireless network there are still components wired together.) And finally, you might also need connectivity devices to attach several computers or networks to each other. We'll look at all of these in the following sections, starting with the component closest in to the "local computer," or the one you're at, and working outward.

Network Interface Cards

You were introduced to the *network interface card (NIC)*, also referred to as a network adapter card, earlier in the chapter. It provides the physical interface between computer and cabling, and prepares data, sends data, and controls the flow of data. It can also receive and translate data into bytes for the CPU to understand. NICs come in many shapes and sizes.

Different NICs are distinguished by the PC bus type and the network for which they are used. The following sections describe the role of NICs and how to evaluate them.

Compatibility

The first thing you need to determine is whether the NIC will fit the bus type of your PC. If you have more than one type of bus in your PC (for example, a combination PCI/PCI Express), use a NIC that fits into the fastest type (the PCI Express, in this case). This is especially important in servers because the NIC can quickly become a bottleneck if this guideline isn't followed.

More and more computers are using NICs that have USB interfaces. For the rare laptop computer that doesn't otherwise have a NIC built into it, these small portable cards are very handy.

A USB network card can also be handy for troubleshooting. If a laptop isn't connecting to the network properly with its built-in card, you may be able to use the USB NIC to see if it's an issue with the card or perhaps a software problem.

Network Interface Card Performance

The most important goal of the NIC is to optimize network performance and minimize the amount of time needed to transfer data packets across the network. The key is to ensure that you get the fastest card that you can for the type of network that you're on. For example, if your wireless network supports 802.11g/n/ac/ax, make sure to get an 802.11ax card because it's the fastest.

Sending and Controlling Data

In order for two computers to send and receive data, the cards must agree on several things:

- The maximum size of the data frames
- The amount of data sent before giving confirmation
- The time needed between transmissions
- The amount of time to wait before sending confirmation
- The speed at which data transmits

If the cards can agree, the data is sent successfully. If the cards cannot agree, the data is not sent.

To send data on the network successfully, all NICs need to use the same media access method (such as CSMA/CD) and be connected to the same piece of cable. This usually isn't a problem, because the vast majority of network cards sold today are Ethernet.

In addition, NICs can send data using either full-duplex or half-duplex mode. *Half-duplex communication* means that between the sender and receiver, only one of them can transmit at any one time. In *full-duplex communication*, a computer can send and receive data simultaneously. The main advantage of full-duplex over half-duplex communication is performance. NICs (Gigabit Ethernet NICs) can operate twice as fast (1 Gbps) in full-duplex mode as they do normally in half-duplex mode (500 Mbps). In addition, collisions are avoided, which speeds up performance as well. Configuring the network adapter's duplexing setting is done from the Advanced tab of the NIC's properties, as shown in Figure 5.14.

FIGURE 5.14   A NIC's Speed & Duplex setting

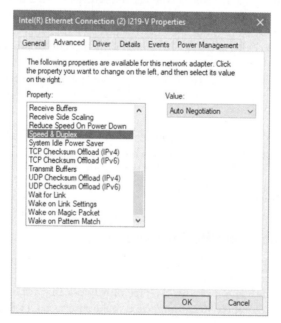

Normally, you aren't going to have to worry about how your NIC sends or controls data. Just make sure to get the fastest NIC that is compatible with your network. Do know that the negotiations discussed here are happening in the background, though.

NIC Configuration

Each card must have a unique hardware address, called a *Media Access Control address* or *MAC address*. (Remember earlier in the chapter we said you didn't need to know the OSI model for the exam, but you should know it anyway? Here's an example of why. Now you can piece together that this is a physical address that is referenced at Layer 2.) If two NICs on the same network have the same hardware address, neither one will be able to communicate. For this reason, the IEEE has established a standard for hardware addresses and assigns blocks of these addresses to NIC manufacturers, who then hardwire the addresses into the cards.

MAC addresses are 48 bits long and written in hexadecimal, such as 40–61–86–E4–5A–9A. An example is shown in Figure 5.15 from the output of the `ipconfig /all` command executed at the Windows command prompt. On a Mac or in Linux, the analogous command is `ifconfig`.

FIGURE 5.15   Physical (MAC) address

```
Command Prompt                                           –  □  ×
C:\Users\Q>ipconfig /all

Windows IP Configuration

    Host Name . . . . . . . . . . . . : DESKTOP-EF0DRK1
    Primary Dns Suffix  . . . . . . . :
    Node Type . . . . . . . . . . . . : Hybrid
    IP Routing Enabled. . . . . . . . : No
    WINS Proxy Enabled. . . . . . . . : No
    DNS Suffix Search List. . . . . . : home

Ethernet adapter Ethernet:

    Media State . . . . . . . . . . . : Media disconnected
    Connection-specific DNS Suffix  . :
    Description . . . . . . . . . . . : Realtek PCIe GBE Family Controller
    Physical Address. . . . . . . . . : 40-61-86-E4-5A-9A
    DHCP Enabled. . . . . . . . . . . : Yes
    Autoconfiguration Enabled . . . . : Yes

Wireless LAN adapter Local Area Connection* 9:

    Media State . . . . . . . . . . . : Media disconnected
    Connection-specific DNS Suffix  . :
    Description . . . . . . . . . . . : Microsoft Hosted Network Virtual Adapter
    Physical Address. . . . . . . . . : C0-C1-C0-6C-92-4A
    DHCP Enabled. . . . . . . . . . . : Yes
    Autoconfiguration Enabled . . . . : Yes
```

Although it is possible for NIC manufacturers to produce multiple NICs with the same MAC address, it happens very rarely. If you do encounter this type of problem, contact the hardware manufacturer.

NIC Drivers

In order for the computer to use the NIC, it is very important to install the proper device drivers. These drivers are pieces of software that communicate directly with the operating system, specifically the network redirector and adapter interface. Drivers are specific to each NIC and operating system, and they operate in the Media Access Control (MAC) sublayer of the Data Link layer of the OSI model.

To see which version the driver is, you need to look at the device's properties. There are several ways to do this. A common one is to open Device Manager (click Start, type **Device**, and click Device Manager under Best Match), and find the device, as shown in Figure 5.16.

FIGURE 5.16   Device Manager

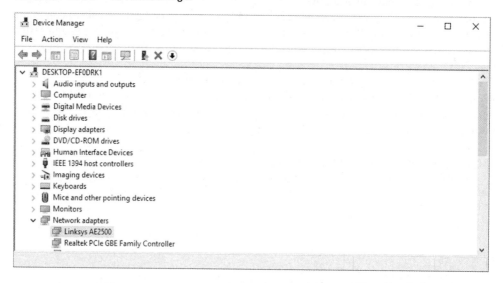

Right-click the device, click Properties, and then go to the Driver tab, as shown in Figure 5.17. Here you can see a lot of information about the driver, update it, or roll it back if you installed a new one and it fails for some reason. You can also update the driver by right-clicking the device in Device Manager and choosing Update Driver from the menu.

The best place to get drivers is always the manufacturer's website. When you click Update Driver, Windows will ask you if you want to search for the driver on the Internet or provide a location for it. The best course of action is to download the driver first, and then tell Windows where you put it.

FIGURE 5.17 NIC properties Driver tab

Remember that for the exam, network interface cards are listed in the exam objectives. There is quite a bit to know about a seemingly simple adapter!

Cables and Connectors

When the data is passing through the OSI model and reaches the Physical layer, it must find its way onto the medium that is used to transfer data physically from computer to computer. This medium is called the *cable* (or in the case of wireless networks, the air). It is the NIC's role to prepare the data for transmission, but it is the cable's role to move the data properly to its intended destination. The following sections discuss the three main types of physical cabling: coaxial, twisted pair, and fiber-optic. (Wireless communication is covered in Chapter 7.)

Coaxial Cable

Coaxial cable (or coax) contains a center conductor core made of copper, which is surrounded by a plastic jacket with a braided shield over it (as shown in Figure 5.18). Either Teflon or a plastic coating covers this metal shield.

FIGURE 5.18   Coaxial cable

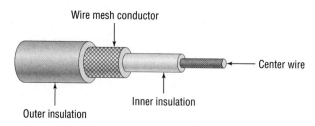

Wire mesh conductor

Center wire

Outer insulation

Inner insulation

Common network cables are covered with a plastic called *polyvinyl chloride (PVC)*. Although PVC is flexible, fairly durable, and inexpensive, it has a nasty side effect in that it produces poisonous gas when burned. An alternative is a Teflon-type covering that is frequently referred to as a *plenum-rated* coating. That simply means that the coating does not produce toxic gas when burned and is rated for use in the ventilation plenum areas in a building that circulate breathable air, such as air-conditioning and heating systems. This type of cable is more expensive, but it may be mandated by electrical code whenever cable is hidden in walls or ceilings.

Plenum rating can apply to all types of network cabling.

Coax Cable Specifications

Coaxial cable is available in various specifications that are rated according to the Radio Guide (RG) system, which was originally developed by the U.S. military. The thicker the copper, the farther a signal can travel—and with that comes a higher cost and a less flexible cable. Coax is uncommonly seen in computer networking today because it's painfully slow; its heyday was a few decades ago.

When coax cable was popular for networking, there were two standards that had high use: RG-8 (thicknet) and RG-58A/U (thinnet). Thicknet had a maximum segment distance of 500 meters and was used primarily for network backbones. Thinnet was more often used in a conventional physical bus. A thinnet segment could span 185 meters. Both thicknet and thinnet had impedance of 50 ohms. Table 5.2 shows the different types of RG cabling and their uses. Although coax is an A+ exam objective, no specific coax cabling standards are currently specified on the exam objectives. The ones that used to be named on the A+ exam objectives were RG-6 and RG-59.

TABLE 5.2   Coax RG types

RG #	Popular name	Ethernet implementation	Type of cable
RG-6	Satellite/cable TV, cable modems	N/A	Solid copper
RG-8	Thicknet	10Base5	Solid copper
RG-58 U	N/A	None	Solid copper

RG #	Popular name	Ethernet implementation	Type of cable
RG-58 A/U	Thinnet	10Base2	Stranded copper
RG-59	Cable television	N/A	Solid copper

Explaining Ethernet Naming Standards

In Table 5.2, you will notice two terms that might be new to you: *10Base5* and *10Base2*. These are Ethernet naming standards. The number at the beginning tells you the maximum speed that the standard supports, which is 10 Mbps in this case. The word *Base* refers to the type of transmission, either baseband (one signal at a time per cable) or broadband (multiple signals at the same time on one cable). Legend has it that the 5 and the 2 refer to the approximate maximum transmission distance (in hundreds of meters) for each specification. Later in the chapter, you will see *10BaseT*, which refers to twisted pair cabling.

Coaxial networking has all but gone the way of the dinosaur. The only two coaxial cable types you might see today are RG-6 and RG-59. Of the two, RG-6 has a thicker core (1.0 mm), can run longer distances (up to 304 meters, or 1,000 feet), and can support digital signals. RG-59 (0.762 mm core) is considered adequate for analog cable TV but not digital and has a maximum distance of about 228 meters (750 feet). The maximum speed for each depends on the quality of the cable and the standard on which it's being used. Both have impedance of 75 ohms.

Coax Connector Types

Thicknet was a bear to use. Not only was it highly inflexible, but you also needed to use a connector called a *vampire tap*. A vampire tap is so named because a metal tooth sinks into the cable, thus making the connection with the inner conductor. The tap is connected to an external transceiver that in turn has a 15-pin AUI connector (also called a *DIX* or *DB-15* connector) to which you attach a cable that connects to the station. The transceiver is shown in Figure 5.19. On the right side, you will see the thicknet cable running through the portion of the unit that contains the vampire tap. DIX got its name from the companies that worked on this format—Digital, Intel, and Xerox.

Thinnet coax was much easier to use. Generally, thinnet cables used a *BNC connector* (see Figure 5.20) to attach to a T-shaped connector that attached to the workstation. The other side of the T-connector would either continue on with another thinnet segment or be capped off with a terminator. It is beyond the scope of this book to settle the long-standing argument over the meaning of the abbreviation BNC. We have heard Bayonet Connector, Bayonet Nut Connector, and British Naval Connector—among others. What is relevant is that the BNC connector locks securely with a quarter-twist motion.

FIGURE 5.19   Thicknet transceiver and cable inside a vampire tap

Thicknet transceiver licensed Under CC BY-Sa 2.5 via Wikimedia Commons. `http://commons.wikimedia.org/wiki/File:ThicknetTransceiver.jpg#/media/File:ThicknetTransceiver.jpg`

FIGURE 5.20   Male and female BNC connectors, T-connector, and terminator

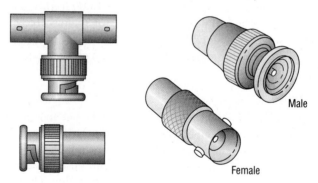

Male

Female

Another type of connector that you will see in use with coax is a *splitter*. As its name implies, a splitter takes a single signal (say that three times fast) and splits it into multiple replicas of the same signal. You might use this for cable TV—one line may run into your house, but the signal ultimately needs to get split for three televisions. This type of configuration will work for cable TV or cable Internet. Figure 5.21 shows a one-to-two coax splitter. You can also buy splitters that split one input into three or more outputs.

FIGURE 5.21 A coax splitter

Keep in mind that a coax signal is designed to go from one sender to one receiver, so splitting it can cause some issues. Splitting the signal causes it to weaken, meaning that signal quality could be lower, and it might not travel the same distance as a non-split signal. To avoid problems, don't over-split the cable, and purchase a good-quality or amplified splitter.

The last type of coax connector we will cover is called an *F-connector* (referred to in exam objectives as an *F type* connector, shown in Figure 5.22), and it is used with cable TV. You'll see it on the end of an RG-6 or possibly an RG-59 cable. The exposed end of the copper cable is pushed into the receptacle, and the connector is threaded so that it can screw into place.

FIGURE 5.22 An F-connector

Twisted Pair Cable

Twisted pair is the most popular type of cabling to use because of its flexibility and low cost. It consists of several pairs of wire twisted around each other within an insulated jacket, as shown in Figure 5.23.

FIGURE 5.23 Unshielded twisted pair cable

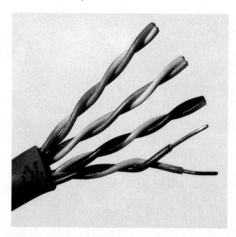

There are two different types of twisted pair cables: *shielded twisted pair (STP)* and *unshielded twisted pair (UTP)*. Both types of cable have two or four pairs of twisted wires going through them. The difference is that STP has an extra layer of braided foil shielding surrounding the wires to decrease electrical interference, as shown in Figure 5.24. (In Figure 5.24, the individual wire pairs are shielded as well.) UTP has a PVC or plenum coating but no outer foil shield to protect it from interference. In the real world, UTP is the most common networking cable type used. STP has been used less frequently, but the newer Cat 7 and Cat 8 standards rely on shielding and offer higher frequencies to deliver ultra-fast transmission speeds.

FIGURE 5.24 Shielded twisted pair cable

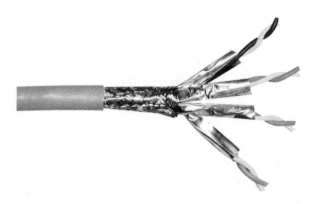

You will often hear people refer to UTP cables as Ethernet cables. As you learned earlier in this chapter, Ethernet is an access method based on the IEEE 802.3 standard and not related to a specific cable type. So while technically it's incorrect, there's no harm in using the term to refer to the cable.

Twisted Pair Cable Specifications

Twisted pair cabling has been in use, at least with old analog telephone lines, for a few generations now. Over time, the need for higher transmission speeds required faster cabling, and the cable manufacturers have been up to the challenge. Now you can find twisted pair in several grades to offer different levels of performance and protection against electrical interference:

Category 1 (Cat 1) contains two twisted pairs. It is for voice-only transmissions, and it is in many legacy phone systems today.

Category 2 (Cat 2) is the lowest-grade cable that can have four pairs of wires. (Every other Cat rating since Cat 2 has four pairs.) It can handle data transmission at speeds up to 4 Mbps.

Category 3 (Cat 3) is able to transmit data at speeds up to 10 Mbps. It was popular for 10BaseT installations before Cat 5 came out.

Category 4 (Cat 4) is able to transmit data at speeds up to 16 Mbps.

Category 5 (Cat 5) is able to transmit data at speeds up to 100 Mbps.

Category 5e (Cat 5e) is able to transmit data at speeds up to 1 Gbps. The enhancement over Cat 5 is that the four twisted pairs of copper wire are physically separated and contain more twists per foot. This provides better interference protection.

Category 6 (Cat 6) is able to transmit data at speeds up to 10 Gbps, but only up to a distance of 55 meters. Its four twisted pairs of copper wire are oriented differently than in Cat 5e. This is the lowest grade of cable you should ever use as a backbone to connect different parts of a network together, such as those on different floors of a building.

Category 6a (Cat 6a) can also handle 10 Gbps speed, but at longer distances (up to 100 meters) than Cat 6 can.

Category 7 (Cat 7) is an incremental upgrade over Cat 6a. Its most notable feature is that every wire pair is shielded, which provides better resistance to crosstalk and external noise. It can handle 10 Gbps at up to 100 meters. You might hear it also called Class F cabling.

Category 8 (Cat 8) improves upon Cat 7 by offering speeds of 25 Gbps or 40 Gbps at up to 30 meters, and it supports 10 Gbps at 100 meters. It's always shielded, just as Cat 7 is. There are two types of Class 8 cable. Class I Cat 8 (also known as Cat 8.1) uses RJ-45 connectors and is backward-compatible with all other twisted pair installations using RJ-45 connectors. Class II Cat 8 (Cat 8.2) uses different connectors, and is not compatible with RJ-45 installations.

For as long as twisted pair has existed, every technician has needed to memorize its standard maximum transmission distance of 100 meters (328 feet). You should burn that into your brain, too. Note, however, that some newer standards have shorter maximum distances. For example, if you want to run 10GBaseT over Cat 6, you won't get that much distance—about 55 meters under ideal conditions. Cat 8 (which isn't an exam objective) can provide up to 40 Gbps but only at 30 meters.

A Few Notes on Twisted Pair Cabling

CompTIA (and many others) usually shortens the word *category* to Cat and, for example, uses the form Cat 5 to refer to Category 5. This is a common way to refer to these categories, and you can feel free to use these terms interchangeably. If you are buying cable today, you shouldn't buy anything older than Cat 5e.

Before the Cat 6a standard was finalized, several cable vendors started selling Cat 6e cable. Much like Cat 5e was an enhanced version of Cat 5, Cat 6e was supposed to be an enhanced version of Cat 6. The thing is, an official Cat 6e specification was never officially established; if you see Cat 6e, there is no guarantee of the type of performance that you will get. The official standard is Cat 6a.

For the exam, you need to know the specifications for Cat 5, Cat 5e, Cat 6, and Cat 6a. In real life, you should be familiar with all standards Cat 5e and newer.

Twisted Pair Connector Types

Twisted pair cabling uses a connector type called an *RJ (registered jack)* connector. You are probably familiar with RJ connectors. Most landline phones connect with an *RJ-11* connector. The connector used with UTP cable is called *RJ-45*. The RJ-11 has room for two pairs (four wires), and the RJ-45 has room for four pairs (eight wires).

In almost every case, UTP uses RJ connectors; a crimper is used to attach an RJ connector to a cable. Higher-quality crimping tools have interchangeable dies for both types of connectors. (Crimpers are discussed in Chapter 12, "Hardware and Network Troubleshooting.") Figure 5.25 shows an RJ-11 connector and an RJ-45 connector.

You will also find RJ-45 splitters (often called *Ethernet splitters*) in the marketplace. The idea is similar to a coax splitter, but functionally they are very different. Coax signals are carried over one wire, while twisted pair uses either two pairs of wires (for 100 Mbps or slower connections) or all four pairs of wires (for Gigabit Ethernet and faster). An Ethernet splitter will take the incoming signal on two pairs and then split it, so on the output end it produces two sets of signals using two pairs each. Because of this, Ethernet splitters are limited to 100 Mbps connections.

FIGURE 5.25 RJ-11 and RJ-45 connectors

 It is not recommended that you use Ethernet splitters on a network. If you need to connect multiple computers together using UTP, use a hub or a switch. We talk about both of these devices later in this chapter.

Punchdown Blocks

Some twisted pair installations don't use standard RJ-45 connectors. Instead, the cable is run to a central panel called a *punchdown block*, often located in a server room or connectivity closet. In a punchdown block, the metal wires are connected directly to the block to make the connection. Instead of a crimper, a punchdown tool is used. Figure 5.26 shows a closeup of wires connected to an older-style 66 block, frequently used in analog telephone communications. Networks that use blocks today are more likely to use a 110 block, which has a higher density of connectors and is designed to reduce crosstalk between cables.

Wiring Standards

Twisted pair cables are unique in today's network environment in that they use multiple physical wires. Those eight wires need to be in the right places in the RJ-45 connector or it's very likely that the cable will not work properly. To ensure consistency in the industry, two standards have been developed: *T568A* and *T568B*.

Older implementations using UTP used only two pairs of wires, and those two pairs were matched to pins 1, 2, 3, and 6 in the connector. Newer applications such as Voice over IP (VoIP) and Gigabit Ethernet use all four pairs of wires, so you need to make sure that they're all where they're supposed to be.

FIGURE 5.26   Cables in a punchdown block

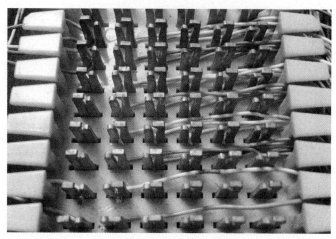

By Z22 - Own work, CC BY-SA 4.0, `https://commons.wikimedia.org/w/index.php?curid=34324171`

If you're creating a regular network *patch cable* to connect a computer to a hub or switch, both sides need to have the same pinout. For that, follow either the T568A standard shown in Figure 5.27 or the T568B standard shown in Figure 5.28. Although there are no differences in terms of how the standards perform, some companies prefer one to the other.

FIGURE 5.27   T568A standard

Pin	Pair	Wire		Color
1	3	1		white/green
2	3	2		green
3	2	1		white/orange
4	1	2		blue
5	1	1		white/blue
6	2	2		orange
7	4	1		white/brown
8	4	2		brown

If you are going to create a cable to connect a computer to another computer directly, or you're going to make a connection from hub to hub, switch to switch, hub to switch, or a computer directly to a router, then you need what's called a *crossover cable*. In a crossover cable, pin 1 to pin 3 and pin 2 to pin 6 are crossed on *one side of the cable only*. This is to get the "send" pins matched up with the "receive" pins on the other side, and vice versa. For easier visualization, look at Figure 5.28.

FIGURE 5.28   T568B standard

Pin	Pair	Wire	Color
1	2	1	white/orange
2	2	2	orange
3	3	1	white/green
4	1	2	blue
5	1	1	white/blue
6	3	2	green
7	4	1	white/brown
8	4	2	brown

The key thing to remember is that a patch (straight-through) cable is the same on both ends. A crossover cable is different on each end. You should know the order of the colors for both standards.

Direct Burial

Occasionally you will run into situations where network cable needs to be run outside or buried underground. For these types of installations, use *direct burial* cable. Direct burial cable is STP with an extra waterproof sheathing.

Whenever you run cables in an area where they can be stepped on (and it's not recommended you do), be aware that no amount of shielding will totally protect the cable from damage. It's best to use a cable guard of some sort to provide protection. We can't count the number of times we've seen people use duct tape or something similar to keep a cable in a high-traffic area from moving around—don't do it. The tape will work to keep it in place, but does nothing to protect the cable.

An alternative may be to bury the cable underground. The recommended distance is 6" to 8" below the ground, and away from any lines that carry electrical current. Also, it's recommended that you use a conduit, such as PVC pipe, to further protect the cable.

Fiber-Optic Cable

Fiber-optic cabling has been called one of the best advances in cabling. It consists of a thin, flexible glass or plastic fiber surrounded by a rubberized outer coating (see Figure 5.29). It provides transmission speeds from 100 Mbps to 10 Gbps over a maximum distance of several miles. Because it uses pulses of light instead of electric voltages to transmit data, it is immune to electrical interference and to wiretapping.

FIGURE 5.29   Fiber-optic cable

Optical fiber cable by Buy_on_turbosquid_optical.jpg: Cable master derivative work: Srleffler (talk) - Buy_on_
turbosquid_optical.jpg http://commons.wikimedia.org/wiki/File:Optical_fiber_cable.jpg#/media/
File:Optical_fiber_cable.jpg

While it's gaining ground rapidly, fiber-optic cable is still not as popular as UTP for local area networks, however, because of its high cost of installation. Fiber-optic cabling is great for networks that need extremely fast transmission rates or transmissions over long distances or in networks that have had problems with electrical interference in the past. Fiber is also becoming more common as backbones to telecommunication systems, and in many places fiber-optic cables can be used to deliver high-speed Internet connections to businesses and homes. We'll talk more about this in Chapter 7.

Fiber-Optic Cable Specifications

Fiber-optic cable comes in two varieties: single-mode or multimode. The term *mode* refers to the bundles of light that enter the fiber-optic cable. *Single-mode fiber (SMF)* cable uses only a single mode (or path) of light to propagate through the fiber cable, whereas *multimode fiber (MMF)* allows multiple modes of light to propagate simultaneously. In multimode fiber-optic cable, the light bounces off the cable walls as it travels through the cable, which causes the signal to weaken more quickly.

Multimode fiber is most often used as horizontal cable. It permits multiple modes of light to propagate through the cable, which shortens cable distances but delivers more available bandwidth. Devices that use MMF cable typically use light-emitting diodes (LEDs) to generate the light that travels through the cable; however, lasers with multimode fiber-optic cable are now being used in higher-bandwidth network devices, such as Gigabit Ethernet. MMF can transmit up to 10 Gbps for up to 550 meters (1,804 feet, or just over one-third of a mile), depending on the standard used.

Single-mode fiber cable is commonly used as backbone cabling. It is also usually the cable type used in phone systems. Light travels through single-mode fiber-optic cable using only a single mode, meaning that it travels straight down the fiber and does not bounce off the cable walls. Because only a single mode of light travels through the cable, single-mode fiber-optic cable supports lower bandwidth at longer distances than does multimode fiber-optic cable. Devices that use single-mode fiber-optic cable typically use lasers to generate the light that travels through the cable. SMF can transmit up to 10 Gbps for up to 40 kilometers (25.85 miles), depending on the standard used.

We have talked about several different types of cables, and it's possible that you will be asked to know maximum distances and transmission speeds on the A+ exam. Table 5.3 summarizes the most common cable types, the specifications with which they are used, and their characteristics.

 For the real world, you should be familiar with all of the standards in Table 5.3. The A+ exam only lists coax, Cat 5, Cat 5e, Cat 6, Cat 6a, and the general term *fiber* as exam objectives. To be safe, it may be best to be able to explain the basic features and purposes of all the cable types listed in the table.

TABLE 5.3   Common cable types and characteristics

Cable type	Ethernet specification	Maximum speed	Maximum distance	Notes
RG-6 coax	*	*	304 meters	Digital cable/satellite television
RG-59 coax	a	a	228 meters	Analog cable TV
Cat 5 UTP or STP	100BaseT	100 Mbps	100 meters	100 Mbps and less use two pairs of wires.
Cat 5e UTP	1000BaseT	1 Gbps	100 meters	1 Gbps and higher use four pairs of wires.
Cat 6 UTP	10GBaseT	10 Gbps	55 meters	Can support 1 Gbps up to 100 meters.
Cat 6a UTP	10GBaseT	10 Gbps	100 meters	
Cat 7 UTP	10GBaseT	10 Gbps	100 meters	Every wire pair is individually shielded.
CAT 8 UTP	25GBaseT or 40GBaseT	40 Gbps	100 meters at 10 Gbps	25 Gbps or 40 Gbps at 30 meters
MMF fiber	1000BaseLX or 1000BaseSX	1 Gbps	550 meters	For fiber, maximum length depends on fiber size and quality.
MMF fiber	10GBaseSR or 10GBaseSW	10 Gbps	300 meters	
SMF fiber	10GBaseER or 10GBaseEW	10 Gbps	40 kilometers	

a *   RG-6 and RG-59 coax cables can be used with many different specifications, and the maximum speed depends on cable quality and specification.

Fiber-Optic Connector Types

There are literally dozens of fiber-optic connectors out there because it seemed that every producer wanted its proprietary design to become "the standard." Three of the most commonly used ones are ST, SC, and LC.

The *straight tip (ST)* fiber-optic connector, developed by AT&T, is probably the most widely used fiber-optic connector. It uses a twist-and-lock attachment mechanism that makes connections and disconnections fairly easy. The ease of use of the ST is one of the attributes that make this connector so popular. Figure 5.30 shows ST connectors.

FIGURE 5.30 ST connectors

The *subscriber connector (SC)*, also sometimes known as a *square connector*, is shown in Figure 5.31. SCs are latched connectors, making it virtually impossible for you to pull out the connector without releasing its latch, usually by pressing a button or release. SCs work with either single-mode or multimode optical fibers. They aren't as popular as ST connectors for LAN connections.

FIGURE 5.31 A sample SC

The last type of connector with which you need to be familiar is the *Lucent connector (LC)*, sometimes also called a *local connector*, which was developed by Lucent Technologies. It is a mini form factor (MFF) connector, especially popular for use with Fibre Channel adapters, fast storage area networks, and Gigabit Ethernet adapters (see Figure 5.32).

FIGURE 5.32 LC fiber connector

The prices of network cables differ dramatically between copper and fiber cables. Exercise 5.1 asks you to investigate the difference for yourself.

EXERCISE 5.1

Pricing Network Cables

1. Visit a major electronics retailer website of your choice or use an Internet search.

2. Search for a Cat 6 patch cable.

3. Price the difference between a 7-foot, 25-foot, and 50-foot cable.

4. Search for the same lengths of Cat 7 patch cables.

   Note the price difference. (As of this writing, Cat 7 cables cost a few dollars more than Cat 6 cables.)

5. Search for fiber-optic cables.

   Notice, first, that most of them are much shorter in length than commercially available UTP cables. What is the price difference? Do you notice price differences between fiber-optic cables with different types of connectors?

There are quite a few network cables and connectors exam objectives to remember for the A+ exam. To summarize, know:

- Copper cables such as coaxial, UTP, and STP, including Cat 5, Cat 5e, Cat 6, Cat 6a, direct burial, and the RJ-11, RJ-45, F type, and punchdown block connectors

- Plenum cable and where it's used

- The T568A and T568B wiring standards

- Fiber-optic cable, its characteristics, and the ST, SC, and LC connectors

Networking Components

Network cabling can link one computer to another, but most networks are far grander in scale than two simple machines. There are a variety of networking devices that provide connectivity to the network, make the network bigger, and offer auxiliary services to end users.

In the following sections, we're going to classify additional networking components into two broad categories: connectivity devices and auxiliary devices. We'll also touch on software-defined networking, a concept that turned classical networking on its head.

Connectivity Devices

We all know that if you want to be part of a computer network, you need to attach to that network somehow. Using network cables is one way to accomplish this, but not everyone is in a position to just plug a cable in and go. In addition, if you want to grow your network beyond a few simple connections, you need to use a special class of networking devices known as *connectivity devices*. These devices allow communications to break the boundaries of local networks and really provide the backbone for nearly all computer networks, regardless of size.

There are several categories of connectivity devices. These connectivity devices make it possible for users to connect to networks and to lengthen networks to almost unlimited distances. We will now discuss the most important and frequently used connectivity devices.

Modems

If you want to connect to a network or the Internet using plain old phone lines and a dial-up connection, a *modem* is the device you'll need. Modems got their name because they modulate and demodulate (mo-dem) digital signals that computers use into analog signals that can be passed over telephone lines. In the early to mid-1990s, modems were practically the only device available to get onto the Internet. Many companies also used them to allow users who were not in the office to dial into the local network.

While modems did provide flexibility, you needed to be near a phone line, and speed was an issue. The fastest modems transferred data at 56 Kbps. At the time that felt lightning quick, but fortunately our species has moved well beyond that technology. It's horrifically slow by today's standards and therefore rarely used.

Modems are fortunately no longer in the A+ exam objectives. We still include a brief description as a point of reference and to give you a sense for how far technology has come since Internet access started becoming common.

Cable/Digital Subscriber Line (DSL) Modems

The traditional modem is essentially obsolete—most homes and many businesses now access the Internet through the use of a *cable modem* or *digital subscriber line (DSL) modem*. The primary difference between the two is the infrastructure they connect to. Cable modems use television cable lines, and DSL modems use telephone lines.

Both cable and DSL modems are digital and therefore aren't technically modems because they don't modulate and demodulate analog signals. We'll cover cable Internet and DSL technologies in more detail in Chapter 7.

Optical Network Terminal (ONT) Modem

Fiber-optic connections to businesses and homes are becoming more and more common, as communications providers race to install fiber all over the country. If there is fiber in your work or home neighborhood, you need a different type of modem to connect to the ISP for Internet access. Such a device is called an *optical network terminal (ONT)* modem.

Much like cable and DSL modems, an ONT isn't truly a modem either, as it doesn't deal with analog-to-digital modulation. It is closer to a modem in a sense though because it takes optical signals and changes them into electrical ones for your internal home or business network. ONTs are typically located out of sight in a wiring closet or at the junction box on the outside of the building, where the optical cabling comes to an end.

Access Points

Technically speaking, an *access point* is any point that allows a user on to a network. On a wired network, this means a hub or a switch, both of which we will cover shortly. The term is commonly used in reference to a *wireless access point*, which lets users connect to your network via an 802.11 technology. We'll get deeper into wireless access points and how to configure them in Chapter 7.

Repeaters and Extenders

A *repeater*, or *extender*, is a small, powered device that receives a signal, amplifies it, and sends it on its way. The whole purpose of a repeater is to extend the functional distance of a cable run. For example, you know that UTP is limited to 100 meters, but what if you need to make a cable run that is 160 meters long? (One answer could be to use fiber, but pretend that's not an option.) You could run two lengths of cable with a repeater in the center, and it would work. Repeaters and extenders work at the Physical layer (Layer 1) of the OSI model. They don't examine the data or make any changes to it—they just take what they receive and send it along its merry way.

Hubs

A *hub* is a device used to link several computers together. Hubs are very simple devices that possess no real intelligence. They simply repeat any signal that comes in on one port and copy it to the other ports (a process that is also called *broadcasting*). You'll sometimes hear them referred to as multiport repeaters. They work at Layer 1 of the OSI model, just as repeaters do.

There are two types of hubs: active and passive. *Passive hubs* connect all ports together electrically but do not have their own power source. Think of them as a multiport repeater. *Active hubs* use electronics to amplify and clean up the signal before it is broadcast to the other ports. Active hubs can therefore be used to extend the length of a network, whereas passive hubs cannot.

Patch Panels

A *patch panel* is essentially a large hub that is rack mounted. It houses multiple cable connections but possesses no network intelligence. Its sole purpose is to connect cables together. Short patch cables are used to plug into the front-panel connectors, and there are longer, more permanent cables on the back. Figure 5.33 shows three rack-mounted devices. The top one is a 24-port patch panel. Underneath that is a 24-port switch, and then a Dell server is shown.

FIGURE 5.33   A patch panel, switch, and server

Switches

Switches work at Layer 2 and they provide centralized connectivity, just like hubs. A *switch* often looks similar to a hub, so it's easy to confuse them. There are big performance differences, though. Hubs pass along all traffic, but switches examine the Layer 2 header of the incoming packet and forward it properly to the right port and only that port. This greatly reduces overhead and thus improves performance because there is essentially a virtual connection between sender and receiver. The only downside is that switches forward broadcasts because they are addressed to everyone. Switches come in two varieties: unmanaged and managed. We've already explained the functionality of an *unmanaged switch*—it connects two or more computers, and passes along all traffic sent to a MAC address to its port. A *managed switch* adds the ability to configure ports, manage traffic, and monitor traffic for issues. For management, the switch will use a network protocol, such as Simple Network Management Protocol (SNMP). (We'll talk about SNMP in depth in Chapter 6.) Managed switches cost more but provide features such as quality of service (QoS), redundancy, port mirroring, and virtual LANs (VLANs). Here's a description of each:

QoS   QoS allows administrators to prioritize certain network traffic by assigning a higher priority to it. Higher-priority traffic may come from a specific server or a specific application. This is used a lot with Voice over IP (VoIP)—telephone calls over a computer network—to ensure that the voice data gets through and the connection doesn't sound garbled.

Redundancy   Redundancy in networking terms means having multiple paths to get data from point A to point B. Administrators can use multiple switches to provide redundant paths, which add a layer of fault tolerance to the network. Managed switches use the Spanning Tree Protocol (STP) to implement redundancy.

Port Mirroring   This is a troubleshooting feature that is used in conjunction with a network monitor. A port can be configured to mirror another port. When traffic is sent to one, it's also sent to the mirror. A network monitor attached to the mirrored port can then analyze the traffic, without taking the network or device on the original port offline.

VLANs   In a virtual LAN (VLAN), computers attached to the same physical switch can be segmented into multiple logical networks. This reduces network traffic on each virtual LAN, because the traffic is isolated from other virtual LANs. Computers on one virtual LAN can still communicate with those on another virtual LAN, if the switch is configured properly. VLANs can also be completely isolated from each other, adding an additional level of security.

Nearly every hub or switch that you will see has one or more status indicator lights on it. If there is a connection to a port of the switch, a light either above the connector or on an LED panel elsewhere on the device will light up. If traffic is crossing the port, the light may flash, or there may be a secondary light that will light up. Many devices can also detect a problem in the connection. If a normal connection produces a green light, a bad connection might produce an amber light.

While it's common practice to refer to switches as Layer 2 devices, some do work at Layer 2 and Layer 3. A Layer 2 switch concerns itself with MAC addresses only and doesn't pay attention to IP addresses. A Layer 3 switch will also work with IP addresses and can handle routing functionality between VLANs.

Routers

Routers are highly intelligent devices that connect multiple network types and determine the best path for sending data. They can route packets across multiple networks and use *routing tables* to store network addresses to determine the best destination. Routers operate at the Network layer (Layer 3) of the OSI model. Because of this, they make their decisions on what to do with traffic based on logical addresses, such as an IP address.

Routers have a few key functions:

- They connect multiple networks to each other, which none of the other devices we have discussed do.

- Routers do not forward broadcasts. (Switches and bridges break up collision domains, whereas routers break up broadcast domains.)

- Routers are normally used to connect one LAN to another. Typically, when a WAN is set up, at least two routers are used.

In the last decade or so, wireless routers have become common for small business and home networks. They possess all the functionality of routers historically associated with networking, but they are relatively inexpensive. We'll talk more about these routers in Chapter 7.

Auxiliary Devices

The devices we just talked about are specialized to provide connectivity. This next group of devices adds in features outside of connectivity that can help network users, specifically by protecting them from malicious attacks, providing network connections over power lines, and providing power over Ethernet cables.

Firewall

A *firewall* is a hardware or software solution that serves as your network's security guard. They're probably the most important devices on networks that are connected to the Internet. Firewalls can protect you in two ways: they protect your network resources from hackers lurking in the dark corners of the Internet, and they can simultaneously prevent computers on your network from accessing undesirable content on the Internet. At a basic level, firewalls filter packets based on rules defined by the network administrator.

Firewalls can be stand-alone "black boxes," software installed on a server or router, or some combination of hardware and software. Most firewalls will have at least two network connections: one to the Internet, or *public side*, and one to the internal network, or *private side*. Some firewalls have a third network port for a second semi-internal network. This port is used to connect servers that can be considered both public and private, such as web and email servers. This intermediary network is known as a *screened subnet* (formerly called a *demilitarized zone [DMZ]*).

A screened subnet is a semi-public network segment located between a perimeter router and an internal router on your network. It is used for web servers, FTP servers, and email relay servers.

Firewalls can be network based in that they protect a group of computers (or an entire network), or they can be host based. A host-based firewall (such as Windows Defender Firewall) protects only the individual computer on which it's installed.

A firewall is configured to allow only packets that pass specific security restrictions to get through. By default, most firewalls are configured as *default deny*, which means that all traffic is blocked unless specifically authorized by the administrator. The basic method of configuring firewalls is to use an *access control list (ACL)*. The ACL is the set of rules that determines which traffic gets through the firewall and which traffic is blocked. ACLs are typically configured to block traffic by IP address, port number, domain name, or some combination of all three.

We'll cover firewalls in more depth in Chapter 7 when we show you how to set up a network.

Ethernet over Power

Occasionally, you will find yourself in a spot where it's not possible to run cables for a network connection and wireless is a problem as well. For example, perhaps you are installing a device that only has a wired RJ-45 port but you can't get a cable to it. *Ethernet over Power* can help make that connection by using electrical outlets; an adapter is shown in Figure 5.34.

FIGURE 5.34   Ethernet over Power adapter

For Ethernet over Power to work, both devices must be on the same electrical circuit, such as would be the case for a house or a small building. To connect the devices, plug both in and then press a button on the side of each device. They will search the electrical circuit for the signal from the other and negotiate the connection. As you can see in Figure 5.34, an Ethernet cable also connects to the device. You can plug that cable into a device directly or into a connectivity device, such as a hub or a switch.

Power over Ethernet

If you can run an Ethernet signal over power lines, why can't you run electricity over network cables? As it turns out, you can—with *Power over Ethernet (PoE)*. This technology is extremely useful in situations where you need a wireless access point in a relatively remote location that does not have any power outlets. For it to work, the access point and the device it plugs into (such as a switch) both need to support PoE. In a configuration such as this, the switch would be considered an *endspan* PoE device, because it's at the end of the network connection. If the switch in question doesn't support PoE, you can get a device that sits between the switch and the access point (called a *midspan* device) whose sole purpose is to supply power via the Ethernet connection. Appropriately, these midspan devices are called *Power over Ethernet injectors*.

The first PoE standard was IEEE 802.3af, released in 2003, and it provided up to 15.4 W of DC power to connected devices. This was enough for wireless access points as well as basic surveillance cameras and VoIP phones, but not enough for videoconferencing equipment, alarm systems, laptops, or flat-screen monitors. Enhancements to the standard have been made over the years to support more power-hungry devices. Table 5.4 lists the standards you should be familiar with.

TABLE 5.4 PoE standards

Name	Year	IEEE standard	Max power	Supported devices
PoE	2003	802.3af	15.4 W	Wireless access points, static surveillance cameras, VoIP phones
PoE+	2009	802.3at	30 W	Alarm systems, PTZ (point/tilt/zoom) cameras, video IP phones
PoE++	2018	802.3bt (Type 3)	60 W	Multi-radio wireless access points, video conferencing equipment
PoE++	2018	802.3bt (Type 4)	100 W	Laptops, flat-screen monitors

Software-Defined Networking (SDN)

Talking about *software-defined networking (SDN)* in a section on networking hardware honestly feels a bit odd, because SDN is essentially setting up a network virtually, without the physical hardware connectivity devices that most people are used to. In a sense, it's a network without the network hardware. When it came out, it was radical enough to blow the minds of many networking professionals. It's all enabled by the cloud, which we will cover more in Chapter 8. For now, though, to help illustrate what SDN is, let's first look at a relatively simple network layout, such as the one shown in Figure 5.35.

FIGURE 5.35 A sample network

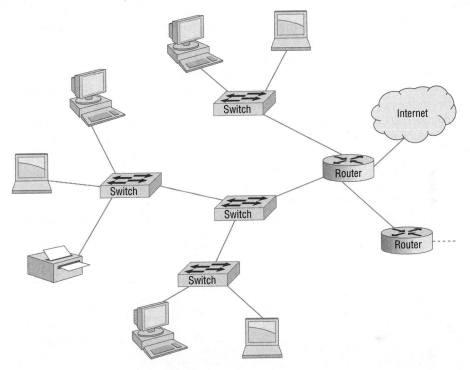

The network in Figure 5.35 has two routers, including one that connects the corporate network to the Internet. Four switches manage internal network traffic, and client devices connect to the switches. New network clients can attach to existing switches, and if the switches run out of ports, more can be added. Of course, in today's environment, we should draw in wireless access points and their clients as well. The wireless access points will connect to a switch or router with a network cable. Adding additional switches, routers, or other network control devices requires purchasing and installing the device and some configuration, but it's nothing that a good net admin can't handle.

Large enterprise networks are significantly more complex and include more routers and perhaps load balancers, firewalls, and other network appliances. Adding to the network becomes more complicated. In particular, adding more routers requires a lot of reconfiguration so that the routers know how to talk to each other.

Routers play a critical role in intra-network communications. The router's job is to take incoming data packets, read the destination address, and send the packet on to the next network that gets the data closer to delivery. There are two critical pieces to the router's job:

- The physical connections and internal circuitry that makes routing happen

- A logical component called a *routing table*, which is a database it uses to determine where to send the packets

In a traditional networking environment, each router is responsible for maintaining its own table. While almost all routers have the ability to talk to their neighbor routers for route updates, the whole setup is still pretty complicated for administrators to manage. The complexity can really become a problem when you are troubleshooting data delivery problems.

Enter SDN. The goal of SDN is to make networks more agile and flexible by separating the forwarding of network packets (the infrastructure layer) from the logical decision-making process (the control layer). The control layer consists of one or more devices that make the decisions on where to send packets—they're the brains of the operation. The physical devices then just forward packets based on what the control layer tells them. Figure 5.36 illustrates the logical SDN structure.

FIGURE 5.36   Software-defined networking

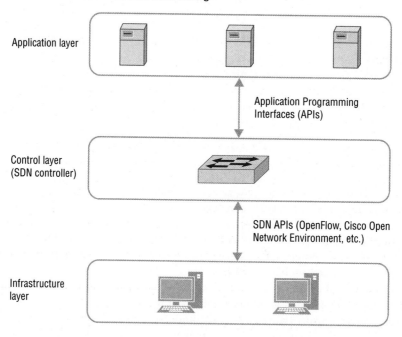

In addition to agility and flexibility, a third advantage to using SDN is centralized network monitoring. Instead of running monitoring apps for each individual piece of network hardware, the SDN software can monitor all devices in one app.

The SDN controller acts as an abstraction layer. Applications that need to use the network actually interface with the SDN controller, thinking that they are working directly with the networking hardware. In the end, data still gets from point A to point B, so any distinction between how that happens isn't important. Because the abstraction layer exists, though, the underlying network hardware and configuration can change, and it won't affect how the applications work. It's the job of the SDN controller to understand how to talk to the infrastructure.

That's Abstract

Database systems make use of abstraction layers all the time. They act as translators between apps and the database itself, reducing the cost and complexity of reconfiguring data systems. They can also act as a security mechanism of sorts, blocking data from those who don't need to see it.

For example, say that your company has four different frontend applications that access a common database. There is a website where customers place orders, an app for the Accounts Receivable department to bill customers, an app for the warehouse to pull orders and check inventory, and a dashboard so that management can see sales performance.

Because of a change in data management policies, the database structure needs to be changed. If each of the apps interfaced directly with the database, then all four apps would need to be recoded to work properly. This could require a significant investment of time and money and may jeopardize business performance. Instead, if an abstraction layer exists, it's the only thing that needs to be recoded before you can use the new database structure. As far as the apps are concerned, nothing has changed.

In addition, say that the management dashboard has sales and profit information. The customers certainly shouldn't see that from the website, but the customers do need to be able to see if something is in stock. The abstraction layer can help protect the sensitive information, acting as a security layer to ensure that sales and profit data doesn't get passed to the web app, while passing through inventory data.

So although an abstraction layer might appear to increase complexity—and it can—know that there are good reasons to use one. It can help improve system agility, provide a layer of security, and ultimately keep costs down.

To make things even more fun, SDN can be used to create virtual networks without any hardware at all. Imagine having five logical servers running in a cloud, all using the same hardware. If they want to talk to each other, they will send data the way they know how to—that is, to their network cards for delivery on the network, likely through a switch or router. But if they are using the same hardware, then they all have the same network adapter.

That makes things weird, right? Well, not really, because SDN manages the communications between the servers. Each server will be assigned a logical NIC and communicate to the others via their logical NICs. SDN manages it all, and there are no communication issues.

Networking hardware to remember for the A+ exam includes routers, switches (managed and unmanaged), access points, patch panels, firewalls, PoE, hubs, cable modems, DSL modems, optical network terminals (ONTs), and NICs. And last but not least, know what SDN does!

Summary

In this chapter, we covered a broad variety of networking topics. This chapter contains everything that you need to get you ready for the networking questions on the A+ 220-1101 exam. At the same time, the A+ exam (and consequently this chapter) barely scratches the surface of the things that you can learn about networking. If making computers talk to each other effectively is an area of interest to you, we suggest that you consider studying for the CompTIA Network+ exam after you pass your A+ tests.

First, we started with networking fundamentals. Much of the discussion of fundamentals was about understanding the concepts behind networking so that you know how to set them up. Topics included LANs versus WANs; clients, servers, and resources; network operating systems; peer-to-peer and server-based resource models; network topologies, such as bus, star, and ring; and theoretical networking models and standards, such as the OSI model and IEEE standards.

Next, you learned about hardware devices used in networking. Each computer needs a network adapter (NIC) of some sort to connect to the network. On a wired network, cables are required, and there are several different types, including coaxial, STP, UTP, and fiber-optic. Each cable type has its own specific connector.

Finally, we discussed various types of network connectivity hardware and auxiliary devices and their use. Some users may need a cable modem, DSL modem, ONT, or access point to get onto the network. All wired computers will plug into a connectivity device, such as a hub or a switch, which in turn is connected to another connectivity device, which is often a router. Other devices on the network, such as firewalls, Ethernet over Power, and PoE injectors, provide additional services. And software-defined networking virtualizes all the network hardware rather than using physical devices.

Exam Essentials

Know the difference between LANs, WANs, PANs, MANs, SANs, and WLANs.   A LAN is a local area network, which typically means a network in one centralized location. A WAN is a wide area network, which means several LANs in remote locations connected to each other. A PAN is a small Bluetooth network. A network that spans an area such as a city or a campus is a MAN. A SAN is designed specifically for storage, and a WLAN is like a LAN but wireless.

Know how computers connect to a network.   It might seem simple, but remember that all computers need a NIC to connect to the network. There's a lot of configuration that happens automatically, and you may need to reconfigure the NIC or update drivers if things don't work properly.

Know about the different types of copper cable.   The three types of copper cable you should know about are coaxial, unshielded twisted pair (UTP), and shielded twisted pair (STP). UTP comes in various types, including Cat 5, Cat 5e, Cat 6, and Cat 6a (among others, but these are the current standards in the exam objectives). For outdoor use, go with direct burial cable.

Understand the difference between a patch (straight-through) cable and a crossover cable.   Patch cables are used to connect hosts to a switch or a hub. Crossover cables switch pins 1 and 3 and 2 and 6 on one end. They are used to connect hubs to hubs, switches to switches, hosts to hosts, and hosts to routers.

Memorize the T568A and T568B cable standards.   As painful as it might sound, you should memorize the pin order for these two standards. The T568A order is white/green, green, white/orange, blue, white/blue, orange, white/brown, brown. T568B is white/orange, orange, white/green, blue, white/blue, green, white/brown, brown. If it helps, note that the blue and brown pairs do not change; only the green and orange pairs do.

Know what a plenum cable is used for.   Plenum cables do not release toxic gas when burned and therefore are required in spaces that circulate air (plenums) within buildings.

Understand performance characteristics of fiber-optic cable.   Fiber can support higher transmission rates and longer distances than copper cable can. It's also immune to electrical interference.

Know which types of connectors are used for the different types of network cables. Coaxial cable uses F type or BNC connectors. Twisted pair uses RJ-11 or RJ-45 connectors or can be terminated at a punchdown block. Fiber connectors include straight tip (ST), subscriber connector (SC), and Lucent (or local) connector (LC).

Know which networking devices are used to connect to the Internet.   Internet connections used to be made through modems on plain old telephone lines. Digital connections today are made through cable modems and DSL modems, and optical connections through optical network terminals (ONTs).

Know what hubs, switches, access points, patch panels, and routers are.   These are all network connectivity devices. Hubs and switches are used to connect several computers or groups of computers to each other. Switches can be managed or unmanaged. An access point is any port where a computer plugs into a network, but the term typically refers to wireless access points. Patch panels are rack-mounted devices with multiple (usually dozens of) wired access points. Routers are more complex devices that are often used to connect network segments or networks to each other.

Know what a firewall and Power over Ethernet (PoE) provides. A firewall is a security device that blocks or allows network traffic to pass through it. PoE provides for electricity over Ethernet cables.

Understand the premise of software-defined networking (SDN). SDN is a cloud service that virtualizes network hardware. Instead of requiring a physical switch or router, SDN can replicate their services through software.

Review Questions

The answers to the chapter review questions can be found in Appendix A.

1. _____ is immune to electromagnetic or radio-frequency interference.
   A. Twisted pair cabling
   B. CSMA/CD
   C. Broadband coaxial cabling
   D. Fiber-optic cabling

2. Which of the following is a type of connector used with coaxial cable?
   A. RJ-11
   B. RJ-45
   C. F type
   D. SC

3. You need to put a connector on the end of an Ethernet crossover cable. The existing end has a white and green colored wire at pin 1. What color do you need to make pin 1 on the new end?
   A. White/green
   B. Green
   C. White/orange
   D. Orange

4. _____ is the type of media access method used by NICs that listen to or sense the cable to check for traffic and send only when they hear that no one else is transmitting.
   A. T568A/T568B
   B. CSMA/CD
   C. CSMA/CA
   D. Demand priority

5. What is the lowest grade of UTP that is rated for 100 Mbps transmission?
   A. Cat 5
   B. Cat 5e
   C. Cat 6
   D. Cat 6a

6. A physical star topology consists of several workstations that branch off a central device called a _____.
   A. NIC
   B. Bridge
   C. Router
   D. Hub

7. Of all the network cabling options, _____ offers the longest possible segment length.

   A. Unshielded twisted pair

   B. Coaxial

   C. Fiber-optic

   D. Shielded twisted pair

8. What devices transfer packets across multiple networks and use tables to store network addresses to determine the best destination?

   A. Routers

   B. Firewalls

   C. Hubs

   D. Switches

9. Which of the following networking hardware devices is capable of creating VLANs?

   A. Firewall

   B. Patch panel

   C. Unmanaged switch

   D. Managed switch

10. Which of the following wireless communication standards is often described in terms of a wireless personal area network?

   A. Bluetooth

   B. Infrared

   C. Cellular

   D. Ethernet

11. Your ISP has just finished running fiber-optic cable in your neighborhood, and you want to switch from cable Internet to a faster fiber-optic connection. Which of the following statements is true about how you will get an Internet connection?

   A. You will continue to use your cable modem.

   B. You need to switch to using a DSL modem.

   C. You need to switch to using an ONT.

   D. You need to switch to using PoE.

12. If you are going to run a network cable in the space above the drop ceiling in your office, which type of cable should you use?

   A. Plenum

   B. PVC

   C. Coaxial

   D. Fiber-optic

13. Which of the following connector types is an MFF connector?

    A. BNC

    B. ST

    C. SC

    D. LC

14. What Ethernet specification would you be running if you needed to make a connection of 10 Gbps over a distance of 5 kilometers?

    A. 10GBaseER

    B. 10GBaseT

    C. 10GBaseSR

    D. 10GBaseLR

15. Which of the following are advantages to using a SAN? (Choose two.)

    A. More storage space on the network

    B. More efficient data storage

    C. Faster data access

    D. Automated data backups

16. You are installing a network at a friend's house, and it's impossible to run a network cable from one point in the house to another. Your friend does not want to use wireless networking. Which of the following is the best option to get network connectivity between the two points?

    A. Power over Ethernet injector

    B. Power over Ethernet switch

    C. Ethernet over Power

    D. Router

17. What type of device will block unwanted traffic from your network using a set of rules called an ACL?

    A. Router

    B. Firewall

    C. Switch

    D. NAS

18. What type of coaxial cable is recommended for digital television cable signals?

    A. RG-6

    B. RG-8

    C. RG-58

    D. RG-59

19. Which of the following devices works with MAC addresses to determine what to do with network traffic?

   A. Hub

   B. Router

   C. Patch panel

   D. Switch

20. Transmitting at 10 Gbps, how far can signals on an MMF cable travel?

   A. 100 meters

   B. 550 meters

   C. 1 kilometer

   D. 40 kilometers

Performance-Based Question

You will encounter performance-based questions on the A+ exams. The questions on the exam require you to perform a specific task, and you will be graded on whether or not you were able to complete the task. The following requires you to think creatively in order to measure how well you understand this chapter's topics. You may or may not see similar questions on the actual A+ exams. To see how your answer compares to the authors', refer to Appendix B.

Look at the pictures of network cable connectors and label each one.

MARGIN ICON

Chapter

6

Introduction to TCP/IP

THE FOLLOWING COMPTIA A+ 220-1101 EXAM OBJECTIVES ARE COVERED IN THIS CHAPTER:

✓ **2.1 Compare and contrast Transmission Control Protocol (TCP) and User Datagram Protocol (UDP) ports, protocols, and their purposes.**

- Ports and protocols
  - 20/21—File Transfer Protocol (FTP)
  - 22—Secure Shell (SSH)
  - 23—Telnet
  - 25—Simple Mail Transfer Protocol (SMTP)
  - 53—Domain Name System (DNS)
  - 67/68—Dynamic Host Configuration Protocol (DHCP)
  - 80—Hypertext Transfer Protocol (HTTP)
  - 110—Post Office Protocol 3 (POP3)
  - 137/139—Network Basic Input/Output System (NetBIOS)/NetBIOS over TCP/IP (NetBT)
  - 143—Internet Mail Access Protocol (IMAP)
  - 161/162—Simple Network Management Protocol (SNMP)
  - 389—Lightweight Directory Access Protocol (LDAP)
  - 443—Hypertext Transfer Protocol Secure (HTTPS)
  - 445—Server Message Block (SMB)/Common Internet File System (CIFS)
  - 3389—Remote Desktop Protocol (RDP)
  - TCP vs. UDP
    - Connectionless
      - DHCP
      - Trivial File Transfer Protocol (TFTP)
    - Connection-oriented
      - HTTPS
      - SSH

✓ **2.5 Given a scenario, install and configure basic wired/wireless small office/home office (SOHO) networks.**

- Internet Protocol (IP) addressing
    - IPv4
        - Private addresses
        - Public addresses
    - IPv6
    - Automatic Private IP Addressing (APIPA)
    - Static
    - Dynamic
    - Gateway

✓ **2.6 Compare and contrast common network configuration concepts.**

- DNS
    - Address
        - A
        - AAAA
    - Mail exchange (MX)
    - Text (TXT)
        - Spam management
            - DomainKeys Identified Mail (DKIM)
            - Sender Policy Framework (SPF)
            - Domain-based Message Authentication, Reporting, and Conformance (DMARC)
- DHCP
    - Leases
    - Reservations
    - Scope
- Virtual LAN (VLAN)
- Virtual private network (VPN)

Networking protocols are a lot like human languages in that they are the languages that computers speak when talking to each other. If computers don't speak the same language, they won't be able to communicate. To complicate matters, there are dozens of different languages that computers can use. Just like humans, computers can understand and use multiple languages. Imagine that you are on the street and someone comes up to you and speaks in Spanish. If you know Spanish, you will likely reply in kind. It doesn't matter if both of you know English as well because you've already established that you can communicate. On the other hand, it's going to be a pretty futile conversation if you don't know Spanish. This same concept applies to computers that are trying to communicate. They must have a network protocol in common in order for the conversation to be successful.

Throughout the years, hundreds of network protocols have been developed. As the use of networking exploded, various companies developed their own networking hardware, software, and proprietary protocols. Some were incorporated as an integral part of the network operating system, such as Banyan VINES. One-time networking giant Novell had IPX/SPX. Microsoft developed NetBEUI. Apple created AppleTalk. Others included DECnet, SNA, and XNS. While a few achieved long-term success, most have faded into oblivion. The one protocol suite that has survived is TCP/IP. Although it has some structural advantages, such as its modularity, it didn't necessarily succeed because it was inherently superior to other protocols. It succeeded because it is the protocol of the Internet.

This chapter focuses on the TCP/IP protocol suite. It is the protocol suite used on the Internet, but it's also the protocol suite used by nearly every home and business network today. We'll start by taking a quick look at the history of TCP/IP and the model on which it's based. Then we'll dive deeper into TCP/IP structure and the individual protocols it comprises. From there, we'll spend some time on IP addressing, including IPv4 and IPv6. Entire books have been written on TCP/IP—so there's no way we could cover it entirely in one chapter. Nor do you need to know every last detail right now. Instead, we'll give you the foundation that you need to understand it well, work effectively with it in the field, and pass the A+ exam.

Understanding TCP/IP

As we mentioned in the introduction, computers use a protocol as a common language for communication. A *protocol* is a set of rules that govern communications, much like a language in human terms. Of the myriad protocols out there, the key ones to understand are the protocols in the TCP/IP suite, which is a collection of different protocols that work together to deliver connectivity. Consequently, they're the only ones listed on the A+ exam objectives. In the following sections, we'll start with a look at its overall structure and then move into key protocols within the suite.

TCP/IP Structure

The *Transmission Control Protocol/Internet Protocol (TCP/IP)* suite is the most popular network protocol in use today, thanks mostly to the rise of the Internet. While the protocol suite is named after two of its hardest-working protocols, *Transmission Control Protocol (TCP)* and *Internet Protocol (IP)*, TCP/IP actually contains dozens of protocols working together to help computers communicate with one another.

TCP/IP is robust and flexible. For example, if you want to ensure that the packets are delivered from one computer to another, TCP/IP can do that. If speed is more important than guaranteed delivery, then TCP/IP can provide that too. The protocol can work on disparate operating systems, such as UNIX, Linux, macOS, Windows, iOS, and Android. It can also support a variety of programs, applications, and required network functions. Much of its flexibility comes from its modular nature.

You're familiar with the seven-layer OSI model that we discussed in Chapter 5, "Networking Fundamentals." Every protocol that's created needs to accomplish the tasks (or at least the key tasks) outlined in that model. The structure of TCP/IP is based on a similar model created by the U.S. Department of Defense—that is, the *Department of Defense (DoD) model*. The DoD model (sometimes referred to as the TCP/IP model) has four layers that map to the seven OSI layers, as shown in Figure 6.1.

FIGURE 6.1   The DoD and OSI models

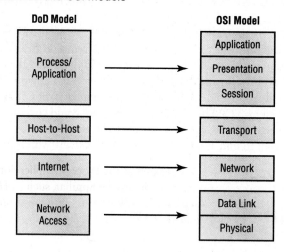

The overall functionality between these two models is virtually identical; the layers just have different names. For example, the Process/Application layer of the DoD model is designed to combine the functionality of the top three layers of the OSI model. Therefore, any protocol designed against the Process/Application layer would need to be able to perform all the functions associated with the Application, Presentation, and Session layers in the OSI model.

TCP/IP's modular nature and common protocols are shown in Figure 6.2.

FIGURE 6.2   TCP/IP protocol suite

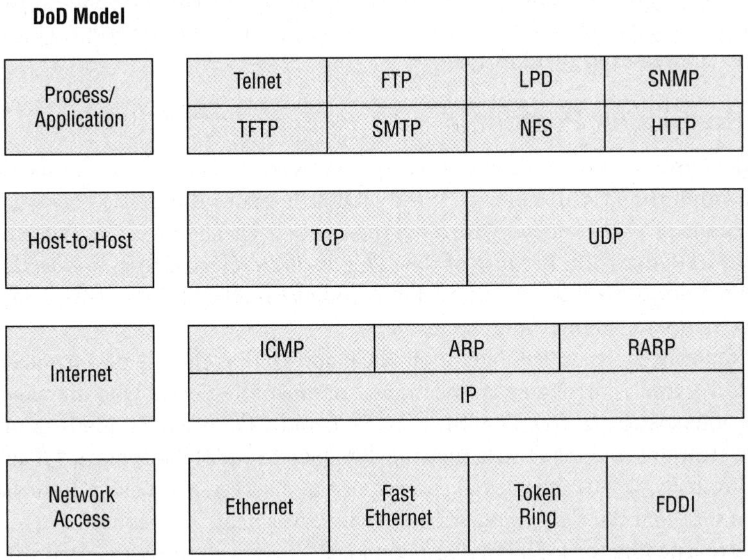

DoD Model

| Process/Application | Telnet | FTP | LPD | SNMP |
| | TFTP | SMTP | NFS | HTTP |

| Host-to-Host | TCP | | UDP | |

| Internet | ICMP | ARP | | RARP |
| | IP | | | |

| Network Access | Ethernet | Fast Ethernet | Token Ring | FDDI |

Working from the bottom up, you'll notice that the Network Access layer doesn't have any protocols, as such. This layer describes the type of network access method that you are using, such as Ethernet, Wi-Fi, or others.

The most important protocol at the Internet layer is IP. This is the backbone of TCP/IP. Other protocols at this layer work in conjunction with IP, such as *Internet Control Message Protocol (ICMP)* and *Address Resolution Protocol (ARP)*.

At the Host-to-Host layer, there are only two protocols: TCP and *User Datagram Protocol (UDP)*. Most applications will use one or the other to transmit data, although some can use both but will do so for different tasks.

The majority of TCP/IP protocols are located at the Process/Application layer. These include some protocols with which you may already be familiar, such as *Hypertext Transfer Protocol (HTTP)*, *File Transfer Protocol (FTP)*, *Simple Mail Transfer Protocol (SMTP)*, *Post Office Protocol (POP)*, and others. Let's take a look at each of the layers in more detail.

Internet Layer Protocols

At the Internet layer, there's one key protocol and a few helpful support protocols. The main workhorse of TCP/IP is the Internet Protocol (IP), and it can be found at this layer. IP is responsible for managing logical network addresses and ultimately getting data from point A to point B, even if there are dozens of points in between. We cover IP addressing in depth in the "Understanding IP Addressing" section later in this chapter.

There are three support protocols you should be aware of at this layer as well. *Internet Control Message Protocol (ICMP)* is responsible for delivering error messages. If you're familiar with the ping utility, you'll know that it utilizes ICMP to send and receive packets. *Address Resolution Protocol (ARP)* resolves logical IP addresses to physical MAC addresses built into network cards. This function is critical because in order to communicate, the sender ultimately needs to know the MAC address of the receiver. Reverse ARP (RARP) resolves MAC addresses to IP addresses.

Host-to-Host Layer Protocols

Next up is the Host-to-Host layer, and it has the fewest protocols. At this layer there are two alternatives within the TCP/IP suite: TCP and UDP. The major difference between the two is that TCP guarantees packet delivery through the use of a virtual circuit and data acknowledgments and UDP does not. Because of this, TCP is often referred to as *connection-oriented*, whereas UDP is *connectionless*. Because UDP is connectionless, it does tend to be somewhat faster, but we're talking about milliseconds here.

Another key concept to understand about TCP and UDP is the use of *port numbers*. Imagine a web server that is managing connections from incoming users who are viewing web content and others who are downloading files. TCP and UDP use port numbers to keep track of these conversations and make sure that the data gets to the right application and right end user. Conversely, when a client makes a request of a server, it needs to do so on a specific port to make sure that the right application on the server hears the request. For example, web servers are listening for HTTP requests on port 80, so web browsers need to make their requests on that port.

A good analogy for understanding port numbers is cable or satellite television. In this analogy, the IP address is your house. The cable company needs to know where to send the data. But once the data is in your house, which channel are you going to receive it on? If you want sports, that might be on one channel, but weather is on a different channel, and the cooking show is on yet another. You know that if you want a cooking show, you need to turn to channel 923 (or whatever). Similarly, the client computer on a network knows that if it needs to ask a question in HTTP, it needs to do it on port 80.

There are 65,536 ports, numbered from 0 to 65535. Ports 0 through 1023 are called the *well-known ports* and are assigned to commonly used services, and 1024 through 49151 are called the *registered ports*. All the ports from 49152 to 65535 are free to be used by application vendors. Fortunately, you don't need to memorize them all.

TCP/IP applications combine the host's IP address with the port number in order to communicate. This combination is known as a *socket*. You might see it written as something like 192.168.2.115:80.

Table 6.1 shows the ports used by some of the more common protocols. You should know each of these for the A+ exam.

TABLE 6.1   Common port numbers

Service	Protocol	Port(s)
FTP	TCP	20, 21
SSH	TCP	22
Telnet	TCP	23
SMTP	TCP	25
DNS	TCP/UDP	53
DHCP	UDP	67, 68
TFTP	UDP	69
HTTP	TCP	80
POP3	TCP	110
NetBIOS/NetBT	TCP	137, 139
IMAP4	TCP	143
SNMP	UDP	161, 162
LDAP	TCP	389
HTTPS	TCP	443
SMB/CIFS	TCP	445
RDP	TCP	3389

A complete list of registered port numbers can be found at `iana.org` and several other sites, such as Wikipedia.

Process/Application Layer Protocols

As we mentioned earlier in the chapter, most of the protocols within the TCP/IP suite are at the Process/Application layer. This is the layer of differentiation and flexibility. For example, if you want to browse the Internet, the HTTP protocol is designed for that. FTP is optimized for file downloads, and Simple Mail Transfer Protocol (SMTP) is used for sending email.

Before we get into the protocols themselves, let's take a quick look into a few key points on the TCP/IP suite's flexibility. There are literally dozens of protocols at the Process/Application layer, and they have been created over time as networking needs arose. Take HTTP, for example. The first official version was developed in 1991, nearly 20 years after TCP/IP was first implemented. Before this protocol was created, there weren't any effective client-server request-response protocols at this layer. HTTP let the client (web browser) ask the web server for a page, and the web server would return it. Going one step further, there was a need for secure transactions over HTTP—hence, the creation of HTTPS in 1994. As new applications are developed or new networking needs are discovered, developers can build an application or protocol that fits into this layer to provide the needed functionality. They just need to make sure that the protocol delivers what it needs to and can communicate with the layers below it. The following sections describe some of the more common Process/Application protocols and their ports—and the ones listed in the A+ exam objectives.

Port 20/21—File Transfer Protocol (FTP)

The *File Transfer Protocol (FTP)* is optimized to do what it says it does—transfer files. This includes both uploading and downloading files from one host to another. FTP is both a protocol and an application. Specifically, FTP lets you copy files, list and manipulate directories, and view file contents. You can't use it to execute applications remotely.

Whenever a user attempts to access an FTP site, they will be asked to log in. If it's a public site, you can often just use the login name *anonymous* and then provide your email address as the password. Of course, there's no rule saying that you have to give your real email address if you don't want to. If the FTP site is secured, you will need a legitimate login name and password to access it. If you are using a browser such as Chrome, Firefox, or Edge to connect via FTP, the correct syntax in the address window is `ftp://username:password@ftp.ftpsite.com`.

The big downside to FTP is that it's unsecure. It transmits usernames and passwords in plain text. If a potential hacker is monitoring network traffic, this information will come through quite clearly. Be aware of this when using FTP, and make sure the FTP password is something not used to log into any other services. For secure file transfers, there are other options including Secure FTP (SFTP) and FTP Secure (FTPS).

 In Windows, you can type a URL such as the one in the FTP example into the Run box to connect as well.

Port 22—Secure Shell (SSH)

Secure Shell (SSH) is a connection-oriented protocol that can be used to set up a secure Telnet session for remote logins or for remotely executing programs and transferring files. Because it's secure, it was originally designed to be a replacement for the unsecure `telnet` command. A common client interface using SSH is called OpenSSH (`www.openssh.com`).

Port 23—Telnet

Speaking of *Telnet*, it seems that it has been around since the beginning of time as a terminal emulation protocol. Someone using Telnet can log into another machine and "see" the remote computer in a window on their screen. Although this vision is text only, the user can manage files on that remote machine just as if they were logged in locally.

The problem with Telnet and other unsecure remote management options (such as RCP [remote copy] and FTP) is that the data they transmit, including passwords, is sent in plain text. Anyone eavesdropping on the line can intercept the packets and thus obtain usernames and passwords. SSH overcomes this by encrypting the traffic, including usernames and passwords.

Port 25—Simple Mail Transfer Protocol (SMTP)

This is the first of three protocols we'll look at devoted to email. *Simple Mail Transfer Protocol (SMTP)* is the protocol most commonly used to send email messages. Because it's designed to send only, it's referred to as a *push protocol*. SMTP is the protocol used to send email from mail server to mail server as well as from a mail server to an email client. An email client locates its email server by querying the DNS server for a mail exchange (MX) record. After the server is located, SMTP is used to push the message to the email server, which will then process the message for delivery.

We will cover DNS servers and MX records in more depth later in this chapter, in the "Understanding DHCP and DNS" section.

Port 53—Domain Name System (DNS)

You probably use *Domain Name System (DNS)* every day whether you realize it or not. Its purpose is to resolve hostnames to IP addresses. For example, let's say that you open your web browser and type in a Uniform Resource Locator (URL) such as `https://www.wiley.com`. Your computer needs to know the IP address of the server that hosts that website in order for you to connect to it. Through a DNS server, your computer resolves the URL to an IP address so communication can happen. DNS is so critical that we have an entire section dedicated to it later in this chapter.

You will find some debate about what DNS stands for. The official name, according to the Internet Engineering Task Force (IETF), is Domain Name System. However, you may see others reference it as Domain Name Server as well. Regardless, the important thing to remember is what DNS does, which is resolving hostnames to IP addresses.

Port 67/68—Dynamic Host Configuration Protocol (DHCP)

Dynamic Host Configuration Protocol (DHCP) dynamically assigns IP addresses and other IP configuration information to network clients. Configuring your network clients to receive their IP addresses from a DHCP server reduces network administration headaches. We'll cover the mechanics of how DHCP works later in this chapter when we talk about IP addressing.

Port 69—Trivial File Transfer Protocol (TFTP)

You already learned about FTP, and *Trivial File Transfer Protocol (TFTP)* is its lighter-weight cousin. It can transfer files much like FTP, but it's much simpler and faster. Table 6.2 highlights a few other key differences.

TABLE 6.2   TFTP vs. FTP

Feature	TFTP	FTP
Authentication	None required	Username/password (although you may be able to use *anonymous*)
Protocol used	UDP (connectionless)	TCP (connection-oriented)
Number of commands	5	About 70
Primary use	Transmitting configurations to and from network devices	Uploading and downloading files

Port 80—Hypertext Transfer Protocol (HTTP)

HTTP was once the most used Process/Application layer protocol. It manages the communication between a web server and client, and it lets you connect to and view all the content that you enjoy on the Internet. All the information transmitted by HTTP is plain text, which means that it's not secure. Therefore, it's not a good choice for transmitting sensitive or personal information, such as usernames and passwords, or for transmitting banking information. Because of that, it's been supplanted by HTTPS (covered later).

Port 110—POP3

For a long time, *Post Office Protocol 3 (POP3)* was the preferred protocol for downloading email. It's been replaced in most installations by IMAP4 (covered later) because IMAP4 includes security and more features than POP3.

Port 137/139—Network Basic Input/Output System (NetBIOS)/NetBIOS over TCP/IP (NetBT)

Network Basic Input/Output System (NetBIOS) is an application programming interface (API) that allows computers to communicate with each other over the network. It works at Layer 5 of the OSI model. Consequently, it needs to work with another network protocol to handle the functions of Layer 4 and below. NetBIOS running over TCP/IP is called *NetBT*, or NBT. Specifically, NetBIOS provides three services:

- Naming service, for name registration and resolution
- Datagram distribution service, for connectionless communication
- Session management service, for connection-oriented communication

For many years, Microsoft network clients were configured with a NetBIOS name, which was their network name. To communicate with another computer on the network, the NetBIOS name would need to be resolved (matched) to an IP address. This was done with a WINS (Windows Internet Name Service) server or LMHOSTS file and could not be performed across any routed connection (which includes the Internet).

If you're familiar with hostnames, they were somewhat analogous and could be one and the same or totally different. (If you're *not* familiar with hostnames and DNS, we cover it later in this chapter.) The big differences are that hostnames are resolved with a DNS server (or HOSTS file) and can work across the Internet. WINS was far inferior to DNS for name resolution, so Microsoft ended up adopting DNS like the rest of the industry.

Port 143—Internet Message Access Protocol (IMAP)

Internet Message Access Protocol (IMAP) is a secure protocol designed to download email. Its current version is version 4, or IMAP4. It's the client-side email management protocol of choice, having replaced the unsecure POP3. Most current email clients, such as Microsoft Outlook and Gmail, are configured to be able to use either IMAP4 or POP3. IMAP4 has some definite advantages over POP3. They include:

- IMAP4 works in connected and disconnected modes. With POP3, the client makes a connection to the email server, downloads the email, and then terminates the connection. IMAP4 allows the client to remain connected to the email server after the download, meaning that as soon as another email enters the inbox, IMAP4 notifies the email client, which can then download it.

- IMAP4 also lets you store the email on the server, as opposed to POP3, which requires you to download it.

- IMAP4 allows multiple clients to be simultaneously connected to the same inbox. This can be useful for smartphone users who have both Outlook on their workstation and their smartphone email client operational at the same time or for cases where multiple users monitor the same mailbox, such as on a customer service account. IMAP4 allows each connected user or client to see changes made to messages on the server in real time.

 The A+ exam objectives incorrectly spell out IMAP as Internet Mail Access Protocol. As we've stated previously, focus on what the acronym "does" instead of what it specifically stands for and you'll be in good shape.

Port 161/162—Simple Network Management Protocol (SNMP)

Simple Network Management Protocol (SNMP) gathers and manages network performance information.

On your network, you might have several connectivity devices, such as routers and switches. A management device called an *SNMP server* can be set up to collect data from these devices (called *agents*) and ensure that your network is operating properly. Although SNMP is mostly used to monitor connectivity devices, many other network devices are SNMP-compatible as well. The most current version is SNMPv3.

Port 389—Lightweight Directory Access Protocol (LDAP)

The *Lightweight Directory Access Protocol (LDAP)* is a directory services protocol based on the X.500 standard. LDAP is designed to access information stored in an information directory typically known as an LDAP directory or LDAP database.

On your network, you probably have a lot of information, such as employee phone books and email addresses, client contact lists, and infrastructure and configuration data for the network and network applications. This information might not get updated frequently, but you might need to access it from anywhere on the network, or you might have a network application that needs access to this data. LDAP provides you with the access, regardless of the client platform from which you're working. You can also use access control lists (ACLs) to set up who can read and change entries in the database using LDAP. A common analogy is that LDAP provides access to and the structure behind your network's phone book.

Port 443—Hypertext Transfer Protocol Secure (HTTPS)

To encrypt traffic between a web server and client securely, *Hypertext Transfer Protocol Secure (HTTPS)* can be used. HTTPS connections are secured using either *Secure Sockets Layer (SSL)* or *Transport Layer Security (TLS)*.

From the client (web browser) side, users will know that the site is secure because the browser will display a small padlock icon next to the address name.

 Real World Scenario

How Secure Is It?

You have probably heard before that you should not enter personal information (such as a credit card number) into an unsecure website. But what does that really mean?

First, know what to look for. If you were to enter information into a website with an address beginning with just http://, you would be asking for someone to steal the information! The HTTP protocol transmits data in plain text, meaning that there is no encryption at all between your computer and the server. On the other hand, HTTPS encrypts the data transmissions as they cross the wire.

To use HTTPS, the website needs to obtain an SSL/TLS certificate from a reputable certificate authority, which verifies the identity of the website. So the good news is that if you are accessing a site with https:// in the header, you know that the site is what it says it is (and not a fake site or Trojan horse) and that transmissions between your computer and that site are encrypted. Once the data is on the website's server, though, HTTPS is no longer relevant and other protection methods are needed to keep your data secure.

Occasionally, you might visit a website that uses HTTPS and get a pop-up error message saying that the certificate has expired or could not be validated. This is most likely a case of the certificate legitimately expiring, but it could be that it's a Trojan horse website. Proceed with caution!

Port 445—Server Message Block (SMB)/Common Internet File System (CIFS)

Server Message Block (SMB) is a protocol originally developed by IBM but then enhanced by Microsoft, IBM, Intel, and others. It's used to provide shared access to files, printers, and other network resources and is primarily implemented by Microsoft systems. In a way, it can function a bit like FTP only with a few more options, such as the ability to connect to printers, and more management commands. It's also known for its ability to make network resources easily visible through various Windows network apps (such as Network in File Explorer).

Common Internet File System (CIFS) is a Microsoft-developed enhancement of the SMB protocol, which was also developed by Microsoft. The intent behind CIFS is that it can be used to share files and printers between computers, regardless of the operating system that they run. It's the default file and print sharing protocol in Windows.

Port 3389—Remote Desktop Protocol (RDP)

Developed by Microsoft, the *Remote Desktop Protocol (RDP)* allows users to connect to remote computers and run programs on them. When you use RDP, you see the desktop of the computer you've signed into on your screen. It's like you're really there, even though you're not.

When you use RDP, the computer at which you are seated is the client and the computer you're logging into is the server. RDP client software is available for Windows, Linux, macOS, iOS, and Android. Microsoft's RDP client software is called *Remote Desktop Connection*. The server uses its own video driver to create video output and sends the output to the client using RDP. Conversely, all keyboard and mouse input from the client is encrypted and sent to the server for processing. RDP also supports sound, drive, port, and network printer redirection. In a nutshell, this means that if you could see, hear, or do it sitting at the remote computer, you could see, hear, or do it at the RDP client too.

Services using this protocol can be great for telecommuters. It's also very handy for technical support folks, who can log into and assume control over a remote computer. It's a lot easier to troubleshoot and fix problems when you can see what's going on and "drive."

For the exam, remember that you will need to be able compare and contrast TCP and UDP ports, protocols, and their purposes. This includes all of the protocols and ports we just covered, as well as what it means to be connectionless or connection-oriented.

Understanding IP Addressing

To communicate on a TCP/IP network, each device needs to have a unique IP address. Any device with an IP address is referred to as a *host*. This can include servers, workstations, printers, routers, and other devices. If you can assign it an IP address, it's a host. As an administrator, you can assign the host's IP configuration information manually, or you can have it automatically assigned by a DHCP server. On the client, this is done through the network adapter's TCP/IP properties. You'll see in Figure 6.3 that the system is set to receive information automatically from a DHCP server. We'll look at how to configure this in more depth in Chapter 7, "Wireless and SOHO Networks."

FIGURE 6.3   TCP/IP Properties

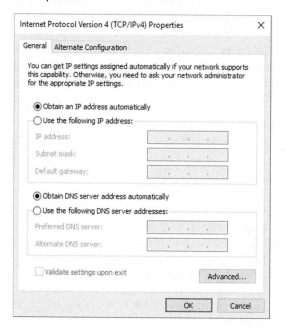

 This section will cover IPv4. IPv6 will be covered in its own section.

An IPv4 address is a 32-bit hierarchical address that identifies a host on the network. It's typically written in dotted-decimal notation, such as 192.168.10.55. Each of the numbers in this example represents 8 bits (or 1 byte) of the address, also known as an *octet*. The same address written in binary (how the computer thinks about it) would be 11000000 10101000 00001010 00110111. As you can see, the dotted-decimal version is a much more convenient way to write these numbers.

The addresses are said to be hierarchical, as opposed to "flat," since the numbers at the beginning of the address identify groups of computers that belong to the same network. Because of the hierarchical address structure, we're able to do really cool things, such as route packets between local networks and on the Internet.

A great example of hierarchical addressing is your street address. Let's say that you live in apartment 4B at 123 Main Street, Anytown, Kansas, USA. If someone sent you a letter via snail mail, the hierarchy of your address helps the postal service and carrier deliver it to the right place. First and broadest is USA. Kansas helps narrow it down a bit, and Anytown narrows it down more. Eventually we get to your street, the right number on your street, and then the right apartment. If the address space were flat (for example, Kansas didn't mean anything more specific than Main Street), or you could use any name you wanted for your state, it would be really hard to get the letter to the right spot.

Take this analogy back to IP addresses. They're set up to organize networks logically in order to make delivery between them possible and then to identify an individual node within a network. If this structure weren't in place, a huge, multi-network space like the Internet probably wouldn't be possible. It would simply be too unwieldy to manage.

Another example of a hierarchical addressing scheme is telephone numbers. The first three digits, the area code, group all telephone numbers with that area code into one logical network. The second grouping of three numbers defines a local calling area, and the last grouping of numbers is the unique identifier within that local calling area.

A Quick Binary Tutorial

As we mentioned earlier, each IP address is written in four octets in dotted-decimal notation, but each octet represents 8 bits. A binary bit is a value with two possible states: on equals 1 and off equals 0. If the bit is turned on, it has a decimal value based upon its position within the octet. An off bit always equals 0. Take a look at Figure 6.4, which will help illustrate what we mean.

FIGURE 6.4   Binary values

Position in octet	8	7	6	5	4	3	2	1
Bit on	1	1	1	1	1	1	1	1
Has the decimal value of . . .	128	64	32	16	8	4	2	1
Mathematically	2^7	2^6	2^5	2^4	2^3	2^2	2^1	2^0

If all the bits in an octet are off, or 00000000, the corresponding decimal value is 0. If all bits in an octet are on, you would have 11111111, which is 255 in decimal.

When you're working with IPv4 addressing, all numbers will be between 0 and 255.

Where it starts to get more entertaining is when you have combinations of zeroes and ones. For example, 10000001 is equal to 129 (128 + 1), and 00101010 is equal to 42 (32 + 8 + 2).

As you work with IPv4 addresses, you'll see certain patterns emerge. For example, you may be able to count quickly from left to right in an octet pattern, such as 128, 192, 224, 240, 248, 252, 254, and 255. That's what you get if you have (starting from the left) 1, 2, 3, and so forth up to 8 bits on in sequence in the octet.

It's beyond the scope of this book to get into too much detail on binary-to-decimal conversion, but this primer should get you started.

If you want more information on binary, here are two helpful resources. A network binary math lesson can be found at `https://learningnet work.cisco.com/s/blogs/a0D3i000002SKMwEAO/network-binary-math-explained`, and you'll find a binary-to-decimal converter at `https://www.rapidtables.com/convert/number/decimal-to-binary.html`.

Parts of the IP Address

Each IP address is made up of two components: the *network ID* and the *host ID*. The network portion of the address always comes before the host portion. Because of the way IP addresses are structured, the network portion does not have to be a specific fixed length. In other words, some computers will use 8 of the 32 bits for the network portion and the other 24 for the host portion, whereas other computers might use 24 bits for the network portion and the remaining 8 bits for the host portion. Here are a few rules that you should know about when working with IP addresses:

- All host addresses on a network must be unique.

- On a routed network (such as the Internet), all network addresses must be unique as well.

- Neither the network ID nor the host ID can be set to all 0s. A host ID portion of all 0s means "this network."

- Neither the network ID nor the host ID can be set to all 1s. A host ID portion of all 1s means "all hosts on this network," commonly known as a *broadcast address*.

Computers are able to differentiate where the network ID ends and the host address begins through the use of a *subnet mask*. This is a value written just like an IP address and may look something like 255.255.255.0. Any bit that is set to a 1 in the subnet mask makes the corresponding bit in the IP address part of the network ID (regardless of whether the bit in the IP address is on or off). When setting bits to 1 in a subnet mask, you always have to turn them on sequentially from left to right, so that the bits representing the network address are always contiguous and come first. The rest of the address will be the host ID. The number 255 is the highest number you will ever see in IP addressing, and it means that all bits in the octet are set to 1.

Here's an example based on two numbers that we have used in this chapter. Look at the IP address of 192.168.10.55. Let's assume that the subnet mask in use with this address is 255.255.255.0. This indicates that the first three octets are the network portion of the address and the last octet is the host portion; therefore, the network portion of this ID is 192.168.10 and the host portion is 55. If the subnet mask were 255.255.0.0, the computer would see its network address as 192.168 and its host address as 10.55. As you can see, the subnet mask can make the exact same address appear as though it's on a different network. If you're ever dealing with network communication issues, the IP address and subnet mask are among the first things you should check.

To communicate using IPv4, each computer is *required* to have an IP address and correct subnet mask. A third component, called a *default gateway*, identifies the IP address of the device that will allow the host to connect outside of the local network. This is typically your router, and it's required if you want to communicate with computers outside of your local network. An example configuration is shown in Figure 6.5.

FIGURE 6.5   Manual TCP/IP configuration with an IP address, subnet mask, and default gateway

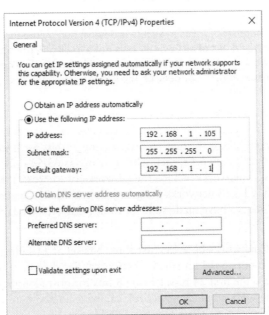

IPv4 Address Classes

The designers of TCP/IP designated classes of networks based on the first 3 bits of the IP address. As you will see, classes differ in how many networks of each class can exist and the number of unique hosts that each network can accommodate. Here are some characteristics of the three classes of addresses that you will commonly deal with:

Class A   Class A networks are defined as those with the first bit set as 0 (decimal values from 0 to 127) and are designed for very large networks. The default network portion for Class A networks is the first 8 bits, leaving 24 bits for host identification. Because the network portion is only 8 bits long (and 0 and 127 are reserved), there are only 126 Class A network addresses available. The remaining 24 bits of the address allow each Class A network to hold as many as 16,777,214 hosts. Examples of Class A networks include the networks for telecommunications giants Comcast and AT&T and organizations such as General Electric, IBM, Hewlett-Packard, Apple, Xerox, Ford, and the U.S. Department of Defense. Most Class A blocks are assigned to regional Internet registries, who allocate IP addresses to a specific region of the world. All possible Class A networks are in use; no more are available.

NOTE   The number of networks available is determined by the formula 2^n, where n represents the number of bits being used. In the Class A example, 7 bits are available by default (because the first one is always set as 0 by design), so there are 2^7 networks available, which is 128. However, the network addresses of 0 and 127 are also reserved, so it's really 126.

The number of hosts available is determined by the formula $2^n - 2$, because a host address of all 0s or all 1s is not allowed. Remember, all 0s means "this network" and all 1s are broadcast addresses. So, in a default Class A network, there can be $2^{24} - 2$ hosts, or 16,777,214.

Class B   Class B networks always have the first 2 bits set at 10 (decimal values from 128 to 191) and are designed for medium-sized networks. The default network portion for Class B networks is the first 16 bits, leaving 16 bits for host identification. This allows for 16,384 (2^{14}) networks, each with as many as 65,534 ($2^{16} - 2$) hosts attached. Examples of Class B networks include the networks of Microsoft, ExxonMobil, and Purdue University. Class B networks are generally regarded as unavailable, but address-conservation techniques have made some of these addresses available from time to time over the years.

Class C   Class C networks have the first three bits set at 110 (decimal values from 192 to 223) and are designed for smaller networks. The default network portion for Class C networks is the first 24 bits, leaving 8 bits for host identification. This allows for 2,097,152 (2^{21}) networks, but each network can have a maximum of only 254 ($2^8 - 2$) hosts. Most companies have Class C network addresses. A few class C networks are still available.

The address assignment examples in this chapter refer to addresses that are used on the Internet. For example, Apple has the network address of 17.0.0.0. No one else on the Internet can use addresses in that network's range (17.0.0.0–17.255.255.255). But if you are using IP addresses on an internal network that never connects to the Internet, you are free to use whatever addresses you would like.

Table 6.3 shows the IPv4 classes, their ranges, and their default subnet masks.

TABLE 6.3   IPv4 address classes

Class	First octet	Default subnet mask	Comments
A	1–127	255.0.0.0	For very large networks; 127 reserved for the loopback address
B	128–191	255.255.0.0	For medium-sized networks
C	192–223	255.255.255.0	For smaller networks with fewer hosts
D	224–239	N/A	Reserved for multicasts (sending messages to multiple systems)
E	240–255	N/A	Reserved for testing

The network addresses 0 and 127 are reserved and not available for use. Specifically, the address 127.0.0.1, called the *loopback address*, is used for troubleshooting network adapters. We'll talk more about this in Chapter 12, "Hardware and Network Troubleshooting."

The IP address can be written in shorthand to show how many bits are being used for the network portion of the address. For example, you might see something like 10.0.0.0/8. The /8 on the end indicates that the first 8 bits are the network portion of the address, and the other 24 are the host portion. Another example is 192.168.1.0/24, which is a Class C network with a default subnet mask.

Classless Inter-Domain Routing

The default subnet masks for each class of address are by no means the only subnet masks that can be used. In fact, if they were, it would severely limit the number of possible TCP/IP networks available. To resolve this and provide additional addressing flexibility, there is *classless inter-domain routing (CIDR)*. This is just a fancy of way of saying, "You don't have to use the default subnet masks." From a practical standpoint, CIDR minimizes the concept of IP address classes and primarily focuses on the number of bits that are used as part of the network address.

Taking a look at the defaults can help illustrate how CIDR works. If you have a Class A default mask of 255.0.0.0, that is 11111111.00000000.00000000.00000000 in binary. A Class B default mask of 255.255.0.0 is 11111111.11111111.00000000.00000000 in binary. There's no rule that says you have to use an entire octet of bits to represent the network portion of the address. The only rule is that you have to add 1s in a subnet mask from left to right. What if you wanted to have a mask of 255.240.0.0 (11111111.11110000.00000000.00000000); can you do that? The answer is yes, and that is essentially what CIDR does. Table 6.4 shows you every available subnet mask and its equivalent slash notation.

TABLE 6.4 CIDR values

Subnet mask	Notation
255.0.0.0	/8
255.128.0.0	/9
255.192.0.0	/10
255.224.0.0	/11
255.240.0.0	/12
255.248.0.0	/13
255.252.0.0	/14
255.254.0.0	/15
255.255.0.0	/16
255.255.128.0	/17
255.255.192.0	/18
255.255.224.0	/19
255.255.240.0	/20
255.255.248.0	/21
255.255.252.0	/22
255.255.254.0	/23
255.255.255.0	/24

Subnet mask	Notation
255.255.255.128	/25
255.255.255.192	/26
255.255.255.224	/27
255.255.255.240	/28
255.255.255.248	/29
255.255.255.252	/30

Earlier, we said that CIDR minimizes the impact of classes, but there are still some restrictions. The /8 through /15 notations can be used only with Class A network addresses; /16 through /23 can be used with Class A and B network addresses; /24 through /30 can be used with Class A, B, and C network addresses. You can't use anything more than /30, because you always need at least 2 bits for hosts.

Now that you know that you *can* do it, the question is, *why* would you do it? The answer is that it provides you with the flexibility to configure your network.

Here's an example. Say that your default network address is 10.0.0.0/8. That means that you have 24 bits left for hosts on that one network, so you can have just over 16.7 million hosts. How realistic is it that one company will have that many hosts? It's not realistic at all, and that doesn't even bring up the issue that the network infrastructure wouldn't be able to handle physically having that many hosts on one network. However, let's say that you work for a large corporation with about 15 divisions and some of them have up to 3,000 hosts. That's plausible. What you can do is to set up your network so that each division has its own smaller portion of the network (a subnet) big enough for its needs. To hold 3,000 hosts and have a bit of room for expansion, you need 12 bits ($2^{12} - 2 = 4,094$), meaning that you have 20 bits left over for the network address. Thus, your new configuration could be 10.0.0.0/20.

Public vs. Private IP Addresses

All the addresses that are used on the Internet are called *public addresses*. They must be purchased, and only one computer can use any given public address at one time. The problem that presented itself was that the world was soon to run out of public IP addresses while the use of TCP/IP was growing. Additionally, the structure of IP addressing made it impossible to "create" or add any new addresses to the system.

To address this, a solution was devised to allow for the use of TCP/IP without requiring the assignment of a public address. The solution was to use private addresses. *Private addresses* are not routable on the Internet. They were intended for use on private networks only. That private addresses weren't intended for use on the Internet freed us from the requirement that all addresses be globally unique. This essentially created an infinite number of IP addresses that companies could use within their own network walls.

Although this solution helped alleviate the problem of running out of addresses, it created a new one. The private addresses that all of these computers have aren't globally unique, but they need to be in order to access the Internet.

A service called *Network Address Translation (NAT)* was created to solve this problem. NAT runs on your router and handles the translation of private, nonroutable IP addresses into public IP addresses. There are three ranges reserved for private, nonroutable IP addresses, as shown in Table 6.5. You should memorize these ranges and be able to identify them on sight.

TABLE 6.5   Private IP address ranges

Class	IP address range	Default subnet mask	Number of hosts
A	10.0.0.0–10.255.255.255	255.0.0.0	16.7 million
B	172.16.0.0–172.31.255.255	255.240.0.0	1 million
C	192.168.0.0–192.168.255.255	255.255.0.0	65,536

 Real World Scenario

Private IP Addresses and Subnet Masks

When you look at the default subnet masks for the private IP address ranges, you might think, "Wait a minute. Those masks aren't the same as the default subnet masks for the address class," and you'd be correct.

To understand how TCP/IP addresses work, it's often helpful to start with the concept of address classes, because it helps you break the information into chunks, making it easier to understand. In the real world, though, most network administrators don't think in terms of classes, and routers certainly don't operate based on classes. Communication and routing on a network all happens in binary. Experienced network admins will think in terms like, "I am dealing with a 10.0.0.0/16 network." They know the address and the length of the subnet mask.

Earlier in this chapter, you learned about the concept of CIDR, which basically ignores the artificial boundaries of address classes. It uses a concept called *variable length subnet masking (VLSM)*, which might sound complicated, but it just means that the length of the subnet mask determines the structure of the network. (And by structure, we mean the network addresses and the number of networks and hosts that you can have on a network.)

How does this relate back to private IP address ranges? You'll notice that the Class A address range is 10.0.0.0/8, which has a "default" mask for a Class A address. 172.16.0.0/12 is an address in the Class B range, but it does not use the "default" /16 mask. If it did use a /16 mask, then the administrator would have only the remaining 16 bits to use for additional subnets and hosts. As it is, the administrator has 20 bits to play with, which provides much greater flexibility in designing the network. The same concept applies to 192.168.0.0/16. The administrator has 16 free bits to create subnets and host ranges, whereas the "default" /24 mask would leave only 8 bits and not a lot of flexibility.

There are three things that you should take away from this sidebar:

- Know the subnet masks in Table 6.5 and understand that they are different from the default masks for that class of address.

- Know that you are not limited to using the default masks or class rules.

- It's all about the binary.

The A+ exam may test you on the basics of IP addressing and subnetting, which we have covered in this book. If you pursue more advanced certifications, such as the CompTIA Network+ or the Cisco series of certifications, you will be expected to know IP addressing and subnetting in depth. If you are interested in learning more (after you pass the A+ exam, of course), check out *CompTIA Network+ Study Guide*, by Todd Lammle.

These private addresses cannot be used on the Internet and cannot be routed externally. The fact that they are not routable on the Internet is actually an advantage because a network administrator can use them essentially to hide an entire network from the Internet.

This is how it works: The network administrator sets up a NAT-enabled router, which functions as the default gateway to the Internet. The external interface of the router has a public IP address assigned to it that has been provided by the ISP, such as 155.120.100.1. The internal interface of the router will have an administrator-assigned private IP address within one of these ranges, such as 192.168.1.1. All computers on the internal network will then also need to be on the 192.168.1.0 network. To the outside world, any request coming from the internal network will appear to come from 155.120.100.1. The NAT router translates all incoming packets and sends them to the appropriate client. This type of setup is very common today.

By definition, NAT is actually a one-to-one private-to-public IP address translation protocol. There is a type of NAT called *NAT Overload*, also known as *Port Address Translation (PAT)*, which allows for many private IP addresses to use one public IP address on the Internet. You probably don't need to have this depth of knowledge for the A+ exam, but it's good stuff to be aware of.

You may look at your own computer, which has an address in a private range, and wonder, "If it's not routable on the Internet, then how am I on the Internet?" Remember, the NAT router technically makes the Internet request on your computer's behalf, and the NAT router is using a public IP address.

 Don't make the mistake of thinking that your internal network can't be hacked if it is using private addresses through NAT. It can. Hackers just have to use more tools and try a little harder to uncover your internal structure. Even if you're using NAT, you still need protective features such as firewalls and anti-malware software.

 For the A+ exam, you will need to know about IPv4 public and private addresses and the default gateway.

Understanding DHCP and DNS

Two critical TCP/IP services you need to be aware of are *Dynamic Host Configuration Protocol (DHCP)* and *Domain Name System (DNS)*. Both are services that need to be installed on a server, and both provide key functionality to network clients.

DHCP

A DHCP server is configured to provide IP configuration information to clients automatically (dynamically), in what is called a *lease*. It's called that because the information is not permanently granted to the client computer, and the client must periodically request a renewed lease or a new lease. The following configuration information is typically provided in a lease:

- IP address
- Subnet mask
- Default gateway (the "door" to the outside world)
- DNS server address

Scopes and Reservations

DHCP servers can provide a lot more than the items on the previous list, but these are the most common. The list of parameters that the DHCP server can provide is configured as part of a *scope*. DHCP servers can have one or more scopes to service clients on different subnets or network segments. The following items are typically included within the scope:

Address Pool   This is the range of addresses that the server can give out to clients. For example, the pool may be configured to give out addresses in the range from 192.168.0.100 to 192.168.0.200. If all of the addresses are given out, then the server can't provide addresses to any new potential clients. If the network is using IPv4 addresses, the address pool configuration will also include the subnet mask.

Lease Durations   IP addresses given out by the DHCP server are leased to clients, and the lease has an expiration time. Before the lease expires, the client (if it's online) will typically renegotiate to receive a new lease. If the lease expires, then the address becomes available to assign to another client. If you have a situation where there are limited IP addresses but a lot of clients coming on and off the network frequently (say, a traveling sales force), you might want to shorten the lease times. The downside is that it will generate a bit more network broadcast traffic, as we will explain in just a bit.

Address Reservations   Some IP addresses can be reserved (it's appropriately named a DHCP *reservation*) for specific clients, based on the client's MAC address. This is particularly useful for devices that need to have a static IP address, such as printers, servers, and routers.

Scope Options   These provide extra configuration items outside of the IP address and subnet mask. The most common items are the address of the default gateway (the router) and DNS servers. Other items might include the addresses of servers providing other functions, such as time synchronization, NetBIOS name resolution, telephony services, or the domain name (whatever.com) for the client to use.

 **Real World Scenario**

TCP/IP Configuration Choices

When configuring TCP/IP on a network, you have three choices for assigning IP addresses: manually (also called *static addressing*), automatically using a DHCP server (also called *dynamic addressing*), and a hybrid approach.

The manual option takes the most work, and it really only works for smaller networks. The administrator needs to keep track of all the addresses that have been assigned so that the same address doesn't end up being accidentally assigned to multiple computers. Duplicate addresses will cause communication problems. Most administrators have better things to do than manage IP addresses manually.

DHCP is extremely convenient. The administrator sets up a scope and options and lets the server automatically manage all the IP addresses. For devices that need a static address, such as printers, servers, and routers, the administrator can configure address reservations based on their MAC addresses. That way, every time a specific printer comes online, it always receives the same address. This takes a bit of setup in the beginning, or when a new device is added, but it's worth it in the long run. The DHCP server is then the single point of management for all IP addresses on the network. That makes administration and trouble-shooting much easier.

The hybrid option is a combination of manual assignments and DHCP. For example, devices that need static IP addresses can be assigned manually, whereas clients get their information from a DHCP server. In a situation like this, the administrator might set a DHCP client pool address range for 192.168.0.100 to 192.168.0.200 and then use addresses 192.168.0.1 to 192.168.0.99 for static devices. The problem with this approach is that it requires extra administrative effort to manage the static addresses and ensure that the same address isn't assigned multiple times. In addition, say another administrator looks at the DHCP server and sees the scope. That administrator might or might not know that addresses lower than .100 are being used for static assignments and could increase the scope to include those addresses. Doing so will cause the DHCP server to hand out addresses that could conflict with devices that have been manually configured. So hybrid is an option, but it's not recommended.

The best option is to use the DHCP server to automatically manage all IP addresses on the network.

How DHCP Works

DHCP clients need to be configured to obtain an IP address automatically. This is done by going into the network card's properties and then the TCP/IP properties, as was shown previously in Figure 6.3.

When the client boots up, it will not have an IP address. To ask for one, it will send a DHCP DISCOVER broadcast out on the network. If a DHCP server is available to hear the broadcast, it will respond directly to the requesting client using the client's MAC address as the destination address. The process is shown in Figure 6.6.

FIGURE 6.6   The DHCP request process

Notice that the DHCP DISCOVER and DHCP REQUEST messages are broadcasts, which means two important things. First, every computer on the network segment receives and needs to process the broadcast message. It's like snail mail that's addressed to "the current resident" at an address, and the computer is compelled to read it. Excessive broadcasts can dramatically slow network performance. Second, broadcasts do not go through routers. Thus, if the client and the DHCP server are on opposite sides of a router, there will be a problem. There are two resolutions. First, make the router the DHCP server. Second, install a *DHCP relay agent* on the subnet that doesn't have the DHCP server. It will be configured with the address of the DHCP server, and it will forward the request directly to the DHCP server on behalf of the client.

Automatic Private IP Addressing

Automatic Private IP Addressing (APIPA) is a TCP/IP standard used to automatically configure IP-based hosts that are unable to reach a DHCP server. APIPA addresses are in the 169.254.0.0–169.254.255.255 range, with a subnet mask of 255.255.0.0. If you see a computer that has an IP address beginning with 169.254, you know that it has configured itself.

Typically, the only time that you will see this is when a computer is supposed to receive configuration information from a DHCP server but for some reason that server is unavailable. Even while configured with this address, the client will continue to broadcast for a DHCP server so that it can be given a real address once the server becomes available.

APIPA is also sometimes known as *zero configuration networking* or *address autoconfiguration*. Both of these terms are marketing efforts, created to remove the perceived difficulty of configuring a TCP/IP network. While TCP/IP has generally been considered difficult to configure (compared to other protocols), APIPA can make it so that a TCP/IP network can run with no configuration at all! For example, say that you are setting up a small local area network that has no need to communicate with any networks outside of itself. To accomplish this, you can use APIPA to your advantage. Set the client computers to receive DHCP addresses automatically, but don't set up a DHCP server. The clients will configure themselves and be able to communicate with each other using TCP/IP. The only downside is that this will create a little more broadcast traffic on your network. This solution is only really effective for a nonrouted network of fewer than 100 computers. Considering that most networks today need Internet access, it's unlikely that you'll run across a network configuration like this.

Real World Scenario

Help! I Can't Get to the Internet!

This is something that you will probably hear a lot: A user on your network calls and complains that they can't get their email or get to the Internet. Everything was fine yesterday, but since this morning they have had no connectivity. Of course, they haven't done anything to or changed their computer at all! No one else on the network appears to be affected.

If the computer is otherwise running normally, the first step should always be to run an `ipconfig` command to look at the IP address configured on the system. More often than not, the user will report back that their IP address is "169 dot 254 dot something dot something." The last two somethings don't really matter—it's the first two numbers that should have your attention. It's APIPA.

Knowing that the computer is a DHCP client, you know that it's not connecting to the DHCP server for some reason. After getting to the workstation, check the easy stuff first. Are the cables plugged in (if it's wired)? Are there lights on the NIC? Even if they appear to be plugged in, unplug and reconnect them. If that doesn't work, try a different cable. Those simple steps will solve the vast majority of these types of problems. If not, then it's on to more advanced troubleshooting steps! (More TCP/IP troubleshooting is covered in Chapter 12.)

DNS

DNS has one function on the network: to resolve hostnames to IP addresses. This sounds simple enough, but it has profound implications.

Think about using the Internet. You open your browser, and in the address bar, you type the name of your favorite website, something like www.google.com, and press Enter. The first question your computer asks is, "Who is that?" Your machine requires an IP address to connect to the website. The DNS server provides the answer, "That is 64.233.177.106." Now that your computer knows the address of the website you want, it's able to traverse the Internet to find it.

    Each DNS server has a database where it stores hostname-to-IP-address pairs. If the DNS server does not know the address of the host you are seeking, it has the ability to query other DNS servers to help answer the request.

Think about the implications of that for just a minute. We all probably use Google several times a day, but in all honesty how many of us know its IP address? It's certainly not something we are likely to have memorized. Much less, how could you possibly memorize the IP addresses of all the websites that you regularly visit? Because of DNS, it's easy to find resources. Whether you want to find Coca-Cola, Toyota, Amazon, or thousands of other companies, it's usually pretty easy to figure out how. Type in the name with a .com on the end of it, and you're usually right. The only reason this is successful is because DNS is there to perform resolution of that name to the corresponding IP address.

DNS works the same way on an intranet (a local network not attached to the Internet) as it does on the Internet. The only difference is that instead of helping you find www.google.com, it may help you find Jenny's print server or Joe's file server. From a client-side perspective, all you need to do is configure the host with the address of a legitimate DNS server and you should be good to go.

The DNS Server

If a company wants to host its own website, it also needs to maintain two public DNS servers with information on how to get to the website. (Two servers are required for redundancy.) An advantage of using ISPs or web hosting companies to host the website is that they are then also responsible for managing the DNS servers.

Each DNS server has a database, called a *zone file*, which maintains records of hostname to IP address mappings. Within a zone file, you will see information that looks something like this:

```
mydomain.com. IN   SOA    ns.mydomain.com.     ;Start of Authority record
mydomain.com. IN   NS     ns.mydomain.com.     ;name server for mydomain.com
mydomain.com. IN   MX     mail.mydomain.com.   ;mail server for mydomain.com
mydomain.com. IN   A      192.168.1.25         ;IPv4 address for mydomain.com
              IN   AAAA   2001:db8:19::44      ;IPv6 address for mydomain.com
ns            IN   NS     192.168.1.2          ;IPv4 address for ns.mydomain.com
www           IN   CNAME  mydomain.com.        ;www.mydomain.com is an
                                                           alias for mydomain.com
www2          IN   CNAME  www                  ;www2.mydomain.com is another
                                                           alias for mydomain.com
mail          IN   A      192.168.1.26         ;IPv4 address for
                                                           mail.mydomain.com
```

Five columns of information are presented. From left to right, they are as follows:

- The name of the server or computer, for example, www.
- IN, which means Internet. (There are other options for this field, but for our purposes, we will focus on Internet.)
- The record type. This example has SOA, NS, MX, A, AAAA, and CNAME. Table 6.6 explains some of the common record types.
- The address of the computer.
- Comments, preceded by a semicolon. In a file like this, the computer disregards everything after a semicolon. It's used to make notes for the administrator without affecting functionality.

TABLE 6.6 Common DNS record types

Type	Meaning
SOA	Start of Authority. It signifies the authoritative DNS server for that zone.
NS	Name Server. It's the name or address of the DNS server for that zone.
MX	Mail Exchange. It's the name or address of the email server.
A	IPv4 host record.

(continues)

TABLE 6.6   Common DNS record types *(continued)*

Type	Meaning
AAAA	Called "quad A," it's the host record for IPv6 hosts.
CNAME	Canonical Name. It's an alias; it allows multiple names to be assigned to the same host or address.
TXT	Text record. Used to enter human-readable or machine-readable data. Today, text records are used primarily for email spam prevention and domain ownership verification.

The DNS server uses the zone file whenever a computer makes a query. For example, if you were to ask this DNS server, "Who is mydomain.com?" the response would be 192.168.1.25. If you ask it, "Who is www.mydomain.com?" it would look and see that www is an alias for mydomain.com and provide the same IP address.

If you are the DNS administrator for a network, you will be required to manage the zone file, including entering hostnames and IP addresses, as appropriate.

Spam Management

Email spam is a problem. The only people who don't agree with this are the spammers themselves. One of the tricks that spammers use is to spoof (or fake) the domain name they are sending emails from. DNS, through the use of TXT records, can help email servers determine if incoming messages are from a trusted source rather than a spoofed one.

Three standards used to battle email spam are *Sender Policy Framework (SPF)*, *Domain Keys Identified Mail (DKIM)*, and *Domain-based Message Authentication, Reporting, and Conformance (DMARC)*. Each one can be used in a DNS TXT record to help thwart malicious users from using a company's domain name to send unauthorized emails.

SPF is the simplest of the three. It authenticates an email server based on its IP address. In an SPF TXT record, the administrator specifies all servers that are legitimate email senders for that domain, based on their IP addresses. Note that we're not referring to client computers sending email, but the addresses of the email servers that are legitimate. When a receiving email server gets a message, it sends a query back to the supposed sending server via the sending domain's return-path value, which is found in the email's headers. The sending domain's DNS servers will provide a list of approved senders' IP addresses. If the original sending machine's IP address is on the list, the email is accepted. If not, the email is rejected.

DKIM is a bit more involved, as it authenticates using encryption through a public-private key pair. Each email sent by the server includes a digital signature in the headers, which has been encrypted by the server's private key. When the receiving email server gets the message, it finds the server's registered public key, which is used to decrypt the message. If the key pair is incorrect, the message is flagged as a fake.

DMARC builds on both SPF and DKIM and essentially combines them together into one framework. It's not an authentication method per se—rather, it allows a domain owner to decide how they want email from their domain to be handled if it fails either an SPF or a DKIM authentication. Options include doing nothing (letting the email through), quarantining the email (i.e., sending it to a spam folder), or rejecting the email. In addition, it allows the domain owner to see where emails that claim to come from their domain actually originate from.

> Setting up and configuring the previous three TXT records is beyond the scope of the A+ exam, because it's a relatively advanced DNS management concept. Do know that the three types of records exist, that they help protect against spam email, and the basics of how each one does its job.

DNS on the Internet

The Internet is really big—so big that there's no way one DNS server could possibly manage all of the computer name mappings out there. The creators of DNS anticipated this, and they designed it in a way that reduces potential issues. For example, let's say that you are looking for the website www.wiley.com. When the DNS server that your computer is configured to use is queried for a resolution, it will first check its zone file to see if it knows the IP address. If not, it then checks its cache to see if the record is in there. The cache is a temporary database of recently resolved names and IP addresses. If it still doesn't know the answer, it can query another DNS server asking for help. The first server it will ask is called a *root server*.

If you look back at the sample zone file shown earlier, you might notice that the first few rows contained mydomain.com. (the dot at the end, the "trailing dot," is intentional). The Internet name space is designed as a hierarchical structure, and the dot at the end is the broadest categorization, known as "the root." At the next level of the hierarchy are the top-level domains, such as .com, .net, .edu, .jp, and others. Below that are the second-level domains, like Google, Microsoft, and Yahoo. Below that there are subdomains (which are optional) and hostnames. Moving down, the levels in the hierarchy get more and more specific, until the name represents an exact host. Figure 6.7 shows an example.

FIGURE 6.7   Internet name hierarchy

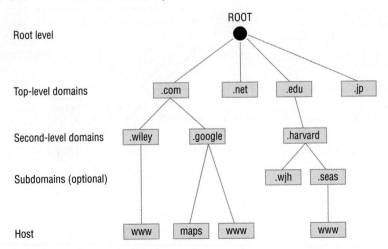

The Dot at the End of the Internet

You've probably used the Internet for quite some time, and you may be thinking, "Where did that trailing dot come from? I've never typed it into my browser." You're right.

As we said, the dot at the end represents the root. Without it, a domain name is not considered a *fully qualified domain name (FQDN)*, fit for Internet use. However, the dot is a convention that's implied when Internet browsers are used; users don't need to type it in. Even though it's omitted, the browser understands that it's technically looking for www.yahoo.com. and not www.yahoo.com with no terminal period. The Internet is an amazing place, isn't it?

There are 13 global root servers. All DNS servers should be configured to ask a root server for help. The root server will return the name of a top-level domain DNS server. The querying DNS server will then ask that server for help. The process continues, as shown in Figure 6.8, until the querying DNS server finds a server that is able to resolve the name www.wiley.com. Then the querying DNS server will cache the resolved name so that subsequent lookups are faster. The length of time that the name is held in cache is configurable by the DNS administrator.

FIGURE 6.8   The DNS name resolution process

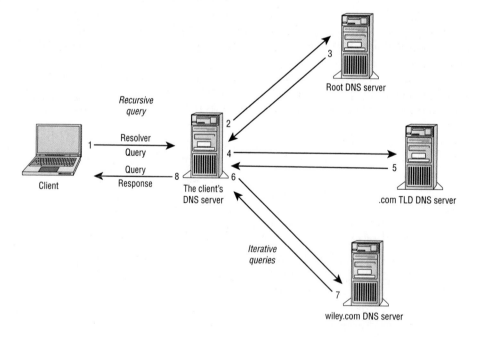

If you're curious, the list of root servers is maintained at `http://www` `.iana.org/domains/root/servers`, among other places.

After looking at Figure 6.8, you might be amazed that the Internet works at all. If nothing else, it should explain why, if you visit a website you've never visited before, it can sometimes take longer than normal to load (provided no one else who uses your DNS server has visited the site recently either). The next time you visit that site, it will probably appear faster, if the name resolution is still held in cache.

Concepts to remember for the A+ exam include the following:

- DNS addresses such as A, AAAA, MX, TXT
- Special TXT addresses DKIM, SPF, and DMARC
- DHCP concepts of leases, reservations, and scope
- The differences between static and dynamic IP addressing
- When and how APIPA is used

IPv6

The present incarnation of TCP/IP that is used on the Internet was originally developed in 1973. Considering how fast technology evolves, it's pretty amazing to think that the protocol still enjoys immense popularity about 50 years later. This version is known as *IPv4*.

There are a few problems with IPv4, though. One is that we're quickly running out of available network addresses, and the other is that TCP/IP can be somewhat tricky to configure.

If you've dealt with configuring custom subnet masks, you may nod your head at the configuration part, but you might be wondering how we can run out of addresses. After all, IPv4 has 32 bits of addressing space, which allows for nearly 4.3 billion addresses! With the way it's structured, only about 250 million of those addresses are actually usable, and all of those are pretty much spoken for.

A new version of TCP/IP has been developed, called *IPv6*. Instead of a 32-bit address, it provides for 128-bit addresses. That provides for 3.4×10^{38} addresses, which theoretically should be more than enough that they will never run out globally. (Famous last words, right?)

IPv6 also has many standard features that are optional (but useful) in IPv4. While the addresses may be more difficult to remember, the automatic configuration and enhanced flexibility make the new version sparkle compared to the old one. Best of all, it's backward compatible with and can run on the computer at the same time as IPv4, so networks can migrate to IPv6 without a complete restructure.

Understanding IPv6 Addressing

Understanding the IPv6 addressing scheme is probably the most challenging part of the protocol enhancement. The first thing you'll notice is that, of course, the address space is longer. The second is that IPv6 uses hexadecimal notation instead of the familiar dotted decimal of IPv4. Its 128-bit address structure looks something like what is shown in Figure 6.9.

FIGURE 6.9   IPv6 address

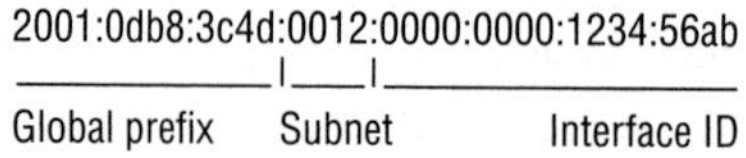

```
2001:0db8:3c4d:0012:0000:0000:1234:56ab
_____|___|_____
Global prefix    Subnet        Interface ID
```

The new address is composed of eight 16-bit fields, each represented by four hexadecimal digits and separated by colons. The letters in an IPv6 address are not case sensitive. IPv6 uses three types of addresses: *unicast*, *anycast*, and *multicast*. A unicast address identifies a single node on the network. An anycast address refers to one that has been assigned to multiple nodes. A packet addressed to an anycast address will be delivered to the closest node. Sometimes you will hear this referred to as one-to-nearest addressing. Finally, a multicast address is one used by multiple hosts, and is used to communicate to groups of computers. IPv6 does not employ broadcast addresses. Multicasts handle that functionality. Each network interface can be assigned one or more addresses.

Just by looking at unicast and anycast addresses, it's impossible to tell the difference between them. Their structure is the same; it's their functionality that's different. The first four fields, or 64 bits, refer to the network and subnetwork. The last four fields are the interface ID, which is analogous to the host portion of the IPv4 address. Typically, the first 56 bits within the address are the routing (or global) prefix, and the next 8 bits refer to the subnet ID. It's also possible to have shorter routing prefixes, though, such as 48 bits, meaning that the subnet ID will be longer.

The Interface ID portion of the address can be created in one of four ways. It can be created automatically using the interface's MAC address, procured from a DHCPv6 server, assigned randomly, or configured manually.

Multicast addresses can take different forms. All multicast addresses use the first 8 bits as the prefix.

Working with IPv6 Addresses

In IPv4, the subnet mask determines the length of the network portion of the address. The network address was often written in an abbreviated form, such as 169.254.0.0/16. The /16 indicates that the first 16 bits are for the network portion and that corresponds to a subnet mask of 255.255.0.0. While IPv6 doesn't use a subnet mask, the same convention for stating the network length holds true. An IPv6 network address could be written as 2001:db8:3c4d::/48. The number after the slash indicates how many bits are in the routing prefix.

Because the addresses are quite long, there are a few ways that you can write them in shorthand; in the world of IPv6, it's all about eliminating extra zeroes. For example, take the address 2001:0db8:3c4d:0012:0000:0000:1234:56ab. The first common way to shorten it is to remove all of the leading zeroes. Thus it could also be written as 2001:db8:3c4d:12:0:0:1234:56ab. The second accepted shortcut is to replace consecutive groups of zeroes with a double colon. So now the example address becomes 2001:db8:3c4d:12::1234:56ab. It's still long, but not quite as long as the original address.

> The double-colon shortcut can be used only once in an address. For example, in the 2001:db8:3c4d:12::1234:56ab address, you can count the number of fields (six) and know that the double colon represents two fields of all zeroes. If, for example, you tried to write an address like 2001::1ab4::5468, you would have a big problem. You would know that there are five fields of zeroes, but you would have no way to identify where exactly the 1ab4 portion of the address falls in relation to the all-zero fields.

A fairly common occurrence today is a mixed IPv4-IPv6 network. As mentioned earlier, IPv6 is backward compatible. In the address space, this is accomplished by setting the first 80 bits to 0, the next 16 bits to 1, and the final 32 bits to the IPv4 address. In IPv6 format, the IPv4 address looks something like ::ffff:c0a8:173. You will often see the same address written as ::ffff:192.168.1.115 to enable easy identification of the IPv4 address.

There are a few more addresses you need to be familiar with. In IPv4, the autoconfiguration (APIPA) address range was 169.254.0.0/16. IPv6 accomplishes the same task with the *link local* address fe80::/10. Every IPv6-enabled interface is required to have a link local address, and they are nonroutable. The IPv4 loopback address of 127.0.0.1 has been replaced with ::1/128 (typically written as just ::1). Global addresses (for Internet use) are 2000::/3, and multicast addresses are FF00::/8. Figure 6.10 shows the output of an ipconfig command, and you can see the IPv4 address configuration as well as the IPv6 link local address. Table 6.7 summarizes the IPv6 address ranges you should be familiar with.

TABLE 6.7   IPv6 address ranges

Address	Use
0:0:0:0:0:0:0:0	Equals ::, and is equivalent to 0.0.0.0 in IPv4. It usually means that the host is not configured.
0:0:0:0:0:0:0:1	Also written as ::1. Equivalent to the loopback address of 127.0.0.1 in IPv4.
2000::/3	Global unicast address range for use on the Internet.
FC00::/7	Unique local unicast address range.
FE80::/10	Link local unicast range.
FF00::/8	Multicast range.

FIGURE 6.10   `ipconfig` output with IPv4 and IPv6 addresses

```
Command Prompt                                                    —    □    ×

C:\>ipconfig

Windows IP Configuration


Ethernet adapter Ethernet:

   Media State . . . . . . . . . . : Media disconnected
   Connection-specific DNS Suffix  . :

Wireless LAN adapter Local Area Connection* 9:

   Media State . . . . . . . . . . : Media disconnected
   Connection-specific DNS Suffix  . :

Wireless LAN adapter Wi-Fi:

   Connection-specific DNS Suffix  . : Home
   Link-local IPv6 Address . . . . . : fe80::3c06:76ff:c44:7e24%6
   IPv4 Address. . . . . . . . . . . : 192.168.1.142
   Subnet Mask . . . . . . . . . . . : 255.255.255.0
   Default Gateway . . . . . . . . . : 192.168.1.1
```

Remember that IPv6 is an exam objective. CompTIA doesn't provide any details under IPv6, but be able to recognize some basic IPv6 addresses. Also know the differences between unicast, multicast, anycast, and link local addresses.

Understanding Virtual Networks

As you learned earlier in this chapter, the subnet mask on an IPv4 network determines the network address. Said differently, it's the mechanism by which networks are defined. Computers configured to be on different networks talk to each other through a router, which sends packets from one network to another. Therefore, the router is the physical device that divides logical networks from each other. In addition to physical and logical networks, one additional term you need to be familiar with is the virtual network. There are two types of virtual networks we'll cover here: virtual local area networks and virtual private networks.

Virtual Local Area Networks

One of the limitations of typical routed network configurations is that computers on the same side of the router can't easily be broken into multiple networks and still communicate with each other. This is because if a sending computer knows that the destination IP address is on another network, it sends its data directly to the router—its default gateway. Other computers on the physical segment will ignore the message because it's not addressed to them. The router then takes a look at the real destination address and sends it out one of its ports, other than the one it came in on, to reach the destination network.

The *virtual local area network (VLAN)* is designed to help segment physical networks into multiple logical (virtual) networks. You may recall from Chapter 5 that VLANs are created by using a managed switch. The switch uses *Spanning Tree Protocol (STP)* to manage configurations and to ensure that there are no infinite network loops. (That's when data gets sent out and bounces between two or more switches, never getting to a destination. Loops are bad.) A VLAN can provide the following benefits:

Broadcast traffic is reduced.   Physical network segments can be logically subdivided, reducing broadcast traffic and speeding network performance.

Security is increased.   Computers on the same physical network can be isolated from each other to provide an additional layer of security. For example, imagine that the Research and Development team is working on several secret projects. R&D computers can be placed on one virtual segment, and the rest of the company on others. Traffic to and from other R&D computers won't be intermingled with other office traffic.

Computers in multiple locations can belong to the same VLAN.   This is one major thing that routers can't do with subnetting. With multiple switches configured appropriately, computers at different physical locations can be configured to be on the same VLAN.

Reconfiguring networks is easier.   With VLANs, if someone moves physical desk locations, their VLAN membership can carry with them, so there is less network reconfiguration needed. Similarly, if someone doesn't move desk locations but changes jobs, they can be assigned to a new VLAN without needing to physically reconfigure the network.

Figure 6.11 shows two potential VLAN configurations. In the first one, computers on one switch are assigned to different VLANs. In the second, the concept is extended to include multiple switches.

One of the questions often asked is, "What's the difference between a VLAN and a subnet?" First, let's look at the key similarity—both are capable of breaking up broadcast domains on a network, which helps reduce network traffic. Also, if you are using both, the recommended configuration is that subnets and VLANs have a 1:1 relationship, one subnet per VLAN. You can configure multiple subnets to be on one VLAN—it's called a *super scope*—but it gets trickier to manage.

Beyond separating broadcast domains, VLANs and subnets are almost entirely different. Recall that VLANs are implemented on switches, and routers are needed to subnet. Consequently, VLANs work at Layer 2 of the OSI model and deal with physical MAC addresses. Routers work at Layer 3, and work with logical IP addresses.

FIGURE 6.11   Two VLAN configurations

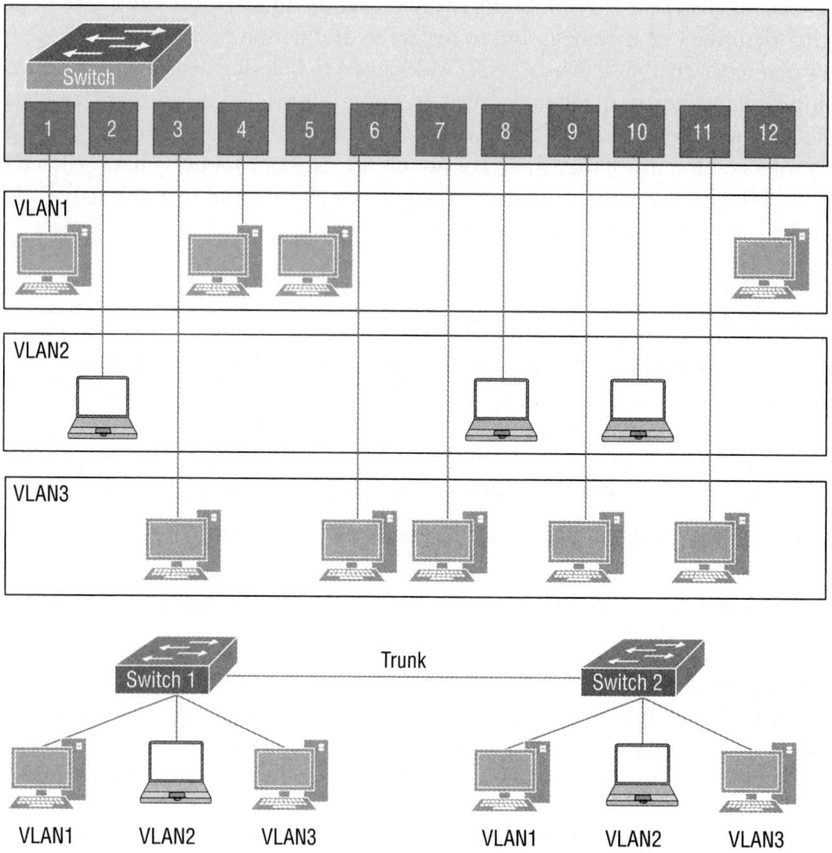

Virtual Private Networks

As networks grow beyond simple physical limitations (such as an office or a building) to include clients from all over the world, the need to secure data across public connections becomes paramount. One of the best methods of addressing this is to tunnel the data. Tunneling sends private data across a public network by placing (encapsulating) that data into other packets. Most tunnels are a *virtual private network (VPN)*. A sample VPN is shown in Figure 6.12.

A VPN is a secure (private) network connection that occurs through a public network. The private network provides security over an otherwise unsecure environment. VPNs can be used to connect LANs together across the Internet or other public networks, or they can be used to connect individual users to a corporate network. This is a great option for users who work from home or travel for work. With a VPN, the remote end appears to be connected to the network as if it were connected locally. From the server side, a VPN requires dedicated hardware or a software package running on a server or router. Clients use specialized VPN client software to connect, most often over a broadband Internet link. Windows 10 comes with its own VPN client software (shown in Figure 6.13) accessible through Start ➤ Settings ➤ Network & Internet ➤ VPN, as do some other operating systems, and many third-party options are also available.

FIGURE 6.12   A VPN

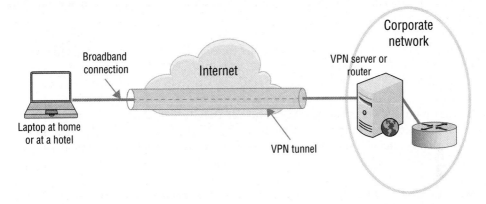

FIGURE 6.13   Windows 10 VPN client

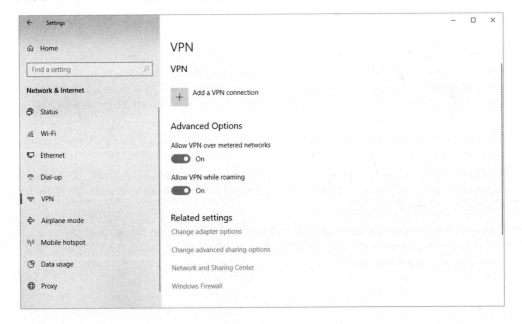

For the A+ exam, be able to describe, compare, and contrast VLANs and VPNs and when each would be used.

Summary

In this chapter, you learned about the protocol suite used on the Internet, TCP/IP. It's by far the most common protocol in worldwide use today. We started with TCP/IP structure. It's a modular suite that follows the DoD model, with different protocols performing unique tasks at each layer. We looked at individual protocols and their functions at the Internet, Host-to-host, and Process/Application layers. We also discussed ports and well-known port numbers for common protocols.

Next you learned about IP addressing. We started with a brief tutorial on converting binary numbers to decimal to make them easier to read. Then we looked at the different address classes, CIDR, public versus private IP addresses, and NAT. Then we followed with details on DHCP, APIPA, and DNS. Each of these services and concepts plays a unique role in managing TCP/IP on your network.

Next, you learned about the next generation of TCP/IP, IPv6. We talked about the seemingly infinite number of addresses as well as the fact that addresses are written in hexadecimal, which might take some getting used to—even for experienced technicians. Finally, we looked at working with IPv6 addresses, including shorthand notation and special addresses to be aware of.

We finished the chapter by looking at two types of virtual networks: VLANs and VPNs.

Exam Essentials

Understand how IPv4 addressing works.   IP addresses are 32-bit addresses written as four octets in dotted-decimal notation, such as 192.168.5.18. To communicate on an IP network, a host also needs a subnet mask, which may look something like 255.255.255.0. If the host needs to communicate outside the local network, it also needs a default gateway, which is normally the internal address of the router.

Addresses can be static (manual) or dynamic (from a DHCP server). If a DHCP server is not available, a network client may use an APIPA address starting with 169.254.

Be able to identify IP address classes.   Know how to identify Class A, B, and C IP addresses. Class A addresses will have a first octet in the 1 to 126 range. B is from 128 to 191, and C is from 192 to 223.

Understand the differences between TCP and UDP.   TCP is a connection-based protocol that attempts to guarantee delivery. UDP is connectionless, which makes it a bit faster, but it doesn't guarantee packet delivery.

Know common TCP/IP ports.   Some common protocol and port pairings that you should know are FTP (20 and 21), SSH (22), Telnet (23), SMTP (25), DNS (53), DHCP (67, 68), TFTP (69), HTTP (80), POP3 (110), NetBIOS/NetBT (137, 139), IMAP (143), SNMP (161, 162), LDAP (389), HTTPS (443), SMB/CIFS (445), and RDP (3389).

Know the private IP address ranges.   Private IP addresses will be in one of three ranges: 10.0.0.0/8, 172.16.0.0/12, or 192.168.0.0/16.

Know what NAT does.   Network Address Translation (NAT) translates private, non-routable IP addresses into public IP addresses. It allows computers on a private network to access the Internet.

Know what DHCP does.   A DHCP server provides IP addresses and configuration information to network hosts. The configuration is provided as a lease, and all lease information is configured in a scope on the DHCP server. Clients that need to have the same address at all times can be configured using a reservation, which grants an address based on a MAC address.

Know about the APIPA range.   IP addresses in the 169.254.0.0/16 range are APIPA addresses.

Know what DNS does.   A DNS server resolves hostnames to IP addresses.

Be familiar with common DNS address classes.   Addresses include A (for IPv4) and AAAA (IPv6), MX (mail exchange), and TXT (text). Special TXT addresses to help combat spam are DKIM, SPF, and DMARC.

Understand how IPv6 addressing works.   IPv6 addresses are 128-bit addresses written as eight fields of four hexadecimal characters, such as 2001:0db8:3c4d:0012:0000:0000:1234:56ab. Using shorthand conventions, this address can also be written as 2001:db8:3c4d:12::1234:56ab.

Addresses can be static or dynamic. APIPA does not exist in IPv6 but has been replaced by a link local address.

Know the difference between unicast, anycast, and multicast in IPv6.   Unicast addresses are for a single node on the network. Anycast can represent a small group of systems. An anycast message will be delivered to the closest node. Multicast messages are delivered to all computers within a group.

Recognize the special classes of IPv6 addresses.   The loopback address is ::1. Global unicast addresses are in the 2000::/3 range. Unique local unicast addresses are in the FC00::/7 range, link local addresses are FE80::/10, and FF00::/8 addresses are multicast.

Understand the differences between a VLAN and a VPN.   A virtual local area network (VLAN) is a logical network configured through a managed switch. A virtual private network (VPN) is a secure point-to-point connection over a public network.

Review Questions

The answers to the chapter review questions can be found in Appendix A.

1. You have just set up a network that will use the TCP/IP protocol, and you want client computers to obtain IP configuration information automatically. Which type of server do you need for this?

    A. DNS

    B. DHCP

    C. NAT

    D. IP configuration server

2. Which of the following protocols was designed to access information stored in an information directory, such as employee phone books?

    A. FTP

    B. LDAP

    C. RDP

    D. CIFS

3. Which TCP/IP protocol uses port 80?

    A. HTTP

    B. HTTPS

    C. Telnet

    D. POP3

4. What is the maximum number of IPv6 addresses that can be assigned to one IPv6 interface?

    A. One (unicast)

    B. Two (unicast and anycast)

    C. Three (unicast, anycast, and multicast)

    D. None of the above

5. Which of the following are valid examples of IPv6 addresses? (Choose all that apply.)

    A. 2001:0db8:3c4d:0012:0000:0000:1234:56ab

    B. ::ffff:c0a8:173

    C. 2001:db8:3c4d:12::1234:56ab

    D. 2001::1ab4::5468

6. Which of the following IP addresses would not be valid for a DNS server on the Internet?

    A. 10.25.11.33

    B. 18.33.66.254

    C. 155.118.63.11

    D. 192.186.12.2

7. The workstations on your network are configured to use a DHCP server. One of the workstations can't communicate with other computers. Its IP address is 169.254.1.18. What could be the problem?

   A. The subnet mask is wrong.

   B. It has a private IP address.

   C. The default gateway is wrong.

   D. It can't reach the DHCP server.

8. Which of the following protocols is responsible for sending email?

   A. IMAP4

   B. POP3

   C. SMTP

   D. SNMP

9. What port does the RDP protocol work on?

   A. 53

   B. 143

   C. 389

   D. 3389

10. An email administrator wants to help protect against their server being spoofed to send spam. They were told that they can do this with a TXT record in their DNS server. If they want to authenticate emails using an encrypted security key, which TXT record would be most appropriate?

    A. DMARC

    B. VLAN

    C. SPF

    D. DKIM

11. What are advantages that TCP has over UDP? (Choose two.)

    A. Acknowledged delivery

    B. Faster delivery

    C. Lower overhead

    D. Virtual circuits

12. Your friend is concerned about the security of making an online purchase. What should you tell them to look for in the address bar of the web browser?

    A. HTTP

    B. HTTPS

    C. SSH

    D. TLS

13. You are manually configuring a TCP/IP host. Another administrator gives you the router's IP address. What is the TCP/IP term for this?

   A. Default gateway

   B. Subnet mask

   C. DNS server

   D. DHCP server

14. Your network is running IPv4. Which of the configuration options are mandatory for your host to communicate on the network? (Choose two.)

   A. IP address

   B. Subnet mask

   C. Default gateway

   D. DNS server address

15. Which of the following protocols is used for secure retrieval of email?

   A. SMTP

   B. SNMP

   C. POP3

   D. IMAP4

16. Which of the following is the name of a secure point-to-point connection made over a public network?

   A. NAT

   B. APIPA

   C. VLAN

   D. VPN

17. Which network protocol is used for administration of networking devices such as routers and switches, and which port(s) does it use?

   A. SNMP, 161 and 162

   B. SNMP, 25

   C. SMTP, 25

   D. SMTP, 161 and 162

18. Which of the following is an IPv6 broadcast address?

   A. ::1

   B. FE80::

   C. FF00::

   D. ::FFFF

   E. None of the above

19. You are setting up a small network that will not connect to the Internet. You want computers to be able to locate each other by using hostnames. What service will do this?

   A. DNS

   B. DHCP

   C. FTP

   D. APIPA

20. Which of the following protocols is responsible for resolving IP addresses to hardware addresses?

   A. DNS

   B. DHCP

   C. ARP

   D. RARP

Performance-Based Question

You will encounter performance-based questions on the A+ exams. The questions on the exam require you to perform a specific task, and you will be graded on whether or not you were able to complete the task. The following requires you to think creatively in order to measure how well you understand this chapter's topics. You may or may not see similar questions on the actual A+ exams. To see how your answers compare to the authors', refer to Appendix B.

Match the following protocols (services) below to their respective ports in the table:

SMTP, FTP, TFTP, RDP, Telnet, LDAP, DHCP, HTTPS, IMAP, NetBIOS/NetBT, POP3, DNS, SNMP, HTTP, SMB/CIFS, SSH

Protocol (service)	Port(s)
	20, 21
	22
	23
	25
	53
	67, 68
	69
	80
	110
	137–139
	143
	161, 162
	389
	443
	445
	3389

Chapter

7

Wireless and SOHO Networks

THE FOLLOWING COMPTIA A+ 220-1101 EXAM OBJECTIVES ARE COVERED IN THIS CHAPTER:

✓ **2.3 Compare and contrast protocols for wireless networking.**

- Frequencies
  - 2.4GHz
  - 5GHz
- Channels
  - Regulations
  - 2.4GHz vs. 5GHz
- Bluetooth
- 802.11
  - a
  - b
  - g
  - n
  - ac (WiFi 5)
  - ax (WiFi 6)
- Long-range fixed wireless
  - Licensed
  - Unlicensed
  - Power
  - Regulatory requirements for wireless power
- NFC
- Radio-frequency identification (RFID)

✓ **2.5 Given a scenario, install and configure basic wired/wireless small office/home office (SOHO) networks.**

- Internet Protocol (IP) addressing
  - IPv4
    - Private addresses
    - Public addresses
  - IPv6
  - Automatic Private IP Addressing (APIPA)
  - Static
  - Dynamic
  - Gateway

✓ **2.7 Compare and contrast Internet connection types, network types, and their features.**

- Internet connection types
  - Satellite
  - Fiber
  - Cable
  - DSL
  - Cellular
  - Wireless Internet service provider (WISP)

Over the last two chapters, we've talked a lot about foundational networking knowledge. We've discussed theoretical networking models, physical topologies, cables and connectors, and connectivity devices. We also spent an entire chapter devoted to the most common protocol of all, TCP/IP. The one critical technology that we haven't covered yet is wireless networking.

Because of the unique technology of wireless networking and its huge popularity, it feels appropriate to talk about it as a separate entity. That said, it's important to remember that wireless networking is just like wired networking, only without the wires. You still need to figure out how to get resources connected to each other and give the right people access while keeping the bad people at bay. You're now just playing the game with slightly different rules and many new challenges.

We'll start this chapter with the last of our key networking "theory" discussions, this time on the categories of wireless networking standards. From there, we'll move on to picking out an Internet connection type and setting up and configuring small networks. This is really where the rubber meets the road. Understanding the theory and technical specifications of networking is fine, but the true value in all this knowledge comes in being able to make good recommendations and implement the right network for your client's needs.

Understanding Wireless Networking Technologies

Wireless networking is so common today that it's taken for granted. When first introduced, wireless networking was slow and unreliable, but it's now fast and pretty stable, not to mention convenient. It seems like everywhere you go there are Internet cafes or fast-food restaurants with wireless hotspots. Nearly every mobile device sold today has Internet capabilities. No matter where you go, you're likely just seconds away from being connected to the Internet.

The most common term you'll hear thrown around referring to wireless networking today is *Wi-Fi*. While the term was originally coined as a marketing name for 802.11b, it's now used as a nickname referring to the family of IEEE 802.11 standards. That family comprises the primary wireless networking technology in use today, but other wireless technologies are out there, too. We'll break down wireless technologies into four groups: 802.11, Bluetooth, long-range fixed wireless, and radio frequency. Each technology has its strengths and weaknesses and fills a computing role.

As a technician, it will fall to you to provide users with access to networks, the Internet, and other wireless resources. You must make sure that their computers and mobile devices can connect, that users can get their email, and that downtime is something that resides only in history books. To be able to make that a reality, you must understand as much as you can about wireless networking and the technologies discussed in the following sections.

802.11 Networking Standards

In the United States, wireless LAN (WLAN) standards are created and managed by the Institute of Electrical and Electronics Engineers (IEEE). The most commonly used WLAN standards are in the IEEE 802.11 family. Eventually, 802.11 will likely be made obsolete by newer standards, but that is some time off. IEEE 802.11 was ratified in 1997 and was the first standardized WLAN implementation. There are over 20 802.11 standards defined, but you will only hear a few commonly mentioned: 802.11a, b, g, n, ac, and ax. As previously mentioned, several wireless technologies are on the market, but 802.11 is the one currently best suited for WLANs.

In concept, an 802.11 network is similar to an Ethernet network, only wireless. At the center an Ethernet network is a connectivity device, such as a hub, switch, or router, and all computers are connected to it. Wireless networks are configured in a similar fashion, except that they use a wireless router or wireless access point instead of a wired connectivity device. In order to connect to the wireless hub or router, the client needs to know the *service-set identifier (SSID)* of the network. SSID is a fancy term for the wireless network's name. Wireless access points may connect to other wireless access points, but eventually they connect back to a wired connection with the rest of the network.

802.11 networks use the *Carrier Sense Multiple Access/Collision Avoidance (CSMA/CA)* access method instead of Ethernet's Carrier Sense Multiple Access/Collision Detection (CSMA/CD). Packet collisions are generally avoided, but when they do happen, the sender will need to wait a random period of time (called a *back-off time*) before transmitting again.

Since the original 802.11 standard's publication in 1997, several upgrades and extensions have been released. The primary characteristics that define them are speed, maximum distance, frequency (which includes channels), and modulation technique.

Speed and distance are networking concepts that you should be familiar with. *Frequency* is the audio range in which the technology broadcasts—fortunately the waves are far outside of the range of human hearing. *Channels*, which we will cover in more depth later, are subdivisions within a frequency. Finally, there is *modulation*, which refers to how the computer converts digital information into signals that can be transmitted over the air. There are three types of wireless modulation used today:

Frequency-Hopping Spread Spectrum   *Frequency-hopping spread spectrum (FHSS)* accomplishes communication by hopping the transmission over a range of predefined frequencies. The changing, or hopping, is synchronized between both ends and appears to be a single transmission channel to both ends.

Direct-Sequence Spread Spectrum   *Direct-sequence spread spectrum (DSSS)* accomplishes communication by adding the data that is to be transmitted to a higher-speed transmission. The higher-speed transmission contains redundant information to ensure data accuracy. Each packet can then be reconstructed in the event of a disruption.

Orthogonal Frequency Division Multiplexing   *Orthogonal frequency division multiplexing (OFDM)* accomplishes communication by breaking the data into subsignals and transmitting them simultaneously. These transmissions occur on different frequencies, or subbands.

The mathematics and theories of these transmission technologies are beyond the scope of this book and far beyond the scope of this exam. We bring them up because as we talk about different Wi-Fi standards, we might note that they use such-and-such modulation. Knowing the basics of how they are different helps you understand why those standards are not compatible with each other. If the sending system is using FHSS and the receiving system is expecting DSSS (or OFDM), they won't be able to talk to each other. With that, let's dive into each of the 802.11 standards you need to know.

802.11

The original *802.11* standard was ratified in 1997 and defines WLANs transmitting at 1 Mbps or 2 Mbps bandwidths using the 2.4 GHz frequency spectrum. The frequency-hopping spread spectrum (FHSS) and direct-sequence spread spectrum (DSSS) modulation techniques for data encoding were included in this standard.

There were never any 802.11 (with no letter after the 11) devices released—it's a standards framework. All in-market versions of 802.11 have a letter after their name to designate the technology.

802.11a

The *802.11a* standard provides WLAN bandwidth of up to 54 Mbps in the 5 GHz frequency spectrum. The 802.11a standard also uses a more efficient encoding system, orthogonal frequency division multiplexing (OFDM), rather than FHSS or DSSS.

This standard was ratified in 1999, but devices didn't hit the market until 2001. Thanks to its encoding system, it was significantly faster than 802.11b (discussed next) but never gained widespread popularity. They were ratified as standards right around the same time, but 802.11b devices beat it to market and were significantly cheaper. It would be shocking to see an 802.11a device in use today.

802.11b

The *802.11b* standard was ratified in 1999 as well, but device makers were much quicker to market, making this the de facto wireless networking standard for several years. 802.11b provides for bandwidths of up to 11 Mbps (with fallback rates of 5.5, 2, and 1 Mbps) in the 2.4 GHz range. The 802.11b standard uses DSSS for data encoding. You may occasionally still see 802.11b devices in use, but they are becoming rare. If you encounter them, encourage the users to upgrade to something faster. They will appreciate the increase in speed!

The 802.11b and 802.11a standards are incompatible for two reasons: frequency and modulation. 802.11b operates in the 2.4 GHz frequency and uses DSSS. 802.11a runs at 5 GHz and uses OFDM.

802.11g

Ratified in 2003, the *802.11g* standard provides for bandwidths of 54 Mbps in the 2.4 GHz frequency spectrum using OFDM or DSSS encoding. Because it operates in the same frequency and can use the same modulation as 802.11b, the two standards are compatible. Because of the backward compatibility and speed upgrades, 802.11g replaced 802.11b as the industry standard for several years, and it is still somewhat common today.

Devices that can operate with both 802.11b and 802.11g standards are labeled as *802.11b/g*.

As we mentioned, 802.11g devices are backward compatible with 802.11b devices, and both can be used on the same network. That was initially a huge selling point for 802.11g hardware and helped it gain popularity very quickly. However, there are some interoperability concerns of which you should be aware. 802.11b devices are not capable of understanding OFDM transmissions; therefore, they are not able to tell when the 802.11g access point is free or busy. To counteract this problem, when an 802.11b device is associated with an 802.11g access point, the access point reverts back to DSSS modulation to provide backward compatibility. This means that all devices connected to that access point will run at a maximum of 11 Mbps. To optimize performance, administrators would upgrade to all 802.11g devices and configure the access point to be G-only.

Today, both 802.11b and 802.11g are considered legacy devices. So to really optimize performance for today's bandwidth-hungry devices, replace all legacy wireless devices (anything older than 802.11n) with 802.11ac or 802.11ax devices.

One additional concept to know about when working with 2.4 GHz wireless networking is channels. We've said before that 802.11b/g works in the 2.4 GHz range. Within this range, the Federal Communications Commission (FCC) has defined 14 different 22 MHz communication channels. This is analogous to a 14-lane audio wave highway, with each lane being 22 MHz wide. An illustration of this is shown in Figure 7.1.

FIGURE 7.1   2.4 GHz communication channels

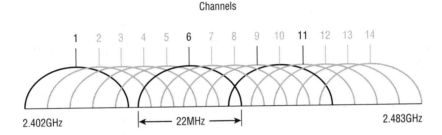

Although 14 channels have been defined for use in the United States, you're allowed to configure your wireless networking devices only to the first 11. When you install a wireless access point and wireless NICs, they will all auto-configure their channel, and this will probably work okay for you. If you are experiencing interference, changing the channel might help. And if you have multiple overlapping wireless access points, you will need to have nonoverlapping channels to avoid communications problems. (We'll talk about this more in the "Installing and Configuring SOHO Networks" section later in this chapter.) Two channels will not overlap if there are four channels between them. If you need to use three nonoverlapping channels, your only choices are 1, 6, and 11. Notice in Figure 7.1 that those three channels are highlighted.

There are many other commercial devices that transmit at the frequencies at which 802.11 operates, which can result in a lot of interference. Older Bluetooth devices, cordless phones, cell phones, other WLANs, and microwave ovens can all create interference problems for 802.11 networks, particularly in the 2.4 GHz range.

802.11n

Continuing the evolution in Wi-Fi is *802.11n*, which was ratified in 2010. The standard claims to support bandwidth up to 600 Mbps, but in reality the typical throughput is about 300–450 Mbps. That's still pretty fast. It works in both the 2.4 GHz and 5 GHz ranges.

802.11n achieves faster throughput in a couple of ways. Some of the enhancements include the use of wider 40 MHz channels, multiple-input multiple-output (MIMO), and channel bonding. Remember how 802.11g uses 22 MHz channels? 802.11n combines two channels to double (basically) the throughput. Imagine being able to take two garden hoses and combine them into one bigger hose. That's kind of what channel bonding does. MIMO means using multiple antennas rather than a single antenna to communicate information. (802.11n devices can support up to eight antennas, or four streams, because each antenna only sends or receives.) Channel bonding also allows the device to communicate simultaneously at 2.4G Hz and 5 GHz and bond the data streams, which increases throughput.

One big advantage of 802.11n is that it is backward compatible with 802.11a/b/g. This is because 802.11n is capable of simultaneously servicing 802.11b/g/n clients operating in the 2.4 GHz range as well as 802.11a/n clients operating in the 5 GHz range.

Not As Much Freedom As You Might Think

In the 5 GHz spectrum, there are 25 nonoverlapping 20 MHz communications channels, 24 of which can be used for Wi-Fi networks. On the surface, this sounds much better than the three non-overlapping channels available in the 2.4 GHz spectrum.

To increase throughput, 802.11n (and 802.11ac, discussed in the next section) bond channels together. When 20 MHz channels are bonded into 40 MHz channels, this reduces the number of nonoverlapping channels to 12. To complicate matters further, weather, commercial, and military radar operate in the 5 GHz range as well, and Wi-Fi needs to avoid conflicting with them.

To avoid conflicts, wireless routers use a technology named *dynamic frequency selection (DFS)*, which will detect radar interference and dynamically adjust to a different frequency range to avoid the problem. If your installation is in an area that does not receive interference from radar signals, you will have 12 nonoverlapping 40 MHz channels; otherwise, only four nonoverlapping, non-DFS 40 MHz channels remain available for bonding.

If you're curious (and it's highly unlikely that you will be tested on this), the four nonoverlapping, non-DFS 40 MHz channels are numbered 36 and 40, 44 and 48, 149 and 153, and 157 and 161. We explain this a bit more in the section on 802.11ac, and Figure 7.2 illustrates what we just discussed.

FIGURE 7.2 Channel availability in the 5 GHz spectrum

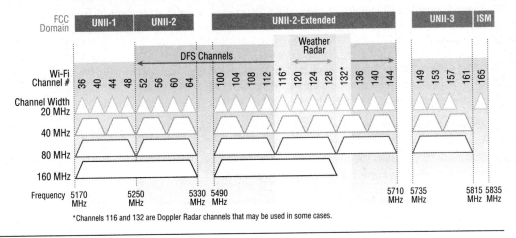

*Channels 116 and 132 are Doppler Radar channels that may be used in some cases.

802.11ac

Technology is always marching forward and getting faster and cheaper, and wireless networking is no different. In January 2014, *802.11ac* was approved, and you will often see it marketed as Wi-Fi 5. In many ways, it's a more powerful version of 802.11n in that it carries over many of the same features while adding in only a few new ones. It's the first commercial wireless standard that claims to offer the speed of Gigabit Ethernet.

802.11n introduced channel bonding and MIMO, and 802.11ac takes those concepts further. Instead of bonding two channels, 802.11ac can bond up to eight for a 160 MHz bandwidth. This results in a 333-percent speed increase. And 802.11ac greatly enhances MIMO. First, it doubles the MIMO capabilities of 802.11n to eight streams, resulting in another 100 percent speed increase. Second, it introduces multi-user MIMO (MU-MIMO) for up to four clients. MU-MIMO allows multiple users to use multiple antennae for communication simultaneously, whereas MIMO only allowed for one such connection at a time on a device.

The theoretical maximum speed of 802.11ac is 6.9 Gbps, but most 802.11ac devices peak at about 1.3 Gbps. Common maximum throughput is just under Gigabit Ethernet speeds, at around 800 Mbps. You might see devices in the marketplace that claim to offer speeds over 2 Gbps, but the reality is that you're unlikely to get those speeds in anything less than pristine, laboratory-like conditions with all top-of-the-line hardware. In other words, it's fast, but don't count on it being *that* fast.

Back to DFS

Remember that Wi-Fi installations using the 5 GHz range need to steer clear of radar signals to avoid conflicts. Radar for airplanes and weather stations has priority over your Wi-Fi network. (Sorry!)

802.11ac obtains its fast performance mostly through channel bonding. If you will recall, 802.11n can bond 20 MHz channels into 40 MHz channels, whereas 802.11ac can take the same channels and bond them further into either 80 MHz or 160 MHz channels.

Ignoring DFS for a moment, a maximum of six nonoverlapping 80 MHz channels and two nonoverlapping 160 MHz channels are available in the 5 GHz spectrum. You can't ignore DFS, though, and it takes the maximum number of nonoverlapping 80 MHz channels down to two and eliminates any possible 160 MHz channels.

Why is this important to know? Well, mostly because it explains why you're probably not going to get gigabit speeds out of 802.11ac. And for companies or other organizations that want to upgrade to 802.11ac, there are only two nonoverlapping channels to use at 80 MHz. This makes it difficult (if not impossible) to deploy in anything other than a relatively small office. The other option is to use 40 MHz channels just like 802.11n, but then the performance boost of 802.11ac is small and not likely to justify the higher cost of equipment. Figure 7.2 illustrates the available channels in the 5 GHz frequency. The channels in the UNII-1 and UNII-3 are the ones that are completely available for Wi-Fi network use. UNII-2 and UNII-2 Extended channels are the DFS ones. (UNII stands for Unlicensed National Information Infrastructure and is sometimes abbreviated as U-NII.)

The most important new feature of 802.11ac is *beamforming*, which can allow for range increases by sending the wireless signal in the specific direction of the client, as opposed to broadcasting it omnidirectionally. Beamforming helps overcome the fact that the range for a 5 GHz signal is inherently shorter than one for a 2.4 GHz signal. Not all 802.11ac routers support beamforming, however, so you might have some range limitations, depending on your hardware. And even if the router does support the technology, the maximum distance still won't be any more than what you will get out of 802.11n.

802.11ax

The newest version of Wi-Fi was released in 2019 and is known as Wi-Fi 6. The technical specification is *802.11ax*. It gives network users what they crave—more speed. It also allows for more simultaneous users of any given access point, which is a big bonus as well.

> ### Playing the Name Game
>
> Wi-Fi 6 is purely a marketing name—it has nothing to do with speed or any other technical improvements. Several years ago, the Wi-Fi Alliance decided that the common public would be confused with the existing Wi-Fi naming conventions, so they needed to make it easier to understand. At the time, 802.11n was given the moniker Wi-Fi 4, and 802.11ac was designated Wi-Fi 5. So of course, the newest generation of Wi-Fi should be Wi-Fi 6, and that's what we have.

Speed is, of course, the major reason that newer versions of technology get produced and accepted. Wi-Fi 6 has a few other advantages over its predecessor, though. Here's a list of enhancements versus Wi-Fi 5:

Faster—Much Faster   Let's get the most user-noticeable one out of the way first. The theoretical maximum speed of Wi-Fi 6 goes from 6.9 Gbps to 9.6 Gbps. Earlier we said that even with Wi-Fi 5's theoretical maximum, in practice it was hard to get anything above 1 Gbps. With Wi-Fi 6 it's very possible to breach that threshold, albeit at pretty short distances (say, 50 feet or less).

Better Connection Management   Wi-Fi 6 introduces a new modulation technique called *Orthogonal Frequency Division Multiple Access (OFDMA)*, which is an enhancement over the previously used OFDM. While OFDM was fast, it had a limitation that it could only transmit to one recipient at a time. OFDMA can handle communications with several clients at once.

In addition, the Wi-Fi 5 implementation of MU-MIMO was only for downlink connections—the router could send signals to multiple receivers. With Wi-Fi 6, MU-MIMO works for uplink connections, too, meaning the router can also simultaneously receive data from multiple clients at once. This lowers latency (time spent waiting) and allows for more simultaneous devices on one network.

Less Co-channel Interference   As we noted with Wi-Fi 5, the channel bonding needed to achieve higher speeds was problematic in that it severely limited the number of nonoverlapping channels available. A network with multiple wireless access points should have their ranges overlap so users never hit Wi-Fi dead spots. Those ranges need to be on different, nonoverlapping channels to avoid interference. If there are only one or two channel options, then there's a problem.

In Wi-Fi 6, a feature called *Basic Service Set (BSS) coloring* adds a field to the wireless frame that distinguishes it from others, reducing the problems of co-channel interference. Specifically, the 802.11ax access point has the ability to change its color (and the color of associated clients) if it detects a conflict with another access point on the same channel. It's a very cool feature sure to be underappreciated by network users, but not network administrators.

Simultaneous Use of Frequencies   Wi-Fi 6 can operate at the 2.4 GHz and 5 GHz frequencies at the same time, which also increases performance.

Improved Battery Life and Power Consumption for Connected Devices   Finally, Wi-Fi 6 has improvements in the technology that allow for client devices to essentially "sleep" while not directly communicating with the access point. This improves battery life and reduces power consumption for client Wi-Fi devices.

With all of these enhancements, it might be tempting to run out and upgrade all of your wireless routers to Wi-Fi 6. You could, but there are three reasons to think long and hard about it before you do:

- They likely will be more expensive than their Wi-Fi 5 counterparts for several years.

- You won't get total speed increases until all devices on the network use Wi-Fi 6, including network cards.

- You might not get the full benefit of the technology unless you have a gigabit Internet connection. Otherwise, your Internet connection will definitely be the bottleneck to the internal network.

Table 7.1 summarizes the 802.11 standards we discussed here. You'll notice that 802.11ac operates in the 5 GHz range and uses OFDM modulation, meaning that it is not backward compatible with 802.11b. That's okay, though—as we said earlier, it's probably best to retire those old and slow devices anyway. Many 802.11ac wireless routers are branded as dual-band, meaning they can operate in the 2.4 GHz frequency as well for support of older 802.11g and 802.11n devices. Keep in mind, though, that dual-band 802.11ac routers can only operate in one frequency at a time, which slows performance a bit. If you are running a mixed environment and want to upgrade to an 802.11ac router, check the specifications carefully to see what it supports.

TABLE 7.1   802.11 standards

Type	Frequency	Maximum throughput	Modulation	Indoor range	Outdoor range
—	2.4 GHz	2 Mbps	FHSS/DSSS	20 meters	100 meters
a	5 GHz	54 Mbps	OFDM	35 meters	120 meters
b	2.4 GHz	11 Mbps	DSSS	40 meters	140 meters
g	2.4 GHz	54 Mbps	DSSS/OFDM	40 meters	140 meters
n	5 GHz/2.4 GHz	600 Mbps	OFDM/DSSS	70 meters	250 meters
ac	5 GHz	6.9 Gbps	OFDM	35 meters	140 meters
ax	5 GHz/2.4 GHz	9.6 Gbps	OFDMA	35 meters	140 meters

The Long and Short on Wi-Fi Ranges

The ranges provided in Table 7.1 are approximate and may differ based on your environment. For example, thick walls and steel beams will dramatically reduce your range. In addition, the maximum data rates for 802.11n and newer standards can be debated. Some equipment (and experts) will quote the theoretical maximum, whereas others will give more realistic throughput numbers. This wasn't an issue pre-802.11n, but the newer technologies use fancier techniques to achieve maximum speeds, and we don't always have hardware that can produce the speeds that scientists can draw up on a whiteboard.

Also keep in mind that when discussing ranges, the farther away from the WAP you get, the lower your connection speed will be. For example, to get 54 Mbps out of an 802.11g router, you need to be within about 100 feet of it. At the far end of its range, your throughput will be only about 6 Mbps. Another key is how many clients are attached to the WAP. More clients means less bandwidth for each client. If you have ever used the Wi-Fi in an airport or a busy hotel, you know exactly what we mean. These principles hold true for all 802.11 technologies. 802.11ax resolves many of these, but it will take several years for it to be widely implemented.

802.11 Devices

If you think about a standard wired network and the devices required to make the network work, you can easily determine what types of devices are needed for 802.11 networks. Just as you do on a wired network, you need a wireless network card and some sort of central connectivity device.

Wireless network cards come in a variety of shapes and sizes, including PCI, PCIe, and USB. As for connectivity devices, the most common are wireless routers (as shown in Figure 7.3) and a type of switch called a *wireless access point (WAP)*. WAPs look nearly identical to wireless routers and provide central connectivity like wireless routers, but they don't have nearly as many features. The main one most people worry about is Internet connection sharing. You can share an Internet connection among several computers using a wireless router but not with a WAP.

Most wireless routers and WAPs also have wired ports for RJ-45 connectors. The router shown in Figure 7.3 has four wired connections—in the figure you can't see them all, but they're available. The connected cable in this example is plugged into the port labeled Internet, which in this case goes to the DSL modem providing Internet access. We'll talk much more about installing and configuring a wireless router in the "Configuring Wireless Routers and Access Points" section later in this chapter.

FIGURE 7.3 Wireless router

What's Next in Wi-Fi?

Like all other computer technologies, Wi-Fi keeps getting faster. When 802.11b was first introduced, gigabit wireless speeds were nothing but a distant dream. Two decades and three versions later, 802.11ac made it a reality. So now that users are sucking up gigabit wireless bandwidth, what's next?

802.11ax (Wi-Fi 6) is in the market and is starting to take hold, theoretically providing close to 10 Gbps connections through the air, if all devices on the network support Wi-Fi 6. Even though Wi-Fi 6 is still new, Wi-Fi 6E is making inroads. In 2020, the United States Federal Communications Commission (FCC) opened up the 6 GHz frequency for Wi-Fi use. This will add 14 new 80 MHz and 7 new 160 MHz channels for Wi-Fi—promising huge new bandwidth capabilities—and Wi-Fi 6E is positioned to take advantage of them.

As of early 2022, though, there aren't a lot of Wi-Fi 6E devices on the market, but they are coming. Keep in mind that if you're using the newly available 6 GHz spectrum on a Wi-Fi 6E network, older Wi-Fi devices can't use that frequency. So, what's next? More speed. A lot more speed. If you're willing to pay for it.

For the A+ exam, you need to be familiar with several Wi-Fi concepts. They include:

- 802.11 versions a, b, g, n, ac (Wi-Fi 5), and ax (Wi-Fi 6)
- Frequencies used, including 2.4 GHz and 5 GHz
- Channels available in the 2.4 GHz and 5 GHz spectrums, and regulations on licensed channels

Bluetooth Networking

We introduced Bluetooth in Chapter 5, "Networking Fundamentals," in the context of a wireless personal area network (PAN). It was released in 1998 and is an industry standard, much like 802.11. However, Bluetooth is not designed to be a WLAN and therefore does not directly compete with Wi-Fi. In other words, it's not the right technology to use if you want to set up a wireless network for your office. It is, however, a great technology to use if you have wireless devices that you want your computer to be able to communicate with. Examples include smartphones, mice, keyboards, headsets, and printers.

Nearly every laptop comes with built-in Wi-Fi capabilities, and most also come Bluetooth-enabled. If not, install a USB Bluetooth adapter to have it communicate with Bluetooth devices. It's a safe bet to say that all smartphones and other mobile devices today support Bluetooth.

Like several versions of Wi-Fi, Bluetooth uses the unlicensed 2.4 GHz range for communication. To avoid interference, Bluetooth can "signal hop" at different frequencies to avoid conflicts with devices using other technologies in the area. Thanks to technology improvements, interference with Wi-Fi is unlikely, but it can still occur.

Bluetooth Versions

Several Bluetooth standards have been introduced. Newer versions have increased speed and compatibility with technologies such as Wi-Fi, LTE, IPv6, and Internet of Things (IoT) devices, along with reduced power requirements and increased security. The newest version is Bluetooth v5.3, which was introduced in 2021. Table 7.2 provides a high-level overview of the major versions and some key features.

TABLE 7.2   Bluetooth major versions and features

Version	Basic Rate (BR)	Enhanced Data Rate (EDR)	High Speed (HS)	Low Energy (LE)	Slot Availability Masking (SAM)
1.x	X				
2.x	X	X			
3.x	X	X	X		
4.x	X	X	X	X	
5.x	X	X	X	X	X

Now let's talk about what some of these features mean:

Basic Rate (BR)   All Bluetooth devices since version 1.0 have supported a basic data transfer rate of 1.0 Mbps. After overhead, actual data transfer is actually 721 Kbps. That is incredibly slow today, but it was sufficient for early keyboards, mice, and speakers.

Enhanced Data Rate (EDR)   Version 2.0 supported EDR, which delivered bit throughput of 3.0 Mbps. After overhead, it goes down to 2.1 Mbps. EDR consumes more power than BR consumes.

High Speed (HS)   With version 3.0 came the HS enhancement, which allowed Bluetooth to transmit over available 802.11 signals. This boosted the data transfer rate to 24 Mbps. Keep in mind, of course, that this requires Wi-Fi to be nearby, and using HS requires considerably more power than EDR.

Low Energy (LE)   Version 4.0 introduced a low energy mode, which sacrifices data transfer rate (270 Kbps) but maintains transmission distance while using less energy. Devices using LE will consume somewhere between 1 percent and 50 percent of power compared to a device operating in Classic mode. The primary intent was to make this compatible with IoT devices. Version 4.2 was the first to include specific features for IoT.

> **NOTE**   Bluetooth devices operate in either Classic mode (BR/EDR) or low energy mode. Classic modes have higher data throughput but require more power. LE sacrifices throughput to save power. Computer peripherals are more likely to use Classic mode, whereas IoT devices, Bluetooth beacons, and things like activity monitors will probably use LE.

Slot Availability Masking (SAM)   One potential issue with Bluetooth is interference on its communication channels—it uses the same unlicensed 2.4 GHz frequency that Wi-Fi does—and SAM is designed to help reduce problems. SAM can detect and prevent interference by switching bands within that frequency spectrum to help maintain throughput.

Bluetooth v5 has several new features over its predecessor, v4.2. Along with introducing SAM, and better security, it is capable of doubling the throughput and achieving four times the maximum distance, up to about 240 meters (800 feet) outdoors with line-of-sight, when in LE mode. That drops to about 40 meters (133 feet) indoors. (Remember, when distances are stated, that's the theoretical maximum under ideal conditions.) It can't do both at once, though. It can increase throughput at a shorter distance, or it can go up to longer distances at a lower data rate. It's the first version that truly challenges other IoT technologies in that space. Subsequent improvements on v5 (v5.1, v5.2, and v5.3) have added features such as Angle of Arrival (AoA) and Angle of Departure (AoD), used to locate and track devices, better caching, improved LE power control and LE audio, and enhanced encryption. All versions of Bluetooth are backward compatible with older versions. Of course, when using mixed versions, the maximum speed will be that of the older device.

One of the key features of Bluetooth networks is their temporary nature. With Wi-Fi, you need a central communication point, such as a WAP or router. Bluetooth networks are formed on an ad hoc basis, meaning that whenever two Bluetooth devices get close enough to each other, they can communicate directly with each other. This dynamically created network is called a *piconet*. Bluetooth-enabled devices can communicate with up to seven other devices in one piconet. One device will be the primary, and the others will be secondaries. The primary controls communication between the devices. Multiple piconets can be combined together to form a *scatternet*, and it's possible for a primary of one piconet to be a secondary in another. In a scatternet, one of the Bluetooth devices serves as a bridge between the piconets.

> Bluetooth devices can be configured to have an effectively permanent
> connection when they are within range of each other. This is convenient
> for smartphones and hands-free headsets or phones and automobile
> communications systems. To do this, the devices need to be paired. We
> will cover the process of pairing Bluetooth devices in Chapter 10, "Mobile
> Connectivity and Application Support."

Bluetooth Devices

As mentioned earlier, Bluetooth devices have classically been computer and communications peripherals—keyboards, mice, headsets, and printers being common. Of course, smartphones and other mobile devices support Bluetooth as well. With the newest versions, we may see more IoT devices with Bluetooth capabilities as well.

One such device is a Bluetooth beacon, which is a small hardware transmitter that uses Bluetooth LE. It's broadcast only and transmits its unique identifier to nearby Bluetooth-enabled devices, such as smartphones. It can be used to send information such as marketing materials or coupons to someone with a smartphone in the vicinity of a product, or as a short-range navigation system.

There are four classes of Bluetooth devices, which differ in their maximum transmission range and power usage; the specifications are shown in Table 7.3. Most computer peripheral Bluetooth devices are Class 2 devices, which have a range of 10 meters (33 feet) and power usage of 2.5 mW. Most headsets are also Class 2, but some Class 1 headsets exist as well. Right now you might be confused, recalling from the standards discussion that Bluetooth v5 has a maximum range of 240 meters outdoors. That is for a Class 1 device running in LE mode only; devices running in classic BR or EDR modes will have shorter ranges.

When studying Bluetooth, it's easy to get the versions and classes mixed up. Remember that they are independent of each other. Most devices you see will be Class 2, regardless of the Bluetooth version they support.

TABLE 7.3   Bluetooth device classes and specifications

Class	Distance	Power usage
1	100 meters	100 mW
2	10 meters	2.5 mW
3	1 meters	1 mW
4	0.5 meters	0.5 mW

Bluetooth networking is an A+ exam objective, so be sure you're familiar with its purpose, performance, and standards.

Long-Range Fixed Wireless

Bluetooth and Wi-Fi are short-range networking technologies. The most common implementations of Bluetooth extend about 10 meters, and besides, Bluetooth isn't designed for WLAN communications. The newest generations of Wi-Fi can transmit over 100 meters or so, but that's under ideal conditions, and at those longer distances, bandwidth is greatly reduced. In situations where the distance is too far for Wi-Fi but high-speed wireless network connectivity is needed, long-range fixed wireless could be the solution. Examples could include networking from building to building in a city or on a campus, bringing Internet access to a remote residence on a lake or in the mountains where wires can't be run, or providing Internet to boats and ships.

Long-range fixed wireless is a point-to-point technology that uses directional antennas to send and receive network signals. An antenna typically looks like a small satellite dish, usually only about 1 meter wide, and can usually send and receive signals for 10 to 20 kilometers. Different dishes will support different technologies. For example, some may support Wi-Fi 5 or 6, whereas others may support those plus cellular networking, too. As the technology is point-to-point, the sending and receiving devices must be pointed at each other—misalignment will cause network failure—and obstructions such as trees or other buildings will cause problems, too.

Unlicensed and Licensed Frequencies

As you learned in the discussion on 802.11, Wi-Fi operates on the *unlicensed frequencies* of 2.4 GHz and 5 GHz. In 2020, 6 GHz was opened up to Wi-Fi in the United States as well. Other unlicensed frequencies include 900 MHz and 1.8 GHz and are used by devices such as walkie-talkies and cordless telephones.

The good news about unlicensed frequencies is that they are free to use. The bad news is that since everyone can use them, they are more susceptible to interference from other signals or eavesdropping. Take the Wi-Fi in your home, for example. If you live nearby other people, it's certain that you can see the Wi-Fi networks belonging to several of your neighbors. Hopefully they (and you) have secured them, but the signals are visible. The same concept applies to long-range fixed wireless. The difference is that here, the beams are directional, fairly narrow, and pointed at a specific receiver. For someone to eavesdrop, they would need to get within the range of the field, which could be challenging but is not impossible.

Other frequencies are *licensed frequencies*, meaning that use of them is granted by a governmental body. In the United States, it's the FCC. Think of AM and FM radio, for example. To operate on those frequencies, radio stations must be granted permission. Some companies may choose to pursue a licensed frequency for long-range fixed wireless as well. If access is granted, then that company is the only one that can use the frequency within a certain geographical area. This type of setup is uncommon.

Power over Long-Range Fixed Wireless

In addition to network signals, power can be transmitted over long-range fixed wireless as well. It's analogous to the Power over Ethernet (PoE) technology you learned about in Chapter 5, but of course it's wireless. A common name for the technology is wireless power transfer (WPT).

The transmitting station generates the power and then transmits it via microwave or laser light toward the receiver. The receiving station gets the signal and converts it back to electricity. It's the exact same principle used by other radio transmissions. The difference is that in radio (for example, terrestrial FM radio) the power produced and received is miniscule. In this application, the power transmitted is much greater. A small-scale example of wireless power transfer is wireless charging pads for mobile devices.

Efficiency is an issue with current WPT implementations. The amount of energy lost can vary; some commercial providers claim to have 70 percent efficiency, which is far lower than copper cables. They may need to improve on that before it becomes commercially viable in large scales. Still, this is an exciting emerging field that could have significant implications for how power gets generated and transmitted in the future. WPT technology is currently regulated in the United States by the FCC.

> Long-range fixed wireless is an A+ exam objective. Be familiar with licensed versus unlicensed frequency use, power over wireless, and regulatory requirements for wireless power.

Radio Frequency Networking Standards

The final group of networking standards we will look at is radio frequency. Technically speaking, all of the networking technologies we've discussed so far in this chapter use radio frequencies to communicate, so perhaps we're taking a bit of creative license here. The two technologies in this section are radio frequency identification and a subset of it called near field communication.

Radio Frequency Identification

Radio frequency identification (RFID) is a communications standard that uses radio waves to facilitate communication. There are three types of RFID, based on the frequency used. This also affects the maximum distance that the waves can travel. Table 7.4 shows the three versions of RFID.

TABLE 7.4   RFID frequencies and characteristics

Name	Frequency	Distance
Low frequency (LF)	125–134 kHz	10 centimeters
High frequency (HF)	13.56 MHz	30 centimeters
Ultra-high frequency (UHF)	856–960 MHz	100 meters

The primary purpose of RFID is to identify items. Those items can be inventory in a store or warehouse, people, or even fast-moving things, such as race cars. An RFID system is made of three components: tag, reader, and antenna. Let's discuss what each component does:

Tag   An RFID tag is fastened to the item that needs to be tracked. This can be temporary, such as an access badge an employee carries around, or it can be permanently affixed to an item. The RFID tag contains identifying information, such as an employee ID, product number, inventory number, or the like.

There are passive RFID tags and active RFID tags. Passive tags do not have a power source and draw their power from radio waves emitted by the RFID reader. This works only across short distances, typically about 25 meters or less. An active tag has its own power source (often a small battery) and may have its own antenna as well. Because it has power to generate a signal, the range for active tags is about 100 meters.

Reader   The reader's job is to read information from tags. Readers have a power source and antenna. Once they get within 100 meters of an active tag or 25 meters of a passive tag, they can detect its presence. Readers can be mobile, such as a handheld inventory tracker, or static. An example of a static reader is the security gates that line the entrances of many retail stores. The products in the store have an RFID tag, and if an active tag passes through the scanners, an alarm sounds to notify the store personnel that someone may be attempting to steal an item.

Antenna   An antenna boosts the distance an RFID signal can travel. Readers may have multiple antennae, depending on the model.

RFID is simplistic in networking terms. Its function is to identify items within a relatively short range. Two-way communication is pretty limited.

Near-Field Communication

A subset of RFID is a very short distance technology known as *near-field communication (NFC)*. NFC is designed to facilitate information sharing and, in particular, contactless payment. It transmits at 13.56 MHz, which is the same frequency as HF RFID.

The field of mobile contactless payment has made NFC explode in popularity over the last several years. Since Apple's introduction of the iPhone 6 back in 2014, nearly every smartphone manufacturer today equips its phones with NFC. Many tablets have NFC as well. Apple got into the NFC payment arena in 2014 with the launch of Apple Pay, which can be used from iPhones, iPads, and the Apple Watch. In 2015, Google introduced Android Pay, which is an update to the older Google Wallet app. No longer do users need to carry around credit cards—their phone and their fingerprint are all they need to complete a purchase.

NFC uses radio frequency (RF) signals, and NFC devices can operate in three different modes:

NFC Card Emulation Mode   This lets the device act as a smartcard. This is useful for making payments at the site of a merchant that uses NFC.

NFC Reader/Writer Mode   This allows the device to read information stored in an NFC tag on a label or poster.

NFC Peer-to-Peer Mode   This allows for ad hoc data transfer between two NFC-enabled devices.

Data rates are rather slow compared to other wireless methods, as NFC operates at 106 Kbps, 212 Kbps, and 424 Kbps. NFC always involves an initiator and a target. Let's say that you wanted to read an NFC tag in a poster. You would move your phone close to the tag, and the phone would generate a small RF field that would power the target. Data could then be read from the tag. Tags currently hold up to about 8 KB of data, which is more than enough to store a URL, phone number, or other date and time or contact information.

In peer-to-peer mode, NFC data is transmitted in the NFC Data Exchange Format (NDEF), using the Simple NDEF Exchange Protocol (SNEP). SNEP uses the Layer 2 Logical Link Control Protocol (LLCP), which is connection-based, to provide reliable data delivery.

To use NFC, a user simply moves their device within range (about 10 centimeters or 4") of another NFC-enabled device. Then, using an app, the device will be able to perform the desired transaction, such as making a payment, reading information, or transferring data from one device to another.

NFC uses two different coding mechanisms to send data. At the 106 Kbps speed, it uses a modified Miller coding (delay encoding) scheme, whereas at faster speeds it uses Manchester coding (phase encoding). Neither method is encrypted, so it is possible to hack NFC communications using man-in-the-middle or relay attacks. (We'll go into detail about specific types of attacks in Chapter 17, "Security Concepts.") Because of the limited distance of the RF signals, though, hacking is pretty hard to do. The potential attacker would need to be within a meter or so to attempt it.

Because of the popularity of mobile payments, it's likely that NFC will be around for quite a few years.

Understanding Infrared

Infrared (IR) waves have been around since the beginning of time. They are longer than light waves but shorter than microwaves. The most common use of infrared technology is the television remote control, although infrared is also used in night-vision goggles and medical and scientific imaging.

In 1993 the *Infrared Data Association (IrDA)* was formed as a technical consortium to support "interoperable, low-cost infrared data interconnection standards that support a walk-up, point-to-point user model." The key terms here are *walk-up* and *point-to-point*, meaning you need to be at very close range to use infrared and it's designed for one-to-one communication. Infrared requires line-of-sight, and generally speaking, the two devices need to be pointed at each other to work. If you point your remote control away from the television, how well does it work?

Some laptops have a built-in infrared port, which is a small, dark square of plastic, usually black or dark maroon. For easy access, infrared ports are located on the front or sides of devices that have them. Figure 7.4 shows an example of an infrared port.

FIGURE 7.4   Infrared port

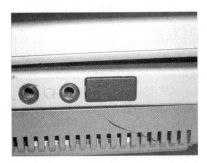

Current IrDA specifications allow transmission of data up to 1 Gbps. Because infrared does not use radio waves, there are no concerns of interference or signal conflicts. Atmospheric conditions can play a role in disrupting infrared waves, but considering that the maximum functional range of an IrDA device is about 1 meter, weather is not likely to cause you any problems.

Security is not an issue with infrared. The maximum range is about 1 meter with an angle of about 30 degrees, and the signal does not go through walls, so hacking prospects are limited. If someone is making an attempt to intercept an infrared signal, it's going to be pretty obvious. The data is directional, and you choose when and where to send it.

You might have read the 1-meter distance limitation and thought, "But my television remote works at longer distances than that," and you are right. Television and other consumer electronics remote controls are not governed by IrDA. They use a different infrared technology, based on the RC-5 protocol developed by Philips in the late 1980s. The maximum functional distance of these remote controls is about 4–6 meters (13–20 feet), depending on the device.

As a networking technology, Infrared seems to be fading from the spotlight (and it's no longer an A+ exam objective, although it's still listed in the acronym list). The slow speed, range limitation, and point-to-point nature of IR are pretty restrictive. Other technologies are simply better for networking.

NFC and radio-frequency identification (RFID) are A+ exam objectives. Be familiar with the uses and performance characteristics of each.

Installing and Configuring SOHO Networks

You already know that for computers to talk to each other, they need to be connected in some way. This can be with physical wires or through the air with one of several wireless technologies. The type of connection you choose depends on the purpose of the connection and the needs of the user or users.

Nearly every small office has a network, and it seems like most homes these days have one or more computers that need access to the Internet. As a technician, you may be asked to set up or troubleshoot any number of these types of networks, often collectively referred to as *small office, home office (SOHO) networks*. This part of the chapter will give you the background you need to feel comfortable that you can get the job done. Most of the principles we talk about apply to larger networks as well, so they're helpful if you're in a corporate environment, too.

Before we get into installation and configuration, though, it's critical to introduce a topic that permeates this whole discussion: *planning*. Before installing a network or making changes to it, *always* plan ahead. When planning ahead, consider the user's or company's needs for today and the future. There is no sense in going overboard and recommending a top-of-the-line expensive solution if it's not needed, but if the network is likely to expand, a little up-front planning can save a lot of money and hassle in the long run.

In the following sections, we will look at how to plan and set up a SOHO network. Be advised that most of what we'll discuss from here on out isn't specifically listed as an A+ exam objective. However, we encourage you to read and understand it for two reasons. One, it has tangible real-life implications if you plan on working with computers. Two, even though the subject matter might not be a specific test objective, it will be related to subjects that are. For example, we'll touch on things like wireless channels when talking about setting up routers, how firewalls work, and differences between cable types, all of which are included in the official exam objectives. In other words, think of this next section as a combination of new material, connecting the dots on concepts you've already learned, and real-world application. With that, let's start by planning a network.

Keys to Planning a Network

Before you run your first cable or place your first wireless router, know exactly where everything is supposed to go on the network. The only way you'll be able to do this is to plan ahead. If you have planned the installation before you begin, the actual physical work of installing the network will be much easier.

Every network is going to be somewhat different. If you are installing a home-based network, the planning is usually pretty simple: figure out where the Internet connection comes in, set up a wireless router, and configure wireless devices, such as laptops, smartphones, and home automation devices, to get on the network. If the network is going to be more complex, however, you should keep the following things in mind as you go through the planning process:

Understand relevant regulations.   If you are installing a home office network, this is probably not needed. But if you are installing a network in an office building, there are likely local building codes that need to be followed.

Make a map.   Understand the layout of the space in which you're installing the network. Get a map of the office or draw one yourself. Add distances or a scale, if possible, so that you can determine how far you'll need to run cables or how many switches or wireless access points you'll need. Label power locations and their capacity. Mark any potential obstacles or hazards that you may run into when you try to run cable, such as fluorescent lights, water pipes, or cinder block walls.

Locate the server(s).   When installing a small network, you may not have to worry about this. But if you have a network with one or more dedicated servers, decide where they will be located. They need to be in a secured location where only authorized people have access to them. This can be anything from a small closet to an elaborate server room with raised antistatic floors. Just make sure that it's temperature-controlled because server closets tend to get very hot, and we know that heat and computers don't mix well.

Identify where client computers will be.   If you are setting up an office in a cubicle farm, just assume one computer (or more, depending on the cubicle type) per cube. This will help you determine where you need shared network resources as well as cable placement.

Locate network resources.   Network users may need to share resources such as printers, so where will they be located? If there are dozens or even hundreds of users, you may need multiple printer locations or *printer banks*. Locate these and other shared resources in enough places so that users don't have to walk from one end of the office to the other just to pick up printouts.

Determine how users will connect.   If network users will all connect wirelessly, you can start figuring out how many wireless routers or access points you'll need. The best way to do this is to perform a wireless site survey. The rule of thumb for Wi-Fi 5 and older is no more than 30 users per access point. Wi-Fi 6 can handle more, but you will still cause performance issues if you cram too many people into one access point.

If you are going to have wired connections, start determining how long the cable runs will be. Remember that UTP has a maximum segment distance of 100 meters. If you have to go up from a patch panel, into a ceiling, and down through a wall or conduit, take that into account, too.

Designate additional connectivity areas, if needed.   If you are running cables and some systems are outside of your maximum cable length, you will need to install a repeater of some sort. The best choice is probably a switch, which repeats signals.

If you have several hundred computers, though, and you want to separate out networks, then a router is the best choice. These connectivity locations can be just a small closet. Other times, if no space is available, some administrators will put the switch in the drop ceiling. Although there is nothing wrong with this (as long as it's secured), it can be challenging to find power up there, and it does make it more difficult to add to that switch. Finally, if there's no way to run power into the area where you need the switch, you could buy one that uses *Power over Ethernet (PoE)*, which is covered in Chapter 5. Generally the number of ports these devices support is limited, but it beats having no connectivity at all.

Choosing an Internet Connection

While it may be apparent to you, your clients might not realize that in order to get on the Internet, computers need an Internet connection. Internet connections can be broadly broken into two categories: dial-up and broadband. It used to be that you had to weigh the pros and cons and figure out which one was best for your situation. Today, the choice is easy. Go broadband. The only time you would want to use dial-up is if broadband isn't available, and if that's the case, we're sorry!

Your Internet connection will give you online service through an *Internet service provider (ISP)*. The type of service you want will often determine who your ISP choices are. For example, if you want cable Internet, your choices are limited to your local cable companies and a few national providers. We'll outline some of the features of each type of service and discuss why you might or might not recommend a specific connection type based on the situation.

Dial-Up/POTS

One of the oldest ways of communicating with ISPs and remote networks is through dial-up connections. Even though dial-up Internet is a horribly antiquated service (and not an exam objective), we feel the need to cover it just in case you run into it. The biggest problem with dial-up is limitations on modem speed, which top out at 56 Kbps. Dial-up uses modems that operate over regular phone lines—that is, the *plain old telephone service (POTS)*—and cannot compare to speeds possible with DSL, cable modems, or even cellular. Reputable sources claim that dial-up Internet connections dropped from 74 percent of all U.S. residential Internet connections in 2000 to 3 percent in 2016. As of 2021, estimates are that about 2 million Americans still use dial-up Internet, which is slightly less than 1 percent of the U.S. population. Most of the people who still use dial-up do it because it's cheaper than broadband or high-speed access isn't available where they live.

The biggest advantage to dial-up is that it's cheap and relatively easy to configure. The only hardware you need is a modem and a phone cable. You dial in to a server (such as an ISP's server), provide a username and a password, and you're on the Internet.

Companies also have the option to grant users dial-up access to their networks. As with Internet connections, this option used to be a lot more popular than it is today. Microsoft offered a server-side product to facilitate this, called the Routing and Remote Access Service (RRAS), as did many other companies. ISPs and Remote Access Service (RAS) servers would use the Data Link layer Point-to-Point Protocol (PPP) to establish and maintain the connection.

> The historical term for a dial-up server is a *RAS* (pronounced like "razz") server, as used in the preceding paragraph. When Microsoft launched Windows 2000, it added routing to its RAS capabilities and renamed it RRAS. Industrywide, however, the term *RAS* is still widely used.

It seems that dial-up is a relic from the Stone Age of Internet access. But there are some reasons it might be the right solution:

- The only hardware it requires is a modem and a phone cord.
- It's relatively easy to set up and configure.
- It's the cheapest online solution (usually $10 to $20 per month).
- You can use it wherever there is phone service, which is just about everywhere.

Of course, there are reasons a dial-up connection might not be appropriate. The big one is speed. If your client needs to download files or has substantial data requirements, dial-up is probably too slow. Forget about video or audio streaming. In addition, with limited bandwidth, it's good only for one computer. It *is* possible to share a dial-up Internet connection among computers by using software tools, but it's also possible to push a stalled car up a muddy hill. Neither option sounds like much fun. If broadband isn't available in a certain location, satellite is probably a better option than dial-up.

DSL

One of the two most popular broadband choices for home use is *digital subscriber line (DSL)*. It uses existing phone lines and provides fairly reliable high-speed access. To utilize DSL, you need a DSL modem (shown in Figure 7.5) and a network card in your computer. The ISP usually provides the DSL modem, but you can also purchase them in a variety of electronics stores. You use an Ethernet cable with an RJ-45 connector to plug your network card into the DSL modem (see Figure 7.6) and the phone cord to plug the DSL modem into the phone outlet. If you need to plug a landline into the same phone jack as your DSL modem, you will need a DSL splitter (such as the one shown in Figure 7.7) and plug the splitter into the wall.

> Instead of plugging your computer directly into the DSL modem, you can plug your computer into a router (such as a wireless router) and then plug the router into the DSL modem. Phone companies may tell you that you can't (or shouldn't) do this, but if you want to connect multiple computers to the Internet and don't mind sharing the bandwidth, there is no reason not to.

FIGURE 7.5 A DSL modem

FIGURE 7.6 The back of the DSL modem

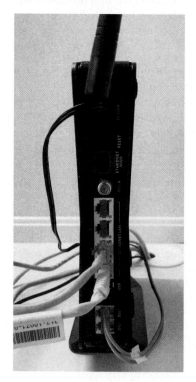

FIGURE 7.7   A DSL splitter

There are several different forms of DSL, including *high bit-rate DSL (HDSL)*, *symmetric DSL (SDSL)*, *very high bit-rate DSL (VDSL)*, and *asymmetric DSL (ADSL)*. Table 7.5 summarizes the general speeds of each. Keep in mind that the maximum speeds decrease as the installation gets farther away from the phone company's equipment.

TABLE 7.5   DSL standards and approximate speeds

Standard	Download speed	Upload speed
ADSL	Up to 8 Mbps	Up to 1 Mbps
SDSL	Up to 2.5 Mbps	Up to 2.5 Mbps
HDSL	Up to 42 Mbps	Up to 8 Mbps
VDSL	Up to 52 Mbps	Up to 16 Mbps

ADSL was the most popular form of DSL for many years. It's asymmetrical because it supports download speeds that are faster than upload speeds. Dividing up the total available bandwidth this way makes sense because most Internet traffic is downloaded, not uploaded. Imagine a 10-lane highway. If you knew that 8 out of 10 cars that drove the highway went south, wouldn't you make eight lanes southbound and only two lanes northbound? That is essentially what ADSL does.

ADSL and your voice communications can work at the same time over the phone line because they use different frequencies on the same wire. Regular phone communications use frequencies from 0 to 4 kHz, whereas ADSL uses frequencies in the 25.875 kHz to 138 kHz range for upstream traffic and in the 138 kHz to 1,104 kHz range for downstream traffic. Figure 7.8 illustrates this.

FIGURE 7.8 Voice telephone and ADSL frequencies used

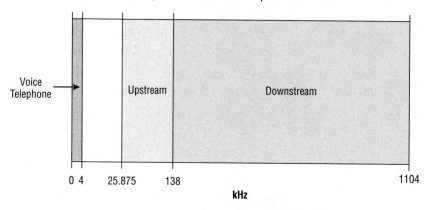

The first ADSL standard was approved in 1998 and offered maximum download speeds of 8 Mbps and upload speeds of 1 Mbps. The newest standard (ADSL2+, approved in 2008) supports speeds up to 24 Mbps download and 3.3 Mbps upload. Most ADSL communications are full-duplex.

Many ISPs have moved from ADSL to VDSL, which offers 52 Mbps downloads and 16 Mbps uploads over telephone wires. In practice, service providers will offer many plans with different speeds, starting at about 10 Mbps to 12 Mbps download and 1 Mbps upload. If you want more speed, you will pay more for it. In addition, just because you pay for a certain speed doesn't mean you will get it. The farther away you are from the phone exchange, the slower your speed. Line quality also affects speed, because poorer lines have more attenuation (signal loss).

 You will probably see Internet providers offering broadband speeds of 1 Gbps or more, and they might call it DSL. Technically, though, speeds that fast are fiber-optic connections, which are covered later. Over the last few years, the lines between DSL and fiber-optic have blurred considerably. It used to be that you ordered one or the other. Today, it's more common to order a broadband speed and the provider figures out if they will give it to you via traditional copper wires (DSL) or fiber-optic.

One major advantage that DSL providers tout is that with DSL you do not share bandwidth with other customers, whereas that may not be true with cable modems.

To summarize, here are some advantages to using DSL:

- It's *much* faster than dial-up.
- Your bandwidth is not shared with other users.
- It's generally very reliable (depending on your ISP).

There are some potential disadvantages as well:

- DSL may not be available in your area. There are distance limitations as to how far away from the phone company's central office you can be to get DSL. Usually this isn't a problem in metro areas, but it could be a problem in rural areas.

- DSL requires more hardware than dial-up: a network card, network cable, a DSL modem, a phone cord, and sometimes a splitter. A DSL modem package usually comes with a network cable and splitter, but many ISPs will make you pay for that package.

- The cost is higher. Lower-speed packages often start off at around $20 to $30 per month, but the ones they advertise with the great data rates can easily run you $100 per month or more.

- If you are in a house or building with older wiring, the older phone lines may not be able to support the full speed you pay for.

That said, DSL is a popular choice for both small businesses and residential offices. If it's available, it's easy to get the phone company to bundle your service with your landline and bill you at the same time. Often you'll also get a package discount for having multiple services. Most important, you can hook the DSL modem up to your router or wireless router and share the Internet connection among several computers.

 To see if DSL is available in your area, go to www.dslreports.com. You can also talk to your local telephone service provider.

With many people using their cell phones as their home phones and landlines slowly fading into history, you may wonder if this causes a problem if you want DSL. Not really. Many phone providers will provide you with DSL without a landline (called *naked DSL*). Of course, you are going to have to pay a surcharge for the use of the phone lines if you don't already use one.

Cable

The other half of the popular home-broadband duet is the *cable modem*. These provide high-speed Internet access through your cable service, much like DSL does over phone lines. You plug your computer into the cable modem using a standard Ethernet cable, just as you would plug into a DSL modem. The only difference is that the other connection goes into a cable TV jack instead of the phone jack. Cable Internet provides broadband Internet access via a specification known as Data Over Cable Service Interface Specification (DOCSIS). Anyone who can get a cable TV connection should be able to get the service.

As advertised, cable Internet connections are usually faster than DSL connections. You'll see a wide variety of claimed speeds; some cable companies offer packages with download speeds up to 50 Mbps, 100 Mbps, or up to 400 Mbps and various upload speeds as well. If it's that fast, why wouldn't everyone choose it? Although cable generally is faster, a big caveat to these speeds is that they are not guaranteed and they can vary. And again, with many phone companies not really differentiating between DSL and fiber-optic, it can be difficult to understand exactly what you're comparing.

One of the reasons that speeds may vary is that you are sharing available bandwidth within your distribution network. The size of the network varies, but it's usually between 100 and 2,000 customers. Some of them may have cable modems too, and access can be slower during peak usage times. Another reason is that cable companies make liberal use of bandwidth throttling. If you read the fine print on some of their packages that promise the fast speeds, one of the technical details is that they boost your download speed for the first 10 MB or 20 MB of a file transfer, and then they throttle your speed back down to your normal rate.

To see how this could affect everyone's speed on the shared bandwidth, consider a simplified example. Let's say that two users (Sally and John) are sharing a connection that has a maximum capacity of 40 Mbps. For the sake of argument, let's assume that they are the only two users and that they share the bandwidth equally. That would mean normally each person gets 20 Mbps of bandwidth. If Sally gets a boost that allows her to download 30 Mbps, for however long, that leaves John with only 10 Mbps of available bandwidth. If John is used to having 20 Mbps, that 10 Mbps is going to seem awfully slow.

Although it may seem as though we are down on cable modems, you just need to understand exactly what you and your customers are getting. In practice, the speeds of a cable modem are pretty comparable to those of DSL. Both have pros and cons when it comes to reliability and speed of service, but a lot of that varies by service provider and isn't necessarily reflective of the technology. When it comes right down to it, the choice you make between DSL and cable (if both are available in your area) may depend on which company you get the best package deal from: phone and DSL through your telephone company or cable TV and cable modem from your cable provider. The company's reputation for quality and customer service may also play a role.

To summarize, here are the advantages to using cable:

- It's *much* faster than dial-up, and it can be faster than DSL (particularly for uploads).

- You're not required to have or use a telephone landline.

- It's generally very reliable (depending on your ISP).

As with anything else, there are possible disadvantages:

- Cable may not be available in your area. In metro areas this normally isn't a problem, but it could be in rural areas.

- Cable requires more hardware than dial-up: a network card, a network cable, and a cable modem. Most ISPs will charge you a one-time fee or a monthly lease fee for the cable modem.

- Your bandwidth is shared with everyone on your network segment, usually a neighborhood-sized group of homes. Everyone shares the available bandwidth. During peak times, your access speed may slow down.

- The cost is higher. Lower-speed packages often start off at around $20 to $30 per month, but the ones they advertise with the great data rates can easily run you $100 or more per month.

Cable modems can be connected directly to a computer but can also be connected to a router or wireless router just like a DSL modem. Therefore, you can share an Internet connection over a cable modem.

For detailed information about cable Internet availability and performance, check out www.highspeedinternet.com.

Fiber-Optic Internet

Fiber-optic cable is pretty impressive with the speed and bandwidth it delivers. For nearly all of fiber-optic cable's existence, it's been used mostly for high-speed telecommunications and network backbones. This is because it is much more expensive than copper to install and operate. The cables themselves are pricier, as is the hardware at the end of the cables.

Technology follows this inevitable path of getting cheaper the longer it exists, and fiber is really starting to embrace its destiny. Some phone and media companies are now offering fiber-optic Internet connections for home subscribers.

An example of one such option is Fios by Verizon. It offers *fiber-to-the-home (FTTH)* service, which means that the cables are 100 percent fiber from their data centers to your home. As of this writing, Fios offered basic packages at 200 Mbps download and 200 Mbps upload, and the fastest speeds are 940 Mbps down and 880 Mbps up. Near-gigabit speeds mean you can download a two-hour HD movie in just over one minute. That's ridiculously fast. Other providers will offer similar packages.

Yet another service you may see is called *fiber-to-the-curb (FTTC)*. This runs fiber to the phone or cable company's utility box near the street and then runs copper from there to your house. Maximum speeds for this type of service are around 25 Mbps. These options are probably best suited for small businesses or home offices with significant data requirements, unless online gaming is *really* important to you.

Some cable companies promise a high-speed, fiber-optic connection for your TV cable as well as cable Internet service. In many cases, the connection is *fiber-to-the-node (FTTN)*, and the fiber runs only from their network to the junction box at the entrance to your neighborhood or possibly to your curb. From there, the cable is coaxial copper. This means that speeds will be significantly slower than advertised. If you're paying for a fiber connection, be sure you're actually *getting* a fiber connection.

Connecting to fiber-based Internet requires an optical network terminal (ONT), which we talked about in Chapter 5. From the ONT, you will have a copper network cable running to a router of some sort (say, a wireless router), and then the computers will connect to the router to get to the Internet.

Are there any downsides to a fiber Internet connection? Really only two come to mind. The first is availability. It's still a little spotty on where you can get it. The second is price.

That great gigabit connection can easily cost you $200 per month after any special introductory pricing wears off.

Satellite

Moving on from wired Internet connections, let's talk about wireless ones. One type of broadband Internet connection that does not get much fanfare is *satellite Internet*. Instead of a cabled connection, it uses a satellite dish to receive data from an orbiting satellite and relay station that is connected to the Internet. Satellite connections are typically a little slower than wired broadband connections, with downloads often maxing out at around 125 Mbps and uploads around 3 Mbps. To compare plans and prices, visit satelliteinternet.com.

The need for a satellite dish and the reliance on its technology is one of the major drawbacks to satellite Internet. People who own satellite dishes will tell you that there are occasional problems due to weather and satellite alignment. You must keep the satellite dish aimed precisely at the satellite or your signal strength (and thus your connection reliability and speed) will suffer. Plus, cloudy or stormy days can cause interference with the signal, especially if there are high winds that could blow the satellite dish out of alignment. Receivers are typically small satellite dishes (like the ones used for DirecTV or Dish Network) but can also be portable satellite modems (modems the size of a briefcase) or portable satellite phones.

Another drawback to satellite technology is the delay (also called *propagation delay*), or *latency*. The delay occurs because of the length of time required to transmit the data and receive a response via the satellite. This delay (between 250 and 350 milliseconds) comes from the time it takes the data to travel the approximately 35,000 kilometers into space and return. To compare it with other types of broadband signals, cable and DSL have a delay between customer and ISP of 10 to 30 milliseconds. With standard web and email traffic, this delay, while slightly annoying, is acceptable. However, with technologies like VoIP and live Internet gaming, the delay is intolerable.

> Online gamers are especially sensitive to propagation delay. They often refer to it as *ping time*. The higher the ping time (in milliseconds), the worse the response time in the game. It sometimes means the difference between winning and losing an online game.

Of course, satellite also has advantages; otherwise, no one would use it. First, satellite connections are incredibly useful when you are in an area where it's difficult or impossible to run a cable, or if your Internet access needs are mobile and cellular data rates just don't cut it, at least not until you get cellular 5G.

The second advantage is due to the nature of the connection. This type of connection is called *point-to-multipoint* because one satellite can provide a signal to a number of receivers simultaneously. It's used in a variety of applications, from telecommunications and handheld GPSs to television and radio broadcasts and a host of others.

Here are a few considerations to keep in mind regarding satellite:

It's expensive compared to other broadband access, and you might get limited data.   Packages usually start around $50 per month for about 25 Mbps downloads. That kind of download speed will cost you only about $30 for DSL or cable. The low-end satellite packages, with download speeds of around 5 Mbps, will run you around $20 to $30 per month. And, many providers set thresholds on the amount of data you can download per month. For an example, a popular 25 Mbps package for $50 per month limits you to 10 GB of data per month (as of this writing). Unlimited plans may be closer to $70 per month. Going over that amount can result in extra charges and/or speed throttling. Your speed will be decreased for a certain period, and you will pay more for that data as well.

Installation can be tricky.   When installing a satellite system, you need to ensure that the satellite dish on the ground is pointed at precisely the right spot in the sky. This can be tricky to do if you're not trained, but some have a utility that helps you see how close you are to being right on (you're getting warmer. . .warmer).

Line-of-sight is required.   Satellite communications require *line-of-sight*. A tree between you and your orbiting partner will cause problems. Rain and other atmospheric conditions can cause problems as well.

Latency can be a problem.   Because of the long distance the message must travel, satellites can be subject to long latency times. While it happens with wired connections, it disproportionately affects satellite transmissions. Have you ever watched a national news channel when a reporter is reporting from some location halfway across the world? The anchor behind the desk will ask a question, and the reporter will nod, and nod, and finally about five excruciating seconds after the anchor is done, the reporter will start to answer. That's latency.

 **Real World Scenario**

All in the Name of Entertainment

Several years ago as a teenager, one of the authors worked for a local television station during the summers. Each summer, the television station would broadcast a Senior PGA golf tournament that was held on a nearby mountain course.

Before the tournament, the crew would spend three days setting up the control truck, cameras, and link back to the station. (It was a network with TV cameras instead of workstations.) Because of the remote location, the crew had to set up a satellite uplink to get the signals back to civilization. From the control truck, a transmitter was pointed at a relay station on the side of the mountain, which in turn was pointed at a satellite orbiting the earth. It took a team of four engineers to set it up. Two engineers would stay at the truck, and two others would board ATVs and journey up the remote mountainside. Once in position, they would set up the relay station, which looked a lot like a keg of beer with a few antennas. The engineers at the truck would adjust their directional microwave transmitter until the relay station received a strong signal. Then the engineers on the mountainside would perform the arduous task of pointing their transmitter at the satellite.

It was a long and tedious process, and that's really the point of the story. Satellite was the *only* option available to complete the network, but satellite networks can be a challenge to set up and configure.

Cellular

It seems that everyone—from kindergarteners to 80-year-old grandparents—has a smartphone today, and of course almost all of them have persistent Internet access. The industry has revolutionized the way we communicate and, some say, contributed to furthering an attention deficit disorder–like, instant gratification–hungry society. In fact, the line between cell phones and computers has blurred significantly with all the smartphones on the market. It used to be that the Internet was reserved for "real" computers, but now anyone can be online at almost any time.

You're probably at least somewhat familiar with cellular Internet—it's what smartphones, many tablets, and older cellular (or cell) phones use. You might not have thought of it in terms of networking, but that's really what it is. There's a central access point, like a hub, which is the cellular network tower. Devices use radio signals to communicate with the tower. The tower, in turn, is connected via wires to a telecommunications backbone, which essentially talks to all the other commercial telecom networks in the world. It's a huge network.

For years, this network was pretty slow, especially by today's standards. The most advanced cell standard when the Internet started becoming a thing was 3G. (There were also 1G and 2G standards before that.) Initially, it had the bandwidth to carry only voice conversations, which consume little bandwidth. Then texting was supported, and after several enhancements it could in theory support downloads of 7 Mbps, although actual data rates varied by carrier, equipment, the number of users connected to the tower, and the distance from the tower. The more current standards are 4G and 5G.

Fourth Generation (4G)

In 2008, the next generation beyond 3G, appropriately named *fourth generation (4G)*, made its appearance. To be specific, 4G refers to a generation of standards for mobile devices (such as phones and tablets) and telecommunication services that fulfill the International Mobile Telecommunications Advanced (IMT-Advanced) specifications as adopted by the International Telecommunication Union (ITU). In more practical terms, it's simply the next-in-line standard for wireless telephone, Internet, video, and mobile TV that replaced 3G.

To meet IMT-Advanced standards, the service must provide peak data rates of at least 100 Mbps for high-mobility communication (such as trains or cars) and 1 Gbps for low-mobility communication. One major difference between 4G and 3G is that 4G is designed to use IP instead of traditional telephone circuits. It's designed to provide mobile broadband access.

The first 4G devices that came on the market did not offer anything close to the speeds specified by the ITU. Mobile manufacturers branded them 4G anyway, and there wasn't much the ITU could do to stop it. The result was that the world became inundated with 4G advertising.

In the early days of 4G, there were two competing standards—WiMAX and Long-Term Evolution (LTE). WiMAX was the marketing name given to the IEEE 802.16 standard for wireless MAN technology. While it was initially promising and had higher speeds than its competing standard, LTE was what the mobile providers latched onto. And as already mentioned, they advertised a lot. For years, whenever you turned on the TV, you couldn't help but be bombarded with commercials from cell providers pitching the fastest or widest or whatever-est 4G LTE network.

The biggest enhancement of 4G LTE over 3G is speed. Whereas with true 3G technology you were limited to about 500 Kbps downloads, some 4G LTE networks will give you download speeds of 10–20 Mbps and upload speeds of 3–10 Mbps. (The theoretical maximum for LTE is 300 Mbps download and 75 Mbps upload.) The range of 4G LTE depends on the tower and obstructions in the way. The optimal cell size is about 3.1 miles (5 km) in rural areas, and you can get reasonable performance for about 19 miles (30 km).

Fifth Generation (5G)

New ITU mobile specifications come out about every 10 years, so it stands to reason that we're now on 5G. Even though the first 5G modem was announced in 2016, it took until late 2018 for cellular providers to test-pilot 5G in several cities. Rollout expanded in earnest in 2019, and now it's fairly widespread, though it's not everywhere yet.

The *fifth generation (5G)* of cellular technology is a massive improvement over 4G—some users will be able to get sustained wireless speeds in excess of 1 Gbps. The theoretical maximum peak download capacity is 20 Gbps, but, of course, that would require pristine conditions, which don't occur in real life.

The technical specifications for 5G divide it into three categories:

- Enhanced Mobile Broadband (eMBB), which will be used for cell phones and mobile communication

- Ultra Reliable Low Latency Communications (URLLC) for autonomous vehicles and industrial applications

- Massive Machine Type Communications (mMTC) for sensors, which is designed to support IoT devices

Initially the focus has been on eMBB and developing the infrastructure to support mobile devices for consumers. Two versions of eMBB will take hold: fixed wireless broadband in densely populated areas and LTE for everywhere else.

Let's start with LTE, because we've already talked about it some. 5G's version of LTE is similar to 4G LTE, just with faster speeds. It will use existing LTE frequencies in the 600 MHz to 6 GHz range. Browsing speeds for 5G are about seven to nine times faster than 4G (490 Mbps on average), and most users can get 100 Mbps download speeds, compared to 8 Mbps on their 4G LTE network. So, in general, expect 5G LTE to be about seven to ten times faster than a comparable 4G connection.

The really exciting feature of eMBB is fixed wireless broadband. This technology uses millimeter wave bands (called *mmWave*) in the 24 GHz to 86 GHz range. With mmWave, 5G users should expect gigabit speeds over a wireless connection. This great performance comes with a catch, though. (Doesn't it always?)

Very short radio waves such as the ones used in mmWave can carry a lot of data, but there are two inherent problems:

- The first is distance. They're limited to about half a mile.

- The second is obstruction. mmWave can be blocked by just about anything, including walls, trees, and even a user's hand.

To overcome the first challenge, transmitters need to be placed very close together. This shouldn't be too much of a problem in urban areas, because 4G transmitters are already packed close together and providers can simply attach a 5G transmitter in the same place.

The second challenge is a bit trickier. Engineers found a way to take advantage of signal bounce—the fact that signals blocked by buildings actually bounce off the buildings—to ultimately bounce the signal to the end user's device. It slows down transmission speeds a bit, but it's still a lot faster than 4G technology. Due to the limitations, however, the fastest 5G connections will be available only in densely populated urban areas.

The promise of 5G performance is intoxicating. With it, users can stream 8K movies over cellular connections with no delays, and it can also enable virtual reality and augmented reality over cell connections. 5G users in urban areas may never need to connect to a Wi-Fi network again, because their cellular connections will be just as fast. Wireless plans may truly become unlimited because of the bandwidth capacity that mmWave creates. For these reasons, some experts have called 5G a revolution, not an evolution.

Wireless Internet Service Provider

One final type of wireless Internet connection is that provided by a *Wireless Internet service provider (WISP)*. In very broad terms, a WISP is an ISP that grants access using a wireless technology. Specifically, though, the industry uses the term to refer to providers that offer fixed point-to-point, relatively short-distance broadband Internet.

That differs from the 5G we mentioned in the last section, because while 5G is point-to-point, the receiver (someone's smartphone) is not generally in a fixed location. The receiver for a WISP-based Internet connection will be a fixed receiver, often a small dish or an antenna.

WISPs can operate over unlicensed channels such as 900 MHz, 2.4 GHz, 5 GHZ, 24 GHz, and 60 GHz, or they might offer service in a licensed frequency in the 6 GHz to 80 GHz range. WISP connections require line-of-sight and can be subject to interference and delay. Table 7.6 summarizes the connection types we have discussed in this chapter.

TABLE 7.6 Common Internet connection types and speeds

Connection type	Approximate basic package cost	Download speed range	Description
Dial-up	$10–$20	Up to 56 Kbps	Plain old telephone service. A regular analog phone line
DSL	$20–$30	Up to 50 Mbps	Inexpensive broadband Internet access method with wide availability, using telephone lines.
Cable	$20–$30	Up to 100 Mbps	Inexpensive broadband Internet access method with wide availability, using cable television lines.
Fiber	$40–$50	Up to 1 Gbps	Incredibly fast and expensive.
Satellite	$30–$40	Up to 25 Mbps	Great for rural areas without cabled broadband methods. More expensive than DSL or cable.
Cellular	$30–$50	Up to 100 Mbps with 5G LTE or 1 Gbps with mmWave	Great range; supported by cell phone providers. Best for a very limited number of devices.
WISP	$40–$150	6 Mbps to 50 Mbps	Fast connection for rural areas without cabled broadband methods.

 **Real World Scenario**

Sometimes, the Choices Are Limited

Before deciding which broadband connection sounds the most appealing, you should also factor in something very important: what is available in your area. DSL is available at different rates of connectivity based on distance from a central station. If you live far enough from a central station, or near a central station that has not been updated lately (such as in the middle of rural America), DSL may not be an option.

Similarly, not all cable providers are willing to take the steps necessary to run a connection in all situations. One of the authors once had a small business in a section of an old industrial building. The cable provider said the office where the modem was desired was too far from their nearest pole and that nothing could be done about it. He offered to pay the expense to have an additional pole placed closer to the location, but they would not discuss it further.

Make certain you know the available options—not just the technological options—before you spend too much time determining what is best for you.

For the exam, be sure to know six different Internet connection types. They are DSL, cable, fiber, satellite, cellular, and wireless Internet service provider (WISP).

Choosing Internal Network Connections

Along with deciding how your computers will get to the outside world, you need to think about how your computers will communicate with each other on your internal network. The choices you make will depend on the speed you need, distance and security requirements, and cost involved with installation and maintenance. It may also depend some on the abilities of the installer or administrative staff. You may have someone who is quite capable of making replacement Cat 6 cables but for whom making replacement fiber-optic cables is a much more daunting task. Your choices for internal connections can be lumped into two groups: wired and wireless.

Many networks today are a hybrid of wired and wireless connections. Understand the fundamentals of how each works separately; then you can understand how they work together. Every wireless connection eventually connects back to a wired network point.

Wired Network Connections

Wired connections form the backbone of nearly every network in existence. Even as wireless becomes more popular, the importance of wired connections still remains strong. In general, wired networks are faster and more secure than their wireless counterparts.

When it comes to choosing a wired network connection type, you need to think about speed, distance, and cost. You learned about several types of wired connections in Chapter 5, such as coaxial, UTP, STP, and fiber-optic, but the only two you'll want to go with today are twisted pair and fiber. You'll run one of the two (or maybe a combination of the two), with UTP by far the most common choice, as an Ethernet star network. Table 7.7 shows a summary of the more common Ethernet standards along with the cable used, speed, and maximum distance. The ones you need to know for the exam are Cat 5, Cat 5e, Cat 6, and Cat 6a, but it's good to be familiar with the others as well.

TABLE 7.7 Common Ethernet standards

Standard	Cables used	Maximum speed	Maximum distance
10BaseT	UTP Cat 3 and above	10 Mbps	100 meters (~300 feet)
100BaseTX	UTP Cat 5 and above	100 Mbps	100 meters
100BaseFX	Multi-mode fiber	100 Mbps	2,000 meters
1000BaseT	UTP Cat 5e and above	1 Gbps	100 meters
10GBaseT	UTP Cat 6 and above	10 Gbps	55 meters (Cat 6) or 100 meters (Cat 6a, 7, an 8)
25GBaseT or 40 GBaseT	UTP Cat 8	25 Gbps or 40 Gbps	30 meters
10GBaseSR	Multi-mode fiber	10 Gbps	300 meters
10GBaseLR	Single-mode fiber	10 Gbps	10 kilometers (6.2 miles)
10GBaseER	Single-mode fiber	10 Gbps	40 kilometers (~25 miles)

Looking at Table 7.7, you might have noticed that the number in the standard corresponds to the maximum speed in megabits (unless it says 10G, where the G is for gigabits). This can help you remember what the standard's maximum speed is without a lot of rote memorization. For example, if you see 100Base anything, you know the maximum speed is 100 Mbps. The letter *T* always indicates twisted pair, and *F* is always fiber.

The first question you need to ask yourself is, "How fast does this network need to be?" There really is no point installing a 10BaseT network these days because even the slowest wireless LAN speeds can deliver that. For most networks, 100 Mbps is probably sufficient. If the company has higher throughput requirements, then look into Gigabit Ethernet (1 Gbps) or faster (10 Gbps).

The second question is then, "What is the maximum distance I'll need to run any one cable?" In most office environments, you can configure your network in such a way that 100 meters will get you from any connectivity device to the end user. If you need to go longer than that, you'll definitely need fiber for that connection unless you want to mess with repeaters.

As you're thinking about which type of cable to use, also consider the hardware you'll need. If you are going to run fiber to the desktop, you need fiber network cards, routers, and switches. If you are running UTP, you need network cards, routers, and switches with RJ-45 connectors. If you're going to run Gigabit, all devices that you want to run at that speed need to support it.

The third question to ask is, "How big of a deal is security?" Most of the time, the answer lies somewhere between "very" and "extremely." Copper cable is pretty secure, but it does emit a signal that can be intercepted, meaning people can tap into your transmissions (hence, the term *wiretap*). Fiber-optic cables are immune to wiretapping. Normally this isn't a big deal, because copper cables don't exactly broadcast your data all over, as a wireless connection does. But if security is of the utmost concern, then fiber is the way to go.

Fourth, "Is there a lot of electrical interference in the area?" Transmissions across a copper cable can be ravaged by the effects of electromagnetic interference (EMI). Fiber is immune to those effects.

Finally, ask yourself about cost. Fiber cables and hardware are more expensive than their copper counterparts. Table 7.8 summarizes your cable choices and provides characteristics of each.

TABLE 7.8   Cable types and characteristics

Characteristics	Twisted pair	Fiber-optic
Transmission rate	Cat 5: 100 Mbps Cat 5e: 1 Gbps Cat 6/6a and 7: 10 Gbps Cat 8: 25 Gbps or 40 Gbps	100 Mbps to 10 Gbps
Maximum length	100 meters (328 feet) is standard Cat 6 10 Gbps is 55 meters. Cat 8 25 Gbps or 40 Gbps is 30 meters.	About 25 miles
Flexibility	Very flexible	Fair
Ease of installation	Very easy	Difficult
Connector	RJ-45 (Cat 8.2 uses non-RJ-45 connectors)	Special (SC, ST, and others)
Interference (security)	Susceptible	Not susceptible
Overall cost	Inexpensive	Expensive
NIC cost	100 Mbps: $15–$40	$100–$150; easily $600–$800 for server NICs
10-meter cable cost	Cat 5/5e: $8–$12 Cat 8: Up to $50	Depends on mode and connector type, but generally $20–$40
8-port switch cost	100 Mbps: $30–$100	$300 and up

Understand that the costs shown in Table 7.8 are approximate and are for illustrative purposes only. The cost for this equipment in your area may differ, and costs also decrease as technologies mature. Fiber has gotten considerably cheaper in the last 5–10 years, but it's still far more expensive than copper.

Fiber-optic cabling has some obvious advantages over copper, but, as you can see, it may be prohibitively expensive to run fiber to the desktop. What a lot of organizations will do is use fiber sparingly, where it is needed the most, and then run copper to the desktop. Fiber will be used in the server room and perhaps between floors of a building as well as any place where a very long cable run is needed.

Wireless Network Connections

People love wireless networks for one major reason: convenience. Wireless connections enable a sense of freedom in users. They're not stuck to their desks; they can work from anywhere! (We're not sure if this is actually a good thing.) Wireless isn't typically as fast and it tends to be a bit more expensive than wired copper networks, but the convenience factor far outweighs the others.

When you are thinking about using wireless for network communications, the only real technology option available today is IEEE 802.11. The other wireless technologies we discussed earlier in the chapter can help mobile devices communicate, but they aren't designed for full wireless LAN (WLAN) use. Your choice becomes which 802.11 standard you want to use.

If network users have a specific need, such as Bluetooth printing or managing IoT devices, you will want to integrate an appropriate technology for that into your design as well.

So how do you choose which one is right for your situation? You can apply the same thinking you would for a wired network in that you need to consider speed, distance, security, and cost. Generally speaking, though, with wireless it's best to start with the most robust technology and work your way backward.

Security concerns about wireless networks are similar, regardless of your choice. You're broadcasting network signals through air; there will be some security concerns. It comes down to range, speed, and cost.

In today's environment, it's silly to consider 802.11n or older. Deciding that you are going to install an 802.11n network from the ground up at this point is a bit like saying you are going to use 10BaseT. You could try, but why?

That brings us to your most likely choices: 802.11ac (Wi-Fi 5) and 802.11ax (Wi-Fi 6). 802.11ac is plenty fast and will be cheaper, but 802.11ax gives better performance, especially in densely crowded networks. It will come down to cost. Network cards will run you anywhere from $20 to $100, and you can get wireless access points and wireless routers for as little as $20 to $40. Shop around to see what kind of deal you can get. Exercise 7.1 has you do just that.

EXERCISE 7.1

The Cost of Networking

1. Visit the website for an electronics store. If you're unfamiliar with any, try www.bestbuy.com.

2. Find an 802.11ax (Wi-Fi 6) wireless router. How much is it?

3. Find an older standard. See if you can find an 802.11n router. If not, go for 802.11ac. How much is it? (You might have to try a site like eBay.com to find older devices.)

4. Now price wired network cards. Find a fiber-optic card and compare its price to an Ethernet card that offers similar speeds. Also look at the price of a 25-meter Cat 6 (or Cat 5) cable versus a 5-meter fiber-optic cable. How much difference is there?

Installing the Network Infrastructure

Once all your plans are complete, you've double-checked them, and they've been approved by the client or boss, you can begin physical installation. As we've said before (but can't overstate), having good plans up front saves time and money. The approval process is critical too, so the people in charge are informed and agree to the plans. Here we'll look at installation of three groups of items: network cards, cables, and connectivity devices.

Installing an Internal NIC

Before you can begin communicating on your network, you must have a NIC installed in the device. External USB NICs are super easy to install—you literally plug it in and it will install its driver and be ready to go. Installing an internal NIC is a fairly simple task if you have installed any expansion card before; a NIC is just a special type of expansion card. In Exercise 7.2, you will learn how to install an internal NIC.

EXERCISE 7.2

Installing an Internal NIC in Windows 10

Before working inside a computer case, be sure to understand and follow safety procedures, including preventing electrostatic discharge (ESD).

1. Power off the PC, remove the case and the metal or plastic blank covering the expansion slot opening, and insert the expansion card into an open slot.

2. Secure the expansion card with the screw provided.

3. Put the case back on the computer and power it up. (You can run software configuration at this step, if necessary.)

If there are conflicts, change any parameters so that the NIC doesn't conflict with any existing hardware.

Note that these first three steps may not be necessary if you have an onboard NIC.

4. Install a driver for the NIC for the type of operating system that you have. Windows Plug and Play (PnP) will recognize the NIC and install the driver automatically.

Windows may also ask you to provide a copy of the necessary driver if it does not recognize the type of NIC you have installed. If Windows does not start the installation routine immediately, you can add it manually:

a. Click Start ➤ Settings (it looks like a gear) ➤ Devices ➤ Bluetooth & Other Devices.

b. Click the plus sign next to Add Bluetooth Or Other Device, as shown in Figure 7.9. That will bring up the Add A Device window (Figure 7.10).

c. Click Everything Else.

d. When Windows finds the NIC, choose it and continue the installation.

FIGURE 7.9 Add Bluetooth or Other Device

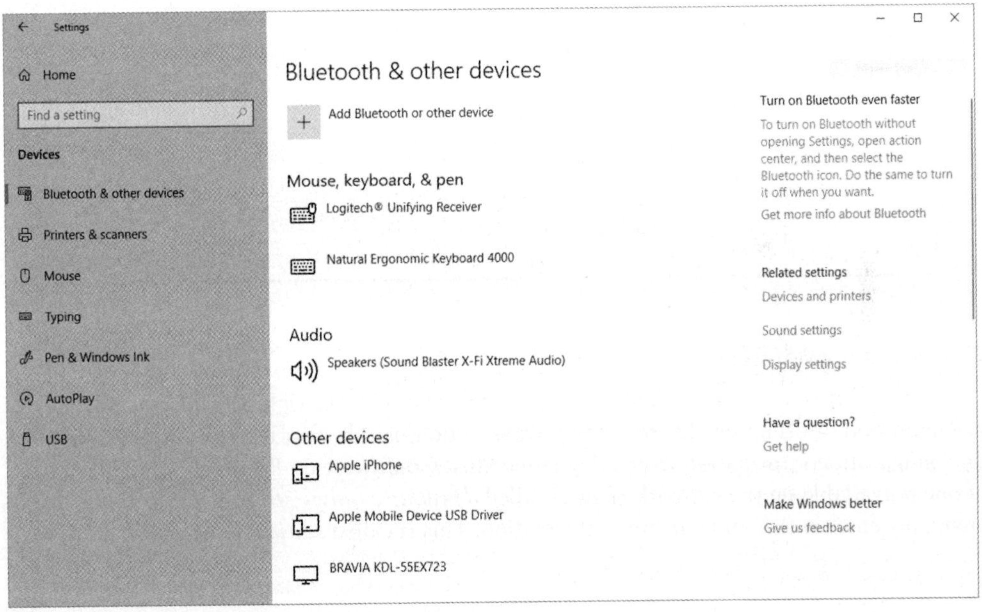

(continues)

5. After installing a NIC, you must hook the card to the network using the appropriate cable (if using wired connections). Attach this patch cable to the connector on the NIC and to a port in the wall (or connectivity device), thus connecting your PC to the rest of the network.

FIGURE 7.10   Add a Device

Configuring a Wired NIC

Now that your NIC is installed, it's time to configure it with the right IP address and TCP/IP configuration information. There are two ways to do this. The first is to automatically obtain IP configuration information from a Dynamic Host Configuration Protocol (DHCP) server, if one is available on the network. This is called *dynamic configuration*. The other way is to manually enter in the configuration information. This is called *static configuration*.

 **Real World Scenario**

Easy Configuration

Imagine that you have a small network of no more than 10 computers and do not have a DHCP server. You want to minimize the administrative hassle of configuring TCP/IP, so you want your computers to configure themselves automatically. What do you do?

The answer is to set the NIC up to get its IP information from the DHCP server anyway. Microsoft Windows operating systems will automatically configure themselves with an Automatic Private IP Addressing (APIPA) address (with the format 169.254.x.x) if they are unable to locate a DHCP server. With an APIPA address, computers on the local network will be able to communicate with one another. The limitation is that the computers will *not* be able to communicate with any remote devices (those not on the local network) and will not be able to get on the Internet.

To configure your NIC in Windows 10, open Control Panel and view by small icons or large icons. Click Network and Sharing Center to see basic network information, as shown in Figure 7.11. From here, there are a few ways you can get to the TCP/IP settings. The first is to click the network name link to the right of Connections. That will open a network status window. Click the Properties button to see the properties, as shown in Figure 7.12. The second way is to click Change Adapter Settings in the left pane of the Network and Sharing Center. You'll see the name of a connection, such as Local Area Connection. Right-click that and then click Properties. This will take you to the screen shown in Figure 7.12.

FIGURE 7.11   Network and Sharing Center

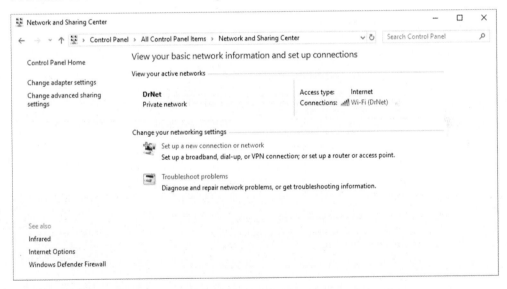

On that screen, highlight Internet Protocol Version 4 (TCP/IPv4) and click Properties. This will take you to a screen similar to the one shown in Figure 7.13.

FIGURE 7.12 Wi-Fi Properties

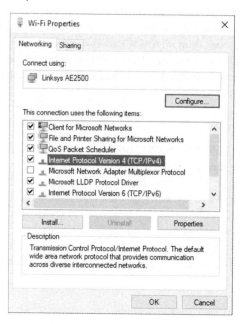

FIGURE 7.13 TCP/IP Properties

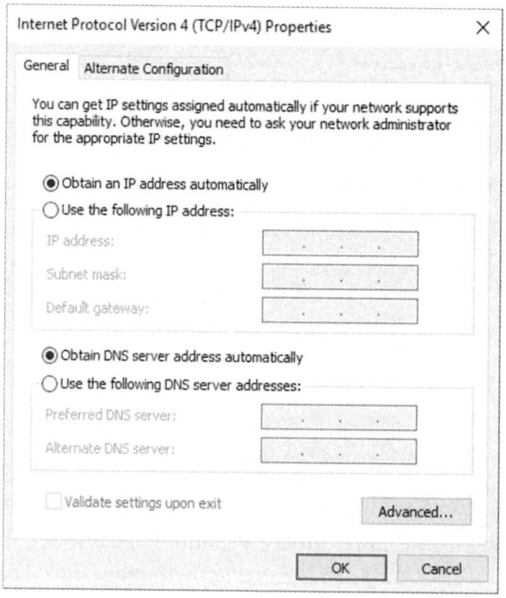

As you can see in Figure 7.13, this computer is configured to obtain its information automatically from a DHCP server. (If you have a wireless router, as many people do on their home networks, it can function as a DHCP server. We'll talk more about that in a few sections.) If you wanted to configure the client manually, you would click Use The Following IP Address and enter the correct information. To supply the client with a DNS server address manually, click Use The Following DNS Server Addresses.

If you manually configure the IP address, you must also manually configure the DNS server address. Otherwise, the client will not have access to a DNS server and won't be able to use the Internet effectively. Client computers can broadcast to find a DHCP server, but they cannot broadcast to find a DNS server. In addition, don't forget the default gateway, which is the address to the router that takes the network to the outside world. Without the gateway, the computer won't have Internet access!

For the A+ exam, be familiar with configuring clients on a SOHO network. This includes public and private addresses, APIPA, static and dynamic configuration, and the gateway.

Bear in mind that these are general steps. Always consult the documentation that comes with the hardware to ensure that there isn't a special step unique to that card.

Configuring a Wireless NIC

Installing an internal NIC is the same whether the card is wired or wireless. Of course, the big difference is how the card connects to the network. A wireless card needs to know the name of the wireless network, or the Security Set Identifier (SSID).

To configure a wireless connection, you can simply bring a Windows (XP or newer) laptop or computer within range of a wireless access point, and Windows will detect and alert you to the presence of the access point. Alternatively, if you would like control over the connection, in Windows 10, you can choose Start ≻ Settings ≻ Network & Internet to bring up the Network Status screen, as shown in Figure 7.14. Click Show Available Networks, and you will get a screen similar to the one shown in Figure 7.15.

If you have a wireless signal strength indicator in the notification area next to the clock, you can click it to see the same screen shown in Figure 7.15.

FIGURE 7.14   Network Status

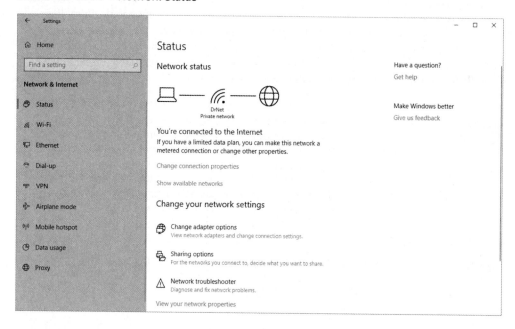

FIGURE 7.15   Available wireless connections

From this screen, you can view the SSIDs of the available wireless networks, including the one to which you are connected (the one that says "Connected" next to it). The icon to the left of the network name indicates the relative signal strength of each connection. Stronger (and faster) connections will have more bars.

> If the connection says Secured or shows a lock icon next to the signal indicator (depending on the OS), it is a secured wireless network and you will need to enter some sort of password to gain access to it. It can be dangerous to join unsecured networks; you have no way of knowing who is on them or their intentions. Wireless attacks on unsecured networks are becoming more common, so be careful with joining unsecured networks!

To connect to any network, click it and choose the Connect button, and Windows will try to connect. Once you are connected, Windows will display "Connected" next to that connection.

> The weaker the signal, the longer the connection will take. Authentication will also slow down the initial connection time.

Installing Network Cables

Network cables are not the most fun things to install. Proper installation of network cables generally means running them through ceilings and walls and making a mess of the office. Thank goodness for wireless!

> Be sure to use plenum cable if you are running cables through spaces where there is air ventilation, such as drop ceilings. PVC-coated cables produce poisonous gas when burned. Also, be sure that you have the proper permission to run the cables and that you aren't violating any building codes.

If you are installing a wired network in an existing office space, you may want to look into hiring out the cable installation to a third party. Many companies have the tools to properly install a wired network.

When installing a wired network yourself, always be aware of the maximum cable lengths, as outlined in Table 7.7. In addition, utilize cable troughs in ceilings and walls or another conduit in walls to keep your cables organized. Figure 7.16 shows a cable trough; they come in a variety of lengths and quality.

Finally, if you must run cables across the floor in a walkway (which isn't recommended), use a floor cable guard to avoid creating a trip hazard and to protect your cables. A floor cable guard is shown in Figure 7.17.

FIGURE 7.16 Cable trough

FIGURE 7.17 Floor cable guard

When running cables through a ceiling, never run the cables directly across fluorescent lights. These lights emit electromagnetic radiation (EMI) that can interfere with network communications. Utilize your cable troughs to keep cables in one place and away from lights. Also remember that fiber-optic cables are immune to EMI.

When installing cables, always be sure to label both ends! That way, you know which cable you're dealing with and where the cable should theoretically go.

Installing and Configuring Connectivity Devices

In this network installation section, we started with the local computer (the NIC) and then moved on to cabling, which, of course, is needed if the network is wired. Continuing our trek away from the local computer, we now need to look at devices that help you connect to other computers. Broadly speaking, we can break these connectivity devices into two categories: those that make connections to the Internet and those that make connections to other local computers. In the first category, we have DSL and cable modems; in the second category, we have switches, wireless routers, and wireless access points.

To be fair, devices that connect computers to other local computers may also get all the computers onto the Internet. For example, your laptop might connect to a wireless router, which lets you talk to a printer on your local network as well as access the Internet.

Installing and Configuring DSL and Cable Modems

We covered the basic installation of DSL and cable Internet service earlier in the chapter, but since we're talking about network installation, now is a good time to review.

To access the outside world, the DSL modem (again, remember it's not *really* a modem, but that's the colloquial term) connects to a telephone line. The cable modem connects to the outside world through cable television lines. The ISP manages the connection for you. Internally, the DSL or cable modem can be connected directly to a computer using a UTP cable, or it can connect to a switch, router, or wireless connectivity device so that multiple users can share the connection.

For the most part, there is little to no configuration you can perform on a DSL or cable modem. The ISP must initiate the connection to the Internet from their end. Sometimes they need to send a technician to your location to enable it, but other times they just ship the device and you plug it in. Don't forget to plug in the power cord! Beyond that, most ISPs don't want you touching any settings on the modem. If something is wrong, you need to reach out to their tech support people for assistance.

Some DSL and cable modems have built-in wireless router capabilities. If so, it's possible that the ISP will want to charge you more per month for that feature. If the modem is so enabled, you may be able to configure basic settings through a web-based interface. Configuring one of these is very similar to configuring a stand-alone wireless router, which we'll cover in detail later in this chapter.

Installing and Configuring Switches and Hubs

Wired switches and hubs are fairly easy to install. Plug in the power, and plug in the network cables for client computers. Hubs don't typically have configuration options—they just pass signals along. Unmanaged switches are similar to hubs in the sense that there's not much to configure. Managed switches will have configuration settings for VLANs and other options. For more information on the services that managed switches can provide, refer to Chapter 5.

When installing switches and hubs, remember to always take maximum cable lengths into consideration.

Installing Wireless Access Points and Routers

Instead of using switches and hubs, wireless networks use either a *wireless access point (WAP)* or a *wireless router* to provide central connectivity. A WAP functions essentially like a wireless hub, whereas a wireless router provides more functionality, similar to that of a wired router. Based on looks alone, they are pretty much identical, and physically installing them is similar. The differences come in configuring them because they will have different options.

We're going to talk about installing and configuring WAPs and wireless routers inter-changeably; just remember that a lot of the features available in a wireless router may not be available in a WAP.

After unwrapping the device from its packaging (and reading the instructions, of course), you must choose a place for it. If it is supplying wireless access to your home network and the Internet, locate it where you can receive access in the most places. Keep in mind that the more walls the signal has to travel through, the lower the signal strength.

In addition, you may choose to have some computers plug directly into the device using a UTP cable. If so, it makes sense to locate the device near the computer or computers you will want to physically connect.

Place the WAP in the center of your home, close to a network connection. Or if you have only one computer, place it close to the broadband Internet connection you are using (i.e., the cable modem or DSL line).

In many offices, WAPs and wireless routers are often placed in the ceiling, with the antennae pointed downward through holes in the ceiling tiles. You can purchase metal plates designed to replace ceiling tiles to hold these devices. The plates have holes precut in them for the antennae to stick through, are designed to securely hold the device and easily open for maintenance, and often lock for physical security. You can also purchase Wi-Fi ceiling antennas that basically look like a little dome hanging from the ceiling.

For wireless connectivity devices placed in a ceiling (or other places with no easy access to an electrical outlet), *Power over Ethernet (PoE)* is a very handy technology to supply both power and an Ethernet connection.

Once you have chosen the location, plug the unit into a wall outlet and connect the two antennae that come with the unit (as needed; many newer devices contain built-in antennae). They will screw onto two bungs on the back of the unit. Once the unit is plugged in, you need to connect it to the rest of your network.

If you are connecting directly to the Internet through a cable modem or DSL or to a wired hub or router, you will most likely plug the cable into the Internet socket of the device, provided that it has one. If not, you can use any of the other wired ports on the back of the device to connect to the rest of your network. Make sure that you get a link light on that connection.

At this point, the device is configured for a home network, with a few basic caveats. First, the default SSID (for example, Linksys) will be used, along with the default administrative password and the default IP addressing scheme. Also, there will be no encryption on the con-nection. This is known as an *open access point*. Even if you have nothing to protect except for the Internet connection, you shouldn't just leave encryption turned off. It makes you an easy and inviting target for neighbors who want to siphon off your bandwidth or even worse. Many wireless manufacturers have made their devices so easy to configure that for most networks it is Plug and Play.

WARNING   If you have personal data on your home network and more than one computer, you should never keep the default settings. Anyone could snoop your access point from the road in front of or behind your house and possibly get on your home network. It's too easy for identity theft!

From a computer on the home network, insert the device's setup media (flash drive or optical media) into the computer. It will automatically start and present you with a wizard that will walk you through setting the name of the SSID of this new access point as well as changing the default setup password, setting any security keys for this connection, and generally configuring the unit for your network's specific configuration. Then you're done!

Configuring Wireless Routers and Access Points

Each wireless manufacturer uses different software, but you can usually configure their parameters with the built-in, web-based configuration utility that's included with the product. While the software is convenient, you still need to know which options to configure and how those configurations will affect users on your networks. The items that require configuration depend on the choices you make about your wireless network. We will divide the configuration section into two parts: basic configuration and security options, which apply to both routers and access points, and then additional services that are normally router-only.

NOTE   In the next section, we will refer to wireless routers, but know that the basic configuration options are often available on wireless access points as well.

Basic Configuration

The Wi-Fi Alliance (www.wi-fi.org) is the authoritative expert in the field of wireless LANs. It lists five critical steps to setting up a secured wireless router:

1. Change the router's SSID.
2. Change the administrator username and password. Make sure it's a strong password.
3. Select AES or WPA2, or WPA3. (We'll discuss these shortly.)
4. Choose a high-quality security passphrase.
5. From the clients, select WPA2 (or WPA3) and enter the security passphrase to connect.

The parameter that needs immediate attention is the SSID. An SSID is a unique name given to the wireless network. All hardware that is to participate on the network must be configured to use the same SSID. Essentially, the SSID is the network name. When you are using Windows to connect to a wireless network, all available wireless networks will be listed by their SSID when you click Show Available Networks.

When you first install the wireless network, the default SSID is used and no security is enabled. In other words, it's pretty easy to find your network (Linksys), and anyone within range of your signal can get on your network with no password required. This is obviously a security risk, so you want to change that.

For the rest of this example, we'll use a Linksys MR9000 wireless router. First, you need to log into your device. The default internal address of this router is 192.168.1.1, so to log in, open Microsoft Edge (or your preferred Internet browser) and type **192.168.1.1** into the address bar. (Some routers use 192.168.0.1 as a default; check your router's documentation if you are unsure about what your router uses.) You'll get a screen similar to the one shown in Figure 7.18.

FIGURE 7.18   Logging into the wireless router

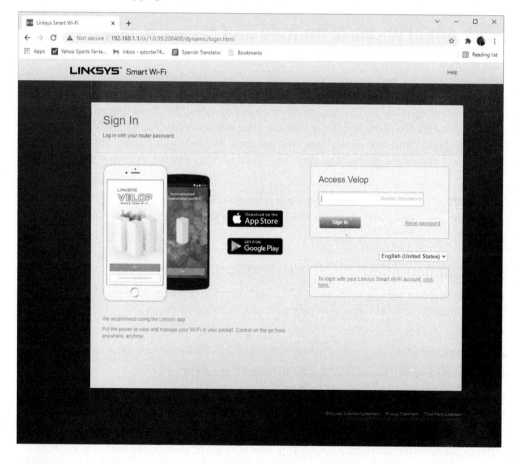

 Some wireless router installation programs install an icon on your desktop to use for management. Clicking the icon will take you to the management program.

You should have already set up the username and password using the installation media provided with the device. If not, look in the documentation for the default username and password. You'll definitely want to change these as soon as possible. Once you're logged in, the first screen you'll see is similar to the one shown in Figure 7.19. You can see sections along the left side that allow you to configure various router settings. On this router, the Connectivity section has an Internet Settings tab that identifies how you configure your incoming connection from the ISP. In most cases, your cable or DSL provider will just have you use DHCP to get an external IP address from its DHCP server, but there are options to configure this manually as well.

FIGURE 7.19   Basic setup screen

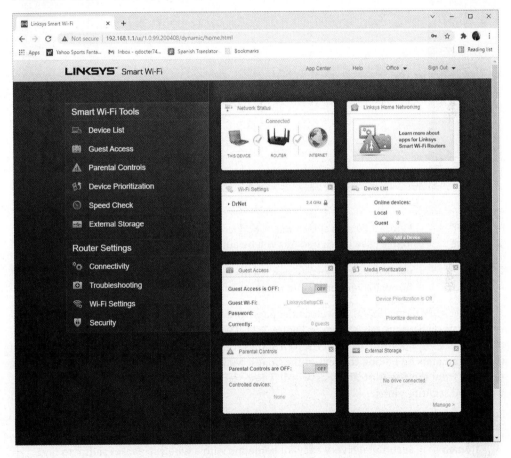

Next, configure the parameters that are crucial for operation according to the Wi-Fi Alliance. On this router, the admin password is configured on the Basic tab of the Connectivity settings, as shown in Figure 7.20.

FIGURE 7.20   Basic wireless settings tab

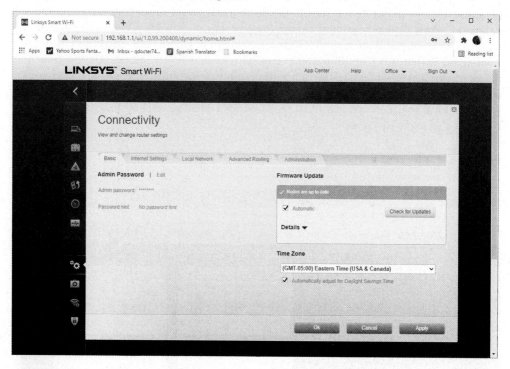

Figure 7.20 also shows the option to check for firmware updates, and in this case those updates will be automatic. After you install a router, change the SSID and passwords, and set up security, you should update the firmware to ensure that it's the most current version. Using older firmware versions could present security risks.

The network name (SSID) as well as the password required by clients to join the network is on the Wi-Fi Settings tab, shown in Figure 7.21. (We blocked out the password for pretty obvious reasons, because this router screen shows it in plain text.) You can change either of these parameters by editing the text in the boxes. Make sure the passwords to join are very different from the administrator password! These steps take care of the SSID, admin password, and security phrase.

Hiding your SSID (by not broadcasting it) does *not* increase network security! It's very easy for someone with a wireless packet sniffer to find an SSID whether it's hidden or not. Hiding the SSID only makes it more difficult for clients to find and connect to the network.

FIGURE 7.21   Wi-Fi settings

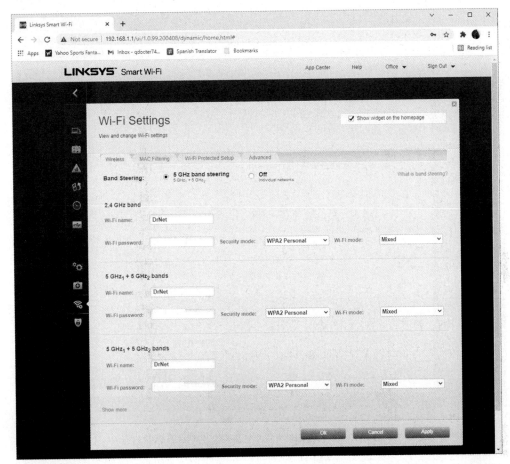

Let's pop back to Connectivity for a minute to configure the internal network settings on the Local Network tab, as shown in Figure 7.22.

Here, you configure your router's hostname, internal IP address (in this case, 192.168.1.1), and subnet mask. On this router, DHCP is also configured on this screen. If you want the device to act as a DHCP server for internal clients, enable it here, specify the starting IP address, and specify the maximum number of DHCP users. Disabling DHCP means that clients will have to use a static IP address.

Most wireless routers (like the one used in this example) have a help section to describe each setting on the configuration pages. If you're not totally sure what a setting does, click the Help link (at the top of the screen in this case) to find out what the setting does. If not, there's always the manual or online help.

FIGURE 7.22   Local Network Settings screen

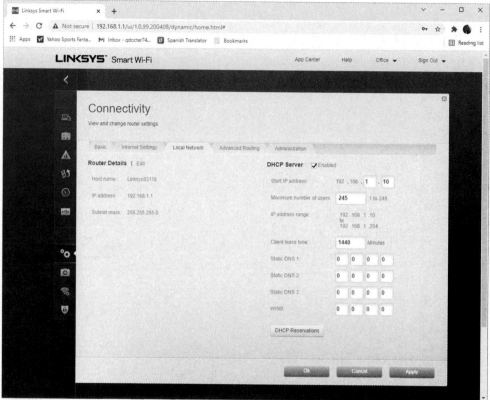

The last critical setting you need to make is to enable wireless *encryption*. If you don't do this, all signals sent from the wireless router to client computers will be in plain text and anyone can join the network without a security password. It's a really bad thing to leave disabled. Before we look at how to set up encryption on our wireless router, let's cover the details on three encryption options.

Wired Equivalent Privacy   *Wired Equivalent Privacy (WEP)* was one of the first security standards for wireless devices. WEP encrypts data to provide data security. It uses a static key; the client needs to know the right key to gain communication through a WEP-enabled device. The keys are commonly 10, 26, or 58 hexadecimal characters long.

You may see the use of the notation WEP.*x*, which refers to the key size; 64-bit and 128-bit are the most widely used, and 256-bit keys are supported by some vendors (WEP.64, WEP.128, and WEP.256). WEP.64 uses a 10-character key. WEP.128 uses 26 characters, and WEP.256 uses 58.

The protocol has always been under scrutiny for not being as secure as initially intended. WEP is vulnerable due to the nature of static keys and weaknesses in the encryption algorithms. These weaknesses allow the algorithm to potentially be cracked in a very short amount of time—no more than two or three minutes. This makes WEP one of the more vulnerable protocols available for security.

Because of security weaknesses and the availability of newer protocols, WEP should not be used widely. You will likely see it as the default security setting on many routers, even with all its shortcomings. It's still better than nothing, though, and it does an adequate job of keeping casual snoops at bay.

Wi-Fi Protected Access   *Wi-Fi Protected Access (WPA)* is an improvement on WEP that was first available in 1999 but did not see widespread acceptance until around 2003. Once it became widely available, the Wi-Fi Alliance recommended that networks no longer use WEP in favor of WPA.

This standard was the first to implement some of the features defined in the IEEE 802.11i security specification. Most notably among them was the use of the *Temporal Key Integrity Protocol (TKIP)*. Whereas WEP used a static 40- or 128-bit key, TKIP uses a 128-bit dynamic per-packet key. It generates a new key for each packet sent. WPA also introduced message integrity checking.

When WPA was introduced to the market, it was intended to be a temporary solution to wireless security. The provisions of 802.11i had already been drafted, and a standard that employed all the security recommendations was in development. The upgraded standard would eventually be known as WPA2.

WPA, WPA2, and WPA3 (discussed next) have two variants: Personal and Enterprise. For a small office or home office network with just one wireless router or access point, Personal is the choice to make. With Personal, the device itself handles the authentication. For larger networks, Enterprise is recommended because it consolidates authentication administration. Enterprise requires the use of a separate central authentication server, such as a Remote Authentication Dial-in User Service (RADIUS) server.

Wi-Fi Protected Access 2   Even though their names might make you assume that WPA and WPA2 are very similar, they are quite different in structure. *Wi-Fi Protected Access 2 (WPA2)* is a huge improvement over WEP and WPA. As mentioned earlier, it implements all the required elements of the 802.11i security standard. Most notably, it uses Counter Mode CBC-MAC Protocol (CCMP), which is a protocol based on the *Advanced Encryption Standard (AES)* security algorithm. CCMP was created to address the shortcomings of TKIP; consequently, it's much stronger than TKIP.

The terms *CCMP* and *AES* tend to be interchangeable in common parlance. You might also see it written as *AES-CCMP*.

Wi-Fi Protected Access 3   The newest and strongest wireless encryption is *Wi-Fi Protected Access 3 (WPA3)*. It was released in 2018 and is mandatory for all new Wi-Fi–certified devices as of July 2020. It offers more robust authentication and increased cryptographic strength to ensure more secure networks.

WPA3-Personal offers increased security even if users choose passwords that don't meet normal complexity requirements through a technology called Simultaneous Authentication of Equals (SAE). SAE is resistant to dictionary attacks, which are brute-force methods of guessing passwords.

WPA3-Enterprise has a plethora of new security features, including multiple authentication methods, enhanced encryption with 128-bit Advanced Encryption Standard Counter Mode with Cipher Block Chaining Message Authentication (AES-CCMP 128), more robust 256-bit security key derivation and confirmation, and 128-bit frame protection. Finally, there's also a 192-bit WPA-3 mode that increases the strength of all features already mentioned. It's way more than you will need to know for the A+ exam (and WPA3 isn't yet an objective), but if cybersecurity is of interest to you, check it out.

Since 2006, wireless devices have been required to support WPA2 to be certified as Wi-Fi compliant. Of the wireless security options available today, it provides the strongest encryption and data protection.

On this particular router, it would make sense to configure security via the Security section, but that's not true. (Who says things need to be logical?) On this particular router, the encryption method is selected on the same page the SSID and network password are configured. It's in the Wi-Fi settings section, Wireless tab that was shown in Figure 7.21.

This router happens to be 802.11ac, so it has sections for both a 2.4 GHz and a 5 GHz network. If there were only devices of one type, it would make sense to disable the other network. In this case, though, we are talking about security, and you can see that it's set to WPA2-Personal. To change the setting, click the down arrow next to Security mode. The other WPA2 choice you generally have is WPA2-Enterprise, which is more secure than Personal. For a business network, regardless of the size, Enterprise is the way to go. In order to use Enterprise, though, you need a separate security server called a RADIUS server.

 Another tab shown on Figure 7.21 is the *MAC Filtering* tab. On that tab, you can configure the router to allow connections only from clients with certain MAC addresses. (Recall that MAC addresses are hardware addresses built into NICs.) This is a light-duty security measure you can use on your network, though an attacker capable of spoofing a MAC address can easily defeat it.

For your wireless router to use WPA2 or WPA3-Enterprise, remember that you need to have a RADIUS server on your network. Remember it this way: WPA-Personal means the local (personal) device handles security, whereas WPA-Enterprise means some other machine on the network (enterprise) does. The A+ exam won't test you on how to configure RADIUS. For now, just know what it is, which is an authentication server. Other exams, such as Network+, will test you on how to configure RADIUS.

With that, the basic router-side setup recommendations have been taken care of. Now it's just a matter of setting up the clients with the same security method and entering the passphrase.

 Real World Scenario

Sharing an Internet Connection

Wireless routers have many advantages over wireless access points. One of the biggest advantages is the ability to share an Internet connection. By sharing a connection, you pay for only one connection, but you can connect as many computers as you would like (or as many as are reasonable) to your wireless router. Here's how to do that.

First, ensure that your DSL modem or cable modem is connected properly. Then, connect your wireless router to your cable modem or DSL modem using a UTP cable (Cat 5e or better). In most cases, the wireless router will have a wired Internet port on the back. Connect the cable here and plug it into your broadband modem. Finally, you can connect computers to your wireless router.

Some ISPs, in an attempt to prohibit this sort of behavior, will restrict access through the modem to one MAC address. This isn't a problem. You can do one of two things. The first option is, when you first make your connection to the ISP, just make sure your computer is already connected through your router. The ISP will see the MAC address of the router and assume that is your computer. The second option is that most wireless routers will allow you to clone your computer's MAC address (see Figure 7.23). Your router will simply tell the ISP that it has the same MAC address as your computer, which was previously connected directly to the cable or DSL modem. ISPs may not like it, but sharing a wireless Internet connection is a very economical option for a small office or home network.

FIGURE 7.23   Option to clone a MAC address

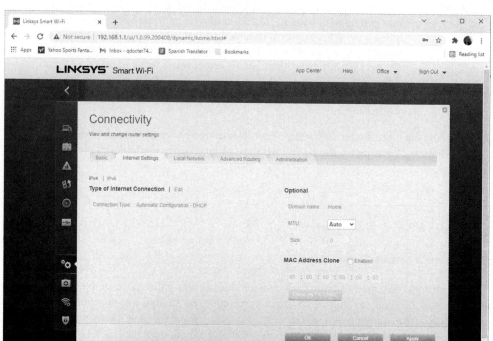

Wireless Channels

Earlier in the chapter, in the section on 802.11g, we brought up the concept of wireless channels. There are 11 configurable channels in the 2.4 GHz range, which is what 802.11b/g uses to communicate. Most of the time, channel configuration is automatically done, so you won't need to change that.

However, let's say you have too many users for one WAP to adequately service (about 30 or more for Wi-Fi 5 or older routers) or your physical layout is too large and you need multiple access points. Now you need to have more than one access point. In a situation like this, here's how you should configure it:

1. Set up the WAPs so that they have overlapping ranges.

    The minimum overlap is 10 percent, and 20 percent is recommended. This way, if users roam from one area to another, they won't lose their signal.

2. Configure the WAPs with the same SSID.

3. Configure the WAPs with nonoverlapping channels.

2.4 GHz channels need to be at least five numbers apart to not overlap. So, for example, channels 2 and 7 do not overlap, nor do channels 4 and 10. There are 11 configurable channels, so you can have a maximum of three overlapping ranges on the same SSID, configured with channels 1, 6, and 11, and not have any interference. Wireless clients are configured to auto-detect a channel by default, but they can be forced to use a specific channel as well.

Some wireless routers allow you to configure the channels used. For example, Figure 7.24 shows a wireless router configuration page where you can configure the 5 GHz network. In this case, you can choose from 20 MHz or 40 MHz channel widths, as well as choose the channel. Each of the 20 MHz channels shown is nonoverlapping.

FIGURE 7.24   5 GHz channels available to select

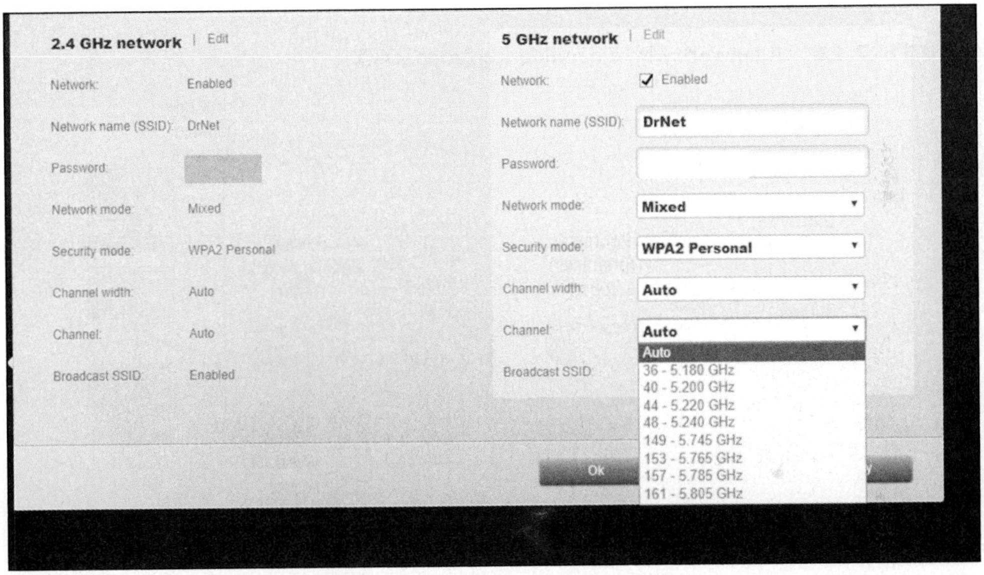

Additional Wireless Router Services

Wireless routers offer many more services than access points offer. Most of those services fall under the umbrella of configuring your router as a firewall. Firewalls are an important networking concept to understand, so we'll first give you a primer on what firewalls are and what they do, and then we'll look at specific configuration options.

Understanding Firewall Basics

Before we get into configuring your wireless router as a firewall, let's be sure you know what firewalls can do for you. A *firewall* is a hardware or software solution that serves as your network's security guard. For networks that are connected to the Internet, firewalls are probably the most important device on the network. Firewalls can protect you in two ways.

They protect your network resources from hackers lurking in the dark corners of the Internet, and they can simultaneously prevent computers on your network from accessing undesirable content on the Internet. At a basic level, firewalls filter packets based on rules defined by the network administrator.

Firewalls can be stand-alone "black boxes," software installed on a server or router, or some combination of hardware and software. Most firewalls have at least two network connections: one to the Internet, or *public side*, and one to the internal network, or *private side*. Some firewalls have a third network port for a second semi-internal network. This port is used to connect servers that can be considered both public and private, such as web and email servers. This intermediary network is known as a screened subnet, formerly called demilitarized zone (DMZ), an example of which is shown in Figure 7.25. Personal software-based firewalls will run on computers with only one NIC.

FIGURE 7.25 A network with a demilitarized zone (DMZ)

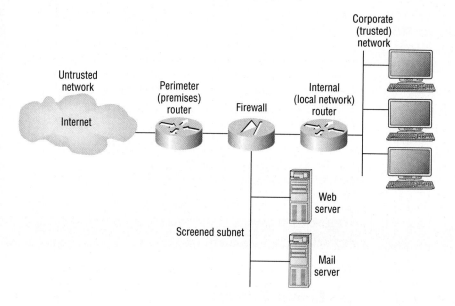

Types of Firewalls

We've already stated that firewalls can be software- or hardware-based or a combination of both. Keeping that in mind, there are two general categories of firewalls: network-based and host-based.

Network-Based Firewalls A *network-based firewall* is what companies use to protect their private network from public networks. The defining characteristic of this type of firewall is that it's designed to protect an entire network of computers instead of just one system. It's generally a stand-alone hardware device with specialized software installed on it to protect your network.

Host-Based Firewalls   In contrast to network-based firewalls, a *host-based firewall* is implemented on a single machine, so it protects only that one machine. This type of firewall is usually a software implementation because you don't need any additional hardware in your personal computer to run it. All current Windows client operating systems come with Windows Defender Firewall (or just Windows Firewall), which is a great example of a host-based solution. Norton Security and many other security products come with software firewalls too. Host-based firewalls are generally not as secure as network firewalls, but for small businesses or home use, they're an adequate, cheap solution.

How Firewalls Work

Firewalls are configured to allow only packets that pass specific security restrictions to get through them. They can also permit, deny, encrypt, decrypt, and proxy all traffic that flows through them, most commonly between the public and private parts of a network. The network administrator decides on and sets up the rules a firewall follows when deciding to forward data packets or reject them.

The default configuration of a firewall is generally *default deny*, which means that all traffic is blocked unless specifically authorized by the administrator. While this is very secure, it's also time consuming to configure the device to allow legitimate traffic to flow through it. The other option is *default allow*, which means all traffic is allowed through unless the administrator denies it. If you have a default allow firewall and don't configure it, you might as well not have a firewall at all.

You will also encounter the terms whitelist and blacklist in relation to network and firewall security. A *whitelist* (or *allow list*) allows access to nobody (so its default is deny) except those users or computers on the whitelist. A *blacklist* (or *block list*) allows access to everyone (default allow) except those on the blacklist.

The basic method of configuring firewalls is to use an *access control list (ACL)*. The ACL is the set of rules that determines which traffic gets through the firewall and which traffic is blocked. ACLs are typically configured to block traffic by IP address, port number, domain name, or some combination of all three.

Packets that meet the criteria in the ACL are passed through the firewall to their destination. For example, let's say you have a computer on your internal network that is set up as a web server. To allow Internet clients to access the system, you need to allow data on port 80 (HTTP) and 443 (HTTPS) to get to that computer.

Another concept you need to understand is *port triggering*. It allows traffic to enter the network on a specific port after a computer makes an outbound request on that specific port. For example, if a computer on your internal network makes an outbound RDP request (port 3389), subsequent inbound traffic destined for the originating computer on port 3389 would be allowed through.

Configuring Your Wireless Firewall

Nearly every wireless router sold today provides you with some level of firewall protection. On the router used in this example, the firewall options are on two separate tabs. Enabling the firewall and setting a few basic options is done from the Security section, as shown in Figure 7.26. More advanced options, such as configuring port forwarding and port triggering, are on the DMZ and Apps and Gaming tabs. (Remember that DMZs are also called screened subnets.)

FIGURE 7.26   Enabling the firewall

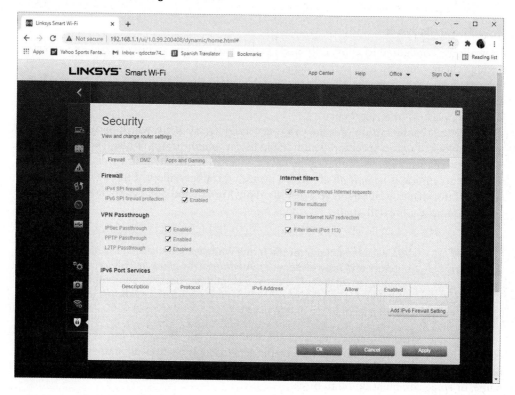

Network Address Translation

Network Address Translation (NAT) is a very cool service that translates a private IP address on your internal network to a public IP address on the Internet. If you are using your wireless router to allow one or more clients to access the Internet but you have only one external public IP address, your router is using NAT.

Most routers have NAT enabled by default, and there might not be any specific configuration options for it. That's true in the case of the router we've been using as an example. You can enable or disable it on the Advanced Routing tab in Connectivity, but otherwise the only options you can configure are the internal IP addresses that the router hands out to clients.

To be technically correct, NAT is specifically a one-to-one translation of a private IP address to a public IP address. If you have multiple client computers with private addresses accessing the Internet using one public address (called many-to-one), that is a specific form of NAT known as *overloading*, Port Address Translation (PAT), or *port forwarding*. The A+ exam does not test you on the differences between NAT and PAT, but other tests do, such as the Network+ exam.

Another type of NAT is called *Dynamic Network Address Translation (DNAT)*, which translates a group of private addresses to a pool of routable addresses. This is used to make a resource that's on a private network available for consumption on public networks by appearing to give it a publicly available address. For example, if a web server were behind a NAT-enabled router and did not have its own public IP address, it would be inaccessible to the Internet. DNAT can make it accessible.

Universal Plug and Play

Universal Plug and Play (UPnP) is a standard designed to simplify the process of connecting devices to a network and enable those devices to automatically announce their presence to other devices on the network. If you remember when Plug and Play was new to computers, it was revolutionary. You simply plugged in a peripheral (such as a USB network card or mouse) and it was detected automatically and it worked. UPnP is the same idea, but for networking. From a standards standpoint, there's not a lot to configure. The client needs to be a DHCP client and the service uses UDP port 1900.

The concept is great. It lets devices connect to the network and discover each other automatically with the Simple Service Discovery Protocol. It can be used for any networked device you can think of, from routers and printers to smartphones and security cameras.

The problem is, UPnP has no authentication mechanism. Any device or user is trusted and can join the network. That is obviously a problem. The security consulting firm Rapid7 did a six-month research study in early 2013 and found that over 6,900 network-aware products, made by 1,500 different companies, responded to public UPnP requests. In total, they found nearly 81 million individual devices responded to requests. The U.S. Department of Homeland Security and many others immediately began requesting people to disable UPnP.

Since that time, the UPnP forum (www.openconnectivity.org) has released statements saying that the security holes have been patched and that the system is more secure than ever. Even though the issues were discovered several years ago, as of this writing, skeptics still abound and UPnP does not appear to be a safe option. Regardless of if and when it gets fixed, the reputation of UPnP is not a good one.

The biggest risk is for open UPnP connections to be exploited by unknown systems on the Internet. Therefore, you should configure your router to not allow UPnP connections from its external connection. Many ISPs have also taken steps to help prevent issues. In summary, the best bet is to leave it disabled.

Real World Scenario

Knowing How to Install and Configure a SOHO Router

If you are given the scenario in real life or on the A+ exam, you should know how to install and configure a SOHO router. In today's environment, most installations for small offices and home networks will involve wireless routers. Throughout this chapter, you have learned everything you need to know to purchase the best device for different situations and how to set it up once you get it out of the box. Let's review here.

The first decision to make is which router technology to purchase. With wireless, it's generally best to go with the best technology available because speeds have been increasing rapidly over the last several years. It seems like 802.11ax provides amazing speed, but you might not be able to use all of its capacity if you don't have gigabit Internet access. Therefore, 802.11ac might be just fine, and possibly cheaper.

Next, how will the office get on the Internet? The two most obvious choices are DSL and cable Internet. Find the best solution (which often means the least expensive), and set it up through the service provider. In fact, you may want to do this first, because it will probably take the provider at least a few days to get it set up on their end and you want it to be ready when you install the network.

Then, as needed, plan the internal network layout. Is it all wireless, or will there be wired connections? Do you need to run cables? Will there be a server closet or other central connectivity point? Once you're certain of your configuration, you can begin installation.

When installing the router, always remember these key steps:

1. Change the default SSID.

2. Change the administrator username and password to something highly secure.

3. Configure the best security possible, such as WPA3.

4. Set a strong passphrase for clients to join the network.

After completing these steps, you can configure the clients to join the network by setting their security appropriately, finding the SSID, and entering the passphrase. By following these guidelines, you will be able to properly install a network, regardless of the scenario presented.

Summary

In this chapter, you learned about wireless networking and configuring a small office, home office (SOHO) network. We started with wireless networking. We introduced the key wireless networking standards 802.11a, 802.11b, 802.11g, 802.11n, 802.11ac (Wi-Fi 5), and 802.11ax (Wi-Fi 6), and talked about their characteristics, such as speed, distances, frequencies, channels, and modulation. Then we moved on to Bluetooth networking, long-range fixed wireless, and, finally, RFID and NFC.

Next, you learned the fundamentals of installing a small network. We started by looking at network planning, which is the critical first step. Don't be the one who forgets that!

Then, we covered the myriad possibilities for Internet connections, from the archaic dial-up to wired broadband options, such as DSL, cable modems, and fiber-optic, and wireless choices: satellite, cellular, and a wireless Internet service provider (WISP). Then we talked about choosing internal network connections in both wired and wireless environments.

From there, we dove into installing network infrastructure. If you did a good job planning, this part should be problem-free. We covered installing and configuring NICs (including IP addressing for clients), cables, and connectivity devices.

Finally, we looked at how to configure a router. The Wi-Fi Alliance has some great practical steps on how to configure a secure wireless network, such as changing the SSID, setting passwords, and enabling encryption, such as WEP, WPA, WPA2, and WPA3. We also looked at other basic configuration options, such as DHCP and communication channels. Then we looked at your wireless router as a firewall, including NAT and UPnP.

Exam Essentials

Know the different 802.11 standards.   Standards you should be familiar with are 802.11a, 802.11b, 802.11g, 802.11n, 802.11ac (Wi-Fi 5), and 802.11ax (Wi-Fi 6). Know the frequencies (2.4 GHz and 5 GHz) that each one uses, as well as performance characteristics of each, such as relative distance and speed.

Know the three nonoverlapping 2.4 GHz wireless channels.   If you need three nonoverlapping channels, you must use channels 1, 6, and 11.

Understand Bluetooth networking.   Bluetooth isn't used for wireless LAN like 802.11 is but for small personal area networks. It's best for peripheral connectivity such as headsets, keyboards, mice, and printers.

Understand how long-range fixed wireless works.   Long-range fixed wireless is a point-to-point wireless connection. It can operate over licensed or unlicensed channels. It can also transmit power through the air, and there are regulatory requirements for doing so.

Understand the difference between RFID and NFC.   Both use radio signals. RFID is used to track the presence or location of items. NFC uses high-frequency RFID signals and can be used for touchless payment systems.

Know the different types of available broadband connections.   Broadband connections include DSL, cable, fiber, satellite, cellular, and wireless Internet service provider (WISP).

Know the various cellular networking standards.   Understand the differences between 4G and 5G, and also how 5G has LTE and mmWave.

Know how to configure a network client to use IP addressing.   Clients can be configured with static IP information, or dynamically through a DHCP server. To communicate on the Internet, clients need an IP address, subnet mask, and gateway. On an internal network, you can use private IP addresses as long as they go through NAT to get to the Internet. APIPA is available as a fallback if a DHCP server is not available.

Understand the three encryption protocols used for wireless networking.   Listed in order from least to most secure, the common wireless security protocols include WEP, WPA, and WPA2. WPA uses TKIP, and WPA2 uses AES. (WPA3 is the most secure, but it's not yet an exam objective.)

Know the different types of available broadband connections.   Broadband connections include DSL, cable, satellite, ISDN, cellular, and fiber-optic.

Review Questions

The answers to the chapter review questions can be found in Appendix A.

1. Which of the following wireless IEEE standards operate on the 2.4 GHz radio frequency and are directly compatible with each other? (Choose two.)

   A. 802.11a

   B. 802.11b

   C. 802.11ac

   D. 802.11g

2. What is the primary function of the SSID?

   A. To secure communication between a web server and a browser

   B. To secure communication between a server and a remote host

   C. To serve as a parameter used to identify a network and configure a wireless connection

   D. To serve as a type of password used to secure a wireless connection

3. Which of the following are features that allow 802.11ac to achieve higher data throughput? (Choose two.)

   A. MIMO

   B. Beamforming

   C. Channel bonding

   D. Code division multiplexing

4. Which of the following is the most secure wireless encryption standard for 802.11 networks?

   A. WEP

   B. WPA

   C. WPA2

   D. SAFER+

5. You are upgrading a wireless network from Wi-Fi 5 over to Wi-Fi 6. Which of the following statements is *not* correct?

   A. Users should get faster speeds.

   B. Network range will be similar.

   C. Fewer users will be able to use each access point.

   D. Devices may have lower power usage while connecting to the network.

6. You have just installed a wireless router on your home network. Which of the following should you do to make it highly secure? (Choose all that apply.)

    A. Change the default administrator name and password.

    B. Change the SSID.

    C. Enable WEP.

    D. Configure it to channel 11.

7. You are setting up a small office network for a client. Which Internet service would you recommend to provide the best speed?

    A. DSL

    B. Cable

    C. Satellite

    D. Fiber

8. Which service allows users with private IP addresses to access the Internet using a public IP address?

    A. DHCP

    B. DNS

    C. DSL

    D. NAT

9. You are installing a single 802.11g wireless network. The office space is large enough that you need three WAPs. What channels should you configure the WAPs on to avoid communication issues?

    A. 2, 5, and 7

    B. 1, 8, and 14

    C. 1, 6, and 11

    D. 3, 6, and 9

10. You are setting up a wireless network. Which wireless standards would give the users over 40 Mbps throughput? (Choose all that apply.)

    A. 802.11ac

    B. 802.11b

    C. 802.11g

    D. 802.11n

11. You have been asked to configure a network for a small office. The wireless router is installed, and now you need to connect the client computers. What do you enter on the client computers to connect to the router?

    A. The administrator password

    B. The security passphrase

    C. The client's MAC address

    D. The default router password

12. Which of the following technologies can operate in the 125 kHz to 134 kHz range?

   A. Bluetooth

   B. RFID

   C. NFC

   D. LTE

13. Due to channel interference, you are upgrading a wireless network from Wi-Fi 5 to Wi-Fi 6. Which feature of Wi-Fi 6 reduces channel interference?

   A. OFDMA

   B. BSS coloring

   C. MU-MIMO

   D. DFS

14. Which of the following security standards was the first to introduce a dynamic 128-bit per-packet security key?

   A. WEP

   B. TKIP

   C. AES

   D. CCMP

15. You are running an 802.11g wireless router in mixed mode. You have three 802.11g wireless NICs using the router. A new user connects using an 802.11b wireless NIC. What will happen?

   A. The user with 802.11b will access the network at 11 Mbps, while the users with 802.11g will access the network at 54 Mbps.

   B. The user with 802.11b will not be able to communicate on the network.

   C. The user with 802.11b will access the network at 11 Mbps. The users with 802.11g will access the network at 54 Mbps, unless they are communicating with the 802.11b device, which will be at 11 Mbps.

   D. All users will access the network at 11 Mbps.

16. When enabled, which feature of a wireless router allows only specified computers to access the network?

   A. Port forwarding

   B. WPS

   C. SSID

   D. MAC filtering

17. A firewall operates by using a set of rules known as what?

   A. SLA

   B. ACL

   C. NAT

   D. APIPA

18. You have set up a wireless router on your network and configured it to use AES. What configuration option do you need to choose on the client computers?

  A. WEP

  B. WPA

  C. WPA2

  D. TKIP

19. Besides 802.11 standards, which wireless communication methods may also work in the 2.4 GHz range? (Choose all that apply.)

  A. Bluetooth

  B. Satellite

  C. Long-range fixed wireless

  D. mmWave

  E. NFC

20. You are configuring a SOHO client to use TCP/IP. Which parameter is needed to tell the client where to communicate to get on the Internet?

  A. Static address

  B. Dynamic address

  C. APIPA

  D. Gateway

Performance-Based Question

You will encounter performance-based questions on the A+ exams. The questions on the exams require you to perform a specific task, and you will be graded on whether or not you were able to complete the task. The following requires you to think creatively in order to measure how well you understand this chapter's topics. You may or may not see similar questions on the actual A+ exams. To see how your answers compare to the authors', refer to Appendix B.

You just purchased a new PCIe network card for a Windows 10 desktop computer. How would you install it?

Chapter

8

Network Services, Virtualization, and Cloud Computing

THE FOLLOWING COMPTIA A+ 220-1101 EXAM OBJECTIVES ARE COVERED IN THIS CHAPTER:

✓ **2.4 Summarize services provided by networked hosts.**

- Server roles

  - DNS

  - DHCP

  - Fileshare

  - Print servers

  - Mail servers

  - Syslog

  - Web servers

  - Authentication, authorization, and accounting (AAA)

- Internet appliances

  - Spam gateways

  - Unified threat management (UTM)

  - Load balancers

  - Proxy servers

- Legacy/embedded systems

  - Supervisory control and data acquisition (SCADA)

- Internet of Things (IoT) devices

✓ **4.1 Summarize cloud-computing concepts.**

- Common cloud models

- Private cloud
- Public cloud
- Hybrid cloud
- Community cloud
- Infrastructure as a service (IaaS)
- Software as a service (SaaS)
- Platform as a service (PaaS)
- Cloud characteristics
  - Shared resources
  - Metered utilization
  - Rapid elasticity
  - High availability
  - File synchronization
- Desktop virtualization
  - Virtual desktop infrastructure (VDI) on premises
  - VDI in the cloud

✓ 4.2 Summarize aspects of client-side virtualization.

- Purpose of virtual machines
  - Sandbox
  - Test development
  - Application virtualization
    - Legacy software/OS
    - Cross-platform virtualization
- Resource requirements
- Security requirements

Networks are often complicated structures. When users get on a network, they have expectations that certain services will be delivered, and most of the time they are unaware of the underlying infrastructure. As long as what they want gets delivered, they are content. In client-server networks, which you learned about in Chapter 5, "Networking Fundamentals," there are one or more servers that play unique roles in fulfilling client requests.

The traditional delivery method for services has been that the servers are on the same network as the clients. They might not be on the same LAN, but they are certainly administered by one company or one set of administrators. If clients on the network need a new feature, the network architects and administrators add the necessary server. This is still the most common setup today, but there's been a sharp growth in cloud computing and virtualization in the last several years. In essence, cloud computing lets networks break out of that model and have services provided by a server that the company doesn't own, and so it's not under the company's direct control. Virtualization is an important technology in cloud computing because it removes the barrier of needing one-to-one relationships between the physical computer and the operating system.

In this chapter, we will talk about some key network services you need to be familiar with as a technician. Servers provide some services, and stand-alone security devices or Internet appliances provide others. After that, we will dive into the world of cloud computing and virtualization, because it's a hot topic that is becoming increasingly important.

Understanding Network Services

As you learned in Chapter 5, networks are made up of multiple types of devices operating together. There are different types of networks, such as peer-to-peer and client-server, and they are categorized based on the types of devices they support. Very simple, small networks can be peer-to-peer, where there are no dedicated servers. However, most networks that you encounter in the business world will have at least one server, and enterprise networks can easily have hundreds or even thousands of servers.

New computer technicians won't be expected to manage large server farms by themselves, but they should be aware of the types of servers and other devices that will be on the network and their basic functions. Experienced technicians may be in charge of one or more servers, and they will need to be intimately familiar with their inner workings. As you gain more experience, you will find that there are advanced certifications in the market to prove your knowledge of servers and show off your skills to potential employers. For the A+ exam, you will need to know various server roles, the features of a few Internet security appliances, the impact of legacy and embedded systems, and the features of Internet of Things (IoT) devices.

Server Roles

Servers come in many shapes and sizes, and they can perform many different roles on a network. Servers are generally named for the type of service they provide, such as a web server or a print server. They help improve network security and ease administration by centralizing control of resources and security; without servers, every user would need to manage their own security and resource sharing. Not everyone has the technical ability to do that, and even if they did, those types of responsibilities might not be part of what they are being asked to deliver at work. Servers can also provide features such as load balancing and increased reliability.

Most server operating systems, such as the Windows Server series, come with built-in software that allows them to play one or more roles. The administrator simply needs to enable the service (such as DHCP or DNS) and configure it properly.

Some servers are dedicated to a specific task, such as hosting websites, and they are called *dedicated servers*. *Nondedicated servers* may perform multiple tasks, such as hosting a website and serving as the administrator's daily workstation. Situations like this are often not ideal because the system needs more resources to support everything it needs to do. Imagine that you are the user of that computer and there is heavy website traffic. Your system could slow down to the point where it's difficult to get anything done. In addition, that kind of setup could introduce additional security risks. Servers can also perform multiple server-specific roles at the same time, such as hosting websites and providing file and print services. As you read through the descriptions of server roles, you will see that it makes more sense to combine some services than it does to combine others.

One important decision network architects need to make when thinking about designing a network is where to place the server or servers. In Chapter 7, "Wireless and SOHO Networks," we introduced the concept of a *screened subnet* (formerly called a *demilitarized zone [DMZ]*), which is a network separated from the internal network by a firewall but also protected from the Internet by a firewall. Figure 8.1 shows two examples of screened subnets.

The network on the left in Figure 8.1 shows a screened subnet managed by what is called a *three-pronged firewall*—so named because it has three network interfaces. You can see that the firewall has an Internet interface, an internal interface, and a screened subnet interface. Another common configuration is a two-pronged firewall (shown on the right of Figure 8.1), with the screened subnet in the middle of the two. In that setup, if an attacker wants to get to your internal network, they have to go through two separate firewalls. Hopefully, you have your firewalls set up to make that task difficult for potential hackers!

FIGURE 8.1   Screened subnets

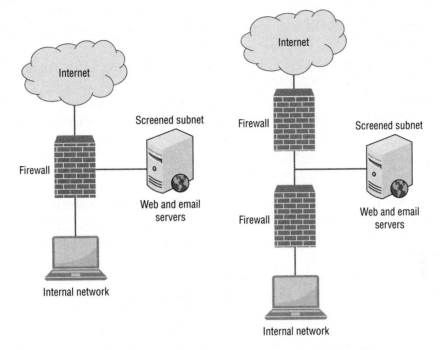

In Figure 8.1, you see that the web and mail servers are in the screened subnet and not on the internal network. This configuration can make it easier to manage the network but still provide great security. As a rule of thumb, any server that needs to be accessed by the outside world should be in the screened subnet, and any server that does not need to be accessed from the Internet should be on the internal network, which is more secure. By the way, servers can play the role of firewalls, too. It's not, however, on the list of objectives as a server role, and in practice it's best to separate other server roles from firewalls. In other words, if you intend to use a server as a firewall, then don't use it for any other types of services. Having services on the firewall itself just makes it easier for hackers to get to. There's no sense in making things easier for them. Now it's time to talk about specific server roles on a network.

DNS

We discussed *Domain Name System (DNS)* servers in Chapter 6, "Introduction to TCP/IP," so we won't go into a lot of depth here. Instead, we'll provide a quick review:

- DNS servers resolve hostnames to IP addresses. An example would be resolving www
  .google.com to 72.14.205.104 so that communication can begin.

- If a company wants to host its own website, it also needs to maintain two public DNS servers with information on how to get to the website. (Two servers are required for redundancy.) An advantage of using ISPs or web hosting companies to host the website is that they are then also responsible for managing the DNS servers.

- Each DNS server has a database, called a *zone file*, which maintains records of hostname to IP address mappings.

- If a DNS server doesn't have an address in its zone file or its cache, it is configured to ask another, higher-level DNS server called the *root server*.

- Within the zone file, some key record types are A (IPv4 host), AAAA (IPv6 host), MX (mail exchanger), and TXT (text).

DNS servers for intranet use only can be located on the internal network (inside the network firewalls). If the DNS server is being used for Internet name resolution, it's most effective to place it in the screened subnet. DNS uses UDP or TCP port 53.

DHCP

Dynamic Host Configuration Protocol (DHCP) servers were also covered in Chapter 6, so there's no sense in repeating all the same material. A review is more appropriate:

- DHCP servers are configured to provide IP configuration information automatically to clients, such as an IP address, subnet mask, default gateway, and the address of a DNS server.

- DHCP servers are configured with a *scope*, which contains the information that the server can provide to clients. DHCP servers need at least one scope, but they can also have more than one.

- Scopes contain an IP address pool, lease duration, address reservations, and scope options such as the default gateway and DNS server address.

- If a client is on a different subnet than the DHCP server, the client's network segment needs to have a *DHCP relay agent*, which will pass along the DHCP request.

- If a Windows-based DHCP client is unable to reach a DHCP server, it will configure itself with an Automatic Private IP Address (APIPA) address. Those addresses have the format 169.254.*x.x*.

DHCP servers should be located on the internal network. If the network has clients that are connecting via remote access, then a device with DHCP capabilities (such as the Remote Access Service [RAS]) can be placed in the screened subnet. DHCP uses UDP ports 67 and 68.

Fileshare or File Server

A *fileshare* or *file server* provides a central repository for users to store, manage, and access files on the network. There are a few distinct advantages to using file servers:

- Ease of access to files for collaboration

- Centralized security management

- Centralized backups

Fileshares come in a variety of shapes and sizes. Some are as basic as Windows-, macOS-, or Linux-based servers with a large amount of internal hard disk storage space. Networks can also use *network-attached storage (NAS)* devices, which are stand-alone units that contain hard drives, come with their own file management software, and connect directly to the network. If a company has extravagant data storage needs, it can implement a *storage area network (SAN)*. A SAN is basically a network segment, or collection of servers, that exists solely to store and manage data.

Since the point of a fileshare is to store data, it's pretty important to ensure that it has ample disk space. Some dedicated file servers also have banks of multiple optical drives for extra storage (letting users access files from optical media) or for performing backups. Processing power and network bandwidth can also be important to manage file requests and deliver them in a timely manner.

As far as location goes, fileshares will almost always be on the internal network. You might have situations where a fileshare is also an FTP server, in which case the server should be on the screened subnet. In those cases, however, you should ensure that the server does not contain highly sensitive information or other data that you don't want to lose.

Print Server

Print servers are much like file servers, except, of course, they make printers available to users. In fact, file servers and print servers are combined so often that you will see a lot of publications or tools refer to *file and print servers* as if they were their own category.

On its own, a *print server* makes printers available to clients over the network and accepts print requests from those clients. A print server can be a physical server like a Windows- or Linux-based server, a small stand-alone device attached to a printer (or several printers), or even a server built into the printer itself. Print servers handle the following important functions:

- Making printers available on the network
- Accepting print requests
- Managing print requests (in the print queue)
- In some cases, processing and storing print jobs

Figure 8.2 shows a simple stand-alone print server. It has an RJ-45 network connection and four USB ports to connect printers. Wireless print servers are easy to find as well.

FIGURE 8.2   A D-Link print server

Although the specific functionality will vary by print server, most of the time administrators will be able to manage security, time restrictions, and other options, including if the server processes the files and if the print jobs are saved after printing. An example is shown in Figure 8.3. Print servers should be located on the internal network.

FIGURE 8.3   Printer management options

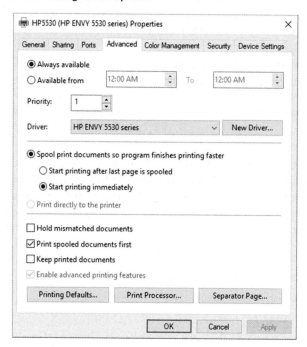

Mail Server

Email is critical for communication, and mail servers are responsible for sending, receiving, and managing email. To be a *mail server*, the computer must be running a specialized email server package. Some popular ones are Microsoft Exchange, Sendmail, Postfix, and Exim, although there are dozens of others on the market.

Clients access the mail server by using an email client installed on their systems. The most common corporate email client is Microsoft Outlook, but Apple Mail, HCL Notes (formerly IBM Notes and Lotus Notes), Gmail, and Thunderbird are also used. Mobile and Internet email clients (which are more popular than their corporate cousins) include the iPhone, iPad, and Android email clients; Gmail; Outlook, Apple Mail, and Yahoo! Mail.

In addition to sending and receiving email, mail servers often have antispam software built into them as well as the ability to encrypt and decrypt messages. Email servers are most often located in the screened subnet. Table 8.1 lists the most important protocols for sending and receiving email.

TABLE 8.1   Important email protocols

Protocol	Port	Purpose
SMTP	25	Sending email and transferring email between mail servers.
POP3	110	Receiving email.
IMAP4	143	Receiving email. It's newer and has more features than POP3.

SMTP is a push (send) protocol, whereas POP3 and IMAP4 are pull (receive) protocols.

Syslog

Network administrators need to know what's happening on their network at all times. The challenge is that there may be hundreds or thousands of devices on the network, with thousands of users accessing resources locally and remotely. Keeping track of who is logging in where, what resources users are accessing, who is visiting the web server, the status of the router, the printer's online status, and innumerable other events could be an administrative nightmare. Fortunately, *syslog* is available to help manage it all.

Syslog works as a client-server model, where the clients generate messages based on the triggering of certain conditions, such as a login event or an error with a device, and send them to a centralized logging server, also known as the *syslog server*. Syslog uses UDP port 514 by default. Consequently, the term *syslog* can be applied to a standard or system for event monitoring, the protocol, or the actual server that collects the logged messages.

Syslog got its start in the UNIX world and is used extensively with Linux-based networking systems and devices. Microsoft operating systems don't natively support syslog—Windows comes with its own event logger called Event Viewer, which we cover in Chapter 15, "Windows 10 Administration"—but it's easy to find packages that let Windows servers participate in a syslog environment. Let's take a look at clients and servers in a syslog system.

Syslog Clients

Many different types of devices, such as servers, routers, and printers, support syslog as a client across a wide variety of operating systems. The primary job of the client (in syslog terms) is to send a message to the syslog server if certain conditions are met. For example, an authentication server can send a message whenever there is a successful or failed login attempt, or a router can send the status of its used or available bandwidth.

Messages have the following three components:

A Facility Code   The *facility code* is a number between 0 and 23 that identifies the type of device sending the message. For example, facility code 0 is for operating system kernel messages; code 2 is used by email servers; code 4 is for security messages; and code 6 is used by printers. Don't worry about memorizing the facility codes. Just know that they tell the server where the message came from.

A Severity Level   The *severity level* lets the administrator know how urgent the issue is. Table 8.2 illustrates the syslog severity levels. The lower the level, the more urgent the message is. Facility codes and error levels can be helpful when sorting events on a syslog server, and they can also be used to send the administrator an alert if something catastrophic happens. Facility codes and severity levels are required message components.

TABLE 8.2   Syslog severity levels

Level	Severity	Description
0	Emergency	A panic condition when the system is unusable
1	Alert	Immediate action needed
2	Critical	Major errors in the system
3	Error	"Normal" error conditions
4	Warning	Warning conditions, usually not as urgent as errors
5	Notice	Normal operation but a condition has been met
6	Information	Provides general information
7	Debug	Information used to help debug programs

A Text Description   The final portion of the message is the text description of the message itself. The description may be in easy-to-read language, or it could be nonsensical ranting. It really depends on the device developer and what they program it to be. There is no standardized format for the description, so it can come in any number of formats. Most messages do come with an IP address or device name included, but the lack of standardization can make understanding messages a fun and entertaining challenge.

Syslog Servers

The syslog server's job is to collect and store messages. Most syslog servers are made up of three components: the listener, a database, and management and filtering software.

Syslog servers listen on UDP port 514 by default. Remember that UDP is a connectionless protocol, so the delivery of packets is not guaranteed. The default implementation of syslog is also not secure. However, you can secure it by running syslog over Transport Layer Security (TLS) and TCP port 6514. Regardless of whether you secure it or not, always place the syslog server behind your firewall and on the internal network.

Even on small networks, devices can generate huge numbers of syslog messages. Therefore, most syslog implementations store messages in a database for easier retrieval and analysis.

Finally, most syslog servers will have management software that you can use to view messages. The software should also have the ability to send the administrator a console message or text (or email) if a critical error is logged. Dozens of syslog packages are available. Some popular packages are Kiwi Syslog by SolarWinds (shown in Figure 8.4), Splunk, syslog-ng, and Syslog Watcher.

FIGURE 8.4   Kiwi Syslog

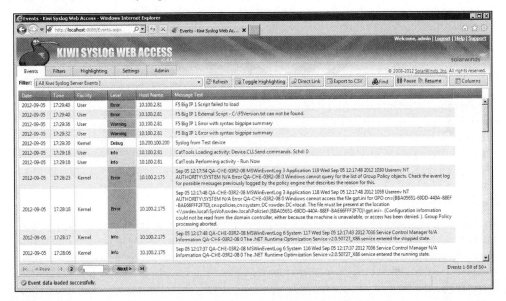

Web Server

Whenever you visit a web page, you are making a connection from your device (the client) to a *web server*. To be more specific, a connection is requested by your Internet software (generally, a web browser) using the *Hypertext Transfer Protocol Secure (HTTPS)* of the TCP/IP protocol suite. Your client needs to know the IP address of the web server, and it will make the request on port 443.

The web server itself is configured with web hosting software, which listens for inbound requests on port 443. Two of the most common web server platforms are the open source Apache and Microsoft's Internet Information Services (IIS), although there are a few dozen different packages available for use. Web servers provide content on request, which can include text, images, and videos, and they can also do things like run scripts to open additional functions, such as processing credit card transactions and querying databases.

> Web servers often function as download servers, too, meaning that they also use FTP. FTP works on TCP ports 20 and 21.

Individuals or independent companies can manage web servers, but more often than not an Internet service provider or web hosting company that manages hundreds or thousands of websites manages them. In fact, one web server can be configured to manage dozens of smaller websites using the same IP address, provided that it has sufficient resources to handle the traffic. On the flip side, huge sites, such as Amazon.com and Google, are actually made up of multiple web servers acting as one site. It's estimated that Google has over 900,000 servers, and Microsoft claims to have over 1 million servers!

If a company wants to host its own web server, the best place for it is in the screened subnet. This configuration provides ease of access (after all, you *want* people to hit your web server) and the best security. The firewall can be configured to allow inbound port 443 requests to the screened subnet but not to allow inbound requests on those ports to make it to the internal corporate network.

Contrast this to a situation where the web server is on the internal network. The firewall then has to let inbound port 443 connections through to the internal network so that Internet-based clients can get to the web server. However, that also means that inbound requests on port 443 can be sent to all internal computers, including non-web servers and even client computers. Hackers could then potentially take advantage of exploits using port 443 to attempt to gain illegitimate access to the network.

Authentication, Authorization, and Accounting (AAA)

The ultimate goal of a security system is to protect resources by keeping the bad people out and letting the good people in. It would be really easy to configure a system such that no one could access anything, and it would be equally simple to let everyone have open access. The first extreme defeats the purpose of having a network, and the second is just begging for trouble. The challenge then is to find a happy medium, where resources are available to those who should have them and nobody else.

In information security, there's a framework for access control known as *triple A*, meaning *authentication, authorization, and accounting (AAA)*. Occasionally auditing is added to the mix, making it *quad A*. And even further, nonrepudiation, or the assurance that something can't be denied by someone, is also sometimes lumped in. Regardless, triple A is the umbrella term for describing systems of access control. AAA servers are gatekeepers and critical components to network security, and they can be implemented on a dedicated server machine, wireless router or access point, Ethernet switch, or a remote access server.

A common term that you will hear in the Windows Server world is *domain controller*, which is a centralized authentication server. Other types of servers that handle all aspects of AAA are *Remote Access Service (RAS)*, *Remote Authentication Dial-In User Service (RADIUS)*, *Terminal Access Controller Access-Control System Plus (TACACS+)*, and *Kerberos*. Authentication servers may be stand-alone (e.g., a "Kerberos server"), or the authentication service may be built into a more well-known OS. For example, Windows Server uses Kerberos.

The AAA process will differ slightly between servers, but generally what happens is the user (or computer) trying to access the network presents credentials. If the credentials are deemed appropriate, the authentication server issues the user a security code or a ticket that grants them access to resources. When the owner of the security code or ticket tries to access a resource, authorization comes into play. And finally, accounting tracks all of it. In the following sections, we will describe the principles of authentication, authorization, and accounting.

Authentication

To implement security, it's imperative to understand who or what is accessing resources on a computer or network. User *authentication* happens when the system being logged into validates that the user has proper credentials. Essentially, the authentication server asks the question, "Who are you?" Oftentimes, this is as simple as entering a username and password, but it could be more complex. There are two categories of authentication:

Single-Factor Authentication The simplest form of authentication is *single-factor authentication*. A single-factor system requires only one piece of information beyond the username to allow access. Most often, this is a password. Single-factor authentication is quite common, but it's not the most secure method out there.

Multifactor Authentication To increase security, your computer or network might require *multifactor authentication*, which as the name implies requires multiple pieces of information for you to log in. Generally speaking, in addition to a username, multifactor authentication requires you to provide two or more pieces of information out of these four categories: something you know, something you have, something you are, or somewhere you are.

You may also hear multifactor authentication referred to by the specific number of factors required, such as two-factor authentication or three-factor authentication.

As mentioned already, most authentication systems require just a password, which is an example of something you know. If you forget your password, a website might ask you to provide answers to security questions that you selected when you registered. These are questions such as the name of your elementary school, father's middle name, street you grew up on, first car, favorite food, musical artist, and so forth.

One-time passwords can be generated by sites to give you a limited time window to log in. These are far more secure than a standard password because they are valid for only a short amount of time, usually 30 minutes or less. The password will be sent to you via text or email or possibly a phone call.

Something you have can be one of a few different things, such as a smartcard or a security token. A smartcard is a plastic card, similar in dimensions to a credit card, which contains a microchip that a card reader can scan, such as on a security system. Smartcards often double as employee badges, enabling employees to access employee-only areas of a building or to use elevators that go to restricted areas, or as credit cards.

Smartcards can also be used to allow or prevent computer access. For example, a PC may have a card reader on it through which the employee has to swipe the card, or that reads the card's chip automatically when the card comes into its vicinity. Or, they're combined with a PIN or used as an add-on to a standard login system to give an additional layer of security verification. For someone to gain unauthorized access, they have to know a user's ID and password (or PIN) and also steal their smartcard. That makes it much more difficult to be a thief!

A security token, like the one shown in Figure 8.5, displays an access code that changes about every 30 seconds. When received, it's synchronized with your user account, and the algorithm that controls the code change is known by the token as well as your authentication system. When you log in, you need your username and password, along with the code on the token.

FIGURE 8.5   RSA SecurID

Security tokens can be software-based as well. A token may be embedded in a security file unique to your computer, or your network may use a program that generates a security token much like the hardware token does. Figure 8.6 shows an example of PingID, which works on computers and mobile devices. This type of token saves you from having to carry around yet another gadget.

FIGURE 8.6   PingID

A system might also require you to log in from a specific location. For example, perhaps users are allowed to log in only if they are on the internal corporate network. Or, maybe you are allowed to connect from your home office. In that case, the security system would know a range of IP addresses to allow in based on the block of addresses allocated to your ISP. This is an example of somewhere you are.

Finally, the system could require something totally unique to you (something you are) to enable authentication. These characteristics are usually assessed via biometric devices, which authenticate users by scanning for one or more physical traits. Common types include fingerprint recognition, facial recognition, and retina scanning.

Authorization

Once it's determined who the user is, the next step in access control is determining what the user can do. This is called *authorization*. Users are allowed to perform only specific tasks on specific objects based on what they are authorized to do. Most computers grant access based on a system of *permissions*, which are groups of privileges. For example, a user might be able to make changes to one file, whereas they are only allowed to open and read another.

One of the key foundations of an authorization system is the principle of *least privilege*. This states that users should be granted only the least amount of access required to perform their jobs, and no more. This principle applies to computers, files, databases, and all other available resources.

Accounting

After users have been authenticated and authorized, it's time to think about tracking what the users did with their access. This is where *accounting* comes in. The principle of accounting seeks to keep a record of who accessed what and when, and the actions they performed.

The most common method of tracking user actions is through the use of logs. Nearly all operating systems have built-in logs that track various actions. For example, Windows-based systems contain Windows Logs, which are part of Event Viewer. To open Event Viewer, click Start and type **Event**. Click Event Viewer in Best Matches when it appears. Windows has logs that track application events, security events, and system events. Figure 8.7 shows the Security log. In an environment where multiple users log in, those logins will be shown here.

Another action that is frequently tracked is web browsing history. Web browsers retain a historical account of the sites that have been visited. To see viewing history in Microsoft Edge, click the Hub (it looks like a star, near the upper-right corner) and then History, as shown in Figure 8.8. There's an option to clear the history as well. Note that this action clears it from the browser, but it won't clear it from any servers (such as a proxy server) that caches web requests. To view the history in Chrome, click the More menu (the three vertical dots) and then History, or just open Chrome and press Ctrl+H.

FIGURE 8.7   Security log in Event Viewer

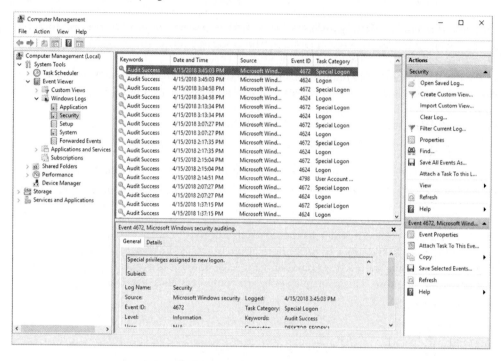

FIGURE 8.8   Microsoft Edge site-viewing history

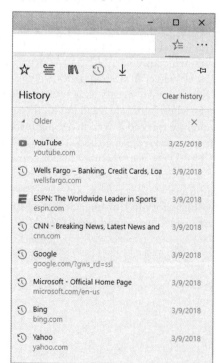

Internet Appliances

The definition of an *Internet appliance* is a device that makes it easy to access the Internet. Taking a slightly broader view, Internet appliances can also help users safely access the Internet by protecting against some of the dangers that lurk there. The CompTIA A+ 220-1101 exam objectives list four items under Internet appliances: spam gateways, unified threat management (UTM), load balancers, and proxy servers. Let's take a look at each one.

Spam Gateways

Spam email is pervasive today. If you use email, it's likely you get spam, and a lot of it. What might be hard to believe is that you would get significantly more if there weren't antispam devices protecting you. A *spam gateway* is an appliance—most likely a software installation or virtual appliance—that blocks malicious emails from entering a network. They go by other names as well, such as antispam gateways (which sound more appropriate), spam blockers, and email gateways.

Antispam gateways can be located in two places: on the cloud or on an internal network, meaning internal to where the firewall is placed. The intent is that emails inbound to a corporate email server will first go through the gateway. If the gateway checks the email and verifies it's not spam, it passes the mail through to the server. Flagged emails get sent to a spam folder, quarantined, or deleted.

Emails that contain certain keywords, have malicious links, or come from domains that are known to send spam are most likely to get flagged. On occasion, legitimate emails will get flagged too, but these appliances get far more right than they get wrong.

Some spam gateways will also handle outbound emails. Hopefully your users aren't spammers, but if they are, the gateway will put an end to it. In most cases, a company sending spam email is accidental. A hacker could be sending emails from your company's domain by spoofing it or by other tricks which might not be immediately visible. A good spam gateway will block these outbound messages and notify the administrator.

Unified Threat Management (UTM)

The Internet is a wondrous place, but it's a scary one as well. It seems like for every video of puppies or kittens doing cute things, there are 10 hackers lurking in dark corners trying to steal identities or crash servers. It's an unfortunate reality of the Internet age. Software and hardware solutions have sprung up in response to various types of threats and managing all of them can be a challenge. For example, a network needs a firewall, antimalware and antispam software, and perhaps content filtering and intrusion prevention system (IPS) devices as well. It's a lot to deal with.

Detecting and Preventing Network Intrusions

When marketing unified threat management (UTM) systems, many vendors will talk about how their system combines an *intrusion detection system (IDS)* or *intrusion prevention system (IPS)* with other features. Both devices are closely related to each other, and both devices monitor network traffic and look for suspicious activity that might be the sign of a network-based attack. You can think of them as being somewhat analogous to antivirus (AV) programs. AV programs examine individual files looking for telltale signs of malicious content (called a *signature*). IDSs and IPSs look for signatures as well, but in network traffic patterns.

Both IDSs and IPSs are different from firewalls. Firewalls have specific sets of rules that allow or deny packets to enter a network, based on criteria such as the packet's origination or destination address, the protocol being used, or the source or destination port. Their primary function is to block malicious traffic from entering the network in the first place. Firewalls may also have IDS or IPS software built in, or IDS and IPS devices can be stand-alone hardware devices.

An IDS is a passive device. It watches network traffic, and it can detect anomalies that might represent an attack. For example, if an attacker were to try to flood a network with traffic on a specific port, the IDS would sense that the additional traffic on that port was unusual. Then the IDS would log the anomaly and send an alert to an administrator. Note that it does nothing to prevent the attack; it simply logs relevant information pertaining to the attack and sends an alert.

By contrast, an IPS is an active device. It too monitors network traffic, but when it detects an anomaly, it can take actions to attempt to stop the attack. For example, if it senses suspicious inbound traffic on a specific IP port, it can shut down the port, block the sender, or reset the TCP connection. If the malicious stream of data is intended for one computer, it can prevent the attacking host from communicating with the intended victim computer or prevent the attacker from communicating with any computer. The specific actions it can take will depend on the device.

Both types of devices come in network-based varieties (NIDS and NIPS) and host-based varieties (HIDS and HIPS). As you might expect based on their names, the network-based versions are designed to protect multiple systems, whereas the host-based ones protect only one computer.

The goal of *unified threat management (UTM)* is to centralize security management, allowing administrators to manage all their security-related hardware and software through a single device or interface. For administrators, having a single management point greatly reduces administration difficulties. The downside is that it introduces a single point of failure. If all network security is managed through one device, a device failure could be problematic.

UTM is generally implemented as a stand-alone device (or series of devices) on a network, and it will replace the traditional firewall. A UTM device can generally provide the following types of services:

- Packet filtering and inspection, like a firewall
- Intrusion prevention service
- Gateway antimalware
- Spam blocking
- Malicious website blocking (either prohibited or nefarious content)
- Application control

UTM has become quite popular in the last several years. Many in the industry see it as the next generation of firewalls.

Load Balancing

Imagine you want to do some online shopping. You open your browser, type **amazon .com** into the address bar, and the site appears. You've made a connection to the Amazon server, right? But is there only one Amazon server? Considering the millions of transactions Amazon completes each day, that seems highly unlikely. In fact it's not the case. Amazon has dozens if not hundreds of web servers, each of them capable of fulfilling the same tasks to make your shopping experience as easy as possible. Each server helps balance out the work for the website, which is called *load balancing*.

Load-balancing technology can be implemented with local hardware or on the cloud. If implemented on a local network, a hardware device, conveniently named a load balancer, essentially acts like the web server to the outside world. When a user visits the website, the load balancer sends the request to one of many real web servers to fulfill the request. Cloud implementations have made load balancing easier to configure and expand, since the servers can be virtual instead of physical.

Common Load Balancing Configurations

We already shared one example of load balancing with an online retailer. In that example, all servers are identical (or very close to identical) and perform the same tasks. Two other common load-balancing configurations are cross-region and content-based.

In a cross-region setup, all servers likely provide access to the same types of content, much like in our Amazon example. The big feature with this setup is that there are servers local to each region—proximity to the users will help speed up network performance. For example, say that a company has a geo-redundant cloud and users in North America, Asia, and Europe. When a request comes in, the load balancer senses the incoming IP address and routes the request to a server in that region. This is illustrated in Figure 8.9. If all servers in that region are too busy with other requests, then it might be sent to another region for processing.

FIGURE 8.9   Cross-region load balancing

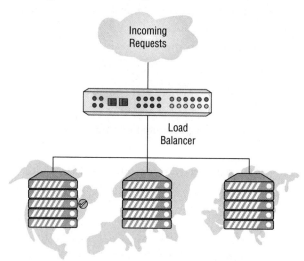

Another common way to load-balance is to split up banks of servers to handle specific types of requests. For example, one group of servers could handle web requests, while a second set hosts streaming video and a third set manages downloads. This type of load balancing is called content-based load balancing and is shown in Figure 8.10.

FIGURE 8.10   Content-based load balancing

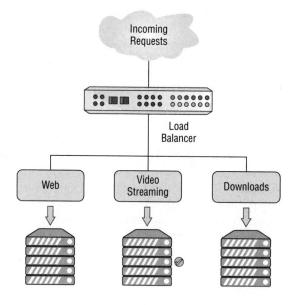

Load Balancing Benefits

Load balancing has performance benefits for high-traffic networks and heavily used applications. Scalability and reliability are important benefits as well. Let's give a few examples of each.

Performance   The Amazon example we used earlier is probably the best example of this, but not all companies provide massive online shopping services. Smaller companies can benefit from performance enhancements as well. Servers that are specialized to handle a specific content type are often more efficient than multipurpose ones. And, the global load balancing example can be applied to distributed sites within a country as well.

Scalability   If using cloud-based load balancing, services are easily scalable. For example, let's say that your company sells products online, and has two servers dedicated to that task. For the majority of the year, the two servers can handle the traffic without a problem. On the busiest shopping day of the year—Cyber Monday—those servers are overwhelmed. With cloud-based load balancing, traffic spikes can be handled by quickly provisioning additional virtual servers to handle the traffic. When the capacity is no longer required, the servers are turned off.

Reliability   Imagine a company that uses a business-critical application for remote salespeople. What happens if the server hosting that application crashes? It wouldn't be good.

With load balancing, different servers can host the application, even in different regions. Perhaps a hurricane wipes out the data center in Florida. The load balancer can direct users to other data centers in different regions, and the business can continue to generate revenue.

Proxy Server

A *proxy server* makes requests for resources on behalf of a client. The most common one that you will see is a web proxy, but you might run into a caching proxy as well. Exercise 8.1 shows you where to configure your computer to use a web proxy server in Windows 10.

EXERCISE 8.1

Configuring Windows 10 to Use a Proxy Server

1.   Click Start ➤ Settings (it looks like a gear) ➤ Network & Internet.

2.   On the left side, click Proxy, as shown in Figure 8.11.

continues

3. Enter the address of the proxy server in the Address box.

Note that you can also enter in exclusions in the box below. Sites entered here would be accessed directly and not through the proxy server.

4. Click Save, and you are finished.

FIGURE 8.11 Enabling a client to use a proxy server in Windows 10

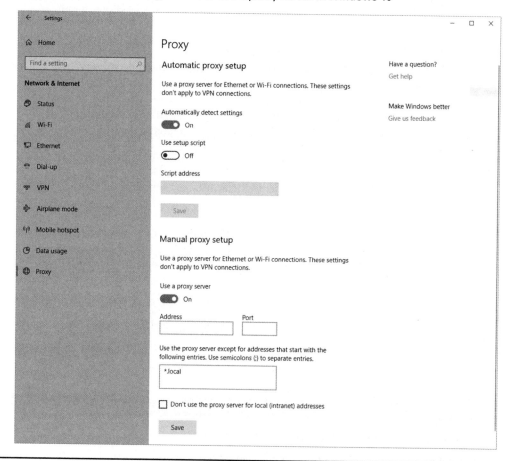

You can get to the same page shown in Figure 8.11 from within Edge. Follow these steps:

1. Click More Actions (the three horizontal dots in the upper-right corner) ➢ Settings ➢ View Advanced Settings ➢ Open Proxy Settings.

a. If you're a Chrome user, or have a Windows OS older than Windows 10, the screen looks slightly different. In Chrome, click More (the three vertical dots in the upper-right corner) ➤ Settings ➤ Advanced ➤ Open Proxy Settings.

The Connections tab of the Internet Properties window will open.

2. Click LAN Settings, and then check the box for the Proxy Server, as shown in Figure 8.12.

FIGURE 8.12 Alternate method of configuring a proxy client

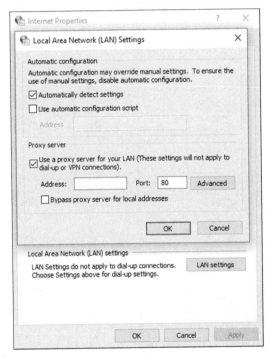

3. Enter the address in the Address box. (In Internet Explorer, click Tools ➤ Internet Options and then the Connections tab.)

The proxy settings apply to all browsers on the client computer, so you don't need to configure it in multiple places if you use multiple browsers.

Let's use an example of a web proxy to illustrate how the proxy server process works. The user on the client computer opens a web browser and types in a URL. Instead of the request going directly to that website, it goes to the proxy server. The proxy then makes the request of the website, and it returns the requested information to the client computer. If it sounds to you like this slows down Internet browsing, you're right—it does. But there are three strong potential benefits to using a proxy.

First, the proxy server can cache the information requested, speeding up subsequent searches. (This is also the only function of a caching proxy, but caching-only proxies are most commonly configured to work on a local intranet.) Second, the proxy can act as a filter, blocking content from prohibited websites. Third, the proxy server can modify the requester's information when passing it to the destination, blocking the sender's identity and acting as a measure of security; the user can be made anonymous.

Keep in mind that if all of the traffic from a network must pass through a proxy server to get to the Internet, that can really slow down the response time. Make sure the proxy or proxies have ample resources to handle all the requests. Figure 8.13 shows an example of a proxy server on a network.

FIGURE 8.13 A proxy server on a network

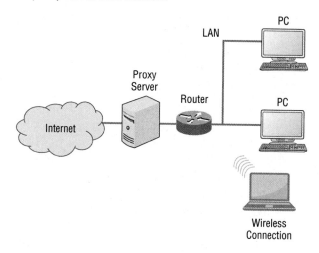

Legacy/Embedded Systems

In regular human terms, legacies are considered a good thing. Most of us want to leave a legacy of some kind, whether it's within a community or organization or within our own families. A legacy is something that lives on far beyond a human life span.

If you mention the term *legacy system* in the computer world, though, you are likely to be met with groans and eye rolls. It means that the system is old and hopelessly outdated by today's computing standards. Legacy systems are usually defined as those using old technology in one or more of the following areas:

- Hardware
- Software (applications or operating system)
- Network protocols

Many legacy systems were state of the art when they were originally implemented in the 1970s or 1980s, but they haven't been upgraded or replaced. Today, though, they are old and slow, and specialized knowledge is required to maintain and operate them. For example, someone might need to know the Pick operating system (which came out in the 1970s), how to operate an IBM AS/400 or manage VAX, or how to configure the IPX/SPX network protocol. (Google these topics sometime!)

It's not just the really old stuff, though. Even technologies that have been invented after the turn of the century can now be considered legacy. For example, Microsoft no longer supports the Windows XP and Windows 7 operating systems. Security and other updates will no longer be provided for these OSs, which could introduce security risks. On the hardware side, the wireless networking 802.11b standard is definitely legacy today, and if 802.11g isn't already legacy, it should be. It's really hard to find new components that include these standards.

 An *embedded system* is one that is critical in a process; other systems or processes depend upon it. For purposes of this section, we will treat legacy and embedded systems as one and the same, because administrators face similar issues with both.

So why don't companies replace legacy systems? It's complicated:

- First, most companies don't have large IT budgets, and replacing legacy systems can be very expensive. This is especially true for many companies that see the systems providing reliable (if a bit slow) service. Why fix what's not broken?

- Second, the cost of failure of an upgrade could be catastrophic. The world's global financial systems are in many places supported by legacy systems. Messing up a migration in that context could be a career-limiting move.

- Third, the time it would take to test the new system, verify functionality, and roll out the implementation could be extensive. Time is money, and we already stated that IT budgets are generally tight.

Furthermore, it's challenging to find technicians and consultants who understand legacy systems. People move from company to company, or consultants retire and take their specialized knowledge with them. Someone who was a mid-20s computer whiz in 1975 is now in their 70s and probably retired. The cost to find someone knowledgeable on these systems can be high.

Speaking of high costs, finding replacement hardware can be difficult to impossible while being expensive at the same time. Eventually, the cost of maintenance might outweigh the cost of upgrading, but then again it might not.

A great example of critical legacy systems is a category known as *supervisory control and data acquisition (SCADA)*. SCADA systems are high-level management systems that are used to control manufacturing machines and processes; manage large-scale infrastructure settings, such as power grids, oil and gas pipelines, and water treatment facilities; and run components in buildings, such as heating and air conditioning. In other words, they're everywhere, and they manage some very important things. But, most SCADA systems are extremely old and were designed to be open access, so they are huge security holes. Hackers have been exploiting those holes faster than developers have been able to patch them.

Real World Scenario

A Fun Example of a Legacy System

Every once in a while, you will come across an article online discussing the use of a legacy system and the challenges faced because of that system. Check out this site to see one that came out a few years ago:

`http://www.popularmechanics.com/technology/infrastructure/a16010/`
`30-year-old-computer-runs-school-heat`.

After reading the story, you will understand why we included it. The article does a great job of outlining the issues that network administrators face in the real world—namely, if it isn't broke, don't fix it!

So what's a network administrator to do? If possible, replacing or repurposing legacy systems can provide long-term benefits to a company. But also recognize the risk involved. If replacement isn't an option, then the best advice that we can give is to learn as much as you can about them. Hopefully, the system is based on established standards, so you can look them up on the Internet and learn as much as possible. If not, see what operating manuals you can track down, or pick the brain of those who understand how they operate. As challenging as legacy systems can be, you can make yourself quite valuable by being the expert on them.

A common administrative option is to try to isolate the legacy system as much as possible so that its lack of speed doesn't affect the rest of the network. This is usually much easier to do with hardware or protocols than with software. For example, the network might be set up with one segment that hosts the legacy systems or protocols.

One technology that is helping replace and update legacy systems is virtualization, which can obviate the need for one-to-one hardware-to-software relationships. We cover virtualization later in the chapter, in the "Concepts of Virtualization" section.

Internet of Things Devices

The *Internet of Things (IoT)* has been growing rapidly for the last several years. Home automation systems and IoT-based security systems are becoming increasingly popular and will likely continue to become more pervasive. IoT also has a place in the manufacturing world, as companies seek to contain costs.

IoT networks will often have a central controller or coordinating device, like a computer switch but dedicated specifically to IoT devices. The administrator will have an app, usually on a smartphone, that provides them with a Wi-Fi or Bluetooth connection to the controller. Settings the administrator enters are then communicated to the end devices via the controller. Many IoT devices can be configured manually as well, but what's the fun in that? One of the key features of IoT is to control devices and see their status without needing to be physically present at each one. It could take an entire book to cover the different types of IoT devices, but we'll look at few popular ones here.

Thermostats

A thermostat is a device connected to a heating or cooling system that allows users to control the temperature of a room, home, or building. Programmable thermostats that allow you to set the temperature based on time and day have been around for more than 20 years. The next step in the evolution is a smart thermostat (shown in Figure 8.14) that's remotely accessible and can do some basic learning based on the weather and your preferences. Smart thermostats usually have a touch screen, often have their own app, and can be controlled by a central coordinator.

FIGURE 8.14   Nest smart thermostat

By Raysonho @ Open Grid Scheduler/Grid Engine. CC0, https://commons.wikimedia.org/w/index.php?curid=49900570

Smart thermostats have the options you would expect, such as setting the temperature, detecting humidity levels, and configuring schedules to save energy when no one is home. The advanced features are what make these devices especially interesting. Examples include:

- Remote sensors, which can be placed on air vents for more accurate reading and control
- The capability to create energy reports

- Voice activation
- Integration with outdoor weather conditions to adjust internal conditions appropriately
- Geofencing, which allows the thermostat to adjust the temperature based on who it detects in the home and their preferences

Different models offer different features, so you're sure to find one that meets your needs as well as your budget.

Home Security and Automation

Home security systems have been around for a long time, and security cameras are an integral part of them. With IoT-based cameras, security systems are more customizable and smarter than ever.

The security camera can be stand-alone but most often is part of a series of cameras connected to a home security system. That central system will often have a touch screen as well as an app. The system can be activated in several ways, such as by the ringing of an integrated doorbell or by motion sensors. Most systems will provide for the recording of video in the event that they're triggered by motion. Video footage may be stored on local storage, such as an SD card, or on the cloud. Configuration options often include when to activate (for example, when motion is detected), how to notify the user (such as a text or email), and how long to record and store footage.

 Important features to consider when buying a smart security camera include its movement capability, field of view, resolution, night vision, waterproofing, audio capabilities (microphone and/or speakers), and motion detection. Cost may also be a factor.

Home security and automation systems may also control door locks and light switches.

Door Locks

Smart door locks are a feature often integrated into home security systems. They will typically be accompanied by a camera and linked to a doorbell. Many will also have a number pad so that you can enter a code to unlock the door instead of needing a key. Figure 8.15 shows a Schlage smart door lock.

In addition to offering security, smart door locks can provide convenience. For example, perhaps you are expecting a delivery. Someone rings the doorbell. With a smart security system that includes a doorbell and door locks, you can instantly see who it is on your smartphone and talk to them. If you feel comfortable, you can unlock the door and tell them to place the package inside. Once they are done, you can lock the door again. Or, you can tell them to set the package down and you'll come get it in a few minutes, whether you're on the other side of the house or the other side of the country.

FIGURE 8.15 Schlage smart door lock

Light Switches

Smart light switches help control lights in the house. Many are designed to replace existing light switches in the wall, whereas others simply mount to the wall. An example of a Lutron switch is shown in Figure 8.16. In addition to having manual controls, many will have their own app or can be controlled through a coordinator.

Features of a smart light switch are fairly straightforward. They can turn lights on or off and dim the lights. They can perform tasks based on a schedule, and some have geofencing or motion sensors to detect when someone enters a room. Some brands will work only with certain types of lights, so make sure to check compatibility.

Voice-Enabled Smart Speakers/Digital Assistants

Smartphones ushered in the widespread use of voice-enabled digital assistants. It started with Siri on the iPhone, and Google Now ("Okay, Google") soon followed for the Android OS. Microsoft even got into the act with Cortana, which was used with its now defunct Windows Phone OS and is also integrated into Windows 10 and Windows 11. Amazon wanted in on the act, too, but they don't have a smartphone OS. So instead, they created a voice-enabled smart speaker called the Echo with a virtual assistant known simply as Alexa. Google, not to be outdone in the digital assistant market, created Google Home, which uses Google Assistant, which evolved from Google Now. The market for these devices is very competitive.

FIGURE 8.16   Lutron smart light switch

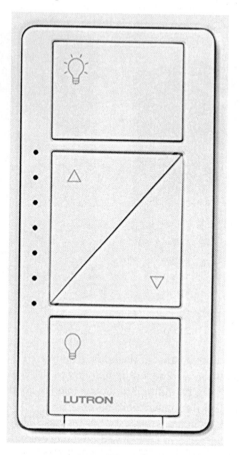

Siri is proprietary to Apple devices, but smart speakers made by other companies will support Alexa or Google Assistant, or both.

The first smart speakers on the market were Wi-Fi–enabled speakers that would listen for you to activate them. Once you said their name, they would listen to your question and use their Internet connection to perform a search and deliver an answer. They were incredibly handy for asking the weather for the day, to play a song, or to answer an obscure trivia question at a party. Newer smart speakers may have integrated video screens as well, up to about 8" or 10" in size. This makes them larger and more conspicuous but lets users view their integrated security cameras, see music videos and movies, and more.

While the features of a smart speaker/digital assistant are appealing to many, there are some potential concerns and risks as well. For example, unless you turn it off, the device is always listening. This is unnerving to some people, and others have even suggested it could be used to eavesdrop on its users. Device manufacturers have gone to lengths to protect users' privacy but know that this could be an issue.

A famous story of misuse comes from late-night television. During a late-night show in 2017, comedian Jimmy Kimmel decided to pull a prank on all of his viewers who had an Amazon Echo or similar device. With the audience quiet, he loudly instructed Alexa (the name that the Amazon digital assistant responds to) to order $500 worth of foam swim "pool noodles." Urban legend has it that multiple viewers were affected by this and sent the product. (To be fair, there are conflicting reports of if it actually worked or not. If it did, Amazon would have accepted the return and reversed the charge.) Of course, this problem could be avoided by turning off automatic voice ordering from Amazon, which is a feature of its digital assistants. Finally, some flaky smart speaker units have been known to speak when not spoken to or even to start laughing for no apparent reason. While this is definitely creepy, it's not necessarily a security threat.

For the A+ exam, be sure you are familiar with the following objectives:

- Server roles: DNS, DHCP, fileshare, print servers, mail servers, syslog, web servers, and authentication, authorization, and accounting (AAA)
- Internet appliances: spam gateways, unified threat management (UTM), load balancers, and proxy servers
- Legacy/embedded systems, including supervisory control and data acquisition (SCADA)
- Internet of Things (IoT) devices

Understanding Virtualization and Cloud Computing

The computer industry is one of big trends. A new technology comes along and becomes popular, until the next wave of newer, faster, and shinier objects comes along to distract everyone from the previous wave. Thinking back over the past 20 to 30 years, there have been several big waves, including the rise of the Internet, wireless networking, and mobile computing.

Within each trend, there are often smaller ones. For example, the Internet was helped by modems and ISPs in the middle of the 1990s, and then broadband access took over. Wireless networking has seen several generations of faster technology, from the 11 Mbps 802.11b, which at the time it came out was pretty cool, to 802.11ax, delivering gigabit wireless. Mobile computing has been a long-lasting wave, first with laptop computers becoming more popular than desktops, and then with handheld devices (namely, smartphones and tablets) essentially functioning like computers.

The biggest recent wave in the computing world is cloud computing. Its name comes from the fact that the technology is Internet-based; in most computer literature, the Internet is represented by a graphic that looks like a cloud. It seems like everyone is jumping on the cloud (pun intended, but doesn't that sound like fun?), and technicians need to be aware of what it can provide and its limitations. The most important core technology supporting cloud computing is virtualization. We will cover both topics in the following sections.

Concepts of Cloud Computing

You hear the term a lot today—*the cloud*. What exactly is the cloud? The way it's named, and it's probably due to the word *the* at the beginning, it sounds like it's one giant, fluffy, magical entity that does everything you could ever want a computer to do. Only it's not quite that big, fluffy, or magical, and it's not even one thing.

Cloud computing is a method by which you access remote servers to store files or run applications for you. There isn't just one cloud—there are hundreds of commercial clouds in existence today. Many of them are owned by big companies, such as Microsoft, Google, HP, Apple, and Amazon. Basically, they set up the hardware and/or software for you on their network, and then you use it.

Using the cloud sounds pretty simple, and in most cases it is. From the administrator's side, though, things can be a little trickier. Cloud computing involves a concept called *virtualization*, which means that there isn't necessarily a one-to-one relationship between a physical server and a logical (or virtual) server. In other words, there might be one physical server that virtually hosts cloud servers for a dozen companies, or there might be several physical servers working together as one logical server. From the end user's side, the idea of a physical machine versus a virtual machine doesn't even come into play, because it's all handled behind the scenes. We'll cover virtualization in more depth later in this chapter.

There are many advantages to cloud computing, and the most important ones revolve around money. Cloud providers can get economies of scale by having a big pool of resources available to share among many clients. It may be entirely possible for them to add more clients without needing to add new hardware, which results in greater profit. From a client company's standpoint, the company can pay for only the resources it needs without investing large amounts of capital into hardware that will be outdated in a few years. Using the cloud is often cheaper than the alternative. Plus, if there is a hardware failure within the cloud, the provider handles it. If the cloud is set up right, the client won't even know that a failure occurred. Other advantages of cloud computing include fast scalability for clients and ease of access to resources regardless of location.

The biggest downside of the cloud has been security. The company's data is stored on someone else's server (off premises), and company employees are sending it back and forth via the Internet. Cloud providers have dramatically increased their security over the last several years, but this can still be an issue, especially if the data is highly sensitive material or personally identifiable information (PII). Also, some companies don't like the fact that they don't own the assets.

Now let's dive into the types of services clouds provide, the types of clouds, cloud-specific terms with which you should be familiar, and some examples of using a cloud from the client side.

Cloud Services

Cloud providers sell everything "as a service." The type of service is named for the highest level of technology provided. For example, if computing and storage is the highest level, the client will purchase infrastructure as a service. If applications are involved, it will be software as a service. Nearly everything that can be digitized can be provided as a service. Let's take a look at the three most common types of services offered by cloud providers, from the ground up:

Infrastructure as a Service   Let's say that a company needs extra network capacity, including processing power, storage, and networking services (such as firewalls) but doesn't have the money to buy more network hardware. Instead, it can purchase *infrastructure as a service (IaaS)*, which is a lot like paying for utilities—the client pays for what it uses. Of the three major cloud services, IaaS requires the most network management expertise from the client. In an IaaS setup, the client provides and manages the software.

Platform as a Service   *Platform as a service (PaaS)* adds a layer to IaaS that includes software development tools such as runtime environments. Because of this, it can be very helpful to software developers; the vendor manages the various hardware platforms. This frees up the software developer to focus on building their application and scaling it. The best PaaS solutions allow for the client to export their developed programs and run them in an environment other than where they were developed. Examples of PaaS include Google App Engine, Microsoft Azure, Red Hat OpenShift, Amazon Web Services (AWS) Elastic Beanstalk, Engine Yard, and Heroku.

Software as a Service (SaaS)   The highest of these three levels of service is *software as a service (SaaS)*, which handles the task of managing software and its deployment, and includes the platform and infrastructure as well. This is the one with which you are probably most familiar, because it's the model used by Google Docs, Microsoft Office 365, and even storage solutions such as Dropbox. The advantage of this model is to cut costs for software ownership and management; clients typically sign up for subscriptions to use the software and can renew as needed.

Figure 8.17 shows examples of these three types of services. SaaS is the same as the Application layer shown in the figure.

Although not included in the A+ objectives, the following other service levels also exist:

- *Hardware as a service (HaaS)*, which is similar to IaaS but is more likely related specifically to data storage
- *Communications as a service (CaaS)*, which provides things like Voice over IP (VoIP), instant messaging, and video collaboration
- *Network as a service (NaaS)*, which provides network infrastructure

- *Desktop as a service (DaaS)*, which provides virtual desktops so that users with multiple devices or platforms can have a similar desktop experience across all systems

- *Data as a service (also DaaS)*, which provides for multiple sources of data in a mash-up

- *Business processes as a service (BpaaS)*, which provides business processes such as payroll, IT help desk, or other services

- *Anything/everything as a service (XaaS)*, which is a combination of the services already discussed

The level of responsibility between the provider and the client is specified in the contract. It should be very clear which party has responsibility for specific elements, should anything go awry.

FIGURE 8.17   Common cloud service levels

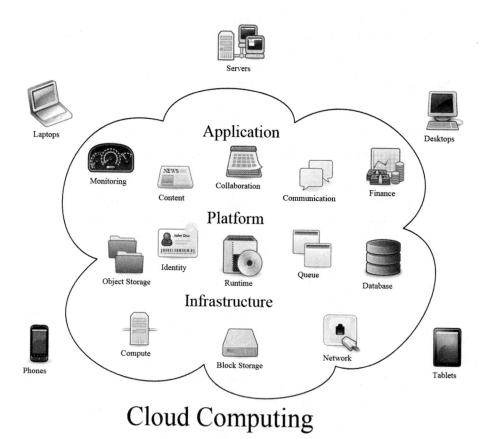

Types of Clouds

Running a cloud is not restricted to big companies offering services over the Internet. Companies can purchase virtualization software to set up individual clouds within their own network. That type of setup is referred to as a *private cloud*. Running a private cloud pretty much eliminates many of the features that companies want from the cloud, such as rapid scalability and eliminating the need to purchase and manage computer assets. The big advantage, though, is that it allows the company to control its own security within the cloud.

The traditional type of cloud that usually comes to mind is a *public cloud*, like the ones operated by the third-party companies we mentioned earlier. These clouds offer the best in scalability, reliability, flexibility, geographical independence, and cost effectiveness. Whatever the client wants, the client gets. For example, if the client needs more resources, it simply scales up and uses more. Of course, the client will also pay more, but that's part of the deal.

Some clients have chosen to combine public and private clouds into a *hybrid cloud*. This gives the client the great features of a public cloud while simultaneously allowing for the storage of more sensitive information on the private cloud. It's the best of both worlds.

The last type of cloud to discuss is a *community cloud*. These are created when multiple organizations with common interests combine to create a cloud. In a sense, it's like a public cloud but with better security. The clients know who the other clients are and, in theory, can trust them more than they could trust random people on the Internet. The economies of scale and flexibility won't be as great as with a public cloud, but that's the trade-off for better security.

Important Cloud Characteristics

We've discussed several important cloud features to this point. The National Institute of Standards and Technology (NIST), a group within the U.S. Department of Commerce, has defined the following five essential characteristics of cloud computing:

On-Demand Self-Service   This is one of the cloud's best features from an end user's standpoint. With on-demand self-service, users can access additional storage, processing, and capabilities automatically, without requiring intervention from the service provider.

Broad Network Access   This means that cloud capabilities are accessible over the network by different types of clients, such as workstations, laptops, and mobile phones, using common access software such as web browsers. The ability for users to get the data they want, when they want, and how they want is sometimes referred to as *ubiquitous access*.

Resource Pooling   The idea of *resource pooling* is closely linked with virtualization, which we will cover shortly. It's essentially the same as the concept of *shared resources* (which is explicitly called out in the A+ exam objectives). The provider's resources are seen as one large pool that can be divided up among clients as needed, and each client pays for the fraction of those resources they use. Clients should be able to access additional resources as needed, even though the client may not be aware of where the resources are physically located. Typical pooled resources include network bandwidth, storage, processing power, and memory.

> With the exception of private clouds, all cloud types use resource pooling or shared resources. In a private cloud, one company controls all the resources.

Rapid Elasticity   We've talked about the ability to scale up resources as needed, and that is elasticity. In most cases, clients can get more resources instantly (or at least very quickly), and that is called *rapid elasticity*. For the client, this is a great feature because they can scale up without needing to purchase, install, and configure new hardware. Elasticity can also work backward; if fewer resources are required, the client may be able to scale down and pay less without needing to sell hardware. You will hear some subscriptions with built-in elasticity referred to as *pay-as-you-grow services*.

Measured Service   Most cloud providers track clients' usage and then charge them for the services used. This type of setup is called *metered service* or *measured service*. Resource usage is monitored by the provider and reported to the client in a transparent fashion.

In addition to those characteristics, the A+ exam objectives list two more: file synchronization and high availability. File synchronization is straightforward enough—it makes sure that the most current copy is on the cloud as well as on a local device. If changes are made to one, the other copy gets updated accordingly. *High availability* refers to uninterrupted and responsive service. When we say uninterrupted, though, we should probably clarify that by saying it's *mostly* uninterrupted. The level of uptime guaranteed by the cloud service provider (CSP) will be specified in a document called the service level agreement (SLA).

Service availability is measured in terms of "nines," or how many nines of uptime the provider guarantees. For example, "three nines" means that the service will be available 99.9 percent of the time, whereas "four nines" will be up 99.99 percent of the time. More nines means more money, and different aspects of your service contract might require different levels of uptime. For example, a critical medical records database might need more guaranteed uptime than would a word processing application. The level of service you should get depends on how much risk your company is willing to take on and the trade-off with cost. Table 8.3 shows how much downtime is acceptable based on the number of nines of guaranteed uptime.

TABLE 8.3   Availability downtime

Availability	Downtime per year	Downtime per day
Three nines (99.9%)	8.77 hours	1.44 minutes
Four nines (99.99%)	52.6 minutes	8.64 seconds
Five nines (99.999%)	5.26 minutes	864 milliseconds
Six nines (99.9999%)	31.56 seconds	86.4 milliseconds

Guaranteeing that services will be available with the possible exception of less than one second per day seems pretty impressive, as is the case with five nines. You might see other combinations, too, such as "four nines five," which translates into 99.995 percent availability, or no more than 4.32 seconds of downtime per day. The majority of CSPs will provide at least three nines or three nines five.

This section referred to the cloud characteristics as defined by the U.S. government agency tasked with promoting technical innovation. It's important to understand these characteristics because that's how cloud providers often refer to their services. Keep in mind that the A+ exam objectives specify a few different services and may use slightly different terms for the same services. We don't share both to confuse you, but rather to make sure you're familiar with industry terminology. For example, if one provider offers you measured service and another offers metered utilization, you should be able to recognize that they're the same thing. The five to know for the exam are shared resources, metered utilization, rapid elasticity, high availability, and file synchronization.

Using Cloud-Based Services

Up to this point, we have primarily focused on the characteristics that make up cloud computing. Now let's turn our attention to some practical examples with which users will probably be more familiar. The two types of cloud interaction we will cover are storage and applications. The next two sections will assume the use of public clouds and standard web browser access.

Cloud-Based Storage

Storage is the area in which cloud computing got its start. The idea is simple—users store files just as they would on a hard drive, but with two major advantages. One, they don't need to buy the hardware. Two, different users can access the files regardless of where they are physically located. Users can be located in the United States, China, and Germany; they all have access via their web browser. This is particularly helpful for multinational organizations.

There is no shortage of cloud-based storage providers in the market today. Each provider offers slightly different features. Most of them will offer limited storage for free and premium services for more data-heavy users. Table 8.4 shows a comparison of some of the better-known providers. Please note that the data limits and prices can change; this table is provided for illustrative purposes only and doesn't include every level of premium service available. Most of these providers offer business plans with unlimited storage as well for an additional cost.

TABLE 8.4   Cloud providers and features

Service	Free	Premium	Cost per year
Dropbox	2 GB	3 TB	$199
Apple iCloud	5 GB	2 TB	$120
Box	10 GB	100 GB	$60
Microsoft OneDrive	5 GB	100 GB	$24
Google Drive	15 GB	2 TB	$100

Which one should you choose? If you want extra features, such as web-based applications, then Google or Microsoft is probably the best choice. If you just need data storage, then Box or Dropbox might be a better option. Some allow multiple users to access a personal account, so that might figure into your decision as well.

 Nearly all client OSs will work with any of the providers, with the exception of Linux, which natively works only with Dropbox.

Most cloud storage providers offer synchronization to the desktop, which makes it so that you have a folder on your computer, just as if it were on your hard drive. And it's important to note that folder will almost always have the most current edition of the files stored in the cloud. The *synchronization app* typically runs in the background and has configurable options, including what, when, and how often to synchronize.

Accessing the sites is done through your web browser. Once you are in the site, managing your files is much like managing them on your local computer. In Figure 8.18, you can see the Google Drive interface, with a few files and folders in it.

You have a few options for sharing a folder with another user. One way is to right-click the folder and choose Share. You'll be asked to enter their name or email address and to indicate whether they can view or edit the file (Figure 8.19). You can also choose Get Link, which will copy a URL link to your Clipboard to paste into a message. Be mindful that the default behavior is that anyone who has the link can view the folder. This might be okay, but it could also be a security risk. You can change the sharing settings by performing the following steps:

1. Right-click the folder and choose Get Link.

2. In the Get Link window that appears (Figure 8.20), click the down arrow next to Anyone With The Link.

   Options include:

   - Restricting the file to people you specify

   - Letting anyone on the Internet with the link view the file (or enabling them to comment or edit, which you specify by clicking the drop-down arrow next to Viewer)

FIGURE 8.18   Google Drive

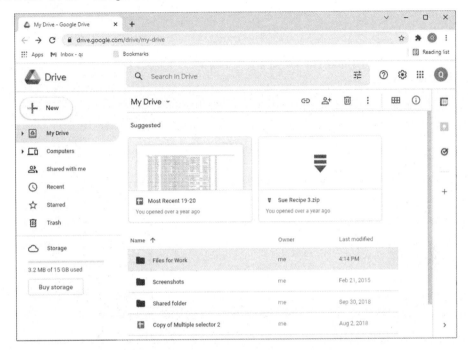

FIGURE 8.19   Sharing a folder on Google Drive

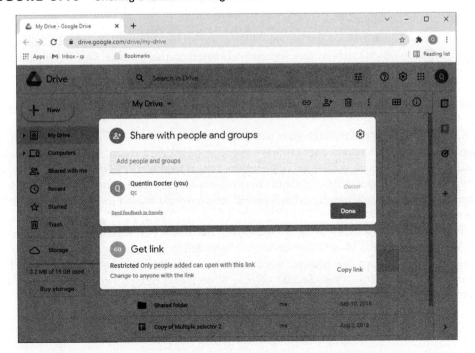

FIGURE 8.20 Share with others settings

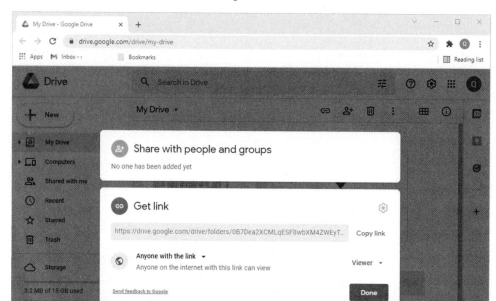

Cloud-Based Applications

Google really popularized the use of web-based applications. After all, the whole Chromebook platform, which has been very successful, is based on this premise. Other companies have gotten into the cloud-based application space as well, such as Microsoft with Office 365. The menus and layout are slightly different from PC-based versions of Office, but if you're familiar with Office, you can easily use Office 365—and all of the files are stored on the cloud.

Cloud-based apps run through your web browser. This is great for end users for a couple of reasons. One, your system does not have to use its own hardware to run the application; you are basically streaming a *virtual application*. Two, different client OSs can run the application (usually) without worrying about compatibility issues. Applications can often work across platforms as well, meaning that laptops, desktops, tablets, and smartphones can all use various apps.

To create a new document using Google Docs, you click the New button, as shown on the left side of Figure 8.18, and then choose the application from the menu. If you choose Google Docs, it opens a new browser window with Google Docs, as shown in Figure 8.21. Notice that near the top, it says *Saved to Drive*. When it says this, you know that the document has been saved automatically.

FIGURE 8.21   Google Docs

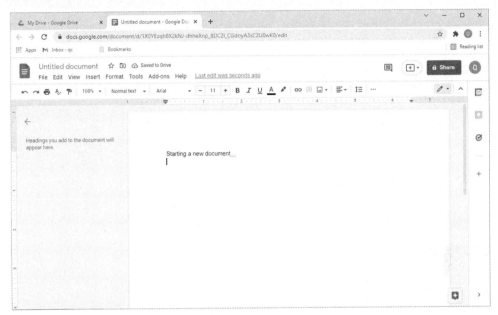

When choosing a cloud provider, you may use any one you like. In fact, it's better if you experience the differences in how providers store files and let you manage and manipulate them before making your choice. Exercise 8.2 will give you experience with using cloud-based storage and applications—specifically, Google Drive and its associated apps. This exercise will work best if you have someone you can work with. For example, in a classroom setting, you can partner with someone. If you are studying at home, you can create multiple accounts and get the same experience. You will just need to log out and in with your other account to see the shared files.

EXERCISE 8.2

Using Google's Cloud Services

1. Open Google at www.google.com.

    If you do not already have a Google account, you will need to create one. With it, you use Google's online apps and storage as well as a Gmail account.

2. If you are doing this exercise on your own, create a second account to share files and folders with.

continues

3.   Once you're logged in, click the Apps icon in the upper-right corner. It's the one that has nine small dots in a square pattern (see Figure 8.22).

FIGURE 8.22   Google Apps icon

This will open Apps, as shown on the right in Figure 8.23.

FIGURE 8.23   Google Apps

4.   In Apps, click Drive. This will open Google Drive (refer to Figure 8.18).

5.   Create a folder by clicking New ➢ Folder and share it with another account.

6. Also create a document or spreadsheet using Google's online software.

How easy or difficult was it?

7. If necessary, log out and log in to the other account that you created to access the resources that were shared for you.

How easy or difficult was it?

The newest trend in web applications and cloud storage is the streaming of media. Companies such as Netflix, Amazon, Pandora, Apple, and others store movies and music on their clouds. You download their client software, and for a monthly subscription fee, you can stream media to your device. It can be your phone, your tablet, your computer, or your home entertainment system. Before the advent of broadband network technologies, this type of setup would have been impossible, but now it is poised to become the mainstream way that people receive audio and video entertainment.

> Many companies have scrapped internal email management and moved to cloud-based email. By using an *off-site email application*, such as Gmail, a company can use their .com email address and Gmail as the client. This relieves administrative burden—all that's required is to call Google to set it up properly. There's a monthly fee, but it's often cheaper than managing an email server internally. And, users can easily access their email from anywhere with an Internet connection. This is an example of SaaS because the cloud provider is hosting the email server and users access it using a browser, which is simply the client.

Concepts of Virtualization

Perhaps the easiest way to understand virtualization is to compare it to more traditional technologies. In the traditional computing model, a computer is identified as being a physical machine that is running some combination of software, such as an operating system and various applications. There's a one-to-one relationship between the hardware and the operating system.

For the sake of illustration, imagine that a machine is a file server and now it needs to perform the functions of a web server as well. To make this happen, the administrator would need to ensure that the computer has enough resources to support the service (CPU, memory, network bandwidth), install web server software (Microsoft Internet Information Services [IIS] or Apache HTTP Server, for example), configure the appropriate files and permissions, and then bring it back online as a file and web server. These would be relatively straightforward administrative tasks.

But now imagine that the machine in question is being asked to run Windows Server and Linux at the same time. Now there's a problem. In the traditional computing model, only one OS can run at one time, because each OS completely controls the hardware resources in the computer. Sure, an administrator can install a second OS and configure the server to dual-boot, meaning the OS to run is chosen during the boot process, but only one OS can run at a time. So if the requirement is to have a Windows-based file server and a Linux-based Apache web server, there's a problem. Two physical computers are needed.

Similarly, imagine that there is a Windows-based workstation being used by an applications programmer. The programmer has been asked to code an app that works in Linux, or Apple's iOS, or anything other than Windows. When the programmer needs to test the app to see how well it works, what do they do? Sure, they can configure their system to dual-boot, but once again, in the traditional computing model, they are limited to one OS at a time per physical computer. Their company could purchase a second system, but that quickly starts to get expensive when you have multiple users with similar needs.

This is where virtualization comes in. The term *virtualization* is defined as creating virtual (rather than actual) versions of something. In computer jargon, it means creating virtual environments where "computers" can operate. We use quotation marks around the word *computers* because they don't need to be physical computers in the traditional sense. Virtualization is often used to let multiple OSs (or multiple instances of the same OS) run on one physical machine at the same time. Yes, they are often still bound by the physical characteristics of the machine on which they reside, but virtualization breaks down the traditional one-to-one relationship between a physical set of hardware and an OS.

 Virtualization has been around in the computer industry since 1967, but it has only recently exploded in popularity thanks to the flexibility that the Internet offers.

The Purpose of Virtual Machines

We have already hit on the major feature of virtualization, which is breaking down that one-to-one hardware and software barrier. The virtualized version of a computer is appropriately called a *virtual machine (VM)*. Thanks to VMs, it is becoming far less common to need dual-boot machines today than in the past. In addition, VMs make technology like the cloud possible. A cloud provider can have one incredibly powerful server that is running five instances of an OS for client use, and each client is able to act as if it had its own individual server. On the flip side, cloud providers can pool resources from multiple physical servers into what appears to the client to be one system, effectively giving clients unlimited processing or storage capabilities (assuming, of course, that the provider doesn't physically run out of hardware).

 Virtual OSs can be powered on or off individually without affecting the host OS or hypervisor—we'll talk about what those are in the upcoming section "The Hypervisor."

Virtual machines have a wide variety of applications, many of which are cloud-based services. Here are three specific uses you should pay particular attention to:

Virtual Sandbox   Imagine a scenario where you have an application that you want to test out in an OS, but you don't want any negative effects to happen to the computer system doing the testing. One way to do this is to test the app in a *sandbox*, which is a temporary, isolated desktop environment. Think of it as a temporary, somewhat limited virtual machine. Any app in the sandbox will act as it would in a full version of the chosen OS, with one big difference. Files are not saved to the hard drive or memory, so the physical machine should never be affected by anything the app in the sandbox does. When the sandbox gets shut down, so does the app and any data associated with it.

There are several sandboxing software solutions on the market, including Sandboxie, Browser in the Box, BufferZone, SHADE Sandbox, and ToolWiz Time Freeze. Some of them are designed for app testing, whereas others will literally sandbox your whole system unless you authorize changes to specific files on the computer. Last but not least, Microsoft is in on the action with Windows Sandbox as well.

Test Development   We already gave an example of *test development* in a virtual machine, with a developer looking to create and test applications as they are works in progress. Apps can be tested in virtualized versions of the same OS that the developer is working on, or in a different OS virtualized on the same computer.

Application Virtualization   *Application virtualization* is a common use of virtual machines as well. It usually takes one of two forms. The first is virtualizing *legacy software* or a legacy OS. We introduced legacy software earlier in the chapter—it's basically old, outdated software. The problem is that legacy apps often only run on legacy OSs, so you need to either virtualize the app in a newer OS and tweak it like crazy to get it to work, or virtualize it in an older OS that has no business running on its own server either.

The second use is *cross-platform virtualization*. It allows programs coded for one type of hardware or operating system to work on another that it's not designed to work on. For example, an app designed for macOS could work in a virtualized version of that OS within a Windows-based server.

The underlying purpose of all of this is to save money. Cloud providers can achieve economies of scale, because adding additional clients doesn't necessarily require the purchase of additional hardware. Clients don't have to pay for hardware (or the electricity to keep the hardware cool) and can pay only for the services they use. End users, in the workstation example we provided earlier, can have multiple environments to use without needing to buy additional hardware as well.

The Hypervisor

The key enabler for virtualization is a piece of software called the *hypervisor*, also known as a *virtual machine manager (VMM)*. The hypervisor software allows multiple operating systems to share the same host, and it also manages the physical resource allocation to those virtual OSs. As illustrated in Figure 8.24, there are two types of hypervisors: Type 1 and Type 2.

A *Type 1 hypervisor* sits directly on the hardware, and because of this, it's sometimes referred to as a *bare-metal hypervisor*. In this instance, the hypervisor is basically the operating system for the physical machine. This setup is most commonly used for server-side virtualization, because the hypervisor itself typically has very low hardware requirements to support its own functions. Type 1 is generally considered to have better performance than Type 2, simply because there is no host OS involved and the system is dedicated to supporting virtualization. Virtual OSs are run within the hypervisor, and the virtual (guest) OSs are completely independent of each other. Examples of Type 1 hypervisors include Microsoft Hyper-V, VMware ESXi, and Citrix Hypervisor (formerly XenServer). Figure 8.25 shows the Hyper-V interface. Exercise 8.3 walks you through the steps to enable Hyper-V in Windows 10.

FIGURE 8.24   Type 1 and Type 2 hypervisors

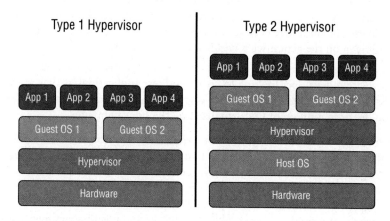

FIGURE 8.25   Microsoft Hyper-V

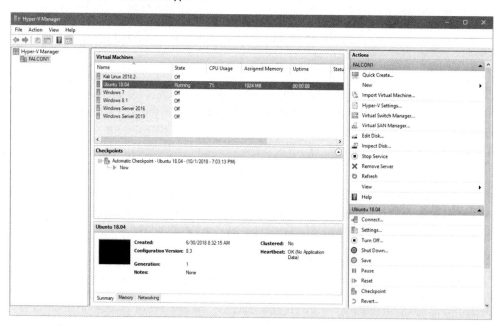

EXERCISE 8.3

Enabling Hyper-V in Windows 10

To enable Microsoft Hyper-V, perform the following steps:

1. Check for minimum system requirements

   - Windows 10 Enterprise, Pro, or Education

   - 64-bit processor with Second Level Address Translation (SLAT)

   - CPU support for VM Monitor Mode Extension (VT-c on Intel CPUs)

   - 4 GB of RAM or more

2. If requirements are met, then right-click the Windows (Start) button.

3. Click Apps And Features.

4. Click Programs And Features.

5. Click Turn Windows Features On Or Off.

6. Select the Hyper-V check box (Figure 8.26), and click OK.

FIGURE 8.26   Enabling Hyper-V

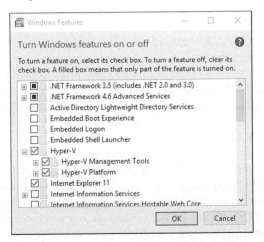

7. After installation, restart your computer.

A *Type 2 hypervisor* sits on top of an existing operating system, called the *host OS*. This is most commonly used in *client-side virtualization*, where multiple OSs are managed on the client machine as opposed to on a server. An example of this would be a Windows user who wants to run Linux at the same time as Windows. The user could install a hypervisor and then install Linux in the hypervisor and run both OSs concurrently and independently. The downsides of Type 2 hypervisors are that the host OS consumes resources, such as processor time and memory, and a host OS failure means that the guest OSs fail as well. Examples of Type 2 hypervisors include Microsoft's Windows Virtual PC and Azure Virtual Server, Oracle VM VirtualBox, VMware Workstation, and Linux KVM.

Hypervisors aren't specifically listed as an objective on the A+ exam. It's one of those technologies that you pretty much need to know how it works, though, given the prevalence of the cloud (and local instances of virtualization) in the world today.

Client-Side Virtualization Requirements

As you might expect, running multiple OSs on one physical workstation can require more resources than running a single OS. There's no rule that says a workstation being used for virtualization is required to have more robust hardware than another machine, but for performance reasons, the system should be well equipped. This is especially true for systems running a Type 2 hypervisor, which sits on top of a host OS. The host OS will need resources, too, and it will compete with the VMs for those resources. Let's talk about specific requirements.

Resource Requirements

The primary resources here are the same as you would expect when discussing any other computer's performance: CPU, RAM, hard drive space, and network performance. From the CPU standpoint, know that the hypervisor can treat each core of a processor as a separate virtual processor, and it can even create multiple virtual processors out of a single core. The general rule here is that the faster the processor the better, but really, the more cores a processor has, the more virtual OSs it can support in a speedy fashion. Within the hypervisor, there will most likely be an option to set the allocation of physical resources, such as CPU priority and amount of RAM, to each VM.

Some hypervisors require that the CPU be specifically designed to support virtualization. For Intel chips, this technology is called *virtualization technology (VT)*, and AMD chips need to support *AMD-V*. Pretty much every processor today supports virtualization, but you might run across older ones that do not. In addition, many system BIOSs/UEFIs have an option to turn on or turn off virtualization support. If a processor supports virtualization but the hypervisor won't install, check the BIOS/UEFI and enable virtualization. The specific steps to do this vary based on the BIOS/UEFI, so check the manufacturer's documentation. An example of what this might look like is shown in Figure 8.27.

Memory is always a big concern for computers, and virtual ones are no different. When you're installing the guest OS, the hypervisor will ask how much memory to allocate to the VM. This can be modified later if the guest OS in the VM requires more memory to run properly. Always remember, though, that the host OS requires RAM, too. Thus, if the host OS needs 4 GB of RAM and the guest OS needs 4 GB of RAM, the system needs to have at least 8 GB of RAM to support both adequately.

FIGURE 8.27   Enabling virtualization in the BIOS/UEFI

```
                  Phoenix TrustedCore(tm) Setup Utility
         Advanced

     Advanced Processor Configuration              Item Specific Help

  CPU Mismatch Detection:          [Enabled]    When enabled, a VMM
  Core Multi-Processing:           [Enabled]    (Virtual Machine
  Processor Power Management:      [Disabled]   Monitor) can utilize
  Intel(R) Virtualization Technology [Enabled]  the additional hardware
  Execute Disable Bit:             [Enabled]    capabilities provided
                                                by Vanderpool
  Adjacent Cache Line Prefetch:    [Disabled]   Technology.
  Hardware Prefetch:               [Disabled]
  Direct Cache Access              [Disabled]   If this option is
                                                changed, a Power Off-On
                                                sequence will be
  Set Max Ext CPUID = 3            [Disabled]   applied on the next
                                                boot.


  F1   Info   ↑↓  Select Item  -/+  Change Values    F9   Setup Defaults
  Esc  Exit   ←→  Select Menu  Enter Select ▶ Sub-Menu F10  Save and Exit
```

Hard disk space works the same way as RAM. Each OS will need its own hard disk space, and the guest OS will be configured via the hypervisor. Make sure that the physical computer has enough free disk space to support the guest OSs.

Finally, from a networking standpoint, each of the virtual desktops will typically need full network access, and configuring the permissions for each can sometimes be tricky.

The virtual desktop is often called a *virtual desktop infrastructure (VDI)*, a term that encompasses the software and hardware needed to create the virtual environment. VDIs can be on premises in the same building as the company using it, or in the cloud. The VM will create a *virtual NIC* and manage the resources of that NIC appropriately. The virtual NIC doesn't have to be connected to the physical NIC; an administrator could create an entire virtual network within the virtual environment where the virtual machines just talk to each other.

That's not normally practical in the real world, though, so the virtual NIC will be connected to the physical NIC. Configuring a virtual switch within the hypervisor normally does this. The virtual switch manages the traffic to and from the virtual NICs and logically attaches to the physical NIC (see Figure 8.28). Network bandwidth is often the biggest bottleneck when you are running multiple virtual OSs. If the network requirements are that each of four VMs on one physical machine get Gigabit Ethernet service all the time, one physical Gigabit Ethernet NIC isn't going to cut it.

With Type 1 hypervisors, virtual desktops are often used with remote administration. This can allow a remote administrator to work on the workstation (to perform maintenance, for example) with or without the knowledge of the user sitting in front of the machine.

FIGURE 8.28 Virtual NICs connecting to a physical NIC

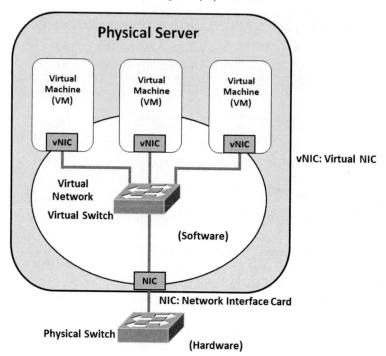

Emulator Requirements

Virtual machines are created to exist and function just like a physical machine. Thus, all the requirements that a physical machine would have need to be replicated by the hypervisor, and that process is called *emulation*. The terms *hypervisor* and *emulator* are often used interchangeably, although they don't mean the same thing. The hypervisor can support multiple OSs, whereas technically, an emulator appears to work the same as one specific OS. As for requirements, the emulator and the hypervisor need to be compatible with the host OS. That's about it.

Some incredibly popular mobile-based games do not have PC equivalents. In other words, you need to run them from iOS or Android. Android is based on open source code, meaning that there are Android emulators on the market. One such free emulator is Andy (www.andyroid.net). People can install Andy on their desktops or laptops, and then install Android apps within Andy. That way, they can play their favorite mobile games on their desktop or laptop computers.

Security Requirements

In the early days of the cloud, a common misconception was that virtual machines couldn't be hacked. Unfortunately, some hackers proved this wrong. Instead of attacking the OS in the VM, hackers have turned their attention to attacking the hypervisor itself. Why just hit one OS when you can hit all of them on the computer at the same time? A number of virtualization-specific threats focusing on the hypervisor have cropped up, but updates have fixed the issues as they have become known. The solution to most virtual machine threats is to always apply the most recent updates to keep the system(s) current.

At the same time, all the security concerns that affect individual computers also apply to VMs. For example, if Windows is being operated in a VM, that instance of Windows still needs antimalware software installed on it.

 Real World Scenario

Setting Up and Using Client-Side Virtualization

If given a scenario on the A+ exam or faced with the situation in real life, you should be able to set up and show someone how to use client-side virtualization. Here are some sample steps to follow:

1. Determine the client's needs for virtualization.

   For example, do they have a Windows or Mac client and need to run Linux? Or perhaps they have a Windows computer and want to run macOS at the same time? Determine their needs, and then secure the additional OSs (including licenses, as appropriate) before beginning the installation.

2. Evaluate the computer to ensure that it can support the VM.

   - Does the processor support virtualization?

   - How much RAM does the computer have? Is it enough to meet the minimum requirements of all installed OSs?

   - How much free hard drive space is there? It should be enough to install the hypervisor and the guest OS as well as to store any files that need to be stored from within the guest OS.

   - Does the system have a fast enough network connection if the guest OS needs access to the network?

3. Consider which hypervisor to use. Is there a version of the hypervisor that's compatible with the host OS?

4. Consider security requirements. If the guest OS will be on the Internet, will proper security software be installed?

5. After all conditions are deemed sufficient, you can install the hypervisor and the guest OS.

It will not affect the host OS, but it's always a good idea to back up the system before installing any new major software packages!

Exercise 8.4 will give you hands-on experience installing a hypervisor and a guest OS.

Now that we have covered the key concepts behind client-side virtualization, it's time to practice. Exercise 8.4 walks you through installing the Oracle VirtualBox hypervisor on a Windows 10 computer and then installing Lubuntu (a distribution of Linux). Normally, installing a second OS involves a relatively complicated process where you need to dual-boot your computer. You're not going to do that here. Instead, you will use the VirtualBox hypervisor that allows you to create a new virtual system on your hard drive and not affect your existing Windows installation. We promise you that this exercise will not mess up Windows on your computer! And when you're finished, you can just uninstall VirtualBox, if you want, and nothing will have changed on your system. This exercise is admittedly a bit long because there are a lot of steps, and it's also probably more "advanced" than typical A+ materials. That said, we encourage you to try it—it usually ends up being one of our students' favorite exercises during training classes.

EXERCISE 8.4

Installing VirtualBox and Lubuntu on Windows 10

The first two steps are for preparation only. You need to download Oracle VirtualBox and a version of Lubuntu. Really, any version of Linux is fine, but we'll point you to Lubuntu, which is a good choice. Depending on your network speed, the download could take an hour or more. These directions are based on VirtualBox version 6.1.28. If you have a different version, the wording on some of the screens might be slightly different, but the following steps should still work.

Obtaining VirtualBox and Lubuntu

1. Download Oracle VirtualBox from `http://www.virtualbox.org/wiki/Downloads`. As you can see in Figure 8.29, the current version as of this writing was 6.1.28.

FIGURE 8.29   Download VirtualBox

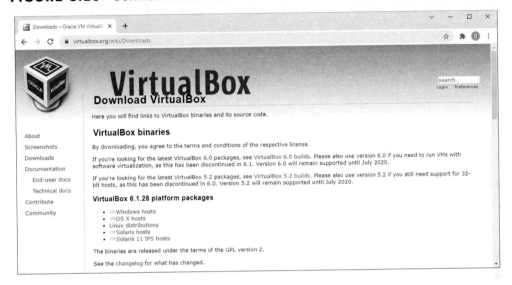

2.   Select the VirtualBox platform package for Windows hosts, unless, of course, you have
     a Mac, and then you need the one for macOS hosts.

3.   Save it to your desktop for ease of access.

4.   Download Lubuntu from `http://lubuntu.me/downloads`. There is a link on the
     page for Lubuntu Desktop 64-bit. Choose the most current one. It will download a zip
     file with an `.iso` extension.

     You will need that ISO file later; it will essentially act as a bootable optical disc for your
     OS installation. Note that this file is nearly 2 GB, so it could take some time to down-
     load.

Installing VirtualBox

Now you can begin the installation of VirtualBox.

1.   Double-click the VirtualBox icon. If you get a security warning, click the Run button.

2.   Click Next on the Setup Wizard screen.

3.   On the Custom Setup screen, click Next and then Next again.

     It will give you a warning about your network interfaces.

4.   Click Yes. (Your network connections will come back automatically.)

continues

EXERCISE 8.4 *(continued)*

5. Click Install.

    This may take several minutes. You may also need to clear a Windows User Account Control security pop-up warning box by clicking Yes to allow Oracle Corporation to install a device driver. There may also be another Windows Security box to clear as well by clicking Install.

6. Once the install is complete, click Finish.

Configuring VirtualBox

It's time to configure VirtualBox.

1. You might get a VirtualBox warning telling you that an image file is not currently accessible. That's fine. Click Ignore.

    You should see a screen similar to the one shown in Figure 8.30.

FIGURE 8.30   Welcome to VirtualBox!

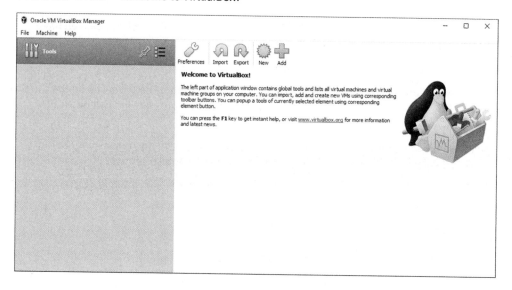

2. Click the blue New icon to create a new virtual machine, and give it a name.

    The Type and Version boxes aren't critical; they don't affect anything. If you type in **Lubuntu** for a name, it will automatically set Type to Linux and Version to Ubuntu (64-bit). Again, these boxes don't affect anything tangible.

3. Click Next.

4. On the Memory Size screen, set the memory size (or leave it at the default), and then click Next.

5. On the Hard Disk screen, the default option is Create A Virtual Hard Disk Now. Leave that option selected and click Create.

You will be prompted for what hard disk file type you want to create.

6. Leave it on VDI and click Next.

On the next screen, you can choose to make the virtual disk a fixed size or allow its size to be dynamically allocated based on need.

7. If you are low on disk space, go with Fixed Size, and click Next. Otherwise, Dynamically Allocated is good. Choose that and click Next.

8. On the File Location And Size screen, it's probably best to leave it at the default size of 10 GB. Definitely don't make it any smaller.

9. Click Create.

Now you will see a screen like the one shown in Figure 8.31.

Great! You now have a virtual machine on your hard drive.

FIGURE 8.31   Virtual machine created

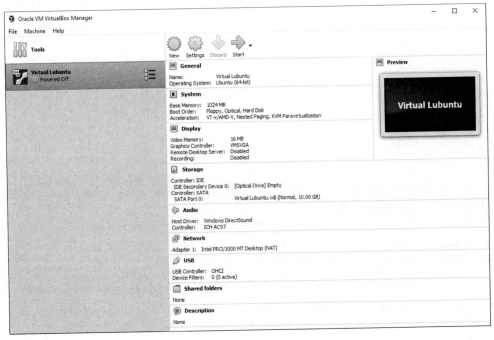

continues

Installing the OS

Now you just need to put something on it—more specifically, an OS.

1. Click the Settings button.

2. In the Settings window for your virtual machine, click the Storage icon on the left.

3. Under one of your controllers, you should see something that looks like a disc icon that says Empty. It should look like Figure 8.32. Click Empty.

   On the very right side of the window, you will have another disc icon with a little down arrow on it.

FIGURE 8.32   Storage tab in Settings

4. Click the down arrow. A menu will pop up.

5. Select Choose/Create Virtual Optical Disk. The Optical Disc Selector window will appear.

6. In the Optical Disk Selector window that pops up, click Add. This will open Windows Explorer. Navigate to the directory where you stored the Lubuntu ISO file that you downloaded.

7. Highlight the file, and then click Open.

That will take you back to the Optical Disk Selector window. The ISO file you selected should be highlighted. Click Choose, as shown in Figure 8.33.

FIGURE 8.33 Choosing the ISO file

8. In the Settings window, click OK.

Now you are back to the Oracle VirtualBox Manager screen.

9. With the Lubuntu VM on the left highlighted, click the green Start arrow.

This will begin the installation of Lubuntu.

10. Follow the Lubuntu installation process.

During the installation, you may get to a screen asking you for an installation type. It looks scary, but choose the Erase Disk And Install Lubuntu option.

This will install Lubuntu on the virtual disk that you created earlier with VirtualBox. It will not wipe out your entire hard drive. If you don't get this screen, then no big deal.

11. Continue with the installation process. When in doubt, choose the default and move to the next step.

continues

When the installation is complete, you may need to click the Restart Now button. If no button appears, Lubuntu will start automatically. It will look something like Figure 8.34. Notice there are two information messages at the top. Click the X at the right side of each to clear them.

Now that the installation is complete, play around in your new operating system! Some suggested additional exercises are included in this chapter's performance-based question.

FIGURE 8.34   Lubuntu running in Oracle VM VirtualBox

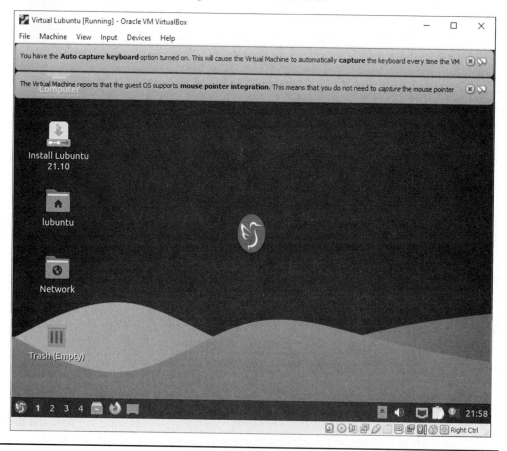

For the A+ exam, you will need to be able to summarize cloud computing concepts and aspects of client-side virtualization. Things to know include:

- Cloud models: private, public, hybrid, and community
- Services such as infrastructure as a service (IaaS), software as a service (SaaS), and platform as a service (SaaS)
- Cloud characteristics: shared resources, metered utilization, rapid elasticity, high availability, and file synchronization
- Virtual desktop infrastructure (VDI) on premises and in the cloud
- The purpose of virtual machines, including sandboxing, test development, and application virtualization for legacy software/OSs and cross-platform virtualization
- Client-side resource and security requirements for virtualization

Summary

In this chapter, you learned about different server roles and technologies that work on local networks as well as ones that work on the Internet to make the cloud possible.

First, you learned about specific server roles. Options include DNS, DHCP, file (fileshare), print, mail, syslog, web, and AAA servers. We talked about what each one of these does as well as where they should be located on the network, either inside the secure network or in the screened subnet. In addition to servers, many networks will have Internet appliances dedicated to security, such as spam gateways and UTM devices, as well as load balancers and proxy servers to manage traffic. Some networks also support legacy or embedded systems, such as SCADA. Although these systems are old and outdated, they often provide critical functionality on the network. We also looked at some examples of IoT devices.

The next topic was cloud computing. Cloud computing has been one of the hottest topics in IT circles for several years now and will likely continue to be so for several more years. Cloud providers sell several different types of services, such as IaaS, PaaS, and SaaS. There are also different types of clouds, such as public, private, community, and hybrid. Cloud features include shared resources, metered utilization, rapid elasticity, high availability, and file synchronization. You can use cloud services for storage, virtual applications (such as email or word processing), or both. Cloud computing is dependent on virtualization.

Virtualization removes the barrier of there being a one-to-one relationship between computer hardware and an operating system. You learned about what virtualization does and the core piece of software, called the hypervisor. You learned the purpose of virtual machines, which includes sandboxing, test development, and application virtualization for legacy software and OSs and cross-platform virtualization, as well as requirements for client-side virtualization. The chapter finished with a long exercise on installing a hypervisor and Lubuntu on a Windows computer.

Exam Essentials

Know the various roles that servers can play on a network.   Roles include DNS, DHCP, file (fileshare), print, mail, syslog, web, and AAA servers. File servers (fileshares) store files for users, and may have optical media and perform backups too. Print servers host printers. Mail servers store, send, and receive email. A syslog server is used to log system events. Web servers host web pages that users access across a network. AAA servers validate user credentials, and then allow users to access resources and track access.

Know what DNS servers do.   DNS servers resolve hostnames to IP addresses. Without DNS servers, finding your favorite websites on the Internet would be an incredibly challenging task. DNS servers have a zone file with hostname to IP address mappings.

Understand how DHCP servers work.   DHCP servers assign IP addresses and configuration information to client computers. Clients request the information via broadcast. Each DHCP server has a scope with a configured range of available IP addresses. The server may also provide additional configuration information, such as the address of the default gateway (a router) and a DNS server.

Understand what spam gateways and UTM systems do.   Spam gateways help email servers detect and deal with unwanted spam email. Unified threat management (UTM) systems centralize security management and often replace traditional firewalls.

Know what load balancers and proxy servers do.   Both types of servers help manage network traffic. Load balancers do so by sending incoming requests to different, typically identical servers to spread out the workload. Proxy servers make requests on behalf of clients.

Know what legacy and embedded systems are.   Legacy systems are older technology no longer supported by the manufacturer. Embedded systems are those that are critical to a process. SCADA is an example of a legacy and embedded system.

Know some examples of services provided by Internet of Things (IoT) devices.   Some device types include thermostats, home security and automation, and voice-enabled speakers and digital assistants.

Understand the four different types of clouds.   A cloud can be public, private, hybrid, or community.

Know the differences between SaaS, IaaS, and PaaS.   All of these are cloud terms. In infrastructure as a service (IaaS), the provider supplies the network infrastructure. In platform as a service (PaaS), software development tools and platforms are also provided. The highest level is software as a service (SaaS), where the provider supplies the infrastructure and applications.

Understand cloud concepts of shared resources, metered utilization, rapid elasticity, high availability, and file synchronization.   All clouds use shared resources, which can be internal or external. A pool of resources is purchased and each participant in the cloud pays for part of it. Metered utilization shows how much a client has used and will be billed for. Rapid elasticity means that a client can quickly get more (or fewer) resources as needed. High availability means that services are always or almost always available, such as three nines five. Cloud file storage services include iCloud and Google Cloud, and in most cases have synchronization apps to sync to the mobile device.

Understand the purpose of virtual machines and what they require.   Virtual machines are designed to save providers and users money. They allow for multiple OSs to be installed on one computer. VMs can provide sandboxing, test development, and application virtualization for legacy software and OSs and cross-platform virtualization. A virtual machine requires certain levels of resources, an emulator, security, and a network connection.

Understand what virtual desktops and virtual NICs are.   A virtual desktop is the collection of software and hardware needed to create a virtual environment. Sometimes it's called a virtual desktop infrastructure (VDI). The virtual NIC, which is controlled by the virtual machine, controls access to other virtual machines on the same system as well as access to the physical NIC.

Review Questions

The answers to the chapter review questions can be found in Appendix A.

1. Your company hosts its own web server, and it allows consumers to make purchases via the server. The help line has been getting complaints that users are unable to access the website. You open the site from an internal workstation and it seems fine. What is the most likely cause?

   A. The firewall is blocking TCP port 23.

   B. The firewall is blocking TCP port 443.

   C. The security module of the web server is malfunctioning.

   D. The web server is down.

2. Your manager wants you to install a networked Internet appliance that prevents network traffic–based attacks and includes antimalware and antispam software. What should you install?

   A. Spam gateway

   B. Load balancer

   C. UTM

   D. Proxy server

3. You are installing a file server for the accounting department. Where should this file server be located on the network?

   A. Outside of the firewall

   B. In the screened subnet

   C. In the secure network

   D. On the router

4. You have been asked to identify the right type of cloud service to help the team of developers to provide programming elements such as runtime environments. Which service do you recommend?

   A. PaaS

   B. IaaS

   C. SaaS

   D. DaaS

5. Which of the following are services that a print server should provide? (Choose two.)

   A. Accepting print jobs from clients

   B. Turning off printers on demand

   C. Providing clients with the appropriate printer driver during installation

   D. Notifying users when the print job is complete

6. You are setting up a cloud contract with a provider. Your team needs the ability to quickly increase capacity to meet peak demands. What do you request?

 A. Rapid elasticity

 B. High availability

 C. Resource pooling

 D. Metered utilization

7. Which type of server is responsible for preventing users from accessing websites with objectionable content?

 A. Proxy

 B. Web

 C. DHCP

 D. DNS

8. Your company wants to move to a cloud provider to be able to scale resources quickly, but it is concerned about the security of confidential information. Which of the following types of cloud models might be the most appropriate for your company?

 A. Public

 B. Private

 C. Community

 D. Hybrid

9. What does a DHCP server need to be configured with to operate properly?

 A. DNS server

 B. Scope

 C. Range

 D. DHCP relay agent

10. You have been asked to advise a group of several universities that want to combine research efforts and store data in the cloud. Which type of cloud solution might be best for them?

 A. Public

 B. Private

 C. Community

 D. Hybrid

11. When configuring a DNS server, administrators must create which of the following?

 A. Zone file

 B. Hosts file

 C. Scope file

 D. DNS proxy

12. Your manager wants to use the cloud because everyone seems to be talking about it. What should you include when you are listing the benefits of using the cloud? (Choose all that apply.)

  A. Increased security

  B. Increased scalability

  C. Lower cost

  D. Improved reliability

13. You are configuring two email servers on your company's network. Which network protocol do the servers use to transfer mail to each other?

  A. POP3

  B. IMAP4

  C. SNMP

  D. SMTP

14. You have been asked to configure a client-side virtualization solution with three guest OSs. Each one needs Internet access. How should you configure the solution in the most cost-effective way?

  A. Three physical NICs

  B. One physical NIC, three virtual NICs, and one virtual switch

  C. One physical NIC, one virtual NIC, and three virtual switches

  D. One physical NIC, three virtual NIC, and three virtual switches

15. You have five web servers that manage requests for online purchases. An administrator notices that one of the servers is always busy while another is idle, and the company is getting some online complaints about the slow website. Which of the following servers will help fix this?

  A. DNS

  B. DHCP

  C. Proxy

  D. Load balancer

16. You have been asked to install Linux in a VM on a Windows 10 client. The Windows 10 client needs 4 GB of RAM, and Linux needs 2 GB of RAM. How much RAM does the system need at a minimum?

  A. 4 GB

  B. 6 GB

  C. 8 GB

  D. Unable to determine from the question

17. A computer using which of the following would be considered a legacy device? (Choose all that apply.)

A. A 386 processor

B. The IPX/SPX protocol

C. An application developed in 1983

D. 1 GB of RAM

18. You have been asked to set up client-side virtualization on an office computer. The host OS is Windows 10, and there will be three Windows 10 guest OSs. Which of the following is true about the need for antivirus security?

A. The host OS needs an antivirus program, but virtual machines can't be affected by viruses.

B. The host OS antivirus software will also protect the guest OSs on the VMs.

C. Installing antivirus software on the virtual switch will protect all guest OSs.

D. The host OS and each guest OS need their own antivirus software installed.

19. You need to set up a temporary operating system environment to quickly test a piece of software your manager wants to install on the network. Which should you use?

A. AAA server

B. Sandbox

C. SCADA

D. Application virtualization

20. You have been asked to set up client-side virtualization on a computer at work. The manager asks for a Type 2 hypervisor. What is the disadvantage of using that type of hypervisor?

A. The guest OS will compete for resources with the host OS.

B. The guest OS will be forced to a lower priortity with the CPU than the host OS.

C. The guest OS will be forced to use less RAM than the host OS.

D. The virtual guest OS will not be able to get on the physical network.

Performance-Based Question

You will encounter performance-based questions on the A+ exams. The questions on the exam require you to perform a specific task, and you will be graded on whether or not you were able to complete the task. The following requires you to think creatively in order to measure how well you understand this chapter's topics. You may or may not see similar questions on the actual A+ exams. To see how your answer compares to the authors', refer to Appendix B.

Describe the steps needed to enable Hyper-V in Windows 10.

Chapter 9

Laptop and Mobile Device Hardware

THE FOLLOWING COMPTIA A+ EXAM 220-1101 OBJECTIVES ARE COVERED IN THIS CHAPTER:

✓ **1.1 Given a scenario, install and configure laptop hardware and components.**

- Hardware/device replacement
  - Battery
  - Keyboard/keys
  - Random-access memory (RAM)
  - Hard disk drive (HDD)/solid-state drive (SSD) migration
  - HDD/SSD replacement
  - Wireless cards
- Physical privacy and security components
  - Biometrics
  - Near-field scanner features

✓ **1.2 Compare and contrast the display components of mobile devices.**

- Types
  - Liquid crystal display (LCD)
    - In-plane switching (IPS)
    - Twisted nematic (TN)
    - Vertical alignment (VA)
  - Organic light-emitting diode (OLED)
- Mobile display components
- WiFi antenna connector/placement
- Camera/webcam

- Microphone
- Touch screen/digitizer
- Inverter

✓ **1.3 Given a scenario, set up and configure accessories and ports of mobile devices.**

- Connection methods
  - Universal serial bus (USB)/USB-C/microUSB/miniUSB
  - Lightning
  - Serial interfaces
  - Near-field communication (NFC)
  - Bluetooth
  - Hotspot
- Accessories
  - Touch pens
  - Headsets
  - Speakers
  - Webcam
- Docking station
- Port replicator
- Trackpad/drawing pad

In 1943, the president of IBM, Thomas Watson, was quoted as saying, "I think there is a world market for maybe five computers." Somewhat more recently, in 1977, Ken Olsen, the founder of one-time computer industry giant Digital Equipment Corporation, stated, "There is no reason anyone would want a computer in their home." Four years later the personal computer was introduced, ironically by IBM. It's about 80 years past the first quote and about 50 years past the second, but looking back at the history of computers, it's amazing to see how far the industry has come.

As recently as the early 1990s, portable computers were luxuries that were affordable to only the wealthy or the select few businesspeople who traveled extensively. As with all other technologies, though, portable systems became smaller, lighter (more portable), more powerful, and less expensive. Because the technology and price disparity between the two platforms has decreased significantly, laptops have outsold desktops since the mid-2000s. For about 20 years, laptop computers enjoyed a status as the most popular mobile computing device available. Desktop computers still were more powerful and cheaper, but with a laptop, users weren't tethered to a desk.

Technology continued its inevitable progression, and smaller mobile devices came into play. Tablets, smartphones, and even wearable devices obtained enough power and features to be considered computers. Laptop sales have been flat since about 2012, whereas smartphones and wearables have continued to increase in market share. Further, smartphones overtook laptops as the most popular device to access the Internet as of 2015. In stark contrast to the computers of yesteryear, today's most popular computing devices can be so small that the likelihood of misplacing them is a real and ongoing concern.

Every indication is that the movement toward mobile computing will continue, so you definitely need to be well versed in portable technologies, which contain both nifty features and frustrating quirks. In this chapter, you will learn about the features and quirks of laptop and mobile device hardware. There are some differences—for example, the majority of hardware on a laptop is more similar to that of a desktop than to that of a smartphone, but there are similarities as well. The display of a laptop (and to be fair, most desktop-sized monitors) is a lot like those in smaller devices. Throughout the chapter, we will cover laptops and smaller mobile devices as though they are similar, and call out specific differences where appropriate. We will start with installing and configuring laptop hardware and components, including details on display technologies. Then we'll finish with setting up and configuring accessories and ports on mobile devices.

Working with Laptop and Mobile Device Hardware

Hardware in all computing devices needs to perform the same tasks. There are devices that control input and output, processing, short-term and long-term storage, displaying information, and connecting to other computers. This is true regardless of the size of the device. Granted, smaller devices are space-constrained, so the hardware components that do these tasks need to be smaller and consume far less energy.

Working with hardware, then, should be similar across devices, and for the most part it is. Maybe instead of having a physical keyboard you'll have a virtual one (and you can't exactly replace it, per se), but at least you know how to input to the device. Or maybe the screen is smaller, but it and the video card still perform the same tasks that their larger counterparts do. In the following sections, we will look at the specifics regarding working with hardware in laptops and smaller devices.

Understanding the Differences between Device Types

The first personal computers developed were more similar to today's desktop computers than they were to laptops or mobile devices. The smaller devices do trace their ancestry back to the desktop, though, so it makes sense to compare them to their bigger counterparts. Here, we'll take a high-level look at what makes laptops and mobile devices unique.

Laptops vs. Desktops

Laptops are similar to desktop computers in architecture in that they contain many parts that perform similar functions. However, the parts that make up a laptop are completely different from those in desktop computers. The obvious major difference is size; laptops are space challenged. Another primary concern is heat. Restricted space means less airflow, meaning parts can heat up and overheat faster.

To overcome space limitations, laptop parts are physically much smaller and lighter, and they must fit into the compact space of a laptop's case. It might not sound like much, but there really is a major difference between a 4-pound laptop and a 5-pound laptop if you're hauling it around in its carrying case all day. Also, laptop parts are designed to consume less power and to shut themselves off when not being used, although many desktops also have components such as video circuitry that go into a low-power state when not active. Finally, most laptop components are proprietary—the motherboard is especially proprietary, and the *liquid crystal display (LCD)* screen from one laptop will not necessarily fit on another.

Manufacturers have also pushed out smaller and smaller portables that are laptop adjacent. For example, in 2007 the first netbooks were introduced. A *netbook* is an extremely small laptop computer that is lighter in weight and more scaled down in features than a standard laptop. The term *netbook* is rarely used today, but Chromebooks are an example of that type of technology. Users are attracted to Chromebooks because of their enhanced portability and affordability. The features that remain are ideal for Internet access and emailing. However, many users would find them insufficient for mainstream business usage. Tablets are even smaller yet, but they are typically characterized as a mobile device, so we'll hold off on talking about them just yet.

If you've shopped for a laptop, you have no doubt noticed that the prices of desktop PCs are often quite a bit lower than those for laptop computers, yet the desktops are usually faster and more powerful. If you've ever wondered what makes a laptop so much different from a PC, here are the primary differences between laptops and desktops:

Portability   This is probably the most obvious difference. Laptops are designed to be portable. They run on batteries, so you aren't tied to one spot at home or at the office. Networking options are available that allow you to connect to a network wirelessly and do work from just about anywhere, including malls, airports, coffee shops, and so on. As anyone who has tried to bring their mini-tower PC to a LAN party can tell you, desktops just aren't that portable.

Cost   Laptops tend to cost more than desktop computers with similar features. The primary reason is that portability requires small components and unique proprietary designs so that those components fit into the small size necessary. Miniature versions of components cost more money than standard-sized (desktop) versions. The cost discrepancy between desktops and laptops has shrunk considerably in the last several years, but it still exists.

Performance   By and large, laptops are always going to lose out somewhere in the performance department. Compromises must often be made between performance and portability, and considering that portability is the major feature of a laptop, performance is what usually suffers. While it is possible to have a laptop and a desktop with comparable performance, the amount of money one would have to spend for a "desktop replacement" laptop is considerable. This is not to say that a laptop can't outperform a desktop—it's just that the "bang for the buck" factor is higher in a desktop.

Expandability   Because desktop computers were designed to be modular, their capabilities can be upgraded quite easily. It is next to impossible to upgrade the processor or motherboard on most laptops. Other than memory and hard drives, most laptop upgrades consist of adding an external device through one of the laptop's ports, such as a USB port.

Quality of Construction   Considering how much abuse laptops get, it is much more important that the materials used to construct the laptop case and other components be extremely durable. Durability is important in a desktop too, but it won't be tested as much as in a laptop.

Building Your Own

This anecdote comes from one of the authors: "During an A+ course, I gave the class the assignment to go out on the web and put together the most powerful and complete computer they could for under a thousand dollars. The class was for non-degree-seeking adults, so nothing was graded; it was simply to provide experience with spec'ing out and pricing the parts that go into making a complete system.

"One of the students had her eye on a new laptop for personal use. Because she noticed the trend toward being able to build a desktop computer for less than she could buy one, the student assumed the same about laptops. Unfortunately, I had not specifically mentioned the fact that there are no standards for building complete laptop clones, unlike with desktops.

"You can't reliably build your own laptop. Because laptop components are designed to exacting specifications to fit properly inside one manufacturer's case, there generally are no universal motherboards, video boards, and so on for laptops. Memory and hard drives are the exception. You can get different brands of memory and hard drives for laptops, but you can't buy a motherboard from one company and the video circuitry from another."

Characteristics of Mobile Devices

If you were asked to define the primary characteristic of mobile devices, you would probably answer, "They are small," and you wouldn't be wrong. There are three overarching characteristics of mobile devices that make working with them unique versus working with laptops or desktops: field servicing and upgrading, input methods, and secondary storage. We'll discuss each one in turn.

Field Servicing and Upgrading

Ever since the dawn of the portable computer, manufacturers and service providers have based a percentage of their success on warranties and "house calls" to repair devices on the fritz. It's a fact that quasi-permanent components, such as displays and motherboards, are widely considered replaceable only with identical components in laptops and smaller devices. However, technically minded users could take it upon themselves to expand the capabilities of their own system by, for instance, upgrading the hard drive, increasing RAM, using expansion cards and flash devices, and attaching wired peripherals.

Although the ability to repair and expand the functionality of portable devices in the field has become all but obviated, it has been shown with current and past generations of mobile devices that users are not averse to giving up expandability and replaceable parts as long as functionality and convenience outshine the loss.

Although many Android and other non-Apple devices allow the replacement of batteries and the use of removable memory cards as primary storage, even this basic level of access is removed in Apple's mobile devices, including its iPad line of tablet computers. In an effort to produce a sleeker mobile phone, even Android devices have been developed without user access to the battery. For Apple, however, in addition to producing a nice compact package, it is all part of keeping the technology as closed to adulteration as possible. Supporters of this practice recognize the resulting long-term quality. Detractors lament the lack of options.

To service closed mobile devices of any size, you may have to seek out an authorized repair facility and take or send your device to them for service. Attempting your own repairs can void any remaining warranty, and it can possibly render the device unusable. For example, a special screwdriver-like tool is required to open Apple's devices. You cannot simply dig between the seams of the case to pop the device open. Even if you get such a device to open, there is no standard consumer pipeline for parts, whether for repair or upgrading. If you want to try the repair yourself, you could be on your own. You may be able to find helpful videos on YouTube or www.ifixit.com to provide some guidance, though.

Anyone who has been around the business for more than just a few years has likely seen their fair share of components and systems with no user-serviceable parts. For these situations, an authorized technician can be dispatched to your location, home or work, with the appropriate tools, parts, and skills to field-service the system for you. On a slightly different, perhaps subtler note, the bottom line here is that many of today's mobile devices, including some of the larger tablet-style devices, have no field-serviceable parts inside, let alone user-serviceable parts. In some extremes, special work environments similar to the original clean manufacturing environment have to be established for servicing.

Input Methods

With decreased size comes increased interaction difficulties. Human interfaces can become only so small without the use of projection or virtualization. In other words, a computer the size of a postage stamp is fine as long as it can project a full-sized keyboard and a 60" display, for example. Using microscopic real interfaces would not sell much product. Thus, the conundrum is that users want smaller devices, but they do not want to have to wear a jeweler's loupe or big-screen virtualization glasses to interact with their petite devices.

As long as the size of the devices remains within the realm of human visibility and interaction, modern technology allows for some pretty convenient methods of user input. Nearly all devices, from tablet size down, are equipped with touch screens, supplying onscreen keyboards and other virtual input interfaces. On top of that, more and more of the screens are developing the capability to detect more than one contact point.

 We discuss touch screens more in the section "Input Devices," later in this chapter.

Generically, this technology is referred to in the industry as multitouch, and it is available on all Apple devices with touch input, including the touchpads of the Apple laptops. Apple, through its acquisition of a company called FingerWorks, holds patents for the capacitive multitouch technology featured on its products. Today, multitouch is more about functionality than novelty. Nevertheless, the markets for both business and pleasure exist for multitouch.

Certainly, touch screens with the capability to sense hundreds of separate points of contact can allow large-scale collaboration or fun at parties. Imagine a coffee table that can allow you to pull out a jigsaw puzzle with the touch of an icon, remembering where you and three friends left off. Imagine all of you being able to manipulate pieces independently and simultaneously and being able to send the puzzle away again as quickly as you brought it out so that you can watch the game on the same surface. This technology exists, and it is for sale today. Early examples were built on Microsoft's PixelSense technology, including the Samsung SUR40. Companies like Ideum build multitouch platform tables, including a monster 86" 4K ultra-high-definition (UHD) display with 100 touch points, allowing up to eight people to use it simultaneously.

On a smaller scale, our mobile devices allow us to pinch and stretch images on the screen by placing multiple fingers on that screen at the same time. Even touchpads on laptops can be made to differentiate any number of fingers being used at the same time, each producing a different result, including pointing and clicking, scrolling and right-clicking, and dragging—all one-handed with no need to press a key or mouse button while gesturing.

HTC created an early touch screen software interface called TouchFLO that has matured into HTC Sense, and it is still in use today on its Android-based mobile devices. TouchFLO is not multitouch capable, nor does it specify the physical technology behind the touch screen, only the software application for it. Theoretically, then, TouchFLO and multitouch could be combined.

The primary contribution of TouchFLO was the introduction of an interface that the user perceives as multiple screens, each of which is accessible by an intuitive finger gesture on the screen to spin around to a subsequent page. On various devices using this concept, neighboring pages have been constructed side by side or above and below one another. Apple's mobile devices employ gestures owing to the contributions of TouchFLO, bringing the potential of combining TouchFLO-like technology and multitouch to bear.

Users of early HTC devices with resistive touch screen technology met with difficulty and discord when flowing to another screen. The matte texture of the early resistive screens was not conducive to smooth gesturing. Capacitive touch screen technology is a welcome addition to such a user interface, making gestures smooth and even more intuitive than ever.

> Resistive touch screens use pressure from a stylus or finger to register the contact. Capacitive touch screens use electrical conductivity, which makes the human finger the perfect stylus. Resistive touch screens allow for more granularity because they can account for more sensors per square inch. Capacitive touch screens are more responsive and better suited to multitouch applications, but they generally don't work if the user is wearing gloves, which can block the finger's electrical current. If you need help remembering the difference, think of resistive screens as providing resistance or needing pressure. And for capacitive screens, think of a capacitor, which stores electricity (and capacitive touch screens utilize conductivity).

Secondary Storage

Computers of all sizes and capabilities use similar forms of RAM for primary storage—the storage location for currently running instructions and data. Secondary storage—the usually nonvolatile location where these instructions and data are stored on a more permanent basis—is another story.

The primary concern with smaller devices is the shock they tend to take as the user makes their way through a typical day. Simply strapping a phone to your hip and taking the metro to work presents a multitude of opportunities for a spinning disk to meet with catastrophe. The result would be the frequent loss of user information from a device counted on more and more as technology advances.

Just as many telephony subscribers have migrated from a home landline that stays put to a mobile phone that follows them everywhere, many casual consumers are content to use their mobile device as their primary or only computing system, taking it wherever they go. As a result, the data must survive conditions more brutal than most laptops because laptops are most often shut down before being transported.

The most popular solution is to equip mobile devices with very small solid-state drives (SSDs) in place of larger magnetic or solid-state drives. There are no moving parts, the drive stays cooler and resists higher temperature extremes, and SSDs require less power to run than their conventional counterparts.

Now that we've illustrated the primary differences between laptops, mobile devices, and desktops, let's examine some principles for taking laptops apart and putting them back together.

Disassembling and Reassembling Laptops

Desktop computers often have a lot of empty space inside their cases. This lets air circulate and also gives the technician some room to maneuver when troubleshooting internal hardware. Space is at a premium in laptops, and rarely is any wasted. With a desktop computer, if you end up having an extra screw left over after putting it together, it might not be a big deal. With laptops, every screw matters, and you'll sometimes find yourself trying to identify visually miniscule differences between screws to make sure that you get them back into the right places.

Even though repairing a laptop poses unique issues, most of the general troubleshooting and safety tips that you use when troubleshooting a desktop still apply. For example, always make sure that you have a clean and well-lit workspace and be cautious of electrostatic discharge (ESD). General safety tips and ESD prevention are covered in Chapter 21, "Safety and Environmental Concerns." For now, our general advice is to use antistatic mats or wrist straps if they're available.

Throughout this section, we'll use the word *laptop* almost exclusively. The principles covered here apply to nearly all portable devices, though, even tablets and smartphones.

One of the key principles for working with laptops is using the right tools to tear the thing apart. It's doubtful that any technician goes into a job thinking, "Hey, I'm going to use the wrong tools just to see what happens." With laptops, though, it's especially important to ensure that you have exactly the tools you'll need for the job. The two main camps of materials you need are the manufacturer's documentation and the correct hand tools. We'll also emphasize the importance of organization.

Using the Manufacturer's Documentation

Most technicians won't bat an eye at whipping out their cordless screwdriver and getting into a desktop's case. The biggest difference between most desktops is how you get inside the case. Once it's opened, everything inside is pretty standard fare.

Laptops are a different story. Even experienced technicians will tell you to not remove a single screw until you have the documentation handy unless you're incredibly familiar with that particular laptop. Most laptop manufacturers give you access to repair manuals on their websites. Table 9.1 lists the service and support websites for some of the top laptop manufacturers.

TABLE 9.1   Laptop manufacturers' service and support websites

Company	URL
Apple	`https://support.apple.com/mac`
Asus	`https://www.asus.com/support`
Dell	`https://www.dell.com/support`
HP	`https://support.hp.com`
Lenovo	`https://support.lenovo.com`
Sony	`https://www.sony.com/electronics/support`

If the site you need isn't listed, a quick Google search should do the trick. Once you are at the right website, search for the manual using the laptop's model number.

WARNING   Some laptop manufacturers have a policy that if you open the case of a laptop, the warranty is voided. Be sure to understand your warranty status and implications of cracking the case open before you do it.

Using the Proper Hand Tools

Once you have the manual in hand or on your screen, you need to gather the proper hand tools for the job. For some laptops, you only need the basics, such as small Phillips-head and flat-head screwdrivers. For others, you may need a Torx driver. Gather the tools you need and prepare to open the case. A small flashlight might also come in handy. Small PC technician toolkits are readily available online or from your favorite electronics retailer. They may have a few different sizes of screwdrivers, hex drivers, Torx drivers, tweezers, a screw grabber, and a few other assorted goodies, all in a convenient carrying case. An example is shown in Figure 9.1. Find one you like and never leave home without it.

FIGURE 9.1 PC technician toolkit

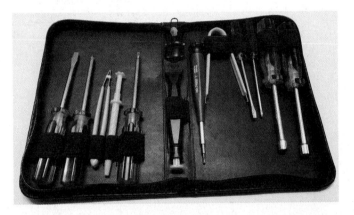

The Consequences of Using the Wrong Tools

It's been said once, but it's important to say it again: always use the right tool for the job when repairing laptops. If the documentation says that you need a T-10 Torx driver, make sure that you have a T-10 Torx driver.

Not using the right tools can result in the stripping of the screw head. If you strip a screw head in a desktop, you might have alternative methods of removing the screw. Laptops are far less forgiving. If you strip a screw head and are unable to turn the screw, you may never be able to remove it. That could result in needing to scrap the device.

Organization and Documentation

Before you crack open the case of your laptop, have an organization and documentation plan in place. Know where you are going to put the parts. Have a container set aside for the screws. You can purchase small plastic containers that have several compartments in them with lids that snap tightly shut, into which you can place screws. You can also use containers designed to organize prescription pills or fishing tackle. The bottom of an egg carton works well too, provided that you don't need to transport the screws from place to place. You don't want the screws falling out and getting lost!

For documentation, many technicians find it handy to draw a map of the computer they're getting into, such as the one shown in Figure 9.2. It can be as complex as you want it to be, as long as it makes sense to you. Taking pictures with your phone is also a smart move, provided that you're allowed to use your phone and don't violate any security or privacy policies.

FIGURE 9.2   Laptop repair road map

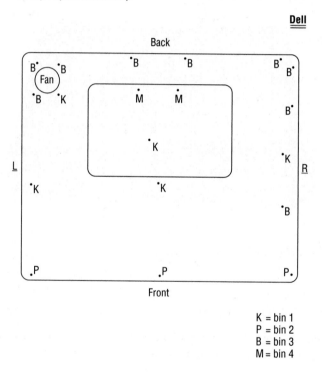

The drawing in Figure 9.2 shows the locations of the screws, and it also calls out where the screws should be placed once they're removed. Again, this type of documentation can be as simple or complex as you want it to be, as long as it makes sense and helps you stay organized.

Now that we've covered some key principles, let's take a look at specific components, technologies involved, and how to install and configure them.

Installing and Configuring Laptop Hardware

In the following sections, you will learn about the various components that make up laptops and how they differ from desktop computer components. These sections deal specifically with laptops, because smaller devices generally don't have field-replaceable components (or you can get specialized training on how to repair them). If you don't remember exactly what each component does, it may help you to refer back to earlier hardware chapters occasionally as you read this chapter.

Laptop Case

A typical laptop case is made up of three main parts:

- The display—usually an LCD or *organic light-emitting diode (OLED)* display

- The case structure, which is the metal reinforcement inside the laptop that provides rigidity and strength and to which most components are mounted

- The case, or the plastic or aluminum cover that surrounds the components and provides protection from the elements

Most cases are typically made of some type of plastic (usually ABS plastic or ABS composite) to provide for reduced weight as well as strength.

 Some laptops have cases made of a strong, lightweight metal, such as aluminum or titanium. However, the majority of laptop cases are made of plastic.

Laptop cases are made in what is known as a *clamshell design*. In a clamshell design, the laptop has two halves, hinged together at the back. The display portion, called the top half, often includes a webcam, microphone, and Wi-Fi antenna. All other components, including the motherboard, memory, storage, keyboard, battery, cooling fan, and speakers, are in the bottom half.

Occasionally, part of the laptop's case or the device's frame will crack and need to be replaced. However, you usually can't just replace the cracked section. Most often, you must remove every component from inside the laptop's case and swap the components over to the new one. This is a labor-intensive process because the screws in laptops are often very small and hard to reach.

Often, repairing a cracked case may cost several hundred dollars in labor alone. Most times, people who have cracked laptop cases wait until something else needs to be repaired before having the case fixed. Or, they just wait until it's time to upgrade to a new system. The decision on when to repair or replace the laptop boils down to a few factors. The primary one is if the user can live with the damage. While they can be annoying, most case problems don't inhibit the operation of the machine. The secondary factor is money. The user (or company) needs to decide if it's really worth spending the money needed to fix the issue immediately.

One of the components you may need to service is the speakers, which are generally built into the bottom part of the case. Exercise 9.1 will provide an example of removing speakers from a Dell Inspiron 13 7000 laptop. We'll use that model for an example throughout this chapter. We realize that this specific model is a few years old and you might not have access to one, but the exercises can help you understand the process. Besides, it would be impractical to list the specific replacement steps for all makes and models out there. If you have a different model, download its service manual and perform the necessary steps.

To get the most out of the exercises in this chapter, it's best if you're able to perform them on a laptop. However, we realize that not everyone has access to a laptop they can tear apart. If you don't have a laptop you can perform surgery on, here are a few options you can try:

- Download a service manual for the laptop you have (or another model that seems interesting). Look for directions on how to remove or replace the components we describe so that you can get a feel for how you would perform the tasks.

- Visit a local computer repair shop and ask if they have any old laptops that they are going to take to recycling. Explain that you are studying for the A+ exam and would like to get experience taking apart a laptop. See if they will let you take one apart at their facility. (You never know until you ask!)

- Visit YouTube or www.ifixit.com and look up videos for how to replace components on your laptop or another model that seems interesting.

Before we get to Exercise 9.1, we want to remind you of a few safety steps to take before working on a laptop. We're not going to repeat these instructions before every exercise, but always perform these steps before beginning digging into a laptop (or a desktop, for that matter):

1. Turn off the computer.

2. Disconnect all external peripherals and cables, such as keyboards, mice, monitors, and network cables.

3. Unplug it from the power source.

4. Ensure that your workspace is free of clutter and well lit.

5. Have the manual or help videos handy, just in case.

6. Make sure you have the proper tools readily available. (This might include a phone to take pictures with.)

7. Ground yourself with an ESD wrist strap or other antistatic protection.

EXERCISE 9.1

Removing Speakers from a Laptop

1. Remove the bottom cover. As shown in Figure 9.3, this model requires removing nine screws to take the cover off.

FIGURE 9.3   Removing nine screws to take off the bottom cover

2.   Make a mental note of the key components and their location, or better yet, take a picture with your phone like the one in Figure 9.4.

FIGURE 9.4   Inside the Inspiron 13 7000

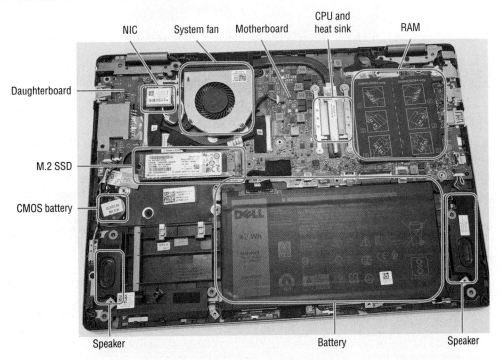

(continues)

3. Disconnect the speaker cable from the motherboard, as shown in Figure 9.5.

FIGURE 9.5   Disconnecting the speaker cable

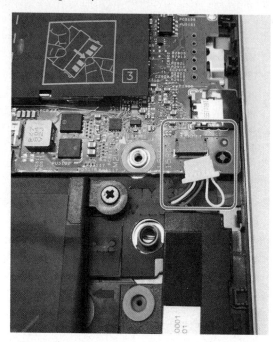

4. Remove the speaker cable from the wire routing guides on the base assembly.

Figure 9.6 shows the speaker wire that travels from the left speaker to the right speaker.

FIGURE 9.6   The speaker wire

5. Remove the rubber grommets that hold the speakers in.

   Figure 9.6 shows the two from the right speaker. The left speaker has three.

6. Carefully remove both speakers from the base assembly.

To replace the speakers, follow the steps in reverse order. Insert the new speakers, replace the grommets, run the speaker wire through the guides, and connect the speaker to the motherboard.

Removing the speakers from the Dell Inspiron 13 7000 was relatively easy. On some laptops, the speakers or speaker wire are completely buried underneath several other components, and you need to remove those first. As we move through this chapter, you will see situations where you need to remove several components before you can get to the one you want.

Laptop Displays

The display system is the primary component in the top half of the clamshell case. (The wireless antenna often resides here too, and we'll get to that in just a bit.) Much like all other laptop components, the display is more or less a smaller version of its desktop counterpart. What is unique to laptop displays, though, is that for some time, the technology used in them was actually more advanced than what was commonly used in desktops. This is due to LCD technology.

Before LCD technology, computer displays used cathode-ray tube (CRT) technology (like old-school televisions) and were big, bulky, and hardly mobile. We introduced LCD and *organic light-emitting diode (OLED)* concepts in Chapter 3, "Peripherals, Cables, and Connectors," but we'll do a quick refresher in the "Screen" section later. Let's focus now on the different components that are required to make these types of displays work on a laptop.

 Some laptops feature screens that rotate orientation depending on how they are held (much like smartphones and tablets), or the screens themselves will rotate horizontally or be entirely removable. Rotating and removable screens cost more money, so consider your needs or the needs of the user when recommending such features.

Video Card

The video card in a laptop or desktop with an LCD monitor does the same thing, regardless of what type of machine it's in. It's responsible for generating and managing the image sent to the screen. LCD monitors are digital, so laptop video cards generate a digital image. Laptop manufacturers put video cards that are compatible with the given display in a laptop, and most laptop manufacturers choose to integrate the LCD circuitry on the motherboard to save space.

Odds are that the laptop you're using has an integrated video card. If the video card fails, you're likely looking at a motherboard replacement. Very few laptops have a replaceable video card. For those that do, replacing or upgrading it will probably resemble replacing system memory.

Video Memory Sharing

If your video card is built into your motherboard, it likely won't have its own memory but will share system memory with the processor. Note that there is nothing wrong with this type of setup; in fact, it often brings the cost of the laptop down. It's just that instead of having 8 GB of RAM and 2 GB of video RAM (for example), you would have only 8 GB total. So if your video card were using 2 GB, the system would be left with only 6 GB. That will slow everything down.

How much of a difference does all of this make? Well, it depends on what you're doing with your laptop. If you're using it for the Internet and light work, probably not much difference. If you're working with more video-intensive applications, using a computer with shared memory might slow things down to an unacceptable level. This usually brings up two questions: What's the optimal balance? And where do I change this?

To answer the first question, again, it depends on what you are doing. If you perform more video-intensive operations (or if you're gaming), then you might want to set aside more memory for the video card. If you're not as concerned with rapid pixilation, then less is fine. Which brings us to the second question: Where do you set it? Shared memory is configured in the system BIOS/UEFI. Each BIOS/UEFI is different, so be sure to consult your owner's manual if you have any questions. Keep in mind that some BIOSs/UEFIs will allow you to set aside only a certain amount of memory—say, 512 MB—for video memory.

How does this affect your computer when you upgrade the memory? First, keep in mind that some of your memory will be taken by the video card, so you might want to upgrade to more memory than you originally had planned, if the laptop supports it. Second, after upgrading the memory, you will need to go into the BIOS/UEFI and reconfigure how much memory you want allocated to the video card.

Backlight

LCD displays do not produce light, so to generate brightness, LCD displays have a backlight. A *backlight* is a small lamp placed behind, above, or to the side of an LCD display. The light from the lamp is diffused across the screen, producing brightness. The typical laptop display uses a *cold cathode fluorescent lamp (CCFL)* as its backlight. As their name implies, they are fluorescent lights, and they're generally about 8" long and slimmer than a pencil. You might see laptops claiming to have 2-CCFL, which just means that they have two backlights. This can result in a laptop with a brighter screen. CCFLs generate little heat, which is always a good thing to avoid with laptops.

Another backlight technology uses LEDs instead of CCFLs. Instead of CCFL tubes, they have strips of LED lights, and most LEDs do not need an inverter. Smaller devices, such as tablets and phones, almost exclusively use LED backlighting, which is smaller and consumes less power than CCFLs.

Inverter

Fluorescent lighting, and LCD backlights in particular, require fairly high-voltage, high-frequency energy. Another component is needed to provide the right kind of energy, and that's the *inverter*.

The inverter is a small circuit board installed behind the LCD panel that takes DC current and inverts it to AC for the backlight. If you are having problems with flickering screens or dimness, it's more likely that the inverter is the problem, not the backlight itself.

There are two things to keep in mind if you are going to replace an inverter. First, they store and convert energy, which means they have the potential to discharge that energy. To an inexperienced technician, they can be dangerous. Second, make sure the replacement inverter was made to work with the LCD backlight that you have. If they weren't made for each other, you might have problems with a dim screen or poor display quality.

 WARNING   Inverters can discharge energy, which can cause severe injury to you. Be careful when working with them!

Screen

The screen on a laptop does what you might expect—it produces the image that you see. The overall quality of the picture depends a lot on the quality of the screen and the technology your laptop uses. Current popular options include variants of LCD and OLED. We introduced these technologies in Chapter 3, but here's a quick review:

Liquid Crystal Display   First used with portable computers, LCDs are based on the electrical property that when a current is passed through a semi-crystalline liquid, the crystals align themselves with the current. Transistors are then combined with these liquid crystals to form patterns, such as numbers or letters. LCDs are lightweight and have low power requirements.

Liquid crystals do not produce light, so LCD monitors need a lighting source to display an image—the backlight that we already discussed. If you see a laptop advertised as having an LED display, it's an LCD monitor with LED backlighting.

There are three popular variants of LCD monitors in use today: *in-plane switching (IPS)*, *twisted nematic (TN)*, and *vertical alignment (VA)*. All three employ LCD technology—that is, they use liquid crystals and transistors to form patterns. They do it in different ways, by aligning the crystals in a different manner.

- TN is the oldest of the three technologies. It has somewhat restricted viewing angles and not the best color reproduction. Colors may appear washed out or too blended together. On the bright side, they have very little lag and can handle high refresh rates such as 240 Hz with ease. That makes them a popular choice for competitive gamers. They're not the best choice for high-end video needs, but they are inexpensive, which also makes them good for everyday office use.

- IPS followed TN into the market. They have the best viewing angles and color reproduction of all LCD monitors. They usually have a bit more lag than TN monitors do, but the difference is minimal in higher-end models. IPS monitors are ideal for those seeking the best color experience, such as graphic designers and video artists. They are also the best choice for someone who wants to mount them vertically, like a lot of programmers do.

- VA has the best contrast ratios of the three, meaning the difference between the dark and bright colors is the best. Color reproduction tends to be good but not quite as good as IPS, and VA monitors do have a bit more lag (but we're talking milliseconds here). It's more a jack-of-all-trades technology than the other two options.

Organic Light-Emitting Diode   OLED displays are the image-producing parts of the display *and* the light source. An organic light-emitting compound forms the heart of the OLED, and it is placed between an anode and a cathode, which produce a current that runs through the electroluminescent compound, causing it to emit light. An OLED, then, is the combination of the compound and the electrodes on each side of it. The electrode in the back of the OLED cell is usually opaque, allowing a rich black display when the OLED cell is not lit. The front electrode should be transparent, to allow the emission of light from the OLED.

If thin-film electrodes and a flexible compound are used to produce the OLEDs, an OLED display can be made flexible, which is not only cool, but it allows it to function in places where other display technologies could never work.

Because OLEDs create the image in an OLED display *and* supply the light source, there is no need for a backlight, so power consumption is less than it is in LCD panels. Additionally, the contrast ratio of OLED displays exceeds that of LCD panels, meaning that in darker surroundings, OLED displays produce better images than LCD panels produce. Generally speaking, OLED monitors are the highest-quality monitors you will find on the market today. OLED is found in smaller devices such as smartphones as well.

Are OLEDs Better than QLEDs?

When shopping for laptops (or TVs) you may see yet another display option, the quantum light-emitting diode (QLED), created by Samsung. (Samsung says it stands for quantum dot LED TV.) Is it better or worse than an OLED?

QLEDs use a backlight like an LED does, technically, thousands of small LED backlights. Over the top of the backlight is a film made of quantum dots (tiny nanoparticles) that enhance the brightness and color of the display. QLEDs will provide better color representation and more brightness, have a longer life span, and are cheaper to make than OLEDs. Large QLEDs will generally be less expensive than OLEDs. On the flip side, OLEDs have a better viewing angle, better black levels, and use less power. So which is better? It's hard to say. Both technologies can deliver high-quality displays, so choosing between them is matter of personal preference.

Digitizer

A *digitizer* is a device that can be written or drawn on, and the content will be converted from analog input to digital images on the computer. Digitizers take input from a user's finger or a writing utensil, such as a stylus. When built into the display, they might be the glass of the display itself, or they might be implemented as an overlay for the display. For touch-screen devices, the digitizer might be the primary method of input. For other devices, such as a laptop with a touch screen, users might find the digitizer helpful for capturing drawings or handwritten notes.

 Other types of digitizers are not built into the screen and may be pads on the palm rest of a laptop or next to the touchpad or peripheral USB devices that look like notepads.

Webcam and Microphone

Webcams are nearly universal on laptops today. The most common placement is right above the display on the laptop, although some are below the screen. Most laptops with webcams will also have a smaller circle to the left of the lens, which has a light that turns on to illuminate the user when the webcam is on. Some people are a bit paranoid about their webcams, and they will put a piece of tape over the camera when it's not in use.

If you're going to use a webcam to conduct a video call with someone, it helps if they can hear you too. That's where the *microphone* comes into play. Microphones are often built into the display unit as well. The webcam shown in Figure 9.7 has the illumination light to the left and the microphone inputs on both sides of the lens. Microphones can also be built into the bottom half of the clamshell, either above the keyboard or somewhere on the front bezel.

Wi-Fi Antenna

Practically all laptops produced today include built-in Wi-Fi capabilities. Considering how popular wireless networking is today, it only makes sense to include 802.11 functionality without needing to use an expansion card. With laptops that include built-in Wi-Fi, the *Wi-Fi antenna* is generally run through the upper half of the clamshell case. This is to get the antenna higher up and improve signal reception. The wiring will run down the side of the display and through the hinge of the laptop case and plug in somewhere on the motherboard.

FIGURE 9.7   Webcam and microphone

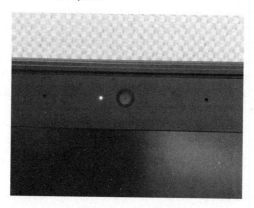

The Wi-Fi antenna won't affect what you see on the screen, but if you start digging around in the display, know that you'll likely be messing with your wireless capabilities as well.

> It's worth repeating again that the Wi-Fi antenna wiring usually runs through one of the hinges of the laptop case. Damage to a hinge can cause Wi-Fi problems. Later in the "Other Internal Components" section, we have an exercise on removing the Wi-Fi card, in which you will disconnect the antenna wires.

Replacing Components within a Laptop Display

While going through the exercises in this chapter, you've probably noticed that the inside of a laptop is tight and complex, and navigating it can be a challenge. Laptop displays are the same way. There are not as many components as compared to the bottom half of a laptop, but space is even tighter. Within a display, the components you might need to replace include the screen (or touch screen/digitizer, which some manufacturers call the display panel), Wi-Fi antenna, webcam, microphone, and inverter.

In most cases, servicing components within the display means removing the display assembly from the base assembly. Exercise 9.2 shows you how to do that.

EXERCISE 9.2

Removing the Display Assembly

1. Remove the bottom cover.

2. Remove the wireless NIC from the base assembly.

3. Open the latch for the display cable and disconnect it from the motherboard. It's the left connector shown in Figure 9.8.

4. Disconnect the touch-screen board cable from the motherboard. It's the right connector shown in Figure 9.8.

FIGURE 9.8   Display cable and touch-screen board cable connectors

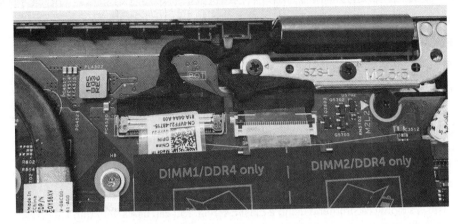

5. Open the computer so that the display assembly is parallel with the base assembly, and lay it screen side down on a flat surface.

    We recommend that you place it on a soft surface to avoid scratching the screen.

6. Remove the screws that secure the display assembly to the base assembly. There are two screws for each hinge, and they are highlighted in Figure 9.9.

FIGURE 9.9   Display assembly hinge screws

7. Lift the display assembly off of the base assembly.

    Note that the NIC antenna wires, display cable and connector, and touch-screen board cable and connector will go with the display assembly.

If you're replacing the entire display unit, all you need to do is get the new unit and reverse the steps you followed in Exercise 9.2. If you're replacing a component within the display unit, you need to go further. To get to the Wi-Fi antenna, webcam, microphone, and inverter, you must also remove the display panel. Exercise 9.3 gives you the general steps needed to accomplish this.

EXERCISE 9.3

Removing the Display Panel

1. Remove the bottom cover.

2. Remove the display assembly.

3. Remove the display cable from the routing guides inside the hinge covers.

4. Use a plastic scribe to pry apart the back of the display assembly and the display panel.

   Step 4 is a tricky step. There's not much of a gap between the display panel and the back of the display assembly. It's generally best to try to start prying it apart near the center of one of the sides of the panel—that's where you're likely to get the most separation to get the scribe in there.

   Also, we highly recommend using a plastic scribe. You can use a very thin flat screwdriver, but the metal is more likely to mark up or damage the case than the plastic scribe. Once you start getting separation, gently work your way around the edge of the display panel to separate the whole thing.

5. Identify the component you need to replace, and remove it.

   Figure 9.10 shows a Lenovo ThinkPad with the display bezel removed. You can see wires running along the side and top. Some of the wires go to the webcam, and others are for the wireless antenna. As always, consult the laptop's documentation to identify the proper components.

FIGURE 9.10   Wires inside a laptop display

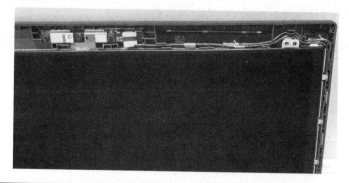

For the exam, be able to compare and contrast display components of mobile devices. This includes the following:

- Types: LCD, IPS, TN, VA, OLED
- Mobile display components
- Wi-Fi antenna connector/placement
- Camera/webcam
- Microphone
- Touch screen/digitizer
- Inverter

Motherboards and Processors

As with desktop computers, the motherboard of a laptop is the backbone structure to which all internal components connect. However, with a laptop, almost all components must be integrated onto the motherboard, including onboard circuitry for the USB, video, expansion, and network ports of the laptop. With desktop systems, the option remains to not integrate such components. Because of the similarities between laptop and desktop components, some material in the next few sections will be familiar to you if you have read Chapter 1, "Motherboards, Processors, and Memory."

Laptop Motherboards

The primary differences between a laptop motherboard and a desktop motherboard are the lack of standards and the much smaller form factor. As mentioned earlier, most motherboards are designed along with the laptop case so that all the components will fit inside. Therefore, the motherboard is nearly always proprietary, and that's what we mean by "lack of standards." They use the technologies you're used to, such as USB and Wi-Fi, but it's very unlikely that you're going to be able to swap a motherboard from one laptop to another, even if both laptops are from the same manufacturer. Figure 9.11 shows an example of a laptop motherboard. Its unusual shape is designed to help it fit into a specific style of case with the other necessary components.

To save space, components of the video circuitry (and possibly other circuits as well) may be placed on a thin circuit board that connects directly to the motherboard. This circuit board is often known as a *riser card* or a *daughterboard*; an example is shown in Figure 9.12. We also labeled them in the Dell in Figure 9.4. They're harder to see when they're in the case with other components, but you may be able to tell that they have very different shapes from those in Figure 9.11 and Figure 9.12.

Dell happens to call this daughterboard an input/output board, or I/O board. This model also has another daughterboard. If you were ordering parts, you'd want to specify I/O board or daughterboard, but for general purposes, the term daughterboard is applicable.

FIGURE 9.11   A laptop motherboard

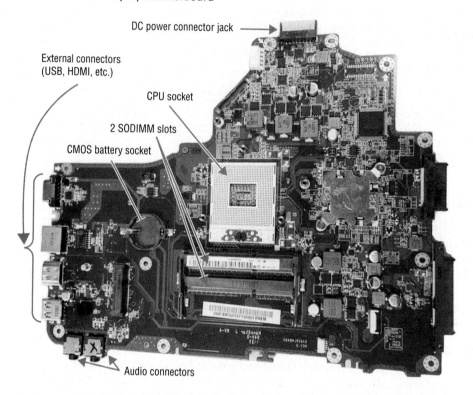

DC power connector jack

External connectors
(USB, HDMI, etc.)

CPU socket

2 SODIMM slots

CMOS battery socket

Audio connectors

FIGURE 9.12   A laptop daughterboard

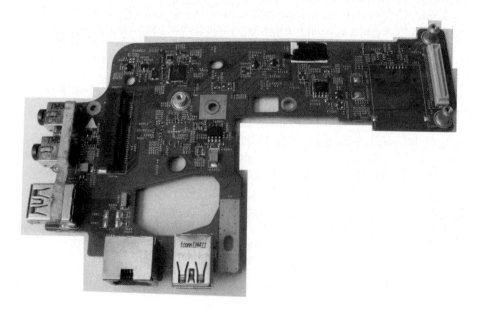

Having components performing different functions (such as video, audio, and networking) integrated on the same board is a mixed bag. On one hand, it saves a lot of space. On the other hand, if one part goes bad, you have to replace the entire board, which is more expensive than just replacing one expansion card. Exercise 9.4 walks you through the steps to remove the motherboard from the Dell Inspiron 13 7000. As you'll see, you need to remove several components and disconnect several connectors before you can get the motherboard out.

EXERCISE 9.4

Removing the Motherboard from a Laptop

1. Remove the bottom cover.

2. Remove the battery.

3. Remove the fan.

4. Remove the heat sink.

5. Remove the solid-state drive.

6. Disconnect all the connectors plugged into the motherboard.

   Be careful, because two of them (for the I/O cable and the display cable) have a latch that needs to be released first. By our count, there are nine connectors. We've highlighted them in Figure 9.13. The two with latches have rectangles around them, and the rest have ovals.

FIGURE 9.13   Disconnecting the motherboard connectors

(continues)

7. Remove the two screws from the system board bracket. They're shown in Figure 9.14 with circles around them.

FIGURE 9.14 Removing the screws

8. Remove the system board bracket.

9. Remove the three screws that hold the motherboard to the base assembly. In Figure 9.14, they are highlighted with squares around them.

10. Lift the motherboard off the base assembly.

To replace the motherboard, follow the steps in reverse order.

Laptop Processors

Just as with desktop computers, the central processing unit (CPU) is the brain of the laptop computer. And just like everything else, compared to desktop hardware devices, laptop hardware devices are smaller and not quite as powerful. The spread between the speed of and number of cores in a laptop CPU and that of a desktop model can be significant. Fortunately, the gap has closed over the years, and laptop processors today are pretty fast—most people think they perform just fine. It's up to the user to determine if the difference in speed hurts their usage experience.

Laptops have less space than desktops, and therefore the CPU is usually soldered onto the motherboard and is not upgradable. You can see the processor of the Dell we've been working on in Figure 9.14—it's the small silver square to the left of the RAM. Within confined computing spaces, heat is a major concern. Add to that the fact that the processor is the hottest-running component, and you can see where cooling can be an issue. To help combat this heat problem, laptop processors are engineered with the following features:

Streamlined Connection to the Motherboard   Nearly all desktop processors mount using pin connectors, whether on the CPU or on the motherboard (as is the case with LGA sockets). Pins and sockets are big and bulky, meaning they're not a laptop's friends. Laptop processors are generally either soldered directly to the motherboard or attached using the Micro-FCBGA (Flip Chip Ball Grid Array) standard, which uses balls instead of pins. In most cases, this means that the processor cannot be removed, meaning no processor upgrades are possible.

Lower Voltages and Clock Speeds   To combat heat, you can either slow the processor down (run it at a lower speed) or give it less juice (run it at a lower voltage). Again, performance will suffer compared to a desktop processor, but lowering heat is the goal here.

Active Sleep and Slowdown Modes   Most laptops will run the processor in a lower power state when on battery power to extend the life of the battery. This is known as *processor throttling*. The motherboard works closely with the operating system to determine if the processor really needs to run at full speed. If it doesn't, it's slowed down to save energy and to reduce heat. When more processing power is needed, the CPU is throttled back up.

While many portable computers will have processors that have just as many features as their desktop counterparts, others will simply use stripped-down versions of desktop processors. Although there's nothing wrong with this, it makes sense that components specifically designed for laptops fit the application better than components that have been retrofitted for laptop use. Consider an analogy to the automobile industry: it's better to design a convertible from the ground up than simply to cut the top off an existing coupe or sedan.

Memory

Laptops don't use standard desktop computer memory chips, because they're too big. In fact, for most of the history of laptops, there were no standard types of memory chips. If you wanted to add memory to your laptop, you had to order it from the laptop manufacturer. Of course, because you could get memory from only one supplier, you got the privilege of paying a premium over and above a similar-sized desktop memory chip.

Fortunately, the industry seems to have settled on one form factor, which is the *small outline dual inline memory module (SODIMM)*, which we introduced in Chapter 1. Recall that they're much smaller than standard DIMMs, measuring 67.6 millimeters (2.6") long and 32 millimeters (1.25") tall. SODIMMs are available in a variety of configurations, including older 32-bit (72-pin and 100-pin) and 64-bit (144-pin SDRAM, 200-pin DDR/DDR2,

204-pin DDR3, 260-pin DDR4, and 262-pin DDR5) options. Different standards of DDR SODIMMs are only a few millimeters longer or shorter than other versions. You probably won't be able to tell the difference unless they are right next to each other, or unless you try to install them and they don't fit in the socket. (You should never have the latter problem, though, because you will check the documentation first!) Figure 9.15 shows a laptop DDR3 SODIMM under a desktop DDR2 DIMM for a size comparison.

FIGURE 9.15   Desktop DIMM and laptop SODIMM

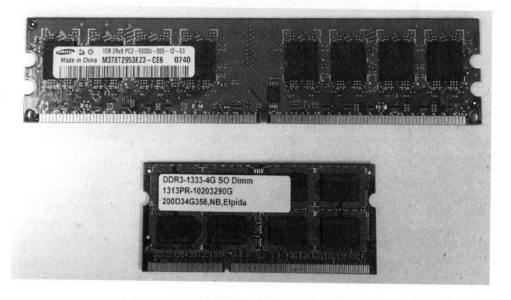

   Laptop manufacturers may still opt to go the proprietary route due to design considerations that favor a custom solution. In fact, many ultra-thin laptop models will have the RAM soldered onto the motherboard to save space. In such systems, the memory is not upgradable. To see what kind of memory your laptop uses, check either the manual or the manu-facturer's website. You can also check third-party memory producers' websites (such as www.crucial.com).

Just as with desktop computers, make sure the SODIMM you want to put into the laptop is compatible with the motherboard. The same standards that apply to desktop memory compatibility apply to laptops. This means that you can find DDR, DDR2, DDR3, DDR4, and DDR5 SODIMMs for laptops. DDR has topped out at 1 GB per module, while DDR2 and DDR3 SODIMM modules can be purchased in sizes up to 8 GB and DDR4 up to 32 GB and DDR5 up to 64 GB (at the time this book was being written). Exercise 9.5 shows you how to replace SODIMMs in a laptop.

EXERCISE 9.5

Replacing Laptop Memory

1. Remove the bottom cover.

2. Remove the battery.

3. Locate the system memory.

   In the Dell Inspiron 13 7000, the two RAM modules are under Mylar flaps.

4. Pull a Mylar flap back to reveal the RAM, as shown with one of the SODIMMs in Figure 9.16.

FIGURE 9.16   SODIMM in a laptop

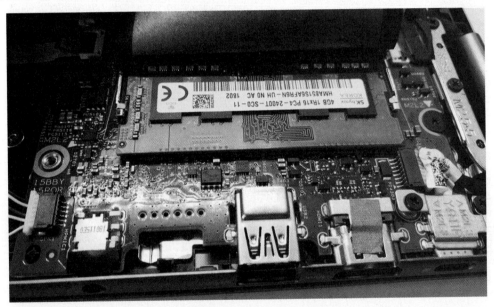

5. Carefully spread apart the metal securing clips on each end of the memory module. It will pop up as shown in Figure 9.17.

(continues)

FIGURE 9.17   Removing a SODIMM

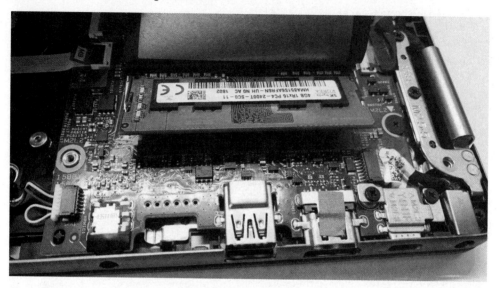

6.   Lift the memory module out of the slot.

When replacing the SODIMM, be sure to align the notch, and insert the module at the approximate angle it was at when it popped up after being released. Slowly press down on the module until it clicks into place. If it doesn't click into place, it's not inserted properly.

For several years, a laptop memory form factor called MicroDIMM enjoyed some popularity. The MicroDIMM is over 50 percent smaller than a SODIMM—only about 45.5 mm (about 1.75") long and 30 mm (about 1.2", a bit bigger than a U.S. quarter) wide. Another major difference is that the MicroDIMM does not have any keying notches on the bottom. Figure 9.18 shows a 172-pin MicroDIMM; notice that it's a lot closer to being square-shaped than the RAM shown in Figure 9.15, in addition to being a lot smaller. It was designed for the ultralight and portable subnotebook style of computer. Common MicroDIMM form factors included 64-bit modules with 172 or 214 pins for DDR2/DDR3. DDR4 and DDR5 MicroDIMMs have not been produced. Replacing a MicroDIMM is just like replacing a SODIMM.

FIGURE 9.18 172-pin MicroDIMM

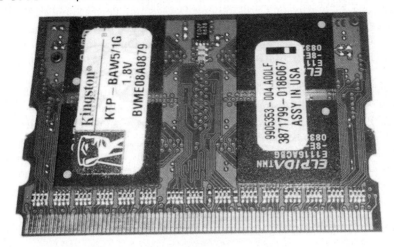

Storage

Storage is important for every computer made. If you can't retrieve important files when you need them, the computer isn't very useful. While the trend is moving toward storing more data online (in the cloud), there's still considerable need for built-in storage.

Laptop Hard Drives

Laptops don't have the room for the full-sized 3.5" hard drives that desktop computers use. Smaller form factor drives at 2.5" or 1.8" that are less than ½" thick are more appropriate. These drives share the same controller technologies as desktop computers; however, they use smaller connectors. Figure 9.19 shows an example of a standard 3.5" hard drive compared to a 2.5" laptop hard drive.

FIGURE 9.19 A desktop hard drive (left) compared to a laptop hard drive (right)

To save space and heat, most laptops today use a *solid-state drive (SSD)*, which we introduced in Chapter 2, "Expansion Cards, Storage Devices, and Power Supplies." Recall that, unlike conventional magnetic hard drives, which use spinning platters, SSDs have no moving parts. They use the same solid-state memory technology found in the other forms of flash memory. Otherwise, they perform just like a traditional magnetic HDD, except they're a lot faster.

Connecting a regular SSD in a desktop is usually just like connecting a regular HDD; they have the same Parallel Advanced Technology Attachment/Serial Advanced Technology Attachment (PATA/SATA) and power connectors. Laptops often have a specialized connector and a single cable that handles both data and power, as shown in Figure 9.20. Most manufacturers also make them in the same physical dimensions as traditional hard drives, even though they could be made much smaller, like removable flash drives. (This is probably to preserve the "look" of a hard drive so as to not confuse consumers or technicians.)

FIGURE 9.20   2.5" SSD, motherboard connector, and cable

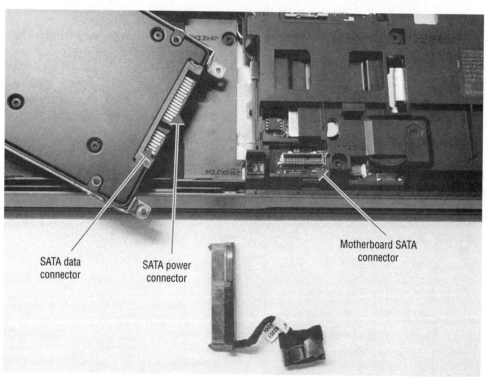

Newer SSDs may come in the even smaller M.2 form factor. In fact, the Dell Inspiron we've been working on in this chapter has an M.2 SSD. Figure 9.21 shows the SSD and the M.2 connector it plugs into. Exercise 9.6 walks you through removing an M.2 SSD from a laptop.

FIGURE 9.21   M.2 SSD and M.2 connector

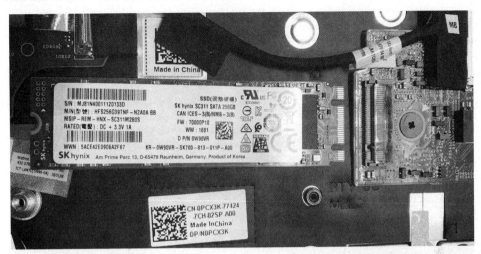

Removing an M.2 SSD from a Laptop

1. Remove the bottom cover.

2. Remove the screw that holds the SSD to the base assembly.

   The drive will pop up slightly. The screw is highlighted in Figure 9.22.

FIGURE 9.22   Removing an M.2 SSD

3. Slide the drive directly out of the connector.

Removing 2.5" or 1.8" SSDs from a laptop will require a few more steps than Exercise 9.6 did. First, disconnect the drive cable from the motherboard (refer to Figure 9.20), and then remove the two to four screws that hold the drive or its mounting bracket in place. Figure 9.23 shows an example of an SSD in a Lenovo ThinkPad that uses three screws— we've already removed them but highlighted the holes for you. Then lift out the drive (and bracket as needed). We show the disconnected drive next to the laptop in Figure 9.24.

FIGURE 9.23   2.5" SATA SSD

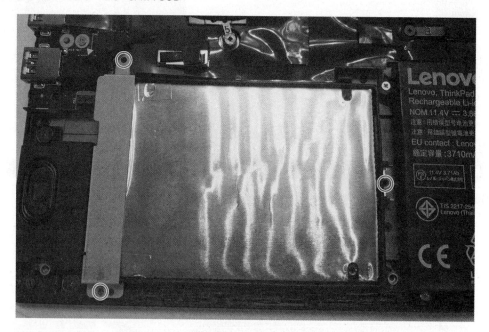

FIGURE 9.24   Disconnected SATA SSD

SSDs are perfect for laptops because they are faster, produce less heat, and are more shock resistant than conventional hard drives. They are more expensive per gigabyte, but that's the trade-off you have to make for better performance.

Hard Drive Data Migration

After replacing a hard drive or upgrading a laptop to a newer model, it may be necessary to get all of the user's data from the old drive (or laptop) onto the new one. Doing so is often referred to as data *migration* or hard drive migration. When setting up for a migration, there are two key questions to ask. The first is, what needs to be migrated? There's a big difference between moving someone's data and moving operating system settings and configurations. The second is, will the old drive be accessible when the new one is up and running? If so, there are more options to perform a migration. The answers to these will help determine which of the migration methods are preferable—either manual file copying or using migration software.

Copying Files Manually   If all that's needed is to get user data from the old device to the new one, then manually copying files is usually an easy option. If the old drive will be inaccessible after the replacement, then files can be copied from the old drive to the cloud or to an external hard drive first. The drive replacement can be made, and then the files copied from the cloud or external drive to the new hard drive. If the old drive will still be accessible, then files can be copied across a network (if conditions permit) or copied from computer to computer with a transfer cable.

The downside to this method is that it doesn't transfer any settings or configurations (such as a user's desktop, color scheme, installed printers, etc.), and it normally doesn't work for apps. Apps will need to be reinstalled on the new drive, and the user will have to reconfigure their settings.

Using Migration Software   Migration software can move files, settings, configurations, and apps from one drive to another. In most cases for this to work, both drives need to be accessible. For example, the old drive needs to be in a different operational computer, in a second expansion slot on the new computer, or otherwise connected, such as through a USB port using a USB-to-SATA adapter. If the connection is available, the migration software can work its magic.

There are several different migration apps available on the market. For example, Laplink PCmover (`http://web.laplink.com`) works with Windows computers. It has several versions, including the Home edition, which is good for normal users, and a Professional version that can copy multiple user profiles. Macrium Reflect (`http://macrium.com`) is another option for Windows-based systems, and SuperDuper (`http://shirtpocket.com`) works for macOS. All of these apps feature a graphical interface, where you choose what you want to migrate and the software takes it from there.

Laptop Optical Drives

Nearly all laptops have a hard drive, but rarely does a laptop made today have an internal optical drive. There just isn't room for one. If you need one, you can attach an external optical drive via an expansion port such as USB. It might be a bit slower than an internal drive, but it's better than not having one at all.

 CD, DVD, and Blu-ray burners are great to have with laptops as backup devices. Simply copy the contents of the hard drive (or just important files) to the optical discs and store them in a safe location.

Input Devices

Because of the small size of laptops, getting data into them presents unique challenges to designers. They must design a keyboard that fits within the case of the laptop. They must also design some sort of pointing device that can be used with graphical interfaces like Windows. The primary challenge in both cases is to design these peripherals so that they fit within the design constraints of the laptop (low power and small form factor) while remaining usable.

Keyboards

A standard-sized desktop keyboard wasn't designed to be portable. It wouldn't fit well with the portable nature of a laptop. That usually means laptop keys are not normal size; they must be smaller and packed together more tightly. People who learned to type on a typewriter or a full-sized keyboard often have a difficult time adjusting to a laptop keyboard.

Keyboards may need to be replaced if keys are missing or are stuck and won't function. If a user has spilled a beverage onto their keyboard, it could cause problems that necessitate a replacement. On most laptop keyboards, you can't replace just one key; the whole board must be replaced to fix a malfunctioning key.

Laptop keyboards are built into the lower portion of the clamshell. Sometimes, they can be removed easily to access peripherals below them, like memory and hard drives, as in the Lenovo ThinkPad series. Other times, removing the keyboard is one of the most challenging tasks, because nearly all other internal components need to be removed first. Exercise 9.7 illustrates the joy of removing the keyboard from the Dell Inspiron 13 7000.

EXERCISE 9.7

Removing a Laptop Keyboard

1. Remove the bottom cover.

2. Remove the battery.

3. Remove the SSD.

4. Remove the wireless card.

5. Remove the fan.

6. Remove the heat sink.

7. Remove the display assembly.

8. Remove the I/O board.

9. Remove the power adapter port.

10. Remove the motherboard.

11. Remove the speakers.

12. Remove the 14 screws that hold the keyboard shield to the base assembly.

13. Lift the keyboard from the base assembly.

As you can see, it was necessary to remove 11 components before we got to the keyboard. With a laptop like this, replacing the keyboard is not a quick-service item.

Pointing Devices

In addition to using the keyboard, you must have a method of controlling the onscreen pointer in the Windows (or other graphical) interface. Most laptops today include multiple USB ports for connecting a mouse, and you can choose from a wide range of wired or wireless full-sized or smaller mice. There are several additional methods for managing the Windows pointer. Here are some of the more common ones:

- Trackball

- Touchpad

- Point stick

- Touch screen

 Because of different pointing-device preferences, some laptops include multiple pointing devices to appeal to a wider variety of people.

Trackball Many early laptops used trackballs as pointing devices. A *trackball* is essentially the same as a mouse turned upside down. The onscreen pointer moves in the same direction and at the same speed that you move the trackball with your thumb or fingers.

Trackballs are cheap to produce. However, the primary problem with trackballs is that they do not last as long as other types of pointing devices; a trackball picks up dirt and oil from operators' fingers, and those substances clog the rollers on the trackball and prevent it from functioning properly.

Touchpad   To overcome the problems of trackballs, a newer technology that has become known as the touchpad was developed. *Touchpad* is actually the trade name of a product. However, the trade name is now used to describe an entire genre of products that are similar in function.

A touchpad is a device that has a pad of touch-sensitive material. The user draws with their finger on the touchpad, and the onscreen pointer follows the finger motions. Included with the touchpad are two buttons for left- or right-clicking (although with some touchpads, you can perform the functions of the left-click by tapping on the touchpad, and Macs have one button). Figure 9.25 shows a touchpad.

FIGURE 9.25   Laptop touchpad

One problem people have with a touchpad is the location. You'll notice that the touch-pad is conveniently placed right below the laptop keyboard, which happens to be where your palms rest when you type. Sometimes this will cause problems, because you can inadvertently cause your mouse cursor to do random things like jump across the screen. Most touchpads today have settings to allow you to control the sensitivity, and they will also differentiate between a palm touching them and a finger. In addition, if you have a sensitive touchpad that is giving you trouble, you can disable it altogether. Exercise 9.8 shows you how to do that in Windows 10. The specific steps to disable the touchpad will differ by manufacturer—you will almost always be able to disable it through the operating system, and some laptops have a function key to disable it as well. The steps in Exercise 9.8 were performed on a Lenovo ThinkPad laptop. Consult the laptop documentation if you are unable to locate the setting.

EXERCISE 9.8

Disabling a Touchpad in Windows 10

1. Open the Mouse app within Control Panel. You can do so by clicking Start, typing **Control**, and then clicking Control Panel when it appears under Best Match.

2. Set Control Panel to view by large icons or small icons so that you can see the Mouse app.

3. Click the ThinkPad tab, as shown in Figure 9.26.

   The tab might have a different name, or could be Properties, depending on how the manufacturer set it up.

4. Remove the check from the Enable TouchPad box to disable the touchpad.

   Notice there are options to enable and disable the TrackPoint as well. The TrackPoint (also known as a point stick) is the button in the middle of the keyboard, between the G, H, and B keys.

5. To examine additional settings, click the Settings button.

   You may have more options, such as the ones shown in Figure 9.27.

6. Click OK to save the settings.

FIGURE 9.26   Mouse Properties

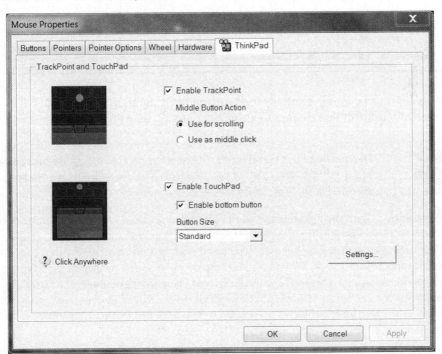

(continues)

FIGURE 9.27   Additional touchpad configuration options

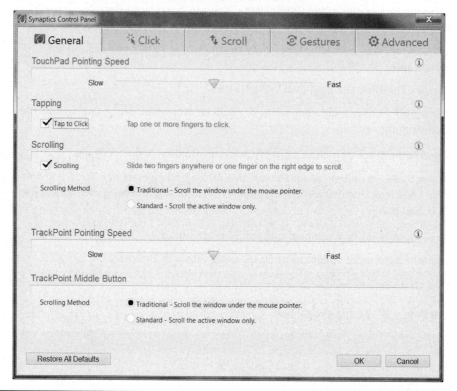

Although touchpads are primarily used with laptop computers, you can also buy external touchpads that connect to a computer just as you would connect a mouse.

> The touchpad can be replaced if it becomes defective, just like most other laptop components. Before you replace it, first be sure that it's not just disabled in the operating system.

Point Stick   With the introduction of the ThinkPad series of laptops, IBM introduced a new feature known as the *Touchpoint*, generically known as a *point stick*. (Think-Pads are now produced by Lenovo.) The point stick is a pointing device that uses a small rubber-tipped stick. When you push the point stick in a particular direction, the onscreen pointer goes in the same direction. The harder you push, the faster the onscreen pointer moves. The point allows fingertip control of the onscreen pointer, without the reliability problems associated with trackballs. Figure 9.28 shows a point stick.

FIGURE 9.28   Point stick

Point sticks have their own problems, however. Often, the stick does not return to center properly, causing the pointer to drift when not in use. You might also notice the rubber cover for the stick becoming a bit gummy with extended use. Most manufacturers supply replacement covers of varying textures with new systems. Some later systems employ a concave version of the cover and updated workings that tend to minimize a lot of these concerns.

Touch Screen   *Touch screens* are standard fare for smartphones and tablets and many laptop computers as well. We've already introduced the technology as a display device, so here we'll cover it as an input device. The idea is pretty simple: it looks like any other display device, but you can touch the screen and the system senses it. It can be as simple as registering a click, like a mouse, or it can be more advanced, such as capturing handwriting and saving it as a digital note.

Although the technical details of how touch screens work are beyond the scope of this chapter, there are a few things to know:

- Some touch screens work with any object touching them, whereas others require a conductive input, such as your finger. iPhones are a great example of this, to which anyone who lives in cold climates and wears gloves can attest.

- Some touch screens are coated with a film that is sensitive to touch. Cleaning these screens with regular glass cleaner can ruin the touch screen nature of the device. It's best to clean those devices only with a damp cloth, as needed.

- Some touch screens need to be calibrated in order to properly interpret the user's input. See the manufacturer's documentation for details.

User options to configure touch screens are often limited to calibrating the screen for touch input or pen input. If the touch screen seems to be sensing input incorrectly or not detecting input from the edges of the screen, it might be time to recalibrate it. In Windows, open Control Panel ➢ Tablet PC Settings, and then click Calibrate. Windows will ask the user to specify pen or touch input. Once that's specified, the user will be able to draw on the screen with their desired input tool, and the system will sense it. (In most cases, there will be a crosshairs on the screen and the user needs to touch where it is.) At the end, the user needs to save the calibration data for it to take effect.

Many laptops sold today are advertised as 2-in-1 devices, meaning that the top portion of the clamshell that holds the display folds completely over, effectively turning the laptop into a glorified tablet. These devices use touch screens, and when they are in tablet mode, the keyboard is disabled. Some will also automatically change the screen orientation to landscape or portrait, depending on how it's being held, just like a smartphone or tablet.

Internal Expansion

Although laptop computers are less expandable than their desktop counterparts, many can be expanded to some extent. The two primary forms of internal expansion used in laptops today are Mini PCIe and M.2.

Mini PCIe

Since around 2005, *Mini PCIe* has been the most common slot for laptop expansion cards. We introduced PCIe in Chapter 2, and mini PCIe is just like the full version except the connectors are smaller. These cards reside inside the case of the laptop and are connected via a 52-pin card edge connector. Mini PCIe cards come in two sizes. The full-sized cards are 30 mm wide and 51 mm long. Half-sized cards (one is shown in Figure 9.29, with the connector at the bottom) are 30 mm wide and 27 mm long. Mini PCIe cards support USB and PCIe x1 functionality, and at the same speeds. Additionally, Mini PCIe cards have the 1.5V and 3.3V power options.

M.2

We also introduced M.2 in Chapter 2, so we won't go into a great amount of detail here. Figure 9.21 earlier in this chapter shows an M.2 hard drive and slot. For purposes of comparing it to Mini PCIe, know that it uses a narrower connector (22 mm vs. 30 mm) that has more pins (66-pin vs. 52-pin). M.2 supports USB 2.0 and newer. The slowest M.2 slots support PCIe x2 and M-keyed slots support PCIe x4, making it much faster than Mini PCIe. Most M.2 expansion cards focus on communications or storage. Common types of cards you will see in the market include the following:

- Wi-Fi network cards
- Bluetooth cards
- Cellular cards
- SSDs

Many laptops don't come with any free internal expansion slots, either M.2 or Mini PCIe. For example, the Dell we've been working on has two M.2 slots, but both are filled. One has the SSD, and the other is used by the Wi-Fi card. Be sure to check the documentation before you buy an expansion card for a laptop, to see what it supports.

FIGURE 9.29   Mini PCIe card in a laptop

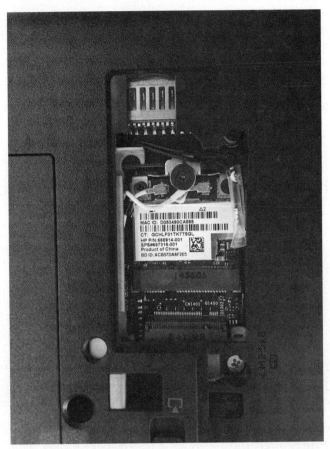

Batteries and Power Adapters

Because portable computers have unique characteristics as a result of their portability, they have unique power systems as well. Portable computers can use either of two power sources: batteries or adapted power from an AC or DC source. Regardless of the source of their power, laptops utilize DC power to energize their internal components. Therefore, any AC power source needs to be rectified (converted) to DC. Most laptop display backlights, on the other hand, require high-voltage, low-amperage AC power. To avoid a separate external AC input, an inverter is used to convert the DC power that is supplied for the rest of the system to AC for the backlight. In case it's not obvious, converters and inverters perform opposite functions, more or less.

Batteries

There are many different battery chemistries that come in various sizes and shapes. Nickel cadmium (NiCd), lithium-ion (Li-ion), and nickel-metal hydride (NiMH) have been the most popular chemistries for laptop batteries. A newer battery chemistry, lithium-polymer (Li-poly), has been gaining in prominence over recent years for smaller devices. Figure 9.30 is a photo of a removable Li-ion battery for an HP laptop.

FIGURE 9.30   A removable laptop Li-ion battery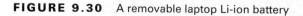

A removable battery is very easy to replace in the event of a battery failure. However, most laptops today make use of an internal battery, such as the one shown in Figure 9.31. This particular battery is very thin—only 5 mm (1/4") thick. Exercise 9.9 shows you how to remove an internal laptop battery.

EXERCISE 9.9

Removing an Internal Laptop Battery

1. Remove the bottom cover.

2. Disconnect the battery from the motherboard.

   Its connector is highlighted with a rectangle in Figure 9.31.

3. Remove the four screws holding the battery in place.

   In Figure 9.31, the screws are highlighted with circles.

FIGURE 9.31   Internal laptop battery

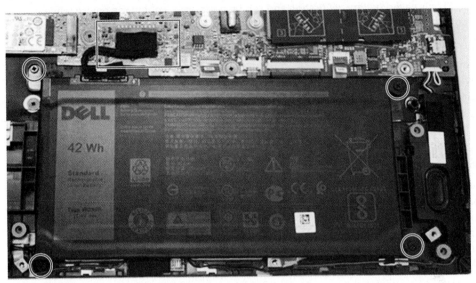

4.   Lift the battery out of the base assembly.

Even though replacing an internal battery requires slightly more effort than replacing an external battery, it's still generally a simple operation.

Battery chemistries can be compared by energy density and power density. Energy density measures how much energy a battery can hold. Power density measures how quickly the stored energy can be accessed, focusing on access in bursts, not prolonged runtime. An analogy to the storage and distribution of liquids might help solidify these concepts. A gallon bucket has a higher "energy density" and "power density" than a pint bottle; the bucket holds more and can pour its contents more quickly. Another common metric for battery comparison is rate of self-discharge, or how fast an unused battery reduces its stored charge.

 Real World Scenario

Is That Battery Really Dead?

Some batteries, such as nickel cadmium (NiCd) batteries, suffer from a performance-affecting chemical memory loss. Others, such as lithium-ion (Li-ion), don't suffer from this affliction but do suffer from so-called digital memory loss that plagues the built-in gauges that monitor the charge left in the battery. This effect can be observed in software gauges that read the battery's charge level. The digital memory effect manifests itself as a sudden loss of power when the gauges register, say, 30 percent remaining capacity. The fix, much like the fix for chemical memory in NiCd batteries, is to allow a full discharge once a month or so. This is called *battery calibration* and can be performed right in the device while it's using the battery.

Other than this occasional full discharge, Li-ion batteries last longer when you partially discharge them and then recharge them, making them ideal for laptops and personal handheld devices, such as smartphones, that tend to get used sporadically on battery power before being plugged back in to charge.

Power Adapters

Most laptop computers can also use AC power with a special adapter (called an *AC adapter*) that converts AC power input to DC output. The adapter can be integrated into the laptop, but more often it's a separate "brick" with two cords: one that plugs into the back of the laptop and another that plugs into a wall outlet. Figure 9.32 is a photo of the latter.

FIGURE 9.32   A laptop AC adapter

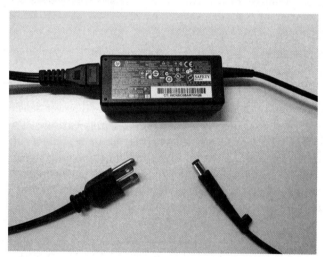

Another power accessory that is often used is a *DC adapter*, which allows a user to plug the laptop into the round *DC jack* power source (usually called an *auxiliary power outlet*) inside a car or on an airplane. An example is shown in Figure 9.33. These adapters allow people who travel frequently to use their laptops while on the road.

FIGURE 9.33   A DC jack in a car

Use caution when selecting a replacement AC adapter for your laptop. You should choose one rated for the same or higher wattage than the original. You must also pay special attention to the polarity of the plug that interfaces with the laptop. If the laptop requires the positive lead to be the center conductor, for instance, then you must take care not to reverse the polarity. Look for symbols like the ones shown in Figure 9.34, and make sure the new power supply is the same as the old one.

FIGURE 9.34   Polarity symbols

positive polarity   negative polarity

Regarding the input voltage of the adapter, care must also be taken to match the adapter to the power grid of the surrounding region. Some adapters have a fixed AC input requirement. Purchasing the wrong unit can result in lack of functionality or damage to the laptop. Other adapters are autoswitching, meaning that they are able to switch the input voltage they expect automatically based on the voltage supplied by the wall outlet. These units are often labeled with voltage-input ranges, such as 100V to 240V, and frequency ranges, such as 50Hz to 60Hz, and are able to accommodate deployment in practically any country around the world. Nevertheless, you should still ascertain whether some sort of converter is required, even for autoswitching adapters.

Other Internal Components

There are a few internal components we've referenced in chapter exercises, but we haven't given explicit details on how to remove them. That's what this section is for. Note that these components aren't currently on the exam objectives, but it helps to know how to remove them anyway. The four components we'll examine are the fan, heat sink, wireless NIC, and CMOS battery. And since we'll be talking about CMOS, which is related to the BIOS/UEFI, we'll look at how to upgrade (or flash) the BIOS/UEFI as well. Exercise 9.10 shows you how to remove the system fan.

EXERCISE 9.10

Removing the System Fan

1. Remove the bottom cover.

2. Remove the two screws that hold the system fan in place. They are highlighted in Figure 9.35.

3. Lift the fan away from the base assembly.

FIGURE 9.35   Removing the system fan

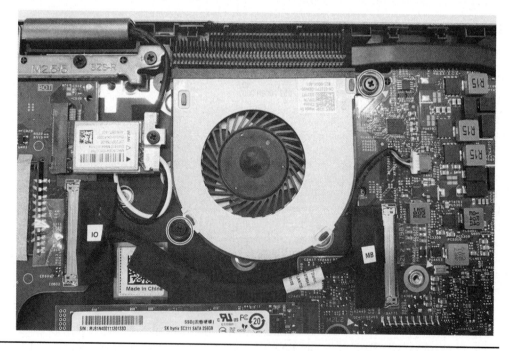

Now that the fan is removed, Exercise 9.11 shows you how to remove the CPU heat sink.

Removing the CPU Heat Sink

1. Remove the bottom cover.

2. Remove the system fan.

3. Loosen the four screws holding the heat sink in place, as highlighted in Figure 9.36.

    The screws will not completely come out of the heat sink bracket.

4. Lift the heat sink straight up off the processor.

    It might stick a bit, since most are adhered with a thermal compound.

FIGURE 9.36   Removing the heat sink

Exercise 9.12 shows you how to remove the wireless NIC. Perhaps ironically, it actually does have wires, but those are for the antenna that runs up into the display.

EXERCISE 9.12

Removing the Wireless NIC

1. Remove the bottom cover.

2. Remove the screw holding the wireless card bracket in place. It's circled in Figure 9.37.

3. The wireless card will pop up, as shown in Figure 9.38.

FIGURE 9.37   Removing the wireless NIC

FIGURE 9.38   Disconnect the two antenna wires.

4. Disconnect the two antenna wires that are attached to the end of the card.

5. Pull the wireless NIC straight out of the M.2 socket.

When you're reconnecting the wireless card, the white antenna cable will go on the main post, which is indicated by a white triangle. The black antenna cable attaches to the auxiliary connector, which is marked with a black triangle.

Exercise 9.13 shows how to remove the CMOS battery. In most laptops, the CMOS battery is covered by a black rubber coating.

EXERCISE 9.13

Removing the CMOS Battery

1. Remove the bottom cover.

2. Disconnect the connector from the motherboard. It's highlighted with a box in Figure 9.39.

3. Peel the battery off the base assembly.

   Odds are good that it's been glued into place, so you might have to pull hard.

FIGURE 9.39   Disconnect the CMOS battery.

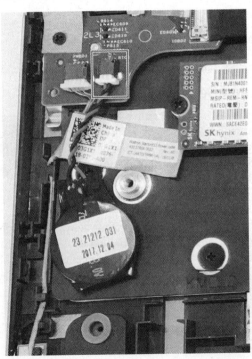

Replacement batteries often come with a small amount of adhesive to secure the new battery in place.

Flashing the system BIOS/UEFI is usually a pretty straightforward process. You can download a BIOS/UEFI update from the manufacturer's website and then run the program. Exercise 9.14 shows sample steps for flashing the BIOS on a Dell laptop.

EXERCISE 9.14

Flashing the System BIOS

1. Turn on the computer.

2. Visit http://www.dell.com/support.

3. Navigate to Drivers & Downloads.

4. Select the operating system installed on your laptop.

5. Find the BIOS section.

6. Select the file and click Download to download the BIOS.

7. After the download is complete, locate the file on your laptop.

8. Double-click the file to run it and begin the BIOS update process. Follow the onscreen instructions.

Physical Privacy and Security Components

Mobile devices are mostly self-contained units, which aids in their portability. One downside to the portability is that mobile devices can easily be carried away by someone other than their rightful owner. And, if a user is doing work on a laptop in a public place, others could shoulder surf and see things they're not supposed to. The use of physical privacy and security components can help deter these unwanted behaviors.

Cable Locks

One way that you can help to physically secure your laptop is through the use of a physical laptop lock, also known as a *cable lock*. Essentially, a cable lock anchors your device to a physical structure, making it nearly impossible for someone to walk off with it. Figure 9.40 shows a cable with a number combination lock. With others, small keys are used to unlock the lock. If you grew up using a bicycle lock, these will look really familiar.

Sometimes a cable lock is called a *Kensington lock* (named after a company that makes them) or a *K-lock*.

FIGURE 9.40   A cable lock

Here's how it works. First, find a secure structure, such as the permanent metal supports of your workstation at work. Then, wrap the lock cord around the structure, putting the lock through the loop at the other end. Finally, secure the lock into your cable lock hole on the back or side of your laptop (Figure 9.41), and you're secure. If you forget your combination or lose your key, you're most likely going to have to cut through the cord, which will require a large cable cutter or a hack saw.

FIGURE 9.41   Cable lock insertion point

If someone wants your laptop bad enough, they can break the case and dislodge your lock. Having the lock in place will deter most people looking to make off with it, though.

Biometrics

Many mobile devices allow you to log in or unlock the screen through *biometrics*, or the use of a body part. For example, you can unlock your smartphone by enabling the facial recognition feature, or some older models have a fingerprint scanner for the same purpose. Other options for higher-end security systems include voice recognition and retinal scanning.

Laptops may have a fingerprint scanner built into the keyboard, such as the square one shown to the right of the Intel sticker in Figure 9.42. Others may be a rectangle or a circle.

If a laptop doesn't have a biometric scanner and you want to add one, there are many USB options available.

FIGURE 9.42   Laptop fingerprint scanner

The use of biometrics can increase device security. Someone may be able to guess your password or see you type it in and can hack you that way. But fingerprints and other biometric features are unique. You may have seen movies where a super-secret spy ring replicates someone's fingerprint to gain access to a system, but in real life that type of thing is virtually unheard of.

Privacy Screens

To keep curious and prying eyes from viewing a laptop (or desktop) monitor, users can install a privacy screen over the front of their display. It's a thin sheet of semi-transparent plastic that reduces the viewing angle so that a display can be read only by someone directly in front of it. An example is shown in Figure 9.43.

FIGURE 9.43   Laptop privacy screen

Some laptops will have a built-in privacy screen setting that can be activated by the function (Fn) keys. For example, it would be Fn+F2 on the laptop keyboard shown in Figure 9.44. In our experience, the built-in privacy screens aren't quite as effective at cutting down the viewing angle as add-on privacy screens are, but they are better than nothing.

FIGURE 9.44   Fn+F2 enables the privacy screen.

Near-Field Scanner Features

In Chapter 7, "Wireless and SOHO Networks," we introduced the concept of near-field communication (NFC). NFC is used extensively today for mobile payment systems because it's fast and convenient. Because NFC is a wireless communications method, the signals sent to and from NFC devices could be intercepted by a malicious third device. Of course, the maximum distance for NFC is about 10 centimeters (about 4"), so it would be pretty difficult for someone to intercept NFC data without the sender and receiver knowing it, but it's not impossible. The key thing to remember is, if using NFC for payment, be aware of your surroundings and keep an eye out for potentially suspicious-looking electronic devices.

There's a ton of information presented in this chapter regarding installing and configuring laptop hardware components. For the A+ exam, the list of hardware you should be able to install and configure if given a scenario is a little (but not much) shorter. Know how to install and configure:

- Battery
- Keyboard/keys
- RAM
- HDD and SSD, including migration
- Wireless cards

Also understand concepts related to physical privacy and security components, such as biometrics and near-field scanner features.

Setting Up and Configuring Accessories and Ports

Other than needing to plug in and charge for a while, laptops and mobile devices don't require anything to be plugged into them to provide a user with full functionality. With that said, there are a number of accessories that can be used to enhance functionality. These include touch pens, headsets, speakers, webcams, trackpads/drawing pads, docking stations, and port replicators. We'll examine each one of them after we take a quick look at accessory connection methods.

Connection Methods

Smaller mobile devices such as smartphones and tablets generally don't have very many physical ports on them. One or two at the most is all you're going to get. That of course limits expandability unless you are connecting the accessory using wireless methods. Laptops often give you more physical connectors—you're likely to have at least a few USB ports to play with, along with an audio jack and the power port.

We've covered all the connection methods listed in the A+ exam objective 1.3 for exam 220-1101 in previous chapters with the exception of hotspot. Because of that, here we'll just do a quick refresh of the ones you need to know.

USB   USB absolutely lives up to its name of being universal. There are multiple USB types to know, including microUSB, miniUSB, and the new oval-shaped USB-C. Just about any type of accessory you could possibly want will come with a USB adapter.

Lightning   Proprietary to Apple devices, the Lightning connector is usually the only external connector you'll find on iPhones and iPads. Macs and MacBooks might or might not have Lightning ports as well—if they do, they are intended mostly for device charging.

Serial Interfaces   Serial is a very broad category. USB is a serial connection, as are Thunderbolt, HDMI, and others. Then of course there's the old-school DB-9 serial port as well. It's kind of funny to think about a DB-9 port on a smartphone or tablet—you won't find them there of course—and we'd be stunned if you found one on a laptop as well. For this exam objective, just be aware that many laptops will have an available serial connection or two—USB of course and perhaps HDMI or Thunderbolt, depending on the model. Common serial accessories include displays, external hard drives, and input and output devices.

Near-Field Communication   NFC is primarily used for mobile commerce and applications like scanning RFID tags, but it could be used for accessories as well. It's wireless, and remember that it has a very limited range (about 10 centimeters, or 4").

Bluetooth   As far as mobile accessories go, Bluetooth is a very popular connection technology. Mobile headsets, speakers, keyboards, and mice are all commonly connected to mobile devices using Bluetooth. Do keep in mind that if you have enabled Bluetooth on a small device such as a smartphone, it will eat up battery life a lot faster.

Hotspot   We mentioned hotspots in passing in Chapter 3, but didn't go into any depth. A *hotspot* is a location where people can get Internet access on a wireless network, typically in a public location such as a restaurant or library. Some mobile plans will also allow you to set up a smartphone as a wireless hotspot so that you can connect a laptop or other device to the Internet through it. A hotspot won't be used for traditional accessory attachment, per se, but it will be for Internet access.

Mobile Accessories

There are dozens of mobile accessories in the marketplace, including security devices, input/ output tools, communication enablers, and mobile commerce endpoints. Here, we will cover a few input tools and communication enablers.

Input Accessories

We could spend an entire chapter talking about input and output devices, given how many exist in the market. For purposes of the A+ exam, though, you only need to know about two: touch pens and trackpads/drawing pads.

A *touch pen*, also known as a *stylus*, is a pen-shaped accessory used to write with or as a pointer. Touch pens come in a variety of shapes and sizes, although most have either a narrow tip (like a pen) or a soft rubber ball-like tip, kind of like a pencil eraser. The idea is that a touch pen will act as an input device on a touch screen, enabling freeform writing, drawing, or clicking through answers to a questionnaire, such as at a medical office. Several touch pens are shown in Figure 9.45.

FIGURE 9.45   Several touch pens

Craig Spurrier, CC BY 2.5 `https://creativecommons.org/licenses/by/2.5`, via Wikimedia Commons

Another accessory designed for freeform input, often in conjunction with a touch pen, is a *trackpad* or drawing pad. You're probably familiar with the touchpad on a laptop, right underneath the keyboard. A trackpad or drawing pad is basically the same thing, only bigger and attached through a USB port. The purpose is to allow people to take notes or create drawings that are displayed on a computer screen and stored in a digital format. Some have buttons, like the one shown in Figure 9.46, to provide additional functionality such as on-pad menu management or erase and undo features.

FIGURE 9.46   Drawing pad accessory with stylus

Wacom_Pen-tablet_without_mouse.jpg: by Tobias Rütten, CC BY-SA 3.0 `https://creativecommons.org/licenses/by-sa/3.0`, via Wikimedia Commons

Communication Accessories

In the last few years, especially thanks to the global pandemic, more and more people have been working remotely. Even those who are still working from offices are affected by this trend, as more meetings become virtual. To make these meetings effective without distracting coworkers or roommates, headsets are a crucial accessory. And of course, if you need to be on camera, a webcam is needed too.

Headsets come in a variety of shapes and sizes. They will connect through the USB port or audio jack. Most laptops will detect the device as it's plugged in, configuring it automatically for you. If instead of a headset you want speakers, either to listen to music or a podcast or to let others hear audio from your system, those will also connect through one of the same two ports.

Nearly all laptops today come with a webcam, but sometimes they break or are of poor quality. In addition, some laptops come with webcams that are below the display as opposed to above it. They work fine, but when the person on video is typing, it looks like their fingers are huge and in your face. We're not fans. For any of those situations, an external webcam can be purchased and connected via USB.

Docking Stations and Port Replicators

Most laptops are designed to be desktop replacements. That is, they will replace a standard desktop computer for day-to-day use and are thus more fully featured than other laptops. These laptops often have a proprietary docking port. A docking port (as shown in Figure 9.47) is about 1" to 2.5" wide and is used to connect the laptop to a special laptop-only peripheral known as a *port replicator*, or a similar device called a *docking station*.

FIGURE 9.47   A docking port

A port replicator reproduces the functions of the ports on the back of a laptop so that peripherals that don't travel with the laptop—such as monitors, keyboards, and printers—can remain connected to the dock and don't all have to be unplugged physically each time the laptop is taken away. A docking station (shown in Figure 9.48) is similar to a port replicator but offers more functionality. Docking stations also replicate ports but can contain things like full-sized drive bays, expansion bus slots, optical drives, memory card slots, and ports that are not otherwise available on a laptop. For example, a laptop might have only two USB ports and an external HDMI port, but its docking station might have eight USB ports along with DVI and DisplayPort for external monitors as well.

Docking ports and docking stations are *proprietary*. That is, the port works only with docking stations designed by the laptop's manufacturer, and vice versa.

For the A+ exam, understand how to set up and configure accessories and ports of mobile devices. Connection methods to know include USB in all its forms, Lightning, serial interfaces, NFC, Bluetooth, and hotspot. Accessories to know include touch pens, headsets, speakers, webcams, docking stations, port replicators, and trackpads/drawing pads.

FIGURE 9.48   The back and front of a docking station

Summary

In this chapter, you learned about laptop and mobile device hardware. We discussed differences between laptops, mobile devices, and desktops, including the various components that make up smaller devices and how they differ in appearance and function from those on a desktop. We also talked about principles for disassembling and reassembling smaller devices in order to not lose parts.

We broke the chapter into several sections to discuss different components. We started with the case, and then moved on to displays, motherboards and processors, memory, storage, input devices, internal expansion, batteries and power adapters, physical privacy and security, other internal components, and external peripherals. In each section, we covered specifics related to laptop versions of these components and included exercises to show you how to service them.

The chapter puts particular emphasis on the components of a display, including the type of display (LCD or OLED), the screen (which may be a touch screen or include a digitizer), Wi-Fi antenna placement, webcam, microphone, and inverter.

Finally, we ended the chapter by examining accessories and their connection methods. Connection methods included USB, Lightning, serial, NFC, Bluetooth, and hotspot. Accessories to remember include touch pens, trackpads/drawing pads, headsets, speakers, webcams, and docking stations and port replicators.

Exam Essentials

Understand how to install and configure laptop components. Components include the battery, keyboard, RAM, hard drives and solid-state drives, and wireless cards.

Know how to migrate data from an old hard drive to a new one. Options include manually copying files or using specialized migration software.

Know laptop physical privacy and security components. They include biometrics and near-field scanner features.

Understand the components that make up a display in a mobile device. Display components include the screen, which may be a touch screen or include a digitizer; Wi-Fi antenna; camera or webcam; microphone; and inverter.

Know the main types of mobile device displays. The two main types of mobile displays are liquid crystal display (LCD) and organic light-emitting diode (OLED). Within LCD, there are in-plane switching (IPS), twisted nematic (TN), and vertical alignment (VA).

Know how to connect mobile device accessories. Connection methods include USB, Lightning, serial, near-field communication (NFC), Bluetooth, and hotspot.

Be familiar with mobile device accessories. Ones to know include touch pens, trackpads/drawing pads, headsets, speakers, webcams, docking stations, and port replicators.

Review Questions

The answers to the chapter review questions can be found in Appendix A.

1. A client has a laptop with which you are unfamiliar. You are asked to perform a memory upgrade. How can you obtain the service manual for this laptop computer?

    A. By pressing F1 while in Windows

    B. By pressing F2 while the system is booting up

    C. By reading the paper copy that comes with the laptop

    D. By searching the manufacturer's website

2. Your manager tells you to replace the inverter on a broken laptop. Where will you find this component?

    A. Underneath the keyboard

    B. In the display

    C. Next to the heat sink and fan

    D. Near the CPU

3. You need to replace an LCD on a defective laptop. Which of the following are components of an LCD? (Choose all that apply.)

    A. Inverter

    B. Screen

    C. Wi-Fi card

    D. Backdrop

4. A user complains that their mouse cursor randomly jumps to different places on the screen when they type. Which device might you want to disable to prevent this from happening?

    A. Touchpad

    B. Mouse

    C. Point stick

    D. Trackball

5. One of the users on your network needs to travel and wants to work on the airplane. Which laptop accessory will allow them to power their laptop from the airplane?

    A. AC adapter

    B. DC adapter

    C. Battery converter

    D. Airplane mode

6. You need to replace defective DDR4 memory in a laptop. How many pins will the replacement memory module have?

A. 200

B. 204

C. 260

D. 288

7. A user complains that their 2-in-1 laptop screen does not properly detect where they place their finger on the screen. What should you do first to resolve the issue?

A. Replace the touch screen

B. Replace the touchpad

C. Recalibrate the touch screen

D. Recalibrate the touchpad

E. Degauss the touch screen

F. Degauss the touchpad

8. You need to wirelessly connect two accessories to a smartphone. Which of the following could be valid options to connect these wireless accessories? (Choose two.)

A. USB

B. Lightning

C. NFC

D. Bluetooth

9. There has recently been a string of hardware thefts in your office building. What should you recommend that your users do to help avoid this problem?

A. Enable GPS tracking

B. Use a docking station

C. Use a cable lock

D. Use the screensaver lock

10. Which of the following describes the job of an inverter in a laptop?

A. It changes the screen orientation when the laptop is rotated.

B. It converts AC power into DC power for the display backlight.

C. It converts DC power into AC power for the display backlight.

D. It allows the laptop display to function in tablet mode.

11. A user is getting a new laptop. Which of the following is *not* a valid option to get the user's files and data from the old hard drive to the new hard drive?

A. Manually copy files from the old drive to the cloud, and then to the new drive

B. Manually copy files from the old drive to an external hard drive, and then to the new drive

C. Use a hard drive migration app

D. Use the NFC disk transfer utility

12. A user on your network wants to be able to draw images on a screen and have the laptop capture them. What type of device needs to be installed on the user's laptop?

A. Inverter

B. Capturer

C. Digitizer

D. Touchpad

13. A user has requested a laptop memory upgrade. The technician attempts to put in new memory, but the memory module is a bit too wide for the slot. What is the most likely scenario?

A. The technician is trying to install DDR4 into a motherboard with DDR3 slots.

B. The technician is trying to install DDR3 into a motherboard with DDR4 slots.

C. The technician is trying to install MicroDIMMs into SODIMM slots.

D. The technician is trying to install DIMMs into SODIMM slots.

14. You have a user who needs to keep desktop devices such as keyboard, monitor, and mouse permanently connected so that they can be used by an attached laptop. What type of device do you recommend that they use?

A. Docking station

B. Keyboard, video, mouse (KVM) switch

C. Input/output virtual server

D. USB hub

15. The process by which the processor slows down to conserve power is officially called
_____.

A. Underclocking

B. Cooling

C. Disengaging

D. Throttling

16. You need to replace a failed AC adapter for a client's laptop. When replacing the adapter, which of the following purchases is acceptable to obtain the same or better results?

A. An AC adapter with a higher voltage rating than the original

B. An AC adapter with a higher wattage rating than the original

C. A DC adapter with the same voltage rating as the original

D. An AC adapter with a lower voltage and wattage rating than the original

17. What should you do for a Li-ion battery that appears to charge fully but does not last as long as the battery's meter indicates that it will last?

A. Replace the battery

B. Exercise the battery

C. Calibrate the battery

D. Short the terminals to discharge the battery

18. You are giving a seminar to new technicians on replacing laptop hard drives. A student asks how laptop hard drives differ from desktop hard drives. What do you tell them?

A. Laptop hard drives use completely different standards from those used by desktop hard drives for communication with the host.

B. Laptop hard drives are solid-state, whereas desktop hard drives have spinning platters.

C. Laptop hard drives require a separate power connection, whereas desktop hard drives are powered through the drive interface.

D. The most common form factor for laptop hard drives is smaller than that of a desktop hard drive.

19. One of your network users has an older laptop with no Bluetooth support. They recently received a Bluetooth headset that they need to use with their laptop. What is the quickest and cheapest way to make the headset compatible with the user's laptop?

A. Buy a Wi-Fi–compatible headset

B. Buy a USB Bluetooth adapter

C. Buy a Mini PCIe Bluetooth adapter

D. Replace the laptop

20. A user wants their laptop to have a full-sized optical drive and external hard drive. Which of the following accessories is most likely to have full-sized bays for these devices?

A. Laptop base

B. Port replicator

C. Docking station

D. Mini PCIe dock

Performance-Based Question

You will encounter performance-based questions on the A+ exams. The questions on the exam require you to perform a specific task, and you will be graded on whether or not you were able to complete the task. The following requires you to think creatively in order to measure how well you understand this chapter's topics. You may or may not see similar questions on the actual A+ exams. To see how your answer compares to the authors', refer to Appendix B.

The hard drive on a Dell Inspiron 13 7000 computer failed. You have an extra hard drive of the exact same type. What would you do to replace it?

Chapter

10

Mobile Connectivity and Application Support

THE FOLLOWING COMPTIA A+ 220-1101 EXAM OBJECTIVES ARE COVERED IN THIS CHAPTER:

✓ **1.4 Given a scenario, configure basic mobile-device network connectivity and application support.**

- Wireless/cellular data network (enable/disable)
    - 2G/3G/4G/5G
    - Hotspot
    - Global System for Mobile Communications (GSM) vs. code-division multiple access (CDMA)
    - Preferred Roaming List (PRL) updates
- Bluetooth
    - Enable Bluetooth
    - Enable pairing
    - Find a device for pairing
    - Enter the appropriate PIN code
    - Test connectivity
- Location services
    - Global Positioning System (GPS) services
    - Cellular location services
- Mobile device management (MDM)/mobile application management (MAM)
    - Corporate email configuration
    - Two-factor authentication
    - Corporate applications

- **Mobile device synchronization**
    - **Recognizing data caps**
    - **Microsoft 365**
    - **ActiveSync**
    - **Calendar**
    - **Contacts**
    - **Commercial mail application**

Devices that fit into the palm of your hand today are substantially more powerful than the bulky desktop systems of the 1990s, and those were exponentially more powerful than the room-sized supercomputers of the 1960s. This movement toward smaller devices creates new needs, specifically in the area of interaction with the devices—and that relates directly to the operating system and hardware. Remember that the OS is the interface between the hardware and the user, meaning that the OS needs to interpret user input and translate that into an action for the underlying hardware. We won't cover the details of mobile OSs in this chapter—that's taken care of in Chapter 13, "Operating System Basics." For this chapter, you just need to remember that Android and iOS are the two dominant mobile operating systems in the market. We'll discuss connectivity and synchronization options for each.

In addition, small mobile devices just don't have room for traditional desktop or laptop hardware. Smartphones don't come with built-in keyboards and mice, nor do small devices have the storage capacity of their larger cousins. Yet with all of their physical space constraints, mobile devices are still expected to perform many of the same tasks as laptops or desktop computers, particularly network connectivity and data storage.

You already know that mobile devices can get on a network and store data. They just do it in a different way than larger systems do. In addition, because of their limited storage capacities, mobile devices can greatly benefit from the syncing of data to a larger storage system, such as a desktop, the cloud, or even an automobile. This chapter focuses on the details of mobile device connectivity, with a particular emphasis on email, as well as device synchronization.

Understanding Mobile Connectivity

Mobile devices like smartphones, tablets, and wearable devices basically exist for their convenience and ability to connect to a network. No one is using their small mobile devices to crunch spreadsheets, create detailed presentations, or perform other tasks that are better suited for larger PCs and Macs. On the other hand, mobile devices are great for surfing the Internet, messaging friends, taking pictures and sending them to friends and family, listening to music and watching videos, and even monitoring our health. Each of these tasks requires a network connection, either wired or wireless, at some point.

Of course, mobile devices are well known for their cellular connectivity, including the ability to access data services over the cellular network. Many subscribers pay a premium for data access, and going over your limit on a data plan can be a very expensive mistake (unless your plan offers unlimited data). To ease the expense involved in data-network access, nearly all manufacturers provide alternate access methods in their devices. For example, the service provider levies no additional expense for Wi-Fi or Bluetooth data access.

There are other cellular options on mobile devices with which you may be less familiar, though, such as hotspots and tethering and updating the firmware. In the following sections, we'll dive into those topics in some detail.

Connecting to a Wi-Fi network gives the mobile device access to resources on the network, such as printers, with the added bonuses of Internet access (assuming the wireless network has it), free texting, and perhaps Wi-Fi phone calls. Not only will this likely give the mobile user faster speeds than cellular, it also has the benefit of not counting against the data plan.

Bluetooth access to other devices is designed mainly for short-range communications, such as between the mobile device and a nearby computer with which it can exchange or synchronize data. Other applications of Bluetooth generally do not involve the exchange of data but rather the use of a nearby resource such as a printer to make a hard copy of a document or a headset to make hands-free phone calls.

As you can see, there is a distinct advantage to being able to connect your mobile device to a noncellular network. Mobile devices will use Wi-Fi when connected instead of cellular for data operations. Android devices will ask you during an important update if you would like to use Wi-Fi only or if cellular is okay to use. Figure 10.1, for example, shows the Google Play Store Settings screen on an Android device that clearly states that apps will be auto-updated over Wi-Fi only. (Other options are to not auto-update, or to update over any network, and data charges may apply.)

FIGURE 10.1   Google Play Store Settings screen

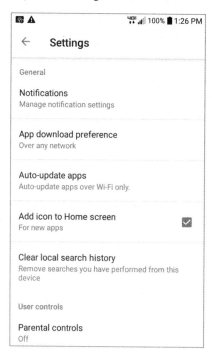

The following sections detail concepts relating to cellular networking and attaching to noncellular networks on iPhones and Android devices. After that, you will be introduced to the tasks required to establish email connectivity over these mobile units to corporate and ISP connections as well as integrated commercial providers.

Understanding Cellular Networking Standards

Most of the networking technologies we cover in this book are relatively short range. Wi-Fi and Bluetooth signals can stretch a few hundred meters at best, and NFC is even more limited than that. Cellular is by far the longest-range of the wireless networking technologies available today.

We introduced fourth generation (4G) and fifth generation (5G) in Chapter 7, "Wireless and SOHO Networks." We'll review those two here, but also introduce a few of their predecessors.

Third Generation (3G)

Two major cell standards dominated the industry for the formative years of the mobile phone evolution. The *Global System for Mobile Communications (GSM)* was the most popular, boasting over 1.5 billion users in 210 countries. The other standard was *code-division multiple access (CDMA)*, which was developed by Qualcomm and available only in the United States.

Both were *third generation (3G)* mobile technologies, and each had its advantages. GSM was introduced first, and when CDMA was launched, it was much faster than GSM. GSM eventually caught up, though, and the two ended up with relatively similar data rates. The biggest issue was that GSM and CDMA were not compatible with each other. Whatever technology you got was based on the provider you signed up with. Sprint (which has since merged with T-Mobile) and Verizon used CDMA, and AT&T and T-Mobile used GSM. That meant that if you had a CMDA phone through Verizon, you couldn't switch (with that phone) to AT&T. And your CDMA phone wouldn't work outside the United States.

When 3G was first introduced in 1998, it specified a minimum data download rate of 200 Kbps. Data rates increased over time, and some carriers claimed to deliver over 7 Mbps downloads—although technically that was with 3.5G. Really, data rates varied by carrier, the equipment installed in the area, the number of users connected to the tower, and the distance from the tower.

Prior to 3G there was a 2G digital standard and a 1G analog standard as well. 1G was launched in 1979, and 2G became commercially available in 1991. New standards appear about every 10 years. After several enhancements, 2G had a maximum data rate of 64 Kbps and with it you could send text messages, read emails, and in theory access the Internet. It was very slow and had limited network range, which is why 3G was greatly appreciated when it launched.

Fourth Generation (4G)

In 2008 *fourth generation (4G)* came into the market. Again, we have already introduced 4G so we won't go into too much depth here, but simply review the key points:

- 4G is designed to use IP instead of traditional telephone circuits, like 3G did. It's designed to provide mobile broadband access.
- In the early days of 4G, there were two competing standards—WiMAX and Long-Term Evolution (LTE). WiMAX initially had higher speeds, but cell phone providers got behind LTE, which won out.
- The biggest enhancement of 4G LTE over 3G is speed. Some 4G LTE networks claim to give you download speeds of 10–20 Mbps and upload speeds of 3–10 Mbps. (The theoretical maximum for LTE is 300 Mbps download and 75 Mbps upload.)
- The range of 4G LTE depends on the tower and obstructions in the way. The optimal cell size is about 3.1 miles (5 km) in rural areas, and you can get reasonable performance for about 19 miles (30 km).

Fifth Generation (5G)

The first *fifth generation (5G)* modem was announced in 2016, but it took until late 2018 for cellular providers to start test piloting 5G. At that point they had a substantial monetary investment in 4G and weren't yet sure of how to best implement the newer standard. As of this writing it's fairly widespread but not available everywhere yet. Because we've already covered 5G in Chapter 7, we'll just review the highlights here:

- Some users will be able to get sustained wireless speeds in excess of 1 Gbps. The theoretical maximum peak download capacity is 20 Gbps.
- There are three 5G classifications:
  - Enhanced Mobile Broadband (eMBB), which is for cell phone and mobile communication
  - Ultra-Reliable Low-Latency Communications (URLLC) for autonomous vehicles and industrial applications
  - Massive Machine Type Communications (mMTC) for sensors, which is designed to support IoT devices
- The early focus was on developing eMBB infrastructure and mobile devices. Two versions of eMBB are available: fixed wireless broadband in densely populated areas and LTE for everywhere else.
  - 5G LTE is like 4G LTE but about seven to ten times faster. Browsing speeds for 5G are about 490 Mbps on average, and most users can get 100 Mbps downloads.
  - 5G uses existing LTE frequencies in the 600 MHz to 6 GHz range.
  - eMBB fixed wireless is revolutionary, offering gigabit speeds using millimeter wave (mmWave) technology in the 24 GHz to 86 GHz range.
  - mmWave is limited to about half a mile and is easily blocked by obstructions.

Having the ability to get gigabit performance over a cellular connection is exciting. Right now, it's hard to imagine how anyone could want or need more, but technology will continue to evolve. Ten or 20 years from now we'll look back and laugh at standards that only gave us a paltry gigabit per second and wonder who was able to survive on speeds that slow.

For now, though, gigabit through 5G is as good as it gets. Now that you're familiar with the standards, let's take a look at how to set up cellular data connections on mobile devices.

Using Cellular Data Connections

Nearly every user of a mobile device knows how to get on the Internet. iOS users have the built-in Safari browser, and Android users have Google Chrome available. Getting online when you have a cellular connection is easy to do if the device has a data plan. Another great feature of mobile devices is that they can share their cellular data connections with other devices. It's basically the exact opposite of joining a mobile phone to a Wi-Fi network, which we will talk about later in this chapter. Next, we will provide details on using and config-uring hotspots and tethering, using airplane mode, and how data network updates are han-dled on mobile devices. We'll also cover a few key acronyms you need to know.

Using Mobile Hotspots and Tethering

We talked about mobile hotspots in Chapter 9, "Laptop and Mobile Device Hardware," and as an exam objective it's a topic that appears in a few places. Because it's an important con-cept for mobile device connectivity, we'll talk about it here as well.

 Real World Scenario

Where Is That Setting?

Throughout this chapter, we will use iOS 14.8.1 and Android 11 One UI Core 3.1 as example OSs for screenshots. Recognize that new versions of iOS and Android come out nearly every year, and the locations of features and settings for new OSs may change slightly. The point of showing screenshots in examples isn't for you memorize exactly where everything is, but rather to give you familiarity enough to accomplish the tasks you'll need to do.

In the real world, if the setting isn't exactly where you expect it to be, or if you're not very familiar with the OS you're working on, you can always Google the answer. It's an option that works for almost every hardware or software problem you run across.

Unfortunately, you can't use Google while sitting for the A+ exam. The good news is, Comp-TIA isn't going to test you on the differences between iOS 14.8.1 and iOS 15. What they may do is give you a screenshot of a settings page and ask you to configure something such as setting up corporate email. By understanding the concept of what you need to do—for example, toggling on email, setting the right protocol, and entering the email server name or address—you should be able to get the answer right. The example screen they give you might not be identical to what we showed here, but it should be close enough that you'll be able to accomplish the task with relative ease.

Recall that a *mobile hotspot* lets you share your cellular Internet connection with Wi-Fi-capable devices. A Wi-Fi-enabled laptop, for example, would look for the mobile phone's Wi-Fi network, join it, and then have Internet access. To enable an iPhone to be a mobile hotspot, go to Settings ≻ Personal Hotspot. Figure 10.2 shows the personal hotspot screen. Simply slide the toggle to the On position to enable it. A password to join the network is provided (and can be changed) as well as instructions on how to join.

FIGURE 10.2   Personal hotspot screen in iOS

 If the wireless plan does not allow that device to be a hotspot, then Settings ≻ Personal Hotspot will not exist. Instead, go to Settings ≻ Cellular. Tap the Set Up Personal Hotspot link as shown in Figure 10.3 to begin the process of setting it up.

FIGURE 10.3   Setting up a personal hotspot

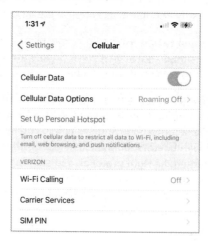

Also recall that there are three potential challenges with using a smartphone as a mobile hotspot: speed, cost, and security. Cellular connections are usually slower than Wi-Fi, so having multiple devices trying to get on the Internet via one cellular link can be slow. From a cost standpoint, you could go over your data plan quite easily by using a hotspot, or the provider might charge you extra just to use it. Finally, there is security. iOS 7 and newer use WPA2, and the iPhone 11 and newer support WPA3, so security is less of an issue, but wireless networks are inherently unsecure due to the fact that the signals are transmitted through the air.

On the Android OS, a mobile hotspot is also enabled under Settings ➤ Connections ➤ Mobile Hotspot And Tethering (see Figure 10.4). On Android, when you turn mobile hotspot on, it automatically turns Wi-Fi off.

FIGURE 10.4 Enabled mobile hotspot in Android

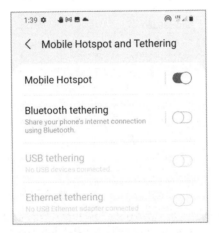

Tapping Mobile Hotspot will show the network name (SSID) and hotspot password (Figure 10.5), and tapping Configure takes you to the screen to change these options and additional settings (Figure 10.6). Figure 10.6 also shows the security choice—the only option available on this phone is WPA2 PSK.

In Android, a mobile hotspot uses WPA2 encryption by default, but that can be turned off so the device is an open portal. It's highly recommended to always leave the encryption on! You can also change the network name and password associated with the hotspot.

Some mobile providers limit the number of devices that can join the mobile hotspot. For example, Verizon limits it to 10 devices for 4G LTE phones, and the Android phone used in the example allows a maximum of 15 devices.

FIGURE 10.5   Android hotspot network name and password

Finally, mobile providers sell small devices that are specifically used as mobile hotspots. Figure 10.7 shows an example of a Verizon Wireless MiFi hotspot. These types of devices will either use your existing mobile contract or will need to have an activation of their own.

Tethering is when you have connected a device to a mobile hotspot. The term used to be reserved only for when you connected via USB cable, as opposed to connecting via wireless. Some devices will not function as a mobile hotspot but will allow you to tether a laptop (or other device) to it so that the mobile device can share the cellular Internet connection.

FIGURE 10.6   Android hotspot configuration options

FIGURE 10.7   Verizon Wireless MiFi hotspot

Enabling and Disabling Wireless/Cellular Connections

Each type of wireless connection can be individually enabled or disabled under Settings. For example, if you look back at Figure 10.3, you can see that in iOS under Settings ➤ Cellular, you can toggle off Cellular Data. You can similarly turn off Wi-Fi under Settings ➤ Wi-Fi. Turning off one connection at a time serves its purpose—for example, disabling Bluetooth to save battery life—but there's also an option to disable all wireless connections at once. It's called airplane mode.

The *airplane mode* feature was named so because, for many years, no network signals were allowed on airplanes. Today, some airlines allow for in-flight Wi-Fi (for a nominal fee, of course), but the name of the feature still sticks. It's not restricted to airplane use, though. If you're in a public area and suspect that someone is trying to hack your phone through the Wi-Fi or Bluetooth connection, airplane mode will quickly shut down all your external connections. Android and iOS both make it easy to enable airplane mode and give you a few ways to get to it.

There are two quick ways to enable airplane mode in Android. The first is to swipe down from the top to open the notifications area. There you may see the quick settings icons, as shown in Figure 10.8. If not, swipe down again to open quick settings. The airplane mode icon looks like an airplane, conveniently enough. Tap it to turn it on or off.

FIGURE 10.8 Android airplane mode in quick settings

The second way is to open Settings ➤ Connections. Swipe the switch to the right to On to enable airplane mode (see Figure 10.9). Notice that an airplane icon also appears in the top-right corner next to the battery indicator. When you turn airplane mode back off, the wireless connections you previously had turned on will be enabled again.

iOS also provides access to airplane mode in two easy ways. One is to open Settings, and it's the first option (see Figure 10.10). When you slide it on, notice how all the other connections are turned off.

The other way is to access it from the Control Center. You can do this from both the lock screen and the Home screen. Simply swipe your finger down from the top bottom of the iPhone's touch screen, and you will get to the Control Center, similar to what's shown in Figure 10.11. Tap the airplane icon in the upper-left corner to enable airplane mode.

FIGURE 10.9   Android airplane mode in Settings

FIGURE 10.10   Airplane mode in iOS

In older versions of iOS, enabling airplane mode turned off Bluetooth as well. In newer versions, Bluetooth will stay on when airplane mode is turned on, but it can be manually disabled by tapping the Bluetooth icon.

FIGURE 10.11 Airplane mode in iPhone Control Center

Understanding Cellular Updates

When most people think of cellular updates, they probably think of an update to the operating system. Perhaps a new Android version is available or iTunes is alerting them to download the latest incarnation of iOS. Those updates are normal, and completing them takes the active participation of the user. Other updates can occur too, and many of these are transparent to the user.

Before we talk about what those updates are, though, you must first understand that mobile phones don't just have one operating system. This might come as a surprise, but most mobile phones have three operating systems. Duties are split up among the operating systems, simply because there are so many specialized tasks for the phone to perform.

The first OS is pretty obvious. The other two are specialized OSs that handle specific functions for the device. These two OSs are very small, typically only a few hundred kilobytes in size, and they are referred to as *real-time operating systems (RTOSs)*. They are designed to be lightweight and fast, and "real-time" refers to their ability to minimize lag in data transfers.

First, there is a *baseband OS* that manages all wireless communication, which is handled by a separate processor. Some people call the wireless communications chips in a mobile phone the radio or the modem. Consequently, you might hear about *radio firmware*, a *radio firmware update*, or a *modem update*. The last two terms are interchangeable with *baseband update*, which simply means an update of the baseband OS.

 Real World Scenario

Why Phones Need a Baseband OS

One question many students ask is, "Why does a mobile phone need three OSs?" It would seem that phones perform fewer functions than PCs perform, and PCs run on one OS.

The answer is that it increases flexibility and reduces software development issues. Think about how many different types of mobile devices are on the market, and then think about how many versions of each are available. We don't know the exact answer, but it's a large number. Without the baseband OS, the primary OS would need to know how to talk to every single type of radio hardware on the market. And when new hardware comes out, which happens frequently, the primary OS would need to know how to talk to it as well. This isn't feasible. Therefore, phones were designed with one additional layer, which is the baseband OS. The baseband OS knows how to talk to the radio hardware, but it also knows how to talk to the primary OS. When a new hardware chipset is deployed, the developers just need to make the new baseband OS talk to iOS or Android on one side and the new hardware on the other side.

Desktop OSs face similar issues, but Windows, macOS, Linux, and others deal with this by using software drivers.

Second, a *subscriber identity module (SIM) OS* manages all data transfers between the phone and the SIM chip, which is a small memory chip that stores user account information, phone identification, and security data, and it is generally tied to a specific carrier.

These RTOSs are normally updated when a user updates an operating system, but occasionally the carrier will update them when the phone is not otherwise busy. Apple currently provides no way to update either RTOS manually on iOS devices. (Users can find information on how to jailbreak the phone online, but that voids all warranties and is not recommended.) There's more information available on how to update an RTOS on Android phones because Android is open source. Users or companies can provide newer versions of the baseband RTOS, and others can download and install them. Some will say that updating your baseband firmware can result in better reception, faster data throughput, and reduced battery usage. There is much Internet debate about the rewards versus the risks, though.

WARNING A discussion of performing a manual update of an RTOS requires three warnings:

- Be sure that the upgrade comes from a reputable source. Look for reviews or comments to be sure that it delivers what you expect it to provide.

- Understand that performing this update will most likely void any warranty that you have.

- Always be sure to allow the updates to complete. Interrupting a firmware update in the middle is a nearly surefire way to *brick* your phone—that is, to make it inoperable.

Two other updates of which you should be aware are *product release instruction (PRI) updates* and *preferred roaming list (PRL) updates*. The PRI contains settings for configuration items on the device that are specific to the network that it's on. The PRL is the reference guide the phone uses to connect to the proper cell phone tower when roaming. Both PRI updates and PRL updates also normally happen when the primary OS on the phone is updated. Some carriers make these two easier to update manually than the RTOS on Android phones, though. For example, Verizon users can dial *228 for a manual PRL update. As always, check with the carrier before attempting to perform these updates and to determine the exact procedure.

NOTE Of all the updates we just covered, only PRL updates are listed in the exam objectives. We cover the others to help round out your knowledge of how mobile devices work behind the scenes.

Key Acronyms to Know

The last section introduced a few new acronyms to know, such as PRI and PRL. There are a few others you might see in relation to mobile phones that you should know too:

International Mobile Equipment Identity   The *International Mobile Equipment Identity (IMEI)* is a 15-digit serial number that is unique to each phone. If a phone is reported stolen, the IMEI will be declared invalid and the phone disabled. The IMEI can be displayed on most phones by dialing *#06#. AT&T and T-Mobile were the first networks to use IMEI.

Mobile Equipment Identifier   The *mobile equipment identifier (MEID)* is an alternate form of a serial number. It's identical to the first 14 numbers of the IMEI. Sprint (now T-Mobile) and Verizon were the first to use MEIDs.

International Mobile Subscriber Identity   The *international mobile subscriber identity (IMSI)* is a unique 15-digit identifier that describes a specific mobile user and their network. It's composed of the following three elements:

Mobile Country Code   The *mobile country code (MCC)* is a three-digit code, such as 310 for the United States and 234 for the United Kingdom.

Mobile Network Code   The *mobile network code (MNC)* is a two- or three-digit code that identifies the carrier. Many carriers have multiple codes. For example, in the United States, 006 is a Verizon code, and 170 and 410 (among others) are AT&T codes.

Mobile Station Identifier Number   The *mobile station identifier number (MSIN)* is a sequential serial number.

Integrated Circuit Card Identifier   The *integrated circuit card identifier (ICCID)* is a 19- or 20-digit identifier for each SIM chip globally. It's like a serial number for the SIM card.

Secure Element Identifier   The *secure element identifier (SEID)* is a very long hexadecimal code that uniquely identifies the phone. It is used in security applications, NFC, and features like Apple Pay.

Within iOS, you can find many of these numbers by choosing Settings ➤ General ➤ About and scrolling to the bottom, as shown in Figure 10.12. To find the same information in Android, go to Settings ➤ About Phone ➤ Status Information (see Figure 10.13). Tap IMEI information to get the IMEI number.

FIGURE 10.12   iOS phone information

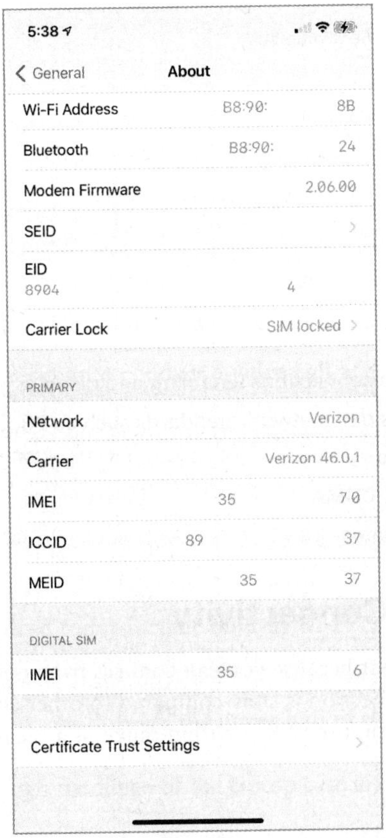

FIGURE 10.13   Android IMEI and other identifiers

For the A+ exam, be sure you are comfortable with:

- Wireless connections (enabling and disabling)
- Wireless data network standards such as 2G, 3G, 4G, and 5G
- Hotspots
- GSM vs. CDMA
- PRL updates

Establishing Wi-Fi Connectivity

Using a cellular network is great because you can connect from nearly anywhere. The downsides, though, are that the connection is slow compared to other connectivity methods, and you have to pay for the data you use. When within range of a secured Wi-Fi network, take advantage of the device's ability to use that network instead. Not only will the connection be faster, it will be free.

Before you can transfer data over a Wi-Fi network, you have to attach to the network in the same manner you would attach a laptop, for instance, to the same wireless network. You have to find the network by its service-set identifier (SSID), or you have to enter the SSID if it is not being broadcast. You must then satisfy any security requirements that might be in place, such as using WPA3 or having the right security keys. Exercise 10.1 steps you through the procedure on an iPhone.

EXERCISE 10.1

Connecting an iPhone to a Wi-Fi Network

1. Tap the Settings app on the Home screen.

2. Tap Wi-Fi on the Settings menu.

3. On the Wi-Fi menu, swipe the Wi-Fi switch to the right to turn it on, as shown in Figure 10.14.

FIGURE 10.14   Turning on Wi-Fi in iOS

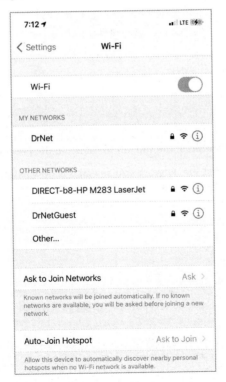

(continues)

Tapping switches also works to toggle them to the opposite state.

4. In the Choose A Network list, tap the name of the wireless network that you want to join.

5. Enter the password or key for the wireless network, if you are asked for one, and then tap the Join button.

   If it connects, it will move the network name under the Wi-Fi switch and put a check next to it, as shown in Figure 10.15. Also note the Ask To Join Networks option near the bottom. Tapping it gives you the options of Off, Notify, and Ask. Turning this off means that you will never be interrupted with offers to join new wireless networks that are in range of the device. Regardless of the setting of this switch, the device will still automatically reconnect to remembered Wi-Fi networks as they come into range. Otherwise, it will join if the other network has a stronger signal and then notify you (Notify) or ask if it should join the new network (Ask).

FIGURE 10.15   Wi-Fi settings with a network that's been joined

6. Tap the Settings back button at the top left to return to the previous screen.

   Notice on this screen that the network you selected is now listed on the Settings page, as shown in Figure 10.16. If not, you are not connected to a Wi-Fi network.

7. Close Settings.

FIGURE 10.16 Settings page with Wi-Fi network connected

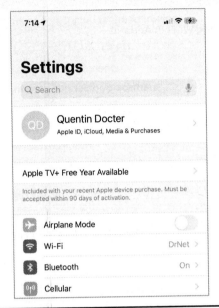

 On iPhones older than the iPhone X, you can use the Home button to return to the Home screen at any time, but the app you leave will continue to remain open in the same screen you left it in unless you restart the iOS device or manually force the app to end. The same can be accomplished on an iPhone X by swiping up from the Home bar (the horizontal bar at the bottom of the screen).

 Throughout this chapter, the practice of tapping successive back buttons in the upper-left corner of the screen, instead of clicking the Home button or swiping up from the Home bar, will be referred to as *backing out of the app*.

A similar series of tasks is required when attaching an Android phone to the same type of network. Exercise 10.2 details that procedure.

EXERCISE 10.2

Connecting an Android Phone to a Wi-Fi Network

1. Tap the Settings app to open it, and then tap Connections.

2. Slide the Wi-Fi switch to the On position, as shown in Figure 10.17.

(continues)

EXERCISE 10.2 *(continued)*

FIGURE 10.17   Enabling Wi-Fi in Android

3. Tap Wi-Fi to see the list of available networks, as shown in Figure 10.18.

FIGURE 10.18   List of available networks

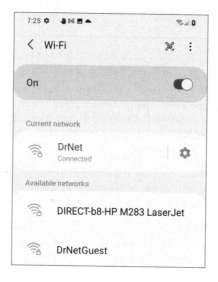

4. Tap the network you want to join.

5. Enter the password for the network and tap Connect.

    The device will go back to the list of Wi-Fi networks, showing that it's connected (see Figure 10.19).

6. Close the Settings app.

FIGURE 10.19   Connected to a network

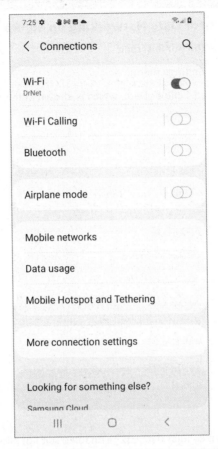

When your phone is connected to a Wi-Fi network, you don't need to use a cellular connection for data transfers—apps will use the Wi-Fi connection for data. But if the connection gets dropped or you move out of Wi-Fi range, the device will use the cellular connection. This might be fine, but it also might not be what you want. If you want to ensure that the phone does not use cellular for data connections, you can disable that option. Exercise 10.3 walks you through the steps of how to do that on an iPhone. When the device is connected to a Wi-Fi network or when paired with a Bluetooth peer, data access will be possible; otherwise, no data-network access will occur.

EXERCISE 10.3

Disabling Cellular Use for Data Networking on an iPhone

1. Tap the Settings app on the home screen.

2. Select Cellular from the Settings menu.

3. Turn off the switch labeled Cellular Data, which is shown in the On position in Figure 10.20.

FIGURE 10.20   iOS Cellular settings

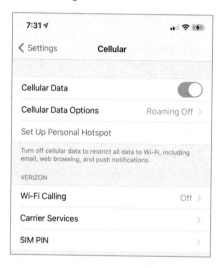

4. If you would like to keep cellular data usage enabled but not allow roaming into other providers' data networks, you can tap Cellular Data Options, which will bring up the options shown in Figure 10.21.

FIGURE 10.21   Cellular data options

5. Here you have the options to disable voice and/or data roaming, as well as configure how voice and data is handled, such as whether to use LTE or 3G. Configuring Low Data Mode can help reduce cellular data usage.

6. If you wish to disable cellular use just for a specific function or app, scroll down in the Cellular settings (or look for the app in the Settings page). You may be able to turn off the use of cellular data for that function or app alone.

For example, Figure 10.22 shows the Use Cellular Data switch for several apps; most of which are currently enabled and three are disabled. This page also shows you how much cellular data each app has used in the current period.

FIGURE 10.22   Cellular data for individual apps

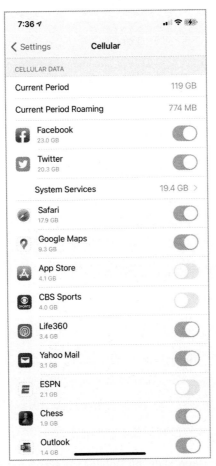

7. Back out of the Settings app or close it.

Exercise 10.4 shows you how to disable cellular data on an Android-based device.

EXERCISE 10.4

Disabling Cellular Use for Data Networking in Android OS

1. Open the Settings app, and then tap Connections.

2. Tap Data Usage.

   It will bring up a screen similar to the one shown in Figure 10.23.

FIGURE 10.23   Data usage in Android OS

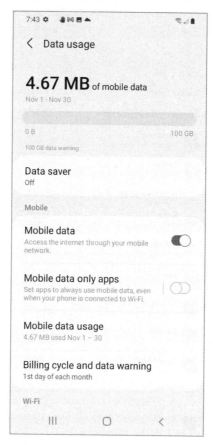

3. To disable cellular data usage, slide the Mobile Data switch to the Off position.

Note that you can leave cellular data enabled but limit the amount that can be used during a specified time period. The dates can be customized to match the billing period used by the mobile carrier. However, be warned that the carrier may track usage slightly differently from the phone, so it might not be a foolproof way to avoid excess data charges.

4. (Optional) To see how much data each app has used in the current period, scroll down and tap Wi-Fi data usage (see Figure 10.24).

FIGURE 10.24   Viewing app data usage in Android OS

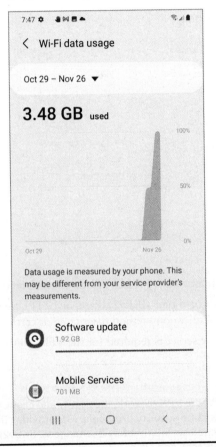

The final setting we will look at in relation to Wi-Fi networks is the *virtual private network (VPN)* configuration. A VPN is a secured network connection made over an unsecure network, such as the Internet. For example, if you wanted to connect your phone to your corporate network over the Internet in order to read email, but you also wanted to secure the connection, you could use a VPN. To set up a VPN on an iPhone, perform the following steps:

1. Select Settings ➢ General ➢ VPN. (Note that if this device has previously connected to a VPN, the VPN can be enabled under the main screen of Settings. Refer back to Figure 10.10 to see the toggle.)

    You will see a screen similar to the one shown in Figure 10.25. You can see that there are four VPNs already configured on this device but that VPN is turned off.

FIGURE 10.25   VPN settings

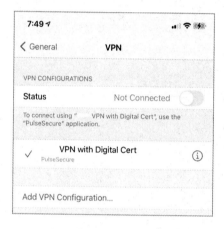

2. To add a new VPN connection, tap Add VPN Configuration (Figure 10.26).
3. Choose the security protocol type (IKEv2, IPsec, or L2TP), then provide a server name and remote ID, an authentication method (username or certificate), and a password.
4. If going through a proxy server is required for the VPN, configure that at the bottom of the screen.

In order for the VPN to work, the server and client must be configured to use the same security protocols. iOS provides three VPN security protocol choices: Internet Key Exchange v2 (IKEv2), Internet Protocol Security (IPsec), and Layer 2 Tunneling Protocol (L2TP). IKEv2 and L2TP are both extensions of the IPsec protocol suite (which is in turn part of the TCP/IP suite you learned about in Chapter 6, "Introduction to TCP/IP"). IKEv2 is the most secure and the fastest, but it isn't supported by as many operating systems as L2TP.

FIGURE 10.26   Adding a VPN connection

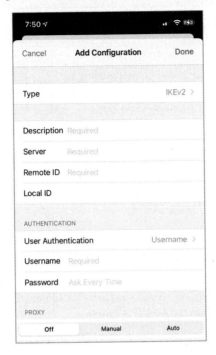

Once you have enabled the VPN, a new VPN option will appear on your Settings page, as previously shown in Figure 10.25. This will allow you to easily enable, disable, or configure the VPN.

VPN connections can be made over cellular as well as over Wi-Fi.

Exercise 10.5 shows you the steps required to set up a PPTP or L2TP VPN connection in Android.

EXERCISE 10.5

Setting Up a VPN in Android

1. Open Settings ➤ Connections ➤ More Connection Settings (Figure 10.27). Tap VPN.

(continues)

FIGURE 10.27   More connection settings

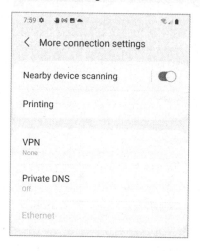

2. If there are no VPNs configured, it will say No VPNs. Tap the three dots icon in the upper-right corner and then tap Add VPN Profile.

    A screen similar to the one shown in Figure 10.28 will appear.

FIGURE 10.28   Edit VPN network

3. Enter the server's VPN configuration information, such as the name, security type (PPTP, L2TP, IPsec, or IKEv2), and address, as well as the security certificate information or username and password (depending on the security method chosen).

4. Tap Save.

   That will take you back to the Add VPN screen, with the new VPN listed (Figure 10.29).

FIGURE 10.29   VPN saved

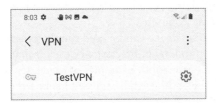

5. Tap the name of the VPN, which will open the Connect To VPN screen.

6. If required (again, depending on the security type chosen), enter the username and password, and tap Connect.

Mobile Phone Security

This is beyond what you need to know for the A+ exam, but you might find it interesting anyway. The security options on Android devices are likely different from iOS-based options. For example, the phone we use in Exercise 10.5 supports Point-to-Point Tunneling Protocol (PPTP), which is a predecessor to L2TP (and far less secure).

Android devices may also show options such as L2TP/IPsec PSK or L2TP/IPsec RSA. Pre-shared Key (PSK) is a security key that's generated by the server and shared with the client. It's susceptible to brute-force attacks and not recommended for highly secure environments. Rivest, Shamir, Adleman (RSA) is a somewhat more secure algorithm that uses asymmetric security keys. It's a better choice than PSK but needs to be administered from an RSA server.

Android also supports many apps that allow you to configure VPN connections, such as TunnelBear (www.tunnelbear.com) owned by McAfee and Hola Free VPN (http://hola.org).

The most secure VPN standard (as of this writing) is called OpenVPN. If your network uses an OpenVPN server, know that you have to install a third-party app (such as OpenVPN Connect) to create the VPN connection. Android does not natively support OpenVPN.

Establishing Bluetooth Connectivity

The IEEE 802.15 standard specifies wireless personal area networks (WPANs) that use Bluetooth for data-link transport. The concept is that certain paired devices will be capable of exchanging or synchronizing data over a Bluetooth connection, such as between a mobile device and a desktop or laptop computer.

In other cases, the Bluetooth *pairing* can be used simply to control one device with another, allowing information to flow bidirectionally, even if that transfer does not result in its permanent storage on the destination. Examples of this latter functionality include a Bluetooth headset for a smartphone, a Bluetooth-attached keyboard and mouse, and pairing a smartphone or MP3 player with a vehicle's sound system.

In general, connecting a mobile device to another device requires that both devices have Bluetooth enabled. Pairing subsequently requires that at least one of the devices be discoverable and the other perform a search for Bluetooth devices. Once the device performing the search finds the other device, a sometime-configurable pairing code must often be entered on the device that performed the search. The code must match the one configured on the device that was found in order for the pairing to occur. In some cases, this pairing will work in one direction only. Usually, it is the mobile device that should search for the other device. If both devices have the same basic capability and will be able to exchange data readily, then it's not as important which device performs the search. Regardless, the pairing code must be known for entry into the device that requests it.

The truth about pairing mobile devices with conventional computers is that the results are hit or miss. There's never any guarantee that a given pairing will be successful to the point of data transfer capability. Both devices must agree on the same Bluetooth specification. This turns out to be the easy part because devices negotiate during the connection. The part that is out of your control is what software services the manufacturer decided to include in their devices. If one device is not capable of file transfers over Bluetooth, then the pairing may go off without a hitch, but the communication process will stop there.

It sometimes takes a few tries to get the pairing or file transfer to work, so always be willing to try a few times. In the worst-case scenario, if it's still not working, look for documentation online to help. Exercise 10.6 shows the steps to connect an Android device to a Windows 10 laptop over Bluetooth and then to transfer a file back and forth between the two. This exercise is split into three sections so that you can concentrate on individual stages of the pairing and file sharing processes.

Exercise 10.7 steps through the process of pairing an iPhone with a vehicle in order to stream music to the vehicle's sound system. Note that the procedures shown in these exercises are based on the specific non-mobile devices used—a Windows 10–based HP laptop and a 2019 Honda. The procedure is roughly the same with other remote devices but will likely vary in the fine details.

EXERCISE 10.6

Pairing an Android Device with a Windows Laptop

Enabling Bluetooth and Pairing

1. On the laptop, enable Bluetooth in Settings ➢ Bluetooth & Other Devices, as shown in Figure 10.30. (To get to Settings, tap the Start button and click the gear icon.)

FIGURE 10.30 Enabling Bluetooth in Windows 10

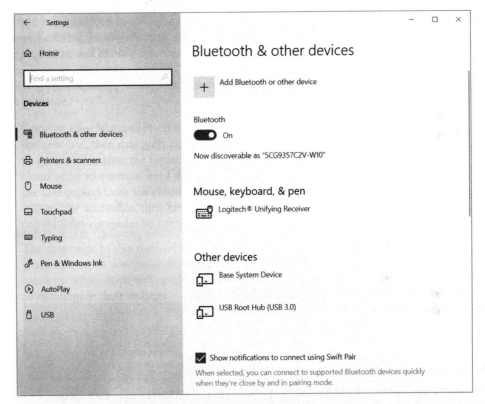

2. On the Android device, tap Settings ➢ Connections ➢ Bluetooth, and turn on Bluetooth.

   Under Available Devices (Figure 10.31), you should see the name of the laptop, provided you are within range. If no devices appear, tap Scan near the top to re-scan for devices.

   (continues)

FIGURE 10.31   Available Bluetooth devices

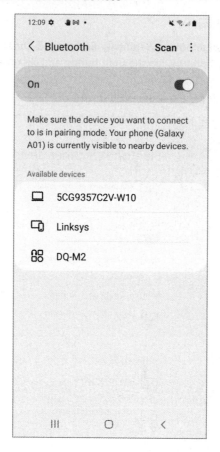

3.   Tap the name of the laptop to connect to.

It will begin pairing. A passkey will appear, as shown in Figure 10.32. Be sure the passkey matches the one shown on the laptop, and tap Pair. Note that you might also need to confirm the passkey on the laptop.

FIGURE 10.32   Bluetooth pairing request

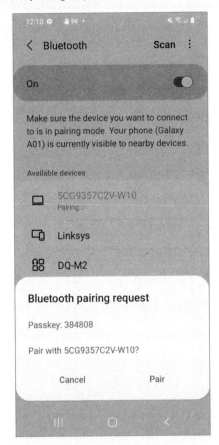

Once the devices are paired, a gear icon will appear in Android, as shown in Figure 10.33.

(continues)

EXERCISE 10.6 *(continued)*

FIGURE 10.33   Paired Bluetooth device with gear

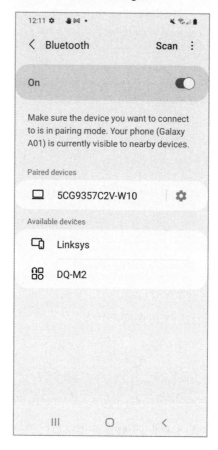

4. (Optional) To unpair the devices, tap on the gear and tap Unpair.

    You can also rename the paired device in this screen.

Transferring Files—Sending to Android

1. In Windows, open Settings ➤ Bluetooth & Other Devices.

2. Scroll down until you see the Send Or Receive Files Via Bluetooth option (Figure 10.34).

3. Click the Send Or Receive Files Via Bluetooth link.

    A screen will open (Figure 10.35), asking if you want to send or receive files.

FIGURE 10.34   Send or receive files via Bluetooth.

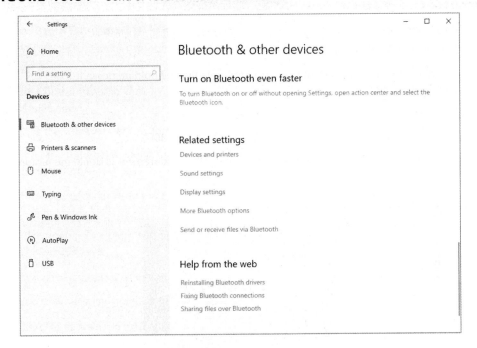

FIGURE 10.35   Bluetooth file transfer

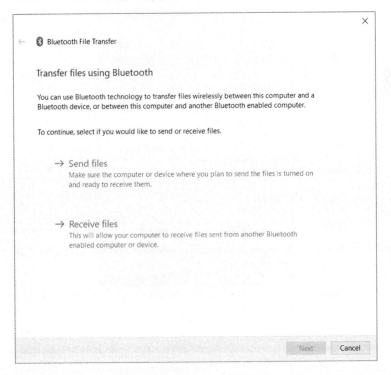

(continues)

4. Click Send Files.

5. Choose the paired device to send files to and click Next.

6. Browse for the files to send. You can send multiple files by holding down the Ctrl key while clicking files.

7. Click Next.

8. On the Android device, click the Accept button (Figure 10.36).

    On the laptop, there will be a transfer status bar. When the transfer is done, the laptop will say File Successfully Transferred.

FIGURE 10.36 Accept the file transfer

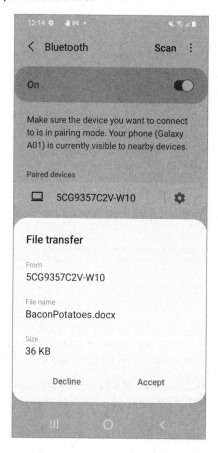

9. Click Finish.

10. In Android, open My Files ➤ Documents.

The files will be in the Download folder by default (Figure 10.37).

FIGURE 10.37 Received file in Android

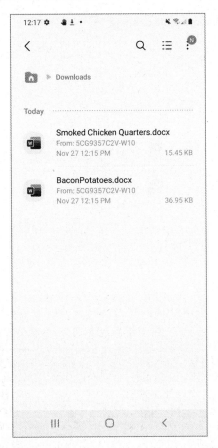

Transferring Files—Receiving from Android

1. In Windows, open Settings ➤ Bluetooth & Other Devices.

2. Scroll down until you see the option Send Or Receive Files Via Bluetooth.

3. Click or tap the Send Or Receive Files Via Bluetooth link.

It will open a screen asking if you want to send or receive files.

4. Click Receive Files.

The next window that appears will tell you the laptop is waiting for a connection.

(continues)

5. On the Android device, find the file you want to share. Hold down on the filename to highlight it (tapping it just once will open up an app to view the file).

6. Tap Share (Figure 10.38) and then Bluetooth.

FIGURE 10.38   Choosing the file to share

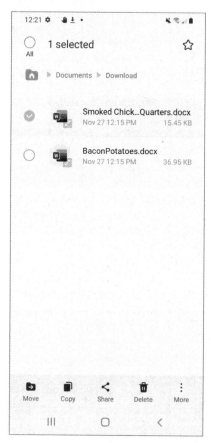

7. Tap the name of the device to share with.

    On the laptop, a status bar will appear as the file is being received.

8. The laptop will ask for a location to save the file. Choose a location, as shown in Figure 10.39.

FIGURE 10.39   Choose a location to save the file.

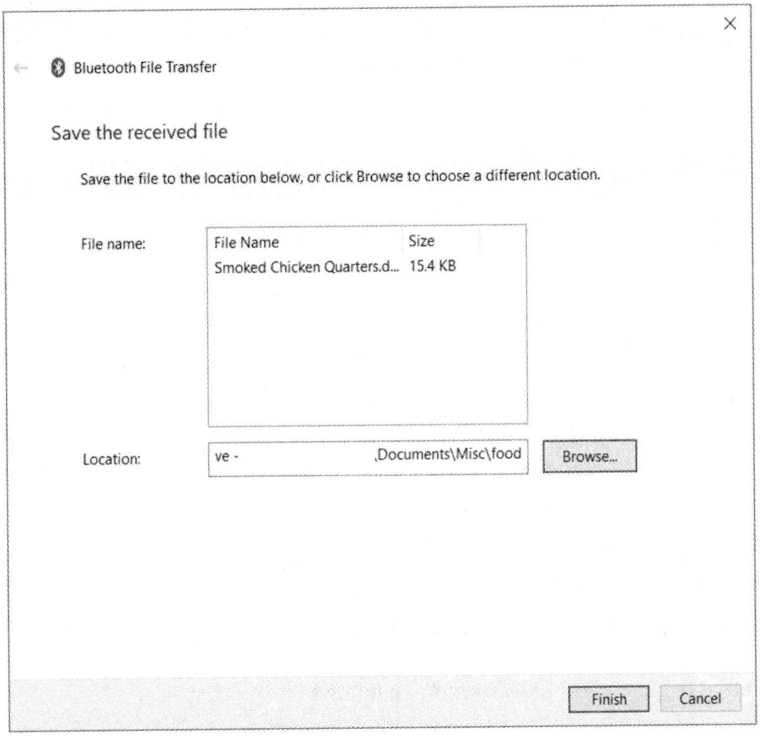

9.   Click Finish.

If you plan on doing a lot of file transfers between a mobile device and a laptop or other paired device, it might make sense to get an app to make that job easier. The devices still need to be paired, but the app makes the transfer process easier. Bluetooth File Transfer is one example, and it's available in the Google Play Store. The iOS App Store has several options available as well if you search for Bluetooth file transfer.

The procedure in Exercise 10.7 is performed from the perspective of an iPhone pairing with a 2019 Honda vehicle. The exact process for Bluetooth pairing will differ based on your mobile OS and the device to which you are connecting. In general, though, remember that these are the steps:

1.   Turn on the Bluetooth hands-free device.

   a.   Enable Bluetooth.

   b.   Enable pairing.

2.   Use your mobile device to locate and select the Bluetooth device.

3. Enter the Bluetooth device's passcode.

4. Confirm pairing on the Bluetooth device by pressing a button or a combination of buttons.

5. Test the connectivity.

EXERCISE 10.7

Pairing an iPhone with a Vehicle's Sound System

1. Enable Bluetooth pairing in the vehicle. It will often involve using menu or voice commands to begin the process.

2. Confirm that the vehicle's hands-free power is enabled.

   Hands-free power might be referred to in other ways, including simply as Bluetooth. Alternatively, the Bluetooth module in certain vehicles might be "always on" and not configurable. The key is to make sure that the vehicle is ready to accept incoming Bluetooth requests.

3. When the vehicle is ready, go into Settings ➢ Bluetooth on the iPhone, and slide the switch to enable Bluetooth.

   It found the car's multimedia system as "HandsFreeLink" under Devices (Figure 10.40).

FIGURE 10.40   Enabling Bluetooth on an iPhone

Bluetooth pairings in this list can be Connected, Not Connected (even if pairing was, however, successful), or Not Paired.

4. Tap the HandsFreeLink device in Other Devices. It will attempt to pair.

The pairing screen will appear on both devices. The iPhone screen is shown in Figure 10.41.

FIGURE 10.41   Bluetooth pairing

5. If the code matches the one on the vehicle screen, tap Pair. You may also need to do the same on the vehicle's touch screen.

Both devices will likely confirm that the pairing was successful. (Although in practice, we've had the devices say that pairing failed, yet steps 6 and 7 below still work, indicating that the pairing was in fact successful. Sometimes this process can be finicky.) The paired device will appear on the iPhone (Figure 10.42).

FIGURE 10.42   Bluetooth device is paired

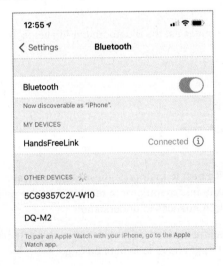

(continues)

EXERCISE 10.7 *(continued)*

6. Confirm the iPhone's connection from the vehicle's perspective.

   If the vehicle has the ability to use the iPhone for voice calls, this feature might be presented to you automatically after pairing is complete. If so, this is a perfect way to confirm connectivity.

7. Switch to the vehicle's Bluetooth audio mode.

   The iPhone might still need to be "connected" for this use. The pairing allows you to select the connection feature in the vehicle and see the iPhone as a connection option. Depending on the vehicle, selecting the iPhone should cause music to begin playing either from its default playlist or the last position where playback was stopped over another output source, including the iPhone's internal speaker or headset jack.

Future connections to the iPhone from this vehicle should be automatic when the vehicle's Bluetooth mode is selected, and the iPhone should begin playing from the point where it last stopped playing over any output source. The specific initial and subsequent interactions between the vehicle and iPhone may vary from this description.

Bluetooth Pairing Steps

The CompTIA A+ exam objectives list the Bluetooth pairing steps as follows:

1. Enable Bluetooth.

2. Enable pairing.

3. Find a device for pairing.

4. Enter the appropriate PIN code.

5. Test connectivity.

For purposes of the exam, it's best to memorize these steps. However, you might have noticed that in the exercises in this chapter (or in real life if you've paired your own devices), there are some slight nuances to understand:

- Usually, the ability to pair is enabled if Bluetooth is enabled. Therefore, step 2 might not be needed, but you might need to initiate pairing.

- It used to be that one device generated a PIN and you entered it into the other. Today, it's more common to have both devices display a PIN, and you confirm on both devices that the PIN matches.

You will also need to understand Bluetooth pairing for the 220-1102 exam, because Bluetooth connectivity issues are part of that exam's objective 3.4 as well.

Understanding Mobile App Support

Mobile devices give users the ability to roam practically anywhere they want to and still be connected to the world. Whether this is a good or bad thing can be up for debate, but here we'll focus on the positive aspects of this freedom. One of the compelling features of mobile devices is to help you pinpoint where you are and help you get from where you are to where you want to be. This is accomplished through location services, which we will cover in this section.

Another positive of mobile devices is of course their size. Small devices are far more portable than bulky desktops or even laptops—you're unlikely to fit a laptop into your pocket. While mobile devices aren't great for editing spreadsheets or documents, they are more than adequate for sending and receiving email, managing calendars, and storing business and personal contacts. And for larger data storage needs, mobile devices easily connect to the cloud or desktop/laptop computers for synchronization. We'll cover all of these topics in this section on mobile app support as well.

Understanding Location Services

Location services identify where you are and can help give you a route to where you want to be. Two different technologies combine to form what we know as location services, and they are GPS and cellular location services.

Understanding GPS

Global Positioning System (GPS) is a satellite-based navigation system that provides location and time services. It's great technology for those who are perpetually lost, want to know the best way to get somewhere, or want or need to track down someone else.

The most common commercial use for GPS is navigation; you can get your current location and directions to where you want to go. Other uses include tracking; law enforcement can monitor inmates with location devices, or parents can locate their children via their smartphones. Oil and gas companies use GPS in their geological surveys, and farmers can use GPS-enabled machines to plant crops automatically. There are three major components to GPS: the satellite constellation, the ground control network, and the receiver. The ground control network monitors satellite health and signal integrity. We'll look at the other two components next.

GPS Satellites

The U.S. Department of Defense (DoD) started developing GPS in the early 1970s, with the goal of creating the best navigation system possible. The first GPS satellite launched in 1978, and today the U.S. government manages 32 total GPS satellites covering the globe. Twenty-four are active satellites for the service, and the rest are backups. Satellites are launched into an orbit of about 12,550 miles above the earth, and old satellites are replaced with new ones when an old one reaches its life expectancy or fails. GPS is free to use for commercial purposes.

There are additional global satellite-based navigation systems managed by other government entities. Collectively, they are called Global Navigation Satellite Systems (GNSSs). All of the systems are outlined in Table 10.1; as you might expect, no two systems are compatible with each other.

TABLE 10.1 Global Navigation Satellite Systems

Name	Managed by	Number of satellites
Global Positioning System (GPS)	United States	24
Global Navigation Satellite System (GLONASS)	Russia	24
Galileo Positioning System	European Space Agency	30
BeiDou Navigation Satellite System (BDS)	China	35
Indian Regional Navigation Satellite System (IRNSS)	India	7

At first glance, it might seem like there are an excessive number of satellites required to run a navigation service. GPS systems were designed to require multiple satellites. Receivers use a process called *triangulation* to calculate the distance between themselves and the satellites (based on the time it takes to receive a signal) to determine their location. They require input from four satellites to provide location and elevation or from three satellites to provide location. Most GNSSs provide two levels of service, one more precise than the other. For example, GPS provides the following two levels:

- Standard Positioning Service (SPS) for civil use, accurate to within 100 meters horizontally and 156 meters vertically. Uses Coarse Acquisition (C/A) code.

- Precise Positioning Service (PPS) for Department of Defense and ally use, accurate to within 22 meters horizontally and 27.7 meters vertically. Uses Precise (P) code.

NOTE   The accuracy numbers listed in this section are the official specifications of GPS, which were calculated when the service was launched. For many years, GPS used a feature called Selective Availability (SA), which was an intentional degradation of public signals, implemented for national security reasons. (The government didn't want potential enemies to be able to use GPS.) In 2000, the United States government discontinued the use of SA. Now, commercial GPS is accurate to within about 10–15 meters in most cases. Under ideal conditions, it can be accurate to within a centimeter. Much of the accuracy depends on the quality of the receiver.

The two service levels are separated by transmitting on different frequencies, named L1 and L2. L1 transmits at 1,575.42 MHz, and it contains unencrypted civilian C/A code as well as military P code. L2 (1,227.60 MHz) only transmits encrypted P code, referred to as Y code. In the United States, SPS is free to use; the receiver just needs to manage C/A code. PPS requires special permission from the U.S. DoD as well as special equipment that can receive P and Y code and decrypt Y code. Galileo, in the European Union, provides free open (standard) service, but charges users a fee for the high data throughput commercial (premium) service. Both offer encrypted signals with controlled access for government use.

GPS Receivers

GPS receivers come in all shapes and sizes. Common forms are wearable watches and wristbands, stand-alone GPS devices (like the Garmin device shown in Figure 10.43), and ones built into automobiles. Most smartphones and tablets support GPS as well (Apple products use the name Location Services), and more and more laptops are coming with built-in GPS capabilities. You can also find GPS devices that come on a collar for pets. Most stand-alone GPS devices feature capacitive touch screens. The Garmin device shown in Figure 10.43 has a 4.5" touch screen; 5" to 7" devices are common as of this writing. It also contains an SD memory card slot for expansion. Popular brands of automobile GPS devices are Garmin, TomTom, and Magellan.

FIGURE 10.43   Garmin Nuvi GPS

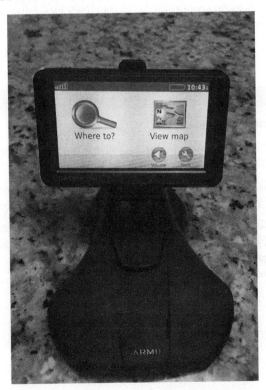

Understanding Cellular Location Services

Cellular location services is designed to do the same thing GPS does, such as provide a user's location or help navigate a route to a destination. While it uses triangulation just like GPS, the rest of the mechanics are different.

First, while commercial GPS services are free, cellular location services is not. It's provided via subscription from a mobile carrier such as Verizon, T-Mobile, AT&T, and others. Second, instead of using satellites, it uses cell phone towers for its triangulation points. This means that if a user doesn't have cell phone reception, then cellular location services won't work. Cellular location services is also less precise than GPS. Recall that GPS is accurate within 100 meters (although it's really often within 10 meters, as we discussed earlier), but cellular location services is only accurate within about 1,000 meters. If a user's phone is within range of multiple cell towers, that precision can increase substantially and get close to GPS performance. However, the rule of thumb is that GPS is more accurate than cellular when locating devices.

Setting precision aside, which technology do mobile devices use for location services? The answer is a combination of GPS and cellular, provided of course the device can find the satellites or cell towers. In fact, mobile devices can use Wi-Fi signals for location purposes as well, so it's really a combination of all three, depending on the circumstance.

Configuring Location Services

Knowing how to turn location services on or off on a GPS receiver or a mobile device is a valuable skill. The specific settings depend on the operating system, of course, but we can provide general guidance here. Exercise 10.8 shows you how to configure Location Services in iOS 12.

EXERCISE 10.8

Configuring Location Services in iOS

1. Click Settings ➤ Privacy ➤ Location Services. You will see a screen similar to the one shown in Figure 10.44.

2. At the top, there is a slider to enable Location Services. Slide it to the on position to enable it (like in Figure 10.44), and off to disable it.

    Note that if you disable it, none of the apps on the device will be able to use the feature, except for Find My iPhone. When on, each app's capability to use Location Services is configured individually.

FIGURE 10.44   iOS location services

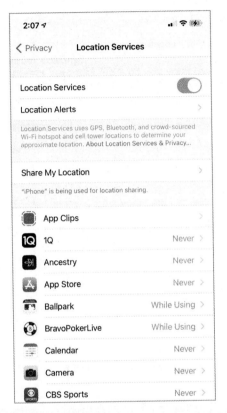

3. To change an individual app, tap on it. There will be four choices:

■   Never

■   Ask Next Time

■   While Using the App

■   Always

4. Configure each app as desired.

In the Android OS, GPS is configured through Settings as well:

1. Tap Settings ➤ Location. You will see a screen similar to the one shown in Figure 10.45.

2. Move the slider to the on position, as shown, to enable GPS.

    You can also configure things such as individual app permissions, and the ability to use Bluetooth and Wi-Fi to improve accuracy (by tapping Improve Accuracy), and location services for emergency purposes.

FIGURE 10.45   Android GPS settings

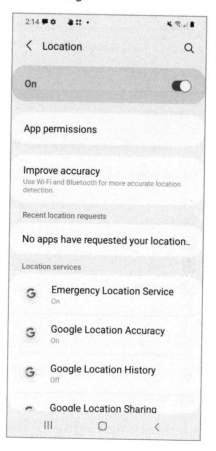

3. Tap App permissions to set location services for each app (Figure 10.46). Options include:

    ▪ Allow All The Time

    ▪ Allow Only While Using The App

    ▪ Ask Every Time

    ▪ Deny

4. Configure apps as you would like, and close Settings.

For the A+ exam, remember that you need to understand location services, which includes GPS and cellular location services.

FIGURE 10.46   Location services app permissions

Understanding Mobile Device and App Management

The use of mobile devices on corporate networks has increased exponentially over the past several years, and it will likely continue to increase over time. So many people work remotely or travel that it just makes sense for them to be able to manage email or perform tasks such as order placement and management from their mobile devices. Of course, these usage cases can give network administrators nightmares, as every additional device connected to the network represents another security risk. And when devices are small and easily misplaced or stolen, that elevates the security risk to a whole new level.

To help with mobile device security, many companies use a combination of mobile device management and mobile application management and can also implement two-factor authentication. We'll look at those in the upcoming sections, and deep dive into the most common corporate use of mobile devices, which is sending and receiving email.

Mobile Device Management and Mobile Application Management

Imagine that you are a network administrator for a corporate network, and the company implements a new policy where mobile devices should be granted network access. As we mentioned earlier, if done incorrectly this can pose a massive security risk to the company, so, no pressure, right? With security in mind, you may want to explore implementing a *mobile device management (MDM)* solution.

An MDM is a software package residing on a server. The key purpose of an MDM is to enroll mobile devices on the corporate network, and once those devices are enrolled, to manage security. This is done through security policies as well as the ability to remotely track, lock, unlock, encrypt, and wipe mobile devices as needed. Now if someone's smartphone is misplaced or stolen, an administrator can wipe it remotely and the security threat is mitigated.

Although this is a good solution for device-level security, there's a big piece missing—the software. That's where *mobile application management (MAM)* comes into play. Typically implemented in conjunction with an MDM, an MAM allows network administrators to remotely install, delete, encrypt, and wipe corporate applications and related data from mobile devices. In an MAM, administrators can specify software packages that are allowed to be installed on the mobile device and prohibit others that could pose security risks. When enrolled in the MAM, users may have a corporate app store that functions similarly to Apple's App Store or Google Play. Figure 10.47 shows an example of some apps in a corporate app store, managed by VMware AirWatch.

FIGURE 10.47   Corporate app store

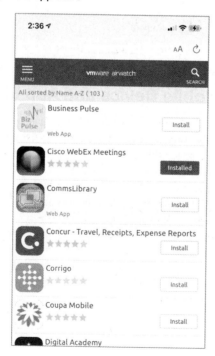

Managing Apps in a BYOD Environment

To reduce costs needed to provide employees with mobile devices, many companies have adopted a bring your own device (BYOD) plan. Under the plan, employees can use their personal smartphones, as long as the phone meets certain security requirements, and install corporate applications. In situations like these, the MDM will be responsible for granting the phone access to the network. If the phone gets lost, however, it may be impractical to use an MDM to wipe it because it would erase all of the user's personal files (photos, music, apps, etc.) as well. With the use of an MAM, though, the corporate applications and data on the lost phone can be remotely wiped, eliminating the security risk for the company.

Two-Factor Authentication

We've talked about authentication several times in this book so far, including multifactor authentication in Chapter 8, "Network Services, Virtualization, and Cloud Computing." Recall that single-factor authentication means a user needs just one piece of information beyond their username, typically a password. Multifactor means they need more than one, such as a password and an additional credential.

Two-factor authentication helps increase security for mobile devices by requiring that additional piece of information. A common implementation is to require a PIN from a security token, which changes every 30 seconds. We showed an example of one back in Figure 8.5. Another way to implement a security token is through a software package such as PingID (as shown in Figure 10.48). Here's a brief overview of how it works:

FIGURE 10.48

1. PingID is installed on the mobile device as well as the user's laptop or desktop computer.
2. The devices are paired.

3. When the user attempts to access an app on their smartphone that requires two-factor authentication, they will first present their username and password.

4. After the username and password have been validated, the smartphone will ask for the PIN.

5. The user opens the PingID software on their laptop or desktop and retrieves the current PIN.

6. The user enters the PIN on the security screen on the smartphone.

7. If the PIN is correct, the user is granted access to the app.

The second factor could also be something such as a one-time password generated by a security server, biometrics, or detection of location of a specific IP address.

Configuring Email Accounts

Accessing email is the most common corporate use for mobile devices. Usually, the most difficult part is finding the server settings that are used only during establishment of the connection, which tends to occur only once for each device. The other big challenge is when users have the same devices and accounts for many years; since they have not configured them in some time, it might be difficult for them to remember their usernames and passwords, if needed.

When configuring mobile devices to access email, you will be attaching to one of the following two types of services:

- An integrated commercial provider, which includes iCloud, Google/Inbox (Gmail), Exchange Online, and Yahoo Mail

- A corporate or ISP-based email service

Generally speaking, connecting to an integrated commercial provider is quite easy and nearly automatic. Connecting to a corporate or ISP-based account usually involves a few more steps, but it shouldn't be too tricky if you know the proper server settings. In the following sections, we'll look at configuring email on a mobile device and settings to know for manual email configuration.

Mobile Internet Email Configuration Options

If your email is on a common web-based service, such as iCloud, Google/Inbox (Gmail), Exchange Online, or Yahoo, configuring the email feature is pretty easy. Usually, your email address and password are all that are required. However, if you have a corporate or ISP account or a custom domain, even if it's hosted and accessible through Gmail, Outlook.com, or the other popular services, you may need to take a few more steps to make a connection. For the purposes of trying out a commercial service, you can always make a dummy account on the service's website and play around with that if it helps you complete these exercises. Exercise 10.9 and Exercise 10.10 detail the basic steps required to configure a commercial email account on an iPhone and on an Android standard email client, respectively.

EXERCISE 10.9

Email Account Configuration on an iPhone

1. From the home screen, tap Settings ➤ Mail ➤ Accounts. You will see a screen similar to the one shown in Figure 10.49.

FIGURE 10.49   Email accounts

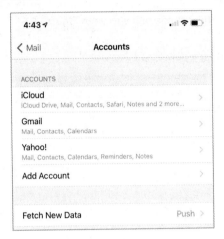

2. Tap Add Account.

A screen similar to the one shown in Figure 10.50 will appear.

FIGURE 10.50   Adding an account

(continues)

EXERCISE 10.9 *(continued)*

Note that if you have an email account with any of the listed services, you can tap it to configure your client. You will be asked for your username and password. After entering this information, you should be done. It's as easy as that to add an account for a commercial provider. For this example, complete the following steps:

a. Tap Other ➢ Add Mail Account.

You will get a screen similar to the one shown in Figure 10.51.

FIGURE 10.51   Creating a new email account

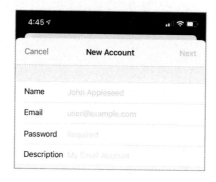

b. Add your name, email address, password, and an optional description.

c. Tap Next.

3. In the New Account screen (see Figure 10.52), choose IMAP or POP.

We will get into the differences between the two in the next section, but if your server supports it, IMAP is preferable.

4. Here you also configure the names of the incoming and outgoing mail servers.

Many organizations will have one server handle both functions.

5. Once you have entered the correct information, tap Next.

The iPhone will make connections to the server(s) to verify the username and password. If the username and password are successful, you will get a screen asking which content you want to receive, such as mail, contacts, and calendars.

6. Tap Save, and it will add your account.

Now you can use the Mail icon on the home page to retrieve email. Note that you can have several email accounts configured to receive email in this app (as was the case in Figure 10.49).

FIGURE 10.52 New Account screen

7. (Optional) To delete an account, repeat steps 1 and 2 in this exercise. On the Passwords & Accounts screen, tap the account that you want to delete.

8. (Optional) Tap Delete Account to remove it from this client.

Exercise 10.10 details the steps required for configuring an email account on an Android standard email client. If the Android device does not have the email app on the home screen, you can add it or run it directly from the All Apps list.

EXERCISE 10.10

Email Account Configuration in Android

1. Tap Settings ➤ Accounts And Backup ➤ Manage Accounts (see Figure 10.53).

FIGURE 10.53 Accounts in Android

2. Tap Add Account.

3. Tap the type of account that you want to add. For this example, choose Personal (IMAP).

4. Enter an email account name and tap Next. (For purposes of this exercise, you can make up fake credentials—the rest of the exercise will work through step 9 with them.)

5. Enter a password and tap Next.

   You will get a screen similar to the one shown in Figure 10.54.

6. Tap Next to validate the server settings.

   The information we entered is obviously fake, so the validation will fail. (Hopefully yours succeeds if you used real credentials!) You will get a warning saying that email security is not guaranteed. Click Edit Settings. Having the validation fail gives us a chance to talk about additional options.

FIGURE 10.54 Incoming Server Settings

Since the validation failed, Android tries to help out by suggesting we try updating the port or security type (see Figure 10.55). Notice that near the bottom of the screen, the port is 143 because we chose IMAP in step 3. Continue with the following steps:

(continues)

FIGURE 10.55 Email port setting

7. Tap anywhere on the setting under Security Type, and you can change the security to SSL/TLS.

   Options are shown in Figure 10.56. Changing the type to SSL/TLS will automatically change the port number to 993. (We will discuss SSL/TLS shortly.)

FIGURE 10.56   Email security options

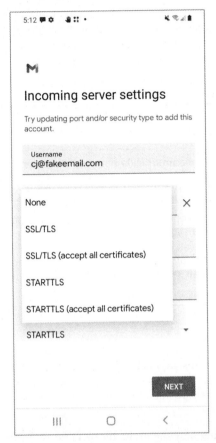

8. Tap Next. Android will contact the server and verify the server settings.

    After verifying a connection to the server, you may be able to choose account options, such as sync frequency and email notification settings.

9. Choose your settings (if applicable) and tap Next.

    You may get an account confirmation page, where you can edit the account name that gets displayed as well as the name that gets displayed on outgoing messages.

10. Tap Next.

    The new account will appear in your accounts list in Settings.

11. Access your email through the Email app on the home page.

Manual Email Configuration Options

In situations when you find that your email client cannot automatically configure your email account for you, there are often manual settings for the protocols required for sending and receiving emails. Table 10.2 details these protocols and their uses. These should look familiar to you if you recall Chapter 6.

TABLE 10.2   TCP/IP mail protocols

Mail protocol	Description	Default port number
Simple Mail Transfer Protocol (SMTP)	Used to communicate between client and server and between servers to send mail to a recipient's account. The key word is *send*, as this is a push protocol.	TCP 25
Post Office Protocol (POP)	Used to communicate between a client and the client's mail server to retrieve mail with little interaction.	TCP 110
Internet Message Access Protocol (IMAP)	Used to communicate between a client and the client's mail server to retrieve mail with extensive interaction.	TCP 143

In Table 10.2 and for the rest of this section, we refer to the POP and IMAP protocols. In practice, the current versions of each are POP3 and IMAPv4. For brevity, we will refer to them as just POP and IMAP—the version numbers do not affect the port numbers and relevant configuration information.

In a TCP/IP network using only the protocols in Table 10.2 (there are other, less common options), you must always use SMTP for sending mail. You must decide between the use of POP and IMAP for interacting with the mail server to retrieve your mail with the client. When supported, IMAP is a clear choice because of its extensive interaction with the server, allowing the client to change the state or location of a mail item on the server without the need to download and delete it from the server.

Conversely, POP limits client interaction with the server to downloading and deleting items from the server, not allowing their state to be changed by the client. In fact, the use of POP as your receive-mail protocol can lead to confusion because copies of the same items appear in multiple client locations, some marked as read and others unread. Additionally, where IMAP changes the state of a mail item on the server and leaves the item on the server for later access by the same or a different client, POP settings must be configured *not* to delete the item from the server on download to each client. This, however, is what leads to the choice of multiple copies among the clients or only one client being able to download the item.

Most, if not all, Internet mail services require secure connections. SMTP, POP, and IMAP are all unsecure protocols, so this poses a problem. One solution is to use *Secure Sockets Layer (SSL)* or *Transport Layer Security (TLS)* on top of these protocols. You might recognize SSL and TLS from their use on TCP port 443 for the HTTPS protocol. When using these protocols to secure the email protocols, mail servers and clients need to communicate on ports other than the ones shown in Table 10.2. These are outlined in Table 10.3.

TABLE 10.3 Secure mail ports

Mail protocol	TCP port number
SMTP with SSL	465
SMTP with TLS	587
IMAP with SSL/TLS	993
POP with SSL/TLS	995

Using STARTTLS

It was mildly obnoxious to have to memorize multiple port numbers (although you should for the exam), as well as program email clients and servers to recognize different ones. A different solution exists, called *STARTTLS*. (You saw it as an option in Figure 10.56.)

STARTTLS secures email communications over the three common email protocols, but it does not change their port numbers. And despite its name, STARTTLS doesn't exclusively use TLS—it can use SSL as well. Some email software supports it, whereas others do not, so be aware of its existence and know what it does. It's not a test objective, but it's something you may run into in the real world.

Additionally, you will need to know the server names for your service. Sometimes they are the same for inbound and outbound mail handling, but they may be different. Table 10.4 lists the servers in the United States for iCloud, Gmail, Exchange Online, and Yahoo Mail. Unless otherwise specified, the ports in Table 10.3 should be used for the protocols listed in Table 10.4.

TABLE 10.4   Secure mail servers for common email services

Service	Direction and protocol	Server name
iCloud	Outbound on SMTP with SSL	`smtp.mail.me.com`
	Inbound on IMAP with SSL	`imap.mail.me.com`
Google/Inbox (Gmail)	Outbound on SMTP with SSL or TLS	`smtp.gmail.com`
	Inbound on IMAP with SSL	`imap.gmail.com`
	Inbound on POP with SSL	`pop.gmail.com`
Exchange Online	Outbound on SMTP with TLS	`smtp.office365.com`
	Inbound on IMAP with SSL	`outlook.office365.com`
	Inbound on POP with TLS	`outlook.office365.com`
Yahoo Mail	Outbound on SMTP with SSL	`smtp.mail.yahoo.com`
	Inbound on IMAP with SSL	`imap.mail.yahoo.com`
	Inbound on POP with SSL	`pop.mail.yahoo.com`

For the A+ exam, be familiar with the differences between MDM and MAM and how MAM is used to manage corporate applications. Also understand two-factor authentication and the principles behind configuring corporate and commercial email clients.

Configuring Mobile Device Synchronization

While some users are content to have a mobile device only, many others do not consider their mobile devices to be islands unto themselves. Instead, they treat their mobile devices as extensions of their primary computing devices that, even if they happen to be portable, stay at work or at home while the mobile devices go on the road with the users. However, because many of the same changes to a user's calendar, contacts, and personal files can be made from the mobile device as easily as from the primary computer, frequent synchronization of the two devices is in order. *Synchronization* is the act of mirroring all unique changes and additions from one device to the other.

In most cases, there are multiple options as to how the mobile device will connect to the computer system it is syncing to. Some connections allow synchronization; others do not. Common connections include over USB, across Wi-Fi, over Bluetooth, and through a cellular connection. Although the wired connections tend to be the most reliable, the convenience of wireless connections and their automatic unattended synchronizations cannot be ignored. When syncing, you can either sync to a local computer (such as a laptop, desktop, or networked server) or to the cloud. Keep in mind that when you sync a mobile device to the cloud or are using certain synchronization utilities, you may run into data caps that only allow you to sync a certain amount of data.

 Real World Scenario

Understanding Data Caps

Syncing a mobile device to a local computer or the cloud is smart mobile device management. Mobile devices can easily be misplaced or broken, yet many of them have apps and data that would be hard to replace, or photos that would be impossible to replace. Where you choose to sync to is a matter of personal preference.

If you sync to the cloud or use a cellular connection to sync, you can run into a problem with data caps. The sync itself might not consume too much data if you have a limited data plan, but when added to email downloads, streamed videos and music, and GPS use, the caps may prove to be too restricting. Here are some tips to see if you have data caps and if so, things you can do about it:

- Research your contracts with your cellular provider and ISP to see if there are data caps, and if so, if your monthly usage comes close to getting capped out.

  - Most ISPs have an app you can use to track usage. On mobile devices, iOS device users can go to Settings ➤ Cellular to see how much data has been used, and Android device users can do the same under Settings ➤ Connections ➤ Data Usage ➤ Mobile Data Usage.

- Research current and other providers to see if they have caps, and the cost associated with plans that don't have caps.

- Change settings to help preserve data. For example, do you need to stream videos in 4K on your tablet? Lowering the video quality will consume less data, and most streaming services have options to do so.

- Take advantage of off-peak hours. Some providers allow for extra data during early morning hours when fewer people are on their devices. If you can, that's a perfect time to schedule a major download or data sync.

With a little legwork and planning, you can avoid data caps and any negative effects they might have on your mobile device experience. Or if nothing else, spend a little more and upgrade your plan to an unlimited one if it's available.

Because each manufacturer of mobile devices must approach synchronization of data in the best manner for their devices, generalized discussions of data to be synchronized can *only* include the common types. Here's a list of the most common types of data to be synchronized by all such utilities:

- Contacts
- Applications
- Email
- Pictures
- Music
- Videos
- Calendar
- Bookmarks
- Documents
- Location data
- Social media data
- E-books
- Passwords

In the following sections, we will look at how to synchronize using Microsoft utilities as well as how to sync iOS and Android devices.

Syncing Using Microsoft Utilities

Microsoft provides several software utilities that enable synchronization between devices. Two that we will focus on here, because they are included as exam objectives, are Microsoft 365 and ActiveSync.

Using Microsoft 365

Microsoft 365 is a subscription service that provides access to the Office suite of apps from Microsoft, including Word, Excel, PowerPoint, and others. With the subscription, users also get storage space in Microsoft's cloud. That cloud storage space can also be used to sync devices with one another.

Imagine a scenario where a user has a desktop and laptop computer, and they want to ensure the operating environment is always identical between the two. Windows 10 users with a Microsoft 365 account can easily sync settings between multiple computers with their subscription. Simply open Start ➤ Settings ➤ Accounts ➤ Sync Your Settings (Figure 10.57), and slide Sync Settings to On. The key things to note about using this are:

- Only settings such as desktop themes, passwords, language preferences, and Windows configuration settings will be synced; this does *not* sync files between computers.
- Sync needs to be enabled on each computer to be synchronized.
- The sync will link back to the email account specified at the top of the Sync Your Settings screen.

FIGURE 10.57   Sync Your Settings

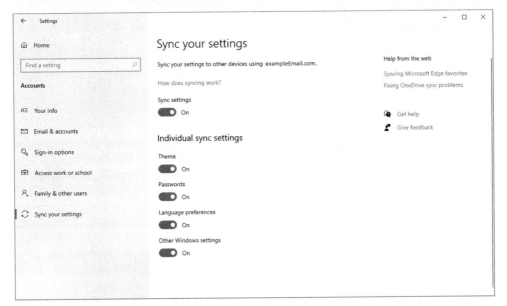

If synchronization is no longer desired, the user can remove the settings from the cloud by taking the following steps:

1. Turn off Sync settings on all synced computers.
2. Go to `http://account.microsoft.com/devices`.
3. Scroll to the bottom of the page and select Clear Stored Settings.

Syncing files and data between Windows-based computers is a bit more involved. It requires a Microsoft SharePoint server in addition to the Windows 365 subscription. Once the server and client are configured, synced files will be accessible through File Explorer. Typically, a user's Documents folder is set up to be synced, and whenever a file is modified, the updated version is saved to both systems. Various third-party synchronization software packages are also available that provide similar functionality.

Using ActiveSync

ActiveSync is a protocol used by Microsoft Exchange Server that allows users to access email, calendar, contacts, and tasks from a mobile device such as a smartphone or a tablet. From the server side, ActiveSync also allows administrators to remotely wipe, enforce password policies, and enable encryption on mobile devices. To set up ActiveSync on a mobile device, the user needs to have a Microsoft Exchange account. Exercise 10.11 shows you how to enable ActiveSync on an iPhone.

EXERCISE 10.11

Enabling ActiveSync in iOS

1. Open Settings ➤ Mail ➤ Accounts.

2. Tap Add Account and then choose Exchange. You will see a screen similar to Figure 10.58. Enter the email address and (optionally) a description. Tap Next.

FIGURE 10.58   Adding an Exchange account

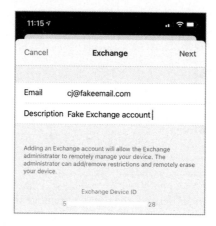

3. Enter the email server name, domain, username, and password into the screen like the one in Figure 10.59, and tap Next.

4. After connecting to the server and verifying the account credentials, you can configure sync options, as shown in Figure 10.60.

FIGURE 10.59   Exchange account parameters

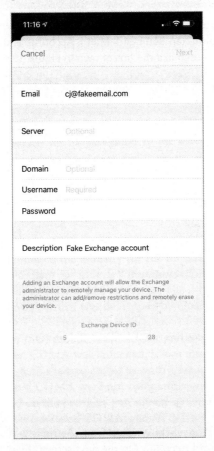

FIGURE 10.60   Exchange account sync options

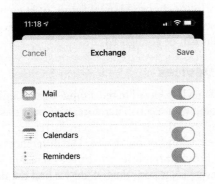

(continues)

5.   If at any time you want to change those options, configure how many days of email to sync, or delete the account, tap Settings ➤ Mail ➤ Accounts and choose the Exchange account. You will see a screen like the one shown in Figure 10.61.

FIGURE 10.61   Changing Exchange options

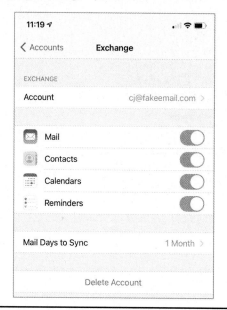

Android devices can use ActiveSync as well. Go to Settings ➤ Accounts And Backup ➤ Manage Accounts and tap Add Account. On the next screen (Figure 10.62), choose Microsoft Exchange ActiveSync. On the following screen (Figure 10.63), enter the email address and password, and tap Sign In (or choose Manual Setup to set configuration options such as the type of security to use). Once connection is made to the server, sync options such as email, contacts, and calendar can be configured.

Syncing Apple iOS Devices

Due to their size, Apple iOS devices have limited storage space, and they also have the potential to get lost (or stolen) somewhat easily. Therefore, it's smart to synchronize your device to a desktop or laptop computer (they will be collectively referred to as *desktop* in the rest of this section) and/or make backups of the device. The differences between the two concepts aren't that large. Synchronization means that the exact same copy of the data (music, pictures, contacts, or whatever) is on both the iOS device and the desktop. Backing up means taking whatever is on the phone at that time and ensuring that a duplicate is stored elsewhere. Synchronization can often happen both ways, whereas backups are a one-way process. Apple provides two options for syncing and backing up: sync to a desktop (using iTunes) and back up to the cloud (using iCloud).

FIGURE 10.62   Adding ActiveSync in Android

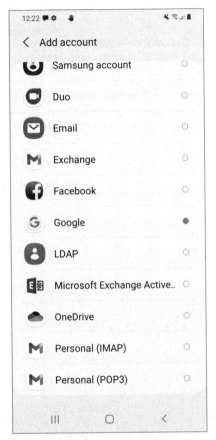

Using iTunes

To sync a device with a desktop, you must have the iTunes app installed on your computer. It's installed by default on Macs and can be found at https://www.apple.com/itunes for non-Apple OSs. Figure 10.64 shows the Summary page of iTunes for an iOS device when it's connected. Notice that the Backups section has options to back up to iCloud or to This Computer. In this section, we will focus on local backups.

By default, iOS devices will automatically sync each time they are connected by USB, and Wi-Fi in some cases, and they are recognized under the Devices section in the left frame of iTunes. The exception is when iTunes is set to prevent automatic synchronization. Figure 10.65 shows the dialog box from iTunes attained by clicking Edit ➢ Preferences ➢ Devices. (You might need to press the Alt key to get the Edit menu to appear.) Notice that syncing is set to occur automatically because the Prevent iPods, iPhones, And iPads From Syncing Automatically check box is cleared.

FIGURE 10.63   Enter email address and password

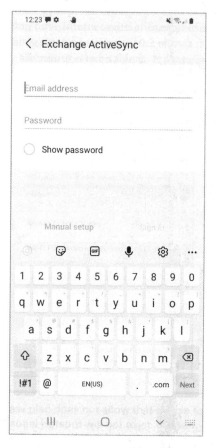

 The iTunes options shown in this section are for version 12.12. Different versions may have slightly different configurations or menus.

When synchronizing with a desktop, both the iOS device and the desktop authenticate each other. This two-way authentication, called *mutual authentication*, lets multiple services on the iOS device communicate with the appropriate services on the desktop.

The selection of what is to be synchronized is a task unto itself, but iTunes provides specific tabs on the left side of the interface for each class of data, as shown back in Figure 10.64, under the Settings section.

FIGURE 10.64 iTunes Summary page

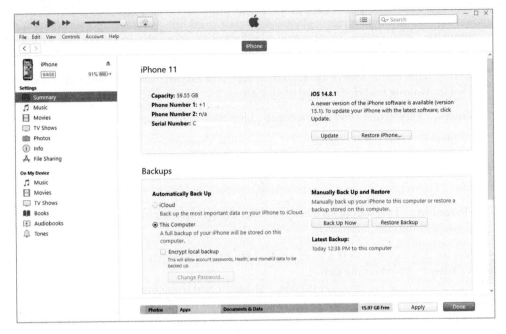

FIGURE 10.65 Devices Preferences in iTunes

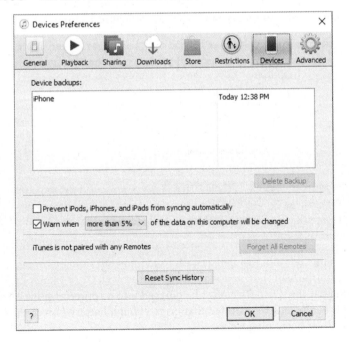

You can make very granular choices about what you want to sync. The following list gives the basic characteristics of each tab:

Summary   This setting contains general information about the device, backup settings, and general sync options.

Music   This setting shows music to be synced and playlist, artist, album, and genre sections for making selections in partial syncing.

Movies   This setting shows movies and video clips to be synced.

TV Shows   This setting displays TV shows to be synced.

Photos   This setting shows photos to be synced.

Info   This setting shows contacts, calendars, mail, and bookmarks to be synced.

File Sharing   This setting specifies apps that can transfer documents between the iPhone and the computer.

Below the Settings section is a section called On My Device that allows you to view what's currently stored on the device.

If the iOS device is running iOS version 5 or higher and the computer it syncs with is running iTunes version 10.5 or higher, you can sync your iOS device by using Wi-Fi. Besides these minimum version requirements, a few things have to come together before this will work. The following list outlines these requirements:

- You must enable Sync with this iPhone over Wi-Fi within iTunes. This is done from the Options section of the Summary tab, as shown in Figure 10.66.

FIGURE 10.66   Enabling sync over Wi-Fi

- Apple states that the iOS device must be plugged into a source of power before a sync will occur. It has been demonstrated that given enough battery power, the iOS device will sync without being plugged in.

- The iOS device should not be plugged into the USB port of the computer with which it syncs. USB synchronization overrides Wi-Fi synchronization.

- The iOS device and the computer with which it syncs must be on the same Wi-Fi network, which means that the SSID of the Wi-Fi network to which they are attached is the same and you are sure that the wireless network is not misconfigured to produce a false positive result, such as with two unconnected WAPs configured with the same SSID.

- The computer with which the iOS device syncs must have iTunes running. Otherwise, the Sync Now button on the iOS device will be dimmed. When in this state, however, once iTunes is opened and all other requirements are met, Wi-Fi sync will begin automatically, if not disabled in Devices Preferences.

You can tell when the device is syncing because the eject arrow to the right of the device name changes to the rotating sync icon, like the one in Figure 10.67. (Compare it to the eject icon to the right of the phone name back in Figure 10.64.) In Figure 10.67, you can also tell that this device is connected to the computer because the battery indicator is displayed. If it were syncing via Wi-Fi, the battery indicator would not be shown.

FIGURE 10.67   Device is syncing

If automatic synchronization is disabled in Devices Preferences, you can start the manual synchronization of an iOS device by selecting the iOS device above the left frame in iTunes and then clicking the Sync button at the bottom-right corner of its Summary tab.

Using iCloud

So far, we've talked about syncing with the desktop, but we haven't mentioned storing data on the cloud. Apple's version of the cloud is called iCloud, and it is available to all iOS users. This is the only real option for users who have ditched their desktops, and a convenient option for those who haven't.

When a user creates an Apple ID, it's used to log into the iTunes store, but it can also be used for an iCloud account. Apple recommends that the same username be used for both, but it is not required. On the iOS device, it's easy to get to iCloud settings. Open the Settings app, tap the Apple ID at the top of the page, and then choose iCloud. The configuration page is shown in Figure 10.68.

FIGURE 10.68 iCloud configuration settings

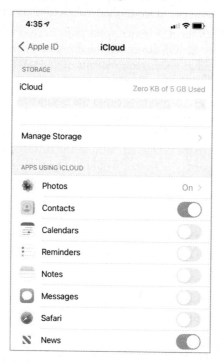

At the top of the iCloud settings, it will show you the space available for that Apple ID and which types of data you are syncing or backing up. Simply slide the switch from off to on to turn on synchronization or backups. The default amount of free storage space is 5 GB. Tapping Manage Storage will give you an option to purchase more space if needed, such as 50 GB, 200 GB, or 2 TB, and manage backups. Synchronization and backups will happen when the phone is plugged into a power source, locked, and connected to Wi-Fi.

Syncing Android Devices

Just as with Apple's devices, mobile devices built for the Android operating system can be synced to a traditional computer. Apple's iTunes is proprietary and has been designated as the application that performs synchronization of iOS devices. In a similar way, manufacturers of Android devices have their own syncing utilities. Because this software and the connection methods allowed vary widely from one manufacturer to another, it is difficult to predict exactly what one manufacturer will offer in its utility and whether each Android device it produces will interact the same way and over the same connections.

 Android devices often use Google Drive as the preferred cloud storage location. Manufacturers will have their own backup and sync tools, such as Samsung SideSync, LG PC Suite (also known as LG PC Sync), and HTC Sync Manager.

Let's use a Samsung phone as an example. If you want to configure backups using Google Drive, tap Settings ➤ Accounts And Backup ➤ Back Up Data (it's under Google Drive). You will see a screen like the one shown in Figure 10.69. In this instance, backup is enabled and the device is automatically backed up. To run a manual backup, tap the Back Up Now button.

FIGURE 10.69 Google Drive backup

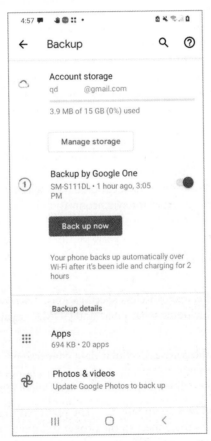

Common items available for synchronization include contacts, applications, email, pictures, music, videos, calendars, bookmarks, documents, location data, social media data, e-books, and passwords. Of course, specific options will depend on the software used.

 NOTE   For the exam, you will need to recognize data caps, understand Microsoft 365 and ActiveSync as they relate to synchronization, and know that two common types of data to sync are calendars and contacts.

Summary

This chapter introduced you to key features of mobile devices: network connectivity and synchronization. Establishing network connectivity means enabling cellular, Wi-Fi, or Bluetooth connections and configuring them properly.

Key cellular concepts to understand are hotspots and tethering, PRI/PRL/baseband, radio firmware, and IMEI/IMSI. When using Bluetooth, you need to pair the device with another Bluetooth device for connectivity.

Next, we covered mobile app support. A popular feature of mobile devices is location services, which can help locate you or your phone and give directions. We then moved into mobile device management and application management, including email configuration, two-factor authentication, and corporate applications.

Finally, we looked at synchronization. Synchronizing a mobile device to a desktop/laptop or the cloud is a good way to ensure that data is saved to a secure or permanent location. Types of data that are synchronized include contacts, applications, email, pictures, music, videos, calendars, bookmarks, documents, location data, social media data, e-books, and passwords. Common connection types for synchronization include Wi-Fi, USB, and cellular.

Exam Essentials

Understand the differences between wireless specifications.   Know basic differences between 2G, 3G, 4G, and 5G, including what GSM and CDMA are and why they weren't compatible.

Know how to enable or disable wireless/cellular data connections.   Wireless connections are individually disabled through the Settings app on most phones or through a quick access screen. Airplane mode disables all wireless signals on Android and all but Bluetooth on iOS.

Understand what PRL is and how to update it.   The preferred roaming list (PRL) is the reference guide the phone uses to connect to the proper cell phone tower when roaming. It's updated when you update a mobile OS. Depending on the OS and carrier, it may be updated manually.

Understand the steps needed to configure Bluetooth. You need to enable Bluetooth, enable pairing, find a device for pairing, enter the appropriate PIN code (or confirm the PIN), and test connectivity.

Know the differences between GPS and cellular location services. GPS is a free service provided by the government and uses satellites. Cellular location services use cell phone towers and require an account with a carrier.

Know the purposes of MDM and MAM. Mobile device management (MDM) is primarily used to determine which mobile devices are allowed on a network and to set policies for access. MDM also provides mechanisms for remotely locking and wiping devices. Mobile application management (MAM) is for managing corporate applications on mobile devices.

Know which protocols are used for email and which ports they use. POP3 (port 110) and IMAP (port 143) are used to receive email, and SMTP (port 25) is used to send email. None of these protocols are inherently secure. They can be secured with SSL or TLS. SMTP over SSL uses port 465, and SMTP over TLS uses port 587. IMAP over SSL/TLS uses port 993, and POP over SSL/TLS uses port 995.

Know what two-factor authentication is. Two-factor authentication requires an additional piece of information beyond the username and password for access to be granted. Often this is a PIN generated by a security token, but it can also be a one-time password or biometrics.

Be familiar with four commercial email providers and required configuration items. Common commercial email providers are iCloud, Google/Inbox, Exchange Online, and Yahoo Mail. Each provider has its own inbound and outbound servers, but most of the time that configuration information is automatically provided when you try to connect to them with an email client.

Know which types of data are often synchronized. Common data types for synchronization include contacts, applications, email, pictures, music, videos, calendars, bookmarks, documents, location data, social media data, e-books, and passwords.

Understand the differences between two Microsoft synchronization utilities. Microsoft 365 can sync Windows settings between two Windows devices. It can also sync files, but a SharePoint server is also required. ActiveSync is used by Exchange Server to sync email, contacts, calendars, and notes between a mobile device and an Exchange email server.

Review Questions

The answers to the chapter review questions can be found in Appendix A.

1. A friend asks you why she would ever disable cellular data networking. Which of the following is *not* a valid reason to disable cellular data networking?

   A. You have a limited amount of data in your monthly plan.

   B. You have access to a reliable Wi-Fi signal.

   C. You are about to download an update to your phone.

   D. Your phone calls are going out over your carrier's cellular network.

2. You need to pair two Bluetooth devices with each other. Which of the following is true regarding Bluetooth pairing?

   A. Bluetooth connections support wireless device control but not file transfers.

   B. Bluetooth is not yet a fully standardized protocol.

   C. Bluetooth connections do not reach as far as Wi-Fi connections.

   D. You must reboot the paired devices to complete the connection.

3. A technician is configuring a mobile client to use email through an ISP. Which port number should they configure to use SMTP?

   A. 25

   B. 110

   C. 143

   D. 995

4. You need to configure email for a mobile client. Their device has a setting referring to port 587. Which mail protocol is likely using this protocol?

   A. SMTP with SSL

   B. SMTP with TLS

   C. IMAP4 with SSL/TLS

   D. POP3 with SSL/TLS

5. You are enabling email on a mobile client. Which of the following is *not* a standard integrated commercial provider for email?

   A. iCloud

   B. Hotmail

   C. Yahoo Mail

   D. Exchange Online

6. If a user wanted to disable Location Services on an iPhone, where would they do that?

   A. Settings ➤ Location Services

   B. Settings ➤ Communications

   C. Settings ➤ Privacy

   D. Settings ➤ GPS

7. A mobile device is having intermittent communications issues. Which software component of a mobile phone is most likely responsible for these issues?

   A. Either iOS or Android OS

   B. SIM OS

   C. Baseband OS

   D. Wireless OS

8. An administrator needs to be able to control which apps are installed on the corporate network's mobile devices, and update or delete them and their data as necessary. Which type of service do they need?

   A. MAM

   B. MDM

   C. Location services

   D. Device synchronization

9. You need to synchronize Windows desktop settings between two laptop computers. Which service is designed to do this?

   A. Microsoft 365

   B. MAM

   C. MDM

   D. ActiveSync

10. You are pairing a Bluetooth headset to a mobile device. On the mobile device, after finding the device for pairing, what is the next step to take?

   A. Enable Bluetooth

   B. Test connectivity

   C. Enter the appropriate PIN code

   D. Enable pairing

11. Which of the following are universally common items that are synced between a mobile device and a larger computer? (Choose all that apply.)

   A. Office documents

   B. Contacts

   C. Operating system files

   D. Calendar

   E. Configuration settings

   F. Apps

12. Which of the following location services typically provides the best accuracy when detecting a user's location?

   A. Cellular

   B. GPS

   C. MAM

   D. MDM

13. Which of the following statements about configuring email access on a mobile device is true?

   A. Most Internet mail services offer an Exchange option.

   B. The TCP ports used for configuring access are usually standard port numbers.

   C. Most ports used for access are UDP ports.

   D. You must download third-party apps for connecting to email services.

14. Which of the following are disabled on an Android device when airplane mode is switched on? (Choose all that apply.)

   A. Cellular

   B. Wi-Fi

   C. Bluetooth

   D. Settings app

   E. Lock screen

15. You need to enable clients to synchronize their mobile devices to their laptops. Which of the following are common connection types to enable laptop synchronization? (Choose all that apply.)

   A. Cellular

   B. Bluetooth

   C. Wi-Fi

   D. USB

   E. Tethering

16. You connect two Bluetooth devices together that have been previously connected. What is the process called that each device uses to verify the other's identity?

   A. MAM

   B. Synchronization

   C. Mutual authentication

   D. Pairing

17. Which of the following most accurately describes what a PRL is?

   A. The list of cell phone towers a mobile device should connect with while roaming

   B. The description of the user and mobile network

   C. The mobile carrier code

   D. The configuration settings of the network the mobile device is on

18. A network administrator wants to be able to remotely wipe everything off of corporate smartphones if they are lost or stolen. What type of service do they need?

    A. MAM

    B. MDM

    C. Two-factor authentication

    D. Location services

19. A user needs to synchronize their iPhone to another platform. Which two options are the default ones for them to choose? (Choose two.)

    A. Google Drive

    B. SharePoint

    C. iCloud

    D. iTunes

20. A mobile user is having cellular connectivity problems when roaming but not when near their home. They are told by their carrier that they need to update their settings. Which of the following settings do they most likely need to update?

    A. PRI

    B. PRL

    C. Baseband

    D. IMEI

Performance-Based Question

You will encounter performance-based questions on the A+ exams. The questions on the exam require you to perform a specific task, and you will be graded on whether or not you were able to complete the task. The following requires you to think creatively in order to measure how well you understand this chapter's topics. You may or may not see similar questions on the actual A+ exams. To see how your answers compare to the authors', refer to Appendix B.

Explain how to establish Wi-Fi connectivity on an Apple iPhone.

Chapter 11

Troubleshooting Methodology and Resolving Core Hardware Problems

THE FOLLOWING COMPTIA A+ 220-1101 EXAM OBJECTIVES ARE COVERED IN THIS CHAPTER:

✓ **5.1 Given a scenario, apply the best practice methodology to resolve problems.**

- Always consider corporate policies, procedures, and impacts before implementing changes

- 1. Identify the problem

  - Gather information from the user, identify user changes, and, if applicable, perform backups before making changes

  - Inquire regarding environmental or infrastructure changes

- 2. Establish a theory of probable cause (question the obvious)

  - If necessary, conduct external or internal research based on symptoms

- 3. Test the theory to determine the cause

  - Once the theory is confirmed, determine the next steps to resolve the problem

  - If the theory is not confirmed, re-establish a new theory or escalate

- 4. Establish a plan of action to resolve the problem and implement the solution

  - Refer to the vendor's instructions for guidance

- 5. Verify full system functionality and, if applicable, implement preventive measures
- 6. Document the findings, actions, and outcomes

✓ **5.2 Given a scenario, troubleshoot problems related to motherboards, RAM, CPU, and power.**

- Common symptoms
  - Power-on self-test (POST) beeps
  - Proprietary crash screens (blue screen of death [BSOD]/pinwheel)
  - Black screen
  - No power
  - Sluggish performance
  - Overheating
  - Burning smell
  - Intermittent shutdown
  - Application crashes
  - Grinding noise
  - Capacitor swelling
  - Inaccurate system date/time

Mentioning the words *troubleshooting theory* to many technicians can cause their eyes to roll back in their heads. It doesn't sound glamorous or sexy, and a lot of techs believe that the only way to solve a problem is just to dive right in and start working on it. Theories are for academics. In a way, they're right—you do need to dive in to solve problems because they don't just solve themselves. But to be successful at troubleshooting, you must take a systematic approach.

You may hear people say, "Troubleshooting is as much of an art as it is a science," and our personal favorite, "You just need to get more experience to be good at it." While there is an art to fixing problems, you can't ignore science. And if you need experience to be any good, why are some less experienced folks incredibly good at solving problems while their more seasoned counterparts seem to take forever to fix anything? More experience is good, but it's not a prerequisite to being a good troubleshooter. Again, it's all about applying a systematic approach.

There's one more detail to understand before getting into the details of specific problems: in order to troubleshoot anything, you need to have a base level of knowledge. For example, if you've never opened the hood of a car, it will be a bit challenging for you to figure out why your car won't start in the morning. If you're not a medical professional, you might not know why that body part hurts or how to make it feel better. In the same vein, if you don't know how data is stored and accessed on a computer, it's unlikely that you'll be able to fix related computer problems. So before you get too heavy into troubleshooting, make sure you understand how the systems on which you are working are supposed to function in the first place.

Because this chapter comes after the hardware and networking chapters, we're going to assume that you've read them already. Therefore, we're not going to get into a lot of detail about how things work—it's assumed that you know those details by now. (If you're still not certain, this book is a great reference manual!) Instead, we'll talk more about what happens when things don't work the way they're supposed to: what signs to look for and what to do to fix the problem.

After discussing the theory, this chapter covers troubleshooting core hardware components, including motherboards, RAM, CPUs, and power. The remainder of the Hardware and Network Troubleshooting objective is covered in Chapter 12, "Hardware and Network Troubleshooting."

Using the Troubleshooting Best Practice Methodology

No matter how skilled you may be at troubleshooting, always consider corporate policies, procedures, and impacts before implementing any changes. Don't perform any actions that would get you or the users into trouble, or that would otherwise cause harm to the company.

When troubleshooting, you should assess every problem systematically and try to isolate the root cause. Yes, there is a lot of art to troubleshooting, and experience plays a part too. But regardless of how "artful" or experienced you are, haphazard troubleshooting is doomed to fail. Conversely, even technicians with limited experience can be effective troubleshooters if they stick to the principles. The major key is to start with the issue and whittle away at it until you can narrow it down and pinpoint the problem. This often means eliminating, or verifying, the obvious.

Although everyone approaches troubleshooting from a different perspective, a few things should remain constant:

Creating a Backup   First, always back up the data before making major changes to a system. Hardware components can be replaced, but data often can't be. For that reason, always be vigilant about making data backups. Be sure to validate your backups by performing a test restore after you set them up. The only thing worse than not having a backup is thinking you have a backup only for it to fail.

Prioritizing Tasks   Second, establish priorities—one user being unable to print to the printer of their choice isn't as important as a floor full of accountants unable to run payroll. Prioritize every job and escalate it (or de-escalate it) as you need to.

Documenting Your Process   Third, but perhaps most important, document everything—not just that there was a problem but also the solution that you found, the actions that you tried, and the outcome of each.

In the next few sections, we'll take you through each step of the troubleshooting process.

Step 1: Identify the Problem

There's a famous quote attributed to Albert Einstein that states, "If I had an hour to solve a problem, I'd spend 55 minutes on the problem and 5 minutes on the solution." Whether or not he said that may be debatable, but the premise behind the quote is spot on because while this may seem obvious, it can't be overlooked: if you can't define the problem, you can't begin to solve it. This is true not only with computers but with every facet of life!

Sometimes, problems are relatively straightforward, but other times they're just a symptom of a bigger issue. For example, if a user isn't able to connect to the Internet from their computer, it could indeed be an issue with their system. But if other users are having similar problems, then the first user's difficulties might just be one example of the real problem.

 Ask yourself, "Is there a problem?" Perhaps "the problem" is as simple as a customer expecting too much from the computer or not understanding how it's supposed to work.

Problems in computer systems generally occur in one (or more) of four areas, each of which is in turn made up of many pieces:

- A *collection of hardware pieces* integrated into a working system. As you know, hardware can be quite complex, what with motherboards, hard drives, video cards, and other components. The good news is that most hardware devices are dedicated to performing a single task, so at times troubleshooting it can be easy. Other hardware issues are more complex. For example, to get on a wired network, the computer needs a NIC and a cable, and there's the hardware at the other end too.

- An *operating system*, which in turn is dependent on the hardware. Operating systems contain several major, often interdependent modules. OS issues can masquerade as hardware issues, and vice versa.

- An *application or software program* that is supposed to do something. Programs such as Microsoft Word and Microsoft Excel are bundled with a great many features. Software issues can be quite perplexing. They may be as simple as a problem with a specific app but can also be related to the OS or even the hardware.

- A *computer user*, ready to take the computer system to its limits (and beyond). A technician can often forget that the user is a very complex and important part of the puzzle.

Talking to the Customer or User

Many times, you can define the problem by asking questions of the user. One of the keys to working with your users or customers is to ensure, much like a medical professional, that you have a good bedside manner. Most people are not as technically savvy as you, and when something goes wrong, they become confused or even fearful that they'll take the blame. Assure them that you're just trying to fix the problem but that they can probably help because they know what went on before you got there. It's important to instill trust with your customer—believe what they are saying, but also believe that they might not tell you everything right away. It's not that they're necessarily holding back information; they just might not know what's important to tell.

⊕ **Real World Scenario**

Is the Power On?

It's a classic IT story that almost sounds like a joke, but it happened. A customer calls technical support because their computer won't turn on. After 20 minutes of trouble-shooting, the technician is becoming frustrated. . .maybe it's a bad power supply? The technician asks the user to read some numbers off the back of their computer, and the user says, "Hold on, I need to get a flashlight. It's dark in here with the power out."

Help clarify things by having the customer show you what the problem is. The best method we've seen of doing this is to say, "Show me what 'not working' looks like." That way, you see the conditions and methods under which the problem occurs. The problem may be a simple matter of an improper method. The user may be performing an operation incorrectly or performing the operation in the wrong order. During this step, you have the opportunity to observe how the problem occurs, so pay attention.

Here are a few questions to ask the user to aid in determining the problem:

Can you show me the problem?   This question is one of the best. It allows the user to show you exactly where and when they experience the problem.

How often does this happen?   This question establishes whether this problem is a one-time occurrence that can be solved with a reboot or whether a specific sequence of events causes the problem to happen. The latter usually indicates a more serious problem that may require software installation or hardware replacement.

Has any new hardware or software been installed recently?   Infrastructure changes can cause problems. For example, new hardware or software can mean compatibility problems with existing devices or applications. A newly installed device may want to use the same resource settings as an existing device. This can cause both devices to become disabled. When you install a new application, that application is likely to install several support files. If those support files are also used by an existing application, then there could be a conflict.

Has the computer recently been moved?   Environmental changes can also have an impact. Moving a computer can cause things to become loose and then fail to work. Perhaps all the peripherals of the computer didn't complete—or weren't included in—the move, meaning that there's less functionality than the user expects.

Has someone who normally doesn't use the computer recently used it?   That person could have mistakenly (or intentionally) done something to make the computer begin exhibiting the irregular behavior.

Have any other changes been made to the computer recently?   If the answer is yes, ask if the user can remember approximately when the change was made. Then ask them to tell you approximately when the problem started. If the two happened closely together, there's a good chance that the problem is related to the change. If it's a new hardware component, check to see that it was installed correctly.

Be careful of how you ask questions so that you don't appear accusatory. You can't assume that the user did something to mess up the computer. Then again, you also can't assume that they don't know anything about why it's not working.

 Real World Scenario

The Social Side of Troubleshooting

When you're looking for clues as to the nature of a problem, no one can give you more information than the person who was there when it happened. They can tell you what led up to the problem, what software was running, and the exact nature of the problem ("It happened when I tried to print"), and they can help you re-create the problem, if possible.

Use questioning techniques that are neutral in nature. Instead of saying, "What were you doing when it broke?" be more compassionate and say, "What was going on when the computer decided not to work?" Frame the question in a way that makes it sound like the computer did something wrong, not the person. It might sound silly, but these things can make your job a lot easier.

Although it's sometimes frustrating dealing with end users and computer problems, such as the user who calls you up and gives you the "My computer's not working" line (okay, and what *exactly* is that supposed to mean?), even more frustrating is when no one was around to see what happened. In cases like this, do your best to find out where the problem is by establishing what works and what does not.

Gathering Information

Let's say that you get to a computer and the power light is on and you can hear the power supply fan whirring but there is no video and the system seems to be unresponsive. At least you know that the system has power, and you can start investigating where things start to break down. (We sense a reboot in your future!)

The whole key to this step is to identify, as specifically as possible, what the problem is. The more specific you can be in identifying what's not working, the easier it will be for you to understand why it's not working and how to fix it. If you have users available who were there when the computer stopped working, you can try to gather information from them. If not, you're on your own to gather clues. It's like *CSI* but not as gory.

So now instead of having users to question, you need to use your own investigative services to determine what's wrong. The questions you would have otherwise asked the user are still a good starting point. Does anything appear amiss or seem to have been changed recently? What is working and what is not? Was there a storm recently? Can I reboot? If I reboot, does the problem seem to go away? Is there any information in system or application logs that provides clues?

If a computer seems to have multiple problems that appear to be unrelated, identify what they are one at a time and fix them one at a time. For example, if the sound is not working and you can't get on the Internet, deal with those separately. If they seem related, such as not being able to get on the Internet or access a network file server, then one solution might solve both problems.

The key is to find out everything that you can that might be related to the problem. Document exactly what works and what doesn't and, if you can, why. If the power is out in the house, as in the story related earlier, then there's no sense in trying the power cord in another outlet.

Determining if the Problem Is Hardware- or Software-Related

This is important because it determines the part of the computer on which you should focus your troubleshooting skills. Each part requires different skills and different tools.

To determine whether a problem is hardware- or software-related, you can do a few things to narrow down the issue. For instance, does the problem manifest itself when the user uses a particular piece of hardware (an external optical drive or a USB hard drive, for example)? If it does, the problem is more than likely hardware-related.

Determining if the issue is hardware- or software-related relies on personal experience more than any of the other troubleshooting steps. Without a doubt, you'll run into strange software problems. Each one has a particular solution. Some may even require reinstallation of an application or the operating system. If that doesn't work, you may need to resort to restoring the entire system (operating system, applications, and data) from a data backup done when the computer was working properly.

Determining Which Component Is Failing (for Hardware Problems)

Hardware problems are usually pretty easy to figure out. Let's say that the sound card doesn't work. You've tried new speakers that you know do work, and you've reinstalled the driver. All the settings look right, but the sound card just won't respond. The sound card is probably the piece of hardware that needs to be replaced.

With many newer computers, several components such as sound, video, and networking cards are integrated into the motherboard. If you troubleshoot the computer and find a hardware component to be bad, there's a good chance that the bad component is integrated into the motherboard and the whole motherboard must be replaced—an expensive proposition, to be sure.

Laptops and a lot of desktops have components (network card, sound card, video adapter) integrated into the motherboard. If an integrated component fails, you may be able to use an expansion device (such as a USB network adapter) to give the system full functionality without a costly repair.

Identifying the Issue at Hand

To summarize, step 1 of the best practice methodology is to identify the problem. This includes the following steps:

- Gather information from the user, identify user changes, and, if applicable, perform backups before making changes.

- Inquire regarding environmental or infrastructure changes.

We feel that making backups isn't an appropriate step at this point—identifying the problem is all about asking questions and gathering information—but understand that this is where CompTIA places it in the exam objectives. In real life, yes, you want to make backups, but you do so before implementing changes that could impact data.

Step 2: Establish a Theory

In your middle school or junior high school years, you probably learned about the scientific method. In a nutshell, scientists develop a hypothesis, test it, and then figure out if their hypothesis is still valid. Troubleshooting involves much the same process.

Once you have determined what the problem is, you need to develop a theory as to why it is happening. First question the obvious. Forgetting to check the obvious things can result in a long and unnecessary troubleshooting process. No video? It could be something to do with the monitor or the video card. Can't get to your favorite website? Is it that site? Is it your network card, the cable, your IP address, DNS server settings, or something else? Once you have defined the problem, establishing a theory about the cause of the problem—what is wrong—helps you develop possible solutions to the problem.

Eliminating Possibilities

Theories can state either what can be true or what can't be true. However you choose to approach your theory generation, it's usually helpful to take a mental inventory to see what is possible and what is not. Start eliminating possibilities, and eventually the only thing that's left is what's wrong. This type of approach works well when it's an ambiguous problem; start broad and narrow your scope. For example, if data on the hard drive is inaccessible, there is likely one of three culprits: the drive itself, the cable it's on (if applicable), or the connector on the motherboard. Try plugging the drive into another connector or using a different cable. Narrow down the options.

 A common troubleshooting technique is to strip the system down to the bare bones. In a hardware situation, this could mean removing all interface cards except those that are absolutely required for the system to operate. In a software situation, this usually means booting up in Windows Safe Mode so that most of the drivers do not load.

Once you have isolated the problem, slowly rebuild the system to see if the problem comes back (or goes away). This helps you identify what is really causing the problem and determine if there are other factors affecting the situation. For example, we have seen memory problems that are fixed by moving the memory modules from one slot to another.

Using External and Internal Resources

Sometimes, you can figure out what's not working, but you have no idea why or what you can do to fix it. That's okay. In situations like these, it may be best to fall back on an old trick called reading the manual. As they say, "When all else fails, read the instructions." The service manuals are your instructions for troubleshooting and service information. Virtually every computer and peripheral made today has service documentation on the company's website. Don't be afraid to use it!

 Before starting to eliminate possibilities, check the vendor's website for any information that might help you. For example, typing in a specific error message on a vendor's website or a search engine might take you directly to specific steps to fix the problem.

If you're fortunate enough to have experienced, knowledgeable, and friendly coworkers, be open to asking for help if you get stuck on a problem. Trading knowledge between coworkers not only builds the skill level of the team, but can also build camaraderie.

 Step 2 of the best practice methodology is to establish a theory of probable cause (question the obvious). This includes conducting external or internal research based on symptoms, if necessary.

Step 3: Test the Theory

You've eliminated possibilities and developed a theory as to what the problem is. Your theory may be specific, such as "the power cable is fried," or it may be a bit more general, like "we can't access the hard drive" or "there's a connectivity problem." No matter your theory, now is the time to start testing it. Again, if you're not sure where to begin to find a solution, the manufacturer's website is a good place to start!

Check the Simple Stuff First

This step is the one that even experienced technicians overlook. Often, computer problems are the result of something simple. Technicians overlook these problems because they're so simple that the technicians assume they *couldn't* be the problem. Here are some simple questions to ask:

Will restarting the computer help?   It's amazing how often a simple computer restart can solve a problem. Restarting the computer clears the memory and starts the computer with a clean slate. Whenever we perform phone support, we always ask the customer to restart the computer and try again. If restarting doesn't work, try powering down the system completely and then powering it up again (rebooting). More often than not, that will solve the problem.

Are the cables plugged in?   And plugged in at both ends? Cables must be plugged in at *both ends* to function correctly. Cables can easily be tripped over and inadvertently pulled from their sockets.

Are the computer and peripherals turned on?   This one seems the most obvious, but we've all fallen victim to it at one point or another. Computers and their peripherals must be turned on to function. Most have power switches with LEDs that glow when the power is turned on.

Is the system ready?   Computers must be ready before they can be used. *Ready* means that the system is ready to accept commands from the user. An indication that a computer is ready is when the operating system screens come up and the computer presents you with a menu or a command prompt. If that computer uses a graphical interface, the computer is ready when the mouse pointer appears. Printers are ready when the Online or Ready light on the front panel is lit.

Do the chips and cables need to be reseated?   You can solve some of the strangest problems (random hang-ups or errors) by opening the case and pressing down on each socketed chip, known as *reseating*. (Of course, make sure the system is off and the components have had a bit of time to cool down first.) This remedies the chip-creep problem, which happens when computers heat up and cool down repeatedly as a result of being turned on and off, causing some components to begin to move out of their sockets. In addition, you should reseat any cables to make sure that they're making good contact.

Always be sure that you're grounded before operating inside the case. If you're not, you could create an electrostatic discharge (ESD) that could damage components. For more information on mitigating ESD, see Chapter 21, "Safety and Environmental Concerns."

Is the problem user error?   User error is common but preventable. If a user can't perform a common computer task, such as printing or saving a file, the problem is likely due to user error. As soon as you hear of a problem like this, you should begin asking questions to determine if the solution is as simple as teaching the user the correct procedure. A good question to ask is, "Were you *ever* able to perform that task?" If the answer is no, it means that they are probably doing the procedure wrong. If they answer yes, then you must ask additional questions to get at the root of the problem.

If you suspect user error, tread carefully in regard to your line of questioning, to avoid making the user feel defensive. User errors provide an opportunity to teach the users the right way to do things. Again, what you say matters. Offer a "different" or "another" way of doing things instead of the "right" way.

 Real World Scenario

"Is It Plugged in?" and Other Insulting Questions

Think about how you would feel if someone were to ask you this question. Your likely response would be, "Of course, it is!" After all, you're not an idiot, right? You'll often get the same reaction to similar questions about the device being turned on. The problem is, making sure that it's plugged in and turned on are the first things that you should always do when investigating a problem.

When asking these types of questions, it's not what you say but how you say it. For example, instead of asking if it's plugged in, you could say something like, "Can you do me a favor and check to see that the cable is plugged in tightly? Maybe it got bumped." That generally gets the user at least to look at it without making them feel dumb. For power, something like, "What color are the lights on the front of the router? Are any of them blinking?" can work well.

Remember to ask neutral and nonthreatening questions. Make it sound like the computer is at fault, not the user. These types of things will help you build rapport and you'll be able to get more information so that you can solve problems faster.

Next Steps

After you test the theory to determine the cause, one of two things will happen. Either the theory will be confirmed or it won't be. Said differently, you were right or wrong. There's nothing wrong with having an initial theory turn out to be incorrect—it just means going back to the drawing board and looking for another explanation. More explicitly, here's what to do next:

- If the theory is confirmed, determine the next steps to resolve the problem. (This is covered in the "Establish a Plan of Action" section, next.)
- If the theory is not confirmed, reestablish a new theory or escalate the problem.

As we just said, it's okay to be wrong with your first guess on the cause of the problem. We can't count the number of times we've said, "Huh, maybe that wasn't the problem—weird," or some variation thereof. It happens—some problems are very complicated. Focus on isolating the issue to narrow down the possible culprits, and double-check manuals or online resources if needed.

If you've tried everything you can think of, or perhaps are in a tense situation that's time-sensitive and you feel in over your head, don't be afraid to escalate the problem. Asking for help can be hard, because sometimes it feels like you've failed in some way. Don't feel bad about it—sometimes getting a second opinion makes all the difference.

Testing Your Theory

Step 3 of the best practice methodology is test the theory to determine the cause of the problem. This includes:

- Once the theory is confirmed, determine the next steps to resolve the problem.
- If the theory is not confirmed, re-establish a new theory or escalate the problem.

Step 4: Establish a Plan of Action

If your theory was right and the fix worked, then you're brilliant! If not, you need to look for the next option. After testing the theory, establish a plan of action to resolve the problem and implement the solution. This may take one of the following three paths:

- Verify full system functionality.
- If the first fix didn't work, try something else.
- If needed, implement the fix on other computers.

Reboot First, Ask Questions Later

If you're running into a software problem on a computer, the first step (after understanding what the problem is and writing down any relevant error messages or capturing them in a screen grab) should always be to reboot. Many times, the problem will go away, and your work there is done.

If the solution worked, and there are no other affected computers, verify full system functionality. We'll discuss that after we talk about what to do if the first fix didn't work, or you need to apply the fix to multiple systems.

Try, Try Again

So you tried the hard drive with a new (verified) cable and it still doesn't work. Now what? Your sound card won't play and you've just removed and reinstalled the driver. Next steps? Move on and try the next logical thing in line.

> When trying solutions to fix a problem, make only one change to the computer at a time. If the change doesn't fix the problem, revert the system back to the way it was and then make your next change. Making more than one change at a time is not recommended for two reasons: one, you are never sure which change actually worked, and two, by making multiple changes at once, you might accidentally cause additional problems.

When evaluating your results and looking for that golden "next step," don't forget about other resources that you might have available. Use the Internet to look at the manufacturer's website. The vendor's instructions could prove invaluable. Read the manual. Talk to your friend who knows everything about obscure hardware (or arcane versions of Windows). When fixing problems, two heads can be better than one.

Spread the Solution

If the problem was isolated to one computer, this step doesn't apply. But some problems that you deal with may affect an entire group of computers. For example, perhaps some configuration information was entered incorrectly into the DHCP server, giving everyone the wrong DNS server address. The DHCP server is now fixed, but all the clients need to renew their IP addresses. Or, maybe a software update that was pushed to all client computers messed up a configuration, and you happened to be first on the scene. Now it's time to resolve it for all computers that are affected.

> Step 4 of the best practice methodology is to establish a plan of action to resolve the problem and implement the solution. This includes referring to the vendor's instructions for guidance.

Step 5: Verify Functionality

After fixing the system, or all the systems affected by the problem, go back and verify full functionality. For example, if the users couldn't get to any network resources, check to make sure they can get to the Internet as well as to internal resources.

Some solutions may accidentally cause another problem on the system. For example, if you update software or drivers, you may inadvertently cause another application to have problems. There's obviously no way that you can or should test all applications on a computer after applying a fix, but know that these types of problems can occur. Just make sure that what you've fixed works and that there aren't any obvious signs of something else not working all of a sudden.

Another important thing to do at this time is to implement preventive measures, if possible. If it was a user error, ensure that the user understands ways to accomplish the task that won't cause the error to recur. If a cable melted because it was too close to a space heater under someone's desk, resolve the issue. If the computer overheated because an inch of dust was clogging the fan. . .you get the idea.

 Step 5 of the best practice methodology is to verify full system functionality and, if applicable, implement preventive measures.

Step 6: Document Findings

A lot of people can fix problems. But can you remember what you did when you fixed a problem a month ago? Maybe. Can one of your coworkers remember something you did to fix the same problem on that machine a month ago? Unlikely. Always document your work so that you or someone else can learn from the experience. Good documentation of past troubleshooting can save hours of stress in the future.

Documentation can take a few different forms, but the two most common are personal and system-based.

We always recommend that technicians carry a personal notebook and take notes during the troubleshooting process. Some problems are long and complex, and it may be hard to remember which setting you changed 15 steps ago. The type of notebook doesn't matter—it can be digital or paper, big or small—use whatever works best for you. Take pictures with your phone if it will be helpful (if it's allowed). The notebook can be a lifesaver, especially when you're new to a job. Write down the problem, what you tried, and the solution. The next time you run across the same or a similar problem, you'll have a better idea of what to try. Eventually, you'll find yourself less and less reliant on your notebook, but it's incredibly handy to have.

System-based documentation is useful to both you and your coworkers. Many facilities have server logs of one type or another, conveniently located close to the machine. If someone makes a fix or a change, it gets noted in the log. If there's a problem, it's noted in the log. It's critical to have a log for a couple of reasons:

- If you weren't there the first time the problem was fixed, you might not have an idea of what to try, and it could take you a long time using trial and error.

- If you begin to see a repeated pattern of problems, you can make a permanent intervention before the system completely dies.

We've seen several different forms of system-based documentation. Again, the type of log doesn't matter as long as you use it. Often, it's a notebook or a binder next to the system or on a nearby shelf. If you have a rack, you can mount something on the side to hold a binder or notebook. For desktop computers, one way is to tape an index card to the top or side of the power supply (don't cover any vents), so if a tech has to go inside the case, they can see if anyone else has been in there fixing something too. Companywide electronic knowledge bases or incident repositories are also commonly used. It is just as important to contribute to these systems as to use them to help diagnose problems.

The sixth and final step of the best practice methodology—don't ever skip it—is to document findings, actions, and outcomes. Be sure you know all six steps in order!

Troubleshooting Motherboards, CPUs, RAM, and Power Problems

To many who are not familiar with computers, that whirring, humming box sitting on or under their desk is an enigma. They know what shows up on the screen, where the power button is, where to put a thumb drive, and what not to spill on their keyboard, but the insides are shrouded in mystery.

Fortunately for them, we're around. We can tell the difference between a hard drive and a motherboard and have a pretty good idea of what each part inside that box is supposed to do. When the computer doesn't work like it's supposed to, we can whip out our trusty screwdriver, crack the case, and perform surgery. And most of the time, we can get the system running just as good as new.

In the following sections, we're going to focus our troubleshooting efforts on the three key hardware components inside the case: motherboards, RAM, and CPUs, as well as power issues. These four components are absolutely critical to a computer system. Without a network card, you won't be able to surf the web. Without a processor, well, you won't be able to surf the web—or do much of anything else for that matter. So it makes sense to get started with motherboards, CPUs, RAM, and power.

Problems with these separate components can often present similar symptoms, so it's good to discuss them all at the same time. We will look at common symptoms for other hardware devices in Chapter 12.

As you continue to learn and increase your troubleshooting experience, your value will increase as well. This is because, if nothing else, it will take you less time to accomplish common repairs. Your ability to troubleshoot from past experiences and gut feelings will make you more efficient and more valuable, which in turn will allow you to advance and earn a better income. We will give you some guidelines that you can use to evaluate common hardware issues that you're sure to face.

The following sections focus primarily on desktop computers. Mobile device and laptop-specific issues are covered in Chapter 12.

Identifying General Hardware Symptoms and Causes

Before we get into specific components, let's take a few minutes to talk about hardware symptoms and their causes at a general level. This discussion can apply to a lot of different hardware components.

Some hardware issues are pretty easy to identify. If flames are shooting out of the back of your computer, then it's probably the power supply. If the power light on your monitor doesn't turn on, it's the monitor itself, the power cord, or your power source. Other hardware symptoms are a bit more ambiguous. We'll now look at some general hardware-related symptoms and their possible causes.

Grinding and Other Random Noises

Have you ever been working on a computer and heard a noise that resembles fingernails on a chalkboard? If so, you will always remember that sound, along with the impending feeling of doom as the computer stops working.

Some noises on a computer are normal. The POST beep (which we'll talk about in a few pages) is a good sound. The whirring of a mechanical hard drive and power supply fan are familiar sounds. Some techs get so used to their "normal" system noises that if anything is slightly off pitch, they go digging for problems even if none are readily apparent.

A simple rule to remember about *grinding noise* and other random noises is this: for it to make a noise, it has to move. In other words, components with no moving parts (such as RAM, SSDs and CPUs) don't make sounds. Mechanical hard drives have motors that spin the platters. Power supply fans spin. Optical drives spin the discs. If you're hearing a grinding, whirring, scraping, or other noise that you didn't expect, these are the likely culprits.

 Grinding noise is a specific symptom called out in the A+ exam objectives.

If you hear a whining sound and it seems to be fairly constant, it's more than likely a fan. Either it needs to be cleaned (desperately) or replaced. Power supplies that are failing can also sound louder and quieter intermittently because a fan will run at alternating speeds.

The "fingernails on a chalkboard" squealing could be an indicator that the heads in a mechanical hard drive have crashed into the platter. Thankfully, this isn't very common today, but it still happens. (Future generations of technicians will never know this sound, with the prevalence of SSDs today!) Note that this type of sound can also be caused by a power supply fan's motor binding up. A rhythmic ticking sound is also likely to be caused by a mechanical hard drive.

Problems with optical drives tend to be the easiest to diagnose. Those drives aren't constantly spinning unless you put some media in them. If you put a disc in and the drive makes a terrible noise, you have a good idea what's causing the problem.

So what do you do if you hear a terrible noise from the computer? If it's still responsive, shut it down normally as soon as possible. If it's not responsive, then shut off the power as quickly as you can. Examine the power supply to see if there are any obvious problems such as excessive dust, and clean it as needed. Power the system back on. If the noise was caused by the hard drive, odds are that the drive has failed and the system won't boot normally. You may need to replace some parts.

If the noise is mildly annoying but doesn't sound drastic, boot up the computer with the case off and listen. By getting up close and personal with the system, you can often tell where the noise is coming from and then troubleshoot or fix the appropriate part.

Never touch internal components when the case is off and the power is on! Doing so could result in a severe electrical shock to you and/or the components.

Excessive Heat

Electronic components produce heat; it's a fact of life. While they're designed to withstand a certain amount of the heat that's produced, excessive heat can cause overheating and drastically shorten the life of components. There are two common ways to reduce heat-related problems in computers: heat sinks and cooling systems, such as case fans.

Any component with its own processor will have a heat sink. Typically these look like big, finned hunks of aluminum or another metal attached to the processor. Their job is to dissipate heat from the component so that it doesn't become too hot. Never run a processor without a heat sink! Nearly all video cards built today have GPUs with heat sinks as well.

Overclocking—running the processor faster than it was designed to run—causes the CPU to produce more heat. In many cases, this voids the manufacturer's warranty and can shorten the life of the CPU. While it may be exciting to run the system at a faster speed, overclock with caution!

Case fans are designed to take hot air from inside the case and blow it out of the case. There are many different designs, from simple motors to high-tech liquid-cooled models. Put your hand up to the back of your computer at the power supply fan and you should feel warm air. If there's nothing coming out, you either need to clean your fan out or replace your power supply. Some cases come with additional cooling fans to help dissipate heat. If your case has one, you should feel warm air coming from it as well.

Computers are like human beings: they have similar tolerances to heat and cold. In general, anything comfortable to us is comfortable to computers, although they do tend to like it colder than many of us do. They need a lot of clean, moving air in order to keep functioning.

Dust, dirt, grime, smoke, and other airborne particles can become caked on the inside of computers and cause overheating as well. This is most common in automotive and manufacturing environments. The contaminants create a film that coats the components, causing them to overheat and/or conduct electricity on their surface. Blowing out these exposed systems with a can of compressed air from time to time can prevent damage to the components. While you're cleaning the components, be sure to clean any cooling fans in the power supply or on the heat sink.

To clean the power supply fan, blow the air from the inside of the case. When you do this, the fan will blow the contaminants out the cooling vents. If you spray from the vents toward the inside of the box, you'll be blowing the dust and grime inside the case or back into the fan motor.

One way to ensure that dust and grime don't find their way into a desktop computer is to always leave the *blanks* (or slot covers) in the empty slots on the back of the case. Blanks are the pieces of metal or plastic that come with the case and cover the expansion slot openings. They are designed to keep dirt, dust, and other foreign matter from the inside of the computer. They also maintain proper airflow within the case to ensure that the computer doesn't overheat.

 Real World Scenario

Creeping Chips

The inside of a computer is a harsh environment; the temperature inside the case of many computers is well over 100° F! When you turn on your computer, it heats up. Turn it off, and it cools down. After several hundred such cycles, some components can't handle the stress, and they begin to move out of their sockets. This phenomenon is known as *chip creep*, and it can be really frustrating.

Chip creep can affect any socketed device, including integrated circuits (ICs), RAM chips, and expansion cards. The solution to chip creep is simple: open the case and reseat the devices. It's surprising how often this is the solution to phantom problems of all sorts, particularly intermittent device failures, random reboots, and unexpected shutdowns.

Components that overheat a lot will have shorter lifespans. Sometimes they simply fail. Other times, they will cause *intermittent shutdowns* before they fail. A PC that works for a few minutes and then locks up is probably experiencing *overheating* because of a heat sink or fan not functioning properly. To troubleshoot overheating, first check all fans inside the PC to ensure that they're operating, and make sure that any heat sinks are firmly attached to their chips.

Overheating and intermittent shutdowns are specific symptoms called out in the A+ exam objectives.

In a properly designed, properly assembled PC case, air flows in a specific path driven by the power supply fan and using the power supply's vent holes. Make sure that you know the direction of flow and that there are limited obstructions and no dust buildup. Cases are also designed to cool by making the air flow in a certain way. Therefore, operating a PC with the cover removed can make a PC more susceptible to overheating, even though it's "getting more air."

Although CPUs are the most common component to overheat, video cards are also quite susceptible, especially for those with high-end graphics needs such as video producers, graphics designers, and gamers. Occasionally other chips on the motherboard—such as the chipset or chips on other devices—may also overheat. Extra heat sinks, fans, or higher-end cooling systems may be installed to cool these chips.

If the system is using a liquid cooling system, know that they have their own set of issues. The pump that moves the liquid through the tubing and heat sinks can become obstructed or simply fail. If this happens, the liquid's temperature will eventually equalize with that of the CPU and other components, resulting in their damage. Dust in the heat sinks has the same effect as with non-liquid cooling systems, so keep these components as clean as you would any such components. Check regularly for signs of leaks that might be starting and try to catch them before they result in damage to the system.

Burning Smells, Smoke, and Visible Damage

A *burning smell* or smoke coming from your computer is never a good thing. While it normally gets warm inside a computer case, it should never be hot enough inside there to melt plastic components or cause visible damage, but it does happen from time to time. And power problems can sometimes cause components to get hot enough to smoke.

A burning smell is a specific symptom called out in the A+ exam objectives.

If you smell an odd odor or see smoke coming from a computer, shut it down immediately. Open the case and start looking for visible signs of damage. Things to look for include melted plastic components and burn marks on circuit boards. The good news about visible damage is that you can usually figure out which component is damaged pretty quickly. The bad news is that it often means you need to replace parts.

Visible damage to the outside of the case or the monitor casing might not matter much as long as the device still works. But if you're looking inside a case and see burn marks or melted components, that's a sure sign of a problem. Replace damaged circuit boards or melted plastic components immediately. After replacing the part, it's a good idea to monitor the new component for a while too. The power supply could be causing the problem. If the new part fries quickly too, it's time to replace the power supply as well.

Looking for Lights and Messages

Many hardware devices have status indicator lights that can help you identify operational features or problems with a device. Obviously, when you power on a system, you expect the power light to come on. If it doesn't, you have a problem. The same holds true for other external devices, such as wireless routers, external hard drives, and printers. In situations in which the power light doesn't come on and the device has no power, always obey the first rule of troubleshooting: check your connections first!

Beyond power indicators, several types of devices have additional lights that can help you troubleshoot. If you have a switch, hub, or other connectivity device, you should have an indicator for each port that lights up when there is a connection. Some devices will give you a green light for a good connection and a yellow or red light if they detect a problem. A lot of connectivity devices will also have an indicator that blinks or flashes when traffic is going through the port. Sometimes it's the same light that indicates a connection, but at other times it's a separate indicator. The same holds true for NICs. They usually have a connectivity light and a transmission light. If no lights are illuminated, it can indicate a lack of connection.

Many computers also have hard drive activity lights. When disk reads or writes occur, the light will blink; otherwise, it will be off. A hard drive indicator that is constantly on is generally not a good sign; it could indicate that the hard drive is constantly busy or that the system is frozen, either of which is bad.

Most keyboards will have status lights for the Caps Lock and Num Lock keys. If you believe a system is locked up, try pressing the Caps Lock or Num Lock key on the keyboard to see if the lights change. If they don't, that's a sign that the system is unresponsive. If no lights ever illuminate on the keyboard, it could be that the keyboard is disconnected or that there is a system power issue.

In addition to lights, you should look for alerts and error messages when possible. An alert is a message generated by a hardware device. In some cases, the device has a display panel that will tell you what the alert is. A good example of this is an office printer. Many have an LCD display that can tell you if something is wrong.

Other alerts and error messages will pop up on the computer screen. If the device is attached to a specific computer, the alert will generally pop up on that computer's screen. Some devices can be configured to send an alert to a specific user account or system administrator, so the administrator will get the alert regardless of which computer they are currently logged into.

Operating system error messages and alerts are generally logged in an event log, such as Windows Event Viewer. Troubleshooting operating system errors is an objective on the 220-1102 exam, and we cover Event Viewer in Chapter 14, "Windows 10 Configuration."

If you have a device with lights and you're not sure what they mean, or if you're receiving an error message that is confusing, it's best to check the manual or the manufacturer's website to learn about them. The manufacturer's website is generally a great place to go for troubleshooting tips!

Intermittent Device Failure

Intermittent problems are absolutely the worst to deal with. They are frustrating for technicians because the system will inevitably work properly when the tech is there to fix it. The users also get frustrated because they see the problem happen, but, of course, it works fine when the tech shows up!

Treat intermittent failures just as you would a persistent issue, if at all possible. See if there were any error messages, or if it happens when the user tries a certain action. Maybe it occurs only when the system has been on for a while or when a specific application is open. Try to narrow it down as much as possible. In many cases, an intermittent failure means that the device is slowly but surely dying and needs to be replaced. If it's something obvious, such as a network card or a disk read/write failure, you know what to replace. If not, and it's something random like intermittent lockups, it may take trial-and-error to find the right part to replace, especially if there were no error messages. Intermittent or unexpected lockups or shutdowns may be a motherboard, CPU, or RAM problem. If you have nothing else to go on, try replacing one at a time to see if that resolves the issue.

Identifying BIOS/UEFI and POST Routine Problems

Every computer has a Basic Input/Output System (BIOS) or Unified Extensible Firmware Interface (UEFI) that acts as an interface between the computer's hardware and any operating system installed on that hardware. It's the first software (technically, firmware) that loads as a system boots, and as such, it plays a critical role in computer operation. If the BIOS/UEFI doesn't work properly, the user will never get to the point where their operating system starts. In this section, we will cover issues specific to the BIOS/UEFI, as well as the boot process it controls, which is the *power-on self-test (POST)*.

BIOS/UEFI Issues

As already mentioned, the BIOS/UEFI is the layer between the hardware and the operating system. Older systems may have a BIOS; UEFI is newer and has more features.

 In this section, we will refer to the BIOS but don't mention UEFI specifically. All these issues can apply to either a BIOS or UEFI BIOS. We just use the term BIOS here for simplicity.

Out-of-Date BIOS   First, computer BIOSs don't go bad; they just become out of date. This isn't necessarily a critical issue; they will continue to support the hardware that came with the box. It does, however, become an issue when the BIOS doesn't support some component that you would like to install—virtualization, for instance.

Most of today's BIOSs are written to an EEPROM and can be updated through the use of software. This process is called *flashing the BIOS*. Each manufacturer has its own method for accomplishing this. Check the documentation for complete details.

If you make a mistake in flashing the BIOS, the computer can become unbootable. If this happens, your only option may be to ship the box to a manufacturer-approved service center. Be careful!

Losing a Computer's Settings   A fairly common issue with the BIOS is when it fails to retain your computer's settings, such as date/time and hard drive settings. The BIOS uses a small battery (much like a watch battery), called the *CMOS battery*, on the motherboard to help it retain settings when the system power is off. If this battery fails, the BIOS won't retain its settings. Simply replace the battery to solve the problem.

Inaccurate system date/time is a specific symptom called out in the A+ exam objectives.

Checking the Boot Priority   Finally, remember that your BIOS also contains the boot priority (also sometimes called the boot sequence) for your system. You probably boot to the first hard drive in your system (the one that contains the OS boot files), but you can also set your BIOS to boot from a secondary hard drive, an optical drive, a USB port, or the network. If your computer can't find a proper boot device, it could be that it's attempting to boot to an incorrect device. Check the BIOS to see if you need to change the boot sequence. To do this, perform the following steps:

1. Reboot the system and look for the message telling you to press a certain key to enter the BIOS (usually something like F2).

2. Once you're in the BIOS, find the menu with the boot priority (like the one shown in Figure 11.1) and set it to the desired order.

If the changes don't hold the next time you reboot, check the battery.

There may be times that you want to boot to an alternate device, such as a USB drive. During the part of the boot process when the BIOS entry key is shown, most systems will also show you an alternate key to press (such as the spacebar) to boot a different device. This can be very helpful when you're troubleshooting a system that won't load the OS properly, as long as you have the installation medium handy.

FIGURE 11.1   UEFI boot priority settings

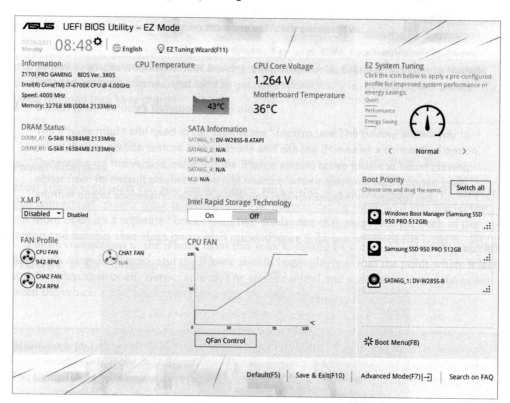

POST Routine Problems

Every computer has a diagnostic program built into its BIOS/UEFI called the POST. When you turn on the computer, it executes this set of diagnostics. Many steps are involved in the POST, but they happen very quickly, they're invisible to the user, and they vary among BIOS/UEFI vendors. The steps include checking the CPU, checking the RAM, checking for the presence of a video card, and verifying basic hardware functionality. The main reason to be aware of the POST's existence is that if it encounters a problem, the boot process stops. Being able to determine at what point the problem occurred could help you troubleshoot.

If the computer doesn't perform the POST as it should, one way to determine the source of a problem is to listen for POST code beeps, also known as a *beep code*. This is a series of beeps from the computer's speaker. A successful POST generally produces a single beep. If there's more than one beep, the number, duration, and pattern of the beeps can sometimes tell you what component is causing the problem. However, the beeps differ depending on the BIOS manufacturer and version, so you must look up the beep code in a chart for your particular BIOS. AMI BIOS, for example, relies on the number of beeps and uses patterns of short and long beeps. Unfortunately, not all computers today give any beep codes because they don't contain the internal piezoelectric speaker.

Power-on self-test (POST) beeps is a specific symptom called out in the A+ exam objectives.

Another way to determine a problem during the POST routine is to use a *POST card*. This is a circuit board that fits into an expansion slot (PCIe, PCI, or USB) in the system and reports numeric codes as the boot process progresses. Each code corresponds to a particular component being checked. If the POST card stops at a certain number, you can look up that number in the manual for the card to determine the problem. Figure 11.2 shows an example of a PCI POST card. USB POST cards are easy to use—you don't have to crack the case to check for POST errors—and they can be used to test laptops as well.

FIGURE 11.2   PCI POST card

POST card 98usd by Rumlin—Own work. Licensed under CC BY-SA 3.0 via Wikimedia Commons.

Motherboard manufacturers tend to use different beep codes to indicate different error messages. If you're getting a beep code during POST, check the Internet for information on what the beep code means. A good reference site is BIOS Central; for example, you can find AMI BIOS beep codes at bioscentral.com/beepcodes/amibeep.htm. You can also visit the BIOS manufacturer's website.

Identifying Motherboard and CPU Problems

Most motherboard and CPU problems manifest themselves by the system appearing to be completely dead. However, "completely dead" can be a symptom of a wide variety of problems, not only with the CPU or motherboard but also with the RAM or the power supply. At other times, a failing motherboard or CPU will cause the system to lock up completely, or "hang," requiring a hard reboot, or the failing motherboard or CPU may cause continuous reboots. A POST card may be helpful in narrowing down the exact component that is faulty.

When a motherboard fails, it's usually because it has been damaged. Most technicians can't repair motherboard damage; the motherboard must be replaced. Motherboards can become damaged due to physical trauma, exposure to electrostatic discharge (ESD), or short-circuiting. To minimize the risk, observe the following rules:

- Handle a motherboard as little as possible, and keep it in an antistatic bag whenever it's removed from the PC case.

- Keep all liquids well away from the motherboard; water can cause a short circuit.

- Wear an antistatic wrist strap when handling or touching a motherboard.

- When installing a motherboard in a case, make sure that you use brass standoffs with paper or plastic washers to prevent any stray solder around the screw holes from causing a short circuit with the metal of the screw.

A CPU may fail because of physical trauma or short-circuiting, but the most common cause for a CPU not to work is overheating, and most overheating issues are due to installation failures. This means that the heat sink and/or fan must be installed properly along with the processor. For example, air gaps in the thermal paste between the CPU and heat sink can cause the processor to run hot and eventually burn up. With a PGA- or LGA-style CPU, ensure that the CPU is oriented correctly in the socket. With an older SECC- or ZIF-style CPU, make sure the CPU is completely inserted into its slot or socket.

I/O Port and Cable Problems

Input/output (I/O) ports are most often built into the motherboard and include USB as well as legacy parallel and serial ports. All of them are used to connect external peripherals to the motherboard. When a port doesn't appear to be functioning, make sure the following conditions are met:

- The cables are snugly connected.

- The port has not been disabled in BIOS Setup.

- The port has not been disabled in Device Manager in Windows.

- No pins are broken or bent on the male end of the port or on the cable being plugged into it.

If you suspect that it's the port, you can purchase a loopback plug to test its functionality. If you suspect that the cable, rather than the port, may be the problem, swap out the cable with a known good one. If you don't have an extra cable, you can test the existing cable with a multimeter by setting it to ohms and checking the resistance between one end of the cable and the other.

Use a pin-out diagram, if available, to determine which pin matches up to which at the other end. There is often—but not always—an inverse relationship between the ends. In other words, at one end pin 1 is at the left, and at the other end it's at the right on the same row of pins. You see this characteristic with D-sub connectors where one end of the cable is male and the other end is female.

Black Screen

Sometimes you will run into a computer with no video output—a *black screen*. This symptom could be the fault of a few different components. Recall that for video to be produced, there needs to be a video card, cable, and a screen, and the screen may have several components such as the screen itself, inverter, backlight, and others. We'll cover it here, though, because with so many motherboards today having video circuitry built into them, it could very well be the motherboard.

If there's no video, as always, check the obvious first. Is the monitor plugged in and turned on? Does it appear to be getting a signal from the video card? Does the light on the monitor make it look like the monitor has gone into sleep mode? If so, perhaps turning the monitor off and back on will do the trick.

If you've checked the usual suspects, try a different monitor and video cable. If there's still no video, then you may try a different video card. On almost all motherboards with built-in video circuitry, the onboard video electronics will be disabled when an expansion video card is installed. Of course, make sure you're plugging the monitor into the new video card and not the video port on the motherboard! (It's happened to all of us, and yes, it can be kind of embarrassing.) If the video circuitry on the motherboard is faulty, either use an expansion card or replace the board.

 Black screen is a specific symptom called out in the A+ exam objectives.

Capacitor Swelling

Many motherboards have capacitors on them, which store electricity. They are short cylindrical tubes. Sometimes, when capacitors fail, they will swell and brownish-red electrolyte residue may seep out of the vents in the top—an example is shown in Figure 11.3. These are called *distended capacitors*, also known as capacitor swelling.

 Capacitor swelling is a specific symptom called out in the A+ exam objectives.

If a capacitor fails, the motherboard will not work. You have a couple of options:

- The first and probably best option is to replace the motherboard. Whatever you do, do *not* touch the residue coming from a distended capacitor! It can cause serious chemical burns.

- The second option is to drain the energy from the failed capacitor and replace it. Do this only if you have specialized training on how to deal safely with capacitors, because they can cause lethal shocks.

FIGURE 11.3   Distended capacitors on a motherboard

By Bushytails at English Wikipedia—Own work, CC BY-SA 3.0

Identifying Memory Issues

Isolating memory issues on a computer is one of the most difficult tasks to do properly because so many memory problems manifest themselves as software issues. For example, memory problems can cause application crashes and produce error messages such as general protection faults (GPFs). Memory issues can also cause a fatal error in your operating system, producing proprietary crash screens such as the infamous *Blue Screen of Death (BSOD)* in Windows or the rotating *pinwheel* in macOS. Sometimes these are caused by the physical memory failing. At other times, they are caused by bad programming, when an application writes into a memory space reserved for the operating system or another application.

Application crashes and proprietary crash screens (blue screen of death [BSOD]/pinwheel) are specific symptoms mentioned in the A+ exam objectives.

In short, physical memory problems can cause app and system lockups, unexpected shutdowns or reboots, or the errors mentioned in the preceding paragraph. They can be challenging to pin down. If you do get an error message related to memory, be sure to write down the memory address if the error message gives you one. If the error happens again, write down the memory address again. If it's the same or a similar address, then it's very possible that the physical memory is failing. You can also use one of several hardware- or software-based RAM testers to see if your memory is working properly. Sometimes switching the slot that the RAM is in will help, but more often than not the RAM needs to be replaced.

Memory issues can also be caused by the virtual memory, which is an area of the hard drive set aside to emulate memory. The operating system creates and manages a paging file (in Windows, it's called `PAGEFILE.SYS`) on the hard drive to act as memory when the system needs more than what the physical RAM can provide; oftentimes, this paging file is dynamic in size. If the hard drive runs out of room for the paging file, memory issues can appear, or the system may have sluggish performance. As a rule of thumb, ensure that at least 10 percent of the hard drive space is free.

This Computer Is SO Slow. . .

Sluggish performance is a specific symptom mentioned in the A+ exam objectives. It's a tricky problem to isolate because it can be caused by many different things. For example, it could be:

- Low physical or virtual memory
- Low available space on the primary hard drive
- Failing motherboard, CPU, or hard drive
- Poorly coded software apps
- Too many apps open at once (causing low memory)
- Malware on the computer

The easy first step to take when troubleshooting a sluggish Windows-based computer is to look at memory usage in Task Manager. There are several ways to open Task Manager, such as pressing Ctrl+Alt+Delete and then choosing Task Manager from the list. Task Manager's Processes page is shown in Figure 11.4. This gives real-time statistics on how busy the CPU, RAM, hard drive, and network connection are. If the CPU, memory, or disk counters are over 80 percent, the system may appear sluggish. Clicking the column header (where the total percent and counter name is) will sort it, so you can see which app or process is causing the most grief. If there are a lot of open apps, closing them may help. If the system isn't running many apps, it may be a background process or a Windows process. Before closing a background or Windows process down, do an Internet search to see what it does—randomly closing processes can limit system functionality (until the computer is rebooted) or cause a system crash.

FIGURE 11.4 Windows Task Manager

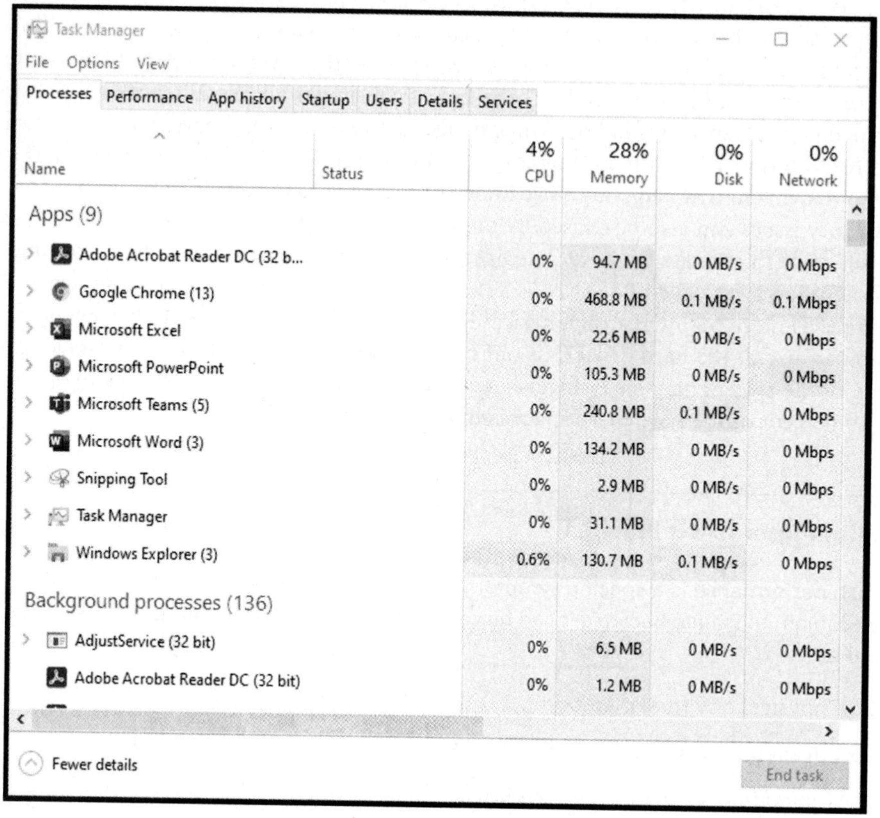

A second thing to check is free disk space. Once the primary drive gets to be under 10 percent free, the system can become slow to respond. Check this by looking at the hard drive properties, as shown in Figure 11.5. If the hard drive is too full, you can use the Disk Cleanup utility to free space. Or, manually delete unneeded files or install a second drive, and copy apps, photos, videos, and other items to the secondary drive.

FIGURE 11.5   Local disk properties

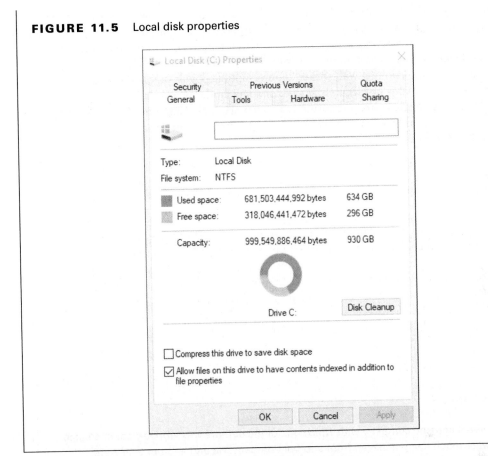

Identifying Power Supply Problems

Power supply problems can manifest themselves in two ways. In the first, you will see an obvious problem, such as an electrical flash or possibly a fire. In the second, the system doesn't respond in any way when the power is turned on. Hopefully you don't have to deal with many of the first type!

Recall from Chapter 2, "Expansion Cards, Storage Devices, and Power Supplies," that power supplies have a voltage switch on the back to change from 110v–120v power to 220v–240v power to meet different countries' power specifications. If a computer has been moved from one country to another, make sure that it's on the right setting before you plug it in and try to power it up.

When the system doesn't respond ("no power") when you try to power it up, make sure the outlet is functional and try a new power cable. If those check out, open the case, remove the power supply, and replace it with a new one. Partial failures, or intermittent power supply problems, are much less simple. A completely failed power supply gives the same symptoms as a malfunctioning wall socket, uninterruptible power supply (UPS), or power strip; a power cord that is not securely seated; or some motherboard shorts (such as those caused by an improperly seated expansion card, memory stick, CPU, and the like). You want to rule out those items before you replace the power supply and find that you still have the same problem as when you started.

 No power is a specific symptom mentioned in the A+ exam objectives.

At other times, the power supply fan might spin but the rest of the system does not appear to get power. This can be a power supply issue or possibly a motherboard issue. (Recall that the power supply plugs into the motherboard, and several devices don't have a power cable but power themselves from the motherboard.) Be aware that different cases have different types of on/off switches. The process of replacing a power supply is a lot easier if you purchase a replacement with the same mechanism.

 Real World Scenario

Hot, Hot, Hot

Several years ago, the company with which one of the authors was working got in a batch of hardware that it had purchased from another company. He and another tech were building Frankensteins out of the plethora of parts they had.

They put RAM into one of the systems and powered it on. Immediately there was an electrical arc from the RAM to the motherboard, so they shut it back off. The arc was present for a split second, and they had the box powered down within a second or two after that.

The RAM module had a pretty obvious burn mark on it, so the author went to take it out and promptly scorched his fingers when he touched it. It was searing hot! They let it cool down for about 20 minutes before going back to take it out. The moral of the story: be careful not to burn yourself on fried components.

Incidentally, they put a new motherboard and new RAM into the same case and powered it up only to see the exact same thing happen. Fried. (Fortunately, the author was smart enough not to burn himself a second time!) The verdict? Bad power supply. After replacing the power supply and trying a third motherboard and RAM combination, they had a functioning system.

If you're curious as to the state of your power supply, you can buy hardware-based power supply testers online starting at about $10 and running up to several hundred dollars. Multimeters are also effective devices for testing your power supplies.

WARNING Never try to repair or disassemble a power supply. They contain capacitors that can store a lethal amount of electricity, even when they are powered off and have been unplugged. The high risk of electrocution and the relatively low cost of a new power supply make working on them something to avoid.

Exercise 11.1 walks you through the steps of troubleshooting a few specific hardware problems. The exercise will probably end up being a mental one for you, unless you have the exact problem that we're describing here. As practice, you can write down the steps that you would take to solve the problem and then check to see how close you came to our steps. Clearly, there are several ways to approach a problem, so you might use a slightly different process, but the general approach should be similar. Finally, when you have found the problem, you can stop. As you go through each step, assume that it didn't solve the issue so you need to move on to the next step.

TIP For additional troubleshooting experience, you can watch videos on YouTube or http://iFixIt.com. There are many great examples for hundreds of different types of problems.

EXERCISE 11.1

Troubleshooting Practice

Issue One: Blank screen on bootup. You turn the computer on, and there's nothing on the screen.

1. Check to make sure the monitor is on. Is its power light on?

   Seriously. Check it. Sometimes 5 seconds of checking the obvious can save you an hour of wasted time.

2. Is the monitor getting a signal?

   Some monitors will go into sleep mode if they don't get a signal. Check the connections. If all the connections are good and you're not getting a signal, it could be the video card.

3. Did the system POST properly? Did you get a POST beep or a beep code?

   No POST likely indicates a bigger problem than just the video card or the monitor. If you do get a POST beep but never see anything, try a different monitor.

(continues)

4. Did you ever see anything on the screen? BIOS information? Did the OS start to load and then go blank?

   The key to troubleshooting an ambiguous situation like this is to ask, "What is the last thing that worked as it was supposed to?" That will help you determine what you need to fix.

Issue Two: The power supply fan spins, but no other devices have power.

1. Did you hear a POST beep or a beep code?

   Odds are you that didn't get any sounds, but it's always good to reboot and double-check.

2. Disconnect all internal and external peripherals so that the only component drawing power is the motherboard (with CPU and RAM, of course). Does it POST then?

   If you disconnect everything and it still doesn't POST, odds are that your motherboard is fried. If it POSTs, then start plugging components back in one at a time, starting with your hard drive and other internal devices and working your way to the external peripherals. You'll eventually get to the part that's causing the problem.

3. If you have a power supply tester or multimeter, now would be a good time to make sure that the power supply is working properly. There's no sense in replacing components, such as the motherboard, if the power supply is just going to fry them!

   Again, with all troubleshooting, it's imperative to narrow down the problem to isolate the cause. If you can do that, then fixing it should be the easy part.

Summary

This chapter addressed the best practice methodology for resolving computer problems as well as troubleshooting core hardware components. In our discussion of troubleshooting theory, you learned that you need to take a systematic approach to problem solving. Both art and science are involved, and experience in troubleshooting is helpful but not a prerequisite to being a good troubleshooter. You learned that in troubleshooting, the first objective is to identify the problem. Many times, this can be the most time-consuming task.

Once you've identified the problem, you need to establish a theory of why the problem is happening, test your theory, establish a plan of action, verify full functionality, and then document your work. Documentation is frequently the most overlooked aspect of working with computers, but it's an absolutely critical step.

Next, we investigated the causes and symptoms of hardware problems, such as noise, excessive heat, burning smells and smoke, visible damage, and intermittent device failure. After the discussion of general hardware, we talked about issues specific to internal components, including the motherboard, CPU, RAM, and power supply.

Exam Essentials

Know the steps to take in troubleshooting computers. First, identify the problem. Then, establish a theory of probable cause, test the theory to determine the cause, establish a plan of action to resolve the problem and implement the solution, verify full system functionality, and, finally, document your findings, actions, and, outcomes.

Understand what happens during the POST routine. During the power-on self-test (POST), the BIOS checks to ensure that the base hardware is installed and working. Generally, one POST beep is good. Any more than that and you might have an error.

Understand problems related to the system BIOS/UEFI. BIOS/UEFI settings are maintained by the CMOS battery when the system is powered off. If the system keeps losing the date and time or boot settings, it could indicate a problem with the CMOS battery.

Know what is likely to cause unexpected shutdowns, system lockups, continuous reboots, and intermittent device failures. All these issues can be caused by a failing motherboard, CPU, or RAM. In the case of other intermittent device failures, it could be that specific device as well. Many times these issues are exacerbated by overheating.

Understand common problems that power supplies can cause. Power supplies can fry components, but they can also cause no power, grinding or squealing noises, spinning fans but no power to other devices, smoke, and burning smells.

Know which devices within a system can make loud noises. Loud noises are usually not welcome, unless you intend for them to come from your speakers. Generally speaking, only devices with moving parts, such as HDDs, power supplies, and fans, can produce unwanted loud noises.

Know how to avoid overheating. Using fans and heat sinks will help to avoid overheating. Also know that overclocking the processor can cause overheating.

Know the proprietary crash screens for Windows and Mac operating systems. Windows has the Blue Screen of Death (BSOD), whereas macOS uses the pinwheel.

Understand what a distended capacitor is. It's when a capacitor swells and possibly bursts, releasing a reddish-brown electrolyte. A motherboard with distended capacitors will likely fail. Don't touch the electrolyte!

Know what causes a black screen.   Black screens are likely the fault of the video card, video cable, or display unit. If the video circuitry is built into the motherboard, it could be a faulty motherboard as well.

Understand causes of sluggish performance.   Generally, sluggish performance is related to the memory or hard drive. If either are being overused, the system will be slower to respond. Overworked CPUs can also cause sluggish performance.

Know what causes application crashes.   App crashes are most likely one of two things: a poorly coded app or faulty memory.

Review Questions

The answers to the chapter review questions can be found in Appendix A.

1. You have discovered a fix for a broken laptop. Before implementing changes, what should you consider, according to the best practice methodology?

    A. The user's budget

    B. Company reputation

    C. Upgrade feasibility

    D. Corporate policies

2. When a user turns on their desktop computer, nothing appears on the screen. They hear three long beeps, followed by three short beeps and three long beeps. What should you do as a next step?

    A. Replace the motherboard.

    B. Replace the RAM.

    C. Replace the CPU.

    D. Look up the beep code on the manufacturer's website.

3. You are identifying the problem while troubleshooting a network issue. Which of the following are proper steps to help identify the problem? (Choose all that apply.)

    A. Inquire regarding infrastructure changes.

    B. Conduct internal or external research based on symptoms.

    C. Refer to the vendor's instructions for guidance.

    D. Determine the next steps to resolve the problem.

    E. Gather information from the user and identify user changes to the computer.

4. A field technician reports back that the computer they are troubleshooting has exposed distended capacitors. Which component has most likely failed?

    A. Power supply

    B. Motherboard

    C. CPU

    D. RAM

5. You are using the best practice methodology to troubleshoot a video problem. During which step should you question the obvious?

    A. Test the theory to determine cause.

    B. Establish a theory of probable cause.

    C. Identify the problem.

    D. Establish a plan of action to resolve the problem.

6. You are solving a problem with a desktop computer that was caused by human error. When is the appropriate time to implement preventive measures, according to the best practice methodology?

   A. When documenting findings, actions, and outcomes

   B. When testing the theory to determine cause

   C. When verifying full system functionality

   D. When questioning the user to identify user changes

7. You are troubleshooting a Windows-based desktop computer that is experiencing unexpected shutdowns. Which of the following would be a good next step to resolve the issue? (Choose two.)

   A. Replace the motherboard, CPU, and RAM to see if it resolves the problem.

   B. Replace the RAM to see if it resolves the problem.

   C. Reinstall Windows to see if it resolves the problem.

   D. Replace the CPU to see if it resolves the problem.

8. When a desktop computer boots up, there is no video on the LCD monitor, just a blank screen. The system makes one beep when it powers on, and air is coming out of the case fan. What is the most likely cause of the problem?

   A. The motherboard has failed.

   B. The video card has failed.

   C. The monitor is disconnected.

   D. The CPU or RAM has failed.

9. You have implemented a solution that resolved an audio problem on a laptop computer. Following the best practice methodology, what is the next step to take?

   A. Document findings, actions, and outcomes.

   B. Verify full system functionality and, if applicable, implement preventive measures.

   C. Establish a plan of action to resolve the problem.

   D. Review system and application logs.

10. You are training a class of new technicians on troubleshooting motherboard issues. Which of the following are issues most likely caused by a failing CMOS battery? (Choose two.)

    A. BIOS time and setting resets

    B. Attempts to boot to the incorrect device

    C. Intermittent device failure

    D. BSOD/pinwheel errors

11. A desktop computer is experiencing continuous reboots. It gets to the BIOS screen and then reboots every time. Which two components are most likely to cause this problem? (Choose two.)

    A. Power supply

    B. RAM

    C. CPU

    D. Motherboard

12. You have fixed a printer problem and verified full functionality. What is the next step to take in the best practice methodology?

    A. Document findings, actions, and outcomes.

    B. Conduct internal or external research.

    C. Review system and application logs.

    D. Establish a theory of probable cause.

13. A user pushes the power button on their desktop computer but nothing happens. They double-check that it is plugged in and that the wall outlet is working properly. Which components are most likely to cause this problem? (Choose two.)

    A. Power supply

    B. Motherboard

    C. Power cord

    D. CPU

    E. RAM

14. A technician who has been troubleshooting a computer tells you that the system is having problems with overheating. Which component is most likely to cause this issue?

    A. Power supply

    B. Motherboard

    C. CPU

    D. RAM

15. You turn on a desktop computer and it fails to boot. You hear a rhythmic ticking coming from inside the case. What is most likely the problem?

    A. Failed hard drive

    B. Failed motherboard

    C. Failed CPU

    D. Failed RAM

    E. A bomb

16. You are using the best practice methodology to troubleshoot a printer. During which phase of the methodology should you use external research based on the symptoms?

   A. Identify the problem.

   B. Establish a plan of action to resolve the problem.

   C. Establish a theory of probable cause.

   D. Implement preventive measures.

17. When you turn on a desktop computer, you hear a loud squealing noise coming from inside the case. Which components are potential culprits for making the noise? (Choose all that apply.)

   A. CPU fan

   B. Power supply fan

   C. HDD

   D. SSD

   E. CPU

   F. RAM

18. A user complains of smoke and a foul odor coming from their desktop computer, so they shut it down. Which component is most likely causing the problem?

   A. Power supply

   B. RAM

   C. CPU

   D. Motherboard

19. A Windows user complains that their computer keeps crashing. What is the proprietary crash screen they are most likely seeing?

   A. Stop sign

   B. Pinwheel

   C. BSOD

   D. Black screen

20. You have been troubleshooting a laptop for an hour and have established a theory of probable cause for the problem. What is the next step you should take?

   A. Test the theory to determine cause.

   B. Document findings, actions, and outcomes.

   C. Verify full system functionality and implement preventive measures.

   D. Establish a plan of action to resolve the problem.

Performance-Based Question

You will encounter performance-based questions on the A+ exam. The questions on the exam require you to perform a specific task, and you will be graded on whether or not you were able to complete the task. The following requires you to think creatively in order to measure how well you understand this chapter's topics. You may or may not see similar questions on the actual A+ exams. To see how your answers compare to the authors', refer to Appendix B.

Place the following steps (and sub-steps) of the best practice methodology in order:

- Verify full system functionality and, if applicable, implement preventive measures.

- Test the theory to determine cause.

- If necessary, conduct external or internal research based on symptoms

- Identify the problem.

- Once the theory is confirmed, determine the next steps to resolve the problem.

- Document the findings, actions, and outcomes.

- Inquire regarding environmental or infrastructure changes.

- Establish a plan of action to resolve the problem and implement the solution.

- Establish a theory of probable cause (question the obvious).

- Gather information from the user, identify user changes, and, if applicable, perform backups before making changes.

- If the theory is not confirmed, reestablish a new theory or escalate.

- Refer to the vendor's instructions for guidance.

Chapter

12

Hardware and Network Troubleshooting

THE FOLLOWING COMPTIA A+ EXAM 220-1101 OBJECTIVES ARE COVERED IN THIS CHAPTER:

✓ **2.8 Given a scenario, use networking tools.**

- Crimper
- Cable stripper
- WiFi analyzer
- Toner probe
- Punchdown tool
- Cable tester
- Loopback plug
- Network tap

✓ **5.3 Given a scenario, troubleshoot and diagnose problems with storage drives and RAID arrays.**

- Common symptoms
    - Light-emitting diode (LED) status indicators
    - Grinding noises
    - Clicking sounds
    - Bootable device not found
    - Data loss/corruption
    - RAID failure
    - Self-monitoring, Analysis, and Reporting Technology (S.M.A.R.T.) failure
    - Extended read/write times

- Input/output operations per second (IOPS)
- Missing drives in OS

✓ **5.4 Given a scenario, troubleshoot video, projector, and display issues.**

- Common symptoms
    - Incorrect data source
    - Physical cabling issues
    - Burned-out bulb
    - Fuzzy image
    - Display burn-in
    - Dead pixels
    - Flashing screen
    - Incorrect color display
    - Audio issues
    - Dim image
    - Intermittent projector shutdown

✓ **5.5 Given a scenario, troubleshoot common issues with mobile devices.**

- Common symptoms
    - Poor battery health
    - Swollen battery
    - Broken screen
    - Improper charging
    - Poor/no connectivity
    - Liquid damage
    - Overheating
    - Digitizer issues
    - Physically damaged ports
    - Malware
    - Cursor drift/touch calibration

✓ **5.6 Given a scenario, troubleshoot and resolve printer issues.**

- Common symptoms
    - Lines down the printed page
    - Garbled print
    - Toner not fusing to paper
    - Paper jams
    - Faded print
    - Incorrect paper size
    - Paper not feeding
    - Multipage misfeed
    - Multiple prints pending in queue
    - Speckling on printed pages
    - Double/echo images on print
    - Incorrect chroma display
    - Grinding noise
    - Finishing issues
        - Staple jams
        - Hole punch
    - Incorrect page orientation

✓ **5.7 Given a scenario, troubleshoot problems with wired and wireless networks.**

- Common symptoms
    - Intermittent wireless connectivity
    - Slow network speeds
    - Limited connectivity
    - Jitter
    - Poor Voice over Internet Protocol (VoIP) quality
    - Port flapping
    - High latency
    - External interference

Hardware problems are sometimes very easy to identify. If you push the power button and nothing happens, you can be pretty confident that it's not the fault of the operating system. Other hardware problems are more complicated. For example, memory issues may cause errors that look like they're the fault of an application, or what appears to be a failing device may be resolved by updating the software driver. So while this chapter focuses on hardware, understand that in many cases you'll need to know how to navigate through apps and software settings to really narrow down the issue.

Network problems introduce even more variables to consider. Instead of just focusing on the local machine, now you need to consider the device at the other end of the connection as well. Perhaps that connection is wired, so it's easy to see if the cable is plugged in and port lights are flashing. If it's wireless, though, the signal travels magically through the air, and you might not have blinking lights to guide the way.

With all of the integration between software applications and hardware components, it can be challenging to understand where one stops and the other starts, or how their interoperation affects one another. To top it all off, you're probably going to be working in an environment that requires you to understand not just one computer but a network full of workstations, servers, switches, routers, and other devices, and how they should play nicely together.

This introduction isn't intended to scare you, but rather to point out that computers are complicated and troubleshooting can be hard. You already know that, but give yourself some latitude in troubleshooting, because it's not always easy. Prepare yourself with a solid foundation of knowledge and never be afraid to consult other resources, such as the Internet or coworkers. Situations will arise that make even the most experienced technicians shake their heads in frustration.

Sometimes, you will hear people say things like, "It just takes practice and experience to become good at troubleshooting." Those words are of little comfort to someone who is relatively new and facing a challenging problem. Yes, experience does help, but even newer technicians can be effective troubleshooters if they understand the fundamentals and follow a logical process.

As you learned in Chapter 11, "Troubleshooting Methodology and Resolving Core Hardware Problems," the best way to tackle any problem is to take a systematic approach to resolving it. This applies to the hardware and networking issues that we'll talk about here as well as the software and security issues that we will cover in Chapter 19, "Troubleshooting Operating Systems and Security."

Recall from Chapter 11 that while experience helps, novice technicians can be effective troubleshooters as well. Troubleshooting becomes a lot easier if you follow logical procedures to help you develop experience. The first thing to do is always to check the easy stuff, such as physical cables and connections. You would be amazed at how many times the simple question "Is it plugged in?" resolves hardware problems. Second, see if anything has recently changed or if there are any recent incidents that might have caused the problem. For example, if someone's laptop won't boot up, you might not have a clue as to why. But if they tell you that they just dropped it down the stairs, you might have a better idea of where to start. Finally, narrow down the scope of the problem. Find out exactly what works and what doesn't. Knowing where the problem starts and stops helps you to focus your troubleshooting efforts.

This chapter finishes the hardware troubleshooting discussion we started in Chapter 11. Specifically, we will look at the following:

- Storage drives and RAID arrays
- Video systems, with an emphasis on projectors and displays
- Mobile devices, including laptops
- Printers
- Wired and wireless networks, including hardware tools and software commands

You may wonder why we broke hardware troubleshooting into multiple chapters. If we're being honest, it's due to the large number of problems that could arise, the volume of A+ exam objectives that creates, and the amount of room it takes to discuss them all. In other words, we didn't want to hit you with a massively long chapter!

Even with breaking it up, though, there's no way that a reasonably sized book could teach you about all the possible issues you could face. Nor would it be logical for you to try to memorize them all. Instead, we focus on some of the common issues and help you think through the process of narrowing down the possibilities so that you can efficiently resolve any problem you encounter. Armed with that knowledge, you should have the confidence to tackle any problem you face, whether it's familiar to you or not.

Troubleshooting Storage Drives and RAID Arrays

Even though storage devices aren't needed, persistent storage is almost universally included in computing devices today. And when they don't work, users tend to get upset. Losing a hard drive's worth of data is incredibly frustrating, especially if there's no suitable backup.

Storage devices present unique problems simply due to their nature—there are multiple technologies in use today. Some of them are devices with moving parts, which means that they are more prone to mechanical failure than a motherboard or a stick of RAM. Others function essentially like RAM and plug directly into a socket instead of needing a cable. If they fail, there's not much you can do besides replace them.

Before we get into common symptoms and solutions, remember that storage system problems usually stem from one of the following three causes:

- The adapter (that is, the SATA, PATA, or other interface) is bad.
- The hard drive (or optical disc) is bad or failing.
- The adapter and disk are connected incorrectly.

The first and last causes are easy to identify, because in either case, the symptom will be obvious: the drive won't work. You won't be able to get the computer to communicate with the disk drive. The way to see which component is at fault is to disconnect and reconnect, or to try the device in another system (or try another drive in the affected system). However, if the problem is a bad or failing disk drive, the symptoms aren't always as obvious. Those are problems we will need to dive deeper into. In the following sections, we'll discuss hard disk problems, including using S.M.A.R.T. technology and RAID arrays. Then we'll finish by taking a quick look at optical drive issues.

Lights and Sounds

While looking at light-emitting diode (LED) status indicators is listed as a subobjective specifically under storage drives, it could be put in several different places as well. A lot of devices have lights that can indicate whether or not a component is working. Storage systems usually have some sort of activity indicator that blinks when the drive is busy either reading or writing data. If the light never comes on, or if the light is on constantly without flickering, there could be a problem.

External network attached storage (NAS) and redundant array of independent (or inexpensive) disks (RAID) storage enclosures have lights as well and may have many more than a standard desktop or laptop computer. For example, many RAID arrays have a light that only illuminates if a drive has failed and needs to be replaced. We'll get into RAID in more detail later in this section. The point is, look for indicator lights and understand what they're communicating to you.

Storage devices that have moving components will make sounds. Mechanical HDDs have a whirring sound as the platters spin, and an irregular ticking or clicking sound when reading and writing. An optical drive spins up when a disc is inserted, and it too will whirr. SSDs have no moving parts, and therefore they do not make sounds. (Well, technically, if one were to get fried it could make an electrical pop. If you hear that, the drive is toast.)

A grinding noise from a storage device is a very bad sign. That means there is a failure in the motor or spindle, or if it sounds more like fingernails on a chalkboard, it means the read/write heads have crashed into the platter and are cutting grooves into it. You'll only need to hear that sound once to remember it forever. If the drive is still operational, get all important data off the drive immediately and replace the drive. A regular, rhythmic ticking or clicking sound is bad too—that usually means the drive is failing or has failed. The solution is the same as for a grinding noise. If you can, get important data off the drive and then replace it.

Talking about hard drive failures is a good time to remind everyone about the importance of regular backups. If the data is irreplaceable, then it needs to be backed up. More frequently updated data needs to be updated more often, for the backups to be current and helpful. On the flip side, after a drive fails is probably not the best time to lecture someone on not having backed up their data. Many years ago, one of the authors took a service call from a third-year PhD student who had a bad hard drive. The student's dissertation—the only copy of it—was on the drive. A bit of empathy was in order, considering the circumstances.

Devices Not Found

If a storage device is plugged in and working, the BIOS/UEFI should detect it first, and then as the operating system loads, it will recognize the drive as well. If someone gives you the symptom that their hard drive isn't being found, the first thing to do is clarify where it's not being found. Is it the BIOS/UEFI, or in the operating system?

Bootable Device Not Found   This could manifest itself in a few different ways, such as a complete failure to boot, the hard drive not being recognized by the BIOS/UEFI, or the OS not being found. Failure to boot at all likely means the drive is not properly connected or it's dead. Do your due diligence and reseat your connections and try different cables, or try the drive in another machine if possible. Most BIOSs/UEFIs today autodetect the hard drive. If that auto-detection fails, it's bad news for the hard drive, unless there's a cable or connection issue.

Finally, a system that boots fine but can't find the OS could indicate a problem with the master boot record (MBR) or boot sector on the hard drive. To fix this in any current version of Windows, boot to bootable media (USB or optical disc) and enter the Windows Recovery Environment (WinRE). In WinRE, you can get to a command prompt and use `bootrec /fixmbr` to fix the MBR and `bootrec /fixboot` to fix the boot sector.

Failed reads and writes from hard drives can also cause the operating system to crash, resulting in a proprietary crash screen (BSOD in Windows or pinwheel in macOS) error.

Missing Drives in OS   Sometimes you have a storage device installed, but you are unable to find it in Windows File Explorer or the Finder in macOS. This could be a connection issue, or perhaps the drive hasn't been properly set up for use. Windows comes with a utility called Disk Management, and Macs have Disk Utility to perform storage device management. If those utilities don't see the drive or mark it as unusable, there are a few things to try:

- Check the connections and try a new cable or port.
- Double-check that the drive is found by the BIOS/UEFI and enabled. If the BIOS/UEFI doesn't see it, the OS won't either.
- Ensure that the drive is found in Disk Management or Disk Utility. If the BIOS/UEFI sees the drive, then the disk utilities should too—but that doesn't necessarily mean the drive is ready for use by File Explorer or the Finder.
- Prepare the drive by initializing it (if needed), allocate space by creating a partition, and assign a drive letter. Without a partition and drive letter, File Explorer and the Finder won't be able to use the space.
- Update the storage device's driver, if possible. This is admittedly a long shot, but it could work, particularly if you're dealing with older hardware.
- Check the drive for bad sectors or other damage. If enough sectors are damaged, the operating system may deem the drive unreadable.

Disk Management is covered in Chapter 14, "Windows 10 Configuration," and other software utilities used to manage hard drives such as chkdsk, format, and diskpart are covered in Chapter 15, "Windows 10 Administration."

Performance Issues

In this category are times when the drive is working, but perhaps not as well as it should or once did. A+ exam objectives that fall into this group include:

- Data loss/corruption
- Extended read/write times
- Input/output operations per second (IOPS)

A failing hard drive might exhibit data loss or corruption or very slow (extended) read/write times. They can also be a symptom of the hard drive being too full. Hard drives move information around a lot, especially temporary files. If the drive doesn't have enough free space (at least 10 percent), it can slow down dramatically. The solution here is to remove files or old applications to free up space and look at defragmenting the hard drive. If problems persist, consider formatting the hard drive and reinstalling the OS. If the issues don't go away, assume that the hard drive is on its last legs.

Input/output operations per second (IOPS), pronounced eye-ops, is an industry standard for how many reads and writes a storage unit can complete. IOPS is frequently quoted on dedicated storage systems such as NAS and RAID devices, but it's so variable and condition-dependent that its usefulness is debatable. Still, if a device's IOPS steadily declines over time or is no longer fast enough to service the user's (most likely the network's) needs, it could be time to replace the device.

The most popular tool used to measure IOPS is Iometer (`sourceforge.net/projects/iometer`); it's open source and it's available for Windows and Linux. Iometer runs simulated disk reads/writes and provides results in a graphical interface (Figure 12.1) and a CSV file. For purposes of the A+ exam, don't worry about memorizing any specific metrics or thresholds for IOPS. Instead, understand what it is, know that it can be measured, and know that if performance decreases over time it could indicate an issue with a storage device.

FIGURE 12.1 Iometer test results

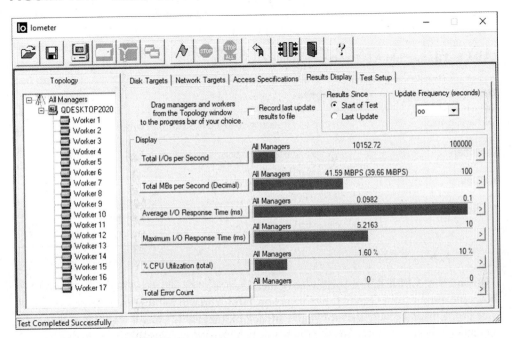

S.M.A.R.T. Diagnostics

As of 2004, nearly every hard drive has been built with *Self-Monitoring, Analysis, and Reporting Technology (S.M.A.R.T.)* software installed. S.M.A.R.T. monitors hard drive reliability and theoretically can warn you in the event of an imminent failure. The idea behind S.M.A.R.T. is great. Who wouldn't want to know when their hard drive was going to fail so they could back up the drive? In practice, though, it seems to help manufacturers locate persistent issues by identifying hard drive design flaws more than it helps end users avoid catastrophic data losses. Helping hard drive manufacturers do a better job isn't a bad thing, but

S.M.A.R.T. hasn't enjoyed widespread commercial success with end users. This can largely be attributed to the following three factors:

- Windows OSs don't come with a built-in graphical utility to parse the data.

- The 70 metrics provided by S.M.A.R.T. aren't always easy to understand, and there has been little guidance as to which metric or metrics are most closely associated with impending drive failure.

- Manufacturers have not consistently defined the metrics among themselves; there are no industrywide analysis applications or standards for this technology.

Let's address the three issues in order. First, you can download one of several graphical tools from the Internet if you want to run S.M.A.R.T. diagnostics on a hard drive. Table 12.1 gives you a few options. Each one has a free option, and they all offer a variety of hard drive diagnostic capabilities.

TABLE 12.1   S.M.A.R.T. software utilities

Name	Website
GSmartControl	http://gsmartcontrol.sourceforge.io
SpeedFan	http://almico.com/speedfan.php
HD Tune	http://hdtune.com
CrystalDiskInfo	http://crystalmark.info/en/software/ crystaldiskinfo

Second, yes, S.M.A.R.T. reports a lot of metrics, not all of which make sense. Figure 12.2 shows the output from GsmartControl version 1.1.3; you can tell that two metrics appear to be problematic because they are highlighted. Pink highlights show a warning, and red highlights indicate a failure. The question is, which metrics are most likely to predict drive failure?

In 2014, Google and cloud service provider Backblaze ran large-scale tests to determine which metrics most strongly correlated with drive failure. Their results showed five metrics, which are highlighted in Table 12.2.

TABLE 12.2   S.M.A.R.T. metrics most correlated with hard drive failure

ID	Attribute name	Description
05	Reallocated sector count	The number of bad sectors that have been found and remapped during read/write processes. Any nonzero number could indicate a problem.
187	Reported uncorrectable errors	The number of errors that could not be recovered using hardware error correction

ID	Attribute name	Description
188	Command timeout	The number of failed hard drive read/write operations due to disk timeout
197	Current pending sector count	The number of unstable sectors waiting to be remapped
198	Uncorrectable sector count	The total number of bad sectors when reading from or writing to a sector

FIGURE 12.2   S.M.A.R.T. report from GsmartControl

ID ▲	Name	Failed	Norm-ed value	Worst	Threshold	Raw value	Type	Flags
1	Raw Read Error Rate	never	112	99	6	46311462	pre-failure	POSR-K
3	Spin-Up Time	never	97	97	0	0	pre-failure	PO---K
4	Start / Stop Count	never	93	93	20	8012	old age	-O--CK
5	Reallocated Sector Count	never	100	100	36	32	pre-failure	PO--CK
7	Seek Error Rate	never	88	60	30	741280327	pre-failure	POSR-K
9	Power-On Time	never	56	56	0	39164	old age	-O--CK
10	Spin-Up Retry Count	never	100	100	97	0	pre-failure	PO--CK
12	Power Cycle Count	never	97	97	20	3997	old age	-O--CK
180	Unknown HDD Attribute	never	100	100	0	267571	pre-failure	PO-R-K
183	Runtime Bad Blocks	never	100	100	0	0	old age	-O--CK
184	End to End Error	never	100	100	97	0	pre-failure	PO--CK
187	Reported Uncorrectable	never	100	100	0	0	old age	-O--CK
188	Command Timeout	never	100	99	0	1	old age	-O--CK
189	High Fly Writes	never	100	100	0	0	old age	-O-RCK
190	Airflow Temperature	never	68	57	45	32 (Min/Max 21/37)	old age	-O---K
194	Temperature (Celsius)	never	32	43	0	32 (0 15 0 0 0)	old age	-O---K
195	Hardware ECC Recovered	never	41	21	0	46311462	old age	-O-RCK
196	Reallocation Event Count	never	100	100	36	32	old age	-O--CK
197	Current Pending Sector Count	never	100	100	0	0	old age	-O--CK
198	Offline Uncorrectable	never	100	100	0	0	old age	----CK

Interestingly enough, metrics related to higher temperatures or the number of reboots did not correlate to drive failure. The old adage that you should leave your computer running to make the hard drive last longer wasn't verified by the research. In addition, over half of the drives in the study failed without recording a sector error, and over 30 percent of the drives failed with no S.M.A.R.T. error whatsoever.

What does that mean for the drive shown in Figure 12.2, which has an error on ID 5? Maybe not much. The same drive passed that ID when scanned with SpeedFan (see Figure 12.3). The safe conclusion is that S.M.A.R.T. can provide useful diagnostics on a hard drive's health, but it's by no means a guaranteed problem finder.

FIGURE 12.3   SpeedFan S.M.A.R.T. output

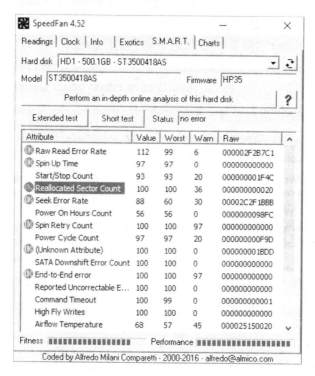

As for the last issue (there being little consistency between hard drive manufacturers), that's an annoyance but not a critical issue. All it really means is that you can't compare data from one drive manufacturer with that of another. It's likely that if you're running S.M.A.R.T. data on a hard drive, you're primarily concerned with that drive's performance, not how it compares to other hard drives. If you have a situation where you're worried about a drive, you can benchmark its performance and track it over time, or you can just replace it.

Exercise 12.1 has you download a S.M.A.R.T. software utility and test your hard drive.

EXERCISE 12.1

Using a S.M.A.R.T. Software Utility in Windows

1. Go to http://almico.com/sfdownload.php and download SpeedFan.

2. Install SpeedFan on your computer.

3. Open SpeedFan.

   Notice that it will begin to collect data on system performance.

4. Click the S.M.A.R.T. tab to see hard drive statistics.

5. Click the Extended Test button to begin an extended test.

6. Look through the list of attributes to see if the drive has any errors.

7. If desired, repeat this process with a different software utility shown in Table 12.1.

RAID Issues

If you are using a redundant array of independent (or inexpensive) disks (RAID) system, you have additional challenges to deal with. First, you have more disks, so the chance of having a single failure increases. Second, you more than likely have one or more additional hard disk controllers, so again you introduce more parts that can fail. Third, there will likely be a software component that manages the RAID array.

Boiling it down, though, dealing with RAID issues is just like dealing with a single hard drive issue, except that you have more parts that make up the single storage unit. If your RAID array isn't found or stops working, try to narrow down the issue. Is it one disk that's failed, or is the whole system down, indicating a problem with a controller or the software? Along with external enclosures, which require a separate connection to the computer, most external RAID systems have status indicators and troubleshooting utilities to help you identify problems. Definitely use those to your advantage.

Finally, the problem could be dependent on the type of RAID you're using. If you are using RAID 0 (disk striping), you actually have more points of failure than a single device, meaning that you're at a greater risk of failure versus using just one hard drive. One drive failure will cause the entire set to fail. RAID 1 (disk mirroring) increases your fault tolerance; if one drive fails, the other has an exact replica of the data. You'll need to replace the failed drive, but unless both drives unexpectedly fail, you shouldn't lose any data. If you're using RAID 5 (disk striping with parity), a minimum of three drives are needed and a single drive failure usually means that your data will be fine, provided that you replace the failed drive.

If two or more drives fail, the RAID 5 array will be lost and you will need to fix the array and then restore the data from backup. RAID 10 is a mirrored striped set that requires at least four drives. As long as one drive in each mirrored pair is functional (just like in RAID 1), you shouldn't lose any data.

> If your hard drive fails completely and you need to get critical data from it, there are third-party companies that provide file recovery software and services. These services are generally very expensive. (And you should have been backing up the drive in the first place!)

Optical Drive Issues

Optical drive (CD, DVD, and Blu-ray) problems are normally media-related. Although optical disc technology is pretty reliable, it's not perfect. One factor to consider is the cleanliness of the disc. On many occasions, if a disc is unreadable, cleaning it with an approved cleaner and a lint-free cleaning towel will fix the problem. The next step might be to use a commercially available scratch-removal kit. If that fails, you always have the option to send the disc to a company that specializes in data recovery.

If the operating system doesn't see the drive, start troubleshooting by determining whether the drive is receiving power. If the tray will eject, you can assume the drive has power. Next, check BIOS/UEFI Setup (SATA or PATA drives) to make sure that the drive has been detected. If not, check the primary/secondary jumper on the drive, and make sure that the PATA adapter is set to Auto, CD-ROM, or ATAPI in BIOS/UEFI Setup. Once inside the case, ensure that both the drive and motherboard ends are securely connected and, on a PATA drive, that the ribbon cable is properly aligned with pin 1, the edge that has the red or pink stripe, being closest to the power connector.

To play movies, a DVD or Blu-ray drive must have Moving Picture Experts Group (MPEG) decoding capability. This is usually built into the drive, video card, or sound card, but it could require a software decoder. If DVD or Blu-ray data discs will read but not play movies, suspect a problem with the MPEG decoding.

If an optical drive works normally but doesn't perform its special capability (for example, it won't burn discs), perhaps you need to install software to work with it. For example, with CD-RW drives, unless you're using an operating system that supports CD writing (and nearly all OSs today do), you must install CD-writing software in order to write to CDs.

> As a reminder, the A+ exam may test you on how to diagnose and fix storage issues. Be familiar with the following common symptoms:
>
> ▪ Light-emitting diode (LED) status indicators
> ▪ Grinding noises
> ▪ Clicking sounds
> ▪ Bootable device not found
> ▪ Data loss/corruption

- RAID failure
- Self-Monitoring, Analysis, and Reporting Technology (S.M.A.R.T.) failure
- Extended read/write times
- Input/output operations per second (IOPS)
- Missing drive in OS

Troubleshooting Video, Projector, and Display Issues

Troubleshooting video problems is usually fairly straightforward because there are only a few components that could be causing the problem. You can sum up nearly all video problems with two simple statements:

- There is either no video or bad video.
- The video card or the monitor/projector/display/cable is to blame.

In the majority of cases when you have a video problem on a desktop computer, a good troubleshooting step is to check the monitor by transferring it to another machine that you know is working. See if it works there. If the problem persists, you know it's the monitor. If it goes away, you know it's the video card (or possibly the driver). Is the video card seated properly? Is the newest driver installed?

The CompTIA A+ exam objectives list 11 symptoms you should understand and know how to fix. We'll break them into three categories:

- Input issues
- Image problems
- Other issues

Let's take a look at each of them now.

Video Input Issues

Imagine you're getting ready for a big presentation. Everyone is gathered in the room, and you connect your laptop to the video projector or external monitors—and there's no display. The audience sighs and people start getting fidgety or multitasking. It's not a great situation. Odds are that if this hasn't happened to you, then you've been on the opposite side—sitting there wishing the presenter could figure it out. What's the best way to resolve this type of issue? Try these three steps:

1. Check the obvious. (Where have you heard this before?) Is everything plugged in and powered on? Look for indicator lights on the projector or external monitor to be sure.

2. Make sure the laptop is set to output video to the right device. On most laptops, you need to press the function key and another key known as the *LCD cutoff switch* (such as F4 or F8) to direct the video output to an external monitor. This is called *toggling*

the display. You might need to do this a few times. Figure 12.4 shows portions of two laptop keyboards—in the top one, F7 is the toggle, and in the bottom one, it's F8. (Later, in Figure 12.7, you will see a monitor icon on F4 that does the same thing.)

FIGURE 12.4   LCD cutoff switches (video toggle keys)

3.   Verify that the monitor or projector is configured for the correct data input source. Having an incorrect data source means that the device won't display anything. Most monitors and projectors have multiple inputs, such as three or four HDMI, DisplayPort, and possibly even VGA ports. There may be a button on the monitor or projector to bring up an onscreen menu and configure the correct source, or you may need to use the device's remote control.

If everything checks out, it's possible there could be physical cabling issues. You can try disconnecting and reconnecting the video cables or another cable if possible.

Video Image Problems

This group of symptoms deals specifically with the image on the screen, or the lack thereof. Here are the ones you should know:

Burned-Out Bulb   This is a projector-specific issue. Projector bulbs have a limited shelf life, and the heat produced by a projector and its bulb can shorten it even further. If the bulb burns out, then clearly there will be nothing displayed. The only resolution is to replace the bulb. Be sure it cools down first before you try to replace it, though—as mentioned, they run hot and they will burn you.

Fuzzy Image   Resolving a fuzzy image problem will differ depending on the display device. For example, projectors have focus mechanisms that allow them to produce images on screens at different distances. A lot of projectors will try to autofocus but will also have onscreen menu options or a knob around the outside of the lens to manually adjust the focus.

A fuzzy image on an LCD screen is an entirely different story. It could be caused by external interference such as fluorescent lights, magnetic devices, and electrical devices such as fans, lamps, and speakers. Check for any of those nearby. If the display uses a cable, it could also be a loose or bad cable. Finally, it could be that the resolution is set for something that the display can't handle, or at least can't handle well. (To be fair, most of the time if the resolution isn't supported, the image will appear warped or stretched and distorted, but it could be fuzzy as well.)

There are a few things you can try to fix it. In Windows, right-click an open area of the desktop and choose Display Settings (Figure 12.5). Once there, you can change the display resolution. Another thing to try is to click Advanced Scaling Settings (Figure 12.6). Turn on the toggle for Let Windows Try To Fix Apps So They're Not Blurry. Custom scaling features, configured on the same page, could cause fuzziness as well.

FIGURE 12.5   Windows Display Settings

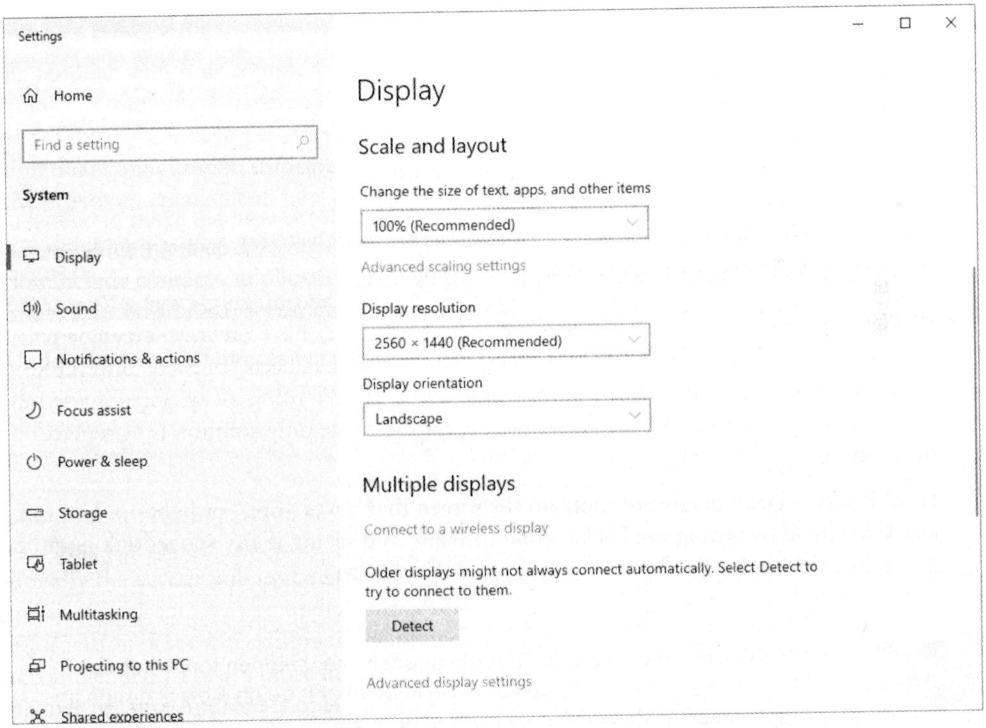

FIGURE 12.6   Advanced Scaling Settings

← Settings	— ☐ ✕

⌂ **Advanced scaling settings**

Fix scaling for apps

Some desktop apps might look blurry when your display settings change. Windows can try to fix these apps so they look better when you open them the next time. This only works for apps on your main display, and it won't work for all apps.

Let Windows try to fix apps so they're not blurry

🔵○ On

Custom scaling

All your displays will be set to the custom scaling size you enter. This can cause some text, apps, and other items to be unreadable if a display doesn't support that size. It might be hard to go back to your original settings.

Enter a custom scaling size between 100% - 500% (not recommended)

100 - 500

Apply

💬 Get help

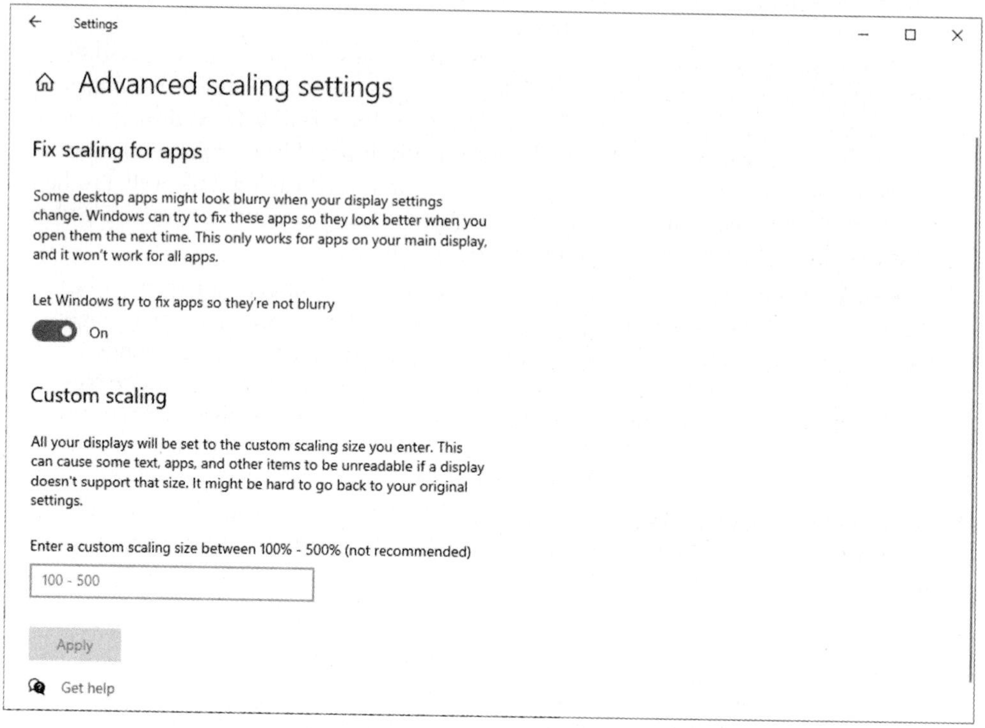

If none of those things work, check the manufacturer's website for similar issues, but it could be that the display itself is bad.

Display Burn-In   When this happens, no matter what you have on your screen, you can still see the outlines of a different image. That image has been "burned" into the monitor (sometimes simply referred to as *burn-in*) and isn't going away. Sometimes you will also hear this referred to as an artifact. Regardless, the only solution is to replace the monitor.

Dead Pixels   Dead pixels are spots on the screen that never "fire," or light up. You can check for these by setting the background to white and seeing if any spots don't light up. The only solution for dead pixels is to replace the monitor.

Dead pixels never light up, but the opposite can happen too, where a pixel is "stuck" in an on position. So instead of it being a black dot on a light screen, it's a lit dot on a black screen. Some suggest that to fix it, you can try to toggle the colors on and off quickly (black screen to white and vice versa), or you can press on the display in that area to get it "unstuck." Personally, we've never had success with either of these two fixes, but they could be worth a shot. If a pixel won't unstick, then the solution is to replace the monitor.

Flashing Screen   Sometimes a display will either subtly flicker or flash off and on. Those two symptoms are caused by different things. Flickering screens are most commonly caused by the backlight starting to fail. In those cases, replace the backlight.

Flashing off and on could be the backlight, but it could also be a loose cable or an unsupported resolution. Try the usual fixes, including checking the cables (if applicable), changing the resolution, or reinstalling the video card driver.

Incorrect Color Display   This can happen when the LCD monitor's controller board starts to fail and doesn't perform color mapping correctly. It also happens on old CRTs. To fix it on an old CRT display, you use a process called *degaussing* (decreasing or eliminating an unwanted magnetic field), which is done through a utility built into the menu on the monitor. Finally, this can also happen if the pins on the connector are damaged or if the connector isn't plugged in all the way. If switching the monitor makes the problems go away, it's probably time to replace the monitor.

Dim Image   If this is a problem with the monitor itself, it's most likely caused by a failing backlight. However, it could also be a configuration setting. On an external monitor, open the onscreen menu and try adjusting the brightness. On a laptop, use the function keys to adjust the brightness. Figure 12.7 shows a laptop keyboard where the keys are F9 and F10. (Back in Figure 12.4, they are F5 and F6 on the top example, and F11 and F12 on the bottom one.) If no amount of adjustment makes the image bright enough for normal use, then replace the backlight.

FIGURE 12.7   Laptop function keys

Other Display Issues

In this final section on video, projector, and display issues, we look at a few symptoms that don't fit nicely into our other sections. This is kind of the grab bag of random video and display problems.

Audio Issues   Many display units today have built-in speakers. The most common reason people have audio problems is because something is muted, but it could also be a cable or connection issue.

First, check the display unit to ensure it's not muted and that the volume is turned up to a reasonable level. This is done on the display's onscreen menu. Next, check to ensure that the computer's audio output is set to the correct device and that it's not muted or the volume isn't turned down. In Windows, right-click the speaker icon on the taskbar, then choose Open Sound Settings (Figure 12.8). Choose the correct device using the drop-down box in the Output section, and ensure that the master volume is turned up.

FIGURE 12.8 Windows sound settings

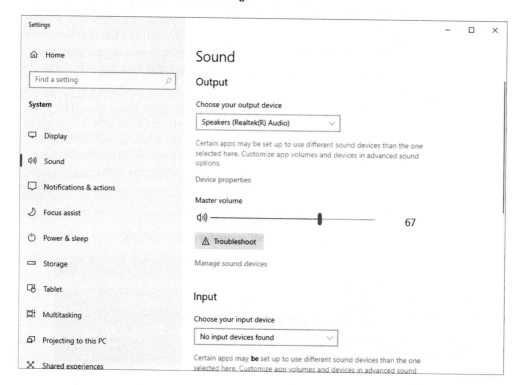

Intermittent Projector Shutdown   We noted earlier that projectors create a lot of heat. When a projector overheats, it will shut itself off to avoid frying components or the bulb. This is the most likely cause of intermittent shutdowns. After the projector cools off, perform a little maintenance cleaning. Most projectors have an air filter to keep dust and debris out of it—check to ensure that's clean and replace it if necessary. Also check to make sure the cooling fan is operational and blowing out warm air.

Monitors can shut down intermittently as well due to overheating. It was more common on older CRT monitors than it is on LCD ones, but it can still happen. Be sure the air vents on the back of the display unit are clear from dust and debris. If the problem persists, it's best to replace the monitor.

Booting into Low-Resolution Mode   Sometimes an operating system refuses to boot into its normal mode and instead boots into a basic video mode. Newer versions of Windows call this "low-resolution" mode, whereas older versions called it VGA mode. This is normally caused by one of two things. One, the video card was set to a resolution it can't handle, or two, there's something messed up with the video card driver. After the OS boots, try reducing the resolution and reboot. If it's still a problem, reinstall the video card driver. If new drivers don't help, consider that the video card is failing.

Other graphics issues can be attributed to the memory installed on the video card. This is the storage location of the screens of information in a queue to be displayed by the monitor. Problems with the memory modules on the video card have a direct correlation to how well it works. It follows, then, that certain unacceptable video-quality issues, such as jerky refresh speeds or lags, can be remedied by adding memory to a video card (if possible). Doing so generally results in an increase in both quality and performance. If you can't add memory to the video card, you can upgrade to a new one with more memory.

 As a reminder, the A+ exam may test you on how to diagnose and fix the following video, projector, and display issues:

- Incorrect data source
- Physical cabling issues
- Burned-out bulb
- Fuzzy image
- Display burn-in
- Dead pixels
- Flashing screen
- Incorrect color display
- Audio issues
- Dim image
- Intermittent projector shutdown

Troubleshooting Common Mobile Device Issues

Mobile devices, for the most part, are essentially the same types of devices as desktops, but troubleshooting the two can feel very different. While the general troubleshooting philosophies never change—steps such as gathering information, isolating the problem, and then testing one fix at a time—the space and configuration limitations can make troubleshooting smaller devices more frustrating. For purposes of the discussion here, the term *mobile devices* includes laptops and anything smaller.

We will look at four areas where mobile devices could have different problems from their desktop counterparts: power and heat, input/output, connectivity, and damage. Much of what we cover will be more closely related to laptops than smaller mobile devices, but the concepts generally apply to mobile computers of all sizes. We'll call out specifics for small mobile devices where applicable.

Working on Laptops and Small Mobile Devices

For whatever reason, it's easier to lose screws and other small pieces when working on laptops than it is with desktops. Don't forget these key concepts when working on laptops:

- Refer to the manufacturer's documentation.

- Use the appropriate hand tools.

- Have a clear organization method for your parts and screws.

- Document and label screw and cable locations.

For a review of these four concepts, see Chapter 9, "Laptop and Mobile Device Hardware."

One of the mobile device issues in exam objective 5.5, Poor/no connectivity, is very similar to the A+ 220-1102 exam objective 3.4, "Given a scenario, troubleshoot common mobile OS and application issues." The implication is that for the A+ 220-1101 exam you will be asked about hardware issues and for the A+ 220-1102 exam it would be OS related. They're similar and often intertwined, so you may see some similar content in Chapter 19. We will do our best to separate out the hardware angle from software-related issues, but as we have stated before, sometimes it's a fine line as to what's really causing the problem.

Power and Heat Issues

Mobile devices are different from desktops in that they're designed to work without a continually plugged-in power source. That freedom introduces complexities that can cause power-related problems, though—specifically, the battery and charging the battery. In addition, because of their compact nature, mobile devices are more prone to overheating. In this section we'll look at battery-related issues as well as overheating problems.

Battery and Charging Issues

Mobile devices are of course meant to be mobile and not plugged in at all times. It's a bit ironic, then, that a good question to ask if a mobile device doesn't seem to power up is, "Is it plugged in?" Everyone hates getting asked that question, but it's a critical question to ask, even with mobile devices. If the device works when it's plugged in but not unplugged, you've narrowed down the problem. You can't assume that the battery is working (or is attached) as it's supposed to be. Always check power and connections first!

Poor Battery Health

If the laptop works while it's plugged in but not while on battery power, the battery itself may be the culprit. As batteries get older, they are not able to hold as much of a charge and, in some cases, are not able to hold a charge at all. That is to say, the battery health may be poor. If the battery won't charge while the laptop is plugged in, try removing the battery and reinserting it. If it still won't charge, you might want to replace the battery.

Another issue that small devices can have is an extremely short battery life. We're not talking about when people complain that their laptop only runs for an hour and a half when they are playing a DVD while surfing the Internet and talking to their friends on their Bluetooth headset over a social media instant messenger. No, that's bound to drain your battery quickly. What we're referring to here is when a laptop battery only lasts for an hour or so after a full charge with normal usage, or if a mobile phone battery is only able to power the device for 30 minutes or so. These things happen.

If it's a laptop, you can try to perform a battery calibration, as we discussed in Chapter 9. For all mobile devices, you can try to drain the battery completely and then charge it fully before turning the device back on. If these options don't work, then it's likely that the battery needs to be replaced.

Improper Charging

Many laptop power adapters have a light indicating that they're plugged in. If there's no light, check to make sure that the outlet is working, or switch outlets. Also, most laptops have a power-ready indicator light when plugged into a wall outlet as well. Check to see if it's lit. If the outlet is fine, try another power adapter. They do fail on occasion.

Smaller mobile devices will have a lightning bolt next to their battery icon or an animated filling battery when charging. If the device doesn't appear to charge, the same culprits apply: it could be the outlet, the adapter, or the device itself.

If you're working on a DC adapter, the same concepts apply. Check for lights, try another adapter if you have one, or try changing plugs, if possible. For example, if you're using a DC outlet in a car, many newer models have secondary power sources, such as ones in the console between the seats.

Another thing to remember when troubleshooting power problems is to remove all external peripherals. Strip your laptop down to the base computer so that there isn't a short or other power drain coming from an external device.

Windows has built-in power management features to help conserve laptop battery life. In Windows, open the Power Options applet in Control Panel. Once there, you can configure different power-saving settings to maximize the battery life of your laptop.

Swollen Battery

The last power issue that we need to discuss is a *swollen battery*. As the term suggests, the battery physically swells in size. It can be caused by a number of things, including manufacturer defects, age, misuse, using the wrong adapter for charging, or leaving the laptop constantly plugged into a wall outlet. Inside the battery, the individual cells become overcharged, causing them to swell. Sometimes the swelling is barely noticeable, but it can cause the device case to crack or pop apart. Other times it's pretty obvious, such as the one shown in Figure 12.9.

FIGURE 12.9   iPhone with a swollen battery

Mpt-matthew at English Wikipedia [GFDL (www.gnu.org/copyleft/fdl.html) or CC BY-SA 3.0 (https://creativecommons.org/licenses/by-sa/3.0)]

If you have a swollen battery, turn the device off immediately and make sure that it's not plugged into a charger. If the battery is removable, you can try to remove it, if you wish, but be very careful. Swollen batteries are more prone to explosions than normal batteries because the casing is already compromised. If you are able to remove it, place it into a safe container, just in case there are further issues. If the battery is not removable, it's time for a new device. In either case, take the battery or device to a proper recycling center to dispose of it. Never just throw it in the trash; it can explode and harm sanitation workers, as well as cause significant damage to the environment.

Overheating

Smaller devices have greater potential to overheat than do their larger brethren. Space is at a premium, so all the components are packed tightly together, which means less room for each component to breathe. Manufacturers realize this, of course, so they use components that generate less heat. Overheating can still be a problem, though. If your mobile device is overheating, turn it off to let it cool down. It could be from overuse, or perhaps it did not have proper ventilation (for example, if it was stuffed into someone's pocket or purse). On laptops, check to ensure that the cooling fan is working and not full of dust or debris. If the overheating is persistent, you have a few options. The first is to test or replace the battery, as that's the most likely culprit. If overheating still happens, you may have to replace the device.

Input Problems

Laptop keyboards aren't as easy to switch out as desktop keyboards. You can, however, very easily attach an external USB keyboard to your laptop if the keys on your laptop don't appear to work.

If the keyboard doesn't seem to respond at all, try pressing the Num Lock and Caps Lock keys to see if they toggle the Num Lock and Caps Lock lights on and off. If the lights don't respond, the keyboard isn't functioning properly. Try rebooting the system. (You will probably have to press and hold the power button for 5 seconds, and the system will shut off. Wait 10 seconds, and press the power button again to turn it back on.) If that doesn't fix the problem, you probably have faulty hardware.

Another problem unique to laptop keyboards is the *Fn key*. (It can be your friend or your enemy.) You can identify it on your laptop keyboard because it's in the lower-left corner and has the letters *Fn* on it (often in blue), as shown in Figure 12.10. If the Fn key is stuck on, the only keys that will work are those with functions on them. If you look at other keys on your laptop, several of them will have blue lettering too. Those are the functions that the keys may perform if you press and hold the Fn key before pressing the function key that you want. If the Fn key is stuck on, try toggling it just as you would a Caps Lock or Num Lock key.

FIGURE 12.10   The Fn key on a laptop

If another key on your laptop keyboard is stuck, you need to determine if the contact is having problems or if the key itself is stuck. If the key is not physically stuck but the laptop thinks it is, rebooting generally solves the problem. If the key physically sticks, you can try blowing out underneath the key with compressed air, or use a cotton swab slightly dampened with water (or rubbing alcohol) to clean underneath the key. Make sure to clean the entire surface underneath the sticking key. If none of this resolves the issue, you might need to replace the keyboard.

One of the conveniences that users often take advantage of in laptops is a built-in pointing device. Most laptops have touchpads or point sticks that function much like a mouse. They're nice because you don't need to carry an external mouse around with you. While these types of devices are usually considered very handy, some people find them annoying. For example, when you are typing your palm might rest on the touchpad, causing erratic pointer behavior. This is referred to as a *ghost cursor* because it seems like the cursor just randomly jumps all over the screen. You can turn the touchpad off through Control Panel. While understanding that you can turn it off on purpose, remember that it can be turned off accidentally as well. Check to make sure that it's enabled. Some laptops allow you to disable or change the sensitivity of the touchpad as well, just as you can adjust the sensitivity of your mouse.

Another potential issue is *cursor drift*, where the mouse cursor will slowly drift in one direction even though you are not trying to make it move. This issue is generally related to the point stick not centering properly after it's been used. If you have cursor drift, try using the point stick and moving it back and forth a few times to get it to re-center itself. You can also try calibrating it within the operating system (most manufacturers make it a tab in Mouse properties), or rebooting. If the problem persists, either disable or replace the point stick.

Finally, here are two issues you may encounter with mobile device displays: digitizer issues and broken screens. Recall from Chapter 9 that a digitizer is a device that can be written or drawn on, typically with the touch from a human finger. Most mobile devices have a digitizer built into the display unit. It may be the glass of the display itself, or it might be implemented as an overlay for the display. Either way, if it's not functioning, that can cause problems. You can probably work around it on a laptop, but a smartphone or tablet with a nonworking digitizer is pretty useless.

In touch-enabled Windows devices, digitizers can be calibrated under Control Panel ➤ Hardware And Sound ➤ Tablet PC Settings ➤ Calibrate The Screen For Pen Or Touch Input. Rebooting may also help. For iOS and Android tablets and phones, if the digitizer isn't working, the only troubleshooting step is to power it off and restart the device. With any device, if the digitizer isn't working, the next step is to replace the screen or the device.

A broken screen, while unfortunate, is all too common with mobile devices. Considering the beating they take on a regular basis, it's a little surprising it doesn't happen more often. First, to help avoid broken screens, make sure all of your mobile users have screen protectors. If a screen does get broken, either replace the screen or replace the device.

Connectivity Issues

Nearly every mobile device sold is equipped with integrated wireless networking, and most have Bluetooth built in as well. In many cases, the wireless antenna is run into the LCD panel. This allows the antenna to stand up higher and pick up a better signal.

If your wireless networking isn't working on a laptop, do the following:

1. Ensure that the network card is turned on. Most laptops have an external switch or button on the front or side or above the keyboard that can toggle the network card on and off. In some cases, it will be a function key. Be sure that this is set to the On position. Figure 12.11 shows a toggle above the keyboard. (It's the one on the left that looks like an antenna.)

FIGURE 12.11 Network card toggle switch above the keyboard

2. Next, make sure the wireless card is enabled through Windows. You generally do this in Windows 10 as follows:

   a. Open Control Panel ➤ Network And Sharing Center.

   b. Click Change Adapter Settings.

   c. Right-click the wireless network connection.

   d. Select Properties to look at the network card properties, as shown in Figure 12.12.

   e. Click the Configure button to open up more Properties, including driver management.

   Some network cards have their own proprietary configuration software as well. You can also often check here by clicking a tab (often called Wireless Networks) to see if you're getting a signal and, if so, the strength of that signal.

FIGURE 12.12   Wireless network connection properties

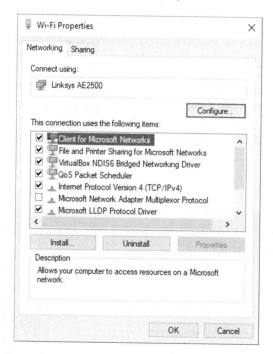

3.   Check the strength of the signal.

A weak signal is the most common cause of intermittent wireless networking connection problems. If you have intermittent connectivity and keep getting dropped, see if you can get closer to the wireless access point (WAP) or remove obstructions between you and the WAP. Failing network cards and connectivity devices can also cause intermittent wireless networking connection failures.

 If you have a USB network adapter, try unplugging it and plugging it back in. Make sure that Windows recognizes the card properly.

If the wireless connection fails but the system has a wired RJ-45 port, try plugging it in. For this, you will need an Ethernet cable and, of course, a wired network to plug it into. But if you get lights on the NIC, you might get on the network.

 Real World Scenario

Potential Wireless and Wired Conflicts

A short time ago, a friend of ours was frustrated because he couldn't get to the network in his office with his laptop plugged into his docking station. He had used the laptop at home the night before and gotten on his wireless network without a problem. But this day, his wired connection would not work. He checked his cables (always your first step) and saw that there were lights (a good sign). He had tried to access both the Internet and intranet sites, but to no avail.

We opened a command prompt and ran `ipconfig`. He didn't have an IP address, but we noticed that his built-in wireless card was listed and active.

What he needed to do was to disable his built-in wireless card. He had enabled the wireless to work at home, and it was still enabled. Because it was enabled, the wireless card was trying to obtain an IP address, and it refused to let the wired "portion" of the card pick up an address from the company DHCP server. (There was no wireless in the building due to strict security policies.) After he disabled his wireless card, his wired connection picked up an IP address, and all was well.

Many laptop network cards have a wired connection in addition to their wireless capabilities. For some of them, the wired connection will not work if the wireless is enabled. It's an attempt to prevent conflicts if both connection types are active.

The principles behind troubleshooting network or Bluetooth connectivity issues on mobile phones and tablets are the same as on laptops. The big difference is that you can't try an external network card if your internal card is failing. We originally looked at some of these settings in Chapter 10, "Mobile Connectivity and Application Support," but now is a good time to review them. The first thing to check is that the network connection or Bluetooth is enabled, which also means double-checking that airplane mode is not turned on. On Android and iOS devices, this is done through Settings. Figure 12.13 shows iOS network settings, and Figure 12.14 shows Android network settings. Toggle the connection off and then back on to reset it; often, that will resolve connectivity issues.

Another way to access network settings in iOS is from the Control Center. You can do this from both the lock screen and the home screen. Simply swipe your finger down from the very top of the iPhone's touchscreen, and you will get the Control Center, similar to what's shown in Figure 12.15. In Android, open the notifications area by swiping down from the top of the screen (you may need to swipe down twice), and network settings will be there as well, as shown in Figure 12.16.

Poor or intermittent connectivity on mobile devices is usually a function of the distance from the access point. Wi-Fi has maximum ranges that can be dramatically shortened by obstructions such as steel or cinder-block walls. Usually, moving closer to the access point will resolve these issues.

FIGURE 12.13 iOS network settings

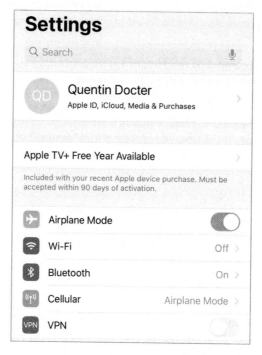

FIGURE 12.14 Android network settings

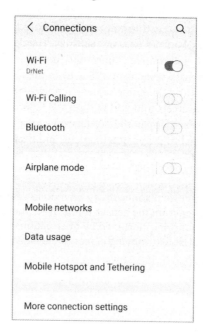

FIGURE 12.15   iPhone Control Center

FIGURE 12.16   Android notifications center

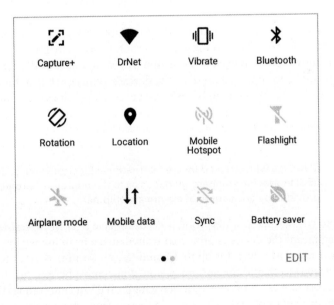

Physical Damage and Malware

Mobile devices take much more of a beating than stationary devices do, which is why cases and screen protectors are needed accessories. Sometimes things happen, though, and a device gets physically damaged. Here we will look at two types of physical damage: liquid damage and physically damaged ports. Then we will take a look at malware and how to avoid issues it can cause.

Physical Device Damage

A device can become damaged in any number of ways, with dropping being the most common. Even if you have a great case on your phone, an airborne expedition down a flight of concrete stairs probably isn't going to have a happy ending. Similarly, liquid can do nasty things to electronics as well.

If a laptop gets doused in a liquid, it's best to turn it off as soon as possible and let it dry out. If it was a spill on the keyboard and no liquid got into ports, the computer is probably salvageable. If liquid got inside the ports, they could be very difficult to clean out and the liquid can cause connectivity problems for those ports.

For significant liquid damage, the laptop can be taken apart and the components—even circuit boards such as the motherboard—can be cleaned with demineralized water and a lint-free cloth. Disassemble the components, clean them with water and the cloth, and let them thoroughly dry. Reassemble, and see if it works. Several years ago, one of our friends had a toddler son who decided to relieve himself on the laptop. The demineralized water and a thorough drying did the trick—the machine still worked. We can't guarantee success in every situation, however!

Mobile devices are much more liquid-friendly than laptops are. Many phones and tablets today are water-resistant, if not entirely waterproof. Every smartphone that is considered water-resistant will have an ingress protection (IP) rating, such as IP67 or IP68. The first digit, which will be from 0–6, represents the device's ability to withstand solid foreign material such as dust. The second digit, which will be from 0–8, shows its moisture resistance. Sometimes you will see a rating such as IPX6, which means the device has not been tested for dust resistance and has a moisture resistance rating of 6.

IP ratings were created by the International Electrotechnical Commission (IEC) to provide standard guidance as to the degrees of protection provided by enclosures of electrical equipment.

For a device to be considered waterproof, it needs to have a moisture resistance rating of 7 or 8. A 7 rating means the device is protected from damage from immersion in water with a depth of up to 1 meter (3.3 feet) for up to 30 minutes. An 8 rating is given to devices that can withstand greater depth and time of immersion, which must be specified by the manufacturer. For the best in protection, buy a device with an IP67 or IP68 rating. Devices with no IP code might or might not survive heavy rain, sprays from water sources, or an accidental dunking.

If you suspect a mobile device has suffered water damage, first, immediately turn it off. Remove the case and anything else that can be removed, such as the SIM card and possibly the battery. Dry everything you can with a lint-free cloth. Then you have a few choices. One is to let it air dry for at least 48 hours. Or you can try the "rice trick." That is, put the device in a sealed container, covered in uncooked rice, and let it sit for 48 hours. The rice should soak up all of the water in the device. Note that professional opinions are divided on the rice trick. Some experts say it works well, others say that residue in the rice can damage electronic components. But if the phone isn't working anyway, how much risk is it to try?

The A+ exam objectives list physically damaged ports as a mobile device symptom. Sometimes the ports are obviously damaged, and other times they simply fail to work. In either case, the only remedy is to replace the port, which usually means replacing several components, including the motherboard on a laptop, or replacing the entire mobile device.

Malware

Malware is malicious software designed to damage, disrupt, or gain unauthorized access to a computer system. Malware infections are one of the most common security risks that you will encounter. Let's look at malware on laptops as well as mobile devices.

Laptops and Malware

Laptops running Windows or macOS have the same vulnerability to malware as their desktop cousins do. To help guard against malware, install antimalware software. These are the four main classes of applications to help protect your system against malware and hackers:

- Antivirus software defends against viruses, worms, and Trojan horses.

- Antispyware software defends against adware and spyware.

- Antispam software reduces the amount of junk email you receive.

- Software firewalls block potentially dangerous network traffic.

There are also suites available that combine multiple security functions; for example, the Norton Security suite includes antivirus, antimalware, and antispam features, along with identity protection tools, a software firewall, a backup tool, and a PC tune-up tool. McAfee's LiveSafe is similar. In addition, there is some overlap between the types of threats each application guards against; for example, an antivirus program may also target some types of non-virus malware.

Even if you have an antimalware application installed, it's not perfect. Occasionally a virus or other malware may get around it, especially a new threat (and especially if you haven't updated your definitions lately). When a system is infected with a virus, a worm, a Trojan horse, or other malicious software, you need to remove it immediately. Here are the five steps to take to remove malware:

1. **Identify malware symptoms.** Before doing anything major, it is imperative first to be sure you are dealing with the right issue. If you suspect malware, then try to identify the type (spyware, virus, and so on) and look for the proof needed to substantiate that it is indeed the culprit.

2. **Quarantine the infected system.** Once you have confirmed that malware is at hand, then quarantine the infected system to prevent it from spreading the malware to other systems. Bear in mind that malware can spread any number of ways, including through a network connection, email, and so on. The quarantine needs to be complete to prevent any spread.

3. **Remediate infected systems.** The steps taken here depend on the type of malware with which you're dealing, but it should include updating antivirus software with the latest definitions and using the appropriate scan and removal techniques.

4. **Schedule scans and updates.** The odds of the system never being confronted by malware again are slim. To reduce the chances of it being infected again, schedule scans and updates to run regularly.

5. **Educate the end user.** Education should always be viewed as the final step. The end user needs to understand what led to the malware infestation and what to avoid, or look for, in the future to keep it from happening again.

Mobile Devices and Malware

Many people believe, incorrectly, that mobile devices running iOS or Android can't get infected with malware. Or, others believe that iOS is totally safe but Android is less so. The second statement is a little closer to the truth, but iOS is still vulnerable to malware. Let's take a look at the four most common ways mobile devices can contract malware:

Malicious Apps   The most common way that malware ends up on mobile devices is through downloading malicious apps. Downloading apps from official sources such as Google Play or the App Store is almost always safe. Apps are vetted and should be good, although Apple is a bit more stringent on developer guidelines than Google is. If someone has jailbroken their phone and is downloading apps from random places though, this is a great way to contract a malware infection.

Operating System Vulnerabilities   If you have a mobile device, it's guaranteed that you've seen the notification to update your OS to a newer version. One of the reasons for that is because developers may have uncovered a vulnerability that hackers can exploit. A general rule of thumb is to always update to the newest version of the mobile operating system that you can.

Suspicious Links   This is the same as it would be on a laptop or a desktop. If you get an email with a suspicious link, don't click it. Clicking it can install malware on your device without your knowledge.

Unsecure Networks   This, too, is the same as it would be for laptops. Using an unsecure network doesn't really pose much of a risk for you downloading malware, but it could easily allow a hacker to read the data transmitted to or from your device. A VPN can help eliminate these issues on unsecured public networks.

A few good rules of practice to avoid malicious apps or malware on a mobile device are:

- Don't jailbreak mobile devices. This compromises built-in security mechanisms.
- Download apps only from official app stores.
- Always update the OS to the most current version.
- Avoid clicking links if you are unsure of the source.
- Use a VPN when on public networks.

Antimalware software such as Norton and Avast can be purchased for iOS and Android as well.

The A+ exam may expect you to troubleshoot the following common symptoms for mobile devices:

- Poor battery health
- Swollen battery
- Broken screen
- Improper charging
- Poor/no connectivity
- Liquid damage
- Overheating
- Digitizer issues
- Physically damaged ports
- Malware
- Cursor drift/touch calibration

Troubleshooting Printer Problems

Even though society is moving away from paper forms, printers are still very common peripherals. Printers are also the most complex peripheral as far as troubleshooting is concerned; this arises from complications in putting ink to paper. There are several different ways that this can be accomplished, but the end result is all pretty much the same.

Recall from Chapter 4, "Printers and Multifunction Devices," that the A+ exam objectives list 3D printers. In the troubleshooting objectives, only 2D printer problems are listed. For a more detailed description of each type of printer's components and inner workings, see Chapter 4.

Different types of printers work in different ways, so you would expect that laser printers might have different issues from impact printers. Because problems are often dependent on the type of printer you're using, we've chosen to break down this discussion by printer type. We'll start with a quick review of the technology and then get into specific issues. At the end, we'll look at the process of managing the print spooler, which is the same regardless of the printer type in use.

Printer manufacturer websites are great places to look to find trouble-shooting information. They often provide descriptions of problems and detailed instructions for resolving the issue. Most printers also come with management software that you can install on your computer, which may be able to assist you in troubleshooting any issues that you have.

Help! I Can't Install My Printer!

Before you can print, you must, of course, install the printer on the computer you want to print from. Sometimes, though, installing the printer can be problematic. The first common issue you will run into is that the printer isn't found during the installation process. If this is the case, check to make sure that the printer is on and connected to either the computer or the network. Wireless network printers are notorious for not being "found." If needed, reseat the connections and try again, or see if you can connect the printer using a different method (for example, USB instead of wireless).

The second common issue is that the printer driver won't install. Be sure that any other instances of that type of printer aren't already installed on the computer. If you just removed the old printer driver, reboot before reinstalling the new one. And, finally, download and install the newest driver from the manufacturer's website.

Impact Printer Problems

Impact printers are so named because they rely on making a physical impact in order to print. These are typically dot-matrix or daisy wheel printers. The impact printer's print head will be activated and forced up against the ink ribbon, making a character or pattern on the paper. Impact printers are relatively simple devices; therefore, only a few problems usually arise. We will cover the most common problems and their solutions here.

Low Print Quality

Problems with print quality are easy to identify. When the printed page comes out of the printer, the characters may be too light or have dots missing from them. Table 12.3 details some of the most common impact print quality problems, their causes, and their solutions.

TABLE 12.3 Common impact print quality problems

Characteristics	Cause	Solution
Consistently faded or light characters	Worn-out printer ribbon	See if you can adjust the print head to be closer to the ribbon. If not (or if it doesn't help), replace the ribbon with a new, vendor-recommended ribbon.
Print lines that go from dark to light as the print head moves across the page	Printer ribbon-advance gear slipping	Replace the ribbon-advance gear or mechanism.
A small, blank line running through a line of print (consistently)	Print head pin stuck inside the print head	Replace the print head.
A small, blank line running through a line of print (intermittently)	A broken, loose, or shorting print head cable	Secure or replace the print head cable.
A small, dark line running through a line of print	Print head pin stuck in the out position	Replace the print head. (Pushing the pin in may damage the print head.)
Printer making a printing noise, but no print appears on the page	Worn, missing, or improperly installed ribbon cartridge	Replace the ribbon cartridge correctly.
Printer printing garbage, such as garbled characters	Cable partially unhooked, wrong driver selected, or bad printer control board (PCB)	Hook up the cable correctly, select the correct driver, or replace the PCB (respectively).

Printout Jams inside the Printer

Printer jams (aka "the printer crinkled my paper") are very frustrating because they always seem to happen more than halfway through your 50-page print job, requiring you to take time to remove the jam before the rest of your pages can print. A paper jam happens when something prevents the paper from advancing through the printer evenly. There are generally three causes of printer jams: an obstructed paper path, stripped drive gears, and using the wrong paper.

Obstructed paper paths are often difficult to find. Usually it means disassembling the printer to find the bit of crumpled-up paper or other foreign substance that's blocking the paper path. A common obstruction is a piece of the "perf"—the perforated sides of tractor-feed paper—that has torn off and gotten crumpled up and then lodged in the paper path. It may be necessary to remove the platen roller and feed mechanism to get at the obstruction.

Stripped drive gears cause the paper to feed improperly, causing it to crinkle and cause jams. Using the wrong paper, such as thick paper when the platen has been set for thin paper, can also cause jams. When loading new paper, always be sure that the platen is properly adjusted.

Impact printers are used for multipart (or multipage) forms. Those forms are typically three or more sheets of paper thick. If the multipage forms are not feeding properly, it could be that the printer is set to receive paper that is too thin or too thick. Check the platen and adjust accordingly.

Use extra caution when printing peel-off labels in impact printers. If a label or even a whole sheet of labels becomes misaligned or jammed, do *not* roll the roller backward to realign the sheet. The small plastic paper guide that most impact printers use to control the forward movement of the paper through the printer will peel the label right off its backing if you reverse the direction of the paper. Once the label is free, it can easily get stuck under the platen, causing paper jams. A label stuck under the platen is almost impossible to remove without disassembling the paper-feed assembly. If a label is misaligned, try realigning the whole sheet of labels *slowly* using the feed roller (with the power off), moving it in very small increments.

Stepper Motor Problems

Printers use stepper motors to move the print head back and forth as well as to advance the paper. The carriage motor is responsible for the back-and-forth motion while the main motor advances the paper. These motors get damaged when they are forced in any direction while the power is on. This includes moving the print head over to install a printer ribbon as well as moving the paper-feed roller to align paper. These motors are very sensitive to stray voltages. If you are rotating one of these motors by hand, you are essentially turning it into a small generator and thus damaging it.

A damaged stepper motor is easy to detect. Damage to the stepper motor will cause it to lose precision and move farther with each step. If the main motor is damaged (which is more likely to happen), lines of print will be unevenly spaced. If the print head motor goes bad, characters will be scrunched together. If a stepper motor is damaged badly enough, it won't move at all in any direction; it may even make grinding or high-pitched squealing noises. If any of these symptoms appear, it's time to replace one of these motors.

Stepper motors are usually expensive to replace—about half the cost of a new printer! Damage to them is easy to avoid; the biggest key is to not force them to move when the power is On.

 Grinding noise is a printer symptom that could occur across all printer types. Remember that to make a noise, a part has to move. So, think about motors, gears, and rollers if you hear grinding. It will probably help to get your ear close to the printer to see if you can tell exactly where it's coming from.

Inkjet Printer Problems

An inkjet printer has many of the same types of parts as an impact printer. In this sense, it's almost as though the inkjet technology is simply an extension of the technology used in impact printers. The parts on an inkjet can be divided into the following four categories:

- Print head/ink cartridge
- Print head carriage, belt, and stepper motor
- Paper-feed mechanism
- Control, interface, and power circuitry

Perhaps the most obvious difference between inkjet and impact printers is that impact printers often use tractor-feed paper, whereas inkjets use normal paper. The differences don't end there, though. Inkjet printers work by spraying ink (often in the form of a bubble) onto a page. The pattern of the bubbles forms images on the paper.

Inkjet printers are the most common type of printer found in homes because they are inexpensive and produce good-quality images. For this reason, you need to understand the most common problems with these printers so that your company can service them effectively. Let's take a look at some of the most common problems with inkjet printers and their solutions.

Print Quality

The majority of inkjet printer problems are quality problems. Ninety-nine percent of these can be traced to a faulty ink cartridge. With most inkjet printers, the ink cartridge contains the print head and the ink. The major problem with this assembly can be described by "If you don't use it, you lose it." The ink will dry out in the small nozzles and block them if they are not used at least once every week or two.

An example of a quality problem is when you have thin, blank lines present in every line of text on the page. This is caused by a plugged hole in at least one of the small, pinhole ink nozzles in the print cartridge. Another common problem is faded printing. Replacing the ink cartridge generally solves these issues.

WARNING   As we warned in Chapter 4, some people try to save money by refilling their ink cartridge when they need to replace it. If you are one of them, stop! Don't refill your ink cartridges! Almost all ink cartridges are *not* designed to be refilled. They are designed to be used once and disposed of (preferably sent to a recycling center). By refilling them, you make a hole in them. Ink can leak out, and the printer will need to be cleaned. The ink will probably also be of the wrong type, and print quality can suffer. Finally, using a refilled cartridge may void the printer's warranty.

If an ink cartridge becomes damaged or develops a hole, it can put too much ink on the page and the letters will smear. Again, the solution is to replace the ink cartridge. (You should be aware, however, that a very small amount of smearing is normal if the pages are laid on top of each other immediately after printing.)

One final print quality problem that does not directly involve the ink cartridge occurs when the print quickly goes from dark to light and then prints nothing. As previously mentioned, ink cartridges dry out if not used. That's why the manufacturers include a small suction pump inside the printer that primes the ink cartridge before each print cycle. If this priming pump is broken or malfunctioning, this problem will manifest itself and the pump will need to be replaced.

TIP   If the problem of the ink quickly going from dark to light and then disappearing ever happens to you and you really need to print a couple of pages, try this trick. First, take the ink cartridge out of the printer. Then squirt some window cleaner on a paper towel and gently tap the print head against the wet paper towel. The force of the tap plus the solvents in the window cleaner should dislodge any dried ink, and the ink will flow freely again. Just be careful to not rub the paper towel across the print head, because this could damage the nozzles.

After you install a new cartridge into many inkjet printers, the print heads in that cartridge must be aligned. *Print head alignment* is the process by which the print head is calibrated for use. A special utility that comes with the printer software is used to do this. Sometimes it's run from the printer itself and other times from the computer the printer is installed on. They vary a bit in how they work. For example, one utility might have the printer print several vertical and horizontal lines with numbers next to them. The utility then displays a screen and asks you to choose the horizontal and vertical lines that are the most "in line." Once you enter the numbers, the software understands whether the print head (s) are out of alignment, which direction, and by how much. The software then makes slight modifications to the print driver software to tell it how much to offset when printing. Other calibration software will print a pattern and then ask you to put the newly printed page on the scanner portion of the printer. It will then scan the pattern to make sure that the heads are properly aligned. Occasionally, alignment must be done several times to get the images to align properly.

Most new inkjet printers automatically align the print head, and no interaction is required on your part. Even if this is the case, your printer software may have an option for you to be able to align the print heads manually.

Color Output Problems

Sometimes when you print a color document, the colors might not be the same colors that you expected based on what you saw on the screen. This is called an incorrect chroma display. A few different issues could cause this problem. First, ink could be bleeding from adjacent areas of the picture, causing the color to be off. A leaking cartridge can cause this, as can using the wrong type of paper for your printer.

If you know that you're using the right paper, try cleaning the print cartridges using the software utility that should have been included with the printer software. Once you do that, print a test page to confirm that the colors are correct. On most color printers, the test page will print colors in a pattern from left to right that mirrors the way the ink cartridges are installed. That brings us to our second potential problem: the ink cartridges are installed in the wrong spot. (This is for printers with multiple color ink cartridges.) That should be easy to check. Obviously, if that's the problem, put the color cartridges where they're supposed to be.

Third, if the ink that comes out of the cartridge doesn't match the label on the cartridge, try the self-cleaning utility. If that doesn't help, replace the cartridge. Finally, if one of the colors doesn't come out at all and self-cleaning doesn't help, just replace the cartridge.

Somewhat related to color problems is speckling on printed pages. This is where the pages have random dots of ink or other material on them as they print. This is most often caused by stuff like paper dust or residue from envelopes, staples, or glue getting into the machinery. Cleaning the printer and blowing it out with compressed air should clear up any speckling. It's possible, but less likely, that speckles could be caused by a leaky ink cartridge.

Paper Jams

Inkjet printers have pretty simple paper paths, so paper jams due to obstructions are less likely than they are on impact printers. They are still possible, however, so an obstruction shouldn't be overlooked as a possible cause of jamming.

Paper jams in inkjet printers are usually due to one of two things:

- A worn pickup roller
- The wrong type of paper

The pickup roller usually has one or two D-shaped rollers mounted on a rotating shaft. When the shaft rotates, one edge of the D roller rubs against the paper, pushing it into the printer. When the roller gets worn, it gets smooth and doesn't exert enough friction against the paper to push it into the printer.

If the paper used in the printer is too smooth, it can cause the same problem. Pickup rollers use friction, and smooth paper doesn't offer much friction. If the paper is too rough, on the other hand, it acts like sandpaper on the rollers, wearing them smooth. Here's a rule of thumb for paper smoothness: paper slightly smoother than a new dollar bill will work fine.

 Creased paper is a common culprit in paper jams. The printer can crease the paper if there are obstructions in the paper path or problems with the paper-feed mechanism.

Paper-Feeding Problems

You will normally see one of two paper-feeding options on an inkjet printer. The first is that the paper is stored in a paper tray on the front of the printer. The second, which is more common on smaller and cheaper models, is for the paper to be fed in vertically from the back of the printer in a paper feeder. Both types may also have manual feed or envelope feed options.

Regardless of the feed style, the printer will have a paper-feed mechanism, which picks up the paper and feeds it into the printer. Inside the paper-feed mechanism are pickup rollers, which are small rubber rollers that rub up against the paper and feed it into the printer. They press up against small rubber or cork patches known as *separation pads*. These help to keep the rest of the paper in the tray so that only one sheet is picked up at a time. A pickup stepper motor turns the pickup rollers.

If your printer fails to pick up paper, it could indicate that the pickup rollers are too worn. If your printer is always picking up multiple sheets of paper, it could be a couple of things, such as problems with the separation pads or your paper being too "sticky," damp, or rough. Some printers that use vertical paper feeders have a lever with which you can adjust the amount of tension between the pickup rollers and the separation pads. If your printer is consistently pulling multiple sheets of paper, you might want to try to increase the tension using this lever.

The final component is the paper-feed sensor. This sensor is designed to tell the printer when it's out of paper, and it rarely fails. When it does, the printer will refuse to print because it thinks it is out of paper. Cleaning the sensor might help, but if not, you should replace the printer.

Stepper Motor Problems

Inkjet printers use stepper motors, just like impact printers. On an inkjet, the print head carriage is the component containing the print head that moves back and forth. A carriage stepper motor and an attached belt (the carriage belt) are responsible for the movement. The print head carriage stays horizontally stable by resting on a metal stabilizer bar. Another stepper motor is responsible for advancing the paper.

Stepper motor problems on an inkjet printer will look similar to the ones on an impact printer. That is, if the main motor is damaged, lines of print will be unevenly spaced, and if the print head motor goes bad, characters will be scrunched together. A lot of damage may cause the stepper motor to not move at all and possibly make grinding or high-pitched squealing noises. If any of these symptoms appear, it's time to replace one of these motors. As with impact printers, stepper motors can be expensive. It may make more economical sense to replace the printer.

Power Problems

Inkjet printers have internal power circuits that convert the electricity from the outlet into voltages that the printer can use—typically, 12V and 5V. The specific device that does this is called the *transformer*. If the transformer fails, the printer will not power up. If this happens, it's time to get a new printer.

Laser Printer Problems

The process that laser printers use to print, called the *electrophotographic (EP) imaging process*, is the most complex process of all commonly used printers. You should have already memorized the seven-step EP process for the 220-1101 A+ exam, but perhaps you've forgotten a bit. Table 12.4 provides a short description of what happens in each step.

TABLE 12.4 The EP imaging process

Step	Action
Processing	The page to be printed gets rendered, one horizontal strip at a time. The image is stored in memory for printing.
Charging	The charging corona gets a high voltage from the high-voltage power supply (HVPS). It uses the voltage to apply a strong uniform negative charge (–600VDC) to the photosensitive drum.
Exposing	The laser scans the drum. Wherever it touches the drum, the charge is reduced from –600VDC to around –100VDC. The pattern formed on the drum will be the image that is printed.
Developing	The developing roller acquires a –600VDC charge from the HVPS and picks up toner, which gets the same –600VDC charge. As the developing toner rolls by the photosensitive drum, the toner is attracted to the lesser-charged (–100VDC) areas on the photosensitive drum and sticks to it in those areas.
Transferring	The charging corona wire or roller acquires a strong positive charge (+600VDC) and transfers it to the paper. As the photosensitive drum with ink on it rolls by, the ink is attracted to the paper.
Fusing	The 350°F fuser roller melts the toner paper and the rubberized pressure roller presses the melted toner into the paper, making the image permanent.
Cleaning	A rubber blade scrapes any remaining toner off the drum, and a fluorescent lamp discharges any remaining charge on the photosensitive drum.

The descriptions in Table 12.4 are summaries of the EP imaging process. For detailed descriptions, see Chapter 4.

Looking at the steps involved in laser printing, it's pretty easy to tell that laser printers are the most complex printers that we have discussed. The good news, though, is that most laser printer problems are easily identifiable and have specific fixes. Let's discuss the most common laser and page printer problems and their solutions.

Don't forget to perform periodic preventive maintenance on your laser printers. It can help eliminate many potential problems before they happen. Preventive maintenance includes cleaning the printer and using manufacturer-recommended maintenance kits.

Power Problems

If you turn on your laser printer and it doesn't respond normally, there could be a problem with the power it's receiving. Of course, the first thing to do is to ensure that it's plugged in.

A laser printer's DC power supply provides three different DC voltages to printer components. These can be checked at a power interface labeled J210, which is a 20-pin female interface. Pin 1 will be in the lower-left corner, and the pins along the bottom will all be odd numbers, increasing from left to right.

You can use a multimeter to test printer voltages.

Using the multimeter, you should find the following voltages:

- Pin 1 +5V
- Pin 5 −5V
- Pin 9 +24V

If none of the voltages are reading properly, then you probably need to replace the fuse in the DC power supply. If one or more (but not all) of the voltages aren't reading properly, then the first thing to do is to remove all optional hardware in the printer (including memory) and test again. If the readings are still bad, then you likely need to replace the DC power supply.

No Connectivity (IP Issues)

You can connect many laser printers directly to your network by using a network cable (such as Category 5, 5e, 6, or 6a) or by using a wireless network adapter with the printer. In cases like these, the printer acts as its own print server (typically, print server software is built into the printer), and it can speed up printing because you don't have a separate print server translating and then sending the directions to the printer.

For printers such as these, no connectivity can be a sign of improperly configured IP settings, such as the IP address. While each printer is somewhat different, you can manually configure most laser printers' IP settings a number of ways:

- Through the printer's LCD control panel. For example, on several HP LaserJet models, you press Menu, navigate to the Network Config menu, select TCP/IP Config, select Manual, and then enter the IP address. You would then also configure the subnet mask and default gateway.

- By using Telnet to connect to the printer's management software from your computer. Note that Telnet is not secure. If you need a secure connection, use Secure Shell (SSH) instead.

- By using the management software that came with your printer.

You can also configure most IP printers to obtain an IP address automatically from a Dynamic Host Configuration Protocol (DHCP) server. When the printer is powered up, it will contact the server to get its IP configuration information, just like any other client on the network. While this may be convenient, it's usually not a good idea to assign dynamic IP addresses to printers. Client computers will have their printer mapped to a specific IP address; if that address is changed, you will have a lot of people complaining about no connectivity. If you are using the DHCP server to manage all of your network's IP addresses, be sure to reserve a static address for the printers.

To see the setting of a printer's IP address, print a configuration page from the printer's control panel. Then post the IP information near the printer so that users can easily connect to it.

Nothing Prints

You tell your computer to print, but nothing comes out of the printer. This problem is probably the most challenging to solve because several different things could cause it. Are you the only one affected by the problem, or are others having the same issue? Is the printer plugged in, powered on, and online? As with any troubleshooting, check your connections first.

Sometimes when nothing prints, you get a clue as to what the problem is. The printer may give you an "out of memory" error or something similar. Another possibility is that the printer will say "processing data" (or something similar) on its LCD display and nothing will print. It's likely that the printer has run out of memory while trying to process the print job. If your printer is exhibiting these symptoms, it's best to power the printer off and then power it back on.

Be aware that large print jobs may cause the printer to say "processing data" for several minutes before the print job starts. There is nothing wrong with this, although it's possible that your printer could stand a memory upgrade. But if the printer exhibits this behavior for a long time, say 20 or 30 minutes, it may be best to cycle the power.

Paper Jams

Laser printers today run at copier speeds. Because of this, their most common problem is paper jams. Paper can get jammed in a printer for several reasons. First, feed jams happen when the paper-feed rollers get worn (similar to feed jams in inkjet printers). The solution to this problem is easy: replace the worn rollers.

Another cause of feed jams is related to the drive gear of the pickup roller. The drive gear (or clutch) may be broken or have teeth missing. Again, the solution is to replace it. To determine if the problem is a broken gear or worn rollers, print a test page, but leave the paper tray out. Look into the paper-feed opening with a flashlight and see if the paper pickup roller(s) are turning evenly and don't skip. If they turn evenly, the problem is probably worn rollers.

 If worn pickup rollers are causing your paper-feed jams, there is something that you can do to get your printer working while you're waiting for the replacement pickup rollers. Scuff the feed rollers with a steel wool pot-scrubber pad (or something similar) to roughen them up. This trick works only once. After that, the rollers aren't thick enough to touch the paper.

Worn exit rollers can also cause paper jams. These rollers guide the paper out of the printer into the paper-receiving tray. If they are worn or damaged, the paper may catch on its way out of the printer. These types of jams are characterized by a paper jam that occurs just as the paper is getting to the exit rollers. If the paper jams, open the rear door and see where the paper is located. If the paper is very close to the exit rollers, they are probably the problem.

The solution is to replace all the exit rollers. You must replace them all at the same time because even one worn exit roller can cause the paper to jam. Besides, they're inexpensive. Don't skimp on these parts if you need to have them replaced.

Paper jams can also be the fault of the paper. If your printer consistently tries to feed multiple pages into the printer, the paper isn't dry enough. If you live in an area with high humidity, this could be a problem. We've heard some solutions that are pretty far out but work (like keeping the paper in a Tupperware-type airtight container or microwaving it to remove moisture). The best all-around solution, however, is humidity control and keeping the paper wrapped until it's needed. Keep the humidity around 50 percent or lower (but above 25 percent if you can, in order to avoid problems with electrostatic discharge).

 **Real World Scenario**

Printer Triage

One of the authors relates the following story. He was in the local hospital ER a while ago having his hand examined. (He had cut it pretty badly on some glass.) The receptionist asked him a few questions, filled out a report in the medical database on her computer, and printed it. When the paper starting coming out of the laser printer, she grabbed it and "ripped" it from the printer, as you might do if the paper were in an old typewriter. The printer's exit rollers complained bitterly and made a noise that made him cringe. She did this for every sheet of paper she printed.

The following week, that printer came in for service because it was jamming repeatedly. The problem? Worn exit rollers.

He had a word with the person in charge of computer repair at that hospital and saved them from many future repairs. The lesson? Printers don't have to be treated with kid gloves, but using them properly can prolong their life and reduce the need for service repairs.

Finally, a grounded metal strip called the *static-charge eliminator strip* inside the printer drains the transfer corona charge away from the paper after it has been used to transfer toner from the EP cartridge. If that strip is missing, broken, or damaged, the charge will remain on the paper and may cause it to stick to the EP cartridge, causing a jam. If the paper jams after reaching the transfer corona assembly, this may be the cause.

Blank Pages

It's really annoying to print a 10-page contract and receive 10 pages of blank paper from the printer. Blank pages are a somewhat common occurrence in laser printers. Somehow, the toner isn't being put on the paper. There are three major causes of blank pages:

Toner Cartridge   The toner cartridge is the source of most quality problems because it contains most of the image-formation pieces for laser printers. Let's start with the obvious. A blank page or faded prints will come out of the printer if there is no toner or low toner in the cartridge. It might sound simple, but some people think these things last forever. Many laser printers give some sort of warning if the toner cartridge is low, but it's easy to check. Just open the printer, remove the toner cartridge, and shake it. You will be able to hear if there's toner inside the cartridge. If it's empty, replace it with a known, good, manufacturer-recommended toner cartridge. If it is not yet empty, shaking it redistributes the toner and may provide better printing for some time.

 When you're shaking a toner cartridge, loose toner can fall out of the cartridge and get on your clothing. Always hold the toner cartridge away from your body when shaking it.

Another issue that crops up rather often is the problem of using refilled or reconditioned toner cartridges. During their recycling process, these cartridges may be filled with the wrong kind of toner (for example, one with an incorrect composition). This can cause toner to be repelled from the EP drum instead of being attracted to it. Thus, there's no toner on the page because there was no toner on the EP drum to begin with. The solution once again is to replace the toner cartridge with the type recommended by the manufacturer.

A third problem related to toner cartridges happens when someone installs a new toner cartridge and forgets to remove the sealing tape that is present to keep the toner in the cartridge during shipping. The solution to this problem is as easy as it is obvious: remove the toner cartridge from the printer, remove the sealing tape, and reinstall the cartridge.

> Most of the time, if you have dust or debris in a printer, you can use compressed air to blow it away. Don't do that with toner, though, because it will make a huge mess. If you have a toner spill, use a specialized toner vacuum to pick it up. Also, never use a damp cloth to try to clean up a toner spill. If a cloth is needed, use a dry one.

Transfer Corona Assembly   The second cause of the blank-page problem is a damaged or missing transfer corona wire or damaged transfer corona roller. If a wire is lost or damaged, the developed image won't transfer from the EP drum to the paper; thus, no image appears on the printout. To determine if this is causing your problem, do the first half of the self-test (described later in this chapter in the "Self-Tests" section). If there is an image on the drum but not on the paper, you know that the transfer corona assembly isn't doing its job.

To check if the transfer corona assembly is causing the problem, open the cover and examine the wire (or roller, if your printer uses one). The corona wire is hard to see, so you may need a flashlight. You will know if it's broken or missing just by looking at it. (It will either be in pieces or just not be there.) If it's not broken or missing, the problem may be related to the high-voltage power supply.

The transfer corona wire (or roller) is a relatively inexpensive part. You can easily replace it by removing two screws and having some patience.

High-Voltage Power Supply   The high-voltage power supply (HVPS) supplies high-voltage, low-current power to both the charging and transfer corona assemblies in laser printers. If it's broken, neither corona will work properly. If the self-test shows an image on the drum but none on the paper, and the transfer corona assembly is present and not damaged, then the HVPS is at fault.

All-Black Pages

Only slightly more annoying than 10 blank pages are 10 black pages. This happens when the charging unit (the charging corona wire or charging corona roller) in the toner cartridge malfunctions and fails to place a charge on the EP drum. Because the drum is grounded, it has no charge. Anything with a charge (like toner) will stick to it. As the drum rotates, all of the toner is transferred to the page and a black page is formed.

This problem wastes quite a bit of toner, but it can be fixed easily. The solution (again) is to replace the toner cartridge with a known, good, manufacturer-recommended one. If that doesn't solve the problem, then the HVPS is at fault. (It's not providing the high voltage that the charging corona needs to function.)

Repetitive Small Marks or Defects

Repetitive marks occur frequently in heavily used (as well as older) laser printers. Toner spilled inside the printer may be causing the problem. It can also be caused by a crack or chip in the EP drum (this mainly happens with recycled cartridges), which can accumulate toner. In both cases, some of the toner gets stuck onto one of the rollers. Once this happens, every time the roller rotates and touches a piece of paper, it leaves toner smudges spaced a roller circumference apart.

The solution is relatively simple: clean or replace the offending roller. To help you figure out which roller is causing the problem, the service manuals contain a chart like the one shown in Figure 12.17. (Some larger printers also have the roller layout printed inside the service door.) To use the chart, place the printed page next to it. Align the first occurrence of the smudge with the top arrow. The next smudge will line up with one of the other arrows. The arrow it lines up with tells you which roller is causing the problem.

FIGURE 12.17 Laser printer roller circumference chart

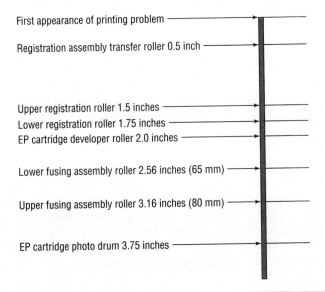

First appearance of printing problem

Registration assembly transfer roller 0.5 inch

Upper registration roller 1.5 inches
Lower registration roller 1.75 inches
EP cartridge developer roller 2.0 inches

Lower fusing assembly roller 2.56 inches (65 mm)

Upper fusing assembly roller 3.16 inches (80 mm)

EP cartridge photo drum 3.75 inches

Remember that the chart in Figure 12.17 is only an example. Your printer may have different-sized rollers and thus need a different chart. Check your printer's service documentation for a chart like this. It is valuable in determining which roller is causing a smudge.

Vertical White Lines on the Page

Vertical white lines running down all or part of the page are a relatively common problem on older printers, especially ones that don't see much maintenance. Foreign matter (more than likely toner) caught on the transfer corona wire causes this. The dirty spots keep the toner from being transmitted to the paper (at those locations, that is), with the result that streaks form as the paper progresses past the transfer corona wire.

The solution is to clean the corona wires. Many laser printers contain a small corona wire brush to help with this procedure. It's usually a small, green-handled brush located near the transfer corona wire. To use it, remove the toner cartridge and run the brush in the charging corona groove on top of the toner cartridge. Replace the cartridge, and then use the brush to remove any foreign deposits on the transfer corona. Be sure to put it back in its holder when you're finished.

Vertical Black Lines on the Page

A groove or scratch in the EP drum can cause the problem of vertical black lines running down all or part of the page. Because a scratch is lower than the surface, it doesn't receive as much (if any) of a charge as the other areas. The result is that toner sticks to it as though it were discharged. The groove may go around the circumference of the drum, so the line may go all the way down the page.

Another possible cause of vertical black lines is a dirty charging corona wire. A dirty charging corona wire prevents a sufficient charge from being placed on the EP drum. Because the charge on the EP drum is almost zero, toner sticks to the areas that correspond to the dirty areas on the charging corona.

The solution to the first problem is, as always, to replace the toner cartridge (or EP drum, if your printer uses a separate EP drum and toner). You can also solve the second problem with a new toner cartridge, although that would be an extreme solution. It's easier to clean the charging corona with the brush supplied with the cartridge.

Image Smudging

If you can pick up a sheet from a laser printer, run your thumb across it, and have the image come off on your thumb, then you have a fuser problem. The fuser isn't heating the toner and fusing it into the paper. This could be caused by a number of things—but all of them can be handled by a fuser replacement. For example, if the halogen light inside the heating roller has burned out, that would cause the problem. The solution is to replace the fuser. The fuser can be replaced with a rebuilt unit, if you prefer. Rebuilt fusers are almost as good as new ones, and some even come with guarantees. Plus, they cost less.

The whole fuser may not need to be replaced. Fuser components can be ordered from parts suppliers and can be rebuilt by you. For example, if the fuser has a bad lamp, you can order a lamp and replace it in the fuser.

A similar problem occurs when small areas of smudging repeat themselves down the page. Dents or cold spots in the fuser heat roller cause this problem. The only solution is to replace either the fuser assembly or the heat roller.

Ghosting

Ghosting (or echo images) is what you have when you can see faint images of previously printed pages on the current page. This is caused by one of two things: a broken cleaning blade or bad erasure lamps. A broken cleaning blade causes old toner to build up on the EP drum and consequently present itself in the next printed image. If the erasure lamps are bad, then the previous electrostatic discharges aren't completely wiped away. When the EP drum rotates toward the developing roller, some toner sticks to the slightly discharged areas.

If the problem is caused by a broken cleaner blade, you can replace the toner cartridge. If it's caused by bad erasure lamps, you'll need to replace them. Because the toner cartridge is the least expensive cure, you should try that first. Usually, replacing the toner cartridge will solve the ghosting problem. If it doesn't, you will have to replace the erasure lamps.

Printer Prints Pages of Garbage

This has happened to everyone at least once. You print a one-page letter, but instead of the letter you have 10 pages of what looks like garbage (or garbled characters) or many more pages with one character per page come out of the printer. This problem comes from one of two different sources:

Printer Driver   The correct printer driver needs to be installed for the printer and operating system. For example, if you have an HP LaserJet Pro MFP M148 and a Windows computer, then you need to install an HP LaserJet Pro MFP M148 driver made for Windows. Once the driver has been installed, it must be configured for the correct page-description language: PCL or PostScript. Most HP LaserJet printers use PCL (but can be configured for PostScript). Determine which page-description language your printer has been configured for, and set the printer driver to the same setting. If this is not done, you will get garbage out of the printer.

    Most printers that have LCD displays will indicate that they are in Post-Script mode with a *PS* or *PostScript* somewhere in the display.

If the problem is the wrong driver setting, the garbage that the printer prints will look like English. That is, the words will be readable, but they won't make any sense.

Formatter Board   The other cause of several pages of garbage being printed is a bad formatter board. This circuit board turns the information the printer receives from the computer into commands for the various components in the printer. Usually, problems with the formatter board produce wavy lines of print or random patterns of dots on the page.

Replacing the formatter board in a laser printer is relatively easy. Usually, this board is installed under the printer and can be removed by loosening two screws and pulling it out. Typically, replacing the formatter board also replaces the printer interface, which is another possible source of garbage printouts.

Finishing Issues

Many laser printers today are multifunction devices that include copying and scanning. Some devices come with finishers, which add touches like collating, stapling papers together, or hole punching output. If one of those functions is not working properly, it's an issue with the finisher. More often than not, it's a simple cleaning that takes care of the issue. For example, if documents are not being stapled, it could be a jam in the stapling mechanism that needs to be cleared. Or, of course, the printer may be out of staples.

Example Printer Testing: HP LaserJet

Now that we've defined some of the possible sources of problems with laser printers, let's discuss a few of the testing procedures that you use with them. We'll discuss HP LaserJet laser printers because they are the most popular brand of laser printer, but the topics covered here apply to other brands of laser printers as well.

We'll look at two ways to troubleshoot laser printers: self-tests and error codes (for laser printers with LCD displays).

Self-Tests

You can perform three tests to narrow down which assembly is causing the problem: the engine self-test, the engine half self-test, and the secret self-test. These tests, which the printer runs on its own when directed by the user, are internal diagnostics for printers, and they are included with most laser printers.

The self-tests explained here are for illustrative purposes only. Information on the tests available for any given printer will be found in the printer's manual, which can be obtained from the printer manufacturer's website.

Engine Self-Test   The engine self-test tests the print engine of the LaserJet. This test causes the printer to print a single page with vertical lines running its length. If an engine self-test can be performed, you know that the laser print engine can print successfully. To perform an engine self-test, you must press the printer's self-test button, which is hidden behind a small cover on the side of the printer (see Figure 12.18). The location of the button varies from printer to printer, so you may have to refer to the printer manual. Using a pencil or probe, press the button. The print engine will start printing the test page.

FIGURE 12.18 Print engine self-test button location. The location will vary on different printers.

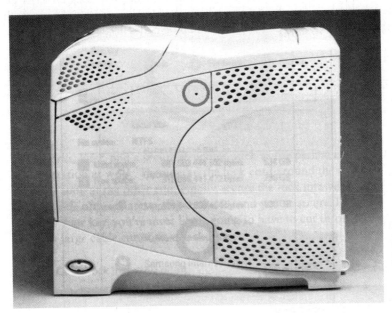

Half Self-Test   A print engine half self-test is performed the same way as the self-test, but you interrupt it halfway through the print cycle by opening the cover. This test is useful in determining which part of the print process is causing the printer to malfunction. If you stop the print process and part of a developed image is on the EP drum and part has been transferred to the paper, then you know that the pickup rollers, registration rollers, laser scanner, charging roller, EP drum, and transfer roller are all working correctly. You can stop the half self-test at various points in the print process to determine the source of a malfunction.

Secret Self-Test   To activate this test, you must first put the printer into service mode. To accomplish this, turn on the printer while simultaneously holding down the On Line, Continue, and Enter buttons. (That's the first secret part, because nobody knows it unless somebody tells them.) When the screen comes up blank, release the keys and press, in order, Continue and then Enter. The printer will perform an internal self-test and then display 00 READY. At this point, you are ready to initiate the rest of the secret self-test. Take the printer offline by pressing the On Line button, press the Test button on the front panel, and hold the button until you see the 04 SELF TEST message. Then release the Test button. This will cause the printer to print one self-test page. (If you want a continuous printout, instead of releasing the Test button at the 04 SELF TEST message, keep holding the Test button. The printer will print continuous self-test pages until you power it off or press On Line, or until it runs out of paper.)

Error Codes

In addition to the self-tests, you have another tool for troubleshooting HP laser printers. Error codes are a way for the LaserJet to tell the user (and a service technician) what's wrong. Table 12.5 details some of the most common codes displayed on an HP LaserJet.

TABLE 12.5   HP LaserJet error messages

Message	Description
00 READY	The printer is in standby mode and ready to print.
02 WARM UP	The fuser is being warmed up before the 00 READY state.
04 SELFTEST or 05 SELFTEST	A full self-test has been initiated from the front panel.
11 PAPER OUT	The paper tray sensor is reporting that there is no paper in the paper tray. The printer will not print as long as this error exists.
13 PAPER JAM	A piece of paper is caught in the paper path. To fix this problem, open the cover and clear the jam (including all pieces of paper causing the jam). Close the cover to resume printing. The printer will not print as long as this error exists.
14 NO EP CART	There is no EP cartridge (toner cartridge) installed in the printer. The printer will not print as long as this error exists.
15 ENGINE TEST	An engine self-test is in progress.
16 TONER LOW	The toner cartridge is almost out of toner. Replacement will be necessary soon.
50 SERVICE	A fuser error has occurred. This problem is most commonly caused by fuser lamp failure. Power off the printer, and replace the fuser to solve the problem. The printer will not print as long as this error exists.
51 ERROR	There is a laser-scanning assembly problem. Test and replace, if necessary. The printer will not print as long as this error exists.
52 ERROR	The scanner motor in the laser-scanning assembly is malfunctioning. Test and replace as per the service manual. The printer will not print as long as this error exists.
55 ERROR	There is a communication problem between the formatter and the DC controller. Test and replace as per the service manual. The printer will not print as long as this error exists.

When There Is No Display

Several times in the printer troubleshooting section, we have mentioned the LCD screen or printer display. Nearly every laser printer and many inkjet printers have them. They are useful for configuring the device as well as relaying information to you. But what about when the screen itself doesn't work?

The screen assembly on a laser printer needs several components to work properly, including the formatter board, engine controller board, and cables connecting the display to each. If any of those components have failed, you could end up with a blank display. It could also be a failed low-voltage power supply (LVPS).

The way to troubleshoot this is to run an engine self-test, which we have already discussed. If there is no output from the engine self-test, then you have a problem with the power supply. If the test works, the device will print a page of lines, and you know that the LVPS is fine. Then it's most likely the display itself, the printer's memory (DIMMs), or the formatter board causing the problem.

Troubleshooting Tips for HP LaserJet Printers

Printer technicians usually use a set of troubleshooting steps to help them solve HP LaserJet printing problems. Let's detail each of them to bring our discussion of laser printer troubleshooting to a close:

Is the exhaust fan operational?   The exhaust fan is the first component to receive power when the printer is turned on. If you can feel air coming out of the exhaust fan, this confirms that AC voltage is present and power is turned on, that +5VDC and +24VDC are being generated by the AC power supply (ACPS), and that the DC controller is functional. If there is no power to the printer (no lights, fan not operating), the ACPS is at fault. Replacement involves removing all printer covers and removing four screws. You can purchase a new ACPS module, but it is usually cheaper to replace it with a rebuilt unit.

Do the control panel LEDs work?   If so, the formatter board can communicate with the control panel. If the LEDs do not light, it could mean that the formatter board is bad, the control panel is bad, or the wires connecting the two are broken or shorting out.

Does the main motor rotate at power-up?   Turn off the power. Remove the covers from the sides of the printer. Turn the printer back on and carefully watch and listen for main motor rotation. If you see and hear the main motor rotating, this indicates that a toner cartridge is installed, all photo sensors are functional, all motors are functional, and the printer can move paper (assuming that there are no obstructions).

Does the fuser heat lamp light after the main motor finishes its rotation?   You will need to remove the covers to see this. The heat lamp should light after the main motor rotation and stay lit until the control panel says 00 READY.

Can the printer perform an engine test print?   A sheet of vertical lines indicates that the print engine works. This test print bypasses the formatter board and indicates whether the print problem resides in the engine. If the test print is successful, you can rule out the engine as a source of the problem. If the test print fails, you will have to troubleshoot the printer further to determine which engine component is causing the problem.

Can the printer perform a control panel self-test?   This is the final test to ensure printer operation. If you can press the Test Page control panel button and receive a test printout, this means that the entire printer is working properly. The only possibilities for problems are outside the printer (interfaces, cables, and software problems).

If you are into electronics, you can probably rebuild the ACPS yourself simply and cheaply. The main rectifier is usually the part that fails in these units; it can easily be replaced, if you know what you're doing.

Most printers will print a test page, which contains both colors and patterns, based on their capabilities. Although the exact style of pattern may vary, the idea is the same for all printers. You're checking to ensure that the printer can do what it's capable of. Many test patterns will measure gradients and resolution as well as letter qualities at various font sizes. Color printers will also print color sections, whereas black-and-white printers will often produce patterns in grayscale. If you are experiencing print-quality issues, running a test pattern is a good way to check to see what's wrong with the printer.

Managing Print Jobs

Most people know how to send a job to the printer. Clicking File and then Print, or pressing Ctrl+P on your keyboard, generally does the trick. But once the job gets sent to the printer, what do you do if it doesn't print?

Keep in mind that in a networked environment, users need the proper permissions both to install and to print to the printer. Not having permission will result in an "access denied" message (or something similar) and the inability to print.

When you send a job to the printer, that print job ends up in a line with all other documents sent to that printer. A series of print jobs waiting to use the printer is called the *print queue*. In most cases, the printer will print jobs on a first-come, first-served basis. (There are exceptions if you've enabled printing priorities in Printer Properties.) Once you send the job to the printer in Windows, a small printer icon will appear in the notification area in the lower-right corner of your desktop, near the clock. By double-clicking it (or by right-clicking it and selecting the printer name), you will end up looking at the jobs in the print queue, like the one shown in Figure 12.19.

FIGURE 12.19 Print jobs in the print queue in Windows

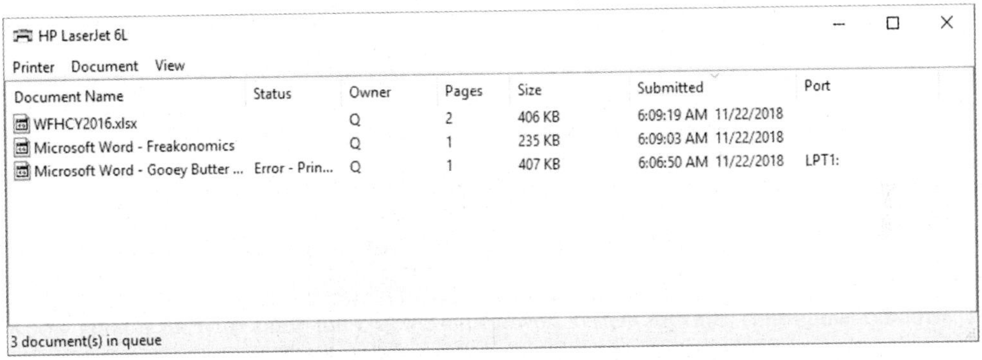

In Figure 12.19, you can see that the first document submitted (at the bottom of the list) has an error, which may explain why it hasn't printed. All the other documents in the queue are blocked until the job with the error is cleared. You can clear it one of two ways. Either right-click the document and choose Cancel, or from the Document menu, shown in Figure 12.20, choose Cancel.

FIGURE 12.20 Printer Document menu in Windows

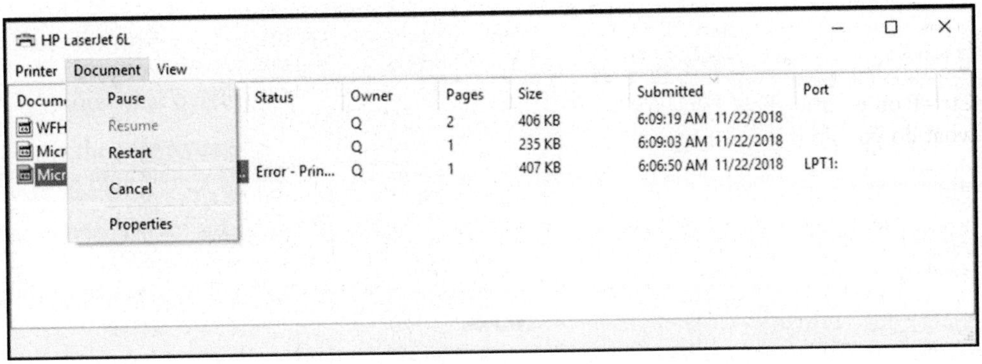

Note that from the menu shown in Figure 12.20, you can pause, resume, restart, and cancel print jobs as well as see properties of the selected print job. If you wanted to pause or cancel all jobs going to a printer, you would do that from the Printer menu, as shown in Figure 12.21.

FIGURE 12.21   Printer menu in Windows

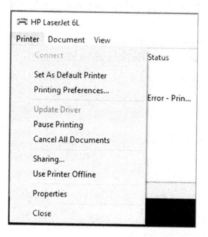

Once you have cleared the print job causing the problem, the next job will move to the top of the queue. It should show its status as Printing, like the one shown in Figure 12.22. But what if it shows that it's printing but it still isn't working? (We're assuming that the printer is powered on, connected properly, and online.) It could be a problem with the print spooler.

FIGURE 12.22   Print job printing correctly

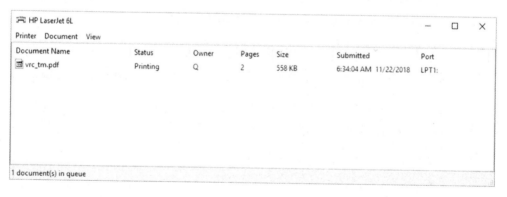

If print jobs are processed very slowly, or if you are continually seeing "low memory" error messages, it might be a good time to upgrade the memory in the printer.

Managing the Print Spooler

The *print spooler* is a service that formats print jobs in a language that the printer understands. Think of it as a holding area where the print jobs are prepared for the printer. In Windows, the spooler is started automatically when Windows loads.

If jobs aren't printing and there's no apparent reason why, it could be that the print spooler has stalled. To fix the problem, you need to stop and restart the print spooler. Exercise 12.2 walks you through stopping and restarting the spooler in Windows 10.

EXERCISE 12.2

Stopping and Restarting the Print Spooler in Windows 10

1. Open the Services app by clicking Start and typing **Services**. The Services app will appear under Best Match.

2. In the right pane, find the Print Spooler service, which is selected in Figure 12.23.

3. Stop the spooler. There are several ways to do this. You can right-click the service name and choose Stop, click the Stop square above the list of services, or click Stop under where it says Print Spooler to the left of the services list.

4. Restart the spooler by right-clicking the service name and choosing Start or by clicking the Start arrow above the list of services. After the spooler has restarted, the service's Status column should display Started.

5. Close Computer Management.

FIGURE 12.23   Locating the Print Spooler service

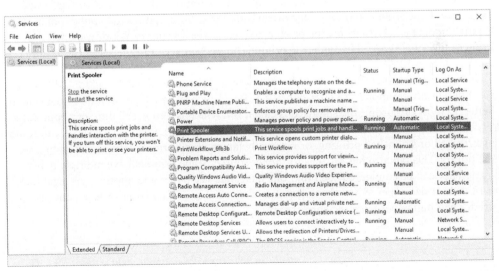

If you have a different version of Windows, the steps to stop and restart the spooler are the same as in Exercise 12.2; the only difference might be in how you get to Computer Management.

 If you have multiple failed print jobs in logs, such as in Windows Event Viewer, stopping and restarting the print spooler is a good solution to try. If the printer is wireless, the failed jobs could also be a sign of intermittent connectivity issues.

Printing a Test Page

If your printer isn't spitting out print jobs, it may be a good idea to print a test page to see if that works. The test page information is stored in the printer's memory, so there's no formatting or translating of jobs required. It's simply a test to make sure that your printer hears your computer.

When you install a printer, one of the last questions you're asked is whether to print a test page. If there's any question, go ahead and do it. If the printer is already installed, you can print a test page from the printer's Properties window (right-click the printer and choose Printer Properties). Just click the Print Test Page button, and it should work. If nothing happens, double-check your connections and stop and restart the print spooler. If garbage prints, there is likely a problem with the printer or the print driver.

Managing Print Options

Printers can print to paper of various sizes, as well as multiple orientations. If a print job is not coming out correctly, such as the output is squeezed into a smaller area than a regular sheet of 8.5 × 11 paper, it may be that the paper size is improperly set. Or, if the right side or bottom is cut off, it could be a page orientation issue. Both options are configured in the Printing preferences settings for the printer. To change the settings in Windows, open the Printers & Scanners app. Highlight the printer, choose Manage, and then select Printing Preferences (Figure 12.24).

In Figure 12.24, there is an option for paper sizes. (Note that this tab will look different for different printer models.) Letter paper is 8.5 × 11 inches, which is common in the United States. In most of Europe, the standard is called A4, which is 210 × 297 mm, or about 8.3 × 11.7 inches. Setting a printer to print to A4 when it should be Letter, or vice versa, can result in stretched or scrunched printing, or unusually larger than normal margins, depending on the printer. This tab also has settings for paper source. Some printers have multiple paper trays. They can be configured such that one has letter size paper and another has legal (8.5 × 14 inches) size paper. When the user prints, they need to specify letter or legal, and the printer will pull paper from the correct tray.

FIGURE 12.24 Paper/Quality options for a printer

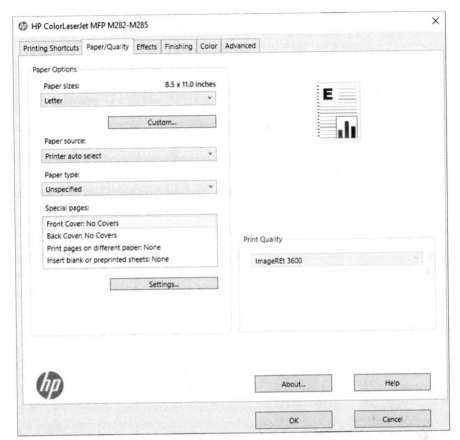

On this specific printer, the paper orientation is handled on the Finishing tab, shown in Figure 12.25. The two options are portrait (taller than it is wide) or landscape (wider than it is tall). Note as well that this printer has options for printing on both sides, a booklet layout, and number of pages per sheet. Again, different printers will have different options—you may just need to click on a few different tabs to find the setting you're looking for, if it's available on that printer.

As a reminder, the A+ exam may test you on how to troubleshoot and resolve the following printer issues:

- Lines down the printed pages
- Garbled print
- Toner not fusing to paper

- Paper jams
- Faded print
- Incorrect paper size
- Paper not feeding
- Multipage misfeed
- Multiple prints pending in queue
- Specking on printed pages
- Double/echo images on the print
- Incorrect chroma display
- Grinding noise
- Finishing issues, including staple jams and hole punch
- Incorrect page orientation

FIGURE 12.25   Finishing tab, including orientation

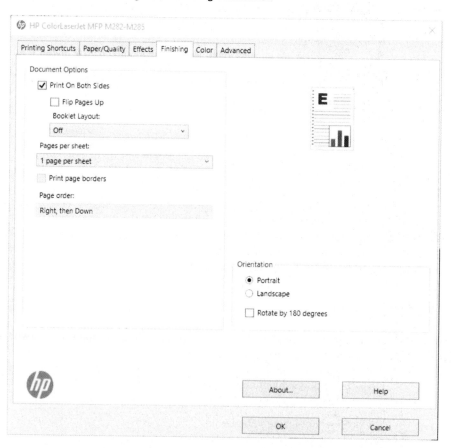

Troubleshooting Networking Problems

As a technician, you are going to be called on to solve a variety of issues, including hardware, software, and networking problems. Networking problems can sometimes be the most tricky to solve, considering that it could be either a software or a hardware problem or a combination of the two causing your connectivity issue.

The first adage for troubleshooting any hardware problem is to check your connections. That holds true for networking as well, but then your troubleshooting will need to go far deeper than that in a hurry. As with troubleshooting anything else, follow a logical procedure and be sure to document your work.

Nearly all the issues tested by CompTIA have something to do with connectivity, which makes sense because that's what networking is all about. Connectivity issues, when not caused by hardware, are generally the result of a messed-up configuration. And because the most common protocol in use today, TCP/IP, has a lot of configuration options, you can imagine how easy it is to configure something incorrectly.

In the following sections, we'll look at connectivity issues and how to resolve them. But first, we will introduce you to several hardware tools and software commands you should know about, as they are essential to network troubleshooting.

CompTIA 220-1101 objective 5.7 combines wired and wireless networking. We'll cover them together and note when specific differences exist.

Using Network Troubleshooting Tools

Networks are so specialized that they have their own set of troubleshooting tools. This includes hardware and software tools. Knowing how to use them can make the difference between a quick fix and a lengthy and frustrating troubleshooting session. The CompTIA A+ exams will test you on both hardware and software tools. Hardware tools are covered in exam 220-1101, whereas the software commands are part of exam 220-1102 objective 1.2. Because both are critical to resolving network issues, we will cover them all here. We'll then review the software tools again in Chapter 15.

Hardware and Cabling Tools

We covered several different types of cables and their properties in Chapter 5, "Networking Fundamentals." Here, we will look at some tools that can be used to make or test network cables, as well as a few tools to troubleshoot network connectivity issues.

Multimeter   Multimeters are versatile electronic measuring tools. A *multimeter* can measure voltage, current, and resistance on a wire. There are many different types and qualities on the market, everywhere from economical $10 versions to ones that cost several thousand dollars. Figure 12.26 shows a basic multimeter. Note that of the tools we cover, the multimeter is the only one that's not on the exam objectives. In real life, they are very useful.

FIGURE 12.26   A basic multimeter

Crimpers and Cable Strippers   A *crimper* is a very handy tool for helping you put connectors on the end of a cable. Most crimpers are combination tools that strip and snip wires and crimp the connector onto the end (see Figure 12.27). You can also buy tools that are just *cable strippers* and cable snippers, but usually the point of cutting and stripping a cable is to put a connector on the end of it, so why not just get a crimper that does it all?

Wi-Fi Analyzer   The one hardware tool that we didn't talk much about earlier is the *Wi-Fi analyzer*. Specific tools for locating Wi-Fi networks and analyzing their traffic are indispensable today. A wireless locator or a Wi-Fi analyzer can be either a handheld hardware device, such as the one shown in Figure 12.28, or specialized software that is installed on a laptop and the purpose of which is to detect and analyze Wi-Fi signals. Anyone interested in wardriving (driving around in a car looking for unsecured wireless networks to hack into) will definitely have one of these, but they're also handy for locating wireless hot spots.

FIGURE 12.27   A UTP crimper

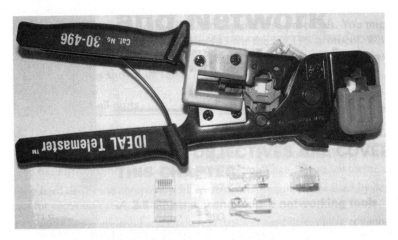

FIGURE 12.28   An RF Explorer handheld Wi-Fi analyzer

Toner Probe   If you need to trace a wire in a wall from one location to another, a *toner probe* (also called a tone generator and probe) is the tool for you. Shown in Figure 12.29, it consists of two pieces: a tone generator and a probe. Because it's so good at tracking, you will sometimes hear this referred to as a "fox and hound."

FIGURE 12.29   A toner probe

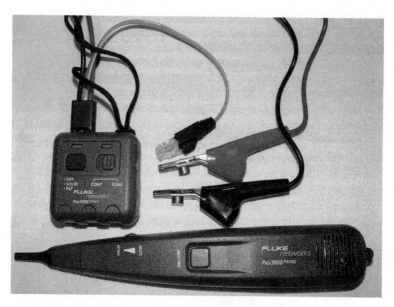

To use a toner probe, attach one end to one end of the cable, such as the end at the computer. Then go to the patch panel with the other end of the probe to locate the cable. These are lifesavers when the cables are not properly labeled.

Punch-Down Tool   If you're working on a larger network installation, you might use a *punch-down tool*. It's not a testing tool but one that allows you to connect (that is, punch down) the exposed ends of a wire into wiring harnesses, such as a 110 block (often used in connectivity closets to help simplify the tangled mess of cables). Figure 12.30 shows the tool and its changeable bit.

FIGURE 12.30   A punch-down tool

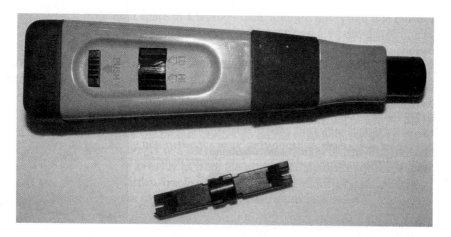

Cable Tester   A *cable tester* is an indispensable tool for any network technician. Usually, you would use a cable tester before you install a cable to make sure it works. Of course, you can test it after it's been run as well. A decent cable tester will tell you the type of cable, and more elaborate models have connectors for multiple types of cables. Figure 12.31 shows a TRENDnet cable tester.

FIGURE 12.31   A TRENDnet cable tester

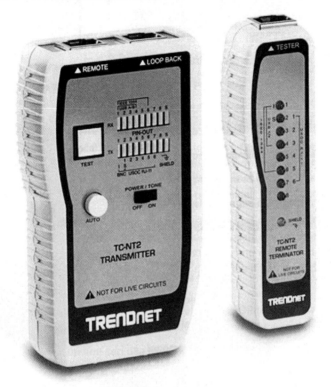

Loopback Plug   A *loopback plug* is for testing the ability of a network adapter to send and receive. The plug gets plugged into the NIC, and then a loopback test is performed using troubleshooting software. You can then tell whether or not the card is working properly. Figure 12.32 shows an Ethernet loopback plug, and they are made for fiber-optic NICs as well.

Network Tap   The final tool we'll cover is indispensable for network troubleshooting. A *network tap* (tap is an acronym for test access port) is a hardware device that creates a copy of network traffic for use by monitoring devices without disrupting normal traffic. Taps have great versatility because they can be moved from one location to another on a network, allowing an administrator to focus on an area that's believed to have problems. They can also detect potential network intrusions, making them helpers for network security as well. In Figure 12.33, you can see where the network cables plug into; the monitor plugs into the back side.

FIGURE 12.32 An Ethernet loopback plug

FIGURE 12.33 A Dualcomm network tap

Networking Tools

As a reminder, the A+ exam may test you on how and when to use the following networking tools:

- Crimper
- Cable stripper

- WiFi analyzer
- Toner probe
- Punchdown tool
- Cable tester
- Loopback plug
- Network tap

Software Commands

Troubleshooting networks often involves using a combination of hardware tools and software commands. Usually, the software commands are easier to deal with because you don't need to dig around physically in a mess of wires to figure out what's going on. The downside to the software commands is that there can be a number of options that you need to memorize. In the following sections, we'll cover the following networking command-line tools, which are all helpful utilities: ipconfig/ip, ping, hostname, tracert, netstat, net, and nslookup.

 Again, these software commands are not specifically listed in the A+ 220-1101 exam objectives, but they are in 220-1102 exam objective 1.2. We include them here because we don't want you to get caught off guard if they do appear on the 220-1101 exam.

ipconfig Command

With Windows-based operating systems, you can determine the network settings on the client's network interface cards, as well as any that a DHCP server has leased to your computer, by typing the following at a command prompt: **ipconfig /all**.

ipconfig /all also gives you full details on the duration of your current lease. You can verify whether a DHCP client has connectivity to a DHCP server by releasing the client's IP address and then attempting to lease an IP address. You can conduct this test by typing the following sequence of commands from the DHCP client at a command prompt:

ipconfig /release
ipconfig /renew

ipconfig is one of the first tools to use when experiencing problems accessing resources because it will show you whether an address has been issued to the machine. If the address displayed falls within the 169.254.x.x category, this means that the client was unable to reach the DHCP server and has defaulted to Automatic Private IP Addressing (APIPA), which will prevent the network card from communicating outside its subnet, if not altogether. Table 12.6 lists useful switches for ipconfig.

TABLE 12.6   `ipconfig` switches

Switch	Purpose
/all	Shows full configuration information
/release	Releases the IP address if you are getting addresses from a Dynamic Host Configuration Protocol (DHCP) server
/release6	Releases the IPv6 addresses
/renew	Obtains a new IP address from a DHCP server
/renew6	Obtains a new IPv6 address from a DHCP server
/flushdns	Flushes the Domain Name System (DNS) server's name resolver cache

In the Linux, UNIX, and macOS worlds, a utility similar to `ipconfig` is `ip`.

Figure 12.34 shows the output from `ipconfig`, and Figure 12.35 shows the output from `ipconfig /all` for one network adapter.

FIGURE 12.34   Output from `ipconfig`

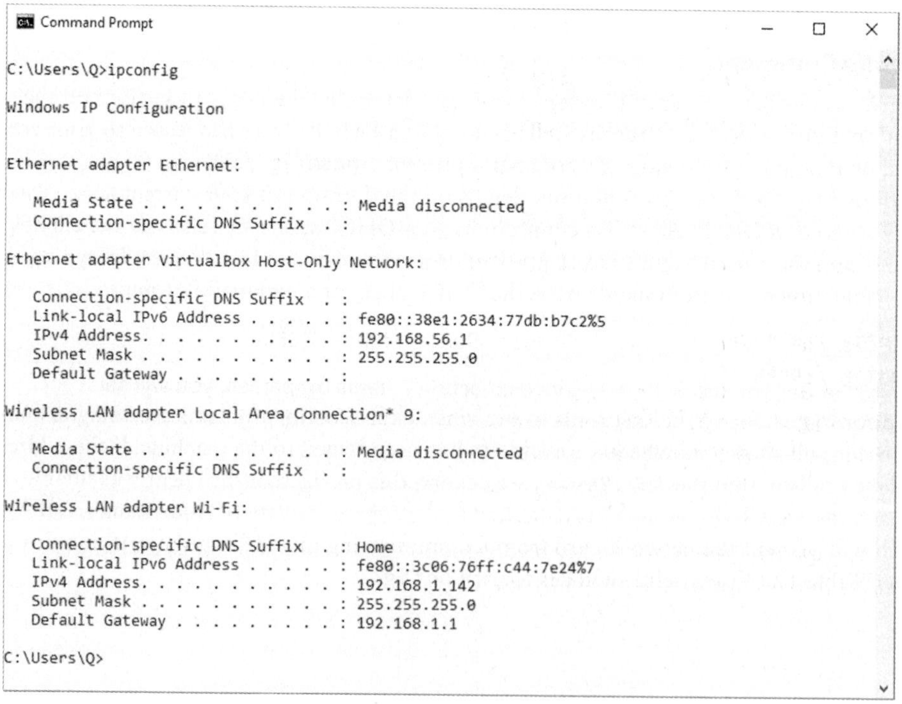

```
Command Prompt                                            —   □   ✕

C:\Users\Q>ipconfig

Windows IP Configuration


Ethernet adapter Ethernet:

   Media State . . . . . . . . . . . : Media disconnected
   Connection-specific DNS Suffix  . :

Ethernet adapter VirtualBox Host-Only Network:

   Connection-specific DNS Suffix  . :
   Link-local IPv6 Address . . . . . : fe80::38e1:2634:77db:b7c2%5
   IPv4 Address. . . . . . . . . . . : 192.168.56.1
   Subnet Mask . . . . . . . . . . . : 255.255.255.0
   Default Gateway . . . . . . . . . :

Wireless LAN adapter Local Area Connection* 9:

   Media State . . . . . . . . . . . : Media disconnected
   Connection-specific DNS Suffix  . :

Wireless LAN adapter Wi-Fi:

   Connection-specific DNS Suffix  . : Home
   Link-local IPv6 Address . . . . . : fe80::3c06:76ff:c44:7e24%7
   IPv4 Address. . . . . . . . . . . : 192.168.1.142
   Subnet Mask . . . . . . . . . . . : 255.255.255.0
   Default Gateway . . . . . . . . . : 192.168.1.1

C:\Users\Q>
```

FIGURE 12.35 Output from `ipconfig /all`

```
Command Prompt                                                    —  □  ×

C:\Users\Q>ipconfig /all

Wireless LAN adapter Wi-Fi:

   Connection-specific DNS Suffix  . : Home
   Description . . . . . . . . . . . : Linksys AE2500
   Physical Address. . . . . . . . . : C0-C1-C0-6C-92-4A
   DHCP Enabled. . . . . . . . . . . : Yes
   Autoconfiguration Enabled . . . . : Yes
   Link-local IPv6 Address . . . . . : fe80::3c06:76ff:c44:7e24%7(Preferred)
   IPv4 Address. . . . . . . . . . . : 192.168.1.142(Preferred)
   Subnet Mask . . . . . . . . . . . : 255.255.255.0
   Lease Obtained. . . . . . . . . . : Wednesday, November 14, 2018 5:46:40 PM
   Lease Expires . . . . . . . . . . : Thursday, November 22, 2018 9:42:30 PM
   Default Gateway . . . . . . . . . : 192.168.1.1
   DHCP Server . . . . . . . . . . . : 192.168.1.1
   DHCPv6 IAID . . . . . . . . . . . : 381731264
   DHCPv6 Client DUID. . . . . . . . : 00-01-00-01-21-CD-E0-62-40-61-86-E4-5A-9A
   DNS Servers . . . . . . . . . . . : 192.168.1.1
   NetBIOS over Tcpip. . . . . . . . : Enabled
   Connection-specific DNS Suffix Search List :
                                       home

C:\Users\Q>
```

In Exercise 12.3, you will renew an IP address on a Windows 10 system within the graphical interface.

EXERCISE 12.3

Renewing an IP Address in Windows 10

1. Open Control Panel by clicking Start and typing **Control**.

2. Click Control Panel under Best Match.

3. In the upper-right corner of Control Panel, set View By to Small Icons or Large Icons.

4. Click Network and Sharing Center to open it.

5. In the left pane, click Change Adapter Settings. This will open a new window displaying your network connections.

6. Right-click your connection and choose Status (Figure 12.36).

    On the General tab of the network connection's status properties, you will see information such as whether you are connected, the speed of the connection, and how long the connection has been active.

7. Click the Details button.

    This expands the information by also showing you the physical (MAC) address and lease information, among other things.

(continues)

8. Look at the information shown, and click Close.

9. Back at the General tab, click the Diagnose button.

    This will diagnose any network problems and attempt to establish or renew the connection. If the network (DHCP) is functioning properly, a notification that it finished will appear in a short time. If not, Windows will attempt to repair the connection.

10. On the General tab, click the Disable button. This will disable the connection and close the Status window.

11. In the Network Connections window, right-click the connection you just disabled and click Enable. It may take a minute to connect.

12. Once it shows the network name, right-click the connection and click Status.

13. Click the Details button and notice the Lease Obtained date. It should be updated to when you just reenabled the connection.

FIGURE 12.36   Network connection status

While Windows provides this interface to troubleshoot connection problems, some administrators still prefer the reliability of a command-line interface. Exercise 12.4 shows you how to perform a similar action using the command line.

EXERCISE 12.4

Renewing an IP Address from the Command Line

This exercise assumes that you are using Windows and dynamic IP assignments from a DHCP server.

1. Open a command prompt (click Start, type **cmd**, and press Enter).

2. Type **ipconfig** and view the abbreviated list of information.

3. Type **ipconfig /all** to see the full list. Notice the date and time on the lease for the IP address.

4. Type **ipconfig /renew** followed by **ipconfig /all**. The date and time on the lease for the IP address should be the current date and time.

5. Close the command-prompt window by typing **exit** and pressing Enter.

---

ping Command

The ping command is one of the most useful commands in the TCP/IP protocol. It sends a series of packets to another system, which in turn sends back a response. This utility can be extremely useful for troubleshooting problems with remote hosts. Pings are also called ICMP echo requests/replies because they use Internet Control Message Protocol (ICMP).

The ping command indicates whether the host can be reached and how long it took for the host to send a return packet. Across WAN links, the time value will be much larger than across healthy LAN links.

The syntax for ping is ping *hostname* or ping *IP address*. Figure 12.37 shows what a ping should look like.

FIGURE 12.37   A successful ping

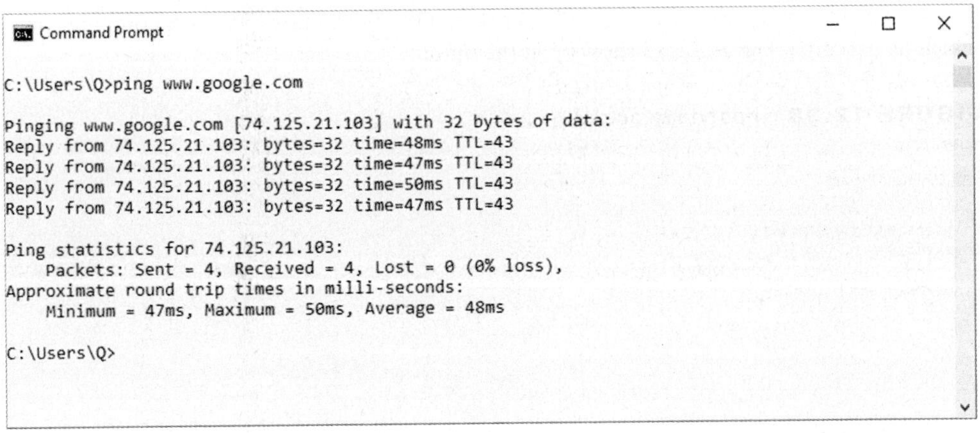

```
Command Prompt                                        —   □   ×

C:\Users\Q>ping www.google.com

Pinging www.google.com [74.125.21.103] with 32 bytes of data:
Reply from 74.125.21.103: bytes=32 time=48ms TTL=43
Reply from 74.125.21.103: bytes=32 time=47ms TTL=43
Reply from 74.125.21.103: bytes=32 time=50ms TTL=43
Reply from 74.125.21.103: bytes=32 time=47ms TTL=43

Ping statistics for 74.125.21.103:
    Packets: Sent = 4, Received = 4, Lost = 0 (0% loss),
Approximate round trip times in milli-seconds:
    Minimum = 47ms, Maximum = 50ms, Average = 48ms

C:\Users\Q>
```

As you can see, by pinging with the hostname, we found the host's IP address thanks to DNS. The time is how long in milliseconds it took to receive the response. On a LAN, you want this to be 10 milliseconds (ms) or less, but 60ms to 65ms for an Internet ping isn't too bad.

The ping command has several options, which you can see by typing **ping /?** at the command prompt. Table 12.7 lists some useful options.

TABLE 12.7   ping options

Option	Function
-t	Persistent ping. Will ping the remote host until stopped by the client (by using Ctrl+C).
-n count	Specifies the number of echo requests to send.
-l size	Specifies the packet size to send.
ping -4 / ping -6	Uses either the IPv4 or IPv6 network, respectively.

NOTE   Some webmasters have configured their routers to block pings in order to avoid problems such as someone trying to eat up bandwidth with a *ping of death* (sending a persistent ping with a huge buffer to overwhelm the recipient). Therefore, if you ping a website, it's possible that you won't get a response even though the site is functional.

hostname Command

The hostname command is a very simple one. It returns the name of the host computer on which its executed. Figure 12.38 shows you the output.

FIGURE 12.38   hostname output

```
Command Prompt                                          —    □    ×

C:\Users\qdoct>hostname
QDesktop2020

C:\Users\qdoct>
```

netstat Command

The netstat command is used to check out the inbound and outbound TCP/IP connections on your machine. It can also be used to view packet statistics, such as how many packets have been sent and received and the number of errors.

When used without any options, the netstat command produces output similar to that shown in Figure 12.39, which shows all the outbound TCP/IP connections.

FIGURE 12.39 Output from netstat

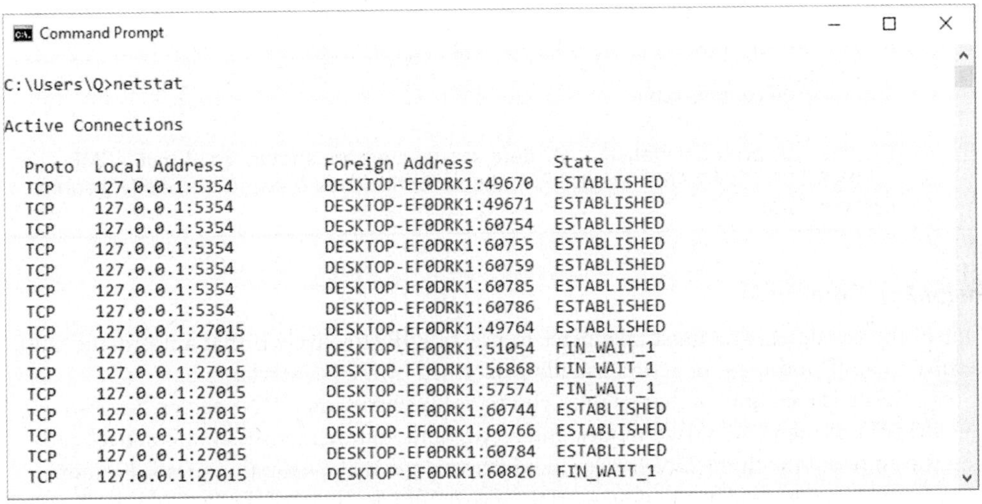

```
Command Prompt                                                    —   □   ×

C:\Users\Q>netstat

Active Connections

  Proto  Local Address          Foreign Address        State
  TCP    127.0.0.1:5354         DESKTOP-EF0DRK1:49670  ESTABLISHED
  TCP    127.0.0.1:5354         DESKTOP-EF0DRK1:49671  ESTABLISHED
  TCP    127.0.0.1:5354         DESKTOP-EF0DRK1:60754  ESTABLISHED
  TCP    127.0.0.1:5354         DESKTOP-EF0DRK1:60755  ESTABLISHED
  TCP    127.0.0.1:5354         DESKTOP-EF0DRK1:60759  ESTABLISHED
  TCP    127.0.0.1:5354         DESKTOP-EF0DRK1:60785  ESTABLISHED
  TCP    127.0.0.1:5354         DESKTOP-EF0DRK1:60786  ESTABLISHED
  TCP    127.0.0.1:27015        DESKTOP-EF0DRK1:49764  ESTABLISHED
  TCP    127.0.0.1:27015        DESKTOP-EF0DRK1:51054  FIN_WAIT_1
  TCP    127.0.0.1:27015        DESKTOP-EF0DRK1:56868  FIN_WAIT_1
  TCP    127.0.0.1:27015        DESKTOP-EF0DRK1:57574  FIN_WAIT_1
  TCP    127.0.0.1:27015        DESKTOP-EF0DRK1:60744  ESTABLISHED
  TCP    127.0.0.1:27015        DESKTOP-EF0DRK1:60766  ESTABLISHED
  TCP    127.0.0.1:27015        DESKTOP-EF0DRK1:60784  ESTABLISHED
  TCP    127.0.0.1:27015        DESKTOP-EF0DRK1:60826  FIN_WAIT_1
```

There are several useful command-line options for netstat, as shown in Table 12.8.

TABLE 12.8 netstat options

Option	Function
-a	Displays all connections and listening ports.
-b	Displays the executable involved in creating each connection or listening port. In some cases, well-known executables host multiple independent components, and in these cases the sequence of components involved in creating the connection or listening port is displayed. In this case, the executable name is in brackets at the bottom. At the top is the components it called, in sequence, until TCP/IP was reached. Note that this option can be time consuming, and it will fail unless you have sufficient permissions.
-e	Displays Ethernet statistics. This may be combined with the -s option.
-f	Displays fully qualified domain names (FQDNs) for foreign addresses.

(continues)

TABLE 12.8   netstat options *(continued)*

Option	Function
-n	Displays addresses and port numbers in numerical form.
-o	Displays the owning process ID associated with each connection.
-p proto	Shows connections for the protocol specified by *proto*; *proto* may be any of the following: TCP, UDP, TCPv6, or UDPv6. If netstat is used with the -s option to display per-protocol statistics, *proto* may be IP, IPv6, ICMP, ICMPv6, TCP, TCPv6, UDP, or UDPv6.
-r	Displays the routing table.
-s	Displays per-protocol statistics. By default, statistics are shown for IP, IPv6, ICMP, ICMPv6, TCP, TCPv6, UDP, and UDPv6; the -p option may be used to specify a subset of the default.

nslookup Command

One of the key things that must take place to use TCP/IP effectively is that a hostname must resolve to an IP address—an action usually performed by a DNS server.

nslookup is a command that enables you to verify entries on a DNS server. You can use the nslookup command in two modes: interactive and noninteractive. In interactive mode, you start a session with the DNS server in which you can make several requests. In noninteractive mode, you specify a command that makes a single query of the DNS server. If you want to make another query, you must type another noninteractive command.

To start nslookup in interactive mode (which is what most admins use because it allows them to make multiple requests without typing nslookup several times), type **nslookup** at the command prompt and press Enter. You will receive a greater than prompt (>) and you can then type the command that you want to run. You can also type **help** or **?** to bring up the list of possible commands, as shown in Figure 12.40. To exit nslookup and return to a command prompt, type **exit** and press Enter.

To run nslookup in noninteractive mode, you would use the nslookup command option you want to run at the command prompt—for example, **nslookup /set timeout=<3>** or **nslookup /view:domain**.

net Command

Depending on the version of Windows you are using, net can be one of the most powerful commands at your disposal. All Windows versions include a net command, but its capabilities differ based on whether it is used on a server or workstation and the version of the operating system.

FIGURE 12.40 Starting nslookup and using help

```
▓ Command Prompt - nslookup                                      —    □    ×

C:\Users\Q>nslookup
Default Server:  Linksys03451
Address:  192.168.1.1

> ?
Commands:   (identifiers are shown in uppercase, [] means optional)
NAME            - print info about the host/domain NAME using default server
NAME1 NAME2     - as above, but use NAME2 as server
help or ?       - print info on common commands
set OPTION      - set an option
    all                 - print options, current server and host
    [no]debug           - print debugging information
    [no]d2              - print exhaustive debugging information
    [no]defname         - append domain name to each query
    [no]recurse         - ask for recursive answer to query
    [no]search          - use domain search list
    [no]vc              - always use a virtual circuit
    domain=NAME         - set default domain name to NAME
    srchlist=N1[/N2/.../N6] - set domain to N1 and search list to N1,N2, etc.
    root=NAME           - set root server to NAME
    retry=X             - set number of retries to X
    timeout=X           - set initial time-out interval to X seconds
    type=X              - set query type (ex. A,AAAA,A+AAAA,ANY,CNAME,MX,NS,PTR,SOA,SRV)
    querytype=X         - same as type
    class=X             - set query class (ex. IN (Internet), ANY)
    [no]msxfr           - use MS fast zone transfer
    ixfrver=X           - current version to use in IXFR transfer request
server NAME     - set default server to NAME, using current default server
lserver NAME    - set default server to NAME, using initial server
root            - set current default server to the root
ls [opt] DOMAIN [> FILE] - list addresses in DOMAIN (optional: output to FILE)
    -a              - list canonical names and aliases
    -d              - list all records
    -t TYPE         - list records of the given RFC record type (ex. A,CNAME,MX,NS,PTR etc.)
view FILE           - sort an 'ls' output file and view it with pg
exit            - exit the program

>
```

While always command line–based, net allows you to do almost anything that you want with the operating system. Table 12.9 shows common net switches.

TABLE 12.9 net switches

Switch	Purpose
net accounts	To set account options (password age, length, and so on)
net computer	To add and delete computer accounts
net config	To see network-related configuration
net continue, net pause, net start, net statistics, and net stop	To control services

(continues)

TABLE 12.9   net switches *(continued)*

Switch	Purpose
net file	To close open files
net group and net localgroup	To create, delete, and change groups
net help	To see general help
net helpmsg	To see specific message help
net name	To see the name of the current machine and user
net print	To interact with print queues and print jobs
net send	To send a message to user(s)
net session	To see session statistics
net share	To create a share
net time	To set the time to that of another computer
net use	To connect to a share
net user	To add, delete, and see information about a user
net view	To see available resources

These commands are invaluable troubleshooting aids when you cannot get the graphical interface to display properly. You can also use them when interacting with hidden ($) and administrative shares that do not appear within the graphical interface.

The net command used with the share parameter enables you to create shares from the command prompt, using this syntax:

net share <share_name>=<drive_letter>:<path>

To share the C:\EVAN directory as SALES, you would use the following command:

net share sales=c:/evan

You can use other parameters with `net share` to set other options. Table 12.10 summarizes the most commonly used parameters, and Exercise 12.5 will give you some experience with the `net share` command.

TABLE 12.10   net share parameters

Parameter	Purpose
/delete	To stop sharing a folder
/remark	To add a comment for browsers
/unlimited	To set the user limit to Maximum Allowed
/users	To set a specific user limit

EXERCISE 12.5

Using the *net share* Command in Windows

In order to create new shared drives with `net share`, you must have administrative privileges at the command prompt. Opening the command prompt normally does not confer administrative privileges. In this exercise, we will open what's called an elevated command prompt, or administrative command prompt.

1. Click the Start button, type **cmd**, and notice that the Command Prompt appears under Best Match.

2. Right-click Command Prompt, and then click Run As Administrator.

3. A User Account Control prompt will appear asking if you want to allow the app to make changes to your device. Click Yes. The elevated command prompt will open.

4. To see what is currently shared on your computer, type **net share** and press Enter.

    You will see output similar to what's shown in Figure 12.41. Notice that the C:\ and E:\ drives are shared by default. This is normal, and they are hidden shares (the $ at the end of the share name makes it hidden), meaning that other users on the network won't see them.

5. You will now share the C:\TEMP folder with the share name *files4u*. To do this, type **net share files4u=c:\temp** and press Enter.

    The system should respond with `files4u was shared successfully`.

(continues)

6. To verify that it was shared, type **net share** and press Enter.

   You can see the new share in Figure 12.42. Users on the network can now access your drive as *computername*\files4u.

7. (optional) To stop sharing files4u, type **net share files4u /delete** at the command prompt and press Enter.

8. (optional) To verify that the folder is no longer shared, type **net share** and press Enter.

FIGURE 12.41   Shares on the local computer

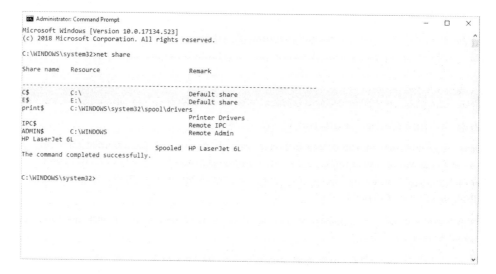

FIGURE 12.42   Output from net share with a new shared drive

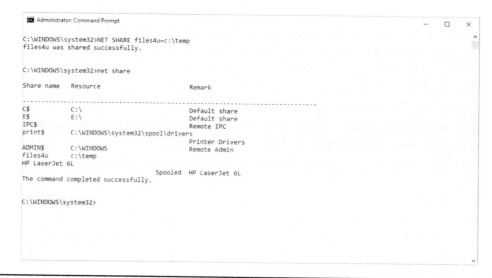

The net /? command is basically a catch-all help request. It will instruct you to use the net command in which you are interested for more information.

tracert Command

tracert (trace route) is a Windows-based command-line utility that enables you to verify the route to a remote host. Execute the command tracert *hostname*, where *hostname* is the computer name or IP address of the computer whose route you want to trace. tracert returns the different IP addresses the packet was routed through to reach the final destination. The results also include the number of hops needed to reach the destination. If you execute the tracert command without any options, you see a help file that describes all the tracert switches.

> The traceroute command can be used on Macs and Linux/UNIX machines; it performs the same task as tracert.

This utility determines the intermediary steps involved in communicating with another IP host. It provides a road map of all the routing an IP packet takes to get from host A to host B.

Timing information from tracert can be useful for detecting a malfunctioning or overloaded router. Figure 12.43 shows the output from tracert. In addition to tracert, there are many graphical third-party network-tracing utilities available on the market.

FIGURE 12.43   Output from tracert

```
Command Prompt                                              —  □  ×

C:\Users\Q>tracert www.apple.com

Tracing route to e6858.dsce9.akamaiedge.net [23.56.211.166]
over a maximum of 30 hops:

  1     1 ms     1 ms     1 ms  Linksys03451 [192.168.1.1]
  2     1 ms     1 ms     1 ms  192.168.200.1
  3    25 ms    25 ms    26 ms  dsl-208-102-195-1.fuse.net [208.102.195.1]
  4    26 ms    25 ms    25 ms  ae1.ev-ptx-1.core.fuse.net [216.68.14.185]
  5    28 ms    25 ms    26 ms  ae1.eve1.core.fuse.net [216.68.14.184]
  6    38 ms    37 ms    40 ms  xe005.atl1.core.fuse.net [216.68.14.133]
  7    38 ms    36 ms    38 ms  ae1-215.cr1-atl1.ip4.gtt.net [173.241.131.161]
  8    40 ms    38 ms    39 ms  a23-56-211-166.deploy.static.akamaitechnologies.com [23.56.211.
166]

Trace complete.

C:\Users\Q>
```

pathping Command

pathping (path ping) combines the best of both worlds from ping and tracert and is a favorite command for many net admins. It acts much like a ping, but it also traces the route to the destination and shows where, if anywhere, packet loss occurs between the sending computer and the remote host. Said differently, pathping first traces the route to the destination host, and then it pings each node between itself and the destination. Figure 12.44 shows the output. A similar command for Linux-based computers is mtr.

FIGURE 12.44   pathping output

```
🖥 Command Prompt                                                         —    □    ×

C:\Users\qdoct>pathping www.sybex.com

Tracing route to www.sybex.com [63.97.118.67]
over a maximum of 30 hops:
  0  QDesktop2020.Home [192.168.1.81]
  1  Linksys03118.Home [192.168.1.1]
  2  192.168.200.1
  3  dsl-208-102-195-1.fuse.net [208.102.195.1]
  4  216.68.14.197
  5  216.68.14.196
  6  et330.ash1.core.fuse.net [216.68.14.149]
  7  et-1-0-23.cr1-was1.ip4.gtt.net [98.124.184.145]
  8  &#10.11.148.204.in-addr.arpa [204.148.11.237]
  9    *        *        *
Computing statistics for 200 seconds...
              Source to Here   This Node/Link
Hop  RTT     Lost/Sent = Pct   Lost/Sent = Pct  Address
  0                                              QDesktop2020.Home [192.168.1.81]
                                0/ 100 =  0%     |
  1    2ms   0/ 100 =  0%       0/ 100 =  0%     Linksys03118.Home [192.168.1.1]
                                0/ 100 =  0%     |
  2    3ms   0/ 100 =  0%       0/ 100 =  0%     192.168.200.1
                                2/ 100 =  2%     |
  3   71ms   4/ 100 =  4%       2/ 100 =  2%     dsl-208-102-195-1.fuse.net [208.102.195.1]
                                0/ 100 =  0%     |
  4   71ms   5/ 100 =  5%       3/ 100 =  3%     216.68.14.197
                                0/ 100 =  0%     |
  5   78ms   4/ 100 =  4%       2/ 100 =  2%     216.68.14.196
                                0/ 100 =  0%     |
  6   89ms   5/ 100 =  5%       3/ 100 =  3%     et330.ash1.core.fuse.net [216.68.14.149]
                                0/ 100 =  0%     |
  7  101ms   2/ 100 =  2%       0/ 100 =  0%     et-1-0-23.cr1-was1.ip4.gtt.net [98.124.184.145]
                                4/ 100 =  4%     |
  8   90ms   6/ 100 =  6%       0/ 100 =  0%     &#10.11.148.204.in-addr.arpa [204.148.11.237]

Trace complete.

C:\Users\qdoct>
```

The top half of the output in Figure 12.44 looks just like tracert. The bottom half is where you see the ping times and packet loss. In this example, there's a little packet loss at each hop from hops 3 through 8. The loss here is low and not a concern. Table 12.11 lists frequently used switches.

TABLE 12.11 pathping switches

Switch	Purpose
-h *number*	Defines the maximum number of hops to search. Useful if, for example, you just want to test connectivity to the ISP.
-n	Does not resolve each hostname. This speeds up the results.
-p *number*	Number of milliseconds to wait between pings. The default is 250. A good choice is 100. Again, speeds up results.
-q *number*	Number of queries per hop. The default is 100, choosing fewer speeds it up. Around 10–20 is usually enough.
-w *number*	Number of milliseconds to wait for each reply. The default is 3 seconds; 500 milliseconds is fine. Speeds up results.

Resolving Connectivity Issues

The whole purpose of using a network is to connect to other resources, right? So when networks don't work like they're supposed to, users tend to get a bit upset. The ubiquity of wireless networking has only made our jobs as technicians more complicated. In the following sections, we'll look at a variety of issues that you might run across and how to deal with them.

No Connectivity

Let's start with the most dire situation: no connectivity. Taking a step back to look at the big picture, think about all the components that go into networking. On the client side, you need a network card and drivers, operating system, protocol, and the right configuration. Then you have a cable of some sort or a wireless connection. At the other end is a switch or wireless router. That device connects to other devices, and so forth. The point is, if someone is complaining of no connectivity, there could be one of several different things causing it. So start with the basics.

The most common issue that prevents network connectivity on a wired network is a bad or unplugged patch cable. Cleaning crews and the rollers on the bottoms of chairs are the most common threats to patch cables. In most cases, wall jacks are placed 4–10 feet away from the desktop. The patch cables are often lying exposed under the user's desk, and from time to time damage is done to the cable, or it's inadvertently snagged and unplugged. Tightly cinching the cable while tying it up out of the way is no better a solution. Slack must be left in the cable to allow for some amount of equipment movement and to avoid altering the electrical characteristics of the cable.

When you troubleshoot connectivity, start with the most rudimentary explanations first. Make sure that the patch cable is tightly plugged in, and then look at the card and check if any lights are on. If there are lights on, use the NIC's documentation to help troubleshoot. More often than not, shutting down the machine, unplugging the patch and power cables for a moment, and then reattaching them and rebooting the PC will fix an unresponsive NIC.

> **NOTE** A properly connected NIC should typically have one light illuminated (the link light). If the link light is not illuminated, it indicates a problem with the NIC, the patch cable, or the device to which the patch cable is connecting (hub, switch, server, and so on). Other lights that may be illuminated include a speed light, duplex light, and/or activity light.

If you don't have any lights, you don't have a connection. It could be that the cable is bad or that it's not plugged in on the other side, or it could also be a problem with the NIC or the connectivity device on the other side. Is this the only computer having problems? If everyone else in the same area is having the same problem, that points to a central issue.

Most wireless network cards also have indicators on them that can help you troubleshoot. For example, a wireless card might have a connection light and an activity light, much like a wired network card. On one particular card we've used, the lights will alternate blinking if the card isn't attached to a network. Once it attaches, the connection light will be solid, and the link light will blink when it's busy. Other cards may operate in a slightly different manner, so be sure to consult your documentation.

If you don't have any lights, try reseating the wireless NIC. If you're using a USB wireless adapter, this is pretty easy. If it's inside your desktop, it will require a little surgery. If it's integrated into your laptop, you could have serious issues. Try rebooting first. If that doesn't help, see if you can use an expansion NIC and make that one light up.

No SSID Found

This is obviously a wireless problem, because wired networks don't use service-set identifiers (SSIDs). If a client can't find an SSID, it won't have network connectivity.

If a client can't find an SSID for a network it had previously joined, the router's SSID may have changed. If you're going to change an SSID, be sure to alert all users or technicians who might be affected. A second potential cause could be that the router is configured to not broadcast SSIDs. Some administrators will stop this broadcast, believing that doing so will increase the network security. It really doesn't, because any semi-decent hacker with a wireless packet sniffer will pick it up. What it does best, though, is to make it difficult for legitimate users to join the network.

A third potential cause is that the user's computer is too far out of range. Get closer to the access point or wireless router, and the signal should appear.

Let's assume that you have lights and that no one else is having a problem. (Yes, it's just you.) This means that the network hardware is probably okay, so it's time to check the configuration. Open a command prompt, type **ipconfig**, and press Enter. You should get an IP address. (If it starts with 169.254. *x*. *x*, that's an APIPA address. We'll talk about those in the "Limited or Local Connectivity" section.) If you don't have a valid IP address, that's the problem.

The Linux, UNIX, and macOS version of ipconfig is ifconfig.

Remember that in order to communicate on a network using TCP/IP (IPv4), you need to have a unique IP address and a valid subnet mask. If you want to communicate on a network outside of your own local network, you also need a default gateway.

If you do have a valid IP address, it's time to see how far your connectivity reaches. With your command prompt open, use the ping command to ping a known, remote working host. If that doesn't work, start working backward. Can you ping the outside port of your router? The inside port? A local host? (Some technicians recommend pinging your loopback address first with ping 127.0.0.1 [or ping ::1 on an IPv6 network] and then working your way out to see where the connectivity ends. Either way is fine. The advantage to starting with the loopback is that if it doesn't work, you know nothing else will either.) Using this methodology, you'll be able to figure out where your connectivity truly begins and ends.

The ping utility is useful for troubleshooting several types of connectivity problems that you might encounter. For example, if you can ping an IP address but not a hostname, then you know it's a DNS error. If you can ping a hostname (such as a remote web server) but you can't get to it with your web browser, then you know it's a problem with your browser or HTTP or port 80, which may possibly involve the router configuration (like a blocked port).

Limited or Local Connectivity

In a way, limited connectivity problems are a bit of a blessing. You can immediately rule out client-side hardware issues because they can connect to some resources. You just need to figure out why they can't connect to others. This is most likely caused by one of two things: a configuration issue or a connectivity device (such as a router) problem.

Check the local configuration first. Use ipconfig /all to ensure that the computer's IP address, subnet mask, and default gateway are all configured properly. After that, use the ping utility to see the range of connectivity. In situations like this, it's also good to check with other users in the area. Are they having the same connectivity issues? If so, it's more likely to be a central problem rather than one with the client computer.

🌐 Real World Scenario

What Can (or Can't) You Get To?

A common refrain from users when they are having network issues is, "I can't get to anything." As a technician, you need to parse that statement to understand what they really can or can't get to, and if it's isolated to their device or occurs on other devices as well. It's best to ask questions to determine which resources are unavailable to them. The two main categories of unavailable resources are local resources and the Internet.

If the user is unable to get to local resources, odds are they can't get to "anything." Local resources include shared drives (aka shares), printers, or their email. In situations like this, treat it like there is no connectivity (or limited connectivity) and troubleshoot appropriately.

If local resources are accessible but the Internet is not, then you know the network card and wireless or wired connectivity is fine. Something is preventing the connection to the outside world. In these situations, there are a few specific things to check. First, check their IP address. If it starts with 169.254, then they have an APIPA address, which means the DHCP server could be having issues. If they seem to have a legitimate IP address, can they ping an Internet website using its IP address? If so, but they can't ping the website name, then it's a DNS issue. If they can't ping the address, try a different one. Other devices that could potentially be blocking the traffic include routers, firewalls, and proxy servers.

APIPA and Link Local Addresses

As we talked about in Chapter 6, "Introduction to TCP/IP," Automatic Private IP Addressing (APIPA) is a service that autoconfigures your network card with an IP address. APIPA kicks in only if your computer is set to receive an IP address from the Dynamic Host Configuration Protocol (DHCP) server and that server doesn't respond. You can always tell an APIPA address because it will be in the format of 169.254.*x*.*x*.

When you have an APIPA address, you will be able to communicate with other computers that also have an APIPA address but not with any other resources. The solution is to figure out why you're not getting an answer from the DHCP server and fix that problem.

Link local addresses are the IPv6 version of APIPA, and link local addresses always start with fe80:: (they are in the fe80::/10 range). They will work to communicate with computers on a local network, but they will not work through a router. If the only IP address that your computer has is a link local address, you're not going to communicate outside of your network. The resolution is the same as it is for APIPA.

IP Address Conflicts

Every host on a network needs to have a unique IP address. If two or more hosts have the same address, communication problems will occur. The good news is that nearly every operating system today will warn you if it detects an IP address conflict with your computer. The bad news is it won't fix it by itself.

The communication problems will vary. In some cases, the computer will seem nearly fine, with intermittent connectivity issues. In others, it will appear as if you have no connectivity.

The most common cause of this is if someone configures a computer with a static IP address that's part of the DHCP server's range. The DHCP server, not knowing that the address has been statically assigned somewhere, doles out the address and now there's a conflict. Rebooting the computer won't help, nor will releasing the address and getting a new lease from the DHCP server—it's just going to hand out the same address again because it doesn't know that there's a problem.

As the administrator, you need to track down the offending user. A common way to do this is to use a packet sniffer to look at network traffic and determine the computer name or MAC address associated with the IP address in question. Most administrators don't keep network maps of MAC addresses, but everyone should have a network map with hostnames. If not, it could be a long, tedious process to check everyone's computer to find the culprit.

Usually the person who manually configured their address didn't intend to cause any problems. This would be a good time to show your professionalism and communication skills and educate the user as to why they shouldn't have done what they did.

Intermittent Connectivity

Intermittent connectivity is when the network sometimes connects, but it's not consistently connected. Sometimes the connection will quickly disappear and reappear, and other times it will be disconnected for longer—minutes can seem like hours when this happens. This category of problems is the most difficult and frustrating to troubleshoot. Getting to why it sometimes behaves but other times does not isn't always easy. Under this heading, we're going to consider intermittent connectivity, slow network speeds, high latency, and related issues, because they are all pretty similar. Terms like "slow network speeds" are fairly straightforward, but not all terms in this section are. Let's define a few, and then get into more detail, because most of these problems have the same causes and resolutions:

- *Latency* is a measure of delay on a network. High latency looks like the connection is intermittent, simply because the delays are so long. If latency is happening on a large data transfer, you might not notice unless the connection terminates. If it happens during video streaming, or on a virtual meeting or a *Voice over Internet Protocol (VoIP)* phone call, you will definitely notice because the person or people on the other end of the line will freeze or completely cut out.

- *Jitter* is variable latency. Think of it as if someone had too much caffeine and they are shaking a bit. Sometimes they are able to hold still, other times they are . . . jittery. Same thing here.

- *Port flapping* is when a switch port opens and closes very quickly. According to Cisco, it's technically when the port opens and closes three or more times in a second for at least 10 seconds. The result is intermittent connectivity.

On a wired network, if you run into slow speeds or intermittent connectivity, it's likely a load issue. There's too much traffic for the network to handle, and the network is bogging down. Solutions include adding a switch, replacing hubs with switches (if your network is using hubs in today's age, it's *really* time to upgrade), and even creating virtual LANs (VLANs) with switches. If the network infrastructure is old (for example, if it's running on Category 3 cable or you only have 10 Mbps switches), then it's definitely time for an upgrade. Remember that your network can only be as fast as its slowest component.

Other wired issues can include bad or poorly connected cables or faulty switch ports. Check to ensure that the cable is properly connected on both ends. Most cables today have a latch that holds them into place, but it's still a good idea to detach and reattach them for good measure. You can always try a different cable, as well, to see if that resolves the problem. If the cable seems to be fine, then perhaps try a different port on the switch or hub, if possible. Finally—and this is rare in today's networking—there could be a speed or duplex mismatch between the sending and receiving devices. Network adapters and connectivity devices can be set to limit the speeds, as a form of backward compatibility. If one device is set too slow, then another transmitting at full speed may have issues connecting with it. With duplex, most NICs are fully capable of sending and receiving at the same time. That's called full duplex. Some older cards were able to operate at only half duplex, meaning they could send or receive, but not both at the same time. Today, nearly all devices autodetect speed and duplex, so this is, as we said, a rare issue. If all else fails, though, it never hurts to check the configuration settings.

Again, the previous steps will fix most issues, but there a few more things to know about VoIP and port flapping:

Fixing Poor VoIP Quality   Most corporate landline telephones today run over an IP network. This is called *Voice over Internet Protocol (VoIP)*. A bad or intermittent network connection will definitely cause poor VoIP quality. Most routers have an option called Quality of Service (QoS) that allows administrators to set priorities for different streams of network traffic. If a network is suffering from poor VoIP quality, the administrator could give it a higher priority. That way, if the network connection is overloaded, higher priority traffic should be less affected.

Dealing with Port Flapping   If confronted with port flapping, the advice given earlier still applies—check the cables, connections, and look for a speed or duplex mismatch. There are two other things to check for as well. First, look at the error logs for the switch. There should be a layer 1 issue on both ends of the link. (Remember the OSI model?) If not, it could be an intermediary device between the ends of the link causing the problem. Second, reseat the small form-factor pluggable (SFP) connectors (one is shown in Figure 12.45). SFPs are pinky-sized, hot-swappable transceivers used in gigabit and faster connections. If reseating doesn't help, switch out the SFPs on the link with ones that are known to work.

FIGURE 12.45   Gigabit SFP

Wireless networks can get overloaded, too. It's recommended that no more than 30 or so client computers use one wireless access point (WAP) or wireless router. (Wi-Fi 6 can handle more but should still be limited to 60–100 at most.) Any more than that can cause intermittent access problems. The most common reason that users on wireless networks experience any of these issues, though, is distance. The farther away from the WAP the user gets, the weaker the signal becomes. When the signal weakens, the transfer rates drop dramatically. For example, the signal from an 802.11ac (Wi-Fi 5) wireless router has a maximum indoor range of about 35 meters (115 feet), barring any obstructions. At that distance, though, 802.11ac will support transfer rates of only about 50 Mbps—far less than the 1.3 Gbps the users think they're getting. External interference, such as from radio signals, microwaves, large motors, and fluorescent lights, as well as physical barriers such as concrete or steel, can greatly reduce the effective range. The solution is to move closer or install more access points. Depending on the configuration of your working environment, you could also consider adding a directional antenna to the WAP. The antenna will increase the distance the signal travels but only in a limited direction.

Network Issues

As a reminder, the A+ exam may test you on how to diagnose and fix the following wired and wireless network issues:

- Intermittent wireless connectivity

- Slow network speeds

- Limited connectivity
- Jitter
- Poor Voice over IP (VoIP) quality
- Port flapping
- High latency
- External interference

Summary

In this chapter, we discussed hardware and network troubleshooting. First, we looked at issues common to storage devices and RAID arrays, such as lights and sounds, devices not found, slow performance, S.M.A.R.T. errors, and optical drive problems. Then, we looked at video issues, such as input and image problems and how to resolve them. Next, we covered problems that are unique to mobile devices and laptop computers. Because of their compact nature, they have unique issues relating to heat and power, input and output, connectivity, and potential damage.

We followed that with a discussion on troubleshooting printers. Specifically, we discussed problems with three major classes of printers, including impact, inkjet, and laser, and then we talked about managing print jobs, the print spooler, printing a test page, and printer configuration options.

Finally, we ended the chapter with a section on troubleshooting issues that are specific to networking. We looked at tools and commands that you can use to troubleshoot network problems, and then finished with symptoms and fixes for a variety of connectivity problems.

Exam Essentials

Understand common issues related to hard drives and RAID arrays.   There are several issues that are hard drive–related. The drive can have a read/write failure or slow performance. If a conventional drive fails, it might produce a loud clicking or scratching noise. Sometimes boot failures are hard drive–related, if the drive can't be found or recognized or the OS isn't found due to a bad boot sector or master boot record. If the OS crashes, it may produce a proprietary crash screen, such as the BSOD in Windows or the pinwheel in macOS. RAID arrays are collections of hard drives and can have similar failures and issues with not being found. All hard drives made today have S.M.A.R.T. diagnostics built into them.

Understand common video, projector, and display symptoms.   Video displays and projectors can have a wide variety of issues. They include overheating and shutting down; no image on the screen; dead pixels; artifacts or display burn-in; incorrect color display; dim, flickering, or distorted images; flashing screen; burned-out bulb; and audio issues.

Understand common mobile device power and heat issues.   Power issues can include a battery not charging, no power, extremely short battery life, overheating, and a swollen battery.

Know what to do to resolve common mobile device input problems.   These can include sticking keys, ghost cursor or pointer drift, num lock lights, or an unresponsive digitizer/touch screen. Be familiar with the laptop Function key and the features it controls, including switching the display to an external monitor.

Know how to set IP addresses on a printer.   The IP address can often be obtained automatically from a DHCP server, but this is not recommended for corporate networks. Instead, use a static IP address (or use a DHCP reservation). You may be able to use the printer's control panel or printer management software to configure the IP address.

Know what could cause the printer to print garbage.   Most often, the print driver causes this. Deleting and reinstalling it should fix the problem. A defective formatter board can also cause it.

Understand what could cause print-quality issues on an impact printer.   Print-quality issues are generally related to either the ribbon or the print head. The specific problem you are having will help determine the culprit.

Know what can cause unevenly spaced lines or characters on a dot-matrix or inkjet printer.   A failing stepper motor usually causes this. For line spacing problems, it's the main stepper motor. For character spacing, it will be the carriage stepper motor.

Know what causes printers to have paper jams.   On an impact printer, jams are usually caused by material getting into the rollers, such as extra "perf" from the tractor-feed paper. On inkjets and laser printers, worn pickup rollers often cause this problem.

Know how to stop and restart the print spooler.   Open the Services applet. Find Print Spooler on the right side. Right-click it and click Stop, or highlight it and click the Stop square above the list of services. To restart the print spooler, right-click it and select Start, or click the Start triangle above the list of services.

Know what to check if your wireless networking card isn't working.   Make sure the card has lights indicating that it's working. You might also have an external toggle switch to turn the card on and off. Finally, if your computer has an external RJ-45 connection, you can plug it in and see if it works when wired.

Understand what various networking hardware tools are used for.   Crimpers are for cutting and stripping cables and putting the connectors on the ends. Cable strippers are similar but don't put connectors on. A Wi-Fi analyzer examines wireless network signals. Toner probes allow you trace a cable from one point to another. Punch-down tools connect wires to frames, such as a 110 block. A cable tester allows you to verify that a cable works; loop-back plugs test the functionality of network cards. A network tap creates a copy of network traffic for use by monitoring devices without disrupting normal traffic.

Know what the `ipconfig`, `ping`, **and** `tracert` **commands are used for.** Admittedly, these are specifically for A+ exam 220-1102, but know what they do. Both `ipconfig` and `ping` are network troubleshooting commands. You can use `ipconfig` to view your computer's IP configuration and `ping` to test connectivity between two network hosts. `tracert` allows you to view the network path a packet takes from the host to the destination.

Know what the `netstat`, `net`, **and** `nslookup` **commands are used for.** These commands need to be understood for exam 220-1102 as well. `netstat` shows network statistics; `net` allows you to perform network-management tasks, such as sharing folders; and `nslookup` allows you to query a DNS server.

Review Questions

The answers to the chapter review questions can be found in Appendix A.

1. If the video on your laptop is not working, what should you do to troubleshoot it? (Choose two.)

    A. Toggle the video function key.

    B. Try using an external monitor.

    C. Remove the display unit and reattach it.

    D. Power the system off and back on.

2. A printer is printing unusually large margins on documents that are sent to it. You suspect that the paper size is set incorrectly. Where should you go to change this?

    A. Print spooler

    B. Paper selection switch on the printer

    C. Printing preferences

    D. Print queue

3. A user tells you that his Android phone case is bulging, and the device has been hot to the touch lately. You suspect a swollen battery. Which of the following is a good next step?

    A. Replace the device.

    B. Leave the device on to drain the battery, and then recharge the device.

    C. Turn the device off, let it cool to room temperature, and then recharge the device.

    D. Use the battery calibration utility.

    E. Freeze the system.

4. A laptop user with an 802.11ac wireless network card just switched desk locations. In the new location, they say that their wireless drops connectivity intermittently and seems to have slow transfer speeds. Which of the following is most likely to resolve these issues?

    A. Replace the network card.

    B. Run `ipconfig` to ensure that they are receiving the right IP address from the DHCP server.

    C. Install a new WAP closer to their new desk.

    D. Use a network monitor to ensure that there are no IP address conflicts.

5. While troubleshooting a client computer, you decide to obtain a new IP address from the DHCP server. After releasing the existing address, which command do you use to get new IP information from the DHCP server?

    A. `ipconfig /refresh`

    B. `ipconfig /renew`

    C. `ifconfig /release`

    D. `ifconfig /start`

6. Users are complaining that their print jobs are not printing. You open the print queue and see 50 jobs lined up. The printer is connected properly and online. What should you do?

   A. Open Printer Troubleshooting and have it diagnose the problem.

   B. Stop and restart the print spooler.

   C. Delete and reinstall the printer.

   D. Delete and reinstall Windows.

7. The display on a laptop computer is continuously flickering. Which of the following are most likely to cause this problem? (Choose two.)

   A. A failing display

   B. Interference from a nearby fan

   C. A failing backlight

   D. A failing inverter

   E. Incorrect video driver

8. You are having problems with the video card in one of your computers. Where could you check for troubleshooting information?

   A. Another computer with the same video card

   B. The video card manufacturer's website

   C. The manual that came with the card

   D. The server log

9. Your laser printer keeps printing vertical black lines on its output pages. What is the most likely cause of the problem?

   A. There is a groove or scratch in the EP drum.

   B. The EP drum-cleaning blade is broken.

   C. The printer is low on toner.

   D. The transfer corona wire is not working properly.

10. The display on your laptop appears warped and fuzzy. You plug in an external monitor, and the image on it is fine. What is the most likely cause of the problem?

   A. The video card

   B. The LCD display

   C. The motherboard

   D. The video driver

11. You have an inkjet printer. Recently, papers are being printed with excessive amounts of ink, and the ink is smearing. What is the most likely cause of the problem?

   A. A faulty ink cartridge

   B. A corrupted print driver

   C. A faulty fuser

   D. Too much humidity in the air

12. You believe that a network card is beginning to fail. Which of the following tools should you use to see if the network card is capable of sending and receiving data from an RJ-45 port?

    A. Toner probe

    B. Loopback plug

    C. Multimeter

    D. Cable tester

13. When you print documents on your laser printer, you see residue from previous images on the output. Which two things are the most likely causes of this problem? (Choose two.)

    A. A faulty transfer corona wire

    B. An overheating printer

    C. A bad erasure lamp

    D. A broken cleaning blade

14. Troubleshooting a network connectivity issue takes you into the wiring closet, where you realize that none of the cables are properly labeled. Several are disconnected. Which tool should you use to determine where the cables run to?

    A. Loopback plug

    B. Punch-down tool

    C. Cable tester

    D. Toner probe

15. You turn on a laptop computer and the hard drive is not recognized. Where should you go to troubleshoot the issue?

    A. S.M.A.R.T. diagnostics

    B. BIOS/UEFI

    C. Windows Device Manager

    D. Boot sector manager

16. You turn a computer on and it doesn't boot up properly. You hear a rhythmic ticking sound coming from inside the case. What is most likely the problem?

    A. The motherboard

    B. The power supply fan

    C. The HDD

    D. The video card

17. You support an old impact printer at work. When the printer prints, there is always a blank horizontal line in the middle of each line of output. What is the most likely cause of the problem?

    A. The print ribbon is old and needs to be replaced.

    B. The print ribbon is not advancing properly.

    C. The print head needs to be replaced.

    D. The wrong print driver is installed.

18. A network cable for a crucial server has failed. There are no premade Ethernet cables available, but there is bulk cable and connectors. Which tool do you need to use to make a new cable?

    A. Crimper

    B. Punch-down tool

    C. Cable tester

    D. Loopback plug

19. A user brings in an iPhone and the touchscreen is not responding. What should you try first to get the device functioning again?

    A. Hold the power button and the sleep/wake button for 10 seconds to reset the device.

    B. Restore the device to factory settings.

    C. Replace the battery in the device.

    D. Hold the power button for 10 seconds to force the device to power off.

20. You are troubleshooting a server and discover that one of the hard drives in the RAID 0 array has failed. Which statement is true?

    A. You need to replace the failed drive, but the data is okay because the drive is configured as a mirror.

    B. You need to replace the failed drive, but the data is okay because the drive is configured as a disk stripe with parity.

    C. You need to replace the failed drive, and the data on the array is lost.

    D. You do not need to replace the failed drive; the system will function normally.

Performance-Based Question

You will encounter performance-based questions on the A+ exam. The questions on the exam require you to perform a specific task, and you will be graded on whether or not you were able to complete the task. The following requires you to think creatively in order to measure how well you understand this chapter's topics. You may or may not see similar questions on the actual A+ exams. To see how your answers compare to the authors', refer to Appendix B.

Your network users are sending print jobs to the printer, but they are stacking up in the queue and not printing. The printer appears to be online and has paper. How would you stop and restart the print spooler in Windows 10?

220-1102

PART

II

Chapter

13

Operating System Basics

THE FOLLOWING CompTIA A+ 220-1102 EXAM OBJECTIVES ARE COVERED IN THIS CHAPTER:

✓ **1.1 Identify basic features of Microsoft Windows editions.**

- Windows 10 editions
  - Home
  - Pro
  - Pro for Workstations
  - Enterprise
- Feature differences
  - Domain access vs. workgroup
  - Desktop styles/user interface
  - Availability of Remote Desktop Protocol (RDP)
  - Random access memory (RAM) support limitations
  - BitLocker
  - gpedit.msc
- Upgrade paths
  - In-place upgrade

✓ **1.7 Given a scenario, apply application installation and configuration concepts.**

- System requirements for applications
  - 32-bit vs. 64-bit dependent application requirements
  - Dedicated graphics card vs. integrated
  - Video random access memory (VRAM) requirements
  - RAM requirements

- Central processing unit (CPU) requirements
- External hardware tokens
- Storage requirements
- OS requirements for applications
  - Application to OS compatibility
  - 32-bit vs. 64-bit OS
- Distribution methods
  - Physical media vs. downloadable
  - ISO mountable
- Other considerations for new applications
  - Impact to device
  - Impact to network
  - Impact to operation
  - Impact to business

✓ 1.8 Explain common OS types and their purposes.

- Workstation OSs
  - Windows
  - Linux
  - macOS
  - Chrome OS
- Cell phone/tablet OSs
  - iPadOS
  - iOS
  - Android
- Vendor life-cycle limitations
  - End-of-life (EOL)
  - Update limitations
  - Compatibility concerns between OSs

The previous chapters focused mainly on the hardware and physical elements of the computing environment. We looked at the physical components, or hardware, of personal computers, laptops, and mobile devices, as well as networking, printers, and troubleshooting procedures. That completes the coverage of the topics on the 220-1101 exam. This chapter marks a departure from that.

In this chapter—and several to come—the focus is on operating systems (OSs). To be specific, the majority of information will be on the Microsoft Windows operating systems, which you must know well for the 220-1102 certification exam. However, the 220-1102 exam also requires basic knowledge of the macOS and Linux operating systems. These are covered in Chapter 16, "Working with macOS and Linux."

Understanding Operating Systems

Computers are pretty much useless without software. A piece of hardware might just as well be used as a paperweight or doorstop if you don't have an easy way to interface with it. Software provides that way. While there are many types of software, or programs, the most important one you'll ever deal with is the operating system. Operating systems have many different, complex functions, but two of them jump out as being critical: interfacing with the hardware and providing a platform on which other applications can run.

Here are three major distinctions of software about which you should be aware:

Operating System   The *operating system (OS)* provides a consistent environment for other software to execute commands. The OS provides users with an interface with the computer so that they can send commands (input) and receive feedback or results (output). To do this, the OS must communicate with the computer hardware to perform the following tasks, as illustrated in Figure 13.1.

- Disk storage and file management
- Device access
- Memory management
- Output formatting

FIGURE 13.1   The operating system interacts with resources.

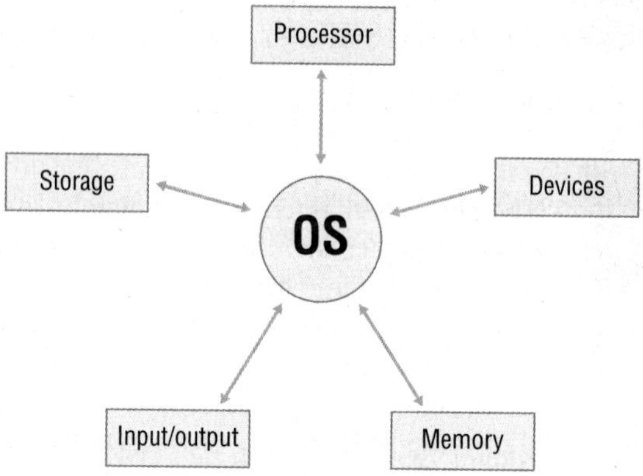

Once the OS has organized these basic resources, users can give the computer instructions through input devices (such as a keyboard or a mouse). Some of these commands are built into the OS, whereas others are issued through the use of applications. The OS becomes the center through which the system hardware, other software, and the user communicate; the rest of the components of the system work together through the OS, which coordinates their communication.

Application   Used to accomplish a particular task, an *application* is software that is written to supplement the commands available to a particular OS. Each application is specifically compiled (configured) for the OS on which it will run. For this reason, the application relies on the OS to do many of its basic tasks. Examples of applications include complex programs, such as Microsoft Word and Microsoft Edge, as well as simple programs, such as a command-line FTP program. Whether they are complex or simple, when accessing devices and memory, the programs can simply request that the OS do it for them. This arrangement saves substantially on programming overhead because much of the executable code is *shared*—that is, it is written into the operating system and can therefore be used by multiple applications running on that OS.

Drivers   *Drivers* are extremely specific software written for the purpose of instructing a particular OS on how to access a piece of hardware. Each modem or printer has unique features and configuration settings, and the driver allows the OS to understand how the hardware works and what it is able to do.

In the following sections, we'll look at some terms and concepts central to all operating systems. Then we'll move into specific discussions of Windows operating systems.

Are These the Only Versions of Windows?

In the workplace, it is likely that you will encounter some different versions of the Windows operating systems beyond just Windows 10, Windows 8/8.1, and Windows 7. Although Windows 7, Windows Vista, and Windows XP are no longer supported by Microsoft, these operating systems can still be found in certain instances. These older operating systems are typically used to support legacy systems, such as kiosks, medical equipment, and many other applications. Windows 10 has become the mainstream operating system for both the workplace and home over the past five or six years, since its release in 2015. It was marketed to be the ongoing version that Microsoft will support in the future. However, Microsoft has recently released the next major version, Windows 11, as of October 2021.

Know that this version of the exam focuses only on the Windows 10/11 operating systems mentioned here, as well as macOS, Linux (both addressed in Chapter 16), Chrome OS, iOS, and iPadOS. We highly recommend that you become familiar with all of the operating systems your job requires, but these are the ones that you will need to know for the A+ certification exam.

Operating System Terms and Concepts

Before we get too far into our discussion of PC operating systems, it will be useful to define a few key terms. The following are some terms that you will come across as you study this chapter and work in the computer industry:

Version   A *version* is a particular revision of a piece of software, normally described by a number that tells you how new the product is in relation to other versions of the product.

Source   The *source code* is the actual code that defines how a piece of software works. Computer operating systems can be *open source*, meaning that the OS can be examined and modified by anyone, or they can be *closed source*, meaning that only an owner or developer can modify or examine the code. As an example, Microsoft and macOS are closed source operating systems and *Linux* is an open source operating system.

    A word often used interchangeably with *closed source* is *proprietary*.

Shell   A *shell* is a program that runs on top of the OS and allows the user to issue commands through a set of menus or another interface (which may or may not be graphical). Shells make an OS easier to use by changing the user interface. Explorer is the name of the shell that has been used with the Windows operating system since Windows 95.

Graphical User Interface   A *graphical user interface*, or *GUI*, is a method by which a person communicates with a computer using graphical images, icons, and methods other than text. GUIs allow a user to use a mouse, touchpad, or another mechanism (in addition to the keyboard) to interact with the computer to issue commands.

Network   A *network* is any group of computers that have a communication link between them. Networks allow computers to share information and resources quickly and securely.

Cooperative Multitasking   *Cooperative multitasking* is a multitasking method that depends on the application itself to be responsible for using the processor and then freeing it for access by other applications. This is the way very early versions of Windows managed multiple applications. If any application locked up while using the processor, the application was unable to free the processor to do other tasks and the entire system locked, usually forcing a reboot.

Preemptive Multitasking   *Preemptive multitasking* is a multitasking method in which the OS allots each application a certain amount of processor time and then forcibly takes back control and gives another application or task access to the processor. This means that if an application crashes, the OS takes control of the processor away from the locked application and passes it on to the next application, which should be unaffected. Although unstable programs still lock, only the locked application will stall, not the entire system. Preemptive multitasking is what is used today in modern operating systems.

Multithreading   *Multithreading* is the ability of a single application to have multiple requests in to the processor at one time. This results in faster application performance because it allows a program to do many things at once.

32-Bit   A *32-bit operating system* is one that can not only run on a 32-bit processor but can utilize the capabilities of the processor fully. While this may sound simple, the truth of the matter is that it took many years after the 32-bit processor became available before operating systems (which were 16-bit at the time) were able to utilize their features. You cannot execute 64-bit software on 32-bit operating systems; the instructions sets are functionally different.

64-Bit   A *64-bit operating system* is one that is written to utilize the instructions possible with 64-bit processors. Originally, these were more common with servers than desktops, but they have now become ubiquitous in the market with both Intel and AMD processors. As mentioned earlier, you cannot mix 64-bit software with 32-bit hardware (but you can run most 32-bit software on 64-bit hardware).

x86   The term *x86* is commonly used to refer to operating systems intended to run on the Intel processor. Intel initially identified its 32-bit processors with numbers ending in 86 prior to switching to the Pentium line.

x64   The term *x64* is commonly used to denote operating systems that can run on 64-bit processors. This is also commonly referred to as *AMD64*, because AMD defined the 64-bit instruction set used today.

ARM   The term *ARM* is commonly used to denote operating systems that can run on Advanced RISC Machine (ARM) processors. ARM operating systems use a *reduced instruction set computing (RISC)* instruction set commonly found on tablet and phone processors. ARMv8-A processors can support 64-bit operating systems, so you will find 32-bit and 64-bit operating systems.

Random Access Memory   The term *random access memory (RAM)* is used to describe the amount of memory installed and accessible for an operating system. The operating system uses RAM to hold its operating system code, as well as the programs you open on the operating system. Each program you install will have a minimum RAM requirement and recommended RAM requirement. Most computer systems on the market today are sold with at least 4 gigabytes (GB) of RAM. PC manufacturers have identified that newer programs are requiring more and more RAM to operate properly, so upgrades of 8 GB of RAM are common and have become the new normal.

A 32-bit operating system has the limitation of addressing only 4 GB of RAM. Most new computer systems on the market today come with a preinstalled 64-bit operating system. The 4 GB limitation will present itself if you are re-installing a computer system that has more than 4 GB of RAM and use a 32-bit version of the operating system. You will find out quickly that you just downgraded the computer.

Operating system vendors implemented a Physical Address Extension (PAE) workaround for the 4 GB limit. For the purposes of the exam, however, you should be aware that 32-bit operating systems have a hard limit of addressing 4 GB of RAM.

Operating Systems

When we think of an operating system, Windows or macOS is probably the first that comes to mind. These operating systems comprise only one category of operating system. We use other operating systems, such as Android and Apple iOS, and don't even realize how much they have become part of our daily life. The CompTIA exam recognized these various operating systems and integrated them into the 220-1102 exam.

Operating System Categories

An operating system category defines the use and function of both the operating system and the hardware. All operating systems fit into one of four different broad categories: *server*, *workstation*, *mobile*, or *cloud-based* operating systems.

Server   Server operating systems allow for the sharing of information and applications by workstation operating systems. The operating system is optimized for background processes used for access by clients, as opposed to the foreground processes, such as the GUI.

Workstation   Workstation operating systems allow end users to access information and applications on server operating systems as well as independently run applications locally. The operating system is optimized for foreground processes, such as the GUI. Background sharing is usually limited to a specific number of users; workstation versions of Microsoft Windows are limited to 10 concurrent users.

Mobile   Mobile operating systems are found on mobile devices such as phones and tablets. The mobile operating system is generally optimized for touch-based devices where one program is used at a time.

Cloud-Based   Cloud-based operating systems are a new breed of operating system that has emerged from the mobile computing era. Cloud-based operating systems are also considered stateless operating systems, since personal data is not primarily stored on the device but in the cloud. Mobile operating systems can be considered cloud-based operating systems. So this category takes on a dual role of defining a category and describing where the data is stored. The Chrome operating system is not a mobile operating system and fits into this category.

Common Operating Systems

Now that you understand the various categories of operating systems you may encounter, we will explore the common operating systems you will find in your everyday work as an A+ technician.

Microsoft Windows   The Microsoft Windows operating system is one of the most popular operating systems adopted by business and personal users. Windows 11, the current version, is considered a workstation operating system.

Apple Macintosh OS   *macOS* is the current version of the operating system for Apple Macintosh laptop and computer hardware platforms. Ironically, macOS is the original operating system name from back in the 1980s. Between 1999 and 2015, the macOS was called Mac OS X. The macOS operating system is considered a workstation operating system.

Linux   Linux was created as a free, open source operating system in 1991 by Linus Torvalds. Linux was created to mimic the design of the MINIX (mini-UNIX) operating system, which was a minimal version of UNIX that was originally used for academic purposes. Today, the Linux kernel (core of the OS) remains a free, open source platform upon which many different Linux distributions have been created, such as Ubuntu, Red Hat, Fedora, CentOS, and Debian, just to name a few. The Linux operating system is considered both a workstation operating system and a server operating system, depending on its installation and configuration.

Microsoft Windows Phone   Microsoft purchased Nokia in 2013 to produce a platform for the Windows Phone furnishing the tile-based Windows 8 operating system. After several years on the market, Microsoft ended the sales of Windows-based phones, and support for the Windows-based phones ended in 2019. The current Microsoft phone is called the Surface Duo and uses a native Android operating system to power the Microsoft 365 suite of applications. Both the original Microsoft Windows phone and the new Surface Duo are considered mobile operating system–based platforms.

Microsoft Windows Tablet   In 2012, with the release of the tile-based Windows 8 operating system, Microsoft released the Surface tablet. The Surface tablet was originally released with an ARM-based processor, but today it is sold mainly with Intel-based processors to compete on the market with *Ultrabooks* (subnotebook computers). The operating system today is a full version of Windows 11 and is considered a mobile operating system.

Android   Google created the *Android* operating system as a tile-based mobile operating system. Android was originally released in 2008 with HTC phones; the release of Android tablets followed in 2011. Android-based phones and tablets have become quite popular in the mobile operating system market. The popularity of Android is attributed to the application ecosystem that the Google Play store creates. The Google Play store enables users to purchase, download, and install applications, books, music, and video for the Android operating system.

iOS   Apple created the iOS operating system as a tile-based mobile operating system. Originally released on the first iPhone in 2007, the operating system was known as the iPhone Operating System (iOS). The release of the iPod Touch followed a few months later, and it also furnished the iPhone Operating System. In 2010, the first iPad was released and it furnished the iPhone Operating System as well. Today, the operating system's name has been shortened to iOS; the current version, as of this writing, is iOS version 15. Apple iOS is a popular mobile operating system in the marketplace today. Its popularity is attributed to Apple's strong support for the accompanying hardware. The Apple App Store also creates a strong ecosystem for downloading, installing, and purchasing applications, books, music, and video for the iOS operating system.

iPadOS   *iPadOS* version 13.1 was released in the fall of 2019 for the Apple iPad. iPadOS is a variant of the popular Apple iOS with better multitasking features and a better home screen. This allows the Apple iPad to behave more like a lightweight laptop than a tablet.

Chrome OS   *Chrome OS* is an operating system that is designed around the Chrome web browser by Google. Chrome OS was released in 2011 on the hardware platform known as the Chromebook, which is considered one of the first Ultrabooks. Chrome OS is a true cloud-based operating system, since all its data is stored in the Google Drive cloud-based storage system. Since the release of the Chromebook, workstation-type devices called Chromeboxes have been released to market. Applications, which are really just web plug-ins, can be installed from the Chrome Web Store. The applications are written in HTML, HTML5, CSS, and JavaScript, which allow cross-platform support between Chrome OS and the Chrome web browser installed on a PC or Mac.

Stateless Operating Systems

The lines have blurred in the past few years with the rapid adoption of the cloud for both enterprise and consumer installations. The workstation-based operating systems, such as Windows 11 and macOS, have embraced the cloud and to some extent have become stateless devices like mobile-based operating systems.

In the enterprise, an operating system can be set up with all the applications a user needs to do their job, along with access to all their files. The installation of applications and the configuration of the applications is managed by mobile device management (MDM) software, such as Intune. Then, if the device breaks, is stolen, or is upgraded to new hardware, a new device can be provisioned in the MDM software and everything gets set up just like their previous device.

Consumer installations have also benefited from the adoption of the cloud. When a consumer purchases a new device to replace their old device, all they have to do is sign into the cloud service and their files and applications will automatically be transferred over and installed. The adoption of the cloud and the new behavior now makes traditional operating systems act more like stateless mobile-based operating systems.

Operating System Life Cycle

An operating system life cycle begins as when an operating system is introduced and ends when the operating system is no longer supported. As a computer technician, you should pay close attention to an operating system's life cycle, because the *end-of-life (EOL)* date for an OS means that it will no longer receive updates.

When an operating system is considered end-of-life, newer features will not be added to the OS in the future. More importantly, security updates will no longer be offered, which will put your operating system and information at risk of compromise.

The network administrator should pay close attention to the dates an operating system is considered end-of-life. If the organization has a support contract for problems, the support of the operating system at the end of life could no longer be honored. Of course, the lack of security updates for a corporate network is more concerning, since the stability of an organization can be compromised.

It has been common practice for network administrators to skip versions of every other operating system. This is mainly attributed to the *long-term support* for the current operating system and the amount of work required to upgrade an entire organization's operating systems. In addition to these factors, many hardware vendors support the current operating system plus the last release. Administrators can purchase a new laptop or PC and request the prior operating system. However, once the next operating system is released, the support for the old operating system will force an upgrade.

 When Windows Vista was released, Windows XP was the dominant corporate operating system. Windows Vista was not highly adopted, but when Windows 7 was released, many administrators planned on the highly anticipated upgrade to Windows 7. We've seen the same trend with Windows 10; many administrators completely skipped rolling out Windows 8 entirely. There is no way to tell what will happen in the future, because Microsoft has changed its naming convention for Windows and released platform upgrades as feature releases.

The following common terminology is used by operating system developers in relation to the life cycle of an OS:

Alpha   An operating system in alpha is a first draft of an operating system. Operating systems that are available in alpha are considered previews. It is common to find these in open source communities, such as Linux operating systems, but it is uncommon to find a corporate-based operating system in alpha.

Beta   An operating system in beta is a second draft of an operating system. This stage of an operating system means most of the bugs have been discovered and are avidly being patched. This stage is typically used to discover missing features and new bugs. Some operating system developers require an opt-in to run a beta operating system, and some require invites to a beta program that mandates participation.

Release Candidate   An operating system that is deemed a release candidate is in the final stage before it is released to market. During the release candidate stage, administrators are urged to install and use the operating system as though it were the final release. The benefit is that the administrator can get a previewed look at the operating system while helping to polish the final product, also called the *release to market (RTM)*. An operating system in this stage is generally stable and has relatively few bugs.

Current   A current operating system, as the term states, is the current release of an operating system. Many operating system developers are on a one- to two-year release cycle for the future version of the current operating system.

Service Pack   Although the term *service pack* is generally associated with updates, it is also used to describe a milestone in the life cycle of an operating system. When a service pack is released for an operating system, it adds major features as well as patches for both security and functionality. Microsoft has replaced this term with the introduction of Windows 8; it is now just called an update. However, many other operating systems still use "service pack."

Mainstream Support   During the *mainstream support* of an operating system, all *hotfixes*, *security updates*, *feature updates*, and general support for the operating system is supported. An operating system developer will usually have a predetermined mainstream support date when the operating system is released. When the mainstream support ends for an operating system, it is either no longer supported or enters into an extended support period.

Extended Support   The *extended support* period, sometimes called the *long-term support (LTS)* period, for an operating system is the final state of an OS's life cycle. For example, during this time, hotfixes and features will no longer be supported, but critical security updates will be supported with Microsoft operating systems. Additional contract purchases may be required if hotfixes are required during this period. An administrator should have all systems upgraded to the current operating system by the end of the extended support date.

Minimum System Requirements

In the upcoming chapters, we'll explore how to install and upgrade each of the operating systems that you need to know for the exam. However, the hardware requirements of the operating system that you are thinking of installing can prevent you from even considering these options. Before you can begin to install an OS, you must consider several items. You must perform the following tasks before you even start to think about undertaking the installation:

1. Determine hardware compatibility and *minimum requirements*.
2. Determine installation options.
3. Determine the installation method.
4. Prepare the computer for installation.

Let's begin our discussion by talking about hardware compatibility issues and the requirements for installing the various versions of Windows.

Determining Hardware Compatibility and Minimum Requirements

Before you can begin to install any version of an operating system, you must determine whether it supports the hardware that you will be using. That is, will the version of the operating system have problems running any of the device drivers for the hardware that you have?

To answer this question, operating system vendors have developed several versions of *hardware compatibility lists (HCLs)*. An HCL is a list of all the hardware that works with the operating system. Microsoft published HCLs for many prior versions of Windows. Since the release of Windows 10, the HCL has disappeared completely and it is now the responsibility of the vendor to certify the compatibility of the hardware with Microsoft. However, many other operating system vendors still have a recommended HCL.

The point is, before installing an operating system, you should check all your computer's components against an HCL or the manufacturer of the component to ensure that they are compatible with the version of operating system you plan to install. If a product is not on the list, that does not mean it will not work; it merely means it has not been tested. The list represents tested software and hardware that vendors have stated are compatible, but it is by no means all-inclusive.

In addition to general compatibility, it is important that your computer have enough "oomph" to run the version of an operating system that you plan to install. For that matter, it is important for your computer to have enough resources to run any software that you plan to use. Toward that end, Microsoft (as well as other software publishers) releases a list of both minimum and recommended hardware specifications that you should follow when installing Windows.

"Minimum specifications" are the absolute minimum requirements for hardware that your system should meet in order to install and run the OS version you have chosen. "Recommended hardware specifications" are what you should have in your system in order to realize usable performance. Always try to have the recommended hardware (or better) in your system. If you don't, you may have to upgrade your hardware before you upgrade your operating system if you're running anything beyond a minimal environment. Table 13.1 lists the minimum hardware specifications for Windows 10 and Windows 11. Note that in addition to these minimum requirements, the hardware chosen must be compatible with the selected version of Windows. Also be aware that additional hardware may be required if certain features are installed (for example, a fingerprint reader is required to use biometric logins). Windows 11 is only available in a 64-bit version and requires a Trusted Platform Module 2.0 and UEFI for added security of the operating system and its applications.

TABLE 13.1   Windows 10 and Windows 11 minimum system requirements

Operating System	Windows 10	Windows 10	Windows 11
Architecture	32-bit	64-bit	64-bit
Processor	1 GHz or faster processor or System on a Chip (SoC)	1 GHz or faster processor or System on a Chip (SoC)	1 GHz or faster processor with 2 or more cores or System on a Chip (SoC)
Memory	1 GB	2 GB	4 GB
Free hard disk space	16 GB	32 GB	64 GB

(continues)

TABLE 13.1   Windows 10 and Windows 11 minimum system requirements *(continued)*

Operating System	Windows 10	Windows 10	Windows 11
Graphics card	Microsoft DirectX 9 or later graphics device with WDDM 1.0 driver	Microsoft DirectX 9 or later graphics device with WDDM 1.0 driver	Microsoft DirectX 12 or later graphics device with WDDM 2.0 driver
Display	800 × 600	800 × 600	High definition 720p
Additional hardware	N/A	N/A	UEFI & TPM 2.0 required

If there is one thing to be learned from Table 13.1, it is that Microsoft is nothing if not optimistic. For your own sanity, though, we strongly suggest that you always take the minimum requirements with a grain of salt. They are, after all, *minimum* requirements. Even the recommended requirements should be considered minimum requirements. The bottom line is to make sure that you have a good margin between your system's performance and the minimum requirements listed. Always run Windows on more powerful hardware rather than less!

Other hardware—sound cards, network cards, modems, video cards, and so on—may or may not work with Windows. If the device is fairly recent, you can be relatively certain that it was built to work with the newest version of Windows. If it is older, however, you may need to find out who made the hardware and check their website to see if there are drivers available for the version of Windows that you are installing.

There's one more thing to consider when evaluating installation methods. Some methods work only if you're performing a clean installation, not an upgrade.

Understanding Applications

An operating system without any applications installed on it isn't very useful. Even back when Windows 1.0 was released 30 years ago, it came with applications, such as Minesweeper, a File Manager, and a simple word processor. In this section, we will explore installing applications for Windows 10/11. However, these concepts can be applied to any operating system.

System Requirements for Applications

Before installing an application, you must collect information on the requirements of the application to make sure that your system can satisfy the requirements. If your system cannot satisfy the requirements for the application, you may have to upgrade the system. You can find application requirements on the vendor's website. For example, if you need to install the Microsoft Power BI Desktop application, you would search Microsoft's site to find the system requirements for this particular application. The documentation would reveal several different requirements, such as the following:

Memory   The most common requirement that needs to be met before installing an application is the memory requirement. Memory is often displayed in the form of total random access memory (RAM) for the operating system.

CPU   The requirement for the *central processing unit (CPU)* required for an application is often displayed in the form of total CPU processing power of the system. It is often expressed in the form of GHz, and other requirements can include the number of physical CPUs, the number of cores, and even the model of processor.

Architecture   The architecture of the CPU and the operating system installed needs to match the application requirements for 32-bit or 64-bit applications. The architecture must meet or exceed the requirements of the application. For example, if the application needs a 64-bit architecture, then the CPU and operating system need to support 64-bit operations. However, if the application requires a 32-bit architecture, then a 32-bit or 64-bit CPU and operating system can accommodate the requirement.

Storage   The requirement for the storage is often displayed in GB or TB, depending on the application. The storage requirement is often the free space required to install the application. However, some software packages that require the storage of user data also display a separate storage requirement for the data.

Prerequisites   A common prerequisite to install an application might be a specific version of the .NET Framework. However, some applications have specific prerequisite requirements, such as a Microsoft SQL Server for data storage.

Display   When data is to be displayed in a specific format, the application designer has formatted the application to a minimum display area. This requirement is often in the form of pixels, such as 1024 × 768. Although pixels are the most common display requirement, another type of requirement is a graphics processing unit (GPU). A specific GPU may be required if the application will process video or graphics.

Video Random Access Memory (VRAM)   VRAM requirements are typically related to applications that are graphic intensive, such as gaming. VRAM is typically much faster than conventional RAM, because it must be accessed faster to sustain the higher bandwidth requirements for the graphics applications being used.

Licensing   When installing an application, the last step is usually licensing the application. The license can come in several different forms, such as a node-locked license tied to a MAC address or drive serial number. A network-based license server allows for concurrent use by several people at once. External hardware tokens license an application with the use of a USB dongle or hardware device that allows the program to run.

Other   In addition to the common requirements, other requirements must be met before an application can be installed. The operating system requirement is one such requirement. Every application will have a minimum operating system on which it can be installed and supported. Other requirements can be for specific hardware, licensing, or drivers.

Additional Application Requirement Considerations

When an application's requirements are published, they are the bare minimum requirements, not the optimal recommended specifications. The requirements are a conservative estimate so that a potential customer is not scared away with expensive hardware upgrades. When extremely low requirements are advertised, we always recommend calling a presales support person. You should describe how the application will be used and seek their recommendations for optimizing the application's performance. You will often find that they are double or triple the advertised bare minimum requirements.

Storage is probably the biggest consideration when evaluating the installation of an application that will store user data. It is extremely difficult to gauge how much storage should be set aside for the application for user data. If too much storage is allocated, the precious commodity might go unused for the life of the application. If too little is allocated, you may have to upgrade the storage—or, worse, you could fill the entire drive up and be forced to do it in a panic.

The most common architectures for CPUs are 32-bit and 64-bit. They are noted as x86 for 32-bit and x64 or AMD64 for 64-bit. The 64-bit CPU extension were adopted from the AMD version of their 64-bit CPU. When installing an operating system, the operating system requirements must be met or exceeded for the CPU architecture type. If you are installing a 64-bit operating system, then you must have at least a 64-bit CPU. If you are installing a 32-bit operating system, you can install it on a 32-bit CPU or 64-bit CPU. However, if you have a 64-bit CPU it always makes sense to install a 64-bit operating system, since it gives you maximum flexibility and you typically can't upgrade to a different architecture.

Operating system compatibility is a consideration for older applications that are still required by organizations. Application compatibility has been incorporated into the Windows operating system since Windows XP. It allows for an application to behave as though the operating system was an older operating system. For example, over the years, Windows has become more restrictive of local permissions on the filesystem. If an application that was written for an older operating system expects to write to a Registry key, application compatibility will allow it to think it's directly writing to the location.

Application Installation

Once the requirements are met for an application and the considerations are investigated, you are ready to install the application. You must now consider how the application will be installed; the number of machines on which the application will be installed will factor into this consideration. This section discusses several different ways that an application can be installed.

Optical Disc

If the installation is a one-off installation, then a CD/DVD drive might be your best option. In recent years, applications have even been shipped on Blu-ray media. If you must install the application on several different PCs, then this method may not be the preferred installation method. When installing from optical media, even the fastest optical drive is slow compared to other methods, such as USB.

ISO Mountable

Although optical discs have been around since the mid-1990s and have been the most popular method of installing applications and operating systems, the optical disk is quickly becoming a relic. When you use a virtualization product such as Hyper-V or VMware Workstation, the optical disc is just too clumsy and slow to use. Mountable ISO images of the physical media has become the new norm. When you need to install an operating system or application, you simply download the media from the vendor, mount the ISO, and install it as if you had a virtual optical drive. ISO sizes will vary from 500 MB to 9.6 GB with normal CD and DVD formats, but Blu-ray discs can be up to 45 GB.

USB Drive

Applications are outgrowing optical media such as CD-ROM and DVD-ROM, so USB drives have become popular. USB drives are faster and bigger than optical media. If a handful of computers require the application, then this might be a better option. However, the disadvantage is that simultaneous installations are limited to the number of flash drives you have with the application loaded. Another common problem with USB drive installations is that the USB drives are lost from time to time or inadvertently overwritten. For this reason, many application vendors lock their drives so they can't be overwritten and repurposed.

Network Installation

When you need to install an application on many different PCs, a network installation should be your first choice. The application is typically uploaded to a file share by the administrator, and then the file share is set to read-only access for the user who is performing the installation. Depending on the speed of the network, this could be the fastest method to install an application on several different PCs simultaneously.

There are several different methods for deploying an application over the network. Each method depends on the number and location of the computers.

User-Initiated Installation

These installations are used when the administrator of the PC will start the installation manually. This method is preferable when the administrator is expected to answer specific questions during the installation, such as where to install the application.

The installation of any application generally requires that the user be an administrator of the operating system or have elevated privileges to install an application. If user-initiated installation is chosen as the method for deploying an application, you must be sure that the user account has the appropriate permissions to install the application.

Automated Installation

Two different types of automated installations can be employed by the administrator: push installations and pull installations. Either installation type is used when the conformity of the installation is required.

Automated installation products, such as Microsoft Endpoint Configuration Manager (MECM), can deploy applications to multiple PCs with a push installation. Microsoft SCCM, formerly called Microsoft System Center Configuration Manager (SCCM), is considered the Swiss Army knife of installation and reporting services. Each client in the network will have the MECM agent installed prior to the push installation of the application. The agent will then be responsible for reporting on the current operating system. This allows you to collect information for determining if you can satisfy the requirements of the application. The agent can then be used as the contact point for the push installation of the application.

Group Policy can also be used to automate the installation of applications. The Group Policy method is a pull-based installation method, where the client will pull the application from the network share. This method contains no agent, so reporting is not available for client resources, installation requirements, or installation status. The benefit is that it requires very little infrastructure if you have Microsoft Active Directory (AD) installed already.

Regardless of the installation type, push- or pull-based, most automated installation methods do not require the user logged in to be an administrator. MECM can be configured to use a system account that has elevated privileges in the target operating system to install the application. Group Policy pull-based installations can also be configured to use a system account that has elevated privileges to install the application.

NOTE Push installations are installations in which the administrator can push an application out to clients. Pull installations are installations in which the client pulls, or queries, for the application to be installed. Group Policy application deployment is a pull type of installation, since the client is responsible for pulling the application and installing it. MECM is a push type installation method. For more information about MECM, visit: https://docs.microsoft.com/en-us/mem/configmgr/core/ clients/deploy/plan/client-installation-methods

Security Considerations

When an application is installed in the operating system, the overall security of the operating system can potentially be compromised. Of course, it is not the intent of the application to weaken the security of the operating system, but vulnerabilities in the application can exist. Application developers realize that their code is not perfect and that vulnerabilities can exist, so many applications now include self-updating capabilities.

Applications weakening the security of the local device should not be your only concern. Applications can actually weaken the security of the entire network, especially if they are not updated frequently. Applications that operate over the network with client-server functionality pose the largest security risks, since they allow for remote exploitation of vulnerabilities. One measure that can be employed with network applications that are not updated frequently is to firewall the services. There are many other active measures, which we will discuss in further detail in Chapter 18, "Securing Operating Systems."

Other Considerations for New Applications

Once the requirements of the application are satisfied, the security of the application is evaluated, and an installation method is chosen, there are several other considerations that should be reviewed before installing a new application. These considerations must be evaluated to ensure that the installation of the application does not impose unintended problems on the organization and network.

Impact to Device   Although the impact to the device should be minimal if the application requirements are satisfied, the impact should still be considered. For example, if you install an application that constantly logs, you could find that the hard drive will fill up quickly and other applications could run more slowly due to the drive activity. Although this is an extreme example, other impacts may be more subtle and manifest over a longer period of time.

Impact to Network   The impact to the network should also be considered. The bandwidth the application needs to operate, and consequently uses, should be evaluated. Although an application at first glance might not appear to use a lot of bandwidth, as more demand is placed on the application, bandwidth will increase. For example, if you installed a network video recorder (NVR), a few cameras might not use too much network. However, as more and more cameras are added, bandwidth usage can sharply increase. If the bandwidth traverses a wide area network (WAN), the application could quickly use all the available bandwidth.

Impact to Operations   Depending on the type of application being installed, the operations of the operating system, or the information system the operating system serves, can be negatively impacted. Therefore, the impact to operations should always be considered before installing an application. For example, if you were to install an Office package on a point-of-sale (POS) system, you could negatively affect the ability of the system to process sales.

Impact to Business   Some applications can have an impact on the business or organization itself. Therefore, the impact on day-to-day business should be evaluated. Examples of applications that could affect business are human resource (HR), customer relationship management (CRM), and sales systems, just to name a few. If these applications were to be changed, they could impact the organization.

Introduction to Windows 10

Microsoft released Windows 10 on July 29, 2015, and offered a free upgrade from Windows 7, Windows 8, and Windows 8.1. The Windows 10 upgrade was initiated by the Get Windows 10 (GWX) upgrade tool, which was installed via a Windows Update. This tool was automatically installed on Windows operating systems that were eligible for the upgrade and just about forced users to upgrade. The free upgrade was to be limited to the first year of the Windows 10 release and expired on July 29, 2016. It has been reported that Microsoft still allows the upgrade and activation of Windows 10/11 for free, but your luck may vary. For these reasons, Windows 10 was rapidly adopted and continues to be adopted as other Windows operating system versions end mainstream support.

Windows Editions

Windows 10 has had a total of 15 editions released, with five of the editions being discontinued (Windows 10 Mobile, Windows 10 Mobile Enterprise, IoT Mobile, Windows 10 S, and Windows 10X). Three of the editions are device-specific editions for IoT (Internet of Things), Holographic, and Windows 10 Team, which is loaded on the Surface Hub (interactive whiteboard). Only two of the 15 editions were made available in the retail channel: Windows 10 Home and Windows 10 Pro. Microsoft has made it easy for the retail consumer to pick the right edition of Windows 10, narrowing down retail choices to the two editions. Technically, there is a third retail edition called Windows 10 Pro for Workstations, which is preinstalled on high-end hardware for *high-performance computing (HPC)* requirements and allows up to 4 CPUs and 6 TB of RAM.

The editions available for Microsoft volume licensing options are Windows 10 Enterprise, Windows 10 Enterprise LTSC (Long-Term Servicing Channel), Windows 10 Education, and Windows 10 Pro Education. Windows 10 volume license editions include features such as AppLocker, BranchCache, and DirectAccess, just to name a few. Windows 10 Enterprise LTSC is an edition that is released every 2–3 years and is supported for 10 years after its initial release. Windows 10 LTSC receives normal Windows updates for security but does not receive feature upgrades. The *Microsoft Store* and bundled apps are also omitted from the Windows 10 Enterprise LTSC edition. Both Windows 10 Enterprise and Windows 10 Education editions have the same features over and above Windows 10 Pro and Windows 10 Home editions. Windows 10 Education editions are made available only to academic institutions and K–12 schools.

Although there are 15 different editions of Windows, the 220-1102 exam focuses on the following four editions:

Windows 10 Home   This edition is sold as a retail product, and it's preinstalled by the hardware vendor. When the operating system is preinstalled, it is referred to as an original equipment manufacturer (OEM) operating system. Windows 10 Home also lacks the key feature of joining a domain that can only be found in Windows 10 Pro or Enterprise.

Windows 10 Pro (Professional)   This is the premier retail edition of the Windows 10 operating system. It is the most common OEM operating system because it allows users to join corporate domains and becomes value-added for the hardware vendor.

Windows 10 Pro for Workstations   This edition is used primarily for high-end computer workstations that require more than two CPUs and that need to address more than 2 TB of memory. Windows 10 Pro for Workstations supports up to four CPUs and 6 TB of memory. In addition, it supports Remote Direct Memory Access and Non-Volatile Dual Inline Memory Modules (NVDIMM).

Windows 10 Enterprise   This edition supports all features of Windows 10 Pro and can be found in mid- to large-sized organizations. It also supports features generally found in mid- to large-sized organizations. Windows 10 Enterprise can only be purchased with a volume license subscription from Microsoft.

More information on Windows 10 editions can be found here:

`https://www.microsoft.com/en-us/windowsforbusiness/compare`

More information on Windows 11 editions can be found here:

`https://www.microsoft.com/en-us/windows/business/compare-windows-11`

There are 32-bit and 64-bit versions available for each of the editions listed except Windows 10 Pro for Workstations, since it is specifically used for high-performance computing. Microsoft released Windows 10 as a successor to Windows 8.1, with the key goal of bridging the gap for cloud-based services while polishing the Windows 8.1 interface. With the introduction of Windows 11, Microsoft only offers Windows 11 in a 64-bit version.

Windows 11

Windows 11 was officially released during the launch of the 220-1102 exam. Objective 1.1 specifically requires you to identify features of the Windows 10 editions. Fortunately, Windows 11 has similar editions to Windows 10 and the features are comparable. This also means that the upgrade paths are similar. However, before upgrading you must make sure that you have the minimum requirements for Windows 11.

Upgrade Paths

If you want to do an upgrade of Windows 10/11 instead of a clean installation, review the recommended upgrade options in Table 13.2. This is a major change from prior upgrade paths, where there were specific restrictions. If you upgrade from Windows 7 Starter to Windows 10/11 Pro, you'll need to provide the new activation key for the higher edition. Although you can switch editions during an upgrade, it is recommended that you use like-to-like editions of Windows. A like-to-like edition is an edition with similar functionality, such as Windows 7 Home Premium to Windows 10/11 Home, or Windows 7 Professional to Windows 10/11 Professional.

TABLE 13.2 Windows 10 recommended upgrade options

Existing operating system	Windows 10/11 Home	Windows 10/11 Pro	Windows 10/11 Education
Windows 7 Starter	Yes	No	No
Windows 7 Home Basic	Yes	No	No
Windows 7 Home Premium	Yes	No	No
Windows 8/8.1 Home Basic	Yes	No	No
Windows 7 Professional	No	Yes	No
Windows 7 Ultimate	No	Yes	No
Windows 8/8.1 Education	No	Yes	Yes
Windows 8/8.1 Pro	No	Yes	No

There are some prerequisites when performing an upgrade to Windows 10/11 and you want to retain settings and applications. The first prerequisite is that you must have at least Windows 7 with Service Pack 1 installed. So, if you have Vista installed, you would need to first perform an in-place upgrade to Windows 7 SP1. Then you could perform an in-place upgrade to Windows 10/11. An in-place upgrade is an upgrade in which you upgrade the current operating system to the desired version.

More information about edition upgrades for Windows 10 can be found here:

```
https://docs.microsoft.com/en-us/windows/deployment/
upgrade/windows-10-upgrade-paths
```

It is also recommended that you upgrade Windows 8 to Windows 8.1 before upgrading to Windows 10/11, but that is not a strict requirement. It is always recommended to have the highest level of service pack or edition prior to performing an upgrade. It minimizes problems later, during the upgrade process.

Another major restriction is that you cannot switch architecture during an in-place upgrade. If you have a 32-bit installation of Windows, then you will need to upgrade to a 32-bit version of Windows 10. You can switch architectures only when performing a clean installation, in which the old operating system is overwritten. This means that you must back up and restore settings, files, and applications. However, the advantages of upgrading to a 64-bit version may outweigh the benefits of bothersome process of reinstalling the applications.

Windows 11 is only available as a 64-bit installation. If you have a preexisting 32-bit version of Windows and want to upgrade to Windows 11, you must reinstall the operating system.

It is always recommended to have a backup of your installation before you begin upgrading. It is equally important to check the application compatibility before upgrading. You should always check with the vendor of the application prior to upgrading to make sure they support Windows 10/11. An upgrade of the application may be required, or a completely new version of the application may be needed.

In addition to checking application compatibility prior to upgrading, you should check the hardware compatibility. Most of the time, a simple upgraded driver is required; however, sometimes you will find that the hardware is not compatible and that new hardware is required. In rare instances, the PC hardware is just not compatible and a new PC is required. However, this is usually the case with laptops, since components are not easily upgradable or upgrades are impossible. So do your homework prior to upgrading and know what to expect after the upgrade process is complete.

Windows Features

Every Windows operating system edition has a set of features that are bundled into the edition being purchased. The difference between the four main editions of the operating system—Home, Pro, Pro for Workstations, and Enterprise—is how the edition is purchased and its accompanying features. Windows 10/11 Home and Windows 10/11 Pro are both available through retail channels and can be purchased off the shelf. Windows 10/11 Pro for Workstations is typically preinstalled on high-performance workstations. Windows 10/11 Enterprise edition is unavailable without a volume license agreement from Microsoft. Table 13.3 compares the features of the four main editions of Windows 10/11.

TABLE 13.3   Windows 10/11 features and editions

Edition	Maximum RAM supported	Maximum physical CPUs supported (multiple cores)	Notes
Home	128 GB	2	Lacks support for Remote Desktop (client only), BitLocker, Windows To Go, Hyper-V, joining to a domain, and participating in Group Policy. This edition is strictly for consumer use.
Pro	2 TB	2	Can join a Windows server domain; includes Remote Desktop Server, BitLocker, Windows To Go, Hyper-V, and participating in Group Policy.
Pro for Workstations	6 TB	4	Includes all features of the Pro edition, with support for 6 TB of RAM and up to 4 physical CPUs.
Enterprise	6 TB	2	Includes BitLocker, support for domain joining and Group Policy, DirectAccess, AppLocker, and BranchCache. This edition is available only through a volume license subscription.

The following is a list of features introduced and associated with the Windows 10/11 operating system that you should know for the exam, along with a brief description of each:

Cortana   The Cortana digital personal assistant allows you to control and search Windows 10 with natural speech. You can now speak to the computer—for example, "Hey Cortana, show me the files I worked on last night." This allows a more natural approach to searching not only the local computer but also the Internet. Cortana can also be used to set reminders and create emails, all via speech. It should be noted that although

Cortana's true potential is unlocked with speech, searching with the keyboard is also supported. Figure 13.2 shows an example of the Cortana interface.

FIGURE 13.2   The Cortana interface

Microsoft Edge   The Microsoft Edge web browser has been developed as a lightweight web browser, as shown in Figure 13.3. Microsoft Edge is the successor to Internet Explorer and has already replaced Internet Explorer as the default web browser on Windows 10/11. The original version of Edge was released on July 29, 2015, for Windows 10. The current version of Edge was released on January 15, 2020, and it was redesigned upon the Chromium source code. Microsoft Edge does not support ActiveX and browser helper objects. Therefore, Internet Explorer 11 will remain an alternate web browser until its end-of-life (EOL) date in mid-2022. No new version of Internet Explorer should be expected in the future, as it is the final version for Internet Explorer.

FIGURE 13.3   The Microsoft Edge web browser

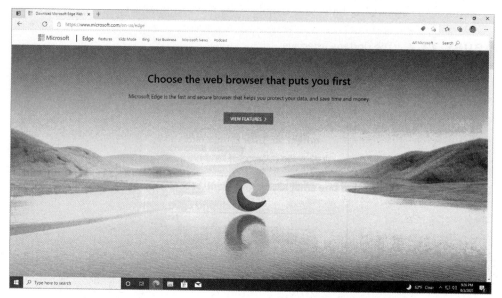

Universal Windows Platform   The Universal Windows Platform (UWP) is a development platform that allows for the development of applications across the various Windows 10 platforms. A developer can now write a UWP application, and the same application can be compiled and run over several different platforms, such as tablets, desktops, Xbox One, and Surface Hub, just to mention a few.

Action Center   The Action Center in Windows 10/11 allows for the quick control of features such as VPN, Settings, and Tablet mode. The Action Center acts as an aggregation for social media, email, and operating system notifications. It is accessed by clicking the notification icon on the rightmost portion of the taskbar. The Action Center will then pop out as a sidebar, allowing for an at-a-glance look at all important messages, as shown in Figure 13.4.

BitLocker   BitLocker allows you to use drive encryption to protect files, including those needed for startup and login, as shown in Figure 13.5. This feature is available in all editions of Windows 10/11, except for Windows 10/11 Home. For removable drives, BitLocker To Go provides the same encryption technology to help prevent unauthorized access to the files stored on them. BitLocker is covered in Chapter 18.

Task View   Task View allows you to have multiple desktops that appear to be virtual sessions inside of the operating system. You are no longer limited to one desktop containing all of your applications. You can now set up several desktops and switch between them. You can even drag an application from one desktop to another. By pressing the Windows key + Tab, you can access the Task View window, as shown in Figure 13.6.

Task View is enabled on the taskbar by default on the Windows 10/11 operating system. If it is not displayed to the right of the Cortana dialog box, you can right-click the taskbar and select the Show Task View button.

FIGURE 13.4   The Windows Action Center

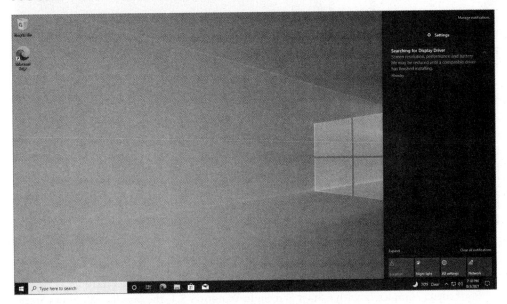

FIGURE 13.5   The BitLocker Control Panel applet

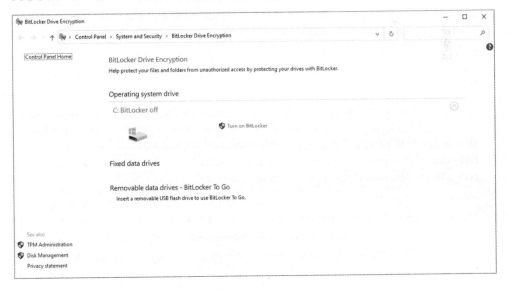

FIGURE 13.6   The Task View window

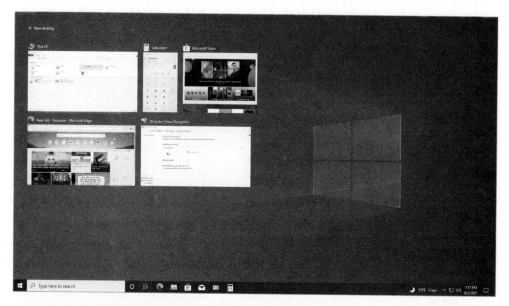

Start Menu   The *Start menu* is back in Windows 10 and has similar functionality to the original Windows 7 Start menu. In Windows 8, Microsoft decided to replace the Start menu completely with a Start Screen. In Windows 8.1, the familiar Windows Start menu flag appeared, but when clicked the Start Screen would appear. In Windows 10, the Start menu also introduced Live Tiles, which could be placed into the Start menu to show the weather, sports, or any other apps installed. In addition to Live Tiles, common application shortcuts can be pinned in the Start menu, as shown in Figure 13.7.

Xbox One   Content from Microsoft Xbox One can be streamed to a Windows 10/11 device or computer. This allows for the access of content as well as recording of games from the Windows 10/11 operating system.

Spotlight   The Spotlight feature displays pictures on the lock screen. You can choose various types of pictures to display, and they are downloaded automatically from Bing and displayed when the lock screen is activated, as shown in Figure 13.8.

You can lock the Windows Desktop several different ways, as follows:

- Press the Windows key + L.
- Press Ctrl+Alt+Delete, then choose Lock.
- Click the Start menu, then select your user icon, and click Lock.

FIGURE 13.7   The Windows 10 Start menu

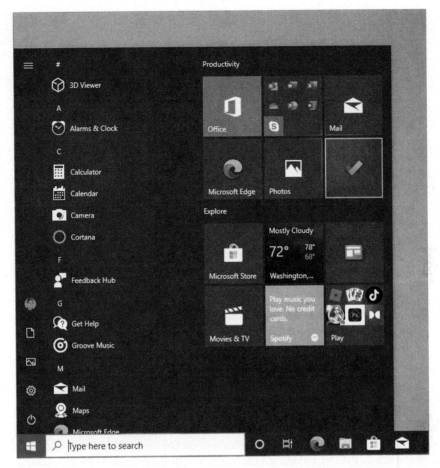

Microsoft Defender Antivirus   Windows 10/11 includes an antivirus and antimalware utility that is built into the operating system. You can always provide your own antivirus or antimalware, but the Microsoft Defender Antivirus allows for protection from the time that Windows is installed. In addition to antivirus/antimalware, Microsoft Defender Antivirus can protect against ransomware, as shown in Figure 13.9.

Settings App   The Settings app is similar to Control Panel in functionality, because you can control many aspects of the operating system. However, any new feature being added to the Windows 10/11 operating system is added to the Settings app in lieu of the creation of new Control Panel applets. At this point, it looks like Control Panel will become a legacy component in future versions of Windows. You can access the Settings app by clicking the Start Menu and selecting the gear on the left-hand side. You can also right-click the Start menu and select Settings from the context menu. The Settings app is shown in Figure 13.10.

FIGURE 13.8   The Windows 10 Lock Screen and Spotlight

Pinning to the Taskbar   The context menu for each application allows you to choose whether you want to pin (add) it to the Start menu, pin it to the taskbar, or remove it if it is already there. You can also uninstall an application with the context menu, as shown in Figure 13.11.

Snap Assist   Windows Snap was first introduced with Windows 7. Snap allows for side-by-side automatic windowing of windows on the screen. All you have to do is move a window over to a side, and the window will resize to half of the screen. Windows 10 introduced Snap Assist, which allows for up to four quadrants of the screen to automatically be adjusted using snapping. When a window is snapped over to a side, a preview in the blank area will show a preview of windows so that you can choose the next window to snap (see Figure 13.12).

FIGURE 13.9   Microsoft Defender Virus & Threat Protection settings

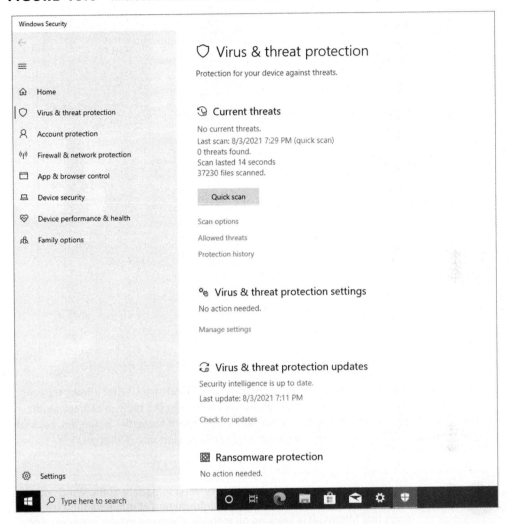

FIGURE 13.10 The Settings app in Windows 10

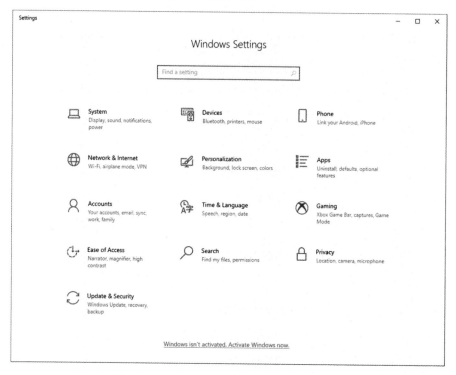

Windows Hello   Windows Hello is a new feature of Windows 10 that allows the user to sign into Windows with biometrics. Windows Hello uses the built-in camera on the laptop or PC so that the device can be unlocked with facial recognition. On devices with a fingerprint reader, you can also use your fingerprint to sign into Windows.

Windows features are added with every version/update of the Windows 10/11 operating system. You can view information about upcoming features that Microsoft is working on with the Windows Insider program. For more information, visit https://insider.windows.com/en-us.

FIGURE 13.11   An application context menu

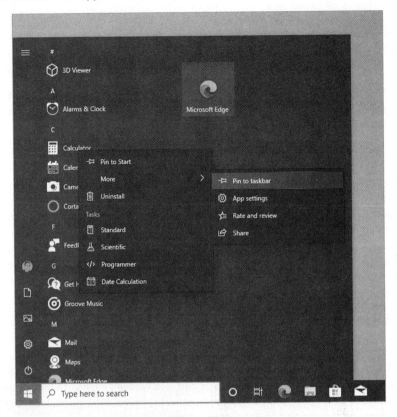

FIGURE 13.12   Windows Snap Assist

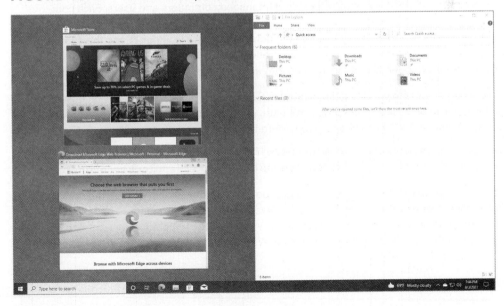

Special Features of Windows

This chapter focuses on the two retail offerings of Windows 10/11 Home and Windows 10/11 Pro. In addition, we will compare features that only exist in Windows 10/11 Enterprise. Windows 10/11 Pro for Workstations supports everything that Windows 10/11 Pro supports.

The 220-1102 exam requires you to know the difference between Windows editions and their features. We've provided additional information on these features so that you can be more familiar with what each of the various features entails:

Domain-joined computers allow for centralized authentication, administration, and auditing of user and computer accounts through Active Directory domain controllers. A single user account can be created that enables the user to log into any computer in the domain of joined computers. This model is often found in corporate networks, because the user can be created when a person is hired. Access levels can then be managed throughout the person's employment with the organization. When the person leaves the organization, their access will also be terminated. Windows 10/11 Home edition does not support domain-joined computer accounts. It is also important to note that Windows 10/11 Home edition does not support Azure AD–joined computers, since Azure AD is the cloud version of the traditional domain.

Group Policy is a feature that is typically used in conjunction with domain-joined computers. The feature allows for policies to be applied to users and computers in the domain. The settings in these policies can be can be a number of different controls for the user or computer. These settings will also be reapplied every 45 minutes. Although Group Policy is typically used with domain-joined computers, it can also be used locally on the computer to control behavior using the `gpedit.msc` command. Windows 10/11 Home lacks the functionality to apply or manage Group Policy through the GPO editor.

Workgroups are a decentralized collection of managed computers and users. Each computer will have local accounts created that can be used for local authentication on the computer. This type of access is useful when the number of users is under 11 and the overhead of maintaining Active Directory domain controllers is not necessary. This is the default mode that all Windows operating systems run under.

AppLocker allows for policies to be created in Group Policy to control the access to applications. This can be based on the program's path, publisher, or hash. This feature is only available in Windows 10/11 Enterprise edition. More information can be found here:

`https://docs.microsoft.com/en-us/windows/security/threat-protection/`
`windows-defender-application-control/applocker/applocker-overview`

Remote Desktop is a client and server application that allows a client to view the desktop of a remote server or workstation. The Remote Desktop feature uses the Remote Desktop Protocol (RDP) to facilitate the remote session. All Windows 10/11 operating systems can act as clients to a Remote Desktop server. However, Windows 10/11 Home cannot act as a server for a Remote Desktop client.

BitLocker is a volume-level encryption method that uses a cryptographic key pair that is stored in the Trusted Platform Module (TPM). The TPM is an encryption chip found on a computer's motherboard. If the integrity of the boot process or the encrypted volume is tampered with in any way, the encrypted volume will not be decrypted during the boot process and a message is displayed. This feature is not available on Windows 10/11 Home.

BranchCache is a Microsoft client-server technology that allows for caching of commonly accessed files at branch office locations. This allows for faster access of documents when the initial request is made. When the user saves the file, it is written to the original file server at the main location and locally cached for any consecutive requests. This feature is only available in Windows 10/11 Enterprise edition. More information can be found here:

```
https://docs.microsoft.com/en-us/windows-server/networking/branch-
cache/branchcache
```

DirectAccess provides an automatic connection for a virtual private network (VPN) between the client and a main office. It is location-aware as well. This provides users who travel with access to corporate resources, just as if they were in the office. This feature is only available in Windows 10/11 Enterprise edition. More information can be found here:

```
https://docs.microsoft.com/en-us/windows-server/remote/remote-
access/directaccess/directaccess
```

The Windows Interface

If you've worked with older versions of Windows (such as Windows 7), you'll notice that it looks similar to the current Windows interface. While there are some differences, most of the basic tasks are accomplished in almost identical fashion on everything from a Windows 95 workstation computer on up. Also, although the tools that are used often vary between the different OSs, the way that you use those tools remains remarkably consistent across platforms.

We will begin with an overview of the common elements of the Windows GUI. We will then look at some tasks that are similar across Windows operating systems. You are encouraged to follow along by exploring each of the elements as they are discussed.

As you follow along, you may notice that there are numerous icons and options that we do not mention. Quite honestly, there are too many to cover, and they're beyond the scope of this chapter. For now, simply ignore them or browse through them on your own, and then return to the text.

The Desktop

The *Desktop* is the virtual desk on which all your other programs and utilities run. By default, it contains the Start menu, the taskbar, and a number of icons. The Desktop can contain additional elements, such as shortcuts or links to web page content. Because the Desktop is the foundation on which everything else sits, the way that the Desktop is configured can have a major effect on how the GUI looks and how convenient it is for users. When you click the lower-left corner of the Desktop, the Start menu appears. (Right-clicking the Windows icon in Windows 8.1 and above displays a set of operating system functions.)

You can change the background patterns, screen saver, color scheme, and size of elements on the Desktop by right-clicking any area of the Desktop that doesn't contain an icon. The menu that appears, similar to the one shown for Windows 10 in Figure 13.13, allows you to do several things, such as create new Desktop items, change how your icons are arranged, or select a special command called Properties or Personalize.

FIGURE 13.13   The Windows 10 Desktop context menu

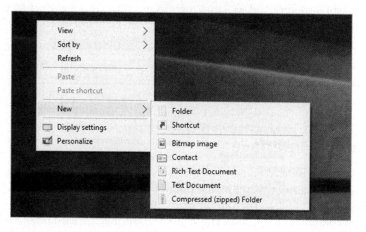

The Three Clicks in Windows

When it comes to interacting with a mouse in Windows, there are three possibilities:

- **Primary mouse click**—A single click (typically the left mouse button) is used to select an object or place a cursor.

- **Double-click**—Two primary mouse clicks in quick succession are used to open a program through an icon or for other application-specific functions.

- **Secondary mouse click (or alternate click)**—Most mice have two buttons. Clicking once on the secondary button (usually the one on the right, although that can be modified) is interpreted differently from a left mouse click. Generally, this click displays a context-sensitive menu in Windows from which you can perform tasks or view object properties.

When you right-click the Desktop in Windows 10 and choose Personalize, you will see the Display Settings screen, as shown in Figure 13.14.

FIGURE 13.14   The Windows 10 Display Settings screen

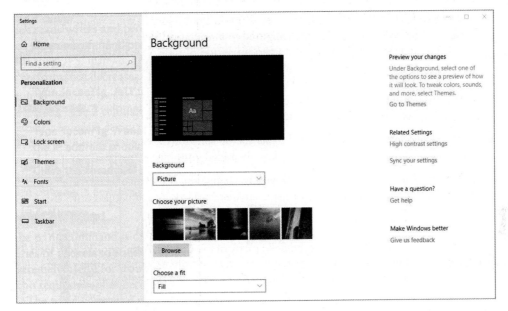

With the rapid adoption of Windows 10, this book will cover the most current version of Windows 10 (21H2), since the CompTIA objectives focus on Windows 10. However, every prior operating system Microsoft has produced has similar settings for personalization. We will cover the main ones in the Display Settings window for Windows 10, but Windows 11 is identical in functionality.

Background   The Background section is used to select a picture to display on the Desktop. In addition to setting a picture, you can select a group of pictures to display as a slideshow or display a static color.

Colors   The Color section allows you to select a color scheme for the Start menu or to change the color or size of other Desktop elements.

Lock Screen   Windows 8 and above allows you to easily change the lock screen wallpaper as well as the applications that are displayed on the lock screen.

Themes   The Themes section allows you to select a theme to customize the look and feel of your machine quickly. Selecting a theme sets several items at once, such as a picture to display on the Desktop, the look of icons, the sounds to use, and so on. All these options can also be selected individually through the other personalization tabs.

Fonts   The Fonts section allows you to review any font installed on the operating system. These fonts are used by applications that allow changing of fonts, such as a Microsoft Office document. In addition, you can uninstall fonts and install new fonts from the Microsoft Store.

Screen Saver   Although the screen saver is not in the Personalization menu, it's worth covering. The screen saver can be configured to automatically display on your screen if your computer has been inactive for a certain period of time. Originally used to prevent burn-in of monitors, screen savers are now generally used for entertainment or to password-protect users' desktops. You can access the screen saver options in Windows 10/11 by clicking Lock Screen under Personalization and then clicking Screen Saver Settings. The Screen Saver Control Panel tab also gives you access to other power settings.

Start   The Start section allows you to set the options for the Start menu, such as to show the most used apps or to show recently added apps, just to name a few.

Taskbar   The taskbar section allows you to change the behavior of the taskbar, such as automatically hiding the taskbar or using smaller buttons, just to name a few.

> Windows 10/11 has replaced many of the Control Panel applets with the Settings app. If you cannot find a setting from a prior operating system in the Control Panel Desktop app, you can find the setting in the new Settings app.

In Exercise 13.1, you will see how to change a screen saver.

EXERCISE 13.1

Changing a Screen Saver in Windows

1. Right-click the Desktop.

2. Choose Personalize from the context menu.

3. Click the Lock screen on the left side.

4. Scroll to the bottom and select Screen Saver Settings.

5. Choose a screen saver from the drop-down menu.

6. Click Preview to view how the screen saver will look.

7. Click OK to exit the Settings window.

The Taskbar

The *taskbar* (see Figure 13.15) is another standard component of the Windows interface. Note that although the colors and feel of the Desktop components, including the taskbar, have changed throughout the operating system versions, the components themselves are the same. In versions prior to Windows 10, the taskbar contains two major items: the Start menu and the notification area, previously called the *system tray* (systray). The Start menu is on the left side of the taskbar and is easily identifiable: it is a button that has the Windows logo or the word *Start* on it, or in the case of Windows 7, it is the large Windows icon. The system tray is located on the right side of the taskbar and contains only a clock by default, but other Windows utilities (for example, screen savers or antivirus utilities) may put their icons there to indicate that they are running and to provide the user with a quick way to access their features.

FIGURE 13.15   The Windows 10 taskbar

Windows also uses the middle area of the taskbar. When you open a new window or program, it gets a button on the taskbar with an icon that represents the window or program as well as the name of the window or program. To bring that window or program to the front (or to maximize it if it was minimized), click its button on the taskbar. As the middle area of the taskbar fills with buttons, the buttons become smaller so that they can all be displayed.

Windows 8/8.1 and Windows 10/11 allow you to pin commonly used programs to the taskbar. The icon will appear on the taskbar, and when the program is running, a line will appear under the icon. You can pin any running task by right-clicking the icon in the taskbar and selecting Pin To Taskbar. You can just as easily remove pinned icons by right-clicking them and selecting Unpin From Taskbar.

You can increase the size of the taskbar as well as move its position on the Desktop. Either of these tasks requires you to first unlock the taskbar, by right-clicking the taskbar and deselecting Lock The Taskbar. (By default, it is enabled.) You can then move the mouse pointer to the top of it and pause until the pointer turns into a double-headed arrow. Once this happens, click the mouse and move it up to make the taskbar bigger, or move it down to make it smaller. You can also click the taskbar and drag it to the top or side of the screen.

In older versions of Windows, the taskbar is not locked by default. Once you've configured the taskbar position and layout to your liking, you can configure it so that it can't be changed accidentally. To do so, right-click the taskbar and select Lock The Taskbar. To unlock the taskbar and make changes, right-click the taskbar and select Lock The Taskbar again.

You can make the taskbar automatically hide itself when it isn't being used (thus freeing that space for use by the Desktop or other windows). In Exercise 13.2, we will show you how to do this.

EXERCISE 13.2

Auto-Hiding the Taskbar

1. Right-click the taskbar.

2. Choose Taskbar Settings to bring up the Settings app for the Personalization options.

3. Click the switch to turn on the Automatically Hide The Taskbar In Desktop Mode option. The taskbar will automatically hide when the mode is turned on.

4. Move the mouse pointer to the bottom of the screen. The taskbar will pop up and be available for normal use.

The Start Menu

Back when Microsoft officially introduced Windows 95, it bought the rights to use the Rolling Stones' song "Start Me Up" in its advertisements and at the introduction party. Microsoft chose that particular song because the Start menu was the central point of focus in the new Windows interface, as it was in all subsequent versions.

To display the Start menu, you can press the Windows key on your keyboard at any time. You can also click the Windows logo button in the taskbar in Windows 10 and 8.1. You'll see a Start menu similar to the one shown in Figure 13.16 for Windows 10. The Windows 11 Start menu is functionally similar. The only difference is that the layout is centered in the screen.

 When Windows 8 was released, the Start menu was replaced with a Start screen. There was considerable backlash from the user community over the removal of the Start menu in Windows 8. A number of third-party vendors developed alternatives and marketed them to fill this demand.

From the Start menu, you can select any of the various options the menu presents. An arrow pointing down on a folder indicates that more items exist in the folder. To select a submenu for an icon, move the mouse pointer over the icon and right-click. The submenu will appear, allowing you to pin, rate, and uninstall an application, just to name a few options.

 To check which OS you are using, press the Windows key and R key at the same time, type **winver.exe**, and then press Enter. The About Windows Application dialog box will display the version and build number of the operating system.

The following sections describe the principal features of the Windows 10/11 Start menu.

FIGURE 13.16 Sample Windows 10 Start menu

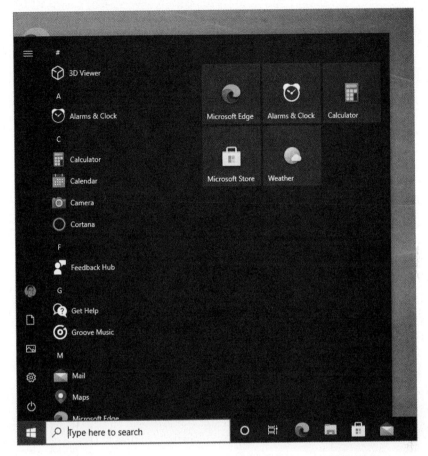

Cortana

Windows 10 introduced Cortana, a personal desktop assistant for the Windows operating system. In Windows 10, Cortana is enabled by default and allows you to search without clicking the Start menu. The search box is located to the right of the Start menu. You just need to start typing. Cortana will search apps installed, documents, and the web. Cortana will even come up with suggestions, as shown in Figure 13.17. You don't even need to type; you can click the microphone in the search box and speak your search. With Windows 11, Cortana has become an app and is no longer integrated with the Start menu.

FIGURE 13.17 The Cortana personal desktop assistant

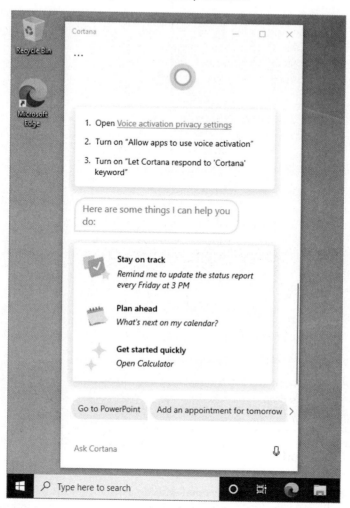

Help and Support

Windows has always included a very good Help system. With the addition of Cortana, Microsoft had originally elected to leave help and support to web searches. However, Microsoft has released the Get Help app in the Microsoft Store, and in later operating systems, it come preinstalled. Hardware vendors may also add a help and support center for the hardware platform.

A quick way to access Help is to press the F1 key. In operating systems before Windows 10, a help and support application would launch. In Windows 10/11, the F1 key launches the web browser.

The Run Command

It is possible to run commands and utilities from the Cortana search box or from the Run dialog box. To access the Run dialog box in Windows 10, simply press the Windows key and the R key at the same time. To execute a particular program, type its name in the Open field. If you don't know the exact path, you can browse to find the file by clicking the Browse button. Once you have typed in the executable name, click OK to run the program.

To open a command prompt, type **command** in the Run box, and then click OK. You might need to run this as Administrator if you want to change system settings. From the Start menu, type **cmd** or **command** in the search field and then press Ctrl+Shift+Enter to run as Administrator.

Applications can easily be started from the Run window. You often will find it faster to open programs this way than to search for their icons in the Start menu maze. In Exercise 13.2, you will see how to start a program from the Run window.

EXERCISE 13.3

Starting a Program from the Run Window

1. Press the Windows key and the R key at the same time.

2. In the Open field, type **notepad**.

3. Click OK. Notepad will open in a new window.

If the program that you want to start has been run from the Run window before, you can find it on the Open field's drop-down list. Click the down arrow to display the list, and then select the program that you want by clicking its name and then OK.

Shut Down Command

Windows operating systems are very complex. At any one time, many files are open in memory. If you accidentally hit the power switch and turn off the computer while these files are open, there is a good chance that they will be corrupted. For this reason, Microsoft has added the Shut Down command under the Start menu. The command appears as an icon of an on/off button without a label. When you select this option, Windows presents you with several choices. The submenu will display Sleep, Shutdown, and Restart.

Icons

Icons are shortcuts that allow a user to open a program or a utility without knowing where that program is located or how it needs to be configured. Icons consist of the following major elements:

- Icon label
- Icon graphic
- Program location or path

The label and graphic of the icon typically tell the user the name of the program and give a visual hint about what that program does. The icon for the Notepad program, for instance, is labeled Notepad, and its graphic is a notepad. By right-clicking an icon once, you make it the active icon and a drop-down menu appears. One of the selections is Properties. Clicking Properties brings up the icon's attributes (see Figure 13.18), and it is the only way to see exactly which program an icon is configured to start and where the program's executable is located. You can also specify whether to run the program in a normal window or maximized or minimized.

FIGURE 13.18 The Properties window of an application

Additional functionality has been added to an icon's properties to allow for backward compatibility with older versions of Windows (known as *compatibility mode*). To configure this, click the Compatibility tab and specify the version of Windows for which you want to configure compatibility. Note that you cannot configure compatibility if the program is part of the version of Windows that you are using. Figure 13.19 shows the settings available for an older program.

FIGURE 13.19   The Compatibility settings possible with an older program

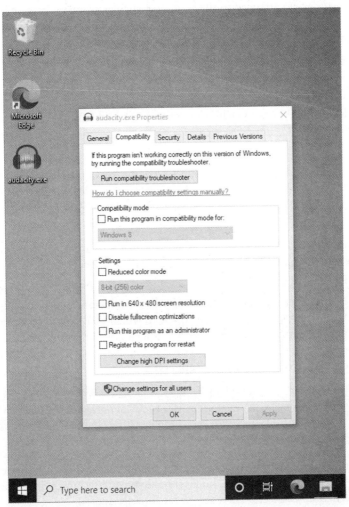

This feature is helpful if you own programs that used to work in older versions of Windows but no longer run under the current Windows version. In addition, you can specify different display settings that might be required by older programs.

Standard Desktop Icons

In addition to the options in your Start menu, a number of icons are placed directly on the Desktop in Windows. The Recycle Bin icon is one of these icons. In the latest version of Windows 10 (21H2), the Microsoft Edge icon can also be found on the Desktop. In older versions of Windows, the Computer icon could also be found on the desktop.

The Computer Icon   If you double-click the Computer icon, it displays a list of all the disk drives installed in your computer. In addition to displaying disk drives, it displays a list of other devices attached to the computer, such as scanners, cameras, and mobile devices. The disk devices are sorted into categories such as Hard Disk Drives, Devices With Removable Storage, Scanners And Cameras, and so on.

You can delve deeper into each disk drive or device by double-clicking its icon. The contents are displayed in the same window.

In addition to allowing you access to your computer's files, the This PC icon on the Desktop lets you view your machine's configuration and hardware, also called the System Properties.

In Windows 8.1 and Windows 10/11, the My Computer icon was renamed This PC. By default, it is not displayed on the Desktop. In Windows 10/11, you can add it by going to Settings ➤ Personalization ➤ Themes and clicking Desktop Icon Settings.

The Network Icon   Another icon in Windows relates to accessing other computers to which the local computer is connected, and it's called Network (known as My Network Places in previous versions).

Opening Network lets you browse for and access computers and shared resources (printers, scanners, media devices, and so on) to which your computer can connect. This might be another computer in a workgroup. It is important to note that network browsing will not operate if the PC is joined to a domain. Network browsing in Windows 7 and above is restricted to the Workgroup mode.

For the exam, know that the two types of networks from which you can choose are Workgroup and Domain. Other chapters in this book focus more on networking specifics and how to set up each type.

Through the properties of Network, you can configure your network connections, including LAN and dial-up connections (should you still live in an area where a now antiquated dial-up connection is required for Internet access).

You can add common Desktop icons by navigating to Settings ➤ Personalization ➤ Themes and clicking Desktop Icon Settings. A dialog box will appear that allows you to add and change the common Desktop icons, as shown in Figure 13.20.

FIGURE 13.20   Common icons can easily be added to the Desktop.

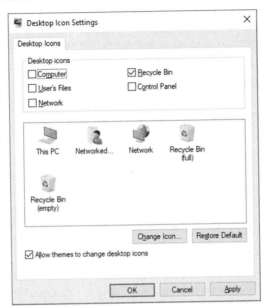

The Recycle Bin   All files, directories, and programs in Windows are represented by icons. These icons are generally referred to as *objects*. When you want to remove an object from Windows, you do so by deleting it. Deleting doesn't just remove the object, though; it also removes the ability of the system to access the information or application that the object represents. Therefore, Windows includes a special folder where all deleted files are placed: the Recycle Bin. The Recycle Bin holds the files until it is emptied or until you fill it. It gives users the opportunity to recover files that they delete accidentally. By right-clicking the Recycle Bin icon, you can see how much disk space is allocated. Some larger files that cannot fit in the Recycle Bin will be erased after a warning.

You can retrieve a file that you have deleted by opening the Recycle Bin and then dragging the file from the Recycle Bin to where you want to restore it. Alternatively, you can right-click a file and select Restore. The file will be restored to the location from which it was deleted.

In versions of Windows that this exam tests you on, the "deleted" files are stored in a folder called \$Recycle.Bin. This was not the case in all previous versions of Windows.

To erase files permanently, you need to empty the Recycle Bin, thereby deleting any items in it and freeing the hard drive space they took up. If you want to delete only specific files, you can select them in the Recycle Bin, right-click, and choose Delete. You can also permanently erase files (bypassing the Recycle Bin) by holding down the Shift key as you delete them (by dragging the file and dropping it in the Recycle Bin, pressing the Del key, or clicking Delete on the file's context menu). If the Recycle Bin has files in it, its icon looks like a full trash can; when there are no files in it, it looks like an empty trash can.

What's in a Window?

We have now looked at the nature of the Desktop, the taskbar, the Start menu, and icons. Each of these items was created for the primary purpose of making access to user applications easier. These applications are, in turn, used and managed through the use of *windows*—the rectangular application environments for which the Windows family of operating systems is named. We will now examine how windows work and what they are made of.

A *program window* is a rectangular area created on the screen when an application is opened within Windows. This window can have a number of different forms, but most windows include at least a few basic elements.

Elements of a Window

Several basic elements are present in a standard window. Figure 13.21 shows the control box, title bar, Minimize/Maximize button, Close button, and resizable border in the text editor Notepad (`notepad.exe`) that has all the basic window elements—and little else.

FIGURE 13.21   The basic elements of a window, as seen in Notepad

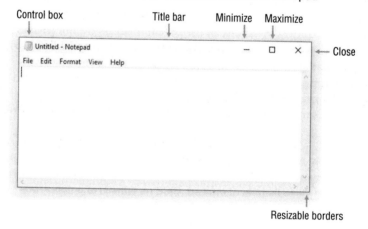

The basic window elements are as follows:

Control Box   Located in the upper-left corner of the window, the control box is used to control the state of the application. It can be used to maximize, minimize, and close the application. Clicking it once brings into view a selection menu. Double-clicking it closes the window and shuts down the application.

Minimize and Maximize/Restore Buttons   Used to change the state of the window on the Desktop. They are discussed in the section "States of a Window" later in this chapter.

Close Button   Used to easily end a program and return any resources that it was using to the system. It essentially does the same thing as double-clicking the control box but with one fewer click.

Title Bar   The area between the control box and the Minimize button. It states the name of the program and, in some cases, gives information about the particular document being accessed by that program. The color of the title bar indicates whether the window is the active window. Clicking and holding on it is an easy way to move the window on the screen.

Menu Bar   Used to present useful commands within an application in an easily accessible format. Clicking one of the menu choices displays a list of related options from which you may choose.

Active Window   The window that is currently being used. It has two attributes. First, any keystrokes that are entered are directed into the active window by default. Second, any other windows that overlap the active window are pushed behind it.

Border   A thin line that surrounds the window in its restored down state and allows it to be resized.

Not every element is found in every window, because application programmers can choose to eliminate or modify each item. Still, in most cases, they will be consistent, with the rest of the window filled in with menus, toolbars, a workspace, or other application-specific elements. For instance, Microsoft Word, the program with which this book was written, adds a Ribbon control. It also has a menu bar, a number of optional toolbars, scroll bars at the right and bottom of the window, and a status bar at the very bottom. Application windows can become quite cluttered.

Notepad is a very simple Windows program. It has only a single menu bar and the basic elements shown in Figure 13.21. It also starts a simple editor, where you can edit a file that already exists or create a new one. Figure 13.22 shows a Microsoft Word window. Both Word and Notepad are used to create and edit documents, but Word is far more configurable and powerful and therefore has many more optional components available within its window.

States of a Window

There is more to the Windows interface than the specific parts of a window. Windows also are movable, stackable, and resizable, and they can be hidden behind other windows (often unintentionally).

FIGURE 13.22 A window with many more components, as seen in Microsoft Word

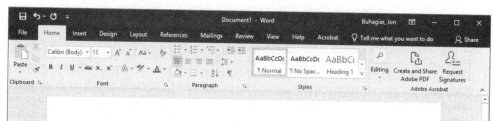

When an application window has been launched, it exists in one of three states:

Maximized   A maximized window takes up all the available space on the screen. When it is in front of other programs, it is the only thing visible—even the Desktop is hidden. It takes up the entire space of the Desktop, and the middle button in the upper-right corner displays two rectangles rather than one. The sides of the window no longer have borders. The window is flush with the edges of the screen. Maximizing a window provides the maximum workspace possible for that window's application, and the user can actively access the window. In general, maximized mode is the preferred window size for most word processing, graphics creation, and other types of user applications.

Restored   A restored window can be used interactively, and it is identical in function to a maximized window, with the simple difference that it does not necessarily take up the entire screen. Restored windows can be very small, or they can take up as much space as maximized windows. Generally, how large the restored window becomes is the user's choice. Restored windows display a Maximize button (the middle button in the upper-right corner) with a single rectangle in it; this is used to maximize the window. Restored windows have a border.

Minimized   Minimized program windows are represented by nothing but an icon and title on the taskbar, and they are not usable until they have been either maximized or restored. The difference between a minimized program and a closed program is that a minimized program is out of the way, but it is still taking up resources and is therefore ready to use if you need it. It also leaves the content of the window in the same place where it was when you minimized it.

When one program is open and you need to open another (or maybe you need to stop playing a game because your boss has entered the room), you have two choices. First, you can close the program currently in use and simply choose to reopen it later. If you do this, however, the contents of the window (your current game, for example) will be lost, and you will have to start over. Once the program has been closed, you can move on to open the second program.

The second option is to minimize the active window. Minimizing the game window, for example, removes the open window from the screen and leaves the program open but displays nothing more than an icon and title on the taskbar. Later, you can restore the window to its previous size and finish the game in progress.

Keep in mind that applications in the background are still running. Therefore, if you minimize your game, you might return to find that you've been eaten by whatever monster you were running from in the game. A program running while minimized can be a good thing, however, if you're running a useful utility, such as a long search or an Internet download.

File Management

File management is the process by which a computer stores data and retrieves it from storage. Although some of the file-management interfaces across Windows may have a different look and feel, the process of managing files is similar across the board.

Files and Folders

In order for a program to run, it must be able to read information off the hard disk and write information back to the hard disk. To be able to organize and access information—especially in larger new systems that may have thousands of files—it is necessary to have a structure and an ordering process.

Windows provides this process by allowing you to create *directories*, also known as *folders*, in which to organize files. Windows also regulates the way that files are named and the properties of files. The filename for each file created in Windows has to follow certain rules, and any program that accesses files through Windows must also comply with these rules:

- Each file has a filename of up to 255 characters.

- Certain characters, such as a question mark (?) and slash (\ or /), are reserved for other uses and cannot be used in the filename. Periods are used to separate the filename from the extension, and the backslash is used to separate the directories in a path from the filename.

- A filename extension (generally three or four characters) can be added to identify the file's type.

- Filenames are not case sensitive. (You can create files with names that use both upper- and lowercase letters, but to identify the file within the filesystem, it is not necessary to adhere to the capitalization in the filename.) Thus, you cannot have a file named working.txt and another called WORKING.TXT in the same folder. To Windows, these filenames are identical, and you can't have two files with the same filename in the same folder. We'll get into more detail on this topic a little later.

In Windows 3.x and DOS, filenames were limited to eight characters and a three-character extension, separated by a period—known as the 8.3 file-naming convention. Windows 95 introduced long filenames, which allowed the 255-character filename convention.

The Windows filesystem is arranged like a filing cabinet. In a filing cabinet, paper is placed into folders, which are internal dividers, which are in a drawer of the filing cabinet. In the Windows filesystem, individual files are placed in subdirectories that are inside directories, which are stored on different disks or different partitions.

Windows also protects against duplicate filenames; no two files on the system can have exactly the same name and path. A *path* indicates the location of the file on the disk; it is composed of the letter of the logical drive on which the file is located and, if the file is located in a folder or subfolder, the names of those directories. For instance, if a file named pagefile.sys is located in the root of the C: drive—meaning it is not within a folder—the path to the file is C:\pagefile.sys. As another example, if a file called notepad.exe is located under Windows under the root of C:, then the path to this file is C:\Windows\notepad.exe.

> The *root folder* of any drive is the place where the hierarchy of folders for that drive begins. On a C: drive, for instance, C:\ is the root folder.

Common filename extensions that you may encounter include .exe (for executable files, aka applications), .dll (for dynamic linked library files), .sys (for system files), .log (for log files), .drv (for driver files), and .txt (for text files). Note that DLL files contain additional functions and commands that applications can use and share. In addition, specific filename extensions are used for the documents created with each application. For example, the filenames for documents created in Microsoft Word have a .doc or .docx extension. You'll also encounter extensions such as .mpg (for video files), .mp3 (for music files), .png and .tif (for graphics files), .htm and .html (for web pages), and so on. Being familiar with different filename extensions is helpful in working with the Windows filesystem.

Capabilities of Explorer

Although it is technically possible to use the command-line utilities provided within the command prompt to manage your files, this generally is not the most efficient way to accomplish most tasks. The ability to use drag-and-drop techniques and other graphical tools to manage the filesystem makes the process far simpler. The *File Explorer* is a utility that allows you to accomplish a number of important file-related tasks from a single graphical interface.

Here are some of the tasks you can accomplish using Explorer:

- View files and directories
- Open programs or data files
- Create directories and files

- Copy objects to other locations
- Move objects to other locations
- Delete or rename objects
- Change file attributes

You can access many of these functions by right-clicking a file or folder and selecting the appropriate option, such as Copy or Delete, from the context menu.

 The File Explorer utility used in Windows 8/8.1 and Windows 10/11 was previously named Windows Explorer. Although the functionality remains almost identical since the introduction of Windows 95, the rebranding was just one of many changes when Windows 8 was released.

Navigating and Using Explorer

Using Explorer is simple. A few basic instructions are all you need to start working with it. First, the Explorer interface has a number of parts, each of which serves a specific purpose. The top area of Explorer is dominated by a set of menus and toolbars that give you easy access to common commands. The main section of the window is divided into two panes: the left pane displays the drives and folders available, which is called the navigation pane, and the right pane displays the contents of the currently selected drive or folder, which is called the results pane. In recent versions of Windows, the Navigation pane is turned off. The following list describes some common actions in Explorer:

Expanding a Folder   You can click a folder in the left pane to expand it (show its subfolders in the left pane) and display its contents in the right pane. Clicking the right-pointing arrow (>) to the left of a folder expands the folder without changing the display in the right pane, as shown in Figure 13.23.

Collapsing a Folder   Clicking the down arrow sign next to a folder collapses it.

Selecting a File   If you click the file in the right pane, Windows highlights the file by marking it with a darker color.

Selecting Multiple Files   The Ctrl or Shift keys allow you to select multiple files at once. Holding down Ctrl while clicking individual files selects each new file while leaving the currently selected file(s) selected as well. Holding down Shift while selecting two files selects both of them and all the files in between.

Opening a File   Double-clicking a file in the right pane opens the program if the file is an application; if it is a data file, it will open using the application for which the filename extension is configured.

Changing the View Type   Windows has several different view types: Extra Large Icons, Medium Icons, Large Icons, Small Icons, List, Details, Content, and Tiles. The choices vary a bit between the Windows versions. You can move between these views by clicking the View menu and selecting the view that you prefer. In Windows 10, the View menu is a ribbon that will drop down when clicked. The Navigation pane can be turned on from the View tab.

Finding Specific Files   You access this option by using the Search button or bar. You can search for files based on their name, file size, file type, and other attributes.

FIGURE 13.23   Windows 10 File Explorer

When you're searching, you can also use wildcards. *Wildcards* are characters that act as placeholders for a character or set of characters, allowing, for instance, a search for all files with a .txt filename extension. To perform such a search, you'd type an asterisk (*) as a stand-in for the filename: *.txt. An asterisk takes the place of any number of characters in a search. A question mark (?) takes the place of a single number or letter. For example, autoex??.bat would return the file autoexec.bat as part of its results.

Creating New Objects   To create a new file, folder, or other object, navigate to the location where you want to create the object, and then right-click in the right pane (without selecting a file or folder). In the menu that appears, select New and then choose the object that you want to create.

Deleting Objects   Select the object and press the Del key on the keyboard, or right-click the object and select Delete from the menu that appears.

 The simplicity of deleting in Windows makes it likely that you or one of the people you support will delete or misplace a file or a number of files that are still needed. In such a case, the Recycle Bin (mentioned earlier) is a lifesaver.

Besides simplifying most file-management commands as shown here, Explorer allows you to complete a number of disk-management tasks easily. For example, you can format and label removable media, which is discussed further in Chapter 15, "Windows Administration."

Preparing for the Exam

Future chapters will delve further into operating systems and the tools, utilities, and features available with each. There is also additional coverage, as applicable, in the chapters on troubleshooting. For purposes of exam study, Table 13.4 offers a complete list of the features for each of the Windows operating systems that you need to know for the exam. It also details which chapter(s) in this book has more coverage of that particular topic.

TABLE 13.4   Windows features

Feature	Purpose	More Information
BitLocker	Encrypts drives; available in each OS but not in every edition	Chapter 18
Domain access vs. workgroup	Shared security for computers and users	Chapter 15
Desktop styles/user interface	Customization of the desktop and the user interface	Chapter 14
Remote Desktop Protocol (RDP)	Allows users and administrators to connect remotely to obtain a desktop session	Chapter 20
Group Policy	A mechanism inside of Active Directory that allows for the management of user and computers	Chapters 14, 17

Summary

In this chapter, you learned about the basic operating systems, application installation, and the Windows 10/11 features. Additionally, we covered the basics of the Windows structure and window management. Because Windows is a graphical system, the key to success in learning to use it is to explore the system to find out what it can do. You will then be better prepared to decipher later what a user has done.

First, we explored the various operating systems you may encounter, along with their characteristics, such as their life cycles, categories, and minimum requirements.

Next, we discussed applications as they apply to the operating system and underlying architecture, as well as the various factors that should be evaluated before installing the application.

Finally, we introduced Windows 10/11 and its various editions. We then covered some basic Windows management concepts, including file management, as well as the folder structure. We also discussed using approved hardware and updating Windows.

With the basic knowledge gained in this chapter, you are now ready to learn how to interact with the most commonly used tools, the subject of the following chapter.

Exam Essentials

Know the RAM limitations between operating system architectures.   32-bit operating systems have a RAM limitation of 4 GB, whereas 64-bit operating systems can address over 4 GB of RAM.

Understand an operating system's life cycle.   When development is started on an operating system, it is considered alpha or beta code. Release candidates precede the release to market (RTM) of an operating system. The end of mainstream support generally means only security updates will continue to be supported during the extended support period.

Know the various operating system types and the common operating systems.   The four basic types of operating systems are server, workstation, mobile, and cloud-based. Windows, macOS, and Linux can be used as server, workstation, and mobile operating systems, whereas Google Chrome is primarily a cloud-based operating system.

Know the various editions of Windows 10 and their limitations.   The four most common Windows 10 editions are Windows 10 Home, Pro, Pro for Workstations, and Enterprise. Windows 10 Home does not allow joining of domains and has many premium features. Windows 10 Pro is the most flexible edition because it allows for domain joining. Windows 10 Pro for Workstations allows for up to 4 CPUs and 6 TB of RAM. Windows 10 Enterprise is a volume licensed edition of Windows 10 that offers premium features.

Know the various requirements for applications.   The system requirements for an application can be architecture, such as 32-bit versus 64-bit, dedicated graphics cards versus integrated, VRAM and RAM requirements, CPU requirements, the use of external licensing dongles or hardware tokens, storage requirements, and application compatibility.

Understand how to manage files in Windows.   Nearly all file management—including moving, copying, renaming, and deleting files and changing file attributes—is accomplished through Windows File Explorer.

Know where files are located.   The various versions of Windows that you need to know for this exam store files in multiple locations. You should be able to identify the location of those files mentioned in this chapter and be able to identify items such as where the Recycle Bin files are on each Windows operating system.

Review Questions

The answers to the chapter review questions can be found in Appendix A.

1. Which of the following can you type in the Start menu in Windows to open a command prompt? (Choose two.)
   - **A.** run
   - **B.** cmd
   - **C.** command
   - **D.** open

2. Which part of the operating system can be described as extremely specific software written for the purpose of instructing the OS on how to access a piece of hardware?
   - **A.** Source code
   - **B.** Application
   - **C.** Kernel
   - **D.** Driver

3. How do you increase the size of the taskbar?
   - **A.** Right-click the mouse and drag the taskbar.
   - **B.** Left-click the mouse and double-click the taskbar.
   - **C.** Move the mouse pointer to the top of the taskbar, pausing until the pointer turns into a double-headed arrow, and then click and drag.
   - **D.** Highlight the taskbar and double-click in the center.

4. Which of the following installation methods would you use if you wanted to install a program on a virtual machine? (Choose the best method.)
   - **A.** ISO
   - **B.** USB
   - **C.** Optical disk
   - **D.** ZIP files

5. The Windows File Explorer program can be used to do which of the following? (Choose two.)
   - **A.** Browse the Internet
   - **B.** Copy and move files
   - **C.** Change file attributes
   - **D.** Create backup jobs

6. What is the maximum allowable length for the name of a file in Windows?

   A. 8 characters

   B. 32 characters

   C. 64 characters

   D. 255 characters

7. Which of the following is a program that runs on top of the OS and allows the user to issue commands through a set of menus or some other graphical interface?

   A. Taskbar

   B. Shell

   C. Desktop

   D. Source

8. If a program doesn't have a shortcut on the Desktop or in the All Apps submenu, you can start it by which of the following methods? (Choose the best answer.)

   A. Using the shutdown command

   B. Typing the program name in the Start box

   C. Using the run command and typing in the name of the program

   D. Typing `cmd` in the Start box followed by the program name

9. Which operating system feature offers the ability for a single application to have multiple requests into the processor at one time?

   A. Multiuser mode

   B. Dystopia

   C. Preemption

   D. Multithreading

10. In Windows, a deleted file can be retrieved using which of the following?

   A. My Computer icon

   B. Recycle Bin

   C. Control Panel

   D. Settings app

11. To turn off a Windows 10/11 operating system gracefully, you should do which of the following?

   A. Run the turnoff command at a command prompt.

   B. Turn off the switch and unplug the machine.

   C. Press Ctrl+Alt+Del.

   D. Select Start, then the power icon, and then choose Shut Down.

12. What is the minimum amount of memory required for a 32-bit installation of Windows 10?

A. 128 MB

B. 256 MB

C. 512 MB

D. 1 GB

13. What is the minimum amount of free hard drive space required for the installation of Windows 10 64-bit?

A. 1.5 GB

B. 15 GB

C. 32 GB

D. 60 GB

14. What is the minimum required memory for a 64-bit installation of Windows 10?

A. 512 MB

B. 1 GB

C. 2 GB

D. 4 GB

15. In Windows, a quick way to access Help is to press which keyboard key?

A. F12

B. The Windows key on the keyboard

C. F1

D. Alt

16. Which of the following was a major change with the introduction of Windows 8?

A. Start screen

B. Gadgets

C. Sidebar

D. System tray

17. Which of the following is located on the rightmost portion of the taskbar?

A. Start menu

B. Quick Launch

C. Notification area

D. Shutdown options

18. In addition to right-clicking the Desktop, how else can you access the Display Properties settings?

A. By clicking the Settings gear in the Start menu

B. By clicking the System icon under Control Panel

C. By pressing Ctrl+Alt+Esc

D. By pressing Ctrl+Alt+Tab

19. Which of the following allows you to navigate file/folder structures in Windows?

A. Start menu

B. File Explorer

C. KDE

D. GNOME

20. What is the minimum required processor speed for a 64-bit installation of Windows 10?

A. 2.2 GHz

B. 3.3 GHz

C. 1.0 GHz

D. 2.3 GHz

Performance-Based Question

You will encounter performance-based questions on the A+ exams. The questions on the exam require you to perform a specific task, and you will be graded on whether or not you were able to complete the task. The following requires you to think creatively in order to measure how well you understand this chapter's topics. You may or may not see similar questions on the actual A+ exams. To see how your answer compares to the authors', refer to Appendix B.

Your organization is planning to upgrade its operating system to Windows 10. Currently all of the laptops used in your organization use Windows 8.1 Pro. The organization eventually wants to roll out the Windows 10 feature of BranchCache. How should you proceed to accommodate the upgrade and the future feature needs?

Chapter 14

Windows Configuration

THE FOLLOWING COMPTIA A+ 220-1102 EXAM OBJECTIVES ARE COVERED IN THIS CHAPTER:

✓ **1.3 Given a scenario, use features and tools of the Microsoft Windows 10 operating system (OS).**

- Task Manager
  - Services
  - Startup
  - Performance
  - Processes
  - Users
- Microsoft Management Console (MMC) snap-in
  - Event Viewer (eventvwr.msc)
  - Disk Management (diskmgmt.msc)
  - Task Scheduler (taskschd.msc)
  - Device Manager (devmgmt.msc)
  - Certificate Manager (certmgr.msc)
  - Local Users and Groups (lusrmgr.msc)
  - Performance Monitor (perfmon.msc)
  - Group Policy Editor (gpedit.msc)
- Additional tools
  - System Information (msinfo32.exe)
  - Resource Monitor (resmon.exe)
  - System Configuration (msconfig.exe)
  - Disk Cleanup (cleanmgr.exe)
  - Disk Defragment (dfrgui.exe)
  - Registry Editor (regedit.exe)

✓ **1.4 Given a scenario, use the appropriate Microsoft Windows 10 Control Panel utility.**

- **Internet Options**
- **Devices and Printers**
- **Programs and Features**
- **Network and Sharing Center**
- **System**
- **Windows Defender Firewall**
- **Mail**
- **Sound**
- **User Accounts**
- **Device Manager**
- **Indexing Options**
- **Administrative Tools**
- **File Explorer Options**
    - **Show hidden files**
    - **Hide extensions**
    - **General options**
    - **View options**
- **Power Options**
    - **Hibernate**
    - **Power plans**
    - **Sleep/suspend**
    - **Standby**
    - **Choose what closing the lid does**
    - **Turn on fast startup**
    - **Universal Serial Bus (USB) selective suspend**
- **Ease of Access**

✓ **1.5 Given a scenario, use the appropriate Windows settings.**

- Time and Language
- Update and Security
- Personalization
- Apps
- Privacy
- System
- Devices
- Network and Internet
- Gaming
- Accounts

✓ **1.8 Explain common OS types and their purposes.**

- Various filesystem types
    - New Technology File System (NTFS)
    - File Allocation Table 32 (FAT32)
    - Third extended filesystem (ext3)
    - Fourth extended filesystem (ext4)
    - Apple File System (APFS)
    - Extensible File Allocation Table (exFAT)

✓ **1.9 Given a scenario, perform OS installations and upgrades in a diverse OS environment.**

- Partitioning
    - GUID [globally unique identifier] Partition Table (GPT)
    - Master boot record (MBR)
- Drive format

The previous chapter introduced the basic components of the Windows operating systems. This chapter builds on that and focuses on the configuration of the Windows 10 operating system.

Interacting with Operating Systems

In the following sections, we will look at the Microsoft GUI from the ground up. In Chapter 13, "Operating System Basics," we took a detailed look at its key components, and we will build on that with an exploration of basic tasks for Windows 10/11. Although the exam objectives are focused on Windows 10/11, most of these configuration concepts can be applied to Windows 8.1, 8, and even Windows 7 in many cases.

 Windows 11 was released to the public on October 5, 2021. This edition of Windows is the next major edition of Microsoft Windows that will be supported in the future. However, the objectives for the CompTIA exam are all based on Windows 10. Most of the knowledge you gain by reading this book is transferable to Windows 11.

Microsoft has included a number of tools with each iteration of Windows to simplify system configuration. Although some tools have specific purposes and are used only on rare occasions, you will come to rely on a number of tools and access them on a regular basis. It is this latter set that we will examine in the following sections.

Task Manager

Task Manager lets you shut down nonresponsive applications selectively in all Windows versions. In current versions of Windows, it can do so much more, allowing you to see which processes and applications are using the most system resources, view network usage, see connected users, and so on. To display Task Manager, press Ctrl+Alt+Delete and click the Task Manager button or option. You can also right-click an empty spot in the taskbar and choose Task Manager from the context menu.

 To get to Task Manager directly in any of the Windows versions that include it, you can press Ctrl+Shift+Esc.

Depending on the Windows version, Task Manager has various tabs. Figure 14.1 shows the common default display in Windows 10/11, but other versions vary from the seven tabs shown here: Processes, Performance, App History, Startup, Users, Details, and Services.

FIGURE 14.1   The default Task Manager in Windows

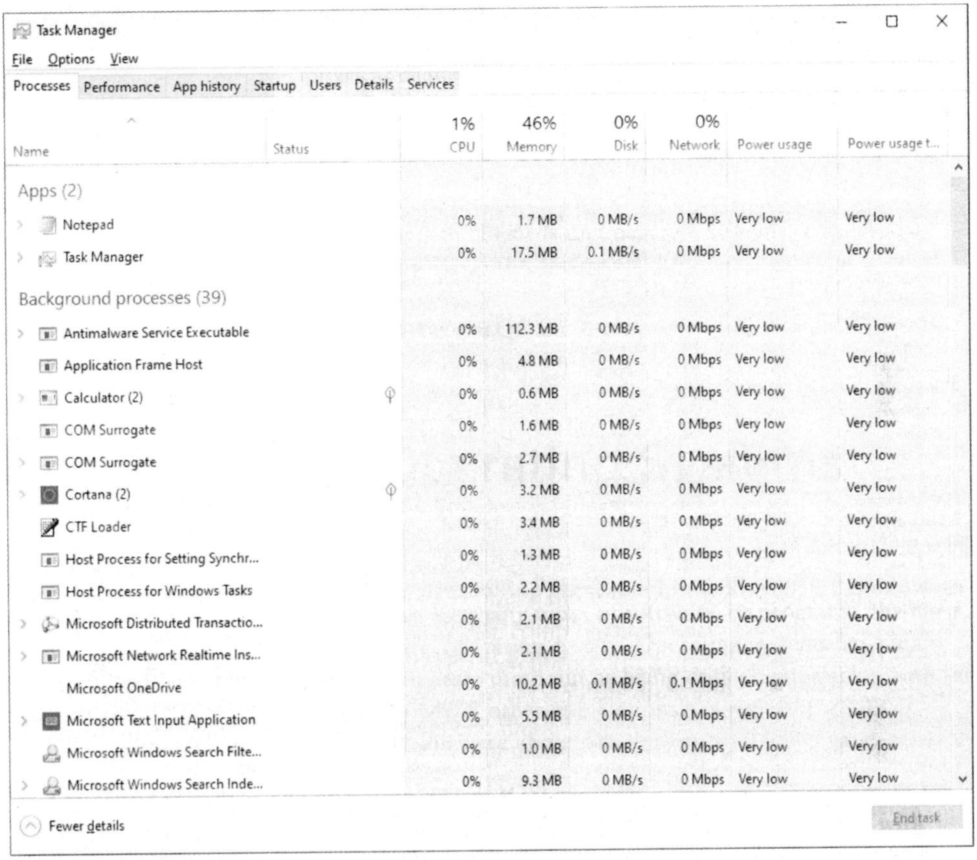

Let's look at these tabs in more detail:

Processes   The Processes tab lets you see which tasks are open on the machine. You also see the status of each task, which can be either Running or Not Responding. If a task/application has stopped responding (that is, it's hung), you can right-click the task in the list and click End Task. Doing so closes the program, and you can try to open it again. Often, although certainly not always, if an application hangs, you have to reboot the computer to prevent the same thing from happening again shortly after you restart the application. You can also use the Processes tab to switch to a different task or create new tasks. In Windows 10/11, many of the elements that appear in Processes are copied between the Processes and Details tabs; an App History tab was added that, as the name implies, displays usage settings for applications and the currently logged-in user account.

Details   In Windows 10/11 the Details tab, shown in Figure 14.2, gives you more detail than the Processes tab. The Details tab can display a multitude of metrics and details, such as Program ID (PID), Status, User Name, and UAC Virtualization Status, and these are just the defaults. You can select the columns you want to see by right-clicking on the header and selecting the various metrics, as shown in Figure 14.3.

FIGURE 14.2   The Details tab of Task Manager

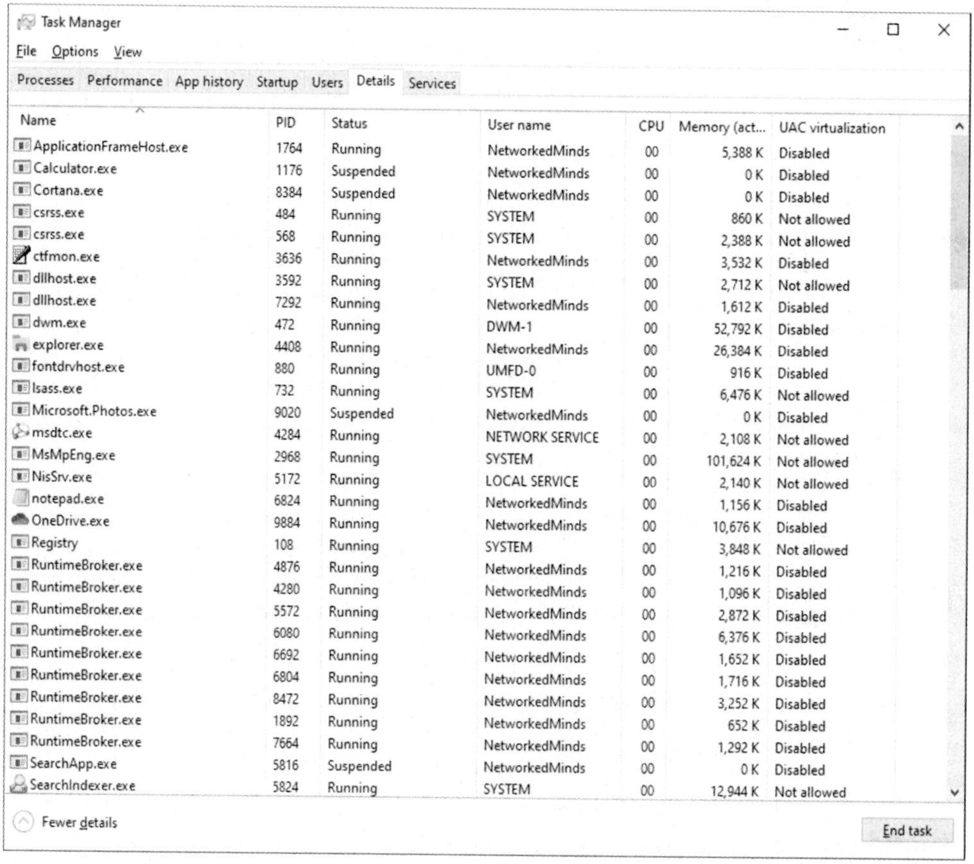

To end a process, right-click it in the list and click End Task. Be careful with this choice, because ending some processes can cause Windows to shut down. If you don't know what a particular process does, you can look for it in any search engine and find a number of sites that explain it.

FIGURE 14.3   The various metrics for the Details tab

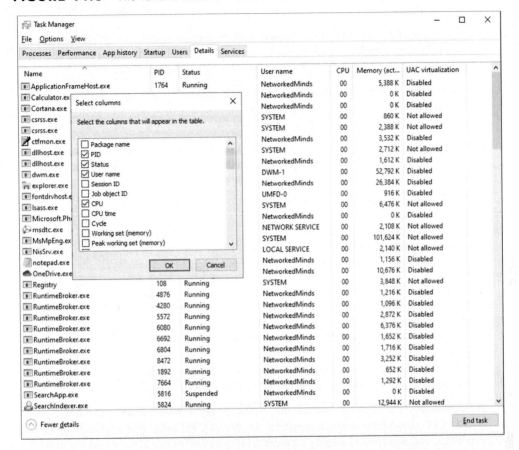

You can also change the priority of a process in Task Manager's Details tab by right-clicking the name of the process and choosing Set Priority. The six priorities, from lowest to highest, are as follows:

Low   For applications that need to complete sometime but that you don't want interfering with other applications. On a numerical scale from 0 to 31, this equates to a base priority of 4.

Below Normal   For applications that don't need to drop all the way down to Low. This equates to a base priority of 6.

Normal   The default priority for most applications. This equates to a base priority of 8.

Above Normal   For applications that don't need to boost all the way to High. This equates to a base priority of 10.

High   For applications that must complete soon, when you don't want other applications to interfere with the applications' performance. This equates to a base priority of 13.

Realtime   For applications that must have the processor's attention to handle time-critical tasks. Applications can be run at this priority only by a member of the Administrators group. This equates to a base priority of 24.

If you decide to change the priority of an application, you'll be warned that doing so may make it unstable. You can generally ignore this option when changing the priority to Low, Below Normal, Above Normal, or High, but you should heed this warning when changing applications to the Realtime priority. Realtime means that the processor gives precedence to this process over all others—over security processes, over spooling, over everything—and this is sure to make the system unstable.

Task Manager changes the priority only for that instance of the running application. The next time the process is started, priorities revert back to that of the base (typically, Normal).

Services   The Services tab lists the name of each running service as well as the process ID associated with it and its description, status, and group. A button labeled Open Services appears on the bottom of this screen. Clicking it will open the *Microsoft Management Console (MMC)* snap-in for Services, where you can configure each service. Within Task Manager, right-clicking a service will open a context menu listing six choices: Start, Stop, Restart, Open Services (which opens the Service MMC), Search Online, and Go To Details (which takes you to the Processes or Details tab).

Performance   The Performance tab displays a variety of information, including overall CPU usage percentage, a graphical display of CPU usage history, the number of processes, and a graphical display of physical memory. This tab also provides you with additional memory-related information, such as physical and kernel memory usage as well as the total number of handles, threads, and processes. Total, limit, and peak commit-charge information also appears, as shown in Figure 14.4.

Some of the items are beyond the scope of this book, but it's good to know that you can use the Performance tab to keep track of system performance. Note that the number of processes, CPU usage percentage, and commit-charge information always appear at the bottom of the Task Manager window, regardless of which tab you have currently selected.

Users   The Users tab provides you with information about the users logged into the local machine. You'll see the username, status, CPU usage, memory usage, disk usage, and network usage. You can right-click the name of any connected user to perform a variety of functions, including viewing active processes, sending the user a message, signing off the user, switching accounts, and initiating a remote-control session to the user's machine, if they are connected remotely.

FIGURE 14.4   The Performance tab of Task Manager

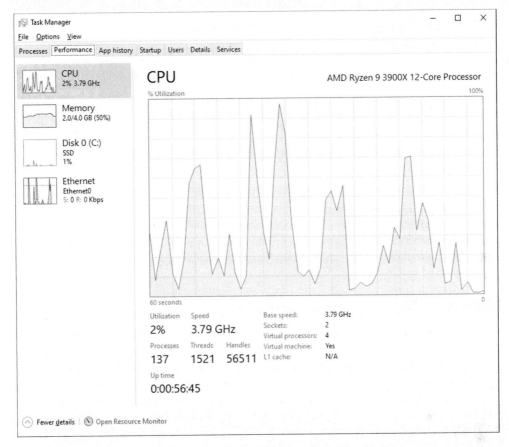

Startup   The Startup tab lists the names of services configured to begin at startup as well as the publisher, status, and startup impact. From this tab, you can select any service listed and choose to disable it. This functionality was provided by the msconfig command in prior versions of Windows, such as Windows 7.

Use Task Manager whenever the system seems bogged down by an unresponsive application.

EXERCISE 14.1

Working with Task Manager

1. Select Start, type **notepad**, and then press Enter.

2. Right-click an empty portion of the taskbar and select Task Manager.

(continues)

3. In the lower-left corner of the window, select More Details.

4. Find Notepad in the Processes tab, right-click, and select Go To Details.

5. Right-click on notepad.exe on the Details tab that opened and select Set Priority, then Above Normal.

6. Confirm the change by clicking Change Priority in the dialog box that opens to confirm your change.

7. Right-click on the column header and choose Select Columns from the drop-down context menu.

8. Scroll through the list and select the Base Priority check box, then click OK.

9. Observe the status of notepad.exe.

10. Right-click notepad.exe and select End Task.

11. Confirm the ending of the task by clicking End Process in the dialog box that displays.

Microsoft Management Console

Microsoft created the Microsoft Management Console (MMC) interface as a frontend in which you can run administrative and configuration tools. Many administrators don't even know that applications they use regularly run within an MMC. In the following sections, we will cover many of the different MMC snap-ins you will use in your day-to-day administration and configuration of the operating system. You can start the MMC by pressing Windows + R to open Run, typing mmc in the box, and then clicking OK. Once the MMC is started, you can create a custom MMC, adding the snap-ins discussed below. Click File ➤ Add Or Remove Snap-ins, and then select which snap-ins to add. For more information about the MMC, visit https://docs.microsoft.com/en-us/troubleshoot/windows-server/system-management-components/what-is-microsoft-management-console.

Computer Management

Windows includes a piece of software to manage computer settings: the Computer Management console. The Computer Management console can manage more than just the installed hardware devices; it can manage all the services running on a computer in addition to Device Manager, which functions almost identically to the one that has existed since Windows 9x. It also contains Event Viewer, which shows any system errors and events as well as methods to configure the software components of all the computer's hardware.

To access the Computer Management console, right-click the Start menu and select it from the context menu. (In Windows 8, it's on the Start screen.)

After you are in Computer Management, you will see all the tools available, as shown in Figure 14.5. This is one power-packed interface and includes the following system tools:

FIGURE 14.5   Computer Management

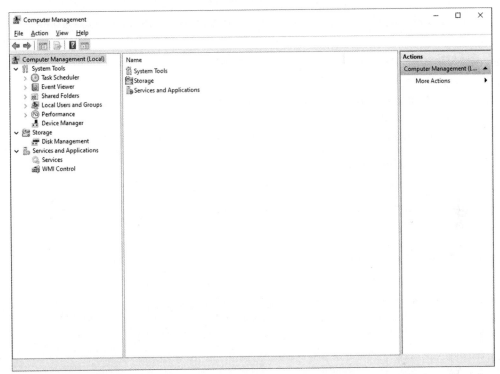

Task Scheduler   Allows for the scheduling of tasks using a simple command, script, or external program. Many of the operating system's functions are tasks such as checking for updates.

Event Viewer   A link to the tool that allows you to view application error logs, security audit records, and system errors.

Shared Folders   Allows you to manage all your computer's shared folders. You can also view active remote sessions and open files from this console.

Local Users and Groups   Allows you to create and manage local user and group accounts.

Performance   Shows you how your system hardware is performing and alerts you if system performance goes under a threshold that you set.

Device Manager   Allows you to manage hardware devices and perform tasks such as updating drivers, disabling devices, and uninstalling devices. Device Manager is the first place to visit if a device is physically installed but not working.

Storage   Allows you to perform basic disk management on the operating system.

Services and Applications   Allows you to control services in the operating system.

Event Viewer

Event Viewer (`eventvwr.msc`) is an MMC snap-in that shows a lot of detailed information about what is running on your operating system. You can start it in several different ways—for example, by clicking Start, typing Event Viewer, and selecting the Event Viewer app, or by right-clicking the Start button and selecting Event Viewer from the context menu. In addition, you can add it as a snap-in inside the MMC or press Windows key + R, type **eventvwr.msc**, and press Enter.

Event Viewer should be the first place you look when you are trying to solve a problem whose solution is not evident. The system and applications will often create an entry in Event Viewer that can be used to verify operation or diagnosis problems, as shown in Figure 14.6.

FIGURE 14.6   Event Viewer

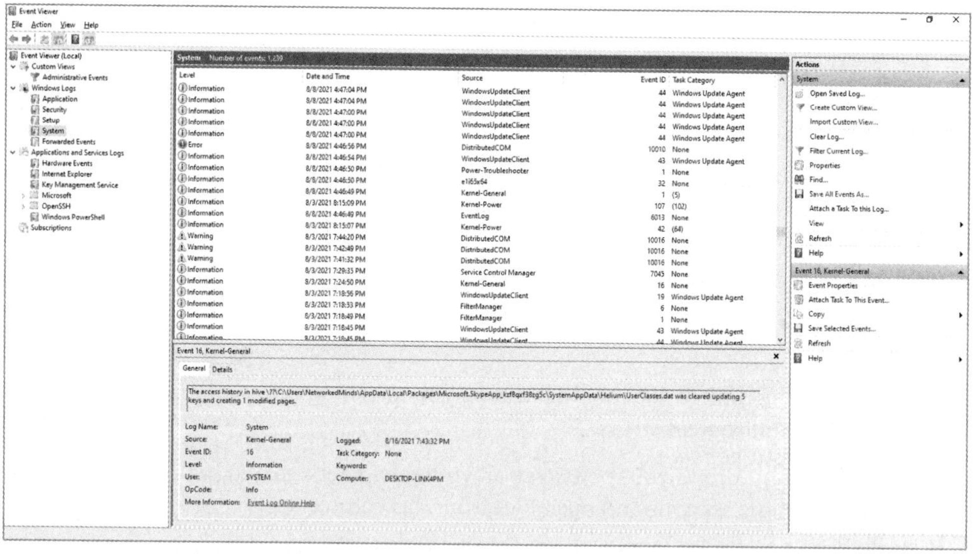

Table 14.1 highlights the three main event logs that you should be concerned with for the exam. Each feature in Windows has the ability to store its events in specific log files, in application and service logs.

TABLE 14.1   Event Viewer logs

Event Log	Description
Application	Events generated by applications installed on the operating system
Security	Events generated by the Security Reference Monitor in the Executive kernel
System	Events generated by the operating system

Although you might think that all the security-related information is in the Security log, you're only half right. The Security log is used by the Security Reference Monitor inside the *Executive kernel*. It is responsible for reporting object audit attempts. Examples of object audit attempts include file access, group membership, and password changes.

Most of the useful security-related information will be in the application and system logs. Using these logs, you can see errors and warnings that will alert you to potential security-related problems. When you suspect an issue with the operating system or an application that interacts with the operating system, you should check these logs for clues. The event log won't tell you exactly what is wrong and how to fix it, but it will tell you if there is an issue that needs to be investigated.

Disk Management

The Disk Management (`diskmgmt.msc`) snap-in is used to view disk information, such as volumes configured on the physical disk and the *filesystems* that are formatted on the volume. Disk Management, shown in Figure 14.7, isn't used just to view information; you can also use it to partition volumes on a new or existing disk, format filesystems, and mount volumes to drive letters. These are just a few configuration tasks; we will cover Disk Management later in this chapter.

Task Scheduler

Task Scheduler (`taskschd.msc`), accessible beneath Computer Management or Administrative Tools in Control Panel, allows you to configure an application to run automatically or at any regular interval (see Figure 14.8). A number of terms are used to describe the options for configuring tasks: *action* (what the task actually does), *condition* (an optional requirement that must be met before a task runs), *setting* (any property that affects the behavior of a task), and *trigger* (the required condition for the task to run).

For example, you could configure a report to run automatically (action) every Tuesday (trigger) when the system has been idle for 10 minutes (condition), and only when requested (setting).

FIGURE 14.7   Disk Management

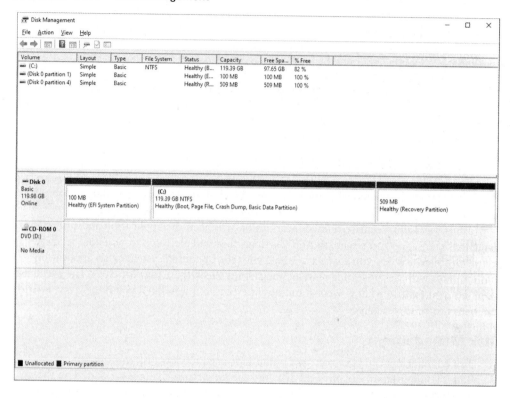

FIGURE 14.8   Task Scheduler

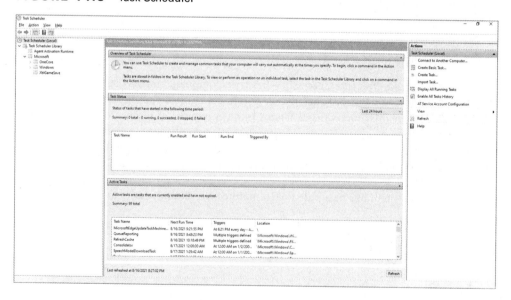

Device Manager

Device Manager (`devmgmt.msc`) is an indispensable tool for the management of peripherals and components attached to the computer. You can view all the devices in the system, as shown in Figure 14.9. Device Manager has been around since Windows 95, and it hasn't changed all that much. Because computer systems have evolved and all newer computer systems are plug-and-play capable, this tool is usually only used when you are in doubt that a component is working or you're troubleshooting a problem, or when you want to check the driver. Device Manager was used in the past a lot more since most peripherals had to be manually configured.

FIGURE 14.9 Device Manager

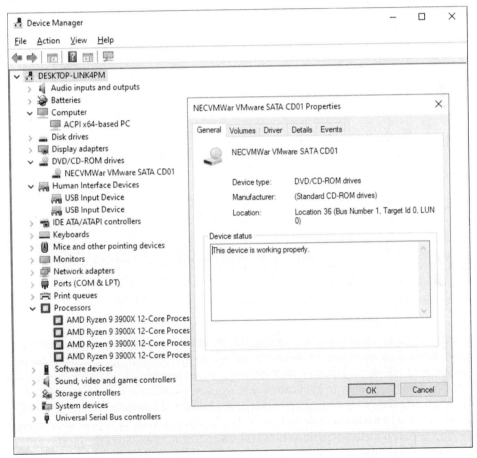

Device Manager allows you to manually update the driver for a device, roll back a driver to a prior version, uninstall a device, and disable a device. Some peripherals, such as the network card, allow you to configure if you want the device to wake the computer. Some peripherals, such as a disk drive or USB device, can be configured to fall asleep if they are not used for a specified period of time.

Certificate Manager

Certificate Manager (`certmgr.msc`) is used to view and manage certificates used by the web browser and the operating system, as shown in Figure 14.10. Certificates are used for a number of reasons; the most common are encryption and digital signatures that provide trust.

FIGURE 14.10   Certificate Manager

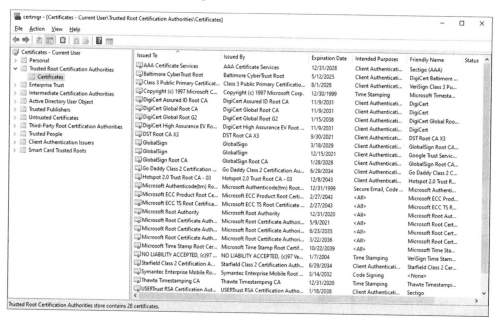

Certificate Manager allows you to manage certificates for your user account, a service account, or the computer account. When you choose to manage your user account, the certificates managed can be used only by your account. So, the certificates are only relevant while you are logged in and using an application that requires a certificate from the certificate store. When you choose to manage certificates for a particular service account, the certificate is only relevant to that specific service, such as a virtual private network (VPN) service. When you choose to manage certificates for the computer account, these certificates are relevant only for the operating system, even if someone is not logged in. This configuration mode is commonly used when configuring a certificate for the Internet Information Services (IIS) web server.

Local Users and Groups

The Local Users and Groups (`lusrmgr.msc`) MMC snap-in allows for granular control over local user accounts and groups for the Windows operating system. You can access the Local Users and Groups MMC by right-clicking the Start menu and choosing Computer Management. You can also press the Windows key + R, type **lusrmgr.msc**, and press Enter. When the tool launches, if you click Users you will see several built-in user accounts, all of which are disabled (depicted with the down arrow), as shown in Figure 14.11. The only active account on a brand-new Windows 10/11 operating system is the first account setup.

FIGURE 14.11   Local Users and Groups

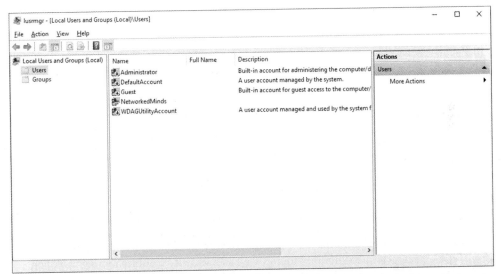

The MMC extension is divided into the following two parts:

- The Users section allows for the viewing, creation, and modification of individual users. You can also access disabled users, such as the built-in Administrator account and Guest account.

- The Groups section allows for the viewing, creation, and modification of groups. The User Accounts Control Panel applet only allows assignment of the administrator group with a radio button–type dialog box. However, from this MMC extension, you can assign many different groups. Each group assigns more permissions to a user.

Performance Monitor

Performance Monitor (`perfmon.msc`) varies a bit in different versions of Windows, but it has the same purpose throughout: to display performance counters, as shown in Figure 14.12. The tool collects counter information and then sends that information to a console or event log.

FIGURE 14.12   Performance Monitor

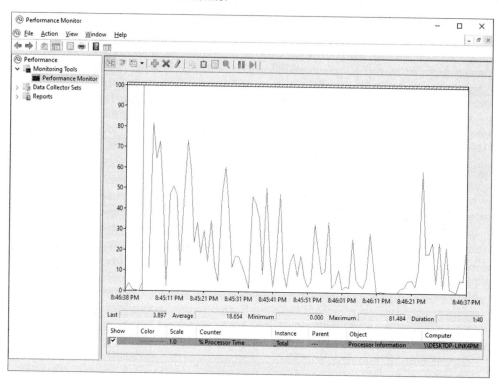

Performance Monitor's objects and counters are very specific; you can use Performance Monitor as a general troubleshooting tool as well as a security troubleshooting tool. For instance, you can see where resources are being used and where the activity is coming from. In Exercise 14.2, you see how to work with Performance Monitor.

EXERCISE 14.2

Working with Performance Monitor

1. Select Start, type **perfmon**, and then press Enter.

   Make sure that you select Performance Monitor, as opposed to System Monitor or another default that may come to the forefront.

2. Choose the Performance Monitor section under Monitoring Tools.

3. Click the plus sign (+) or right-click in the graphical display area and select Add Counters.

4. Expand the Processor section, and then select the %Processor Time object.

5. Click Add and then click OK.

6. Open Windows File Explorer, click the C: drive, type * into the search box, and then press Enter.

7. Quickly change to Performance Monitor and watch the impact of this search on the processor.

   This action is time consuming and therefore will help you notice the changes that take place in Performance Monitor.

8. Run the same operation again. This time, however, change your view within Performance Monitor to the histogram bar by clicking the button directly to the left of the plus sign.

9. Run the same operation again, changing your view within Performance Monitor to Report.

10. Exit Performance Monitor.

Group Policy Editor

The Group Policy Editor (gpedit.msc) tool allows you to edit the local Group Policy for the operating system. *Group Policy* is a mechanism that allows an administrator to set various settings to customize the operating system. These settings can restrict the operating system in a number of ways, such as removing the settings tab from a built-in application. Group Policy can also control aspects of security for the operating system. Group Policy also contains a mechanism to enforce these settings by reapplying the settings periodically in the event they are changed.

The Group Policy Editor divides all settings between computer settings and user settings. The computer settings affect the operating system and how it behaves. The user settings affect the user logged onto the operating system. If you open the Group Policy Editor by typing **gpedit.msc** in the Run dialog box and pressing Enter, the tool will open and display a tree of settings, as shown in Figure 14.13.

There is another way to open the Group Policy Editor in which you can edit the Group Policy for a specific user, administrators, or all non-administrators. You must first start the MMC tool by typing **mmc** in the Run dialog box and then pressing Enter. Then, add the snap-in Group Policy Object Editor. After it is selected, another dialog box will pop up where you can browse to select a specific user or group or a special group of users, as shown in Figure 14.14.

FIGURE 14.13 Group Policy Editor

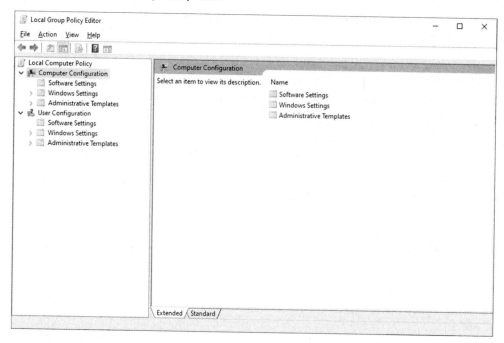

FIGURE 14.14 Group Policy Editor browse dialog box

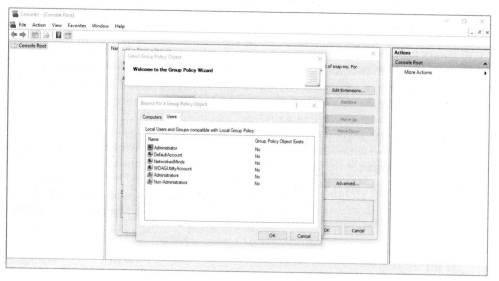

Additional Tools

When the Microsoft Management Console (MMC) was first introduced with Windows 2000, it was to be a single pane of glass for monitoring and configuration of the Windows operating system. Over 20 years later, we still use a mixture of tools outside the MMC to monitor and configure Windows. Next, we discuss some of these additional utilities and tools.

System Configuration Tool

The System Configuration (`msconfig.exe`) tool allows you to configure how Windows 10/11 starts up, as well as launching additional tools. The tabs of the System Configuration tool differ a bit based on the Windows version you are running. The main tabs are General, Boot, Services, Startup, and Tools. Figure 14.15 shows the General tab for Windows 10. From here, you can configure the startup options.

FIGURE 14.15   System Configuration General tab in Windows 10

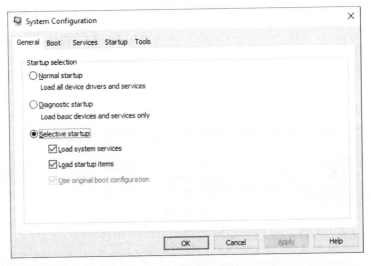

Figure 14.16 shows the Boot tab for Windows 10. Note that from here, you can configure the next boot to be a safe boot, and you can turn on the boot information so that you can see drivers as they load—which is quite useful when a system keeps hanging during boot. Although the option is titled Safe Boot, this is classically referred to as booting into Safe mode.

Figure 14.17 shows the Services tab for Windows 10. On this tab, you can view the services installed on the system and their current status (running or stopped). You can also enable or disable services.

FIGURE 14.16   System Configuration Boot tab in Windows 10

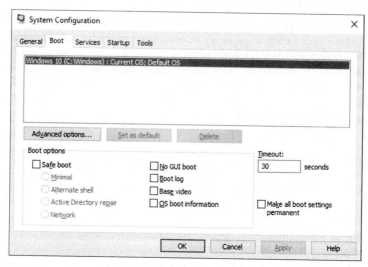

FIGURE 14.17   System Configuration Services tab in Windows 10

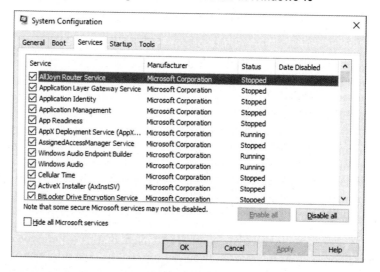

In Windows 7 and earlier, the Startup tab allowed you to configure applications that start up when any user logs in. In Windows 8/8.1 and Windows 10/11, the Startup tab redirects you to the Startup tab in Task Manager, where these tasks can be performed, as shown in Figure 14.18.

FIGURE 14.18   System Configuration Startup tab and Task Manager Startup tab

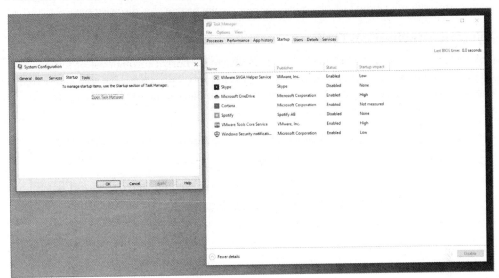

Figure 14.19 shows the Tools tab for Windows 10. On this tab, you can launch a number of administrative tools to configure various Windows features.

FIGURE 14.19   System Configuration Tools tab in Windows 10

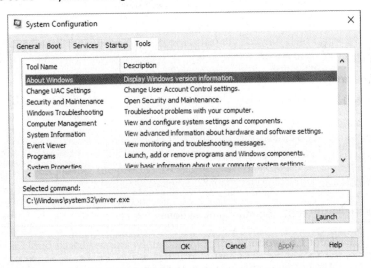

Keep in mind that the tabs differ slightly based on the operating system version. We walked through the CompTIA objectives related to this tool in this discussion.

System Information Tool

The System Information (`msinfo32.exe`) tool displays a fairly thorough list of settings on the machine (see Figure 14.20). You cannot change any values here, but you can search, export, and save the output. Several command-line options can be used when starting msinfo32; Table 14.2 summarizes them.

FIGURE 14.20   The Msinfo32 interface shows configuration values for the system.

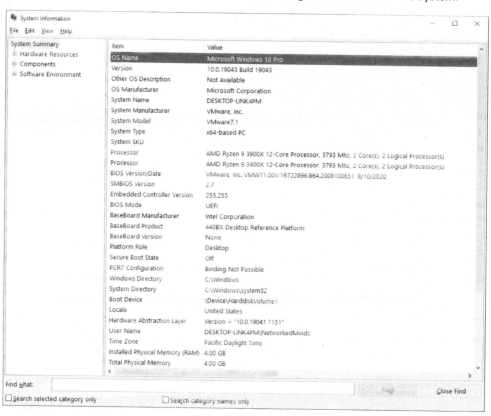

TABLE 14.2   msinfo32 command-line options

Option	Function
/computer	Allows you to specify a remote computer on which to run the utility
/nfo	Creates a file and saves it with an .nfo extension
/report	Creates a file and saves it with a .txt extension

Resource Monitor

Resource Monitor (`resmon.exe`) is used to identify resource utilization of CPU, disk, network, and memory on Windows. The utility was originally introduced in Windows Vista and has been included with all new releases of Windows. The utility can be launched a few different ways. The first is by entering the command **resmon.exe** in the Run dialog box. Another way to open the Resource Monitor is from inside Task Manager. At the lower left of the Performance tab is the option Open Resource Monitor; clicking it will launch Resource Monitor in a new window. Figure 14.21 shows Resource Monitor and the four tabs for each resource.

FIGURE 14.21   Resource Monitor

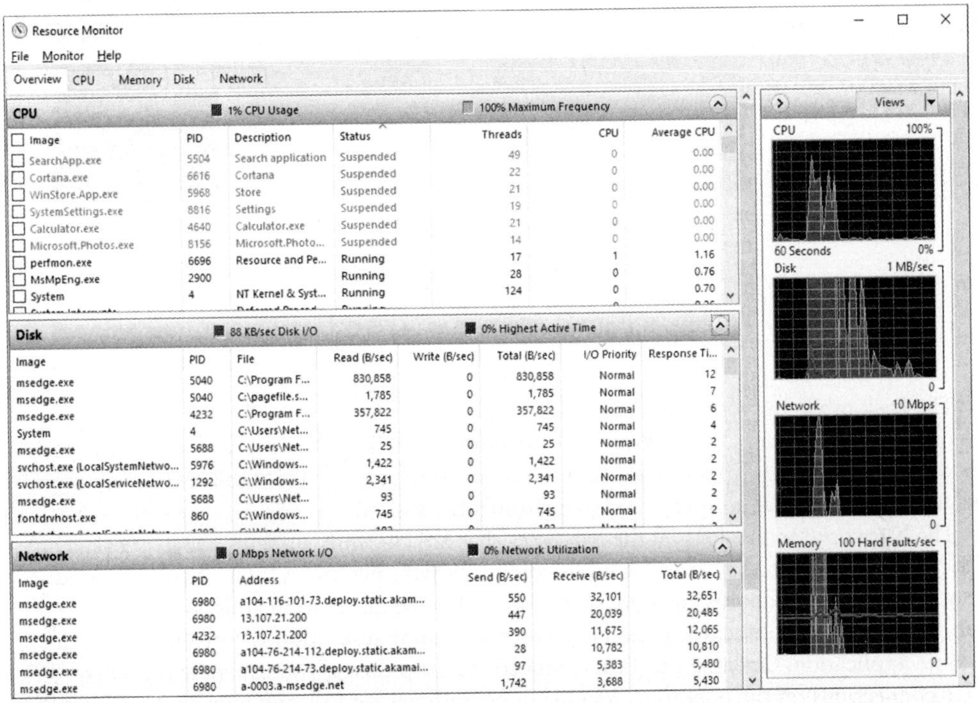

The CPU tab allows you to identify the process with the highest amount of CPU utilization on the operating system. Each column can be sorted; it is as simple as clicking the CPU column to sort the column and find the process with the highest CPU utilization. When you do find the process, you can right-click the entry and choose to end the process, suspend the process, and even search the process online.

The Memory tab displays detailed memory usage of the processes running on the operating system, as shown in Figure 14.22. This tab can help you identify memory in use, memory reserved by hardware, and memory available by the operating system and processes.

FIGURE 14.22   Resource Monitor Memory tab

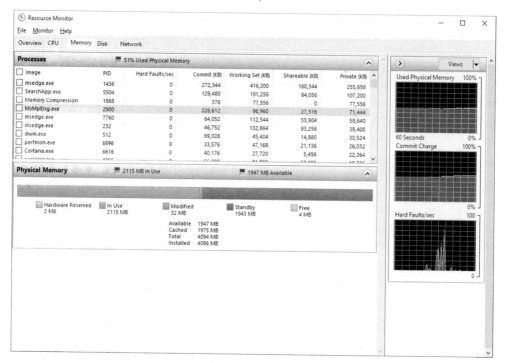

The Disk tab helps you identify a process that is overusing the hard drive with a high amount of read requests, write requests, or overall usage. The Disk tab will also allow you to identify the I/O priority of processes and their response time. This tab is extremely useful when you suspect that a process is slowing down the system.

The Network tab displays all the processes that are currently utilizing the network. The processes can be sorted by send, received, and total bytes per second. The Network tab does a lot more than just displaying activity; it also shows the destination addresses for each process. This is valuable information if you suspect name resolution is a problem with the remote application. Opening the TCP Connections drop-down, you can view the active TCP connections on the operating system, along with packet loss and latency. Normally this active view of network traffic can only be performed with a packet capture tool or another third-party tool. The Network tab is not just useful for information on outgoing applications, it can also display processes listening on TCP and UDP ports. The Resource Monitor tool will also display *firewall* status for the processes listening on the operating system.

Disk Cleanup

Storage space is finite in a computer, and it is inevitable that it will be consumed over time. It can be consumed by a number of files, such as the operating system, downloaded programs, temporary files, updates, deleted files, and of course your data files. The Disk Cleanup (cleanmgr.exe) tool can clean up operating system files to free up space without affecting your data files. Disk Cleanup, shown in Figure 14.23, can be launched by entering the command **cleanmgr.exe** in the Run dialog box, or by right-clicking the C: drive, selecting Properties, and then clicking Disk Cleanup.

FIGURE 14.23   Disk Cleanup

Once Disk Cleanup is launched, you can select the various files you want to clean up on the system drive. The categories you can delete are Downloaded Program Files, Temporary Internet Files, DirectX Shader Cache, Delivery Optimization Files, Recycle Bin, Temporary Files, Thumbnails, Windows Update Files, Windows Defender Antivirus, and countless other files. For some categories, you can view the files that you can potentially delete; two such categories are Temporary Internet Files and Downloaded Program Files. However, there are other categories in which you can view the individual files. After selecting the categories you want to delete, you can purge them from the disk, thus freeing up space.

Control Panel

Although, for the most part, Windows is functional from the time it is installed, Microsoft realized that if someone were going to use computers regularly, they would probably want to be able to customize their environment so that it would be better suited to their needs—or at least more fun to use. As a result, the Windows environment has a large number of utilities that are intended to give you control over the look and feel of the operating system.

This is, of course, an excellent idea. It is also a bit more freedom than some less-than-cautious users seem to be capable of handling. You will undoubtedly serve a number of customers who call you to restore their configuration after botched attempts at changing one setting or another.

More than likely, you will also have to reinstall Windows yourself a few times because of accidents that occur while you are studying or testing the system's limits. This is actually a good thing, because no competent computer technician can say that they have never had to reinstall because of an error. You can't really know how to fix Windows until you are experienced at breaking it. So, it is extremely important to experiment and find out what can be changed in the Windows environment, what results from those changes, and how to undo any unwanted results. To this end, we will examine the most common configuration utility in Windows: Control Panel, as shown in Table 14.3, which describes some popular applets. Also, not all applets are available in all versions.

TABLE 14.3   Selected Windows Control Panel applets

Applet name	Function
Device Manager	Adds and configures new hardware
Programs and Features	Changes, adds, or deletes software
Administrative Tools	Performs administrative tasks on the computer
Folder Options	Configures the look and feel of how folders are displayed in Windows File Explorer
Internet Options	Sets a number of Internet connectivity options
Network and Sharing Center	Sets options for connecting to other computers
Power Options	Configures different power schemes to adjust power consumption
Devices and Printers	Configures printer settings and print defaults
System	Allows you to view and configure various system elements (discussed in more detail later in this chapter)
Windows Defender Firewall	Configures basic firewall exemptions
Mail	Configures the Outlook mail profile
Sound	Configures audio
User Accounts	Configures local accounts on the operating system
Indexing Options	Configures the folders to index for search capabilities
Ease of Access	Allows for accessibility options for users

In the current version of Windows, when you first open Control Panel, it appears in Category view, as shown in Figure 14.24. Control Panel programs have been organized into various categories, and this view provides you with the categories from which you can choose. When you choose a category and pick a task, the appropriate Control Panel program opens. Or, you can select one of the Control Panel programs that is part of the category.

FIGURE 14.24   The Windows Control Panel in Category view

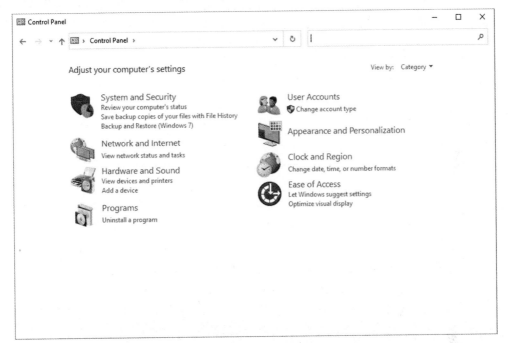

You can change this view to Classic view (or Small/Large Icons in Windows 10/11, Windows 8/8.1, and Windows 7), which displays all the Control Panel programs in a list, as in older versions of Windows. The specific wording of the CompTIA objective (1.4) for this exam reads, "Given a scenario, use the appropriate Microsoft Windows 10 Control Panel utility." The items are organized by category and not by large icons in Windows by default. Therefore, we *strongly* suggest that administrators change to this view. To do so, select Large Icons in the View By drop-down box in the right corner of Control Panel. Throughout this chapter, when we refer to accessing Control Panel programs, we will assume that you have changed the view to the Large Icons view.

For a quick look at how the Control Panel programs work, in Exercise 14.3, you'll examine some of the settings in the Date and Time applet (`timedate.cpl`).

NOTE   Filenames appearing in parentheses, such as `timedate.cpl` in the preceding paragraph, can be used to start the utility without needing to go through the Control Panel dialog boxes.

The Date and Time applet is used to configure the system time, date, and time zone settings, which can be important for files that require accurate time stamps (or for users who don't wear a watch). Because Date and Time is a simple program, it's a perfect example to use. Current versions of Windows have an Internet Time Settings tab, which enables you to synchronize time on the computer with an Internet time server (the options in Windows 10/11 are shown in Figure 14.25). By default, the Internet time server is set to `time.windows.com`.

FIGURE 14.25   Windows Date and Time/Internet Time Settings

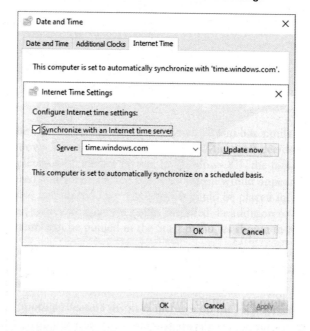

EXERCISE 14.3

Changing the Time Zone

1. Click Start, type **Control Panel** or **`timedate.cpl`**, and then select the appropriate result from the search.

2. From Control Panel, double-click the Date and Time icon. (By default, the programs are listed alphabetically.)

3. Click the Time Zone tab, and from the drop-down menu, select (GMT –03:30) Newfoundland.

4. Hop a plane to Newfoundland, secure in the knowledge that you will know what time it is once you get there.

5. If you skipped step 4, change the time zone back to where it should be before closing the window.

Microsoft is slowly moving away from Control Panel in favor of the Settings app. Many of the same settings appear in both Control Panel and the Settings app. Some settings can only be set in the Settings app, such as Windows Update settings, whereas others, such as BitLocker, can only be set in the classic Control Panel.

Regional and Language Options

You can configure regional settings through the Control Panel applet Region in Windows 10/11 and 8/8.1. Using this applet (`intl.cpl`), you can choose which format is used for numbers (see Figure 14.26), your geographic location, and the language to be used for non-Unicode programs. In Windows 10/11, the Settings app is also used to set the layout of the keyboard you are using as well as set the regional settings previously mentioned.

FIGURE 14.26   Windows Region Control Panel applet

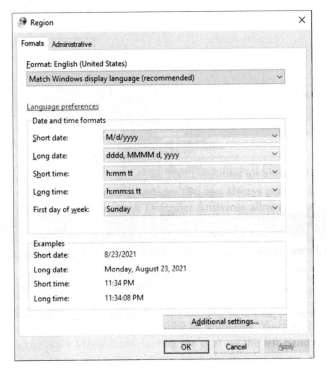

The ability to support so many languages is provided through the use of the *Unicode* standard. In Unicode, and the Unicode Character Set (UCS), each character has a 16-bit value. This allows the same character to be interpreted/represented by 65,536 different entities.

If you click Additional Settings, you can go beyond the date and time formats and also configure number and currency, as shown in Figure 14.27.

FIGURE 14.27   Windows Additional Settings Region Control Panel applet

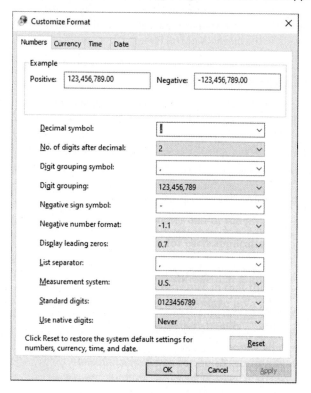

Internet Options Applet

The Internet Options applet (inetcpl.cpl) brings up the Internet Properties dialog box, as shown in Figure 14.28. The tabs include General, Security, Privacy, Content, Connections, Programs, and Advanced. Use this applet to configure the browser environment for Internet Explorer 11 and specify such things as the programs used to work with files found online.

FIGURE 14.28   Windows 10 Internet Options Control Panel applet

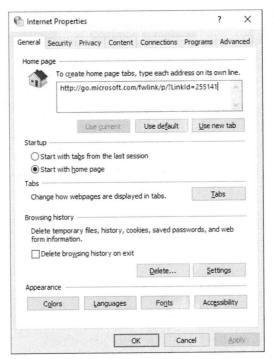

 It's important to note that in Windows 10, Internet Explorer exists alongside the Microsoft Edge browser. However, the Microsoft Edge browser is not controlled by these settings. Microsoft has incorporated an Internet Explorer mode for Microsoft Edge; this will allow a smoother transition to Edge. The sunset date for Internet Explorer is June 15, 2022, and Windows 11 does not include Internet Explorer.

File Explorer Options Applet

The File Explorer Options applet will open to the General tab, as shown in Figure 14.29. Using this tab, you can change the default opening pane for File Explorer. The Quick Access option, the default, displays frequently used folders and recent files. The This PC option displays the common folders found under This PC, along with devices and drives. In addition, you can control how folders open, such as opening folders in the same window or opening folders in their own new windows. You can change how items are opened, such as single-click or double-click. This tab also lets you change privacy settings, such as showing recently used file folders in the Quick Access view. By default, Windows 10/11 will be helpful by showing these recently used files and folders, but you may want to shut that behavior off. After doing so, you should clear the File Explorer history by clicking the Clear button in the General tab of the Folder Options applet.

FIGURE 14.29 Windows 10 File Explorer General Options

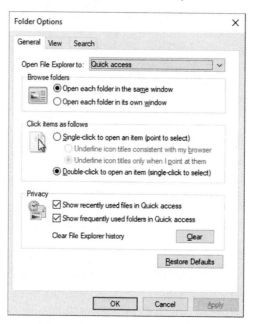

The View tab in the File Explorer Options applet allows you to change how files and folders are viewed in File Explorer. There are a number of settings on this tab that will allow you to change the way File Explorer is viewed. The settings range from always show-ing menus to showing all folders in the Navigation pane. One of the first settings that is usually changed is Hide Extensions For Known File Types, because seeing the extensions is really handy.

 In later versions of Windows 10/11, the ability to see extensions is the default. This was changed because many malicious files can hide their extensions in an attempt to be executed or opened.

Some of the more important files that you will need to work on are hidden by default as a security precaution. To make certain folders or files visible, you need to change the display properties of Windows File Explorer, as shown in Figure 14.30. You learn how to do this in Exercise 14.4.

FIGURE 14.30   Windows 10 File Explorer View Options

EXERCISE 14.4

Showing Hidden Files and Folders

1. Open Windows File Explorer on a Windows system.

2. Browse to the root of the C: drive and note the entries that are there.

3. If it is available, choose View and select the Hidden Items option so that they are now visible.

4. Note the entries that now appear but that did not previously.

5. Open the File Explorer Options applet from Control Panel and select the View tab, if needed.

6. Deselect Hide Protected Operating System Files (Recommended).

7. Deselect Hide File Extensions For Known File Types.

8. Click OK.

You will now be able to see the Windows system files discussed in the following sections. For security reasons, you should set these attributes back to the defaults after you've read this chapter.

The Search tab in the Folder Options applet controls the Search and Index feature in Windows 10/11. You can turn off using the search feature and change the behavior of non-indexed locations.

System Applet

The System applet in Control Panel is one of the most important applets, and technically it's not an applet. In most recent versions of Windows 10/11, the System applet in Control Panel will open the Settings app to the About screen. From within the Settings app panel, you can make a large number of configuration changes to a Windows machine. If you click Advanced System Settings, the classic System Properties (`sysdm.cpl`) will open. (See Figure 14.31 for the Windows 10/11 classic System Properties applet.) You can perform a number of functions in this applet, which can include some of the following options:

- Network Identification
- Device Manager
- Hardware
- User Profiles
- Environment Variables
- Startup and Recovery
- Performance
- System Protection
- Remote
- Computer Name
- Advanced

FIGURE 14.31   Windows System Properties Control Panel applet

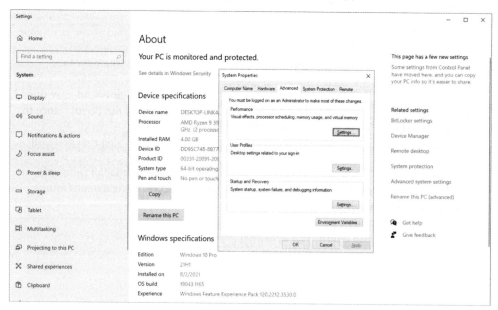

In the following sections, we will look more closely at the functionality of the tabs.

Computer Name

This tab is used to define whether the machine is in a workgroup or a *domain* environment. We talk more about networking in Chapter 15, "Windows Administration," but in general terms, here's the difference between a workgroup and a domain:

Workgroup   Loosely associated computers, each of which is its own security authority, that share a common *workgroup* name. Often used for 10 or fewer computers/workstations that do not require a server computer.

Domain   A group of computers that are tightly connected or associated and that share a common domain name. Has a single authority (called a *domain controller*) that manages security for all the computers. Often used for 10 or more computers/workstations that connect to one or more server computers.

Hardware

This tab includes a number of tools that enable you to change how the hardware on your machine is used. The most useful is the ability to open the Device Manager directly from this tab. The other setting on this tab is how Windows behaves when you plug in devices. By default, Windows will automatically download *drivers*, *apps*, and custom icons from the devices plugged in. When you purchase a hardware device, odds are that it's been in the box for a while. By the time it gets made, packaged, stored, delivered to the store, stored again at the retailer, and then purchased by you, it's entirely likely that the company that made the device has updated the driver—even possibly a few times if there have been a lot of reported problems.

Advanced

The Advanced tab has several subheadings, each of which can be configured separately, as shown in Figure 14.32. The following options are among those on this tab.

PERFORMANCE

Although it is hidden in the backwaters of Windows' system configuration settings, the Performance option holds some important settings that you may need to configure on a system. To access it, on the Advanced tab, click Settings in the Performance area.

In the Performance window, you can set the size of your virtual memory and how the system handles the allocation of processor time. In Windows, you also use Performance to configure visual effects for the GUI.

How resources are allocated to the processor is normally not something that you will need to modify. It is set by default to optimize the system for foreground applications, making the system most responsive to the user who is running programs. This is generally best, but it means that any applications (databases, network services, and so on) that are run by the system are given less time by the system.

FIGURE 14.32   Windows System Properties Advanced Tab

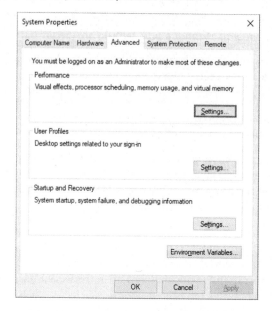

 If the Windows machine will be working primarily as a network server, you may want to change the Performance option to Background Services. You can find this in the Performance Options on the Advanced tab. Otherwise, leave it as is.

ENVIRONMENT VARIABLES

There are two types of *environment variables* (as shown in Figure 14.33), and you can access either one by clicking the Environment Variables button in the System Properties window.

User Variables   Specify settings for an individual user and do not affect others who log into the machine.

System Variables   Set for all users on the machine. System variables are used to provide information needed by the system when running applications or performing system tasks.

 System and user variables were extremely important in the early days of DOS and Windows. Their importance has lessened with recent Windows versions, but this is the interface where TEMP variables, the location of the OS, and other important settings for Windows can be found.

FIGURE 14.33   Windows environment variables

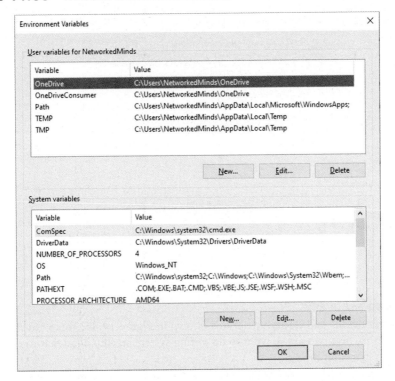

USER PROFILES

In Windows, every user is automatically given a *user profile* when they log into the workstation. This profile contains information about their settings and preferences. Although it does not happen often, occasionally a user profile becomes corrupted or needs to be destroyed. Alternatively, if a particular profile is set up appropriately, you can copy it so that it is available for other users. To do either of these tasks, use the User Profiles settings to select the user profile with which you wish to work. You will be given three options, as shown in Figure 14.34.

Change Type   The Change Type option enables you to configure a profile as local (the default) or roaming. If a user works at two machines, each machine will use a different profile. Updates to one machine will not be reflected on the other. If you have a network, roaming profiles can be configured to allow a user to have a single profile anywhere on the network. Further discussion of this topic is beyond the scope of this book.

Delete   The Delete option removes the user's profile entirely. When that user logs in again, they will be given a fresh profile taken from the system default. Any settings that they have added will be lost, as will any profile-related problems that they have caused.

Copy To   The Copy To option copies a profile from one user to another. Often the source profile is a template set up to provide a standard configuration.

FIGURE 14.34   Windows User Profiles Settings

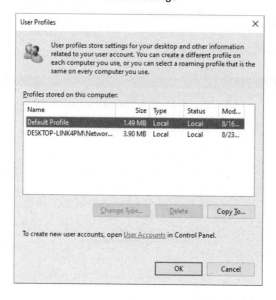

STARTUP AND RECOVERY

The Windows Startup And Recovery options, shown in Figure 14.35, are relatively straightforward. They involve two areas: what to do during system startup and what to do in case of unexpected system shutdown.

FIGURE 14.35   Windows Startup And Recovery options

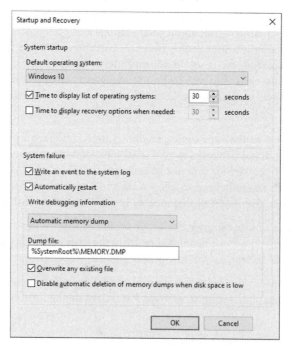

System Startup   The System Startup option defaults to the Windows OS you installed, but you can change this default behavior if you like. Unless you are *dual-booting*, only one option is available; however, if you have another OS installed, you can change the Windows boot manager to load that as the default. You can also reduce the time the menu (time to display list of operating systems or recovery options) is displayed or remove the menu entirely.

> **WARNING**   If you choose to disable the menu completely on a dual-boot system, you will find that doing so may cause you annoyance in the future when you want to boot into a different OS but no longer have a choice to do so. Thus, you should always let the boot menu appear for at least 2–5 seconds if you are dual-booting.

System Failure   A number of options are available in the Startup And Recovery dialog box for use in case of problems. These include writing an event about the problem, sending an alert to the network, and saving information about the problem to disk. These options come into play only in case of a major system problem.

System Protection

The System Protection tab lets you disable/enable and configure the System Restore feature, as shown in Figure 14.36. When System Restore is enabled on one or more drives, the operating system monitors the changes that you make on your drives. From time to time, it creates what is called a *restore point*. Then, if you have a system crash, it can restore your data back to the restore point. You can turn on System Restore for all drives on your system or for individual drives. Note that turning off System Restore on the system drive (the drive on which the OS is installed) automatically turns it off on all drives.

FIGURE 14.36   Windows System Protection Options

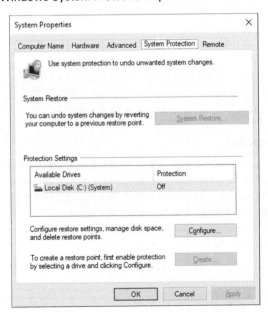

Remote

The Remote tab lets you enable or disable Remote Assistance and Remote Desktop, as shown in Figure 14.37. Remote Assistance permits people to access the system in response to requests issued by the local user using the Windows Remote Assistance tool. Remote Desktop permits people to log into the system at any time using the Remote Desktop Connection tool. This can help an administrator or other support person troubleshoot problems with the machine from a remote location.

FIGURE 14.37 Windows Remote options

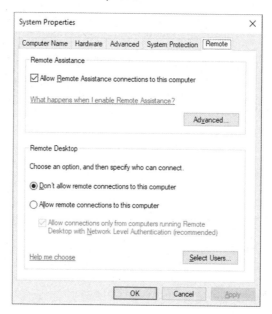

Remote Assistance is enabled by default. It is handled at two levels. Having just Remote Assistance turned on allows the person connecting to view the computer's screen. To let that person take over the computer and be able to control the keyboard and mouse, click Advanced, and then, in the Remote Control section, click Allow This Computer To Be Controlled Remotely. You can also configure Remote Desktop here.

User Accounts Applet

The User Accounts applet allows you to view and create accounts for the Windows operating system. You can change the account name that appears on the Welcome and Start screen. You can also change the account type by selecting the Standard or Administrator radio button. In Windows 10, the Settings app for Accounts allows you to change the picture that is displayed along with your username. In Windows 8/8.1 and Windows 7, the user picture can be selected from the User Accounts applet.

In addition to the management of user accounts, the User Accounts applet allows you to change the *User Account Control (UAC)* settings for the operating system, as shown in Figure 14.38.

FIGURE 14.38   Windows User Accounts applet

Power Options Applet

The Power Options applet (`powercfg.cpl`) allows you to choose a power plan of Balanced, Power Saver, or High Performance, as shown in Figure 14.39. Each power plan dictates when devices—namely, the display device and the computer—will turn off or be put to sleep.

FIGURE 14.39   Windows Power Options applet

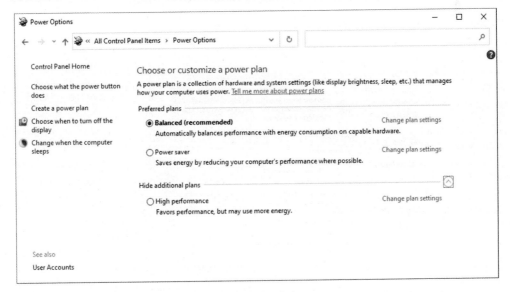

When you click Change Plan Settings, you can change how fast the display is turned off and how fast the computer is put to sleep, as shown in Figure 14.40.

FIGURE 14.40 Windows Edit Plan Settings

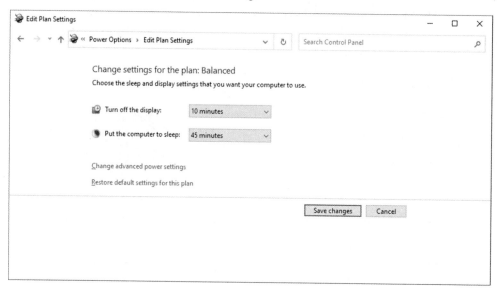

Clicking Change Advanced Power Settings allows you to configure a number of settings based on power, as shown in Figure 14.41. These settings include specifying when the hard drive turns off, turning off the wireless adapter, specifying Internet options for JavaScript Timer Frequency, and determining the system cooling policy. The applet allows you to tweak your power policy, and you can always restore the plan defaults.

FIGURE 14.41 Windows Advanced Power Settings

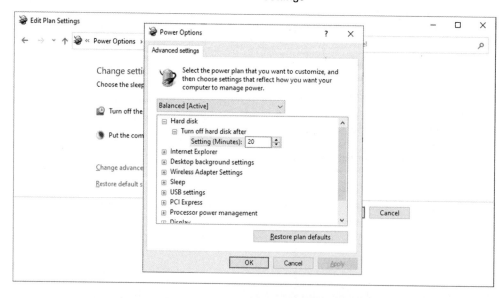

Power Management

The power plan configured in Windows will interface with the Advanced Configuration and Power Interface (ACPI). The ACPI must be supported by the system BIOS/UEFI in order to work properly. However, most computer hardware made in the last decade will support the ACPI. The ACPI on the computer hardware provides the operating system with the necessary methods for controlling the hardware. This is in contrast to Advanced Power Management (APM), which gave only a limited amount of power to the operating system and let the BIOS do all the real work. Because of this, it is not uncommon to find legacy systems that can support APM but not ACPI.

There are four main states of power management common in most operating systems:

Hibernate   This state saves all the contents of memory to the hard drive, preserves all data and applications exactly where they are, and allows the computer to power off completely. When the system comes out of hibernation, it returns to its previous state by restoring the contents of memory from the hard drive. This power state consumes the least amount of power and the system will appear to be completely off in this state. This power state is usually only available on laptops and not desktops.

Sleep/Suspend   In some operating systems, *Sleep* is used interchangeably with *Hibernate*, but that should not be the case. In Windows, Sleep puts the system in a low-power state, whereas Hibernate turns the system off, or at least it appears to be off.

Standby   The *standby* state might appear to be identical to the sleep mode, as it restores the system quickly. However, it is not really a power state. Standby mode typically reduces power and turns the screen off.

Shutdown/Turn Off   As the name implies, this shuts down everything and then turns off the system. You can shut down the system and have it stay off, or you can shut down the system and have it power back on (Restart). The latter option is often used when updates need to be applied.

Advanced Power Savings

If you are interested in saving power with a system that is not accessed often, one option is to employ Wake on LAN (WoL). Wake on LAN is an Ethernet standard implemented via a card that allows a "sleeping" machine to awaken when it receives a wakeup signal. Wake on LAN cards have more problems than standard network cards. In our opinion, this is because they're always on. In some cases, you'll be unable to get the card working again unless you unplug the PC's power supply and reset the card.

Another power-saving feature is to choose what happens when you close the lid of your laptop. This option is only available on laptop devices that have a lid closure sensor. The option can be found on the left-hand side of the Power Options Control Panel applet, and it's labeled Choose What Closing The Lid Does. When the dialog box opens, you will see drop-down menus for pressing the power button or sleep button and closing the lid, as shown in Figure 14.42. Depending on whether the laptop is plugged in or on battery power, you can choose a different option.

FIGURE 14.42   Windows Advanced Power System Settings

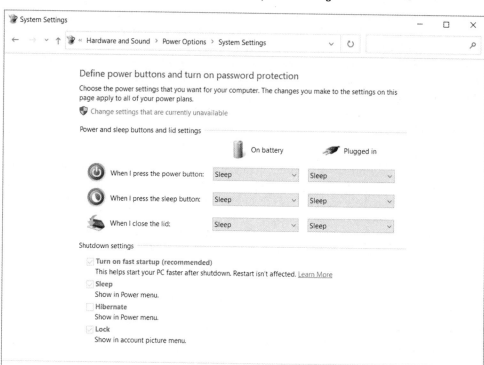

Windows Fast Startup is another advanced feature that was originally introduced with Window 8 as Fast Boot. The feature allows the system to hibernate during shutdown so that the system will appear to start up more quickly. The Fast Startup feature will attempt to know when a cold boot is required, such as when installing a program. If a cold boot is required, you have two options. The first option is to turn Fast Startup off in the Power Options System Settings, as shown in Figure 14.42. You can also use the shutdown /s /t 0 command; the /s switch will shut down the system and the /t 0 switch will do it immediately. The shutdown command also allows for shutdown of remote computers with the command shutdown /m \\computername /s /t 0.

The Universal Serial Bus (USB) selective suspend feature will allow the USB hub on the motherboard to suspend power to a device via the USB port. This is a handy feature to save battery power on a laptop if an external hard drive, a mouse, or some other device that requires power is not being used. However, this feature can also be problematic if you have a communication device connected via USB. You can turn this feature off on the Power Management tab of the device inside Device Manager, as shown in Figure 14.43.

FIGURE 14.43 Device Properties, Power Management tab

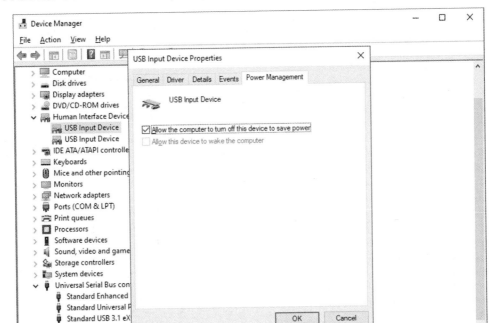

There is a lot more going on than just powering off a USB port with the USB selective suspend feature. The operating system communicates to the device via the device driver and signals the device itself to power down. The system or the device can then send a wake-up signal to restore operations. You can find more information at `https://docs .microsoft.com/en-us/windows-hardware/drivers/usbcon/usb-selective-suspend`.

Credential Manager Applet

The Credential Manager applet allows you to manage stored credentials for applications such as the Internet Explorer and Microsoft Edge browsers, as well as the operating system itself. The Credential Manager service built into Microsoft operating systems stores username and password credentials in an encrypted database. The applet allows you to interact with the service to make changes to the stored credentials, as shown in Figure 14.44.

FIGURE 14.44 Windows Credential Manager applet

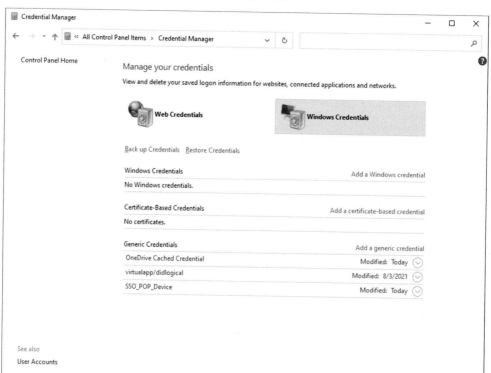

Programs and Features Applet

The Programs and Features applet (`appwiz.cpl`) allows you to view and uninstall desktop applications that are installed in Windows, as shown in Figure 14.45. You can also see the installed updates by clicking View Installed Updates on the left side of the applet.

The Programs and Features applet also allows you to install and remove features in Windows. When you click Turn Windows Features On Or Off on the left side, a dialog box will appear with a list of OS features that can be selected or deselected. Features are different from desktop applications because they are an integral part of the operating system. Examples include *Hyper-V*, Internet Explorer 11, and Windows PowerShell 2.0, just to name a few.

Devices and Printers Applet

The Devices and Printers applet allows you to manage external devices such as external hard drives, printers, and webcams. From Control Panel, you can discover and add new devices that are connected to your network. Devices and Printers is shown in Figure 14.46.

FIGURE 14.45   Windows Programs and Features applet

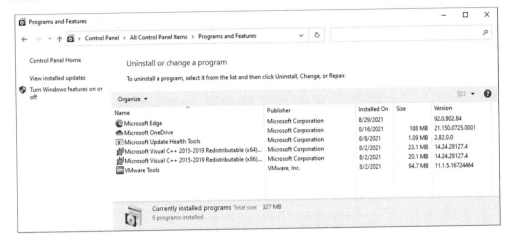

FIGURE 14.46   Windows Devices and Printers applet

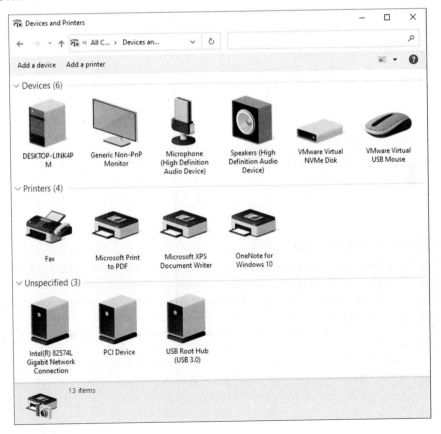

Sound Applet

The Sound applet (`mmsys.cpl`) allows you to view and change the default playback and recording device for sound on the system. By right-clicking the device and choosing Properties, you can view and modify the properties of a playback or recording device. The changes will vary by the device and the vendor of the device—common options are playback and recording levels and enhancements to the playback and recording levels. In addition, the Sound applet enables you to change the operating system's sound scheme, allowing you to change the various sounds, as shown in Figure 14.47.

FIGURE 14.47   Windows Sound applet

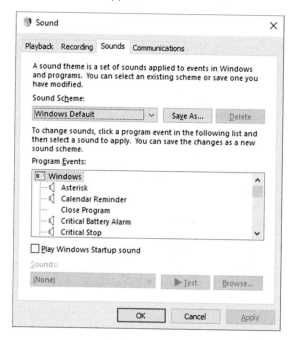

Troubleshooting Applet

The Troubleshooting applet does exactly what its name says it does—it allows troubleshooting of Programs, Hardware and Sound, Network and Internet, and System and Security, as shown in Figure 14.48. Troubleshooting has one notable feature: application compatibility troubleshooting. When this feature identifies any application that is problematic, the Troubleshooting wizard will appear and Windows will try to troubleshoot the application compatibility.

FIGURE 14.48   Windows Troubleshooting applet

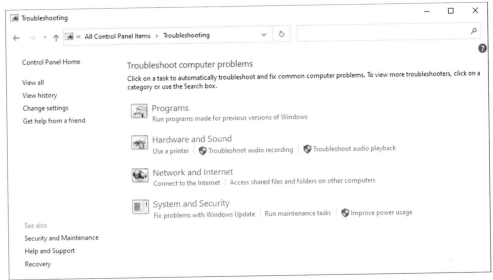

Network and Sharing Center Applet

The Network and Sharing Center applet allows you to view and change the active network connections for the operating system, as shown in Figure 14.49. The applet displays the current network profile that the computer has been placed into by the Windows Firewall service. From the main page of the applet, you can click Change Adapter Settings to see the classic network adapter view, which allows the adapters to be configured manually. From the main page of the applet, you can also click Change Advanced Sharing Settings on the left side. This allows you to change network discovery options for the network profile chosen as well as turn on or off file and printer sharing globally for the operating system.

Device Manager Applet

The Device Manager applet (`hdwwiz.cpl`) was first introduced in Windows 95 and has hardly changed since its introduction over 20 years ago. If the applet looks familiar, it is the same as the MMC Device Manager (`devmgmt.msc`). Device Manager allows you to view and change hardware devices on the operating system, as shown in Figure 14.50. This applet allows the administrator to load and update third-party drivers as well as drivers in the Windows Catalog. Device Manager is usually the first place you should check if a hardware device does not function after installation.

FIGURE 14.49 Windows Network and Sharing Center applet

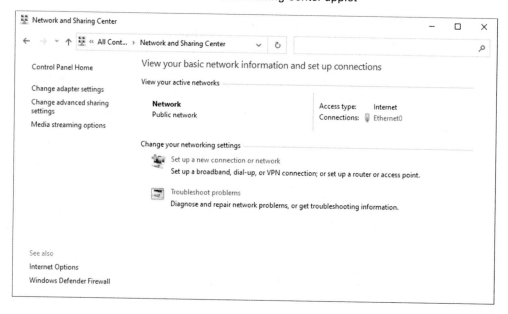

FIGURE 14.50 Windows Device Manager

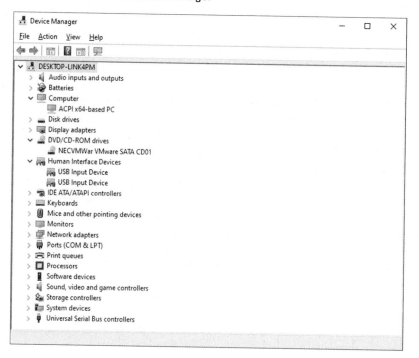

BitLocker Applet

BitLocker drive encryption is a low-level full-disk encryption feature that can be controlled from the BitLocker Drive Encryption applet, as shown in Figure 14.51. The BitLocker Drive Encryption applet also allows you to turn on BitLocker drive encryption on removable media devices.

FIGURE 14.51   Windows BitLocker Drive Encryption applet

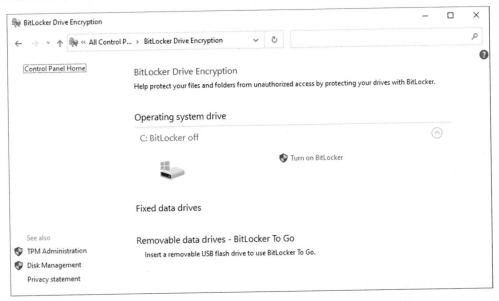

Windows Defender Firewall

The Windows Firewall (`firewall.cpl`), which in Windows 10 is named Windows Defender Firewall, is used to block access from the network (be it internal or the Internet). While *host-based firewalls* are not as secure as other types of firewalls, this was a great move in the right direction. It first appeared in Windows XP Service Pack 2 but was released as a polished product in Windows Vista.

Figure 14.52 shows the opening screen of Windows Defender Firewall in Windows 10/11. Windows Defender Firewall is turned on by default. It also blocks incoming traffic by default.

Clicking Advanced Settings on the left opens the Windows Defender Firewall with Advanced Security MMC, as shown in Figure 14.53. This MMC allows great control of the Windows Defender Firewall controls for inbound and outbound rules. Inbound rules can be created to allow and deny network traffic inbound to applications and the operating system. Outbound rules can be created to allow and deny network traffic leaving the operating system. Only inbound firewall rules are restricted by default. When an application attempts to listen to specific network traffic, the operating system will display a dialog box asking you to confirm the network activity. This dialog box will automatically create an inbound rule for the application's traffic. The Windows Defender Firewall with Advanced Security MMC allows you to pre-create the rule. In addition, you can create connection security rules for authenticating and encrypting traffic.

FIGURE 14.52   Windows Defender Firewall in Windows 10

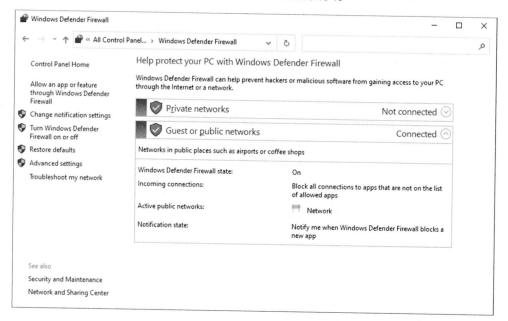

Mail Applet

When Microsoft Outlook is installed in Windows, it is configured through the Mail applet. If you do not have Microsoft Outlook installed, the icon will simply not show up in Control Panel. The Mail applet is how you configure an email account, additional data files (OST files), RSS feeds, SharePoint lists, Internet calendars, published calendars, and address books, as shown in Figure 14.54. In the main dialog box you can even set up different profiles for different accounts. If more than one profile is configured, you will be prompted when Outlook launches to specify the profile you want to use.

Outlook will usually configure itself automatically by asking a series of questions when it first launches. The initial configuration will be stored and can be accessed by launching the Mail applet.

FIGURE 14.53   Windows Defender Firewall with Advanced Security in Windows

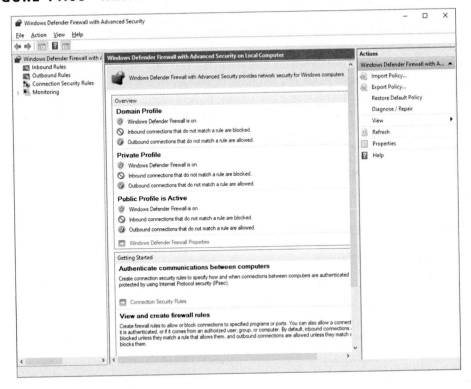

FIGURE 14.54   Outlook Mail applet

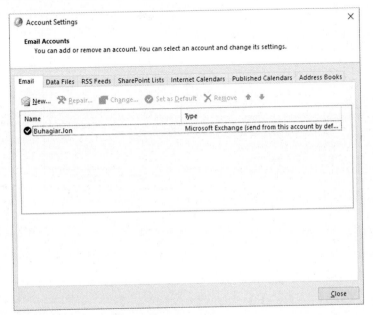

Indexing Options Applet

The Indexing service was introduced as a desktop search engine with Windows NT 4.0. Today the Indexing service is an integral part of Windows 10/11. It's an exceptional feature that is a requirement for today's volume of data. The Indexing service will systematically index files such as Microsoft Office documents, PDFs, text files, and many other files types. When searching for a word using File Explorer in a folder that is indexed, the Indexing service is queried directly, thus returning fast results. If the folder is not indexed, then the search process grinds through each file in the folder and produces results at a much slower pace.

You access the Indexing Options dialog box, shown in Figure 14.55, by using the Index Options applet in Control Panel. The default locations indexed are Internet Explorer History, Start Menu, and the Users folder (excluding AppData files). You can add locations to be indexed if you store files outside the normal Documents or Desktop locations that are contained inside the Users folder.

FIGURE 14.55   Indexing Options dialog box

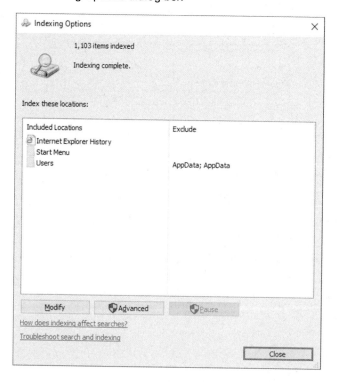

By clicking Advanced in the Indexing Options dialog box, you open the dialog box shown in Figure 14.56. There you can choose to index encrypted files and to treat words with diacritics (accents) as different words. You can also rebuild the index in an attempt to fix missing documents from your search. This dialog box also allows you to relocate the index database. The File Types tab allows you to add various file types to index. It contains a very inclusive range of file types, but by default many are set to index just metadata on the file. Important file types like DOCX and PDF are set to index the contents.

FIGURE 14.56   Advanced Options for indexing

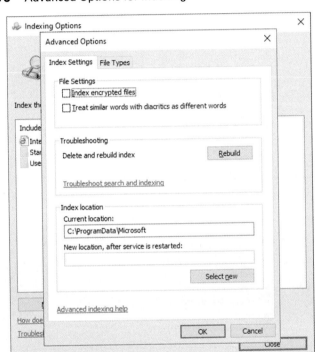

Ease of Access Center Applet

The Ease of Access Center applet contains various settings that make it easier to use Windows for motor and sensory impaired users, as shown in Figure 14.57. There is a wide range of tools, such as a magnifier, narrator, on-screen keyboard, and a high-contrast color scheme. In the many versions of Windows over the years, the accessibility tools have become expansive. Microsoft has continually added tools and settings to this applet to allow anyone with an impairment to use the operating system to its fullest.

FIGURE 14.57   Ease of Access Center applet

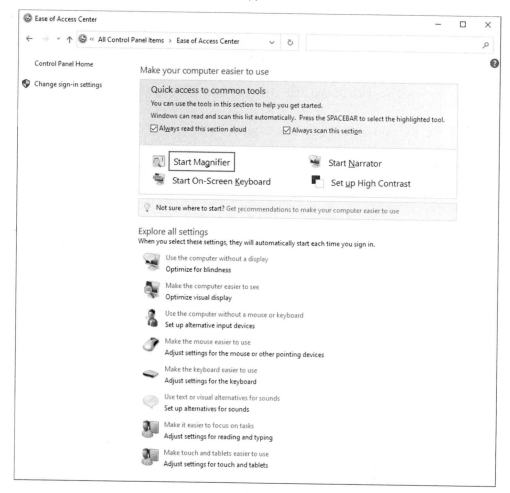

Administrative Tools Applet

The Administrative Tools applet isn't really an applet at all; it is like a shortcut to various tools, as shown in Figure 14.58. These tools all have a common theme: administering the operating system. Many of these tools can be accessed in other ways, such as right-clicking the Start button or using the Start menu and expanding Windows Administrative Tools.

In this array of tools, you can configure component services, clean up and defragment the disk, set up iSCSI connections, edit the local security policy, set up Open Database Connectivity (ODBC) connectors, create recovery media, schedule tasks, and perform memory diagnostics. These are just a few tasks that we haven't already covered.

FIGURE 14.58　Administrative Tools applet

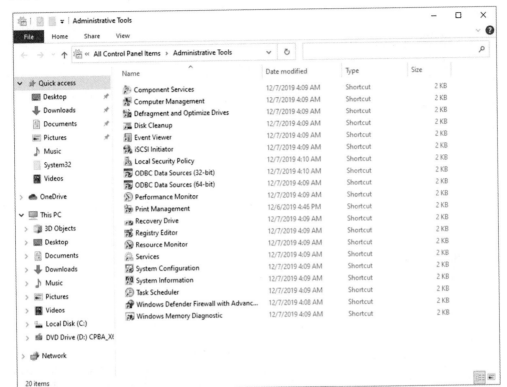

Windows Settings

The Windows Settings app first made its debut in Windows 8. It was Microsoft's attempt to make configuring Windows simpler for end users. Many of the configuration tasks formerly performed in Control Panel have been either duplicated in the Settings apps or replaced entirely. The appearance of the Settings app has created anxiety for both end users and administrators alike, because it's a change (albeit unwanted) from the Control Panel that has been around since Windows 95.

You can open the Settings app by clicking the Start menu and selecting the gear on the left-hand side. The Settings app will open to the screen shown in Figure 14.59. Here, you can search for the setting you need, or you can choose from various categories. The search capability has been a welcomed feature, since every release of Windows introduces new settings.

FIGURE 14.59 Windows 10 Settings app

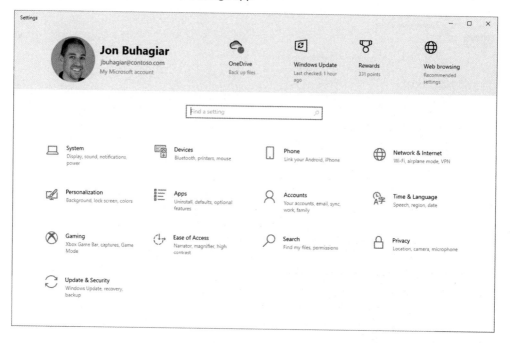

Many of the settings that are covered in this section have also been covered in the Control Panel section, as per the objectives of the CompTIA 220-1102 exam. It is good to know both ways to access settings, since many of the settings in Control Panel have not been moved over to the Settings app. Likewise, many of the settings in the Settings app can only be found in the app, because they are entirely new settings.

Time and Language

The Time and Language screen in the Settings app allows you to change settings related to the date and time in Windows 10/11, as shown in Figure 14.60. Click Time & Language to change anything that you can change in Control Panel.

The Set Time Automatically switch is set by default and synchronizes with Network Time Protocol (NTP) server of time.windows.com. You can choose to have Windows adjust the time zone automatically, or you can manually change the time zone. This dialog box also allows for customized calendars in the taskbar.

FIGURE 14.60   Date & Time settings

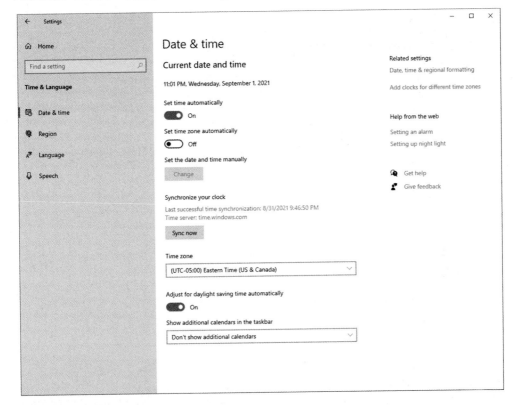

On the left side, under Time & Language, select Region. Changing the Country or Region setting allows Windows to deliver content relevant to the area where you reside. This dialog box also allows you to change the way values such as money, time, and date are formatted. If you select Language from the left side, you can set the Windows display language as well as the preferred language, as shown in Figure 14.61. In addition, you can set the keyboard language and speech language preferences.

Update and Security

The Update and Security category is where you can access all settings related to Windows updates and security, as shown in Figure 14.62. Windows 10 removed the option to control Windows updates from Control Panel and forces you to configure Windows updates in the Settings app.

FIGURE 14.61 Language settings

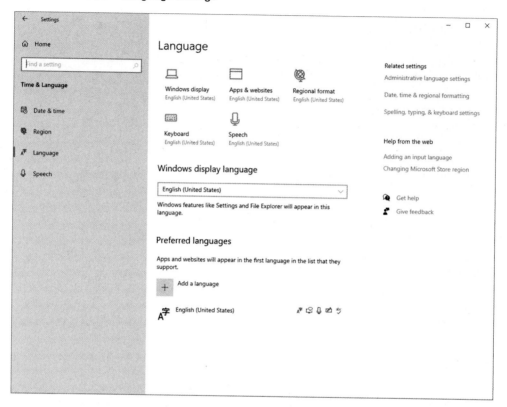

From this initial screen, you can check for Windows updates, as well as control downloads and installation, view the optional updates, pause updates, change your active hours, view update history, and set advanced options. Advanced options allow you to specify whether you want to receive updates for other Microsoft products, download updates over metered connections, determine how soon Windows is restarted after updates are applied, update notifications, and whether to pause updates until a certain date.

If you click Delivery Optimization on the Advanced Options screen for the Windows Update settings, you can change where Windows receives updates. By default, Windows will attempt to download updates from other PCs on the local network in order to conserve bandwidth. If the updates are not available, then Windows will download the updates from the Windows Update service.

FIGURE 14.62   Windows Update settings

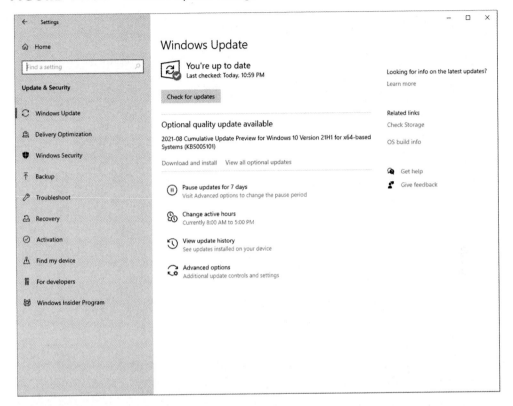

The Windows Security option on the left side of the screen allows you to change a number of security-related items, as shown in Figure 14.63. From this screen, you can view Virus & Threat Protection, Account Protection, Firewall & Network Protection, App & Browser Control, Device Security, Device Performance & Health, and Family Options. The Windows Security screen is a one-stop shop for everything security-related for the operating system.

In addition to Windows Updates and security-related configuration. the Update & Security screen allows you to access several other options. The Backup section allows you to back up files to OneDrive, back up using File History, and open the prior Backup and Restore utility. The Backup screen is shown in Figure 14.64.

FIGURE 14.63 Windows Security settings

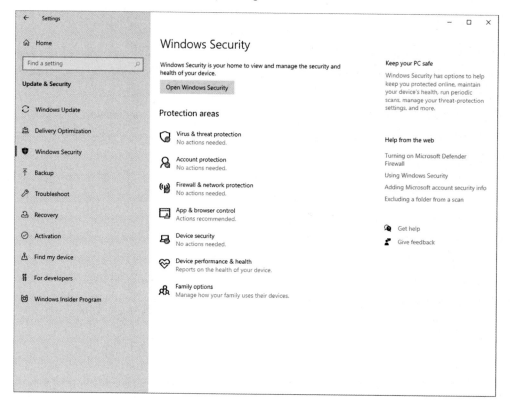

The Troubleshoot section allows you to specify how Windows will run the trouble-shooting recommendations. Also, you can view troubleshooting history and run additional troubleshooters. The Recovery section allows you to reset the operating system back to the original state by using the Reset This PC option. You can also use advanced startup options by clicking Restart Now under Advanced Startup, as shown in Figure 14.65.

FIGURE 14.64   Windows Backup settings

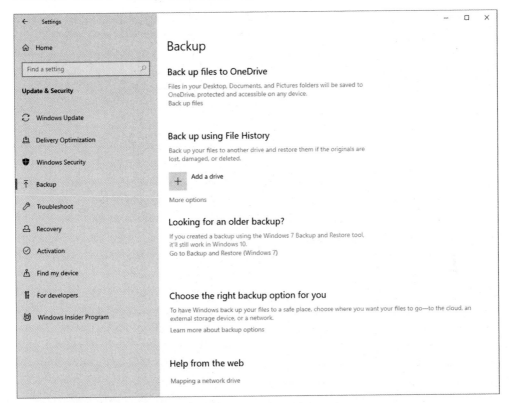

The Activation section allows you to activate Windows 10/11 or change the product key. The Find My Device section lets you track your device, if you misplace or lose the device. For Developers allows you to change how the operating system behaves, such as allowing apps to be installed from files, device discovery, and other developer-friendly settings for File Explorer, as shown in Figure 14.66.

The last section in the Update & Security screen is the Windows Insider Program. Here you can enroll in the Windows Insider Program to get the most advanced set of features that Microsoft is developing for Windows.

FIGURE 14.65 Windows Recovery settings

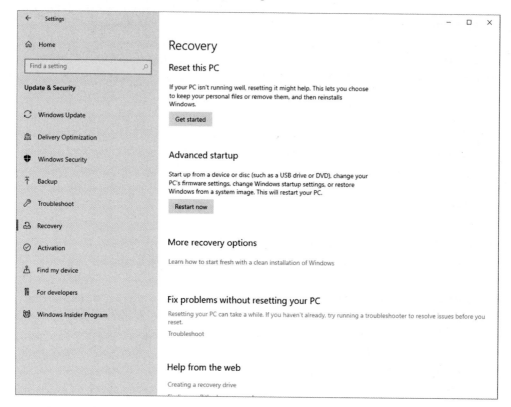

Personalization

The classic Display applet has been removed from the Windows 10 Control Panel. You can now change display settings in the Personalization screen, shown in Figure 14.67. You can configure the background, formerly known as the wallpaper.

The Colors section allows you to change the colors for the Windows controls and application controls. Lock Screen allows you to configure how the lock screen looks and what is displayed on the screen when it is locked. By default, the background is set to Windows Spotlight. The Spotlight feature downloads pictures from Bing and displays them on the lock screen. You can also configure which applications will display their status on the lock screen. As with prior versions of Windows, the theme can be changed using the Themes section. Changing the theme will change the background, colors, sounds, and mouse cursor. You can even download more themes from the Microsoft Store. The Fonts section allows you to view all the installed fonts on Windows, as well as install new fonts by dragging and dropping them. The Fonts section also contains a link to open the Microsoft Store so you can download additional fonts. The Start section allows you to personalize the Start menu, as shown in Figure 14.68. You can change a number of settings, such as displaying the app list in the Start menu, showing recently added apps, and showing the suggestions, just to name a few settings.

FIGURE 14.66   Windows For Developers settings

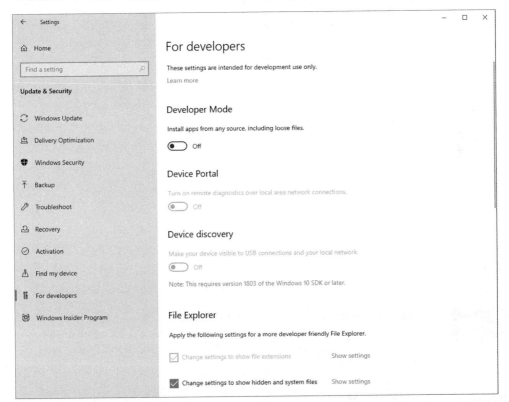

The Taskbar section allows you to change a number of settings. You can lock the taskbar from changes, automatically hide the taskbar, use small taskbar buttons, turn on Peek to preview when the mouse cursor hovers over an application, change the orientation of the taskbar on the screen, and a number of other settings.

FIGURE 14.67 Windows 10 Personalization settings

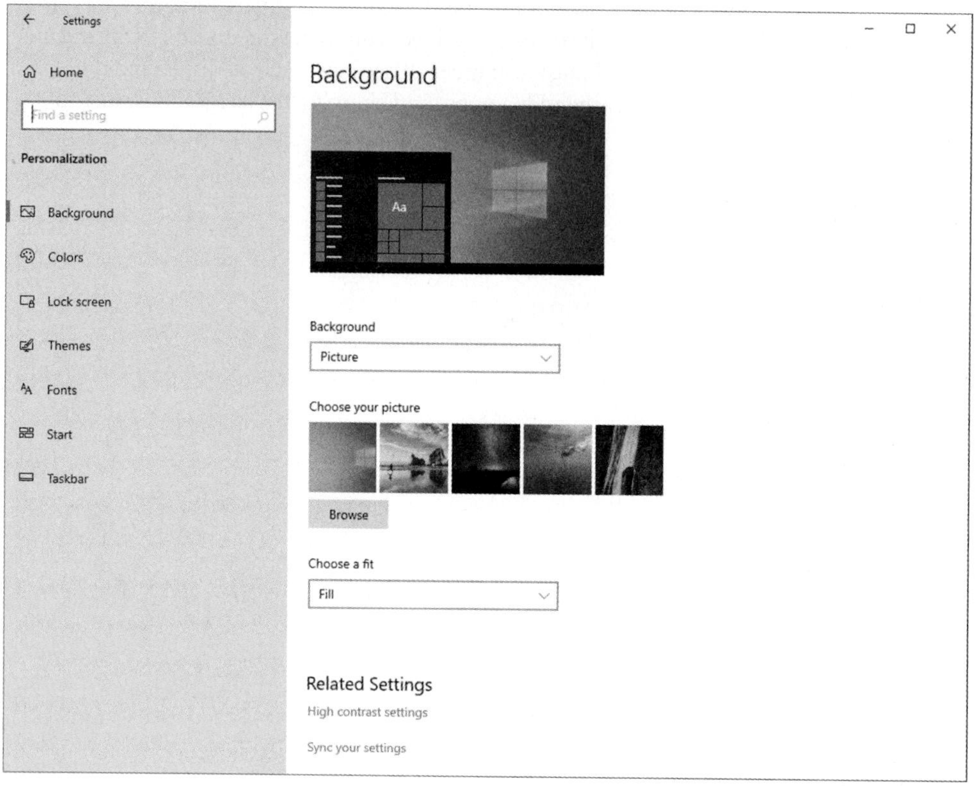

← Settings		− □ ✕
⌂ Home	**Background**	
[find a setting 🔍]		
Personalization		
▭ Background		
◈ Colors		
⬚ Lock screen	**Background**	
⬚ Themes	[Picture ∨]	
ᴬᴬ Fonts	Choose your picture	
⬚ Start		
▭ Taskbar	[Browse]	
	Choose a fit	
	[Fill ∨]	
	Related Settings	
	High contrast settings	
	Sync your settings	

Windows 8/8.1 and Windows 10/11 do not support changing the depth of color from 32-bit to 16-bit. If an application requires a color depth of 16-bit, use the Application Compatibility tab in the application's Properties dialog box to set 16-bit color.

Apps

The Apps section will eventually replace the Program and Features Control Panel, since it performs many of the same functions. This section opens to the Apps & Features subsections, as shown in Figure 14.69. This section will allow you to change the source of apps in relation to the Microsoft Store. You can also uninstall apps by right-clicking the app and selecting Uninstall. By clicking Optional Features, you can choose to uninstall a feature or add a new one.

FIGURE 14.68   Windows 10 Start settings

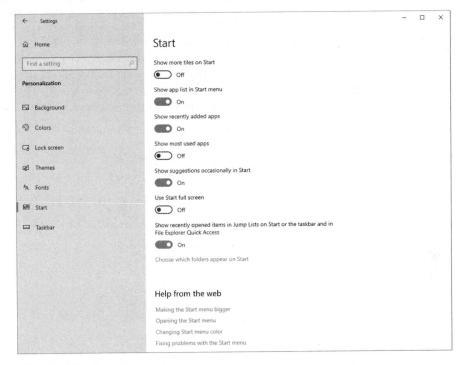

FIGURE 14.69   Windows 10 Apps & Features settings

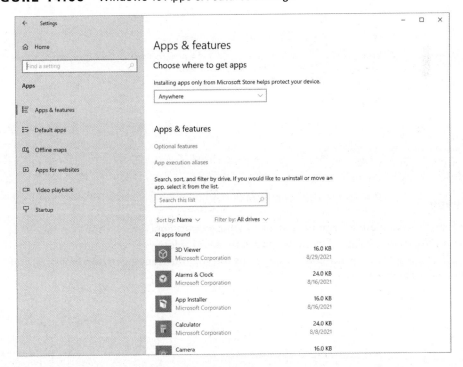

In the Default Apps section, you can select the default app for email, maps, music, photos, videos, and websites. You also have the option to set the default app by the file type of the file or the network protocol being used. Offline Maps allows you to download maps, as well as update the already downloaded maps. Use the Apps For Websites section to associate an app with a website. Doing so causes the app to "spring into action" when a website is visited, making it a seamless experience. The Video Playback section allows you to tweak how a video will look when played back on Windows. Use the Startup section to specify which applications start in the background, as shown in Figure 14.70.

FIGURE 14.70   Windows 10 Start settings

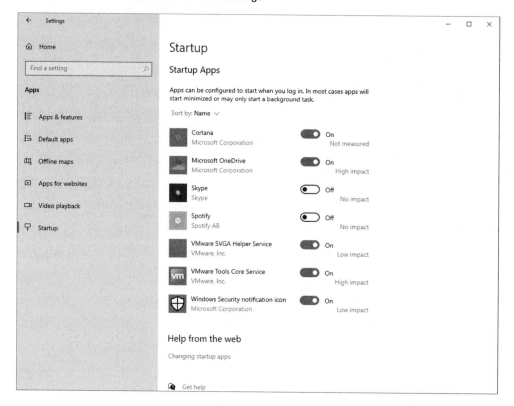

Privacy

The Privacy section allows you to control all your privacy concerns with Windows 10/11. The opening section, General, is shown in Figure 14.71. Here you can control your advertising ID, how websites make content decisions for you, the tracking of app launches, and suggested content settings.

FIGURE 14.71   Windows 10 General Privacy Settings

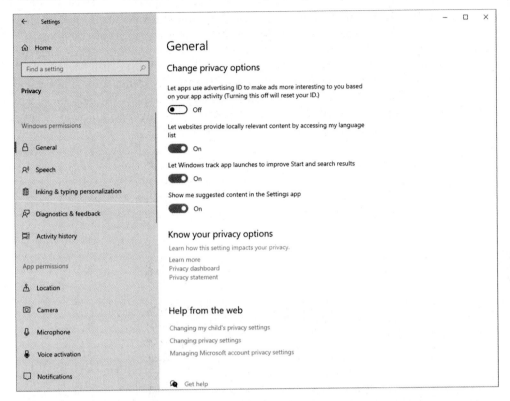

The Speech section allows you to control how your voice is used for speech recognition with Microsoft's online speech recognition technology. Inking & Typing Personalization allows you to control whether your handwriting is used to build a personal dictionary of words. In Diagnostic & Feedback, you control how your personal information is used to provide diagnostic and feedback statistics to Microsoft. The Activity History section lets you control if your activity is stored and tracked on the device. This setting is useful if you want to view recent documents; press the Windows key + Tab and Windows will show you all your previous documents. You can clear history and turn off all tracking.

In addition to the aforementioned Windows permission settings, you can view and control App permissions. The various permissions that can be viewed and controlled are as follows: Location, Camera, Microphone, Voice Activation, Notifications, Account Info, Contacts, Calendar, Phone Calls, Call History, Email, Tasks, Messaging, Radios, Other Devices, Background Apps, App Diagnostics, Automatic File Downloads, Documents, Pictures, Videos, and File System. This is quite an exhaustive list, and you can review and control each of these permissions for a particular application.

System

The System section allows you to change a multitude of settings that pertain to the operating system, as shown in Figure 14.72. In the Display section, you can arrange your monitors, if you have more than one. You can also change how the additional monitors operate, such as extending or duplicating your desktop. You can also turn on the feature called Night Light that restricts the blue light the display normally emits. The Display section also allows you to tune the Windows high dynamic range (HDR) of colors on your display. The most important settings are probably the display resolution and Scale And Layout settings, which allow you to get the most out of your display.

FIGURE 14.72 Windows 10 System settings

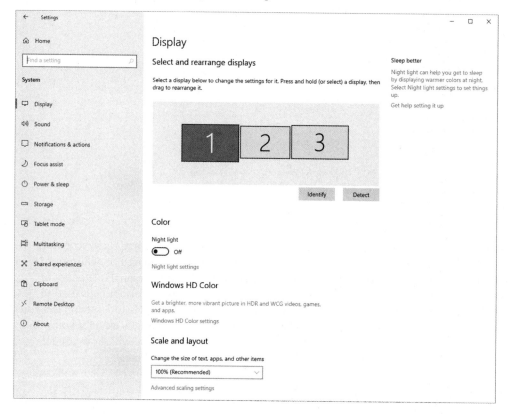

In the Sound section, you select your output and input devices, as shown in Figure 14.73. You can also click the Troubleshoot button to help you identify sound issues. The Sound section is similar to the Sounds Control Panel applet, because it allows you to change the sound devices and control volume levels.

FIGURE 14.73 Windows 10 Sound settings

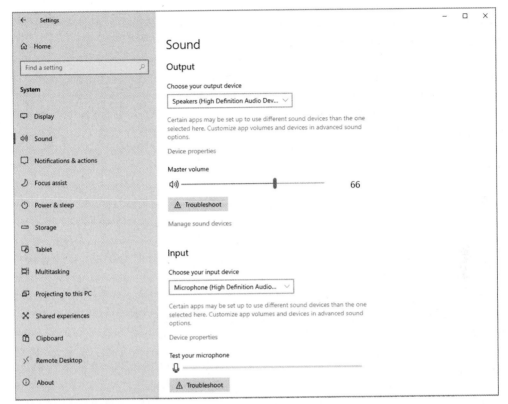

The Notifications & Actions section allows you to change the way the operating system notifications behave. You can control all operating system notifications, change lock screen notifications, control reminder and incoming VoIP calls on the lock screen, and specify whether notifications play sounds, among other settings. The Focus Assist section allows you to control which notifications come to your attention and when they notify you; you can, for example, choose to suppress notifications when you are playing a video game. The Power & Sleep section is identical to the Power Control Panel applet. Here you can change when the screen turns off and when the operating system enters sleep mode. The Storage section provides a graphical overview of space used on the local disk, as shown in Figure 14.74. Clicking each category of storage brings up a different view of the storage. For example, Apps & Features displays all the applications you can uninstall on the operating system, and Temporary Files displays all the various temporary files on the operating system (you can then choose to remove them). A feature called Storage Sense can be turned on, which automatically frees up space on the local disk by removing unneeded files.

FIGURE 14.74 Windows 10 Storage settings

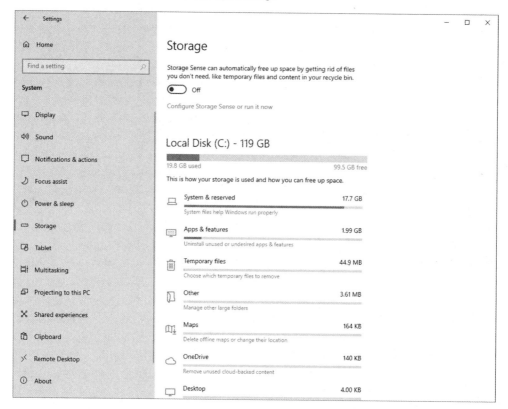

The Tablet section lets you control how the device performs when you remove the keyboard and convert it to a tablet. Use the Multitasking section to control Snap Assist, which is how an application or window snaps into a corner of the screen. You can also change the way the Alt + Tab keys display applications. In addition, you can configure how virtual desktops are used in Windows 10/11. The Projecting To This PC section allows you to control how other devices project their displays to Windows 10/11. The protocol used is called Miracast, which is a technology that allows screen sharing across devices. The Shared Experiences section allows you to control how apps are shared across multiple devices. You can start a task on one device and finish it on another device, if you are logged into both devices and have the feature turned on. The Clipboard section allows you to control how the clipboard operates. You can turn on features like Clipboard History, which enables you to have multiple items in your clipboard. You can even sync clipboards across multiple devices. Use the Remote Desktop section to enable and disable the Remote Desktop feature, which allows you to connect remotely to the PC. The last section, About, allows you to view information about the PC and rename it, if you want.

Devices

The Devices section allows you to view, control, and configure all devices connected to the PC. This section will eventually replace the Devices and Printers Control Panel applet. The opening screen of Bluetooth & Other Devices allows you to view and configure devices that are directly connected to the system, connected via Bluetooth, or connected via another wireless technology, as shown in Figure 14.75. On this screen, you can add a Bluetooth device with a pairing process.

FIGURE 14.75   Windows 10 Devices settings

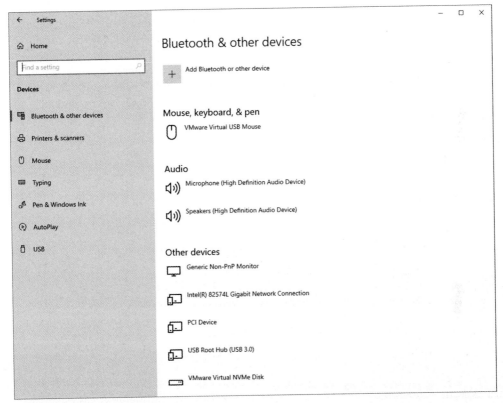

The Printers & Scanners section allows you to view and configure all of the installed printers and imaging devices on the operating system. You can allow Windows to manage the default printer, and Windows will select the most recently used printer as your default. You also have the option to add additional printers or scanners. The Mouse section lets you change how the mouse behaves on the operating system. You can change settings like which button on the mouse is your primary button, your cursor speed, how the scroll wheel advances, and other mouse-related settings. Use the Typing section to control whether spell check is enabled and whether suggestions are turned on as you type. The Pen & Windows Ink section contains settings related to handwriting, such as the font to use when converting handwriting. The AutoPlay section allows you to control how AutoPlay works for media and devices connected to Windows. You can choose a default action for removable drives or memory cards inserted. The USB section allows you to control notifications if a USB device is not working correctly or has issues.

Network & Internet

Use the Network & Internet section to view and control network settings for Windows, as well as Internet settings. The opening screen is the Status screen, and it displays the current network status for the Network connection, as shown in Figure 14.76. On this screen you can click Properties and change various properties of the network connection, such as the public or private firewall posture, metered connection setting, and IP addressing. A newer feature lets you view the data usage for each application, which makes it easy to find an application that uses a lot of bandwidth.

FIGURE 14.76   Windows 10 Network & Internet settings

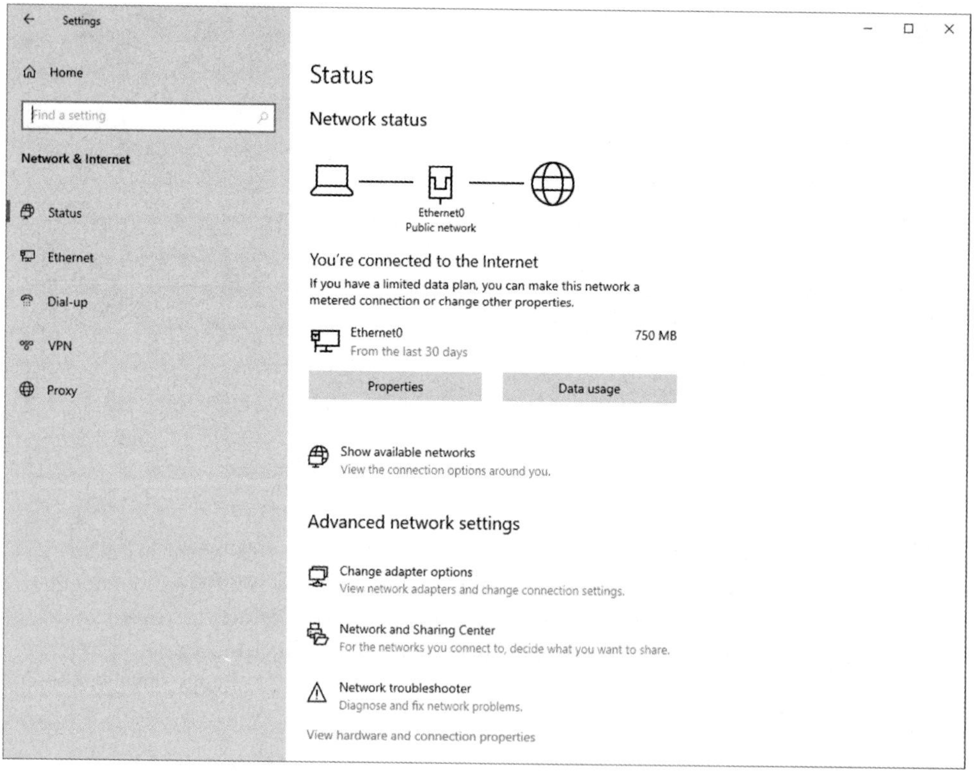

In addition to viewing and changing basic properties for the network connection, you can open the traditional view of network adapters, access the Network and Sharing Center, and open the Network Troubleshooter. The Ethernet section allows you to open the traditional view of network adapters as well. Use this section to configure advanced sharing options, such as network discovery and file and printer sharing. This section also lets you specify a shortcut to open the Network and Sharing Center as well as the Window Firewall.

Although it's unlikely you have a dial-up connection, the Network & Internet section includes a screen for configuring dial-up connections. This section, just like the Ethernet section, provides a way to open the traditional view of network adapters, access the Network and Sharing Center, and turn on Windows Firewall.

Use the VPN (virtual private network) section to view and configure settings for VPN connections, as shown in Figure 14.77. You can add a VPN connection or change advanced options, such as allowing VPN over metered networks or allowing VPN connections while roaming if a cellular modem is being used. The same shortcuts to adapter settings, Advanced Sharing Options, Network and Sharing Center, and the Windows Firewall are also available.

FIGURE 14.77   Windows 10 VPN settings

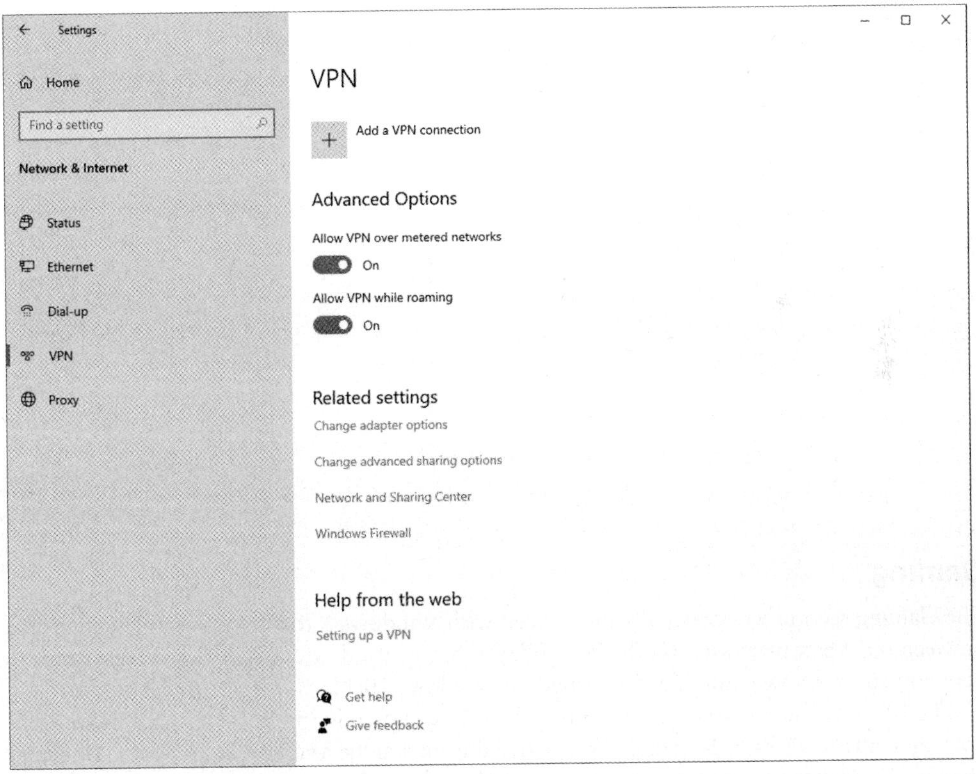

The last section is Proxy, where you can configure a proxy for the currently logged-on user, as shown in Figure 14.78. Here you set the proxy that Internet Explorer 11 and Microsoft Edge will use. Other applications that use the common Microsoft web controls will also use the proxy server. By default, Automatically Detect Settings is enabled, but you can elect to use a setup script instead. It is a common task to manually set a proxy server, which will be in the form of an IP address or *fully qualified domain name (FQDN)*, along with the port and a bypass list of addresses.

FIGURE 14.78   Windows 10 Proxy settings

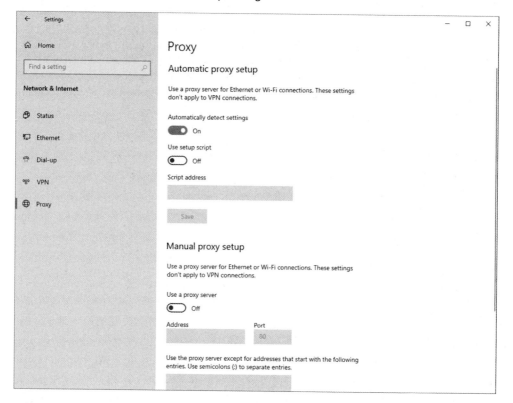

Gaming

The Gaming section was originally introduced with Windows 8 to create a seamless interface between the Xbox platform and the PC. Today, it has evolved into a very rich feature, and here you control how gaming is performed on Windows 10/11.

The Xbox Game Bar section is the opening screen, shown in Figure 14.79. In this section, you can control whether the game bar is active during a game and how it launches. You can change any of the shortcut keys related to the Xbox Game Bar.

FIGURE 14.79   Windows 10 Gaming settings

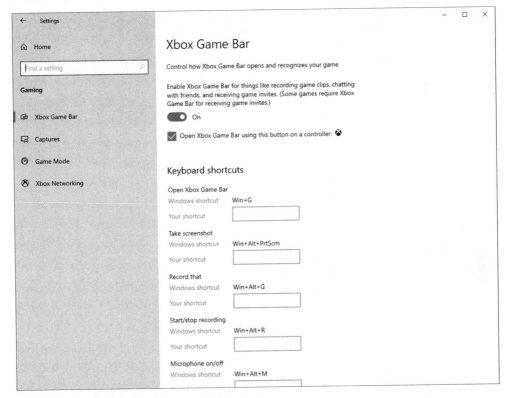

The most important key sequence is the Windows + G key, which launches the Xbox Game Bar, as shown in Figure 14.80. However, if you have an Xbox controller, the Xbox key will launch the game bar.

The Captures section allows you to configure where screenshots and recorded captures are saved. You can manage all aspects of the capture in this section, such as recording length, recording audio, audio quality, microphone and system volume levels, recorded frames per second, and overall video quality. Use the Game Mode section to control the game mode, which turns off Windows updates so they don't interrupt gameplay. You can also adjust the quality of gameplay to deliver the best frame rate, and manually change the Graphics settings for performance of either desktop apps or Microsoft Store apps.

The last section in the Gaming setting is the Xbox Networking section, which helps an Xbox Live player diagnose problems with gameplay and networking. This section automatically checks Internet connectivity, Xbox Live services, your latency to these services, and packet loss. It displays the latency, packet loss, the type of NAT your router is using, and local server connectivity. The type of NAT and local service connectivity setting affect others wishing to connect to your computer for multiplayer games.

FIGURE 14.80 Windows 10 Xbox Game Bar

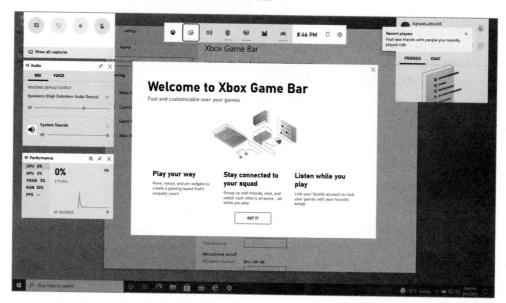

Accounts

The Accounts section allows you to view and configure all the settings for your user account, as well as other accounts on the operating system. The default screen is the Your Info screen, and it will display all of the information about your account, such as name, email address, and account type, as shown in Figure 14.81. You also have the option of managing your Microsoft account online.

The Email & Accounts section enables you to add an email account that is used for email, calendar, and contact information. You can also change accounts used by other apps, such as the Microsoft Store app, that require a login. This section also allows you to change the default apps associated with files and actions, such as viewing a movie, listening to music, or browsing the web.

Use Sign-in Options to change the way you log into Windows. The Windows Hello feature is configured on this screen, as shown in Figure 14.82. Windows Hello allows you to substitute your face, fingerprint, PIN, security key, or picture password for your actual password. The Hello feature works by storing your real credentials, such as your username and password, in Credential Manager. Credential Manager is then locked with this process. When you attempt to log in with a picture of your face, Windows Hello will unlock the credentials stored in Credential Manager and pass the actual username and password to the operating system. Dynamic Lock is another feature that can be configured in this section. Dynamic Lock will dynamically lock your computer when you walk away with a device that is paired to the laptop, such as a mobile device.

FIGURE 14.81   Windows 10 Accounts, Your Info

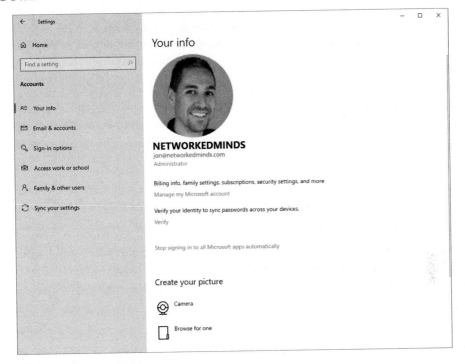

FIGURE 14.82   Windows 10 Hello

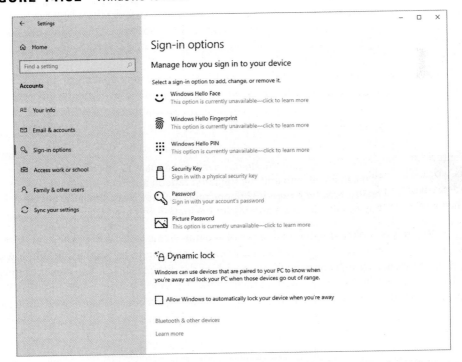

The Access Work Or School section is used to connect the operating system with a corporate or school account. These accounts usually contain mobile device management (MDM) settings. This passes some or all of the control of the operating system to the organization responsible for the account. The enrollment of the operating system into an MDM system can be performed with a provisioning package to help simplify the enrollment process. You can also export management log files for analysis if something is not functioning properly with the MDM control. You can set up an account for test taking, which locks the operating system down when it is logged into.

The Family & Other Users section allows you to add family member accounts. You can then limit time, apps, appropriate websites, and games. In addition, you can add others to log into the operating system who are not controlled via your family group. Windows 10/11 also has the ability to be set up as a kiosk. You launch a wizard that will create a local account, and you can then choose a kiosk app. When the kiosk mode is enabled, the operating system will boot up, automatically login as the local user created, and the configured app with run.

The last section, Sync Your Settings, allows you to choose what is synced from one Windows system to another Windows system. You can sync your theme, passwords, language preferences, and other Windows settings.

The Windows Registry

Windows configuration information is stored in a special configuration database known as the *Registry*. This centralized database contains environmental settings for various Windows programs. It also contains registration information that details which types of filename extensions are associated with which applications. So, when you double-click a file in Windows File Explorer, the associated application runs and opens the file that you double-clicked.

The Registry was introduced with Windows 95. Most operating systems up until Windows 95 were configured through text files, which could be edited with almost any text editor. However, the Registry database is contained in a special binary file that can be edited only with the Registry Editor provided with Windows.

 Current versions of Windows have what appear to be two applications that can be used to edit the Registry: regedit and regedt32 (with no i). In reality, however, regedt32 opens regedit. They work similarly, but each has slightly different options for navigation and browsing.

The Registry is broken down into a series of separate areas called *hives*. The keys in each hive are divided into two basic sections—user settings and computer settings. In Windows, a number of files are created corresponding to each of the different hives. The names of most of these files do not have extensions, and their names are SYSTEM, SOFTWARE, SECURITY, SAM, and DEFAULT. One additional file, whose name does have an extension, is NTUSER.DAT.

The basic hives of the Registry are as follows:

HKEY_CLASSES_ROOT   Includes information about which filename extensions map to particular applications.

HKEY_CURRENT_USER   Holds all configuration information specific to a particular user, such as their desktop settings and history information.

HKEY_LOCAL_MACHINE   Includes nearly all configuration information about the actual computer hardware and software.

HKEY_USERS   Includes information about all users who have logged into the system. The `HKEY_CURRENT_USER` hive is actually a subkey of this hive.

HKEY_CURRENT_CONFIG   Provides quick access to a number of commonly needed keys that are otherwise buried deep in the `HKEY_LOCAL_MACHINE` structure.

Modifying a Registry Entry

If you need to modify the Registry, you can modify the values in the database or create new entries or keys. You will find the options for adding a new element to the Registry on the Edit menu. To edit an existing value, double-click the entry and modify it as needed. You need administrator-level access to modify the Registry.

WARNING   Windows uses the Registry extensively to store all kinds of information. Indeed, the Registry holds most, if not all, of the configuration information for Windows. Modifying the Registry in Windows is a potentially dangerous task. Control Panel and other configuration tools are provided so that you have graphical tools for modifying system settings. Directly modifying the Registry can have unforeseen—and unpleasant—results. You should modify the Registry only when told to do so by an extremely trustworthy source or if you are absolutely certain that you have the knowledge to do so without wreaking havoc.

Restoring the Registry

Windows stores Registry information in several files on the hard drive. In Windows 7 and earlier, you could restore this information using the Last Known Good Configuration option on the F8 start menu. With later versions, you would have to restore the files from a backup for the `systemroot\repair` directory by using the Windows Backup program. Repairing the Registry from a backup overwrote the Registry files in `systemroot\system32\config`.

The Last Known Good Configuration option no longer exists at boot time in Windows 8/8.1 and Windows 10/11. If the operating system suffers two consecutive failed attempts to boot into Windows, the Windows Recovery Environment (WinRE) will automatically boot. From the WinRE, the operating system will try to automatically fix common issues. However, the only way to recover a blue screen on boot is to choose Reset This PC in the WinRE and select Keep My Files. More information on WinRE can be found here:

```
https://support.microsoft.com/en-us/help/4026030/how-to-
use-windows-recovery-environment-winre-to-troubleshoot-
common-s
```

Real World Scenario

Beware of Editing the Registry

Just in case it hasn't sunk in yet: be careful editing the Registry! There is no Undo button, nor do you have the safety net of choosing not to save your edits before you close. Once you make the change, it's made—for better or for worse.

There have been countless examples throughout our careers of people going in to edit the Registry without really knowing what they were doing. In many cases, making small changes to the Registry, without having a viable backup, means having to reinstall Windows. At the very least, this is inconvenient.

Windows can help in this regard if you are in a networked environment with Windows-based servers. You can create system policies that prevent users from performing certain tasks, and the most important task to restrict is running Registry editors.

Remember that a system restore will restore the Registry to the state it was in when a restore point was saved. As a very last-resort option for system recovery, Windows uses the Windows Recovery Environment (WinRE) to do a complete PC reset. It is your goal to make sure that you never need to use this.

Disk Management

Where there are files, there are disks. That is, all the files and programs that we've talked about so far reside on disks. Disks are physical storage devices, and they also need to be managed. There are several aspects to disk management. One is concerned with getting disks ready to be able to store files and programs; another deals with backing up your data; and yet another involves checking the health of disks and optimizing their performance. We'll look at these aspects in more detail.

Getting Disks Ready to Store Files and Programs

In order for a hard disk to be able to hold files and programs, it has to be partitioned and formatted. *Partitioning* is the process of creating logical divisions on a hard drive. A hard drive can have one or more partitions. *Formatting* is the process of creating and configuring a file allocation table (FAT) and creating the root directory. The *New Technology Filesystem (NTFS)* is available with all the versions of Windows you need to know about for the exam, but others are also recognized and supported. The file table for the NTFS is called the *Master File Table (MFT)*.

The following is a list of the major filesystems that are, or have been, used and the differences among them:

File Allocation Table   *FAT* is the acronym for the file table used to keep track of where files are within the filesystem. It's also the name given to this type of filesystem, introduced in 1981. The filesystems for many OSs have been built on the design of FAT but without its limitations. A FAT filesystem uses the *8.3 naming convention* (eight letters for the name, a period, and then a three-letter file identifier). This later became known as *FAT16* (to differentiate it from FAT32) because it used a 16-bit binary number to hold cluster-numbering information. Because of that number, the largest FAT disk partition that could be created was approximately 2 GB.

Virtual FAT   *Virtual Fat (VFAT)* is an extension of the FAT filesystem that was introduced with Windows 95. It augmented the 8.3 file-naming convention and allowed filenames with up to 255 characters. It created two names for each file: a long name and an 8.3-compatible name so that older programs could still access files. When VFAT was incorporated into Windows 95, it used 32-bit code for improved disk access while keeping the 16-bit naming system for backward compatibility with FAT. It also had the 2 GB disk partition limitation.

FAT32   The *FAT32* filesystem was introduced along with Windows 95 OEM Service Release 2. As disk sizes grew, so did the need to be able to format a partition larger than 2 GB. FAT32 was based more on VFAT than on FAT16. It allowed for 32-bit cluster addressing, which, in turn, provided for a maximum partition size of 2 terabytes (2,048 GB). It also included smaller cluster sizes to avoid wasted space. FAT32 support is included in current Windows versions.

New Technology Filesystem   Introduced along with Windows NT, *New Technology Filesystem (NTFS)* is available with all current versions of Windows. NTFS is a much more advanced filesystem in almost every way than all versions of the FAT filesystem. It includes such features as individual file security encryption and compression, disk quotas, and RAID support, as well as support for extremely large file and partition sizes and disk transaction monitoring. It is the filesystem of choice for higher-performance computing.

Compact Disc File System   Although not a filesystem that can be used on a hard drive, *Compact Disc File System (CDFS)* is the filesystem of choice for CD media. It has been used with 32-bit Windows versions since Windows 95. A CD mounted with the CDFS driver appears as a collection.

Extended File Allocation Table   Created by Microsoft, *Extended File Allocation Table (exFAT)* is a proprietary filesystem of choice for flash drives where NTFS cannot be used (because of overhead) and FAT32 is not acceptable (due to filesystem limitations). Although exFAT is a proprietary filesystem, it is being adopted by third-party device vendors to overcome the filesystem limitations of FAT32. It is ideal for SD cards that hold a lot of information, and it is supported in all current versions of Windows. exFAT is the default filesystem on USB flash drives over 32 GB in size.

Network File System   Network File System (NFS) was created by Sun Microsystems a number of decades ago and is widely used in UNIX and *Linux* environments. Starting with Windows 7, Microsoft includes support for NFS with Windows (but it is not always installed). Windows versions prior to Windows 7 (Vista) can install Windows Services for UNIX (SFU) to gain this support.

Extended File System   Not natively supported with Windows, ext3 (Third Extended File System) became the default filesystem for many distributions of Linux due to its journaling capabilities. Enhancements were added to it to create *ext4* (Fourth Extended File System), which is used with Android and other operating systems. It is possible to use ext4 with Windows, but doing so requires making some sacrifices in features for the sake of compatibility.

Hierarchical File System   *Hierarchical File System (HFS)* is a proprietary filesystem that was developed by Apple for the Mac OS back in 1985. The filesystem was originally created so that the filesystem could scale for larger disks. HFS+ eventually replaced the original HFS filesystem and it was the primary filesystem on which macOS operated prior to macOS Sierra 10.12.4, iOS 10.3, and tvOS 10.2. Windows operating systems cannot read drives formatted in HFS.

Apple File System   *Apple File System (APFS)* is a proprietary filesystem that was developed by Apple to replace HFS and HFS+. The filesystem was mainly developed to introduce new features with *solid-state storage drives (SSD)*, such as compression, encryption, and snapshots, just to name a few. APFS also fixed some core issues with the HFS+ filesystem, such as the number of files and data integrity. The filesystem is the default filesystem for macOS Sierra 10.12.4, iOS 10.3, and tvOS 10.2 and later. Windows operating systems cannot read drives formatted in APFS.

Swap Partition   Swap partitions, which are found only within Linux and UNIX installations, are the equivalent of the page file (`pagefile.sys`) in Windows, except that they are their own partition type. They are used for *virtual memory* when the physical memory is exhausted.

When you're installing Windows 10/11, the installer defaults to NTFS. However, you can use the partitioning tool to format the partition with FAT32. It's really unnecessary, since NTFS is a much better filesystem with respect to stability, avoiding corruption, and security. When you are formatting a storage drive, you can format it with FAT or NTFS. Storage devices formatted in FAT can be read by other operating systems, but when they are formatted in NTFS the operating system must explicitly support NTFS.

To format a partition from the command line, use the `format` command, which is available with all versions of Windows. You can run `format` from a command prompt or by right-clicking a drive in Windows File Explorer and selecting Format. However, when you install Windows, it performs the process of partitioning and formatting for you if a partitioned and formatted drive does not already exist.

You can usually choose between a *quick format* and a *full format*:

- With a quick format, a new file table is created on the hard disk, but files are not fully overwritten or erased from the disk.

- A quick format is much faster since the normal format fully erases any and all existing data on the hard disk (a time-consuming process).

 Be extremely careful with the `format` command! When you format a drive, treasured data can be lost. Before using the `format` command, make sure that you back up the data you want to save.

Disk Management MMC

In Windows, you can manage hard drives through the Disk Management console. To access Disk Management in Windows 10, right-click the Start menu and then click Disk Management. Alternatively you could start the Disk Management MMC by typing **diskmgmt.msc** in the Run dialog box.

The Disk Management screen lets you view a lot of information about all the drives installed in your system, including CD/DVD-ROM drives (see Figure 14.83).

Given a scenario, there are many instances in which an administrator would turn to Disk Management during the course of trying to find the right storage solution. The Disk Management administrative console allows you to review all the logical partitions (volumes) configured and physical drives (disks) that are connected to the computer.

The logical volume is displayed in the upper portion of the Disk Management console. This view allows you to see at a glance all the configured volumes on the operating system. Details about the volume letter or type, the layout type, the type of disk (basic vs. *dynamic*), filesystem, status, capacity, and free space can be seen in this logical view.

The physical layout, displayed below the logical view, allows you to see the layout of the physical disks in a graphical format. Using both views, you can see the layout of a physical disk and its corresponding logical layout. The physical layout allows you to view the status of the drive, the size of the drive, and its health, in addition to the layout of volumes on the physical disk.

FIGURE 14.83   Disk Management MMC in Windows 10

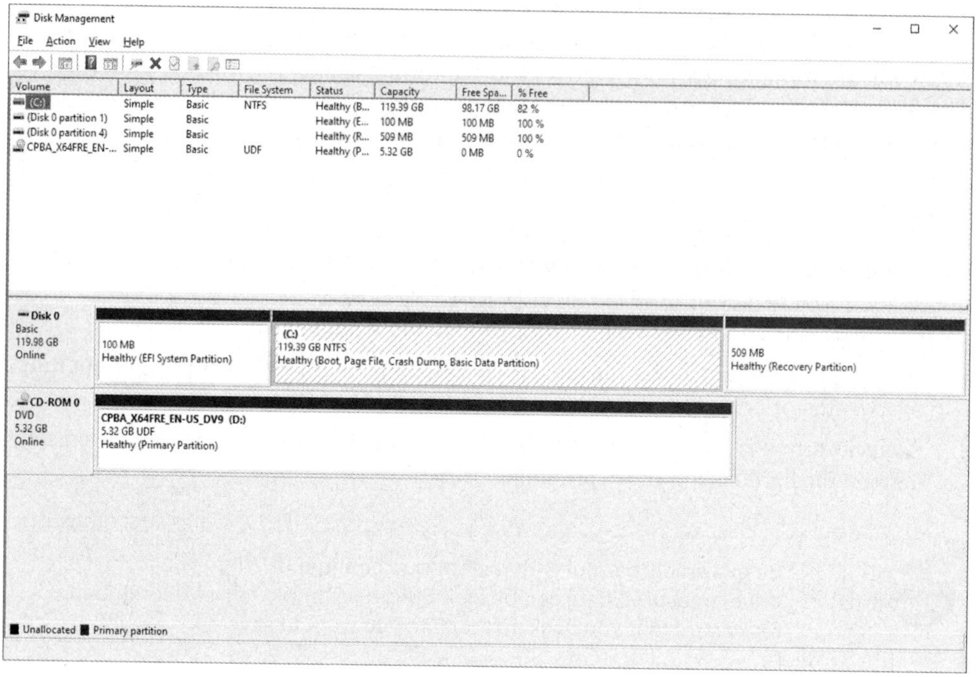

Windows supports three types of partition styles: Basic, GPT, and Dynamic. Partition styles are also known as partition schemes; the terms are used to describe the underlying structure of the partitioning of the physical disk.

Basic Disks   *Master Boot Record (MBR)* is the standard BIOS partition table used and predates GPT. MBR disk storage can have a maximum of four primary partitions or three primary partitions and one extended partition containing multiple logical partitions, for a maximum of 26 logical partitions. The partition from which the operating system boots must be designated as active and must be a primary partition. Only one partition on a disk can be marked active.

GPT Disks   *GUID Partition Tables (GPT)* is the current partition table specification used with *Unified Extensible Firmware Interface (UEFI)* BIOS. GPT partition tables allocate 64-bit logical block addressing for larger partitions. If you need to create partitions 2 TB or larger, it is required. A GPT disk can contain up to 128 primary partitions. The large number of primary partitions supported eliminates the need to create extended/logical partitions.

Dynamic Disks   *Dynamic disks* are proprietary to Windows operating systems. Dynamic disks can contain up to 2,000 volumes. All the dynamic disks installed in the operating system contain an identical 1 MB database (partition table) that describes all the other disks installed. The true benefit of this 1 MB database is moving fault-tolerant disks to another Windows operating system. The operating system will automatically recognize that the disks work together, and the *Logical Disk Management (LDM)* will configure itself according to the layout in the 1 MB database.

> The terms *partition* and *volume* are interchangeable; they both mean the same thing. They are logical subdivisions of a physical disk. Dynamic disks use the terminology of volumes, and MBR and GPT use the terminology of partitions. Sometimes partitions will be referred to as volumes, such as when you use the diskpart command-line utility.

Right-clicking any volume opens a context menu that allows you to change the drive letter or paths, format, extend, shrink, delete, or add a mirror. Right-clicking any drive opens a context menu that allows you to create a new spanned, striped, mirrored, or RAID-5 volume. You can also convert to a dynamic or GPT disk.

Let's discuss the features and functions in further detail:

Initializing Disks   The phrase *initializing a disk* means different things depending on if it is a hardware initialization or, in this case, a Windows initialization. When you initialize a disk in Windows, you are allowing the LDM to recognize the disk. When you initialize a disk in hardware disk systems, you are erasing the partition table and even the data. To initialize a disk, right-click the drive and select Initialize. This needs to be performed only once.

Mounting Partitions   Once a partition (volume) is created, you need to make it available to the operating system for use. You have two basic options. The first option is to assign the volume a drive letter. The second option is to mount the volume in an empty NTFS folder. So you can mount an entire volume in a specific folder. You can perform this task by right-clicking a partition and selecting Change Drive Letter And Paths.

Extending Partitions   When you install an operating system on a disk, you will more than likely use the entire disk for the installation of the operating system. However, if you ever fill it all up and buy a bigger drive, when you clone it over to the new larger disk, you will find that the partition is the same size. This is where extending a partition comes in handy. It is also very common for virtualized operating systems, since adding space to a virtual disk can be done on the fly. As long as there is unallocated space on the disk, you can right-click the partition (volume) and choose Extend Volume.

Shrinking Partitions   Shrinking a partition, also known as splitting a partition, is not a common task, but it is done from time to time. It is usually performed when an installation is not using a fraction of the physical disk storage and another partition is required. You can perform this action by right-clicking the partition (volume) and choosing Shrink Volume.

Extending partitions and shrinking partitions require that you perform the task on the last partition (volume) created on the drive. This is not always the case. These functions will not always work from within the operating system. An open source tool called SystemRescueCD contains a tool called GParted. This tool allows you to reconfigure the disk layout and move partitions around, as well as shrink and extend partitions.

Adding Drives   When you add a disk to the system, you normally have to power the computer down to attach the disk. However, servers have the capability to add drives on the fly, called *hot swap disks*. When a disk is added to the operating system, the operating system needs to know it. You can make the operating system take inventory of its disks by selecting Rescan Disks from the Action menu in the Disk Management console.

Adding Arrays   Arrays of disks are multiple disks working together for a specific purpose. These are also known as a *Redundant Array of Independent (or Inexpensive) Disks (RAID)*. They are used for fault tolerance so that in the event of a disk failure, the system will continue to function. They can also be used to add performance to a system by using multiple disks. Striped disks, also known as *RAID-0*, require two or more disks and are used for performance; they do not offer any fault tolerance. A mirror, also known as *RAID-1*, is the most basic type of fault tolerance; it creates an identical mirror of the information on another disk. Striped disks with parity, also known as *RAID-5*, offer performance and fault tolerance and require three or more disks. Windows is unique in that it allows volumes to participate in array groups, rather than requiring the entire disk. A combination of mirroring (*RAID-1*) and striping (*RAID-0*) can be used together as *RAID-10*. *RAID-10* offers both fault tolerance of a mirrored disk and the performance of striping across the mirrors. *RAID-10* requires a minimum of four disks to operate.

Windows can create RAID groups of 0, 1, and 5, but RAID 10 is not directly supported. There are various tricks to making a RAID 10 volume, such as creating two mirrors and then striping across the mirrors. However, this adds a level of complexity, and we recommend that if you need RAID 10 you purchase a hardware solution such as a dedicated RAID card.

Storage Spaces   This Windows feature was initially introduced in Windows Server 2012 and Windows 8. It allows for a group of drives to be placed into a pool of storage that can be configured for fault tolerance. The benefit is that more disks can be added later to extend a storage pool dynamically. The one caveat is that the hard drives can either be managed by the Disk Management MMC or Storage Spaces, but not both.

The *Storage Spaces* feature lets you manage a variety of hard drives. A unique feature is its capability to create a storage pool using two or more external (USB-attached) hard drives. Storage Spaces is not exclusive to external hard drives; internal hard drives can be used as well.

In Storage Spaces, you can create a two-way mirror, a three-way mirror, or parity resiliency of your data. A two-way mirror is identical in functionality to a *RAID-1* mirror. A three-way mirror is similar to a RAID-1 mirror in that it duplicates the data on two other drives; unlike RAID-1, however, you can lose two hard drives and retain data. A parity resiliency type is identical in functionality to a *RAID-5* (striping with parity). You can also use Storage Spaces without resiliency, which is called a *simple volume*, as shown in Figure 14.84.

FIGURE 14.84   Windows 10 Storage Spaces

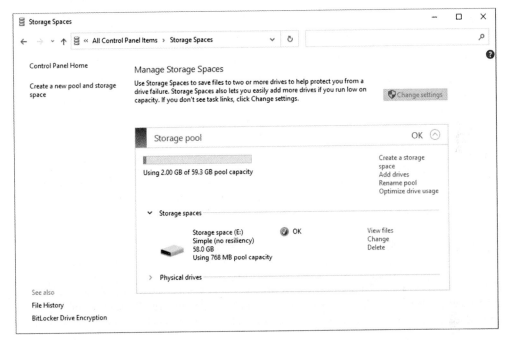

Checking the Health of Hard Disks and Optimizing Their Performance

As time goes on, it's important to check the health of Windows computers' hard disks and to optimize their performance. Windows provides you with several tools to do so, some of which we've already mentioned in this chapter. One important tool is Disk Defragmenter, which has existed in almost all versions of Windows.

When files are written to a hard drive, they're not always written contiguously, or with all the data in a single location. Files are stored on the disk in numbered blocks, similar to PO boxes. When they are written, they are written to free blocks. As a result, file data is spread out over the disk, and the time it takes to retrieve files from the disk increases.

Defragmenting a disk involves analyzing the disk and then consolidating fragmented files and folders so that they occupy a contiguous space (consecutive blocks). This increases performance during file retrieval, since the hard drive arm in mechanical hard disks needs to travel less to retrieve the blocks. Defragmentation of the filesystem is not required on solid-state drives (SSDs), since the fragmentation of data blocks does not slow down the retrieval of the memory locations.

To access Disk Defragmenter, follow these steps:

1. Click Start ➤ Windows Administrative Tools ➤ Defragment and Optimize Disk.

2. In the list of drives, select the drive that you want to defragment, and then click Analyze. When the analysis is finished, Disk Defragmenter tells you how much the drive is fragmented and whether defragmentation is recommended.

3. If defragmentation is recommended, click Defragment.

Be aware that for large disks with a lot of fragmented files, this process can take quite some time to finish.

In Windows, you can also access Disk Defragmenter through the properties of any partition listed in Disk Management (or, even easier, any disk root under This PC in Windows File Explorer). Select the Tools tab, and then click Defragment.

Summary

In this chapter, you learned about some of the tools that can be used with Windows. We covered basic Windows management concepts, including managing disks, using filesystems, and understanding directory structure. Keeping your computer healthy will save you a lot of stress.

With the basic knowledge gained in this chapter, you are now ready to learn how to interact with the most popular operating systems in use today. These topics are covered in the next four chapters.

Exam Essentials

Know which filesystems are available in Windows and the differences between them.   The most commonly used filesystem on Windows hard drives is NTFS. FAT32 is older and perhaps a bit quicker for smaller hard drives and USB thumb drives, but NTFS adds a plethora of important features, including security and auditing. exFAT is a filesystem Microsoft adopted to address large filesystems that FAT32 had problems addressing. Additionally, you should know that the ext3, ext4, and APFS filesystems are not compatible with Windows without third-party software.

Know which Windows Control Panel utility to use for a given scenario. A number of Control Panel applets allow you to change Windows' functionality. With the introduction of Windows 10, some of the functionality is split between the Settings app and the classic Control Panel applets. You should be proficient with both for a given scenario in which changes to the operating system need to be made.

Know which Windows settings section is used for a given scenario. The Settings app is slowly replacing Control Panel as the main method of configuring Windows. You should know the major categories of the Settings app and the various settings each of them contain.

Know the main administrative tools. You should know the primary graphical tools for troubleshooting Windows and configuring the operating system. These include the disk management tools, Administrative Tools, Device Manager, Task Manager, System Information, System Restore, and Task Scheduler.

Know the various disk management concepts. You should know the various concepts related to disk management to initialize and mount a drive to assign a drive letter; the concepts of extending, splitting, and shrinking partitions (volumes); fault tolerance arrays; and Storage Spaces. GPT should be used with UEFI BIOS, addressing 2 TB and larger drives, or if more than 26 logical volumes are required.

Review Questions

The answers to the chapter review questions can be found in Appendix A.

1. Which MMC snap-in allows you to start a program based on a condition?

   A. Programs and Features

   B. Task Scheduler

   C. Disk Management

   D. Group Policy Editor

2. In Windows, which of the following is the filesystem of choice for CD media?

   A. NTFS

   B. EFS

   C. FAT32

   D. CDFS

3. Which utility can be used to schedule a remote shutdown?

   A. `taskmgr`

   B. `kill`

   C. `shutdown`

   D. `netstat`

4. Which event log should be checked if you suspect that the computer has rebooted unexpectedly?

   A. Application

   B. Boot

   C. Security

   D. System

5. Which of the following filesystems is a proprietary filesystem created by Microsoft for use with large flash drives?

   A. GPT

   B. NFS

   C. ext3

   D. exFAT

6. Which section in the Settings app lets you configure backups?

   A. System

   B. Devices

   C. Apps

   D. Update and Security

7. Which of the following filesystems is a proprietary filesystem created by Apple that offers SSD support?

   A. HFS

   B. ext4

   C. APFS

   D. exFAT

8. Which Control Panel applet would you use to join the operating system to a domain?

   A. System

   B. User Accounts

   C. Internet Options

   D. Programs and Features

9. What can you do if a program is not responding to any commands and appears to be locked up?

   A. Open the System Control Panel applet and choose Performance to see what process is causing the problem.

   B. Add more memory.

   C. Press Ctrl+Alt+Delete to reboot the computer.

   D. Open Task Manager, select the appropriate task, and then click End Task.

10. Which command will start the Event Viewer snap-in?

   A. `eventviewer.exe`

   B. `eventvwr.msc`

   C. `lusrmgr.msc`

   D. `devmgmt.msc`

11. You need to configure an iSCSI connection; where will you find iSCSI settings?

   A. Storage Spaces applet

   B. Disk Management snap-in

   C. Administrative Tools

   D. Device Manager snap-in

12. Which type of resources do you configure in Device Manager?

   A. Hardware

   B. Files and folders

   C. Applications

   D. Memory

13. What should be periodically done with mechanical hard drives to speed up performance when launching and saving files?

   A. Free up space

   B. Empty Recycle Bin

   C. Defragment

   D. Trim

14. You have a number of files with a `.des` extension and you want to be able to search each file's metadata; which applet should this be configured in?

   A. Internet Options applet

   B. File Explorer Options applet

   C. Indexing Options applet

   D. Ease of Access Center applet

15. Which of the following partitions is specifically the partition from which the operating system boots?

   A. Primary partition

   B. Extended partition

   C. Dynamic partition

   D. Logical partition

16. Which of the following Registry hives contains information about the computer's hardware?

   A. `HKEY_CURRENT_MACHINE`

   B. `HKEY_LOCAL_MACHINE`

   C. `HKEY_MACHINE`

   D. `HKEY_RESOURCES`

17. Which of the following replaces the MBR in 64-bit versions of the Windows operating system?

   A. LILO

   B. NFS

   C. GPT

   D. GRUB

18. Which of the following utilities will rearrange the files on your hard disk to occupy contiguous chunks of space?

   A. Disk Defragmenter

   B. Windows File Explorer

   C. Scandisk

   D. Windows Backup

19. Which power mode will write the contents of the RAM to the disk?

    A. Hibernate

    B. Standby

    C. Sleep

    D. Suspend

20. Which partition style allows up to 2,000 volumes to be partitioned on a physical disk?

    A. GPT

    B. MBR

    C. Dynamic Disk

    D. Basic Disk

Performance-Based Question

You will encounter performance-based questions on the A+ exams. The questions on the exam require you to perform a specific task, and you will be graded on whether or not you were able to complete the task. The following requires you to think creatively in order to measure how well you understand this chapter's topics. You may or may not see similar questions on the actual A+ exams. To see how your answers compare to the authors', refer to Appendix B.

You are working at a company that has standardized on Windows 10 workstations for all. The phone rings, and it is your supervisor. He tells you that his workstation is running incredibly slowly, almost to the point where is it is unusable. When you ask what he is running, he reports that he has exited out of everything but the operating system. You suspect there are background processes tying up the CPU and memory. Which utility can you have him use to look for such culprits?

FIGURE 14.85   Windows Task Manager

Name	Status	56% CPU	60% Memory	48% Disk	0% Network	Power usage	Power usage t...
System		12.5%	0.1 MB	0.6 MB/s	0 Mbps	Moderate	Low
Microsoft OneDrive (64 bit) Setup		11.7%	6.2 MB	38.4 MB/s	0 Mbps	Moderate	Low
WaasMedic Agent Exe		11.1%	2.3 MB	15.5 MB/s	0 Mbps	Moderate	Low
wsappx		5.3%	8.4 MB	0.1 MB/s	0 Mbps	Low	Very low
Service Host: Windows Update		3.1%	18.6 MB	0.3 MB/s	0 Mbps	Low	Very low
Antimalware Service Executable		2.3%	137.7 MB	0.1 MB/s	0 Mbps	Very low	Very low
System interrupts		2.2%	0 MB	0 MB/s	0 Mbps	Very low	Very low
Microsoft Content		2.2%	10.9 MB	0.1 MB/s	0 Mbps	Very low	Very low
Host Process for Windows Tasks		1.4%	7.1 MB	0.1 MB/s	0.1 Mbps	Very low	Very low
Service Host: Remote Procedure...		0.8%	7.8 MB	0.1 MB/s	0 Mbps	Very low	Very low
Task Manager		0.5%	19.7 MB	0.1 MB/s	0 Mbps	Very low	Very low
Service Host: State Repository S...		0.5%	7.4 MB	0 MB/s	0 Mbps	Very low	Very low
Service Host: DCOM Server Proc...		0.5%	8.8 MB	0.1 MB/s	0 Mbps	Very low	Very low
Windows Explorer		0.5%	25.5 MB	0.1 MB/s	0 Mbps	Very low	Very low
Microsoft Windows Search Inde...		0.3%	6.4 MB	0 MB/s	0 Mbps	Very low	Very low
Shell Infrastructure Host		0.3%	5.1 MB	0.1 MB/s	0 Mbps	Very low	Very low
Service Host: Web Account Ma...		0.2%	2.7 MB	0.1 MB/s	0 Mbps	Very low	Very low
Windows Security Health Service		0.2%	2.5 MB	0.1 MB/s	0 Mbps	Very low	Very low
Xbox Game Bar (4)		0.2%	27.3 MB	0.2 MB/s	0 Mbps	Very low	Very low

Chapter

15

Windows Administration

THE FOLLOWING COMPTIA A+ 220-1102 EXAM OBJECTIVES ARE COVERED IN THIS CHAPTER:

✓ **1.2 Given a scenario, use the appropriate Microsoft command-line tool.**

- **Navigation**
  - **cd**
  - **dir**
  - **md**
  - **rmdir**
  - **Drive navigation inputs**
    - **C:\ or D:\ or x:**
- **Command-line tools**
  - **ipconfig**
  - **ping**
  - **hostname**
  - **netstat**
  - **nslookup**
  - **chkdsk**
  - **net user**
  - **net use**
  - **tracert**
  - **format**
  - **xcopy**
  - **copy**

- robocopy
- gpupdate
- gpresult
- shutdown
- sfc
- [command name] /?
- diskpart
- pathping
- winver

✓ **1.6 Given a scenario, configure Microsoft Windows networking features on a client/desktop.**

- Workgroup vs. domain setup
  - Shared resources
  - Printers
  - File servers
  - Mapped drives
- Local OS firewall settings
  - Application restrictions and exceptions
  - Configuration
- Client network configuration
  - Internet Protocol (IP) addressing scheme
  - Domain Name System (DNS) settings
  - Subnet mask
  - Gateway
  - Static vs. dynamic
- Establish network connections
  - Virtual private network (VPN)
  - Wireless
  - Wired
  - Wireless wide area network (WWAN)
- Proxy settings

- ⬚ **Public network vs. private network**
- ⬚ **File Explorer navigation—network paths**
- ⬚ **Metered connections and limitations**

✓ **1.9 Given a scenario, perform OS installations and upgrades in a diverse OS environment.**

- ⬚ **Boot methods**
    - ⬚ **USB**
    - ⬚ **Optical media**
    - ⬚ **Network**
    - ⬚ **Solid-state/flash drives**
    - ⬚ **Internet-based**
    - ⬚ **External/hot-swappable drive**
    - ⬚ **Internal hard drive (partition)**
- ⬚ **Types of installations**
    - ⬚ **Upgrade**
    - ⬚ **Recovery partition**
    - ⬚ **Clean install**
    - ⬚ **Image deployment**
    - ⬚ **Repair installation**
    - ⬚ **Remote network installation**
    - ⬚ **Other considerations (Third-party drivers)**
- ⬚ **Upgrade considerations**
    - ⬚ **Backup files and user preferences**
    - ⬚ **Application and driver support/backward compatibility**
    - ⬚ **Hardware compatibility**
- ⬚ **Feature updates**
    - ⬚ **Product life cycle**

The previous chapter introduced the basic components of Windows operating systems and discussed the various tools used to configure Windows. This chapter builds on the previous chapters and focuses on Windows administration. In this chapter you will learn how to install and upgrade Windows 10/11 and learn various command-line tools. We'll also explore advanced concepts, such as Microsoft networking and design. All the content is generic to the Windows operating systems you'll be tested on during the 220–1102 exam. The content can be applied to any of the previous Windows operating systems.

Installing and Upgrading Windows

Windows 10, released on July 29, 2015, was the successor to Windows 8.1. Actually, for many people who never upgraded from Windows 7, it was their direct upgrade to Windows 10. The user interface (UI) looked to be the same, and it was a well-needed upgrade. Microsoft also made the upgrade notification so irritating that many were forced to upgrade just to escape the notifications.

Regardless of the motivation to upgrade to Windows 10, its adoption was successful because of its meager system requirements. The hardware requirements for Windows 10 are identical to prior versions of Windows. Starting with Windows 11 requirements have been scaled up for performance, as shown in Table 15.1. The meager hardware requirements were one of the driving factors for many to just hit the upgrade button.

TABLE 15.1   Windows 10/11 system requirements

Component	Windows 10 Requirement	Windows 11 Requirement
Processor	1 GHz or faster	1 GHz or faster (2 or more cores) 64-bit
RAM	1 GB (32-bit) or 2 GB (64-bit)	4 GB (64-bit)
Hard drive space	16 GB (32-bit) or 32 GB (64-bit)	64 GB (64-bit)
Graphics card	DirectX 9 with WDDM 1.0 or higher driver	DirectX 12 with WDDM 2.0 driver

If you are planning to install Windows 10 on a computer, it must meet the specifications in Table 15.1, which are pretty easy to meet or exceed. However, sometimes you'll find that your organization's computers are older than you think. Windows 11 requires a realistic amount of computing power, RAM, and storage. In addition to these requirements, a UEFI firmware that is Secure Boot capable and a TPM 2.0 is required by Windows 11. To learn more about Windows 10 and Windows 11 system requirements, visit `https://docs.microsoft.com/en-us/windows-hardware/design/minimum/minimum-hardware-requirements-overview`.

Checking Hardware Compatibility

In the past, Microsoft published a hardware compatibility list (HCL) for Windows XP and prior Windows operating systems. With the introduction of Windows Vista, Microsoft went away from a published list of vendors in a static document and moved to the Windows Catalog, which listed not only compatible hardware but compatible applications as well. Today, we find that the list of compatible hardware and software has changed again: you can access the Windows Compatible Products List at `https://partner.microsoft.com/en-us/dashboard/hardware/search/cpl`. However, the best way to check is to verify with the manufacturer that drivers exist and that the hardware is compatible with Windows 10/11.

Sometimes you need to deploy Windows 10/11 to a group of computers. There are several tools that can be used to collect information about the hardware of the current operating system. The easiest tool to use is the System Information utility. To access this utility, you simply log in and select System Information from the Start menu. You can use System Information to investigate the processor, RAM, hard drive, and video card, as well as specifics about each of the peripherals connected (see Figure 15.1). You can also access System Information by pressing Windows key + R, typing **msinfo32.exe**, and clicking OK.

You can also use System Information remotely. Select View and then choose Remote Computer from the drop-down menu and select the remote computer. You can also access this utility from the command line by typing **msinfo32.exe**. The `msinfo32.exe` command allows remote collection of information to a flat text file using the following command:

`msinfo32.exe /computer computername /report c:\report.txt`

The `msinfo32.exe` command can also be used to output the information to its native format using the following command:

`msinfo32.exe /computer computername /nfo c:\report.nfo`

FIGURE 15.1   System Information

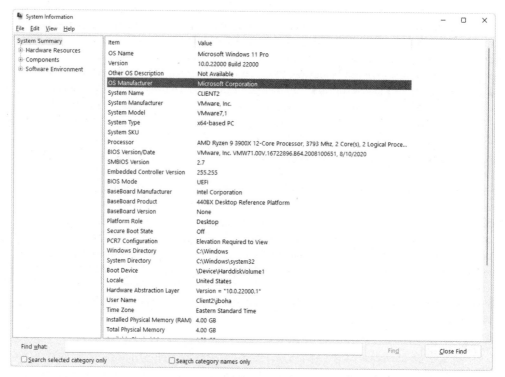

However, this NFO file will need to be opened with the System Information utility, which might be difficult if there are more than 10 or so machines.

An alternative to the System Information (`msinfo32.exe`) utility is the Microsoft Assessment and Planning Toolkit (MAP), which can be downloaded from the Microsoft Download Center (`www.microsoft.com/downloads`). The MAP Toolkit allows for the automated inventory collection of hardware and software from the current operating systems. The MAP Toolkit can then produce a report from the collection of data and provide the administrator with the readiness of current hardware for Windows 10/11. The MAP Toolkit requires the installation of a SQL database, which is included in the installation of the MAP Toolkit. The MAP Toolkit requires a dual-core 1.5 GHz processor, 2 GB of RAM, and a minimum of 1 GB of free hard drive space.

Windows Installation Options

Windows 10/11 can be installed as an upgrade or as a clean installation. When you choose Custom, you can decide whether or not to format the hard disk. If you choose not to format the hard disk, the old operating system is placed in a folder called `WINDOWS.OLD`. When you choose to format the hard disk, it will erase your files, programs, and settings.

When installing Windows 10, you have the option to install it on *Basic Input/Output System (BIOS)*-based hardware or *Unified Extensible Firmware Interface (UEFI)*-based hardware. When installing Windows 11, you must install it on UEFI-based hardware. The hardware must support the newer standard of UEFI to install it in this fashion. UEFI hardware provides a feature called *Secure Boot*. Secure Boot operates by checking the signatures of the hardware, including the UEFI drivers (also called option ROMs), EFI applications, and, finally, the operating system. If the signatures are verified, the operating system is then given control of the boot process and the hardware. Windows 11 also requires that the hardware is Secure Boot–capable and a TPM 2.0 module is installed.

For a UEFI installation, the partitioning of the drive will be laid out like Figure 15.2. The Recovery partition holds a bootable copy of the Windows Recovery Environment (WinRE) and is roughly 500 MB in size. The *EFI System Partition (ESP)* is a System partition used to hold the *Boot Configuration Data (BCD)* for the booting of the boot partition containing the *Windows kernel*.

FIGURE 15.2 Windows default disk layout

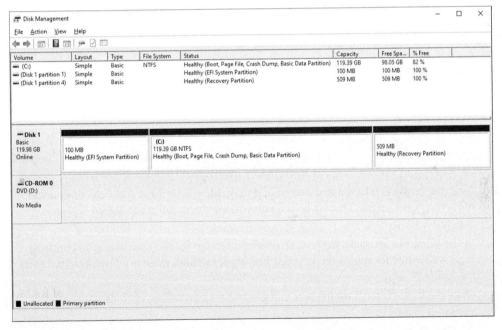

 The Windows Recovery Environment (WinRE) is a bootable environment used by Windows for recovery of the operating system. WinRE is automatically booted when the operating system does not start properly after two consecutive boots. WinRE can also be booted into by restarting the operating system and holding down the Shift key. However, this process assumes that you can successfully boot the operating system.

The Installation Process

The installation of Windows 11 is almost identical to the installation of Windows 10, Windows 8/8.1, and Windows 7. For that matter, it is similar to most operating systems, such as macOS or Linux. There are several common elements during the setup process that must be addressed, such as *locale* and where to install the operating system.

The installation of Windows 11 can be performed from a Windows 11 installation DVD-ROM. However, optical media such as DVD-ROM is rarely used because most laptops and tower computers no long include optical drives. Universal Serial Bus (USB) installation media is a preferred method with most computer vendors. The installation media is created with the Windows 11 Media Creation Tool, which can be downloaded from:

`www.microsoft.com/software-download/windows11`

 Windows XP was the last operating system to support CD-ROM installation media. Starting with Windows Vista, the size of every Windows release has grown and required DVD media for the installation. In addition to using the media creation tool to create USB media, you can download ISO files. The files can then be burned to DVD or used with a virtual machine by mounting the ISO file.

If you are performing an upgrade from within another operating system and the installation does not begin immediately, look for the `setup.exe` file and run it. The following example shows the setup of Windows 11 with the latest installer (21H2) and a clean installation:

1. Start by booting the computer and directing it to boot from the physical media. Each computer will have a different way of entering the one-time boot menu, such as pressing the F12 key or the Esc key, or sometimes by initiating it from the BIOS/UEFI.

2. After the media is selected and detected, it may ask you to press a key to continue with the setup of the media. Once it boots, you will see the initial setup screen shown in Figure 15.3.

3. In the Windows Setup dialog box, select the language for the installation to continue in as well as the format of the keyboard or input method; these are often referred to as the *locale*.

Once the locale is set, a dialog box will present you with three options to proceed, as shown in Figure 15.4:

- The first option is the most obvious: to install the operating system.

- The second option is to enter into recovery mode by selecting Repair Your Computer.

- The third option is less obvious: to exit the installation by pressing the X in the upper-right corner of the dialog box.

FIGURE 15.3 Windows Setup dialog box

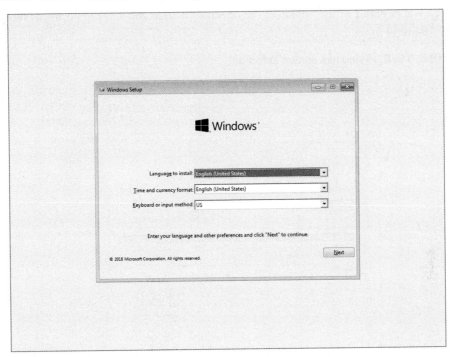

FIGURE 15.4 Windows setup options

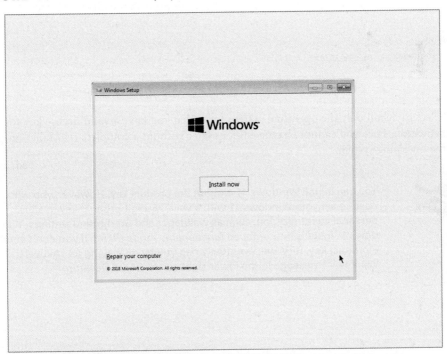

4. Click Install Now.

You will be asked which version of the operating system you want to install, as shown in Figure 15.5.

FIGURE 15.5 Windows edition selection

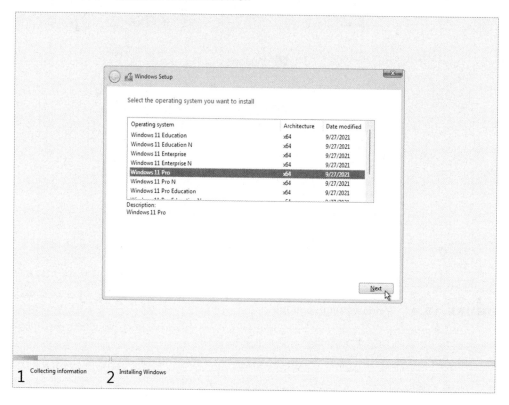

5. Select to install only the operating system for which you have a valid license key for activation, since you cannot change editions later without a complete reinstallation of the operating system.

> **NOTE** You can install Windows 11 without the product key. However, you will need to activate Windows 11 with a valid 25-digit product key to allow personal customization, such as wallpaper and Start menu settings. Windows 11 installs into *reduced functionality mode (RFM)*. If you don't enter a product key, RFM will eventually nag you by displaying an "Activate Windows" message in the lower-right corner of the Desktop.

After selecting the edition, you will be prompted with the *end-user license agreement (EULA)*, as shown in Figure 15.6.

FIGURE 15.6   Windows end-user license agreement

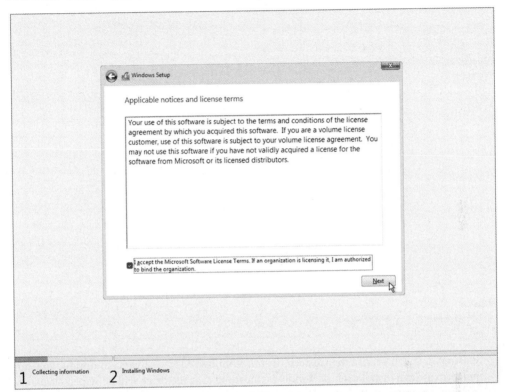

6. To continue, check the "I accept the Microsoft Software License Terms" check box, and then click Next.

    The next screen asks you which type of installation you want. There are two options, as shown in Figure 15.7.

    Upgrade   If you choose Upgrade: Install Windows And Keep Files, Settings, And Applications, you must have a compatible version of Windows for the upgrade (as we'll discuss in the next section). Choosing this option upgrades the current operating system to Windows 11 and places the old operating system in the C:\WINDOWS.OLD folder. You have 30 days to roll back to the prior operating system if you do not want to keep Windows 11.

FIGURE 15.7   Windows installation options

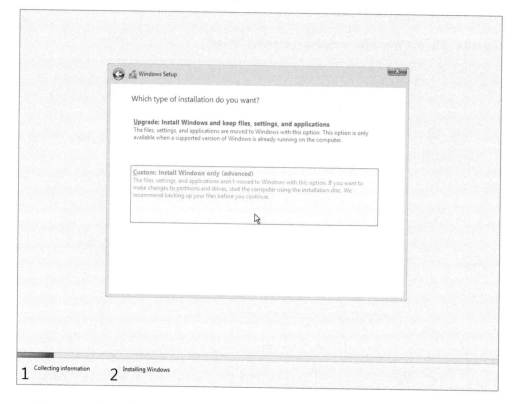

Custom   If you choose the Custom: Install Windows Only (Advanced) option, you can perform a clean installation of Windows, meaning that the drive will be wiped clean. Always remember that *custom* means a clean installation with Windows.

7. Choose Custom: Install Windows Only (Advanced). This is also known as a clean installation, because it will format the installation drive.

The next screen asks where you want to install the new operating system. You can delete, create, and extend partitions. However, most of the time if a partition exists and you are not upgrading, then deleting the existing partitions is the most common task. In rare instances where no drives show up, you may need to install custom drivers specified by the vendor. You can perform that task from this screen as well by selecting Load Driver, as shown in Figure 15.8.

FIGURE 15.8   Windows installation partitioning

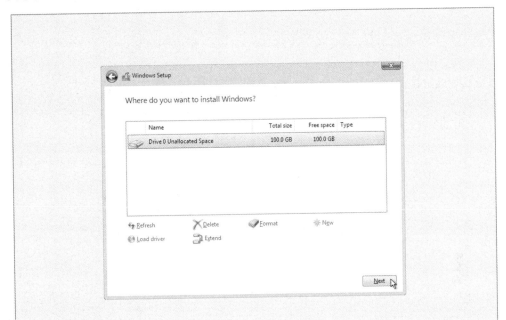

8.   Select the drive for the installation of Windows 11, and then click Next.

Once you have gone past this point, there is no going back. The Windows installation will begin, as shown in Figure 15.9.

This step is where the filesystem is formatted, the boot files are copied, and the operating system's files are applied to the disk. After this stage completes, the files are on the hard drive but the operating system is not generalized to your computer; that happens in the next boot. After the computer reboots, it will detect hardware and run through what is called a *generalize pass*. The screen showing that device drivers are being detected (along with a percentage) will flash by, and then you'll see a Getting Ready screen, as shown in Figure 15.10. This is the point where the operating system is adjusting itself to the computer hardware.

FIGURE 15.9   Windows installation progress

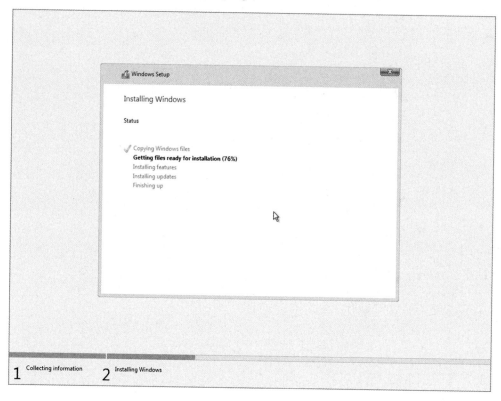

FIGURE 15.10   Windows Getting Ready screen

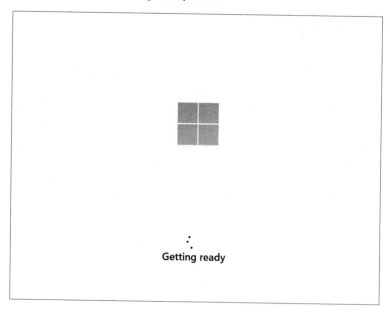

Once the drivers are detected, the operating system will reboot again. During this boot, the drivers detected in the prior stage will be instantiated and the *specialize pass* will begin. In this pass, the locale (region) of the operating system will be chosen, as well as the keyboard layout. You can even choose a second keyboard layout, if you're switching out a keyboard.

9. Confirm the region by clicking the Yes button, as shown in Figure 15.11.

FIGURE 15.11   Operating system locale (region) setting

10. Confirm the keyboard layout by clicking the Yes button, as shown in Figure 15.12. It will also ask you if you want to add a second keyboard layout; just click Skip.

The Windows installation will check for updates after the selection of the locale, keyboard layout, and additional keyboard layout question. The operating system will do some background work and the screen will assure you that something is going on in the background, as it changes with its message.

FIGURE 15.12   Operating system keyboard layout setting

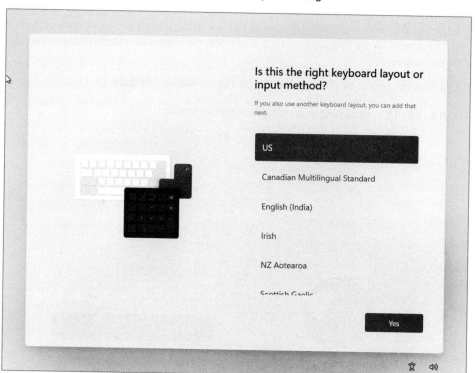

11. Windows 11 allows you to name your device during the setup, as shown in Figure 15.13. This different from older operating systems, such as Windows 10 and Windows 8/8.1, where a random name was created for you.

    The operating system will reboot after you confirm the name of the system. You will then see a Just a Moment screen while the operating system boots, as shown in Figure 15.14.

12. The next set of screens will set up the first user account as well as the first administrator of the operating system. This is considered the OOBE pass, or the *out-of-box experience pass*, where the first account is set up for the operating system. You have the choice of logging in with a Microsoft account by choosing Set Up For Personal Use. This is great if you have the account combined with a Microsoft 365 subscription, since the licensing of the Office products are all streamlined when performing a login of this nature. However, if you want to join the computer to an organization's Intune mobile device management (MDM) service, you can select Set Up For Work or School, as shown in Figure 15.15.

FIGURE 15.13 Operating system name

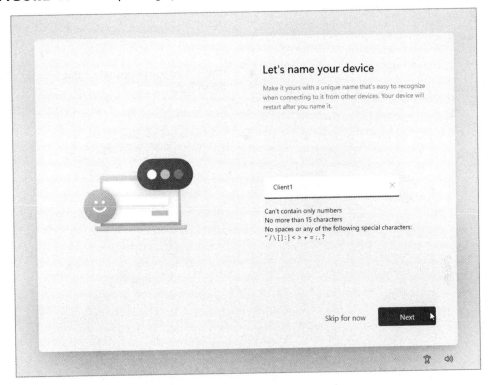

FIGURE 15.14 Just A Moment screen

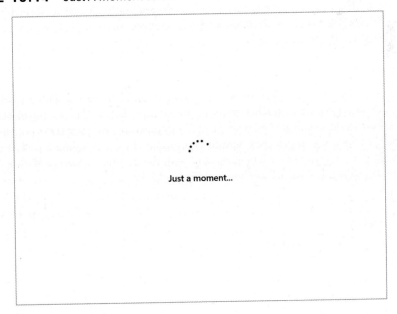

FIGURE 15.15   Windows account options

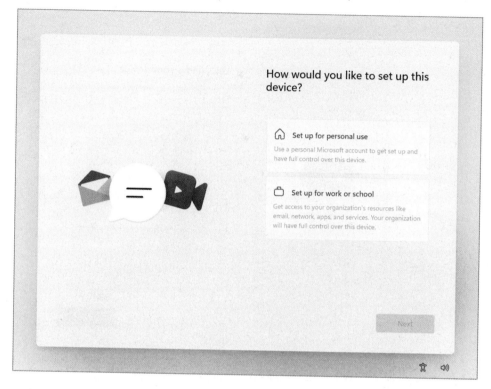

If you click Set Up For Personal Use, you will be asked to sign in with a Microsoft account so that your apps, files, and services will sync to the device, as shown in Figure 15.16. Alternately you can click Sign-in Options and you will be presented with the options to sign in with a security key, create an offline account, or retrieve your username, as shown in Figure 15.17. Creating an offline account is similar to the local accounts created on previous operating system versions.

If you choose Set Up For Work or School, you'll be asked to sign in with a work account or school account that is attached to an Intune service. This will give control of the device over to the organization, where it will be controlled by the MDM policies in Intune. Alternately, you can click Sign-in Options, as shown in Figure 15.18. If you select Sign-in Options you will be presented with the options to Sign In With A Security Key or Domain Join Instead, as shown in Figure 15.19.

FIGURE 15.16   Microsoft account for personal use

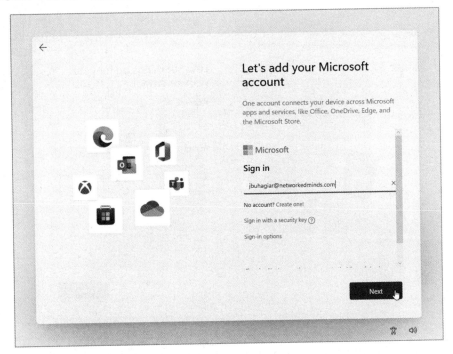

FIGURE 15.17   Microsoft account options for personal use

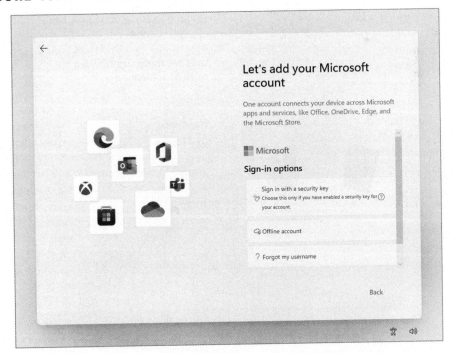

FIGURE 15.18 Microsoft account for work or school

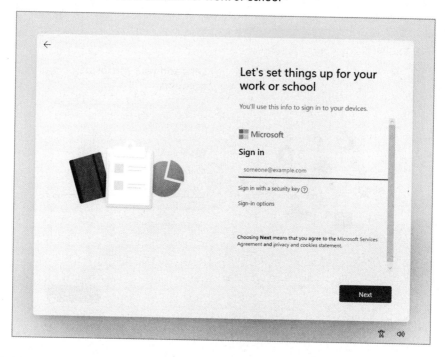

FIGURE 15.19 Microsoft account options for work or school

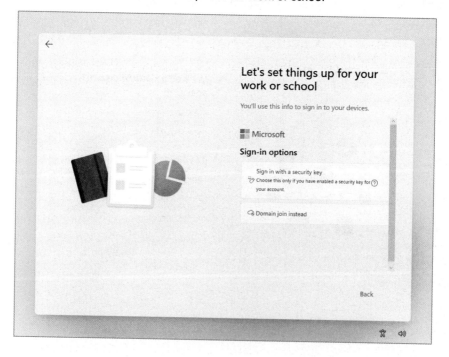

13. We will install using a Microsoft account, so select the Set Up For Personal Use option and sign in with your Microsoft account.

14. After successfully logging into your Microsoft account, you will be asked to create a PIN to log into the computer with, as shown in Figure 15.20.

FIGURE 15.20   Create a PIN screen

The PIN will replace your password for *only* this installation. By setting a PIN, you protect your Microsoft account password. If someone shoulder surfs your PIN, they won't have your Microsoft account password—they would only have access to the local computer if it is left unattended.

Type the PIN for the account, then enter it again and click OK, as shown in Figure 15.21.

15. Next you're asked if you are restoring this operating system or setting the operating system up as a new device, as shown in Figure 15.22. If you select restore from the prior device, then OneDrive files, apps, and preferences will be restored. If you select Set Up As New Device, then OneDrive files will be merged to this operating system, but apps and preferences will not be synced over.

FIGURE 15.21 Set up a PIN screen

FIGURE 15.22 Restore from prior device or Set up as new device

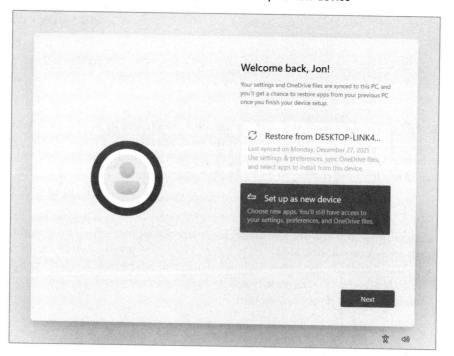

16. The next screen offers what are known as *telemetry* options, as shown in Figure 15.23. Choose the level of privacy on the device as well as features like Location, Find My Device, Diagnostic Data, and other features that transmit to Microsoft's cloud. Once you have made your selection, click Accept to continue.

FIGURE 15.23 Windows telemetry options

17. Next, you're asked to customize your experience, as shown in Figure 15.24. The options you select will not limit what you can do on the device; you'll only customize the tips and recommendations for features, products, and services. For this step, just select Skip.

18. One of the key features of using a Microsoft account is the ability to back up your files with OneDrive. This screen confirms that you will back up your Desktop, Documents, and Pictures folder on this device, as shown in Figure 15.25. Or you can select Only Save Files To This PC, which will not use OneDrive (and files will not be backed up automatically). Click Next.

FIGURE 15.24   Windows experience customization

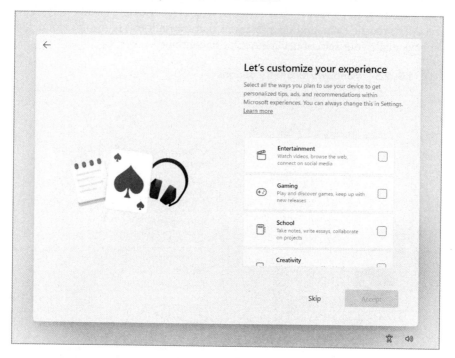

FIGURE 15.25   OneDrive confirmation screen

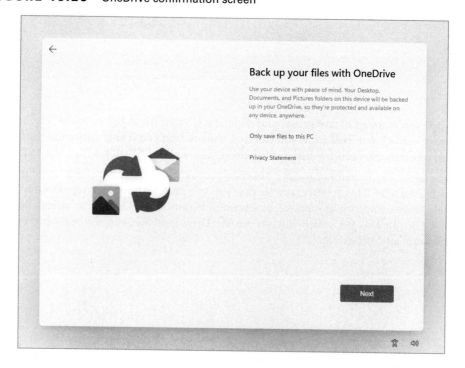

19. The next screen allows you to claim a free trial of a Microsoft 365 subscription that allows access to Microsoft Word, Excel, PowerPoint, OneNote, and Outlook. You also have the option to enter a product key to activate the installation. Click No, Thanks.

20. The next screen allows you to sign up for the Xbox Game Pass. The Game Pass allows you to play over 100 PC games and it also gives you addition perks if you are a gamer. Click Skip For Now.

21. At this step of the installation, it may look like nothing is happening, but a lot is going on in the background. The installation process is setting up and syncing your user account. While this happens in the background, you will see the screen shown in Figure 15.26.

FIGURE 15.26   This Might Take a Few Minutes screen

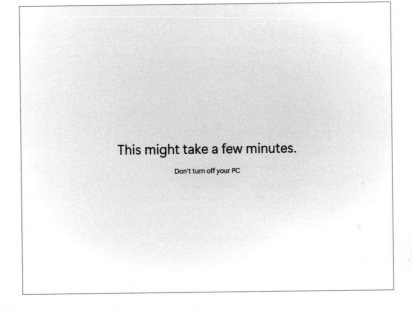

At this point, you are pretty much done. The next screen you will see is the Windows 11 Desktop. However, throughout the entire setup, you were never asked for your time zone. The time zone is automatically calculated based on your IP address. If it is incorrect, then the following procedure will manually adjust it.

To manually adjust the time, perform the following steps:

1. Right-click the clock in the lower-right corner of the Desktop.

2. Select Adjust Date and Time.

This will open the Date & Time screen, as shown in Figure 15.27.

3. Turn off Set Time Automatically if you want to change the time. If you want to change the time zone, turn off Set Time Zone Automatically if it is turned on.

FIGURE 15.27   Date & Time

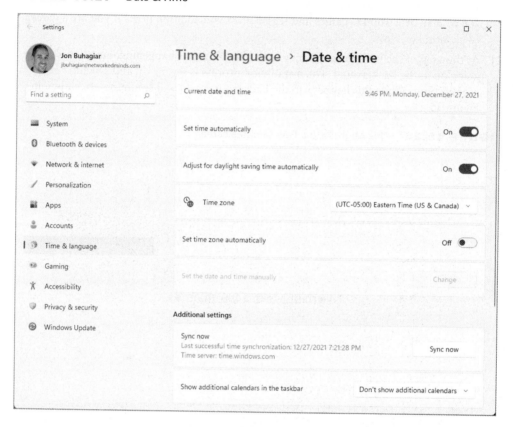

 This installation was based on the current version of Windows 11, version 21H1 as of this writing. Although each version introduces new screens and features, the basic setup does not change.

The Upgrade Process

Now let's take a look at the in-place upgrade process for a Windows 10 operating system to Windows 11. It is recommended that you start by performing all of the current *Windows Updates* first. Then you can start the upgrade process itself by inserting the Windows 11 media or connecting to a network share that contains the media and launching `setup .exe`. This will require answering a User Access Control (UAC) prompt. When the setup process starts, it will give you the option to change how Windows Setup downloads updates, as shown in Figure Figure 15.28, or you can just click Next at this point. The default is to proceed with the download of Windows Updates for the installation.

FIGURE 15.28   Install Windows 11 screen

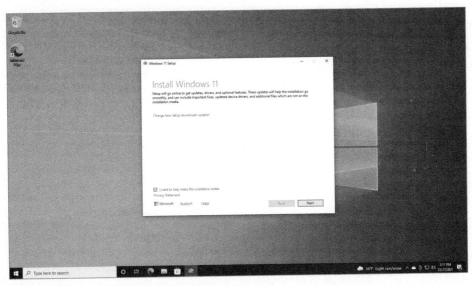

Before proceeding, you must accept the end-user license agreement (EULA), also known as the license terms, as shown in Figure 15.29.

FIGURE 15.29   Windows 11 end-user license agreement

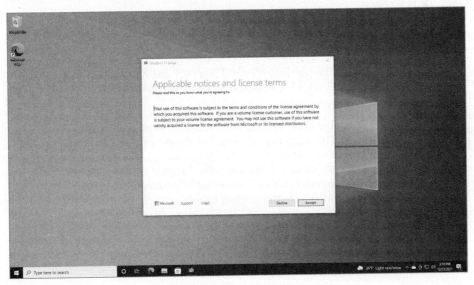

The installer will check and download updates necessary for the installation before continuing, as shown in Figure 15.30. This will ensure that you are secure and the upgrade process is smooth and without complication.

FIGURE 15.30   Windows 11 update check

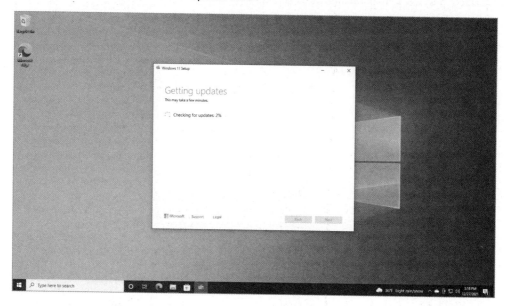

The next screen you will then see is the Ready To Install screen shown in Figure 15.31. This confirms the edition detected and also confirms that personal files and apps will be kept. You have the option to change what is kept during the upgrade process by clicking Change What To Keep.

The upgrade process will begin, and you will see the familiar progress percentage in the upper-left corner of the screen, as shown in Figure 15.32. The computer will reboot, and Setup will continue with a different progress screen, as shown in Figure 15.33. The computer will reboot several times during this process. As mentioned earlier, device drivers will be detected, and a reboot is required for the drivers to be properly loaded and instantiated.

The Windows 11 (21H2) upgrade process is almost identical to the Windows 10 (21H2) upgrade process. The Windows 11 upgrade process has omitted the possibility of choosing the wrong edition of Windows 11, by automatically detecting the currently installed edition. The Windows 11 upgrade process has also omitted the telemetry settings screen, inheriting the settings from the original install.

FIGURE 15.31   Windows 11 Ready To Install screen

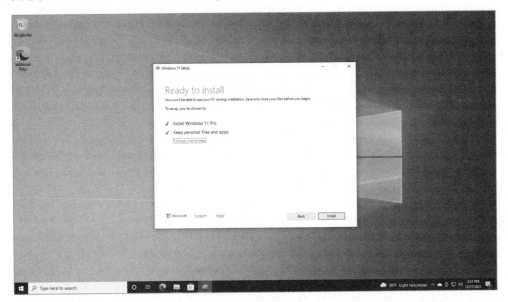

FIGURE 15.32   Windows 11 upgrade percentage

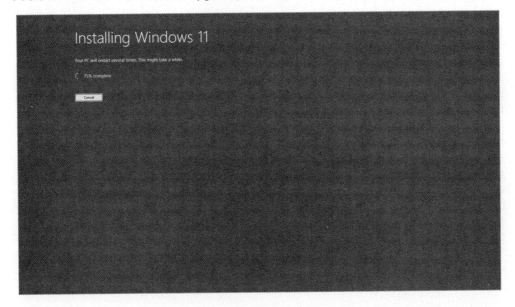

FIGURE 15.33   Windows 11 upgrade percentage after reboot

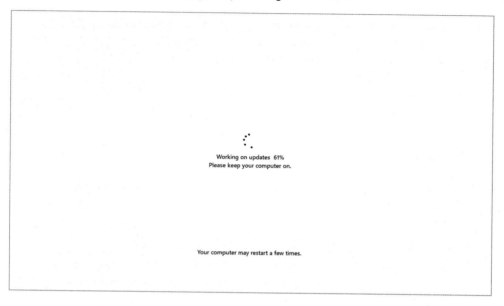

Working on updates 61%
Please keep your computer on.

Your computer may restart a few times.

Repair Installation

A *repair installation* is used when you want to reinstall the operating system without losing personal data files, application settings, or applications you've installed. The installation is similar to an upgrade, as described in the previous section, except that Windows 10/11 will detect that it is installed already. You will be presented with the option Keep Personal Files And Apps. The setup process will then reinstall the OS without affecting your personal files, applications, and their corresponding settings. It will, however, reinstall the operating system files, so it is considered a *repair* installation.

Another option for reinstalling Windows 10/11 is to reset the operating system with the Reset This PC option. This option is used to reset the operating system back to its original state. It provides another way to fix the operating system when it looks to be corrupted. This method should be used as a last resort. It does allow you the choice to keep personal files or completely erase them along with the operating system. On Windows 10, you can reset the operating system with the Reset This PC option by clicking Start, clicking the Settings gear, clicking Update & Security, clicking Recovery, and then choosing the Get Started option under Reset This PC. On Windows 11, you can reset the operating system with the Reset This PC option by clicking Start, clicking the Settings gear, clicking, clicking Recovery, and then choosing the Reset PC option under Reset This PC.

Recovery Partition

Some vendors will supply a recovery partition that contains the original image for the OS the system came installed with. In the event the operating system is corrupted, the recovery partition can be used to reimage the device back to the factory image. When vendors started to include the recovery partition, the image could be restored by booting the computer into the recovery partition, and a third-party utility would be used to reimage the device. However, with Windows 10/11 the use of third-party utilities is no longer needed—Windows has a provision for locally installing the image via WinRE.

Side-by-Side Upgrading Windows 10/11

Side-by-side upgrades require additional hardware, since the original operating system will not be modified during the upgrade. The new hardware will be the hardware that is installed from scratch with Windows 10/11. The user settings and data will then be migrated over from the previous operating system to the new one.

Side-by-side upgrades are the best way to upgrade when you need to upgrade a system but the current system is in use. When dealing with one system, side-by-side upgrades are great because you don't have to worry about backups of the OS. However, applications must be reinstalled, so this approach does have its disadvantages. When multiple systems require upgrading, a *rolling upgrade* can be performed. A rolling upgrade is a variation on the side-by-side upgrade that allows the decommissioned equipment to be used to upgrade the next user, and this creates a cycle. In other words, as you complete the upgrade of one user, their old system becomes the next user's new system, and the process continues until you get to the last user.

There are a few ways of migrating the user data from the old device to the new device, depending on how your deployment is configured. If the devices are using OneDrive to back up users' data folders, then users can simply sync their data onto their new devices. This method will work for data files and *Microsoft Store* apps, but OneDrive will not back and restore Win32 applications.

If you are not using OneDrive, then you can migrate user data with Windows 10/11 using the Microsoft Windows User State Migration Tool (USMT). The USMT allows you to migrate user file settings related to the applications, Desktop configuration, and accounts from one computer to another computer. The migration can be performed via a network connection or a hard drive. USMT is compatible with Windows 10 and Windows 11, but it is currently available only as part of the Windows 11 Assessment and Deployment Kit (ADK). Although the USMT is not part of the CompTIA objectives for the 220-1102 exam, it is important to know that a tool like the USMT exists, because the migration of user information is a component of an upgrade.

Additional information about the USMT can be found here:

https://docs.microsoft.com/en-us/windows/deployment/usmt/usmt-what-does-usmt-migrate

Using the USMT requires an investment of time. If you are performing only a few side-by-side upgrades, you can copy the user's profile directory manually. Then, when the new computer is ready, you can copy over the various folders, such as videos, pictures, and documents.

Image Deployment

Upgrading operating systems takes time and complex steps to complete, such as running Windows Upgrade, installing updates, upgrading the OS, and installing programs. These steps can take a tremendous amount of time, but if you have fewer than a dozen devices to upgrade, then you could manually upgrade the devices. However, if you have more than a dozen, there are alternatives such as image deployment.

The image deployment process is simple in concept. It starts with a base operating system on a reference computer utilizing real hardware or a virtual machine. The software is then installed on the operating system, an answer file is created using the Windows 11 Assessment and Deployment Kit (ADK), and the Sysprep tool is run on the operating system. The last step is to use a tool like Windows Deployment Services (WDS) to create an image of the operating system. Once the image is captured, it can be deployed to the other computers using the Windows Preinstallation Environment (WinPE).

Upgrading Editions of Windows

Windows 10/11 has the ability to upgrade at any time from one edition of the operating system to a higher one (for example, from Windows 10/11 Home to Windows 10/11 Pro). This can easily be accomplished by entering the appropriate activation product key. You can access the activation menu by clicking the Start menu, typing **Activation**, then clicking the Activation shortcut. You can only upgrade editions; downgrading of retail editions is not supported. However, downgrading of volume license editions, such as Windows 10/11 Enterprise to Windows 10/11 Pro, can be achieved. Downgrading of Windows 10/11 Education to Windows 10/11 Pro can also be done. Downgrading of volume license editions is not formally supported by Microsoft but can be accomplished.

Security and Feature Updates

The Windows platform has always had security updates and feature updates. In older versions of Windows such as XP, the features were subtle additions to the operating system. However, with the introduction of Windows 10 entire releases have been dedicated to major feature releases, such as the Creators update and the Anniversary update. Since then, the features have not been so dramatic, but Windows continues to get feature updates with every major/minor update.

Windows versions change twice a year (semi-annually) and have done so since the introduction of Windows 10. They just haven't been obvious, because they were downloaded as a Windows Update. The original version of Windows 10 is 1507, which was released in July 2015.

You may have noticed the pattern. The version is a *date code*, consisting of the last two digits of the year (15) and the two-digit month (07). So, it's simple to calculate when the last major update was released and what is currently installed. With the October 2020 release of Windows 10, Microsoft deviated from this naming convention, using H1 for first half and H2 for second half of the year. For example, version 21H1 was released in the first half of 2021. Windows 11 also follows the same date code with its initial release in October 2021; its date code is 21H2.

Versions are updated twice a year (semi-annually), usually in spring and fall. They are often referred to as the Windows 10 Spring Update or Windows 10 Fall Update, respectively. They also have a theme, such as the Fall Creator Update, which bundles content-creation tools, or the Anniversary Update, which bundles new features. As of this writing, the current Windows 10 version is 21H2 and the Windows 11 version is 21H2. They were both used in the development of this book. Using `winver.exe`, you can see the actual version of the operating system, as shown in Figure 15.34.

FIGURE 15.34   Discovering your version of Windows 11

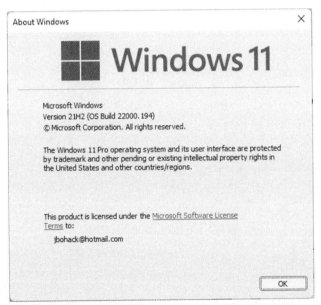

The life cycle of a Windows product has an end date for support, generally a year to two years after the product has been released. Once the end date is met, Microsoft will no longer support that version of Windows. The retirement date of Windows is generally 10 to 12 years, depending on the operating system's popularity. When the product reaches its retirement date, security updates are no longer furnished for the operating system. Therefore, you should be planning OS upgrades on a consistent schedule.

Probably the biggest change to Windows 10/11 is the way updates are delivered to the operating system. The end user no longer has the option to choose if they want to set up Windows Updates; they are mandatory and unavoidable. You can pause updates for up to 7 days on the main Windows Update screen, or pause all updates for up to 35 days, but inevitably they will be installed. To pause Windows Updates, click the Start menu, select the Settings gear, click Updates & Security, choose Advanced Options, and then click Select Date and choose a date up to 35 days later. Figure 15.35 shows the advanced options.

FIGURE 15.35   Advanced options for Windows Updates

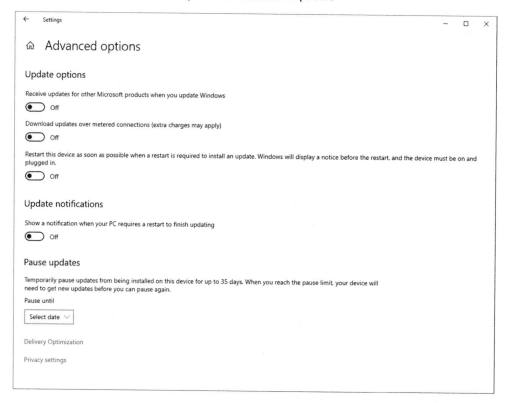

Windows 11 has identical controls for pausing Windows Updates. To pause Windows Updates, click the Start menu, select the Settings app, click Windows Update, and then choose 1 to 5 weeks (35 days) in the drop-down for the Pause Updates section.

Windows 10/11 has three different build branches of code (updates) that will be installed on a regular basis with automatic updates. The branches are as follows:

General Availability Channel   This is the default servicing channel for Windows 10/11 devices, with the exception of Windows 10/11 Enterprise LTSC (Long-Term Servicing Channel).

Insider Program   The Insider Program allows you to get the latest product updates from Microsoft before they are available for the targeted release. You must enroll your organization first, and then you can enroll your device to get the latest updates from the Windows Insider Program build channel.

Long-Term Servicing Channel   Only users of the Windows 10/11 Enterprise LTSC Edition can select this channel for updates. The operating system will receive monthly updates via Windows Updates, but no new features will be added over the lifetime of the product.

Table 15.2 details the list of the various Windows 10/11 editions and the options for changing their service update channels.

TABLE 15.2   Windows servicing channel options

Windows 10/11 Edition	General Availability Channel	Insider Program	Long-Term Servicing Channel
Home	Yes	Yes	No
Pro	Yes	Yes	No
Enterprise	Yes	Yes	No
Enterprise LTSC	No	No	Yes
Education	Yes	Yes	No

With the introduction of Windows 10 and the new Windows Update servicing channel options, Microsoft has introduced the concept of Windows as a Service (WaaS). A deeper dive on Windows servicing channels can be viewed here:

`https://docs.microsoft.com/en-us/windows/deployment/` `update/waas-overview`

Installation/Upgrade Boot Options

You can begin the installation or upgrade process by booting from a number of sources. There are three sources in particular with which you should be familiar: optical disc (CD-ROM/DVD), USB flash drive, and network boot (PXE). The one most commonly used for an attended installation is the CD-ROM/DVD boot. (They are identical in functionality.) Because Windows 10/11 only comes on DVD, though, the CD-ROM option applies to older operating systems, not this one.

You can boot a PC over the network (rather than from a DVD, USB, or hard disk) with *Windows Preinstallation Environment (WinPE)*, which is a stub operating system that creates a *Pre-boot Execution Environment (PXE)*. A stub operating system is characterized as a scaled-down version of the primary operating system. A stub operating system usually has basic functionality to perform a basic task, such as the installation of the Windows OS. When Windows 10 is installed with this method, it is considered a *remote network installation*.

You can install or upgrade Windows with traditional installation media, such as DVD, USB flash drives, and network boot (PXE), but they all tend to be a bit slow. An alternate method of installation and upgrade of Windows is from an external/hot-swappable drive, such as a USB hard drive. You can even use an external hot-swappable drive, such as an eSATA. However, the top speed on eSATA is 6 Gbps, compared to the top speed of USB 3.1 at 10 Gbps.

There is one other final option for installing Windows that is often used for reinstallation of the operating system by the original equipment manufacturer (OEM). That option is an internal hidden partition that contains the installation media. The OEM will often include this partition on the hard drive to allow the user to easily reinstall the operating system in the event of problems. In recent years, OEMs have moved away from an internal hard drive partition in favor of the Reset Your PC option in Windows.

Considerations

With every great plan there are unplanned consequences; we call them *considerations*. When installing Windows 10/11 or upgrading to Windows 10/11, there are several considerations surrounding the applications you need to use and the hardware Windows 10/11 is being installed on.

When you upgrade an operating system, you have the potential for data loss. Therefore, it is always advisable to back up files and user preferences before starting an upgrade. Depending on the user you are upgrading in your organization, if files are lost it could cause catastrophic loss of sales, payments, and most importantly time. Whenever possible, perform a full-drive backup, because settings may be in a spot you wouldn't normally back up. If a full-drive backup cannot be performed, then perhaps replace the drive with another one. Label the original drive *removed* and recycle it after you confirm that everything is acceptable with the end user.

The applications must be supported on Windows 10/11. You may think that if it runs, then it's supported, but you'd be wrong. Just because a program runs on Windows 10/11 doesn't mean that it was meant to be run on the operating system. It is up to the discretion of the software vendor if they will support you on the latest operating system. This is often discovered in the event you need help from them. So always check if the application is supported on the latest OS before upgrading. In many cases you'll find that software vendors require the latest version of their product purchased or installed for it to be supported on the latest OS. Applications are also backward compatible with older operating systems, because not everyone will be on the latest and greatest operating system.

The hardware that Windows 10/11 is running on is another consideration. Many motherboards and peripherals need third-party drivers. These drivers must be supported on Windows 10/11 or they may not function correctly. Older network interface cards (NICs) are notorious for not being supported on Windows 10/11. So, always check the hardware vendor's website before upgrading to Windows 10/11.

Command-Line Tools

Although the exam focuses on the Windows operating systems, it tests a great number of concepts that carry over from the Microsoft Disk Operating System (MS-DOS). MS-DOS was never meant to be extremely user friendly. Its roots are in Control Program for Microcomputers (CP/M), which, in turn, has its roots in UNIX. Both of these older OSs are command line–based, and so is MS-DOS. In other words, they all use long strings of commands typed in at the computer keyboard to perform operations. Some people prefer this type of interaction with the computer, including many folks with technical backgrounds. Although Windows has left the full command-line interface behind, it still contains a bit of DOS, and you get to it through the command prompt.

Although you can't tell by looking at it, the Windows command prompt is actually a Windows program that is intentionally *designed* to have the look and feel of a DOS command line. Because it is, despite its appearance, a Windows program, the command prompt provides all the stability and configurability you expect from Windows. You can access a command prompt by running cmd.exe.

A number of diagnostic utilities are often run at the command prompt. They can be broken into two categories: networking and operating system. The utilities associated with networking appear in other chapters, but the focus here is on the utilities associated with the operating system.

The OS command-line tools that you are expected to know for the exam are *cd*, *dir*, *md*, *rmdir*, *ipconfig*, *ping*, *hostname*, *netstat*, *nslookup*, *chkdsk*, *net user*, *net use*, *tracert*, *format*, *xcopy*, *copy*, *robocopy*, *gpupdate*, *gpresult*, *shutdown*, *sfc*, *diskpart*, *pathping*, *winver*, and [*command name*] */?*. They are discussed in the sections that follow, along with the commands available with standard privileges, as opposed to those with administrative privileges.

Navigation

The power of the command line comes from the level of detail that can be attained with simple commands. There are several commands that allow you to extract a high level of detail. However, the command line is an unforgiving user interface that requires specific commands, whereas with the GUI you just need to know how to point and click, but it lacks the high level of detail. In the following section we will cover basic navigation at the command line.

dir Command

The dir command is used to display a list of the files and folders/subdirectories within a directory. When you use it without any parameters, dir will show you not only that information but also the volume label and serial number, along with the amount of free space, in bytes, remaining on the disk.

Wild cards can be used with the command to list all files that begin with a certain letter or end with certain letters. An example is typing **dir *.txt** to list all the text files in a directory. A plethora of parameters are available that can be used to customize the results or the display. Table 15.3 lists some of the most common switches available for dir.

TABLE 15.3   Common dir switches

Switch	Purpose
/a	Allows you to specify the attributes of files you are seeking (hidden, system, and so on).
/o	Allows you to specify a different display order (alphabetic is the default).
/l	Returns the results unsorted and in lowercase format.
/s	Recursively searches through subdirectories as well as the current directory.
/t	Sorts the files according to time order.
/p	Displays the results one page/screen at a time.
/q	Shows file ownership.

cd, md, rd Commands

The cd, md, and rmdir commands are used to change (or display), make, and remove directories, respectively. The commands cd, md, and rd are shorthand versions of the chdir, mkdir, and rmdir commands, respectively. Table 15.4 lists their usage and switches.

TABLE 15.4   cd/md/rd usage and switches

Command	Purpose
cd [path]	Changes to the specified directory.
cd /d [drive:] [path]	Changes to the specified directory on the drive.

Command	Purpose
cd ..	Changes to the directory that is up one level.
cd \	Changes to the root directory of the drive.
md [drive:] [path]	Makes a directory in the specified path. If you don't specify a path, the directory will be created in your current directory.
rmdir [drive:] [path]	Removes (deletes) the specified directory.
rmdir /s [drive:] [path]	Removes all directories and files in the specified directory, including the specified directory itself.
rmdir /q [drive:] [path]	Quiet mode. You won't be asked whether you're sure you want to delete the specified directory when you use /s.

Drive Navigation

So far, you've seen the basics of looking at directories with the dir command, changing directories, making directories, and removing them. However, up to this point we have assumed you are on the same partition. The cd command will change directories within a drive letter, such as the C: drive, but it will not change drive letters unless you supply the /d switch. To change drives without using the dir command, just enter the drive letter and append a semicolon to it. For example, if you want to change to the D: drive, enter **d:** at the command prompt. You can then use the cd command followed by the drive letter, and if you want to change back, enter **c:** at the command prompt.

Now that you've learned how to navigate the command prompt to look at files, let's use that knowledge in Exercise 15.1.

EXERCISE 15.1

Command-Line Directory Management

1. Open a command prompt by click Starting, typing **cmd** in the Open field, and clicking OK.

2. Change to the root of your C: drive by typing **cd /d C:** and pressing Enter.

   Note: If you are already in C:, all you have to do is type **cd ** and press Enter.

3. Create a directory called C14 by typing **md C14** and pressing Enter.

(continues)

4. Change to the C14 directory by typing **cd C14** and pressing Enter.

5. Create several layers of subdirectories at once. Type **md A1\B2\C3\D4** and press Enter. Notice that these commands create each of the directories that you specified. You now have a directory structure that looks like this: C:\C14\A1\B2\C3\D4.

6. Change back to your root directory by typing **cd **.

7. Attempt to delete the C14 directory by typing **rd C14** and pressing Enter.

    Windows won't let you delete the directory because the directory is not empty. This is a safety measure. Now let's really delete it.

8. Delete the C14 directory and all of its subdirectories by typing **rd /s C14** and pressing Enter.

    You will be asked whether you're sure that you want to delete the directory.

9. If you are, type **Y** and press Enter.

10. To close the command prompt window, type **exit**.

    Note that if you had used the /q option in addition to /s, your system wouldn't have asked whether you were sure; it would have just deleted the directories.

Network Connectivity Tools

Windows is a network operating system, which means that the operating system and its principal user relies on the network for connectivity to information. This is where the command line becomes really useful to the administrator of the PC. The command line will return a large amount of data that is normally not suited for a graphical user interface (GUI). The following is a short list of commands that can help you diagnose network connectivity issues from the command line.

ipconfig Command

The ipconfig command is a network administrator's best friend—it assists in the diagnosis of network problems with the operating system. The ipconfig command without any switches displays basic information, such as the IP address, subnet mask, default gateway, and DNS suffix. The command ipconfig /all lists adapters and each one's assigned IP address, subnet mask, default gateway, DNS suffix, DNS server(s), *DHCP server*, and MAC address, just to name the most important elements. Viewing these assignments can help you diagnose the current network status of the connection.

In addition to verifying the status of a network connection's assignments, you can release and renew DHCP-assigned IP addresses. The /release switch releases the IP address, and the /renew switch renews the lease of an IP address.

The ipconfig command also allows you to view the local DNS cache with the /dis-playdns switch. You can flush the local DNS cache with the /flushdns switch. These switches come in handy when a DNS entry has changed and you want to immediately flush the cache and verify any cached entries.

ping Command

Next to the ipconfig command, the ping command is the runner-up as the network administrator's best friend. The ping command allows you to verify network connectivity via *Internet Control Message Protocol (ICMP)* packets. A common troubleshooting step used by network administrators is to ping the default gateway. If it returns a ping, then the network connectivity problem is probably beyond that device or your subnet mask is incorrect. However, after a successful ping, you can verify that your computer has basic connectivity to it. An example of a successful ping is as follows:

```
C:\Users\Sybex>ping 172.16.1.1

Pinging 172.16.1.1 with 32 bytes of data:
Reply from 172.16.1.1: bytes=32 time<1ms TTL=64
Reply from 172.16.1.1: bytes=32 time<1ms TTL=64
Reply from 172.16.1.1: bytes=32 time<1ms TTL=64
Reply from 172.16.1.1: bytes=32 time<1ms TTL=64

Ping statistics for 172.16.1.1:
    Packets: Sent = 4, Received = 4, Lost = 0 (0% loss),
Approximate round trip times in milli-seconds:
    Minimum = 0ms, Maximum = 0ms, Average = 0ms


C:\Users\Sybex>
```

tracert Command

The tracert command allows the network administrator to verify the path a network packet travels to its destination. As the diagnostic packet passes through the internetwork, each router responds with a response time. This enables you to locate a fault in an internetwork. Here's an example:

```
C:\Users\Sybex>tracert 8.8.8.8

Tracing route to google-public-dns-a.google.com      [8.8.8.8]
over a maximum of 30 hops:
  1    <1 ms    <1 ms    <1 ms  pfsense.Sybex.local  [172.16.1.1]
  2    13 ms    12 ms    17 ms  96.120.62.213
```

```
 3     15 ms     15 ms     12 ms  te04012.comcast.net  [68.86.101.141]
 4     13 ms     19 ms     12 ms  162.151.152.153
 5     12 ms     13 ms     20 ms  96.108.91.78
 6     22 ms     14 ms     20 ms  96.108.91.121
 7     21 ms     24 ms     20 ms  be-7016-cr02.comcast.net  [68.86.91.25]
 8     20 ms     20 ms     26 ms  be-10130-pe04.comcast.net  [68.86.82.214]
 9     20 ms     20 ms     21 ms  as040-2-c.comcast.net  [75.149.229.86]
10     22 ms     21 ms     20 ms  108.170.240.97
11     20 ms     23 ms     21 ms  108.170.226.85
12     20 ms     22 ms     18 ms  google-public-dns-a.google.com  [8.8.8.8]

Trace complete.

C:\Users\Sybex>
```

pathping Command

pathping, another command-line tool, combines the benefits of tracert and ping. The tool can be used to diagnose packet loss (or suspected packet loss) to a destination website. It is invaluable to network administrators to help prove to their ISP that packet loss is a problem on their network.

The tool will first trace the entire path to a destination IP address or DNS host. Then, each of the hops will be tested with ICMP for packet loss and round-trip time. It easily identifies router hops that are causing the delay or packet loss. The following is an example of a pathping to my provider's DNS server:

```
C:\Users\Sybex>pathping 75.75.75.75

Tracing route to cdns01.comcast.net [75.75.75.75]
over a maximum of 30 hops:
 0 Wiley.sybex.local [172.16.1.101]
 1 pfSense.sybex.local [172.16.1.1]
 2 96.120.62.213
 3 te-0-5-0-12-sur02.pittsburgh.pa.pitt.comcast.net [69.139.166.77]
 4 be-11-ar01.mckeesport.pa.pitt.comcast.net [68.86.147.109]
 5 be-7016-cr02.ashburn.va.ibone.comcast.net [68.86.91.25]
 6 ae-4-ar01.capitolhghts.md.bad.comcast.net [68.86.90.58]
 7 ur13-d.manassascc.va.bad.comcast.net [68.85.61.242]
 8 dns-sw01.manassascc.va.bad.comcast.net [69.139.214.162]
 9 cdns01.comcast.net [75.75.75.75]
```

```
Computing statistics for 225 seconds...
        Source to Here   This Node/Link
Hop RTT  Lost/Sent = Pct Lost/Sent = Pct Address
 0                          Wiley.sybex.local [172.16.1.101]
                 0/ 100 = 0%  |
 1  0ms   0/ 100 = 0%   0/ 100 = 0% pfSense.sybex.local [172.16.1.1]
                 0/ 100 = 0%  |
 2  14ms  0/ 100 = 0%   0/ 100 = 0% 96.120.62.213
                 0/ 100 = 0%  |
 3  15ms  0/ 100 = 0%   0/ 100 = 0% te-0-5-0-12-sur02.pittsburgh.pa.pitt.
comcast.net [69.139.166.77]
                 0/ 100 = 0%  |
 4  15ms  0/ 100 = 0%   0/ 100 = 0% be-11-ar01.mckeesport.pa.pitt.comcast.net
[68.86.147.109]
                 0/ 100 = 0%  |
 5  23ms  0/ 100 = 0%   0/ 100 = 0% be-7016-cr02.ashburn.va.ibone.comcast.net
[68.86.91.25]
                 0/ 100 = 0%  |
 6  23ms  0/ 100 = 0%   0/ 100 = 0% ae-4-ar01.capitolhghts.md.bad.comcast.net
[68.86.90.58]
                 0/ 100 = 0%  |
 7  25ms  0/ 100 = 0%   0/ 100 = 0% ur13-d.manassascc.va.bad.comcast.net
[68.85.61.242]
                 0/ 100 = 0%  |
 8  24ms  0/ 100 = 0%   0/ 100 = 0% dns-sw01.manassascc.va.bad.comcast.net
[69.139.214.162]
                 0/ 100 = 0%  |
 9  23ms  0/ 100 = 0%   0/ 100 = 0% cdns01.comcast.net [75.75.75.75]

Trace complete.

C:\Users\Sybex>
```

netstat Command

The netstat command allows you to view listening and established network connections for the operating system. Several switches can be used with the netstat command. One of the most useful is the -b switch, which displays the name of the application and its current established connections. Adding the -a switch displays all the listening connections in addition to the established connections. A basic example follows:

```
C:\Users\Sybex>netstat
```

```
Active Connections

  Proto  Local Address        Foreign Address        State
  TCP    127.0.0.1:49750      view-localhost:50912   ESTABLISHED
  TCP    127.0.0.1:50912      view-localhost:49751   ESTABLISHED
  TCP    172.16.1.181:49208   104.20.60.241:https    ESTABLISHED
  TCP    172.16.1.181:49599   172.67.181.149:https   ESTABLISHED
  TCP    172.16.1.181:49600   52.167.17.97:https     TIME_WAIT
  TCP    172.16.1.181:49602   20.50.80.210:https     ESTABLISHED
  TCP    172.16.1.181:49603   a104-75-163-105:http   TIME_WAIT
  TCP    172.16.1.181:56759   151.101.1.140:https    ESTABLISHED
  TCP    172.16.1.181:64151   iad23s96-in-f10:https  CLOSE_WAIT
  TCP    172.16.1.181:64152   iad66s01-in-f13:https  CLOSE_WAIT
  TCP    172.16.1.181:64154   iad23s96-in-f10:https  CLOSE_WAIT

C:\Users\Sybex>
```

nslookup Command

DNS is one of the most important network services that an operating system and user relies on for resolution of www.sybex.com to an IP address. Without DNS, we just couldn't remember the millions of IP addresses; it would be like trying to remember the phone number of every person you've ever met or are going to meet.

When DNS problems arise, the nslookup command allows you to verify that DNS is working correctly and that the correct results are being returned. The simplest way to use DNS is to use an inline query, such as **nslookup www.sybex.com**. This will return the IP address associated with the *fully qualified domain name (FQDN)* of www.sybex.com. The nslookup command can also be used in the interactive mode by typing **nslookup** and pressing Enter. This mode allows you to query more than the associated IP address, depending on the type of DNS record you are trying to diagnose. By default, the record looked up with the nslookup command is the A or CNAME DNS records. These records are the most commonly looked up DNS records for diagnosing connectivity issues. By specifying the -type argument, you can change the default record queried. The following is an example of retrieving the IP address for the FQDN of www.sybex.com, as well as the use of the -type argument:

```
C:\Users\Sybex>nslookup www.sybex.com
Server:  pfsense.wiley.local
Address:  172.16.1.1

Non-authoritative answer:
Name:    www.sybex.com
Address:  63.97.118.67
```

```
C:\Users\Sybex>nslookup -type=mx sybex.com
Server: pfSense.wiley.local
Address: 172.16.1.1

Non-authoritative answer:
sybex.com    MX preference = 20, mail exchanger = cluster1a.us.messagelabs.com
sybex.com    MX preference = 10, mail exchanger = cluster1.us.messagelabs.com

C:\Users\Sybex>
```

hostname Command

The hostname command allows the administrator to keep their sanity. The command returns the hostname of the computer that you have the command prompt open on. It can get pretty confusing for the administrator when they jump from one computer to another and remain in the command line. So by typing the command **hostname**, you can positively identify the system you are about to execute a command on. The following is an example of the command's use:

```
C:\Users\Sybex>hostname
Wiley-023432

C:\Users\Sybex>
```

Other Network Tools

There are several other command-line tools just as useful as the connectivity tools we've discussed, but they are used for various other purposes. The following tools are part of the objectives for the 220-1102 exam, and they are commonly used by Windows administrators.

gpupdate Command

Active Directory refreshes local and Active Directory–based policies every 90 minutes in what is called a *background refresh cycle*. When the background refresh happens, policies are reapplied, forcing the settings that the administrator has configured in the Group Policy settings.

The gpupdate command is used to update Group Policy settings. It refreshes, or changes, both local and Active Directory–based policies and replaces some of the functionality that previously existed with the secedit command.

The gpupdate command can force the refresh cycle immediately with the /force switch. In addition, you can target the computer or the user, which is particularly useful when trying to diagnose a problem with Group Policy Objects (GPOs). The following is an example of forcing a refresh for the computer GPO settings:

```
C:\Users\bohack>gpupdate /force /target:computer
Updating policy...
```

```
Computer Policy update has completed successfully.

C:\Users\bohack>
```

gpresult Command

The gpresult command is used to show the Resultant Set of Policy (RSoP) report/values for a remote user and computer. Bear in mind that configuration settings occur at any number of places: they are set for a computer, a user, a local workstation, the domain, and so on. Often one of the big unknowns is which set of configuration settings takes precedence and which is overridden. With gpresult, it is possible to ascertain which settings apply.

A number of switches can be used in conjunction with the gpresult command. The most useful switches are the /r and /z switches. The /r switch allows you to see the RSoP summary of GPOs applied. This allows you to quickly verify if a policy is being applied. You can then use the /z switch to turn on super-verbosity, which allows the output to display the exact settings being applied.

net Command

The net command can be used with several different subcommands. Most of the subcommands have been deprecated with the last few releases of Windows.

net use The net use subcommand is still widely used by administrators to map drive letters to network shares. The syntax for mapping a drive of Z: to the network location of \\server\share is as follows:

```
net use Z: \\server\share
```

net user The net user is another subcommand widely used by administrators. This command allows an administrator to list all the local accounts on a Windows installation by entering **net user**. It can also be used to list local accounts or domain accounts by supplying some arguments to the command. If you wanted to create a local account of usertwo with a password of *Passw0rd*, you would use the following syntax:

```
net user usertwo Passw0rd /add
```

Disk Commands

There are several commands for the administration of drives and folders. In this section, we will cover the common command-line tools that you will use in day-to-day administration of Windows. All of these tools can be accessed in the GUI as well, but the advantage to using the command line is avoiding clicks and potential mistakes.

format Command

The format command is used to wipe data off disks and prepare them for new use. Before a hard disk can be formatted, it must have partitions created on it. (Partitioning was done in the DOS days with the fdisk command, but that command does not exist in current versions of Windows, having been replaced with `diskpart`.) The syntax for `format` is as follows:

`format [volume] [switches]`

The *volume* parameter describes the drive letter (for example, `D:`), mount point, or volume name. Table 15.5 lists some common `format` switches.

TABLE 15.5   format switches

Switch	Purpose
/fs:[*filesystem*]	Specifies the type of filesystem to use (FAT, FAT32, or NTFS)
/v:[*label*]	Specifies the new volume label
/q	Executes a quick format

There are other options as well—to specify allocation sizes, the number of sectors per track, and the number of tracks per disk size. However, we don't recommend that you use these unless you have a very specific need. The defaults are just fine.

Thus, if you wanted to format your D: drive as NTFS, with a name of HDD2, you would type the following:

format D: /fs:ntfs /v:HDD2

> Before you format any drive, be sure that you have backed it up (or are prepared to lose whatever is on it).

copy Command

The copy command does what it says: it makes a copy of a file in a second location. (To copy a file and then remove it from its original location, use the move command.) Here's the syntax for copy:

`copy [filename] [destination]`

It's pretty straightforward. There are several switches for copy, but in practice they are rarely used. The three most commonly used switches are /a, which indicates an ASCII text file; /v, which verifies that the files are written correctly after the copy; and /y, which suppresses the prompt asking whether you're sure that you want to overwrite files if they exist in the destination directory.

> The copy command cannot be used to copy directories. Use xcopy for that function.

One useful tip is to use wild cards. For example, at the command prompt, the asterisk (*) is a wild card that means *everything*. So, you could type **copy *.exe** to copy all files that have an .exe filename extension, or you could type **copy *.*** to copy all files in your current directory. The other popular wild card is the question mark (?), which does not mean everything but instead means one thing. For example, copy ABC?.exe would copy only .exe files with four-letter names, of which the first three letters are ABC.

xcopy Command

If you are comfortable with the copy command, learning xcopy shouldn't pose too many problems. It's basically an extension of copy with one notable exception—it's designed to copy folders as well as files. The syntax is as follows:

xcopy [source] [destination][switches]

There are 26 xcopy switches. Some commonly used ones are listed in Table 15.6.

TABLE 15.6   xcopy switches

Switch	Purpose
/a	Copies only files that have the Archive attribute set and does not clear the attribute (useful for making a quick backup of files while not disrupting a normal backup routine).
/e	Copies directories and subdirectories, including empty directories.
/f	Displays full source and destination filenames when copying.
/g	Allows copying of encrypted files to a destination that does not support encryption.
/h	Copies hidden and system files as well.
/k	Copies attributes (by default, xcopy resets the Read-Only attribute).
/o	Copies file ownership and ACL information (NTFS permissions).
/r	Overwrites read-only files.
/s	Copies directories and subdirectories but not empty directories.
/u	Copies only files that already exist in the destination.
/v	Verifies the size of each new file.

Perhaps the most important switch is /o. If you use xcopy to copy files from one location to another, the filesystem creates new versions of the files in the new location without changing the old files. In NTFS, when a new file is created, it inherits permissions from its new parent directory. This could cause problems if you copy files. (Users who didn't have access to the file before might have access now.) If you want to retain the original permissions, use xcopy /o.

robocopy Command

The robocopy.exe (Robust File Copy) utility is included with recent versions of Windows and has the big advantage of being able to accept a plethora of specifications and keep NTFS permissions intact in its operations. The /mir switch, for example, can be used to mirror a complete directory tree.

An excellent resource on how to use robocopy can be found at https://docs.microsoft.com/en-us/windows-server/administration/windows-commands/robocopy. The robocopy utility is the Swiss army knife of file and folder copy utilities. It can copy files and their attributes to include NTFS attributes.

diskpart Command

The diskpart.exe utility shows the partitions and lets you manage them on the computer's hard drives. You can perform the same functions in the diskpart utility as you can perform in the GUI, which is discussed later in this chapter. Because of the enormous power that diskpart holds, membership in the Administrators local group (or equivalent) is required to run diskpart.

chkdsk Command

You can use the Windows chkdsk.exe utility to create and display status reports for the hard disk. chkdsk can also correct filesystem problems (such as cross-linked files) and scan for and attempt to repair disk errors. You can manually start chkdsk by right-clicking the problem disk and selecting Properties. This will bring up the Properties dialog box for that disk, which shows the current status of the selected disk drive.

By clicking the Tools tab at the top of the dialog box and then clicking the Check button in the Error-checking section, you can start chkdsk. Exercise 15.2 walks you through starting chkdsk in the GUI, and Exercise 15.3 does the same from the command line.

EXERCISE 15.2

Running chkdsk within Windows

1. Open Windows File Explorer by holding down the Windows key and pressing E.

2. Right-click C: and choose Properties.

3. Click the Tools tab, and then click the Check button.

4. Choose Scan Drive.

5. Once the drive is scanned for errors, you can click Close.

   In operating systems prior to Windows 10, you can choose options such as Automatically Fix Filesystem Errors and/or Scan For And Attempt Recovery Of Bad Sectors.

EXERCISE 15.3

Running chkdsk at the Command Line

1. Open an administrative command prompt in Windows 10/11 by clicking the Start menu and typing **cmd**, and then press Ctrl+Shift+Enter.

   You can also right-click on the result and run cmd with administrator privileges from the context menu.

2. Type **chkdsk /f** and press Enter.

   The system will now scan for, and fix, filesystem errors.

Miscellaneous Command-Line Tools

There are lots of other command-line tools, so many that we could dedicate a book to all of them. However, for the 220-1102 exam, there are specific command-line tools that CompTIA wants you to know. In the following, we will cover all the other miscellaneous command-line tools that don't fit into one of the previously mentioned categories.

shutdown Command

The shutdown.exe utility can be used to schedule a shutdown (complete or a restart) locally or remotely. You can even have the computer enter into a hibernation power state. In addition, shutdowns of the computer can be logged with a variety of reasons, from unplanned to application maintenance. A message can also be specified and announced to users for the shutdown. The syntax of the command is as follows:

```
shutdown [/i | /l | /s | /sg | /r | /g | /a | /p | /h | /e | /o] [/hybrid] [/
soft] [/fw] [/f] [/m \\computer][/t xxx][/d [p|u:]xx:yy [/c "comment"]]
```

There are a lot of different switches, as you can see from the previous usage syntax. Table 15.7 lists the most important switches for the shutdown command.

TABLE 15.7   shutdown **switches**

Switch	Purpose
/s	Shut down the computer.
/sg	Shut down the computer. On the next boot, restart any registered applications.
/r	Do a full shutdown and restart the computer.
/g	Do a full shutdown and restart the computer. After the system is rebooted, restart any registered applications.

Switch	Purpose
`/a`	Abort a system shutdown.
`/h`	Hibernate the local computer.
`/o`	Go to the advanced boot options menu and restart the computer. Must be used with the `/r` option.
`/m \\ computer`	Specify the target computer.
`/t xxx`	Set the timeout period before shutdown to *xxx* seconds. The valid range is 0–315360000 (10 years), with a default of 30. If the timeout period is greater than 0, the `/f` parameter is implied.

sfc Command

The System File Checker (`sfc.exe`) is a command line–based utility that checks and verifies the versions of system files on your computer. If system files are corrupted, `sfc` will replace the corrupted files with correct versions.

The syntax for the `sfc` command is as follows:

```
sfc [switch]
```

Table 15.8 lists the switches available for `sfc`.

TABLE 15.8   sfc switches

Switch	Purpose
`/scanfile`	Scans a file that you specify and fixes problems if they are found.
`/scannow`	Immediately scans all protected system files and replaces corrupted files with cached copies.
`/verifyonly`	Scans protected system files and does not make any repairs or changes.
`/verifyfile`	Identifies the integrity of the file specified and makes any repairs or changes.
`/offbootdir`	Repairs an offline boot directory.
`/offwindir`	Repairs an offline Windows directory.

To run sfc, you must be logged in as an administrator or have administrative privileges. If the System File Checker discovers a corrupted system file, it will automatically overwrite the file by using a copy held in another directory. The most recent Windows versions store the files in a large number of discrete folders beneath C:\WINDOWS\WINSXS (where they are protected by the system and only TrustedInstaller is allowed direct access to them—the cache is not rebuildable). TrustedInstaller is a service in Windows 10/11 that enables the installation, removal, and modification of system components.

> The C:\WINDOWS\SYSTEM32 directory is where many of the Windows system files reside.

If you attempt to run sfc from a standard command prompt, you will be told that you must be an administrator running a console session in order to continue. Rather than opening a standard command prompt, on Windows 10/11 click the Start menu, type **cmd**, and then press Ctrl+Shift+Enter. On Windows 8.1 and below, choose Start ➤ All Programs ➤ Accessories, and then right-click Command Prompt and select Run As Administrator. The UAC will prompt you to continue, and then you can run sfc without a problem.

winver Command

winver.exe is not a command-line tool but a useful tool to glean information about the operating system. The command will display a GUI dialog box. The command's sibling at the command line is ver.exe. This command has its roots all the way back to DOS, and it's still active in the latest version of Windows 10. Using the command will return the version of Windows, as shown in the following:

```
C:\Users\NetworkedMinds>ver.exe

Microsoft Windows [Version 10.0.19043.1237]

C:\Users\NetworkedMinds>
```

help and /? Commands

The help command does what it says: it gives you help. If you just type **help** and press Enter, your computer gives you a list of system commands that you can type. To get more information, type the name of a command that you want to learn about after typing **help**. For example, if you type **help rd** and press Enter, you will get information about the rd command.

You can get the same help information by typing /? after the command.

> The /? switch is slightly faster and provides more information than the help command. The help command provides information for system commands only. (It does not include network commands.) For example, if you type **help ipconfig** at a command prompt, you get no useful information (except to try /?); however, typing **ipconfig /?** provides the help file for the ipconfig command.

Commands with Standard Privileges vs. Administrative Privileges

By default, any user can open a command prompt and begin typing the names of command-line commands. Certain commands, however, can be dangerous when run and, as a safety precaution, require administrative privileges. The sfc command was mentioned earlier, for example, as requiring administrative privileges.

With Windows 7, rather than opening a standard command prompt, choose Start ➤ All Programs ➤ Accessories, right-click Command Prompt, and then choose Run As Administrator. The UAC will prompt you to continue, and then you can run sfc without a problem. With Windows 8, there are two choices on the Start menu; the latter allows you to open the command prompt with administrative privileges. Windows 10/11 behaves similarly to Windows 7; you can right-click the Command Prompt search result and choose Run As Administrator, as shown in Figure 15.36.

FIGURE 15.36   Opening a command prompt with admin privileges in Windows 10

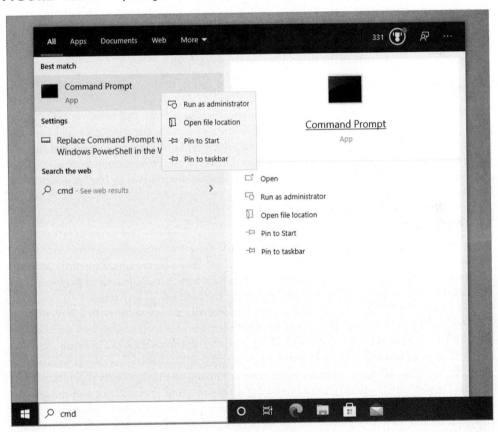

In most cases, if you try to run a utility that requires administrative privileges and you are not currently in a console session that has them, an error message will notify you of this.

Networking in Windows

CompTIA expects you to know a number of topics related to networking and Windows. This section covers the various scenarios in which you will deploy Windows in a network. First, we'll cover small office, home office (SOHO) deployments, and then we'll scale it out to an enterprise network. Many of these options are identical in Windows 8/8.1, with the exception of a few new features that we will highlight as specific to Windows 10/11.

Networking Models

There are several different networking models that you can use to facilitate Windows authentication. There is no single way to implement a network model; it all depends on the needs of the organization to share the resources. Each model has its advantages and disadvantages. This section covers the three most popular methods.

HomeGroup

The *HomeGroup* feature is available in Windows 10 version 1709 and prior, as well as Windows 8/8.1 and Windows 7. The HomeGroup feature allows for the sharing of files and printers with a single password. You can choose which types of resources are shared, such as pictures, documents, music, videos, and printers. However, the HomeGroup feature has been removed as of Windows 10 version 1803. We will discuss alternatives to HomeGroups in the following sections.

Workgroups

The *workgroup* networking model has existed in the Windows operating system since it was first introduced. Windows can function as both a client and a server simultaneously. When an operating system can function as both a client and a server, it is considered *peer-to-peer networking*. Clients can join the network and leave the network at any time.

The core of the Windows operating system is essentially the same for both a server and workstation. There are a few differences between the two—for instance, servers normally give priority to background services like file and printer sharing versus the desktop. The second and most limiting is the restriction of connecting 20 simultaneous clients to a single workstation. After 20 simultaneous connections are made, all others clients will return an "Access Denied" error—that is, until one of the 20 connections is closed out and the session is terminated. This takes some time on the workstation side, so if you have more than 20 clients, you should plan to deploy an actual server system running software such as Windows Server 2019 or Windows Server 2022.

Workgroups are normally used in SOHO environments or in situations that do not require the infrastructure of a dedicated server for authentication. They should be kept to a maximum of 20 clients, with the expectation that each client will maintain its own resources (files and printer sharing). Many small offices use this networking model and never need anything more.

A typical situation where a workgroup is effective is when a printer needs to be shared from a single computer. The disadvantage is that the computer must be on in order for the clients to use the printer. Another disadvantage with workgroups is user authentication, which we will discuss in detail later in this chapter.

When you install Windows 10/11, by default it is joined to the workgroup named Workgroup. However, there may be instances in which you want to join another workgroup. To join another workgroup, perform the following steps:

1. Click the Start menu.

2. Click the Settings gear.

3. Click System.

4. Click About.

5. Click the Advanced System Settings, related setting.

6. Click Change Settings under the heading of Computer Name, Domain, and Workgroup Settings.

7. Click Change Next to Rename This Computer or Change Its Domain Or Workgroup.

8. Change the Workgroup option to the desired workgroup.

9. Click OK.

10. Click OK.

11. Reboot the computer.

Domains

Domain functionality has existed since Microsoft Windows 3.51 (mid-1990s). Unlike the workgroup networking model, the domain networking model requires that clients be joined to a domain. Joining a domain creates a trust between the client (Windows client, for example) and the authentication server (Windows Server 2019 running Active Directory, for example). Joining a client to a domain allows users with an account in the domain to log into the client. To join a domain in Windows 10/11, perform the following steps:

1. Click Start ➢ Settings ➢ Accounts ➢ Access Work or School ➢ Connect ➢ Join This Device To A Local Active Directory Domain. You will be prompted to enter a domain name, as shown in Figure 15.37.

2. Enter your credentials on the domain when prompted, which allows the joining of the operating system, as shown in Figure 15.38.

3. Reboot the operating system for the changes to take effect.

FIGURE 15.37   Windows 11 Settings app for joining a domain

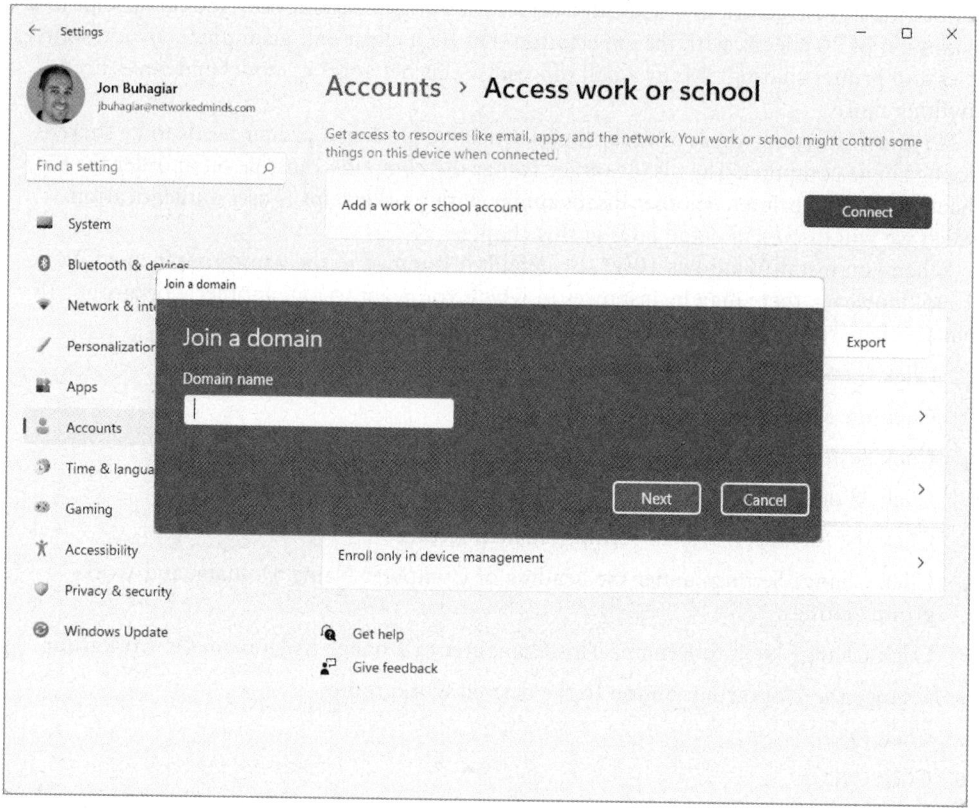

An alternate way of joining a domain is through the System Properties dialog box. To do so:

1. Right-click Start.
2. Click System.
3. Under Related choose Advanced System Settings.
4. Under Computer Name, Domain, And Workgroup Settings, select Change Settings.
5. Click Change.
6. Select the Domain radio button under Member Of.
7. Enter the domain name and click OK, as shown in Figure 15.39.

The next dialog box will prompt you to enter your credentials on the domain that allows the joining of the operating system. You will then need to reboot the operating system for the changes to take effect. This method of joining an operating system to a domain has been supported since Windows XP.

FIGURE 15.38   Windows 11 domain credentials prompt

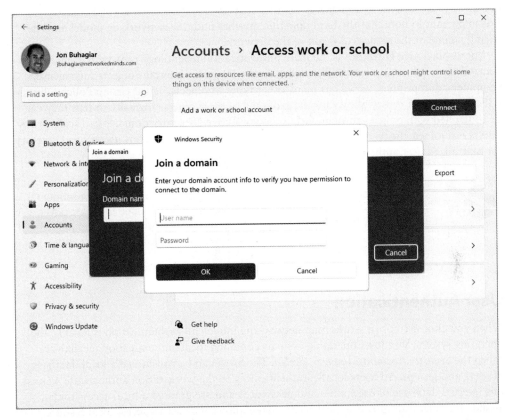

FIGURE 15.39   Windows domain joining

Domains also allow for files and printers to be secured with domain credentials. The key takeaway in the benefit to domains is centralized authentication for users and computers. It is important to note that the term *domain* describes both the networking model and the friendly name of the security domain of the network.

Microsoft Active Directory is the main authentication technology used with domain controllers in a domain networking model. Active Directory contains objects such as users, computers, and printers, as well as many other types of objects, called Group Policy Objects (GPOs). Active Directory allows for the grouping of these objects logically so that they can be controlled with policies through Group Policy. Active Directory domains can scale to any number of joined clients and user credentials. Many large organizations use Active Directory for centralized user authentication, because it is very scalable.

> **NOTE** Group Policy is a component of Active Directory as well as a component of the client-side operating system. Group Policy is used to create policies that can be applied to groups of users and a group of computers. Group Policy is considered enforced, since it reapplies policies every 90 minutes.

User Authentication

When you choose to use a workgroup networking model, all authentication is local to the operating system. Windows operating systems contain a local authentication mechanism called the *Security Account Manager (SAM)*. The SAM can be considered a local database of users and groups. All users locally authenticating to the workstation authenticate against this internal database of usernames and passwords and are granted a local access token, as shown in Figure 15.40. The local access token allows the user to access local resources secured with the user's identity.

FIGURE 15.40 Windows local authentication

When clients are joined to a domain, a user with credentials on the domain can log into the workstation. When this happens, they are authenticating against an Active Directory *domain controller*. An Active Directory domain controller retains information about all access rights for all users and groups in the network. When a user logs into the system, AD issues the user a *globally unique identifier (GUID)*, also known as an *access token*. Applications that support Active Directory can use this access token to provide access control. When a client is joined to a domain, users can still log into the local operating system using the SAM, as if they have a local account (see Figure 15.41). However, local logins are normally restricted to administrators once a client is joined to the domain.

FIGURE 15.41   Windows domain authentication

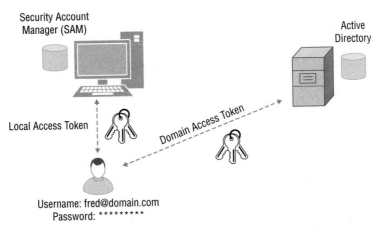

Active Directory simplifies the sign-on process for users and lowers the support requirements for administrators. Access can be established through groups, and it can be enforced through group memberships. Active Directory can be implemented using a Windows Server (such as Windows Server 2019 or Windows Server 2022) computer. All users will then log into the Windows domain using their centrally created AD accounts.

> Azure AD is a cloud-based alternative to hosting a traditional AD domain in a physical location. There are different benefits depending on the requirements, such as the Microsoft 365 platform. There is also a monthly cost to maintain the licensing.

One of the big problems that larger systems must deal with is the need for users to access multiple systems or applications. This may require a user to remember multiple accounts and passwords. The purpose of a *single sign-on (SSO)* is to give users access to all the applications and systems that they need when they log in.

SSO operates on the principle that the resource trusts the authentication server. When a user logs in initially, they will authenticate against the authentication server for their organization. When the user then visits the resource, which is normally a cloud-based resource, it will prompt the authentication server to provide a claim on behalf of the user, as shown in Figure 15.42.

FIGURE 15.42   Single sign-on

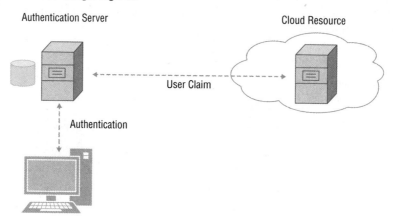

The claim normally contains basic information about the user, such as first and last name, email address, or any other attribute. At no time is the user's password sent, because they authenticated once already. Although we've oversimplified SSO in this example, it really is this simple, without the layers of encryption and complicated trust rules. As we adopt more and more cloud resources, it is becoming the number one way to provide authentication for our users because we never transmit the actual username and password.

> Single sign-on is both a blessing and a curse. It's a blessing in that once the user is authenticated, they can access all the resources on the network and browse multiple directories. It's a curse in that it removes the doors that otherwise exist between the user and various resources. This creates a security risk, because if an attacker gets the username and password for the user, they have access to all the resources.

Establishing a Network Connection

A key element to a successful network is the connection that connects the computer to the actual network. There are a number of different ways to connect to the network that we will cover in the following section. The key takeaway is that the network system will function identically, regardless of the connection. For example, if you have a computer joined to an organization's domain, the login process will function identically with a wireless versus a wired connection.

The type of connection you choose is based on your convenience and the requirements of the connection. As an example, wireless is extremely convenient, but it requires you to be within distance of an access point (AP), and the further you are away from the AP the slower the connection. If your requirement is consistent high bandwidth for a Voiceover IP (VoIP) call, then a wired connection is your best choice and wireless would be problematic.

Wired   A wired network is most common in organizations with desktop computers. Unfortunately, a wired connection means that there is no mobility for the connection; you are literally wired to a desk.

Wired connections are the most reliable and arguably easiest to diagnose when there are problems. The network link light gives you a visual indicator that you have a network connection. Windows 10/11 will also place a visual notification of a computer with a cable in the notification area when a wired connection is detected.

Wireless   A wireless connection is found in networks where mobility is required. Wireless is often used in small office/home office (SOHO) networks settings. It can also be found in small and large organizations that require workers to move around, such as a factory setting, sales workforce, or medical setting, just to name a few.

Connecting to wireless networks is not as straightforward as making a wired connection. There is rarely a visual identifier that you have a wireless connection, such as the link light with a wired connection. Windows 10/11 will display the notification tray icon as a radio wave. If the radio wave is grayed out with an asterisk at the upper left, then there are wireless connections detected and you are not connected to any of them. If you click the wireless icon, all of the wireless networks available will be displayed, along with their security status, as shown in Figure 15.43.

FIGURE 15.43   Wireless connectivity

You can then choose a wireless network and select Connect. If the wireless network requires additional security, such as a preshared key (PSK) or a corporate login to a *captive portal*, the operating system will direct you. By default, wireless networks that you connect to will automatically reconnect when you are in range. When the wireless connection is established, the notification tray icon will appear as a white radio wave. As you move further away from the AP, the wireless indicator will act as a signal strength meter.

Virtual Private Network (VPN)   In recent years, *virtual private networks (VPNs)* have become the rage of network privacy for browsing. These applications provide encryption to an anonymous server from which you can browse the Internet. However, the 220-1102 exam is based on traditional VPN technology that provides a secure connection between the two endpoints in an organization.

The VPN connection is an overlay network on top of an established network connection called the underlay network. So, you will need an established Internet connection before a VPN can connect. The VPN connection will provide two distinct features to the end user. The first feature it provides is an entry point to the organization's private network. The second feature it provides is end-to-end encryption for everything transmitted over the connection between the client and the organization's private network.

Establishing a VPN connection will require information from the organization's VPN appliance or server. You will need the VPN protocol, server address, and the sign-in info. You can create a VPN connection by navigating the Start button ➢ Settings gear ➢ Network & Internet ➢ VPN; from here you can add a VPN connection, as shown in Figure 15.44.

Wireless Wide Area Network (WWAN)   A wireless wide area network (WWAN) connection is a connection that is created with a cellular data provider, such as Sprint, Verizon, or AT&T, just to name a few. The mobile device will require a special card called a WWAN adapter, or most mobile devices will have a built-in card. You will then need to register the connection with the cellular provider to activate the connection; this process usually requires a monthly billing for data and the connection is often metered.

A metered connection is a connection in which you pay for a specific amount of data to be downloaded. Once the amount of data is reached, you generally pay for overages per gigabyte. Many features in Windows, such as Windows Updates, will work differently depending on whether the connection is a metered connection. Windows Updates will not download over a metered connection, so the features don't use all your precious data over the metered connection. The cellular option of connectivity is not the only connection that can be classified as a metered connection; each of the methods of connectivity in this section can be set as a metered connection. It is just more common to find cellular connection as a metered connection.

FIGURE 15.44   VPN connectivity

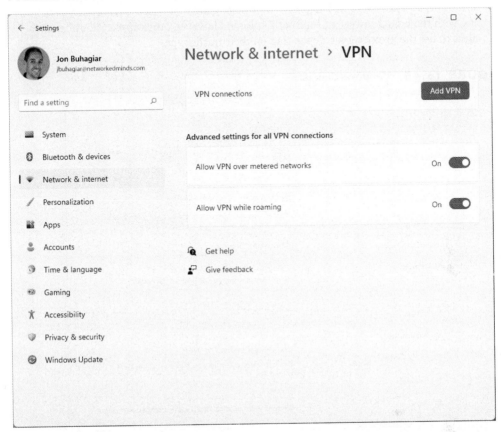

Once the connection is registered, you can connect via the wireless notification tray icon and select the cellular network you wish to connect to. You can also connect to the cellular network by navigating the Start button ➢ Settings gear ➢ Network & Internet ➢ Cellular, as shown in Figure 15.45. If your device does not support a WWAN device, then the Cellular section will not appear on the Network & Internet screen. After selecting Cellular, you can then configure roaming options, as well as the preference of cellular over Wi-Fi, and you can tell Windows to treat the connection as a metered connection.

Proxy Settings   In addition to establishing a connection, you may need to set a proxy server depending on your organization's policies. In many organizations, the web browser is not allowed to directly request web pages from the destination web server. An intermediary called a *proxy server* is used to request the web page on behalf of the user.

The use of a proxy server allows for caching of frequently accessed web pages, as well as the ability to filter content. The proxy is primarily for web-based traffic, such as browsing with the Edge browser or Internet Explorer. However, other applications can also elect to use the proxy server, depending on their traffic type.

FIGURE 15.45   Windows Cellular

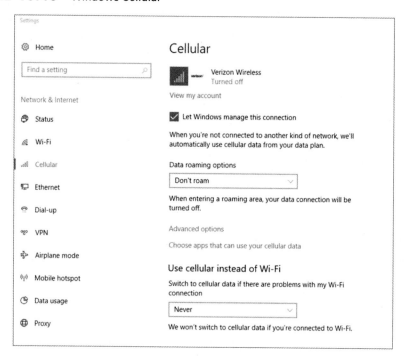

To configure the proxy settings for Microsoft Edge and Internet Explorer, click the Start button ➤ Settings gear ➤ Network & Internet ➤ Proxy. From the proxy screen you can configure the operating system to automatically use a setup script (JavaScript) by clicking the switch for Use Setup Script and specifying the script address, as shown in Figure 15.46.

You can also specify a manual proxy setup, which is a common configuration task. You will simply click the switch Use A Proxy Server and then enter the address and port. Specific websites often require direct access and will not work with a proxy server. You can enter exceptions into the lower section and separate servers with a semicolon. You can also use wild cards, if you want to exclude an entire namespace.

FIGURE 15.46   Windows Proxy settings

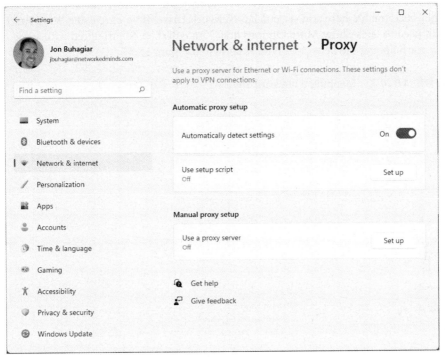

Accessing Resources

Now that you understand networking models, authentication, and how to connect to the network, let's focus on the resources that users will access. This section covers the most common types of resources.

Network Shares

A *network share* is a type of resource sharing that allows access to file and folder resources over a network from a file server. File Explorer is used to access network shares, but you can also use command-line commands to access the resources, as you will see in the following sections. As the name implies, network shares are those that exist on the network; however, they can be mapped to appear as if they are local. The `net use` command can be used to establish network connections at a command prompt, for example. If you want to connect to a shared network drive and make it your M: drive, the syntax is **net use M: ** *server\share*. The *server\share* portion of the command is called the *Universal Naming Convention (UNC)* path. The UNC path is a standard way to describe the server and fileshare to the Windows operating system.

In addition to using the command line, you can use the GUI to map a network share. After browsing to the server by typing *servername* in the Windows File Explorer address bar, right-click the fileshare and select Map Network Drive. If you are using Windows 11, you will need to click Show More Options first. You will then be prompted with some options for mapping the network share, as shown in Figure 15.47.

FIGURE 15.47   Mapping a network drive

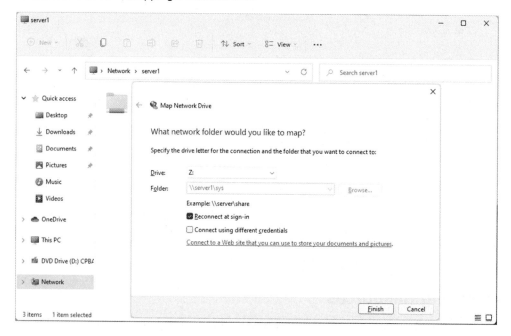

 By default, the Reconnect At Sign-In option is selected. In order to ensure that the mapped drive is reconnected when the user signs in, this option must be selected.

Printer Shares

Another common type of network resource is printing. Although we often need to access files and folders, at some point we will probably need to print. You can use the same command to connect to a shared printer; the syntax of `net use lpt1: \\server\` `printername` will map a printer to the LPT1 device. As in the prior example, you can make the printer act as if it is locally connected to the operating system. You can also use the GUI method of connecting a printer by right-clicking the printer after browsing to the server and then selecting Connect, as shown in Figure 15.48.

FIGURE 15.48   Connecting to printers

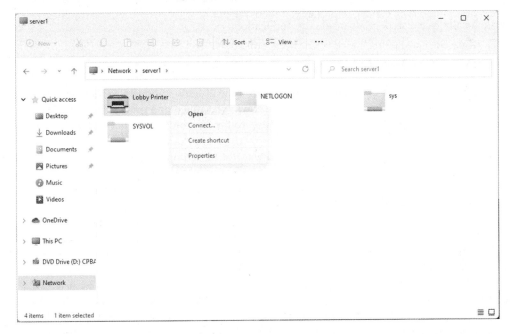

 Sharing printers was one of the primary reasons why networking became popular in the workplace, and it still continues to be an important reason today. Know that you can map to any printer on the network, but it still must be shared in order for you to be able to use it.

Administrative Shares

Administrative shares are automatically created for administrative purposes on Windows. These shares can differ slightly based on which operating system is running, but they end with a dollar sign ($) to make them hidden. There is one for each volume on a hard drive (C$, D$, and so forth), as well as admin$ (the root folder—usually C:\WINDOWS), and print$ (where the print drivers are located). These are created for use by administrators and usually require administrator privileges to access. It's important to note that they are hidden shares and that any shared folder created with a trailing $ will be hidden from the users as well. Unless you know they exist, they will not be visible.

Shared Resources

Although you can access shares on file servers and printers that are shared, there are many other shared resources that can be shared and accessed. Files and printers are just the common resources that make up the file and print sharing service that Windows has had built in, arguably since the inception of MS-DOS. Application sharing is one example of a shared resource. Scanners and faxes are other examples of hardware-based shared resources.

These examples only scratch the surface; the cloud is full of applications and shared resources. All these resources can be authenticated with domain-based authentication or separate locally based credentials inside the application.

Firewall Settings

Microsoft Windows has come with a preinstalled firewall since Windows XP Service Pack 2. The addition of the Windows Firewall feature was welcomed at a time in history when the Internet could be described as the *Wild West*. Today Windows Defender Firewall is an integral part of Windows. Surprisingly the interface has not changed all that much from its debut with Windows XP. The original firewall was not turned on by default, but with the introduction of Windows Vista the firewall was on by default in the inbound direction. The firewall is never configured in an outbound direction, but if needed it has the ability.

Windows Defender Firewall is scalable as a host-based firewall, because an average user can configure the firewall. However, if more complicated firewall rules need to be composed, the advanced interface allows for an administrator to intervene. The configuration of the firewall is really straightforward; you can access the basic firewall controls by clicking Start ➢ Windows System ➢ Control Panel ➢ Windows Defender Firewall, or you can click Start and start typing the word *firewall* until it appears in the search results. Launching it will display the dialog box shown in Figure 15.49. The basic Windows Defender Firewall dialog box allows you to perform basic firewall tasks, such as turning off the firewall, changing user notification, restoring defaults, and most importantly, allowing an app or feature through the firewall.

FIGURE 15.49 Windows Defender Firewall

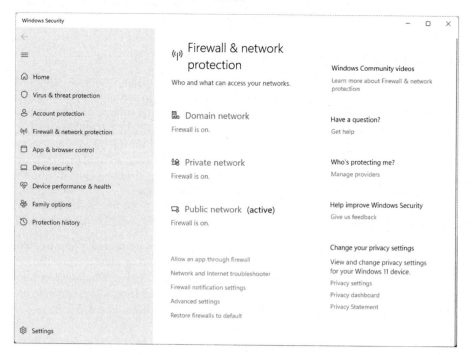

There are a number of applications and services that are preconfigured in the firewall. For example, when you share a folder, the ports associated with filesharing are automatically enabled. Another mechanism exists to allow the firewall to easily configure itself; when a program is launched that listens to a port, an Allow Access or Cancel notification is sent to the user, as shown in Figure 15.50. If the user selects Allow Access, a rule is added to the firewall for the specific application.

FIGURE 15.50   Windows Defender Firewall notifications

Along with the automated mechanism in which firewall rules can be added, you can specify which network profile they are active in. Network profiles are identified by the MAC address of the default gateway. The firewall will learn the internal network of your home by making a note of the MAC address of your router. If the MAC address has not been seen before by the network operating system, then the firewall will ask if the network is private or public. This way the firewall can behave differently in your home than if you were in an airport or another public setting. There are three different network profiles that firewall rules can be active for: public, private, and domain. You can control if your laptop is public or private, but if a domain controller exists and the laptop is joined to a domain, then the domain profile becomes active.

The individual rules can be examined or individually configured with the Windows Defender Firewall with Advanced Security MMC, as shown in Figure 15.51. You can see each of the rules along with its effective profile of public, private, domain, or all.

Adding rules manually allows for maximum granularity but comes with the price of complexity. You can add a rule based on a program, port, predefined rule, or something totally custom. For example, if you wanted to only allow an incoming port of 2233 via TCP to a specific application awaiting its request for a specific network profile, this interface will allow you to do so. If you are the administrator of a domain, you can also create rules inside a Group Policy Object (GPO) and deploy the rules out to a large group of computers.

FIGURE 15.51   Windows Defender Firewall with Advanced Security

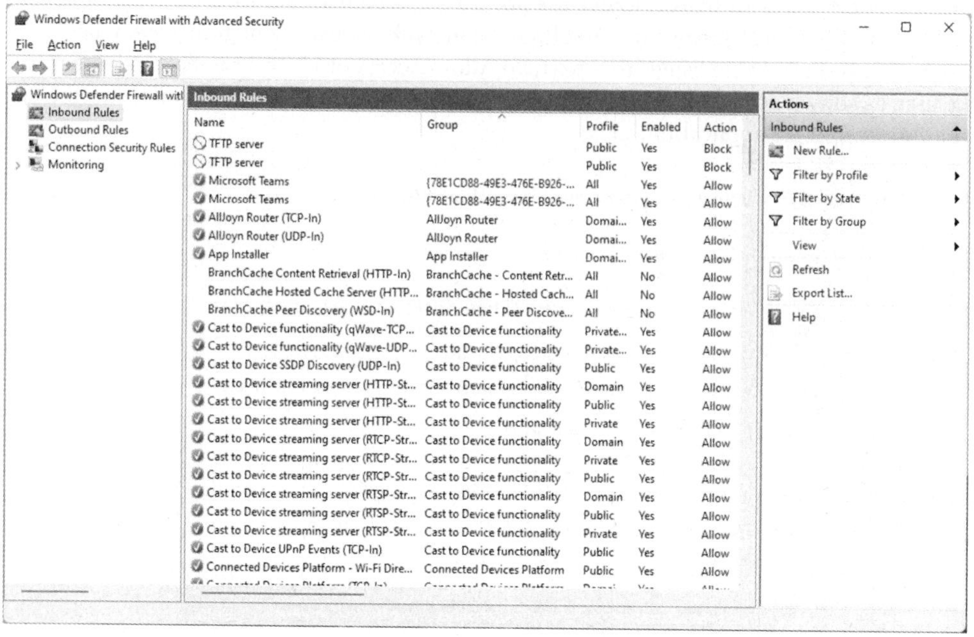

A Group Policy Object (GPO) is a collection of Group Policy settings. GPO allows an administrator to change the behavior and appearance of the operating system and control certain aspects of the user.

Client Network Configuration

If you have a router or a server that supports the Dynamic Host Configuration Protocol (DHCP), the client will automatically configure itself with an IP address, subnet mask, default gateway, and the appropriate Domain Name System (DNS) servers. This is the default behavior for all devices, because it is trouble-free from a user's point of view. For example, if you turn on your laptop at home, your router will serve all the information necessary to get on the home network and the Internet. If you pick up your device and go to work, this process will also happen at your workplace to allow you to connect to servers or the Internet.

Configuration of a Static IP Address

If you need to statically configure your network settings, that will require some planning and manual configuration. The first thing you will need is an IP address that is not used by another computer in the network. The subnet mask will also need to match the network you will configure the computer in. If you want to communicate outside the immediate network, you will need a default gateway, which is your router's IP address. A DNS address is also required if you want to translate simple domain names to IP addresses. There are two ways to configure the static IP address: by using the new Settings app and by using the legacy Control Panel applet. You should be familiar with both ways, as the legacy Control Panel applet offers more features, such as alternate IP address configuration.

Settings App   You can configure the network addressing via the Settings app by clicking Start ➤ Settings gear ➤ Network & Internet ➤ Properties, and then clicking Edit under IP Settings. You can then choose Manual from the drop-down menu to open two switches for IPv4 and IPv6. You can then click the switch for IPv4 and enter the IP address, subnet mask, gateway, and DNS settings, as shown in Figure 15.52.

FIGURE 15.52   Settings App network configuration

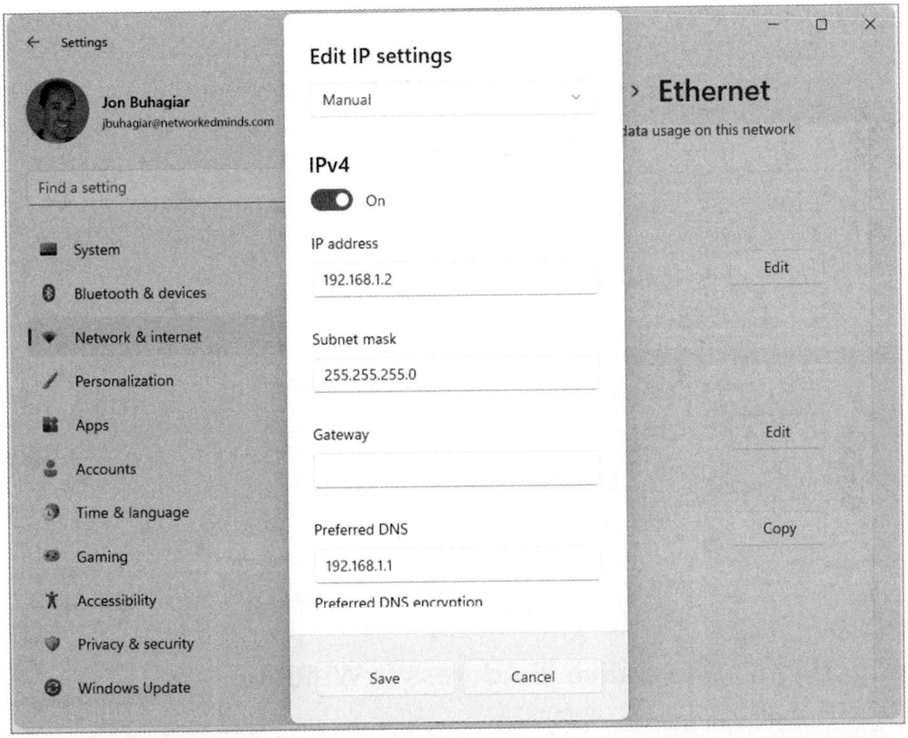

Control Panel Applet   The original Control Panel applet has been around since Windows NT 4.0, and you can get there a number of ways. To open the dialog, first open the Control Panel, then click Network And Sharing Center. When the dialog box opens, select Change Adapter Settings from the left side and then right-click the network adapter and select Properties. You can then double-click Internet Protocol Version 4

(TCP/IPv4). From here you can select Use The Following IP Address and manually enter the IP address, subnet mask, and gateway, as shown in Figure 15.53. As you can see, this method is not easier to get to, but it is familiar to a seasoned professional.

FIGURE 15.53   Control Panel network configuration

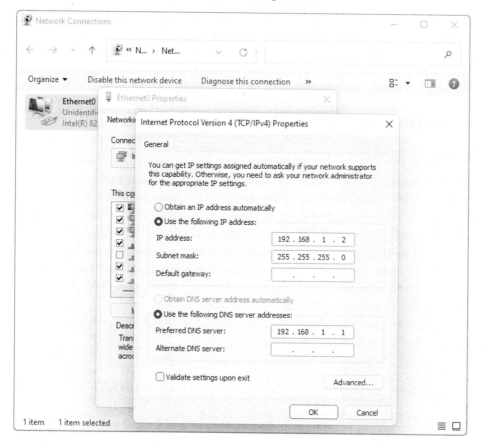

Configuring an Alternative IP Address in Windows

Windows 11 and prior versions of Windows also allow for the use of an alternate IP address—that is, an address configured for the system to use in the event the first choice is not available. In order for an alternate configuration to be set, the first choice has to be dynamic; the tab becomes visible only when the General configuration is set to Obtain An IP Address Automatically (as shown in Figure 15.53), and the alternate is used only if the primary address cannot be found/used, such as when the DHCP server is down. The Alternate IP address configuration is only available with the Control Panel applet.

IP Addressing   Two radio buttons exist on the Alternate Configuration tab: Automatic Private IP Address and User Configured (see Figure 15.54). The first option is the default, meaning that the alternate address used is one in the APIPA range (169.254. *x*.*x*). Selecting User Configured requires you to enter a static IP address to be used in the IP Address field. The entry entered must be valid for your network in order for it to be usable.

FIGURE 15.54   Alternate Configuration tab

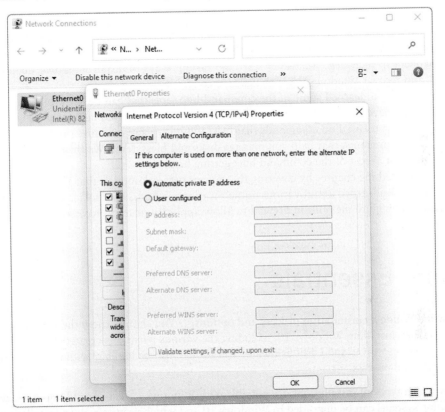

Subnet Mask   When the User Configured radio button is selected on the Alternate Configuration tab, you must enter a value in the Subnet Mask field. This value must correspond with the subnet values in use on your network and work with the IP address you enter in the IP Address field.

DNS   When the User Configured radio button is selected on the Alternate Configuration tab, you should enter values in the Preferred DNS Server and Alternate DNS Server fields. These entries are needed in order to translate domain names into IP addresses.

Gateway   When the User Configured radio button is selected on the Alternate Configuration tab, you must enter a value in the Default Gateway field. This value must correspond with the subnet values and the IP address that you enter. This address identifies the router to be used to communicate outside the local network.

Summary

In this chapter, you learned the various options for the installation and upgrade of Windows. Both the installation and the upgrade process were covered in great detail, so you could see what happens in each step. We also covered the various ways to install Windows, deploy images, and recover Windows when things go wrong.

In addition, you learned some of the command-line tools that can be used to administer Windows. We covered basic Windows commands to view, create, and navigate files and folders. We then focused on commands that help administer and diagnose the network. We also covered commands that help you manage disks and filesystems. We then explored the most important aspect of the command line: getting help.

We concluded the chapter by covering the various network models that Windows is deployed in. You learned about various authentication methods, how to access resources, and how to configure the built-in firewall to allow applications to be accessed via the network.

Exam Essentials

Know the Windows installation process and options.   You should know the various options when installing Windows 10, including the various partitions created and the differences between BIOS and UEFI firmware. You should also be familiar with the Windows 10 installation process.

Know which types of installations are possible with Windows.   You should know which operating systems can be upgraded to Windows 10 and which require a clean installation.

Understand upgrading to Windows.   You should know that a custom installation either wipes the old system or replaces the existing system, putting the old files into WINDOWS .OLD. Applications then have to be reinstalled, and user data has to be migrated from the old system using tools such as USMT. An upgrade preserves the existing applications and the user data, moving them into the new operating system.

Understand what each of the command-line utilities does.   Many utilities allow you to perform various functions at the command line. These include cd, dir, md, rmdir, ipconfig, ping, hostname, netstat, nslookup, chkdsk, net user, net use, tracert, format, *xcopy, copy, robocopy, gpupdate, gpresult, shutdown, sfc, diskpart, pathping,* and *winver*. The cmd command opens a command prompt, where you can type the rest of the commands. If you're not sure how to use a particular utility, using the /? switch at the end of the command will provide information about how to use it.

Understand networking in Windows.   You should understand the different networking models in which a Windows operating system can participate: HomeGroup, workgroups, and domains. You should also understand the basic user authentication methods used with each of these networking models, as well as common methods for accessing networking resources.

Know the various ways to establish a connection.   You should know how to connect and diagnose wired and wireless connections to a network. In addition, you should understand how a WWAN is configured and how VPN networks are used and configured.

Know the various ways to access resources.   You should know how to connect to network shares and printer shares using the UNC path of the resource. In addition, you should know the other types of resources, such as administrative shares and other hardware-based resources that you may encounter.

Review Questions

The answers to the chapter review questions can be found in Appendix A.

1. Which installation type should you choose if you want a clean installation of Windows?
   - **A.** Custom
   - **B.** Upgrade
   - **C.** Repair
   - **D.** Refresh

2. What is the name of the pass that detects hardware and installs drivers?
   - **A.** Generalize
   - **B.** OOBE
   - **C.** Specialization
   - **D.** WinPE

3. Which partition contains the recovery utility in the event of a problem?
   - **A.** BCD
   - **B.** System
   - **C.** ESP
   - **D.** WinRE

4. Which tool is used to create an operating system image for deployment?
   - **A.** WDS
   - **B.** MAP toolkit
   - **C.** USMT
   - **D.** sysprep

5. Which command will allow copying of all data to include NTFS permissions?
   - **A.** xcopy
   - **B.** copy
   - **C.** chkdsk
   - **D.** robocopy

6. Which Windows Update branch for Windows will install features as they are released to the general public?
   - **A.** Semi-Annual Channel
   - **B.** General Availability
   - **C.** Long-Term Servicing Channel
   - **D.** Insider Program

7. Which edition of Windows 10 will not allow for Insider Program branch releases?

    A. Home

    B. Pro

    C. Education

    D. Enterprise

8. You used the `winver.exe` utility and it reported Windows 10 Version 1703 (OS Build 15063.145). What is the current date of the last update?

    A. 63rd day of 2015

    B. 145th day of 2015

    C. March of 2017

    D. The version needs to be looked up at `Microsoft.com`.

9. Which command is used to measure packet loss as a packet travels to a destination address?

    A. `ping`

    B. `nslookup`

    C. `pathping`

    D. `tracert`

10. Which tool allows you to report a remote computer's inventory of hardware?

    A. `regedit.exe`

    B. `msinfo32.exe`

    C. `msconfig.exe`

    D. `dxdiag.exe`

11. Which command will allow you to check a volume for corruption?

    A. `diskpart`

    B. `format`

    C. `chkdsk`

    D. `sfc`

12. Which restriction will be imposed on Windows users until they activate the operating system?

    A. They won't be able to launch applications.

    B. They won't be able to run Windows Updates.

    C. They won't be able to change the wallpaper.

    D. They won't be able to browse the Internet.

13. What is the name of the pass that configures and creates the user environment during the setup process?

    A. Generalization

    B. OOBE

    C. Specialization

    D. WinPE

14. When installing Windows, you can control telemetry data. In which step during setup is this configured?

   A. Privacy settings

   B. Cortana options

   C. Partitioning options

   D. Account creation

15. You want to upgrade from Windows Vista Home Basic edition to Windows 10. What are your options?

   A. Upgrade to Windows 10 Home.

   B. Upgrade to Windows 10 Pro.

   C. Upgrade to Windows 10 Enterprise.

   D. Upgrade first to Windows 7 Home Basic.

16. You want to upgrade from 32-bit Windows 7 Professional to a 64-bit version of Windows 10. What are your options?

   A. Upgrade directly to Windows 10 Pro 64-bit.

   B. Upgrade first to Windows 10 Pro 32-bit, and then upgrade to 64-bit.

   C. Upgrade to Windows 8.1 64-bit, and then upgrade to Windows 10 64-bit.

   D. You must perform a clean installation of Windows 10 Pro 64-bit.

17. Where is the Boot Configuration Data stored on a Windows installation utilizing EFI?

   A. EFI System Partition

   B. WinRE partition

   C. Secure Boot partition

   D. `C:\WINDOWS`

18. Which command is used to identify ports in use by applications and the operating system?

   A. `netstat`

   B. `ipconfig`

   C. `pathping`

   D. `nslookup`

19. Which type of connection is configured in the Cellular screen in the Settings app?

   A. Wired

   B. Wireless

   C. WWAN

   D. VPN

20. What is the maximum number of concurrent connections that can be made to a Windows workstation?

A. 10 connections

B. 15 connections

C. 20 connections

D. 25 connections

Performance-Based Question

You will encounter performance-based questions on the A+ exam. The questions on the exam require you to perform a specific task, and you will be graded on whether or not you were able to complete the task. The following requires you to think creatively in order to measure how well you understand this chapter's topics. You may or may not see similar questions on the actual A+ exam. To see how your answers compare to the authors', refer to Appendix B.

You need to join a Windows 11 workstation to an Active Directory domain. What are the steps you need to follow to complete the task?

Chapter

16

Working with macOS and Linux

THE FOLLOWING COMPTIA A+ 220-1102 EXAM OBJECTIVES ARE COVERED IN THIS CHAPTER:

✓ **1.10 Identify common features and tools of the macOS/ desktop OS.**

- ▪ Installation and uninstallation of application
  - ▪ File types
    - ▪ .dmg
    - ▪ .pkg
    - ▪ .app
  - ▪ App Store
  - ▪ Uninstallation process
- ▪ Apple ID and corporate restrictions
- ▪ Best practices
  - ▪ Backups
  - ▪ Antivirus
  - ▪ Updates/patches
- ▪ System Preferences
  - ▪ Displays
  - ▪ Networks
  - ▪ Printers
  - ▪ Scanners
  - ▪ Privacy
  - ▪ Accessibility
  - ▪ Time Machine

- Features
  - Multiple desktops
  - Mission Control
  - Key Chain
  - Spotlight
  - iCloud
  - Gestures
  - Finder
  - Remote Disc
  - Dock
- Disk Utility
- FileVault
- Terminal
- Force Quit

✓ 1.11 Identify common features and tools of the Linux client/desktop OS.

- Common commands
  - ls
  - pwd
  - mv
  - cp
  - rm
  - chmod
  - chown
  - su/sudo
  - apt-get
  - yum
  - ip
  - df

CompTIA has acknowledged that system administrators and technicians are increasingly dealing with more than just Windows on a daily basis. Therefore, they have included objectives based on *macOS* and *Linux*.

This chapter looks at the non-Windows operating systems from the standpoint of what you need to know to pass the exam. All the topics relevant to objectives 1.10 and 1.11 of the 220-1102 exam are covered.

macOS and Linux

In the beginning there was UNIX. UNIX System 5 (version 5) is an operating system originally created and licensed by AT&T Labs. The UNIX operating system is considered to be the root of all UNIX-based operating systems. In the mid-1970s, the University of California at Berkeley (UC Berkeley) licensed UNIX from AT&T for their computer systems and expanded on the tools shipped in the original version of UNIX. These tools became the foundation of UNIX as it is today, but UC Berkeley only licensed the operating system for specific machines. The students quickly became upset and developed and released a version of UNIX called the Berkeley Software Distribution (BSD). The term *distribution* is used today with UNIX/Linux operating systems to define the operating system and its ecosystem for application management, patching, and upgrades.

Although it began with UNIX, BSD became very popular because it was an open source license. This allowed everyone to use the operating system on any computer system they wished. In the mid-1980s, Steve Jobs created a company called NeXT and built computers that furnished the NeXTSTEP operating system. The NeXTSTEP operating system was originally built from BSD version 4.3. Unfortunately, the NeXT computer company never really took off. However, the NeXTSTEP operating system was acquired by Apple and eventually became the macOS we know today.

Linux has a very different origin story from macOS. Actually, Linux has nothing to do with the original codebase of UNIX. In the mid-1990s a Finnish student named Linus Torvalds set out to create a completely open source operating system for the world to use. Linux was the result of his efforts; it was designed from scratch, so it was completely free for anyone to use or incorporate into their own products. Today you can find a great number of Linux distributions, such as *Ubuntu, Debian, Arch Linux, Gentoo, Red Hat*. . .and the list goes on.

Although Linux has a completely different codebase from BSD and UNIX, the operating system itself functions similarly. Only the kernel and interworkings of the OS are different. Many of the applications that were created by students on the BSD platform were ported over to Linux. Functionally, the operating systems are very similar in design and usability.

 The complete history of UNIX is vast and interesting; we have covered only the big events in the UNIX timeline. Many different organizations were involved, spanning all the way back to the 1960s. Learn more about the history of UNIX here: https://unix.org/what_is_unix/history_timeline.html.

Applications on macOS

The applications that are available or installed on an operating system indirectly define an OS by extending functionality to the end user. As with the case of UNIX, BSD, Linux, and macOS, all of the basic command-line applications are similar in functionality, as you will learn in this chapter. These command-line applications are preinstalled with the OS distribution. When you need functionality that isn't part of the base OS, you have a few different ways to install applications.

Installing Applications from the App Store

macOS contains an application ecosystem called the *App Store*, shown in Figure 16.1. From the App Store you can download and buy applications for macOS. Some applications might be free from the App Store, but they contain in-app purchases. They are called *freemium* games and applications, and they typically use this feature.

Applications installed through the App Store do not function any differently from legacy downloaded applications. Unfortunately, not all applications are available through the App Store. The developer of an application must publish it on the App Store, and not every vendor will submit their application. This is mainly due to the costs related to publishing an app to the App Store.

The benefit of using the App Store to install applications for macOS is if you purchase an app and have two devices, then you need to purchase the application only once. This is assuming you are logged in with the same Apple ID that purchased the application. Also, updates for the applications are automatically installed, compared to downloading applications from the developer directly. The Updates section in the App Store will show you all the applications containing updates.

When you first turn on your Apple device and run through the installation, it will ask for an *Apple ID*. You really can't move on with the setup without an Apple ID. The Apple ID is your digital identity on the device, and it's what also ties your Apple Wallet to the App Store for purchases. The Apple ID will contain credit card information that can be used for purchases.

FIGURE 16.1   macOS App Store

An organization may use mobile device management (MDM) software to control the installation of applications from the App Store or any software installations in general. An organization might also use the App Store as a distribution point for applications that its employees are expected to use. The organization's MDM software is associated with the employee's Apple ID, which is usually the employee's email address. These features were introduced in macOS starting with version 10.9. New features are introduced in every version of macOS.

Installing Downloadable Applications

Installing downloadable applications on macOS is not much different from the same process in Windows. The process consists of three steps: providing the installation to the operating system, mounting the installation, and then installing the applications.

The first step requires you to provide the application's installation files to the operating system. This step is normally done nowadays as a download, since we always want the latest updated applications. The process is pretty routine, as you can imagine; you navigate to a web page and download the app. However, providing the application might also be a simple as plugging in a USB drive or loading a DVD. macOS will automatically mount the USB drive or DVD onto the desktop and open the root folder.

The second and third step in the installation process is to launch the file you downloaded and install the application. When you launch the file, what will happen next depends on the type of file. There are a number of different file types that can be downloaded from the Internet, such as ZIP, ISO, DMG, PKG, or APP, just to name a few. The most common files for macOS applications are as follows:

APP Files   The APP file will end in *.app* and it is used to contain the application. The APP file is actually a container for various resource files and folders, and it also contains the executable for launching the application. You will rarely download an APP directly from the Internet. The APP file will often be found inside a ZIP, DMG, or ISO file or physical media.

DMG Files   A DMG file will end in *.dmg* and it stands for disk imaging file. The DMG file is directly comparable to ISO or ZIP files. The DMG file contains a file structure, and the file can be mounted as a disk on the macOS desktop. DMG files used for application installation will normally contain two files: the application itself and a shortcut to the Applications folder. This allows you to drag (copy) the APP file into the Applications folder, and doing so will install the application.

PKG Files   A PKG file will end in *.pkg* and it is an automated package installer. The PKG file is comparable to the application installation programs that are commonly found in Windows. When the PKG file is launched, it will ask the user a series of questions about the installation. PKG files are found inside DMG, ZIP, and physical media. These files are used when the installation requires customization by the end user.

In Exercise 16.1, you will install an application on macOS, to understand the process.

EXERCISE 16.1

Installing Applications on macOS

1. Open the Safari app from the Dock.

2. When Safari opens, type **sublimetext.com** in the address bar and press Return.

3. When the web page loads, choose the download option of OS X (10.7 or later is required).

4. A prompt will ask you to allow downloads from www.sublimetext.com; click Allow.

5. The download is stored in the Downloads folder located on the right side of the Dock. Click the Downloads folder and select the application Sublime Text Build 3211.dmg.

6. After macOS mounts the DMG as a drive and opens the folder, drag the Sublime Text icon over the Applications shortcut and release it.

7. You can then eject the Sublime Text mount on the desktop by selecting the folder and clicking Finder ➤ File ➤ Eject.

8. Press Shift+Command+A to open the Applications folder.

Managing Applications

The Applications folder contains all the applications installed on macOS, as shown in Figure 16.2. You can view and manage applications inside this folder. The two most common methods of launching the folder are using the *Finder app* and selecting Go ➤ Applications or pressing Shift+Command+A. This key sequence will also launch the Applications folder and requires no shuffling of applications to get to the Finder app.

FIGURE 16.2   macOS Applications folder

From the Applications folder, you can delete user-installed applications. However, pre-installed applications in this folder cannot be deleted by the user, since they are technically part of the operating system. These applications are similar to the built-in applications on Windows.

To delete a user-installed application, select the folder; then on the Finder menu, select File ➤ Move To Trash. This will place the application into the Trash and remove it from the operating system. Another method is to select the application and press Command+Delete. In Exercise 16.2 you will uninstall an application, to understand the process better.

EXERCISE 16.2

Uninstalling Applications on macOS

1. Press Shift+Command+A to open the Applications folder.

2. Select the Sublime Text application.

3. On the Finder menu, click File ➤ Move To Trash.

4. Open the Trash folder from the right side of the Dock and observe that the Sublime Text application is there.

Creating Shortcuts

The last and most important topic we will cover about applications is the availability of the application. Creating shortcuts is an essential part of your overall workflow. You should be able to launch an application in as few clicks as possible. To create a shortcut, launch the Applications folder by pressing Shift+Command+A and drag the application to the *Dock*.

Best Practices

Regardless of the operating system, there are a number of best practices that an administrator should always follow. Depending on the operating system (and distribution, version, edition, and so on), it may be possible to perform operations with the utilities provided, or third-party utilities may be needed.

Scheduled Backups

Backups are duplicate copies of critical information, ideally stored in a location other than the one where the information is currently stored. Backups include both paper and computer records. Computer records are usually backed up using a backup program, backup systems, and backup procedures.

The primary starting point for disaster recovery involves keeping current backup copies of important data files, databases, applications, and paper records available for use. Your organization must develop a solid set of procedures to manage this process and to ensure that all critical information is protected.

Computer files and applications should be backed up on a regular basis. Here are some examples of critical files that should be backed up:

- Applications
- Appointment files

- Audit files
- Customer lists
- Database files
- Email correspondence
- Financial data
- Operating systems
- Prospect lists
- Transaction files
- User files
- User information
- Utilities

This list isn't all-inclusive, but it provides a place for you to start.

In most environments, the volume of information that needs to be stored is growing at a tremendous pace. Simply tracking this massive growth can create significant problems.

 NOTE An unscrupulous attacker can glean as much critical information from copies as they can from the original files. Make sure that your storage facilities are secure, and it is a good idea to add physical security to the backup media as well.

You might need to restore information from backup copies for any number of reasons. Some of the more common reasons are as follows:

- Accidental deletion
- Application errors
- Natural disasters
- Physical attacks
- Server failure
- Virus/malware infection
- Workstation failure

Types of Storage Mechanisms

The information that you back up must be immediately available for use when needed. If a user loses a critical file, they won't want to wait several days while data files are sent from a remote storage facility. Several types of storage mechanisms are available for data storage:

Working Copies Working copy backups, sometimes referred to as *shadow copies*, are partial or full backups that are kept at the computer center for immediate recovery purposes. Working copies are frequently the most recent backups that have been made.

Typically, working copies are intended for immediate use. They are usually updated on a frequent basis.

> Working copies aren't usually intended to serve as long-term copies. In a busy environment, they may be created every few hours.

Many filesystems used on servers include journaling. A *journaled file system (JFS)* includes a log file of all changes and transactions that have occurred within a set period of time (such as the last few hours). If a crash occurs, the operating system can check the log files to see which transactions have been committed and which transactions have not.

This technology works well, allowing unsaved data to be written after the recovery, and the system is usually successfully restored to its pre-crash condition.

On-Site Storage   *On-site storage* usually refers to a location on the site of the computer center that is used to store information locally. On-site storage containers are available that allow computer cartridges, tapes, and other backup media to be stored in a reasonably protected environment in the building.

> As time goes on, tape as a medium for backups is losing its popularity to other technologies, such as cloud storage.

On-site storage containers are designed and rated for fire, moisture, and pressure resistance. These containers aren't fireproof in most situations, but they are *fire-rated*. A *fireproof container* should be guaranteed to withstand damage regardless of the type of fire or temperature, whereas fire ratings specify that a container can protect the contents for a specific amount of time in a given situation.

If you choose to depend entirely on on-site storage, make sure that the containers you acquire can withstand the worst-case environmental catastrophes that could happen at your location. Make sure, as well, that they are in locations where you can easily find them after the disaster and access them (near exterior walls, on the ground floor, and so forth).

> General-purpose storage safes aren't usually suitable for storing electronic media. The fire ratings used for safes generally refer to paper contents. Because paper does not catch fire until 451° Fahrenheit, electronic media are typically ruined well before paper documents are destroyed in a fire.

Off-Site Storage   *Off-site storage* refers to a location away from the computer center where paper copies and backup media are kept in the event the primary site suffers a catastrophe. Off-site storage can involve something as simple as keeping a copy of backup media at a *remote office*, or it can be as complicated as a nuclear-hardened high-security storage facility. The storage facility should be bonded, insured, and inspected on a regular basis to ensure that all storage procedures are being followed.

Your determination of which storage mechanism to use should be based on the needs of your organization, the availability of storage facilities, and your budget. Most off-site storage facilities charge based on the amount of space required and the frequency of access needed to the stored information.

Although it is easy to see the need for security at any location where your files are stored, don't overlook the need for security during transportation as well.

Scheduled Disk Maintenance

When files are written to a hard drive, they're not always written contiguously or with all the data located in a single location. When discussing Windows, we talked about Disk Defragmenter, which has existed in almost all versions of Windows, and its ability to take file data that has become spread out over the disk and put it all in the same location, a process known as *defragmenting*. This process decreases the time it takes to retrieve files.

As opposed to FAT- and NTFS-based filesystems, the filesystems used on macOS and Linux rarely, if ever, need to be defragmented. The ext3 and ext4 filesystems are common to Linux, and Apple File System (APFS) is common to macOS. They all have on-the-fly defragmentation methods and implement file allocation strategies differently from their traditional Windows counterparts.

System Updates/App Store

It is important to keep the operating system current and updated. Like Windows, many other operating systems include the ability to update automatically, and almost all can look for updates and tell you when they are available. In the Apple world, the *App Store* represents a location where you can also find updates.

For example, Figure 16.3 shows that a new version of iOS is available on an iPhone. By clicking on Learn More, you display the reasons the new version has been released, allowing you to read about the changes and decide whether you want to upgrade. The update notification usually includes a Learn More option and a link to Apple's release page for the iOS update.

FIGURE 16.3   Apple iOS software update

To access the Software Update area on an iPhone or iPad, choose Settings ➢ General ➢ Software Update. However, when an update is available, you will generally see a prompt on your home screen. To access the Software Update section on macOS, choose System Preferences from the Apple menu, and then click Software Update. In most cases, unless a production device would be negatively impacted, you should keep systems updated with the latest releases.

Patch Management

As a general rule, updates fix a lot of issues and patches fix a few; multiple patches are rolled into updates. You can't always afford to wait for updates to be released and should install patches—particularly security-related patches—when they are released. Bear in mind that if all the security patches are not installed during the OS installation, attackers can exploit the weaknesses and gain access to information.

A number of tools are available to help with patch management, although the intentions of some are better than others. For example, rather than probe a service remotely and attempt to find a vulnerability, the Nessus vulnerability scanner (`https://www.tenable.com/downloads/nessus`) will query the local host to see if a patch for a given vulnerability has been applied. This type of query is far more accurate (and safer) than running a remote check. Since remote checks actually send the exploit in order to check to see if it is applicable, this can sometimes crash a service or process.

Depending on the variant of Linux you are running, *APT (Advanced Package Tool)* can be useful in getting the patches from a repository site and downloading them for installation on Debian and Ubuntu (just to name a few). The most common command used with this tool is `apt-get`, which, as the name implies, gets the package for installation, as shown in Figure 16.4. *The Yellowdog Updater, Modified (YUM)* tool is used with *Red Hat Package Manager (RPM)*-based Linux distributions, such as *CentOS*, Fedora, and Red Hat, and works in a similar way to APT.

FIGURE 16.4   Ubuntu apt-get tool

```
login as: user
Server refused our key
user@172.16.1.161's password:
Welcome to Ubuntu 14.04.5 LTS (GNU/Linux 3.13.0-32-generic x86_64)

 * Documentation:  https://help.ubuntu.com/

  System information as of Sun Sep  9 19:04:53 EDT 2018

  System load:  0.0              Processes:         245
  Usage of /:   11.5% of 17.34GB Users logged in:   0
  Memory usage: 9%               IP address for eth0: 172.16.1.161
  Swap usage:   0%

  Graph this data and manage this system at:
    https://landscape.canonical.com/

*** System restart required ***
Last login: Sun Sep  9 19:04:53 2018
user@sparkle:~$ sudo apt-get update
[sudo] password for user:
Ign http://us.archive.ubuntu.com trusty InRelease
Hit http://us.archive.ubuntu.com trusty-updates InRelease
Hit http://us.archive.ubuntu.com trusty-backports InRelease
Hit http://us.archive.ubuntu.com trusty Release.gpg
Hit http://us.archive.ubuntu.com trusty-updates/main Sources
Hit http://security.ubuntu.com trusty-security InRelease
Hit http://us.archive.ubuntu.com trusty-updates/restricted Sources
Hit http://us.archive.ubuntu.com trusty-updates/universe Sources
Hit http://us.archive.ubuntu.com trusty-updates/multiverse Sources
Hit http://security.ubuntu.com trusty-security/main Sources
Hit http://us.archive.ubuntu.com trusty-updates/main amd64 Packages
Hit http://us.archive.ubuntu.com trusty-updates/restricted amd64 Packages
Hit http://us.archive.ubuntu.com trusty-updates/universe amd64 Packages
```

Driver/Firmware Updates

With any operating system, it is essential to keep the drivers and *firmware* updated. Always remember to back up your configurations (such as for routers) before making any significant changes—in particular, a firmware upgrade—in order to provide a fallback in case something goes awry.

Many network devices contain firmware with which you interact during configuration. For security purposes, you must authenticate in order to make configuration changes and do so initially by using the default account(s). Make sure that the default password is changed after the installation on any network device; otherwise, you are leaving that device open for anyone recognizing the hardware to access it using the known factory password.

Updating firmware for macOS is performed via software updates. During the software update process, the firmware and the software that corresponds to it are updated. Updating firmware for the hardware installed on Linux computers will vary significantly, depending on the type of hardware. Many enterprise Linux vendors, such as Red Hat, include firmware updates in their software updates. As a rule, however, firmware is not part of the Linux software update process.

Antivirus/Antimalware Updates

At one point in time, there were so few viruses outside the Windows world that users not running Windows felt safe without protection on their systems. A significant reason for the low amount of non-Windows *malware* was that the authors of such devious programs were focusing on Windows simply because it had the lion's share of the market; they wanted to inflict as much harm as possible with their code.

As other operating systems have increased in popularity, so too have the number of malware items written for them or that can affect them. Because of this, today it is imperative to have protection on every machine. Additionally, this protection—in the form of definition files—must be kept current and up-to-date. Antivirus and antimalware definitions are released by the hour as new viruses and malware are identified. Most operating systems check daily for updates to definitions. Chapter 17, "Security Concepts," discusses security and antivirus/antimalware in more detail.

Tools

There are a number of tools to be aware of in macOS and Linux. Most of these have counterparts in the Windows world, and we'll make comparisons where they apply. Tools are released on a daily basis, but the following are the most important for the CompTIA objectives and daily maintenance:

Restore/Snapshot   *Snapshots* are archives of key files and settings as they exist at a moment in time. It is possible to take snapshots and restore them as needed. The macOS Time Machine feature performs a backup of your data to the external drive connected to the system. However, the external drive may not always be connected to the system, so local snapshots are also created. These local snapshots allow you to restore files using the local filesystem. To use local snapshots, simply start Time Machine, and if the external storage device is not connected, you'll be presented with the local snapshots.

Image Recovery   As a general rule, images are typically larger than snapshots. You can take a snapshot of a project, and that will include all the files associated with the project, whereas an image would include the project files and all files on the system at the time. Again, this is only a general rule, since images can be granular as well. Typically, however, snapshots are thought of as subsets of images.

The macOS *Disk Utility* can be used to create an image of the macOS operating system, and the image can be directed to an external storage device. Linux can use a multitude of open source tools to create an image of the operating system. The most common is the dd command.

Disk Maintenance Utilities   A number of disk maintenance utilities are available with, or for, macOS and Linux. The most important utilities you should know are du, which shows how much disk space is in use; df, which shows how much space is free; and fsck, which checks and repairs disks. Although these command-line tools are available on both macOS and Linux, Disk Utility is available only on macOS. The Linux operating system can use a variety of open source disk utilities.

> You can use the man (manual) command to learn more about any command-line utility. The man command is covered later in this chapter.

FileVault   The *FileVault* tool allows you to provide full-disk encryption to prevent unauthorized access to the information contained on the device during startup. FileVault uses XTS-AES-128 with a 256-bit key. The feature first appeared in OS X 10.3 (2003), and it is currently on its second release (FileVault 2). It can be enabled by navigating to System Preferences ➢ Security & Privacy ➢ FileVault, and from there you can click Turn On FileVault.

Shell/Terminal   The command-line interface in Linux is usually reached through a Terminal session (though that need not always be the case). It is in this Terminal session that you interact with the *shell*—the interpreter between the user and operating system. The most popular shell for Linux today is *Bash (an acronym for Bourne Again Shell)*, but csh (C-shell), ksh (Korn shell), and a number of others are also in use. In the macOS/iOS world, *OpenSSH (open shell)* is often downloaded and installed. The macOS Terminal utility is accessible by going to Finder ➢ Devices ➢ Applications ➢ Utilities ➢ Terminal.

Screen Sharing   This feature, built into macOS, enables you to share your screen with others. While your screen is shared, the user of the other computer sees what you see, and they can open, move, and close files as well as restart your system. It requires a *Virtual Network Computing (VNC)* connection client.

> The Internet offers numerous versions of VNC connection clients— many are free, and some have unique features that you must pay for. An example of a free VNC connection client is TightVNC (https://www .tightvnc.com/download.php).

Force Quit   Sometimes an application can become unresponsive. When that happens in macOS, you can use *Force Quit* to force the application to close. The Force Quit dialog box can be accessed by pressing Option+Command+Esc. This is similar to pressing Ctrl+Alt+Delete on Windows. Alternatively, you can choose Force Quit from the Apple menu in the upper-left corner of the screen. Most devices, whether running macOS or iOS, offer similar options. With an iPad, for example, if you press the Home button twice quickly, a list of apps will appear at the bottom of the screen. Swipe to get to the app in question, and then swipe up on its preview to close it.

System Preferences

Like any other modern-day operating system, macOS is highly customizable. macOS has a feature called System Preferences that allows you to customize the operating system, similar to the Windows 10/11 Settings app and Control Panel applets. In this section, we will cover the most important System Preferences. After this section, you'll understand how to configure macOS and personalize it for your needs.

All preferences are accessed through the System Preferences screen, shown in Figure 16.5. The System Preferences screen can be accessed in a number of ways. The easiest way to launch it is from the Dock, but you can also launch it by clicking the Apple icon in the upper left of the screen and selecting System Preferences.

FIGURE 16.5   macOS System Preferences

The number of icons on the System Preferences screen depends on the applications installed on the operating system and if they are configurable. Let's explore the various System Preferences that you need to know for the CompTIA exam:

Displays   The Displays preference is primarily used to adjust display resolution and brightness, as shown in Figure 16.6. The Display tab will also allow you to adjust the operating system if you have multiple monitors connected. You can also adjust the color tones the display produces by selecting the Color tab and calibrating the display profile. This preference is generally used when editing graphic artwork is the primary function of the device. The Night Shift tab is used to adjust colors at night so that you can get a better night's sleep. This feature is primarily used with laptops, since, for example, you may check the news or catch up on emails before you fall asleep. The device will automatically make the system colors warmer so that it is easier to fall asleep afterward.

FIGURE 16.6   Displays preference

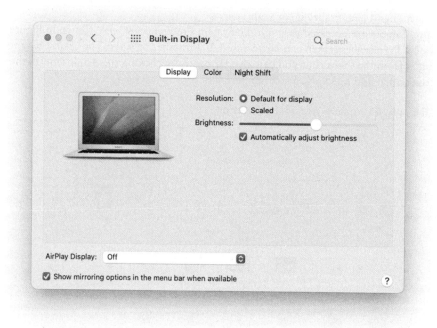

The Displays preference also allows for configuration of the AirPlay Display setting. By default, AirPlay Display is set to off, but if an AirPlay device is detected you can select it in the drop-down list and turn it on. Your display will then be mirrored on the AirPlay Device.

AirPlay allows you to share media, such as videos, photos, music, and other streaming services to a smart device that supports AirPlay. Many different smart devices support AirPlay, such as Apple TV, Smart TVs, and speaker/radio systems, just to name a few.

Network   The Network preference contains settings pertaining to the network connectivity for the device, as shown in Figure 16.7. In the figure, Wi-Fi (wireless) is the main connectivity method. If the device used a wired connection, the connectivity method would be Ethernet. You can open the Network preference by clicking the Apple icon in the upper left of the desktop and selecting System Preferences and then Network.

FIGURE 16.7   Network preference

The Network preference allows you to create location-based preferences. You can make a number of changes to the network settings and assign the changes to a location. For example, you could have a location of work and home. At work you might turn off Bluetooth and at home Bluetooth might be on.

The Network preference is also where you can join wireless networks and change how you join wireless networks. By default, the device will automatically join the network selected. However, there are circumstances where you would not want to automatically join the network, such as if you were directly connecting to a wireless device like a camera that broadcasts its own Service Set Identifier (SSID). If the primary wireless network was still set to automatically join, the device would keep disconnecting from the camera to join the primary network.

If you click Advanced, you can change your primary wireless networks and specify whether they are auto-joined, as shown in Figure 16.8. In addition to changing advanced properties for the wireless connection, you can select the TCP/IP tab and statically set the IP address. The DNS tab allows you to change the DNS servers to be queried. The WINS tab is for a deprecated Windows service, Windows Internet Name Service, that permits network browsing via broadcasts. The 802.1X tab allows you to set up 802.1X profiles for network-level security. The Proxies tab allows you to configure proxy servers for traffic on the device, as well as bypass local and select addresses. Finally, the Hardware tab allows you to set special characteristics based on the device.

FIGURE 16.8 Advanced Network preferences

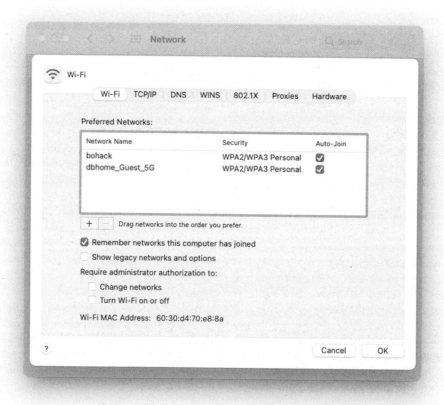

Each device will have various methods for network connectivity. Depending on the various methods, the Network preferences will differ depending on the connection. The Advanced settings may also differ depending on the type of connectivity method for the device.

Printers & Scanners The Printers & Scanners preference, shown in Figure 16.9, is where you can access all settings related to printing and scanning for the device. In the figure, only an HP DeskJet Plus 4100 is connected to the device. However, there could be several different printers simultaneously connected via this System Preference. This would then allow the user to select any of the printers for their use in the desired application.

FIGURE 16.9 Printers & Scanners preference

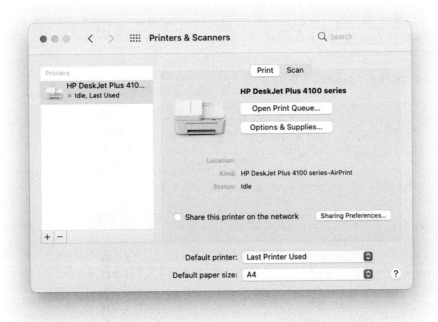

Printers can be added and removed with this System Preference by clicking the + and − on the print preference screen. You can then select the device and open the print queue by clicking Open Print Queue. This will allow you to see all the print jobs currently waiting to be printed from the local device. You can also click Options & Supplies and view the various options for the printer and check the ink or toner supply levels. In addition, you can share the printer by selecting Share This Printer On The Network. You can then configure the Sharing preferences and choose who can print to the printer.

Many printers today can also be purchased as multifunction copiers (MFCs), which means the printer doesn't just print—it can copy and scan as well. If the device is capable of scanning, a Scan tab will be available after you select the device. Depending on the MFC device attached, the Scan tab will allow you to configure various settings. Although MFC devices are becoming common, if a stand-alone scanner was connected to the device, it would show in the Printers & Scanners preferences. The device would have only one tab for scanning.

In addition to changing settings for the printers and scanners attached, you can change the default printer and the default paper size. The default printer is set to the last printer used.

Security & Privacy   The Security & Privacy preference contains a number of settings that apply to the security of the device and the privacy of the user. The General tab allows you to change the password for the current user, as well as configure how long after the screen saver begins the user is asked to enter their password before logging back in, as shown in Figure 16.10. Many advanced settings in Security & Privacy require the system to be unlocked by clicking the lock in the lower left and entering the administrator password.

FIGURE 16.10   Security & Privacy

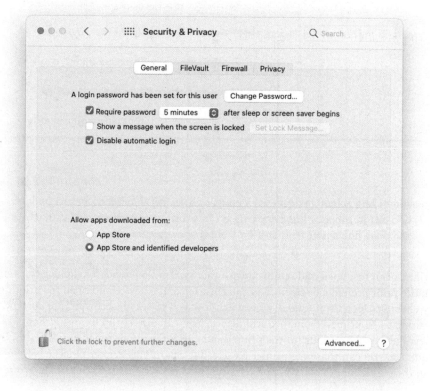

A lock screen message can also be set that displays when the screen is locked. Automatic login is disabled by default, but you can change the setting to allow automatic login of the workstation on boot-up. The applications downloaded on the device can also be controlled; you can select whether apps can be downloaded only from the App Store or from App Store And Identified Developers, which is the default.

The FileVault tab allows you to configure disk-level encryption to protect your files in the event the device is lost. You can turn on the FileVault feature by clicking Turn On FileVault. Once you do, you will need to unlock the disk with the user's password. If there are multiple users configured on the device, they will need to verify their passwords before the encryption is performed.

The Firewall tab allows you to turn on and configure the built-in firewall for macOS. It is not turned on by default, but you can turn it on by clicking Turn On Firewall and then configure the firewall options. You can choose to block all inbound connections by default and create exceptions for only the applications you choose. By default, after turning on the firewall, the operating system allows all inbound connections to applications running on the system. You must choose to block all inbound connections and configure the exceptions.

The Privacy tab allows you to configure settings related to privacy for the user's account, as shown in Figure 16.11. You can control location services that relay information about your location to services like Siri. You can also control the applications that request access to your data, such as Contacts, Calendars, Reminders, and Photos, just to name a few. You can add or remove the applications that need or have access to your data.

Accessibility   The Accessibility preference allows you to customize macOS to support requirements such as vision, hearing, or motor skills, as shown in Figure 16.12. You can turn on VoiceOver, which will provide spoken commands as well as descriptions of items in Braille. Turn on Zoom to allow zooming with the use of the keypad. The Display settings allow you to turn on display features for high contrast as well as reduce motion. The Spoken Content section allows you to configure the operating system to speak announcements, sections, items, and typing feedback. Use the Descriptions section to turn on additional spoken content.

The Audio section allows you to visually indicate when audio alerts are being played so that the user does not miss an alert. The Captions section will display captions (subtitles) for the operating system.

Use the Voice Control section to enable the ability to speak to the computer to display and edit text. The Keyboard section lets you enable sticky keys and slow keys. The Pointer Control section lets you control how the trackpad operates by changing click speed. In the Switch Control section, you can specify that an adaptive device (such as a joystick) be used to control your Mac, enter text, and interact with items on your screen.

The Siri section allows you to configure Siri to accept typed requests in lieu of spoken requests. In the Shortcut section, you can specify that a shortcut list appear when you press Option+Command+F5.

FIGURE 16.11 Privacy tab preferences

Backup/Time Machine As discussed in the previous section, backups are important. In the macOS world, *Time Machine* is a feature that can be used to make backups of various types (incremental, full, and so forth), as shown in Figure 16.13. In order to use Time Machine to back up your data, you will need an external storage device. These devices can be connected via external USB, Thunderbolt, or FireWire, or wirelessly with 802.11. To access Time Machine, select Apple menu ➤ System Preferences ➤ Time Machine. When an external storage device is connected for the first time and Time Machine is not configured, macOS will prompt you to set up Time Machine.

FIGURE 16.12 Accessibility System Preferences

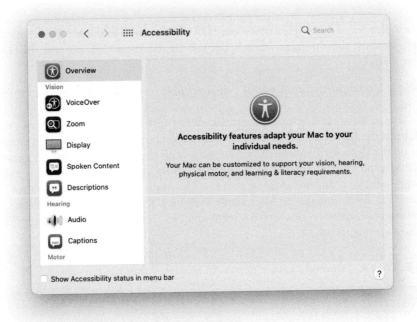

FIGURE 16.13 Time Machine preferences

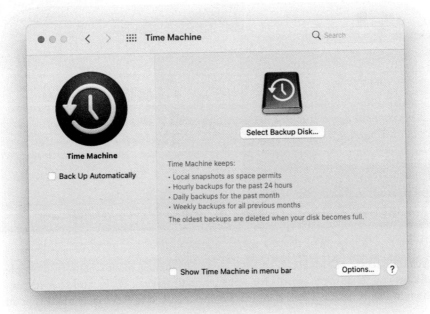

Features

There are a number of macOS features CompTIA wants you to know for the exam. You don't have to know the intricacies of each, but you should know their purpose. Be familiar with these features:

Multiple Desktops/Mission Control   It is possible to run a large number of things at one time, whether those things are apps or desktops. Apple's *Mission Control* is an easy way to see what is open and switch between applications. To access Mission Control, press the Mission Control key on an Apple keyboard, click the Mission Control icon on the Dock (or Launchpad), or swipe up with three or four fingers on a trackpad. Once Mission Control is accessed, all open windows and spaces are shown—grouped by app—and you can choose between them. The Apple macOS Mission Control feature is identical in functionality to Microsoft's Task View feature. It allows you to see all the applications running on one screen so that you can choose the foreground application, as shown in Figure 16.14.

FIGURE 16.14   Viewing multiple apps with Mission Control

Keychain Access   *Keychain Access* is a password management system from Apple. It allows you to store passwords for websites, mail servers, Wi-Fi, and so forth, as shown in Figure 16.15. There is an iCloud variant (iCloud Keychain) that keeps such

information as Safari usernames/passwords and credit card information. Values stored in Keychain Access are kept current (changes are synced) to simplify resource access. To view the current Keychain, select Applications ➤ Utilities ➤ Keychain Access.

FIGURE 16.15   Apple Keychain Access utility

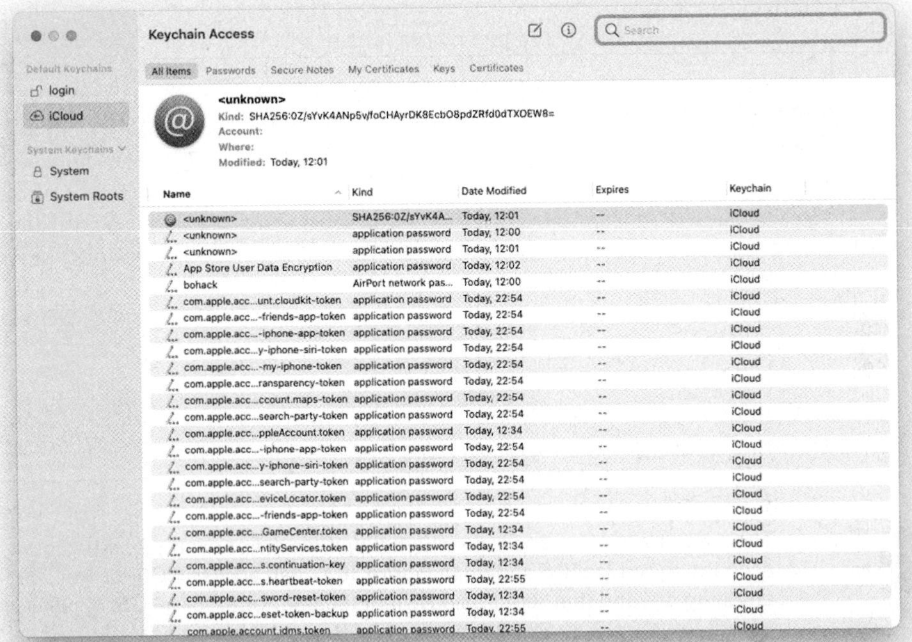

Spotlight   The search feature within macOS is Spotlight, and a magnifying glass icon in the upper-right corner of the menu bar represents it (or you can press Command+spacebar from any app). As you type in the Spotlight utility, the results will display. As shown in Figure 16.16, we have searched for *apple*, and one of the results is the contact info for Apple Inc. Spotlight can search for documents, images, apps, and so on. Recent versions include autocomplete features as well as suggestions for additional results (usually on Wikipedia, *iTunes*, and such).

iCloud   One of the best ways to always have the latest version of files, regardless of the device that you are using to access them, is to have them stored/accessed remotely. iCloud is Apple's answer to remote storage. You can configure your Apple devices to place files there automatically or use it for backup. Figure 16.17 shows iCloud configuration settings on macOS.

FIGURE 16.16 Apple Spotlight utility

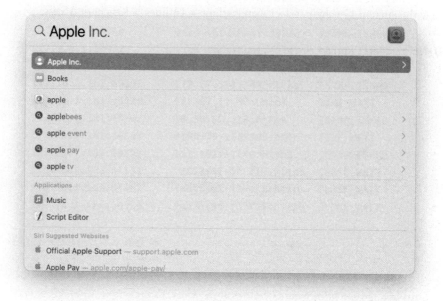

There can be costs associated with using iCloud. For example, the iCloud account on the macOS shown in Figure 16.17 can access 5 GB for free, but anything beyond that requires payment ($0.99/month for 50 GB, $2.99/month for 200 GB, or $9.99/month for 2 TB, as of this writing).

Gestures   With Apple products, it is possible to scroll, tap, pinch, and swipe to interact with the macOS or other products in a way that is intended to be natural and intuitive. You can accept the default actions for these gestures, or you can configure them differently, as shown in Figure 16.18.

To see the basics of gestures on a macOS, visit `https://support.apple.com/en-us/HT204895`.

Finder   To use an analogy, the Finder is to macOS as File Explorer is to Windows. It lets you browse through folders and find files, disks, apps, and so on, as shown in Figure Figure 16.19. You can change the view to see the entries with images, in a list view, in a column view, and so on.

FIGURE 16.17   iCloud configuration settings on macOS

Remote Disc   Officially called *Remote Disc* (disc with a *c*), this macOS feature lets you access files on a CD or DVD installed in one machine on a remote machine, as shown in Figure 16.20. This is handy if you need to retrieve files from a disc and the workstation at which you are sitting does not have a built-in drive. This feature only works on macOS Mojave 10.14 and earlier; the feature was removed on macOS Catalina 10.15 and later.

The computer from which you are accessing a disc need not be running macOS. It is also possible to access discs on a Windows computer if DVD or CD Sharing has been set up. To learn more, visit `https://support.apple.com/en-us/HT203973`.

FIGURE 16.18 Settings for default gestures on macOS

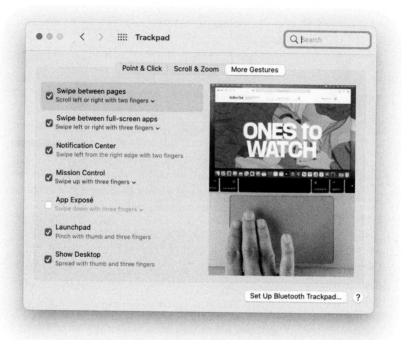

FIGURE 16.19 Apple Finder utility

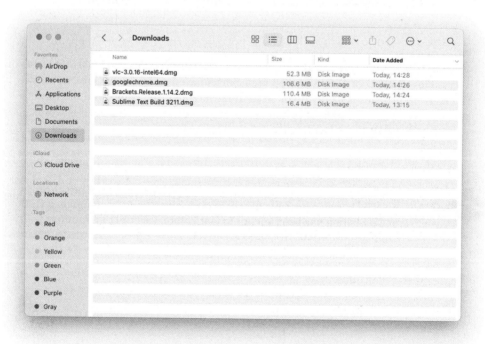

FIGURE 16.20   Apple Remote Disc

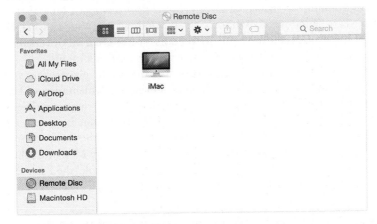

Dock   In macOS, a bar of icons runs along the bottom (or side, if so configured) of your screen, as shown in Figure 16.21. That set of icons, known as the *Dock*, provides easy access to key apps that come with the Mac (such as Safari, Mail, App Store, and Music) or others that you choose to add there. To see the basics of the Dock on a Mac, visit `https://support.apple.com/en-us/HT201730`.

FIGURE 16.21   Apple macOS Dock

There are many other features of macOS that make it a powerful operating system to use. The aforementioned features, however, are the ones that CompTIA wants you to be aware of for the exam. Make sure that you know the purpose of each as you prepare.

Basic Linux Commands

The best way to approach the following commands is to think about Microsoft Windows. That operating system offers a plethora of utilities for configuring the workstation, and just in case they don't work, or you want to go about it the hard way, you can use command-line utilities to accomplish similar tasks. The odds are good that you spend most of your time walking through graphical dialog boxes but you're familiar enough with the command-line utilities that you can use them when you need to.

Linux is the same way. There is an overabundance of graphical utilities that can be used to configure the system, and they differ based on the distribution and the graphical interface being used. In addition to these, command-line utilities are available in every distribution that can be used to get the job done. Those command-line utilities are what we'll focus on here.

There is only one vendor for Windows (Microsoft), but there are many vendors for Linux (Red Hat, SuSE, Ubuntu—to name just three). Also, a new version of Windows is released only every few years (Windows 7, Windows 8/8.1, Windows 10, Windows 11), but with Linux—especially because there are so many vendors—there are a lot of versions. With Ubuntu, for example, the goal is to release a new version every six months.

With all the different distributions and versions, getting to the place where you can run command-line utilities can differ a bit. In almost every implementation of Linux, you can boot into a command-line mode, and the commands entered there can then be run. Better than that, though, the easiest way to get to the command line is to open a terminal (also called a console) window. This allows you to interact with the shell, where you can type commands to your heart's content. The default shell in many Linux distributions is Bash. When you open a terminal window or log in at a text console, the Bash shell is what prompts you for commands. When you type a command, the shell executes your command.

Understanding the Syntax of Shell Commands

Because a shell interprets what you type, knowing how the shell processes the text you enter is important. All shell commands have the following general format (some commands have no options):

```
command [option1] [option2] ... [optionN]
```

On a command line, you enter a command followed by zero or more *options* (also called *arguments*). The shell uses a blank space or a tab to distinguish between the command and options. This means that you must use a space or a tab to separate the command from the options and the options from one another. If an option contains spaces, you put that option inside quotation marks. For example, to search for a name in the password file, enter the following grep command (grep is used for searching for text in files):

```
grep "Jon B" /etc/passwd
```

When grep prints the line with the name, it looks like this:

```
filea:x:1000:100:Jon B:/home/testuser:/bin/bash
```

If you create a user account with your username, type the grep command with your username as an argument to look for that username in the /etc/passwd file. In the output from the grep command, you can see the name of the shell (/bin/bash) following the last colon (:). Because the Bash shell is an executable file, it resides in the /bin directory; you must provide the full path to it.

The number of command-line options and their formats depend on the actual command. Typically, these options look like -X, where X is a single character. For example, you can use the -l option with the ls command. The command lists the contents of a directory, and the option provides additional details. Here is a result of typing ls -l in a user's home directory:

```
total 0
drwxr-xr-x 2 testuser users 48  2018-09-08 21:11 bin
drwx-      2 testuser users 320 2018-09-08 21:16 Desktop
```

```
drwx–      2 testuser users 80   2018-09-08 21:11 Documents
drwxr-xr-x 2 testuser users 80   2018-09-08 21:11 public_html
drwxr-xr-x 2 testuser users 464  2018-09-17 18:21 sdump
```

 The /etc/passwd file contains a list of the usernames and their respective attributes, such as User ID (UID), Group ID (GID), User ID info, home directory, and shell. Interesting enough, it doesn't normally store the user's password; another file, called the shadow file (/etc/shadow), now contains a hashed version of the user's password.

If a command is too long to fit on a single line, you can press the backslash key (\) followed by Enter. Then continue typing the command on the next line. For example, type the following command (press Enter after each line):

**cat **
/etc/passwd

The cat command then displays the contents of the /etc/passwd file.

You can concatenate (that is, string together) several shorter commands on a single line by separating the commands with semicolons (;). For example, the following command changes the *current directory* to your home directory, lists the contents of that directory, and then shows the name of that directory:

cd; ls -l; pwd

You can combine simple shell commands to create a more sophisticated command. For example, suppose you want to find out whether a device file named sdb resides in your system's /dev directory because some documentation says that you need that device file for your second hard drive. You can use the ls /dev command to get a directory listing of the /dev directory, and then browse through it to see whether that listing contains sdb.

Unfortunately, the /dev directory has a great many entries, so you may find it hard to find any item that has sdb in its name. You can, however, combine the ls command with grep and come up with a command line that does exactly what you want. Here's that command line:

ls /dev | grep sdb

The shell sends the output of the ls command (the directory listing) to the grep command, which searches for the string sdb. The vertical bar (|) is known as a *pipe* because it acts as a conduit (think of a water pipe) between the two programs—the output of the first command is fed into the input of the second command.

Discovering and Using Linux Commands

Literally hundreds, if not thousands, of Linux commands exist within the shell and the system directories. Fortunately, CompTIA asks that you know a much smaller number than that. Table 16.1 lists common Linux commands by category.

TABLE 16.1   Essential Linux commands

Command name	Action
Managing files and directories	
cd	Changes the current directory.
chmod	Changes file permissions.
chown	Changes the file owner and group.
cp	Copies files.
ls	Displays the contents of a directory.
mkdir	Creates a directory.
mv	Renames a file and moves the file from one directory to another.
rm	Deletes files.
pwd	Displays the current directory.
Processing files	
cat	Displays the contents of a file.
df	Displays the total disk free (disk free space) for a directory.
dd	Copies blocks of data from one file to another (used to copy data from devices).
find	Searches for text in a file hierarchy.
grep	Searches for regular expressions in a text file.
nano	Text-based editor for files.
Managing files	
apt-get	Downloads files from a repository site.
yum	Downloads files from a repository site.
shutdown	Shuts down Linux.
vi	Starts the visual file editor, which can be used to edit files.

Command name	Action
man	System help for executable files.
Managing users	
passwd	Changes the password.
su	Starts a new shell as another user. (The other user is assumed to be root when the command is invoked without any argument.)
sudo	Runs a command as another user (usually the root user).
Networking	
dig	DNS query utility.
ip	Allows you to display and configure information related to a network interface card (NIC).
ifconfig	Allows you to display and configure information related to a network interface card (NIC).
iwconfig	Similar to ifconfig, but used for wireless configurations.
Quitting	
q	While not a utility, the q command is often used to quit most interactive utilities. It is used, for example, to quit working in the vi editor.
Managing processes	
ps	Displays a list of currently running processes.
kill	Terminates a process.
top	Displays running processes, similar to Windows Task Manager.

Becoming root (Super User)

When you want to do anything that requires a high privilege level (for example, administering your system), you have to become *root*. Normally, you log in as a regular user with your everyday username. When you need the privileges of the *super user*, though, use the following command to become root:

su -

The su command followed by a space and the minus sign (or hyphen) provides an environment similar to what the user would expect by applying the user's environment variables and initial login scripts. Once executed, the shell then prompts you for the root password. Type the password and press Enter.

> When the su command is entered without a username as an option, you will be prompted for the password of the root account, and a Bash shell will open on behalf of the root account. However, you can use the su command followed by any user account name, and as long as you supply the correct password, you will be logged in as that user.

After you've finished with whatever you want to do as root (and you have the privilege to do anything as root), type **exit** to return to your normal username.

Instead of becoming root by using the su – command, you can type **sudo** followed by the command that you want to run as root. In some distributions, such as Ubuntu, you must use the sudo command because you don't get to set up a root user when you install the operating system. If you're listed as an authorized user in the /etc/sudoers file, sudo executes the command as if you were logged in as root. Type **man sudoers** to read more about the /etc/sudoers file.

> As you learn many of the commands in this chapter, you'll realize that it is similar to learning a new language. Therefore, practice makes perfect and we urge you to practice these commands.

Maintaining the Operating System

The Linux operating system is a secure and functional operating system. However, it's inevitable that at some point you will need to obtain updates for security or to extend the functionality by adding packages. Thankfully, every Linux distribution has its own unique repository of security patches and additional packages. When choosing a Linux distribution, you should spend time exploring its benefits. For example, Debian packages are more stable, but the disadvantage is that the packages are older than the current version of packages. Mint Linux is tailored to laptops and desktops, but it is not normally found on servers. These are just a few examples—the lesson is to do your homework before you decide on a Linux distribution.

Once you have chosen and installed a Linux distribution, you'll want to update the repositories and then upgrade the distribution to get the latest security patches. A *repository* is a group of packages that are available for download. The repository contains metadata, such as versions, dates, descriptions, and dependencies, about these packages. When you update the repositories, you are downloading the metadata so that you can search and begin the upgrade process.

Depending on the version, you will have one of two tools: the Advanced Package Tool (APT) or Yellowdog Updater, Modified (YUM). Linux distributions, such as Ubuntu, Debian, and Mint, will use the APT package management tool. In the operating system you can update the repositories by using the `apt` command or the `apt-get` command. In addition to upgrading the operating system, you can install and manage packages. In order to update the operating system, you will need to update the repositories first and then you can upgrade the operating system binaries as shown in the following:

```
user@server:~$ sudo apt-get update
[sudo] password for user:
Hit:1 http://archive.ubuntu.com/ubuntu bionic InRelease
Hit:2 http://archive.ubuntu.com/ubuntu bionic-updates InRelease
Hit:3 http://archive.ubuntu.com/ubuntu bionic-backports InRelease
Hit:4 http://archive.ubuntu.com/ubuntu bionic-security InRelease
Reading package lists... Done
user@server:~$ sudo apt-get upgrade
Reading package lists... Done
Building dependency tree
Reading state information... Done
Calculating upgrade... Done
The following packages have been kept back:
  base-files netplan.io sosreport ubuntu-advantage-tools ubuntu-server
The following packages will be upgraded:
  accountsservice apport apt apt-utils bash bcache-tools bind9-host bsdutils
[ output cut]
  unattended-upgrades update-manager-core update-notifier-common ureadahead
  util-linux uuid-runtime vim vim-common vim-runtime vim-tiny wget xkb-data
241 upgraded, 0 newly installed, 0 to remove and 5 not upgraded.
Need to get 111 MB of archives.
After this operation, 43.2 MB of additional disk space will be used.
Do you want to continue? [Y/n]
```

In the following example, you can see how a package such as `iftop` is installed using the `apt-get` command:

```
user@server:~$ sudo apt-get install iftop
Reading package lists... Done
Building dependency tree
Reading state information... Done
The following NEW packages will be installed:
  iftop
0 upgraded, 1 newly installed, 0 to remove and 246 not upgraded.
Need to get 36.0 kB of archives.
```

```
After this operation, 91.1 kB of additional disk space will be used.
Get:1 http://archive.ubuntu.com/ubuntu bionic/universe amd64 iftop amd64
1.0~pre4-4 [36.0 kB]
Fetched 36.0 kB in 0s (102 kB/s)
Selecting previously unselected package iftop.
(Reading database ... 66991 files and directories currently installed.)
Preparing to unpack .../iftop_1.0~pre4-4_amd64.deb ...
Unpacking iftop (1.0~pre4-4) ...
Setting up iftop (1.0~pre4-4) ...
Processing triggers for man-db (2.8.3-2ubuntu0.1) ...
user@server:~$
```

The YUM package manager is used to update and install packages for Red Hat–based Linux distributions, such as Red Hat Enterprise Server, Fedora, and CentOS, just to name a few. The tool works like the APT tool; the first step is to update the repositories, then you can update the binaries, as shown here:

```
[root@localhost ~]# yum update
CentOS Stream 8 - AppStream      5.6 MB/s | 16 MB 00:02
CentOS Stream 8 - BaseOS         1.6 MB/s |  6 MB 00:02
CentOS Stream 8 - Extras          35 kB/s | 15 kB 00:00
Dependencies resolved.
Nothing to do.
Complete!
[root@localhost ~]# yum upgrade
Last metadata expiration check: 0:01:40 ago on Fri 22 Oct 2021 09:52:10 PM EDT.
Dependencies resolved.
Nothing to do.
Complete!
[root@localhost ~]#
```

The yum command can also be used to install packages. In the following example, we are using yum to install the nano utility:

```
[root@localhost ~]# yum install nano
Last metadata expiration check: 0:45:41 ago on Fri 22 Oct 2021 10:51:16 PM EDT.
Dependencies resolved.
================================================================================
 Package        Architecture      Version              Repository       Size
================================================================================
Installing:
 nano           x86_64            2.9.8-1.el8          baseos          581 k
```

```
Transaction Summary
================================================================================
Install  1 Package

Total download size: 581 k
Installed size: 2.2 M
Is this ok [y/N]:
```

Now that you know how to update the operating system and install packages, it's inevitable that you'll run out of space on the operating system. Fortunately, you can monitor and quickly find out how much space is free on the disk by using the df command, otherwise known as the disk free command. By using the df command you can quickly see the percentage of free space, and if you supply the -h argument you'll get results in human-readable formats of bytes, as shown here:

```
user@server:~$ df -h
Filesystem      Size  Used Avail Use% Mounted on
udev            1.9G     0  1.9G   0% /dev
tmpfs           393M  1.5M  391M   1% /run
/dev/sda2        20G  6.0G   13G  33% /
tmpfs           2.0G     0  2.0G   0% /dev/shm
tmpfs           5.0M     0  5.0M   0% /run/lock
tmpfs           2.0G     0  2.0G   0% /sys/fs/cgroup
/dev/loop0       91M   91M     0 100% /snap/core/6350
/dev/loop1      100M  100M     0 100% /snap/core/11993
tmpfs           393M     0  393M   0% /run/user/1000
user@server:~$
```

Managing Processes

Every time the shell executes a command that you type, it starts a process. The shell itself is a process, as are any scripts or programs that the shell runs. The ps command will show a snapshot of the current processes running as the currently logged-in user. Use the ps ax command to see a list of processes for the entire operating system. When you type **ps ax**, Bash shows you the current set of processes. Here are a few lines of output from the command ps ax -cols 132 (the -cols 132 option is used to ensure that you see each command in its entirety):

```
PID TTY   STAT  TIME COMMAND
1   ?     S     0:01 init [5]
2   ?     SN    0:00 [ksoftirqd/0]
3   ?     S<    0:00 [events/0]
4   ?     S<    0:00 [khelper]
```

```
9     ?   S<    0:00 [kthread]
19    ?   S<    0:00 [kacpid]
75    ?   S<    0:00 [kblockd/0]
115   ?   S     0:00 [pdflush]
116   ?   S     0:01 [pdflush]
118   ?   S<    0:00 [aio/0]
117   ?   S     0:00 [kswapd0]
711   ?   S     0:00 [kseriod]
1075  ?   S<    0:00 [reiserfs/0]
2086  ?   S     0:00 [kjournald]
2239  ?   S<s   0:00 /sbin/udevd -d
[output cut]
6460  ?   Ss    0:02 /opt/gnome/bin/gdmgreeter
6671  ?   Ss    0:00 sshd: testuser [priv]
6675  ?   S     0:00 sshd: testuser@pts/0
6676  p/0 Ss    0:00 -bash
6712  p/0 S     0:00 vsftpd
8002  ?   S     0:00 pickup -l -t fifo -u
8034  p/0 R+    0:00 ps ax-cols 132
```

In this listing, the first column has the heading PID, and it shows a number for each process. PID stands for *process ID (identification)*, which is a sequential number assigned by the Linux kernel. If you look through the output of the ps ax command, you'll see that the init command is the first process and has a PID of 1. That's why init is referred to as the *mother of all processes*.

The COMMAND column shows the command that created each process, and the TIME column shows the cumulative CPU time used by the process. The STAT column shows the state of a process: S means that the process is sleeping, and R means that it's running. The symbols following the status letter have further meanings; for example, < indicates a high-priority process, and + means that the process is running in the foreground. The TTY column shows the terminal, if any, associated with the process.

The process ID, or process number, is useful when you have to stop an errant process forcibly. Look at the output of the ps ax command and note the PID of the offending process. Then use the kill command with that process number to stop the process. For example, to stop process number 8550, type the following command:

kill 8550

The ps command will allow you to see processes currently running at the time you initiate the command. However, if you want to see an interactive display of processes similar to the Windows Task Manager, you can use the top command, shown in Figure 16.22. The top command allows you to sort by columns and scroll through the various processes. You can even kill processes interactively.

FIGURE 16.22 The top command

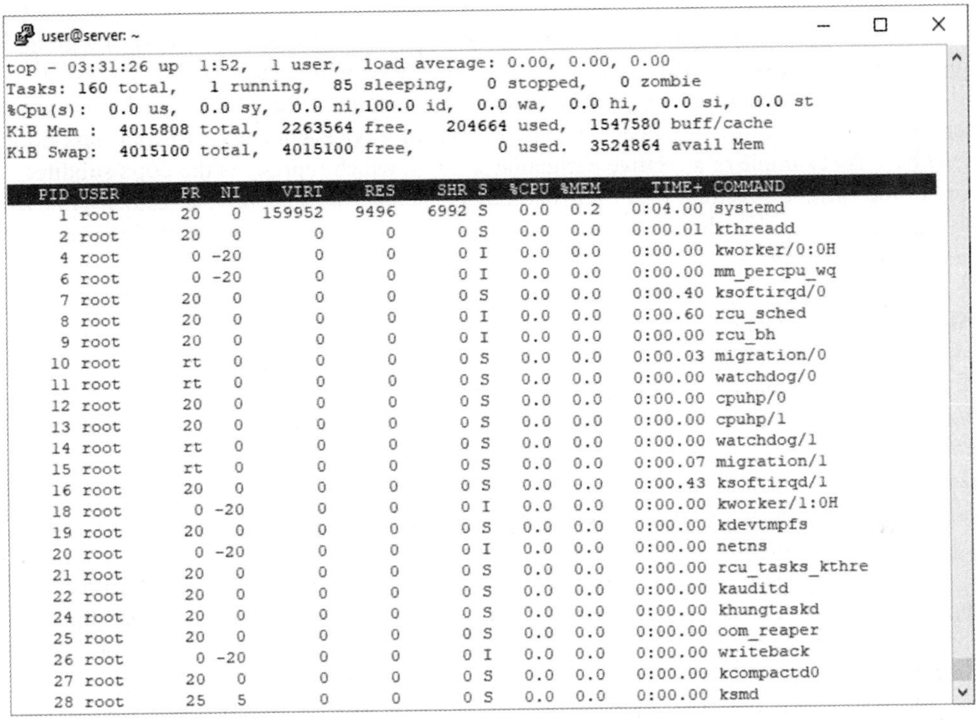

```
user@server: ~                                                    —   □   ×
top - 03:31:26 up  1:52,  1 user,  load average: 0.00, 0.00, 0.00
Tasks: 160 total,   1 running,  85 sleeping,   0 stopped,   0 zombie
%Cpu(s):  0.0 us,   0.0 sy,   0.0 ni,100.0 id,   0.0 wa,   0.0 hi,   0.0 si,   0.0 st
KiB Mem :  4015808 total,  2263564 free,   204664 used,  1547580 buff/cache
KiB Swap:  4015100 total,  4015100 free,        0 used.  3524864 avail Mem

  PID USER      PR  NI    VIRT    RES    SHR S  %CPU %MEM     TIME+ COMMAND
    1 root      20   0  159952   9496   6992 S   0.0  0.2   0:04.00 systemd
    2 root      20   0       0      0      0 S   0.0  0.0   0:00.01 kthreadd
    4 root       0 -20       0      0      0 I   0.0  0.0   0:00.00 kworker/0:0H
    6 root       0 -20       0      0      0 I   0.0  0.0   0:00.00 mm_percpu_wq
    7 root      20   0       0      0      0 S   0.0  0.0   0:00.40 ksoftirqd/0
    8 root      20   0       0      0      0 I   0.0  0.0   0:00.60 rcu_sched
    9 root      20   0       0      0      0 I   0.0  0.0   0:00.00 rcu_bh
   10 root      rt   0       0      0      0 S   0.0  0.0   0:00.03 migration/0
   11 root      rt   0       0      0      0 S   0.0  0.0   0:00.00 watchdog/0
   12 root      20   0       0      0      0 S   0.0  0.0   0:00.00 cpuhp/0
   13 root      20   0       0      0      0 S   0.0  0.0   0:00.00 cpuhp/1
   14 root      rt   0       0      0      0 S   0.0  0.0   0:00.00 watchdog/1
   15 root      rt   0       0      0      0 S   0.0  0.0   0:00.07 migration/1
   16 root      20   0       0      0      0 S   0.0  0.0   0:00.43 ksoftirqd/1
   18 root       0 -20       0      0      0 I   0.0  0.0   0:00.00 kworker/1:0H
   19 root      20   0       0      0      0 S   0.0  0.0   0:00.00 kdevtmpfs
   20 root       0 -20       0      0      0 I   0.0  0.0   0:00.00 netns
   21 root      20   0       0      0      0 S   0.0  0.0   0:00.00 rcu_tasks_kthre
   22 root      20   0       0      0      0 S   0.0  0.0   0:00.00 kauditd
   24 root      20   0       0      0      0 S   0.0  0.0   0:00.00 khungtaskd
   25 root      20   0       0      0      0 S   0.0  0.0   0:00.00 oom_reaper
   26 root       0 -20       0      0      0 I   0.0  0.0   0:00.00 writeback
   27 root      20   0       0      0      0 S   0.0  0.0   0:00.00 kcompactd0
   28 root      25   5       0      0      0 S   0.0  0.0   0:00.00 ksmd
```

Directory Navigation

In Linux, when you log in as root, your home directory is /root. For other users, the home directory is usually in the /home directory. For example, the home directory for a user logging in as testuser is /home/testuser. This information is stored in the /etc/passwd file. By default, only you have permission to save files in your home directory, and only you can create subdirectories in your home directory to organize your files further.

Linux supports the concept of a *current directory*, which is the directory on which all file and directory commands operate. After you log in, for example, your current directory is the home directory. To see the current directory, type the **pwd** command.

To change the current directory, use the **cd** command. To change the current directory to /usr/lib, type the following:

cd /usr/lib

Then to change the directory to the cups subdirectory in /usr/lib, type the following command:

cd cups

Now if you use the pwd command, that command shows /usr/lib/cups as the current directory.

These two examples show that you can refer to a directory's name in two ways: with an absolute pathname or a relative pathname. An example of an absolute pathname is /usr/lib, which is an exact directory in the directory tree. (Think of the absolute pathname as the complete mailing address for a package that the postal service will deliver to your next-door neighbor.) An example of a relative pathname is cups, which represents the cups subdirectory of the current directory, whatever that may be. (Think of the relative directory name as giving the postal carrier directions from your house to the one next door so that the carrier can deliver the package.)

If you type **cd cups** in **/usr/lib**, the current directory changes to /usr/lib/cups. However, if you type the same command in /home/testuser, the shell tries to change the current directory to /home/testuser/cups.

Use the cd command without any arguments to change the current directory back to your *home directory*. No matter where you are, typing **cd** at the shell prompt brings you back home. The tilde character (~) is an alias that refers to your home directory. Thus, you can also change the current directory to your home directory by using the command cd ~. You can refer to another user's home directory by appending that user's name to the tilde. Thus, cd ~superman changes the current directory to the home directory of superman.

A single dot (.) and two dots (..), often referred to as *dot-dot*, also have special meanings. A single dot (.) indicates the current directory, whereas two dots (..) indicate the parent directory. For example, if the current directory is /usr/share, you go one level up to /usr by typing the following:

cd ..

Directory Listings

You can get a directory listing by using the ls command. By default, the ls command, without any options, displays the contents of the current directory in a compact, multi-column format. To tell the directories and files apart, use the –F option (ls –F). The output will show the directory names with a slash (/) appended to them. Plain filenames appear as is. The at sign (@) appended to a listing indicates that this file is a link to another file. (In other words, this filename simply refers to another file; it's a shortcut.) An asterisk (*) is appended to executable files. (The shell can run any executable file.)

You can see even more detailed information about the files and directories with the –l (long format) option. The rightmost column shows the name of the directory entry. The date and time before the name show when the last modifications to that file were made. To the left of the date and time is the size of the file in bytes. The file's group and owner appear to the left of the column that shows the file size. The next number to the left indicates the number of links to the file. (A *link* is like a shortcut in Windows.)

Finally, the leftmost column shows the file's permission settings, which determine who can read, write, or execute the file. This column shows a sequence of nine characters, which appear as rwxrwxrwx when each letter is present. Each letter indicates a specific permission. A hyphen (-) in place of a letter indicates no permission for a specific operation on the file. Think of these nine letters as three groups of three letters (rwx), interpreted as follows:

Leftmost Group   Controls the read, write, and execute permissions of the file's owner. In other words, if you see rwx in this position, the file's owner can read (r), write (w), and execute (x) the file. A hyphen in the place of a letter indicates no permission. Thus, the string rw- means that the owner has read and write permissions but not execute permission. Although executable programs (including shell programs) typically have execute permission, directories treat execute permission as equivalent to *use* permission: a user must have execute permission on a directory before they can open and read the contents of the directory.

Middle Group   Controls the read, write, and execute permissions of any user belonging to that file's group.

Rightmost Group   Controls the read, write, and execute permissions of all other users (collectively thought of as *the world*).

Thus, a file with the permission setting rwx------ is accessible only to the file's owner, whereas the permission setting rwxr--r-- makes the file readable by the world.

An interesting feature of the ls command is that it doesn't list any file the name of which begins with a period. To see these files, you must use the ls command with the -a option, as follows:

```
ls -a
```

Most Linux commands take single-character options, each with a hyphen as a prefix. When you want to use several options, type a hyphen and concatenate (string together) the option letters, one after another. Thus, ls -al is equivalent to ls -a -l as well as to ls -l -a.

Changing Permissions and Ownership

You may need to change a file's permission settings to protect it from others. Use the chmod command to change the permission settings of a file or a directory. To use chmod effectively, you have to specify the permission settings. A good way is to concatenate letters from the columns of Table 16.2 in the order shown (who/action/permission). You use only the single character from each column—the text in parentheses is for explanation only.

TABLE 16.2 Letter codes for file permissions

Who	Action	Permission
u (user)	+ (add)	r (read)
g (group)	− (remove)	w (write)
o (others)	= (assign)	x (execute)
a (all)	s (set user ID)	

For example, to give everyone read access to all the files in a directory, pick a (for *all*) from the first column, + (for *add*) from the second column, and r (for *read*) from the third column, to come up with the permission setting a+r. Then use the set of options with chmod, as follows:

chmod a+r *

On the other hand, to permit everyone to execute one specific file, type the following:

chmod a+x filename

Use ls -l to verify that the change took place.

Sometimes you have to change a file's user or group ownership in order for everything to work correctly. For example, suppose you're instructed to create a directory named *cups* and give it the ownership of user ID *lp* and group ID *sys*. You can log in as root and create the cups directory with the command mkdir as follows:

mkdir cups

If you check the file's details with the ls -l command, you see that the user and group ownership are both assigned to root. To change the owner, use the chown command. For example, to change the ownership of the cups directory to user ID *lp* and group ID *sys*, type the following:

chown lp.sys cups

Working with Files

To copy files from one directory to another, use the cp command. If you want to copy a file to the current directory but retain the original name, use a period (.) as the second argument of the cp command. Thus, the following command copies the Xresources file from the /etc/X11 directory to the current directory (denoted by a single period):

cp /etc/X11/Xresources .

The cp command makes a new copy of a file and leaves the original intact.

If you want to copy the entire contents of a directory—including all subdirectories and their contents—to another directory, use the command cp -ar *sourcedir destdir*.

(This command copies everything in the *sourcedir* directory to the *destdir* directory.) For example, to copy all the files from the /etc/X11 directory to the current directory, type the following command:

cp -ar /etc/X11 .

To move a file to a new location, use the mv command. The original copy is gone, and a new copy appears at the destination. You can use mv to rename a file. If you want to change the name of today.list to old.list, use the mv command as follows:

mv today.list old.list

On the other hand, if you want to move the today.list file to a subdirectory named saved, use the following command:

mv today.list saved

An interesting feature of mv is that you can use it to move entire directories (with all their subdirectories and files) to a new location. If you have a directory named data that contains many files and subdirectories, you can move that entire directory structure to old_data by using the following command:

mv data old_data

To delete files, use the rm command. For example, to delete a file named old.list, type the following command:

rm old.list

Be careful with the rm command, especially when you log in as root. You can inadvertently delete important files with rm.

Sometime you just need to view the contents of a file. To view the contents of a file, use the cat command. The cat command will display the contents of a file as shown in the following example:

```
user@server:~$ cat /etc/hosts
127.0.0.1       localhost.localdomain    localhost
::1             localhost6.localdomain6  localhost6

# The following lines are desirable for IPv6 capable hosts
::1     localhost ip6-localhost ip6-loopback
fe00::0 ip6-localnet
ff02::1 ip6-allnodes
ff02::2 ip6-allrouters
ff02::3 ip6-allhosts
user@server:~$
```

The cat file can also be used to concatenate multiple files. For example, you may have two files that you want to join together. By using the > redirector, you can redirect the output of two or more files into one file, as follows.

```
user@server:~$ cat file1
```

```
file1 contents
user@server:~$ cat file2
file2 contents
user@server:~$ cat file2 file1 > file3
user@server:~$ cat file3
file2 contents
file1 contents
user@server:~$
```

The original text-based editor that came with Linux/UNIX was the vi editor, which was short for visual editor. The original vi editor was not end-user–friendly and it often required a cheat sheet to get anything done. Thankfully, the nano and pico editors were adopted by Linux, which made editing text-based config files much easier. You can launch the nano editor by typing the nano command followed by the file you want to edit, such as **nano file3**. This will launch the editor, as shown in Figure 16.23.

FIGURE 16.23   The nano editor

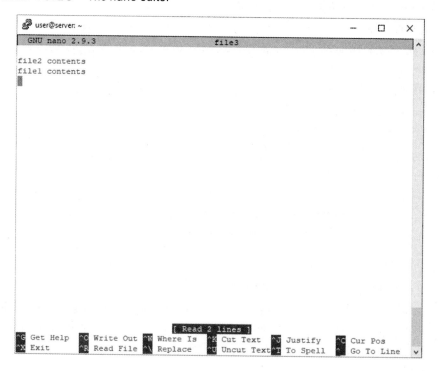

Once the editor is launched, it acts similar to the Windows Notepad utility. You can use the arrow keys to navigate text; find text; replace text; and cut, copy, and paste text.

The editor is also very intuitive; by using the Control key sequences, you can perform all the functions and even get help.

One of the most important functions you can perform on files is finding them. In Windows we can use the familiar Ctrl+F key sequence to search for files in a folder structure. In Linux the `find` command allows you to do the same. You can find a file in a folder structure as shown here:

```
user@server:~$ find -name file4
./folder1/file4
user@server:~$
```

In exercise 16.3 you will work with some basic files on the Linux operating system to get some exposure to working with files.

EXERCISE 16.3

Working with Files

1. Log into a Linux or macOS operating system and open a Terminal.

2. Type **cd** ~ and press Enter. This will change directory to your home folder.

3. Type **cat > file1** and press Enter. Begin typing **this is file1 contents**, then press Control+D.

4. Type **cat > file2** and press Enter. Begin typing **this is file2 contents**, then press Control+D.

5. Type **ls** and press Enter to examine the two files you've created.

6. Type **cat file2 file1 > file3** and press Enter. This will concatenate the two files.

7. Type **cat file3** and press Enter to examine the contents of file3.

In this example we used the `cat` command to redirect console input to a file, such as file1 and file2. We could have used the nano command if it was available to achieve the same outcome. We then used the `cat` command to concatenate the two files.

Working with Directories

To organize files in your home directory, you have to create new directories. Use the `mkdir` command to create a directory. For example, to create a directory named `images` in the current directory, type the following:

mkdir images

After you create the directory, you can use the `cd images` command to change to that directory.

You can create an entire directory tree by using the -p option with the `mkdir` command. For example, suppose your system has a `/usr/src` directory and you want to create the directory tree `/usr/src/book/java/examples/applets`. To create this directory hierarchy, type the following command:

mkdir -p /usr/src/book/java/examples/applets

When you no longer need a directory, use the `rmdir` command to delete it. You can delete a directory only when the directory is empty. To remove an empty directory tree, you can use the -p option, as follows:

rmdir -p /usr/src/book/java/examples/applets

This command removes the empty parent directories of applets. The command stops when it encounters a directory that's not empty.

Networking Utilities

Just as you can use the `ipconfig` command to see the status of IP configuration with Windows, the `ifconfig` command can be used in Linux. You can get information about the usage of the `ifconfig` command by using `ifconfig -help`. The following output provides an example of the basic `ifconfig` command run on a Linux system:

```
eth0 Link encap:Ethernet HWaddr 00:60:08:17:63:A0
inet addr:192.168.1.101 Bcast:192.168.1.255 Mask:255.255.255.0
UP BROADCAST RUNNING MTU:1500 Metric:1
RX packets:911 errors:0 dropped:0 overruns:0 frame:0
TX packets:804 errors:0 dropped:0 overruns:0 carrier:0
collisions:0 txqueuelen:100
Interrupt:5 Base address:0xe400
lo Link encap:Local Loopback
inet addr:127.0.0.1 Mask:255.0.0.0
UP LOOPBACK RUNNING MTU:3924 Metric:1
RX packets:18 errors:0 dropped:0 overruns:0 frame:0
TX packets:18 errors:0 dropped:0 overruns:0 carrier:0
collisions:0 txqueuelen:0
```

In addition to using `ifconfig`, Linux users can use the `iwconfig` command to view the state of their wireless network. By using `iwconfig`, you can view such important information as the link quality, access point (AP) MAC address, data rate, and encryption keys, which can be helpful in ensuring that the parameters in the network are consistent.

The ifconfig utility is slowly being replaced on certain distributions of Linux with the ip utility. Red Hat Enterprise Linux has adopted the ip utility and it's similar to the ifconfig utility. You can configure an address or show the configured IP addresses similar to the ifconfig utility. The output even looks very familiar to the ifconfig utility:

```
root@sybex:~# ip addr add 172.16.1.200/12 eth0
root@sybex:~# ip addr
eth0: <BROADCAST, MULTICAST, UP> mtu 1500 qlen 1000
 link/ether 00:0c:29:e9:08:92 brd ff:ff:ff:ff:ff:ff:ff:ff
 inet 172.16.1.200/12 scope global eth0
    valid_lft forever preferred_lft forever
 inet6 fe80::20c:29ff:fee9:892/64 scope link
    valid_lft forever preferred_lft forever
lo: <LOOPBACK,UP,LOWER_UP> mtu 65536 noqueue
 link/loopback 00:00:00:00:00:00:00:00 brd 00:00:00:00:00:00:00:00
 inet 127.0.0.1/8 scope host lo
    valid_lft forever preferred_lft forever
 inet6 ::1/128 scope host
    valid_lft forever preferred_lft forever

root@sybex:~#
```

The Domain Information Groper (dig) tool is almost identical to the nslookup tool and has become an adopted standard for name resolution testing on Linux/UNIX operating systems. The tool allows you to resolve any resource record for a given host and direct the query to a specific server.

The command does not offer an interactive mode like the nslookup command. The command by default queries A records for a given host, and the output has debugging turned on by default.

In the following example, you see a query being performed on the DNS server of 8.8.8.8 for an MX record of sybex.com. The debugging output shows that one query was given, two answers were retrieved, and nothing was authoritative (not the primary servers). The output also details the query made and the answers returned.

```
root@Sybex:~# dig @8.8.8.8 mx sybex.com

; <<>> DiG 9.9.5-3ubuntu0.13-Ubuntu <<>> @8.8.8.8 mx sybex.com
; (1 server found)
;; global options: +cmd
;; Got answer:
;; ->>HEADER<<- opcode: QUERY, status: NOERROR, id: 49694
;; flags: qr rd ra; QUERY: 1, ANSWER: 2, AUTHORITY: 0, ADDITIONAL: 1
```

```
;; OPT PSEUDOSECTION:
; EDNS: version: 0, flags:; udp: 512
;; QUESTION SECTION:
;sybex.com.              IN    MX

;; ANSWER SECTION:
sybex.com.        899    IN    MX    10 cluster1.us.messagelabs.com.
sybex.com.        899    IN    MX    20 cluster1a.us.messagelabs.com.

;; Query time: 76 msec
;; SERVER: 8.8.8.8#53(8.8.8.8)
;; WHEN: Wed Nov 01 21:43:32 EDT 2017
;; MSG SIZE rcvd: 104


root@Sybex:~#
```

Getting Help

Linux is a great alternative to the Windows operating system, but the command line can be overwhelming. However, once you learn some of these basic commands it can be very rewarding. From time to time you may need help, and this is where the man command comes in handy. The man command, also known as the manual command, allows you to quickly look up the command arguments or usage of a command, as shown in Figure 16.24. Enter the command **man**, followed by the command you need information on, to open the manual page. For example, you can see the manual page for the cat command by entering **man cat** at the command line.

The manual pages are installed with any package that is installed on the system. We will only be concerned with command-line usage, but for programmers, there are manual pages that explain system calls and APIs.

Linux and Windows

The Microsoft Windows operating system has used the Server Message Block (SMB) protocol to connect clients to file servers and printer servers since the introduction of Windows. Linux has primarily used Network File System (NFS) as its protocol of choice for sharing files between Linux systems. Both SMB and NFS are considered filer protocols; they define how one system accesses files on another system over the network.

FIGURE 16.24 The man command

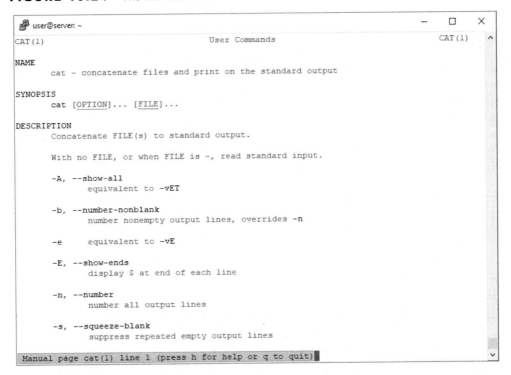

```
🖳 user@server: ~                                                     —  □  ✕
CAT(1)                          User Commands                          CAT(1)  ⌃

NAME
       cat - concatenate files and print on the standard output

SYNOPSIS
       cat [OPTION]... [FILE]...

DESCRIPTION
       Concatenate FILE(s) to standard output.

       With no FILE, or when FILE is -, read standard input.

       -A, --show-all
              equivalent to -vET

       -b, --number-nonblank
              number nonempty output lines, overrides -n

       -e     equivalent to -vE

       -E, --show-ends
              display $ at end of each line

       -n, --number
              number all output lines

       -s, --squeeze-blank
              suppress repeated empty output lines                             ⌄

Manual page cat(1) line 1 (press h for help or q to quit)█
```

Although Microsoft has started to support NFS as an available protocol on Windows for sharing between Windows and Linux, SMB is the protocol of choice if you primarily work from Windows. This is mainly because the SMB file sharing is easier to set up and is native to the Windows operating system. *Samba* is a free open source software (FOSS) package that can be installed on Linux to allow the Linux operating system to share the underlying filesystem via the SMB protocol. By installing the Samba package, you can turn a Linux server into a Windows file server that communicates via SMB. The Samba project is even so advanced that you can use Samba in place of an Active Directory (AD) domain controller (DC).

The Samba installation is simple. If the Linux distribution you are using supports APT package management, then simply issue the command **sudo apt install samba**. If the Linux distribution you are using supports YUM package management, then simply issue the command **sudo yum install samba**. Unfortunately, installing the service is the easy part of the process. Samba offers so many features that the configuration can be pretty complex, depending on what you are trying to achieve.

If you are just setting up a simple file share, then the configuration is pretty straightforward. You will need to edit the smb.conf file in the /etc/samba directory structure by using the command **sudo nano /etc/samba/smb.conf**. The following is a sample configuration of a simple file share.

```
[fileshare]
    comment = Samba on Linux
    path = /opt/fileshare
    read only = no
    browsable = yes
```

The first line, [fileshare], is the file share name. This can be anything, but for this example it is fileshare. The comment that follows is for the administrator to explain the purpose of the share. The path is the local filesystem path that will be shared out; in this example, it is /opt/fileshare. The read only line configures read and write capability for the share. The browsable line configures whether the share is populated in the NetBIOS browsing process.

After saving the configuration, the Samba service will need to be restarted to pick up the new configuration added to the CONF file. Restarting the service can be achieved by entering the following:

sudo service smbd restart

You may also have to add a firewall rule to allow incoming connections. This can be achieved by entering the following:

sudo ufw allow samba

These examples were from an Ubuntu server, using APT package management. However, the process is the same regardless of the operating system or package management. Install Samba, configure Samba, restart the Samba service, and open the firewall.

Summary

This chapter provided an overview of operating systems other than Microsoft Windows. In particular, we looked at macOS and Linux, including the features and various tools included with each that appear on the CompTIA A+ 220-1102 exam.

We covered the installation and uninstallation of applications in macOS. This included the various methods with which an application can be downloaded and installed. We also discussed the basic management of applications, such as creating shortcuts.

We also covered best practices for both macOS and Linux. There are best practices that technicians and administrators should follow regardless of which operating system(s) they are running, such as backup and antivirus.

The chapter concluded with an examination of some basic Linux commands. Many of the commands can be used in a variety of applications. This chapter covered what you need to know for the 220-1102 exam.

Exam Essentials

Know how applications are managed in macOS.   Know that applications can be installed via the App Store or downloadable applications. Know the various file types an application installation can be downloaded on. Know how applications are installed by simply dragging the application to the Applications folder, and be able to describe the uninstallation process of dragging the application to the Trash.

Be able to identify best practices.   Best practices help keep systems and data usable. Among the best practices to follow, it is important to schedule backups, schedule disk maintenance, keep systems up to date, and make sure that antivirus/antimalware definition files are current.

Know the available System Preferences.   You should be familiar with the various System Preferences. Know what each preference offers in the form of configuration for macOS.

Know key macOS tools and features.   There are a number of tools and features included with macOS that make it an attractive operating system to use. Among them are Mission Control, Keychain, Spotlight, iCloud, Gestures, the Finder, Remote Disc, Dock, Disk Utility, File Vault, Terminal, and Force Quit.

Know the basic Linux commands.   Every version and distribution of Linux allows you to get to the command line in one way or another and interact with the shell. From there, you can give commands to navigate around (cd, pwd), to create and change file values (chmod, chown), to run commands (su, sudo), and to do many other tasks.

Review Questions

The answers to the chapter review questions can be found in Appendix A.

1. Within a Linux terminal, you want to see all the files on your system in long format (using the −l option), including any hidden files (which requires the −a option). Which command should you use?

   A. `ls -a | ls -l`

   B. `ls -s; ls -l`

   C. `ls -la`

   D. `ls -a\ls -l`

2. Which of the following allows you to see all running programs in macOS?

   A. Keychain

   B. Mission Control

   C. Finder

   D. Force Quit

3. As part of your training program, you're trying to convince users to make backups on a regular basis. Which Apple app can be used to make backups of various types on a regular basis?

   A. Time Machine

   B. Finder

   C. VSS

   D. Keychain

4. Which of the following Linux commands/utilities can be used to edit a file?

   A. `ps`

   B. `nano`

   C. `rm`

   D. `ls`

5. Which of the following Linux commands/utilities can be used to edit an Ethernet connection's configuration settings?

   A. `dd`

   B. `apt-get`

   C. `ip`

   D. `pwd`

6. Which of the following is a macOS feature for password management?

   A. Spotlight

   B. Keychain

   C. Dock

   D. Gestures

7. The interpreter in Linux between the operating system and the user is known as the _____.

   A. Shell

   B. Translator

   C. Login

   D. GUI

8. What type of backup is kept on site at the computer center for immediate recovery purposes?

   A. On-path attack

   B. Cloud copies

   C. Journal copies

   D. Working copies

9. Which of the following utilities can be used in Linux to download patches for installation on a workstation?

   A. update

   B. Shell/terminal

   C. apt

   D. patch

10. Which of the following commands can be used to change the owner of a file to a new owner in Linux?

    A. cd

    B. chmod

    C. chown

    D. pwd

11. Which Linux utility can be used to check and repair disks?

    A. fsck

    B. chkdsk

    C. du

    D. dumgr

12. Your iPad has an application that will not stop running. What feature/tool can you use to stop it?

    A. kill

    B. Force Quit

    C. Task Manager

    D. Close Quit

13. Which of the following is the most common shell used with Linux?

    A. Tcl/Tk

    B. Terminal

    C. Bash

    D. SSH

14. What is the name of the area at the bottom of a macOS screen where, by default, a bar of crucial icons appears?

    A. Footer

    B. Mission Control

    C. Taskbar

    D. Dock

15. Which key combination can you use to bring up Spotlight from within an app?

    A. Control+Shift

    B. Option+Tab

    C. Command+spacebar

    D. Alt+Home

16. Which Linux command can be used to let you run a single command as another user?

    A. sudo

    B. su

    C. passwd

    D. ifconfig

17. Which of the following Linux commands will show you a list of running processes?

    A. ls

    B. cat

    C. ps

    D. su

18. You are currently in a Linux terminal session and in the /home/testuser/documents/
mail directory. Which command will take you to /home/testuser/documents?

   A. cd .

   B. cd ..

   C. cd . . .

   D. cd ~

19. If the permissions for a file are rwxrw-r--, what permissions apply for a user who is a
member of the group to which the owner belongs?

   A. Read, write, and execute

   B. Read and write

   C. Read only

   D. No access

20. What does the -p option with mkdir do?

   A. Prompts the user before creating files

   B. Prompts the user before creating subfolders

   C. Creates subfolders as well as folders

   D. None of the above

Performance-Based Question

You will encounter performance-based questions on the A+ exams. The questions on the exam require you to perform a specific task, and you will be graded on whether or not you were able to complete the task. The following requires you to think creatively in order to measure how well you understand this chapter's topics. You may or may not see similar questions on the actual A+ exams. To see how your answers compare to the authors', refer to Appendix B.

By default, not all files and folders in a Linux directory are shown when you do an ls listing. Entries that start with a period (.) are considered "hidden" and not shown. Try this command in your home directory, and then compare the result with what you see when you don't use the -a option:

1. Type **cd /** to change to the root directory.
2. Type **ls -F** to see the files and directories in the root directory.
3. Type **ls -aF** to see everything, including hidden files.
4. Type **cd ~** to change to your home directory.
5. Type **ls -l** to see the files and directories in your home directory.
6. Type **ls -al** to see everything, including hidden files.

Chapter

17

Security Concepts

THE FOLLOWING COMPTIA A+ 220-1102 EXAM OBJECTIVES ARE COVERED IN THIS CHAPTER:

✓ **2.1 Summarize various security measures and their purposes.**

- Physical security
    - Access control vestibule
    - Badge reader
    - Video surveillance
    - Alarm systems
    - Motion sensors
    - Door locks
    - Equipment locks
    - Guards
    - Bollards
    - Fences
- Physical security for staff
    - Key fobs
    - Smart cards
    - Keys
    - Biometrics
        - Retina scanner
        - Fingerprint scanner
        - Palmprint scanner
    - Lighting
    - Magnetometers

- Logical Security
  - Principle of least privilege
  - Access control lists (ACLs)
  - Multifactor authentication (MFA)
  - Email
  - Hard token
  - Soft token
  - Short message service (SMS)
  - Voice call
  - Authenticator application
- Mobile device management (MDM)
- Active Directory
  - Login script
  - Domain
  - Group Policy/updates
  - Organizational units
  - Home folder
  - Folder redirection
  - Security groups

✓ **2.3 Given a scenario, detect, remove, and prevent malware using the appropriate tools and methods.**

- Malware
  - Trojan
  - Rootkit
  - Virus
  - Spyware
  - Ransomware
  - Keylogger
  - Boot sector virus
  - Cryptominers

- Tools and methods
  - Recovery console
  - Antivirus
  - Anti-malware
  - Software firewalls
  - Anti-phishing training
  - User education regarding common threats
  - OS reinstallation

✓ **2.4 Explain common social-engineering attacks, threats, and vulnerabilities.**

- Social engineering
  - Phishing
  - Vishing
  - Shoulder surfing
  - Whaling
  - Tailgating
  - Impersonation
  - Dumpster diving
  - Evil twin
- Threats
  - Distributed denial of service (DDoS)
  - Denial of service (DoS)
  - Zero-day attack
  - Spoofing
  - On-path attack
  - Brute-force attack
  - Dictionary attack
  - Insider threat
  - Structured Query Language (SQL) injection
  - Cross-site scripting (XSS)

- Vulnerabilities
  - Non-compliant systems
  - Unpatched systems
  - Unprotected systems (missing antivirus/ missing firewall)
  - EOL OSs
  - Bring your own device (BYOD)

✓ **2.6 Given a scenario, configure a workstation to meet best practices for security.**

- Data-at-rest encryption
- Password best practices
  - Complexity requirements (Length, Character types)
  - Expiration requirements
  - Basic input/output system (BIOS)/Unified Extensible Firmware Interface (UEFI) passwords
- End-user best practices
  - Use screensaver locks
  - Log off when not in use
  - Secure/protect critical hardware (e.g., laptops)
  - Secure personally identifiable information (PII) and passwords
- Account management
  - Restrict user permissions
  - Restrict login times
  - Disable guest account
  - Use failed attempts lockout
  - Use timeout/screen lock
- Change default administrator's user account/password
- Disable AutoRun
- Disable AutoPlay

✓ **2.8 Given a scenario, use common data destruction and disposal methods.**

  ▪ Physical destruction

      ▪ Drilling

      ▪ Shredding

      ▪ Degaussing

      ▪ Incinerating

  ▪ Recycling or repurposing best practices

      ▪ Erasing/wiping

      ▪ Low-level formatting

      ▪ Standard formatting

  ▪ Outsourcing concepts

      ▪ Third-party vendor

      ▪ Certification of destruction/recycling

Think of how much simpler an administrator's life was in the days before every user had to be able to access the Internet, and how much simpler it must have been when you only had to maintain a number of dumb terminals connected to a mini-tower. Much of what has created headaches for an administrator since then is the inherent security risk that comes about as the network expands. As our world—and our networks—have become more connected, the need to secure data and keep it away from the eyes of those who can do harm has increased exponentially.

Realizing this, CompTIA added the Security domain to the A+ exams a number of years back. Security is now a topic that every administrator and technician must not only be aware of and concerned about, but also be actively involved in implementing methods to enforce and monitor. In the world of production, quality may be job one, but in the IT world, it is security.

This chapter, one of two chapters that focus primarily on security, will cover myriad security concepts. First, we will explore the physical aspects of security, and then we will dive deeper into the logical aspects of security. We will then look at how external forces, such as malware, social engineering, and vulnerabilities, can impact security. We will finish this chapter by looking at some common ways that you can safeguard yourself from security breaches. We will cover the proper destruction and disposal methods as well as security measures you can employ in network installations.

NOTE A+ is not the only IT certification that CompTIA offers. Security+ is one of the more popular choices. The topics found in this chapter are a subset of what you need to know for that certification.

Many of the security issues that plague networks today can be solved through the implementation of basic security elements. Some of those elements are physical (e.g., locked doors), and others are digital (e.g., antivirus software), but all share in common the goal of keeping problems out. The following six topic areas are key:

- Physical security
- Digital security
- User education
- The principle of least privilege
- Email security
- Virtual private networks (VPNs)

As you study for the exam, know the types of physical security elements that you can add to an environment to secure it. Know, as well, what types of digital security you should implement to keep malware at bay. Understand that the first line of defense is the user. You need to educate users to understand why security is important, and you must impose the principle of least privilege to prevent them from inadvertently causing harm.

Physical Security Concepts

Physical security is the most overlooked element of security in a network. A simple lock can keep out the most curious prying eyes from a network closet or server room. A more layered approach can be implemented for higher security installations. However, the simple fact is that not a lot of time is spent on physically securing the network. In the following sections, we will cover the CompTIA objectives related to physical security of networks.

Access Control Vestibule

The use of an access control vestibule, also known as a mantrap, helps to prevent nonauthorized users from tailgating. An *access control vestibule* is a small room that has two controlled doors, as shown in Figure 17.1. When a person enters the first door, they are trapped in the room until they have been authorized to enter the second controlled door. The close proximity between people in this confined space makes it uncomfortable both for the authorized user and for the nonauthorized user attempting to tailgate. In this example, the doors are controlled by radio frequency identification (RFID) readers, which we will cover later in this section.

FIGURE 17.1   A common access control vestibule setup

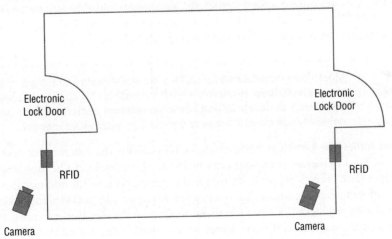

Badge Reader

Identification (ID) badges are used to provide proof of access. Badges can be any form of identification intended to differentiate the holder from everyone else. This can be as simple as a name badge or a photo ID. When the badge contains a photo ID, it is considered the authentication factor of something that you are.

Many ID badges also contain a magnetic strip or RFID provision so that the badge can be used in conjunction with a *badge reader*. When the information is read by the badge reader, it is sent to an access control system for authorization through the controlled door. A benefit of implementing badge readers is that it creates an electronic audit of all access to an area.

Video Surveillance

Video surveillance is the backbone of physical security. It is the only detection method that allows an investigator to identify what happened, when it happened, and, most important, who made it happen. Two types of cameras can be deployed: fixed and *pan-tilt-zoom (PTZ)*. Fixed cameras are the best choice when recording for surveillance activities. Pan-tilt-zoom (PTZ) cameras allow for 360-degree operations and zooming in on an area. PTZs are most commonly used for intervention, such as covering an area outside during an accident or medical emergency. PTZ cameras are usually deployed for the wrong reasons, mainly because they are cool! PTZs are often put into patrol mode to cover a larger area than a fixed camera can. However, when an incident occurs, they are never pointed in the area you need them! It is always best to use a fixed camera or multiple fixed cameras, unless you need a PTZ for a really good reason. They are usually more expensive and require more maintenance than fixed cameras.

Video surveillance can be deployed using two common media types: coaxial cable and Ethernet. Coaxial cable is used typically in areas where preexisting coaxial lines are in place or distances are too far for typical Ethernet. These systems are called closed-circuit television (CCTV). Coaxial camera systems generally use appliance-like devices for recording of video. These CCTV recorders generally have a finite number of ports for cameras and a finite amount of storage in the form of direct-attached storage (DAS).

 Most video installations for CCTV are coaxial cable and Ethernet, as previously described. However, wireless is popular for consumer applications, such as doorbells and home surveillance cameras. These devices generally use cloud storage and require an Internet connection.

Ethernet (otherwise known as IP) surveillance is becoming the standard for new installations. Anywhere an Ethernet connection can be installed, a camera can be mounted. Power over Ethernet (PoE) allows power to be supplied to the camera, so the additional power supplies used with coaxial cameras are not needed. Ethernet also provides the flexibility of virtual local area networks (VLANs) for added security so that the camera network is isolated from operational traffic. IP surveillance uses network video recorder (NVR) software to record cameras. Because NVRs are server applications, you can use traditional storage such as network area storage (NAS) or storage area network (SAN) storage. This allows you to treat the video recordings like traditional data.

Coaxial camera networks can be converted to IP surveillance networks with the use of a device called a *media converter*. These devices look similar to a CCTV recorder. They have a limited number of ports for the coaxial cameras and are generally smaller than the CCTV recorder. This is because they do not have any DAS. The sole purpose of the media converter is to convert the coaxial camera to an Ethernet feed to the NVR.

The use of IP video surveillance allows for a number of higher-end features such as camera-based motion detection, license plate recognition (LPR), and motion fencing. Advanced NVR software allows cameras to send video only when motion is detected at the camera; this saves on storage for periods of nonactivity. LPR is a method of detecting and capturing license plates in which the software converts the plate to a searchable attribute for the event. With motion fencing, an electronic fence can be drawn on the image so that any activity within this region will trigger an alert. Among the many other features are facial recognition and object recognition.

Motion Sensors

There are several different motion sensor types that you can use to detect unauthorized access. Passive infrared (PIR) is the most common motion detection used today, mainly because of price. PIR sensors operate by monitoring the measurement of infrared radiation from several zones. In Figure 17.2, you can see the reflective panel that divides the infrared zones. A PIR sensor will always have this grid pattern on the sensor's face.

FIGURE 17.2   A typical PIR sensor

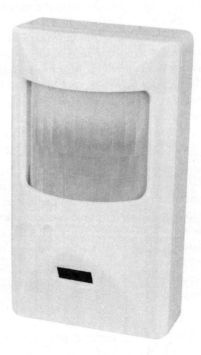

Microwave detectors also look like PIR sensors, but they do not have a reflective panel. Microwave detectors are common in areas where wide coverage is needed. Microwave detectors operate by sending pulses of microwaves out and measuring the microwaves received. These detectors are more expensive than PIR sensors and are susceptible to external interference, but they have a wider area of coverage.

Vibration sensors are another type of sensor used for motion detection. Although you may have seen them in the latest over-the-top heist movie, vibration sensors are really used in physical security systems. They are most often implemented as seismic sensors. They help protect from natural disasters and accidental drilling, or the occasional over-the-top heist.

Alarm System

An alarm system is another type of physical security system. It provides a method to alert security personnel in the event of unauthorized access or a break in. An alarm system can be configured to trigger in the event of an access control system logging unauthorized access to a controlled door. However, it is more common to find alarm systems installed for break-in detection and response.

An alarm system can be configured to use motion sensors, video surveillance, magnetic contacts, and a multitude of other sensors. Each sensor will be installed in a different logical zone. The perimeter of the building might be zone 1, the server room might be zone 2, and so on. There could be many different zones configured for each sensor. The main purpose of the zone is to communicate the location of the sensor being tripped so that law enforcement agents can respond to that location.

A monitoring company is typically contracted with the installation. The purpose of the monitoring company is to act as a buffer between the zone being tripped and a law enforcement agency. The alarm panel will dial out to a monitoring station and it will transmit the account number and the zone that is tripped. The monitoring station can then process its call-down list. The call-down list will typically consist of the phone number of the supervisor of the area, the in-house security personnel, and ultimately a law enforcement agency. The monitoring company can also monitor the health of the alarm panel, depending on the model of alarm panel and its features.

Door Locks

The most common physical prevention tactic is the use of locks on doors and equipment. This might mean the installation of a tumbler-style lock or an elaborate electronic combination lock for the switching closet. If a tumbler-style lock is installed, then the appropriate authorized individuals who require access will need a physical key. Using physical keys can become a problem, because you may not have the key with you when you need it the most, or you can lose the key. The key can also be copied and used by unauthorized individuals. Combination locks, also called cipher locks, can be reprogrammed and do not require physical keys, as shown in Figure 17.3. Combination locks for doors can be purchased as mechanical or electronic.

FIGURE 17.3   A typical combination door lock

 When physical locks use keys, the factor of authentication is considered something that you have—because you must have the key. When physical locks use ciphers, the authentication is considered something you know—because you must know the cipher.

Equipment Locks

There are many different types of *equipment locks* that can secure the information and the device that holds the information. Simply thwarting the theft of equipment containing data and restricting the use of USB thumb drives can secure information. In the following sections, we will cover several topics that are directly related to the physical aspects of information security.

Cable Locks

Cable locks are used to secure laptops and any device with a Universal Security Slot (USS), as shown in Figure 17.4. A cable lock is just that—a cable with a lock at one end. The lock can be a tumbler or a combination, as shown in Figure 17.5. The basic principle is that the end of the lock fits into the USS. When the cable is locked, the protruding slot of metal turns into a cross that cannot be removed. This provides security to expensive equipment that can be stolen due to its portability or size.

FIGURE 17.4 A Universal Security Slot

FIGURE 17.5 A standard cable lock

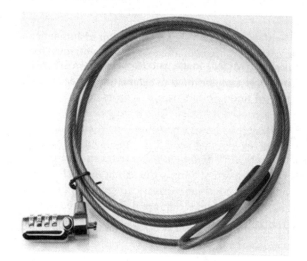

Server Locks

Most servers come with a latch-style lock that prevents someone from opening the server, but the tumbler-style lock is trivial to open. Anyone with a paperclip can open these locks if they have forgotten the keys. Other types of server locks are holes for padlocks that latch through the top cover and the body of the server. However, over the past 10 years, a declining number of servers come with this feature. This is mainly due to the fact that servers can be better secured behind a locked rack-mounted enclosure. Rack-mounted enclosures generally come with a tumbler-style lock that can protect all the servers and network equipment installed in the cabinet, while still providing airflow.

USB Locks

Universal Serial Bus (USB) locks can be put into place to physically lock out USB ports on a workstation or server from use. These devices are extremely rare to find, because most equipment and operating systems allow for the USB ports to be deactivated. USB locks work by inserting a small plastic spacer into the USB port. Once inserted, the spacer latches to the USB detent with plastic teeth. A tool is required to remove the USB spacer.

Security Guards

Physical security begins with personnel—specifically, security-focused personnel, such as security guards. *Security guards* should be responsible for limiting access from the outer perimeter of your installation. Security guards typically use photo IDs, also known as ID badges, to allow access to the installation. Exceptions to this are people on the entry control roster; in some secured buildings, only people on the entry control roster are allowed to enter. In this type of scenario, the ID badge is used only to provide ID. This is common in government and sensitive installations.

Fences

Fences are a physical security barrier to keep unauthorized persons out of a secure area. Exterior fences can be arranged so that they create a choke point where a guard can inspect credentials to allow authorized personnel into the area. Guards can also be replaced with electronic locks and RFID readers to limit access. When installed in conjunction with a video camera system to surveil the area around the entry point, a fence creates a very secure outer layer for your facility. Fences should be considered the outermost security layer of a multiple-barrier system.

In addition to an exterior fence, the building that houses the data should have RFID readers and electronic door locks. The innermost area surrounding the equipment can also be segmented with a fence and additional access controls, such as standard keyed locks or electronic access control. When fences are used in the interior of the data center, air quality can be maintained while preventing unauthorized access, as shown in Figure 17.6. Using multiple barriers as described allows contractors for HVAC systems to maintain their systems, while preventing direct physical access to the servers and equipment.

FIGURE 17.6   Interior data center fences

Bollards

A *bollard* is an architectural structure that acts as a visual indicator for a perimeter. They are also very sturdy, since their second function is to act as a barrier for the perimeter and protect the area. They are commonly found around areas where a truck or other vehicle can cause damage. In Figure 17.7, the bollard is protecting a fiber-optic vault from accidental damage by a vehicle. Bollards can also be found in the interior of a building if there is potential for damage to a protected area from a vehicle, such as a forklift or equipment cart.

Physical Security for Staff

Organizations should authorize and audit staff access for sensitive areas inside a facility. Implementing physical security for staff is one way you can control access to the physical equipment and the data that is stored on the equipment. By limiting access to the equipment and the underlying data, you can prevent service disruptions or loss of data. This section will focus on ways that you can implement physical security for staff.

FIGURE 17.7   A typical bollard

Key Fobs

Key fobs are named after the chains that used to hold pocket watches to clothes. *Key fobs* are embedded *radio frequency identification (RFID)* circuits that fit on a set of keys and are used with physical access control systems, as shown in Figure 17.8. They are often used for access to external and internal doors for buildings. Key fobs are close-proximity devices that authorize the user for entry; an electronic lock is actuated when the device is presented, and the door can be opened. This is an authentication factor of something that you have.

FIGURE 17.8   A key fob

Smartcards and RFID Badges

A *smartcard* is the size of a credit card with an integrated circuit embedded into the card (also called an integrated circuit chip [ICC]). The chip is exposed on the face of the card with surface contacts, as shown in Figure 17.9. Smartcards are used for physical authentication to electronic systems and access control systems and require a PIN or password. A smartcard is considered a multifactor authentication method because it is something you have (card) and something you know (PIN or password). The U.S. military uses smartcards called Common Access Cards (CACs) for access to computer systems and physical access controls.

FIGURE 17.9 A typical smartcard

An RFID badge is a wireless, no-contact technology used with RFID transponders. RFID badges typically work on the 125 kHz radio frequency and are passively powered by the RFID transponder. When an RFID badge is placed in close proximity to the RFID transponder, the radio frequency (RF) energy emitted by the transponder powers a chip in the RFID badge. The RFID chip then varies the frequency back to the transponder in the effort to transmit its electronic signature (number). This type of authentication is considered something you have.

Keys

Physical keys are extremely hard to control and do not allow for the auditing of their usage. A physical key can be lent to someone, copied, stolen, or used by an unauthorized person. Because of the problems surrounding physical keys, their use should largely be avoided.

If keys are absolutely necessary, then a two-person system should be considered. A two-person system requires that two people must use their keys to open one lock, although nothing stops the keys from being lent to the same person to open a door.

Another option is to use an electronic lock box for management of the keys. When a technician needs a particular key, they will log into the key box and check out the key needed. This system allows for auditing controls, but it does not prevent copying of keys.

Biometrics

Biometric devices use physical characteristics to identify the user. This type of authentication is considered something that you are. Such devices are becoming more common in the business environment. Biometric systems include fingerprint/palm/hand scanners, retinal scanners, and soon, possibly, DNA scanners. Figure 17.10 shows a typical biometric device. In recent years, several mobile phones have implemented biometrics in the access control of the mobile device. Several manufacturers have adopted fingerprint access control, and some have even adopted facial recognition via the forward-pointing camera.

FIGURE 17.10   A typical biometric lock

To gain access to resources, you must pass a physical screening process. In the case of a hand scanner, this may include identifying fingerprints, scars, and markings on your hand. Retinal scanners compare your eye's retinal pattern to a stored retinal pattern to verify your identity. DNA scanners will examine a unique portion of your DNA structure to verify that you are who you say you are.

With the passing of time, the definition of biometrics is expanding from simply identifying physical attributes about a person to being able to describe patterns in their behavior. Recent advances have been made in the ability to authenticate someone based on the key pattern that they use when entering their password (how long they pause between keys, the amount of time each key is held down, and so forth). A company adopting biometric technologies needs to consider the controversy they may face. Some authentication methods are considered more intrusive than others. The error rate also needs to be considered, along with an acceptance of the fact that errors can include both false positives, where the reader allows access falsely, and false negatives, where the reader denies access erroneously. Therefore, biometrics is often used with another factor of authentication, such as a PIN number. This approach provides multifactor authentication.

Lighting

Most security cameras work on the principle of collecting light to record a picture. As light levels decrease, the quality of the picture decreases significantly. Therefore, areas in which you have video cameras should have sufficient levels of lighting. In reality any area that is sensitive should have a level of lighting, since threat agents often hide in darker areas to avoid being seen.

Lighting the area doesn't always require a visible light source. Most cameras sensors built in the last 10 years allow for the collection of light from infrared (IR) light sources. This means that even in the dark you can surveil and record an area, although a visible light source does deter unauthorized access.

Magnetometers

The *magnetometer*, also known as a metal detector, uses an electromagnetic field to detect metallic objects. We have all seen these devices at a choke point in the airport or government building. When a metal detector is used for people entering a facility, you can detect weapons, such as guns or knives. When a metal detector is deployed in this fashion, it protects your staff from threat agents with malicious intent.

A metal detector can also be used to monitor people leaving a facility. The metal detector can monitor staff leaving with equipment. When it is used in this way, it will protect against data loss and theft. However, unless your organization is regulated as a highly classified facility, this approach will be hard to enforce and could infringe on your employees' privacy.

Logical Security

Whereas the topic of physical security concepts, from CompTIA's standpoint, focuses on keeping individuals out, logical security focuses on keeping harmful data and malware out as well as on authorization and permissions. This logical security includes devices and methods that protect the environment logically, such as firewalls, antivirus software, and directory permissions, just to name a few. The areas of focus are antivirus software, firewalls, antimalware, user authentication/strong passwords, and directory permissions. Each of these topics is addressed in the sections that follow.

Principle of Least Privilege

The *principle of least privilege* is a common security concept that states a user should be restricted to the fewest number of privileges that they need to do their job. By leveraging the principle of least privilege, you can limit internal and external threats. For example, if a front-line worker has administrative access on their computer, they have the ability to circumvent security; this is an example of an internal threat. Along the same lines, if a worker has administrative access on their computer and receives a malicious email, a bad actor could now have administrative access to the computer; this is an example of an external threat. Therefore, only the permissions required to perform their tasks should be granted to users, thus providing least privilege.

Security is not the only benefit to following the principle of least privilege, although it does reduce the surface area of attack because users have less access to sensitive data that can be leaked. When you limit workers to the least privilege they need on their computers or the network, fewer intentional or accidental misconfigurations will happen that can lead to downtime or help desk calls. Some regulatory standards require following the principle of least privilege. By following the principle of least privilege, an organization can improve on compliance audits by regulatory bodies.

Access Control Lists

Access control lists (ACLs) are used to control traffic and applications on a network. Every network vendor supports a type of ACL method; for the remainder of this section, I will focus on Cisco ACLs.

An ACL method consists of multiple access control entries (ACEs) that are condition actions. Each entry is used to specify the traffic to be controlled. Every vendor will have a different type of control logic. However, understanding the control logic of the ACL system allows you to apply it to any vendor and be able to effectively configure an ACL. The control logic is defined with these simple questions:

- How are the conditions of an ACL evaluated?
- What is the default action if a condition is not met?
- How is the ACL applied to traffic?
- How are conditions edited for an ACL?

Let's explore the control logic for a typical Cisco layer 3 switch or router. The conditions of the ACL are evaluated from top to bottom. If a specific condition is not met for the ACL, the default action is to deny the traffic. Only one ACL can be configured per interface, per protocol, and per direction. When you are editing a traditional standard or extended ACL, the entire ACL must be negated and reentered with the new entry. With traditional ACLs, there is no way to edit a specific ACL on the fly. When editing a named access list, each condition is given a line number that can be referenced so that the specific entry can be edited. For the remainder of this section, we will use named access lists to illustrate an applied access list for controlling traffic.

In Figure 17.11 you can see a typical corporate network. There are two different types of workers: HR workers and generic workers. We want to protect the HR web server from access by generic workers.

FIGURE 17.11   A typical corporate network

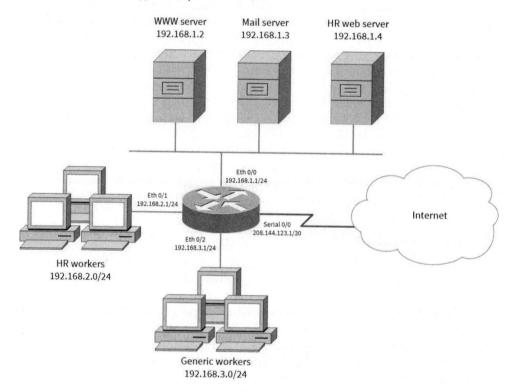

We can protect the HR server by applying an ACL to outgoing traffic for Eth 0/0 and describing the source traffic and destination to be denied. We can also apply an ACL to the incoming interface of Eth 0/2 describing the destination traffic to be denied. For this example, we will build an access list for incoming traffic to Eth 0/2, blocking the destination of the HR server.

```
Router(config)# ip access-list extended block-hrserver
Router(config-ext-nacl)# deny ip any host 192.168.1.4
Router(config-ext-nacl)# permit ip any any
Router(config-ext-nacl)# exit
Router(config)# interface ethernet 0/2
Router(config-if)# ip access-group block-hrserver in
```

This ACL, called block-hrserver, contains two condition action statements. The first denies any source address to the specific destination address of 192.168.1.4. The second allows any source address to any destination address. We then enter the interface of Eth 0/2 and apply the ACL to the inbound direction of the router interface. The rule will protect the HR server from generic worker access while allowing the generic workers to access all other resources and the Internet.

It is important to note that the focus of this section is to understand how ACLs are used to protect resources. It is not important to understand how to build specific ACLs, since commands will be different from vendor system to vendor system.

Authentication Factors

This section discusses various components of physical security that control access. When components are used to control access, they do so based on the authentication of people. Authentication can happen in several different ways, as follows:

Something You Know   This is commonly a username and password or *personal identification number (PIN)*. You can make passwords more complex by requiring uppercase, lowercase, numeric, and symbol combinations.

Something You Have   This is based on something you physically have. This chapter covers several different types of devices, including key fobs, keys, and smartcards, just to name a few.

Something You Are   This authentication factor is based on something that makes you physically unique. Biometrics such as fingerprints, your voice, and retina scans should be the first things that come to mind.

Somewhere You Are   A relatively new factor of authentication is based on somewhere you are. With the proliferation of Global Positioning System (GPS) chips, your current location can authenticate you for a system. This is performed by authentication rules based on the user's location.

Something You Do   Another relatively new factor of authentication for network systems is based on something you do. Although it has been used for hundreds of years for documents and contracts, a signature is something that you do and don't even think about how you do it. It is unique to you and only you, because there is a specific way you sign your name. Typing your name into the computer is something you do and don't think about, but there is a slight hesitation that you make without knowing it.

Multifactor Authentication

All authentication is based on something that you know, have, are, or do, or a location you are in. A common factor of authentication is a password, but passwords can be guessed, stolen, or cracked. A fingerprint can be lifted with tape, a key can be stolen, or a location spoofed. No one factor is secure by itself because it can be compromised easily.

When more than one item (factor) is used to authenticate a user, this is known as *multifactor authentication (MFA)*. It may take two, three, or four factors to authenticate, but as long as it is more than one, as the name implies, it is known as multifactor. One of the most common examples where this is used in everyday life is at an ATM. In order to withdraw money, a user must provide a card (one factor) and a PIN number (a second factor). If you know the PIN number but do not have the card, you cannot get money from the machine. If you have the card but do not have the PIN number, you cannot get money from the machine.

In this section we will cover the most common two-factor (2FA)/multifactor authentication methods use by protected applications. The following methods are generally used in conjunction with a traditional user and password combination. It should be assumed that when we talk about 2FA it provides the same functionality as MFA.

Email

Some applications use email as a 2FA method. However, using email as a 2FA option is probably the least secure method. This is mainly due to the fact that people reuse passwords. If your banking website username and password is compromised (something you know) and you reuse the same credentials on email, it provides no protection. Hopefully the email account is protected with 2FA in a way that it requires something you have.

Email is useful as a notification method when someone logs into a secure login. However, keep in mind the threat agents know this as well. If your email account is compromised, a threat agent will often create a rule in your email box to dump these notifications directly to the trash.

Short Message Service (SMS)

Some applications will allow the use of short message service (SMS) text messages as the 2FA method. When this method is used, a simple text message is sent to the user's phone number. The message will contain a random 5- to 8-digit code that the user will use to satisfy the 2FA requirement. When you first set up this 2FA method, the protected application will request the code before turning on 2FA. This is done to verify that the phone number is correct and that you can receive text messages.

Voice Call

Some applications that are protected by 2FA will allow voice calls to be initiated to the end user. This is usually done if the person does not have a phone that accepts text messages. The voice call will recite a 5- to 8-digit code that the user will use to satisfy the 2FA requirement. This process is similar to SMS, with the difference being it is an automated voice call.

Hardware and Software Tokens

Physical *hardware tokens* are anything that a user must have on them to access network resources. They are often associated with devices that enable the user to generate a one-time password (OTP) to authenticate their identity. SecurID from RSA is one of the best-known examples of a physical hardware token, as shown in Figure 17.12.

FIGURE 17.12   An RSA security key fob

Hardware tokens operate by rotating a code every 60 seconds. This rotating code is combined with a user's PIN or password for authentication. A hardware token is considered multifactor authentication because it is something you have (hardware token) and something you know (PIN or password).

A new type of hardware token is becoming the new standard, and it can be considered a software token or soft token. It operates the same as a hardware token, but it is an application on your cell phone that provides the code. Google Authenticator is one example of these types of applications. Microsoft also has an authenticator application similar to Google Authenticator.

When configuring 2FA on an application, you have two ways of adding an account to the authenticator application. You can take a picture of a quick response (QR) code, or you can enter a security code into the authenticator application. If you use choose to use a QR code, then the application turning the 2FA on will present a QR code that can be scanned by the authenticator application. If you choose to use a setup key, the application turning on the 2FA will provide a key. There is generally a second step before the application is protected by 2FA, where you will be required to enter a code from the authenticator application to the protected application. A lengthy one-time-use backup key is also generated, in case you need to turn 2FA off because your device is lost or stolen.

Mobile Device Management (MDM)

The traditional workforce is slowly becoming a mobile workforce, with employees working from home, on the go, and in the office. Mobile devices such as laptops, tablets, and smartphones are used by employees to connect to the organization's cloud resources. *Bring your own device (BYOD)* has been embraced as a strategy by organizations to alleviate the capital expense of equipment by allowing employees to use devices they already own.

Because employees are supplying their own devices, a formal document called the BYOD policy should be drafted. The BYOD policy defines a set of minimum requirements for the devices, such as size and type, operating system, connectivity, antivirus solutions, patches, and many other requirements the organization will deem necessary.

Many organizations use *mobile device management (MDM)* software that dictates the requirements for the BYOD policy. MDM software helps organizations protect their data on devices that are personally owned by the employees. When employees are terminated or a device is lost, the MDM software allows a secure remote wipe of the company's data on the device. The MDM software can also set policies requiring passwords on the device. All of these requirements should be defined in the organization's BYOD policy.

Active Directory

Microsoft originally released *Active Directory (AD)* with Windows 2000 Server to compete with Novell Directory Services (NDS). Active Directory is a highly scalable directory service that can contain many different objects, including users, computers, and printers, just to name a few. Active Directory uses a protocol called *Lightweight Directory Access Protocol (LDAP)* to quickly look up objects. It's important to understand that Active Directory is *not* the authentication mechanism; it is only the directory for storing and for the lookup of objects. Active Directory works in conjunction with Kerberos, which is the protocol that performed the authentication of users.

Active Directory uses a directory partition called the *schema partition* to describe classes of objects and the attributes that define each object. Each attribute is defined in the schema based on the value it will contain. For example, a user class can have a first name, last name, middle initial, description, and a number of other attributes. A specific user account is then created and configured in the GUI Microsoft Management Console (MMC) called Active Directory Users and Computers. There are also several attributes that don't show up in the management tool, such as when an object was last changed or replicated, as well as many other attributes used by Active Directory for management.

Domain

A domain is a hierarchical collection of security objects, such as users, computers, and policies, among other components. Active Directory domains are named with a Domain Name System (DNS) name. For example, sybex.com would be the root domain; if you wanted to add a new domain, you would append the namespace to the left, as follows: east.sybex .com. Using a DNS namespace is one of the ways that Active Directory is scalable and hierarchical. Many organizations never need anything more than one domain to contain all their security objects.

When a user authenticates against an Active Directory domain, a domain access token is issued, as shown in Figure 17.13. You can consider these to be keys for the various locks (ACLs) on resources. If the user is a member of a particular security group, it will be in their security token. When the user encounters a file that is secured with an ACL, the security token is presented. If there is a matching credential, then the user is granted the associated file permission on the ACL.

FIGURE 17.13   Active Directory security tokens

Organizational Units

A domain can hold security objects, but you need to have some organization to the many different objects that you will create in your domain. Organizational units (OUs) enable you to group objects together so that you can apply a set of policies to the objects. OUs should be designed to group objects by the following criteria:

Object Class   Objects can be organized based on their class or type. You can organize all the computers and users into their respective OUs.

Geographic Location   Objects can be organized based on their location. It is common practice to use airport codes when the organization is spread across a large distance. However, town names can also be used when the organization branches are in relatively close proximity.

Function   Objects can be organized based on their function in the organization, such as servers, workstations, and users. Objects can also be grouped by their job function, such as Sales, Marketing, and HR.

Hybrid   Nothing says that you have to stick to one organization of objects. Depending on how you are planning your domain, you could use a combination. It is not uncommon to see airport codes to represent the various offices, with functions under each airport code, as shown in Figure 17.14.

Group Policy

Group Policy is a feature of Active Directory that enables you to apply policies to control users and computers. Typically, you do not apply policies to individual users or computers but instead to groups of users or computers. A Group Policy Object (GPO) is a type of object in Active Directory that allows you to apply a set of policies against an organizational unit. Group Policy Objects are created, linked, and edited in the Group Policy Management Console (GPMC), as shown in Figure 17.15.

FIGURE 17.14 A hybrid OU structure

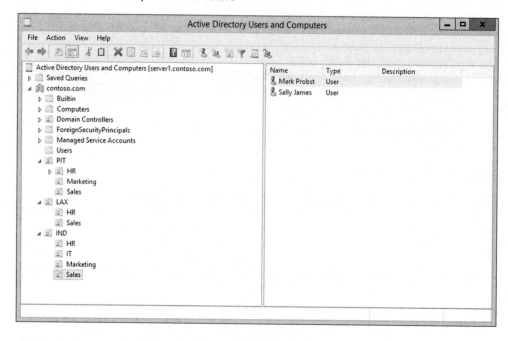

FIGURE 17.15 The Group Policy Management Console

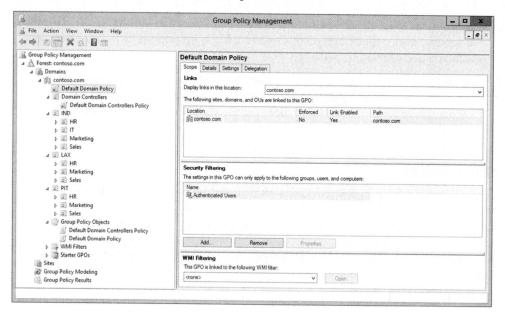

You can control thousands of settings for both the user and computer objects, as shown in Figure 17.16. Policies are hard controls that you can force on an object. Policies are refreshed in the background every 90 minutes. So, if a setting that has a policy applied changes, it will be set back during the refresh cycle. Most of the time, however, settings are grayed out when they are being managed by GPO and cannot be changed at all. Preferences allow for files, Registry, environment variable, and Control Panel items to be modified. Preferences set an initial setting and are applied only during first login, so these settings are a preference, not a policy, and the user can change these settings afterward.

FIGURE 17.16   Group Policy Object settings

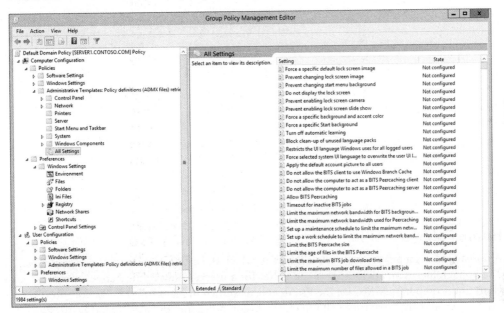

Login Scripts

Login scripts are one of the configurable attributes for a user account. As covered in Chapter 20, "Scripting and Remote Access," you can use VBScript or Windows batch scripts as login scripting languages. Login scripts are useful on an Active Directory network for connecting network-mapped drives and printers, among other administrative tasks. Login scripts also provide uniformity across an enterprise by running the same commands for each user configured with the script. The location of the setting is found on the Profile tab of the user account, as shown in Figure 17.17.

FIGURE 17.17   Profile settings for a user account

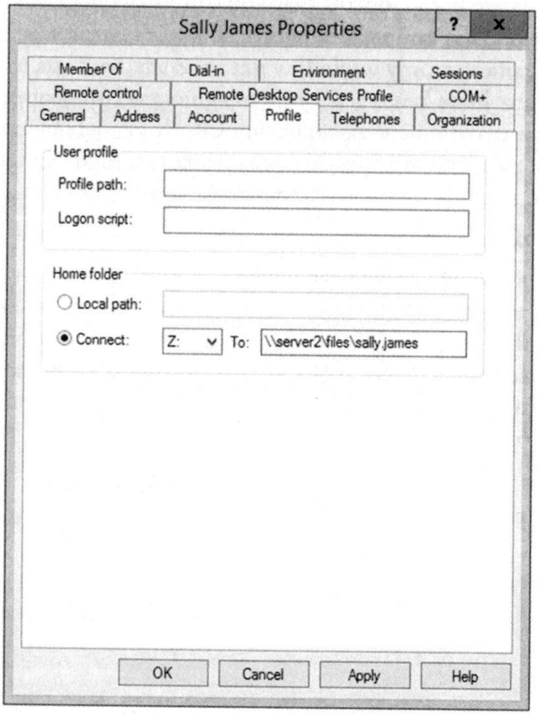

Home Folders

A *home folder* is a private network location in which the user can store their personal files. The home folder is an attribute that can be set for a user account in the Active Directory Users and Computers MMC on the Profile tab, as shown in Figure 17.17. The location can be a local path, if the user will use the same computer, and the files should be stored locally for the user. However, it is most useful when you connect a network drive to a remote file server. This allows for centralized file storage, and you can then perform backups on the data.

Folder Redirection

Normally, when a user logs into the network and a roaming profile exists for the user, the profile is completely downloaded to the computer the user is working on. During logout, all data is written back to the roaming profile location on the network file server. Profiles can become extremely large in size, sometimes even gigabytes, and slow down the login and logout processes.

Folder redirection is a Group Policy setting that allows the redirection of portions of users' profile folders to a network location. When folder redirection is used, the roaming profile is still downloaded. However, the redirected folders are not downloaded; they are simply redirected to the network location. This speeds login and logout times because the entire profile is no longer downloaded (login) and uploaded (logout).

Security Groups

The use of Active Directory domains allows you to adopt a centralized administration model for user accounts. You also have the ability to secure files, printers, and other resources on the domain with these centralized credentials. However, if you secure the resources solely with user accounts, very quickly it will become a daunting task, as more and more people need access to resources. This is a common pitfall of new administrators, because most resources only need to be accessed by a few people initially.

All security should be done using *security groups* for a few reasons. The first reason is a simple one: you want to administer groups of users and not individual users. It is easier to apply permissions to a group of users than individual users. As the resource needs to be shared by more people, you never have to revisit the resource to apply the new permissions if a group is used. All you need to do is add the new users to the group and they will have access.

One additional benefit that accompanies using security groups is the centralized auditing of permissions. If you want to know who has access to a resource, all you have to do is look at the membership of the group associated with the resource. If you need to check if someone specific has permission to the resource, you just have to look at their group membership.

When securing resources, you should always create a new group that is associated with the resource and never reuse a group for multiple resources. For example, if you were securing a main office printer, you should create a group that explains the resource and the level of access, such as creating a group called perm_print_mainprinter. Just by looking at the group you can identify that it is a permissions group, that it allows printing, and that the resource is the main printer.

Malware

Malware is a broad term describing any software with malicious intent. Although we use the terms *malware* and *virus* interchangeably, distinct differences exist between them. The lines have blurred because the delivery mechanisms of malware and viruses are sometimes indistinguishable.

A virus is a specific type of malware, the purpose of which is to multiply, infect, and do harm. A virus distinguishes itself from other malware because it is self-replicating code that often injects its payload into documents and executables. This is done in an attempt to infect more users and systems. Viruses are so efficient in replicating that their code is often programmed to deactivate after a period of time, or they are programmed to only be active in a certain region of the world.

Malware can be found in a variety of other forms, such as covert cryptomining, web search redirection, adware, spyware, and even ransomware, and these are just a few. Today the largest threat of malware is ransomware because it's lucrative for criminals.

Ransomware

Ransomware is a type of malware that is becoming popular because of anonymous currency, such as Bitcoin. Ransomware is software that is often delivered through an unsuspecting random download. It takes control of a system and demands that a third party be paid. The "control" can be accomplished by encrypting the hard drive, by changing user password information, or via any of a number of other creative ways. Users are usually assured that by paying the extortion amount (the ransom), they will be given the code needed to revert their systems back to normal operations. CryptoLocker was a popular ransomware that made headlines across the world (see Figure 17.18). You can protect yourself from ransomware by having antivirus/antimalware software with up-to-date definitions and by keeping current on patches.

FIGURE 17.18   CryptoLocker

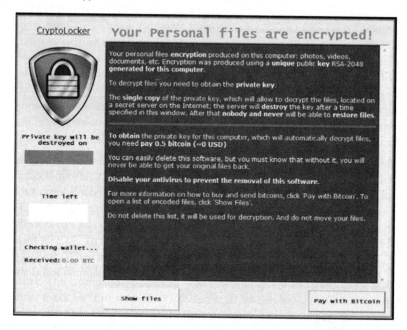

Trojans

Trojan horses are programs that enter a system or network under the guise of another program. A Trojan horse may be included as an attachment or as part of an installation program. The Trojan horse can create a backdoor or replace a valid program during installation. It then accomplishes its mission under the guise of another program. Trojan horses can be used to compromise the security of your system, and they can exist on a system for years before they're detected.

The best preventive measure for Trojan horses is to not allow them entry into your system. Immediately before and after you install a new software program or operating system, back it up! If you suspect a Trojan horse, you can reinstall the original program(s), which should delete the Trojan horse. A port scan may also reveal a Trojan horse on your system. If an application opens a TCP or UDP port that isn't supported in your network, you can track it down and determine which port is being used.

Keyloggers

A *keylogger* is normally a piece of software that records an unsuspecting victim's keystrokes. Keyloggers can stay loaded in memory and wait until you log into a website or other authentication system. They will then capture and relay the information to an awaiting host on the Internet.

Keyloggers don't always have to be in the form of software. Some keyloggers are hardware dongles that sit between the keyboard and computer. These must be retrieved and the data must be downloaded manually, so they are not very common.

Rootkits

Rootkits are software programs that have the ability to hide certain things from the operating system. They do so by obtaining (and retaining) administrative-level access. With a rootkit, there may be a number of processes running on a system that don't show up in Task Manager, or connections that don't appear in a Netstat display of active network connections that may be established or available. The rootkit masks the presence of these items by manipulating function calls to the operating system and filtering out information that would normally appear.

Unfortunately, many rootkits are written to get around antivirus and antispyware programs that aren't kept up-to-date. The best defense you have is to monitor what your system is doing and catch the rootkit in the process of installation.

Spyware

Spyware differs from other malware in that it works—often actively—on behalf of a third party. Rather than self-replicating, like viruses and worms, spyware is spread to machines by users who inadvertently ask for it. The users often don't know they have asked for it but have done so by downloading other programs, visiting infected sites, and so on.

The spyware program monitors the user's activity and responds by offering unsolicited pop-up advertisements (sometimes known as *adware*), gathers information about the user to pass on to marketers, or intercepts personal data, such as credit card numbers.

Cryptominers

With the rise of bitcoin, so came the rise of cryptominers. A cryptominer is typically a purpose-built device that grinds out cryptographic computations. When the computation is balanced a cryptocoin is created and equates to real money, such as Bitcoin, Ethereum, and Dogecoin, just to name a few. A cryptominer does not always have to be a dedicated purpose-built device, it can also be a distributed group of computers called a cryptopool.

Malware in the form of cryptominers became very popular, because it is a very lucrative way for threat agents to make money. The problem is that the threat agents uses your computer to grind out the computations. The most common way a threat agent will run a cryptominer remotely is with JavaScript embedded on a malicious web page. Threat agents have also been known to create viruses in which the payload (cryptominer) uses your video card to grind out the computations. However, the JavaScript variant is more common to find in the wild.

Viruses

Viruses can be classified as polymorphic, stealth, retrovirus, multipartite, armored, companion, phage, and macro viruses. Each type of virus has a different attack strategy and different consequences.

 Estimates for losses due to viruses are in the billions of dollars. These losses include financial loss as well as lost productivity.

The following sections introduce the symptoms of a virus infection, explain how a virus works, and describe the types of viruses you can expect to encounter and how they generally behave. We'll also discuss how a virus is transmitted through a network and look at a few hoaxes.

Symptoms of a Virus/Malware Infection

Many viruses will announce that you're infected as soon as they gain access to your system. They may take control of your system and flash annoying messages on your screen or destroy your hard disk. When this occurs, you'll know that you're a victim. Other viruses will cause your system to slow down, cause files to disappear from your computer, or take over your disk space.

 Because viruses are the most common type of malware, the term *virus* is used in this section.

You should look for some of the following symptoms when determining if a virus infection has occurred:

- The programs on your system start to load more slowly. This happens because the virus is spreading to other files in your system or is taking over system resources.

- Unusual files appear on your hard drive, or files start to disappear from your system. Many viruses delete key files in your system to render it inoperable.

- Program sizes change from the installed versions. This occurs because the virus is attaching itself to these programs on your disk.

- Your browser, word processing application, or other software begins to exhibit unusual operating characteristics. Screens or menus may change.

- The system mysteriously shuts itself down or starts itself up and does a great deal of unanticipated disk activity.

- You mysteriously lose access to a disk drive or other system resources. The virus has changed the settings on a device to make it unusable.

- Your system suddenly doesn't reboot or gives unexpected error messages during startup.

This list is by no means comprehensive. What is an absolute, however, is the fact that you should immediately quarantine the infected system. It is imperative that you do all you can to contain the virus and keep it from spreading to other systems within your network, or beyond.

How Viruses Work

A virus, in most cases, tries to accomplish one of two things: render your system inoperable or spread to other systems. Many viruses will spread to other systems given the chance and then render your system unusable. This is common with many of the newer viruses.

If your system is infected, the virus may try to attach itself to every file in your system and spread each time you send a file or document to other users. Some viruses spread by infecting files that are either transmitted through a network or by removable media, such as backup tapes, USB thumb drives, CDs, and DVDs, just to name a few. When you give removable media to another user or put it into another system, you then infect that system with the virus.

Many viruses today are spread using email. The infected system attaches a file to any email that you send to another user. The recipient opens this file, thinking it's something that you legitimately sent them. When they open the file, the virus infects the target system. The virus might then attach itself to all the emails that the newly infected system sends, which in turn infects the computers of the recipients of the emails. Figure 17.19 shows how a virus can spread from a single user to literally thousands of users in a very short period of time using email.

FIGURE 17.19   A virus spreading from an infected system using email

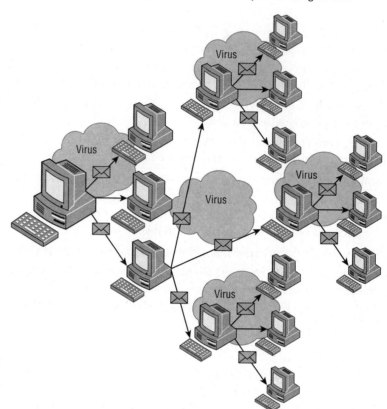

Types of Viruses

Viruses take many different forms. The following list briefly introduces these forms and explains how they work.

    The best defense against a virus attack is up-to-date antivirus/antimalware software installed and running. The software should be on all workstations as well as the server.

These are the most common types of viruses, but this isn't a comprehensive list:

Armored Virus   An armored virus is designed to make itself difficult to detect or analyze. Armored viruses cover themselves with protective code that stops debuggers or disassemblers from examining critical elements of the virus. The virus may be written in such a way that some aspects of the programming act as a decoy to distract analysis while the actual code hides in other areas in the program.

From the perspective of the creator, the more time that it takes to deconstruct the virus, the longer it can live. The longer it can live, the more time it has to replicate and spread to as many machines as possible. The key to stopping most viruses is to identify them quickly and educate administrators about them—the very things that the armor makes difficult to accomplish.

Boot Sector Virus   This virus infects the Master Boot Record (MBR) of a hard disk or floppy disk. This type of virus loads when the computer boots and can re-infect an operating system. Secure Boot is used to verify the entire boot process with digital signatures and identify any part of the boot process that has been modified.

Companion Virus   A companion virus attaches itself to legitimate programs and then creates a program with a different filename extension. This file may reside in your system's temporary directory. When a user types the name of the legitimate program, the companion virus executes instead of the real program. This effectively hides the virus from the user. Many of the viruses that are used to attack Windows systems make changes to program pointers in the Registry so that they point to the infected program. The infected program may perform its dirty deed and then start the real program.

Macro Virus   A macro virus exploits the enhancements made to many application programs. Programmers can expand the capability of applications such as Microsoft Word and Excel. Word, for example, supports a mini-BASIC programming language that allows files to be manipulated automatically. These programs in the document are called *macros*. For example, a macro can tell your word processor to spell-check your document automatically when it opens. Macro viruses can infect all the documents on your system and spread to other systems via email or other methods. Macro viruses are one of the fastest-growing forms of exploitation today.

Multipartite Virus   A multipartite virus attacks your system in multiple ways. It may attempt to infect your boot sector, infect all your executable files, and destroy your application files. The hope here is that you won't be able to correct all the problems and will allow the infestation to continue. The multipartite virus depicted in Figure 17.20 attacks a system's boot sector, infects application files, and attacks Word documents.

FIGURE 17.20   A multipartite virus commencing an attack on a system

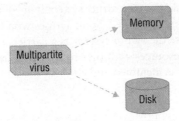

Phage Virus   A phage virus alters programs and databases, and the only way to remove this virus is to reinstall the programs that are infected. If you miss even a single instance of this virus on the victim system, the process will start again and infect the system once more.

Polymorphic Virus   Polymorphic viruses change form to avoid detection. These types of viruses attack your system, display a message on your computer, and delete files on your system. The virus will attempt to hide from your antivirus software. Frequently, the virus will encrypt parts of itself to avoid detection. When the virus does this, it's referred to as mutation. The mutation process makes it hard for antivirus software to detect common characteristics of the virus.

A *signature* is an algorithm or other element of a virus that uniquely identifies it. Because some viruses have the ability to alter their signature, it is crucial that you keep signature files current, whether you choose to download them manually or configure the antivirus engine to do so automatically.

Retrovirus   A *retrovirus attack* bypasses the antivirus software installed on a computer. You can consider a retrovirus to be an anti-antivirus. Retroviruses can directly attack your antivirus software and potentially destroy the virus definition database file. When this information is destroyed without your knowledge, you are left with a false sense of security. The virus may also directly attack an antivirus program to create bypasses for itself.

Stealth Virus   A *stealth virus* attempts to avoid detection by masking itself from applications. It may attach itself to the boot sector of the hard drive. When a system utility or program runs, the stealth virus redirects commands around itself to avoid detection. An infected file may report a file size different from what is actually present. Stealth viruses may also move themselves from file A to file B during a virus scan for the same reason.

Virus Transmission in a Network

Upon infection, some viruses destroy the target system immediately. The saving grace is that the infection can be detected and corrected. Some viruses won't destroy or otherwise tamper with a system; instead, they use the victim system as a carrier. The victim system then infects servers, fileshares, and other resources with the virus. The carrier then infects the target system again. Until the carrier is identified and cleaned, the virus continues to harass systems in this network and spread.

> **Present Virus Activity**
>
> New viruses and threats are released on a regular basis to join the cadre of those already in existence. From an exam perspective, you need only be familiar with the world as it existed at the time the questions were written. From an administrative standpoint, however, you need to know what is happening today.
>
> To find this information, visit the US-CERT Current Activity web page at `https://www .us-cert.gov/ncas/current-activity`. You'll find a detailed description of the most current viruses as well as links to pages on older threats.

Botnets

A *botnet* is a group of zombies, which sounds like a ridiculous beginning to a horror movie. When malware infects a computer, its purpose is often to lie dormant and await a command from a command-and-control server. When this happens, the computer is considered a zombie. When enough infected computers (zombies) check in, the *threat agent* will send a command to the command-and-control server, and the botnet of zombies will work on the task. Often the task is to launch a malicious DDoS attack or to send spam. DDoS will be covered later in this chapter.

Worms

A *worm* is different from a virus in that it can reproduce itself, it's self-contained, and it doesn't need a host application to be transported. Many of the so-called viruses that make the news are actually worms. However, it's possible for a worm to contain or deliver a virus to a target system.

By their nature and origin, worms are supposed to propagate, and they use whatever services they're capable of using to do that. Early worms filled up memory and bred inside the RAM of the target computer. Worms can use TCP/IP, email, Internet services, or any number of possibilities to reach their target.

Mitigating Software Threats

Now that you understand some of the common software threats, let's look at how you can protect yourself from them. This section discusses practical tools and methods that you can use to safeguard yourself from common software-based threats. We will also discuss tactics you can use to mitigate risk as well as ways to recover from security mishaps.

Antivirus

Most malware can be simply prevented with the use of antivirus software. Back when Windows XP came out, the running joke was that you would get a virus before you could get a chance to install antivirus software. To some extent this was true, if you had to get online to retrieve the software.

Microsoft introduced Microsoft Security Essentials as a download for Windows XP, and the Windows Vista operating system started to ship with it installed. Today, Windows comes preinstalled with Windows Virus & Threat Protection, so if you don't purchase antivirus software you are still protected. As a result of these tactics, Microsoft has made the Windows operating system safer than it used to be.

Although Microsoft's antivirus program will work fine for most computing needs, there are some advantages to purchasing antivirus products from third-party vendors. To understand some of the differences, you need to be familiar with the components of antivirus software. Antivirus software comprises two main components: the antivirus engine and the definitions database, as shown in Figure 17.21.

FIGURE 17.21   Antivirus software components

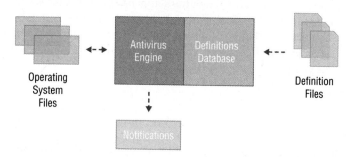

Antivirus Engine   The antivirus engine is responsible for the real-time scanning of operating system files and the notifications to the user. Various antivirus engines will scan operating system files differently. For example, an antivirus engine might recognize when a game is being played, and it will temporarily stop scanning files so that the game loads faster. Notifications can also automatically submit files to the cloud for more extensive scanning.

Definitions Database   The definitions database is why you would select one antivirus product over another. A definitions database's effectiveness is based on two attributes: the frequency of updates and the comprehensiveness of the database signatures. Antivirus definitions, also known as antivirus signatures, are discovered daily and added to the antivirus database. Some antivirus products will download deltas to the initial database every hour, and some will download them once a day.

Antimalware

Malware is a broad term and covers many different software threats that we learned about in this chapter. Antimalware and antivirus are extremely similar in their functionality, and sometimes vendors have a hard time differentiating their products. This is because many antivirus products now check more than just files.

An antimalware software package will not only check the filesystem for threats, like rootkits and trojans, but will also watch incoming email for phishing scams and malicious websites, as shown in Figure 17.22. When these threats are detected, the user gets a notification, and the threat is usually mitigated or avoided completely.

FIGURE 17.22 Antimalware components

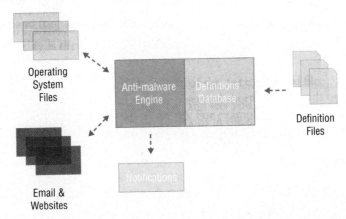

In Exercise 17.1 you will test your antimalware protection with a harmless file called an Eicar file.

EXERCISE 17.1

Testing Your Antimalware

1. Navigate to the Eicar antimalware test file site at `https://www.eicar`
    `.org/?page_id=3950`.

2. Scroll down to the download section.

3. Download a few of the Eicar test files and notice how your antivirus detects
    the malware.

4. Examine the alerts as your antimalware software reports the malware.

The Eicar website contains a totally benign piece of malware that triggers your antimalware engine. Any search for Eicar will produce similar results and the contents are benign.

Recovery Console

A recovery console can perform a number of useful functions for recovery from a security threat. The Windows Recovery Environment (WinRE) is a recovery console that can perform a number of useful functions, as we'll cover in this section. The most useful function is the Reset This PC option, which allows you to refresh the operating system while keeping your data files or remove everything and start from scratch, as shown in Figure 17.23. The latter of the two options assumes you have backups of your data files.

FIGURE 17.23   Windows Recovery Environment

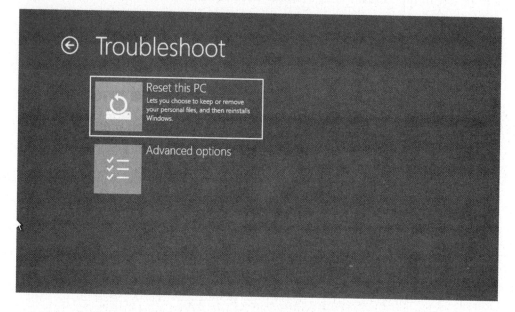

The Windows Recovery Environment also allows you to perform a system restore, whereby you can restore the operating system back to a specific point in time. If a system recovery image exists, you can also recover with the System Image Recovery option. This option will reset the operating system back to the point in the recovery image, which is usually just like the day you turned it on. Figure 17.24 shows the Advanced Options menu.

End-User Education

By far the best prevention of security threats is the education of your end users regarding common threats. For example, the most effective method of preventing viruses, malware, spyware, and harm to data is to teach your users not to open suspicious files and to open only those files that they're reasonably sure are virus/malware free. End users should also be educated on how to identify Trojans and phishing emails scams. The end-user education should also identify guidelines for physical destruction of data, in particular any paperwork that has sensitive information on it. End users should also be educated on the various social engineering threats and how to identify them. An end user who has foresight and who exercises vigilance is more powerful than any antivirus or antimalware product on the market.

FIGURE 17.24 Windows Advanced Options

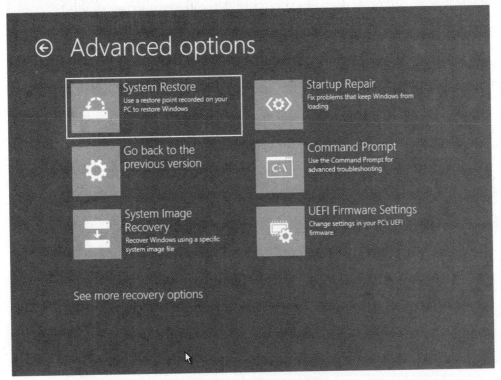

End-user education in an organization is normally part of the employee onboarding process for new hires. However, it should not stop there, because threats change every day. Many organizations revisit the training for their employees once a year in ideal circumstances. This training can be performed in a formal classroom setting or through an online service. Some online services offer educational videos that have interactive questions to verify that the employee has learned the objectives of the video.

Because phishing is such a widespread problem for organizations, special antiphishing training is often mandatory for employees a few times a year. Often organizations will phish their employees with specially crafted emails in an attempt to see how well their training is working. When an employee spots the phishing attempt, they can earn rewards, like a gift card. However, if they get phished, then they must retake the antiphishing training or they may be targeted in the future. A popular month for these tactics is October, because it is the cybersecurity awareness month.

Software Firewalls

"Software firewalls" is a misnomer for this section, since all firewalls are software-based in some way. Sure, you might purchase a piece of equipment that is classified as a hardware firewall, but there is software running on the firewall to protect your network. However, when we discuss firewalls in respect to operating systems, we call them software firewalls, because they are part of the operating system and thus considered software.

Let's look at where we came from and where we are now. A major gamechanger in the history of Microsoft was the release of Windows XP Service Pack 2, which switched on the built-in firewall by default. It was long overdue for the operating system at the time. It was also not well received, because administrators had to learn firewall rules when they installed a new software package that required incoming network traffic. As a result, the firewall was the first thing that got shut off when there was a problem with connectivity.

Throughout the years of new Windows versions, the firewall has received new features and became a polished product. Windows 10 renamed the product Windows Defender Firewall and Windows Defender Firewall with Advanced Security, as shown in Figure 17.25. Both of these configure the same firewall service, with the latter of the two allowing for much more granular control. The inner workings are almost identical to those of the original firewall that shipped with Windows XP SP2.

FIGURE 17.25   Windows Defender Firewall with Advanced Security on Windows 10

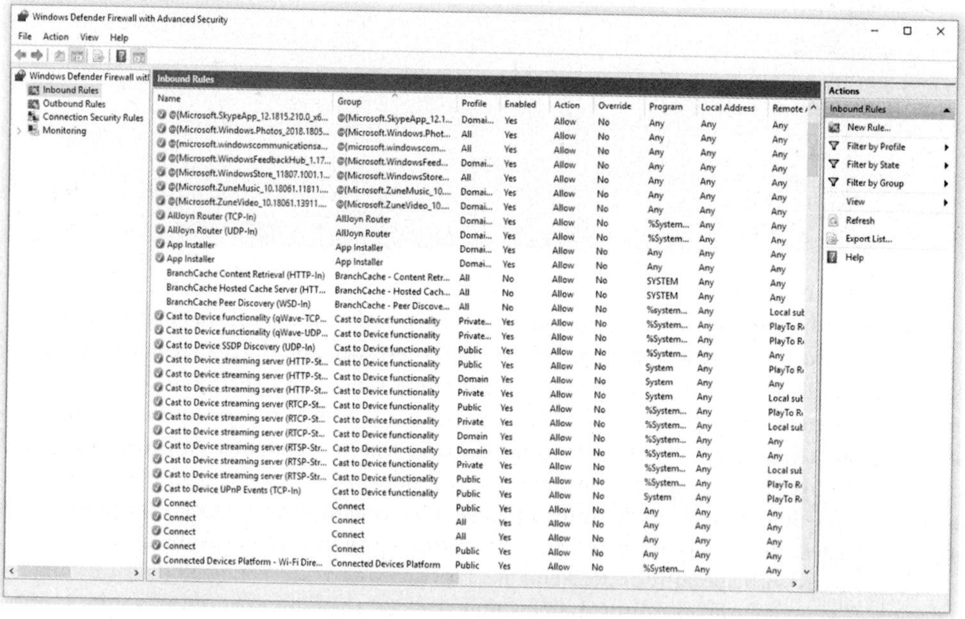

The Windows firewall has achieved its original purpose of protecting the operating system from malicious worms and malicious inbound network connections. By default, the outbound network traffic is allowed and inbound network traffic is blocked, unless a rule exists (see Figure 17.26).

FIGURE 17.26   Windows Defender Firewall with Advanced Security defaults

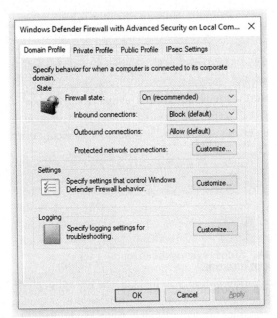

You will also notice that there are three different profiles: Domain, Private, and Public. When the network service starts up, it contacts the default gateway (router) and configures itself to a profile. This allows the operating system to be location-aware and protect itself differently based on your location. If the router has never been seen before, then you'll get prompted with a dialog box asking you to choose if you want to allow your PC to be discoverable, as shown in Figure 17.27. If you answer Yes, then the firewall profile will be configured as Private, and any rules associated with the Private Profile will be active. If you answer No, then any rules associated with the Public Profile will be active. The Domain Profile is automatically selected if the network is the corporate network and the operating system is joined to the domain.

FIGURE 17.27   Windows location dialog box prompt

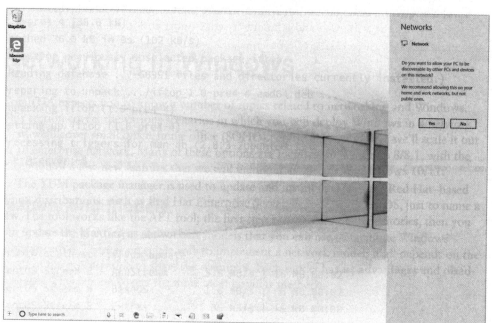

Firewalls are also built into other operating systems, including Linux and macOS. Depending on the distribution of Linux or macOS, the firewall included will vary, as well as the way you would configure it. However, most distributions of Linux, such as Ubuntu and Debian, come with the iptables firewall installed. CentOS and Fedora come with firewalld, which also supports location-based firewall rules.

Regardless of which type of firewall an operating system comes preinstalled with, a third-party firewall can be installed. These firewalls can offer intrusion-detection capabilities that alert you when someone is attacking. In almost all cases, the firewall that comes with the operating system is more than adequate, but you have to keep it on at all times to prevent unwanted connections.

Reinstalling the OS

When you are compromised by a virus or other type of malware, the only way to be sure you have removed it completely is to reinstall the operating system. This may seem like an extreme measure, but virus researchers do not always know what the threat agent embeds in the operating system. The threat agent's mission is to gain access to your operating system and to keep a persistent connection. If that means opening a few other backdoors, then that is what they will embed in their malware.

Fortunately, the Windows operating system makes it easy to reinstall the operating system. The Windows operating system allows you to reset the PC with the use of the recovery console or from the Settings app. Many devices also have a recovery tool embedded in the browser to factory-reset/reimage the device.

Social Engineering Attacks, Threats, and Vulnerabilities

Social engineering is a process in which an attacker attempts to acquire information about your network and system by social means, such as talking to people in the organization. A social engineering attack may occur over the phone, by email, or in person. The intent is to acquire access information, such as user IDs and passwords. When the attempt is made through email or instant messaging, it is known as *phishing* (discussed later), and it's often made to look as if a message is coming from sites where users are likely to have accounts. (Banks, bills, and credit cards are popular.)

These are relatively low-tech attacks and are more akin to con jobs. Take the following example: Your help desk gets a call at 4:00 a.m. from someone purporting to be the vice president of your company. They tell the help desk personnel that they are out of town to attend a meeting, their computer just failed, and they are sitting in a FedEx office trying to get a file from their desktop computer back at the office. They can't seem to remember their password and user ID. They tell the help desk representative that they need access to the information right away or the company could lose millions of dollars. Your help desk rep knows how important this meeting is and gives the user ID and password over the phone. At this point, the attacker has just successfully socially engineered an ID and password that can be used for an attack by impersonating a high-profile person.

Another common approach is initiated by a phone call or email from someone who pretends to be your software vendor, telling you that they have a critical fix that must be installed on your computer system. It may state that if this patch isn't installed right away, your system will crash and you'll lose all your data. For some reason, you've changed your maintenance account password, and they can't log in. Your system operator gives the password to the person. You've been hit again.

In Exercise 17.2, you'll test your users to determine the likelihood of a social engineering attack. The steps are suggestions for tests; you may need to modify them slightly to be appropriate at your workplace. Before proceeding, make certain that your manager knows that you're conducting such a test and approves of it.

EXERCISE 17.2

Testing Social Engineering

1. Call the receptionist from an outside line when the sales manager is at lunch. Tell the receptionist that you're a new salesperson, that you didn't write down the username and password the sales manager gave you last week, and that you need to get a file from the email system for a presentation tomorrow. Does the receptionist direct you to the appropriate person or attempt to help you retrieve the file?

2. Call the human resources department from an outside line. Don't give your real name but instead say that you're a vendor who has been working with this company for years. You'd like a copy of the employee phone list to be emailed to you, if possible. Do they agree to send you the list, which would contain information that could be used to try to guess usernames and passwords?

3. Pick a user at random. Call them and identify yourself as someone who works with the company. Tell them that you're supposed to have some new software ready for them by next week and that you need to know their password to finish configuring it. Do they do the right thing?

The best defense against any social engineering attack is education. Make certain that the employees of your company know how to react to the requests presented here. Social engineering works on the premise that people try to help when they are vested in your efforts, such as a co-worker or if you are trying to help them.

Phishing

Phishing is a form of social engineering in which you ask someone for a piece of information that you are missing by making it look as if it is a legitimate request. An email might look as if it is from a bank and contain some basic information, such as the user's name. These types of messages often state that there is a problem with the person's account or access privileges. The person will be told to click a link to correct the problem. After they click the link, which goes to a site other than the bank's, they are asked for their username, password, account information, and so on. The person instigating the phishing attack can then use this information to access the legitimate account.

One of the best countermeasures to phishing is to mouse over the Click Here link and read the URL. Almost every time, the URL is an adaptation of the legitimate URL, as opposed to a link to the real thing.

The only preventive measure in dealing with social engineering attacks is to educate your users and staff never to give out passwords and user IDs over the phone or via email or to anyone who isn't positively verified as being who they say they are.

When phishing is combined with *Voice over IP (VoIP)*, it becomes known as *vishing*, which is just an elevated form of social engineering. While crank calls have existed since the invention of the telephone, the rise in VoIP now makes it possible for someone to call you from almost anywhere in the world, without the worry of tracing, caller ID, and other features of landlines, and pretend to be someone they are not in order to get data from you.

Two other forms of phishing of which you should be aware are *spear phishing* and *whaling*, which are very similar in nature. With spear phishing, the attacker uses information that the target would be less likely to question because it appears to be coming from a trusted source. Suppose, for example, that you receive a message that appears to be from your spouse that says to click here to see that video of your children from last Christmas. Because it appears far more likely to be a legitimate message, it cuts through your standard defenses like a spear, and the likelihood that you would click this link is higher. Generating the attack requires much more work on the part of the attacker, and it often involves using information from contact lists, friend lists from social media sites, and so on.

NOTE Trust is a key issue with security. There are trusted software sources that you know and work with all the time (such as Microsoft), and there are untrusted sources—and you should differentiate between them. Likewise, there are trusted sites and untrusted sites, and you should similarly differentiate between them. Let common sense be your guide.

Whaling is nothing more than phishing, or spear phishing, for so-called "big" users—thus, the reference to the ocean's largest creatures. Instead of sending out a To Whom It May Concern message to thousands of users, the whaler identifies one person from whom they can gain all the data that they want—usually a manager or business owner—and targets the phishing campaign at them.

Shoulder Surfing

Another form of social engineering is known as *shoulder surfing*. It involves nothing more than watching someone when they enter their sensitive data. They can see you entering a password, typing in a credit card number, or entering any other pertinent information. A privacy filter can be used to block people from looking at your screen from an angle. However, privacy filters do not protect you as you are entering a password, since a shoulder surfer will watch your keystrokes. The best defense against this type of attack is to survey your environment before entering personal data. It is also proper etiquette to look away when someone is entering their password.

Tailgating

Tailgating is another form of social engineering, and it works because we want to be helpful. Tailgating is the act of entering a building that requires a swipe card or other authentication factor by using the person in front of you.

You may be walking toward an entry that requires some authentication, when someone walking the same way introduces themselves as new to the company and shares some stories about their first day. By the time you get to the door, you may hold it open for them and wish them luck. It can even happen without you knowing it, if the door barely closes and they grasp it. Several different tactics, such as access control vestibules and guards, can be used to mitigate this threat. The best prevention is education of your staff to make sure that it does not happen.

Impersonation

Impersonation is prevalent in many different social engineering attacks. The threat agent portrays (impersonates) another employee for many of the attacks to work. Most employees want to help another fellow employee. The threat agent might be impersonating Bill Jones from accounting asking IT to reset his password. Or the threat agent might impersonate the IT department calling Bill Jones and instructing him to type some well-crafted commands into his computer. Many phishing emails also impersonate your bank, an online store, or some other reputable source in an attempt to steal your credentials. The best method for combatting impersonation is end-user training. Training should help users identify suspicious email or phone calls.

Dumpster Diving

Dumpster diving is the act of a person rifling through the trash with the expectation to find information. A strong policy to prevent dumpster diving is the physical destruction of any sensitive data. Destruction can be performed with the use of a mechanical shredder on site or a service that destroys materials off site on behalf of the organization. If an off-site shredding service is performed, always request a signed certificate of destruction to prove that sensitive material was destroyed.

Evil Twin

An *evil twin* attack is a wireless phishing attack in which the attacker sets up a wireless access point to mimic the organization's wireless access points. When a user connects to the evil twin, it allows the attacker to listen in on the user's traffic. Evil twin access points often report a stronger signal to entice the user to connect to the specific access point, as shown in Figure 17.28. The attacker will then create a connection back to the wireless network and passively sniff network traffic as it routes the traffic to the original destination. The best way to mitigate against evil twin attacks is to perform wireless site surveys on a regular basis to ensure that only valid access points are being used.

FIGURE 17.28   Evil twin attack

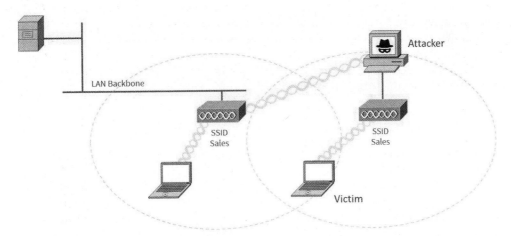

Common Security Threats

A *threat* is a potential danger to the network or the assets of the organization. The potential danger to a network or organization is the attack that a threat agent can carry out. All attacks upon an organization are either technology based or physically based. A technology-based attack is one in which the network and operating systems are used against the organization in a negative way. Physically based attacks use human interaction or physical access, which we previously covered as social engineering attacks. We will now cover several different types of technology-based attacks that are commonly used against networks and organizations.

Denial-of-Service Attacks

A *denial-of-service (DoS)* is an attack launched to disrupt the service or services a company receives or provides via the Internet. A DoS attack is executed with an extremely large number of false requests; because of the attack, the servers will not be able to fulfill valid requests for clients and employees. There are several different types of DoS attacks:

Reflective   A reflective DoS is not a direct attack; it requires a third party that will inadvertently execute the DoS. The attacker will send a request to a third-party server and forge the source address of the packet with the victim's IP address. When the third party responds, it responds back to the victim. There are two victims in this type of DoS attack: the first is the victim the attack is aimed at, and the second is the third-party server used to carry out the attack. Figure 17.29 shows an ICMP-based smurf attack, which is a reflective attack.

FIGURE 17.29   An ICMP-based smurf attack

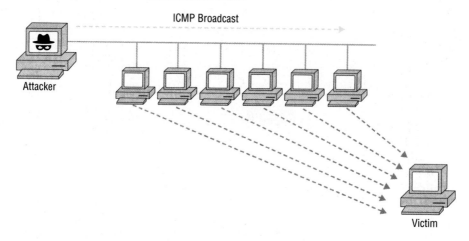

Amplified   An amplified DoS is a variant of a reflective DoS attack. It is carried out by making a small request to the third-party server that yields a larger response to the victim. The most common third-party servers used to carry out the attack are DNS and NTP. For example, an attacker will request a DNS query for a single hostname that contains 20 aliases while forging the source IP address. The victim is then barraged with the 20 answers from the query, as shown in Figure 17.30.

FIGURE 17.30   An amplified attack

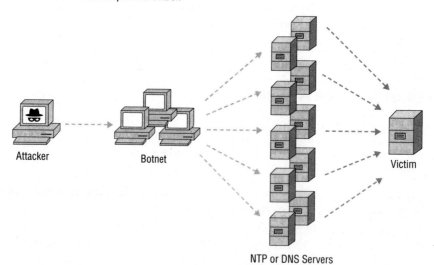

Distributed   A distributed denial-of-service (DDoS) has become the most common type of DoS, because the source of the DoS is varied. It is common for botnets to launch DDoS attacks on organizations. When a single host is used to create a DoS, it can simply be blocked. However, when traffic is coming from millions of different hosts, it is impossible to isolate the DoS and firewall the source. Figure 17.31 shows a DDoS attack.

FIGURE 17.31   A DDoS attack

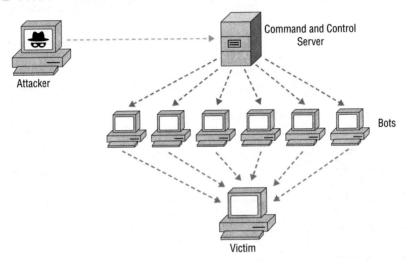

Attacker

Command and Control Server

Bots

Victim

Zero-Day Attacks

When a hole (vulnerability) is found in a web browser or other software, and attackers begin exploiting it the very day it is discovered by the developer (bypassing the one-to-two-day response time that many software providers need to put out a patch once the hole has been found), it is known as a *zero-day* attack (or exploit). It is very difficult to respond to a zero-day exploit. If attackers learn of the weakness the same day as the developer, then they have the ability to exploit it until a patch is released. Often, the only thing that you as a security administrator can do, between the discovery of the exploit and the release of the patch, is to turn off the service. You can do this by isolating or disconnecting the system(s) from the network until a patch is released. Although this can be a costly undertaking in terms of productivity, it is the only way to keep the network safe.

    Several years ago, Stuxnet was found to be using a total of four zero-day vulnerabilities to spread from host to host. You can learn more about Stuxnet here:

```
http://www.symantec.com/connect/blogs/stuxnet-using-three-
additional-zero-day-vulnerabilities
```

Spoofing Attacks

A *spoofing attack* is an attempt by someone or something to masquerade as someone else. This type of attack is usually considered an access attack. A common spoofing attack that was popular for many years on early UNIX and other timesharing systems involved a programmer writing a fake login program. It would prompt the user for a user ID and password. No matter what the user typed, the program would indicate an invalid login attempt and then transfer control to the real login program. The spoofing program would write the login and password into a disk file, which was retrieved later.

The most popular spoofing attacks today are IP spoofing, ARP spoofing, and DNS spoofing. With IP spoofing, the goal is to make the data look as though it came from a trusted host when it didn't (thus spoofing the IP address of the sending host), as shown in Figure 17.32. The threat agent will forge their packet with the victim's source address.

FIGURE 17.32   IP address spoofing attack

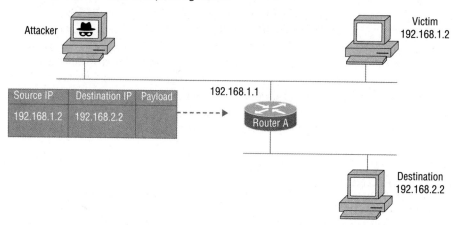

With *ARP spoofing* (also known as *ARP poisoning*), the media access control (MAC) address of the data is faked. By faking this value, it is possible to make it look as though the data came from a networked device that it did not come from. This can be used to gain access to the network, to fool the router into sending to the device data that was intended for another host, or to launch a DoS attack. In all cases, the address being faked is an address of a legitimate user, making it possible to get around such measures as allow/deny lists.

With *DNS spoofing*, the DNS server is given information about a name server that it thinks is legitimate when it isn't. This can send users to a website other than the one to which they wanted to go, reroute mail, or do any other type of redirection for which data from a DNS server is used to determine a destination. Another name for this is *DNS poisoning*.

Always think of spoofing as fooling. Attackers are trying to fool the user, system, and/or host into believing that they're something that they are not. Because the word *spoof* can describe any false information at any level, spoofing can occur at any level of network.

The important point to remember is that a spoofing attack tricks something or someone into thinking that something legitimate is occurring.

On-Path Attack (Previously Known as Man-in-the-Middle Attack)

Many of the attacks we're discussing can be used in conjunction with an *on-path attack*, which was previously known as a man-in-the-middle (MitM) attack. For example, the evil twin attack mentioned earlier allows the attacker to position themselves between the compromised user and the destination server. The attacker can then eavesdrop on a conversation and possibly change information contained in the conversation. Conventional on-path attacks allow the attacker to impersonate both parties involved in a network conversation. This allows the attacker to eavesdrop and manipulate the conversation without either party knowing. The attacker can then relay requests to the server as the originating host attempts to communicate on the intended path, as shown in Figure 17.33.

FIGURE 17.33   On-path attack

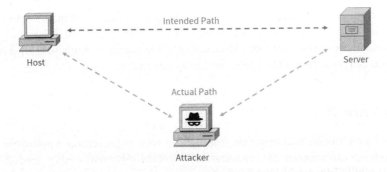

Password Attacks

Password attacks occur when an account is attacked repeatedly. This is accomplished by using applications known as password crackers, which send possible passwords to the account in a systematic manner. The attacks are initially carried out to gain passwords for an access or modification attack. There are several types of password attacks:

Brute-Force Attacks   A *brute-force* attack is an attempt to guess passwords until a successful guess occurs. As an example of this type of attack, imagine starting to guess with *A* and then going through *z*; when no match is found, the next guess series goes from *AA* to *zz*, and then it adds a third value (*AAA* to *zzz*). Because of the nature of this routine, this type of attack usually occurs over a long period of time. To make passwords more difficult to guess, they should be much longer than a few characters. It is recommended that you make the password at least 12 digits and complex. You should also have password lockout policies.

Dictionary Attacks   A *dictionary attack* uses a dictionary of common words to attempt to find the user's password. Dictionary attacks can be automated, and several tools exist in the public domain to execute them. As an example of this type of attack, imagine guessing words and word combinations found in a standard English-language dictionary.

Rainbow Tables   When passwords are stored in the operating system, they are stored in their hashed format. A hash is a one-way cryptographic algorithm. If you have access to the password hash, a rainbow table can be used to find the password. Rainbow tables are databases that have had every permutation run through a hashing algorithm, so the hash can be looked up and cross-referenced back to the password that created it. These databases can be really large. It is not uncommon for a rainbow table to ship on a portable hard drive.

Hybrid Attacks   A *hybrid attack* typically uses a combination of dictionary entries and brute force. For example, if you know that there is a good likelihood that the employees of a particular company are using derivatives of the company name in their passwords, then you can seed those values into the values attempted.

Insider Threat

Insider threats are threats that originate from within your organization. Employees know the organization and can navigate the organization to get the information they need. A disgruntled employee can carry out an attack on the organization by leaking information or selling it. When information is sold to a competitor for profit, it is considered corporate espionage. The inside threat does not always need to be criminal in intent. It can also be as simple as an employee plugging an unauthorized wireless access point into the corporate network.

SQL injection

A *Structured Query Language (SQL) injection* attack occurs when a threat agent enters a series of escape codes along with a well-crafted SQL statement into a URL. The seamlessly harmless page on the backend that is awaiting the request runs the SQL query along with its normal query. For example, a normal post URL might look like this:

```
http://www.wiley.com/phone.php?name=jones
```

The threat agent will add their SQL injection after the normal post query string, such as the following:

```
http://www.wiley.com/phone.php?name=jones; DROP TABLE Users
```

This would generate the following SQL query on the backend and send the malicious query to the SQL database:

```
SELECT FullName, PhoneNum
From Phones
Where FullName Like '%jones%'; DROP TABLE USERS
```

The first two and half lines to the semicolon are generated by the page the query is posted to. The line basically tells the SQL database to return the full name and phone number for anything that contains jones. However, the threat agent appended `DROP TABLE Users` to the query with a semicolon. This will delete the users table and cause disruption. Technically the SQL injection causes a DoS attack. Other malicious queries that are not so obvious and disruptive can be submitted to discover information like table structure and consequently steal data. Many retailers, banks, and online stores, just to name a few, have fallen prey to SQL injection attacks and made front-page news.

The best way to combat this attack is by building input validation into the rendered page on the backend; this is also known as *sanitization*. This mitigation tactic is well outside the scope of the exam, but understanding the attack is the key takeaway.

Cross-Site Scripting (XSS)

Cross-site scripting (XSS) is a tactic a threat agent uses to deliver a malicious script to the victim by embedding it into a legitimate web page. Common delivery methods for XSS are message boards, forums, or any page that allows comments to be posted. The threat agent will submit a post to these types of pages with their malicious script, such as JavaScript. When the victim browses the page, the threat agent's script will execute.

JavaScript and other scripting languages are controlled tightly by the browser, so direct access to the operating system is usually not permitted. However, the script will have access to the web page you are browsing or the cookies the actual page stores. This type of attack is common in hijacking web pages and trying to force the user into installing a piece of malware.

Exploits and Vulnerabilities

Exploits and vulnerabilities both have the same effect of compromising systems. Vulnerabilities are weaknesses in security for an operating system or network product. Vulnerabilities are the reason we need to constantly patch network systems. Exploits are scripts, code, applications, or techniques used in exploiting the vulnerabilities by a threat agent, as shown in Figure 17.34. In the following section we will cover the most common vulnerabilities as they pertain to the CompTIA exam.

FIGURE 17.34   Threat agents, exploits, and vulnerabilities

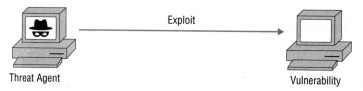

Noncompliant Systems

One of the easiest ways to make your systems vulnerable and expose them to threats is to fail to keep them compliant. As an administrator, you should always follow security regulatory standards as well as compliance standards.

One product that can keep your operating systems compliant is Microsoft Endpoint Configuration Manager (MECM). MECM allows for the publishing of a baseline for the Windows operating system. It will then monitor the baseline against the operating systems in your organization and will remediate them if they fall out of compliance.

MECM is just one of many tools that can be used for compliance, several of which are third-party tools. Third-party compliance solutions provide other unique benefits, such as the compliance of third-party applications in addition to Windows.

Patching and Updates

When operating systems are installed, they are usually point-in-time snapshots of the current build of the operating system. From the time of the build to the time of installation, several vulnerabilities can be published for the operating system. When an OS is installed, you should patch it before placing it into service. Patches remediate the vulnerabilities found in the OS and fixed by the vendor. Updates add new features not included with the current build. However, some vendors may include vulnerability patches in updates. Network devices also have patches and updates that should be installed prior to placing them into service.

After the initial installation of the device or operating system and the initial patches and updates are installed, you are not done! Vendors continually release patches and updates to improve security and functionality, usually every month and sometimes outside of the normal release cycle. When patches are released outside of the normal release cycle, they are called out-of-band patches and are often in response to a critical vulnerability.

Microsoft products are patched and updated through the Windows Update functionality of the operating system. However, when an administrator is required to patch and update an entire network, Windows Server Update Services (WSUS) can be implemented. A WSUS server enables the administrator to centrally manage patches and updates. The administrator can also report on which systems still need to be patched or updated.

Operating Systems Life Cycle

All operating systems have a life cycle of release, support, and eventually end of life. When most operating systems reach their end of life (EOL), the vendor stops supplying security patches. The void of the most current patches creates a giant vulnerability for the organization, since the operating system is no longer protected from the latest vulnerabilities. To combat these vulnerabilities, it is recommended that you keep the operating system current. This is accomplished with continual upgrades to the operating system as new versions are released.

Unprotected Systems

Obviously, an unpatched system presents a huge vulnerability in your network, but an unprotected system is just as vulnerable. A workstation or server without antivirus protection or firewall protection poses a significant risk. A workstation or server without antivirus software can contract malware and potentially infect other computers and ultimately leak data. A missing or misconfigured firewall is equally as vulnerable. The firewall is used to prevent unauthorized connections that could exploit a vulnerability in the operating system. Firewalls are also often used in place of an undesirable patch that causes other issues. For example, turning on a firewall rule that prevents connecting to the Print Spooler service on Windows is a good protection method. It can shield you from print spooler vulnerabilities if the workstation or server is not providing print services. However, if the operating system is not protected by the firewall and an exploit is released, it is consequentially vulnerable.

BYOD

Security is the biggest concern as it applies to BYOD devices. The biggest reason is that the organization has less control over BYOD devices than over devices it issues and owns. BYOD devices come with two inherent risks: data leakage and data portability. Data leakage happens when a device is lost or compromised in some way. There are tactics to mitigate this, such as full device encryption. However, the user's device is then forcefully encrypted by the organization and there could be legal ramifications. Another common tactic is to use mobile device management (MDM) software that creates a partition for company data. This would allow the company to encrypt their data and not affect user data.

Data portability means that the user can cart away organizational data when they leave. Although most of the time this is not a risk, an unscrupulous salesperson may be a big risk to the organization. A line-of-business (LOB) application should be selected that displays only the data on a mobile device and does not allow data storage. Another tactic is to employ MDM software that allows remote wiping of the organization's data. When an employee leaves, the wipe is executed and the organization's data is gone. This type of functionality is also useful if a device is lost, so it also mitigates the risk of data leakage.

Security Best Practices

A best practice is a technique or methodology that has largely been adopted by the professional community. A number of security best practices are techniques that can keep the organization safe and secure. Many of the best practices will mitigate some of the risk from attacks that I previously discussed. The benefits of other best practices might not be immediately apparent, but they will keep an organization safe in the long run.

Data Encryption

To prevent the loss of data, data encryption should be considered—not that the data is really ever lost, but it's no longer within your control. Consider an example of a laptop with sensitive patient record information stored on it. If the laptop were to be stolen, there are a number of utilities that could provide unauthorized access. However, with encryption (such as BitLocker) enabled, both the operating system and the data would remain encrypted and inaccessible.

There are three concepts associated with data encryption: data in use, data in transit, and data at rest, as shown in Figure 17.35. *Data in use* is the concept of data that is in an inconsistent state and/or currently resident in memory. Most of the time, you don't need to be too concerned with data in memory, since that is normally a function of the operating system. However, when data is written to a temporary location, it is considered data in use and therefore should be encrypted. *Data in transit* is information traversing the network and should always be encrypted so that it is not intercepted. Over the past decade, just about every website and application has adopted some form of encryption, so there is no reason not to use encryption in transit.

Data at rest is a point of contention because it is believed that once the data hits the server, it's safe. However, the data is more vulnerable because it's in one spot. If a drive needed to be replaced because it went bad, outside of physical destruction there is no way to assure the data is inaccessible. When used for backup tapes, it is not only a good idea but should be a requirement.

FIGURE 17.35   Data and encryption

Setting Strong Passwords

One of the most effective ways to keep a system safe is to employ strong passwords and educate your users about their best practices. Many password-based systems use a one-way hashing approach. You can't reverse the hash value in order to guess the password. This makes it impossible to reverse the hashes if the database of stored passwords is lifted (stolen) from the operating system. Because the hash is sent over the network in lieu of the actual password, the password is harder to crack.

Passwords should be as long and complex as possible. Most security experts believe that at least 12 characters should be used—20 or more characters if security is a real concern. If you use only the lowercase letters of the alphabet, you have 26 characters with which to work. If you add the numeric values 0–9, you get another 10 characters. Adding uppercase letters, you gain an additional 26 characters. If you go one step further by using symbol characters (such as !"#$%&'()*+,-./:;<=>?@[\]^_`{|} and ~, including a blank space), you have an additional 33 more characters. You then have a pallet of 95 characters for each position in your password. A typical example of a complex password using all these elements might be %s4@7dFs#D2$. If you have a hard time coming up with a strong password on your own, you can always use an online password generator, such as https:// passwordsgenerator.net.

When the *Password Complexity* policy in Group Policy is enabled for the Windows operating system, three of the four categories—lowercase, uppercase, numbers, and symbols—must be used in your password. Windows Server and/or Active Directory can also require a minimum password size, which guarantees a secure password when coupled with complexity.

Most vendors recommend that you use symbols in your password, and some go so far as to require it. Some symbols, however, do not work for web-based applications. Therefore, you may find that a vendor accepts a reduced set of characters. Although this reduces the complexity, using characters in addition to letters and numbers makes the password more secure.

Let's look further at password complexity. If you used a 4-character password, this would be $95 \times 95 \times 95 \times 95$, or approximately 81.5 million possibilities. A 5-character password would give you 95^5, or approximately 7.7 billion possibilities. And a 10-character password would give you 95^{10}, or 5.9×10^{18} (a *very* big number) possibilities. As you can see, these numbers increase exponentially with each position added to the password. A 4-digit password could probably be broken in a fraction of a day, whereas a 10-digit password would take considerably longer and much more processing power.

If your password consisted of only the 26 lowercase letters, the 4-digit password would have 26^4, or 456,000 combinations. A 5-character password would have 26^5, or over 11 million combinations, and a 10-character password would have 26^{10}, or 1.4×10^{14} combinations. The number of combinations is still a big number, but it would take considerably less time to break it compared to a longer password. This is all based on the notion that a brute-force password attack is being performed. If a dictionary attack were being performed, a 4- or 5-digit lowercase password could take less than 5 minutes to crack.

Mathematical methods of encryption are primarily used in conjunction with other encryption methods as part of authenticity verification. The message and the hashed value of the message can be encrypted using other processes. In this way, you know that the message is secure and hasn't been altered.

Requiring Passwords

Make absolutely certain that you require passwords for all accounts. It's such a simple thing to overlook in a small network, but it's not something a malicious user will overlook. By default, Windows will not allow an account to connect over the network if it has a blank password. It will, however, allow a person to log in locally with a blank password. There is a security option in the local Group Policy that specifies this behavior, as shown in Figure 17.36.

FIGURE 17.36   Windows security options

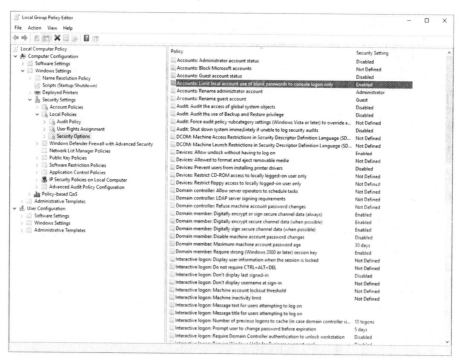

The operating system is not the only place where you should use a password for security. You should also use passwords on the *basic input/output system (BIOS)* and *Unified Extensible Firmware Interface (UEFI)* firmware. If a malicious user has access, they could possibly circumvent your security by booting a live operating system.

You should also change the *default passwords* on system accounts. There are dedicated sites on the web that document default username and password for various vendor devices. A common hacker can easily pull up these sites and find the default username and password for your wireless access point, camera system, or any other system on which you've neglected to change the default password.

Password Expiration

Password expiration should be a consideration because passwords can be compromised as time goes on. Whether passwords are compromised by shoulder surfing or keylogging, or intercepted via the network when a user is logging in, the fact remains they are only one factor of authentication. Therefore, passwords should be set to expire on a monthly, bi-monthly, quarterly, semi-annual, or annual basis. The more sensitive an account is, the more frequently the password should be changed.

Windows has a default password expiration of 42 days, as shown in Figure 17.37. You should put in place a system to expire passwords on a periodic basis, as stated previously. You would then communicate this to your users via the onboarding process when they are hired.

FIGURE 17.37   Password expiration

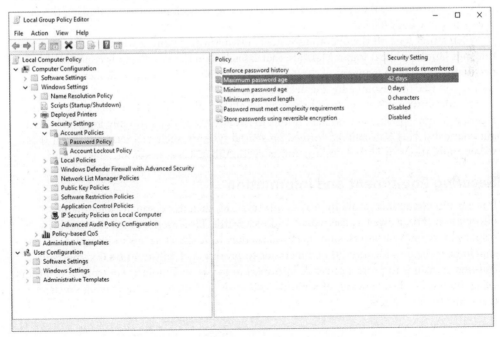

End-User Best Practices

In addition to administrator best practices, there are several different end-user best practices that you should advocate to your users. In the following, we will cover the top end-user best practices covered by the CompTIA exam. However, when it comes to end-user best practices and training, these are just the tip of the iceberg.

Locking Screens

When a user walks away from their computer and leaves themself logged in, anyone who walks up to the computer has the same level of access as the owner of the account. This type of attack requires that the threat agent be physically present. However, leaving a computer logged in also invites insider threats, unauthorized access to information, or even data loss.

Training users to lock their screen when they walk away is the best way to prevent unauthorized access. By simply pressing the Windows key and L, a user can lock their screen as they walk away.

Alternately, the administrator can require a user to use a screen saver lock. For example, the screen saver lock can be set to 15 minutes. After 15 minutes of idle time, the screen saver will turn on. The user will not be able to access the desktop until they enter their password. This setting provides two benefits: first, it provides a visual deterrent to potential threat agents, and second, it prevents threat agents from carrying out an attack.

Logging Off

When users are not utilizing a system, they should be encouraged to log off the system. When users remain logged in, the programs that they were running stay running as well. If there is malware on the system, it will stay running as well, potentially allowing threat agents to carry out attacks.

When a user logs off the operating system, any malware running will terminate and hopefully not launch on next login. Malware that launches on the next login is considered to be persistent. Outside of malware, if the system has a resource that is shared, then having users log off will free the resource for the next person.

The administrator has control at their disposal that allows them to police the user. After a period of time in which the system is idle, the administrator can forcibly log off the user automatically. This is usually performed on shared systems, such as a terminal server that serves applications or virtual desktop infrastructure that serves desktops.

Securing Equipment and Information

It is our job as administrators to protect information, such as personally identifiable information (PII), as well as usernames and passwords. However, we also bestow this responsibility onto our users, since many times they have direct access to information. Users should be trained to identify PII and methods to protect such information. Examples of end-user measures to protect sensitive information can be as simple as controlling printouts, using discretion when viewing information with others around, and destroying sensitive trash, just to name a few.

End users also have portables devices that can contain sensitive data, and these devices should be secured when not in use. Many an organization has made front-page headlines with the loss of a simple laptop containing PII. Locks can be used to secure devices, and most portable devices contain a security slot for a lock. A laptop with sensitive data is not the only device that can be lost or stolen—portable hard drives can also contain PII and thus should be physically controlled, or their use should be prevented.

Account Management

Given a security-related scenario, account management can take into consideration such settings as restricting user permissions, setting login time restrictions, disabling the Guest account, locking an account after a certain number of failed attempts, and configuring a screen lock when the system times out after a specified length of inactivity.

Restricting User Permissions

When assigning user permissions, follow the *principle of least privilege*: give users only the bare minimum that they need to do their job. Assign permissions to groups rather than to users, and make users members of groups (or remove them from groups) as they change roles or positions.

The use of groups is crucial to account management, because when you apply permission on NTFS for the user, you need to visit the resource to identify the permissions granted. When you use a group and apply the NTFS permission to that specific group, you can now look at either the membership of the group or the membership of the user in Active Directory. This allows you to see who has access to the resource without having to visit the resource. Figure 17.38 shows an oversimplified example. A user, Fred, is a member of both the Sales and R&D groups; therefore, he has access to the Sales and R&D folders. In a real-world application, the group would be more descriptive, such as Perm_RW_Sales_ Server1. This naming would describe what the group is used for (permissions), what level of permissions (RW), what resource (Sales share), and on what server (Server1).

FIGURE 17.38   Users, groups, and resources

Setting Time Restrictions

Configure user accounts so that logins can occur only during times that the user can be expected to be working. Preventing logins at 2:00 a.m. can be an effective method of keeping hackers from your systems. This can be performed in Active Directory by clicking the user's account, selecting the Account tab, and then clicking Logon Hours, as shown in Figure 17.39. From this interface, you can configure the permitted hours for logins and denied hours for logins.

FIGURE 17.39 Account restrictions

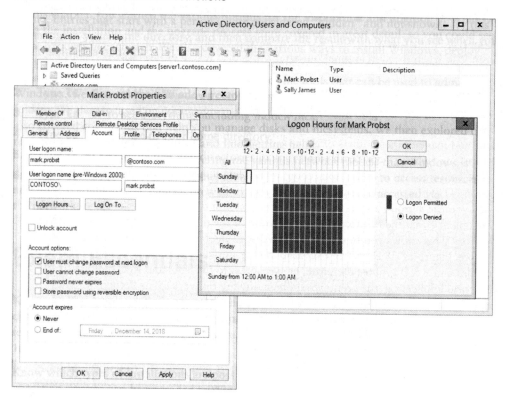

You can also set account expiration on the Properties tab of the user. By default, the account is set to never expire. However, you can add a date at which time the account will expire. This is best used on contractor accounts, where the terms of use can be defined. Because contractor accounts often don't go through typical human resource processes, the accounts can be forgotten about. By adding an account expiration, you can be assured that at the end of the contract the account will be disabled (expired).

Limiting the Number of Failed Login Attempts

Configure user account settings to limit the number of login attempts before the account is locked for a period of time. Legitimate users who need to get in before the block expires can contact the administrator and explain why they weren't able to give the right password three times in a row, and illegitimate users will go away in search of another system to try to enter.

When choosing the number of failed attempts, you need to consider the number of calls you get to the help desk versus the security in having few failed attempts before lockout. You'll find that when you set it to three failed attempts, the help desk will get more calls than necessary, but it allows for better security. Setting the number of failed login attempts to five may be better for users, because many users realize after the third failed attempt that their Caps Lock key was on, but it's less secure than three failed attempts. This setting needs to be evaluated against your security requirement and help desk volume.

You should also consider the length of the lockout. If it's a Monday morning and a person enters their password wrong X number of times and gets locked out, 5 minutes might be appropriate. The time it takes to get a cup of coffee and unlock might be just enough time on a Monday morning to allow the user to wake up. You can specify these settings for an entire domain, as shown in Figure 17.40. As shown here, the user will be locked out for 30 minutes after three failed attempts. By default, there is no account lockout policy set for a domain.

FIGURE 17.40   Account lockout policy settings

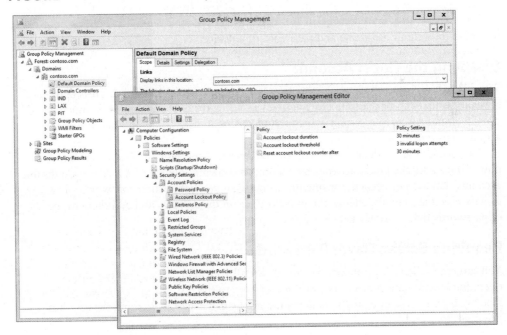

If a password attack is being executed, no protection could easily allow millions of password attempts. By setting a failed login attempt counter and a lockout duration, you slow the progress of the attack.

Changing Default Usernames

Default accounts represent a huge weakness because everyone knows they exist. When an operating system is installed—whether on a workstation or a server—certain default accounts are created. Knowing the names of those accounts simplifies the process of potential attackers accessing them because they only have to supply the password.

The default username should be changed whenever possible. Several websites are dedicated to documenting the default username and password for routers, switches, and other network equipment. These sites are useful, especially when you lose the documentation for the device and have to *factory-reset* it. A login after you have successfully just factory-reset the device is really the only time that it's acceptable to use the default username and password for security. You don't need a website to guess the common administrative accounts on equipment or an operating system. They are usually admin, administrator, root, or sysadmin. Changing the default username makes it more challenging for someone to try to guess the credentials.

Changing the default password to a complex password is also a good practice in hardening the device. However, changing the username will also ensure that a brute-force attack cannot be performed against the default username. There are many different websites dedicated to listing the default credentials for network devices, so it doesn't take tremendous skill to obtain the default username and password of a device.

Disabling the Guest Account

When Windows is installed, one of the default accounts it creates is Guest. This represents a weakness that can be exploited by an attacker. While the account cannot do much, it can provide initial access to a system, which the attacker can use to find another account or acquire sensitive information about the system.

You should disable all accounts that are not needed, especially the Guest account. Windows 10 disables the Guest account by default, as shown in Figure 17.41. After you disable accounts that are not needed, rename the accounts, if you can. (Microsoft won't allow you to rename some.) Finally, change the passwords from the defaults and add them to the list of passwords that routinely get changed.

Requiring Screen Saver Passwords

You can require lengthy, complex passwords for all your users as well as lock down the operating system with passwords, but if a user goes to the restroom or on break without locking their workstation, any person wandering by can access everything the user has privileges to.

FIGURE 17.41   Disabled Guest account

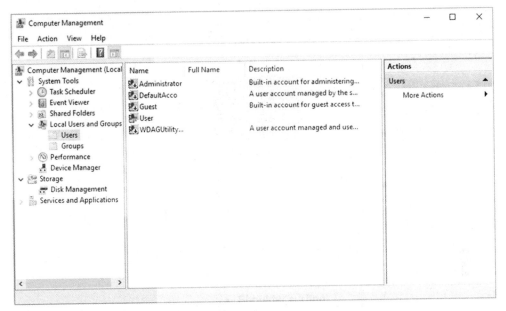

A *screen saver* should automatically start after a short period of idle time, and a password should be required before the user can begin the session again. This method of locking the workstation adds one more level of security. A Group Policy can be put in place to turn on password-protected screen savers. Adding a password-protected screen saver can ensure that if a workstation is left unattended, it will lock and require a password to resume access. You can access this setting on Windows 10/11 by right-clicking an empty portion of the Desktop and selecting Personalize ➢ Lock Screen ➢ Screen Saver Settings. Then, in the Screen Saver Settings dialog box, to manually require a password after a screen saver has activated, select the On Resume, Display Logon Screen check box, as shown in Figure 17.42.

Disable AutoRun

It is never a good idea to put any media in a workstation if you do not know where it came from or what it is. The simple reason is that said media (CD, DVD, USB) could contain malware. This attack is commonly referred to as a *drop attack*. Compounding matters, that malware could be referenced in the `autorun.inf` file, causing it to be summoned when the media is inserted in the machine and requiring no other action. `autorun.inf` can be used to start an executable, access a website, or do any of a large number of different tasks. The best way to prevent a user from falling victim to such a ploy is to disable the *AutoRun* feature on the workstation.

FIGURE 17.42 The Screen Saver Settings dialog box

Microsoft has changed the function on Windows so that it no longer acts as it previously did (prior to Windows 7). The feature is now disabled by default. The reason Microsoft changed the default action can be summed up in a single word: security. That text-based `autorun.inf` file can not only take your browser to a web page, it can also call any executable file, pass along variable information about the user, or do just about anything else imaginable. Simply put, it is never a good idea to plug any media into your system if you have no idea where it came from or what it holds. Such an action opens up the user's system—and the network—to any number of possible risks. An entire business's data could be jeopardized by someone with elevated privileges inadvertently putting a harmful CD into a computer at work.

AutoPlay

The AutoRun feature is disabled by default, so that malicious software does not start automatically. However, the ability to automatically start a video, music, or open a folder when removable media is inserted into the computer is really useful. The functionality of automatically performing an action or asking what should be done when media is inserted is still enabled by default on Windows, via a feature called *AutoPlay*. AutoPlay distinguishes itself from AutoRun, since it does not look at the `autorun.inf` file and does not start an executable unless the user specifically clicks an option that they want to do so.

Destruction and Disposal Methods

Think of all the sensitive data written to a hard drive. The drive can contain information about students, clients, users—about anyone and anything. The hard drive can be in a desktop PC, in a laptop, or even in a printer. Many laser printers above consumer grade offer the ability to add a hard drive to store print jobs. If the drive falls into the wrong hands, you can not only lose valuable data but also risk a lawsuit for not properly protecting privacy. An appropriate data destruction/disposal plan should be in place to avoid any potential problems.

Since data on media holds great value and liability, that media should never simply be tossed away for prying eyes to stumble on. For the purpose of this objective, the media in question is hard drives, and there are three key concepts to understand with regard to them: formatting, sanitation, and destruction. Formatting prepares the drive to hold new information (which can include copying over data already there). Sanitation involves wiping the data off the drive, whereas destruction renders the drive no longer usable.

 Although this objective is heavily focused on hard drives, it is also possible to have data stored on portable flash drives, backup tapes, CDs, or DVDs. In the interest of security, it is recommended that you destroy them before disposing of them.

Recycling or Repurposing Best Practices

For exam purposes, the best practices for recycling or repurposing fall into the categories of low-level formats (as opposed to standard formatting), overwrites, and drive wipes.

Low-Level Format vs. Standard Format

There are multiple levels of formatting that can be done on a drive. A standard format, accomplished using the operating system's format utility (or similar), can mark space occupied by files as available for new files without truly deleting what was there. Such erasing—if you want to call it that—doesn't guarantee that the information isn't still on the disk and recoverable.

A low-level format (typically accomplished only in the factory) can be performed on the system, or a utility can be used to completely wipe the disk clean. This process helps to ensure that information doesn't fall into the wrong hands.

The manufacturer performs a low-level format on integrated device electronics (IDE) hard drives. Low-level formatting must be performed even before a drive can be partitioned. In low-level formatting, the drive controller chip and the drive meet for the very first time and learn to work together. Because controllers are integrated into SATA and IDE drives, low-level formatting is a factory process. Low-level formatting is not operating system–dependent.

WARNING Never perform a low-level format on IDE or SCSI drives! These drives are formatted at the factory, and you may cause problems by using low-level utilities on them.

The main thing to remember for the exam is that most forms of formatting included with the operating system do not actually erase the data completely. Formatting the drive and then disposing of it has caused many companies problems when individuals who never should have seen it retrieve the data using applications that are commercially available.

Hard Drive Sanitation and Sanitation Methods

A number of vendors offer hard drives with *Advanced Encryption Standard (AES)* cryptography built in. However, it's still better to keep these secure hard drives completely out of the hands of others than to trust their internal security mechanisms once their usable life span has passed for the client. Some vendors include freeware utilities to erase the hard drive. If it is a Serial ATA (SATA) drive, you can always run HDDErase, but you are still taking your chances.

Sanitation Utilities

HDDErase is a freeware utility that is included with many different boot images. HDDErase can be downloaded with Hiren's BootCD from www.hirensbootcd.org.

If you were to perform a web search, you would find several other sanitization utilities like HDDErase, but it is important to recognize and acknowledge that many of these do not meet military or GSA specifications. Those specifications should be considered as guidelines to which you must also adhere when dealing with your own, or a client's, data. The only surefire method of rendering the hard drive contents completely eradicated is physical destruction.

Solid-state drives (SSDs) pose a greater problem since the media is flash memory and not mechanical, like conventional hard disk drives (HDDs). Low-level formats can be performed, as mentioned in the preceding section, but the 1s and 0s will still be technically on the flash memory. Therefore, many vendors have a sanitization utility for scrubbing information from SSDs. It is best to check with the vendor, as these tools are specific to the vendor and model of SSD.

Overwrite

Overwriting the drive entails copying over the data with new data. A common practice is to replace the data with 0s. A number of applications allow you to recover what was there prior to the last write operation, and for that reason, most overwrite software will write the same sequence and save it multiple times.

DBAN is a utility that comes with its own boot disk from `https://dban.org`. You can find a number of other software "shredders" by doing a quick web search.

Drive Wipe

If it's possible to verify beyond a reasonable doubt that a piece of hardware that's no longer being used doesn't contain any data of a sensitive or proprietary nature, then that hardware can be recycled (sold to employees, sold to a third party, donated to a school, and so on). That level of assurance can come from wiping a hard drive or using specialized utilities.

If you can't be assured that the hardware in question doesn't contain important data, then the hardware should be destroyed. You cannot, and should not, take a risk that the data your company depends on could fall into the wrong hands.

Physical Destruction

Physically destroying the drive involves rendering it no longer usable. While the focus is on hard drives, you can also physically destroy other forms of media, such as flash drives and CD/DVDs.

Shredder

Many commercial paper shredders are also capable of destroying DVDs and CDs. Paper shredders, however, are not able to handle hard drives; you need a shredder created for just such a purpose. A low-volume hard drive shredder that will destroy eight drives per minute can carry a suggested list price of around $20,000.

Drill/Hammer

If you don't have the budget for a hard drive shredder, you can accomplish similar results in a much more time-consuming way with a power drill. The goal is to physically destroy the platters in the drive. Start the process by removing the cover from the drive—this is normally done with a Torx driver. (Although #8 does not work with all drives, it is a good one to try first.) You can remove the arm with a slotted screwdriver and then the cover over the platters using a Torx driver. Don't worry about damaging or scratching anything—nothing is intended to be saved. Everything but the platters can be tossed away.

As an optional step, you can completely remove the tracks using a belt sander, grinder, or palm sander. The goal is to turn the shiny surface into fine powder. Again, this step is optional, but it adds one more layer of assurance that nothing usable remains. Always wear eye protection and be careful not to breathe in any of the fine particles that are generated during the grinding/destruction process.

Following this, use the power drill to create as small a set of particles as possible. A drill press works much better for this task than trying to hold the drive and drill it with a hand-held model.

Do You Really Want to Do It Yourself?

Even with practice, you will find that manually destroying a hard drive is time consuming. There are companies that specialize in this and can do it efficiently. One such company is Shred-it, which will pick up your hard drive and provide a chain-of-custody assurance and a certificate of destruction on completion. You can find out more about what they offer at www.shredit.com.

Electromagnet (Degaussing)

A large electromagnet can be used to destroy any magnetic media, such as a hard drive or backup tape set. The most common of these is the degaussing tool. *Degaussing* involves applying a strong magnetic field to initialize the media. (This is also referred to as *disk wiping*.) This process helps ensure that information doesn't fall into the wrong hands.

Degaussing involves using a specifically designed electromagnet to eliminate all data on the drive, including the factory-prerecorded servo tracks. You can find wand model degaussers priced at just over $500 or desktop units that sell for up to $30,000.

Incineration

A form of destruction not to be overlooked is fire. It is possible to destroy most devices by burning them up, using an accelerant such as gasoline or lighter fluid to aid the process.

WARNING Be careful with any fire, particularly those in which accelerants are used. Be sure that you are not burning anything capable of releasing toxic fumes and that you have the fire controlled and contained at all times.

Certificate of Destruction

A *certificate of destruction* (or *certificate of recycling*) may be required for audit purposes. Such a certificate, usually issued by the organization carrying out the destruction, is intended to verify that the asset was properly destroyed and usually includes serial numbers, type of destruction done, and so on.

Securing Physical Documents/Passwords/Shredding

The type and amount of information that can be gleaned from physical documents is amazing, even in the age when there is such a push to go paperless. *Dumpster diving* is a common problem that puts systems at risk. Companies normally generate a huge amount of paper, most of which eventually winds up in dumpsters or recycle bins. Dumpsters can contain highly sensitive information (such as a password a user has written on a piece of paper because they haven't memorized it yet).

In high-security and government environments, sensitive papers should either be shredded or burned. Most businesses don't do this. In addition, the advent of "green" companies has created an increase in the amount of recycled paper, which can often contain all kinds of juicy information about a company and its individual employees.

Document-Shredding Services

Many small companies purchase document-shredding equipment and perform this task themselves. Larger companies with a higher volume can contract a shredding service. These services place document receptacles in the offices for workers to dispose of sensitive documents. The service will then come in and dispose of the documents in a controlled fashion, sometimes shredding the documents on the premises with special equipment. These services can sometimes furnish certifications of disposal, depending on the type of destruction you require.

Summary

In this chapter, you learned about the various issues related to security that appear on the A+ 220–1102 exam. Security is a popular topic in computing, and the ways in which a troublemaker can cause harm increase regularly. CompTIA expects everyone who is A+ certified to understand the basic principles of security and be familiar with solutions that exist.

You also learned of security problem areas and issues that can be easily identified. Problem areas include viruses, Trojans, worms, and malware. Security solutions include implementing encryption technology, using authentication, implementing firewalls, and incorporating security at many levels.

Exam Essentials

Know the various security measures and their purpose.   There are several different physical security measures that can be applied to the public and your staff. In addition, there are several different logical security measures, such access control lists (ACLs), multifactor authentication (MFA), and several others discussed in this chapter. Be familiar with their practical application.

Know the various physical security devices.   You should be familiar with the various physical security devices, such as the use of an access control vestibule, badge readers, video surveillance, alarm systems, motion sensors, door locks, equipment locks, guards, bollards, and fences. In addition, you should be able to describe security devices as they relate to staff, such as the use of key fobs, smartcards, keys, biometrics, lighting, and magnetometers.

Know the various logical security methods. You should be familiar with logical methods of security, such as the implementation and use of access control lists (ACLs), implementing principle of least privilege, and multifactor authentication (MFA), including email, hard tokens, soft tokens, short message service (SMS), voice calls, and authenticator applications as factors of authentication.

Be able to describe why antivirus/antimalware software is needed. Antivirus/antimalware software looks at a virus and takes action to neutralize it based on a virus definition database. Virus definition database files are regularly made available on vendor sites.

Understand the need for user education. Users are the first line of defense against most threats, whether physical or digital. They should be trained on the importance of security and how to help enforce it.

Know the types of malware and mitigation. You should be familiar with the various types of malware commonly found, such as Trojan, rootkit, virus, spyware, ransomware, keylogger, boot sector virus, and cryptominers. In addition, you should be familiar with the various ways to mitigate malware with the use of the recovery console, antivirus, antimalware, software firewalls, antiphishing training, user education, and OS reinstallation.

Know the various best practices for security. You should know the best security practices, such as implementing data-at-rest encryption, password complexity, and password expiration, as well as protecting BIOS or UEFI with passwords. In addition, you should know the various end-user best practices, such as using screen saver locks, logging off when a computer or application is not in use, and implementing security and protection of critical hardware as well as security of personally identifiable information (PII) and passwords.

Know how to compare and contrast social engineering, threats, and vulnerabilities. Social engineering variants include shoulder surfing (watching someone work) and phishing (tricking someone into believing they are communicating with a party other than the one with whom they are communicating). Variations on phishing include vishing, shoulder surfing, whaling, tailgating, impersonation, dumpster diving, and evil twin.

Know the various threats to a network. You should be familiar with the various threats to a network, such as distributed denial-of-service (DDoS), denial-of-service (DoS), zero-day attack, spoofing, on-path attacks, brute-force password attacks, dictionary password attacks, insider threats, Structured Query Language (SQL) injection, and cross-site scripting (XSS).

Understand the need for good passwords. Passwords are the first line of defense for protecting an account. A password should be required for every account, and strong passwords should be enforced. Users need to understand the basics of password security and work to keep their accounts protected by following company policies regarding passwords.

Understand the difference between standard and low-level formatting.   Standard formatting uses operating system tools and marks the drive as available for holding data without truly removing what was on the drive (thus, the data can be recovered). A low-level format is operating system–independent and destroys any data that was on the drive.

Understand how to implement appropriate data destruction and disposal methods.   A hard drive can be destroyed by tossing it into a shredder designed for such a purpose, or it can be destroyed with an electromagnet in a process known as degaussing. You can also disassemble the drive and destroy the platters with a drill or other tool that renders the data irretrievable.

Review Questions

The answers to the chapter review questions can be found in Appendix A.

1. Which component of physical security addresses outer-level access control?

    A. Fences

    B. Access control vestibule

    C. Multifactor authentication

    D. Strong passwords

2. Which type of device can detect weapons on a person entering a facility?

    A. Biometrics

    B. Magnetometer

    C. Motion sensor

    D. Badge reader

3. As part of your training program, you're trying to educate users on the importance of security. You explain to them that not every attack depends on implementing advanced technological methods. Some attacks, you explain, take advantage of human shortcomings to gain access that should otherwise be denied. Which term do you use to describe attacks of this type?

    A. Social engineering

    B. IDS

    C. Perimeter security

    D. Biometrics

4. You're in the process of securing the IT infrastructure by adding fingerprint scanners to your existing authentication methods. This type of security is an example of which of the following?

    A. Access control

    B. Physical barriers

    C. Biometrics

    D. Softening

5. Which type of attack denies authorized users access to network resources?

    A. DoS

    B. Worm

    C. Trojan

    D. Social engineering

6. As the security administrator for your organization, you must be aware of all types of attacks that can occur and plan for them. Which type of attack uses more than one computer to attack the victim?

A. DoS

B. DDoS

C. Worm

D. Rootkit

7. A vice president of your company calls a meeting with the IT department after a recent trip to competitors' sites. She reports that many of the companies she visited granted access to the operating system or applications after an employee presented a number that rotated. Of the following, which technology relies on a rotating number for users for authentication?

A. Smartcard

B. Biometrics

C. Geofencing

D. Token

8. You've discovered that credentials to a specific application have been stolen. The application is accessed from only one computer on the network. Which type of attack is this most likely to be?

A. On-path attack

B. Zero-day

C. Denial-of-service (DoS)

D. Smurf

9. A junior administrator comes to you in a panic. After looking at the log files, he has become convinced that an attacker is attempting to use a legitimate IP address to disrupt access elsewhere on the network. Which type of attack is this?

A. Spoofing

B. Social engineering

C. Worm

D. Password

10. Which of the following is different from a virus in that it can reproduce itself, is self-contained, and doesn't need a host application to be transported?

A. Worm

B. Smurf

C. Phish

D. Trojan

11. A reflective attack attempts to use a broadcast ping on a network. The return address of the ping may be that of a valid system in your network. Which protocol does the reflective attack use to conduct the attack?

    A. TCP

    B. IP

    C. UDP

    D. ICMP

12. Which type of attack involves passing a database query with a web request?

    A. Insider threat

    B. Evil twin

    C. SQL injection

    D. Tailgating

13. Which is an example of an authentication method in which you have something?

    A. Password

    B. Key fob

    C. Fingerprint

    D. Place

14. You need to protect your users from potentially being phished via email. Which of the following should you use to protect them?

    A. Antivirus software

    B. End-user education

    C. SecureDNS

    D. The principle of least privilege

15. Your help desk has informed you that they received an urgent call from the vice president last night requesting his login ID and password. When you talk with the VP today, he says he never made that call. What type of attack is this?

    A. Spoofing

    B. Replay

    C. Social engineering

    D. Trojan horse

16. Internal users suspect there have been repeated attempts to infect their systems, as reported to them by pop-up messages from their antivirus software. According to the messages, the virus seems to be the same in every case. What is the most likely culprit?

    A. A server is acting as a carrier for a virus.

    B. A password attack is being carried out.

    C. Your antivirus software has malfunctioned.

    D. A DoS attack is under way.

17. You're working late one night and notice that the hard drive on your new computer is very active even though you aren't doing anything on the computer and it isn't connected to the Internet. What is the most likely suspect?

A. A spear phishing attack is being performed.

B. A virus is spreading in your system.

C. Your system is under a DoS attack.

D. TCP/IP hijacking is being attempted.

18. You're the administrator for a large bottling company. At the end of each month, you routinely view all logs and look for discrepancies. This month, your email system error log reports a large number of unsuccessful attempts to log in. It's apparent that the email server is being targeted. Which type of attack is most likely occurring?

A. Brute-force

B. Backdoor

C. Worm

D. TCP/IP hijacking

19. Your boss needs you to present to upper management the need for a firewall for the network. What is the thesis of your presentation?

A. The isolation of one network from another

B. The scanning of all packets for viruses

C. Preventing password attacks

D. The hardening of physical security

20. Which Active Directory component maps printers and drives during login?

A. Home folders

B. Organizational unit

C. Login script

D. Microsoft Management Console (MMC)

Performance-Based Question

You will encounter performance-based questions on the A+ exams. The questions on the exam require you to perform a specific task, and you will be graded on whether or not you were able to complete the task. The following requires you to think creatively in order to measure how well you understand this chapter's topics. You may or may not see similar questions on the actual A+ exams. To see how your answers compare to the authors', refer to Appendix B.

Calculate the complexity of a simple 8-character alphanumeric password versus a 25-character alphanumeric password with symbols.

Chapter

18

Securing Operating Systems

THE FOLLOWING COMPTIA A+ 220-1102 EXAM OBJECTIVES ARE COVERED IN THIS CHAPTER:

✓ **2.2 Compare and contrast wireless security protocols and authentication methods.**

- Protocols and encryption
    - WiFi Protected Access 2 (WPA2)
    - WPA3
    - Temporal Key Integrity Protocol (TKIP)
    - Advanced Encryption Standard (AES)
- Authentication
    - Remote Authentication Dial-In User Service (RADIUS)
    - Terminal Access Controller Access-Control System (TACACS+)
    - Kerberos
    - Multifactor

✓ **2.5 Given a scenario, manage and configure basic security settings in the Microsoft Windows OS.**

- Defender Antivirus
    - Activate/deactivate
    - Updated definitions
- Firewall
    - Activate/deactivate
    - Port security
    - Application security

- OS updates
- Device encryption
- Remote backup applications
- Failed login attempts restrictions
- Antivirus/Anti-malware
- Firewall
- Policies and procedures
  - BYOD vs. corporate-owned
  - Profile security requirements
- Internet of Things (IoT)

✓ **2.9 Given a scenario, configure appropriate security settings on small office/home office (SOHO) wireless and wired networks.**

- Home router settings
  - Change default passwords
  - IP filtering
  - Firmware updates
  - Content filtering
  - Physical placement/secure locations
  - Dynamic Host Configuration Protocol (DHCP) reservations
  - Static wide-area network (WAN) IP
  - Universal Plug and Play (UPnP)
  - Screened subnet
- Wireless specific
  - Changing the service set identifier (SSID)
  - Disabling SSID broadcast
  - Encryption settings
  - Disabling guest access
  - Changing channels

- Firewall settings
    - Disabling unused ports
    - Port forwarding/mapping

✓ **2.10 Given a scenario, install and configure browsers and relevant security settings.**

- Browser download/installation
    - Trusted sources
        - Hashing
    - Untrusted sources
- Extensions and plug-ins
    - Trusted sources
    - Untrusted sources
- Password managers
- Secure connections/sites – valid certificates
- Settings
    - Pop-up blocker
    - Clearing browsing data
    - Clearing cache
    - Private-browsing mode
    - Sign-in/browser data synchronization
    - Ad blockers

This chapter is the second of two chapters that focus primarily on security. Chapter 17, "Security Concepts," covered myriad security concepts, ranging from physical security to the proper destruction of data storage devices in your organization. In this chapter, we will focus on operating system security and mobile security.

Many organizations are adopting a cloud-first initiative for their line-of-business applications. This has further perpetuated the adoption of mobile devices in the workplace. These initiatives, along with the rapid adoption of mobile devices in our personal lives, has created a tremendous need for security. This chapter will address the concerns of operating system security, mobile device security, and best practices.

Working with Windows OS Security Settings

Every operating system offers security features and settings. While you need to know a little about Linux and macOS, the A+ exams focus primarily on Windows and the OS-specific security settings that you need to know to secure them. The following sections will explore some basic Windows OS security features and settings in more detail.

Users and Groups

A number of groups are created on the operating system by default. The following sections look at the main ones.

Microsoft vs. Local Accounts

During the initial setup of Windows, Microsoft urges the user to log in with a Microsoft account, as shown in Figure 18.1. You can set up a Microsoft account with an email, a phone, or a Skype login, which is actually a Microsoft account. This feature was originally introduced with Windows 8.

Setting up your initial user account is a smart idea, because it allows you to set up tools, such as OneDrive, to back up your files. The most significant feature is it allows setup of synchronization for settings across all of your devices. However, it also allows access to other Microsoft productivity tools and ultimately it is how you access the Microsoft Store and the Store App ecosystem.

FIGURE 18.1 Microsoft account screen

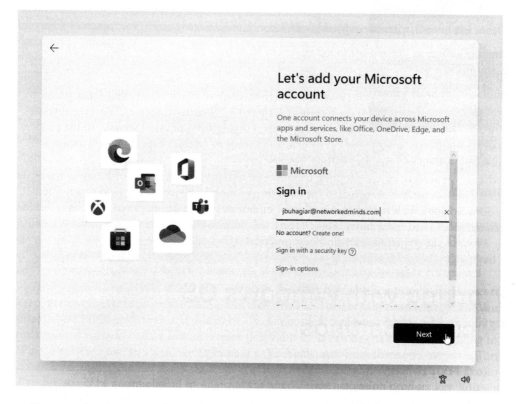

You can also choose to select an offline account, as shown on the lower left of Figure 18.1. When you use an offline account, many of the features we described earlier need to be set up manually. Also, depending on the feature, it may not work as designed. When you elect to create an offline account, you are actually electing to use local accounts on the operating system. Many corporate-owned devices still use local accounts and connect to a traditional Active Directory (AD) domain.

Choosing to sign in with a Microsoft account or local (offline) account depends on what you are trying to achieve. If the device will be used for personal work, then a Microsoft account is the best option. If the device will be used for an organization, then a local account might be the best option. A third option exists that is reserved for organizations, which is the use of a corporately owned email address for enrollment into mobile device management (MDM) software, such as Intune.

In the following we will cover the basic local accounts and local permissions that you should expect to see on the CompTIA exam.

Administrator

The *Administrator* account is the most powerful of all: it has the power to do everything from the smallest task all the way to removing the operating system. Because of the great power the Administrator account holds, and the fact that it is always created, many who want to do harm target this account as the one that they try to breach. To increase security, during the installation of the Windows operating systems in question, you are prompted for the name of a user who will be designated as the Administrator. The power then comes not from being called "Administrator" (the username might now be "buhagiar," "jbuhagiar," or something similar) but from being a member of the *Administrators group*. (Notice the plural for the group and singular for the user.)

Since members of the Administrators group have such power, they can inadvertently do harm (such as accidentally deleting a file that a regular user could not). To protect against this, the practice of logging in with an Administrators group account for daily interaction is strongly discouraged. Instead, we suggest that system administrators log in with a user account (lesser privileges) and change to the Administrators group account (elevated privileges) only when necessary.

Power User

Originally, Microsoft wanted to create a group in Windows whose members were not as powerful as members of the Administrators group, so they created the *Power Users* group. The idea was that members of this group would be given Read and Write permission to the system, allowing them to install most software but keeping them from changing key operating system files. As such, it would be a good group for those who need to test software (such as programmers) and junior administrators.

The group did not work out as planned, and in Windows 7, Windows 8/8.1, and Windows 10/11 the group has no more permissions than a standard user. The group is now kept around only for backward compatibility with Windows XP systems.

Guest

The *Guest user* account is created by default (and should be disabled) and is a member of the Guests group. For the most part, members of the Guests group have the same rights as a standard user, except they can't get to log files. The best reason to make users members of the Guests group is that they can access the system only for a limited time.

 As part of operating system security, it's usually recommended that you rename the default Administrator and Guest accounts that are created at installation.

Standard User

By default, *standard users* belong to the local Users group. Members of this group have Read and Write permission to their own profile. They cannot modify systemwide Registry settings or do much harm outside of their own accounts. Under the principle of least privilege, users should be made members of the Users group only, unless qualifying circumstances force them to have higher privileges.

If you attempt to run some utilities (such as `sfc.exe`) from a standard command prompt, you will be told that you must be an administrator running a console session in order to continue. If your account is in the Administrators group, then the command prompt must be launched with the elevated permissions of the administrator. To do so, choose Start ➤ All Programs ➤ Accessories, and then right-click Command Prompt and choose Run As Administrator. The User Account Control (UAC) will prompt you to continue, and then you can run `sfc.exe` without a problem.

Changing between Account Types

You can change between account types of standard and administrator for your local user account or for other local user accounts by using the legacy Control Panel applet for User Accounts. You simply open Control Panel, select User Accounts, then click Change Your Account Type to change your account type or click Manage Another Account, select the user, then click Change The Account Type. You will be presented with the dialog box in Figure 18.2, where you can change the type of account from Administrator to Standard using the radio buttons.

FIGURE 18.2   Changing the account type

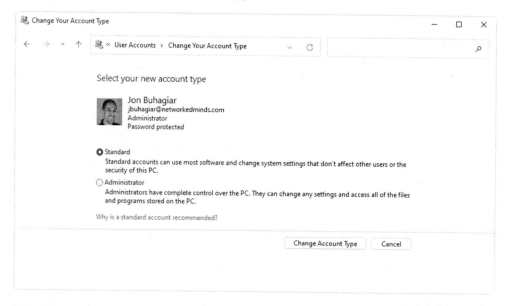

If the Standard option is grayed out and you cannot change the user account to a standard user, then you must make another administrative user. The operating system must have at least one valid administrative account. The operating system will not let you lock yourself out through this set of screens.

User Authentication

Users can log into the local operating system with their username and password, if they have an account, and they will receive a local access token. The *access token* the user is granted is locally significant for the operating system. For example, an administrator (local) who authenticates against the operating system is only an administrator of that operating system and has no further network permissions. Every Windows operating system has a local database and authentication system called the *Security Account Manager (SAM)*, as shown in Figure 18.3.

FIGURE 18.3   Windows authentication

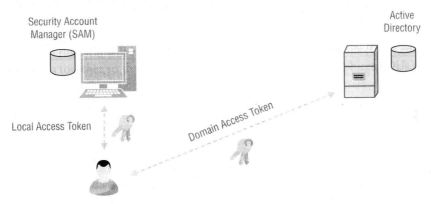

Active Directory simplifies the sign-on process for users and lowers the support requirements for administrators. Access can be established through groups and enforced through group memberships: all users log into the Windows domain using their centrally created Active Directory account. It's important to enforce password changes and make certain that passwords are updated throughout the organization on a frequent basis.

Active Directory uses Kerberos v5. A server that runs Active Directory retains information about all access rights for all users and groups in the network. When a user logs into Active Directory, they are granted a *network access token*, also called a *Kerberos token*. This token can be used to authenticate against other servers and workstations in the domain and is accepted network (domain) wide. This token is also referred to as the user's *globally unique identifier (GUID)*. Applications that support Active Directory for authentication can use this GUID to provide access control.

Single Sign-On

One of the big problems larger networks must deal with is the need for users to access multiple systems or applications. This may require users to remember multiple accounts and passwords. An alternative to this is that the application must support Active Directory authentication, but that creates other considerations.

The purpose of *single sign-on (SSO)* is to give users access to all the applications and systems that they need when they log in. Single sign-on is often used with cloud-based resources. The principle behind SSO is that the resource will trust that the user has already been authenticated. The authentication server performs this by sending a claim on behalf of the user, as shown in Figure 18.4. This claim can contain any number of Active Directory user attributes, such as first name, last name, email, and username, just to name a few. It is important to understand that at no time during the authentication process are the username and password sent to the resource that is requesting authentication. The resource must trust that the user has already been authenticated and accept the claim at face value.

FIGURE 18.4   Claims-based authentication

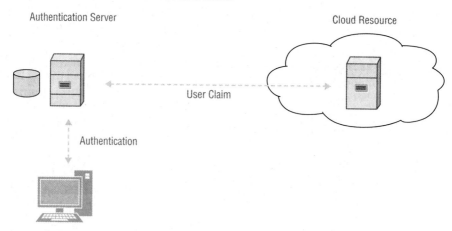

Single sign-on is both a blessing and a curse. It's a blessing in that once users have been authenticated, they can access all the resources on the network and browse multiple folders. Single sign-on is a curse in that it removes the doors that otherwise exist between the user and various resources.

Windows Hello

The problem with traditional usernames and passwords is that they are too complex for the user to consistently type. As administrators we want to make sure that users lock their workstation and type their password when they return to gain access. However, this is a burden on the user, especially if we are constantly changing passwords and making them more complex.

Windows Hello addresses these problems by storing the user's credentials in a secure container called the Credential Manager. The Credential Manager is then locked and unlocked with the authentication of biometrics or a PIN by the user. Once the Credential Manager is unlocked, the credentials can be passed to the operating system to provide the login credentials. Windows Hello can be configured by navigating to Start ➤ Settings App ➤ Accounts ➤ Sign-in Options, and you will be brought to the various ways to configure Windows Hello, as shown in Figure 18.5.

FIGURE 18.5   Windows Hello Sign-in options

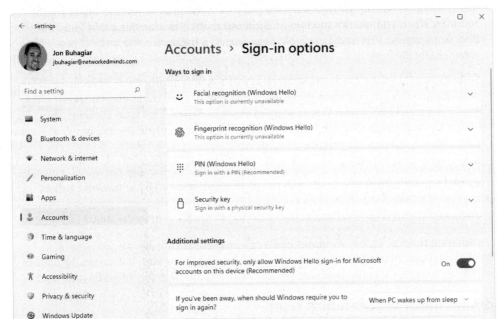

There are several different sign-in options for Windows Hello that will allow for easier login of the device. The available options will depend on your hardware connected to the device. As an example, if you want to use your fingerprint, you will need a fingerprint reader. There are several options as shown in Figure 18.5, but they all basically fall into a few categories:

Biometric Sign-in   Using the Windows Hello Face option will allow you to use your face to unlock the operating system. If your device is equipped with a camera, it will sense you entering the scene and verify your face to unlock the device. You can also use your fingerprint to provide authentication, but you will need a fingerprint reader as previously mentioned. Both of these biometric options authenticate you based on something you are. Because it is coupled with something that you have (the device), the process actually provides two-factor authentication/multifactor authentication (2FA/MFA). Multifactor authentication will be covered later in this chapter.

PIN   The most common option for devices without a camera or fingerprint reader is to use a personal identification number (PIN). The PIN can be a simple password containing numbers such as a PIN you use for your bank. Although you can make this as complex as you wish, its intended purpose is to make it easier to log in for the end user. When you use this method of authentication, it is something that you know. Both knowing the PIN and having physical access to the device, the process provides 2FA/MFA.

Security Key   Using a hardware security key or token is another way of securing Windows Hello. You can configure Windows to log you in after you present a security key, which is a small USB device that is plugged into the device. This is an authentication method of something that you have. By having both the security key and physical access to the device, the process provides 2FA/MFA.

Picture Password   A picture password is similar to a gesture-based password. You can upload a picture, then select points in the picture you must click on to allow authentication. This type of authentication is based on something that you know, and when combined with the physical access to the device, the process provides 2FA/MFA.

In addition to local logins, Windows Hello can be used to authenticate users for a Microsoft account, Active Directory account, and Azure AD account. It can even be used to authenticate users for identity provider services, which is another way of addressing SSO.

Administrator vs. Standard User

Administrators have rights in the operating system that allows them to change the operating system. Standard users do not have these rights and can only make changes to their environment. Because the administrative rights can cause harm to the operating system or introduce security issues, care should be taken in granting your end users administrative permissions. You should exercise the principle of least privilege with granting end-user rights. This means that unless someone needs administrative privileges, they should always log in with a standard user account. This protects the local operating system and potentially the network (if domain authenticated) from the security threats covered in Chapter 17.

User Account Control (UAC) is a feature that was introduced in Windows Vista. It supports the principle of least privilege by logging an administrator in with minimal permissions. This is extremely handy for users who occasionally need administrative rights, such as your home operating system. For example, if extra privileges were required to modify the operating system, a prompt asking if the user wants to continue would be displayed, as shown in Figure 18.6. If the user answers Yes, then the user will receive the administrative token to complete the task. UAC allows the user to run as a standard user with the ability to escalate privileges.

In Exercise 18.1 you will examine the security token for your user account. The exercise assumes that you are the administrator of the operating system.

FIGURE 18.6   UAC prompt

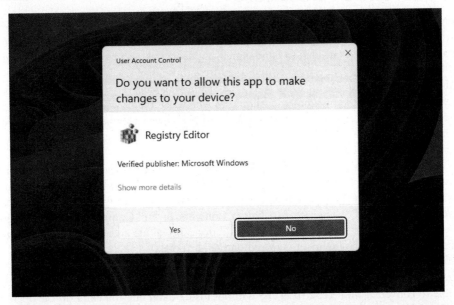

Examining a Security Token

This exercise assumes that you have not turned off the UAC and that you are the administrator of the operating system.

1. Click the Start menu, type **cmd**, and then press Enter.

2. In the command prompt, type **whoami /ALL**, and then press Enter.

3. Record the privileges that you see in the output.

4. Click the Start menu and type **cmd**.

5. Right-click Command Prompt and select Run As Administrator.

6. Answer Yes to the UAC prompt.

7. In the command prompt, type **whoami /ALL**, and then press Enter.

8. Compare the privileges that you see in the output.

When you opened the first command prompt, it was opened with the standard user credentials of your account. When you opened the second command prompt, you selected Run As Administrator. The second command prompt was opened with the administrative security token.

NTFS vs. Share Permissions

The *New Technology File System (NTFS)* was introduced with Windows NT to address security problems. Before Windows NT was released, it had become apparent to Microsoft that a new filesystem was needed to handle growing disk sizes, security concerns, and the need for more stability. NTFS was created to address those issues.

Although the *File Allocation Table (FAT)* filesystem was relatively stable if the systems that were controlling it kept running, it didn't do well when the power went out or the system crashed unexpectedly. One of the benefits of NTFS was a transaction-tracking system, which made it possible for Windows NT to back out of any disk operations that were in progress when it crashed or lost power.

With NTFS, files, folders, and volumes can each have their own security. NTFS's security is flexible and built in. Not only does NTFS track security in ACLs, which can hold permissions for local users and groups, but each entry in the ACL can specify which type of access is given—such as Read & Execute, List Folder Contents, or Full Control. This allows a great deal of flexibility in setting up a network. In addition, special file-encryption programs were developed to encrypt data while it is stored on the hard disk.

Microsoft strongly recommends that all network shares be established using NTFS. Several current operating systems from Microsoft support both FAT32 and NTFS. It's possible to convert from FAT32 to NTFS without losing data, but you can't do the operation in reverse. (You would need to reformat the drive and install the data again from a backup tape.)

> If you're using FAT32 and want to change to NTFS, the convert utility will allow you to do so. For example, to change the E: drive to NTFS, the command is convert E: /FS:NTFS.

Share permissions apply only when a user is accessing a file or folder through the network, as shown in Figure 18.7. *NTFS permissions* and attributes are used to protect the file when the user is local. With FAT and FAT32, you do not have the ability to assign "extended" or "extensible" permissions, and the user sitting at the console effectively is the owner of all resources on the system. As such, they can add, change, and delete any data or file.

With NTFS as the filesystem, you are allowed to assign more comprehensive security to your computer system, as shown in Table 18.1. NTFS permissions can protect you at the file level. Share permissions can be applied to the folder level only, as shown in Table 18.2. NTFS permissions can affect users accessing files and folders across a network or logged in locally to the system where the NTFS permissions are applied. Share permissions are in effect only when the user connects to the resource through the network.

FIGURE 18.7   Network share permissions and NTFS permissions

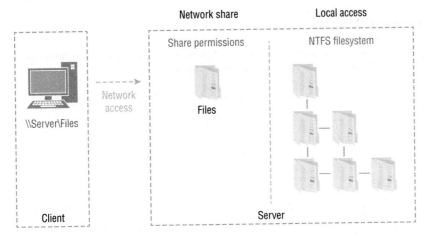

TABLE 18.1   NTFS permissions

NTFS permission	Meaning	Object used on
Full Control	Gives the user all the other choices and the ability to change permissions. The user can also take ownership of the folder or any of its contents.	Folder and file objects
Modify	Combines the Read & Execute permission with the Write permission and further allows the user to delete everything, including the folder.	Folder and file objects
Read & Execute	Combines the Read permission with the List Folder Contents permission and adds the ability to run executables.	Folder and file objects
List Folder Contents	The List Folder Contents permission (known simply as List in previous versions) allows the user to view the contents of a folder and to navigate to its subdirectories. It does not grant the user access to the files in these directories unless that is specified in file permissions.	Folder objects
Read	Allows the user to navigate the entire folder structure, view the contents of the folder, view the contents of any files in the folder, and see ownership and attributes.	Folder and file objects
Write	Allows the user to create new entities within a folder.	Folder and file objects

TABLE 18.2   Share permissions

Share permission	Meaning
Full Control	Gives the user all the other permissions as well as permission to take ownership and change permissions.
Change	Allows the user to overwrite, delete, and read files and folders.
Read	Allows the user to view the contents of the file and to see ownership and attributes.

Allow vs. Deny

Within NTFS, permissions for objects fall into one of three categories: Allow, Deny, or not configured. When viewing the permissions for a file or folder, you can check the box for Allow, which effectively allows the group selected to perform that action. You can also uncheck the box for Allow, which does not allow that group that action, as shown in Figure 18.8. Alternatively, you can check the Deny box, which prevents that group from using that action. There is a difference between not allowing (a cleared check box) and Deny (which specifically prohibits), and you tend not to see Deny used often. Deny, when used, trumps other permissions.

FIGURE 18.8   NTFS folder permissions

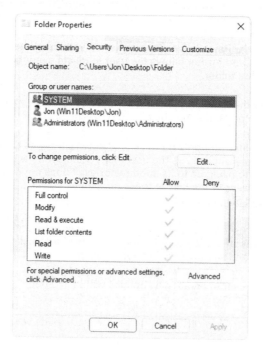

Permissions set on a folder are inherited down through subfolders unless otherwise changed. Permissions are also cumulative; if a user is a member of a group that has Read permission and a member of a group that has Write permission, they effectively have both Read and Write permissions.

Effective Permissions

When a user accesses a file share, both the share permissions and NTFS permissions interact with each other to form the effective permission for the user. Figure 18.9 shows that a user named Fred has logged in and received his access token containing the Sales and R&D groups, since he is a member of both groups. When Fred accesses the Sales file share, the share permissions define that he has read-only access because he is part of the Sales group. You can see that the NTFS permissions are granting him read and write access because of his Sales group membership, as well as full control because he is also in the R&D group. If Fred were to locally log in to this computer, he would effectively have full control of these files. However, because he is accessing these files from the network, he only has read-only access because of the file-share permissions. The opposite is also true: if he had full permission at the share level and read-only permission at the NTFS level, he would effectively have read-only access.

FIGURE 18.9   Effective permissions

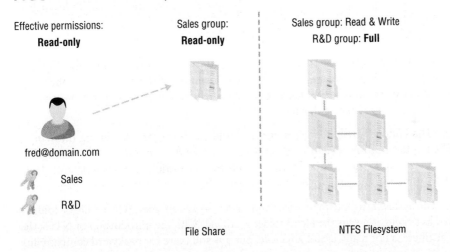

Effective permissions:
Read-only

Sales group:
Read-only

Sales group: Read & Write
R&D group: **Full**

fred@domain.com

Sales

R&D

File Share   NTFS Filesystem

The rule for figuring out effective permissions is simple: if a user is in more than one group for which there are multiple permissions, take the most permissive permission of NTFS and then the most permissive permission of the share; the effective permission is the more restrictive of the two. There are some circumstances that change this rule slightly when the user (or group) is denied. If a user is in any group that is denied permission at the share or the NTFS level, they are denied for that access level. Therefore, when you derive the more restrictive permission, it will always be a deny for the user. A simple way to remember this is that a deny is a deny.

Moving vs. Copying Folders and Files

When you copy a file, you create a new entity. When you move a file, you simply relocate it and still have but one entity. This distinction is important when it comes to understanding permissions. A copy of a file will have the permissions assigned to it that are already in place at the new location of the file, regardless of which permissions were on the original file.

A moved file, on the other hand, will attempt to keep the same permissions as it had in the original location. Differences will occur if the same permissions cannot exist in the new location. For example, if you are moving a file from an NTFS volume to FAT32, the NTFS permissions will be lost. If, on the other hand, you are moving from a FAT32 volume to an NTFS volume, new permissions will be added that match those for newly created entities.

Folder copy and move operations follow guidelines that are similar to those for files.

File and Folder Attributes

Since the introduction of FAT, file and folder *attributes* have existed in the filesystem. The basic set of attributes—Read-only, Hidden, System, and Archive—can still be found in both FAT and NTFS and are very useful for the operating system, as explained in the following list. You can view the file or folder attributes by right-clicking the file or folder and selecting Properties. From there, you can view the Read-only and Hidden attributes.

Read-Only   The Read-only attribute is used to make a file or folder read-only. If the Read-only attribute is present, regardless of the permission of the file or folder, the user cannot write or delete a file or folder. The Read-only attribute is useful for protecting files from being overwritten or deleted.

Hidden   The Hidden attribute makes files and folders disappear when using the Windows File Explorer utility, using the defaults or using the `dir` command. The files still function and are still a part of the filesystem, but they just don't appear by default. The Hidden attribute is useful when you want to hide a file or folder from the average user.

System   The System attribute marks files and folders as system files. When a file or folder is marked as system, it means the file or folder is critical. With the introduction of NTFS, the System attribute is not really useful anymore, but it is still there for backward compatibility.

Archive   The Archive attribute can be used to tell the system whether the file has changed since the last time it was backed up. Technically, it is known as the Archive Needed attribute. If this bit is on, the file or folder should be backed up. If it is not selected, a current version of the file is already backed up.

Only the Read-only and Hidden attributes can be set or cleared from the GUI. The Archive attribute can be accessed from the Advanced Attributes dialog box. The System attribute can be set or cleared only with the `attrib.exe` command.

Windows uses NTFS, which gives you a number of options that are not available on earlier filesystems, such as FAT and FAT32. A number of these options are implemented through the use of the Advanced Attributes dialog box, as shown in Figure 18.10.

FIGURE 18.10   The Advanced Attributes dialog box

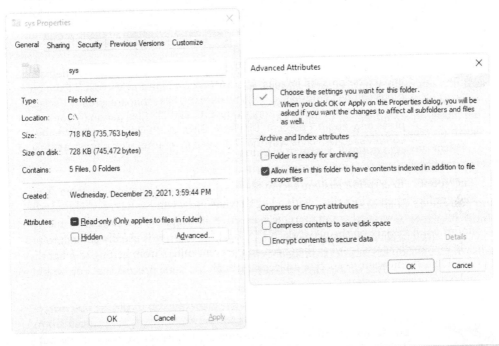

FAT32 does not have as many options as NTFS, such as encryption and compression. These attributes are available only on NTFS partitions.

To reach these options in Windows, right-click the folder or file that you want to modify, and then select Properties from the menu. On the main Properties page of the folder or file, click the Advanced button in the lower-right corner. In the Advanced Attributes window, you have access to the following settings:

Indexing   Windows implements a feature called the *Indexing Service* to catalog and improve the search capabilities of your drive. Once files are indexed, you can search for them more quickly by name, date, or other attributes. Setting the index option on a folder causes a prompt to appear, asking whether you want the existing files in the folder to be indexed as well. If you choose to do this, Windows will automatically reset this attribute on subfolders and files. If not, only new files created in the folder will be indexed.

Compression   The versions of Windows that you need to know for the exam support advanced *compression* options, which were first introduced in Windows NT. NTFS files and folders can be dynamically compressed and uncompressed, often saving a great deal of space on the drive. As with indexing, when you turn on compression for a folder, you'll be prompted as to whether you want the existing files in the folder to be compressed. If you choose to do this, Windows automatically compresses the subfolders and files. If not, only new files created in the folder are compressed.

Compression works best on such files as word processing documents and uncompressed images. Microsoft Word files and Microsoft Paint bitmaps can be compressed up to 80 percent. Files that are already packed well do not compress as effectively; EXE and ZIP files generally compress only about 2 percent. Similarly, GIF and JPEG images are already compressed (which is why they are used in Internet web pages), so they compress a little or not at all.

Encryption   *Encryption* lets you secure files so that no one else can view them. You encrypt files by encoding them with a key to which only you have access. This can be useful if you're worried about extremely sensitive information, but in general encryption is not necessary on the network. NTFS local file security is usually enough to provide users with access to what they need and prevent others from getting to what they shouldn't. If you want to encrypt a file, go through the same process that you would for indexing or compression.

Encryption and compression are mutually exclusive—you can set one but not both features on a file or folder. Not all features are available in all editions of every operating system. If a user forgets their password or is unable to access the network to authenticate their account, they will not be able to open encrypted files. By default, if the user's account is lost or deleted, the only other user who can decrypt the file is the Administrator account.

In Exercise 18.2 you will have the opportunity to view file permissions for both basic and advanced permissions. Make sure that you don't inadvertently add any deny permissions, as you could be prevented from making any further changes.

EXERCISE 18.2

Examining File Permissions

1. Open Windows File Explorer.

2. Right-click a file or folder and choose Properties.

3. Select and then examine the Security tab.

   You'll see the users and/or groups to which permissions have been assigned.

4. Select a user or group in the list, and examine the list of standard permissions. (To add a new user or group, click Add and follow the prompts.)

    Any standard permissions that are checked in the Allow column are applied. If a check box is grayed out, then the permission was inherited.

5. To revoke a set of standard permissions, click the appropriate check box in the Deny column.

    If you click the check box in the Deny column for the Full Control permission, all other standard permissions are also denied.

6. Click Advanced to examine advanced options.

7. Click Cancel twice to close the file or folder's properties.

Be sure that you don't accidentally make any changes that you didn't intend to make. Changing permissions without understanding the ramifications can have negative consequences, such as losing access to files or folders. It is a best practice to assign Deny permissions sparingly. It's better to uncheck Allow. (You may need to turn off Inheritance.)

Shared Files and Folders

You can share folders, and the files beneath them, by right-clicking the file or folder and choosing Give Access To from the context menu and selecting Specific People. In Windows, the context menu asks you to choose with whom you want to share the folder or file, as shown in Figure 18.10. You can then choose who to share it with along with their respective permissions. It is important to understand that when you use this method to share files and folders, the share permissions are set to Full Control for the Everyone group. The dialog box shown in Figure 18.11 will allow you to manipulate the NTFS permissions via the permission level.

You can access the Advanced Sharing settings by right-clicking the folder you want to share, selecting Properties, then clicking the Sharing tab, and finally selecting Advanced Sharing, as shown in Figure 18.12. This file-sharing method is more traditional with network administrators because every aspect of the share can be controlled. Using this method, only the share permissions are set from this dialog box. The NTFS security permissions are set on the Security tab. In addition, you can add other share names to the same location, limit the number of simultaneous connections, and add comments.

Administrative Shares vs. Local Shares

Administrative shares are automatically created on all Windows operating systems on the network for administrative purposes. These shares can differ slightly based on which operating system is running, but they always end with a dollar sign ($) to make them hidden. There is one share for each volume on a hard drive (c$, d$, and so on) as well as admin$ (the root folder—usually C:\WINDOWS) and print$ (where the print drivers are located).

FIGURE 18.11 Choose People To Share With

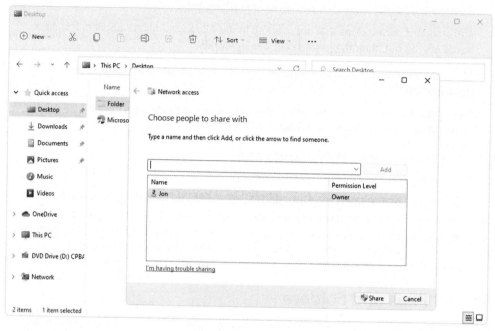

FIGURE 18.12 Advanced file and folder sharing

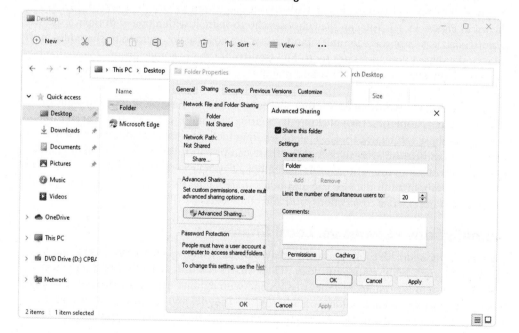

These shares are created for use by administrators and usually require administrator privileges to access.

Local shares, as the name implies, are shares that are created locally by the administrative user on the operating system. The term *local shares* is used to distinguish between automated administrative shares and manually created shares.

Permission Inheritance and Permissions Propagation

Inheritance is the default throughout the permission structure unless a specific setting is created to override it. A user who has Read and Write permissions in one folder will have them in all the subfolders unless a change has been made specifically to one of the subfolders. If a user has the Write permission, which is inherited from the folder above, the removal of permissions cannot be performed unless inheritance is disabled. Only additional permissions can be added explicitly, since this is actually a new permissions entry and not the removal of an existing permissions entry. You can control NTFS inheritance by right-clicking a folder, selecting Properties, then choosing the Security tab, selecting Advanced, and clicking the Disable Inheritance button, as shown in Figure 18.13.

FIGURE 18.13   Disabling inheritance

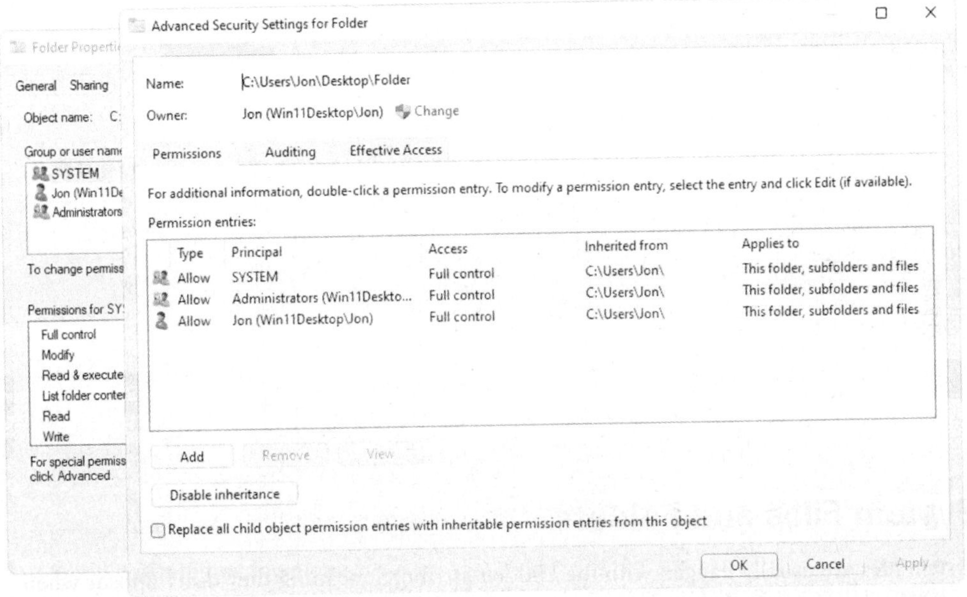

If the Disable Inheritance button is selected, you will be changing the NTFS security settings on the folder. A second dialog box will pop up and you must choose to either keep the existing permissions, by selecting Convert Inherited Permissions To Explicit Permissions On This Object, or to start fresh with no permissions by selecting Remove All Inherited Permissions From This Object. You should use caution when selecting the latter of the two options, because all folders and files below will inherit and propagate the removal of existing permissions.

If you want to make sure that inheritance and permissions for a folder are propagated to all files and folders below, you can use Replace All Child Object Permission Entries With Inheritable Permission Entries From This Object (refer to Figure 18.13). This option will replace every permission in this folder and all the subfolders, regardless of whether explicit permissions were applied further down in the folder structure.

In the Advanced Security Settings, you can also configure permissions entries that only apply to the current folder, current folder and files, all folders and files, or other variations of these, as shown in Figure 18.14. These settings can change the propagation of file permissions to folders and files.

FIGURE 18.14   Permission entry

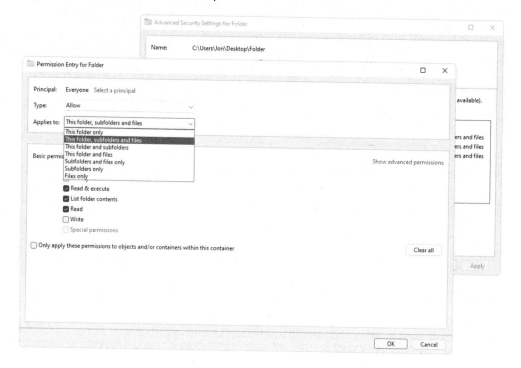

System Files and Folders

System files are usually flagged with the Hidden attribute, meaning they don't appear when a user displays a folder listing. You should not change this attribute on a system file unless absolutely necessary. System files are required in order for the operating system to function. If they are visible, users might delete them (perhaps thinking that they can clear some disk space by deleting files that they don't recognize). Needless to say, that would be a bad thing! Most system files and folders are protected by the operating system and won't allow deletion, but better safe than sorry.

Changing File Attributes

File attributes determine what specific users can do to files or folders. For example, if a file or folder is flagged with the Read-only attribute, then users can read the file or folder but cannot make changes to it or delete it. Attributes include Read-only, Hidden, System, and Archive, as well as Compression, Indexing, and Encryption. Not all attributes are available with all versions of Windows. We'll look at this subject in more detail in a moment.

> Some attributes—such as Read-only, Hidden, System, and Archive—date back to DOS. All others—such as Compression, Indexing, and Encryption—are a part of NTFS.

You can view and change file attributes either by entering **attrib** at the command prompt or by changing the properties of a file or folder. To access the properties of a file or folder, right-click the file or folder and select Properties. You can view and configure the Read-only and Hidden file attributes on the General tab. To view and configure additional attributes, click Advanced, as shown in Figure 18.15.

FIGURE 18.15   Windows file attributes

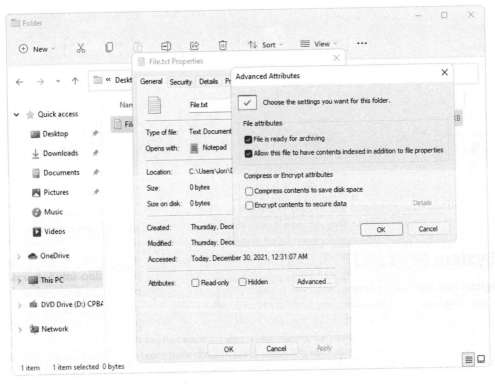

Windows Security Features

Although everything we've covered so far is a Windows security feature, we have focused on the basic elements of authentication and securing resources. In the following section we will cover the common Windows security features that can protect us from external threats, such as malware, malicious network activity, and data loss.

Microsoft Defender

Microsoft Defender, also known as Windows Defender Antivirus, was originally introduced with Windows XP as a downloadable antivirus product. It was later shipped with the Vista operating system, and it has become a pillar of security in the Windows 10/11 operating system. The addition of Microsoft Defender allows the Windows operating system to be protected right out of the box. A user never needs to install anything else to be protected from malware. That being said, there are lots of products on the market that provide security features above and beyond Microsoft Defender.

FIGURE 18.16   Microsoft Defender settings

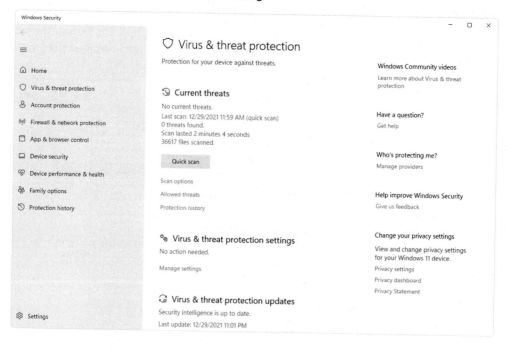

You can view the Microsoft Defender settings by navigating to Start ➤ Settings App ➤ Update & Security ➤ Windows Security ➤ Virus & Threat Protection in Windows 10. In Windows 11, you can view the settings by navigating to Start ➤ Settings App ➤ Privacy & Security ➤ Windows Security ➤ Virus & Threat Protection, as shown in Figure 18.16.

On the Virus & Threat Protection screen you can make a scan of the computer. In addition, the screen will detail how many threats have been found, when it was last scanned, how many files were scanned, and how long the scan lasted. By clicking Scan Options you can select from Quick Scan, Full Scan, Custom Scan, and Microsoft Defender Offline Scan.

Quick Scan   This option will check folders in the system where threats are commonly found.

Full Scan   This option will perform a full scan of the entire operating system.

Custom Scan   This option will allow you to select the folders on the drive you want to scan.

Microsoft Defender Offline Scan   This option will restart the device, reboot into the Windows Recovery Environment (WinRE), and launch a full Microsoft Defender Scan. It is used to remove malware that is difficult to remove while the operating system is running.

You can also change the Microsoft Defender Virus & Threat Protection Settings by clicking Manage Settings on the Virus & Threat Protection screen. This will allow you to manage a number of settings to change the way Microsoft Defender operates, as shown in Figure 18.17.

FIGURE 18.17   Microsoft Defender Virus & Threat settings

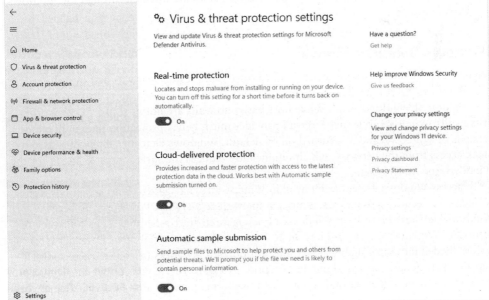

You can toggle off real-time protection when installing certain applications that require that antivirus be off during installation. However, the real-time protection will turn back on automatically after a period of time. You can also toggle Cloud-Delivered Protection, which provides cloud-based data on threats and ultimately faster protection. Turning this setting off might be required for certain regulatory requirements, since it automatically turns on cloud-based sample submission. Automatic Sample Submission can be controlled separately as well and toggled on and off. The Tamper Protection security setting prevents malicious applications from tampering with Microsoft Defender settings. Tamper Protection protects against tampering from third-party processes; even Group Policy settings cannot disable Microsoft Defender when Tamper Protection is turned on.

Controlled Folder Access   The Controlled Folder Access feature can be accessed in the Virus & Threat Protection Settings. The feature is used to prevent ransomware from harming files, folders, and memory areas on the device. By default, it is turned off, but it can be easily turned on by clicking the toggle. Once it is set to the default, folders protected are documents, pictures, videos, music, and favorites. Specific folders can be added, and the defaults can also be removed. You can also exempt an application so that it is allowed to modify the files.

Exclusions   Although it is not common to need to exempt a folder from the antimalware engine, it can be configured from the Virus & Threat Protection Settings. This option allows you to exempt an entire folder from the real-time protection and scans. One use may be performance-impacted applications such as games, but caution should be used.

Update Definitions   An antimalware engine is only as good as its latest definitions, and Microsoft Defender is no different. Therefore, both the Microsoft Defender engine and its definitions are updated quite frequently. Both are updated through the Windows Update process.

Windows Defender Firewall

Windows Defender Firewall is an advanced host-based firewall that was first introduced with Windows XP Service Pack 2. It was integrated and became a security feature with the introduction of Windows Vista. While host-based firewalls are not as secure as other types of firewalls, Windows Defender Firewall provides much better protection than in previous versions of Windows, and it is turned on by default. Windows Defender Firewall is used to block access from the network, which significantly reduces the surface area of attack for the Windows operating system.

To access Windows Defender Firewall in Windows 10, navigate to Start ➤ Settings Apps ➤ Update & Security ➤ Windows Security ➤ Firewall & Network Protection. To access Windows Defender Firewall in Windows 11, navigate to Start ➤ Settings Apps ➤ Privacy & Security ➤ Windows Security ➤ Firewall & Network Protection. Windows Defender Firewall is divided into separate profile settings: for domain networks (if you're connected to a domain), private networks, and public networks. In Figure 18.18, you can see the default protection for a Windows client that is not joined to a domain and is active on a public network.

FIGURE 18.18   Firewall & Network Protection

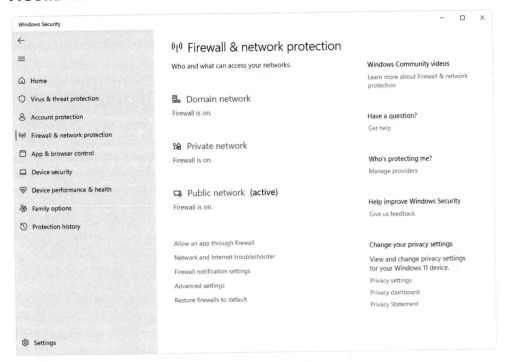

Activate and Deactivate the Firewall   By default, the Windows Defender blocks inbound connections, but outbound connections are not blocked by default. You can temporarily deactivate the Windows Defender Firewall for a network profile by clicking on the network profile in the Firewall & Network Protection screen and toggling the Windows Defender Firewall setting to Off, as shown in Figure 18.19. Deactivating the firewall protection is extremely useful if you are trying to troubleshoot a network connectivity problem. Dropping the firewall temporarily and testing the incoming connection will confirm that a firewall adjustment needs to be made.

Allowing Applications   When applications attempt to listen on a port for an incoming connection, the Windows operating system will display a notification asking if you want to allow access. However, if the notification does not display and you determine that an application needs to be allowed through the firewall, you can click Allow An App Through Firewall in the Firewall & Network Protection screen. This will open the Allowed Apps settings page shown in Figure 18.20. Here you can modify the apps that are allowed through the Windows Defender Firewall, as well as add new ones. You will need administrative access to change any network firewall settings.

FIGURE 18.19   Deactivating Windows Defender Firewall network protection

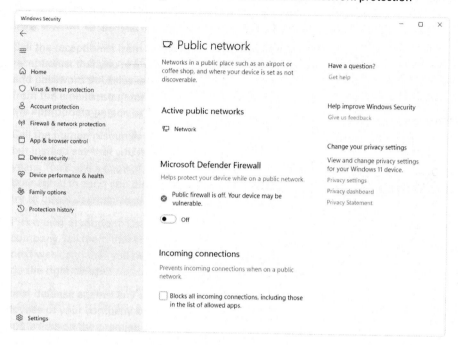

FIGURE 18.20   Windows Defender Firewall Allowed Apps

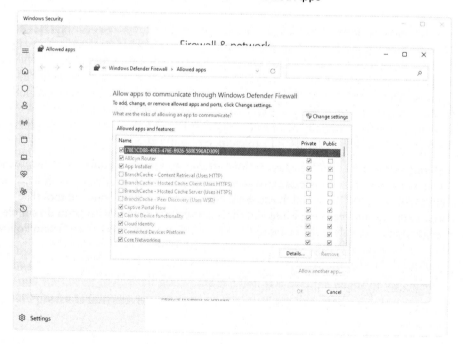

Windows Defender Firewall with Advanced Security When you allow an application to listen for an incoming connection via the notification dialog box, the operating system creates a rule in the firewall to allow the connection. This is all done for you behind the scenes and it shows up neatly as an allowed application. However, you can also manually create a rule in Windows Defender Firewall with the Advanced Security MMC, as shown in Figure 18.21. You can open the MMC by clicking Advanced Settings on the Firewall & Network Protection screen.

FIGURE 18.21 Windows Firewall with Advanced Security

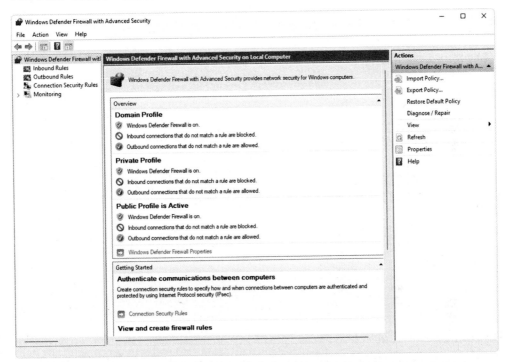

Here you can configure inbound and outbound rules as well as import and export policies and monitor the security of your system. Monitoring is not confined to the firewall; you can also monitor security associations and connection security rules. In short, Windows Defender Firewall with Advanced Security is an incredibly powerful tool that builds on what Windows Vista introduced. Not only can this MMC snap-in do simple configuration, but it can also configure remote computers and work with Group Policy.

Exceptions Manual exceptions, also known as firewall rules, are configured on the Inbound Rules tab in the Windows Defender Firewall with Advanced Security MMC. You can click New Rule and configure a firewall rule based on a program, port, predefined rule, or totally custom rule. A rule based on a program allows all incoming connection to the application. A rule based on a port allows you to configure a specific rule based on a TCP or UDP connection to a specific port or range of ports. A predefined rule allows you to modify a predefined rule. A custom rule allows you to configure a program and specific ports; you can even scope it down to the incoming range of IP addresses you will allow. Any of these settings can also be configured after running the New Rule Wizard, as shown in Figure 18.22.

FIGURE 18.22   Windows Defender Firewall with Advanced Security inbound rules

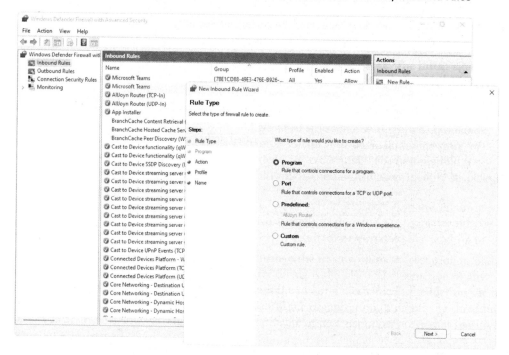

BitLocker

You have to be careful, because CompTIA sometimes refers to the utility as "bit-locker" or "Bitlocker," while it is officially known as *BitLocker*. This tool allows you to use drive encryption to protect files—including those needed for startup and login. This is available only with more complete editions of Windows 10/11 (Pro, Enterprise, Education, Pro for Workstations), Windows 8/8.1 (Pro and Enterprise), and Windows 7 (Enterprise and Ultimate).

Another requirement is the use of a *Trusted Platform Module (TPM)*. The TPM is a chip on the motherboard that safely stores the encryption key so that the key is not stored on the encrypted disk. BitLocker can mitigate the risk of data loss, because if the disk is separated from the computer, it is still encrypted and only the TPM with the encryption/decrypting key can decrypt the disk. This prevents out-of-band attacks on the hard drive, where it would be mounted and examined on a second system. BitLocker can also sense tampering. If it senses tampering, the recovery key must be reentered. The recovery key is either entered from a printout, loaded from a USB drive in which it was originally saved, or recovered from your

Microsoft account. An option of how the recovery key is stored is presented to you when you initially turn on BitLocker.

BitLocker to Go

You can also protect removable drives with *BitLocker to Go*. It provides the same encryption technology BitLocker uses to help prevent unauthorized access to the files stored on them. You can turn on BitLocker to Go by inserting a USB drive into the computer and opening the BitLocker Drive Encryption Control Panel applet, as shown in Figure 18.23. When a USB drive is inserted into a Windows computer that contains BitLocker to Go encryption, the operating system prompts you for the password to unlock the drive. This password is the one you used originally when you set up BitLocker to Go on the USB drive.

FIGURE 18.23   BitLocker Drive Encryption applet

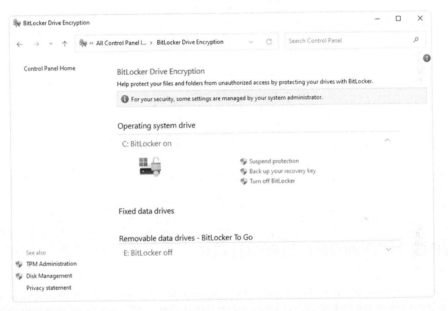

EFS

Encrypting File System (EFS), available in most editions of Windows, allows for the encryption/decryption of files stored in NTFS volumes. EFS uses certificates to encrypt the data, and the private certificate is stored in the user profile. When the first file is encrypted, the operating system automatically generates a key pair. If the computer were joined to an Active Directory domain and a *certificate authority (CA)* existed, the CA would create the key pair. You can encrypt a file or folder by right-clicking the object, selecting Properties, then Advanced, as shown in Figure 18.24.

All users can use EFS, whereas only administrators can turn on BitLocker. EFS does not require any special hardware, whereas BitLocker benefits from having the TPM. As an additional distinction, EFS can encrypt just one file, if so desired, whereas BitLocker encrypts the whole volume and whatever is stored on it. Finally, EFS can be used in conjunction with BitLocker to further increase security.

FIGURE 18.24   Encrypting a file in Windows 10

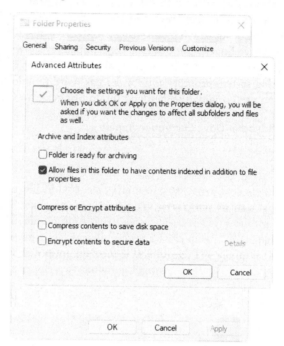

Web Browser Security

The web browser is arguably the most used application on the Window operating system. It is also your portal to the Internet and all the bad things that reside outside of your network. Therefore, it makes sense that there is an entire objective dedicated to web browser security for the CompTIA exam. In this section we will explore various browser security topics. We will primarily focus on the Microsoft Edge browser that comes preinstalled in the Windows 10/11 operating system. However, we will also reference Chrome, as it holds more than 60 percent of the market share worldwide (`https://gs.statcounter.com`) as of this writing.

Browser Download and Installation

Edge is the successor to Internet Explorer and comes preinstalled in the Microsoft Windows 10/11 operating system. Edge is also the default web browser in the Windows 10/11 operating system. Although Edge comes preinstalled in Windows 10/11, there are circumstances when you need to download the Edge web browser and install it in other operating systems. A common scenario is downloading and installing Edge for a server operating system in which it is not preinstalled, such as Windows Server 2019 or another operating system, such as macOS or Linux.

To download the Edge installer, you can often just search for "**Edge download.**" Depending on the search you use, the result can be in the top three results, but malware can also be disguised as the download. Therefore, you need to ensure your download is supplied by a trusted source. You should only download the browser from the vendor, in this case Microsoft. A simple way to check that the source is the vendor is to check the URL in the address bar, as shown in Figure 18.25. If the address bar shows the parent address of Microsoft.com, then you are obviously downloading Edge from a trusted source.

FIGURE 18.25   Downloading Microsoft Edge

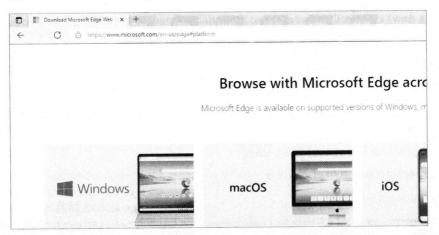

There are two main ways to download most browsers: online and offline. The online version will initially download a small install application (approximately 2 MB) that will download the rest of the installation and install the remaining download. The online version typically can be downloaded from the Microsoft Edge download page, as previously described. An offline installation can be downloaded from Microsoft as well and offers the benefit on not requiring any Internet connectivity. An offline version can be downloaded from www.microsoft.com/en-us/edge/business/download. By downloading the offline version from the Microsoft trusted source, you can be assured that future installations from this install are genuine.

When you store the installation for future installation, you should protect the installer from being tampered with. The best preventive measure is to create a Secure Hash Algorithm (SHA) hash of the executable and store it in another location. Before you run the offline installer, simply run the hashing against the install and check its signature. If the signature matches, then the installer has not been tampered with. If the signature does not match, the tampering could have occurred and it should be treated as being from an untrusted source.

In the following exercise, you will get to use the `Get-FileHash` cmdlet built into PowerShell. If you already have a file hash and it is not in the SHA256 format, you can use the argument of `-Algorithm MD5` or `-Algorithm SHA1` depending on the format you need to verify.

In Exercise 18.3 you will create a hash for a sample file with a PowerShell cmdlet. Then you will slightly modify the file and hash it again and compare the outcomes.

EXERCISE 18.3

Working with File Hashes

1. Open Notepad, type **example**, and save it to the desktop as **example.txt**.

2. Navigate to the desktop, hold the Shift key, right-click, and choose Open PowerShell Window Here.

3. Type `Get-FileHash .\example.txt`.

4. Examine the file hash and make a note of it.

5. Type `Get-FileHash .\example.txt`.

6. Compare the two file hashes; they should be identical.

7. Open the file `example.txt` and make the lowercase e in `example` an uppercase E; then save the file.

8. Navigate back to the PowerShell prompt.

9. Type `Get-FileHash .\example.txt`.

10. Examine the file hash.

11. Change the uppercase E back to a lowercase e, rerun the `Get-FileHash` cmdlet, and compare the two hashes.

Google Chrome and other third-party browsers require download and installation from the vendor sites, just like Microsoft Edge. These practices can and should be employed with any installation, not just web browsers. You should always download installations from a trusted source, then protect them with file hashing to detect tampering.

Extensions and Plug-ins

The best feature in any web browser is the ability to extend its functionality to accommodate your exact needs. By using extensions and plug-ins, you can functionally change the way the web browser works and the web pages it consequently renders. *Extensions* extend the functionality of the web browser that was not originally conceived when it was designed. *Plug-ins* change the way web pages are rendered on the web browser. Each web browser will call these something slightly different—for example, plug-ins might be called add-ons, as in the case of Firefox. Google Chrome refers to both extensions and plug-ins as extensions.

Microsoft refers to both extensions and plug-ins as add-ons. For the remainder of this section, we will refer to all plug-ins and extensions as add-ons.

Most modern web browsers have an ecosystem of add-ons. Google Chrome has an ecosystem called the Chrome Web Store that can be accessed via `https://chrome.google.com/webstore`. Microsoft has an ecosystem called Edge Add-ons that can be access via `https://microsoftedge.microsoft.com`, as shown in Figure 18.26. An add-on ecosystem is a place where the vendor trusts the publisher of an add-on. The add-on ecosystem in turn distributes the add-on for users, and supplies updates and synchronized installations across multiple devices. The add-on ecosystem should always be considered a trusted source for web browser add-ons.

FIGURE 18.26   Microsoft Edge add-ons

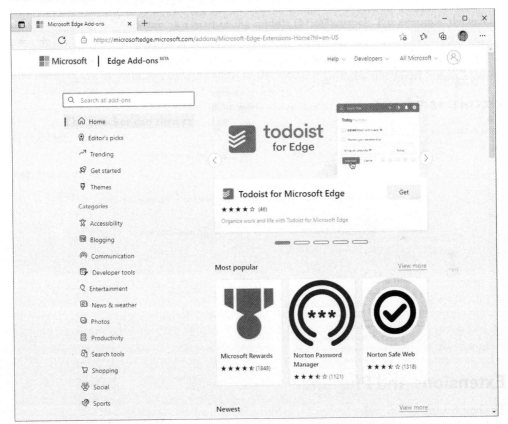

Most web browsers will also allow manual installation of add-ons. This is also called *sideloading*, since you are manually installing the file outside of the ecosystem. This is usually done and allowed by the web browser for development purposes. This type of installation can be found among untrusted applications that the ecosystem doesn't allow. The add-on might look reputable and the web page might explain that manual installation is required, since the developers don't agree to the terms of service (ToS) of the ecosystem. In any case, you should consider these add-ons untrusted and therefore avoid them.

Credentials Managers

As you sign up for websites, they require more complex, lengthier passwords. Sometimes your username might be your favorite nickname, sometimes the nickname might not be available, and sometimes the site might require an email in lieu of a nickname-style username. You should also employ the practice of single-purpose passwords and never reuse a password. So, if your credentials on site A are compromised, then your credentials on site B will not be vulnerable.

No longer can we keep track of all these usernames and passwords. Luckily password managers have come to our rescue. They are built into every operating system and most web browsers. Microsoft Edge and Internet Explorer both use the Microsoft Credential Manager, which was originally introduced with Windows XP. It functions as a password manager and is built into the operating system. In Figure 18.27, you can see some web credentials stored by Microsoft Edge. You can access the Credential Manager by navigating to the Start menu, typing **Control Panel** and selecting it in the results, then clicking Credential Manager.

FIGURE 18.27   Microsoft Credential Manager

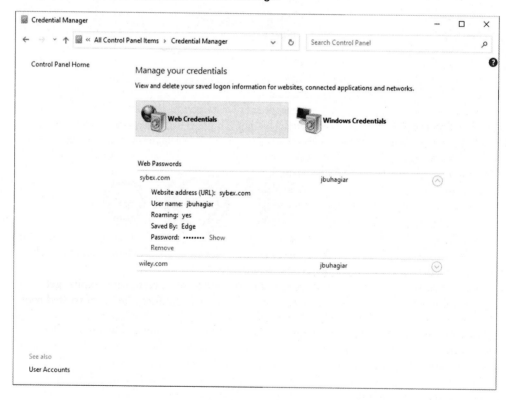

Credentials are stored by successfully logging into a website with a username and password combination. The web browser will ask if you want to save the credentials. Once the credentials are stored, when a website asks for a username and password matching the site in the Credential Manager, the associated credentials are offered to the user for logging into the site. If you are in the Credential Manager and you want to see the password, click Show and enter your credentials for the currently logged-on user. By entering your credentials for the currently logged-on user, you unlock the Credential Manager and it will let you see the password. You also have the option of deleting the credentials by clicking Remove.

Other web browsers, such as Google Chrome and Mozilla Firefox, have a credential manager built-in. These web browsers do not use the Microsoft Credential Manager. They synchronize their usernames and passwords between installations of the web browser on various devices. You can also download and install a third-party stand-alone credential manager. KeePass is one example, and there are several freely available on the Internet.

Secure Data Transfers

Securing data transfers to and from the web browser is critical for the security of day-to-day operations. We use our web browsers for accessing sensitive information at work, doing our personal banking, accessing social media, and the list goes on. So, securing data in transit is a primary concern to manage the risk of eavesdropping from threat agents. The Hypertext Transfer Protocol over Secure Sockets Layer (SSL), also known as HTTPS, is a method for securing web data communications. SSL is a cryptographic suite of protocols that use public key infrastructure (PKI) to provide secure data transfer.

A PKI is a system that provides the key pair of private and public keys, also known as certificates. The certificates are used to validate communication and encrypt communications between web browsers and web servers. The private key (certificate) from the key pair is installed on the web server. The public key (certificate) is available to anyone who wants to validate the data encrypted with the private key that is installed on the server. The web browser will automatically download the public key for the cryptography process.

Because there is a level of trust involved with the public/private key pair, your web browser must initially trust the publisher of the key pair. The publisher of the key pair is known as the certificate authority (CA). Every web browser comes with an initial list of trusted root certificate authorities, which is a beginning of trust for issuing CAs. The issuing CAs are the CAs that actually issue the key pairs. In most cases the web browser will use the operating system's list of trusted root CAs, as shown in Figure 18.28. However, some web browsers maintain a list of their own trusted root CAs.

Each certificate has an expiration date, and from time to time, certificates expire, get replaced, or in some cases get revoked for various reasons. Therefore, the list of trusted root certificate authorities must be updated now and then. The Microsoft Windows platform does this with routine Windows Updates, but browsers may update their own lists with updates of their own.

FIGURE 18.28   Trusted root CAs

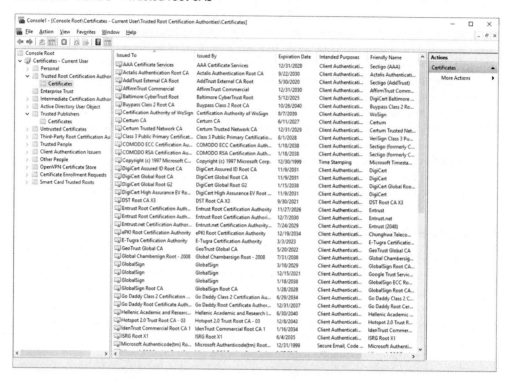

Although the S in HTTPS stands for secure, SSL is the protocol suite used for securing communications. The SSL suite is a suite of protocols that includes the current standard of Transport Layer Security (TLS) 1.3. TLS 1.3 is used for securing websites, as of this writing.

Settings

A lesson on web browser security wouldn't be complete without covering security settings for the web browser. In this final section, we will explore the various security settings you will find on modern-day web browsers. We discuss the most common topics that you will see on the CompTIA exam, but in no way is this a complete list of security settings. The web browser is the most used application for accessing data, and new settings are introduced all the time to combat threat agents.

Pop-up Blocker

Pop-up blockers are used to prevent both pop-ups and pop-unders from appearing when you visit a web page. While older browsers did not incorporate an option to block pop-ups, most current browsers, including the latest versions of Edge and Chrome, have that capability built in.

By default, the pop-up blocker is enabled on all sites globally. However, some sites, such as banking websites, might need to pop up a web page. When this happens, the address bar will notify you that an attempted pop-up occurred. You can then click and allow the specific site to use pop-ups. If you want to view a site's permission for pop-ups, click the lock at the left of the address bar and choose Permissions For This Site, as shown in Figure 18.29.

FIGURE 18.29   Permissions for a site

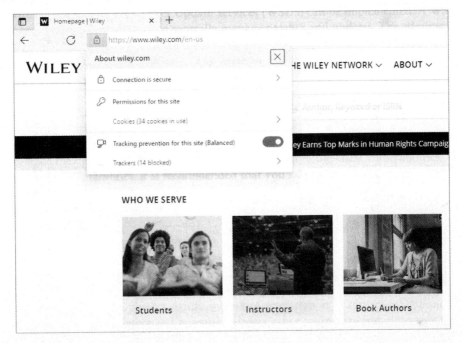

Clearing Browsing Data

Browsing data is a broad term used to describe any data stored while visiting websites. Data that may be considered browsing data is browsing history, download history, cookies, image and file caches, passwords, autofill form data, and site settings. These are just the top categories, so keep in mind that browsing data is a broad term. Browsing history is used by the browser to highlight links you've already visited. Download history allows you to historically see what has been downloaded. Cookies are used to save settings used by the web page, such as themes and login data, to name a few. Passwords are saved for convenience when logging into websites, the same as autofill form data. The site settings are adjustments you've made to the browser to optimally render the web page.

There are various reasons you may want to clear browsing data. The most compelling reason is data privacy. However, it is sometimes necessary to clear browsing data when you are trying to replicate a problem seen with the web browser.

You can clear the browsing data by clicking the three dots in the upper-right corner of the Edge web browser. Then click Settings, choose Privacy, then Search And Services, and scroll down to Clear Browsing Data Now and select Choose What To Clear. You will be presented with a dialog box similar to Figure 18.30. Options for the time range are Last Hour, Last 24 Hours, Last 7 Days, Last 4 Weeks, and All Time. You can also selectively delete the web browsing data that you desire.

FIGURE 18.30   Clearing browsing data

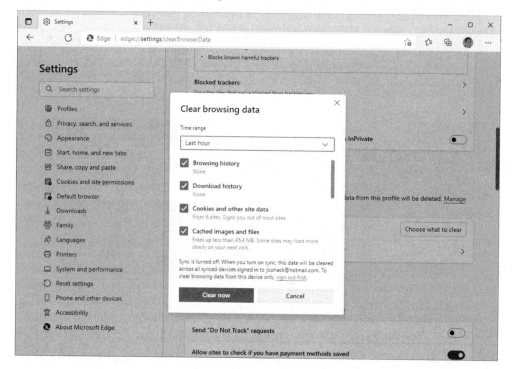

Clearing Cache

When a web browser renders a web page, the files retrieved are cached. This is done so that if you need them again you can quickly retrieve them from storage. This caching mechanism speeds up the web browser and reduces unneeded trips to the Internet. There are times when you need to clear your web browser cache, such as when developing a web page. You will want to retrieve the latest copy of the web page and its assets so that you can verify how it is rendered. The cache images and files are part of the web browsing data that can be cleared. The process is similar to the previously mentioned process for clearing browsing data, except only the cache images and files will be cleared.

Private-Browsing Mode

Private-browsing mode was created primarily to address data privacy while you are web browsing. The most compelling feature of private-browsing mode is that it does not store any web browsing data. Therefore, when you close private-browsing mode, all browsing data is destroyed.

The private-browsing mode on the Edge web browser is called InPrivate browsing; Chrome calls it Incognito mode. One the Edge web browser you can enter InPrivate mode by clicking the three dots in the upper right-hand corner of the window, then selecting New InPrivate Window. Another way is to press Ctrl+Shift+N to open the InPrivate window. In either case, the window explains the mode, as shown in Figure 18.31. The methods to open a private-browsing window on Chrome are identical, except that it is called Incognito mode.

FIGURE 18.31   InPrivate browsing

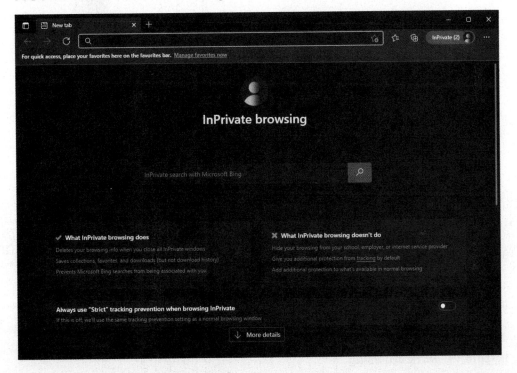

Browser Data Synchronization

On average, we access our web browsers on several devices. You may access them on your home computer, personal laptop, and mobile device, just to name a few. Therefore, the browsing data should follow you, no matter which device you are using. Modern web browsers fortunately support browser data synchronization, which allows you to share your data across many different devices. To sync your device, you just need to make sure that you have signed in and acknowledged that you want to sync browsing data. You can verify this by clicking on your account in the upper-right corner of the web browser. Your account details will be displayed, as shown in Figure 18.32. If you are not syncing, you can click the link Turn On Sync.

FIGURE 18.32   Account details

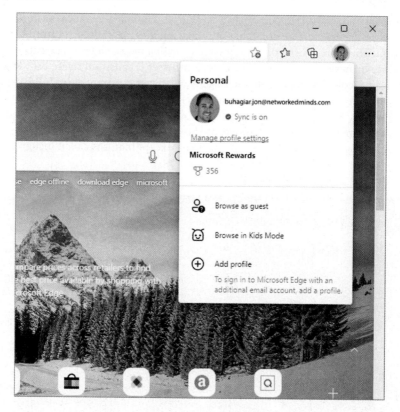

Use caution before syncing your personal web browsing data with your work computer's. You should keep a strict separation between work and leisure. During our leisure time we might search for something that could be misconstrued as mischievous to our coworkers. Therefore, you should maintain different accounts for work and play and never sync your personal account to a work web browser.

Leisure vs. work browsing

During leisure time you may be watching a movie in which someone picks a lock and curiosity may strike you to search "how to pick a lock." That search will now be in your autofill form data (browsing data). Imagine clicking a search box while giving a presentation in front of coworkers and "how to pick a lock" autofills. You know the context of your search, but do your audience and coworkers know? Think of all the other searches you perform in your leisure time.

Ad Blockers

The Internet was originally embraced as a mechanism to share information and bring people together. However, it was equally embraced by commerce as a mechanism to deliver products and services. One such service is the marketing of other services and products; we get these as marketing ads.

You can install an ad blocker add-on for most web browsers to stop a lot of the spammy ads you might receive on a web page. However, entire websites, such as many news sites, subsidize their income with marketing ads. If you don't have a subscription, then you have to allow marketing ads in order to enjoy their content; it seems a pretty fair trade. Most of these sites allows you have directions on how to exempt their site from the ad blocker.

You may wonder why you should install an ad blocker at all if every site allows you to exempt it. Ad blockers are extremely useful as an added layer of insulation from threat actors. Although most sites are legitimate and serve relevant ads, there are plenty of sites that serve malicious ads. An ad blocker helps to block all ads and allows you to judge whether the site is worthy of an exemption.

Securing a SOHO Network (Wireless)

CompTIA wants administrators of small office, home office (SOHO) networks to be able to secure those networks in ways that protect the data stored on them. This objective looks at the security protection that can be added to a wireless SOHO network, while the following section examines similar procedures for a wired network.

A wireless network is not and never will be secure. Use wireless only when absolutely necessary. If you must deploy a wireless network, here are some tips to make improvements to wireless security:

- Change the default SSID.
- Disable SSID broadcasts.
- Disable DHCP or use reservations.
- Use MAC filtering.
- Use IP filtering.
- Use the strongest security available on the wireless access point.
- Change the static security keys every two to four weeks.
- When new wireless protection schemes become available (and are reasonably priced), consider migrating to them.
- Limit the user accounts that can use wireless connectivity.
- Use a preauthentication system, such as RADIUS.
- Use remote access filters against client type, protocols used, time, date, user account, content, and so forth.

- Use IPsec tunnels over the wireless links.
- Turn down the signal strength to the minimum needed to support connectivity.
- Seriously consider removing wireless access from your LAN.

Changing Default Usernames and Passwords

In addition to those created with the installation of the operating system(s), default accounts are also often associated with hardware. Wireless access points, routers, and similar devices often include accounts for interacting with, and administering, those devices. You should always change the passwords associated with those devices and, where possible, change the usernames.

If there are accounts that are not needed, disable or delete them. Make certain that you use strong password policies and protect the passwords with the same security that you use for users and administrators. (In other words, don't write the router's password on an address label and stick it to the bottom of the router.)

Changing the SSID

All radio frequency (RF) signals can be easily intercepted. To intercept 802.11 wireless traffic, all you need is a PC with an appropriate 802.11 card installed. Many networks regularly broadcast their names (known as an *SSID broadcast*) to announce their presence. Simple software on the PC can capture the link traffic in the wireless AP and then process this data to decrypt account and password information.

You should change the SSID—whether or not you choose to disable its broadcast—to keep it from being a value that many outsiders come to know. If you use the same SSID for years, then the number of individuals who have left the company or otherwise learned of its value will only increase. Changing the variable adds one more level of security.

Guest Network Isolation

Most guests in your network never need to connect to the organization's servers and internal systems. When guests connect to your wireless network, it is usually just to get connectivity to the Internet. Therefore, a guest service set identifier (SSID) should be created that isolates guest traffic from production traffic. These guest network SSIDs are usually created by default on consumer wireless devices. On enterprise wireless LAN controllers, the guest network typically needs to be created.

Some considerations for the guest network are what is open to guests, how long they have access, how much bandwidth, the SSID name, and the list goes on, depending on your organization. Guest networks usually don't give totally unrestricted Internet access; certain sensitive ports like TCP port 25 (SMTP) are normally blocked. The length of time they have access is another concern. Generally, a guest is just that, a guest. So, 4 hours, 8 hours, or 24 hours of access seem responsible. You should give this a lot of thought because too short a time will create administrative overhead and too long a window of access allows for abuse of service. If you don't expect guest access to your wireless network, then it should be disabled.

Setting Encryption

It's important to remember that you should always enable encryption for any wireless network that you administer. Choose the strongest level of encryption you can work with. The following are some wireless protocols that you might encounter when securing wireless:

Open Open security is just that—open with no passphrase or authentication protocol. Open security was originally how all wireless access points (WAPs) were shipped to the customer. Open security still has its uses when used in conjunction with guest wireless access.

Wired Equivalent Privacy Shared passphrases are used with Wired Equivalent Privacy (WEP). WEP provides 64- or 128-bit encryption via the shared passphrase. The passphrase can easily be cracked with tools and is no longer used to secure wireless.

Wi-Fi Protected Access Wi-Fi Protected Access (WPA) was standardized by the Wi-Fi Alliance in 2003 in response to the vulnerabilities in Wired Equivalent Privacy (WEP). WPA uses 256-bit keys versus the 64-bit and 128-bit keys WEP used previously. WPA operates in two modes for security: preshared key (PSK), also called personal mode, and enterprise mode. PSK is the most common mode, because it can easily be implemented with a mutual agreed-upon passphrase. Enterprise mode, also called WPA-802.1X, requires a certificate server infrastructure. Enterprise mode uses the 802.1X protocol, RADIUS, and EAP; it is often used in corporate environments.

WPA introduced many improved security features over WEP, such as message integrity checks (MICs), which detect packets altered in transit. WPA also introduced Temporal Key Integrity Protocol (TKIP), which uses the RC4 algorithm for encryption. TKIP provides per-packet keying to prevent eavesdropping on wireless conversations. However, despite the improvements in security, WPA is considered exploitable and is no longer used for wireless security. A common exploit used against WPA is an attack on the helper protocol of Wi-Fi Protected Setup (WPS). WPS is used for consumer ease of setup and should be turned off for security purposes.

Temporal Key Integrity Protocol (TKIP) TKIP uses the RC4 encryption algorithm protocol as its cipher. TKIP seeds the RC4 algorithm with a key that is derived from the MAC address and initialization vector. TKIP also works in conjunction with message integrity checks (MICs) to check the integrity of messages received by the access point. The MIC protocol, also called Michael, is a 32-bit cyclic redundancy check (CRC). If two CRC MICs fail within 60 seconds, the access point requires TKIP to rekey the RC4 seed value.

Wi-Fi Protected Access 2 (WPA2) WPA2, also known as 802.11i, is the successor to WPA. WPA was deprecated in 2006 when WPA2 became a wireless security standard. Just like WPA, WPA2 operates in both personal mode (PSK) and enterprise mode.

WPA2 uses the Advanced Encryption Standard (AES) algorithm to protect data. AES is more secure than the RC4 algorithm used with TKIP. WPA2 replaced TKIP with Counter Cipher Mode (CCM) with Block Chaining Message Authentication Code Protocol (CCMP). However, TKIP can be configured as a fallback for WPA backward compatibility. Like WPA, WPA2 is exploitable if the WPS service is enabled. WPS should be turned off for security purposes.

Counter Cipher Mode with Block Chaining Message Authentication Code Protocol (CCMP)   Advanced Encryption Standard (AES) uses a 128-bit key to seed the AES encryption and a 128-bit cipher block. The prior ciphered text is used to encrypt the next block of text; this type of cipher is called code block chaining (CBC). CCMP-AES also uses a MIC to check the integrity of wireless data received. If the MIC fails, the CCMP-AES rekeys the session.

Wi-Fi Protected Access 3 (WPA3)   This is the successor to WPA2 and became part of the mandatory Wi-Fi Alliance certification process in July 2020. WPA3 introduced 192-bit cryptographic strength in WPA3-Enterprise mode. WPA3 still requires CCMP-128 as a minimum requirement for WPA3-Personal mode. The most significant improvement is the use of the Simultaneous Authentication of Equals (SAE) exchange that replaces the preshared key (PSK) exchange used with WPA and WPA2-Personal mode. SAE was originally introduced with IEEE 802.11s.

Disabling SSID Broadcast

One method of "protecting" the network that is often recommended is to turn off the SSID broadcast. The access point is still there and can still be accessed by those who know about it, but it prevents those who are looking at a list of available networks from finding it. This should be considered a very weak form of security because there are still ways, albeit a bit more complicated, to discover the presence of the access point besides the SSID broadcast.

Wireless MAC Filtering

Most APs offer the ability to turn on MAC filtering, but it is off by default. In the default state, any wireless client that knows of the existence of the AP can join the network. When MAC filtering is used, the administrator compiles a list of the MAC addresses associated with the users' computers and enters them. When a client attempts to connect, an additional check of the MAC address is performed. If the address appears on the list, the client is allowed to join; otherwise, they are forbidden from so doing. On a number of wireless devices, the term *network lock* is used in place of *MAC filtering*, but the two terms are synonymous.

NOTE   Adding port authentication to MAC filtering takes security for the network down to the switch port level and increases your security exponentially.

Frequencies

The frequencies used with wireless local area networks (WLANs) vary by standard. The two main frequencies used are 2.4 GHz and 5 GHz. The 2.4 GHz frequencies are governed by the industrial, scientific, and medical (ISM) radio bands. The 5 GHz frequencies are governed by the Unlicensed National Information Infrastructure (U-NII) radio band. It is important to note that in the future, 6 GHz frequencies will be used with the second release of 802.11ax called Wi-Fi 6E.

To learn more about Wi-Fi 6, visit www.wi-fi.org/discover-wi-fi/wi-fi-certified-6.

2.4 GHz

The 2.4 GHz spectrum is governed by the ISM radio band. The 802.11b/g/n standards operate on 2.4 GHz frequencies. The band consists of 14 channels 22 MHz wide. In North America only the first 11 of the channels can be used for wireless. In Japan all 14 channels can be used, and almost everywhere else in the world the first 13 channels can be used. Only 3 of the 14 channels are considered nonoverlapping, as seen in Figure 18.33. The channels of 1, 6, and 11 are considered prime channels for WLAN because they do not overlap with the other channels in the channel plan.

FIGURE 18.33   The 2.4 GHz channel plan

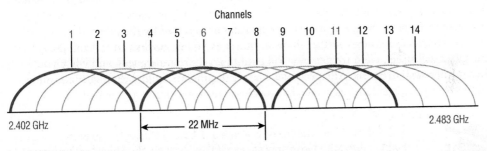

5 GHz

The 5 GHz frequencies are governed by the Unlicensed National Information Infrastructure (U-NII) radio band. The 802.11 a/n/ac/ax standards operate on the 5 GHz frequency spectrum.

   As seen in Figure 18.34, the band consists of 25 nonoverlapping channels. In North America the 802.11a standard can function on 12 channels consisting of 36, 40, 44, 48, 52, 56, 60, 64, 149, 153, 157, and 161. Each regulatory domain restricts the number of channels and specific channels for the region.

   In North America, the 802.11ac standard can use 25 of the nonoverlapping channels. In Europe and Japan, the channels are limited to the U-NII 1, U-NII 2, and U-NII 2E list of channels. The 802.11n standard only allowed the first 24 channels in North America, because channel 165 is in the ISM band.

FIGURE 18.34   The 5 GHz channel plan

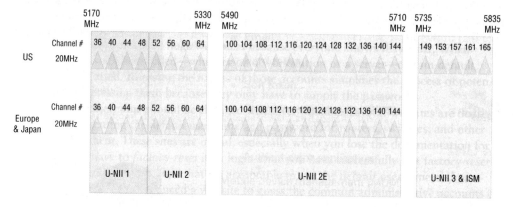

Speed, Coverage, and Security

Speeds will always be higher on 5 GHz wireless, such as the 802.11 a/n/ac standards. The 802.11ac standard can use a maximum of 25 nonoverlapping channels. However, the 802.11 b/g/n standards are restricted to the 2.4 GHz wireless band with three nonoverlapping channels. You should always be aware of the airspace around your AP. If you are overlapping on a channel, you should make every effort to change the channel on your AP. By changing the channel, you will effectively increase the speed of the connection for all your users within the cell.

Lower frequencies will go further in distance, yet as you go further away from the AP your speed will suffer. High frequencies will tend to go shorter distances, and when you move further away from the AP, speed will sharply decline. Using higher frequencies allows you to lower power and decrease the changes of signals traveling to a public place.

> The 802.11 a/n/ac standards operate at 5 GHz exclusively and 802.11 802.11 b/g/n standards operate at 2.4 GHz exclusively. The latest standard of 802.11ax operates at 5 GHz, 6 GHz, and 2.4 GHz. 802.11ax will steer the client to the best frequency band, also known as band steering. The concept remains the same: the higher the frequency, the shorter the distance; the lower the frequency, the longer the distance.

Radio Power Levels

Consider the radio power level, since the wireless access point has better transmitting power than most mobile devices. Let's use the analogy of two people standing in a field. One person is using a bullhorn to ask the other person the time, and the other person only has their voice to respond. Although they can hear the request, they will not be heard when they answer because they don't have a bullhorn. To fix this problem, the wireless access point should have its power level adjusted so that the client needs to be closer to receive data or associate with the SSID.

From a security standpoint, power levels should be adjusted so that they do not travel past the interior of the organization's building. If they do, then someone sitting in the parking lot or an adjoining building could attempt to infiltrate the wireless network. On the chance that the signal is actually traveling too far, some access points include power level controls that allow you to reduce the amount of output provided.

 A great source of information on RF power values and antennas can be found on the Cisco site:

www.cisco.com/c/en/us/support/docs/wireless-mobility/ wireless-lan-wlan/23231-powervalues-23231.html

Antenna and Access Point Placement

Antenna placement can be crucial in allowing clients to reach the access point. For security reasons, you do not want to overextend the reach of the network so that people can get on to the network from other locations (the parking lot, the building next door, and so on). Balancing security and access is a tricky thing to do.

There isn't any one universal solution to this issue—it depends on the environment in which the access point is placed. As a general rule, the greater the distance the signal must travel, the more it will attenuate; however, you can lose a signal quickly in a short space as well if the building materials reflect or absorb it. You should try to avoid placing access points near metal (which includes appliances) or near the ground. They should be placed in the center of the area to be served and high enough to get around most obstacles.

Wireless site surveys can be performed with specialized software that records the strength of the signal on a map you import of the coverage area. Wireless surveys should be performed in your environment before access point placement to help you determine the best placement. They should also be performed after access point placement for fine-tuning of the location and verification of uniform signal strength.

Assign Static IP Addresses

While DHCP can be a godsend, a SOHO network is small enough that you can get by without it issuing IP addresses to each host. The advantage to assigning the IP addresses statically is that you can make certain which host is associated with which IP address and then utilize filtering to limit network access to only those hosts.

WPS

WPS (Wi-Fi Protected Setup) can help to secure the network by requiring new machines to do something before they can join the network. This often requires the user to perform an action in order to complete the enrollment process: press a button on the router within a short time period, enter a PIN number, or bring the new device close-by (so that near-field communication can take place). It should be noted that during this brief period the wireless access point is susceptible to an attack. Anyone with the passcode or the ability to guess the passcode can gain access to your wireless network. Therefore, WPS is not used outside of SOHO networks and is not found in corporate networks.

Authentication

When setting up a wireless network, you are extending a wired network to a wireless network. Therefore, you must consider how users will authenticate to the wireless network. The following are various concepts of authentication that can be used with wireless and wired networks (though they are more commonly used with wireless networks):

Single-Factor Authentication   As previously mentioned, single-factor authentication is weak authentication. It is based on only one of the following factors:

- Something you know
- Something you have
- Something you are
- Somewhere you are
- Something you do

Setting up a wireless network based on a preshared key limits you to a single authentication factor, which everyone consequently shares. The use of a preshared key is a great example of an authentication factor of something that you know. Unfortunately, a preshared key can be compromised because people must share it, and you only have one preshared key per wireless SSID.

Multifactor Authentication   Using single-factor authentication alone allows you to be compromised much more quickly. Therefore, using multifactor authentication is desirable for a higher level of wireless security. *Multifactor authentication* requires two or more single-factor authentication methods to be used to secure the wireless network. A common multifactor authentication implementation is the use of the Extensible Authentication Protocol – Transport Layer Security (EAP-TLS) protocol. EAP-TLS requires that a certificate be installed in the operating system along with a matching password for the computer.

RADIUS   *Remote Authentication Dial-In User Service (RADIUS)* was originally proposed as an Internet Engineering Task Force (IETF) standard. It has become a widely adopted industry standard for authenticating users and computers for network systems.

RADIUS creates a common authentication system, which allows for centralized authentication and accounting.

The origins of RADIUS are from the original ISP dial-up days, as its acronym describes. Today, RADIUS is commonly used for authentication of virtual private networks (VPNs), wireless systems, and any network system that requires a common authentication system. RADIUS operates as a client-server protocol. The RADIUS server controls authentication, authorization, and accounting (AAA). The RADIUS client can be wireless access points, a VPN, or wired switches. The RADIUS client will communicate with the RADIUS server via UDP port 1812 for authentication and UDP port 1813 for accounting.

The RADIUS server can be installed on many different operating systems, such as Linux and Windows. Microsoft Windows Server includes an installable feature, called the Network Policy Server (NPS), that provides RADIUS functionality.

TACACS+   *Terminal Access Controller Access Control System Plus (TACACS+)* is a protocol developed by Cisco, from the original dated protocol of TACACS. Although it was developed by Cisco, it was released as an open standard. The protocol is mainly used for authentication of users on routers and switches to allow management access. It is also used to authenticate users connecting to wireless access points via a centralized database. The TACACS+ protocol is declining in popularity and has largely been replaced by RADIUS.

Kerberos   *Kerberos* is an open standard for authentication developed by the Massachusetts Institute of Technology (MIT). It is also the main authentication protocol used by Microsoft Active Directory. Kerberos can be used as the main authentication method for the Microsoft implementation of a RADIUS server, called the Network Policy Server (NPS). Kerberos can also be used with the 802.1X protocol for direct authentication with the Extensible Authentication Protocol (EAP).

Securing a SOHO Network (Wired)

Although a wired network can be more secure than a wireless one, there are still a number of procedures that you should follow to leave as little to chance as possible. Among them, change the default usernames and passwords to different values and secure the physical environment. You should also disable any ports that are not needed, assign static IP addresses, use IP filtering, and use MAC filtering to limit access to hosts that you recognize.

Changing Default Credentials

When installing a network device, the very first thing you must do is log in to the device. There is often a standardized default username and password for each vendor or each vendor's product line. Most devices make you change the default password upon login to the device.

Changing the default password to a complex password is a good start to hardening the device. However, changing the username will also ensure that a brute-force attack cannot be performed against the default username. There are many different websites dedicated to listing the default credentials for network devices, so it doesn't take tremendous skill to obtain the default username and password of a device.

The hosts in the network are no exception to changing default usernames and passwords. In Windows, the Guest account is automatically created with the intent that it is to be used when someone must access a system but lacks a user account on that system. Because the Guest account is so widely known to exist, you should not use this default account but instead create another account for the same purpose if you truly need one. The Guest account leaves a security risk at the workstation and should be disabled to deter anyone attempting to gain unauthorized access.

Change *every* username and password that you can so that they vary from their default settings.

Upgrading Firmware

When you purchase a network device, you don't know how long it's been sitting on the shelf of a warehouse. In that time, several exploits could have been created for vulnerabilities discovered. It is always recommended that a device's *firmware* be upgraded before the device is configured and put into service.

Most hardware vendors will allow downloading of current firmware. However, some vendors require that the device be covered under a maintenance contract before firmware can be downloaded. It is also best practice to read through a vendor's change log to understand the changes that have been made from version to version of firmware.

Filtering

IP filtering, also known as firewall rules, helps secure the internal network from an external network. The external network could be the Internet, or it could be a network less trusted than the internal network, such as a wireless network. In any case, firewall rules help harden the security of an organization because we can restrict activity from the external network to specific applications.

Firewall rules are normally configured with an implicit deny at the end of the rules set. This means that if an application has not explicitly been allowed, it will automatically (implicitly) be denied. The easy way to remember what *implicit* means is that it implies there is a deny, unless a user or application has been explicitly allowed. This implicit deny operation of a firewall is the default for firewall rule sets.

Although there is an implicit deny at the end of firewall rule sets, you may also need to explicitly deny an application or IP address. An explicit deny is required when another explicit rule follows, allowing access to a wide range of applications or IP addresses. For example, you may want to allow access to all the servers from the client networks. However, you should explicitly deny applications the clients shouldn't have access to, such as Remote Desktop Protocol (RDP) or Secure Shell (SSH).

Disabling Ports

Disable all protocols on the network device that are not required. As an example, many network multifunction printers are preconfigured with a multitude of protocols, such as TCP/IP, Bonjour, and Internet Printing Protocol (IPP), just to name a few. If you don't need them, remove the additional protocols, software, or services, or prevent them (disable them) from loading. Ports on a switch, router, or firewall not in use present an open door for an attacker to enter and should be disabled or disconnected.

 Many of the newer SOHO router solutions (and some of the personal firewall solutions on end-user workstations) close down the ICMP ports by default. Keep this in mind, because it can drive you nuts when you are trying to see if a brand-new station, server, or router is up and running.

MAC Address Filtering

Limiting access to the network by employing IP filtering is not the only way to restrict access. *MAC address filtering* can also be employed to restrict traffic to MAC addresses that are known and to filter out those that are not. Even in a home network, you can implement MAC filtering with most routers and typically have an option of choosing to allow only computers with MAC addresses that you list or deny only computers with MAC addresses that you list.

 If you don't know a workstation's MAC address, you can find it by using `ipconfig /ALL` (on Windows machines; it is listed as *physical address* and `ifconfig` on macOS and Linux machines).

Content Filter

Content filters are useful in networks to restrict users from viewing material that is non–work-related, questionable, or malware. Content filtering is usually dictated by organization policy and management. The content filter operates by watching content and requests from web browsers and other applications. The content filter functions in two ways: The first is content based; when images and text are requested from a website, the content filter can use heuristic rules to filter the content according to administrator-set policies. The second method is URL based, which is much more common since many websites now use SSL/TLS (encryption) and the traffic is encrypted. Content filters are typically purchased with a subscription that provides updates to the categories of material administrators block. Content filters can be hardware solutions or software solutions, although it is common to find them installed as software solutions.

Screened Subnet

The *screened subnet* is also known as the *demilitarized zone (DMZ)*. The DMZ gets its name from the segmentation that is created between the exterior and the interior of the network. This is similar to where borders of two opposing countries meet with military presence on both sides. Between the two sides there is a neutral segment called the DMZ. As it pertains to a network, hosts that serve Internet clients are placed in the DMZ subnet. As shown in Figure 18.35, a network segment called the DMZ sits between an external firewall and the internal firewall. The external firewall contains ACLs to prevent Internet hosts from accessing nonessential services on the server in the DMZ. The internal firewall restricts which hosts can talk to internal servers. A typical rule on the external firewall would allow HTTP access for a web server in the DMZ and would restrict all other ports. A typical rule on the internal firewall would allow only the web server to communicate with the SQL backend database in the internal network.

FIGURE 18.35   A typical DMZ with two firewalls

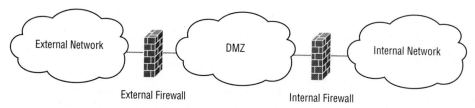

Although the concept of the DMZ is still used today in network design, a screened subnet can be created between any two segments in the network. The subnets don't necessarily need to be external and internal in relation to the network. Routers containing ACLs can be implemented in lieu of firewalls to filter traffic to the screened subnet, as shown in Figure 18.36. In the figure, a network called Network A is segmented from the screened subnet by a router with ACLs filtering traffic. On the other side of the screened subnet is another network called Network B, and it too is segmented by a router with ACLs filtering traffic. Each of these two networks have equal access to the hosts in the screened subnet. These two networks, Network A and Network B, could potentially be a wireless network and the wired network, respectively.

FIGURE 18.36   A typical screened subnet with two routers

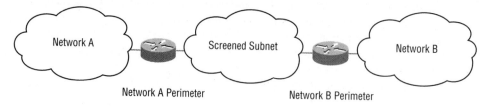

Some screened subnets are just another interface on a single firewall, as shown in Figure 18.37. In this example, the rules for both the Network A subnet and the Network B subnet would be on the same firewall. The benefit of a single firewall is centralized administration of firewall rules. Each interface is placed into a trust zone, and the firewall rules allow incoming and outgoing connections.

FIGURE 18.37 A typical screened subnet with one firewall

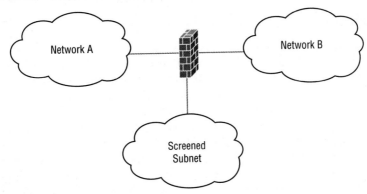

Port Forwarding/Mapping

On the router, the port configuration dictates what traffic is allowed to flow through. The router can be configured to enable individual port traffic in, out, or both; when you implement this type of configuration it is referred to as port forwarding. If a port is blocked (such as port 80 for HTTP or port 21 for FTP), the data will not be allowed through, and users will be affected. *Port forwarding* is also known as *port mapping*, and both are subsets of what a firewall does, and the amount of tweaking they require to get right is about the same.

Port forwarding is required when you are trying to share a network service with the Internet, such as a web server. It is commonly required when gaming, since some games require you to set up an impromptu game server. The players on the Internet will have to connect to the ports on your local machine behind your router, through port forwarding. There are websites dedicated to configuring these port forwarding settings manually; an example is https://portforward.com.

If you need to configure port forwarding frequently, then you might want to skip manually port forwarding altogether. The *Universal Plug and Play (UPnP)* is a network protocol that allows for automatic configuration of port forwarding. Most modern-day routers have the feature turned on, which is a security concern if you are not using any port forwarding. The UPnP protocol operates by the clients initiating a connection to the router and communicating the ports needing to be forwarded to the client. The router then opens the ports and forwards them to the client.

DHCP

Dynamic Host Configuration Protocol (DHCP) is responsible for automatic configuration of IPv4 IP addresses and subnet masks for hosts from a pool of IPv4 addresses. It is also responsible for configuration of such options as default gateways, DNS server addresses, and many other IP-based servers. It performs configuration of the host in a series of network broadcasts and unicasts.

Reservations

When a client requests an IP address from a DHCP server, the client's MAC address is transmitted in the DHCP packet. A rule on the DHCP server called a *DHCP reservation* can tie the client's MAC address to a particular IP address. When a reservation is created for a client, the client is guaranteed to obtain the same IP address every time for the DHCP process. When a reservation is created on the DHCP server, no other hosts can obtain the reservation IP address unless they have the MAC address that matches the reservation. This type of assignment is considered a dynamically static–assigned IP address.

Reservations can be very handy when static IP addresses are too troublesome to configure, such as network printers with poor configuration options. It's common to set a reservation on network printers and move on when faced with a finicky static IP address process. You can save an hour of busy work in the right situation. Reservations can also be useful when you need to make specific firewall rules for a client based on its IP address.

Static

Dynamic IP addressing is the standard in small-to-large networks when configuring client computers. Static IP addressing should only be used under certain circumstances for client computers, since it is not very scalable and a nightmare to keep track of manually. DHCP allows for central management of the IP address space versus static assignment of individual hosts (which is decentralized). Static IP addressing should only be used on internal network resources such as routers, network printers, and servers.

Static IP addressing can be useful for wide area network (WAN) connections, also known as your connection to the Internet. If a server is operating at the location, a static IP address is necessary for clients to be able to connect. Name resolution to the IP address is the biggest driver for static IP addressing. There are work-arounds, such as dynamic DNS services, but the best solution is to purchase a static IP address from the Internet provider.

Physical Security

Just as you would not park your car in a public garage and leave its doors wide open with the key in the ignition, you should educate users to not leave a workstation that they are logged into when they attend meetings, go to lunch, and so forth. They should log out of the workstation or lock it. "Lock when you leave" should be a mantra they become familiar with. A password (usually the same as their user password) should be required to resume working at the workstation.

You can also lock a workstation by using an operating system that provides filesystem security. Microsoft's earliest filesystem was referred to as File Allocation Table (FAT). FAT was designed for relatively small disk drives. It was upgraded first to FAT-16 and finally to FAT-32. FAT-32 (also written as FAT32) allows large disk systems to be used on Windows systems.

FAT allows only two types of protection: share-level and user-level access privileges. If a user has write or change access to a drive or directory, they have access to any file in that directory. This is very unsecure in an Internet environment.

With NTFS, files, directories, and volumes can each have their own security. NTFS's security is flexible and built in. Not only does NTFS track security in access control lists (ACLs), which can hold permissions for local users and groups, but each entry in the ACL can also specify which type of access is given. This allows a great deal of flexibility in setting up a network. It's advisable to use BitLocker to encrypt the device's storage whenever possible. In addition, special file-encryption programs can be used to encrypt data while it is stored on removable hard disk.

Microsoft strongly recommends that all network shares be established using NTFS. While NTFS security is important, however, it doesn't matter at all which filesystem you are using if you log into your workstation and then leave, allowing anyone to sit at your desk and use your account. If the computer is in your home office and it's unlocked, you may come back to find your cat is lying on the Delete key. So, the rule of thumb is lock your operating system when you leave the keyboard.

Last, don't overlook the obvious need for physical security. Adding a cable to lock a laptop to a desk prevents someone from picking it up and walking away with a copy of your customer database. Every laptop case we are aware of includes a built-in security slot in which a cable lock can be added to prevent it from easily being carried off the premises. If this is in your home office, it might deter a burglar from walking away with sensitive information.

When it comes to desktop models, adding a lock to the back cover can prevent an intruder with physical access from grabbing the hard drive or damaging the internal components. You should also physically secure network devices, such as routers, access points, and the like. Place them in locked cabinets, if possible—if they are not physically secured, the opportunity exists for an unauthorized person to steal them or manipulate them to connect to the network.

Mobile Device Security

Apple computers have a pretty decent reputation in the industry for being somewhat resistant to malware. Whether or not this is because of the relatively small installed base or the ease with which hackers penetrate "other" operating systems, this characteristic carries over to Apple's mobile devices. In fact, hackers don't seem to be as interested in attacking the legions of mobile devices as much as they have gone after the Windows operating systems that drive the vast majority of laptops, desktops, and servers in the world. Nevertheless, attacks occur. Coupled with how easy mobile devices are to misplace or steal, it behooves users to have proactive monitoring and contingency plans in place.

The following sections detail the built-in security utilities that are common in today's mobile devices. Furthermore, for threats not covered by the software with which the devices ship, the protection available from third-party utilities is worth discussing.

Screen Locks

Apple and Android mobile devices include a requisite locking mechanism, which is off by default. The user on the go is encouraged to enable a lock. If your device acts primarily as a home computing device and rarely goes with you out the door, there is very little reason to set a lock. However, knowing how to do so is important. The following are types of locks that you can implement to secure your device:

Fingerprint Lock   The *fingerprint lock* is a biometric-type lock that uses your fingerprint to unlock the device. The fingerprint lock is the most secure biometric method for a device. The technology works by placing your finger on a touchpad sensor on the device. On Apple devices, the fingerprint recognition is called *Touch ID*. The technology works exceptionally well, except when your fingers are wet or extremely dirty. When your fingers are wet or extremely dirty, they make different prints from those you originally trained the device to recognize.

Face Lock   The *face lock* is a biometric-type lock that allows you to use your face to unlock your device. There are a high number of false positives that makes the face lock less secure than the fingerprint lock. This means that presumably someone that looks like you could unlock your phone. Almost all mobile devices have a front-facing camera, allowing you to instantly know that you've unlocked the phone seamlessly by looking at your phone. On Apple devices, this technology is called *Face ID*.

Pattern Lock   The *pattern lock* is a type of passcode that allows you to unlock your device. Swipe lock works by displaying nine dots in a matrix of 3 × 3. You then swipe with your finger with the registered pattern to unlock the phone. The swipe lock is the least secure of any locking methods. A grease trail from your fingers can allow someone to derive the swipe pattern.

PIN Lock   The *PIN lock* is by far the most common way to unlock devices. It is typically a 4- or 6 digit-numeric passcode. However, it can also be alphanumeric, depending on the device. Passcode locks suffer from the same problems that passwords are prone to: people can shoulder surf or learn your passcode over time.

Swipe Lock   The *swipe lock* is not really a lock at all. It allows you to unlock the phone easily by swiping on the screen. This lock method is to really prevent pocket dialing of someone by accident.

Exercise 18.4 outlines the steps for creating a code for your iPhone.

Setting the Passcode Lock on an iPhone

1. Tap Settings.

2. Depending on the iOS version, select either Face ID & Passcode or Touch ID & Passcode.

3. Tap Turn Passcode On.

4. Enter a six-digit passcode.

   If you want to use a four-digit passcode, tap Passcode Options to switch to a four-digit numeric code or a custom alphanumeric passcode.

5. Enter the passcode a second time to confirm. Doing so sets the passcode.

   Optionally, you can set the amount of time that must pass while the phone is asleep before the passcode will be required and whether the Erase Data feature should be enabled. Setting the Required Passcode field to Immediately requires entering the passcode each time the device wakes up.

The same general concept for Android phones is illustrated in Exercise 18.5.

Setting the Passcode Lock on an Android Phone

Depending on the Android version, these steps might differ.

1. Swipe up on the home screen.

2. Tap the Settings app.

3. Select Lock Screen and/or Security from the Settings menu.

4. Tap Screen Lock Type on the Lock Screen And Security menu.

5. Select Pattern from the Phone Security list.

6. Use your finger to draw a continuous pattern of four or more dots, and then tap the Continue button.

7. Repeat the same pattern, and then tap the Confirm button.

8. Optionally, tap Secure Lock Settings to lock the phone automatically and adjust the number of wrong swipes before a factory reset occurs.

Remote Wipes and Locator Applications

Should your work or personal mobile device disappear or fall into the wrong hands, it's always nice to have a backup plan to ensure that no company secrets or personal identifiers get misused by anyone who would use the information with ill will. Apple supplies a free app called *Find My iPhone* that, together with iCloud, allows multiple mobile devices and Macs to be located if powered on and connected to the Internet (via cellular, Wi-Fi, Ethernet, and so on). The app allows the device to be controlled remotely to lock it, play a sound (even if audio is off), display a message, or wipe it clean.

Within a newer iPhone's Settings screen, you can find an iCloud settings page and select the Find My iPhone switch. If this switch is off, the Find My iPhone app and iCloud web page will be unable to find your device.

On the login screen for the iPhone app, you must enter the iCloud account information that includes the device you are attempting to control remotely.

Note that when you change the password for your Apple ID, it affects your iCloud account but does not transfer automatically within your device. Always remember to update your iCloud account information on each device when you update the associated Apple ID.

Although iCloud has its own settings page, you can also create an iCloud account—or change the settings—by choosing Settings ⟩ Passwords And Accounts.

The iCloud website's login page (www.icloud.com) calls for the same credentials as the app. You are signing in with HTTPS, so your username and password are not traversing the Internet in the clear. With the switch in the iCloud settings screen set to Off for all devices on your account, when you sign in to the app with your iCloud account credentials, you are met with a disabling switch message.

You do not need to go to the website if you have another device with the Find My iPhone app or can borrow one from someone else. The device forgets your credentials when you log out, so the owner will not be able to control your device the next time they use the app.

After logging into the iCloud website, you can click the icon that matches the icon for the Find My iPhone app in iOS. Assuming that you've made it into the app on another device and your Find My iPhone feature is enabled on your missing device, the Info screen tells you that your device has been found and gives you options for the next step you take.

Tapping the Location button in the upper left shows you a map of where your device is currently located. You have three options for how to view the location: a two-dimensional map, a satellite map, and a hybrid version, where the two-dimensional street-name information is laid over the satellite view.

If you tap the Play Sound or Send Message button on the Info screen, instead of the Location button, the screen that pops up allows you to display a message remotely. You might consider first displaying a message without the sound, which is at maximum volume. Ask in the message to be called at another number. If you hear from someone in possession of your device, the hunt is over. Otherwise, send another message with the tone to get the attention of the nearest person. If you are at the reported location when you generate the sound, it can help you home in on the device.

If you do decide to use the remote-lock feature of the app, you'll have the opportunity to reconsider before locking it. You should have no issue with locking the device. Doing so does not prevent you from using the app further; it simply makes sure that the device is harder to break into.

Should you decide to take the sobering step of destroying the contents of the device remotely, you get a solemn notice allowing you the opportunity to reassess the situation before proceeding. Sometimes there's just no other option.

For Android devices, Google's *Find My Device* app performs many of the same functions as Apple's Find My iPhone app, including playing your ring tone for 5 minutes. When you search Google's web page for "find my device," a map will display the location of your device. Clicking the location will reveal the SSID the phone is connected to, the phone's battery level, and when the phone was last in use at that location. You can then choose to play a sound (ring tone), secure the device, or erase the device. Securing the device will lock the phone and sign you out of your Google account. This option can also allow you to display a message on the lock screen. Erasing the device is the last step when you know it cannot be recovered and you want to be assured your data is removed.

Uh-Oh. Where's My Phone?

After a recent visit to a car dealership, a prospective new car owner named Jimmy departed without his iPhone—at least, that's where Find My iPhone said it was. Luckily, Jimmy had the foresight to set up his free iCloud account and log that phone into it. Upon his return to the dealership, Jimmy was temporarily disheartened to find that no one had seen his phone.

It occurred to him that he had laid his phone down on the counter in the men's room as he was washing his hands. He didn't recall having it after that point. A cursory look around the facilities turned up nothing. The app was not accurate enough to tell him where exactly the phone was at the time it was located on the Find My iPhone website, which he checked from home. However, the app did indicate that the iPhone was still somewhere at the dealership.

Jimmy noticed that the salesperson assisting him had an iPhone, so he asked her if she also used the Find My iPhone app. She did. He asked if he could borrow her phone for a brief instant. She obliged, and Jimmy entered his iCloud credentials into the salesperson's app and then entered the message, "I'm in the showroom." He left the Play Sound switch on and tapped the Send button.

In less than five minutes, a manager who had been back at the loading dock came to the showroom with a story. He said he heard a disturbing noise coming from the dumpster, which was quite full and scheduled to be picked up the next morning. The trash bag containing Jimmy's phone was conveniently right at the top of the heap and easily retrieved by the manager.

Jimmy recalled being in a bit of a fluster as he left the men's room. He was about to finalize the terms of the deal he had been working on for more than an hour. In his haste to get back to the table, apparently his phone slipped from his hand as he was disposing of the paper towels he used to dry his hands. So, the cliché "All's well that ends well" has a shred of truth. Jimmy owed this happy ending to the features of the Find My iPhone app and tells his story to anyone who will listen.

Remote Backup

Apple iOS devices automatically back themselves up either to a computer running iTunes that they sync with or to the iCloud account associated with the device. When a mobile device is connected to a computer containing iTunes, the process of backup is called *synchronization*. iCloud Backup is the most common method of backing up Apple iOS devices, since no computer is necessary. iCloud does require a Wi-Fi connection or cell service. To enable iCloud Backup, navigate to Settings, then tap your name, tap iCloud, and finally tap iCloud Backup. You can create an immediate backup by tapping Back Up Now, or you can wait until the next backup interval.

The Android operating system will automatically synchronize the device to Google Drive. Android phones require a Google account during setup. This account is the account that will synchronize to Google Drive. Google Drive is Google's cloud-based storage product. The backup service will back up Wi-Fi passwords, phone logs, app settings, contacts, messages, pictures, and other related files. A multitude of third-party backup apps can be downloaded from Google's Play Store. Each third-party app offers different features over and above the built-in backup service functionality, such as the capability to remove the bloatware apps that come with the phone.

Both Apple iCloud and Google Drive services allot you a certain amount of storage when you sign up for free. The limited cloud storage used for backups of your settings and data is adequate for most people. However, you can always purchase more storage from Apple and Google.

Failed Login Attempts Restrictions

After you've set a screen lock, an optional step is to set the device to wipe, or factory reset, after a number of failed attempts. This option will wipe local data on the device if incorrect passcodes are entered 10 times in a row, or perform a factory reset depending on the device. While this is recommended for users with devices that contain sensitive data and that are frequently taken into public venues or placed in compromising positions, the casual user should not turn this feature on unless they can be sure that a recent backup will always be available in iTunes or Google.

Imagine a user's child or a mischievous, yet harmless, friend poking away at passcodes until the device informs them that it is being wiped clean; it's not for everyone. Restoring from a backup is easy enough, but will a recent backup be available when disaster strikes? Apple performs a backup to the iCloud or the computer running iTunes that the iOS device syncs with.

Apple imposes cooling-off timeout periods of increasing duration, even if the Erase Data feature is disabled and you or someone else repeatedly enters the wrong code over multiple lockouts. The final penalty with the Erase Data feature disabled is that you cannot unlock the device until it is connected to the computer with which it was last synced.

When a passcode is set, Android devices have a similar approach to failed login attempts as their Apple counterparts. A factory reset will occur after 10 failed attempts.

The difference is that if waiting the timeout period won't help because you've forgotten the pattern or code, this device can tie your access back to the Google account you used when setting it up. This is also the account where you receive purchase notifications from Google Play, and it does not have to be a Gmail account (one of the benefits of the open-source nature of Android). If you remember how to log into that account, you can still get into your phone. Or at least you can investigate the credentials to that account on a standard computer and return to the device to enter those credentials.

Viruses and Malware on Mobile Devices

For the most part, mobile devices have been left alone with viruses and malware, as compared with the Windows platform. However, this is not a reason to let your guard down and not worry about viruses and malware on mobile devices. Mobile devices can contract a virus and malware through the installation of a malicious app.

Most malware installed on mobile devices will spam your device with ads from the Internet. However, some malware can expose your personal information and even subject your device to the control of a malicious individual. Viruses, on the other hand, will use your email application to send copies of itself or turn your device into a zombie.

The extent of the damage from malware or a virus is hard to estimate, but one thing is for sure: protection goes a long way. Antivirus and antimalware software should be installed on your mobile device to thwart malicious attempts to infiltrate your device. All the leading vendors, such as AVG, Norton, and Avast (just to name a few), have offerings of antivirus and antimalware. Most installations of these apps are free, and other services or features can be purchased within the apps.

Trusted Sources vs. Untrusted Sources

You can limit your exposure to malicious apps by only installing apps from trusted sources, such as the Apple's App Store or Google Play. In most cases, the mobile operating system must specifically be configured to accept installations from untrusted sources. So, it's not likely that you will mistakenly install an app from an untrusted source. Examples of untrusted sources include manual installs of Android APK (Android Package Kit) or untrusted Apple IPA (iOS App Store Package) files. These files can be distributed outside of the Google Play and Apple's App Store ecosystems. When files are distributed outside of these ecosystems, consider them untrusted.

Operating System Updates

It's easy to forget that these tiny yet powerful mobile devices we've been talking about are running operating systems that play the same role as the operating systems of their larger siblings. As such, users must be careful not to let the operating systems go too long without updates. Occasionally, mobile devices will notify the user of an important update to the operating system. Too often, however, these notifications never come. Therefore, users should develop the habit of checking for updates on a regular basis.

Not keeping up with software updates creates an environment of known weaknesses and unfixed bugs. Mobile devices operate on a very tight tolerance of hardware and software performance. Not maintaining the device for performance at the top of its game will tend to have more pronounced repercussions than those seen in larger systems.

For the iPhone, iPod Touch, and iPad, you can check for the most important level of updates by tapping Settings ➢ General ➢ Software Update. For the Android operating system, there are multiple updates that can be checked for manually. All of them are accessible by following Menu ➢ Settings ➢ System Updates.

Full-Device Encryption

As discussed previously, BitLocker and BitLocker to Go greatly enhance security by encrypting the data on drives (installed and removable, respectively) and helping to secure it from prying eyes. At a minimum, the same level of protection that you would apply to a desktop machine should be applied to a mobile device, because it can contain confidential and personally identifiable information (PII), which could cause great harm in the wrong hands.

Full-device encryption should be done on laptops and mobile devices, and you should back up regularly to be able to access a version of your files should something happen to the device itself. When full-device encryption is turned on, both the device and the external storage (SD card) are encrypted. The only way to view the information on the SD card is from the encrypting mobile device.

Android devices do not automatically turn on device encryption and encrypt files upon setting a passcode on the device, like iOS devices do.

Multifactor Authentication

Multifactor authentication, mentioned previously in this chapter, involves using more than one item (factor) to authenticate. An example of this would be configuring a BitLocker to Go–encrypted flash drive so that when it is inserted into your laptop, a password and smartcard value must be given before the data is decrypted and available.

Authenticator Applications

An authenticator app works with mobile devices to generate security codes that can keep accounts secure by requiring two-factor authentication (2FA). Once this is set up, your account will require a code from the app in addition to your account password. Authenticator applications are available for download with Apple, Android, and other mobile device operating systems, as well as desktop operating systems. An account is usually added to the authenticator application by entering a secret key or scanning a QR barcode; this creates the account in the authenticator application. Several different authenticator apps can be downloaded; they vary depending on the mobile operating system.

Firewalls

Mobile devices have the same inherent vulnerabilities as desktop operating systems. However, mobile devices are generally not targeted the same as desktop operating systems. When a mobile device starts up, it is configured with an IP address via either the internal cellular radio or the Wi-Fi radio, so the device can be exploited via the network. Therefore, a firewall should be installed and turned on to protect the mobile device.

However, inbound communication is not the only aspect of security you need to be concerned about on mobile devices. Outbound communication also is a primary concern. A mobile device firewall app will allow you to monitor both the inbound and outbound communications on your mobile device. Several third-party firewall apps (both free and for purchase) can be downloaded from either Apple's App Store or Google Play.

Policies and Procedures

With the explosive growth of mobile devices in the workplace, there are many different policies and procedures that may be required for your organization to minimize data loss. This section focuses on the policies and procedures specific to mobile devices that you may have in your organization.

As employees are hired in your organization, a certain amount of initial interaction with the information technology (IT) is required. This interaction, called the *onboarding procedure*, is often coordinated with the Human Resources (HR) department. During the onboarding procedure, the IT representative will help the user log in for the first time and set their password. The password policy is often the first policy discussed with the user. Other policies—such as bring your own device (BYOD), acceptable use policy (AUP), nondisclosure agreement (NDA), and information assurance—should also be discussed during the onboarding procedure. The use of email and file storage and policies should also be covered with the user during the onboarding process. Each organization will have a different set of criteria that make up the onboarding procedures.

Eventually, employees will leave your organization. The *offboarding procedure* ensures that information access is terminated when the employment of the user is terminated. The offboarding procedure will be initiated by the HR department and should be immediately performed by the IT department. This process can be automated via the organization's employee-management system. This procedure can also be performed manually if the employee-management system is not automated. However, the procedure must be performed promptly, since the access to the company's information systems is the responsibility of the IT department.

During the offboarding procedure, email access is removed via the *mobile device management (MDM)* software, the user account is disabled, and IT should make sure that the user is not connected to the IT systems remotely. The offboarding procedure may also specify that the user assume ownership of the terminated employee's voicemail, email, and files.

BYOD vs. Corporate-Owned

The traditional workforce is becoming a mobile workforce, with employees working from home, on the go, and in the office. These employees use laptops, tablets, and smartphones to connect their companies' cloud resources. Organizations have embraced BYOD initiatives as a strategy to alleviate the capital expense of equipment by allowing employees to use devices they already own.

Because employees are supplying their own devices, a formal document called the *BYOD policy* should be drafted. The BYOD policy defines a set of minimum requirements for the devices, such as size and type, operating system, connectivity, antivirus, patches, and many other requirements the organization will deem necessary, as well as the level of service your IT department will support for personally owned equipment.

Many organizations use MDM software, which helps enforce the requirements for the BYOD policy. MDM software helps organizations protect their data on devices that are personally owned by the employees. When employees are terminated or a device is lost, the MDM software allows a secure remote wipe of the company's data on the device. The MDM software can also set policies requiring passwords on the device. All of these requirements should be defined in the organization's BYOD policy.

Corporate-owned mobile devices are also of paramount concern when it comes to security. The equipment is mobile, so these devices sometimes travel and can disappear completely. Luckily, MDM software allows you to not only control the data on these devices, but in many instances even track it via a built-in Global Positioning System (GPS) sensor (if the device supports this functionality). When MDM software is implemented in the capacity of tracing assets, consideration must be given to privacy. Although it may be acceptable to track a corporate-owned mobile device, the end user must be made aware of this policy.

Profile Security Requirements

When you implement an MDM solution to manage mobile devices, part of your implementation is the creation of profile security requirements for the mobile devices you will manage. The profile security requirements allow the management of the mobile devices in a uniform fashion. As an administrator, you can choose settings for mobile devices under your purview and enforce profile security requirements in various ways. In a given scenario, you may want to enforce settings for the entire organization, whereas in other scenarios you may want to differ the settings based on organizational unit, role, or other group type. Among the settings you may want to enforce are those requiring the encryption of drives and the use of complex passwords.

IoT Considerations

The *Internet of Things (IoT)* is an exploding industry. You can now control everything from your lights to your thermostat with a mobile device or computer. The downside to connecting things to the Internet is that they must be patched so that they are not exploitable. Hardware vendors often wire off-the-shelf components into the hardware, and these off-the-shelf components never get frequent updates. So, this is a major security consideration for an organization. Ease of use versus security is the balance beam that you walk when owning IoT devices.

In recent years, attackers have harvested IoT devices for distributed denial-of-service (DDoS) attacks. The Mirai botnet is one such popular botnet that can crush an organization's bandwidth. This can happen when IoT devices in your network are used in a DDoS or are attacked by the botnet. To mitigate inadvertently being used in a DDoS, you can place the IoT devices on an isolated network and police their outbound bandwidth.

Unfortunately, there is not much you can do with IoT devices to prevent being attacked. If an attacker wants to attack your organization with IoT devices, firewalls, ISP controls, and third-party services like Cloudflare can help mitigate these attacks. This is not really an IoT consideration because any botnet can attack you and the mitigations are the same as if you were attacked by an IoT botnet.

Summary

In this chapter, you learned some best practices related to operating system security. We then focused on Windows operating system security settings, such as sensitive accounts and filesystem permissions. We concluded with mobile device security for both Apple devices and Google Android. The mobile device operating systems are changing rapidly, as both consumer and enterprise needs change. However, the objectives on the A+ 220–1102 exam are general enough that a mastery of them will enable you to secure a mobile device today and into the future.

Security, as you've already guessed, is a large part of the CompTIA A+ certification. CompTIA expects everyone who is A+ certified to understand security-related best practices and be able to secure both Windows operating systems and mobile devices.

Exam Essentials

Understand Windows operating system security concepts. You should be able to compare and contrast Microsoft Windows operating system security settings. This should include knowing the various accounts that are created by default and why you need to disable or rename these accounts. You should also have an in-depth understanding of NTFS permissions and share permissions, and their interaction, to form the effective permissions the user has when accessing a share remotely. In addition, you should have a good understanding of authentication and the options to encrypt both the operating system and removable drives.

Know how to compare wireless security protocols and authentication methods. Wireless networks can be encrypted through WEP, WPA, WPA2, and WPA3 technologies. Wireless controllers use service-set identifiers (SSIDs)—32-character, case-sensitive strings—that must be configured in the network cards to allow communications. However, using ID string configurations doesn't necessarily prevent wireless networks from being monitored, and there are vulnerabilities specific to wireless devices.

Understand the basics of antenna placement and radio power levels. Antenna placement can be crucial in allowing clients to reach an access point. Place access points near the center of the area to be served and high enough to get around most obstacles. Know that power level controls allow you to reduce the amount of output provided.

Know how to configure security on SOHO wireless and wired networks in various scenarios. Disable all unneeded protocols/ports. If you don't need them, remove them or prevent them from loading. Ports not in use present an open door for an attacker to enter. MAC filtering allows you to limit access to a network to MAC addresses that are known and filter out (deny access to) those that are not.

Understand mobile device security concepts. You should understand how screen locks operate. Explain why we need remote wipe in the event of a device missing or lost. Understand the risks of viruses and malware on mobile devices, as well as measures that can be taken to mitigate these risks. In addition, you should have a good understanding of the importance of full-device encryption, authentication applications, firewalls, and policies for mobile devices.

Review Questions

The answers to the chapter review questions can be found in Appendix A.

1. Which policy would you create to define the minimum specification if an employee wanted to use their own device for email?

   A. MDM

   B. AUP

   C. BYOD

   D. NDA

2. Which term refers to copying data between a mobile device and a computer system in order to mirror such things as contacts, programs, pictures, and music?

   A. Calibration

   B. Remote wipe

   C. Pairing

   D. Synchronization

3. You want to follow the rules of good security administration as set by CompTIA and vendors. To do so, which account should be disabled on most Windows operating systems for security reasons?

   A. Guest

   B. Print Operators

   C. Power Users

   D. Userone

4. What kind of mobile app is being used when the owner's phone displays a message on the screen and emits an extremely loud tone?

   A. Failed login restriction

   B. Antivirus

   C. Locator

   D. Remote wipe

5. As a best practice, after a set period of inactivity on a Windows workstation, what should happen?

   A. The system should shut down.

   B. The system should restart.

   C. A password-enabled screensaver should automatically start.

   D. The system should log out the user.

6. A new app developed for the Android platform has which extension?

    A. `.sdk`

    B. `.apk`

    C. `.ipa`

    D. `.exe`

7. Which of the following has the goal of allowing a username/password combination to be entered once and then allowing claims to be used for consecutive logins? (Choose the best answer.)

    A. Tokens

    B. Kerberos

    C. Single sign-on

    D. Multifactor authentication

8. Which of these is a password manager?

    A. Edge

    B. Credential Manager

    C. Internet Explorer 11

    D. Active Directory

9. You have a very small network in a home-based office, and you want to limit network access to only those hosts that you physically own. What should you utilize to make this possible?

    A. Static IP addresses

    B. Disabled DNS

    C. Default subnet mask

    D. Empty default gateway

10. Which wireless encryption protocol provides Advanced Encryption Standard (AES) encryption?

    A. Wired Equivalent Privacy (WEP)

    B. Wi-Fi Protected Access (WPA)

    C. Wi-Fi Protected Access 2 (WPA2)

    D. Temporal Key Integrity Protocol (TKIP)

11. Which type of add-on will extend the functionality of the web browser in a way it wasn't originally designed?

    A. Pop-up blocker

    B. Extensions

    C. Plug-in

    D. Ad blocker

12. What is normally performed when an employee is offboarded?

    A. Their user account is deleted.

    B. Their user account is unlocked.

    C. Their user account is created.

    D. Their user account's password is reset.

13. By default, when setting up an Android device, why do you need a Google account?

    A. The device requires email setup.

    B. The account is used for cloud synchronizations.

    C. The account is used for desktop backups.

    D. The device requires registration.

14. You need to secure your mobile device's lock screen with the highest level of protection. Which of the following should you use? (Choose the best answer.)

    A. Fingerprint lock

    B. Face lock

    C. Passcode lock

    D. Swipe lock

15. You need to encrypt a single file on a Windows desktop. Which technology should you use?

    A. EFS

    B. BitLocker

    C. NTFS

    D. BitLocker to Go

16. A user is in both the Sales group and the Marketing group. The Sales group has full permission at the share level, and the Marketing group has Read-only permission. The files on NTFS are secured with the Modify permission for the Sales group and the Read & Execute permission for the Marketing group. Which permissions will the user have?

    A. Full

    B. Modify

    C. Read-only

    D. Read & Execute

17. James just moved a folder on the same partition. What will happen with the permissions for the folder?

    A. The permissions will be the same as they were before the move.

    B. The permissions will be inherited from the new parent folder.

    C. The permissions will be configured as the root folder for the drive letter.

    D. The permissions will be blank until configured.

18. A user is in the Sales group. The Sales group has no permissions at the share level. The files on NTFS are secured with the Modify permission for the Sales group. What permissions will the user have?

   A. The user will have the Modify permission when connecting from the network.

   B. The user will have the Modify permission when logged in locally to the computer.

   C. The user will have no access when logged in locally to the computer.

   D. The user will have Read-only permissions when connecting from the network.

19. You are trying to delete a file on the local filesystem, but the operating system will not let you. What could be the problem? (Choose the best answer.)

   A. The NTFS Modify permission is applied to the file.

   B. The share permissions are not set to Full Control.

   C. The file attributes are set to Read-only.

   D. The file attributes are set to System.

20. You need to enforce profile security requirements on mobile devices. Which should you use to achieve this goal?

   A. AUP

   B. NDA

   C. BYOD

   D. MDM

Performance-Based Question

You will encounter performance-based questions on the A+ exams. The questions on the exam require you to perform a specific task, and you will be graded on whether you were able to complete the task. The following requires you to think creatively in order to measure how well you understand this chapter's topics. You may or may not see similar questions on the actual A+ exams. To see how your answers compare to the authors', refer to Appendix B.

You have been asked to create a working structure for your organization's network. You have three groups: Sales, Marketing, and R&D. You need to set up a network share and NTFS to allow Sales to access Marketing material but not modify it in any way. R&D must be able to write to marketing files and read Sales information. Marketing must only have read access to R&D and Sales. Each group should have the Modify permission to their respective folder. All permissions should be controlled with share permissions. How will you set up the folders for access, NTFS permissions, and share permissions?

Chapter
19

Troubleshooting Operating Systems and Security

THE FOLLOWING COMPTIA A+ 220-1102 EXAM OBJECTIVES ARE COVERED IN THIS CHAPTER:

✓ **3.1 Given a scenario, troubleshoot common Windows OS problems.**

- Common symptoms
  - Blue screen of death (BSOD)
  - Sluggish performance
  - Boot problems
  - Frequent shutdowns
  - Services not starting
  - Applications crashing
  - Low memory warnings
  - USB controller resource warnings
  - System instability
  - No OS found
  - Slow profile load
  - Time drift
- Common troubleshooting steps
  - Reboot
  - Restart services
  - Uninstall/reinstall/update applications
  - Add resources

Chapter 16

- Verify requirements
- System file check
- Repair Windows
- Restore
- Reimage
- Roll back updates
- Rebuild Windows profiles

✓ **3.2 Given a scenario, troubleshoot common personal computer (PC) security issues.**

- Common symptoms
  - Unable to access the network
  - Desktop alerts
  - False alerts regarding antivirus protection
  - Altered system or personal files
    - Missing/renamed files
  - Unwanted notifications within the OS
  - OS update failures
- Browser-related symptoms
  - Random/frequent pop-ups
  - Certificate warnings
  - Redirection

✓ **3.3 Given a scenario, use best practice procedures for malware removal.**

1. Investigate and verify malware symptoms.
2. Quarantine the infected systems.
3. Disable System Restore in Windows.
4. Remediate infected systems.
   a. Update anti-malware software
   b. Scanning and removal techniques (e.g., safe mode, preinstallation environment)

5. Schedule scans and run updates

6. Enable System Restore and create a restore point in Windows

7. Educate the end user

✓ **3.4 Given a scenario, troubleshoot mobile OS and application issues.**

- Common symptoms
    - Application fails to launch
    - Application fails to close/crashes
    - Application fails to update
    - Slow to respond
    - OS fails to update
    - Battery life issues
    - Randomly reboots
    - Connectivity issues
        - Bluetooth
        - WiFi
        - Near-field communication (NFC)
        - AirDrop
    - Screen does not autorotate

✓ **3.5 Given a scenario, troubleshoot common mobile OS and application security issues.**

- Security concerns
    - Android package (APK) source
    - Developer mode
    - Root access/jailbreak
    - Bootleg/malicious application
        - Application spoofing
- Common symptoms
    - High network traffic
    - Sluggish response time

- Data-usage limit notification
- Limited Internet connectivity
- No Internet connectivity
- High number of ads
- Fake security warnings
- Unexpected application behavior
- Leaked personal files/data

Troubleshooting is a major responsibility of an A+ technician's daily job. It may not be as glamorous as we'd like it to be, but it does make up a good percentage of our daily workload. Applying a systematic approach to software troubleshooting is the key to solving all problems. A systematic solution also works well in preventing problems in the first place.

Many of the common software problems that you will spend time solving can be prevented with proper preventive maintenance. Preventive maintenance tends to get neglected at many companies because technicians are too busy fixing problems. Spending some time on keeping those problems from occurring is a good investment of resources.

In this chapter, we'll look at applying the same troubleshooting methodology to common software problems. We'll also apply similar troubleshooting to security issues. First, we'll look at common symptoms of problems and their solutions. We'll then follow up with ways to deal with—and prevent—security-related issues.

Troubleshooting Common Microsoft Windows OS Problems

Windows is mind-bogglingly complex. Other operating systems are complex too, but the mere fact that Windows has nearly 60 million lines of code (and thousands of developers have worked on it!) makes you pause and shake your head. Fortunately, you just need to take a systematic approach to solving software-related issues.

Windows-based issues can be grouped into several categories based on their cause, such as boot problems, missing files (such as system files), configuration files, and virtual memory. If you're troubleshooting a boot problem, it's imperative that you understand the Windows boot process. Some common Windows problems don't fall into any category other than "common Windows problems." We cover those in the following sections, followed by a discussion of the tools that can be used to fix them.

Common Symptoms

There are numerous "common symptoms" that CompTIA asks you be familiar with for the exam. They range from the dreaded *Blue Screen of Death (BSOD)* to spontaneous restarts and everything in between. They are discussed here in the order in which they appear in the objectives list.

Sluggish Performance

The performance of your systems will inevitably slow down over time. This could be due to a multitude of causes, ranging from bad Windows Update patches to malware. Sluggish or slow performance is one of the hardest problems to solve on a Windows operating system, because many of the symptoms are related to each other.

The first step to solving the problem is identifying the component that is impacted by the performance issue. The following is a list of critical components that can be affected by slow performance:

CPU A symptom of poor CPU performance is the slow execution of applications. The operating system GUI will be unresponsive and sluggish. You may also hear your CPU fan running higher than normal if overheating starts to occur. CPU problems can be caused by an application that requires high CPU usage, such as movie rendering.

RAM A symptom of the operating system running out of RAM is high disk activity. As physical memory is used up, the less active pages of memory are swapped out to the hard disk drive (HDD). The symptoms of performance closely resemble CPU-related issues, where applications are slow in loading. RAM problems can be caused by too many applications being open at once or an application that has high RAM requirements, such as a database.

Disk A symptom of poor hard disk drive performance is the thrashing of the drive heads on the platters of the drive. Thrashing occurs when there is excessive movement of the drive arm to locate information on the drive. Disk problems can be caused by excessive fragmentation, high RAM usage, or a high volume of drive usage by applications, such as a video capture.

Network Symptoms of poor network performance are slow loading web pages, network applications that load slowly, and even timeouts. If you are using wireless, network issues can be caused by poor signal strength. If you are connected through Ethernet, poor network performance can be directly related to the local area network (LAN). The problems can also be outside of your network.

Graphics Symptoms of poor graphics (GPU) performance are usually related to slow-running video games and playback of videos. The frames per seconds (FPS) will be excessively low as the computer tries to render the screen. It is not common to have graphics-related issues unless you just downloaded the latest shoot-em-up game. Graphics-related problems are usually the hardest to solve because they require third-party tools by the graphics card vendor.

As you can see from the list of possibly affected components, many of the symptoms are closely related, such as RAM, CPU, and disk. The excessive usage of RAM can create performance symptoms with your hard disk drive. If left for a long period of time, these can both lead to an increase in CPU activity.

There are several tools that you can use to identify the problem area so that you can focus your attention on narrowing down the problem. The first tool you should start up is the

Task Manager, as shown in Figure 19.1. You can launch Task Manager in several different ways, such as right-clicking the Start menu and selecting Task Manager, right-clicking the taskbar and selecting Task Manager, or (my personal favorite) pressing Ctrl+Shift+Esc. The Performance tab will show you four of the five critical areas (detailed previously) on the left side. In this example, you can see that the processor is spiked out at almost 100 percent and all other systems are within tolerance.

FIGURE 19.1   The Performance tab in Task Manager

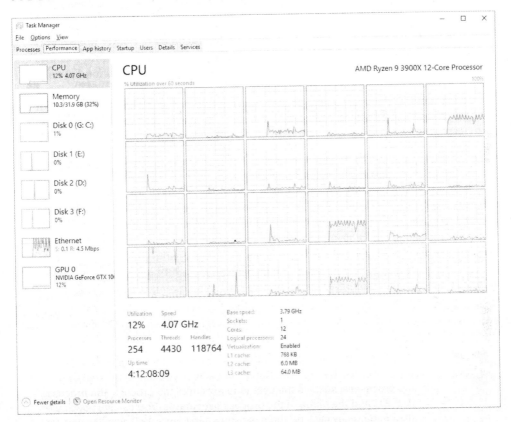

Now that you've isolated the problem to the critical area of CPU, you can narrow it down further by looking at the Processes tab, as shown in Figure 19.2. You can see that Microsoft Windows Malicious Software Removal Process is using nearly 26 percent of the CPU. The other 74 percent is most likely distributed among other processes. By clicking the core area headings of CPU, Memory, Disk, and Network, you can sort usage from high to low or from low to high. In this particular instance, the operating system was caught booting up, so that particular process was displaying high CPU.

FIGURE 19.2   The Processes tab in Task Manager

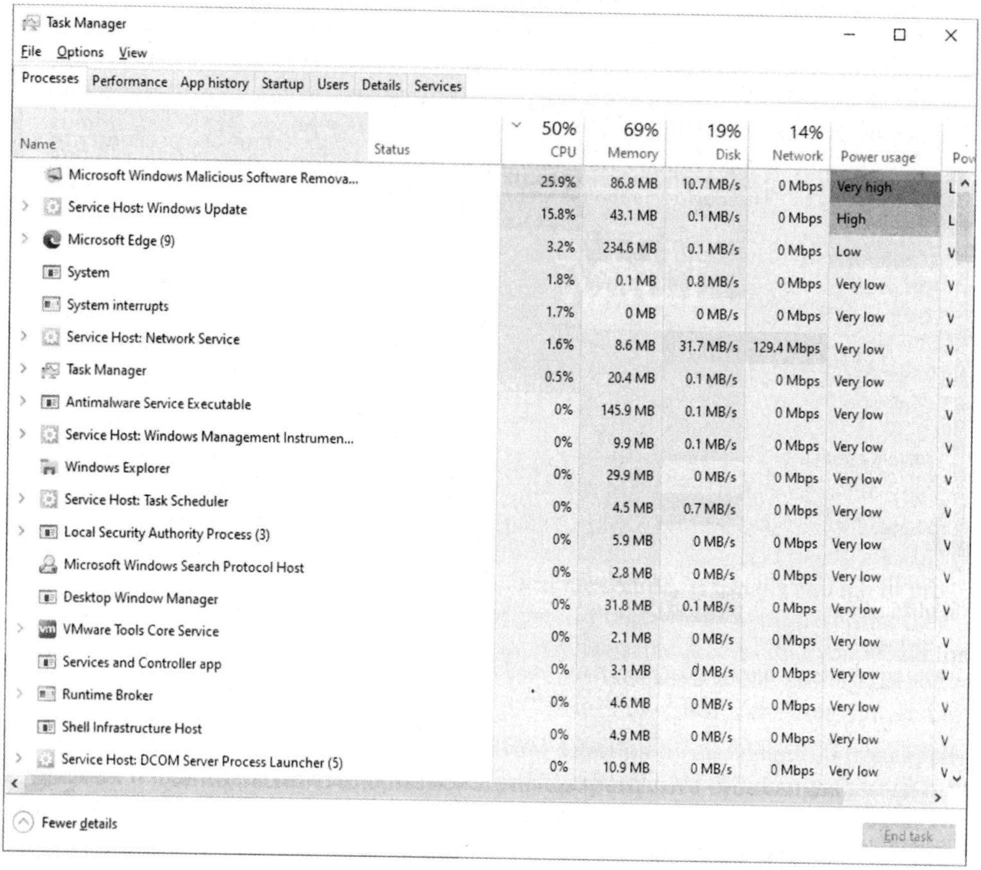

Name	Status	50% CPU	69% Memory	19% Disk	14% Network	Power usage	Pow
Microsoft Windows Malicious Software Remova...		25.9%	86.8 MB	10.7 MB/s	0 Mbps	Very high	L
› Service Host: Windows Update		15.8%	43.1 MB	0.1 MB/s	0 Mbps	High	L
› Microsoft Edge (9)		3.2%	234.6 MB	0.1 MB/s	0 Mbps	Low	V
System		1.8%	0.1 MB	0.8 MB/s	0 Mbps	Very low	V
System interrupts		1.7%	0 MB	0 MB/s	0 Mbps	Very low	V
› Service Host: Network Service		1.6%	8.6 MB	31.7 MB/s	129.4 Mbps	Very low	V
› Task Manager		0.5%	20.4 MB	0.1 MB/s	0 Mbps	Very low	V
› Antimalware Service Executable		0%	145.9 MB	0.1 MB/s	0 Mbps	Very low	V
› Service Host: Windows Management Instrumen...		0%	9.9 MB	0.1 MB/s	0 Mbps	Very low	V
Windows Explorer		0%	29.9 MB	0 MB/s	0 Mbps	Very low	V
› Service Host: Task Scheduler		0%	4.5 MB	0.7 MB/s	0 Mbps	Very low	V
› Local Security Authority Process (3)		0%	5.9 MB	0 MB/s	0 Mbps	Very low	V
Microsoft Windows Search Protocol Host		0%	2.8 MB	0 MB/s	0 Mbps	Very low	V
Desktop Window Manager		0%	31.8 MB	0.1 MB/s	0 Mbps	Very low	V
› VMware Tools Core Service		0%	2.1 MB	0 MB/s	0 Mbps	Very low	V
Services and Controller app		0%	3.1 MB	0 MB/s	0 Mbps	Very low	V
› Runtime Broker		0%	4.6 MB	0 MB/s	0 Mbps	Very low	V
Shell Infrastructure Host		0%	4.9 MB	0 MB/s	0 Mbps	Very low	V
› Service Host: DCOM Server Process Launcher (5)		0%	10.9 MB	0 MB/s	0 Mbps	Very low	V

Fewer details

End task

Starting in Windows 8, the Task Manager gained a few tabs. One of those is called Details. The Details tab allows you to see the details of the processes, such as the user who executed the process, the process ID (PID), and the name of the process executable. You can sort by any of the headings by clicking them, as shown in Figure 19.3, just like you can on the Processes tab. You can even right-click the headings and add columns, such as peak memory usage and the exact command line, just to name a few.

FIGURE 19.3 The Details tab in Task Manager

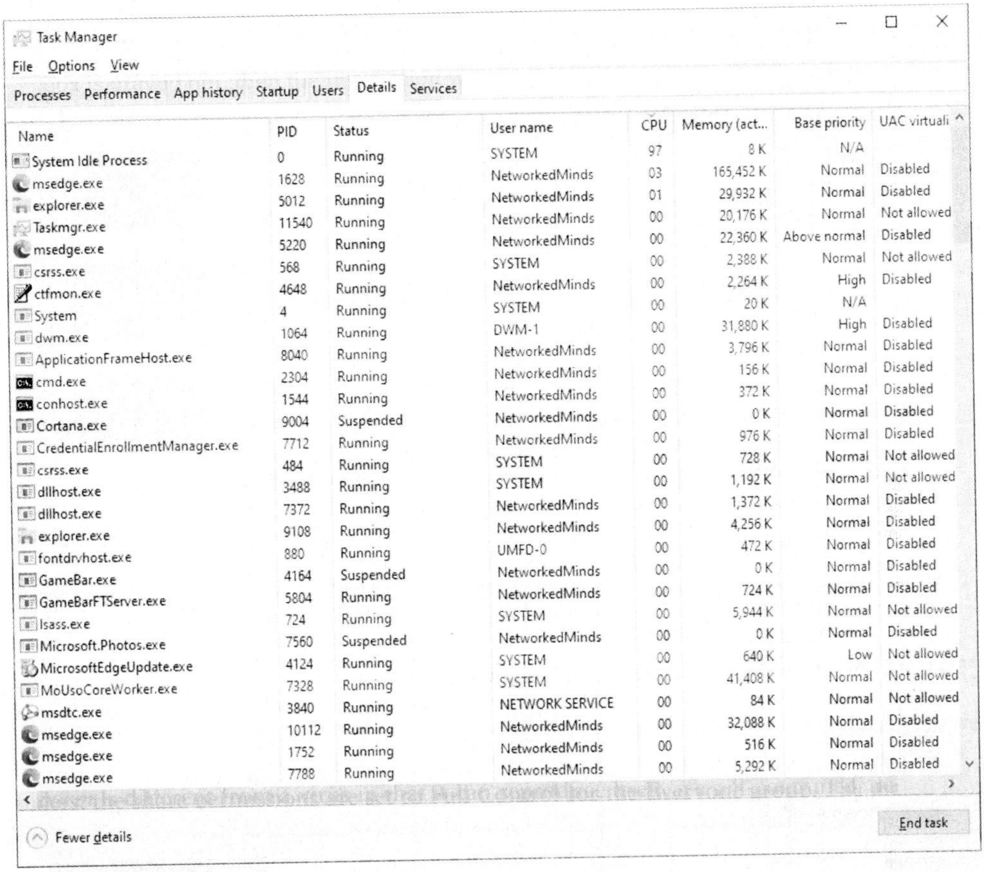

Name	PID	Status	User name	CPU	Memory (act...	Base priority	UAC virtuali
System Idle Process	0	Running	SYSTEM	97	8 K	N/A	
msedge.exe	1628	Running	NetworkedMinds	03	165,452 K	Normal	Disabled
explorer.exe	5012	Running	NetworkedMinds	01	29,932 K	Normal	Disabled
Taskmgr.exe	11540	Running	NetworkedMinds	00	20,176 K	Normal	Not allowed
msedge.exe	5220	Running	NetworkedMinds	00	22,360 K	Above normal	Disabled
csrss.exe	568	Running	SYSTEM	00	2,388 K	Normal	Not allowed
ctfmon.exe	4648	Running	NetworkedMinds	00	2,264 K	High	Disabled
System	4	Running	SYSTEM	00	20 K	N/A	
dwm.exe	1064	Running	DWM-1	00	31,880 K	High	Disabled
ApplicationFrameHost.exe	8040	Running	NetworkedMinds	00	3,796 K	Normal	Disabled
cmd.exe	2304	Running	NetworkedMinds	00	156 K	Normal	Disabled
conhost.exe	1544	Running	NetworkedMinds	00	372 K	Normal	Disabled
Cortana.exe	9004	Suspended	NetworkedMinds	00	0 K	Normal	Disabled
CredentialEnrollmentManager.exe	7712	Running	NetworkedMinds	00	976 K	Normal	Disabled
csrss.exe	484	Running	SYSTEM	00	728 K	Normal	Not allowed
dllhost.exe	3488	Running	SYSTEM	00	1,192 K	Normal	Not allowed
dllhost.exe	7372	Running	NetworkedMinds	00	1,372 K	Normal	Disabled
explorer.exe	9108	Running	NetworkedMinds	00	4,256 K	Normal	Disabled
fontdrvhost.exe	880	Running	UMFD-0	00	472 K	Normal	Disabled
GameBar.exe	4164	Suspended	NetworkedMinds	00	0 K	Normal	Disabled
GameBarFTServer.exe	5804	Running	NetworkedMinds	00	724 K	Normal	Disabled
lsass.exe	724	Running	SYSTEM	00	5,944 K	Normal	Not allowed
Microsoft.Photos.exe	7560	Suspended	NetworkedMinds	00	0 K	Normal	Disabled
MicrosoftEdgeUpdate.exe	4124	Running	SYSTEM	00	640 K	Low	Not allowed
MoUsoCoreWorker.exe	7328	Running	SYSTEM	00	41,408 K	Normal	Not allowed
msdtc.exe	3840	Running	NETWORK SERVICE	00	84 K	Normal	Not allowed
msedge.exe	10112	Running	NetworkedMinds	00	32,088 K	Normal	Disabled
msedge.exe	1752	Running	NetworkedMinds	00	516 K	Normal	Disabled
msedge.exe	7788	Running	NetworkedMinds	00	5,292 K	Normal	Disabled

Using *Resource Monitor*, you can get a much more detailed view than what is displayed in Task Manager. You can open Resource Monitor with the shortcut on the lower left of the Performance tab in Task Manager, as shown in Figure 19.4. This tool allows you to read real-time performance data on every process on the operating system. Resource Monitor also allows you to sort details, the same as Task Manager. You can click each critical area and drill down to the performance issue.

A unique feature of Resource Monitor is the visualization of data. When you select a process on the upper view, Resource Monitor automatically filters the activity of the critical area, as shown in Figure 19.5. As you can see in this example, the Edge browser processes have been selected and then the Network tab can be chosen to display the network activity and connections. The result is the isolation of network activity for this process. This can be done for any of the critical areas.

FIGURE 19.4   Resource Monitor

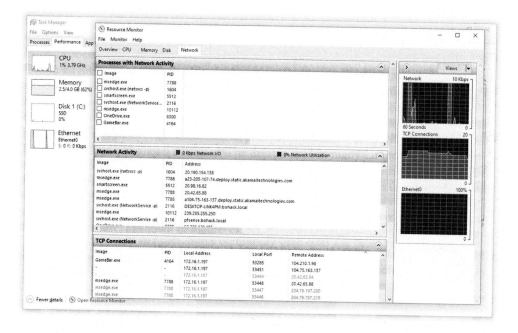

FIGURE 19.5   Selective isolation in Resource Monitor

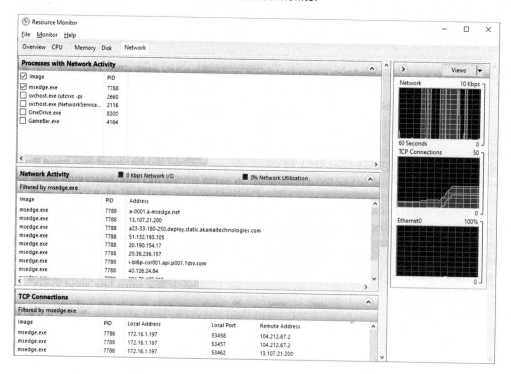

Now that you've isolated the problem to an action or process in the operating system, you need to do the following:

1. Formulate a theory of probable cause.

2. Test the theory to determine the cause.

3. Establish a plan of action to resolve the problem and implement the solution.

4. Verify the full-system functionality and, if applicable, implement preventative measures.

5. Document findings, actions, and outcomes.

The theory of probable cause may be that a hardware upgrade is required due to a new version of the application that demands more resources. Or it could be as simple as the job the application is running is higher than normal in load. Remember to question the obvious and do the simple things, such as rebooting, to see if the problem goes away. It is often joked about that problems always go away after a reboot. It's not too far from the truth. Sometimes a process is hung up and is affecting another process. A reboot sometimes fixes them both and the symptoms go away. More likely than not, the problem will still be there. This is when you need to start testing your theory of probable cause to determine the cause.

You might find that after running a large query the hard drive is extremely stressed. Your action plan might be to upgrade the hard drive or move the workload to a faster machine. In either case, you need to verify that the process is functioning the way the user expects it to.

If you determine that it's a certain report in the database, remind the user that the report takes time and maybe they should schedule it when the computer is not immediately needed. Or schedule the system for an upgrade of hardware to prevent these problems in the future.

Ultimately, you should document your finding so that other technicians do not waste time with the same issue. The more intricate the problem, the more time is wasted when you forget you've solved it already or don't remember the answer. Always document the actions taken, such as upgrades or changes to the process for the user. You should also note the outcome—whether it was successful or showed no immediate performance increase—so that if another technician is working on the same or a similar issue, they can gauge whether the solution is effective.

Boot Problems

With the introduction of Windows Vista, the boot process had changed from prior operating systems of Windows XP, 2000, and NT 4.0. We've used this current boot process introduced with Windows Vista all the way to today with Windows 11. The current boot process allows for the adoption of UEFI firmware.

In order to troubleshoot a failure to boot, you need to understand the complete boot process, starting with either the BIOS or the UEFI. The process is slightly different depending on which firmware you have on the motherboard. However, the outcome is the same: the hardware hands control over to the operating system so that the operating system can boot.

BIOS   Legacy BIOS systems perform a *power-on self-test (POST)*, and then the BIOS bootstrap routine looks at the master boot record (MBR) at the beginning of the disk.

The MBR then reads the boot sector on the first primary partition found. This boot sector then instructs the Boot Manager to load.

UEFI   UEFI firmware will perform a similar POST. Then the UEFI bootstrap begins by loading drivers for the hardware. One of the differences is that UEFI can contain drivers that allow it to boot across a network or other nonstandard devices. Just like the legacy BIOS, the UEFI firmware looks at the MBR in the GUID Partition Table (GPT). The GPT defines a globally unique identifier (GUID) that points to a partition containing the Boot Manager. Therefore, UEFI firmware requires a partitioning scheme of GPT and cannot use the standard MBR partitioning scheme.

The initial boot sequence from hardware control to software control is almost identical in both BIOS and UEFI firmware. UEFI firmware does give you many more options, because UEFI drivers can be loaded before control is handed over to the software. This allows UEFI to treat all locations containing an operating system the same. Up to the point at which the hardware hands control over to the software, there is no difference between a network boot and a hardware boot.

After control is handed over to the software, several files are used to complete the operating system bootup. The most important files are as follows:

Windows Boot Manager   The Windows Boot Manager (BOOTMGR) bootstraps the system. In other words, this file starts the loading of an operating system on the computer.

BCD   The Boot Configuration Data (BCD) holds information about operating systems installed on the computer, such as the location of the operating system files.

winload.exe   winload.exe is the program used to boot Windows. It loads the operating system kernel (ntoskrnl.exe).

winresume.exe   If the system is not starting fresh but resuming a previous session, then winresume.exe is called by BOOTMGR.

ntoskrnl.exe   The Windows OS kernel is the heart of the operating system. The kernel is responsible for allowing applications shared access to the hardware through drivers.

ntbtlog.txt   The Windows boot log stores a log of boot-time events. It is not enabled by default.

System Files   In addition to the previously listed files, Windows needs a number of files from its system folders (for example, SYSTEM and SYSTEM32), such as the hardware abstraction layer (hal.dll), the Session Manager (smss.exe), the user session (winlogon.exe), and the security subsystem (lsass.exe).

Numerous other dynamic link library (DLL) files are also required, but usually the lack of them or corruption of one of these files produces a noncritical error, whereas the absence of hal.dll causes the system to be nonfunctional.

We'll now look at the complete Windows boot process. It's a long and complicated process, but keep in mind that these are complex operating systems, providing you with a lot more functionality than older versions of Windows:

1. The system self-checks and enumerates hardware resources. Each machine has a different startup routine, called the POST (power-on self-test), which is executed by the commands written to the motherboard of the computer. Newer PnP boards not only check memory and processors, but also poll the systems for other devices and peripherals.

2. The master boot record (MBR) loads and finds the boot sector. Once the system has finished its housekeeping, the MBR is located on the first hard drive and loaded into memory. The MBR finds the bootable partition and searches it for the boot sector of that partition.

3. The MBR determines the filesystem and loads BOOTMGR. Information in the boot sector allows the system to locate the system partition and to find and load into memory the file located there.

4. BOOTMGR reads the boot configuration data (BCD) to get a list of boot options for the next step. The BCD contains multi-boot information or options on how the boot process should continue.

5. BOOTMGR then executes winload.exe. This switches the system from real mode (which lacks multitasking, memory protection, and those things that make Windows so great) to protected mode (which offers memory protection, multitasking, and so on) and enables paging. Protected mode enables the system to address all the available physical memory.

6. If Windows is returning from a hibernated (suspended) state, winresume.exe is responsible for reading the hiberfil.sys file into memory and passes control to the kernel after this file is loaded.

7. The OS kernel loads the executive subsystems. *Executive subsystems* are software components that parse the Registry for configuration information and start needed services and drivers.

8. The HKEY_LOCAL_MACHINE\SYSTEM Registry hive and device drivers are loaded. The drivers that load at this time serve as boot drivers, using an initial value called a *start value*.

9. Control is passed to the kernel, which initializes loaded drivers. The kernel loads the Session Manager, which then loads the Windows subsystem and completes the boot process.

10. Winlogon.exe loads. At this point, you are presented with the login screen. After you enter a username and password, you're taken to the Windows desktop.

Now that you understand the boot process, let's look at how you can collect information to identify the problem. We'll consider this in two parts: hardware and software. The hardware process begins with the POST, and the software portion of the bootstrap begins with the BOOTMGR.

You can collect information from the BIOS/UEFI firmware boot with third-party system event log (SEL) viewers. However, it is very unlikely that you have a failure to boot because of a BIOS/UEFI firmware issue. It's not impossible, but it is highly unlikely.

To collect information on the software portion of the boot process loads, you can use boot logging. The ntbtlog.txt file is located at the base of the C:\Windows folder, as shown in Figure 19.6. Boot logging is off by default and needs to be turned on. To enable boot logging, issue the command **bcdedit /set {*current*} bootlog Yes**. You can also use the System Configuration utility (msconfig.exe) by selecting the Boot Log option on the Boot tab, as shown in Figure 19.7. Because the BCD is read by BOOTMGR, this point of the boot process is where logging would begin and the first entries would be the loading of the kernel.

FIGURE 19.6   The ntbtlog.txt file

```
ntbtlog - Notepad                                        —   □   ×
File  Edit  Format  View  Help
Microsoft (R) Windows (R) Version 10.0 (Build 17134)
11 21 2018 14:37:08.500
BOOTLOG_LOADED \SystemRoot\system32\ntoskrnl.exe
BOOTLOG_LOADED \SystemRoot\system32\hal.dll
BOOTLOG_LOADED \SystemRoot\system32\kd.dll
BOOTLOG_LOADED \SystemRoot\system32\mcupdate_AuthenticAMD.dll
BOOTLOG_LOADED \SystemRoot\System32\drivers\msrpc.sys
BOOTLOG_LOADED \SystemRoot\System32\drivers\ksecdd.sys
BOOTLOG_LOADED \SystemRoot\System32\drivers\werkernel.sys
BOOTLOG_LOADED \SystemRoot\System32\drivers\CLFS.SYS
BOOTLOG_LOADED \SystemRoot\System32\drivers\tm.sys
BOOTLOG_LOADED \SystemRoot\system32\PSHED.dll
BOOTLOG_LOADED \SystemRoot\system32\BOOTVID.dll
BOOTLOG_LOADED \SystemRoot\System32\drivers\FLTMGR.SYS
BOOTLOG_LOADED \SystemRoot\System32\drivers\clipsp.sys
BOOTLOG_LOADED \SystemRoot\System32\drivers\cmimcext.sys
BOOTLOG_LOADED \SystemRoot\System32\drivers\ntosext.sys
BOOTLOG_LOADED \SystemRoot\system32\CI.dll
BOOTLOG_LOADED \SystemRoot\System32\drivers\cng.sys
BOOTLOG_LOADED \SystemRoot\system32\drivers\Wdf01000.sys
BOOTLOG_LOADED \SystemRoot\system32\drivers\WDFLDR.SYS
BOOTLOG_LOADED \SystemRoot\system32\drivers\WppRecorder.sys
BOOTLOG_LOADED \SystemRoot\system32\drivers\SleepStudyHelper.sys
BOOTLOG_LOADED \SystemRoot\System32\Drivers\acpiex.sys
BOOTLOG_LOADED \SystemRoot\system32\drivers\mssecflt.sys
BOOTLOG_LOADED \SystemRoot\system32\drivers\SgrmAgent.sys
BOOTLOG_LOADED \SystemRoot\System32\drivers\ACPI.sys
BOOTLOG_LOADED \SystemRoot\System32\drivers\WMILIB.SYS
BOOTLOG_LOADED \SystemRoot\system32\drivers\wd\WdBoot.sys
BOOTLOG_LOADED \SystemRoot\System32\drivers\intelpep.sys
BOOTLOG_LOADED \SystemRoot\system32\drivers\WindowsTrustedRT.sys
BOOTLOG_LOADED \SystemRoot\System32\drivers\WindowsTrustedRTProxy.sys
BOOTLOG_LOADED \SystemRoot\System32\drivers\pcw.sys
BOOTLOG_LOADED \SystemRoot\System32\drivers\msisadrv.sys
BOOTLOG_LOADED \SystemRoot\System32\drivers\pci.sys
BOOTLOG_LOADED \SystemRoot\System32\drivers\vdrvroot.sys
```

FIGURE 19.7   System Configuration options for boot logging

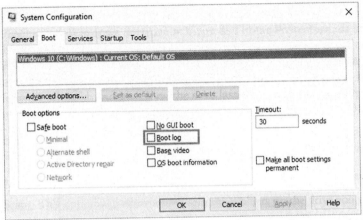

Chances are, if you're having trouble booting into Windows, you won't be able to access the command prompt to issue `bcdedit` commands, nor will you able to access `msconfig` `.exe`. Not to worry. You can still access logging by allowing the operating system to fail two times in a row. The third time, the computer will boot into the recovery console. From there, click Troubleshooting ➢ Advanced Options ➢ Startup Settings ➢ Restart. When the computer restarts, it will boot into the Startup Settings menu, as shown in Figure 19.8. Of course, you won't be able to boot the computer to retrieve the files, but you can use the command prompt in the Windows Recovery Environment.

The idea is to collect information to identify the problem and, above all, to fix the problem. Sometimes you need to let Windows repair itself. The Windows Recovery Environment (WinRE) contains a Startup Repair option. Using the Startup Repair option is similar to issuing `bootrec /rebuildbcd` at the command prompt, which will rebuild the BCD.

If that fails, the ultimate solution might be to use the Reset This PC option in the Windows Recovery Environment or to install the operating system from scratch.

No OS Found

When it's reported that an operating system is missing, or "no OS is found," the first thing to check is that no media is in the machine (USB, DVD, CD, and so on). The system may be reading this media during boot before accessing the hard drive. If that is the case, remove the media and reboot. You should also change the BIOS/UEFI settings to boot from the hard drive before any other media to prevent this issue in the future.

FIGURE 19.8   Startup Settings menu

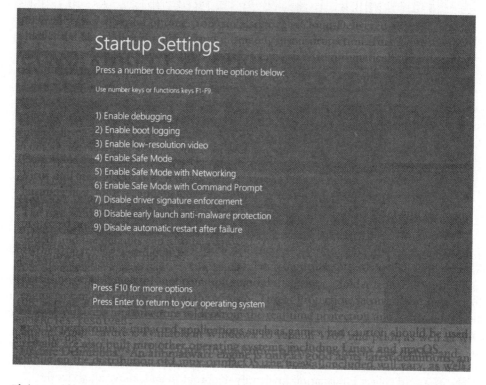

If the problem is not as simple as removing the non-bootable media, then you may have to boot into the Windows Recovery Environment. This may be a challenge, because if the BIOS/UEFI cannot boot to the Windows Boot Manager, then the Windows Recovery Environment cannot be executed. The Boot Manager is responsible for executing the Windows Recovery Environment. You will have possibly two options to fix this. The first option is to use the vendor's recovery console. This option is dependent on the vendor supplying a recovery console that can be accessed via the BIOS/UEFI; not every vendor supplies this tool. The second option is to boot the installation media and choose Repair when it first boots. Choosing this option will launch the Windows Recovery Environment booted from the installation media. You can then choose to repair the operating system by selecting Troubleshoot ➤ Advanced Options ➤ Startup Repair. The Windows Recovery Environment will then attempt to repair the operating system.

Operating System instability

When an *application crashes*, you want to isolate the cause of the crash and solve it. The cause could be a compatibility issue, a hardware issue, or a host of other problems. One step to take early on is to look for updates/patches/fixes to the application released by the vendor. Be sure to try these updates on a test machine before rolling them out to all machines, and verify that they address the problem and do not introduce new problems.

One tool that is extremely helpful in identifying software problems is Reliability Monitor, as shown in Figure 19.9. Reliability Monitor allows you to see application crashes and the times and dates they occurred. It also allows you to see which updates were installed before and after the crashes. You can use Reliability Monitor to narrow down whether other software is causing the issues and what led up to the crashes.

FIGURE 19.9   Windows Reliability Monitor

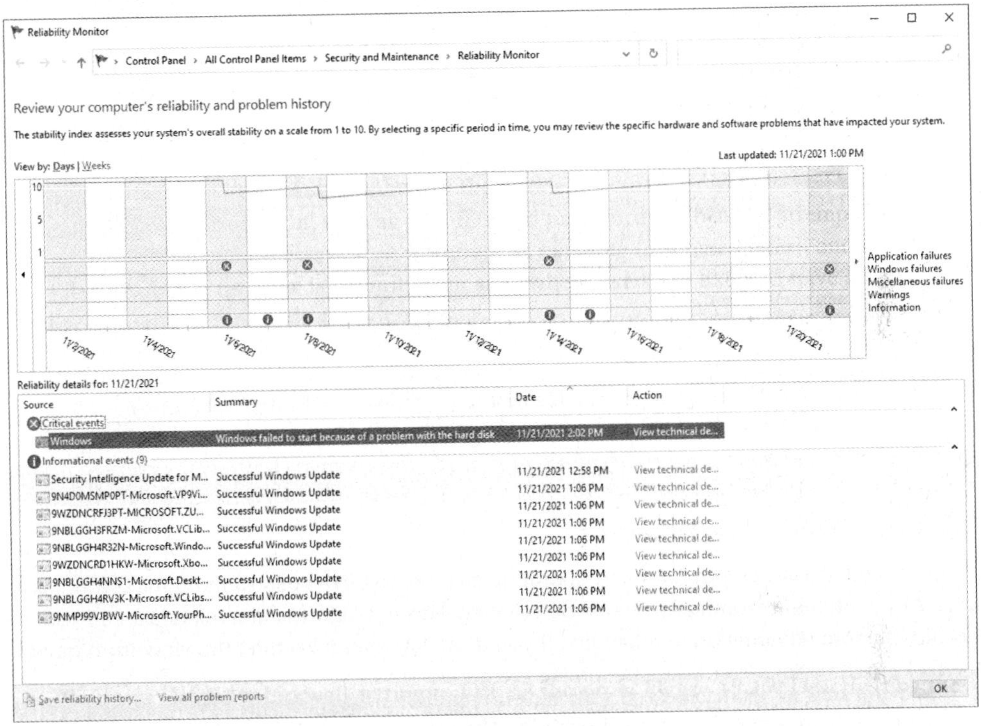

In addition to Reliability Monitor, you can access the Windows event logs in *Event Viewer* for information about Microsoft-based application problems, as shown in Figure 19.10. All third-party vendors should log errors to the Windows event logs, but generally you will only find Microsoft products using these logs. In either case, you might find more information about why an application is crashing by looking at the Application log.

The applications on the operating system are not the only elements captured by Reliability Monitor. Reliability Monitor also captures the overall stability of the operating system. It will allow you to see every reboot caused by a problem and even blue screens. The overall stability of the operating system is drawn as a graphical line inside the Reliability Monitor application. This allows you to historically look back and trace when a problem started.

FIGURE 19.10 Windows event logs in Event Viewer

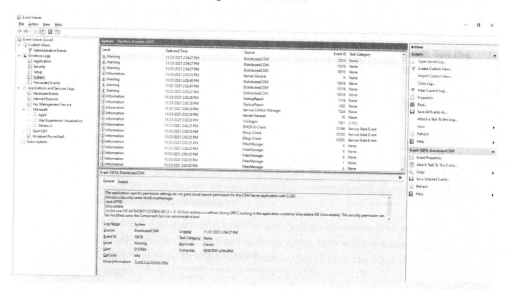

In Exercise 19.1 you will review the Reliability Monitor built into Windows.

EXERCISE 19.1

Reviewing Reliability Monitor

This exercise is best performed on an operating system that has been running for some time. Although the operating system should be flawless and operate at a reliable level, you should see some fluctuation in reliability. If you don't, then try switching the view from days to weeks in the upper left of the app, above the graph.

1. Click the Start menu, type **View Reliability History**, and then click the Control Panel app result.

2. Make note of your current reliability score by looking at the graph on the rightmost section of the graph and comparing the location with the legend on the left side (1 through 10).

3. Make note of if and why your score has gone down over the days shown.

4. If there is a drop in reliability, click on Day and the lower section of the app will display the reliability details.

5. View the details and make note of the action.

As you click through the reliability events, make note of applications that constantly crash or that are problematic. These are the applications you should investigate further. Some of the solutions in the next section will lend some suggestion on how to fix them.

Blue Screen of Death

The Blue Screen of Death (BSOD)—not a technical term, by the way—is another way of describing the blue-screen error condition that occurs when Windows fails to boot properly or quits unexpectedly, as shown in Figure 19.11. If this happens during a boot, it is at this stage that the device drivers for the various pieces of hardware are installed/loaded. If your Windows GUI fails to start properly, more likely than not the problem is related to a misconfigured driver or misconfigured hardware.

FIGURE 19.11   Blue Screen of Death

You can try a few things if you believe that a driver is causing the problem. One is to try booting Windows into safe mode, which you can access via the Startup Settings in the Windows Recovery Environment. In safe mode, Windows loads only basic drivers, such as a standard VGA video driver and the keyboard and mouse. After you've booted into safe mode, you can uninstall the driver that you think is causing the problem.

Another option is to boot into the Windows Recovery Environment and use System Restore, which will revert the system drivers back to the state they were in when the restore point was created. Bear in mind that a System Restore will not affect personal files, but it will remove applications, updates, and drivers.

In Windows 7 and prior operating systems, you can enter the Advanced Boot Options during system startup by pressing the F8 key. The Advanced Boot Options menu contains an option called Last Known Good Configuration. This option will allow you to boot to the last time you had successfully started up and logged in. This option was removed in Windows 8/8.1/10 and Windows 11. You should now be using System Restore. The Windows

Recovery Environment will automatically launch if there are two failed attempts to boot the operating system in 2 minutes.

Frequent Shutdowns

There are many reasons why your computer might randomly turn off or shut down without warning. The problem is almost always related to faulty hardware or a faulty driver, but sometimes it can be as simple as tweaking your advanced power settings.

The first place to check is Event Viewer on the System tab. You should start combing through the logs and looking for the source of Kernel-Boot or Kernel-General. The entries will help you identify if the operating system was shut down properly or it just suddenly lost power. Any time the operating system is shut down, the kernel will log an entry, and when it is powered back up, it will also log an entry. In addition to the Kernel-Boot and Kernel-General sources, you should also investigate the source of EventLog. These entries will be created if the EventLog service detects a dirty shutdown, such as when the power is removed. By checking the Event Viewer logs, you identify whether the problem is a hardware problem or whether the operating system is actually shutting itself down.

If you identify that the problem is a hardware issue, then the first step to resolving the problem is updating drivers. You should remove any autodetected drivers and reinstall the vendor's driver for the specific hardware. If the problem persists, then swapping known good hardware might help narrow down the issue.

If you determine that the operating system is shutting itself down, then the power settings should be checked. You can access the power settings by navigating to the Start menu ➤ Settings App ➤ Power & Sleep. Make sure that the PC is not going into sleep mode when plugged in. From this screen you can access the advanced power settings by clicking Change Plan Settings, then Change Advanced Power Settings. You will need to selectively tweak some of the settings and test your adjustments, such as turning off hard disk sleep, general sleep settings, and processor power management, to name a few. Tweak the timer or adjustment and then monitor the change from the setting to determine the fix.

Services Not Starting

A service's failure to start is directly related either to another application installed with conflicting resources or to a misconfiguration of the service. In either case, the first place to start is the Event Viewer, as shown in Figure 19.12. The System log will display an Event ID of 7000 from the source of the Service Control Manager. The reason for the failure will vary, depending on the problem.

If a service is conflicting with another resource, we recommend that you reinstall the software that installed the service that is failing. Although this might break the conflicting application, it is probably the quickest way to find a conflicting resource.

FIGURE 19.12   Service Control Manager events

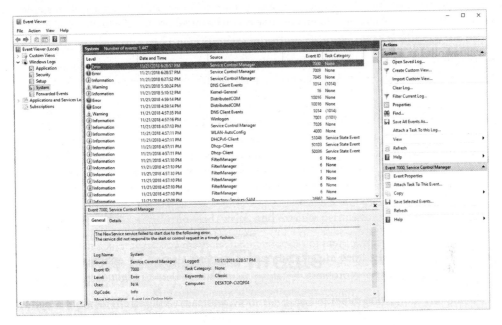

If the service fails to start because of a misconfiguration, the most likely cause is the user account the service is configured to start with. If a misconfigured user account is the problem, you will see an Event ID of 7000 in Event Viewer, and the description will read that the service failed due to a login failure. You can verify the user configured to start the service in the Services properties, as shown in Figure 19.13. You open the properties of the service by right-clicking the Start menu, selecting Computer Management, then Services, right-clicking the service, selecting Properties, and finally selecting the Log On tab.

Make sure that the password for the user account has not changed and that the user account is not locked out. You can manually reset the password for the user and reenter the password in the Services properties. Also make sure that the account has the Log On As A Service right.

 **Real World Scenario**

Did You Reboot Your Computer?

Quick quiz: You just got an error in Windows, and it appears that you are on the verge of a crash (of your application or the whole system). What do you do?

The first thing is to write down any error messages that appear. Then save your work (if possible) and reboot your computer.

Anyone who has called tech support, or who has been a tech support person, knows how demeaning the question, "Did you restart your computer?" can seem. Most people respond with an indignant, "Of course!" In reality, they might or might not have actually done it.

Whenever there's a software problem, always, always reboot the computer before trying to troubleshoot. Often, the problem will disappear, and you'll have just saved yourself half an hour of frustration. If the same problem reappears, then you know that you have work to do.

Why does rebooting help? When an application is running, it creates one or more temporary files that it uses to store information. It also stores information in memory (RAM). If a temporary file or information in RAM becomes corrupted (such as by application A writing its information into application B's memory space), the original application can have problems. Rebooting will clear the memory registers and most often remove problematic temporary files, thus eliminating the issue.

It might sound trite, but the first axiom in troubleshooting software really is to reboot. Even if the user says they did, ask them to reboot again. (Tell them you want to see the opening screen for any possible error messages, or make up another good excuse.) If the problem doesn't come back, it's not a problem. If it does, then you can use your software skills to fix it.

FIGURE 19.13   Services properties

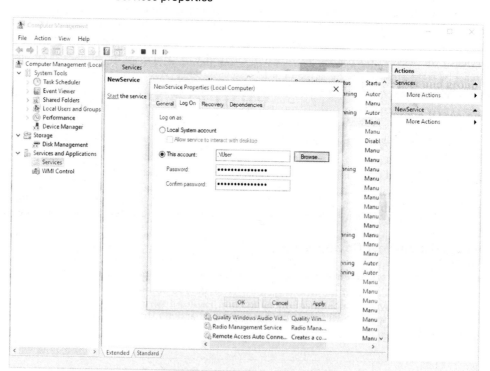

Low Memory Warnings

Random access memory (RAM) is the computer's physical memory. The more RAM you physically have installed in a computer, the more items you can have in the running foreground of the operating system. If you run out of physical memory, then processes that are backgrounded (minimized) will be loaded into the *page file*, or *paging file*, on the hard drive. This is called paging, and it is totally normal to have a certain amount of paging happen during normal activity. The page file is actually hard drive space into which idle pieces of programs are placed while other active parts of programs are kept in or swapped into main memory. The programs running in Windows believe that their information is still in RAM, but Windows has moved the data into near-line storage on the solid-state drive (SSD) or hard drive. When the application needs the information again, it is swapped back into RAM so that the processor can use it.

When system processes are at risk of not having enough memory free, you will see a warning message similar to the one shown in Figure 19.14. When this happens it means one of two things; the first is that you simply don't have enough physical RAM in the computer. The second is that a process is using a large amount of RAM that it normally doesn't need. The operating system is letting you know that it can't swap out any more pages of memory to the page file (virtual memory).

FIGURE 19.14   Low memory warning

The larger the page file, the fewer times the machine has swapped out the contents of what it is holding in memory. The maximum possible size of your page file depends on the amount of disk space that you have available on the drive where the page file is placed. Windows configures the minimum and maximum page file size automatically. If you want Windows to handle the size of the page file dynamically, you have to change the default setting by selecting System Managed Size in the Virtual Memory dialog box. We'll show you how to get there in a moment.

In Windows, the page file is called `pagefile.sys` and is located in the root directory of the drive on which you installed the OS files. The page file is a hidden file; to see the file in Windows File Explorer, you must have the Folder options configured to show hidden files. Typically, there's no reason to view the page file in the filesystem, because you'll use Control Panel to configure it. However, you may want to check its size, and in that case, you'd use Windows File Explorer.

The moral of the story: as with most things virtual, a page file is not nearly as good as actual RAM, but it is better than nothing.

To modify the default virtual memory settings, follow these steps: Click Start, type **Control Panel,** and select it from the results. Click the System icon and select Advanced System Settings from the right panel. In the Performance area, click Settings. Next, click the Advanced tab (yes, another Advanced tab), and then, in the Virtual Memory area, click Change and the Virtual Memory dialog box will open, as shown in Figure 19.15. Note that in addition to changing the page file's size and how Windows handles it, you can specify the drive on which you want to place the file.

FIGURE 19.15 Windows Virtual Memory settings

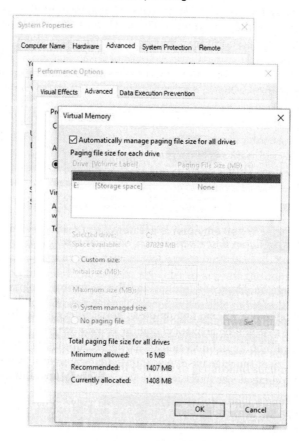

You should place the page file on a drive with plenty of empty space. As a general rule, try to keep 20 percent of your drive space free for the overhead of various elements of the OS, like the page file. Do not set the page file to an extremely small size. If you make the page file too small, the system can become unbootable—or at least unstable. In general, the page file should be at least 1.5x the amount of RAM in the machine.

USB Controller Resource Warnings

The *USB controller* is a hardware component on the motherboard that supplies both power and a data path for the devices connected. It is possible to plug in too many devices and overload the power the port can handle. Most USB 2.0 ports can handle five concurrent loads of 100 mA each, for a total of 500 mA. USB 3.0 can handle six concurrent loads of 150 mA each, for a total of 900 mA. If a device connected draws more than the allotted power, it will malfunction or irradicably disconnect.

The USB controller is also responsible for allotting the number of endpoints for the purpose of accepting data. The endpoints are equivalent to the number of lanes on a highway for cars (data) to travel at any given moment. If you plug in too many devices you can request more ports than are allotted for the USB controller and you will get an error, similar to Figure 19.16.

FIGURE 19.16 USB controller error

The easiest way to fix this issue is to move some USB devices around on the USB ports. You should move any devices that don't need USB 3.0 to USB 2.0 ports, such as keyboards and mice. Then ensure that your devices that require speed support are connected to USB 3.0 ports. If you are using a USB hub, make sure that you have connected it to a similar port. For example, if you are using a USB 2.0 hub, ensure it is connected to a USB 2.0 port and not a USB 3.0 port. More complex solutions are upgrading the driver to the latest driver the vendor supplies for the USB controller or just simply upgrading the hardware to a newer chipset.

Slow-Loading Profiles

A local profile is a group of settings for the user as well as their personal files. Local profiles can be slow to load because of items set to start when the profile is loaded. You can use Task Manager to selectively disable startup items, as shown in Figure 19.17. By the process of elimination and after several logouts and logins, you can narrow down the performance problem caused by slow-loading local profiles.

FIGURE 19.17   Startup items in Task Manager

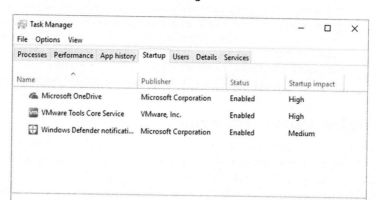

Typically, local profiles will not slow down login tremendously. Roaming profiles that are located on a server typically cause slow loading of the profile. The local profiles don't need to traverse a network during login. Roaming profiles, on the other hand, need to traverse the network during login (load from the server) and logout (write back to the server).

There are some things you can do to alleviate the stress on the network and speed up the load time of network profiles. For example, you can save space by deleting temporary Internet files in both Edge and Internet Explorer. You can also save a tremendous amount of space—sometimes gigabytes—by deleting downloaded files. In addition to space traversing the network, login scripts, Group Policy processing, and services starting upon login can also contribute to slow-loading profiles.

Time Drift

The *real-time clock (RTC)* on the motherboard is responsible for maintaining the correct time. The RTC can drift over time and the computer can become faster or slower. When an operating system is running on a hypervisor, the problem is increased tenfold, since the RTC is actually emulated by the hypervisor. When the *time drifts* too far, you can have authentication problems. If the time drifts too far, certificates can also be invalidated and you'll have problems with web browsers.

Fortunately, the Windows operating system has addressed the problems of time drift by periodically querying a Network Time Protocol (NTP) server. You will need to ensure that the client has the ability to contact the time server of time.windows.com, or you will need to configure a time server the client can reach.

You can verify that the NTP server is reachable by opening the Date & Time Control Panel applet and trying to update time. This can be performed by clicking the Start menu ➤ Windows System ➤ Control Panel ➤ Date & Time, then selecting the Internet Time tab and clicking Change Settings. Be sure that the Synchronize With An Internet Time Server option is selected. Then click Update Now. The operating system will attempt to call out to the NTP server and the results will be displayed in the dialog box, as shown in Figure 19.18.

FIGURE 19.18   Configuration of time

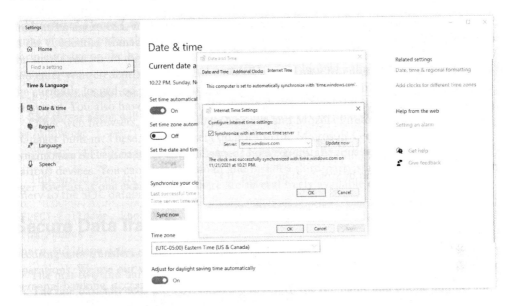

On virtual machines running on a hypervisor, the VMware guest tools or Hyper-V Integration Services will be responsible for emulating the RTC. These additions will also sync the VM's clock to the hypervisor host's time; this way, you only have to worry about the host's synchronization with an NTP server.

Common Troubleshooting Steps

Now that we've covered common symptoms of Microsoft Windows OS problems, let's look at common solutions that you can implement to solve those problems.

Rebooting

Rebooting a system often takes care of problems, for a multitude of reasons. One of the top reasons is that it allows the operating system to terminate hung processes gracefully. After the operating system reboots, the processes are normally restarted. An added bonus is that only the applications the user requires are relaunched. The goal is to fix the user's problem with minimal disruption. A reboot can't be done every time, especially if the user could lose work as a result.

Depending on the circumstances, when reproducing a problem, one of the first things to do is reboot. It serves an important purpose of isolating the problem so that you can reproduce it. For example, if you've isolated the problem to Excel not scrolling properly when a web browser is open, you should reboot and try to replicate the problem. If you discover the reboot fixed the problem, then you've solved the problem. However, if the problem still exists, you've now isolated the problem further by eliminating other programs that could have been hung in the background affecting this problem. The steps of rebooting and then opening Excel can also be used to verify when you've solved the problem.

Restarting Services

Services normally don't need to be restarted. On occasion, however, a change is made that requires that a service be restarted to reflect the change. Services should be restarted if they crash, of course. Although this is rare, it still happens from time to time. If a service crashes, you can restart the service in the Computer Management MMC by selecting Services, then right-clicking Service and choosing Start, as shown in Figure 19.19. You can use the same method to restart a running service.

FIGURE 19.19   Manually starting a service

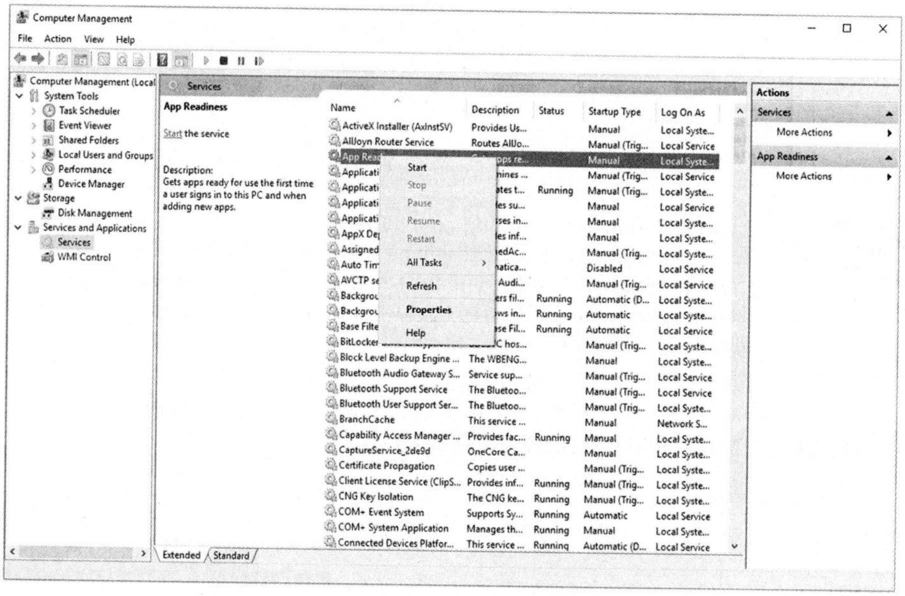

Services can be configured to automatically start in the event of failure on the Recovery tab of the Services properties, as shown in Figure 19.20. For example, by default the Print Spooler service is set to restart on the first and second failure, but after that it will remain stopped. The reset counter can be set for a number of days, and the service can be started after a specific number of minutes after its failure. You can even have the computer restart or run a program in the event a service fails.

FIGURE 19.20 Service recovery

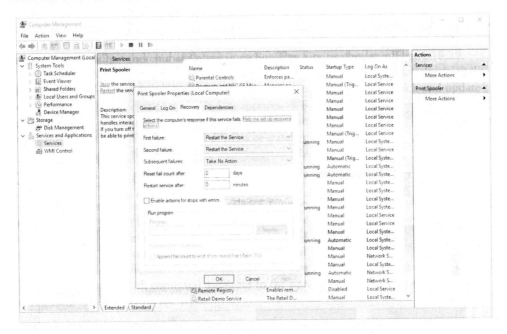

Fixing Application Issues

If an application is crashing and acting erratically, it may be due to another application that has overwritten critical files used by the application, or the files may have become corrupted. In either case, choosing to repair an application will validate that it is installed properly and the process will replace any missing critical files for the application. Data files and configuration files will not be touched while the application is being repaired; only critical files (such as DLLs) will be checked and repaired.

You can repair an application by right-clicking the Start menu, selecting Apps And Features, then Programs And Features (under the Related Settings heading), right-clicking the application, and then selecting Repair, as shown in Figure 19.21. The application's installer will launch and start to repair the application.

If a repair does not fix the application, then you should perform a complete uninstall and reinstallation of the application. When you uninstall the application, the uninstaller should remove configuration files that could be causing the issue. Some applications require you to manually remove the configuration files, which are often in a folder of your profile, such as AppData. You should always contact the vendor for the specific folders to remove to ensure the application has been completely uninstalled. Once you've completely uninstalled the application, you can reinstall the application and test to see if the problem is fixed.

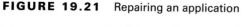

FIGURE 19.21   Repairing an application

If after a repair or uninstall and reinstall, the application is still broken, it could be caused by a bug. You can update the application to get the latest fixes. However, it is always recommended to identify the problem and then cross-reference it with the vendor's change log for the application.

NOTE   Using the attitude "I can't break it any more than it is broke" might work for most applications. However, just blindly updating an application may cause other problems and complicate the original issue. Always try to verify if the problem is a known bug and update the application accordingly.

Application Requirements and Resources

Applications require a certain amount of RAM, storage space, and CPU speed. Some applications may also require an SSD hard drive, or a GPU with a specific speed and amount of VRAM. When searching for a solution for a problem, you should first verify the requirements for the application based on the vendor's requirements. This will establish an expectation of performance for the application on the given hardware. If the requirement is higher than the given hardware, then you will need to scale the hardware up by adding resources.

Although the hardware might meet the requirements of the application, most often the application is not the only application running on the hardware. This must be taken into consideration when trying to solve a problem.

The performance of the application might also need to be addressed. Often vendors will publish the minimum specification for the application requirements. However, when you speak with support their recommendations for your workload might be very different. This is another aspect of the solution that must be taken into consideration.

Computers are built with a finite amount of resources, such as RAM, CPU, and storage. After reviewing the application requirements and weighing the considerations of application coexistence with other applications and the current load of the application in question, you may decide to add more resources. Adding resources such as RAM, CPU, and storage is considered to be scaling up the hardware. Before adding resources, you should document the performance and the utilization of the resources. Then after you've added the resources, you should compare the current performance and utilization of resources by the application.

System File Checks

When a feature of the operating system stops functioning or errs in a manner that makes you suspect corruption, the System File Checker tool can scan and replace critical files. The System File Checker is launched from the command line with the command `sfc.exe` and performs a myriad of functions. For example, you can execute the command `sfc.exe /verifyonly` and the System File Checker will inspect all the critical files and verify integrity only. You can also supply the command `sfc.exe /scannow` and the tool will scan and repair any files that fail the integrity check. You can perform the same task on individual files such as `kernel32.dll`. The System File Checker tool will also allow offline repair and checks.

Using the System File Checker tool on the operating system to be inspected is pretty straightforward, as described previously. However, if the operating system can't boot, you can use the command in offline mode as well. You simply boot the Windows Recovery Environment locally from installation media or some other source. Once the Windows Recovery Environment is booted, select Advanced Options and open a Command Prompt as Administrator. Then enter **sfc.exe /scannow /offbootdir=C:\ /offwindir=C:\Windows**, assuming that Windows is installed on the C: drive.

Repairing Windows

As previously discussed, the System File Checker utility will verify the integrity and replace any corrupted files. However, the utility will only replace files if they fail an integrity check. An alternate method to ensure the operating system is properly installed is to perform a repair installation of Windows. The repair installation will reinstall all files from source media regardless of their integrity. The repair installation will leave all applications and user files in place.

To initiate a repair installation of Windows, you will need to first download a copy of Windows. The easiest way to download Windows is to use the installation media creation tool. You can download the media to a USB flash drive or to an ISO file. If you download the media to a USB flash drive, then all you must do to start the process is launch `setup .exe` and choose to keep all apps and files. If you download an ISO file, you will need to mount the ISO by double-clicking the file. You can then start `setup.exe` and follow the prompts, choosing to keep all apps and files. Either option will begin the reinstallation of the operating system, as shown in Figure 19.22.

FIGURE 19.22   Reinstallation of Windows

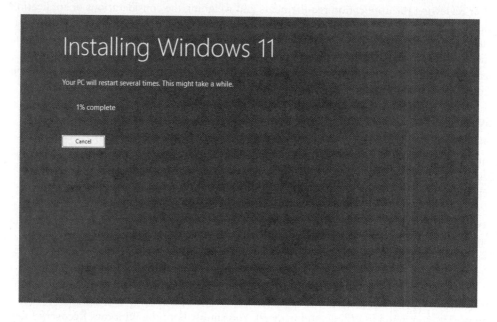

Restoring Windows

Almost everyone, no matter how hard they've tried to keep their computer running properly, will experience a computer crash at some point. Many of the ways to get your computer back up and running (such as reinstalling the operating system) take a lot of time. In Windows, System Restore allows you to create restore points to make recovery of the operating system easier.

A *restore point* is a copy of your system configuration at a given point in time. Restore points are created one of three ways:

▪   Windows creates them automatically by default.

▪   You can manually create them yourself (which is highly recommended before you make any significant changes to the system, such as installing new drivers).

▪   During the installation of some programs, a restore point is created before the installation; that way, if the installation fails, you can "roll back" the system to a preinstallation configuration.

Restore points are useful for when Windows fails to boot but the computer appears to be fine otherwise, or if Windows doesn't seem to be acting right and you think it was because of a recent configuration change.

It's important to note that in Windows 10/11, the automatic system recovery option is disabled by default. It must be turned on manually. We will cover how to do so in Exercise 19.2.

Microsoft is moving toward unifying all settings under the Settings app for Windows 10/11. This differs from prior operating systems and the legacy Control Panel app. System Restore is one of those settings that can be opened only from the legacy Control Panel app. To open System Restore, click Start, type **Control Panel** and select it from the results, and then click System And Security. This will open to a list of Control Panel choices. Select Security And Maintenance, and then Recovery. A screen like the one shown in Figure 19.23 will appear, and you can select from one of several tasks.

FIGURE 19.23   Windows Advanced Recovery Tools

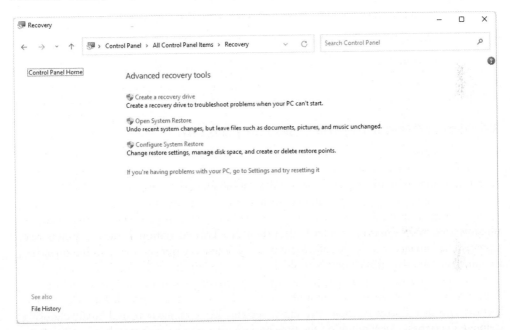

 If you need to use a restore point and Windows won't boot, the system will boot in the *Windows Recovery Environment*, in which a full system restore can be performed.

The Advanced Recovery Tools can be used to configure System Restore settings. You can also get to Advanced Recovery Tools by opening the System Control Panel (right-click Computer and choose Properties) and selecting the System Protection tab.

The other option is to select how much disk space is available for System Restore. The less disk space you make available, the fewer restore points you will be able to retain. If you have multiple hard drives, you can allocate a different amount of space to each drive.

Exercise 19.2 demonstrates how to create a restore point manually in Windows.

Manually Creating a Restore Point in Windows

1. Click the Start menu, type **Control Panel**, and then click the Control Panel app result.

2. Click System And Security, and then click Security And Maintenance, and then Recovery.

3. Click Configure System Restore. The System Properties dialog box will open.

4. Select Local Disk (C:) (System), and then click Configure.

5. Click the Turn On System Protection radio button, and then click OK.

6. Click Create below the Configure button.

7. Type a name for the restore point.

8. When the process is finished, click OK, and then exit out of the Control Panel windows.

Reimaging/Reloading the Operating System

In certain situations, a problem may require you to reinstall software. The time required to uninstall and reinstall the software can sometimes exceed the time it takes to reimage the operating system with the software preinstalled. Reimaging the computer will depend on whether you use operating system images or load each computer by hand.

If your organization does not use a standardized image for its computers, you can use the Windows Recovery Environment and select the Reset This PC option. If the computers have a preinstalled image, you can use the System Image Recovery option to reload the operating system. You can select this option by holding down the Shift key as you reboot the operating system, then choosing Advanced Options after the reboot, then selecting System Image Recovery. You can also reset the computer by opening the Settings app, clicking Update & Security and then Recovery, then selecting Reset This PC (Get Started), and finally choosing Remove Everything. Depending on the type of computer you have, it may have a proprietary process for recovering system images.

A factory recovery partition may exist on a machine. A vendor has a great deal of freedom with what it puts here, but usually it contains copies of drivers and preinstalled programs. This partition—if it exists—may serve as a last resort for stabilizing a system if all else has failed.

Microsoft Updates

Occasionally, applying an update will fix a problem, mainly because that is what updates do: they fix problems. Once you've identified that applying an update is the solution, you need to download, distribute, and install the update. Luckily, by default Windows 10/11 automatically installs updates for the operating system to keep you up to date and problem-free.

In large-scale networks, the organization may employ a corporate patch-management solution. Microsoft offers a free patch-management solution called Windows Server Update Services (WSUS). Microsoft also sells a licensed solution called Microsoft Endpoint Configuration Manager (MECM), which performs many other functions in addition to patch management. If an update is required and your organization uses one of these products, the patch must be approved, downloaded, and deployed. Third-party patch-management solutions may also be used in your organization. Third-party solutions are usually specific to an application or suite of applications, such as Adobe or Autodesk.

In small office, home office (SOHO) environments and small network environments, the update may be a one-off installation for a specific application. In this case, the update just needs to be downloaded and installed, per the vendor instructions. Always make sure to have a plan to roll back from a bad update. Turning on System Protection before the update is a good idea. If an update fails, you can simply use System Restore to restore the operating system to a prior point in time.

Very rarely you will find that a Microsoft or third-party update has created a problem on the operating system. When this happens, it's pretty easy to roll back updates by uninstalling them. Simply open the Settings app, select Update & Security, then View Update History, then Uninstall Updates, and finally select the update and choose Uninstall, as shown in Figure 19.24.

FIGURE 19.24 Uninstalling an update

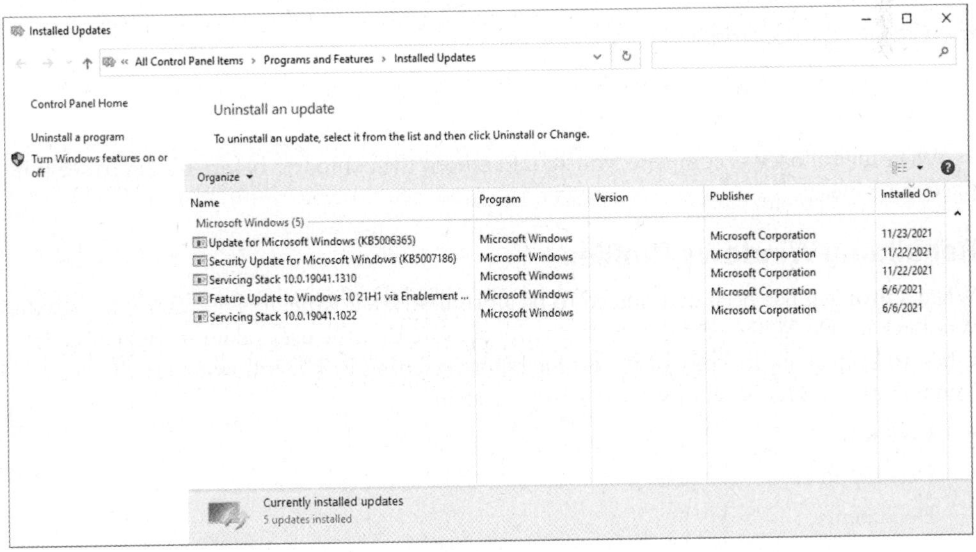

On the left of the Installed Updates screen, you can select Uninstall A Program. This will take you to the Programs And Features – Uninstall Or Change A Program screen. From here, you can uninstall third-party updates. After uninstalling an update, it's a good idea to reboot before testing to see if it fixed the issue.

An alternative to uninstalling an update is to use System Restore to revert to an earlier time before the update. However, System Protection must have been turned on before the update was installed. System Protection in Windows 10/11 is turned off by default. You can turn it on by clicking the Start menu, then type **Recovery** and select it, then click Configure System Restore, select the System drive, click Configure, select Turn On System Protection, and finally click OK.

Rolling Back Device Drivers

When you isolate a hardware problem to a faulty device driver, it is sometimes necessary to roll back the current driver to a prior version. This action will roll back the driver to the original version detected by Windows, also called the *out-of-box driver*. In some cases, it may roll back to a generic driver, which reduces functionality until a proper driver is installed.

This process can be completed with these steps:

1. Right-click the Start menu.
2. Select Device Manager.
3. Select the device.
4. Right-click and select Properties from the context menu.
5. Select the Driver tab.
6. Click Roll Back Driver.
7. Provide the reason for rolling back the driver.
8. Click Yes, as shown in Figure 19.25.

When the rollback is complete, you should reboot the computer before testing to see if it fixed the issue.

Rebuilding Windows Profiles

When a problem has been determined to be a profile-related issue, it is necessary to reset the Windows profile. When performing this action, ensure that the user's data is backed up. It is best to keep an entire copy of the profile before resetting it. The following are the most common places data is kept by the operating system:

- Contacts
- Desktop Items
- Documents

- Favorites

- Links

- Music

- Pictures

- Videos

- Saved Games (optionally)

- Downloads (optionally)

- 3D Objects (optionally)

FIGURE 19.25   Rolling back a driver

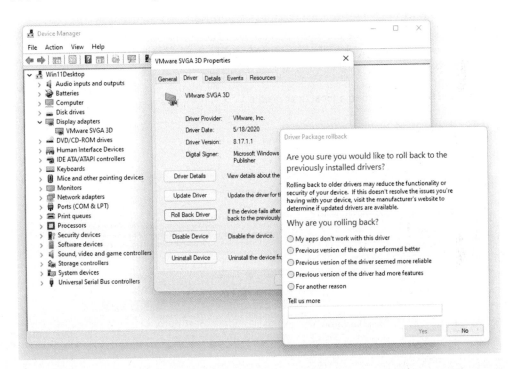

To back up a local profile, log into an administrative account (other than the one you are backing up), and then copy the profile under `C:\Users` to a new location. Do not move the profile, because the operating system references it in the Registry.

You can then reset a local profile on the Advanced tab of System Properties, as shown in Figure 19.26. You can access the User Profiles dialog box by following these steps:

1. Click the Start menu.

2. Type **System**.

3. Select System under Settings.

4. Click Advanced System Settings.

5. Select the Advanced tab.

6. Select Settings (User Profiles).

7. Select the profile you want to reset.

8. Click Delete, and answer Yes to confirm the deletion.

9. Log in as the user. Windows will create a new profile.

The user's files can then be manually copied over. The Profile dialog box also allows you to view the overall size of a user's local or remote profile, so it also helps in the troubleshooting process.

FIGURE 19.26 Deleting a local user profile

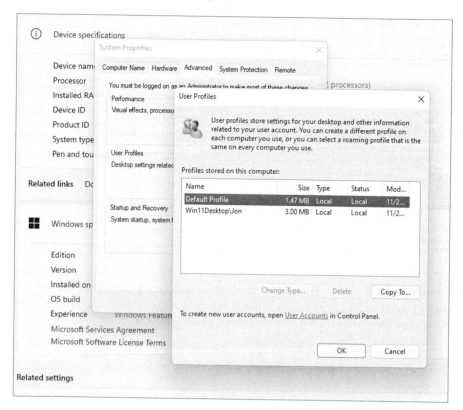

You can also use that procedure to delete a roaming user profile that has been left on the Windows operating system. However, performing the procedure on a roaming profile will not reset the profile. You will only remove the profile to clear space. To reset a network-based roaming profile, perform the following steps:

1. Ensure the user is logged out completely.

2. Delete all local copies of the user's profile left on any machine.

3. Navigate to the network location containing the user's profile and rename the folder.

4. Log the user into the machine on which you have deleted the locally cached copy.

5. Copy any useful items back to the user's profile.

6. Log the user out to ensure the roaming profile is saved back.

> **NOTE** User profile management can become complicated, depending on how it is implemented. For the CompTIA A+ exam, you will need to have a basic understanding. For more information, visit:
>
> https://docs.microsoft.com/en-us/windows/win32/shell/about-user-profiles

Troubleshooting Security Issues

There are a number of topics CompTIA expects you to know for the 220–1102 exam as it pertains to security issues. Many of these issues also appear in other CompTIA certification exams, such as Security+ and other exams that have a security component. Rest assured that for the 220–1102 exam, you do not need to know the depth of content as if you were preparing for the Security+ exam. However, you should be familiar with the following symptoms when determining if a security-related problem has occurred:

- You are unable to access the network.

- Desktop alerts mysteriously appear.

- You receive false alerts regarding antivirus protection.

- Altered system or personal files are discovered.

- Missing or renamed files are discovered.

- Unwanted notifications appear within the operating system.

- Operating systems updates fail.

- You receive random or frequent pop-ups.

- You receive certificate warnings.

- Your browser is redirected to websites.

This list is by no means exhaustive. What is an absolute is the fact that you should immediately rectify the security issue or quarantine the system if you experience even one of these symptoms. In the following sections we will cover the aforementioned security-related symptoms, as well as explore some causes for these symptoms.

It cannot be overstated that establishing security policies and procedures, updating your operating systems, updating your applications, and updating your network devices are all good measures to help eliminate potential security problems.

Common Symptoms

The operating system is by far the largest attack vector for threat agents. The software installed on the operating system and the files that the operating system stores are the perfect mixture of targets. Threat agents can target an unpatched application that contains a vulnerability. A threat agent can also sneak a file that is infected with malware onto the operating system. In the following section we will identify symptoms of common security issues along with their possible causes.

The solutions for the symptoms vary significantly. However, the overall goal is to keep your operating system protected. Protecting the operating system can be achieved by keeping the OS current on all patches. The applications that are installed on the operating system should be kept current with patches as well. Antimalware software should be installed, and best practices should be employed, as previously discussed in past chapters.

Network Connectivity Issues

If your computer is hooked up to a network, you need to know when your computer is not functioning properly on the network and what to do about it. In most cases, the problem can be attributed to either a malfunctioning network interface card (NIC) or improperly installed network software. The biggest indicator in Windows that some component of the network software is nonfunctional is that you can't log in to the network or access any network service. To fix this problem, you must first fix the underlying hardware problem (if one exists) and then properly install or configure the network software.

In some situations, network connectivity issues can be related to security threats. Although you might not seem to have network connectivity, the NIC might be working fine, while the real problem is a malicious program that has crashed or that it is not operating as the creator of the malicious program intends. The malware will act as a *proxy* for the network traffic. This type of malware is usually intent on stealing credentials or banking information. However, it can also be used to inject ads and cause *browser redirection*.

Not all malware that causes network connectivity issues acts as a proxy. Some malware changes network settings, such as your DNS servers. This type of malware will cause browser redirections by controlling what you resolve through its DNS. It is also common for malware to change your system proxy so that all requests go through the threat agent's remote proxy.

False Alerts and Hoaxes

Users have plenty of real viruses and other issues to worry about, yet some people find it entertaining to issue phony threats disguised as security alerts to keep people on their toes. Some of the more popular *hoaxes* that have been passed around are the Goodtimes and the Irina viruses. Millions of users received emails about these two viruses, and the symptoms sounded awful. The mention of these two hoaxes serves to outline the most well-known hoaxes. Since these came out, there have been many different hoaxes, most of which were not as well known as these.

Both of these warnings claimed that the viruses would do things that are impossible to accomplish with a virus. When you receive a virus warning, you can verify its authenticity by looking on the website of the antivirus software you use, or you can go to several public systems. One of the most helpful sites to visit to get the status of the latest viruses is the website for the *CERT organization* (www.cert.org). CERT monitors and tracks viruses and provides regular reports on this site.

> Though the names are similar, there is a difference between http://cert.org and http://us-cert.gov. While the latter is a government site for the U.S. Computer Emergency Readiness Team, the former is a federally funded research and development center at Carnegie Mellon University.

When you receive an email that you suspect is a hoax, check the CERT site before forwarding the message to anyone else. The creator of the hoax wants to create widespread panic, and if you blindly forward the message to coworkers and acquaintances, you're helping the creator accomplish this task. For example, any email that includes "forward to all your friends" is a candidate for research. Disregarding the hoax allows it to die a quick death and keeps users focused on productive tasks. Any concept that spreads quickly through the Internet is referred to as a *meme*.

Identifying a Hoax

Symantec and other vendors maintain pages devoted to bogus hoaxes. Symantec's site is located at:

www.symantec.com/security-center/risks/hoaxes

You can always check there to verify whether an email you've received is indeed a hoax.

Desktop Alerts

A desktop alert is a notification or dialog box that is crafted to look like it was generated by the operating system. This is a crafty way of social engineering the user into becoming a victim. The malware is crafted to generate a pop-up box that states there is a security error detected and that you should call Microsoft or Windows Support right away, as shown in Figure 19.27. When you call the number given, you are calling scammers who will try to sell you software you don't need.

FIGURE 19.27   Malware-generated call-in alert

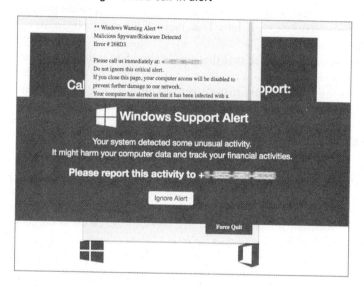

Social engineering is not the only method of a threat agent. The threat agent can generate realistic operating system dialog boxes that coax you into downloading and installing malware, such as shown in Figure 19.28. The average person might just figure it's time to update their software—it even states that, by downloading the software (malware), you agree to the EULA.

FIGURE 19.28   Malware-generated download alert

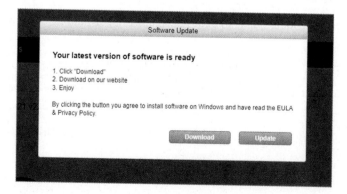

OS Notifications

Another really popular method of distributing malware is by using browser push notification messages. The user will browse to a malicious site and then the user will be coaxed into allowing push notifications for the site. Once this is allowed, the site can push notifications to the operating system and spawn a notification that looks like it's coming from the operating system. Use of the operating system notifications is a well-known attack aimed at coaxing the user into installing malware or pushing advertising to the user.

In some cases, the initial installation of the malware is prompted by a browser push notification. After the user installs the malware, it might start prompting deals of the day or other ads. This type of malware is considered adware, and it is becoming rare compared to other types of malware covered in this chapter.

Outside of user education, antimalware software can be used to prevent this type of threat. However, user education is much more effective. A routine review of sites allowed to send notifications should be performed periodically. A routine review of installed applications should be performed as well to ensure that malware has not been installed at some point.

Rogue Antivirus

One clever way of spreading a virus is to disguise it so that it looks like an antivirus program. When it alerts the user to a fictitious problem, the user then begins interacting with the program and allowing the rogue program to do all sorts of damage. One of the trickiest things for threat agents to do is to make the program look as if it came from a trusted source—such as Microsoft—and mimic the Windows Notification Center interface enough to fool an unsuspecting user. The notification might show that a new download or update is waiting for you to install it. It may even notify you that your antivirus software is disabled and needs attention.

Education is the only way to combat rogue antivirus. You should arm yourself with the knowledge of current antivirus programs. You can achieve this knowledge by reading consumer articles on the latest and greatest antivirus and antimalware applications. You should also pass that education to others in your family and organization. This can easily be achieved by detailing which antivirus and antimalware you have installed. Then there will be no confusion when a notification or pop-up occurs stating it's time to install the rogue antivirus malware.

Threat agents are designing malware to look very realistic and mimic big-name software. If you are unsure of the source and do not trust it, visit the site and redownload the software. Do your homework, as the threat agents are doing their homework.

Renamed System Files/Disappearing Files/Permission Changes/ Access Denied

Threat actors that create malware have a number of methods by which they can wreak havoc on a system. One of the simplest ways is to delete key system files and replace them with malicious copies. When this occurs, the user can no longer perform the operation associated with the file, such as printing, saving, and so on. When malware is embedded on an operating system and gains privilege level access, it is known as a *root kit*. Once the operating system is infected with the malware, the threat actors will comb through files looking for sensitive information that they can ransom.

Just as harmful as deleting files, the malware can rename the files or change the permissions associated with them. This could prevent the user from accessing the files or even copying them off to an uninfected system. When an operating system is infected with *ransomware* the malware will encrypt the files. The files might also disappear from the user's normal view and the ransom request may be placed in the parent directory. The mode of operation for most ransomware is to rename the files with a unique extension as the malware encrypts the files. The ransom note is then placed in every folder so the user has instructions on payment for decrypting the files.

Starting with Windows Vista, Microsoft enabled the User Account Control (UAC) by default. This change to the operating system greatly reduced the number of attempts to use elevated privileges and definitely made it more difficult to change system files. In addition to enabling the UAC, Microsoft removed the Modify NTFS permission from system files for the Administrator account. Only the *Trusted Installer* (Windows Update) has access to modify these files; even the System (operating system) permissions are Read and Execute. If that wasn't enough, a self-healing service watches for files changed and replaces them with trusted versions. The System File Checker (SFC) is a user tool that can be used to manually heal missing or modified system files. Malware can maliciously modify files and, in some cases, cause them to go missing. The System File Checker was covered in Chapter 15, "Windows 10 Administration," and was also discussed earlier in this chapter.

OS Update Failures

Failed updates for Windows—assuming they aren't caused by connectivity issues—can often be traced to misconfigured settings. These settings can also cause the operating system to report that an update needs to be installed when it has already been installed. The best solution is to find the error code being reported in Windows Update Troubleshooter, solve the problem, and download the update.

Recent versions of Windows 10/11 include a troubleshooting utility. To access the utility, click the Start menu and select the Settings app. Once the Setting app opens, select Update & Security, then click Troubleshoot, then Additional Troubleshooters, and finally choose Windows Update.

Microsoft has also published some common problems that should be checked. You can access the document at `https://support.microsoft.com/en-us/windows/troubleshoot-problems-updating-windows-188c2b0f-10a7-d72f-65b8-32d177eb136c`. The solutions Microsoft recommends in the documents are:

- Reboot.

- Verify free space.

- Run Windows Update again.

- Update third-party drivers.

- Disconnect external hardware.

- Check Device Manager for errors.

- Perform a system restore or repair installation.

Browser-Related Symptoms

The web browser is the most used application on the operating system. It's so popular that Google has made an operating system around their Chrome web browser called the ChromeOS. On Windows, the web browser is just an application like any other application on the operating system. However, it is the easiest way a threat agent can access your operating system. Therefore, in this section we will cover some of the most common symptoms you may observe related to the web browser.

Pop-Ups

Pop-ups (also commonly known as popups) are both frustrating and chancy. When a user visits a website and another instance (either another tab or another browser window) opens in the foreground, it is called a pop-up; if it opens in the background, it is called a *pop-under*. Both pop-ups and pop-unders are pages or sites that you did not specifically request and that may only display ads or bring up applets that should be avoided.

Most modern web browsers come standard with a pop-up blocker and by default they block all pop-ups. If you visit a link that contains a pop-up, the browser will notify you that it has blocked it. If the pop-up is on a trusted website, you will have the option to allow pop-ups for the site.

Threat agents have found other creative ways to pop up ads or referred content. Through the use of JavaScript they can serve overlays over the original web page. In older web browsers, the JavaScript could even hold you hostage at the malicious page. However, most newer browsers limit the access of JavaScript and you can always close the web page.

If you continually receive pop-ups or overlays, then you may be infected with malware or a rogue page is minimized serving the pop-ups/overlays. A reboot should clear the problem, but it is also best to scan your operating system with antivirus/antimalware software.

Certificate Issues

There are several problems that plague *digital certificates*. Of the two major problems, one is related to the proper setting of time and date and the other is trust related. The time on the host should always be checked along with the expiration of the SSL certificate. If the certificate is expired, this will cause problems.

On the other hand, when an untrusted SSL certificate is encountered, the web browser will alert you that the SSL certificate is not valid, as shown in Figure 19.29. Every web browser comes with a list of trusted certificate publishers. If a certificate is issued to a website or is not trusted, a warning box will come up preventing you from visiting the site. You can click through the warning prompt and visit the site anyway, but the address bar will still read "Not secure" or display an unlocked lock icon during your visit.

FIGURE 19.29 An untrusted SSL certificate warning

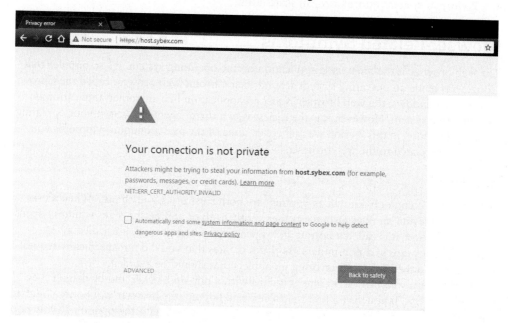

The problem should always be investigated further, since information entered in the site could be intercepted if the site was hacked. The first step to diagnose is checking the hostname in the URL. All certificates must match the hostname in the URL that they are issued for. If you tried accessing the site by the IP address, this warning is benign and can be disregarded. However, if you entered the correct hostname, then the certificate should be inspected. Every web browser is different, but every web browser will let you view the certificate. In Figure 19.30 we can see that the certificate has been self-signed.

Both the Issued To and Issued By fields in the certificate are the same. This is common when the website is in development, but it is not normal once the website has been placed into production. It is also common on network management equipment that allows configuration through a web page. Often the management web page will use a self-signed certificate. For this purpose, the certificate can be imported into your trusted publisher certificate store so that it can be trusted in the future.

FIGURE 19.30 A self-signed certificate

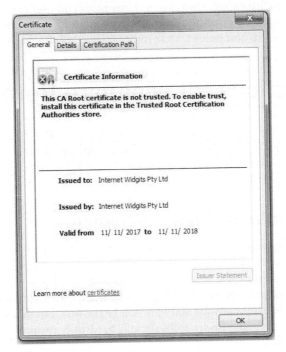

Browser Redirection

Pharming is a form of redirection in which traffic intended for one host is sent to another. This can be accomplished on a small scale by changing entries in the hosts file and on a large scale by changing entries in a DNS server, also known as *DNS poisoning*. In either case, when a user attempts to go to a site, they are redirected to another site. For example, suppose Illegitimate Company ABC creates a site to look exactly like the site for Giant Bank XYZ. The pharming is done (using either redirect method) and users trying to reach Giant Bank XYZ are tricked into going to Illegitimate Company ABC's site, which looks enough like what they are used to seeing that they give their username and password.

As soon as Giant Bank XYZ realizes that the traffic is being redirected, it will immediately move to stop it. But while Illegitimate Company ABC will be shut down, it was able to collect data for the length of time that the redirection occurred, which could vary from minutes to days.

Another form of browser redirection is called affiliate redirection. This type of browser redirection can be very subtle. For example, when you search for a product and click the link in the results, the malware will redirect your browser to the intended site with an affiliate link attached. Now anything you purchase will credit a commission to the person who redirected the browser with the affiliate link. This malware is usually related to an unscrupulous plug-in in the browser.

Because an attacker can use many different tactics to launch browser redirection, the mitigation is not straightforward. However, implementing end-user education, maintaining updates for browsers and operating systems, and ensuring that your antimalware/antivirus software is up-to-date are best practices to protect against browser redirection.

Best Practices for Malware Removal

Best practices for malware removal is a key objective for the 220-1102 exam. The best way to think about this is as a seven-item list of what CompTIA wants you to consider when approaching a possible malware infestation. The following discussion presents the information that you need to know.

1. Identify and Verify Malware Symptoms

Before doing anything major, it is imperative first to be sure that you are dealing with the right issue. If you suspect malware, try to identify the type (spyware, virus, and so on) and look for the proof needed to substantiate that it is indeed the culprit.

You first need to identify the problem. This can be done with a multitude of tools, but hopefully your antivirus/antimalware software will be the first tool that helps to identify the problem. If the antivirus/antimalware software fails to identify the problem, then other third-party tools must be used.

Earlier in this chapter, in the section "Troubleshooting Common Microsoft Windows OS Problems," we introduced you to Resource Monitor to isolate performance problems. A similar tool, called Process Explorer, can be downloaded from Microsoft Sysinternals. This tool allows a different visualization from what Resource Monitor provides, as shown in Figure 19.31. You can see the process list on the operating system; in this case, there is a process called regsvr32.exe. When you look more closely, you can see that it is creating network traffic and is very active on the operating system. The process is actually a ransomware application calling out to command-and-control servers. It is sneakily disguising itself as the regsvr32.exe utility, which is normally used to register DLLs.

Unfortunately, this lone example will not give you the expertise of a professional virus/malware hunter. However, it provides just one of many examples of third-party software that can help you detect and identify viruses and malware running on a computer.

Many built-in tools, such as netstat.exe, can also provide assistance. For example, the netstat -nab command enables you to view all the processes on the operating system and their network connections. Using the netstat -nab command is how it was identified that something looked wrong with the regsvr32.exe process; otherwise, the command would have looked like any other process on the operating system.

In addition to applications that can identify viruses and malware, third-party websites can aid in detection. One such website is VirusTotal (www.virustotal.com). VirusTotal allows users to upload potentially unsafe applications. Their service will scan the applications against more than 70 antivirus engines and report if the signature is found. It's a valuable tool to validate that you've found an application on your operating system that is malicious. Many tools, such as Process Explorer, can even check against the VirusTotal database.

FIGURE 19.31   Process Explorer

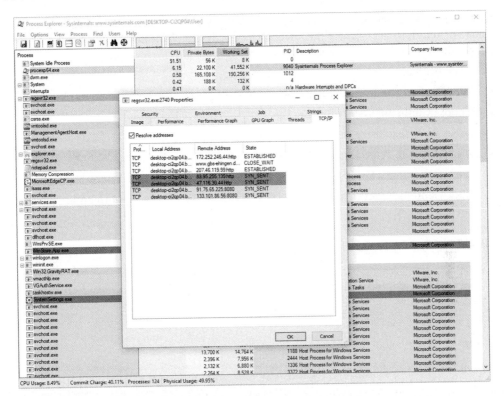

2. Quarantine Infected Systems

Once you have confirmed that a virus or malware is at hand, then quarantine the infected system to prevent it from spreading the virus or malware to other systems. Bear in mind that the virus or malware can spread in any number of ways, including through a network connection, email, and so on. The quarantine needs to be complete enough to prevent any spread.

Ransomware is probably the biggest risk, since it will spread through a network rapidly and encrypt files in its path. The ransom is usually equivalent to the number of files or the total size of files. In either case, over the past eight years it has made headline news, as it has taken down extremely large companies. In one instance, the Petya ransomware even took down most of the computers in Ukraine, along with several other countries.

If an infected system is discovered and needs further analysis, it should be quarantined from the network and put into an isolated network. This hot network is a place where it can be studied further, without repercussions to the operational network.

3. Disable System Restore in Windows

This is a necessary step because you do not want to have the infected system create a restore point—or return to one—where the infection exists. System Protection in Windows 10/11 is turned off by default. You can disable System Protection with these steps:

1. Click the Start menu.
2. Type **Recovery** and select it from the results.
3. Choose Configure System Restore.
4. Select the system drive and click Configure.
5. Disable System Protection.
6. Click Delete (Disk Space Usage).
7. Click Continue (confirmation), then Close, OK, and finally Yes (confirmation), as shown in Figure 19.32.

FIGURE 19.32   System Protection

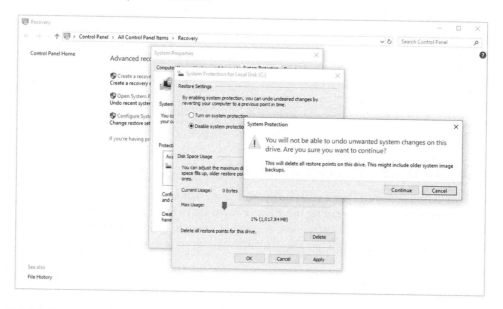

Most ransomware will dump your restore points for you, since you could potentially recover the operating system and then recover files using your previous versions.

4. Remediate Infected Systems

The steps taken here depend on the type of virus or malware with which you're dealing, but they should include updating antivirus and antimalware software with the latest definitions and using the appropriate scan and removal techniques. You can update *Microsoft Defender* from the Microsoft Defender Security Center by clicking the task tray in the lower-right corner of the desktop, then right-clicking the Windows Security shield, and finally clicking Check For Protection Updates, as shown in Figure 19.33.

FIGURE 19.33 Microsoft Defender Security updates

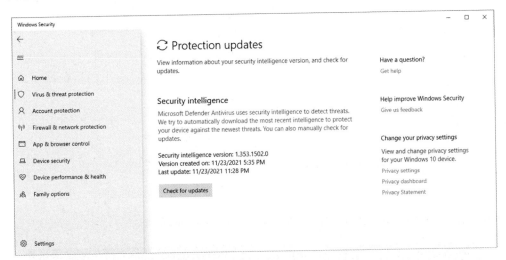

Depending on the type of virus or malware, you may need to boot into safe mode or the Windows Recovery Environment (as discussed earlier in this chapter). However, the remediation of the virus or malware will be different for each situation. Microsoft Defender Security can automatically perform an offline scan. To perform an offline scan, click the task tray in the lower-right corner, then right-click the shield, select View Security Dashboard, click Virus & Threat Protection, click Scan Options, and select Microsoft Defender Offline Scan, as shown in Figure 19.34.

After you confirm that you will save your work by clicking Scan in the confirmation dialog box, the UAC will prompt you to answer Yes, and then Windows will reboot. The Windows Recovery Environment will boot and Windows Defender Antivirus will run, as shown in Figure 19.35.

FIGURE 19.34 Microsoft Defender Offline scan

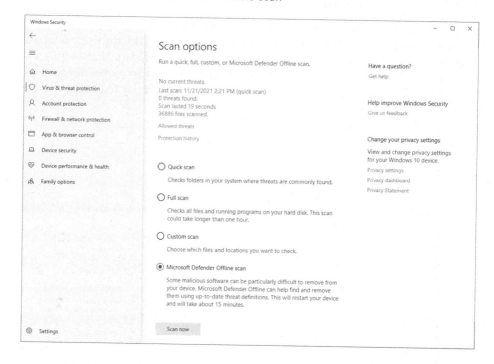

FIGURE 19.35 An offline Microsoft Defender Antivirus scan

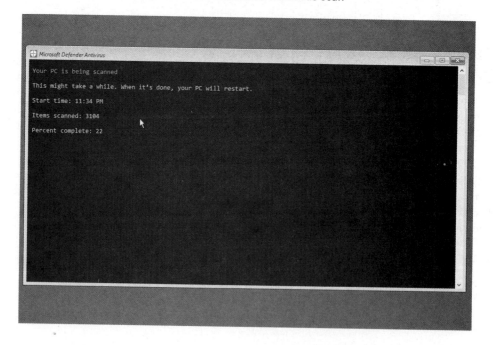

In some situations, such as in a ransomware attack, no remediation can be performed because the user files are encrypted. In these cases, the malware should be removed from the operating system, and then the user data must be restored from a backup. The unfortunate and terrifying fact when it comes to ransomware is that there will be loss of work.

In many instances, remediating the virus or malware is impossible because no one knows for sure what the virus or malware actually does. Antivirus researchers can document the delivery system that a virus or malware uses to enter your system. You can then patch the vulnerability, which is part of the remediation process. What antivirus research cannot do most of the time is document the payload of a virus or malware. This is because most of the time the payload is encrypted and changed, depending on the need of its creator. In these cases, the remediation might be to sanitize the drive and reinstall the operating system from an image or manually install it.

5. Schedule Scans and Run Updates

The odds of the system never being confronted by malware again are slim. To reduce the chances of it being infected again, schedule scans and updates to run regularly. Most anti-malware programs can be configured to run automatically at specific intervals; however, should you encounter one that does not have such a feature, you can run it through Task Scheduler.

Microsoft Defender Security is scheduled to automatically scan the operating system during idle times. However, if you want to schedule a scan, you can use Task Scheduler:

1. Click the Start menu.
2. Type **Task Scheduler** and then select Task Scheduler from the results.
3. Open the Task Scheduler Library.
4. Select Microsoft, then Windows
5. Select Windows Defender, and double-click Windows Defender Scheduled Scan.
6. Select the Triggers tab.
7. Click New on the Triggers tab, then select Weekly and choose the day of the week in the New Trigger dialog box.
8. Click OK, as shown in Figure 19.36. You'll need to click OK again after the New Trigger dialog box closes.

Windows Defender Security is scheduled to automatically download updates during the Windows Update check, which is daily. If you require the latest updates, use either the Check For Updates option in the Windows Update settings or the Check For Updates option in the Microsoft Defender Security Center.

FIGURE 19.36   Creating a Windows Defender Security scheduled scan

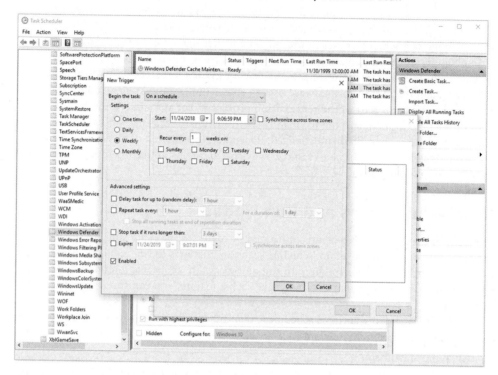

 Microsoft is in the process of rebranding Windows Defender; it will be called Microsoft Defender. Some settings may be under Windows Defender, such as the scheduled tasks discussed in this section. Some settings may also be under Microsoft Defender. Keep this in mind when looking for settings such as scheduled tasks and Group Policy Objects (GPOs).

6. Enable System Restore and Create a Restore Point in Windows

Once everything is working properly, it is important to create restore points again, should a future problem occur and you need to revert back. You can enable System Protection by following these steps:

1. Click the Start menu.
2. Type **Restore** and select it from the results.
3. Click Create A Restore Point.
4. Select the System drive and click Configure.
5. Click Turn On System Protection, and click OK.

You can then manually create a restore point by clicking Create in the System Protection dialog box, typing a description (such as **after remediation - date**), clicking Close (in the confirmation dialog box), and clicking OK to close the System Properties.

7. Educate the End User

Education should always be viewed as the final step. The end user needs to understand what led to the malware infestation and what to avoid, or look for, in the future to keep it from happening again. This training can be formal training in a classroom setting, or it can be an online training in which the user must participate and answer questions.

It is common for large companies to require annual or biannual end-user training for threats. It is becoming more common for training to be done online, and a number of companies offer this as a service. It is not uncommon for a company to send a phishing attempt to their employees. When an employee falls for the phishing attempt, they are automatically signed up for mandatory training. Incentives are also common, such as the first employee who notifies the IT department of the phishing attempt gets a gift card.

Troubleshooting Mobile OS Issues

As mobile devices have been rapidly replacing the desktop and laptop machines that used to rule the workplace, the equipment an administrator must maintain has now evolved to cover a plethora of options. This section focuses on common mobile OS and application issues and some of the tools that can be used to work with them. A subsequent section will look at the same topics with more of a focus on security.

In the following sections, we will cover many common symptoms of problems that are common with mobile OSs and applications. In this section, we cover how to identify application symptoms as they appear in the objectives.

Application Problems

Mobile devices are generally error free and function fine. However, as we install applications to the mobile OS, we introduce potential problems. This happens because a mobile application is generally developed for the nominal platform. The application is also usually only tested on one or two devices as the developer sees fit. The developer can't account for every make and model of mobile device, and this is generally why we see application problems. In this section we will cover the most common application problems you may encounter with mobile devices. You will notice that they are all somewhat connected and usually have the same steps to rectify the problem.

Application Launch Issues

If an application (app) does not load, it could be attributed to a multitude of reasons. One common reason is that the application is still running in the background and is not really loading; it is just becoming a foreground application and becoming the application in focus. When you close an application, it sometimes doesn't close all the way down and free up memory. Instead, it gets moved to the background and is technically still running.

The first thing you should try if an application is not loading is to force-quit the application. To force-quit an application on an Android device, press the tab view (usually the leftmost soft button) and then swipe the application left or right to close. On Apple devices, double-tap the Home button or swipe up on the application you want to close.

Another common problem related to applications not loading is that sometimes the cache associated with the application is corrupted. This usually happens right after an application upgrades itself, which is all the time on mobile devices. On an Android phone, you can clear the application's cache by tapping Settings, tapping Apps, choosing the application, tapping Storage, and finally tapping Clear Cache. On Apple devices, tap Settings, tap General, tap iPhone Storage, choose the application, and finally tap Reset Cache On Next Launch. Clearing the cache will not affect the majority of the application's storage.

In many cases, an application will not allow you to clear its cache. If the option is not there, or after you've cleared the cache the application is still not loading, uninstall and reinstall the application. This option will (should) remove any data associated with the app.

You can remove Android applications by tapping Settings, tapping Apps, choosing the application, and tapping Uninstall. You can then visit the Google Play store and reinstall the application.

Apple is even simpler. All you need to do is tap and hold on an icon until all the icons dance back and forth. An *X* will be displayed in the upper-left corner of the application icon. Simply tap the *X* to uninstall the application. You can then visit the App Store and reinstall the application.

Application Crashes

Another less common problem with applications is that they crash or close out unexpectedly. This issue is less common since most applications run fine, but occasionally you will have a mobile application just close or crash out on you. This is frustrating, because it usually happens when you most need it and it is generally an intermittent problem. This is how this particular problem differentiates itself from an app not loading; it doesn't crash every time.

The recommendations are the same for a crashing or closing application. Ultimately, you need to find the series of events or steps to trigger the bug and crash or close the application. Once you've reproduced the problem, it's time to try to fix the issue by doing one or more of the following:

- Force-quit the application.
- Clear the application cache.
- Clear the application data.
- Uninstall the application.
- Reboot the device.
- Reinstall the application.

If none of these solutions works, then it may be time to check the vendor's site for any similar problems (and solutions) encountered by others. Support for applications on mobile devices is normally forum or community support. However, some paid mobile applications have email-based support. Describe the issue, the device make and model, steps to reproduce the problem, and other applications installed on the device.

Application Fails to Update

You may have one or more applications on your mobile device that fail to update. Generally, the developers will backward support an old application until it doesn't make sense anymore, because of new features. The developer's expectation is that their application will be updated on all the mobile devices so that features still operate as expected. So the user will most likely see crashes, closes, or other erratic behavior if the application is not up to date.

The Google Play store and the Apple App Store manage the purchase, installation, and upgrade of applications. This upgrade maintenance on installed applications happen in the background without the user ever knowing it even happens. However, from time to time you may encounter an application that does not want to upgrade automatically. The first troubleshooting step should be to try to manually upgrade it from the Play Store or the App Store.

If manually updating the application does not work, then there are a few other steps you can take to troubleshoot the application, such as force-quitting the application and rebooting the phone to close any applications that may be stuck in memory. The next step is to temporarily disable any antivirus or antimalware software installed on the device. Then try to upgrade the application manually from the Play Store or the App Store.

Another consideration is to make sure that you are connected to the Internet via Wi-Fi. Most app store applications will treat cellular data as a metered connection and will not automatically update applications. Also make sure that the app store is configured to automatically update applications.

If all else fails and the application still doesn't want to upgrade, you can try to uninstall the application and reinstall it. You can follow the same guidelines for a crashing or closing application. Before uninstalling the application, make sure you check the compatibility for the latest version of the application. You could uninstall the application and find you can't reinstall it, because your device does not meet the minimum specifications. This could also be the original problem, which would explain why the application won't update.

Performance Issues

There are a number of reasons you can have performance issues with a mobile device. Most performance issues are directly related to the applications on the device. For example, an application may use too much processing time and it could cause poor battery life and performance. A group of applications can use all available RAM and starve the unit for processing space. In the following we cover the various performance problems you may encounter with a mobile device.

Slow Performance

Slow performance is almost always related to RAM usage. Mobile operating systems operate the same as conventional desktop or laptop operating systems. The only real difference between traditional operating systems and mobile devices is the default action for an application is not to close it but to put it into the background. As programs are loaded into RAM, they allocate a percentage for their variables and inner workings. When RAM is filled up, the mobile device will swap background memory pages onto the built-in storage; this process is similar to the page file process. This slows down the device because now its focus is on clearing up memory for competing applications.

Fortunately, most mobile devices allow you to see the RAM usage at a glance and over a longer period of time. On an Android device, tap Settings ➤ Battery And Device Care ➤ Memory. You will see the memory usage for the device, along with each application and its own usage. You can also clear up memory from here, which basically just closes the applications. Unfortunately, you cannot monitor RAM usage on an Apple mobile device, but a simple soft reset works just as well.

It is uncommon to have a performance problem attributed to high CPU on a mobile device. That is not to say it doesn't happen; it's just uncommon. To narrow down problems with a particular application performing slowly, reboot the device and launch only that particular application to isolate and monitor its performance.

Frozen System

Frozen is a silly term that technicians use when something is not functioning or responding. It doesn't really describe the temperature, just the functionality—a block of ice.

If the system is frozen (not responding to a single thing), it will appear with the same symptoms as a nonresponsive touchscreen. One of the ways you can differentiate between a frozen system/lockup and a nonresponsive touchscreen is if the device will soft reset. If the device will not soft reset, then a hard reset might need to be performed. The hard reset procedure should be research for the type of device you are trying to hard reset. For example, Apple has several different types of procedures depending on the model and generation of the device. Samsung also has hard reset procedures that differ based upon model of device.

If the restart does not work, plug in the device, let it charge (an hour or more is recommended), and then try to restart it. The power level in the battery can sometimes be so low that performance is turned all the way down and the device will appear unresponsive and frozen.

Random Reboots

Random reboots and restarts could be a symptom of a hardware issue. They can also be related to a problem in the operating system. When a problem is intermittent or random, it is very hard to diagnose. However, by checking the following you can at least rule out some of the most common culprits of random reboots.

Battery Health   The most obvious culprit is the battery that powers the phone. Check to make sure that your phone has a good charge and the battery is not swollen. If your phone allows for the battery to be replaced, you should clean the contacts and replace the battery. Then monitor for reboots.

Update   The operating system should be on the current revision of software. If it isn't, then it should be updated to the latest. Stability issues are often addressed in updates for the operating system.

Storage   Check the storage on the device and make sure that it is not over 90 percent. If it is over 90 percent, then you should clean up some space and monitor the device. You can do this by clearing data from applications, clearing application cache, and uninstalling unused applications.

Running Applications   Check the applications running on the operating system. This should be checked 10 minutes after a reboot so that you can see the applications that are set to automatically start on boot. You should disable or uninstall any application that is rarely used and automatically starts on boot.

Auto Restart   On some Android phones there is an Auto Restart feature that should be turned off by default. This feature should be checked because it could have been erroneously turned on and might causing the random reboots. Apple mobile devices do not have this feature.

Factory Reset   The dreaded factory reset is a last-ditch effort. It will, however, rule out the device's operating system from being the culprit of random reboots. You should also be selective in the software that you reinstall. A cyclical process of install and monitor, then install more and monitor, may help identify an application that is affecting the stability of the device.

OS Fails to Update

When an OS fails to update for a mobile device, there can be a number of reasons for the issue. However, as you will see, the common troubleshooting steps are no different than those for any other application on the mobile device.

Reboot   A reboot of the mobile device is always recommended, since a process could be preventing the update from installing. A reboot of the operating system also allows for memory to be freed up since insufficient memory could be preventing the update.

Compatibility   You should check to make sure that the operating system update is compatible with the mobile device hardware. It is common to find that a hardware device is only supported for 5 to 7 years, at which time it is no longer compatible with future operating system upgrades.

Storage   Make sure that there is enough storage space on the mobile device to accommodate the update. When an update is to be applied to the device, at some point both operating systems will need to exist: the upgrade and the current operating system.

Connectivity   Be sure that you have a Wi-Fi connection and that you are currently connected. Many operating systems will not download the update over a metered connection, such as cellular. A bad Internet connection can also prevent an OS update from completing.

If none of these suggestions allow you to successfully update the mobile device, then you can try to manually install the operating system update via the over-the-air (OTA) update. This will require a computer, and depending on the vendor, this option may not work. The vendor needs to support manual installation of updates with their third-party utility. Apple supports the iTunes application, which will work with the device to upgrade the operating system. For more information; visit `https://support.apple.com/en-us/HT212186`.

Extremely Short Battery Life

Batteries never last as long as you would like. Apple defines battery life as the amount of time a device runs before it needs to be recharged (as opposed to battery life span, which is the amount of time a battery lasts before it needs to be replaced). Tips for increasing battery life include keeping OS updates applied (they may include energy-saving patches), avoiding ambient temperatures that are too high or too low, letting the screen automatically dim, and turning off *location-based services*. You should also disconnect peripherals and quit applications not in use. Wi-Fi, for example, uses power when enabled, even if you are not using it to connect to the network.

Outside of the preceding usage tips, sometimes battery life is attributed to a performance problem. High RAM usage can shorten battery life because power is expended on moving pages of memory in and out of RAM. This is done to keep the foreground applications running.

Overheating

When most mobile devices get too warm, they will tell you that they need to cool down before they can continue to be used, and they will automatically take measures to protect themselves (turning off features, closing apps, and so on).

One of the most concerning reasons is the lithium-ion (Li-ion) battery contained inside these devices. When a Li-ion battery gets too hot, you risk explosion or fire from a situation called *thermal runaway*. This is where the battery starts to get so hot that the separator inside the battery melts and causes a chain reaction.

Luckily, mobile devices shut down when they get too hot from ambient temperatures or internal temperature from the CPU. One of the best ways to prevent overheating is to avoid ambient temperatures that are too hot. Avoid having the device in direct sunlight for extended time periods, in a hot car on a summer day, or on top of a heat source. When the device does overheat, you can often help it cool down quicker by removing any protective case that may be there—and putting it back on later.

Mobile Device Overheating

When a mobile device overheats, be sure to understand why it is overheating. Was the ambient temperature too hot? Was the CPU usage too high and indicative of another problem? Was it a combination of the two, or did you just leave it in the direct hot sun?

When a lithium-ion battery is exposed to heat (even in small amounts), its useful life span will degrade. Most phones today have a built-in battery, which is not user-replaceable. When the battery goes bad, you are either tied to a charger every hour or it's time for a new phone.

Connectivity Issues

We rely heavily on our mobile devices, and the day-to-day functionality of our mobile devices relies heavily on connectivity to the outside world. The connectivity to the provider network (cellular) is generally supported by the provider, such as Verizon, T-Mobile, or AT&T, just to name a few. When you have a problem with the cellular network, make sure that you have coverage and a fresh reboot. However, outside of the obvious you are best to escalate the problem to your provider. The day-to-day connectivity we are responsible for as A+ technicians will be covered in the following section.

Intermittent Wireless

There are a number of reasons why intermittent wireless connections can occur, but the two most common are lack of a good signal and interference. Increasing the number of *wireless access points (WAPs)* for coverage, or being closer to them, can address the lack of a good signal.

Interference can be addressed by reducing the number of devices competing for the same channel. In many instances, however, the interference may be coming from an external source, such as a microwave oven or even a Bluetooth device on the 2.4 GHz band. To avoid common interference of this nature, use an SSID that is dedicated to the 5 GHz band. Using the 5 GHz band won't guarantee you an interference-free connection, since radar operates in this band. However, you will have better odds of selecting a channel without interference. In an effort to reduce interference and speed up wireless connectivity, 802.11ax has been developed to use a 6 GHz band. The Wi-Fi Alliance ratified the standard as Wi-Fi 6E in July 2020.

Another common problem with intermittent wireless is the auto-reconnection feature for the SSID. Your phone normally goes into a sleep mode every so often. This is normal and saves battery life. One of the first devices to sleep for battery conservation is the wireless circuitry. When you power on your phone, the wireless circuitry needs to associate with your WAP, which will happen unless you do not tell it to automatically reconnect. You can verify your wireless SSID and the auto-reconnection settings on Android by tapping Settings, tapping Connections, tapping Wi-Fi, tapping the current SSID, tapping Edit, and then making sure Auto Reconnect is selected. On an Apple device, tap Settings on your Home screen, tap Wi-Fi, tap the blue circled I next to your current SSID, and make sure that Auto-Join is on.

> The auto-reconnect features can open you up to security concerns, such as the evil twin attack. The evil twin attack involves two access points; one is operated by an organization and the other is operated by the threat agent. The threat agent will assign the same SSID to their AP, then they will send disassociation frames to the organization's AP and its clients. This forces the clients to disconnect, and if auto-reconnect is on they will reconnect to the evil twin operated by the threat agent. Information is then relayed to the network and actively sniffed for usernames and passwords.

No Wireless Connectivity

A common cause of a lack of wireless connectivity is that the wireless radio has been turned off. It happens from time to time, when an application that controls the Wi-Fi doesn't turn it back on. On an Android phone, swipe down from the status bar, then tap the wireless icon to make sure it is lit up. On Apple devices tap Settings, then tap Wi-Fi, and make sure that the slider is turned to the right and lit up in green.

Another common cause of a lack of wireless connectivity is for a device to be in *Airplane mode*. When a mobile device is in Airplane mode, all the radios for the cellular network of the provider, Wi-Fi, Bluetooth, and *near-field communication (NFC)* will be turned off. This function was created so that in one tap you could comply with the Federal Aviation Administration (FAA) or the European Aviation Safety Agency (EASA).

> On newer iOS devices, such as iPhones, the Bluetooth is not turned off when you enter Airplane mode.

To make sure that your device is not in Airplane mode, look on the upper status bar that displays your cellular strength. If a plane appears there, then your phone is in Airplane mode. On Android, you can swipe down, then tap the icon of the airplane so that it's no longer lit up. On Apple devices, tap Settings, then Airplane Mode, and then tap the slider so that it is no longer lit up. On both Android and Apple devices, both the cellular service and wireless networks will be restored after Airplane mode is disabled.

Bluetooth Connectivity

The lack of Bluetooth connectivity can also be attributed to the use of Airplane mode, or Bluetooth can just be turned off. So, be sure to check this setting in addition to Airplane mode. On Android devices, you can swipe down, then tap the Bluetooth icon if it is not lit up. On Apple devices, go to Settings, then tap Bluetooth if it is not lit up. Depending on the phone and version of the operating system, the Bluetooth icons will be displayed on your upper status bar and will look similar to Figure 19.37.

FIGURE 19.37   Bluetooth status icons

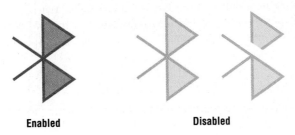

Enabled   Disabled

Lack of Bluetooth connectivity can also be caused when a device is not turned on and/or has an improper setting for pairing. A common pairing issue is not having the proper Bluetooth passcode entered for the device. Each device, when paired, has a specific code from the vendor. Most vendors use a common code, such as 1234, but the code could also be 0000, or any combination, so it's best to check the vendor's documentation for Bluetooth pairing information.

To pair or re-pair a device, first ensure that the device is turned on and that it's discoverable. (Consult the vendor's documentation, as necessary.) On Android devices, tap Settings, then tap Connections, then tap Bluetooth (the phone will immediately start scanning for discoverable devices), select the available device, and enter the passcode from the vendor's documentation. On Apple devices, pairing can be performed by tapping Settings, tapping Bluetooth, tapping the device name, and entering the passcode from the vendor's documentation.

Near-Field Communication (NFC)

Near-field communication (NFC) is a short-distance wireless communication protocol. NFC is built into many mobile devices for the application of payment systems, such as Google Pay and Apple Pay. In addition, NFC is used for data exchange between mobile devices. A use case for this application is the transfer process when a new mobile device is purchased. You can simply tap the two devices together, and the new mobile device pulls the information from the existing mobile device. NFC nominally requires a distance of 4 centimeters or less to operate.

The first thing to check on the mobile device is that Airplane mode is not on. Airplane mode will impede the functionality of NFC, because NFC uses electromagnetic radio fields to enable communications between the phone and the NFC device.

The next thing to check is that it is not the reader. However, when attempting to pay for something and Google Pay or Apple Pay isn't working, anxiety often builds. Troubleshooting between you and the cashier is usually the last thing that comes to mind. However, briefly asking the cashier if anyone else has had an issue today can rule out the reader.

The case on the mobile device can also interfere with NFC communications. If the case is a ruggedized case and has an aluminum back, it could impede the NFC signal. Simply popping it out of the case can rule out the phone case as part of the problem.

Signing out of the mobile payment system will sometimes rectify the problem. In the process of signing back in, it will also validate if the provider's network is down, as this can often be a problem for mobile payment systems. Another troubleshooting step is selecting another credit card in the mobile payment system if you have multiple cards available in the app.

AirDrop

AirDrop is an Apple proprietary protocol used to quickly transfer files between iPhones, iPads, and Macs. AirDrop uses a combination of Bluetooth and Wi-Fi to transfer files, such as photos, documents, and video, just to name a few. Bluetooth is used to broadcast, discover, and negotiate communications between the two devices. Wi-Fi is then used as a point-to-point communication method for the two devices to transfer the file. As you may have noticed already, there are several different processes going on and because of this there can be issues. However, AirDrop between Apple products is a very polished protocol and usually works flawlessly.

The first item to check is that Airplane mode is not on and impeding communications. Airplane mode can turn off the two critical methods of communication that AirDrop requires to function: Bluetooth and Wi-Fi. Newer iOS devices will not turn off Bluetooth automatically in Airplane mode. However, if you turn Bluetooth off while in Airplane mode, your phone will remember this setting. Just as your device must have Bluetooth and Wi-Fi turned on, the other person needs to have both turned on. Also, make sure that both parties involved in the transfer do not have the personal hotspot on. If personal hotspot mode is on, it will impede the point-to-point transfer of the files.

The next obvious item to check is that the other person is within range of your device. Since Bluetooth will broadcast and discover the other person's device, the other person needs to be in range of your Bluetooth. If the person is out of range from your Bluetooth signal, then either the phone won't be discovered or the negotiation for the transfer will not succeed.

After you have checked the connectivity between devices and have ensured that Bluetooth and Wi-Fi are working accordingly, security is the next item to check. When AirDrop first came out as a feature, it lacked security and anyone was able to send files to anyone else. Apple soon developed security, whereas only your contacts can send you a file by default. If the other party is not a contact or you are not their contact, you will not be able to receive or send to the other person (respectively). If they are not in your contacts, then setting AirDrop to receive from everyone will allow you to receive the file. However, this should be a temporary setting, since this allows anyone to send you files via AirDrop. More information on how to use AirDrop can be found here: `https://support.apple.com/en-us/HT204144`.

Autorotate Issues

The autorotate function allows a phone to switch between portrait mode and landscape mode by sensing how you are holding the phone. Autorotate is a feature of convenience, because no matter which way you are holding the phone, you can read the information displayed. This of course is assuming you have the screen facing you.

The first item to check is that you do not have autorotate turned off or locked. On the Android operating system there are several different ways to check this, depending on the vendor and the Android version, so it is best to check your specific model of phone. On Apple devices, this can be checked by swiping down from the top-right corner of your screen. When the Control Center opens, look for the circle with the lock in the middle and make sure it is not enabled. This is the Portrait Orientation Lock button, and if it is set, as shown in Figure 19.38, the screen will not autorotate.

FIGURE 19.38 The Portrait Orientation Lock button

If the autorotate function is not turned off or locked to a specific orientation, then you should suspect an application has possibly locked the orientation. A quick reboot will close out all running applications that could have a lock on the autorotate function. The reboot will also reset the autorotate service, in case it has crashed.

If closing the applications and rebooting the device does not remedy the issue, then you should suspect a hardware issue. There are third-party tools available that allow you to test the sensors. Ultimately, the service center can verify that a sensor is bad and malfunctioning.

Troubleshooting Mobile Security Issues

The preceding section—and its corresponding objectives—looked at mobile devices and focused on common OS and application issues; this section builds on that and focuses on security-related issues. Once again, it looks at security concerns and common symptoms, differing only in that there is more of a focus on security. It needs to be pointed out, though, that CompTIA is stretching the definition of the word *security* to include more scenarios than many would typically consider. A fair number of the issues that appear in this section would have fit easily in the preceding section.

Security Concerns

As it pertains to mobile devices there are a number of security concerns that you should be aware of. These concerns are the same for personal devices as they are for organizationally owned devices. Understanding these concerns will help you secure mobile devices and allow you to be more knowledgeable about the consequences.

Android Package (APK) Source

An Android package (APK) is a developer file format for installation of Android applications. When developing an Android application, the developer will side-load the application, usually using an Android tool such as Android Debug Bridge (ADB). The ADB will allow the developer to install the APK directly onto the device they are testing with.

When the developer wants to release the final version of their application, they will upload the APK to the Google Play store. The Google Play store will then rate the content, make sure that the APK is not malicious, and finally trust it for installation. The application is then distributed from a trusted source—the Google Play app store. If at any time the application changes in a way to break the terms of service (ToS), it will be banned from the Google Play store. Examples of breaking the ToS are malicious content, illegal content, and child endangerment, just to name a few.

When you install an APK from an untrusted source, you run the risk of security concerns. If the APK is not installable from a trusted source such as the Google Play app store, then the publisher might have broken the ToS. Some organizations will block the installation of APKs from untrusted sources to prevent data loss and malicious activity from mobile devices.

Developer Mode

The *developer mode* on Android and Apple devices allows a developer to connect to the device via a USB connection. A developer can then create a bridge from a computer to side-load applications as well as debug. The developer mode on Android offers myriad settings that can be changed, such as viewing running services, staying awake, setting a mock GPS location, and USB debugging, just to name a few. The Android operating system allows you to change and tweak settings that can be security concerns. Because of all these tweaks and settings changes, the developer mode is a security concern. By using the mock GPS locations, you can make your phone think that it is within a geolocation security perimeter and possibly circumvent security.

Apple's latest iOS does not have a developer mode like Android. However, you can perform development functions through the Xcode application on a Mac to help you develop iOS applications.

The development mode on Android can be accessed by navigating to Settings ➤ About Phone ➤ Software Information, then tapping Build Information seven times. The Development menu will be on the parent menu under About Phone.

Root Access/Jailbreak

The terms *root access* and *jailbreak* are synonymous with each other. However, *root access* is normally associated with Android and *jailbreak* is normally associated with Apple iOS. When you attain root access for an Android device, you literally have access as the super user named root. This access allows you to change various aspects of the operating system, such as turning on premium features like hotspot and tethering, and changing the operating system on the device by flashing new firmware.

When you root an Android phone and flash a new firmware, you no longer have the patch management from the parent vendor of the phone. For example, if you root a Samsung phone and install Havoc OS, then you no longer receive the Samsung security policies and updates. The Google Play store will also be affected, since only older versions of the applications will be available for download. This means that patch management will lag behind.

When jailbreaking the Apple iOS, you attain a higher level of access to the iOS, just as you do when you root an Android device. The motivation to jailbreak an iOS device is to access premium features, such as adding photo modes, hiding apps, and installing newer features on old devices. Jailbreaking is a security concern because you are modifying the operating system of the phone. Malicious software can easily be installed, and with the new level of access, it can hide itself.

Many organizations that employ mobile device management (MDM) create policies to prevent rooted and jailbroken devices from attaining access to organization information. This policy might restrict getting email from the device, or it could restrict access to the network in your organization.

It is best to use the operating system that has shipped with your mobile device. In many cases, once a device has been rooted or jailbroken, it cannot be reverted back to stock.

Malicious Applications

A *malicious application* is any application with malicious intent for the user or the user's device. You can find malicious applications on both Android and Apple mobile platforms. You can identify a malicious app by reviewing its permissions and contrasting it with its function—for example, if you download a camera application and it asks to record calls. There should be some suspicion and you should revoke the permissions and potentially uninstall the software.

The obvious security concern for a malicious application is that it has excessive permissions to your data or your organization's data. Periodically you should review the permissions each application installation has on your device. Another rule of thumb is to look before you click and think of the security concerns before installing software.

Bootleg Applications

A *bootleg application* is a premium application that has been cracked or nullified to remove the digital rights management (DRM). Bootleg applications can be found for a number of premium mobile apps; they generally are in the form of an APK. Bootleg applications usually contain malicious software, because that is how the bootlegger makes their money. This obviously goes back to the discussion of verifying the source of the application and being cautious with APK installations.

Application Spoofing

Application spoofing is the act of a malicious application spoofing a legitimate application. Application spoofing is much more prevalent in the mobile application marketplace and can be observed on both Apple and Google mobile platforms.

The security concern for application spoofing is the possibility of installing malicious software on your device. Disguising itself as a legitimate application, it has the same security concern of access to personal data and organizational data. You can prevent application spoofing by verifying the name of the publisher, the icon for the application, and the number of installations. If you are downloading a social media platform and it has only 100 downloads, this should send up a red flag. Another method of validating the application is to read reviews for the application. Again, think before you click and download the software.

Common Symptoms

The following sections discuss common symptoms of problems with mobile operating systems and application-related security issues. As with so many issues involving troubleshooting, common sense is most important. Using logic and a systematic approach, you can often identify and correct small problems before they become large ones.

High Resource Utilization

High resource utilization can be a telltale sign that a device is running more than you think it should be—perhaps the drives are being searched or the camera is recording your every move. Monitor for high resource usage. If you discover it, find out what is causing it and respond appropriately. In this section I will cover some basic components and what you should look out for.

High Network Traffic

A higher than normal amount of traffic can be a symptom of a security issue. Spikes in traffic for extended periods of time can mean that data is being stolen from your device or relayed through your device. You should have an idea of the volume of traffic you would normally expect on your device.

You can start closing applications as you watch the volume of traffic. When the volume of traffic subsides, you probably have your culprit. Then, as covered previously, check the application's permissions to see if the application is malicious or is compromised in some way. Clear cache and data, then uninstall and reinstall the application from a known good source. This procedure may identify the issue or verify that you had a malicious application installed. A telltale sign is if the application is no longer available.

Data-Usage Limit Notification

Exceeding the limits on data plans can also be symptomatic of a security issue. Data usage coincides with the volume of traffic previously discussed. A malicious application running on the device could be used to send *spam* or malware, or to conduct a multitude of other malicious activities from your device. A malicious application can also continually spy on you and your data. All of these activities can rob you of precious data in your data plan, pushing you over your contracted limits.

Excessive malicious use of data on a mobile device can be mitigated with two methods:

- The first method is watching the normal usage of data from month to month. Identifying a normal baseline of usage can alert you when data usage is abnormal.

- The second method is to use a mobile firewall, which limits the traffic leaving the mobile device.

Sluggish Performance

While applications, normal usage, and so on can contribute to *sluggish performance*, another offender could be malware or a virus. When you observe sluggish performance on your device, you need to investigate the symptom, as it could indicate a security issue. Check RAM and CPU usage and if an application is out of control, it could be infected with malware. It is best to run an antivirus/antimalware scan on the device to check it thoroughly.

Not every problem is related to a possible security threat. The normal search for a cellular signal can be just as taxing on the device. However, if you are in the normal locations in your day-to-day travels, such as work and home, and still experience sluggish performance, you may have an application problem (out of memory) or a security threat. In either case, the issue needs to be checked out quickly.

Limited Internet Connectivity

When you have limited Internet connectivity on your mobile device, you should not immediately think that the limited connectivity is a security symptom. Limited Internet connectivity can be a result of many different problems. Mobile devices are very susceptible to limited Internet connectivity because they contain small transceivers for wireless and cellular communications. The radio firmware also plays a big role in choosing the right radio frequency and is often the problem with connectivity.

Taking everything into consideration, if you know nothing has changed in the wireless environment, your firmware is the same, you've rebooted, and no one else is having a problem, you can suspect this is a security symptom. Malicious applications will often monopolize your connection or proxy the connection in an effort to sniff usernames and passwords. Both monopolization of the connection and proxying of the connection can create intermittent Internet connections. If your connection is being monopolized, then you will see high network bandwidth as previously discussed. There are a number of ways that a network connection can be proxied for malicious purposes, such as DNS proxy, network transmission, and wireless, just to name a few. The ideal way to combat this issue is with a mobile device firewall and antimalware software.

No Internet Connectivity

If all the usual causes have been reviewed, then you should suspect no Internet connectivity to be a security-related symptom. In some rare instances, malware will cause the mobile device to have no Internet connectivity. This generally happens because a DNS server that the mobile device is pointed to for malicious reasons has ceased to function. Or the relay server that is proxying the connection has ceased to function. There are a multitude of reasons why no Internet connectivity would be experienced. As previously recommended, a good mobile device firewall and antimalware should be employed.

Complete failure of an Internet connection is easier to diagnose than an intermittent problem. Therefore, a factory reset of the device should aid in figuring out whether the hardware is bad or the problem is software, such as malware, triggering the problem.

High Number of Ads

When a mobile device is experiencing a high number of ads, this is a security-related symptom of adware. Adware is a type of malware that pops up ads for malicious purposes, usually to entice the user to buy something. Adware is usually the result of installing a malicious application on the mobile device. There are two ways to diagnose the problem of adware. The first depends on the number of ads and the frequency of the ads. You can start by uninstalling applications until the ads stop popping up. This method is preferable because it is probably the quickest.

The second method, a factory reset, is much more effective, but it will not identify the malicious application. A factory reset will remove any malware along with all the applications. Of course, you can start installing applications until the ads start. However, resetting a phone is a pretty anxiety-producing process for avid mobile device users frantically trying to sign back into applications. Therefore, the first method may be preferred. Once the application is uninstalled and the device is factory reset, be sure to install antimalware software on the device.

Fake Security Warnings

A *fake security warning* on any system is a big red flag and a security symptom. Mobile devices are not exempt from fake security warnings, although these warnings on full operating systems are more common. Regardless, when a fake security warning is discovered, it should be treated as if malware is installed on the device. The device should be factory reset and antimalware should be installed prior to reinstalling the applications.

Unexpected Application Behavior

Unexpected application behavior is not always an indication that you have been infected with malware or have a security symptom. Applications have unexpected behavior all the time. However, when an untrusted and newly installed application behaves in an unexpected way, this could be a symptom of a security problem with the application.

When you experience unexpected application behavior, you should immediately question the trust of the application. This can be done by reading reviews for the application to determine if others have run into similar problems. Also judge the application by its installer base, which is proportional to the reviews. For example, if an application has 100 installs and only has 5 people commenting that it's a great application, then this app should fall under suspicion.

The first step to be taken is to scan the device for malware. If the application is flagged as malware, then a factory reset should be performed. Then install only the trusted applications that you use daily.

Leaked Personal Files/Data

When authorized users access devices through unintended connections or unauthorized users access stolen devices, they can access the data on the device. Outside of these risks, there is always the risk of loss or theft of the device itself.

Therefore, security for mobile devices should be applied in a layered approach. Antivirus and antimalware software should be installed on the device to protect it from malicious applications. In addition, a mobile firewall should be installed along with the antivirus and antimalware software. Fortunately, there are third-party security suites that can protect you from all these threats.

Mobile device management (MDM) software should also be employed. This software is like the Swiss army knife of security for mobile devices. It can require passcodes, the installation of antivirus, antimalware software, mobile firewalls, current updates, and so much more. One of the most notable features is the ability to remotely wipe the device in the event it is stolen or lost.

In addition, there should be a firm policy that details the encryption of data in use, at rest, and in transit. A written policy should be drafted along with procedures on how to deal with leaks when they occur. These policies are usually drafted with an insurance company in order to protect an organization in case of a data leak of personal information.

Summary

This chapter addressed systematic approaches to working with computer problems as well as troubleshooting operating systems and resolving security-related issues. In our discussion of troubleshooting theory, you learned that you need to take a systematic approach to problem solving. Both art and science are involved, and experience in troubleshooting is helpful but not a prerequisite to being a good troubleshooter. You learned that in troubleshooting, the first objective is to identify the problem. Many times, this can be the most time-consuming task.

Once you've identified the problem, you need to establish a theory of why the problem is happening, test your theory, establish a plan of action, verify full functionality, and then document your work. Documentation is frequently the most overlooked aspect of working with computers, but it's an absolutely critical step.

Next, we discussed operating system–related troubleshooting issues. First, we looked at common symptoms, and then we discussed some tools that can be helpful in solving problems.

Finally, we looked at security-related troubleshooting issues as well as best practices for removing malware. Again, we started by looking at common issues and then how to solve them.

Exam Essentials

Know the common symptoms and solutions for operating system problems. Be able to identify the five critical systems of CPU, RAM, network, disk, and graphics that interact with an operating system. Know the various symptoms that will lead to operating system problems. Also, be able to identify solutions to operating system problems.

Understand the various security issues related to operating systems. Be able to identify common security issues that you will see affecting operating systems. You should also understand the impact of these security issues on both the operating system and the organization, as well as common ways to mitigate and solve these security issues.

Know the process for removing malware. Know the seven steps to remove malware. Be able to identify how to perform these seven steps during the malware-removal process. You should be familiar with the various tools used to identify and remove malware.

Know how to troubleshoot mobile OS and application issues. Be able to identify the common symptoms of application-based issues for mobile devices. Know how to solve mobile issues for applications on both Android and Apple devices.

Understand mobile device security issues. You should have a good understanding of the various mobile device security symptoms, problems, and solutions. Be able to articulate how these issues pose a risk to the organization, as well as how these issues can be mitigated and solved.

Review Questions

The answers to the chapter review questions can be found in Appendix A.

1. In Windows, which utility is responsible for finding, downloading, and installing Windows patches?

   A. Device Manager

   B. Microsoft Management Console

   C. Download Manager

   D. Windows Update

2. Which Startup Setting option allows you to boot with basic drivers?

   A. Enable Debugging

   B. Enable Safe Boot

   C. Disable Driver Signature Enforcement

   D. Enable Low-Resolution Video

3. Which `bootrec` option can be used in Windows to rebuild the boot configuration file?

   A. `/fixboot`

   B. `/rebuildbcd`

   C. `/scanos`

   D. `/fixmbr`

4. What is the first step in malware removal?

   A. Quarantine the infected system.

   B. Identify and verify the malware symptoms.

   C. Remediate the infected system.

   D. Educate the end user.

5. Which tool will allow you to troubleshoot a slow-loading profile?

   A. Profile tab of the Advanced System Properties

   B. Regedit

   C. Windows Recovery Environment

   D. Windows Preinstallation Environment

6. Which of the following components are only used to restore Windows from a suspended state?

   A. BCD

   B. `ntoskrnl.exe`

   C. `winload.exe`

   D. `winresume.exe`

7. One of the users you support has a Windows 10/11 laptop that will not boot up. The user just installed brand-new drivers for a graphics card. They need to access a tax application and their data files. What should you try first?

   A. Use System Restore.

   B. Use Reset This PC.

   C. Reimage the laptop.

   D. Manually reinstall Windows 10.

8. Which partitioning type is required when you have UEFI firmware?

   A. GPT

   B. MBR

   C. POST

   D. Boot Sector

9. Which of the following are used to prevent pop-unders from appearing?

   A. Antimalware utilities

   B. Pop-up blockers

   C. Phishing sites

   D. Antivirus software

10. In general, how often should you update your antivirus definitions?

    A. Weekly

    B. Monthly

    C. Daily

    D. Antivirus definitions do not need to be updated.

11. Which tool can be used to diagnose why Windows 10/11 is slow and sluggish?

    A. Resource Monitor

    B. `msconfig.exe`

    C. Device Manager

    D. Reliability Monitor

12. Which tool will allow you to diagnose why Windows Update keeps failing?

    A. `ntbtlog.txt`

    B. Windows Update Troubleshooter

    C. Windows Recovery Environment

    D. Safe mode

13. Which of the following programs could be considered antimalware?

    A. Microsoft Defender Security

    B. MDM

    C. Windows Action Center

    D. VirusTotal

14. Which of the following tools allows you to manually fix maliciously modified system files?

    A. `regedit`

    B. SFC

    C. `bootrec`

    D. UAC

15. Which of the following can you do to help eliminate security problems? (Select the best answer.)

    A. Establish security policies and procedures.

    B. Optimize drives.

    C. Prevent booting into safe mode.

    D. Prevent booting into Windows Recovery Environment.

16. A mobile device is running out of RAM. What could be the most likely problem?

    A. The device is not charged to capacity.

    B. The digitizer is not functioning properly.

    C. The device is in DND mode.

    D. The device has background applications open.

17. What is a risk of using the auto-reconnect feature on a mobile device?

    A. The device will reconnect to any SSID.

    B. The device could be exploited by an evil twin attack.

    C. The device's battery life could be shortened.

    D. You may exceed your cellular data plan's limits.

18. You notice that the reliability of the operating system has diminished in Reliability Monitor. Where can you find more details on why applications are failing?

    A. Device Manager

    B. Event Viewer

    C. Windows Recovery Environment

    D. `msconfig.exe`

19. Why would the operating system write out large amounts of RAM to the page file?

    A. The CPU is running high on utilization.

    B. This is a normal process of the operating system.

    C. The amount of physical RAM is low.

    D. The page file is faster than conventional RAM.

20. What is one consequence of an overheating mobile device?

    A. Higher RAM usage

    B. Degraded battery life

    C. Inaccurate touchscreen response

    D. Inability to decrypt emails

Performance-Based Question

You will encounter performance-based questions on the A+ exams. The questions on the exam require you to perform a specific task, and you will be graded on whether or not you were able to complete the task. The following requires you to think creatively in order to measure how well you understand this chapter's topics. You may or may not see similar questions on the actual A+ exams. To see how your answers compare to the authors', refer to Appendix B.

List, in order, the seven best practice steps associated with malware removal.

Chapter

20

Scripting and Remote Access

THE FOLLOWING COMPTIA A+ 220-1102 EXAM OBJECTIVES ARE COVERED IN THIS CHAPTER:

✓ **4.8 Identify the basics of scripting.**

- Script file types
    - .bat
    - .ps1
    - .vbs
    - .sh
    - .js
    - .py
- Use cases for scripting
    - Basic automation
    - Restarting machines
    - Remapping network drives
    - Installation of applications
    - Automated backups
    - Gathering of information/data
    - Initiating updates
- Other considerations when using scripts
    - Unintentionally introducing malware
    - Inadvertently changing system settings
    - Browser or system crashes due to mishandling of resources

✓ **4.9 Given a scenario, use remote access technologies.**

- Methods/tools
  - RDP
  - VPN
  - Virtual network computer (VNC)
  - Secure Shell (SSH)
  - Remote monitoring and management (RMM)
  - Microsoft Remote Assistance (MSRA)
  - Third-party tools
    - Screen-sharing software
    - Video-conferencing software
    - File transfer software
    - Desktop management software
- Security considerations of each access method

CompTIA has identified that with the rapid adoption of cloud-based services, system administrators have a need for scripting and remote access now more than ever. Scripting allows you to manage a system as if you have logged in and performed the task yourself, such as purging old log files from a web server to make space. Remote access technologies allow you to connect to these remote systems so that you can manually administer them.

This chapter looks at a variety of scripting languages. After completing this chapter, you may not be an expert at writing scripts—the goal is to familiarize you with the various scripting languages so that you can learn the basics of scripting and their purposes. We'll also look at various remote access methods and their security considerations.

Scripting

Before diving into scripting, we'll begin by discussing the differences between a programming language and a scripting language. When you write a script, you are basically using a high-level programming language. An example of a low-level programming language is assembler, also known as *assembly language*. Figure 20.1 shows what we call the "programming pyramid."

FIGURE 20.1 Programming pyramid

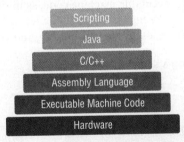

The lowest layer is the actual hardware, which is the central processing unit (CPU). Directly above the hardware layer is the *executable machine code* that interacts with the hardware to make it perform some useful function or process. The operating system is usually programmed in a low- to mid-level programming language, such as C/C++ or even assembly language. It is then *compiled* into executable machine code. Applications are often programmed in high-level languages, such Java, C#, or VB.NET, and are compiled to executable machine code or an intermediate code. Scripts, however, are not compiled; they are interpreted, as we discuss in this section.

Depending on which layer you program on, you gain some advantages, but at the same time you are also capped by some of the limitations of each layer. For example, a program created in assembly language will be quite complex because you will need to perform low-level functions just to add two numbers together. However, because you are at such a low level, you have direct access to the hardware, so you are limitless in your control of the hardware. If you were to use a higher-level language, such as C/C++, the application would be relatively easy to write; adding two numbers is as simple as $c = a + b;$. Because it is a higher-level language, however, you do not have the same lower-level control over the hardware as with assembly language. You have access only to what the compiler will understand and compile to executable machine code, as shown in Figure 20.2.

FIGURE 20.2   Compiling a programming language

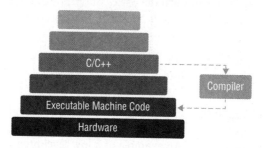

Scripting languages do not need to be compiled. They are interpreted by the shell, command line, or external interpreter, as shown in Figure 20.3. The interpreter reads the script and executes the instructions in the operating system. The big difference is that you do not need to compile scripts to executable machine code, as in the previous example of a C/C++ program. Unfortunately, the higher the level, the less control you have over the process. The benefit is you can create a script rather quickly, and you don't need to compile it.

FIGURE 20.3   Interpreting a scripting language

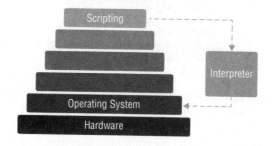

Another big difference between applications and scripts is that scripts require applications to complete their purpose. If an application doesn't exist for a function in your script, then you should evaluate whether a script is the right course of action. For example, if you need to resize pictures, an application must exist that can be called via the command line that will take the appropriate input and resize the pictures. If an application doesn't exist that can resize the picture, then you might need to write an application that resizes a picture in lieu of a script. A script cannot normally create functions of this nature; it can only call on them.

 Java is a compiled language that requires the Java Development Kit (JDK) in order to be compiled to an intermediate code called bytecode. The bytecode is then run on top of the Java runtime, known as the Java Runtime Environment (JRE). This is why you need to install Java to run Java programs on your operating system. JavaScript, on the other hand, is a scripting language that many different web browsers support. JavaScript does not need a JRE since it is interpreted inside the web browser.

Scripting Basics

There are several different types of scripting languages. Each scripting language has its own nuances and syntax. This section discusses some scripting basics that you can apply to any scripting language. You'll only have to adjust the syntax to the scripting language you've selected to get the desired outcome.

Variables

A *variable* is a symbolic word or combination of letters that can be used to hold a value. The value can be defined as a number, text, Boolean, or array. Numbers can be either *integers* or *floating-point*, but the scripting languages you choose must support floating-point math. Floating-point math is a value that contains a decimal number, whereas integers are whole numbers. Text is also called a *string* and has no numeric equivalent. A string containing 30 will not be a value of 30; it will be only be a string of characters containing a 3 and a 0. Mathematical computations cannot be performed on a string. Boolean values are true or false values, and true values and arrays are collections of strings, numbers, and Boolean values.

You might see a programming language described as a strongly typed language. That means that the variable must be defined as to what type of value it will hold and how long the value will be. This is yet another difference between scripting languages and programming languages: scripting languages do not need variables to be defined and are normally not typed. Most of the time, you can just load a variable with a value and it is dynamically typed. This is not the most economical use of memory, but that shouldn't be an issue, because scripts are often simple ways to complete a simple task; therefore, it doesn't matter that loading a variable with a value and having it dynamically typed isn't the most economical use of memory.

The name of a variable should have some meaning and cannot be a reserved word. So if you had a variable that needed to hold a counter, you could simply create a variable called count. However, you would need to ensure that count was not used elsewhere in the program for a function; otherwise, it's a *reserved word* in the scripting language and cannot be used as a variable.

The following is an example of a variable named count being created in the *PowerShell* scripting language and loaded with the value 1. Generally, you load a value by specifying the variable, followed by an equal sign, and then the value. In PowerShell, the syntax dictates that you place a $ in front of the variable in order to notify the interpreter that you are addressing a variable. Each scripting language is slightly different, but the concept remains the same. You can also view the contents of the variable either by typing the variable name and pressing Enter or by using the echo command before the variable.

```
PS C:\Users> $count = 1
PS C:\Users> $count
1
PS C:\Users> echo $count
1
PS C:\Users>
```

Environment Variables

As previously mentioned, variables hold values in scripts so that we can do things such as counting. Environment variables also hold values, but they are used for the environment of either the system or the current user. Environment variables often hold values like the path to an executable or the location of the temporary folder.

Environment variables are inherited in a structured fashion: system, user, and then program. They can be overwritten at any underlying level, but only for that entity. For example, if a script changes the user environment variable for the temporary folder, the change is applicable only for that script unless the user environment is changed—then it will affect all scripts run by a user. Here are the types of variables you will encounter in the operating system:

System Variable   Defined for use by the system, or any user or program

User Variable   Defined for use by a specific user, or any program executing under that specific user

Program Variable   Defined for use inside a script or application and can only be accessed from inside the script or application

Comment Syntax

Your scripts should have a level of end-user readability. The code should describe what is going to happen without external documentation. Although we strive to create eloquent scripts that read like computer poetry, sometimes we need to make comments inside the code.

Each language has a different way to make comments. The following example uses the PowerShell syntax. As you progress through the next section, "Scripting Languages," you will see the way to comment in the various languages. You'll notice in the following code that we've added some commenting that is generally used for script creation. The three basic components of the comments are author name, authored date, and the purpose of the script. Although the following comment block is best practice, it is not required; one-line comments inside the code are allowed also. In this scripting language, PowerShell, the comment is preceded by the # symbol. Other scripting languages have their own syntax, and you'll see the various examples throughout this chapter.

```
# Jon Buhagiar
# 10/16/18
# This script will output a directory listing of the C drive
Get-ChildItem C:\
```

Loops

When writing a script, you may need to create a controlled loop inside the script. An example of a controlled loop is to read a file and then do some things for each line contained in the file. You can use two basic loops in your scripts: for loops and while loops.

A for loop is a stepped loop with a defined beginning and a defined end; each step is defined as well. The following example shows a for loop for PowerShell that starts at 1 and counts to 10. The output is the word *Number* and an incrementing number. You can see that the variable is initially set to 1 with ($count=1), and a test is done to check if the variable is less than or equal to 10 with ($count -le 10). The for loop is stepped by adding 1 to the existing number with ($count++). This is just one example of a for loop, and every scripting language is a bit different in syntax, but the concept is the same.

```
For($count=1; $count -le 10; $count++) {
    Write-Host "Number $count"
    }


[ Output of Script ]


Number 1
Number 2
Number 3
Number 4
Number 5
Number 6
Number 7
Number 8
Number 9
Number 10
```

A while loop continues to loop until either it is exited or a condition is met. The while loop has no defined beginning, only a defined end, and it can be exited without consequence to the function. In the following code, the variable count is set to 0, and then the while loop begins. Inside the while loop, the count variable is incremented by 1 each time it loops with ($count++). The loop will continue as long as count is less than 11 with ($count -lt 11). The output will be identical to the prior example.

```
$count = 1
While ($count -lt 11) {
    Write-Host "Number $count"
    $count++
    }
```

```
[ Output of Script ]

Number 1
Number 2
Number 3
Number 4
Number 5
Number 6
Number 7
Number 8
Number 9
Number 10
```

A while loop and a do while loop are identical in functionality; they both loop until a condition is no longer true. The difference between the two is that a while loop puts the condition before the code in the loop, whereas a do while has the condition after the code in the loop. Each language supports either one loop or the other, and sometimes both types of loop. However, the concept remains the same: the loop will continue until the condition is no longer true.

Branch Logic

Branch logic enables code to deviate, or branch, depending on a condition. The if statement is the most common conditional branch logic found in scripts. The if statement is usually followed by a condition and a then clause. It can even use an else clause. The then clause is executed only if the condition is true; if the condition is not true, the else clause is executed.

In the following example, the string str is set to 1. The if statement then checks the condition of str being equal to 1 with ($str -eq 1). It is true, so the next statement of

`Write-Host "Yes"` is executed. It's important to note that PowerShell implies the `then` clause; only the `else` clause needs to be spelled out. If `str` were anything other than `1`, the condition would be false, executing the `else` clause of `Write-Host "No"`. This is an example for PowerShell, but in the next section, "Scripting Languages," you will find many different examples for each scripting language.

```
$str=1
If ($str -eq 1) { Write-Host "Yes" } Else { Write-Host "No" }


[ Output of Script ]


Yes
```

Scripting Languages

Now that you understand the basic differences between a programming language and a scripting language and some scripting basics, let's look at several different scripting languages you are likely to encounter as a technician. As we cover the various languages, we'll highlight which operating systems they are common to or natively supported on—which is often the biggest deciding factor when you choose a scripting language.

Windows Batch Scripts

Windows batch scripts have been around since the release of Microsoft's Disk Operating System (DOS) back in 1981. The original script interpreter was `command.com`, and since then Windows NT was released, which included an updated command-line interpreter called *Command Prompt*, or `cmd.exe`. The original file extension used with batch scripts was .bat, but today both .bat and .cmd can be used to initiate a batch script because they are both associated with the command-line interpreter `cmd.exe`.

A Windows batch script is probably the fastest way to get something done when all you need is a list of commands run one after the other. For example, say you need to create new user accounts for a school. You can get the usernames in an Excel sheet, and you can create a script from the entries by using an Excel formula, adding in the column of the username. As an example, the formula `="NET USER" & A1 & "PassW0rd /ADD /DOMAIN"` copied into cell B1 will produce the line you need to execute. Then you just need to drag the formula down, and the script will be built. A quick copy and paste, and the script will look similar to the following output. It's a quick and dirty way to create user accounts. Using the combination of an Excel sheet and a copy-and-paste into a batch script is the fastest way to build and execute a laundry list of commands.

```
NET USER UserOne PassW0rd /ADD /DOMAIN
NET USER UserOne PassW0rd /ADD /DOMAIN
NET USER UserOne PassW0rd /ADD /DOMAIN
NET USER UserOne PassW0rd /ADD /DOMAIN
[ Output Cut ]
```

Batch scripts can also contain logic. The following is a simple batch script that tests whether a variable of FLIPFLOP is equal to 0 using an if statement. If FLIPFLOP is equal to 0, the script will proceed to write to the screen the word *Zero*, set FLIPFLOP to a value of 1, and then jump to :LOOP. Because FLIPFLOP is set to 1, it is not equal to 0; so, the else clause in the if statement will be processed, and the word *One* will be printed to the screen, and FLIPFLOP will then be set to 0, and the script will jump to :LOOP again. This will proceed until Ctrl+C is pressed to stop the processing of the script.

```
@ECHO OFF
REM FlipFlop Script
SET /A FLIPFLOP=0
:LOOP
IF %FLIPFLOP% EQU 0 (ECHO Zero && SET /A FLIPFLOP=1) ELSE (ECHO One && SET /A
FLIPFLOP=0)
GOTO :LOOP
```

EXERCISE 20.1

Creating and Running a Windows Batch Script

1. Click the Start menu and type **Notepad**. Select Notepad from the search results.

2. Type the preceding batch script example into Notepad.

3. Choose File ➤ Save As, and then choose to save the batch script to your desktop.

4. Name the file **flipflop.cmd**, and then click Save.

5. Press the Windows key and the R key at the same time, type **cmd.exe**, and then press Enter.

6. Type **cd %userprofile%\desktop** and press Enter.

7. Type **flipflop.cmd**, and then press Enter.

   Notice that your screen display will alternate between *One* and *Zero*.

8. Press Ctrl+C.

   This will display the question Terminate batch job (Y/N)?.

9. Answer Y, and then press Enter.

10. Switch to Notepad and add **REM** in front of the @echo off command.

11. Save the file by choosing File ➤ Save.

12. Switch to the command prompt and rerun flipflop.cmd.

    You will now see the commands as well as the variable contents while the script is running.

13. Press Ctrl+C.

This will display the question `Terminate batch job (Y/N)?`.

14. Answer Y, and then press Enter.

 Another way to open a command prompt to a specific folder is to first browse to the folder, and then hold the Shift key and right-click an empty space in the folder. Select Open PowerShell Window Here on Windows 10/11 or Open Command Windows Here on Windows 8/8.1. If you are on Windows 10/11 and opened a PowerShell window, type **cmd** and then press Enter. This will change your interpreter to cmd.exe.

PowerShell Scripts

PowerShell allows for the automation and management of the Windows operating systems, as well as cloud-related services such as *Microsoft Azure* and *Microsoft 365*. One of the limiting features of any scripting language is its ability to perform a needed task. PowerShell was created to be totally extensible. It was built on the .NET Framework *Common Language Runtime (CLR)*. Any programmable library a .NET application has access to, PowerShell can use, which is what makes it so extensible. It has been used since Windows Server 2008 as a configuration tool for the operating system. In fact, most of the time when you configure a service in the Server Manager tool, you actually run a PowerShell command in the background. Many of the GUI wizards allow you to see the PowerShell script that will be executed so that you can reuse the line in a script of your own.

PowerShell introduced the concept of *cmdlets*. PowerShell has over 100 cmdlets installed, called the core cmdlets. You can always add your own cmdlet by creating a PS1 script and installing it into the PowerShell cmdlet store in the operating system, as you will do in Exercise 20.2. A cmdlet is simply a verb and a noun separated by a dash. Here are a few examples:

Get-Item   Gets an item such as a directory listing, environment variable, or Registry key

Set-Item   Changes the value of an item, such as creating an alias or setting an environment variable

Copy-Item   Copies an item, such as a file or folder

Remove-Item   Deletes an item, such as a file, folder, or Registry key

Move-Item   Moves an item, such as a file, folder, or Registry key

These are just a few of the built-in core cmdlets for PowerShell. Others exist for -Item, such as Rename-Item, New-Item, Invoke-Item, and Clear-Item. Each one performs a corresponding action on the noun following the dash. You can even extend the functionality of a command with your own PS1 cmdlet. There is a Get-Verb command so that you can see all the appropriate verbs that you can use for your own command.

> **NOTE**   To learn more about creating your own cmdlets, visit:
>
> https://docs.microsoft.com/en-us/powershell/
> scripting/developer/cmdlet/how-to-write-a-simple-
> cmdlet?view=powershell-7.2

If you use the `Get-Item` cmdlet and specify a folder, information about that folder will be returned. If you want to see all the other folders contained within that folder, you can use a * wildcard. Or you can use the `Get-ChildItem` cmdlet and specify the directory, as follows:

```
PS C:\Users\UserOne> Get-item c:\*


    Directory: C:\


Mode                 LastWriteTime         Length Name
----                 -------------         ------ ----
d-----        11/28/2017   9:52 PM                Dell
d-----         5/16/2018   9:32 PM                NVIDIA
d-----         4/11/2018   7:38 PM                PerfLogs
d-r---         5/28/2018  10:04 PM                Program Files
d-r---         8/12/2018   5:31 PM                Program Files (x86)
d-r---         5/28/2018   6:11 PM                Users
d-----        10/18/2018  10:17 PM                Windows


PS C:\Users\UserOne> Get-ChildItem c:\


    Directory: C:\


Mode                 LastWriteTime         Length Name
----                 -------------         ------ ----
d-----        11/28/2017   9:52 PM                dell
d-----         5/16/2018   9:32 PM                NVIDIA
d-----         4/11/2018   7:38 PM                PerfLogs
d-r---         5/28/2018  10:04 PM                Program Files
d-r---         8/12/2018   5:31 PM                Program Files (x86)
d-r---         5/28/2018   6:11 PM                Users
d-----        10/18/2018  10:17 PM                Windows
```

When you use the `dir` command in PowerShell to view a directory listing of files, you are actually using something called an *alias*. The alias then calls the `Get-ChildItem` cmdlet. To see all the aliases on the operating system, you can use the `Get-Alias` cmdlet. You can see all the commands mapped over to PowerShell cmdlets, as follows:

```
PS C:\Users\UserOne> get-alias

CommandType       Name
-----------       ----

Alias             % -> ForEach-Object
Alias             ? -> Where-Object
Alias             ac -> Add-Content
Alias             asnp -> Add-PSSnapin
Alias             cat -> Get-Content
Alias             cd -> Set-Location
Alias             CFS -> ConvertFrom-String
Alias             chdir -> Set-Location
Alias             clc -> Clear-Content
Alias             clear -> Clear-Host
Alias             clhy -> Clear-History
Alias             cli -> Clear-Item
Alias             clp -> Clear-ItemProperty
Alias             cls -> Clear-Host
[ Output Cut ]
```

PowerShell also has a great way to develop scripts in what is called an *Integrated Scripting Environment (ISE)*. The ISE allows you to write a script and test it without having to switch back and forth between a text editor and the execution environment. In addition to the writing and execution environment in the same window, there is a type-ahead feature that allows you to pick a command if you remember only the first few letters, as shown in Figure 20.4. You can also use the Tab key to complete a command, which makes writing scripts easy when you know the first couple of letters. Formatting is also automated and makes for easy-to-read scripts. The formatting highlights variables and commands in different colors so that you can differentiate between the two.

Before any script can be executed on the Windows operating system, you must first allow scripts to run. By default, any PowerShell scripts will be blocked. Exercise 20.2 shows you how to "unrestrict" PowerShell scripts using the `Set-ExecutionPolicy` cmdlet.

FIGURE 20.4 PowerShell ISE

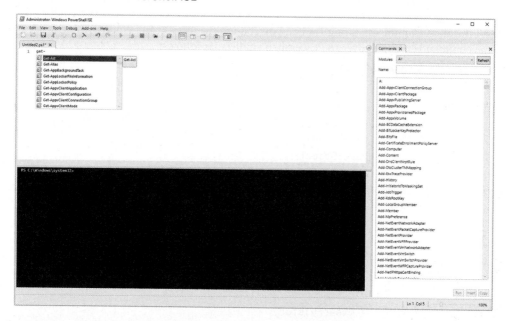

Creating Your First PowerShell Script

1. Click the Start menu, type **PowerShell**, right-click Windows PowerShell ISE in the search results, and select Run As Administrator.

2. Click Yes in the User Account Control dialog box when prompted.

3. In the lower portion of the ISE, type **get-executionpolicy**, and then press Enter.

   You'll notice that it returns Restricted.

4. Type **set-executionpolicy unrestricted**, and then press Enter.

5. Answer Yes to the prompt.

6. Type the following into the top portion of the ISE:

```
#FlipFlop Script
While ($true) {
   If ($FLIPFLOP -eq 0) {
     Write-Host "Zero"
     $ FLIPFLOP=1
     } Else {
     Write-Host "One"
```

```
    $ FLIPFLOP=0
  }
}
```

7. Click File ➤ Save.

    The save dialog box will default to your Documents folder.

8. Rename the file **flipflop.ps1**, and then click Save.

9. In the lower portion of the ISE, type **cd ~\Documents**, and then press Enter.

    Note that you used the ~ character, which represents your home directory, as previously covered in Chapter 16, "Working with macOS and Linux."

10. Type **.\flipflop.ps1**, and then press Enter.

    This will run the script and display the alternating words *Zero* and *One*. To stop it, press Ctrl+C. Alternatively, you can click the red stop button on the ribbon at the top of the window. You can execute the script by clicking the green play button.

11. Type **set-executionpolicy default**, and then press Enter to change the execution policy back to the default setting.

 Microsoft has created a cross-platform version of PowerShell, called *PowerShell Core*, that runs on Linux and macOS. This version will run nearly all the commands that the Windows version of PowerShell offers, with a few platform-specific nuances. More information on this topic can be found at https://docs.microsoft.com/en-us/powershell.

Visual Basic Scripts

Visual Basic scripts—also known as *VBScripts*—are scripts based on Microsoft's Visual Basic language. VBScript technology has been around since Windows 98 and Windows NT, so it is very mature, but it is slowly being replaced by PowerShell, as we'll explain. VBScripts also run only on Windows operating systems, unlike PowerShell scripts.

VBScript technology is based on the *Component Object Model (COM)* to allow interaction with the operating system. Any COM object that can be instantiated can be accessed through a VBScript. As you learned in the preceding section, PowerShell is based on the .NET Framework. The Component Object Model predates the .NET Framework as a way to register programming libraries with the operating system. By default, VBScripts cannot access programming libraries that have been written for the .NET Framework, which is why VBScripts are slowly losing popularity and support by Microsoft.

VBScripts are still extremely useful when it comes to a structured language for creating login scripts. As previously mentioned, scripts are an interpreted language and are not compiled. VBScripts are no different; they require an interpreter to process. There are three main interpreters that can process VBScripts: *Windows Scripting Host (WSH)*, Internet Information Services (IIS) Active Server Pages (ASP), and Internet Explorer. ASP and Internet Explorer are deprecated, so we will focus on WSH.

The Windows Scripting Host is an environment that allows you to run VBScripts from the command line. By default, when a *VBS* script is run, a program called wscript.exe processes the script. Any output will be sent to a Windows message box that you must close by clicking OK. This can be quite annoying if you have multiple lines of output, as each line will pop up a message box you have to close. A VBScript can also be executed with the cscript.exe program. This version of the VBScript processor outputs to a console window—the name stands for console script.

VBScripts are normally edited in Notepad and saved with a .vbs extension. A number of third-party editors allow type-ahead. As previously mentioned, type-ahead is a feature that allows for the completion of code after a few letters have been entered. Microsoft supports an editor called Visual Studio Code, which you can download from https://code.visualstudio.com.

The following VBScript will perform the same output as the two preceding examples. As you can tell, the syntax is a little different.

```
'FlipFlop Script
Do Until FLIPFLOP > 2
  If FLIPFLOP = 0 Then
    Wscript.Echo "Zero"
    FLIPFLOP = 1
  Else
    Wscript.Echo "One"
    FLIPFLOP = 0
  End If
Loop
```

Because of the popularity of Windows PowerShell and its access to the .NET Framework, there will be no future releases of the VBScript processor. Microsoft will maintain the VBScript processor until it is retired. However, Windows batch scripts would probably be deprecated before the VBScript processor.

Shell Scripts

Bash stands for the Bourne Again Shell. Bash is backward compatible with its predecessor, called the *Bourne shell* (or *sh*). Whether you're using the Bash shell or the sh shell, either will perform similar functions for scripting purposes. The shell itself interprets commands for scripting, similar to the Windows DOS shell. However, the Bash and sh shells are much more advanced in their structure and functionality than DOS. Linux/UNIX shell scripts are basically how the operating system boots itself up and starts all the necessary services.

Linux and UNIX scripts often end with the *.sh* extension to signify to the end user that the file contains a script (text) and not an executable code. Shell scripts do not require the .sh extension in order to be executed. They do, however, require execute permissions to be applied. This can be done with the chmod command, as you learned in Chapter 16. Another nuance is that you must specify the relative path using ./ and then the script—for example, ./script.sh.

Shell scripts can be edited in any text-based editor. The vi editor was probably the first editor—and on older systems, your only choice. Today, there is a multitude of editors from which to choose, such as pico/nano, jed, Gedit, and Kate/Kwrite, just to name a few. Any of these editors will do a fine job for the basic editing of scripts. Some people find that opening two consoles is the fastest way to write a script on Linux/UNIX. One console serves as the editing console, with the text editor loaded and saving changes that are made, while the other console serves as the execution environment.

The following is a simple shell script that performs identical functionality to the scripts you have seen throughout this chapter. There are two major things to note with this example. The first is the syntax of the script, which differs slightly from the other examples but basically looks similar. The second thing to note is the directive on the first line. The directive tells the operating system which shell to process the script in. The #! is called a *hashbang*. The hashbang lets the operating system know the path of the script interpreter that will be used to process the script—in this case, it is /bin/bash.

```
#!/bin/bash
#FlipFlop Script
while [ !$FLIPFLOP ]; do
  if [ $FLIPFLOP -eq 0 ]
  then
    echo Zero
    FLIPFLOP =1
  else
    echo One
    FLIPFLOP =0
  fi
done
```

The best way to start scripting with Linux/UNIX shell scripts is to load up Linux and try it out. You can find a great guide to Linux scripting here: https://help.ubuntu.com/community/Beginners/BashScripting

Python Scripts

The *Python* scripting language was first released in 1991, and it started to gain popularity over the past 10 years or so. It is not normally installed by default in any operating system.

If you want to use Python on a Windows or macOS operating system, you need to visit www .python.org to download the latest version, and then install it. If you are running a Linux operating system, you will install Python through the package management system of the operating system.

If you install Python from www.python.org, you will only be prompted to download Python 3.x. However, when installing on Linux, if you do not specify Python 3, you will install the older version, Python 2.x. Python 2 is no longer being supported and has fewer features than the current version, Python 3.x.

The Python installation does not include an *integrated development environment (IDE)*, also known as an *Integrated Scripting Environment (ISE)*. The installation contains only the interpreter and some documentation to get you started. You can use any text editor to create and edit scripts. An extremely popular Python IDE is the Free Community version of PyCharm, by JetBrains. The IDE allows for script development similar to the PowerShell ISE but with many more features, as shown in Figure 20.5.

FIGURE 20.5   The PyCharm IDE

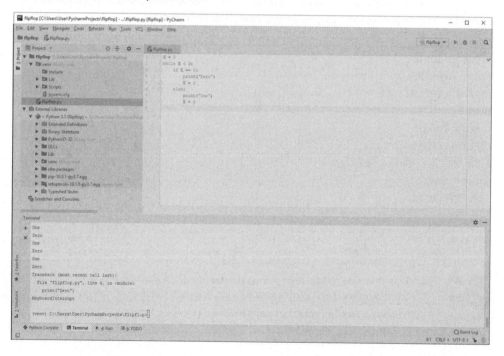

Python was created to be an easy scripting language to learn, and it is very forgiving with syntax. It is probably one of the best languages that we can recommend to start scripting in because it is so forgiving, unlike Bash or Windows batch scripting. Python also doesn't lack in features. Like VBScript and PowerShell, Python is extensible and can use external libraries. One disadvantage to using Python is that it's not been widely adopted in enterprise environments. So you will not be able to build login scripts with it, because the interpreter does not have direct ties into the operating system. You'll often find that your flexibility is limited when you try to integrate a Python script into an enterprise process.

Python scripts normally end with the *.py* extension so that the end user can identify the scripting language used within the file. The `.py` extension also allows the script to be launched on Windows operating systems. With Linux/UNIX and macOS systems, however, the hashbang defines the interpreter to use and generally looks something like `#! /usr/bin/python3`.

The following script was written in Python and follows the same functionality as the previous examples in this chapter. As you can see, the program's readability is similar to the earlier examples and the syntax differs slightly.

```
#FlipFlop Script
FLIPFLOP = 0
while FLIPFLOP < 2:
  if FLIPFLOP == 0:
    print("Zero")
    FLIPFLOP = 1
  else:
    print("One")
    FLIPFLOP = 0
```

JavaScript

JavaScript and the Java programming language have several similarities—for example, they are both object-oriented languages, and their syntax is similar. However, the similarities end there, because Java is a programming language and JavaScript is a scripting language, with the difference being that Java is compiled whereas JavaScript is a scripting language.

JavaScript is mainly interpreted in web browsers to allow for interactive web pages. JavaScript is one of the three core web technologies; the other two are *Hypertext Markup Language (HTML)* and *Cascading Style Sheets (CSS)*. JavaScript can also be adapted to run outside the web browser with a runtime called `Node.js`. Both web browser JavaScript and `Node.js` scripts end in the *.js* extension, which identifies the contents of the file as JavaScript code.

JavaScript can be edited with any text-based editor. Microsoft Visual Studio Code does an excellent job of formatting for Windows-based editing of JavaScript. Brackets is another popular editor for JavaScript and runs on a variety of platforms.

The following is an example of JavaScript code. The example is similar to the previous examples in relation to functionality. This particular script was coded to run in `Node.js`, since JavaScript normally outputs to HTML. The structure is similar to the previous examples. As always, every language differs slightly in syntax.

```
//FlipFlop Script
FLIPFLOP = 0;
while (FLIPFLOP < 2) {
  if (FLIPFLOP == 0) {
    console.log ('Zero');
    FLIPFLOP = 1;
  } else {
    console.log ('One');
    FLIPFLOP = 0;
  }
}
```

 For the 220-1102 exam, CompTIA does not expect you to write scripts. However, you should be able to identify scripts and know their associated extensions.

Scripting Use Cases

Scripting is a fairly new objective for the CompTIA A+ exam, and it may look overwhelming to you. You are not expected to have mastered the skills of writing scripts, such as those included in this chapter. They have been included so that you can visualize the various languages and understand the syntax. You will be required to read and understand what a script is doing, as well as identify the various elements of a script, such as variables, branch logic, basic loops, and the type of variables.

In addition to basic comprehension of scripts, you will need to know the various use cases where you may find yourself scripting something together. The basic rule of thumb should always apply: if the task is repetitious and needs to be completed several times, then a script should be developed. For example, if you needed to create 20 users, then a script is your best choice. Time versus reward should be calculated based on the time it takes to develop the script compared to the time it will take to complete the job. One consideration is how often you must complete the task; if you have three users you need to create every week, then developing a script is a good investment of time.

In this section, we'll examine several different scenarios in which you might find yourself developing scripts to complete.

Automation

The most compelling situation for the use of a script is one that requires some form of automation for a task. Scripts are perfect for *basic automation* tasks, such as creating users, adding users to groups, or even more intricate and sophisticated tasks. When a task is automated with a script, it guarantees that the task will flow the same every time it is executed.

There are two types of scripts that you will most likely create: scripts for automating your own tasks and scripts that automate tasks for others. During your career you will most likely find tasks that you have to do over and over. These tasks should be automated as much as possible, and each repetitive task should have its own script. As a best practice, you should create a folder that contains all the scripts you use on a daily basis. This way, you always know where they are, and when you move to a new computer, you can simply copy them over. Obviously, when you create scripts for others, you won't use them on a daily basis. However, these scripts should also be grouped together in a common folder, since you will probably reuse a part of one script or the entire script for another user.

The following is an example of a task that should be automated. It assumes that you have the Remote Server Administration Tools (RSAT) installed on your system, which includes the `dsquery` and `dsget` commands. The command line will query Active Directory for users with *test* in their name. The output from the initial command of `dsquery user -name *test*` accomplished that task and outputs the distinguished name (DN) of the user. We then pipe that output to the `dsget user -samid -ln -fn -email` command line and that retrieves the username, first name, last name, and email address of each user.

```
C:\sys>dsquery user -name *test* | dsget user -samid -ln -fn -email
  samid          fn            ln          email
  testuser1      user1         test        test.user1@wiley.com
  testuser2      user2         test        test.user2@wiley.com
  testuser3      user3         test        test.user3@wiley.com
C:\sys>
```

This is a handy command line, but typing it in every time you need an answer like this is tedious. Luckily, we can write a simple script where we just need to change one part of the script. Where we had `test`, we simply replace it with `%1` to capture the first argument from the Windows batch script. Then we just start Notepad and copy the line in and save it as `lookup.cmd`.

```
dsquery user -name *%1* | dsget user -samid -ln -fn -email
```

Then when we run it, we get the following output:

```
C:\sys>lookup test
C:\sys>dsquery user -name *test* | dsget user -samid -ln -fn -email
  samid          fn            ln          email
  testuser1      user1         test        test.user1@wiley.com
  testuser2      user2         test        test.user2@wiley.com
  testuser3      user3         test        test.user3@wiley.com
C:\sys>
```

The script works just like before, but each command is echoed to the console. This is easily fixed by editing the file `lookup.cmd` with the following additional lines:

```
@echo off
dsquery user -name *%1* | dsget user -samid -ln -fn -email
```

Now when the file is executed, you won't see the echo of the command actually executed, but only the output of the command, as shown here:

```
C:\sys>lookup test
    samid               fn          ln          email
    testuser1           user1       test        test.user1@wiley.com
    testuser2           user2       test        test.user2@wiley.com
    testuser3           user3       test        test.user3@wiley.com
C:\sys>
```

We can refine the script further to add some branch logic, so if the user doesn't supply an argument, it explains the argument required:

```
@echo off

if {%1}=={} (
echo.
echo You must supply the following.
echo ex. %0 {name of user}
echo.
goto :END
)

dsquery user -name *%1* | dsget user -samid -ln -fn -tel -email

:END
```

The process of refining the script is called the development process. The first script you build will have common parts that you will reuse, such as the error handling when no argument is supplied. In this example we used a Windows batch script, but it's recommended to use whichever scripting language(s) you are comfortable with. There is no right way to develop a script, and the purpose of this example is to show you the thought process involved in writing a script.

Restarting Machines

Another common task might be to restart multiple machines. You can solve this problem in several different ways, and it's all about the end goal of the task. If this is a one-time task, then you could write a simple script, such as the following:

```
shutdown /s /m \\computer1 /t 0
shutdown /s /m \\computer2 /t 0
shutdown /s /m \\computer3 /t 0
shutdown /s /m \\computer4 /t 0
```

If this is a recurring task, then you could develop a script that reads a text file into a variable and restarts each computer. It sounds complex, but it really isn't when you break down the task into smaller pieces. For example, say you need to read a file of computer names, and then walk through each line in the files and restart the computer. For this example, let's switch to PowerShell, since it allows reading of files and parsing them. Start by creating a text file named **list.txt** with four computer names in it: computer1 through computer4. Now we'll test the script by saving it as restartcomps.ps1.

```
$list = Get-Content .\list.txt
ForEach($line in $list) {
  Echo $line
}
```

The script will read the contents of the list.txt file into the variable $list. Then the script will load the variable $line for each entry in the $list collection. When we run the script, we get the following output:

```
PS C:\sys> Set-ExecutionPolicy Unrestricted

Execution Policy Change
The execution policy helps protect you from scripts that you do not trust.
Changing the execution policy might expose you to the security risks described
in the about_Execution_Policies help topic at https:/go.microsoft.com/
fwlink/?LinkID=135170. Do you want to change the execution policy?
[Y] Yes  [A] Yes to All  [N] No  [L] No to All  [S] Suspend  [?] Help (default
is "N"): y
PS C:\sys> ./restartcomps.ps1
computer1
computer2
computer3
computer4
PS C:\sys>
```

Now that we have the first two parts of the script working, we just need to add the functional piece. While we are refining the script, let's also remove the variable and read the lines directly:

```
foreach($line in $(Get-Content .\list.txt)) {
  Write-Output $line
  Restart-Computer -Computer $line
}
```

When the script is run, the output will remain the same, but you'll also be restarting the computers that are written as output to the console. We can make the script fancier by allowing arguments for the file to read, but we think you have the idea behind the script development process. It is a work in progress, and you always have some outstanding code to automate your job.

Remapping Network Drives

Remapping network drives can be done in a multitude of ways with VBScript, PowerShell, Window batch scripts, or some other favorite language. However, Windows batch script and PowerShell are the most common. In the following, we see a script that maps a few drives using a Windows batch script. When we map a drive, we are mounting a remote filesystem through to a drive letter. For example, we can mount the remote filesystem of \\server1\ files to a local drive letter of m:

```
net use m: \\server1\files
net use n: \\server2\files
net use o: \\server3\files
```

The same script can also be developed in PowerShell:

```
New-PSDrive -Name "m" -PSProvider FileSystem -Root "\\server1\files"
New-PSDrive -Name "n" -PSProvider FileSystem -Root "\\server2\files"
New-PSDrive -Name "o" -PSProvider FileSystem -Root "\\server3\files"
```

These scripts don't need to be complex like the previous scripts. We just want to obtain a reproducible result every time the script runs.

Installation of Applications

When scripting is combined with the installation of applications, you can perform a number of functions that are not possible on their own. For example, you can write a script that installs the prerequisites for an installation and then only succeeds if the subsequent installations are successful. A lot of these scenarios are going to be custom to your specific needs and environment. The following is an example of a PowerShell command that will install an application called App.msi:

```
Invoke-CimMethod -ClassName Win32_Product -MethodName Install -Arguments
@{PackageLocation='\\server\installs\App.msi'}
```

A few assumptions are made with the PowerShell example. The first assumption is that you are calling an MSI installer. If you aren't, the code will not work, since every installer has its own methods for invoking an installation. The second assumption is that you are an administrator of the operating system. Writing a PowerShell script will not circumvent Windows security.

Creating a scripted installation of an application is rewarding, but it is also time consuming. You will most likely have to refine your script several times before it works as expected. This means that you will need to install the application many times to get it right. However, if you have an application that requires installation across a number of computers, you can easily reclaim the time spent on the script.

Automated Backups

Backups should be trusted to back up software that is engineered to expire media, rotate media, and generally back up and restore the data and systems that the organization depends on. This type of software is considered off-the-shelf backup software and scripts are not expected to replace this software. However, by using scripts you can automate pieces of the backup process to make the process much more reliable.

A common example of automating backups with scripts is the backup of SQL databases. You can use off-the-shelf backup software to back up the database. However, one common problem is that the agent installed on the SQL server that facilitates the backup will take a snapshot of the database and back it up in whole. This might seem like what we are trying to achieve as an end goal—except when you try to restore it, you'll quickly find that you need to restore the database in whole, even though you only need one table of records.

If you preprocess the database with a script, you can export it to a file. This file can then be backed up and restored to any SQL server, even down to the record level. The following is a maintenance script used with Microsoft SQL to back up the database to a file. The script is written in the SQL scripting language.

```
USE TestRecords
GO
BACKUP DATABASE [TestRecords]
TO  DISK = N'D:\DBBackups\TestRecords.bak'
WITH CHECKSUM;
```

You can automate many other types of backups, such as custom application data, Registry settings, email data, and any other type of data you can address with a script. However, one of the most common backups you will automate with scripts are SQL database backups.

Gathering of Information/Data

Although you can use applications such as Device Manager to gather information about a computer, using the GUI is not scalable when you need to gather information from a large group of computers. This is where scripts come in handy to gather information and even export the information to a file for you. In the following examples, we will look at some simple PowerShell commands for gathering information and exporting the information. However, you can use any scripting language you like and Windows batch scripting is very commonly used as well.

```
PS C:\sys> Get-Service

Status   Name                DisplayName
------   ----                -----------
Running  agent_ovpnconnect   OpenVPN Agent agent_ovpnconnect
Stopped  AJRouter            AllJoyn Router Service
Stopped  ALG                 Application Layer Gateway Service
Stopped  AppIDSvc            Application Identity
Stopped  Appinfo             Application Information
[ Output Cut ]
```

The Get-Service cmdlet will show you all the services running on the operating system. It will output a long list and will display each service's Status, Name, and DisplayName. By piping the output to the Export-Csv cmdlet, we can output a lot more detail and send it directly to a comma-separated values (CSV) file. An example of this is in the following command string:

```
PS C:\sys> Get-Service | Export-Csv .\Services.csv
```

The Get-Service cmdlet isn't the only command you can use to gather data; there are various other commands that let you gather data and export it. Obviously, you can chain these commands together in a script and gather a large amount of data. You can then use scripts to mine the data for specific information, such as a service state or free space.

Initiating Updates

The Windows platform has been automatically patching itself since the release of Microsoft Update and Windows XP. The feature of Microsoft Update and the Windows platform have evolved since the early release. It has turned into a robust feature to keep Windows up to date. However, if you need an immediate result to patch a security hole, then scripting a solution is the best remedy.

There are a number of ways to get patches to immediately install on Windows. The approach you choose depends on your patch management solution, such as Windows Update, Windows Server Update Services (WSUS), Microsoft Endpoint Configuration Manager (MECM), or a third-party patch management solution. For the remainder of this section, we will use the Windows Update solutions for examples.

If you want to script Windows Updates to initiate patching via Windows batch scripting, then the utility of choice is wuauclt.exe. The command can be directed to detect patches with the /detectnow argument. However, don't expect anything elaborate; the utility will not notify you that it is doing anything. If you want to watch the progress, then you'll need to keep an eye on the log file, C:\Windows\WindowsUpdate.log.

An alternative is to use PowerShell and a PSGallery module call PSWindowsUpdate. This module allows you to fully automate the patch management and obtain a great level of detail. For example, after installing the module you can execute the command Get-WindowsUpdate to obtain the pending list of available updates, as shown here:

```
PS C:\sys> Install-Module -Name PSWindowsUpdate

NuGet provider is required to continue
PowerShellGet requires NuGet provider version '2.8.5.201' or newer to interact with NuGet-based repositories. The NuGet
 provider must be available in 'C:\Program Files\PackageManagement\ProviderAssemblies' or
'C:\Users\bohack\AppData\Local\PackageManagement\ProviderAssemblies'. You can also install the NuGet provider by
```

```
running 'Install-PackageProvider -Name NuGet -MinimumVersion 2.8.5.201
-Force'. Do you want PowerShellGet to install
and import the NuGet provider now?
[Y] Yes  [N] No  [S] Suspend  [?] Help (default is "Y"): y


Untrusted repository
You are installing the modules from an untrusted repository. If you trust this
repository, change its
InstallationPolicy value by running the Set-PSRepository cmdlet. Are you sure
you want to install the modules from
'PSGallery'?
[Y] Yes  [A] Yes to All  [N] No  [L] No to All  [S] Suspend  [?] Help (default
is "N"): y
PS C:\sys> Get-WindowsUpdate


ComputerName Status     KB          Size Title
------------ ------     --          ---- -----
CERES        -------    KB5007406   80MB 2021-11 Cumulative Update Preview for
.NET Framework 3.5, 4.7.2 and 4.8 for...
CERES        -------    KB2267602    2GB Security Intelligence Update for
Microsoft Defender Antivirus - KB2267602 (...


PS C:\sys>
```

You can then execute the command Get-WUInstall -AcceptAll -AutoReboot and the operating system will begin to install the updates and automatically reboot. These are just a few ways you can script the installation of Windows Updates.

Script Considerations

Along with the knowledge of scripting comes great power and even greater responsibility. There are several key points that should be considered before scripting a solution and during the development of the script. In the following section we will cover some of these key considerations.

Of course, there may be considerations outside of these CompTIA objectives. The one consideration that has resonated throughout the previous section is the decision between investing time to develop a script or just completing the task. This is something that you will need to take into account before you even begin scripting.

Introducing Security Issues

A common pitfall with scripting is inadvertently introducing a security issue. Security issues come in all different forms when scripting. The most common security issue is the embedding of security credentials in scripts. Regardless of how secure you think the script will be, it's a bad habit and should be avoided at all costs.

That being said, there are instances where embedding a password cannot be avoided. In these situations, you should use mechanisms that are supported in the scripting language to act as a digital locker for your password or methods that encrypt the password. One such mechanism is the ConvertTo-SecureString cmdlet. It means more lines of code, more time, and sometimes more aggravation in getting it to work, but the benefit is a secure system.

Another potential problem is the inadvertent introduction of malware with scripting. This usually happens when you need additional functionality, such as email capability or changing a system setting. Windows batch scripting has its limitations, and it is easy to use a third-party tool to get the last bit of functionality out of the script. However, that third-party tool may have malicious intent, and you could introduce that malicious code to the system in which the script is executed. PowerShell has its own potential malware risks; when you add an untrusted module, the same could happen.

The best way to avoid these pitfalls is to not shortcut the solution. Do your homework and avoid embedding passwords or using untrusted modules or third-party utilities in your scripts. It means more work, but this should be factored into your cost-benefit analysis when taking on developing a script.

Changing System Settings

Scripts are generally created to change various user and system settings. However, sometimes you can inadvertently change a system setting that is not meant to be changed. If this happens, it can adversely affect the system it is executed on. Therefore, it is always best to test the script on a sacrificial computer. A virtual machine is the best option, since it can be reverted to a prior snapshot if something unexpected happens.

An example of a simple mistake is using the setx command incorrectly. The setx command modifies the system environment variables and is used by Windows batch scripting. By using the statement setx path "$path;c:\sys" /m, you could cause irreversible problems. This statement will set the path variable to $path;c:\sys, because the incorrect syntax was used to address the variable of path. The correct statement is actually setx path "%path%;c:\sys" /m. The statement now sets the path variable to the current path variable contents (%path%) and the addition of c:\sys.

The mistake can be as simple as mixing up syntax from one scripting language with syntax from another scripting language. However, some commands are not as forgiving, such as the previous example. When using PowerShell the mistake can be very subtle, since many commands cover both user and system settings. Always test your script before you execute it on a live system. Otherwise, you might be reinstalling an operating system in addition to completing your scripting task.

System Crashes

Scripting allows you to automate processes, which is the main reason we are developing the script in the first place. However, automation can sometimes create problems that we can't foresee during the development of the script. As an example, you can quickly gobble up all the usable RAM resources with the following Windows batch script. The script will launch instances of Notepad until the operating system runs out of memory.

```
:loop
start notepad.exe
goto :loop
```

Although this script is obvious in its intent, it is an extreme example of automation that if left unchecked will crash the system. Windows batch scripting is not the only scripting language where things can go awry; you can do the same with PowerShell. This example will create an HTML-formatted file of the directory structure:

```
Get-ChildItem c:\ -Recurse | ConvertTo-Html | Out-File -FilePath .\output.html
```

The problem with this example is the sheer size of the resulting file. This statement will recursively list all the files from the C: drive down. When the file is launched in the web browser, the browser will quickly run out of memory trying to display the large file. More elaborate scripts may automatically open the web browser and immediately crash it.

To prevent similar problems from happening in your environment, you should test and monitor your scripts. By testing your script solution for errors or conditions that can run the system out of resources unintentionally, you identify and correct problems that would otherwise cripple the system. Monitoring should be performed after the script is in place, such as a script that is started via the Task Scheduler. You want to identify any spikes in resource usage after the solution is in place.

Remote Access

Remote access technologies have been around for as long as networks have been in existence. As a technician, you can't always be in all the places you are needed. Remote access technologies allow you to do just that. You can create a remote connection to a distant computer on the network and change its configuration. In this section, we will discuss several different types of remote access technologies that are covered on the CompTIA 220-1102 exam, as well as their security implications for a network.

Remote Desktop Protocol

Remote Desktop Protocol (RDP) is used exclusively with Microsoft operating systems. An RDP client—the *Remote Desktop Connection client*, also known as the `mstsc.exe` utility—is built into the Microsoft operating system, as shown in Figure 20.6. The Remote Desktop Connection client can provide remote access as though you were sitting in front of the keyboard, monitor, and mouse. The Remote Desktop Connection client and RDP can transport several other resources, such as remote audio, printers, the clipboard, local disks, and video capture devices, as well as any other Plug and Play (PnP) devices.

RDP communicates over TCP port 3389 to deliver the remote screen and connect the local mouse and keyboard for the RDP session. RDP uses Transport Layer Security (TLS) encryption by default, and it provides 128-bit encryption. Microsoft allows one remote user

FIGURE 20.6 The Remote Desktop Connection client

connection or a local connection on desktop operating systems via RDP, but not both at the same time. On server operating systems, Microsoft allows two administrative connections, which can be a combination of local or remote access but cannot exceed two connections.

Microsoft also uses RDP to deliver user desktops and applications via terminal services. When RDP is used in this fashion, a centralized gateway brokers the connections to each RDP client desktop session. Terminal services require terminal services licensing for either each user connecting or each desktop served. RDP can also be used to deliver applications to end users using Microsoft RemoteApp on terminal services. When RemoteApp is used, the server still requires a terminal services license. However, just the application is delivered to the user rather than the entire desktop.

Virtual Private Network (VPN)

A virtual private network (VPN) extends your company's internal network across the Internet or other unsecured public networks. This remote access technology allows clients and branch networks to be connected securely and privately with the company's network. There are several different ways a VPN can be used in your network architecture, and we will cover them in the following sections. A VPN achieves this private connection across a public network by creating a secure tunnel from end to end through the process of encryption and encapsulation. The encryption protocols used vary, and we will cover them as well. Since a tunnel is created from end to end, your local host becomes part of the company's internal network along with an IP address that matches the company's internal network. We don't have to be bound to only TCP/IP across a VPN, since this technology can encapsulate any protocol and carry it through the tunnel.

Site-to-Site VPN

Over the past 10 to 15 years, using high-bandwidth connections to the Internet has become cheaper than purchasing dedicated leased lines. So, companies have opted to install Internet connections at branch offices for Internet usage. These lines can serve a dual purpose: connecting users to the Internet and connecting branch offices to the main office. However, the Internet is a public network and unsecured, but site-to-site VPN connections can fix that. Companies with multiple locations have reaped the benefits of creating VPN tunnels from site to site over the Internet by ditching their leased lines, installing VPN concentrators at each location, and creating VPN tunnels. Site-to-site VPN is also much more scalable than leased lines because locations only need a connection to the Internet and a VPN concentrator to be tied together. Figure 20.7 details two locations tied together with a VPN tunnel. The magic happens all in the VPN concentrator. Since VPN concentrators also have a routing function, when a tunnel is established, a route entry is created in the VPN concentrator for the remote network. When traffic is destined for the branch office with a destination network of 10.2.0.0/16, the router encrypts and encapsulates the information as data and sends it to the other side of the tunnel over the Internet. This is similar to a host-to-site VPN, the difference being the routing is performed in the VPN concentrator. When the packet is received on the other side of the tunnel, the VPN concentrator decapsulates the data, decrypts the packet, and sends the packet to its destination inside the branch network. It is common to find that the appliance performing VPN is also the firewall and router. Firewalls today are sold with VPN software built in and licensed accordingly.

FIGURE 20.7   A typical site-to-site VPN

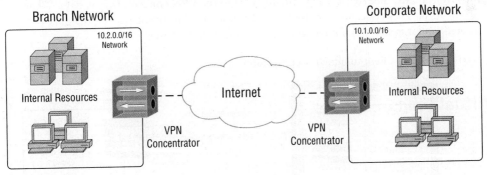

Client-to-Site VPN

Client-to-site VPN connectivity is a remote access strategy for mobile access. It can be used for telecommuters, salespeople, partners, and administrative access to the internal network resources. The key concept is that VPN access is granted on an individual or a group basis for the mobile users. Using the example in Figure 20.8, you can allow salespeople to connect to the corporate network so they can update sales figures or process orders. This can all be done securely over the Internet while the users are mobile and have access to a network connection.

FIGURE 20.8   A typical host-to-site VPN

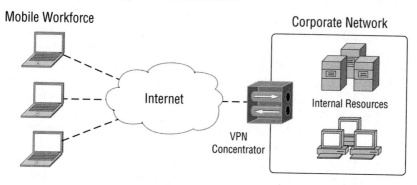

When a client computer establishes a VPN connection, it becomes part of the internal corporate network. This happens by assignment of an IP address from the internal corporate network. In Figure 20.9, you can see a mobile device such as a laptop with a VPN client installed in the operating system. When the connection is established with the VPN concentrator over the Internet, a pseudo network adapter is created by the VPN client. In this example, the pseudo network adapter is assigned an internal IP address of 10.2.2.8/16 from the VPN concentrator. The laptop also has its own IP address of 192.168.1.3/24, which it uses to access the Internet. A routing table entry is created in the operating system for the 10.2.0.0/16 network and through the pseudo network adapter. When traffic is generated for the corporate network, it is sent to the pseudo adapter, where it is encrypted and then sent to the physical NIC and sent through the Internet to the VPN concentrator as data. When it arrives at the VPN concentrator, the IP header is stripped from the packet, the data is decrypted, and it is sent to its internal corporate network resource.

FIGURE 20.9   Client-to-site VPN connection

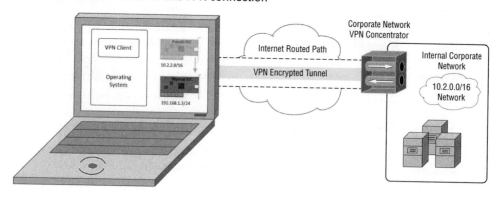

Clientless VPN

There are many different VPN solutions on the market. Each one of them traditionally requires the installation of a VPN client. However, there are a growing number of products that do not require the installation of a client; these products are called clientless VPN solutions. The VPN client is the web browser on the mobile device requiring connectivity back to the corporate network. The VPN appliance acts as a reverse proxy to the various resources internal to the organization.

Virtual Network Computing

Virtual Network Computing (VNC) is a remote control tool for the sharing of desktops. The VNC client normally operates on TCP port 5900. VNC is similar to Microsoft RDP, with the exception that VNC is an open source protocol and typically allows only one console session per operating system. It supports encryption via plug-ins, but it is not encrypted by default.

VNC operates in a client-server model. The server allows for the remote control of the host on which it is installed. It is normally configured with a simple shared password, but it can also be configured with Windows groups. Several different clients can be used, such as RealVNC, TightVNC, and many others, but they all perform similarly.

Many different VNC clients are available for download. To learn more, visit www.realvnc.com and www.tightvnc.com. A simple web search for "VNC clients" will produce a staggering number of results. Each client has its own unique feature set.

Telnet

Telnet is an older remote access protocol for Linux, UNIX, and network device operating systems. Telnet provides an unencrypted remote text console session for remote access purposes, communicating over TCP port 23. It is not considered secure and should not be used, because a malicious user can eavesdrop on the session. Many network devices still use Telnet for configuration purposes. However, SSH, if available, should be configured and used in lieu of Telnet.

Because Telnet is unsecure and deprecated, many operating systems have removed the Telnet client and the server service. Since Windows 7, the Telnet client that comes with the operating system requires installation as a Windows feature. In Windows Server 2016, both the Telnet client and server were removed completely. Telnet has largely been replaced with SSH.

For more information about the `telnet` command, visit:
`https://docs.microsoft.com/en-us/windows-server/administration/windows-commands/telnet`

Secure Shell

Secure Shell (SSH) is commonly used for remote access via a text console for Linux and UNIX operating systems. The SSH protocol encrypts all communications between the SSH client and the SSH server using TCP port 22. The SSH server is also known as the SSH daemon. SSH uses public-private key pair cryptography to provide authentication between the SSH client and server. SSH can also use a key pair to authenticate users connecting to the SSH server for the session, or a simple username and password can be provided.

It is important to understand that both the user and their host computer are authenticated when the user attempts to connect to the server. During the initial connection between the user's host computer and the SSH server, the encryption protocol is negotiated for the user's login, and the cryptography keys are verified. PuTTY, shown in Figure 20.10, is a common SSH client that is free to download and use. PuTTY provides various methods of connecting to a remote device, including Telnet and SSH.

FIGURE 20.10   PuTTY SSH Client

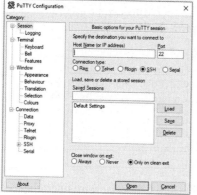
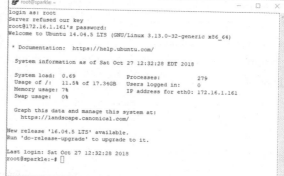

 Microsoft included the OpenSSH client by default in Windows 10 version 1803 and later. The OpenSSH client is located in the C:\WINDOWS\SYSTEM32\OpenSSH folder.

Beyond logging into a Linux or UNIX server for remote access, SSH can provide remote access for applications. Through the use of SSH port forwarding, the application can be directed across the SSH connection to the far end. This allows applications to tunnel through the SSH session. It also encrypts application traffic from the client to the server, because it is carried over the SSH encrypted tunnel. SSH can behave similarly to a VPN connection, but it is more complex to set up.

Remote Monitoring and Management

In the early days of your organization, it may have been simple to monitor and manage all the various systems from one location. However, as your organization's footprint grew across different sites and many employees now work from home (WFH), it is more difficult to monitor and manage the various systems. Systems need patching, must be monitored for disk space, and have hardware and applications installed—and these are just a few of the tasks.

This is where a *remote monitoring and management (RMM)* solution can help IT across your enterprise or multiple enterprises and give you a holistic view of your enterprise. There are several different RMM solutions on the market today. Among the most popular solutions are managed service providers (MSPs) that manage your enterprise for a contracted price. These service providers ultimately use RMM software to monitor and maintain the enterprise. The MSP will require your organization to install an agent that is configured to report back to the MSP's RMM software.

You can also purchase a cloud-based or on-premises solution for maintaining your organization with your own IT department. Every vendor of RMM solutions has their own variation of features, which makes up the product's secret sauce. These solutions also require the installation of an agent that reports back to the RMM solutions. Regardless of which product you choose, there are two main features to RMM: the remote monitoring feature and the management feature.

Remote Monitoring   The remote monitoring feature of an RMM system can monitor a number of different components, such as security, hardware, applications, and even activity on the operating system. These are just a few of the components of the remote monitoring feature found in RMM systems. The list grows depending on the RMM vendor. The most common monitoring is the security of the various systems across your enterprise, such as patch levels, antimalware status, and exploits. Another monitored component is the hardware and applications installed across the enterprise. Monitoring the hardware can identify your assets, as well as identify when upgrades are needed. Application monitoring can identify problems with a specific application or your vulnerability in the event the application needs to be patched. These are just a few monitored components—the list grows with every release of new RMM software by vendors.

Reporting is a major component of the remote monitoring capabilities of RMM systems. The reporting can be active or passive for most systems. In an active reporting system, the RMM software will compile a report periodically and alert you when a major change is discovered. As an example, if over 30 percent of your computers are vulnerable to a new exploit, the system can be configured to alert you. You may also set up a similar threshold alert for disk space. The passive reports can be run and give you an overall picture of your network and are typically in the form of a drill-down report. A drill-down report allows you to view the overall health and drill down to specific areas of interest to a specific detail.

Remote Management   The remote management feature of RMM solutions can also be quite diverse in the type of management they provide. Many RMM vendors offer the management of computers via a form of remote desktop control. This remote desktop control allows you to intervene when a user has a problem. RMM solutions also offer integrated patch management solutions to patch applications and the operating system. In addition to user intervention and security, you may find remote application installation, disk cleanup, and remote antimalware scan features, and these features just scrape the surface of RMM capabilities. Every vendor of RMM systems has their own unique management capabilities based on their product's focus, such as security, asset management, or user productivity.

Remote Access Tools

Since the release of Windows XP, Microsoft has included various tools to allow remote assistance to the Windows operating system. In addition to Microsoft's proprietary remote assistance tools, many vendors have entered the market. As a result, there are a number of third-party remote assistance tools freely available and out on the market, with varying costs. Let's explore some of the built-in capabilities of the Windows product and some of the features of third-party products.

Microsoft Remote Assistance (MSRA)

Microsoft Remote Assistance (MSRA), or `msra.exe`, was released with Windows XP. The tool itself is dated, but it is still available in Windows 11, as shown in Figure 20.11. The interface has not changed much since its original release, nor has the functionality. The MSRA tool allows a trusted helper to assist the user when the user creates a solicited request

FIGURE 20.11   MSRA tool

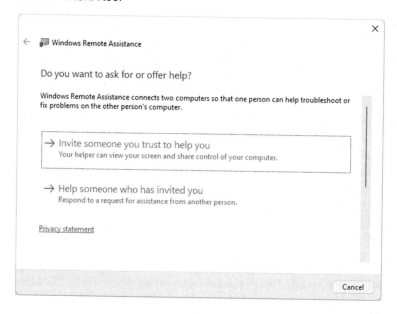

by choosing Invite Someone You Trust to Help You. This option will generate an Invitation .msrcIncident file that you can save as a file or email to the trusted user if you have email set up on the operating system, as shown in Figure 20.12. The third option is Easy Connect, which uses IPv6 and peer-to-peer networking to transfer the request.

FIGURE 20.12   Inviting the helper

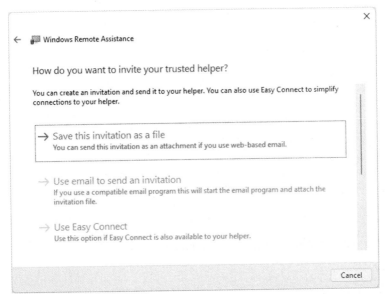

Before the user can send a request, the operating system must allow Remote Desktop connections. You can access this setting by clicking Start ➤ System ➤ About ➤ Advanced System Settings, then choosing the Remote tab, shown in Figure 20.13. You then select Allow Remote Connections To This Computer in the Remote Desktop area and click OK. By default, Allow Remote Assistance Connections To This Computer is already selected.

When the trusted helper gets the Invitation.msrcIncident file, the file will launch the MSRA tool and attempt to connect to the user. The user will then supply the session password to the trusted helper. Once the user and helper are connected and the password is entered on the trusted helper's MSRA tool, the user will be prompted to allow the helper. The result is a remote connection to the user, as shown in Figure 20.14. The default view of the MSRA tool is viewing mode. The trusted helper can request control of the operating system, and the user must allow the helper to control the operating system by answering the prompt. The MSRA tool has a chat feature that allows the trusted helper to communicate with the user.

However, you must keep several items in mind when using the MSRA tool. The first is that you will not find the tool in any menu. The only way to launch the tool is to enter **msra.exe** in a run dialog box. Another consideration is that MSRA only works well inside the organization. The use of routers and firewalls breaks the functionality of MSRA over the Internet. Easy Connect was added to allow IPv6 to be used via an IPv4 network to work around this problem, but Easy Connect is not set up by default. Outside of these considerations, MSRA is a useful tool for technicians.

FIGURE 20.13   Allowing Remote Desktop Connections

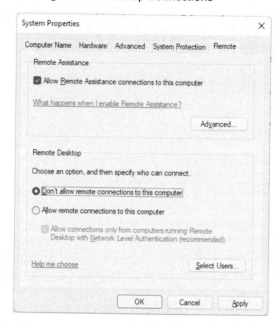

FIGURE 20.14   MSRA tool connected to the user

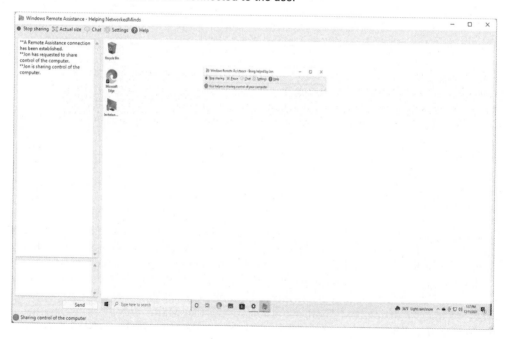

Quick Assist

Microsoft realized the deficiencies in the original MSRA tool and included another remote access tool in Windows 8/8.1 and Windows 10/11 for soliciting help called *Quick Assist*, shown in Figure 20.15. Quick Assist operates similarly to third-party services such as Splashtop, GoToMeeting, and Join.me. These tools allow for remote desktop sharing and assistance for a user through screen sharing. Unfortunately, Quick Assist does not support file transfers. Quick Assist works behind routers and firewalls. The original Remote Assistance tool introduced in Windows XP did not work behind routers and firewalls. Quick Assist is slowly replacing the Remote Assistance application in current Windows versions. Quick Assist even has its own shortcuts for easy access by the user.

FIGURE 20.15 Windows Quick Assist tool

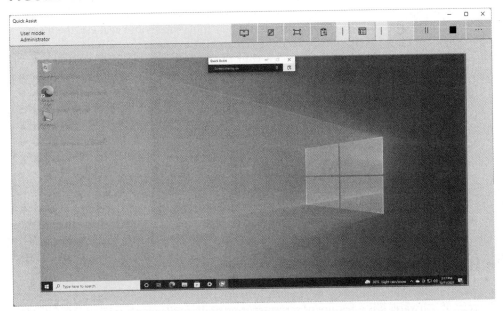

You can launch Quick Assist on Windows 10/11 by clicking the Start menu and typing **Quick Assist**. Once the Quick Assist tool is started on your computer (the assistant), choose Give Assistance. You will then be prompted to log in with a Microsoft account. Once you are signed in, you will be presented with a six-digit number, which will be valid for 10 minutes. On the end user's (person being helped) computer, the end user will launch Quick Assist and select Get Assistance. The end user will need to obtain your six-digit code and enter it into the dialog box when prompted. Once the number is entered on the end user's side, both computers will connect, and you will be asked what type of control you want to provide for the end user: View Only or Full Control. Of course, the end user has to allow the control, but you can provide remote assistance without installing any third-party software.

Quick Assist offers chat functionality to the assistant and the end user in a chat window. You can launch this window by clicking Toggle Instruction Channel on the Quick Assist toolbar. You can also launch Task Manager automatically in later versions of the tool. By clicking the Task Manager item on the Quick Assist toolbar, you can remotely launch Task Manager on the end user's operating system. An annotation tool allows you to draw on the end user's screen to guide them. Select this tool by clicking the Annotate option on the Quick Assist toolbar. However, just like the MSRA tool, Quick Assist does not have a file transfer utility. Any file transfers must be done with a file sharing service, where the user downloads the file from the Internet link you provide.

Third-Party Tools

Third-party tools such as Splashtop, GoToMeeting, and Join.me have their own unique features. Each tool fits into a category of screen sharing, videoconferencing, file transfer, or desktop management. When choosing a third-party tool, you should evaluate the main requirements and the category the software excels at. Let's examine the various categories to help you better identify the best software for your needs.

Screen Sharing   Both the MSRA tool and Quick Assist fit into the category of *screen-sharing* software. Screen-sharing software will share your screen with another user, and it is most often used to troubleshoot problems. Two popular screen-sharing software utilities are Splashtop and TeamViewer. Both allow you to share your screen with another person, similar to the MSRA tool and Quick Assist. However, these tools have other built-in features that the MSRA tool and Quick Assist do not, such as file sharing and screen blanking.

Videoconferencing   The *videoconferencing* category includes any screen-sharing software that allows more than one person to screen-share. The software also has some additional functionality, such as calendar invite, call-in numbers, and attendee management. Microsoft Teams, WebEx, Zoom, and GoToMeeting are all examples of videoconferencing software. These tools are often used to present ideas and collaborate between groups of people.

File Transfer   The ability to file transfer between two computers is not really a category of software; it is a feature of screen-sharing and/or videoconferencing software. *File transfer software* can, however, be a category of remote access software if you are solely looking for that feature. Popular file transfer software includes OneDrive, Dropbox, and Google Drive. These file transfer utilities allow the sharing of files between users and serve a specific purpose for the distribution of files bidirectionally.

Desktop Management   The last category is an extension of some screen-sharing software packages such as Splashtop and TeamViewer. Both of these products can be used in an ad hoc fashion for screen sharing. They also be installed on the operating system and configured to allow an inbound connection. When these tools are installed to await an incoming connection, they are considered to be *desktop management software* solutions. Many of these tools also allow integration with other management tools like Intune and Jamf. This integration gives you complete device management, and a lot of these tools will even show when a device is online and connectable.

Security Considerations

Each of the remote access technologies discussed in this chapter have security considerations. Before implementing a remote access technology, you should determine what type of data is going to be exchanged and whether the level of encryption is sufficient. Telnet, which is not encrypted, might be fine if simple data is being transmitted, such as temperature or humidity readings. However, if passwords, configuration, or any type of sensitive information will be transmitted, then a more secure protocol, such as Secure Shell, should be used.

Beyond the data in transit and the method that provides the transit, there are other security considerations. One of the biggest concerns is any agent that awaits connection and is exposed to the Internet. A threat agent can exploit these software packages and compromise a host via these software packages. To combat this problem, keep your software package up to date, and if multifactor authentication is available, use it.

Videoconferencing packages should be secured so that a password is required to join a meeting. Setting a password will thwart conference bombing, also known as *Zoombombing*. This is the act of a threat agent guessing the meeting ID and joining an otherwise private conversation. This type of security concern isn't really your typical threat, but it is a liability to your organization if not avoided.

Zoombombing became an annoyance on the Internet during the COVID pandemic. Organizations were disbanded from their campuses and employees were sent home to work. Because Zoom conferencing software is a dominant software product for videoconferencing, many organizations used the software to continue doing business. With the higher usage and the relaxation of security by organizations, Internet trolls guessed meeting IDs and joined otherwise private conferences. The trolls mainly caused disruption to the ongoing conferences, but many exposed the participants to unsavory behavior.

Summary

This chapter focused on the basics of scripting and introduced programming concepts such as scripting types, commenting, branch logic, loops, and use cases for scripting. Scripting is a somewhat newer objective for the CompTIA A+ objectives. It is a worthy skill for an A+ technician.

We also introduced you to the various remote access technologies, highlighting their advantages and weaknesses. In addition, we covered remote assistance tools, which allow a remote user to share their screen with you for support purposes.

Exam Essentials

Understand the basics of scripting.   You should understand that a programming language is compiled and a scripting language is interpreted. You should also understand the various elements of a script, such as the comment, interaction of environment variables, branch logic, and loops.

Know the various scripting languages.   You should know the advantages and disadvantages of each scripting language and the use cases for scripting, as well as other security and system considerations. In addition, you should know which operating systems each of the various scripting languages operates on. Be familiar with the various script file types that correspond to each scripting language.

Know the various remote access technologies.   You should know that RDP is a Microsoft protocol used for remote access; Telnet is a cleartext, unsecure console protocol; and SSH is an encrypted, secure console protocol. In addition, Quick Assist is a remote assistance application in Windows, and there are third-party screen-sharing and desktop management tools that function similarly and include file-sharing capabilities, as well as videoconferencing software.

Review Questions

The answers to the chapter review questions can be found in Appendix A.

1. Which statement about scripting languages is true?

   A. Scripting languages require a compiler.

   B. Scripting languages are strongly typed.

   C. Scripting languages are interpreted.

   D. Scripting languages have good memory management.

2. What level are scripting languages considered?

   A. High

   B. Mid

   C. Intermediate

   D. Low

3. Which type of variable will allow decimal math?

   A. Boolean

   B. Integer

   C. Floating-point

   D. String

4. Which environment variable is not inherited?

   A. System variable

   B. User variable

   C. Program variable

   D. String variable

5. Which statement will load a PowerShell variable `xvar` with a value of 2?

   A. `xvar = 2`

   B. `$xvar = 2`

   C. `xvar = 2;`

   D. `set /a xvar=2`

6. Which type of loop has a defined beginning and end, and steps from beginning to end?

   A. `do while` loop

   B. `while` loop

   C. `if` statement

   D. `for` loop

7. Which extension is used with the Windows batch scripting language?

    A. .vbs

    B. .js

    C. .bat

    D. .py

8. Which scripting language allows for the use of the Component Object Model (COM)?

    A. PowerShell

    B. VBScript

    C. Windows batch script

    D. JavaScript

9. Which extension is used with the Python scripting language?

    A. .vbs

    B. .js

    C. .bat

    D. .py

10. Which scripting language is used with Microsoft Azure and Microsoft 365?

    A. PowerShell

    B. VBScript

    C. Windows batch script

    D. JavaScript

11. Which scripting language is used within web pages to allow for interactive content?

    A. PowerShell

    B. Bash

    C. Windows batch script

    D. JavaScript

12. Which extension is used with the Bash scripting language?

    A. .vbs

    B. .sh

    C. .bat

    D. .py

13. What must be done before a Bash script can be executed?

    A. chown permissions must be set.

    B. The execute attribute must be set.

    C. chmod permissions must be set.

    D. An .sh must be added to the end of the script.

14. Which statement will load a JavaScript variable `mvar` with a value of 8?

    A. `$mvar = 8`

    B. `mvar = 8`

    C. `mvar = 8;`

    D. `set /a mvar=8`

15. Which scripting language has its own preinstalled Integrated Scripting Environment (ISE)?

    A. VBScript

    B. Bash

    C. Python

    D. PowerShell

16. Which line would be used to comment JavaScript code?

    A. `//comment`

    B. `'comment`

    C. `REM comment`

    D. `# comment`

17. Which extension is used with the JavaScript scripting language?

    A. `.js`

    B. `.sh`

    C. `.bat`

    D. `.py`

18. Which Microsoft remote protocol allows for local drives to be presented to the remote system?

    A. VCN

    B. RDP

    C. SSH

    D. Telnet

19. On which network protocol and port does SSH operate?

    A. TCP port 3389

    B. TCP port 22

    C. TCP port 23

    D. TCP port 443

20. Which tool is used for screen sharing?

    A. RDP

    B. MSRA

    C. SSH

    D. Telnet

Performance-Based Question

You will encounter performance-based questions on the A+ exams. The questions on the exam require you to perform a specific task, and you will be graded on whether or not you were able to complete the task. The following requires you to think creatively in order to measure how well you understand this chapter's topics. You may or may not see similar questions on the actual A+ exams. To see how your answers compare to the authors', refer to Appendix B.

You have been assigned to write a PowerShell script that will find other scripts in a user profile directory and all its subdirectories. Which PowerShell variable should you use, since %UserProfile% is an environment variable and will not run in PowerShell?

Chapter

21

Safety and Environmental Concerns

THE FOLLOWING COMPTIA A+ 220-1102 EXAM OBJECTIVES ARE COVERED IN THIS CHAPTER:

✓ **4.4 Given a scenario, use common safety procedures.**

- Electrostatic discharge (ESD) straps
- ESD mats
- Equipment grounding
- Proper power handling
- Proper component handling and storage
- Antistatic bags
- Compliance with government regulations
- Personal safety
  - Disconnect power before repairing PC
  - Lifting techniques
  - Electrical fire safety
  - Safety goggles
  - Air filtration mask

✓ **4.5 Summarize environmental impacts and local environmental controls.**

- Material safety data sheet (MSDS)/documentation for handling and disposal
  - Proper battery disposal
  - Proper toner disposal
  - Proper disposal of other devices and assets

- Temperature, humidity-level awareness, and proper ventilation
  - Location/equipment placement
  - Dust cleanup
  - Compressed air/vacuums
- Power surges, under-voltage events, and power failures
  - Battery backup
  - Surge suppressor

✓ **4.6 Explain the importance of prohibited content/ activity and privacy, licensing, and policy concepts.**

- Incident response
  - Chain of custody
  - Inform management/law enforcement as necessary
  - Copy of drive (data integrity and preservation)
  - Documentation of incident
- Licensing/digital rights management (DRM)/end-user license agreement (EULA)
  - Valid licenses
  - Non-expired licenses
  - Personal use license vs. corporate use license
  - Open-source license
- Regulated data
  - Credit card transactions
  - Personal government-issued information
  - PII
  - Healthcare data
  - Data retention requirements

In this chapter, we start by talking about safety, which includes your safety and the safety of your coworkers, as well as environmental concerns. Observing proper safety procedures can help prevent injury to you or to others.

Our discussion about the environment is two-sided. The environment affects computers (via things like dust, sunlight, and water), but computers can also potentially harm the environment. We'll consider both sides as we move through this chapter.

Next, we will cover some legal aspects of operational procedures. These include licensing of software, protection of personally identifiable information, and incident response.

Understanding Safety Procedures

The proliferation of computers in today's society has created numerous jobs for technicians. Presumably that's why you're reading this book: you want to get your CompTIA A+ certification. Many others, who don't fix computers professionally, like to tinker with them as a hobby. Years ago, only the most expert users dared to crack the case on a computer. Often, repairing the system meant using a soldering iron. Today, thanks to the cheap parts, computer repair is not quite as involved. Regardless of your skill or intent, if you're going to be inside a computer, you always need to be aware of safety issues. There's no sense in getting yourself hurt or killed.

As a provider of a hands-on service (repairing, maintaining, or upgrading someone's computer), you need to be aware of some general safety tips, because if you are not careful, you could harm yourself or the equipment. Clients expect you to solve their problems, not make them worse by injuring yourself or those around you. In the following sections, we'll talk about identifying safety hazards and creating a safe working environment.

Identifying Potential Safety Hazards

Anything can be a potential safety hazard, right? Okay, maybe that statement is a bit too paranoid, but there *are* many things, both human-made and environmental, that can cause safety problems when you're working with and around computers.

Perhaps the most important aspect of computers you should be aware of is that not only do they *use* electricity, but they also *store* electrical charge after they're turned off. This makes the power supply and the monitor pretty much off-limits to anyone but a repairperson trained specifically for those devices. In addition, the computer's processor and various parts of the printer run at extremely high temperatures, and you can get burned if you try to handle them immediately after they've been in operation.

Those are just two general safety measures that should concern you. There are plenty more. When discussing safety issues with regard to PCs, let's break them down into four general areas:

- Computer components
- Electrostatic discharge
- Electromagnetic interference
- Natural elements

Computer Components

As mentioned earlier, computers use electricity. And as you're probably aware, electricity can hurt or kill you. The first rule when working inside a computer is always to make sure that it's powered off. If you have to open the computer to inspect or replace parts (as you will with most repairs), be sure to turn off the machine before you begin. Leaving it plugged in is usually fine, and many times it is actually preferred because it grounds the equipment and can help prevent electrostatic discharge.

There's one exception to the power-off rule: you don't have to power off the computer when working with hot-swappable parts, which are designed to be unplugged and plugged back in when the computer is on. Most of these components have an externally accessible interface (such as USB devices or hot-swappable hard drives), so you don't need to crack the computer case.

The Power Supply

Do not take the issue of safety and electricity lightly. Removing the power supply from its external casing can be dangerous. The current flowing through the power supply normally follows a complete circuit; when your body breaks the circuit, your body becomes part of that circuit. Getting inside the power supply is the most dangerous thing you can do as an untrained technician.

The two biggest dangers with power supplies are burning or electrocuting yourself. These risks usually go hand in hand. If you touch a bare wire that is carrying current, you could get electrocuted. A large-enough current passing through you can cause severe burns. It can also cause your heart to stop, your muscles to seize, and your brain to stop functioning. In short, it can kill you. Electricity always finds the best path to ground. And because the human body is basically a bag of saltwater (an excellent conductor of electricity), electricity will use us as a conductor if we are grounded.

Although it is possible to open a power supply to work on it, doing so is *not* recommended. Power supplies contain several capacitors that can hold *lethal* charges *long after they have been unplugged!* It is extremely dangerous to open the case of a power supply. Besides, power supplies are relatively inexpensive and are considered *field replaceable units (FRUs)*. It would probably cost less to replace one than to try to fix it—and much safer.

In the late 1990s, a few mass computer manufacturers experimented with using open power supplies in their computers to save money. We don't know if any deaths occurred because of such incompetence, but it was definitely a very bad idea.

Current vs. Voltage: Which Is More Dangerous?

When talking about power and safety, you will almost always hear the saying, "It's not the volts that kill you; it's the amps." That's mostly true. However, an explanation is in order.

The number of volts in a power source represents its potential to do work. But volts don't do anything by themselves. Current (amperage, or amps) is the force behind the work done by electricity. Here's an analogy to help explain this concept: Say you have two boulders. One weighs 10 pounds and another weighs 100 pounds, and each is 100 feet off the ground. If you drop them, which one will do more work? The obvious answer is the 100-pound boulder. They both have the same potential to do work (100 feet of travel), but the 100-pound boulder has more mass and thus more force. Voltage is analogous to the distance the boulder is from the ground, and amperage is analogous to the mass of the boulder.

This is why you can produce static electricity on the order of 50,000 volts and not electrocute yourself. Even though this electricity has a great potential for work, it does very little work because the amperage is so low. This also explains why you can weld metal with a 110 or 220 volt welder. Welders use only 17 to 45 volts at the tip of the welder, but they also use anywhere from 55 to 590 amps!

If you ever have to work on a power supply, for safety's sake you should discharge all capacitors within it. To do this, connect a resistor across the leads of the capacitor with a rating of 3 watts or more and a resistance of 100 ohms (Ω) per volt. For example, to discharge a 225-volt capacitor, you would use a 22.5kΩ resistor (225V × 100Ω = 22,500Ω, or 22.5kΩ). You can also purchase a tool, known as a *grounding pen* or *discharge pen*, that will discharge any size capacitor. The tools look similar to a pen and have a wire that is connected to ground.

The Monitor

Other than the power supply, the most dangerous component to try to repair is a computer monitor—specifically, older-style *cathode-ray tube (CRT)* monitors. In fact, we recommend that you *not* try to repair monitors of any kind.

To avoid the extremely hazardous environment contained inside the monitor (it can retain a high-voltage charge for hours after it's been turned off), take it to a certified monitor technician or television repair shop. The repair shop or certified technician will know the proper procedures for discharging the monitor, which involve attaching a resistor to the flyback transformer's charging capacitor to release the high-voltage electrical charge that builds up during use. They will also be able to determine whether the monitor can be repaired or whether it needs to be replaced. Remember, the monitor works in its own extremely protected environment (the monitor case) and may not respond well to your desire to try to open it.

WARNING   A CRT is vacuum sealed. Be extremely careful when handling a CRT. If you break the glass, it will implode, which can send glass in any direction.

Even though we recommend not repairing monitors, the A+ exam may test your knowledge of the safety practices to use if you ever need to do so. If you have to open a monitor, you must first discharge the high-voltage charge on it by using a *high-voltage probe*. This probe has a very large needle, a gauge that indicates volts, and a wire with an alligator clip. Attach the alligator clip to a ground (usually the round pin on the power cord). Slip the probe needle underneath the high-voltage cup on the monitor. You will see the gauge spike to around 15,000 volts and slowly reduce to 0 (zero). When it reaches 0, you may remove the high-voltage probe and service the high-voltage components of the monitor.

WARNING   Do *not* use an ESD strap when discharging the monitor. Doing so can lead to a fatal electric shock.

Working with *liquid crystal display (LCD)* monitors—or any device with a fluorescent or LCD backlight—presents a unique safety challenge. These types of devices require an *inverter*, which provides the high-voltage, high-frequency energy needed to power the backlight.

The inverter is a small circuit board installed behind the LCD panel that takes DC power and converts (inverts) it for the backlight. If you've ever seen a laptop or handheld device with a flickering screen or perpetual dimness, it was likely an inverter problem. Inverters store energy even when their power source is cut off, so they have the potential to discharge that energy if you mess with them. Be careful!

The Case

One component that people frequently overlook is the case. Cases are generally made of metal, and some computer cases have very sharp edges inside, so be careful when handling them. You can cut yourself by jamming your fingers between the case and the frame when you try to force the case back on. Also of particular interest are drive bays. Countless technicians have scraped or cut their hands on drive bays when trying in vain to plug a drive cable into the motherboard. You can cover particularly sharp edges with duct tape. Just make sure that you're covering only metal and nothing with electrical components on it.

The Printer

If you've ever attempted to repair a printer, you might have thought that a little monster was inside, hiding all the screws from you. Besides missing screws, here are some things to watch out for when repairing printers:

- When handling a toner cartridge from a laser printer or page printer, do not turn it upside down. You will find yourself spending more time cleaning the printer and the surrounding area than fixing the printer.

- Do not put any objects into the feeding system (in an attempt to clear the path) when the printer is running.

- Laser printers generate a laser that is hazardous to your eyes. Do not look directly into the source of the laser.

- If it's an inkjet printer, do not try to blow in the ink cartridge to clear a clogged opening—that is, unless you like the taste of ink.

- Some parts of a laser printer (such as the *EP cartridge*, which is an *image drum*) will be damaged if you touch them. Your skin produces oils and has a small surface layer of dead skin cells. These substances can collect on the delicate surface of the image drum (EP cartridge) and cause malfunctions. Bottom line: Keep your fingers out of places where they don't belong.

- Laser printers use very high-voltage power sources to charge internal components, which can cause severe injuries.

- Laser printers can get extremely hot in order to fuse the toner to the page. Don't burn yourself on internal components. The fuser can get extremely hot!

 Using an egg carton (or other container with small compartments) is a great way to store and keep track of screws that you take out of a device when you're working on it. If it's an impromptu repair and you don't have a container with compartments, you can use a piece of paper with tape that is looped. This allows you to also write down what the screws were removed from.

When working with printers, we follow some pretty simple guidelines. If there's a messed-up setting, paper jam, or ink or toner problem, we will fix it. If it's something other than that, we call a certified printer repairperson. The inner workings of printers can get pretty complex, and it's best to call someone trained to make those types of repairs.

The Keyboard and Mouse

Okay, we know that you're thinking, "What danger could a keyboard or mouse pose?" We admit that not much danger is associated with these components, but there are a couple of safety concerns that you should always keep in mind:

- If your mouse has a cord, it can catch on something, causing items to fall off a desk, or it might even be long enough that someone can trip over it. So, make sure that it's safely out of the way.

- You could short-circuit your keyboard if you accidentally spill liquid into it. Keyboards generally don't function well with half a can of cola in their innards.

Electrostatic Discharge

So far, we've talked about how electricity can hurt people, but it can also pose safety issues for computer components. One of the biggest concerns for components is *electrostatic discharge (ESD)*. For the most part, ESD won't do serious damage to a person other than provide a little shock. But little amounts of ESD can cause serious damage to computer components, and that damage can manifest itself by causing computers to hang, reboot, or fail to boot at all. ESD happens when two objects of dissimilar charge come into contact with each other. The two objects exchange electrons in order to standardize the electrostatic charge between them. This charge can, and often does, damage electronic components.

CPU chips and memory chips are particularly sensitive to ESD. Be extremely cautious when handling them.

When you shuffle your feet across the floor and shock your best friend on the ear, you are discharging static electricity into their ear. The lowest static voltage transfer that you can feel is around 3,000 volts; it doesn't electrocute you because there is extremely little current. A static transfer that you can *see* is at least 10,000 volts! Just by sitting in a chair, you can generate around 100 volts of static electricity. Walking around wearing synthetic materials can generate around 1,000 volts. You can easily generate around 20,000 volts simply by dragging your smooth-soled shoes across a carpeted floor in the winter. (Actually, it doesn't have to be winter. This voltage can occur in any room with very low humidity—like a heated room in wintertime.)

Relative humidity has a significant impact on the electricity you generate. Walking around can generate 1,500 volts at 65–90 percent relative humidity, but it can produce 35,000 volts if the relative humidity is in the 10–25 percent range.

It makes sense that these thousands of volts can damage computer components. However, a component can be damaged with less than 300 volts! This means that if a small charge is built up in your body, you could damage a component without realizing it.

Do you have long hair or (gasp!) have to wear a tie when fixing computers? Tie it back. Letting long hair or dangling cloth get inside an open computer case is asking for trouble, because both are notorious for carrying and conducting static electricity.

The good news is that there are measures that you can implement to help contain the effects of ESD. The first and easiest item to implement is the antistatic wrist strap, also referred to as an ESD strap. We will look at the antistatic wrist strap, as well as other ESD prevention tools, in the following sections.

Antistatic Wrist Straps

To use an ESD *antistatic strap*, you attach one end to an earth ground (typically, the ground pin on an extension cord) or the computer case and wrap the other end around your wrist. This strap grounds your body and keeps it at a zero charge. Figure 21.1 shows the proper way to attach an antistatic strap. There are several varieties of wrist straps available. The strap shown in Figure 21.1 uses an alligator clip and is attached to the computer case itself, whereas others use a banana clip that attaches to a grounding coupler.

FIGURE 21.1   ESD strap using an alligator clip

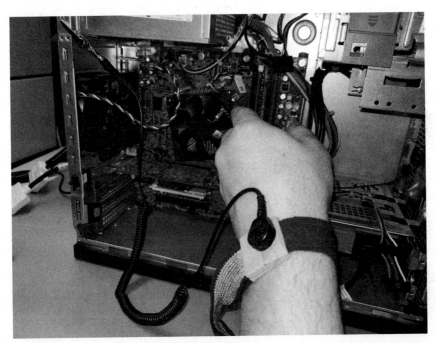

 **Real World Scenario**

ESD Symptoms

Symptoms of ESD damage may be subtle, but they can be detected. One of the authors relates this experience:

"When I think of ESD, I always think of the same instance. Several years ago, I was working on an Apple Macintosh. This computer seemed to have a mind of its own. I would trouble-shoot it, find the defective component, and replace it. The problem was that as soon as I replaced the component, it failed. I thought maybe the power supply was frying the boards, so I replaced both at the same time, but to no avail.

"I was about to send the computer off to Apple when I realized that it was winter. Normally this would not be a factor, but winters where I live are extremely dry. Dry air promotes static electricity. At first I thought my problem couldn't be that simple, but I was at the end of my rope. So, when I received my next set of new parts, I grounded myself with an anti-static strap for the time it took to install the components, and prayed while I turned on the power. Success! The components worked as they should, and a new advocate of ESD prevention was born."

In order for an antistatic wrist strap to work properly, the computer must be plugged in but turned off. When the computer is plugged in, it is grounded through the power cord. When you attach yourself to it with the wrist strap, you are grounded through the power cord as well. If the computer is not plugged in, there is no ground, and any excess electricity on you will just discharge into the case, which is not good.

WARNING An ESD strap is a device that is specially designed to bleed electrical charges away *safely*. It uses a 1 megohm resistor to bleed the charge away slowly. A simple wire wrapped around your wrist will not work correctly, and you could be electrocuted!

WARNING Never wear an ESD strap if you're working inside a monitor or inside a power supply. If you wear one while working on the inside of these components, you increase the chance of getting a lethal shock.

ESD Antistatic Mats

It is possible to damage a device by simply laying it on a benchtop. Therefore, you should have an ESD *antistatic mat* in addition to an ESD strap. An ESD mat drains excess charge away from any item coming in contact with it (see Figure 21.2). ESD mats are also sold as mouse/keyboard pads to prevent ESD charges from interfering with the operation of the computer. Many wrist straps can be connected to the mat, thus causing the technician and any equipment in contact with the mat to be at the same electrical potential and eliminating ESD. There are even ESD bootstraps and ESD floor mats, which are used to keep the technician's entire body at the same potential.

Antistatic Bags for Parts

Antistatic bags, shown in Figure 21.3, are important tools to have at your disposal when servicing electronic components because they protect the sensitive electronic devices from stray static charges. By design, the static charges collect on the outside of these silver or pink bags, rather than on the electronic components.

FIGURE 21.2   Proper use of an ESD antistatic mat

FIGURE 21.3   An antistatic component bag

 Unlike antistatic mats, antistatic bags do not "drain" the charges away, and they should never be used in place of an antistatic mat. These bags conduct a uniform charge, because the surface is somewhat conductive.

You can obtain the bags from several sources. The most direct way to acquire antistatic bags is to go to an electronics supply store and purchase them in bulk. Most supply stores have several sizes available. Perhaps the easiest way to obtain them, however, is simply to hold onto the ones that come your way. That is, when you purchase any new component, it usually comes in an antistatic bag. After you have installed the component, keep the bag. It may take you a while to gather a collection of bags if you take this approach, but eventually you will have a fairly large assortment.

Self-Grounding

We recommend that you include a grounding strap in your toolkit so that you're never without it. But we also realize that things happen and you might find yourself in a situation where you don't have your strap or an ESD mat. In such cases, you should *self-ground*.

Self-grounding is not as effective as using proper anti-ESD gear, but it makes up for that with its simplicity. To self-ground, make sure the computer is turned off but plugged in. Then touch an exposed (but not hot or sharp) metal part of the case. This will drain electrical charge from you. Better yet is if you can maintain constant contact with that metal part. That should keep you at the same bias as the case. Yes, it can be rather challenging to work inside a computer one-handed, but it can be done.

Additional Methods

Another preventive measure that you can take is to maintain the relative humidity at around 50 percent. Don't increase the humidity too far—to the point where moisture begins to condense on the equipment. It is best to check with the manufacturer of the equipment that you are protecting to find the optimal humidity. Also, use antistatic spray, which is available commercially, to reduce static buildup on clothing and carpets.

> If you don't have any antistatic spray, you can always use the "Downy solution." In a spray bottle, combine one part water with one part liquid fabric softener. Mist areas such as carpet and clothing that cause problems. If used regularly, it will keep static away—and keep your office smelling nice.

Vendors have methods of protecting components in transit from manufacture to installation. They press the pins of integrated circuits (ICs) into antistatic foam to keep all the pins at the same potential, as shown in Figure 21.4. In addition, most circuit boards are shipped in antistatic bags, as discussed earlier.

> Antistatic foam looks a lot like Styrofoam. However, there are huge differences between the two. While antistatic foam helps reduce the transfer of electricity, Styrofoam does not. Styrofoam holds a charge on its surface quite easily. Have you ever tried to get some of those small packing "peanuts" off your hands? Be careful to not mix the two up, lest you fry your components.

FIGURE 21.4   Antistatic foam

At the very least, you should be mindful of the dangers of ESD and take steps to reduce its effects. Beyond that, you should educate yourself about those effects so that you know when ESD is becoming a major problem.

Electromagnetic Interference

When compared to the other dangers that we've discussed in this chapter, *electromagnetic interference (EMI)*, also known as *radio-frequency interference (RFI)* when it's in the same frequency range as radio waves, is by far the least dangerous. EMI really poses no threats to you in terms of bodily harm. What it can do is make your equipment or network malfunction.

EMI is an unwanted disturbance caused by electromagnetic radiation generated by another source. In other words, some of your electrical equipment may interfere with other equipment. Here are some common sources of interference:

Network Devices   The popularity of wireless networking devices has introduced the possibility of interference. Some of the most popular wireless networking standards, 802.11b/g/n/ax, use the 2.4 GHz range for transmissions. Bluetooth devices happen to use the same frequency. In theory, they won't interfere with each other because they use different modulation techniques. In practice, however, interference between the two types of devices can happen.

Magnets   Magnets work by generating an electromagnetic field. It might make sense, then, that this field could cause electromagnetic interference. For the most part, you don't need to worry about this unless you have huge magnets at work. Do note, however, that many motors use magnets, which can cause interference. For example, one of our friends used to have his computer on the opposite side of a wall from his refrigerator. Whenever the compressor kicked in, his monitor display would become wavy and unreadable. It was time to move his home office. Another common culprit is a desk fan. Put a desk fan next to a monitor and turn on the fan. What happens to the display? It will become wavy. This is another example of EMI.

Cordless Phones   Cordless phones can operate at a variety of frequencies. Some of the more common frequencies are 900 MHz, 1.9 GHz, 2.4 GHz, and 5.8 GHz. Many of these are common ranges for computer equipment to operate in as well.

Microwave Ovens   Microwave ovens are convenient devices for heating food and beverages. The radiation they generate is typically in the 2.45 GHz range, although it can vary slightly. If a microwave is being used near your computer, you'll often see a distorted display, just as if a fan or motor were being run next to your computer. You may also experience interference with wireless network communications.

Copper wires are susceptible to EMI. Fiber-optic cables, which use light to transmit data, are not susceptible to EMI.

Natural Elements

Computers should always be operated in cool environments and away from direct sunlight and water sources. This is also true when you're working on computers. We know that heat is an enemy of electrical components. Dirt and dust act as great insulators, trapping heat inside components. When components run hotter than they should, they have a greater chance of breaking down faster.

It pretty much should go without saying, but we'll say it anyway: water and electricity don't mix. Keep liquids away from computers. If you need your morning coffee while fixing a PC, make sure that the coffee cup has a tight and secure lid.

 Real World Scenario

Water and Servers Don't Mix

This situation happened at a company where one of the authors used to work. The building needed some roof repairs. Repairs went on for several days, and then the weekend came. It just so happened that the area on which they were working was over the server room. That weekend was a particularly rainy one, and, of course, no one was in the office over the weekend.

Monday morning came, and the IT staff arrived to find that the server room was partially flooded. Rain had come in through weaknesses in the roof caused by the maintenance and had flooded through the drop ceiling and into the server room. Nearly half a million dollars' worth of equipment was ruined.

Although this is an extreme example, it illustrates an important point: always be aware of the environment in which you're working, and be alert to potential sources of problems for your computer equipment.

Creating a Safe Workplace

Benjamin Franklin was quoted as saying, "An ounce of prevention is worth a pound of cure." That sage advice applies to a lot in life and certainly to computer safety. Knowing how to work with and handle computer equipment properly is a good start. It's also important to institutionalize and spread the knowledge, and to make sure that your company has the proper policies and procedures in place to ensure everyone's safety.

Moving Computer Equipment

We've already talked about some of the hazards posed by computer parts. Many times it's the more mundane tasks that get us, though, such as moving stuff around. One of the most common ways that IT employees get hurt is by moving equipment in an improper way. Changing the location of computers is a task often completed by IT personnel. You can avoid injury by moving things the right way.

To ensure your personal safety, here are some important techniques to consider before moving equipment:

- The first thing always to check for is that it's unplugged. There's nothing worse (and potentially more dangerous) than getting yanked because you're still tethered.
- Securely tie the power cord to the device or remove it altogether, if possible.
- Remove any loose jewelry and secure long hair or neckties.
- Lift with your legs, not your back. Bend at the knees when picking something up, not at the waist.
- Do not twist when lifting.
- Maintain the natural curves of the back and spine when lifting.
- Keep objects close to your body and at waist level.
- Push rather than pull, if possible.

The muscles in the lower back aren't nearly as strong as those in the legs or other parts of the body. Whenever lifting, you want to reduce the strain on those lower-back muscles as much as possible. If you want, use a back belt or brace to help you maintain the proper position while lifting.

CRT monitors can be heavy. (Thank goodness for flat screens!) When lifting and carrying any type of monitor, always keep the glass face toward your body. The front of the monitor is the heaviest part, and you want the heavy part closest to your body in order to reduce strain on your muscles.

If you believe that the load is too much for you to carry, don't try to pick it up. Get assistance from a coworker. Another great idea is to use a cart. It will save you trips if you have multiple items to move, and it saves you the stress of carrying components.

If you do use a cart to move the equipment, make sure that you do not overload the cart. Know the cart's weight limitation and estimate the weight of the equipment you will be hauling. Most small, commercial service carts will hold around 100–200 pounds. If you're moving a battery backup unit that requires two people to lift, you may be pushing the limitations of the cart. Also make sure the load is not top heavy. Always place the heaviest items on the lower shelves of a cart.

When moving loads, always be aware of your surrounding environment. Before you move, scout out the path to see whether there are any *trip hazards* or other safety concerns, such as spills, stairs, uneven floors (or ripped carpet), tight turns, or narrow doorways.

Using Appropriate Repair Tools

A big part of creating a safe working environment is having the right tools available for the job. There's no sense implementing a sledgehammer solution to a ball-peen hammer problem. Using the wrong tool might not help fix the problem, and it could very possibly hurt you or the computer in the process.

Most of the time, computers can be opened and devices removed with nothing more than a simple screwdriver. But if you do a lot of work on PCs, you'll definitely want to have additional tools on hand.

Computer toolkits are readily available on the Internet or at any electronics store. They come in versions from inexpensive (under $10) kits that have around 10 pieces to kits that cost several hundred dollars and have more tools than you will probably ever need. Figure 21.5 shows an example of a basic 13-piece *PC toolkit*. All of these tools come in a handy zippered case, so it's hard to lose them.

Figure 21.5 shows the following tools, from left to right:

- Sockets, ranging from 1/4″ and 1/2″
- Screwdriver bits: #1 and #1 Phillips tips, #1 and #2 flat tip, T10, T15, T20 Torx tips, and a 1/4″ drive adapter
- Hex keys
- ESD strap
- Screw container
- Screwdriver
- 1/8″ flat screwdriver
- Tweezers

- Long-nose pliers
- A three-claw retriever
- A #2 Phillips extension
- An integrated circuit (IC) extractor
- Wire strippers

FIGURE 21.5   PC toolkit

A favorite of ours is the three-claw retriever, because screws like to fall and hide in tiny places. While most of these tools are incredibly useful, an IC extractor probably won't be. In today's environment, it's rare to find an IC that you can extract, much less find a reason to extract one.

The following sections look at some of the tools of the PC troubleshooting trade.

Screwdrivers

Every PC technician worth their weight in pocket protectors needs to have a *screwdriver*—at least one. There are three major categories of screwdrivers: flat-blade, Phillips, and Torx. In addition, there are devices that look like screwdrivers, except that they have a hex-shaped indented head on them. They're called *hex drivers*, and they belong to the screwdriver family.

When picking a screwdriver, always keep in mind that you want to match the size of the screwdriver head to the size of the screw. Using a screwdriver that's too small will cause it to spin inside the head of the screw, stripping the head of the screw and making it useless. If the screwdriver is too large, on the other hand, you won't be able to get the head in far enough to generate any torque to loosen the screw. Of course, if the screwdriver is way too big, it won't even fit inside the screw head at all. Common sizes for Phillips-head screws are 000, 00, 0, 1, 2, and 3. When you are dealing with Torx screws, the two most common sizes are T-10 and T-15.

When tightening screws, you don't need to make them so tight that they could survive the vibrations of an atmospheric reentry. Snug is fine. Making them too tight can cause problems when loosening them, which could cause you (or someone else not so strong) to strip the head. Using an electric screwdriver is fine, if you have one. The only problem with them is that they tend to be larger than manual screwdrivers and can be difficult to get inside a case.

Using magnetic-tipped screwdrivers is not recommended. Many computer disks contain magnetically coded information, and the magnetic tip of a screwdriver could cause a problem. Keep a retrieving tool handy instead, just in case you drop a screw.

Antistatic Wrist Straps

We've already talked about these, but they are important, so we'll mention them again. An antistatic wrist strap is essential to any PC technician's arsenal. They don't typically come with smaller PC toolkits, but you should always have one or two handy.

Other Useful Tools

PC techs also commonly carry the following tools:

Pliers   Pliers are useful for a variety of tasks, especially gripping something. Long-nose or needle-nose pliers extend your reach.

Wire Cutters   Wire cutters come in a variety of forms but are primarily used for cutting cables. It's not likely that you'll need any sort of heavy-duty metal cutters.

Wire Strippers   If you are making your own network cables or fixing them, having a cable stripper (and crimper) is essential.

Mirrors   Mirrors are handy inside tight spaces. Many techs like to use a dentist-style mirror because of its compact size and good reach.

Flashlight   Never underestimate the utility of a good flashlight. You never know what your lighting situation will be like when you're at a repair site. Smaller flashlights with good output are great to have because they can fit into tight spaces.

Compressed Air For as much as computers and dust don't get along, it sure seems like they are attracted to each other. In all seriousness, computer components are powered by electricity, which causes the components to have a slight electrical charge. Dust is also electrically charged, so it's attracted to computer components. Compressed air can help you clean off components, especially in hard-to-reach places.

Be judicious about your use of compressed air. Often, you will find yourself just blowing the dust from one part of a computer to another.

Multimeter If you're having power issues, a multimeter is an invaluable tool. It measures electrical current, voltage, and resistance. You'll also hear of voltmeters, and while the two have somewhat different functions, both of them can be used to troubleshoot power problems. You can use a voltmeter to determine whether a computer's power supply is producing the right amount of current for the devices that depend on it.

Air Filter Masks We've mentioned dust, and you will occasionally encounter large amounts of it when working inside computers. If you're using compressed air to blow dust out, it could easily get into your eyes or lungs. You don't want to breathe these airborne particles, and in some environments (like machine shops), you don't know what types of hazardous materials are mixed in with the airborne particles. You don't need a big army-grade gas mask, but a small respirator will help considerably.

Safety Goggles Your eyesight should be a primary concern when working with any type of tools, because accidents happen. You should always wear protective glasses that cover all sides of your eyes. When you think of *safety goggles*, you probably think of the science lab rubberized goggles from high school chemistry class. Safety goggles can be as comfortable as a pair of glasses, if you purchase approved safety glasses.

Fire Safety

Repairing a computer isn't often the cause of an electrical fire. However, you should know how to extinguish such a fire properly. Four major classes of fire extinguishers are available, one for each type of flammable substance: A, for wood and paper fires; B, for flammable liquids; C, for electrical fires; and D (metal powder or NaCl [salt]), for flammable metals, such as phosphorus and sodium.

The most popular type of fire extinguisher today is the multipurpose, or ABC-rated, extinguisher. It contains a dry chemical powder (for example, sodium bicarbonate, mono-ammonium phosphate) that smothers the fire and cools it at the same time. For electrical fires (which may be related to a shorted-out wire in a power supply), make sure the fire extinguisher will work for Class C fires. If you don't have an extinguisher that is specifically rated for electrical fires (Class C), you can use an ABC-rated extinguisher.

The topic of electrical fire safety is a very broad subject. The best prevention method for electrical fires is to follow building codes. If building codes are not followed, your organization could be fined. Every state and locality has a different building code that you should reference with new structures and alterations to existing structures. In addition to state and local building codes, you also need to reference national building codes related to fire prevention. One organization that supplies reference to these codes is the National Fire Protection Association (NFPA) www.nfpa.org/Codes-and-Standards. The U.S. Fire Administration (www.usfa.fema.gov/prevention) is a government organization that provides general training and prevention material.

Creating a Safe Work Environment

We've already talked about some work environment issues. For example, don't put a computer next to the break-room sink, and keep computers out of direct sunlight (even if the desk location is great). A few other things to watch out for are trip hazards, atmospheric conditions, and high-voltage areas.

Cables are a common cause of tripping. If at all possible, run cables through drop ceilings or through conduits to keep them out of the way. If you need to lay a cable through a trafficked area, use a floor cable guard to keep the cables in place and safe from crushing. Floor guards come in a variety of lengths and sizes (for just a few cables or for a lot of cables). Figure 21.6 shows a cable guard.

FIGURE 21.6   Floor cable guard

Another useful tool to keep cables under control is a *cable tie* (see Figure 21.7). It's simply a plastic tie that holds two or more cables together. Cable ties come in different sizes and colors, so you're bound to find one that suits your needs.

FIGURE 21.7   Cable ties

 In a pinch, and without a floor cable guard, you can use tape, such as duct tape, to secure your cables to the floor. This is recommended only as a temporary fix for two reasons. First, it's not much less of a trip hazard than just having the cables run across the floor. Second, duct tape doesn't protect the cables from being crushed if people step on them or heavy objects are moved over them.

Exercise 21.1 is a simple exercise that you can modify and use as needed. Its purpose is to illustrate common office hazards that you may not have realized were there.

EXERCISE 21.1

Finding Trip Hazards

1. Walk around the server room and count how many cables are lying on the floor.

2. Walk around the client areas and see how many cables are lying on the floor or are exposed underneath cubicles.

Maybe you're fortunate and don't find any, but odds are that you found at least one area with exposed cables that should not be exposed. You can reapply this exercise for other dangerous items, such as exposed wires and exposed sharp edges.

Atmospheric conditions you need to be aware of include areas with high static electricity or excessive humidity. Being aware of these conditions is especially important for preventing electrostatic discharge, as we've already discussed.

Finally, be aware of high-voltage areas. Computers do need electricity to run, but only in measured amounts. Running or fixing computers in high-voltage areas can cause problems for the electrical components and problems for you if something should go wrong.

Implementing Safety Policies and Procedures

The *Occupational Safety and Health Act* states that every working American has the right to a safe and healthy work environment. To enforce the act, the *Occupational Safety and Health Administration (OSHA)* was formed. OSHA covers all private-sector employees and U.S. Postal Service workers. Public-sector employees are covered by state programs, and federal employees are covered under a presidential executive order. In a nutshell, OSHA requires employers to "provide a workplace that is free of recognized dangers and hazards."

There are three overarching criteria to a safe work environment:

- The company and its employees have identified all significant hazards in the work setting.

- Preventive measures have been taken to address each significant hazard.

- The company and its employees understand how to respond to accidents or near-miss accidents if or when they occur.

The following sections explore specific responsibilities and how to create a safe work environment plan.

Always ensure that your company's safety policies and procedures comply with all government regulations.

Employer and Employee Responsibilities

Maintaining workplace safety is the responsibility of employers as well as employees. Here are some of the important responsibilities of employers:

- Provide properly maintained tools and equipment.

- Provide a warning system, such as codes or labels, to warn employees of potential hazards or dangerous chemicals.

- Post the OSHA poster in a prominent location.

- Keep records of workplace injuries or illnesses.

- Continuously examine workplace conditions to ensure OSHA compliance.

It's also the responsibility of the employee to help maintain a safe work environment. Specifically, employees are charged with the following tasks:

- Read and understand OSHA posters.

- Follow all employer-implemented health and safety rules and safe work practices.

- Use all required protective gear and equipment.

- Report hazardous conditions to the employer.

- Report hazardous conditions that the employer does not correct to OSHA.

As you can see, employers and employees need to work together to keep the workplace safe. It is illegal for an employee to be punished in any way for exercising their rights under the Occupational Safety and Health Act.

 Real World Scenario

Play It Safe with Common Sense

When you're repairing a PC, do not leave it unattended. Someone could walk into the room and inadvertently bump the machine, causing a failure. Worse, they could step on pieces that may be lying around and get hurt. It is also not a good idea to work on the PC alone. If you're injured, someone should be around to help. Finally, if you're fatigued, you may find it difficult to concentrate and focus on what you are doing. The most important safety measure to remember when you are repairing PCs is to pay close attention to what you are doing.

Safety Plans

We recommend that your company create and follow a workplace safety plan. Having a safety plan can help avoid accidents that result in lost productivity, equipment damage, and employee injury or death.

A good safety plan should include the following elements:

- A written document that states, among other things, who is responsible for implementing and managing the plan
- Systematic periodic inspections to identify workplace hazards
- Procedures for eliminating hazards once identified
- Processes for investigating the cause of accidents, injuries, or illnesses
- A safety and health training program specific to the job duties performed
- A system for employees to communicate safety or health concerns without fear of reprisal
- A system to ensure that employees comply with safety and health rules
- A system to maintain safety and health records, including steps taken to implement accident-prevention initiatives

It might seem like a laundry list of items to consider, but a good safety program needs to be holistic in nature to be effective.

Many companies also incorporate rules against drug or alcohol use in their safety and health plans. Specifically, employees are not allowed to come to work if under the influence of alcohol or illegal drugs. Employees who do come to work under the influence may be subject to disciplinary action up to and including termination of employment.

After your safety plan has been created, you need to ensure that all employees receive necessary training. Have each employee sign a form at the end of the training to signify that they attended, and keep the forms in a central location (such as with or near the official safety policy). In addition to the training record, you should make available and keep records of the following:

- Safety improvement suggestion form
- Accident and near-accident reporting form
- Injury and illness log
- Safety inspection checklist
- Hazard removal form
- Material safety data sheets

Safety rules and regulations will work only if they have the broad support of management from the top down. Everyone in the organization needs to buy into the plan; otherwise, it won't be a success. Make sure that everyone understands the importance of a safe work environment, and make sure that the culture of the company supports safety in the workplace.

Incident Management

Accidents happen. Hopefully, they don't happen too often, but we know that they do. Details on how to handle accidents are a key part of any safety plan so that when an accident does happen, you and your coworkers know what to do. Good plans should include steps for handling a situation as well as reporting an incident. We will cover *incident response* in more detail later in this chapter. Two major classifications of accidents are environmental and human.

When related to computers, environmental accidents typically come in one of two forms: electricity or water. Too much electricity is bad for computer components. If lightning is striking in your area, you run a major risk of frying computer parts. Even if you have a surge protector, you could still be at risk.

The best bet in a lightning storm is to power off your equipment and unplug it from outlets. Make the lightning have to come inside a window and hit your computer directly in order to fry it.

WARNING
Those cheap $10 surge suppressors will fry right along with your computer. And don't be fooled—most power strips do *not* protect against power surges.

Water is obviously also bad for computer components. If there is water in the area and you believe that it will come in contact with your computers, it's best to get the machines powered off as quickly as possible. If components are not powered on but get wet, they may still work after thoroughly drying out. But if they're on when they get wet, they're likely cooked. Water + electronic components = bad. Water + electronic components + electricity = *really* bad.

Many server rooms have raised floors. Although this serves several purposes, one is that equipment stored on the raised floor is less susceptible to water damage if flooding occurs.

Human nature dictates that we are not infallible, so, of course, we're going to make mistakes and have accidents. The key is to minimize the damage caused when an accident happens.

If a chemical spill occurs, make sure that the area gets cordoned off as soon as possible. Then clean up the spill. The specific procedure on how to do that depends on the chemical, and that information can be found on material safety data sheets (MSDSs). Depending on the severity of the spill or the chemical released, you may also need to contact the local authorities. Again, the MSDS should have related information. We cover MSDSs in more detail later in the chapter.

Physical accidents are more worrisome. People can trip on wires and fall, cut or burn themselves repairing computers, and incur a variety of other injuries. Computer components can be replaced, but that's not always true of human parts (and it's certainly not true of lives). The first thing to keep in mind is always to be careful and use common sense. If you're trying to work inside a computer case and you see sharp metal edges inside the case, see whether the metal (or component on which you are working) can be moved to another location until you finish. Before you stick your hand into an area, make sure that nothing is hot or could cut you.

When an accident does happen (or almost happens), be sure to report it. Many companies pay for workers' compensation insurance. If you're injured on the job, you're required to report the incident, and you might also get temporary payments if you are unable to work because of the accident. Also, if the accident was anything but minor, seek medical attention. Just as victims in auto accidents might not feel pain for a day or two, victims in other physical accidents might be in the same position. If you never report the accident, insurance companies may find it less plausible that your suffering was work related.

Understanding Environmental Controls

It is estimated that more than 25 percent of all the lead (a poisonous substance) in landfills today comes from consumer electronics components. Because consumer electronics (televisions, DVRs, Blu-ray players, stereos) contain hazardous substances, many states require that they be disposed of as *hazardous waste*. Computers are no exception. Monitors contain several carcinogens and phosphors as well as mercury and lead. The computer itself may contain several lubricants and chemicals as well as lead. Printers contain plastics and chemicals, such as those in toners and inks, which are also hazardous. All of these items should be disposed of properly.

Remember all those 386 and 486 computers that came out in the late 1980s and are now considered antiques? Maybe you don't, but there were millions of them. Where did they all go? Is there an Old Computers Home somewhere that is using these computer systems for good purposes, or are they lying in a junkyard somewhere? Or could it be that some folks just cannot let go and have a stash of old computer systems and computer parts in the dark depths of their basements? Regardless of where they are today, all of those old components have one thing in common: they are hazardous to the environment.

On the flip side, the environment is also hazardous to our computers. We've already talked about how water and computers don't mix well, and that's just the beginning. Temperature, humidity, and air quality can have dramatic effects on a computer's performance. And we know that computers require electricity; too much or too little can be a problem.

With all these potential issues, you might find yourself wondering, "Can't we all just get along?" In the following sections, we will talk about how to make our computers and the environment coexist as peacefully as possible.

Managing the Physical Environment

Some of our computers sit in the same dark, dusty corner for their entire lives. Other computers are carried around, thrown into bags, and occasionally dropped. Either way, the physical environment in which our computers exist can have a major effect on how long they last. It's smart to inspect the physical environment periodically in order to ensure that there are no working hazards. Routinely cleaning components will also extend their useful life, and so will ensuring that the power supplying them is maintained.

Maintaining Power

As electronics, computers need a power source. Laptops can free you from your power cord leash for a while, but only temporarily. Power is something that we often take for granted until we lose it, and then we twiddle our thumbs and wonder what people did before the Internet. Most people realize that having too much power (a *power surge*) is a bad thing because it can fry electronic components. Having too little power, such as when a *blackout* occurs, can also wreak havoc on electrical circuits.

Obviously, if we lose power, the equipment stops working. We have all experienced blackouts, but there are many other electrical problems we can encounter that will affect our network equipment and interrupt operations:

Sags   An electrical sag is created when the line voltage dips below the nominal operating voltage. Normally the voltage should stay consistent at 90 percent of the voltage specification. An electrical sag is considered an event if the voltage drops within 1/2 second to 3 seconds of a power cycle.

Brownout   An electrical sag where the line voltage dips below the nominal operating voltage for more than 3 seconds of a power cycle. Brownouts are commonly caused by large upstream draws on electrical demand.

Spike   Power spikes are created when the line voltage increases over the nominal operating voltage. A voltage spike can be tens of thousands of volts, but the event only lasts 1 to 2 nanoseconds.

Surges   Power surges are also created when the line voltage spikes over the nominal operating voltage. However, the difference between a spike and a surge is that a surge can last over 3 nanoseconds.

FIGURE 21.8   A simple power strip

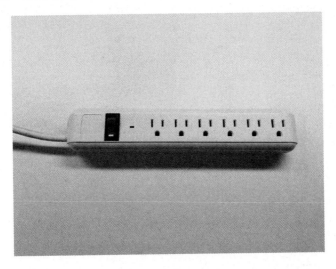

Power strips come in all shapes and sizes and are convenient for plugging multiple devices into one wall outlet. Most of them even have an on/off switch so that you can turn all the devices on or off at the same time. Figure 21.8 shows a simple power strip.

Don't make the mistake of thinking that power strips will protect you from electrical surges, though. If you get a strong power surge through one of these $10 devices, the strip and everything plugged into it can be fried. Some people like to call power strips "surge protectors" or "surge suppressors," but power strips do nothing to protect against or suppress surges.

Devices that actually attempt to keep power surges at bay are called *surge protectors*. They often look similar to a power strip, so it's easy to mistake them for each other, but protectors are more expensive, usually starting in the $25 range. Surge protectors have a fuse inside them that is designed to blow if it receives too much current and not to transfer the current to the devices plugged into it. Surge protectors may also have plug-ins for RJ-11 (phone), RJ-45 (Ethernet), and BNC (coaxial cable) connectors.

Figure 21.9 shows a surge protector, which doesn't look too different from a simple power strip. The key is to read the packaging and the labels on the product. Make sure that the device will protect your electronics from electrical surges. There is usually a printed specification of 200V to 500V. This indicates how much of a surge in voltage the surge protector can handle.

The best device for power protection is called an *uninterruptible power supply (UPS)*. These devices can be as small as a brick, like the one shown in Figure 21.10, or as large as an entire server rack. Some just have a few indicator lights, while others have LCD displays that show status and menus and that come with their own management software.

FIGURE 21.9 A surge protector

Inside the UPS are one or more batteries and fuses. Much like a surge suppressor, a UPS is designed to protect everything that's plugged into it from power surges. UPSs are also designed to protect against *power sags* and even power outages. Energy is stored in the batteries, and if the power fails, the batteries can power the computer for a period of time so that the administrator can then safely power it down. Many UPSs and operating systems will also work together to power down a system automatically (and safely) or switch it to UPS power. These types of devices may be overkill for Uncle Bob's machine at home, but they're critically important fixtures in server rooms.

FIGURE 21.10 An uninterruptible power supply

UPSs can accommodate several different devices; the number depends on the size and power rating. The model shown in Figure 21.11 has four plugs for battery backup and surge protection, and another four outlets for surge protection only. Two of each of the four outlets are controlled by a master switch on the unit.

FIGURE 21.11   The back of a UPS

The UPS should be checked periodically as part of the preventive maintenance routine to make sure its battery is operational. Most UPSs have a test button you can press to simulate a power outage. You will find that batteries wear out over time, and you should replace the battery in the UPS every couple of years to keep the UPS dependable.

Power blackouts are generally easy to detect. Power sags without a complete loss, called a *brownout*, are also very damaging to electrical components but often go unnoticed. Uninterruptable power supplies can prevent this type of damage.

Managing the Environment

Sometimes we can't help how clean—or unclean—our environments are. A computer in an auto body shop is going to face dangers that one in a receptionist's office won't. Still, there are things that you can do to help keep your systems clean and working well. We're going to break these concepts down into two parts. First, we'll look at common issues you should be aware of, and then we'll discuss proper cleaning methods.

Avoiding Common Problems

In a nutshell, water and other liquids, dirt, dust, unreliable power sources, and heat and humidity aren't good for electronic components. Inspect your environment to eliminate as many of these risks as possible. Leaving your laptop running outside in a rainstorm? Not such a good idea. (Been there, done that.)

Computers in manufacturing plants are particularly susceptible to environmental hazards. One technician reported a situation with a computer that had been used on the manufacturing floor of a large equipment manufacturer. The computer and keyboard were covered with a black substance that would not come off. (It was later revealed to be a combination of paint mist and molybdenum grease.) There was so much diesel fume residue in the power supply fan that it would barely turn. The insides and components were covered with a thin, greasy layer of muck. To top it all off, the computer smelled terrible!

Despite all this, the computer still functioned. However, it was prone to reboot itself every now and again. The solution was (as you may have guessed) to clean every component thoroughly and replace the power supply. The muck on the components was able to conduct a small current. Sometimes, that current would go where it wasn't wanted and zap—a reboot. In addition, the power supply fan is supposed to partially cool the inside of the computer. In this computer, the fan was detrimental to the computer because it got its cooling air from the shop floor, which contained diesel fumes, paint fumes, and other chemical fumes. Needless to say, those fumes aren't good for computer components.

Computers and humans have similar tolerances to heat and cold, although computers like the cold better than we do. In general, anything comfortable to us is comfortable to a computer. They don't, however, require food or drink (except maybe a few RAM chips now and again)—keep those away from the computer.

It's bad practice to eat, drink, or smoke around your computer. Smoke particles contain tar that can get inside the computer and cause problems similar to those just described.

Computers need lots of clean moving air to keep them functioning. One way to ensure that the environment has the least possible effect on your computer is always to leave the blanks in the empty slots on the back of your box. These pieces of metal are designed to keep dirt, dust, and other foreign matter out of the inside of the computer. They also maintain proper airflow within the case to ensure that the computer does not overheat.

You can also purchase computer enclosures to keep the dust out—just make sure that they allow for proper air ventilation. Many times these devices use air filters in much the same way a furnace or a car engine does.

Cleaning Systems

The cleanliness of a computer is extremely important. Buildup of dust, dirt, and oils can prevent the various mechanical parts of a computer from operating. Cleaning them with the right cleaning compounds is equally important. Using the wrong compounds can leave residue behind that is more harmful than the dirt that you are trying to remove.

Most computer cases and monitor cases can be cleaned by using mild soapy water on a clean, lint-free cloth. Do *not* use any kind of solvent-based cleaner on monitor screens, because doing so can cause discoloration and damage to the screen surface. Most often, a simple dusting with a damp cloth (moistened with water) will suffice. Make sure that the power is off before you put anything wet near a computer. Dampen (don't soak) a cloth in mild soap solution and wipe the dirt and dust from the case. Then wipe the moisture from the case with a dry, lint-free cloth. Anything with a plastic or metal case can be cleaned in this manner.

WARNING Don't drip liquid into any vent holes on equipment. Monitors in particular often have vent holes in their tops.

Additionally, if you spill anything on a keyboard, you can clean it by soaking it in distilled, *demineralized water* and then drying it off. The extra minerals and impurities have been removed from this type of water, so it will not leave any traces of residue that might interfere with the proper operation of the keyboard after cleaning. The same holds true for the keyboard's cable and its connector.

The electronic connectors of computer equipment, on the other hand, should never touch water. Instead, use a swab moistened in distilled, *denatured isopropyl alcohol* (also known as electronics or contact cleaner and found in electronics stores) to clean contacts. Doing so will take oxidation off the copper contacts.

Finally, the best way to remove dust and debris from the inside of the computer is to use compressed air (not a vacuum). Compressed air can be more easily directed and doesn't easily produce ESD damage, as a vacuum could. Simply blow the dust from inside the computer by using a stream of compressed air. Make sure to do this outside so that you don't blow dust all over your work area or yourself. Also be sure to wear safety goggles and use an air mask. If you need to use a vacuum, a nonstatic *computer vacuum* that is specially made for cleaning computer components is recommended. Their nozzles are grounded to prevent ESD from damaging the components of the computer.

One unique challenge when cleaning printers is spilled toner. It sticks to everything and should not be inhaled—it's a carcinogen. Use an electronics vacuum that is designed specifically to pick up toner. A typical vacuum's filter isn't fine enough to catch all the particles, so the toner may be circulated into the air. Normal electronics vacuums may melt the toner instead of picking it up.

TIP If you get toner on your clothes, use a magnet to get it out. (Toner is half iron.)

Table 21.1 summarizes the most common cleaning tools and their uses.

TABLE 21.1 Computer cleaning tools

Tool	Purpose
Computer vacuum	Sucking up dust and small particles
Mild soap and water	Cleaning external computer and monitor cases
Demineralized water	Cleaning keyboards or other devices that have contact points that are not metal
Denatured isopropyl alcohol	Cleaning metal contacts, such as those on expansion cards
Monitor wipes	Cleaning monitor screens. Do *not* use window cleaner.
Lint-free cloth	Wiping down anything. Don't use a cloth that will leave lint or other residue behind.
Compressed air	Blowing dust or other particles out of hard-to-reach areas

Periodically cleaning equipment is one of the easiest ways to prevent costly repairs, but it's also one of the most overlooked tasks. We're often too busy solving urgent crises to deal with these types of tasks. If possible, block out some time every week for the sole purpose of cleaning your equipment.

Handling and Disposing of Computer Equipment

Each piece of computer equipment that you purchase offers a manual, usually found online. Detailed instructions on the proper handling and use of that component can be found in the manual. In addition, many manuals give information on how to open the device for maintenance or on whether you should even open the device at all.

If you have the luxury of having paper manuals, don't throw them away. Keep a drawer of a file cabinet specifically for hardware manuals (and keep it organized). You can always look up information on the Internet as well, but having paper manuals on hand is useful for two reasons:

- You may need to fix something when Internet access isn't readily available. (Router problems, anyone?)

- Some companies are required to keep hardware documentation, in the event of an audit (such as for ISO 9000–compliant organizations).

In the following sections, we'll cover two topics: using safety documentation and following safety and disposal procedures.

There are several different ISO specifications that an organization can be certified for by the International Organization for Standardization (ISO). Each different ISO certification corresponds to a specific set of policies and procedures that an organization must adhere to. When a company is certified, it means they meet or exceed following the standardized policies and procedures for their organization.

Using Safety Documentation

In addition to your product manuals, another place to find safety information is in material safety data sheets (MSDSs). MSDSs include information such as physical product data (boiling point, melting point, flash point, and so forth), potential health risks, storage and disposal recommendations, and spill/leak procedures. With this information, technicians and emergency personnel know how to handle the product as well as respond in the event of an emergency.

MSDSs are typically associated with hazardous chemicals. Indeed, chemicals do not ship without them. MSDSs are not intended for consumer use; rather, they're made for employees or emergency workers who are consistently exposed to the risks of the particular product.

The U.S. *Occupational Safety and Health Administration (OSHA)* mandates MSDSs only for the following products:

- Products that meet OSHA's definition of *hazardous* (they pose a physical or health hazard)

- Products that are "known to be present in the workplace in such a manner that employees may be exposed under normal conditions of use or in a foreseeable emergency"

One of the interesting things about MSDSs is that OSHA does not require companies to distribute them to consumers. Most companies will be happy to distribute one for their products, but they are under no obligation to do so.

If employees are working with materials that have MSDSs, those employees are required by OSHA to have "ready access" to MSDSs. This means that employees need to be able to get to the sheets without having to fetch a key, contact a supervisor, or submit a procedure request. Remember the file cabinet drawer that you have for the hardware manuals? MSDSs should also be kept readily accessible. Exercise 21.2 helps you find your MSDSs and get familiar enough with them to find critical information.

EXERCISE 21.2

Finding MSDSs

1. Locate the MSDSs in your workplace. You might have to ask a manager. (Do you even have them?)

2. Find an MSDS for a product you're interested in.

(continues)

EXERCISE 21.2 *(continued)*

3. Does the MSDS list any potential health effects for this item? What are they?

4. What is the proper disposal procedure for this item?

It's not likely that you're going to memorize or need to memorize everything on an MSDS. The key things are to know where to find the MSDS and how to find information in it quickly. If you have a spill of a potentially dangerous chemical, the last thing you need to do is spend your time figuring out how to handle the spill without causing injury to yourself or others.

At this point, you might stop to think for a second, "Do computers really come with hazardous chemicals? Do I really need an MSDS?" Consider this as an example: oxygen. Hardly a dangerous chemical, considering we need to breathe it to live, right? In the atmosphere, oxygen is at 21 percent concentration. At 100 percent concentration, oxygen is highly flammable and can even spontaneously ignite some organic materials. In that sense, and in the eyes of OSHA, nearly everything can be a dangerous chemical.

If you are interested in searching for free MSDSs, several websites are available, such as www.msds.com. Many manufacturers of components also provide MSDSs on their websites.

The sections within an MSDS are the same regardless of the product, but the information inside each section changes. Here is a truncated sample MSDS for ammonium hydrogen sulfate:

```
**** MATERIAL SAFETY DATA SHEET ****
Ammonium Hydrogen Sulfate
90009
**** SECTION 1—CHEMICAL PRODUCT AND COMPANY IDENTIFICATION ****
MSDS Name: Ammonium Hydrogen Sulfate
Catalog Numbers:
A/5400
Synonyms:
Sulfuric acid, monoammonium salt; Acid ammonium sulfate; Ammonium
acid sulfate.
**** SECTION 2—COMPOSITION, INFORMATION ON INGREDIENTS ****
CAS# Chemical Name % EINECS#
7803-63-6 Ammonium hydrogen sulfate 100 % 232-265-5
Hazard Symbols: C
Risk Phrases: 34
**** SECTION 3—HAZARDS IDENTIFICATION ****
EMERGENCY OVERVIEW
Causes burns. Corrosive. Hygroscopic (absorbs moisture from the air).
```

Potential Health Effects

Skin:

Causes skin burns.

Ingestion:

May cause severe gastrointestinal tract irritation with nausea, vomiting, and possible burns.

Inhalation:

Causes severe irritation of upper respiratory tract with coughing, burns, breathing difficulty, and possible coma.

**** SECTION 4—FIRST-AID MEASURES ****

Skin:

Get medical aid immediately. Immediately flush skin with plenty of water for at
least 15 minutes while removing contaminated clothing and shoes.

Ingestion:

Do not induce vomiting. If victim is conscious and alert, give 2-4 cupfuls of milk or water. Never give anything by mouth to an unconscious person. Get medical aid immediately.

Inhalation:

Get medical aid immediately. Remove from exposure and move to fresh air immediately.
If not breathing, give artificial respiration. If breathing is difficult, give oxygen.

**** SECTION 5—FIREFIGHTING MEASURES ****

**** SECTION 6—ACCIDENTAL RELEASE MEASURES ****

General Information: Use proper personal protective equipment as indicated in Section 8.

**** SECTION 7—HANDLING and STORAGE ****

Handling:

Wash thoroughly after handling. Wash hands before eating. Use only in a well-ventilated area. Do not get in eyes, on skin, or on clothing. Do not ingest or inhale.

Storage:

Store in a cool, dry place. Keep container closed when not in use.

**** SECTION 8—EXPOSURE CONTROLS, PERSONAL PROTECTION ****

Engineering Controls:

Use adequate general or local exhaust ventilation to keep airborne concentrations below the permissible exposure limits.

Respirators:

Follow the OSHA respirator regulations found in 29 CFR 1910.134 or European Standard EN 149. Always use a NIOSH or European Standard EN 149 approved respirator when necessary.

```
**** SECTION 9—PHYSICAL AND CHEMICAL PROPERTIES ****
Physical State: Solid
Color: White
Odor: Not available
**** SECTION 10—STABILITY AND REACTIVITY ****
Chemical Stability:
Stable under normal temperatures and pressures.
Conditions to Avoid:
Incompatible materials, dust generation, exposure to moist air or water.
**** SECTION 11—TOXICOLOGICAL INFORMATION ****
RTECS#:
CAS# 7803-63-6: BS4400500
**** SECTION 12—ECOLOGICAL INFORMATION ****
**** SECTION 13—DISPOSAL CONSIDERATIONS ****
Products which are considered hazardous for supply are classified as Special
Waste, and the disposal of such chemicals is covered by regulations which may
vary according to location. Contact a specialist disposal company or the local
waste regulator for advice. Empty containers must be decontaminated before
returning for recycling.
**** SECTION 14—TRANSPORT INFORMATION ****
**** SECTION 15—REGULATORY INFORMATION ****
European/International Regulations
European Labeling in Accordance with EC Directives
Hazard Symbols: C
Risk Phrases:
R 34 Causes burns.
Safety Phrases:
S 26 In case of contact with eyes, rinse immediately with plenty of water and
seek medical advice. S 28 After contact with skin, wash immediately with...
**** SECTION 16—ADDITIONAL INFORMATION ****
MSDS Creation Date: 6/23/2004 Revision #0 Date: Original.
```

Following Proper Disposal Procedures

It is relatively easy to put old components away, thinking that you might be able to put them to good use again someday, but doing so is not realistic. Most computers are obsolete as soon as you buy them. And if you have not used them recently, your old computer components will more than likely never be used again.

We recycle cans, plastic, and newspaper, so why not recycle computer equipment? The problem is that most computers contain small amounts of hazardous substances. Some countries are exploring the option of recycling electrical machines, but not all have enacted appropriate measures to enforce their proper disposal.

Some countries are ahead of others on the recycling issue. For example, in 2013, the United Kingdom introduced the Waste Electrical and Electronic Equipment (WEEE) Regulations, which obligates manufacturers to provide disposal methods for items they manufacture. Consumers can insist that manufacturers take back dangerous waste and electrical and electronic equipment. Many local governments also provide e-waste programs and disposal centers.

Regardless of manufacturer or community programs, we can take proactive steps, as consumers and caretakers of our environment, to promote the proper disposal of computer equipment:

- Check with the manufacturer. Some manufacturers will take back outdated equipment for parts (and may even pay you for them).

- Properly dispose of solvents or cleaners (as well as their containers) used with computers at a local hazardous waste disposal facility.

- Disassemble the machine and reuse the parts that are good.

- Check out businesses that can melt down the components for the lead or gold plating.

- Contact the Environmental Protection Agency (EPA) for a list of local or regional waste disposal sites that accept used computer equipment. The EPA's web address is www.epa.gov.

- Check with the EPA or at www.msds.com to see if what you are disposing has an MSDS. These sheets contain information about the toxicity of a product and whether it can simply be disposed of as trash. They also contain lethal-dose information.

- Check with local nonprofit or education organizations that may be interested in using the equipment.

Check out the Internet for possible waste disposal sites. Table 21.2 lists a few websites that we came across that deal with the disposal of used computer equipment. A quick web search will likely locate some in your area.

TABLE 21.2   Computer recycling websites

Site name	Web address
Goodwill	www.goodwillsc.org/donate/computers
Staples	www.staples.com/sbd/cre/marketing/sustainability-center/ recycling-services/electronics
U.S. EPA	www.epa.gov/recycle/electronics-donation-and-recycling
Tech Dump	www.techdump.org

The National Conference of State Legislatures details each state's legislation regarding electronics waste. The site also details state programs to collect electronics waste. For more information, visit:

www.ncsl.org/research/environment-and-natural-resources/
e-waste-recycling-legislation.aspx

Following the general rule of thumb of recycling your computer components and consumables is a good way to go. In the following sections, we'll look at four classifications of computer-related components and the proper disposal procedures for each.

Batteries

The EPA estimates that more than 350 million batteries are purchased annually in the United States. One can only imagine what the worldwide figure is. Batteries contain several heavy metals and other toxic ingredients, including alkaline, mercury, lead acid, nickel cadmium, and nickel metal hydride.

Never burn a battery to destroy it. Doing so will cause the battery to explode and could result in serious injury.

When batteries are thrown away and deposited into landfills, the heavy metals inside them will find their way into the ground. From there, they can pollute water sources and eventually find their way into the supply of drinking water. In 1996, the United States passed the *Mercury-Containing and Rechargeable Battery Management Act* (aka the *Battery Act*) with two goals: to phase out the use of mercury in disposable batteries and to provide collection methods and recycling procedures for batteries.

Several countries around the world have battery-recycling programs. Information on battery recycling in the United States can be found at www.call2recycle.org. You can find information on the Battery Act at:

www.epa.gov/rcra/mercury-containing-and-rechargeable-
battery-management-act-public-law-104-142

Five types of batteries are most commonly associated with computers and handheld electronic devices: alkaline, nickel-cadmium (NiCd), nickel-metal hydride (NiMH), lithium-ion (Li-ion), and *button cell*.

Alkaline Batteries   *Alkaline batteries* have been incredibly popular portable batteries for several decades. Before 1984, one of the major ingredients in this type of battery was mercury, which is highly toxic to the environment. In 1984, battery companies began reducing the mercury levels in batteries, and in 1996, mercury was outlawed in alkaline batteries in the United States. Still, it's strongly recommended that you recycle these batteries at a recycling center. Although newer alkaline batteries contain less mercury than their predecessors, they are still made of metals and other toxins that contaminate the air and soil.

Nickel-Cadmium   *Nickel-cadmium (NiCd)* is a popular format for rechargeable batteries. As their name indicates, they contain high levels of nickel and cadmium. Although nickel is only semi-toxic, cadmium is highly toxic. These types of batteries are categorized by the EPA as hazardous waste and should be recycled.

Nickel-Metal Hydride (NiMH) and Lithium-Ion (Li-ion)   Laptop batteries are commonly made with *Nickel-Metal Hydride (NiMH)* and *lithium ion (Li-ion)*. Unlike the previous types of batteries that we have discussed, these are not considered hazardous waste, and there are no regulations on recycling them. However, these batteries do contain elements that can be recycled, so it's still a good idea to go that route.

Button Cell   These batteries are so named because they look like a button. They're commonly used in calculators and watches as well as portable computers. They often contain mercury and silver (and are environmental hazards due to the mercury) and need to be recycled.

You may have noticed a theme regarding the disposal of batteries: recycling. Many people just throw batteries in the trash and don't think twice about it. However, there are several laws in the United States that require the recycling of many types of batteries, and recycling does indeed help keep the environment clean. For a list of recycling centers in your area, use your local Yellow Pages (under Recycling Centers) or search the Internet.

If you're ever exposed to the electrolyte (the inside "juice") of the battery, immediately flush the exposed area with water. If it gets on your eye, immediately contact a physician and wash the eye for 15 minutes.

Display Devices

Computer monitors (CRT monitors, not LCDs) are big and bulky, so what do you do when it's time to get rid of them? As previously mentioned, monitors contain capacitors that are capable of retaining a lethal electric charge after the monitors have been unplugged. You wouldn't want anyone to set off the charge accidentally and die. But what we didn't mention earlier, which is important now, is that most CRT monitors contain high amounts of lead. Most monitors contain several pounds of lead, in fact. Lead is very dangerous to humans and the environment and must be dealt with carefully. Other harmful elements found in CRTs include arsenic, beryllium, cadmium, chromium, mercury, nickel, and zinc.

If you have to dispose of a monitor, contact a computer-recycling firm. It's best to let professional recyclers handle the monitor for you.

🌐 **Real World Scenario**

How *Not* to Dispose of Your Monitors

This story comes from the technical support division of a now-defunct major computer manufacturer, which used a lot of computers at its own facility. At one time, the company had as many as 500 technicians working the phones. So you can imagine that they burned out a lot of equipment.

Here's how they disposed of dead monitors. An IT staff member would take the monitor out to the dumpster and bring along a sledgehammer. Setting the monitor on its back, he would take one good swing at the glass panel with the hammer to shatter the screen. (This was done, by policy, to ensure that no one would want to go out to the dumpster and try to salvage the dead monitor.) After spraying glass everywhere, he picked up the monitor and threw it in the dumpster.

One employee observed that it probably wasn't good to be spreading glass all over the parking lot by shattering monitors. That advice was taken, and the sledgehammer was retired. Instead, an IT staff member would use a permanent black marker and draw all over the screen (again, so no one would want to try to salvage it), and again, it was thrown in the dumpster.

In our enlightened state today (as opposed to the mid-1990s), we can see how this was not a good plan for disposing of broken monitors. In fact, many states today have laws prohibiting the disposal of computer monitors in trash bins. This is a good law because, with the amount of harmful elements in monitors, they're every bit the environmental hazard that batteries are.

Laser Printer Toner Disposal

Toner cartridges should be recycled as well. PC recycling centers will take old toner cartridges and properly dispose of them. The toner itself is a carcinogen, and the cartridges can contain heavy metals that are bad for the environment.

Toner cartridges are valuable to companies that refurbish and refill these cartridges. It's actually big business to refill these expensive cartridges, and it's environmentally responsible. Most toner is the same for all types and models of laser printers, so a toner refurbishing center will refill and test these cartridges. Then these companies sell the cartridges for a fraction of the price of new toner cartridges. If a new toner cartridge is installed, the old toner cartridge is boxed up and sent back. Even if your organization doesn't contract with one of these services, they would be happy to take the old cartridges off your hands and keep them out of the trash.

Mobile Devices

Cell phones and tablets are considered disposable units, with the average life expectancy of two to four years. Their popularity has outpaced mobile computing and the desktop computer market. These mobile devices are extremely small and fit neatly into the trash. However, mobile devices contain the same toxic metals and chemical compositions as their larger cousins. Every mobile device has a circuit board that contains lead, batteries that contain other heavy metals, and bodies that contain plastics.

These devices should be recycled responsibly. Many big-tag retailers have an anonymous recycling drop bin, where you can recycle a mobile device. There are even automated kiosks where you can get money for a defective device. You simply tell it what is wrong with the device, the device's make and model, and its condition. The kiosk will then offer you a few dollars to recycle it. The company that owns and operates the kiosk refurbishes the device and resells it for a fraction of the cost of a new one.

Before recycling a mobile device, make sure the device is wiped of your personal data with the factory reset function. You never know where the device will end up. It could be refurbished and resold locally or sold for parts to a nefarious market.

Chemical Solvents and Cans

Nearly every chemical solvent that you encounter will have a corresponding MSDS. On the MSDS for a chemical, you will find a section detailing the proper methods for disposing of it. Chemical solvents were not designed to be released into the environment, because they could cause significant harm to living organisms if they're ingested. If in doubt, contact a local hazardous materials handler to find out the best way to dispose of a particular chemical solvent.

Cans are generally made from aluminum or other metals, which are not biodegradable. It's best always to recycle these materials. If the cans were used to hold a chemical solvent or otherwise hazardous material, contact a hazardous materials disposal center instead of a recycling center.

Always be sure that you are following all applicable laws and regulations when disposing of computer equipment.

Understanding Policies, Licensing, and Privacy

Many of the operational procedures that we've discussed up to this point have been about safety—yours, your computer equipment's, and the environment's. We've also touched on regulations, as in always be sure to comply with local government regulations. In the following sections, we focus more on the legal side of things. Not understanding legal requirements is not a justifiable defense in a court of law. Considering that IT professionals often deal with software licensing and personally identifiable information, or sometimes encounter prohibited activity or have to deal with a security incident, you should understand the general principles related to these concepts.

Dealing with Prohibited Content/Activity

This is a situation that no one really wants to deal with, but it happens more often than we would care to admit: a computer you are fixing has content on it that is inappropriate or illegal, or you see someone on your network performing an action that is against policy or laws. How you respond in such a situation can have a significant bearing on your career, the other people involved, and, depending on the situation, the well-being of your organization. The key to dealing with *prohibited content* or activity is to have a comprehensive policy in place that covers appropriate behavior. After that, it's a matter of executing the proper steps per the plan when something happens.

Situations involving prohibited content or activities are not easy to address. The accused person might get angry or confrontational, so it's important always to have the right people there to help manage and defuse the situation. If you feel that the situation is severe enough to worry about your own personal safety, don't be afraid to involve the police. While the situation needs to be handled, there's no sense in putting yourself in direct danger to do so.

Creating a Prohibited Content Policy

Creating a policy is the most important part of dealing with prohibited content or actions. Without a policy in place that specifically defines what is and what isn't allowed, and what actions will be taken when a violation of the policy occurs, you don't really have a leg to stand on when a situation happens.

What is contained in the policy depends on the organization for which you work. Generally speaking, if something violates an existing federal or local law, it probably isn't appropriate for your network either. Many organizations also have strict policies against the possession of pornographic or hate-related materials on the organization's property. Some go further than that, banning personal files such as downloaded music or movies on work computers. Regardless of what is on your policy, always ensure that you have buy-in from very senior management so that the policy will be considered valid.

Here are some specific examples of content that might be prohibited:

- Adult content
- Content that advocates violence against an individual, group, or organization
- Unlicensed copyrighted material
- Content related to drugs, alcohol, tobacco, or gambling
- Content about hacking, cracking, or other illegal computer activity
- Violent or weapons-related content

A good policy will also contain the action steps to be taken if prohibited content or activity is spotted. For example, what should you do if you find porn on someone's work laptop?

The policy should explicitly outline the punishment for performing specific actions or possessing specific content. The appropriate penalty may very well be based on the type of content found. Something that is deemed mildly offensive might result in a verbal or written warning for the first offense and a more severe sentence for the second offense. If your company has a zero-tolerance policy, then employees may be terminated and possibly subject to legal action.

Finally, after the policy has been established, it's critical to ensure that all employees are aware of it and have proper training. In fact, it's highly recommended that you have all employees sign a disclosure saying they have read and understand the policy, and that the signed document be kept in their human resources file. Many organizations also require that employees review the policy yearly and re-sign the affidavit as well.

Incident Response

If you have your policy in place, then your *incident response* plan should be relatively scripted. It might not be easy to deal with, but the steps you should take should be outlined for you. Professionalism should be maintained during the incident. This is a good time to remind you that people will be looking at your reaction as well as your actions, and professionalism will define how you dealt with the incident. If you see prohibited content and start giggling and walk away, that probably doesn't reflect well on you. Always remember that others are watching you. The specific steps that you take will depend on your policy. The following sections describe the best practices for dealing with security incidents.

Detecting the Incident

An incident can be detected in several different ways. The preceding section used the example of pornographic content on a laptop or mobile device. This is a great illustration of an example of passive detection. You were not looking for this material, but you found it, and now you must respond. A full list of incident detections is detailed in the following:

Passive   *Passive detection* is used to clue in on what happened and how it happened. Passive detection can be when you are reviewing logs, content, or events and discover an incident. Another example of passive detection in a physical security context is the use of a video camera. The video camera will show you an event in the past, but it is normally not actively looking for an event. An example of passive detection in a digital context is the use of file hashes. If a file hash does not match the original, then someone or something has tampered with the original content.

Active   *Active detection* is used to actively look for security incidents. This type of detection in a physical security context is similar to having a security guard patrol your premises. A digital example might be the use of an *intrusion detection system (IDS)* running on your firewall that alerts you to an attempted break-in. This type of detection is used to catch a perpetrator in the act of a security incident.

Proactive   *Proactive detection* is the act of proactively securing possible holes in security. *Penetration testing*, also known as *pen testing*, involves someone trying to penetrate either the physical or software defenses of the organization. The exercise is done to strengthen the organization's security for either the physical or digital defenses. Proactive detection normally does not create a security incident, unless the potential for the loss of information was discovered during the process.

Responding to the Incident

Once an incident is detected using the methods mentioned in the preceding section (passive, active, or proactive), or it's detected through dumb luck, it's time to spring into action and respond to the incident. The person responding to the incident, called the *first responder*, should be versed in how to collect evidence in the order of volatility. If the evidence is not collected, for example, from a computer's RAM, and the computer reboots, the evidence will be gone. The *order of volatility* is as follows:

Memory Contents   Evidence of the incident located in the RAM of the computer or system. This evidence can be a file that has not been saved to the filesystem. It can also be a process running in RAM that requires a memory dump for further analysis.

Swap Files/Virtual Memory   Evidence that has been saved out to a swap file/virtual memory, because the process has been backgrounded or is no longer in foreground RAM. The swap file/paging file should be copied to removable media.

Network Processes   Evidence that is part of a network process, such as a browser redirection or spam or active network communications. This is where most of the incidents occur on a network. This information should be saved to removable media.

System Processes   Evidence that is part of a system, such as an exploit that has been rooted into the operating system. This is also a common place for incidents to occur. The information should be separated out of the system and saved to removable media.

Filesystem Information   This evidence is in the form of files on a hard drive. An example of filesystem information is illegal content that has been saved to the filesystem. This information must be preserved in its original form but also copied for evidence purposes.

Raw Disk Blocks   This evidence is in the form of a block-level copy of the data. Once an incident is discovered and all the other volatile evidence has been collected, the last step is to create an image of the affected system. This can be done with a tool called a *write-blocker* (which makes the media read-only) and specialized software that copies data at the block level.

The preceding evidence can be collected with the sophisticated tools that only a highly trained first responder might have on hand. However, not all the tools need to be complex tools. A simple camera can preserve information. For example, if you walk up to a system that displays a ransomware screen, your first reaction should be to take a photo of the screen. If you press a key, the ransomware could crash and disappear. Photo evidence of data and processes that are loaded in RAM is a good alternative to not having any evidence, but having a digital copy of the evidence is preferred.

The act of photographing the scene should not be limited to just the computer screen; anything relevant to the incident should be photographed as evidence. Time and date stamps should be overlaid onto the image. This is normally a function of any camera. However, if you can't digitally record the time stamps, a simple alternative is to include a watch in the frame of the photo.

You should take notes with a pad and pen, recording the initial scene, including time and date. Create a chronology of the discovery and collection of the evidence. Remember, any of this could potentially be used in a court of law. The underlying premise is to record as much evidence as possible before the crime scene is tainted by others.

Following the Right Chain of Custody

The removed materials should be secured and turned over to the proper authorities. Depending on the situation, materials may be held in a safe, locked location at the office, or they may need to be turned over to local authorities. Have a documented procedure in place to follow, given a situation.

The materials that are deemed as evidence should be well documented as to why they are considered evidence. The *chain of custody* documentation should define the following:

- Who obtained the evidence
- Who secured the evidence
- Who controlled the evidence during the entire process

If the evidence is moved, the chain of custody documentation should reflect the following:

- The reasons it was moved
- Who moved it
- How it was secured
- Who controlled it

The chain of custody must be maintained at all times. If a chain of custody of the evidence is not maintained, the evidence may not be admissible in a court of law.

Reporting the Incident

Once you've collected the initial set of evidence and in the order of volatility, it's time to report the incident. The incident should be reported to management and a decision should be made whether to involve law enforcement. Involving law enforcement is of course dependent on the severity of the incident. A piece of malware that has infected a single machine is a bit different than malware that has infected an entire network. Your management might elect not to involve law enforcement at all.

Regardless of the direction management takes, the evidence collected, as well as notes taken during the collection, will help an escalation team or law enforcement to proceed in building a case. The goal of the first responder is to collect evidence that answers the following questions:

- What happened?
- When did it happen?
- How did it happen?
- Who made it happen?
- Why did it happen?

An escalation team or law enforcement's job is to fill in the blanks by using the evidence. If the evidence is complete and concise, it will be used to build a case against the threat agent. The ultimate goal is to stop a future incident from happening.

Recovering from the Incident

Your most important task is to recover from the incident. If your critical ordering system was affected during the incident, it's your job to get it back online. If the incident involved one computer that is used by a task worker, then it's your job to get it back up and running. You might notice a common theme here: it's your job to get things back to normal after the incident. Once you can get the flow of information flowing again, you can move on to remediating the incident.

During the recovery from the incident, you may have to make changes to the network or systems that support the clients. Any changes during the recovery process should be documented thoroughly. Documenting these changes is important if you are submitting claims to insurance, assessing damages, or looking for future reparations.

Remediating the Incident

All components affected by the incident should be remediated to ensure that all traces of the incident have been removed. Remediation can be as simple as adding firewall rules to the firewall, or it can involve formatting a server and reloading it. The steps to remediation should also include steps to prevent the incident from happening in the future.

Documenting the Incident

Before, during, and after the incident, the documentation process should begin. You should collect as much information as possible, as a formal incident report will eventually be formulated defining the following key elements. You will learn about the incident report in Chapter 22, "Documentation and Professionalism."

- Date and time
- Summary
- Root cause

- Actions taken
- Remediation
- Services impacted
- Recommendations

It really doesn't matter how you collect information for documentation purposes. It can be pad and pen or something more elaborate. The only stipulation is that the documentation should not be on a system that can be affected by the incident. An offline laptop is fine, as long as the laptop is never introduced to the network affected by the ongoing incident. This could jeopardize all of the documentation efforts and hinder the outcome.

Reviewing the Incident

The final step for incident response is to review all the documentation and findings of the incident—a process often called a hot-wash meeting. During a hot-wash meeting, the incident response team should talk about what has been done properly during the incident and what procedures should be changed for future incidents. These meetings should be constructive and support standards of excellence for the incident response team.

Another key goal of the review process is to identify threats similar to the characteristics of the incident. If an employee entered credentials into a phishing page, what measures are in place to prevent this from happening to others in the organization? You may have rules in place for this particular phishing email, but are your employees trained for future incidents similar to this? If not, end-user training may be required.

Best Practices for Incident Response

Now that you have a good understanding of the process involved with incident response, let's look at some of the best practices. The following best practices should be applied to all elements of the incident response process:

Follow your policies exactly as they are written.   Yes, we've already said this several times. It's crucial that you do this. Not following the policies and procedures can derail your case against the offender and possibly set you up for problems as well.

If you are the first responder, get a verifier.   Your first priority as the first responder is to identify the improper activity or content. Then you should always get someone else to verify the material or action so that it doesn't turn into a situation of your word against someone else's. Report the situation immediately through the proper channels.

Preserve the data or device.   The data or device should immediately be removed from the possession of the offending party and preserved. This will ensure that the data doesn't mysteriously disappear before the proper parties are notified.

Use documentation.   Document everything that could be relevant to the situation. Many companies have standard documentation that is used in incident response in order to be sure that the responder captures important information and does not forget to ask critical questions or look for vital clues.

Always be sure to follow government regulations as well as corporate end-user policies and security best practices when dealing with sensitive information.

Managing Software Licenses

When you buy an application, you aren't actually buying the application. Instead, you're buying the right to use the application in a limited way, as prescribed by its licensing agreement. Most people don't read these licensing agreements closely, but suffice it to say, they're pretty slanted in favor of the software manufacturer.

Don't like the terms? Too bad. No negotiation is allowed. If you don't accept the *end-user license agreement (EULA)*, your only recourse is to return the software for a refund. (Most vendors will refuse to take back an opened box. Still, the software manufacturer is required to take it back and refund your money if you reject the licensing. This is true of programs purchased online as well.)

 Many companies rely on *digital rights management (DRM)* to protect digital assets, such as online photos or videos. DRM is not as established as licensing agreements are, but you should still respect the property of the owners of digital content.

Although the majority of the applications that you acquire will probably be commercial products, there are a number of alternatives to commercial software sales. Here are some of the license types that you may encounter:

Freeware *Freeware* is software that is completely free. On a small scale, you can get such software from download sites such as www.download.com or from the creator's personal website. Large companies like Google and Microsoft also sometimes offer products for free, because it serves the company's interests to have a lot of people using their software. Examples include Google Chrome and Microsoft Internet Explorer. Freeware doesn't include source code, and users aren't allowed to modify the application.

Open Source Open source software is freer than free: not only is the application free, but the source code (code used by programmers) is also shared to encourage others to contribute to the future development and improvement of the application. OSs such as Linux and applications such as OpenOffice fit this category. Open source software can't be sold, although it can be bundled with commercial products that are sold.

Shareware Shareware is software that provides a free trial, with the expectation that you'll pay for it if you like it and decide to keep it. In some cases, a shareware version isn't the full product; in other cases, it expires after a certain amount of time. Some shareware provides a full and unlimited version, with payment requested on the honor system.

Multiuser   This is commercial software that you're allowed to install on more than one computer. For example, some versions of Microsoft Office allow you to install the same copy on two or three PCs.

Single User   This is commercial software for which the license restricts installation to a single PC. A common misconception is that a single-user license allows you to install the software on more than one computer as long as you use only one instance at a time, but that's not accurate. Commercial products sometimes have activation systems that lock the software to a specific PC once it's installed, so you can't install it elsewhere. Microsoft Office is a good example of commercial software.

Concurrent   This license allows the software to be installed on many PCs but used concurrently by a smaller number. For example, you may have 1,000 computers with the application installed, but only 100 users can use it simultaneously. This is useful in situations in which everyone needs to have an application available but the application gets very little actual use.

Perpetual   A perpetual or non-expiring license is a license that can be purchased for a software product. Many video games still use this license model. You purchase the software and the right to use the software for life. Software vendors that use perpetual licensing will also offer software upgrades or patches for the first year, as customary. However, any upgrades after the first year are generally covered under a support or maintenance fee.

Corporate, Campus, or Site   These are enterprise licenses, which permit an organization to install the application on an agreed-upon number of PCs. For example, a school may buy a site license of an antivirus program and allow all students to download and install it freely to ensure that the school's network remains virus free. Microsoft calls this a volume license key.

Valid License   A valid license is any software license that is current in its term and not counterfeit. As long as the license is not used already, it is valid for activation for the software product it is associated with.

If you buy any sort of commercial software, you will receive a *product key*, which you will need to enter during installation or the first time the application is opened. The product key might be emailed to you, or it could be located on the physical media if you got an installation CD-ROM, DVD, or thumb drive. Figure 21.12 shows an example of a product key.

FIGURE 21.12   A Microsoft product key

In a corporate environment, license management is a critical responsibility. The company may spend thousands or even millions of dollars on software licenses. Money could be wasted on unused licenses, or if the company's computers have unlicensed software, it could result in huge fines. Ignorance is not a legal excuse in this area.

To avoid these problems, it may be best for your company to purchase a software asset management tool, such as Microsoft's Software Asset Management guide (`www.microsoft.com/en-us/download/details.aspx?id=31382`), License Manager by License Dashboard (`www.licensedashboard.com`), or FlexNet Manager by Flexera Software (`www.flexerasoftware.com`). In general, here are the steps to take for proper license management:

1. Build a database of all licenses owned by your company. This includes what type of license it is, license numbers, and expiration dates, if any.

2. Perform an inventory of all licensed software installed on your computers. (This can be quite an effort.)

3. Compare the license list to the installation base.

4. For any gaps where you have unlicensed software, either remove the software or procure licenses.

Because of the potential for heavy fines, many companies prohibit the installation of software on client computers unless specifically authorized by a manager or the IT department.

 Real World Scenario

How Do I Buy the Right Licenses?

Consider this situation: After talking to your boss about software licenses, you decide to investigate the office productivity software on your department's computers. You are unable to find proper documentation that the correct software licenses were purchased, leading you to wonder whether the company has the right licenses. Your boss wants to avoid any potential legal issues and asks you to go buy enough copies of the latest version of Microsoft Office for the 20 users in your department. What do you do?

The first question to ask yourself is, do all 20 people use their computers at the same time? If not, then you might be able to purchase a concurrent license for fewer than 20 users. If there's the possibility of all 20 users needing Office at once, then you'll definitely need licenses for everyone. You might purchase a corporate license as well. Now that you have figured out what to buy, how do you do it?

One option is to go to the local computer store, load up 20 boxes of Office (if they have that many in stock), and trudge up to the cashier. A second option is to go to Microsoft's volume licensing site, at www.microsoft.com/en-us/licensing/default, to learn about purchasing multiple licenses. Microsoft will direct you to an authorized reseller so that you can purchase the licenses. The authorized reseller will register the list of license numbers with Microsoft's licensing center. Now you need just one physical (or downloaded) copy to perform the installation.

Managing Sensitive Information

As an IT manager, you will very likely have access to information that you will need to keep closely guarded. For example, you might have access to username and/or password lists, medical or educational records, addresses and phone numbers, or employee records. It's your responsibility to ensure that sensitive information does not get released into the wrong hands. On the flip side, you may encounter information that's sensitive because it's prohibited or illegal. You need to know how to react in those situations as well.

Much of the data you come into contact with could be regulated outside of the organization's internal policies. Regulated data must be identified as it enters your network, and the proper operating procedures should be followed. The operating procedures for such data should be constructed so that you can adhere to the data's regulatory compliance rules. The regulatory rules for compliance can be at any local, state, or federal level. Many of the regulations in the following sections are at a federal level of compliance.

Personally Identifiable Information

Personally identifiable information (PII) is anything that can be used to identify an individual person on its own or in context with other information. This includes someone's name, address, other contact information; the names of family members; and other details that people would consider private.

PII should always be kept confidential and secure. It seems like every few months or so we see news stories of data breaches at big companies resulting in stolen credit card data or username and contact lists. This information finds its way into hackers' hands and causes millions of people grief and monetary damages. Be sure that this information is properly secured and can be accessed only by authorized personnel.

Personal Government-Issued Information

Any personal information contained in a document issued by a government or state is considered personal government-issued information. Examples of government-issued documents are defined as a birth certificate, Social Security card, identification card, driver's license, resident card, taxpayer ID number, or password, just to name a few. The category of information is very broad and can overlap with other types of protected data, such as protected health information or other PII.

The threat to personal government-issued information being compromised is that the information is how a person is defined by the government. The theft of a Social Security number is a direct theft of identity in the eyes of the government. Tax records to credit information is tied to a Social Security number. Therefore, like any PII, this data should also be kept confidential and secure.

Payment Card Industry Data Security Standard

Payment Card Industry Data Security Standard (PCI DSS) is a standard of processes and procedures used to handle data related to transactions using payment cards. A payment card is any card that allows the transfer of money for goods or services. Types of payment cards include credit cards, debit cards, or even store gift cards.

PCI DSS compliance is not enforced by government entities. PCI DSS compliance is actually enforced by banks and creditors. Merchants must comply with the PCI DSS standard to maintain payment card services. If a merchant does not comply with PCI DSS standards and a breach occurs, the merchant can be fined by the banks. Once a breach of PCI data occurs, then local, state, and federal laws can apply to the merchant. For example, some laws require the merchant to pay for credit-monitoring services for victims after a breach.

General Data Protection Regulation

The *General Data Protection Regulation (GDPR)* is a European Union (EU) law governing how consumer data can be used and protected. The GDPR was created primarily to protect citizens of the European Union. It applies to anyone involved in the processing of data based on the citizens of the European Union, regardless of where the organization is located.

The GDPR recommends that organizations hire a *data protection officer (DPO)*. This person is the point of contact for all compliance with GDPR, as well as any other compliances your organization falls under. The underlying goal is to achieve consent from the end user of your product or service. Consent to collect information must be proven by an organization beyond a shadow of doubt. This means that if someone visits your website from the European Union, you must receive consent in clear language to even place a cookie in their web browser. The DPO is responsible for coordinating this language, as well as the life cycle of any data that is collected.

Protected Health Information

Protected health information (PHI), also known as *personal health information*, refers to any information used in the health care industry to describe a patient or ailment. This information can be considered "the patient chart" you always see on television. However, *electronic health records (EHR)* go way beyond the current condition of a patient; they describe a person from the cradle to the grave.

Electronic health records are used to record a patient's vitals every time the patient visits a doctor's office. They represent historical information about patients, as well as billing information used by health care providers. This makes the EHR extremely valuable to a hacker and represents a large makeup of identity theft.

This type of identity theft is really dangerous! Your diagnosis could be determined based upon vitals, allergies, or conditions that are recorded from a person who assumes your identity. Try to explain to the insurance company that your gallbladder needs to be removed, but their records show they paid to have it taken out already.

PHI can also be used to track the statistics of larger groups of people. However, the data must be anonymized first, before it is put into a publicly addressable database for these statistics and studies. Information such as names, Social Security numbers, phone numbers, health insurance information, account numbers, and specific geographical information must be removed. Interesting enough, geographical information can include only the first three digits of a zip code.

Data Retention Requirements

As you learned, there are all different forms of data and they are regulated for sensitivity and confidentiality purposes. The storage of data is also regulated depending on the type of data. The data to be retained is usually transactional in nature, such as a financial transaction, but it can also be data that has touched your system.

Regulations are not the only governing factor for data retention—your company can also have an internal requirement. An example of an internal retention requirement might be for memorandums, access control records, or even video footage. There are different reasons for adhering to an internal data retention requirement, but they all shield the organization from liability in some way. This is very apparent in legal situations. If you keep all data indefinitely on old backups and there is a lawsuit, you will be liable to restore records in a timely fashion, even if those old systems are no longer supported. If you don't produce the data in a timely fashion, you could default a lawsuit in favor of the plaintiff. These discoveries of information are considered e-discovery by court proceedings.

As an IT professional, it is your responsibility to work with legal counsel in your organization to define data retention periods. However, before you can define the data retention periods, you will need to identify the data to be protected. A document profile should be created that clearly defines the types of data you deal with on a daily basis. This stage of the process is where you can also identify outside governing requirements for retention.

Once the document profile is created, you should start tagging data in your environment with the data types. This may be as simple as naming the email backup job **email data**. You should then set up a hard policy to control how long the data is kept. Keep in mind that holding the data too long is just as bad as not holding the data long enough.

Summary

This chapter covered three areas of operational procedures that you should integrate into your work:

- Safety procedures

- Environmental controls

- Licensing, policies, and sensitive materials

First, we looked at the importance of safety procedures. Safety is about protecting you from harm as well as protecting your computer components from getting damaged. Then, we outlined some methods to apply the policies and procedures for a safe working environment, and identified potential safety hazards. Included were preventing *electrostatic discharge (ESD)* and *electromagnetic interference (EMI)*, creating a safe work environment, and properly handling computer equipment.

Safety involves you and your coworkers, but it also includes environmental issues. The environment can have a harmful effect on computers, but computers can also greatly harm the environment. You need to be familiar with the importance of material safety data sheets (MSDSs) as well as the proper disposal procedures for batteries, display devices, and chemical solvents and cans. These items need to be kept out of the environment because of the damage that they can cause.

Finally, we looked at potential legal issues. Failure to follow certain procedures can expose you or your company to legal proceedings. Make sure that all the software on your computers is legal and licensed and that the computers contain no illegal or prohibited materials. You may also need to protect personally identifiable information, depending on the type of data you have. When incidents happen, you need to know how to respond properly to mitigate the issue.

Exam Essentials

Know which computer components are particularly dangerous to technicians. The most dangerous components are the power supply and the monitor. Both are capable of storing lethal charges of electricity, even when unplugged. You also need to be aware of parts that get incredibly hot, such as the processor, which can cause severe burns if touched.

Understand where to find safety information regarding chemicals.   You can find this information in a material safety data sheet (MSDS). An MSDS might not have come with your purchase, but most suppliers will gladly supply one.

Know which tool to use for which job.   The majority of computer repair jobs can be handled with nothing more than a Phillips-head screwdriver. However, you might need cutters, extra light, or a mirror for some jobs. Avoid using magnetic-tipped tools.

Understand methods to help prevent ESD.   One of the biggest and most common dangers of electronic components is electrostatic discharge (ESD). You can employ several methods to help avoid ESD-related problems, such as grounding yourself; using an antistatic wrist strap, bag, or mat; and controlling the humidity levels.

Know the proper disposal procedures for used computer parts, batteries, and chemical solvents.   The specific disposal procedure depends on the item. However, the safe answer is always to recycle the component, not to throw it in the trash.

Know the differences between license types.   Open source applications don't require a purchased license, whereas commercial applications do require a purchased license. Some licenses are personal licenses, meaning the applications are for use by one person on one computer, whereas others are enterprise licenses, meaning the applications can be used on multiple computers at the same time.

Understand how to handle prohibited content or activity.   Always have policies and procedures in place to deal with prohibited content or activity. When an incident happens, follow the procedures, report through proper channels, preserve the data or device, and follow the chain of custody.

Know the various types of sensitive information.   You should know that personal identifiable information (PII) is any information used to identify an individual. The Payment Card Industry Data Security Standard (PCI DSS) is a standard of policies and procedures used by the payment industry. General Data Protection Regulation (GDPR) is a European Union (EU) law governing how EU citizen data is used. Protected health information (PHI) is any information used to describe a patient or a patient's ailment.

Review Questions

The answers to the chapter review questions can be found in Appendix A.

1. You have dropped a screw into a tight location of a computer. How should you retrieve it?

   A. Use a magnetic-tipped screwdriver.

   B. Use a magnetic grabber.

   C. Use a three-pronged grabber.

   D. Shake the computer until it falls out.

2. You have a failed CRT monitor that you must dispose of safely. Which of the following is used to discharge voltage properly from the unplugged computer monitor?

   A. Antistatic wrist strap

   B. Screwdriver

   C. High-voltage probe

   D. Power cord

3. One of your coworkers just spilled a chemical solvent in a warehouse, and you have been asked to help clean it up. Which of the following must contain information about a chemical solvent's emergency cleanup procedures?

   A. OSHA

   B. MSDS

   C. Product label

   D. CRT

4. You are purchasing an inkjet printer cartridge for home use that you know has an MSDS. How do you obtain the MSDS for this product?

   A. The store is required to give you one at the time of purchase.

   B. It's contained in the packaging of the printer cartridge.

   C. You are not legally allowed to have an MSDS for this product.

   D. You should visit the printer cartridge manufacturer's website.

5. In the interest of a safe work environment, which of the following should you report? (Choose two.)

   A. An accident

   B. A near-accident

   C. Spills on the floor inside a building

   D. Rain forecasted for a workday

6. What is the approximate minimum level of static charge for humans to feel a shock?

    A. 300 volts

    B. 3,000 volts

    C. 30,000 volts

    D. 300,000 volts

7. Your work environment has been unusually dry lately, and several components have been damaged by ESD. Your team has been asked to be extra careful about ESD damage. Which of the following measures can be implemented to reduce the risk of ESD? (Choose two.)

    A. Use an antistatic wrist strap.

    B. Use an antistatic bag.

    C. Spray disinfectant spray.

    D. Shuffle your feet.

8. Which of the following are OSHA requirements for a safe work environment that must be followed by employers? (Choose two.)

    A. Attend yearly OSHA safe work environment seminars.

    B. Provide properly maintained tools and equipment.

    C. Have an OSHA employee stationed within 5 miles of the facility.

    D. Display an OSHA poster in a prominent location.

9. Your office just added 20 new workstations, and your manager has put you in charge of configuring them. The users need to have Microsoft Office installed. What should you do to install Microsoft Office properly on these computers?

    A. Ensure that the company has the proper licenses to install 20 additional copies.

    B. Agree with the open source license agreement during installation.

    C. Use the personal license key from an existing system to install Office on the new computers.

    D. Follow normal installation procedures; nothing else needs to be done.

10. Your office is moving from one floor of a building to another, and you are part of the moving crew. When moving computer equipment, which of the following are good procedures to follow? (Choose two.)

    A. Lift by bending over at the waist.

    B. Carry CRT monitors with the glass face away from your body.

    C. Use a cart for heavy objects.

    D. Ensure that there are no safety hazards in your path.

11. You just removed four AA alkaline batteries from a remote-control device. What is the recommended way to dispose of these batteries?

A. Throw them in the trash.

B. Incinerate them.

C. Take them to a recycling center.

D. Flush them down the toilet.

12. When replacing a hard drive, you discover prohibited material on a user's laptop. What should you do first? (Choose two.)

A. Destroy the prohibited material.

B. Confiscate and preserve the prohibited material.

C. Confront the user about the material.

D. Report the prohibited material through the proper channels.

13. You need to investigate how to protect credit card data on your network. Which information should you research?

A. PCI DSS

B. GDPR

C. PHI

D. PII

14. Which class of fire extinguisher is recommended for use in a wood and paper fire?

A. A

B. B

C. C

D. D

15. Which of the following are common types of screwdrivers? (Choose two.)

A. Circular

B. Phillips

C. Torx

D. Helix

16. Which of the following are elements of a good workplace safety plan? (Choose two.)

A. Periodic workplace inspections

B. A safety and health training program

C. Retribution for employees who report violations

D. An independent third-party auditor of the safety plan

17. What is the recommended use policy on magnetic-tipped screwdrivers inside computers?

    A. Do not use them.

    B. It's okay to use them, but keep them away from the processor.

    C. It's okay to use them, but keep them away from the RAM.

    D. It's okay to use them, but only if they're of the powered variety.

18. Which of the following are usually contained on an MSDS? (Choose two.)

    A. Freezing point

    B. Handling and storage instructions

    C. Personal protection instructions

    D. Salinity levels

19. Which of the following are OSHA requirements for a safe work environment that must be followed by employees? (Choose two.)

    A. Immediately report all accidents to OSHA.

    B. Use protective gear and equipment.

    C. Attend safety training.

    D. Follow all employer-implemented health and safety rules.

20. Which of the following types of batteries are not considered environmental hazards?

    A. Alkaline

    B. Nickel-metal hydride (NiMH)

    C. Nickel-cadmium (NiCd)

    D. Button cell

Performance-Based Question

You will encounter performance-based questions on the A+ exams. The questions on the exam require you to perform a specific task, and you will be graded on whether or not you were able to complete the task. The following requires you to think creatively in order to measure how well you understand this chapter's topics. You may or may not see similar questions on the actual A+ exams. To see how your answers compare to the authors', refer to Appendix B.

One of your office coworkers recently tripped on a power cord and injured himself. What should you do to find potential trip hazards in your office? Once the hazards are identified, what actions should you take?

Chapter

22

Documentation and Professionalism

THE FOLLOWING COMPTIA A+ 220-1102 EXAM OBJECTIVES ARE COVERED IN THIS CHAPTER:

✓ **4.1 Given a scenario, implement best practices associated with documentation and support systems information management.**

- Ticketing systems
  - User information
  - Device information
  - Description of problems
  - Categories
  - Severity
  - Escalation levels
  - Clear, concise written communication
    - Problem description
    - Progress notes
    - Problem resolution
- Asset management
  - Inventory lists
  - Database system
  - Asset tags and IDs
  - Procurement life cycle
  - Warranty and licensing
  - Assigned users

- Types of documents
    - Acceptable use policy (AUP)
    - Network topology diagram
    - Regulatory compliance requirements
        - Splash screens
    - Incident reports
    - Standard operating procedures
        - Procedures for custom installation of software package
    - New-user setup checklist
    - End-user termination checklist
- Knowledge base/articles

✓ **4.2 Explain basic change-management best practices.**

- Documented business processes
    - Rollback plan
    - Sandbox testing
    - Responsible staff member
- Change management
    - Request forms
    - Purpose of the change
    - Scope of the change
    - Date and time of the change
    - Affected systems/impact
    - Risk analysis
    - Risk level
    - Change board approvals
    - End-user acceptance

✓ **4.3 Given a scenario, implement workstation backup and recovery methods.**

- Backup and recovery

    - Full

    - Incremental

    - Differential

    - Synthetic

- Backup testing

    - Frequency

- Backup rotation schemes

    - On site vs. off site

    - Grandfather-father-son (GFS)

    - 3-2-1 backup rule

✓ **4.5 Summarize environmental impacts and local environmental controls.**

- Battery backup

- Surge suppressor

✓ **4.7 Given a scenario, use proper communication techniques and professionalism.**

- Professional appearance and attire

    - Match the required attire of the given environment

        - Formal

        - Business casual

- Use proper language and avoid jargon, acronyms, and slang, when applicable

- Maintain a positive attitude/project confidence

- Actively listen, take notes, and avoid interrupting the customer

- Be culturally sensitive

    - Use appropriate professional titles, when applicable

- Be on time (if late, contact the customer)
- Avoid distractions
  - Personal calls
  - Texting/social media sites
  - Personal interruptions
- Dealing with difficult customers or situations
  - Do not argue with customers or be defensive
  - Avoid dismissing customer problems
  - Avoid being judgmental
  - Clarify customer statements (ask open-ended questions to narrow the scope of the problem, restate the issue, or question to verify understanding)
  - Do not disclose experience via social media outlets
- Set and meet expectations/time line and communicate status with the customer
  - Offer repair/replacement options, as needed
  - Provide proper documentation on the services provided
  - Follow up with customer/user at a later date to verify satisfaction
- Deal appropriately with customers' confidential and private materials
  - Located on a computer, desktop, printer, etc.

Every day at work, we do what it takes to get the job done. As IT professionals, we have millions of facts crammed into our heads about how various hardware components work and what software configuration settings work best for our systems. We know which servers or workstations give us constant trouble and which end users need more help than others. We are counted on to be experts in knowing *what* to do to keep computers and networks running smoothly. And even though we don't tend to think about it overtly, we need to be experts in *how* we get things done as well. Even though the *how* might not be at the top of your mind every day (hopefully you don't go to work every day thinking "Okay, don't get killed by a monitor" or "Let's see if I can be nice to someone today"), but it should be integrated into your work processes. Operational procedures define the *how*, and they provide guidance on the proper ways to get various tasks accomplished.

In this chapter, we will start by talking about documentation used to document the network and the policies that you will encounter and need to enforce. We will then look at change management practices used to make changes to the network that will affect other business units in your organization.

We will also look at disaster prevention and recovery. In the process, we will cover topics such as backup and recovery, power resiliency, and cloud storage versus local storage.

In the final part of this chapter, we'll switch to discussing professionalism and communication and focus on topics that you need to know for your exam study. Applying the skills learned here will help you pass the exam, but on a more practical level, it will help you become a better technician and possibly further advance your career.

Documentation and Support

Creating documentation of the network and systems you work on is the last step to many projects. However, it is the most overlooked, or it is considered secondary to fixing new problems or upgrading to the next system. The documentation produced has positive effects on production and problem solving. It is used so that you don't need to redo the step of discovery the next time you have a problem. Documentation also allows you to have others work on a problem with the same distinctive view you had at the time of documentation.

Some of the documentation you create will help to create policies and procedures that others will need to follow. Throughout this book, we have discussed the hard controls of these policies. For example, when you implement a password policy, you can dictate that a password be complex and of a certain length. A written policy is a soft control that might detail how to create a complex password. In this chapter, we will look at several different policies that you will come across as a technician.

Ticketing Systems

One of the most important functions of the information technology (IT) department is to solve problems and fulfill end-user requests. The core of this function is the ability to receive incoming requests, track progress, and assure that problems and requests are solved and completed. It is common to find a ticketing system at the heart of this function called help desk services or support services. A ticketing system adds other benefits to the function of the help desk, such as accountability, reporting, collaboration, and escalation, just to name some of the important benefits.

There are hundreds of ticketing system vendors on the market today, and each one has some unique features. When choosing a ticketing system, the first decision you must make is to host it on-premises, also known as on-prem, or host it through a cloud option from the vendor. Many ticketing systems can be purchased as a software-as-a-service (SaaS) cloud model. You are charged a monthly fee based on the number of tickets, storage, or the number of agents (help desk personnel), whereas on-prem systems are licensed either per agent or per supported users and storage is not a concern. There are a number of considerations when choosing between on-prem and cloud based. The SaaS option is a great option for a number of reasons, mainly for availability. However, if all of your employees are local to your site, then on-prem might be the best solution. If you are conscientious about keeping the system up to date for security patches, having an on-prem system is another box to patch (so to speak). But if you elect SaaS hosting, the vendor is responsible for patching and keeping the system secure.

Besides the initial hosting options, there are several features that are somewhat standard with any ticketing system. These features include escalation, automated routing, knowledge base, email to open a ticket, ticket management, and real-time reporting, and those are just a few of the features. We will cover many of them in this section.

Entering Tickets

Once you have a ticketing system in place, it's just a matter of having tickets entered into the system. Your users should have no problem finding network issues to create tickets for. There are three main entry methods of generating a ticket: email, portal, and manually.

Email is probably the easiest way to enter a ticket. It is customary when setting up a ticket system to dedicate an email address for entering tickets, such as helpdesk@wiley.com or support@wiley.com. When a user has a problem, they simply have to email the ticketing system and a ticket is automatically generated. Their email address will become the identity for the ticket related to the problem, and IT can converse with them via email. This method of ticket entry is commonly used for external customers, such as product support.

Every ticketing system will have a portal for the users and help desk personnel to log into. This of course means that the users and the help desk personnel need an existing account, or users can sign up for an account when they enter the ticket. These types of ticketing systems are often established for internal issues inside the organization. Once signed into the portal, a user has several fields to fill out in order to submit the ticket. This type of setup is nice for users if they have multiple tickets and want to track them simultaneously.

The manual entry of tickets is a catch-all entry method. A help desk support person is responsible for entering the ticket information manually to create a ticket. This is a common practice when someone calls into the help desk. The entry of the ticket serves two main purposes: The first is that it allows for follow-up or escalation of the problem. The second purpose is that entering a ticket can identify a problem common to your network—for example, if a system has just been upgraded and calls come into the help desk because of a problem with the upgraded system. The user or even your help desk personnel might not know of the recent upgrade. However, the accumulation of tickets for similar issues will allow help desk personnel to identify a systemwide problem. The problem(s) can then be escalated to the party responsible for the problematic upgraded system. There are many other reasons for manually entering a ticket, such as scheduling of help desk staff, identifying specific skills required by help desk staff, and the overall volume of work. These are just a few; each organization has its own reasons.

These are the most common ticket entry methods for ticketing systems. There are many other methods, such as application-triggered entry and interactive voice response (IVR) automation.

Ticket Details

The devil is in the details, as the saying goes, and that is also true when entering a ticket into the ticketing system. There are several elements that need to be entered correctly for the successful resolution of a problem. If a user is self-entering the ticket, then you will have no control over this initial process.

When a user enters a ticket using the portal, it is common for them to be very brief with their problem description. This is usually because the description window is one field of many and the user may feel they have to be brief. Problems that are submitted via email might have more elaborate explanations, because users may feel more comfortable communicating in email. However, other fields may not be filled out, such as severity, contact information, or problem category. The ticketing system generally cannot decipher these elements from a simple email.

When acting as a help desk support person answering the help desk line, we have the most control over manually entering a ticket into the ticketing system. We also directly interface with the user. So, there should be a standardized process for collecting the necessary information, as well as some best practices to be followed. Always keep in mind that your interactions with the user make an impression on the entire department. You should have good interpersonal skills, display empathy, and above all have patience. All of these skills will help both you and the user reach a resolution more quickly.

Another important skill that you should display is actively listening to the user. This skill is often related to the skill that detectives have when interviewing a person. When a user calls into the help desk, the critical information to collect is who they are, how to contact them, and a description of the problem. In addition, you should ask the urgency of the issue.

If you are able to enter information into the ticket entry form as the person is talking to you, do so. If you are unable to type and listen, or you must allow for long awkward pauses as you type, you should use the trusted method of pad and paper. You can always enter the information after the person is off the phone and moves on to their next task, awaiting a response for the problem. Or, if you solved the problem, then you can enter the ticket with the resolution after they are off the phone to act as a follow-up. Always exercise speed and accuracy in obtaining the information, especially if you are not able to help the person and need to escalate the ticket to someone else.

The following is a list of information you should obtain on the initial call with the user as you exercise all of the best practices:

User Information   The first information you want to obtain is the user's name. This is important for your communication with the user. Always use their name throughout the interview about the problem. In addition, you should obtain the best method to contact them, such as their phone number, cell phone number, email address, or physical location. This information is important if you must escalate the problem to another technician.

Description of the Problem   A good description of the problem is the most important information you must gather. During your communications with the user, ask them to describe the exact problem they are having. If the user offers multiple problems, ask to review one at a time. Also, ask the user how you can reproduce the problem, then review the steps to reproduce the problem with the user. After you learn about the problem and the steps to reproduce it, repeat the steps to the user in a calm way to verify that you have clear and concise information.

Device Information   Although the device being used by the user might not be apparent to you as being part of the problem, if the ticket needs to be escalated it may help in solving the problem more quickly. Information to be obtained is the type of device, operating system version, hardware service tag, and method of network access. Another technician might find that a model or version of operating system is a key to the problem.

Severity of the Problem   You may pick up the urgency in the user's voice, and that can serve as an indicator of the severity of the problem. You must communicate this in entering the ticket—often there is a drop-down menu for low, mid, or high severity. Always keep in mind that not everything can be of the utmost urgency; although we would like to make everything an emergency, we often don't have the staff to do so. Communicate with the user about the severity of the issue and agree upon a severity level. Always use patience, empathy, and professionalism in your communications.

Category of the Problem   The category of a problem is a critical element of the ticket. In some cases, the category may automatically route a ticket to a group of people in your support staff. For example, if a user calls in and has a problem with the organization's database and reporting, the ticket may need to be routed to the database administrators for the organization. Likewise, if there is a problem with a phone, the ticket may be routed to the phone administrators for the organization. In addition to automatic routing to a group of administrators, categories are useful for reporting. They help identify categories of problems that see the most tickets, which can be an indication you need more staff or need to adopt a quality control process.

Levels of Support

Every IT department has a structure, and they vary from organization to organization. On a very high level there are typically two main groups of support personnel: network administrators and application/database administrators. However, your organization might have security administrators, application developers, storage administrators, virtualization administrators—and these just scratch the surface.

In each group of support personnel, there are varied levels of experience, support, and responsibilities. The simplest structure is front-office personnel, who interface with the users, and back-office personnel, who interface with the front-office personnel, and make systemwide changes. Depending on the size of your organization, you may also have an intermediate level of personnel who interface with the back-end and front-end personnel. This intermediate level serves as a buffer to keep engineers separated from the day-to-day problems. These levels are often numbered from basic knowledge to expert knowledge, level 1 through level 3.

Regardless of your structure, these various levels are considered escalation points. As an IT technician or even an IT administrator, you are not always expected to have the answer, but you are expected to be able to get the answer. When you don't have the answer and must ask someone more knowledgeable, this process is called escalation. With a ticketing system, if all the information is properly obtained, you can escalate the ticket to a higher level of technician or administrator. The next level up the support chain should be able to read through the ticket notes and work on a resolution. When a ticket is escalated to another person, it is common for that person to own the ticket (problem) and be responsible for communicating with the user.

You may also find that you are the most knowledgeable person about a particular system in your organization, yet you still do not have an answer. This is fine and it happens all the time, but always keep in mind you that are expected to be able to find the answer. This requires an escalation of the problem to a third party, potentially outside your organization. It is also the reason support contracts should be kept current so that you have an escalation point outside of your organization. When an escalation is made outside of your organization, the point of contact (POC) inside your organization will be the owner of the ticket.

Clear Communication

The requirement and benefits of clear communications cannot be overstated enough—not just verbal communications, but also written communications between technicians and users, as well as technicians and their escalation points. Clear, concise written communications can also break down verbal communications problems between regions of the world. There are three stages to any problem where clear, concise written communications are required:

Problem Description   Not only should the problem description be clear and concise to you and the user, but it should communicate the problem to someone not part of the initial communications. Don't use jargon, acronyms, or references to anything that is not clearly defined in the problem description. Always keep in mind that the problem may have to be escalated.

Work-Arounds   When a problem is identified and a solution requires time, a work-around should be communicated to the user. A work-around serves as a temporary way of allowing the user to continue their work by working around the problem. Always communicate that it is a temporary solution and that you will work on a permanent solution.

Progress Notes   The most important part of the ticketing process is the progress of solving the problem. You should adopt the rule of daily communications with the user and communicate where you are in the process of obtaining a resolution. Be as transparent with the user as possible—always keep in mind that the user might ask for a supervisor to review the progress. If the user stops communicating with you on the progress of a resolution, give them a drop-dead date when the ticket will be suspended or closed.

Problem Resolution   The last stage to any problem is the resolution, and you should strive to have a resolution to every problem. The resolution or steps to the resolution should be clear and concise written communications. This also serves as a reference to other technicians with the same problem.

Follow-Up

Although the problem resolution should be where the communication with the user ceases, it is important to follow up with the user to make sure the problem is resolved. This important step should be done right before the ticket is closed. You may learn that the final resolution presented does not work for the user and that they continue to use the work-around that you presented as a temporary fix. This often happens when you must escalate the problem and communications are not clear and concise between the next technician and the user.

The ticket management process should include the steps of entry, resolution, solution, follow-up, and knowledge base. Each ticket that is completed strengthens your technical support for future problems. It also strengthens the faith the users have that the IT department can solve their problems. When you follow up with the user, you verify that all of your efforts and your escalation point's efforts are justified by the solution.

Many ticket systems allow for the entry of a knowledge base article for future users and technicians to self-service their problems. Writing the draft of a knowledge base article should happen after you have identified a successful follow-up with the user.

Asset Management

Asset management is an important part of the IT department's responsibilities, because the IT assets are considered *fixed tangible assets*. Some other examples of fixed tangible assets are land, furniture, and office equipment. When equipment is initially purchased, the accounting department records it as an asset on the company's general ledger, because it adds to the value of the company. Over time, however, the asset will lose its initial value. The accounting department will depreciate the value of the asset based on its perceived lifespan.

The management of these assets benefits the organization in defining the organization's worth. The management of assets also helps the IT department in forecasting upgrades and future expenditures for growth. In this section we will cover the various elements of asset management as it applies to the IT department.

Asset Management Systems

There are a number of ways to manage assets for the organization. Choosing a way to manage assets depends on what needs to be done with the information. Asset management at an organization-wide level is often a module of an accounting package used by the company. This software allows an asset (equipment) to be tracked by associating a number on the asset tag with the condition, business unit, and perceived value of the equipment. Examples of this equipment are desks, land, and even computer equipment. These types of databases work well for reporting on the value of equipment that the organization owns to calculate a net worth for an organization, but they do very little in helping an IT department plan upgrades.

Laptops, desktops, and other devices have variables such as storage, RAM, operating system versions, and other unique variables to the hardware and software of the device. Asset management systems are databases that collect data from the operating system through the use of an agent. This type of asset management is more detailed than a purchasing record from the accounting department. Once the information is collected, reports can be drawn when upgrades are required. For example, a report you may compile in the asset management system might be all operating systems that match Windows 10 and that have less than 4 GBs of RAM and hard drives smaller than 100 GBs. You then have a report of what needs to be upgraded in terms of hardware for an upgrade of the operating system to Windows 11. When using an asset management for an organization that spans a large geographic area, this is invaluable information that otherwise would have taken days to collect.

Asset management systems don't stop at hardware; software packages and their accompanying licensing are considered assets as well. Many asset management systems can also collect a list of the software installed on the devices in your organization. They can also include detailed licensing usage information so that you can gauge where licensing is being used efficiently and where it is not based on usage.

Not all asset management requires databases and asset management systems. When managing a small amount of equipment, an inventory list is more than sufficient. The list can be a simple Microsoft Excel sheet detailing the types of equipment and their associated quantities. These inventory lists work really well when trying to control consumable electronics like mice, keyboards, and monitors. Once the rotating stock of equipment becomes too large in quantity and value, it's time to look at an asset management system.

Asset Tags

All computer and network equipment should be tracked, from the cradle to the grave, by the IT department. When equipment enters the company, it should be labeled with an *asset tag*, as shown in Figure 22.1. The asset tag is often a permanent metallic sticker or metallic plate that is riveted to the equipment. The asset tag often has a *barcode*, which defines the numeric number that identifies the asset. This asset tag should then be entered into the asset management software, by either typing in the number or scanning the bar code.

FIGURE 22.1   An asset tag

Procurement Life Cycle

The entire life cycle for any IT system is cyclical and differs slightly depending on the assets. The typical life cycle for IT systems consists of purchasing, deploying, managing, and retiring. The exact procedures for the IT life cycle will depend on your organization and the goods or services.

The first step is the procurement of the goods or services. This process is typically standardized by your organization's business affairs department or finance department. Just like any process, the procurement process differs from organization to organization. An example of a procurement life cycle is shown in Figure 22.2; yours may differ slightly. Regardless, the procurement life cycle will always start by identifying the need for the goods or services being requested. If it costs money for the organization, then it has to fill a need or solve a problem. This is probably the most important step in the procurement process. If it does not solve an apparent problem or need, then it might not get approved or may be sidelined for another budget cycle.

After the need is identified, it's time to obtain quotes for the goods or services. You should have three comparative quotes for the goods or services being requested. However, depending on the goods or services, achieving that may not be feasible. Examples where comparable quotes are unobtainable are direct purchasing from the vendor, vendor-registered value-added resellers (VARs), and custom goods or services.

The budget approval process will be dependent on the reported needs of the goods or services, as previously explained. The goods or services are submitted for approval for the operational budget (OpeX) or the capital budget (CapX). Items being submitted for the CapX budget will depend on their value and utility. The test is always, can the item be depreciated over the expected life of the product? Examples are servers, workstations, and other equipment. Anything that cannot be depreciated, such as services, will fall into the OpeX budget. It is likely that your organization has a standard characterization of goods and services

FIGURE 22.2   An example of a procurement life cycle

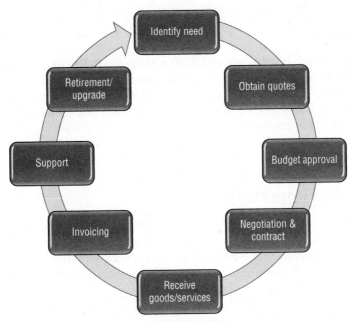

and which budget is applicable. The outcome of the budget approval process will either be approved or denied, but it can also be conditionally approved based on meeting goals or other conditions.

Once the goods or services are approved, then your business affairs department will work with the vendor or reseller to negotiate money, terms and conditions, and the overall contract/scope of work (SOW). Once the purchase is completed, you will receive the goods or services. At this point, the contract or SOW is important, because it will define when the vendor is to be paid. If all the goods are not received or the services are not complete, then the vendor is not entitled to send an invoice for payment or the invoice can be held. Although this sounds like a simple part of the procurement process, it is often overlooked. You should never begin payment until the goods are received or the contract/SOW is satisfied.

During the initial phase of obtaining quotes, you should identify the cost for ongoing support, maintenance, or licensing of the goods or services. These costs should be submitted to the operational expense budget as an ongoing/recurring cost, since these costs are usually a monthly or annual cost. The vendor or VAR might also include 3–5 years of support, maintenance, or licensing in the quote so that it can be submitted to a capital budget. This will be based on your organization's processes. Typically, the vendor will include an initial warranty or license with the original purchase of the product or service.

Every product or service outlives its usefulness. This is where we identify retiring or upgrading the product or service. This retirement or upgrade will then start the procurement process all over again. This time around, identifying the needs is easier, unless the retirement does not necessitate replacing the product.

Assigned Users

When assets are acquired by the organization, they must be managed throughout their life cycle. This typically requires assigning a person to manage the group of assets, such as laptops, servers, and hotspots. This is a critical step in the management of the asset. The person who manages the assets is responsible for identifying users who are assigned to the devices in the event of termination. The responsible person is also required to forecast upgrades and perform accounting for all assets over their life cycles. Each organization has its own requirements, but these are the top requirements for asset management.

Common Documentation

Documentation is extremely important to an IT department, not to mention the entire organization. It serves many different purposes, such as educating new IT workers, recording work performed, highlighting problems, and describing normal functionality. However, documentation is usually one of the functions that suffer the most when projects are hurried and there is a push to start the next project.

In the following sections, we will cover the most common documents that help support the IT department and day-to-day operations. Some of these documents are prepared by collecting information in a specific manner and then detailing the results; examples are site surveys and baseline configurations. However, many of these documents simply detail how the network is connected and how it functions. The documentation process of the existing network components is usually the best way to learn the network.

Acceptable Use Policy

An *acceptable use policy (AUP)* is an internal policy used to protect an organization's resources from employee abuse. Employees use a number of resources to conduct an organization's business. Email is one such example. It is generally not acceptable for an employee to use an organization's email for religious, political, or personal causes; illegal activities; or commercial use outside of the organization's interest.

An organization's legal counsel, human resources department, and IT department are responsible for developing the AUP. The systems that should be included in the AUP are telephone, Internet, email, and subscription services that the organization retains. The AUP might not be exclusive to electronic resources; the organization might also include postage and other nonelectronic resources that could be abused.

Network Topology Diagrams

Documentation should be the last step of the work you perform—we can't stress that enough. When you use documentation in respect to network troubleshooting, the documentation allows you to understand a problem, and documentation is created as you collect information. You gain an understanding of the problem by summarizing what you've learned about a problem into a drawing on a page. This, in turn, allows you to understand how something works and why it works. This type of documentation is called a *scratch diagram*. It is not formal documentation; it's just scratched out with a pen and paper, as shown in Figure 22.3.

FIGURE 22.3   Scratch documentation

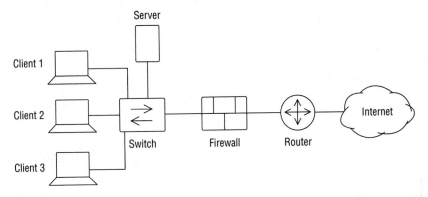

Although a scratch diagram is great for diagnostics, it's not meant to be the final formal documentation of a project or system. A *finish diagram* should be created in a program such as Microsoft Visio or SmartDraw. These are just a few examples of programs used for network documentation; many others are available.

Regardless of which you program you choose, you should create all documentation in the program, and all your staff should have access for modifications. Figure 22.4 shows an example of finished diagram that you might produce from the scratch diagram in Figure 22.3. This documentation is much more refined and would most likely be your final documentation at the end of a project, problem, or implementation of a network system.

FIGURE 22.4   Finish diagram

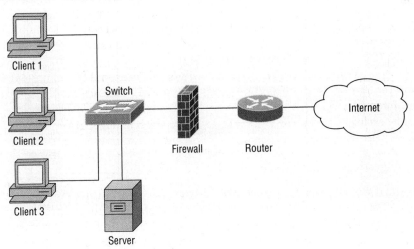

There are some common symbols that you can use when creating either a scratch diagram or a finished diagram. The symbols shown in Figure 22.5 are universally recognized by network professionals. Although you can adapt your own symbols for variation, they should remain similar to those shown here so that someone does not have to ask you what something represents.

FIGURE 22.5 Common networking symbols

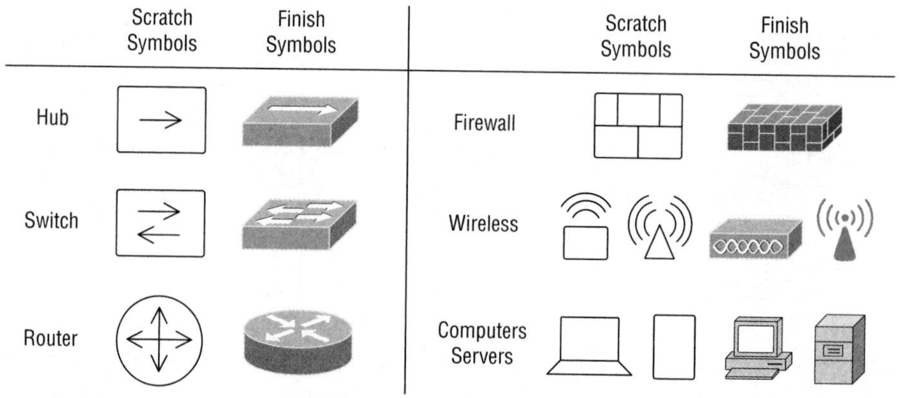

	Scratch Symbols	Finish Symbols		Scratch Symbols	Finish Symbols
Hub	→		Firewall		
Switch	⇄		Wireless		
Router	⊕		Computers Servers		

Logical Diagrams

Logical diagrams are useful for diagnostic purposes and for creating high-level documentation. They allow you to see *how* a network works and represent the logical flow of information. In the logical diagram shown in Figure 22.6, you can see that Client 1 can communicate directly with the other computers on the same network segment. However, if Client 1 wants to communicate with Client 3, it must communicate through the router.

FIGURE 22.6 A logical network diagram

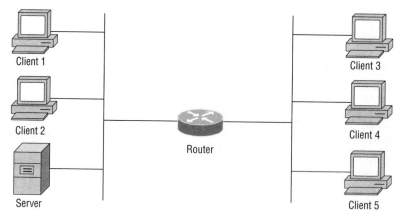

Physical Diagrams

Physical diagrams are also useful for diagnostic purposes and for creating precise documentation. Physical diagrams define a network's physical connections. The physical documentation details *why* a network works by showing exactly how the information will flow. For example, in the physical diagram shown in Figure 22.7, you can see exactly how Client 1 is connected to the network and the devices it will traverse when it communicates with Client 3.

FIGURE 22.7   A physical network diagram

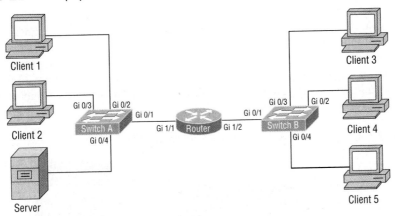

Regulatory and Compliance Policy

You may wonder why it's necessary to follow a certain procedure. The answer sometimes is that the procedure is an outcome of a law, otherwise known as a *regulation*. Laws are created at the federal, state, and local levels. The laws that are externally controlled and imposed on an organization are called regulations. The following are various regulations you may encounter while working in IT:

Sarbanes–Oxley Act   The Sarbanes–Oxley Act (SOX) affects publicly traded companies. It regulates how companies maintain financial records and how they protect sensitive financial data. The Securities and Exchange Commission (SEC) enforces SOX compliance.

Health Insurance Portability and Accountability Act   The Health Insurance Portability and Accountability Act (HIPAA) affects health-care providers and providers that process health records. It regulates how a patient's information is secured and processed during the patient's care. HIPAA regulations are imposed on health-care providers to ensure patient privacy. The Department of Health & Human Services (HHS) enforces HIPAA compliance.

Family Educational Rights and Privacy Act   The Family Educational Rights and Privacy Act (FERPA) affects education providers and organizations that process student records.

FERPA regulates the handling of student records, such as grades, report cards, and disciplinary records. It was created to protect the rights of both students and parents for educational privacy. The Department of Education enforces FERPA compliance.

Gramm–Leach–Bliley Act   The Gramm–Leach–Bliley Act (GLBA) affects providers of financial services. GLBA requires financial institutions that offer products and services, such as loans, investment advice, or insurance, to safeguard customer information and detail the practices for sharing consumer information. It was created to protect consumer information and avoid the loss of consumer information. The Federal Trade Commission (FTC) enforces GLBA compliance.

Your organization must comply with these regulations, or you could risk fines or, in some cases, even jail time. Your organization can comply with regulations by creating internal policies. These policies have a major influence on processes and, ultimately, procedures that your business unit in the organization will need to follow, as shown in Figure 22.8. So, to answer the question of why you need to follow a procedure, it's often the result of regulations imposed on your organization.

FIGURE 22.8   Regulations, compliance, and policies

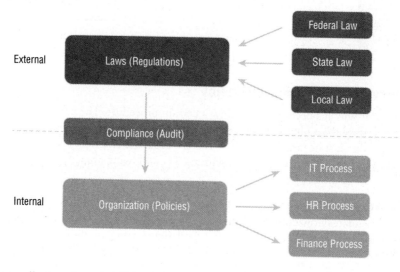

The overall execution of policies, processes, and procedures when driven by regulations is known as *compliance*. Ensuring compliance to regulations is often the responsibility of the compliance officer in the organization. This person is responsible for reading the regulations (laws) and interpreting how they affect the organization and business units in the organization. The compliance officer works with the business unit directors to create a policy to internally enforce these regulations so that an organization is compliant. An audit process is often created so that adherence to the policy can be reported on for compliance.

Once the policy is created, the process can then be defined or modified. A process consists of numerous procedures or direct instructions for employees to follow. Figure 22.9 shows a typical policy for disposing of hazardous waste.

FIGURE 22.9   Policy for disposing of hazardous waste

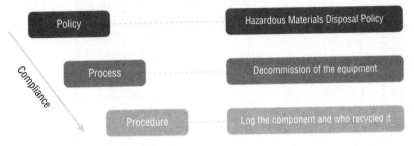

The process of decommissioning network equipment might be one of the processes affected by the policy. Procedures are steps within a process, and these, too, are affected (indirectly) by the policy. As the example shows, a regulation might have been created that affects the handling of hazardous waste. To ensure compliance, a hazardous waste policy was created. The process of decommissioning equipment was affected by the policy. As a result, the procedures (steps) to decommission equipment were affected as well.

Splash Screens

A common documentation method that is widely accepted is the use of splash screens or screen captures to detail a problem, the solution to a problem, or the installation of software. It's a very efficient method because you can quickly illustrate a problem, solution, or installation with simple screen captures. The Windows operating system has a built-in tool called Steps Recorder to assist with obtaining screen captures, as shown in Figure 22.10.

The software will capture mouse clicks and save screen captures, along with some context for what has been clicked. At the end of the screen capture you can review the screens captured, view them as a slide show, and view additional information. You can save everything to a ZIP file containing an MHT (MIME HTML) file that contains all the screen captures in a single file.

Steps Recorder is not the only tool that can be used to capture splash screens. Several third party-applications are available. Each of these has different features that makes it unique. A popular third-party application is Camtasia, which allows the capture of live video screen recording and provides a video editor.

Incident Documentation

An *incident* is any event that is unusual or outside of the normal processes. You may encounter many different types of incidents as a technician: network security incidents, network outage incidents, and even customer service incidents. Regardless of which type of incident transpires, an incident document should be completed so that there is a record of the

FIGURE 22.10   Windows Steps Recorder

event. A record of the incident allows for further review after the incident has subsided so that it is not repeated.

The incident document should be completed as soon as possible so that key details are not forgotten. This document is often used as an executive brief for key stakeholders in the company, such as C-level people—for example, the chief information officer (CIO). The incident document can also be public-facing and used to inform customers of the incident. When used in this fashion, the incident document allows the organization to communicate with transparency about a major incident they allow may have experienced. Chapter 21, "Safety and Environmental Concerns," covered the processes and procedures for incident response in further detail. Here are common elements of a network incident document:

Date and Time   The date and time of the incident is probably the most important element, because several incidents could happen on the same day. The date and time allow you to distinguish between various incidents. The date and time should be referenced using the *Universal Time Code (UTC)* so that someone anywhere in the world does not need to calculate the time offset.

Summary   The incident summary is another important piece of information that should be documented. It will often be the first thing that is looked at because it describes what happened during the incident.

Root Cause   The root cause is the reason the incident occurred. Every incident needs to have a root cause defined; otherwise, the incident could happen over and over again. The network team's first responsibility is to identify the root cause.

Actions Taken   The actions taken are the actions that transpired during the incident to rectify the situation. Most of the time, they are temporary actions so that business can resume.

Remediation   The remediation is the ultimate fix that will repair the root cause of the incident. This could be as simple as installing a patch, or it could be as complex as redesigning a network component.

Services Impacted   The services impacted section details all the network systems and business units that were affected during the incident. This section defines the severity of the incident.

Recommendations   The recommendations section details the next steps to take to remediate the issue. It also explains how to avoid similar incidents in the future.

Although these are the most common elements of an incident document, the document is not limited to these elements. Each organization has different needs for the process of reviewing network incidents. A template should be created so that there is consistency in the reporting of incidents.

Standard Operating Procedures

When organizations create policies, they will outline specific processes to adhere to the policies. Throughout this discussion you may see the words *policy* and *plan*. Policies are also considered plans for the organization; once a plan is ratified, it becomes a policy. Put another way, a policy is a mature and enforced plan of action. Each process derived from the plan or policy contains a list of steps that are called *standard operating procedures (SOPs)*, as shown in Figure 22.11. All of these components are part of the documentation process for a *quality management system (QMS)*. QMSs are created to meet certain International Organization for Standardization (ISO) requirements. A common ISO certification is ISO 9001. When a company is ISO certified, it means that it adheres to strict quality standards for consistent outcomes and has a detailed operation plan. There are many information technology ISO

FIGURE 22.11   Standard operating procedures

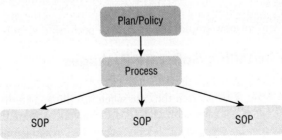

standards that your organization can be certified with. You have probably seen these certifications in a sales manual at some point.

A process in a QMS is just that—a process. A process is defined as taking an input and creating an output. Here's an example: A specific server needs to be decommissioned, which is the input to the process of decommissioning a server, and the output of the process is that the server is wiped clean of corporate information. The process in this example is the decommissioning of a server. (We are oversimplifying the process in this example.) Most processes have an input specification and an output specification.

The SOP in this example outlines how to perform the process of decommissioning the server. The SOP should clearly explain who is responsible and the standard they must achieve for the process. In the example of a decommissioned hard drive, the SOP would define the following:

- Who is responsible for removal of the server from the rack
- Who is responsible for wiping the drives in the server
- What standard should be used to wipe the drives
- Who is responsible for removing DNS entries
- Who is responsible for removing firewall rules
- Who is responsible for clearing the BIOS/UEFI
- In which order the tasks are performed

Several tasks are created from the SOP document. Each task is defined as part of the procedure to achieve the decommissioning of the server. The work instructions serve two primary purposes. The first is to detail how each task should be performed. The exact steps are listed in the work instructions, and for the previous example, they may include the following:

- How to remove the server from the rack
- How to wipe the drives in the server
- How the drives should be wiped
- How to remove the DNS entries
- How to remove the firewall rules
- How to clear the BIOS/UEFI

The second purpose of the work instructions is to provide a training process for new employees. The work instructions are a more detailed portion of the procedure, so it becomes a training item for new employees on how to perform their job.

Procedures for Installing Software Packages

If something is worth doing the first time, then it's worth documenting and chances are it will need to be done again. This is often the case when installing custom software packages. When a new software package is purchased, a technician is often assigned to assist and install the application for the users. It is that technician's responsibility to document the software installation process. This ensures that other technicians will not have to start from scratch to help the next user who needs the software package installed.

Documenting the software installation will save time for consecutive installations. It also allows the initial technician to pass the knowledge on to other teammates. This is obviously important for the rest of the IT team, and it's also important for the initial technician. It is often the case that the original technician will be assigned the consecutive installation, mainly because they are the only ones who know how to install the software. Therefore, documenting the process of installing the software serves two purposes of saving time and passing information on to other teammates.

Onboarding/Offboarding Procedures

As employees are hired in your organization, a certain amount of initial interaction with IT is required. This interaction is called the *onboarding procedure* and is often coordinated with the HR department in your organization. During the onboarding procedure a *new-user setup checklist* should be followed. Examples of the items on the checklist include showing the user how to log in the first time and changing their password. The password policy is often the first policy discussed with the user. Other policies such as bring your own device (BYOD), acceptable use policies (AUPs), and information assurance should also be discussed during the onboarding procedure. Email, file storage, and policies should be covered as well. Each organization has a different set of criteria that make up the onboarding procedures.

Eventually, employees will leave your organization. The offboarding procedure ensures that information access is terminated when the user is terminated. A *user termination checklist* should be followed during the offboarding procedure. The process will be initiated by the HR department and should be immediately performed by the IT department. This process can be automated by using the organization's employee management system. The procedure can also be manually performed if the employee management system is not automated. However, the procedure must be performed promptly, since access to the company's information systems is the responsibility of the IT department. During the offboarding procedure, email access or BYOD access is removed through the use of the mobile device management (MDM) software; the user account is disabled; and IT should make sure the user is not connected to the IT systems remotely. The offboarding procedure may also specify that a supervisor must assume ownership of the terminated employee's voicemail, email, and files.

Knowledge Base/Articles

If time is spent on a problem, it's worth documenting so that the same amount of time is not required by someone else or yourself in the future. A *knowledge base* is a collection of problems with solutions that both your internal customers (IT staff) and external customers (end users) can use to solve common problems. The Microsoft Knowledge Base is a great example of a knowledge base. It contains more than 200,000 public articles and just as many that are private and accessible only by partners. Most helpdesk software allows for the creation of a knowledge base article from the resolution of a problem. A knowledge base can become very large, so many knowledge bases allow keyword searches.

Fortunately, you don't need fancy helpdesk software to create a knowledge base. You can simply have a collection of articles that are accessible to either your colleagues or your end users. A knowledge base article should be clear and easy to understand. Make sure that you define any terms or jargon used within the article so that you don't lose the audience it is intended for. Here are common elements of a typical knowledge base article:

Title   The title should represent the key symptom of the problem and be action based. For example, if the problem is that the Num Lock key stays on after the system boots up, the title could be "Num Lock Enabled After Boot."

Introduction   The introduction should explain, in plain language, what the rest of the article will cover. It should include the thesis of the problem as well as the systems affected by the problem.

Symptoms   The symptoms section explains how to identify the symptoms of the problem. It assists the user in validating that the problem covered in the introduction is affecting their system. This section can include steps to reproduce the problem. For example, after a fresh bootup and login, your Num Lock key stays lit up.

Solution   The solution section contains the steps to fix the issue outlined in the introduction. The solution should not be restricted to just one solution; many solutions can be detailed, as well as work-arounds, if the primary solutions cannot be implemented.

More Information   The more information section contains a list of resources that were used to formulate the solution. This section is important because the symptoms might be similar to those of another problem or an unidentified problem. The resources listed will allow the technician to research the problem deeper.

Date   The date is important because it allows the reader to see if the problem is an old problem or a newer one, to gauge how relevant the solution is to the current problem.

Author   The author section allows for the technician reading the knowledge base to contact the original technician who created the article.

Although these are the most common elements for a knowledge base article, you are not constricted to only these elements. Whichever format you end up using, it is important to be consistent. A template should be drafted so that there is consistency. Consistency allows either the technician or the end user to expect the elements when they review the article.

Change Management Best Practices

When you implement a new system or change an existing system, you affect a lot of people. You also affect business processes and other business units with these changes. Don't underestimate the power of the documentation you produce as a technician. It can and often will be used by change management groups to review the impact of your proposed changes.

Change management is a process often found in large corporations, publicly held corporations, and industries such as financial services that have regulatory requirements. However, change management is not exclusive to these types of organizations. The main purpose of change management is to standardize the methods and procedures used to handle changes in the company. These changes can be soft changes of personnel or processes, or hard changes of network services and systems.

When changes are proposed to a process or set of processes, a document is drafted called the *change management plan document*. This document is used throughout the change management process to evaluate the impact to the business continuity of the organization. In the following section, we will discuss the elements of a change management plan document.

Documented Business Processes

The documented business process is incorporated into the change management plan document. It provides an overview of the business process that the changes are expected to affect. It allows everyone involved in the process both directly and indirectly to understand the entire process.

The documentation specifically defines who interacts with, how they interact with, why they interact with, and when they interact with the process. For example, if your company created widgets, your documentation might detail the process of manufacturing the widget. The document would describe the following:

- How the raw components enter the production line
- Who delivers the raw materials
- When they deliver the raw materials
- Who assembles the raw materials to create a finished product
- Who inspects the finished product
- When and how the product is shipped

Change Rollback Plan (Backout Plan)

The *rollback plan*, also called the backout plan, describes the steps to roll back from a failed primary plan. If it were determined that the primary plan could not be completed, you would either implement an alternate (secondary) plan or a rollback plan, depending on the changes proposed in the change management plan document. Like the primary and alternate plans, the rollback plan should contain the steps to be taken in the event the rollback plan must be executed. The rollback plan should also document any changes to configuration so that it can be reverted back. Most of the rollback plan will consist of the original configuration, with any additional steps to revert it back.

Sandbox Testing

Sandbox testing is extremely useful when you want to test a change before placing it into production. A sandbox can be constructed to match your environment; you can then implement the change and fine-tune your primary plan. The use of a sandbox testing environment allows you to hone your process for the proposed change while observing any potential issues.

The introduction of virtual machines makes it very easy to set up a sandbox for testing. You can clone production servers into an isolated network and then create snapshots on the server in the sandbox and test over and over again, until all the bugs are worked out of the primary plan.

Responsible Staff Member

Every process in the organization must have a person who is assigned to be the *responsible staff member*. This person oversees the process and can answer questions about the process. If there are any changes to the process or changes that can affect the process, this person acts as the main point of contact. They can then facilitate any changes to the process.

As an example, you may assign a person to be the responsible party for the electronics decommissioning process. Any questions about disposal of electronics should be directed to this person. If your organization is choosing a new e-waste company, it will affect the decommissioning process. Therefore, this person should be included in the decision as a stakeholder. Any changes can then be adjusted or integrated into the decommissioning process, and this person can facilitate the changes.

Request Forms

The change management process often begins with a *request form* that details the proposed change. The exact elements in the request form will differ slightly depending on your organization's requirements. The following lists the most common elements found on the change management request form. Some of the information found on the request form is preliminary; the information will be expanded upon as the request form transitions into the change control document.

Item to Be Changed   This is the item that is being requested for a change. Examples are software, hardware, firmware, configuration, or documentation.

Reason   The reason the item is being submitted for a change. Examples are legal, marketing, performance, software bug, or process problem.

Priority   The urgency, or priority, of the change is documented in this section of the form, although this should also be conveyed in the reason for the change. The priority is often a separate field on the change control form. Examples are emergency, urgent, routine, or a specific date.

Change Description/Plan   The description or plan for the change is documented in this section. For changes in configuration, you would detail the changes to the configuration and why each part of the configuration is being changed. Firmware changes would list the version being upgraded from and the version being upgraded to.

Change Rollback Plan   The rollback plan describes the steps to roll back from a failed primary plan. If it was determined that the primary plan could not be completed, you would implement either an alternate plan or a rollback plan depending on the changes proposed.

Technical Evaluation   In this section of the form, you document why the primary plan will succeed. The changes should be tested in a lab environment closest to the production environment and documented in this section. When you're creating the technical evaluation, outline specific objective goals along with the metrics with which they can be measured.

Duration of Changes   Here, you document the estimated duration of the change process. Any service outages will be documented in this section.

Purpose of Change

The *purpose of change* is the reason the change management process starts. Either your business unit requires a change that will affect others, or another business unit requires a change that can affect your business unit indirectly. A change to any part of the process, such as the intake of raw materials, could affect the end result. Change is an essential component of a business, and it should be expected. If your company only created widgets and never evolved, you would eventually be out of business.

Unfortunately, not all changes support the company's product line directly. Some changes are imposed on the company, because IT systems are constantly changing. As a technician, you are constantly upgrading and patching systems and equipment. These upgrades and patches are considered changes that can affect the entire business process.

This section of the change management plan document should explain why the change is necessary. It needs to include any vendor documentation explaining the change to the product. For example, if the proposed change were to install a Microsoft Windows security patch, the purpose of the change would be the security of the Windows operating system. The vendor documentation in this example would be the knowledge base article that normally accompanies Windows security patches. Other examples of purposes of change might be legal, marketing, performance, capacity, a software bug, or a process problem that requires a change.

Scope of Change

The *scope of change* details how many systems the proposed change will affect. The scope could involve only one system, or it could be all the systems in an entire enterprise. The scope of change is not limited to the number of systems that will be changed. The scope can also describe how many people a proposed change will affect. For example, if you propose to change lines of code in an ordering system, the change could affect your salespeople, customers, and delivery of the products. The scope of this change could impact the business continuity directly if something goes wrong during the change.

When creating this section of the change management plan documentation, be sure to document which systems the proposed change will affect, the number of systems the proposed change will affect, the number of people the proposed change will affect, as well as whether anyone will be directly or indirectly affected. In addition, you should include the proposed date and time of the change and how long the change will take. Keep in mind that this section allows the change management team to evaluate how big the proposed change is. The scope should answer the following questions:

- Who will the change affect?
  - IT resources
  - Other departments
  - Business units
  - Partners
  - Customers
- What will the change affect?
  - IT systems
  - Sites/locations
  - Processes/procedures
  - Availability of systems
  - Outage duration
- What will be impacted?
  - Other proposed changes
  - System performance
  - System capacity
  - Other resources (personnel, security, etc.)
- When is the proposed change?
  - Date and time of the change
  - Duration of the change

Risk Analysis

Whenever a change is made to a system or equipment, there is the potential for the system or equipment to fail. The change could even cause another system or piece of equipment to fail. In some circumstances, the change might be successful but inadvertently cause problems elsewhere in the business process. For example, if a change to an ordering system causes confusion in the ordering process, sales might be inadvertently lost.

Risk analysis is the process of analyzing the proposed changes for the possibility of failure or undesirable consequences. Although you will include this section in the initial change management plan document, your sole risk analysis will be narrow in perspective, because you will focus on the process from the IT aspect. A change advisory board will perform a much larger risk analysis. This team will have a much larger perspective, since they come from various business units in the organization. From this analysis, a proper risk level to the organization can be determined. The risk level will dictate how much time is spent on the possibility of failure or undesirable consequences from the change.

Plan for Change

The plan for change section of the change management plan document explains how the proposed change will be executed. Steps should be detailed on the changes and the order of the changes. If changes were to be made in configuration files, switches, or routers, you would document the changes to the configuration and why each part of the configuration is being changed. Firmware changes would list the version being upgraded from and the version being upgraded to. The idea is to provide as much detail as possible about the documented changes to be made to the systems or equipment.

When a change is implemented or planned, there is always the potential for problems, or you may identify a consideration in the execution of the plan. The plan for change section should detail those considerations. It's common for a primary plan to be drafted as well as an alternate plan in the event the primary plan cannot be executed. For example, if the primary plan is to move a server from one rack to another so that it can be connected to a particular switch, the alternate plan could be to leave it in the rack and use longer cables. Be sure to have multiple plans; once the change is approved, the plan(s) outlined in this document must be executed closely.

You should also document why the primary plan will succeed. The changes should be tested in a lab environment closest to the production environment (if possible) and documented in this section as well. When creating the plan, you should outline specific, objective goals, along with the metrics with which they can be measured. For example, if you are planning to make a change because there is a high error rate on an interface, then the metric measure to be compared would be the error rate on the interface. You would document what you expect the error rate to be after the change is made so that you can measure the success of the change.

Change Board

The change board, also known as the *change advisory board*, is the body of users who will ultimately evaluate and then approve or deny the change you propose. This group of people often meets weekly to discuss the changes detailed in the change management plan documents. The goal of the change advisory board is to evaluate the proposed changes in order to reduce the impact on day-to-day operations of the organization.

It is common practice for the meetings of the change advisory board to be held via a conference call at a set time every week. This allows key stakeholders in an organization to be available regardless of where they are in the world. Because it's at a set time every week, there are no excuses for not being available during the change control meetings.

It is likely that if you are the technician proposing the change, you will be on the call for questions or clarification. The key to getting a change approved is to know your audience and communicate clearly in the change control plan document. Remember, the change advisory board is often composed of various stakeholders from the entire organization, not just IT. You should not assume that the change you are proposing is as clear to them as it is to you. Some change advisory boards are made up strictly of IT stakeholders, so you must understand who will review the proposed changes and choose your wording appropriately.

The change management document must be approved by the majority of change advisory board members or by specific board members. The approval of the proposed change should be documented in the change control policy for the organization. Only approved changes can be executed. If other changes need to be made outside of the original submission, additional approvals must be acquired.

> Each organization is different, and each change management documentation process will be slightly different. However, the sections described here are the most common elements found on these documents.

User Acceptance

Although the CompTIA A+ exam does not focus on application development testing and approval, *user acceptance* is an objective on the exam as it pertains to the change management process. It should be noted that user acceptance is not solely used for application development; it is also used when there is a significant update to an interface or a process, such as a service pack or upgrade to an operating system.

When a change is to be made in which the user's interaction will be impacted, it is common practice to beta-test the change. This is also known as user testing or just plain application testing. You can achieve user acceptance two different ways:

In-Person Testing   The person responsible for testing dedicates time and performs testing in person with the developer.

Self-Paced Testing   This has its advantages, since the user will be relaxed in their own environment during testing.

Regardless of which method of testing you choose, a strict time frame must be communicated to the user testing the change.

Once user acceptance is obtained, it should be documented in the user acceptance section of the change management documentation. The methods of testing, the users and groups involved in testing, and the time invested in testing should be included in this section as well. Remember that the goal is the approval and successful implementation of the changes, so it is important that you are convincing and, more importantly, convinced that the change will succeed without repercussions.

Disaster Prevention and Recovery

As a technician you're responsible for preventing disasters that could impact the organization. You're also responsible for recovering from uncontrolled disasters. Luckily, you can prevent disasters by taking the proper precautions, as we will discuss in the following sections.

When you take steps to prevent disaster, you'll find that you're prepared when disaster strikes and can restore business continuity that much more quickly. This section discusses the following types of disasters:

- Data loss

- Power-related issue

Both of these types of disasters have the potential for data loss and work stoppage.

Data Backups

When we think of data backups, we usually relate them to disasters. However, data backups are not just used to restore from disaster; we often use data backups when a user inadvertently deletes files they shouldn't have deleted. Data backups are also used when users overwrite files or just plain forget where they put them in the first place. Regardless of how the data was lost, the underlying reason we create data backups is to recover from data loss.

Because you can't choose the disaster or situation that causes the loss of data, you should adopt a layered strategy, starting with the user and expanding outward to the infrastructure. The following sections cover several different types of strategies that can protect you from data loss.

File Level Backups

Most of the time, your users will need to restore a single file or perhaps a few files, but definitely not the entire server or server farm. Therefore, you should make sure that one of the layers of protection allows for the restoration of individual files. You can implement this type of strategy several different ways. Depending on your resources, you should use them all.

Volume Shadow Copy

Volume Shadow Copy, also known as the *Volume Snapshot Service (VSS)*, has been an integral part of the Windows Server operating system since the release of Windows 2000. Volume Shadow Copy can be enabled on a volume-by-volume basis. Once it's turned on, all the shares on the volume are protected. You can access Volume Shadow Copy by right-clicking a volume and selecting Properties. You can then configure it by using the Shadow Copies tab, as shown in Figure 22.12.

Volume Shadow Copy has one amazing advantage: it empowers the user to restore their own files. All the user needs to do is right-click the file or empty space in the shared folder, select Properties, and then in the Properties window, select the Previous Versions tab. This will open a list of snapshots, as shown in Figure 22.13. The user can then double-click the snapshots to open them as if they were currently on the filesystem. This allows the user to evaluate what they are looking for. Once they find what they are looking for, they can either click the Restore button or drag the files over to the current folder.

One limitation to Volume Shadow Copies is the number of snapshots that can be active. Only 64 snapshots can be active at one time. The oldest snapshot is deleted when a new snapshot is created to maintain a running total of 64 snapshots. By default, Volume Shadow

FIGURE 22.12 The Shadow Copies tab

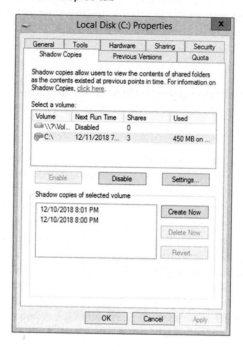

FIGURE 22.13 The Previous Versions tab

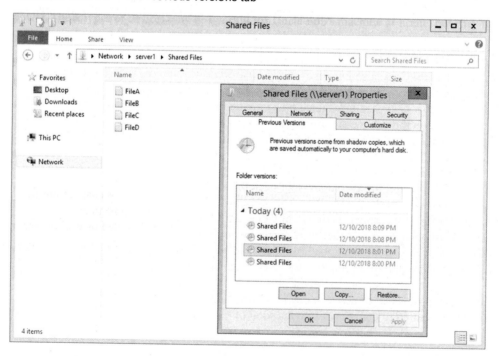

Copy is not enabled. When it is enabled, the default schedule creates a snapshot twice a day, at 7 a.m. and 12 p.m. It's advisable to set a schedule that creates a snapshot every hour during normal business hours. This will give the user the last 64 hours of work, which could be well over a week and a half, if you were open 9–5.

File-Based Backups

File-based backups are a common type of backup in organizations today and have been since the introduction of backup software. The Windows Server operating system includes a backup program capable of protecting the local server, as shown in Figure 22.14. It is somewhat limited, because it only supports a file-based destination and does not offer options for data tapes. It also only allows for the management of the local server. However, the product is free and is included with the Server operating system, so there is no reason not to have some type of backup.

FIGURE 22.14 Windows Server Backup

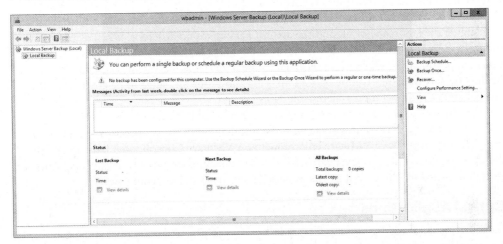

Advanced backup software, such as Veeam Backup & Replication and Veritas Backup Exec, allows for the centralized management of all backups. Multiple backup jobs can be created for various groups of servers and can be directed to various destinations. For example, the accounting servers might back up to a tape library unit, whereas the sales servers back up to a disk storage unit. We'll discuss media type later in this chapter, but the key takeaway is that multiple jobs can be created and executed at the same time.

Advanced backup software often requires a licensed agent to be installed on each server. Depending on the type of agent purchased, the agent might just allow for a simple backup of files, or it might allow for open files to be backed up while they are in use. Some agents even allow for the snapshot of all files so that a point-in-time image can be made of the filesystem. The backup is then created from the snapshot. This type of backup is common in financial institutions, where an end-of-day cutoff needs to be created.

Advanced backup software normally performs a pull of files from the selected source server and directs the information to the selected media. This is called the pull backup method, and it is probably the most common type of backup you will encounter. However, there are also push backup methods, in which the backup software directs the selected source server to push the files to the destination media using the backup server. This reduces the utilization on the backup server and speeds up the backup process, also known as the backup window.

Image-Based Backups

Image-based backups allow for a complete server to be backed up. This type of backup is also called a *bare-metal backup*. It's called a bare-metal backup because if the server hardware were to fail, you would restore the backup to a new server (bare-metal) and restore it completely. The inherent problem with these types of restorations is that they require administrator intervention. However, the technology is impressive and spares you from reinstalling the server from scratch.

Virtualized environments are where image-based backups really add value. Virtualization is changing the landscape of IT, and the area of backups is no different. When a server is virtualized, the guest virtual machine consists of configuration files, a virtual filesystem file, and other supporting files. When access is given to the underlying filesystem where the files can be directly accessed, they can be backed up. This allows for an image to be created for the current state of an operating system—files and all.

Most enterprise backup software supports image-based backups for an additional license fee. It normally requires an agent to be installed on the host operating system, such as Microsoft Hyper-V. In VMware environments, a VMware Consolidated Backup (VCB) proxy is required. This application proxy allows the backup software to create snapshots for the guest virtual machines and assists in backing up the virtual machine files.

Critical Applications

So far, we've discussed how to use file server backups to protect an organization. However, an organization does not rely solely on file servers; there are many other types of servers in an organization. Examples include Microsoft SQL, for databases, and Microsoft Exchange, for email. In addition, there are several other types of applications that might be custom to an organization.

Just like file servers, Microsoft SQL and Microsoft Exchange have custom agents that are licensed. These agents allow for the data contained in the proprietary data stores to be backed up to your backup media. In addition to the backup of data, the agent starts a maintenance process at the end of a backup. This maintenance process checks the consistency of the current data store by replaying transaction logs, also called *tlogs*.

Critical applications for an organization do not have to be on site. As organizations adopt a cloud-based approach to IT, they push critical applications out of the network and into the cloud. Providers such as Amazon Web Services (AWS) and Microsoft Azure can provide not only the critical applications but also backup services that are contained in the cloud.

Data Restoration Characteristics

When discussing the restoration of data, two characteristics dictate when you back up and how you back up. The concept of the *recovery point objective (RPO)* defines the point in time that you can restore to in the event of a disaster. The RPO is often the night before, since backup windows are often scheduled at night. The concept of the *recovery time objective (RTO)* defines how fast you can restore the data.

Backup Media

When creating a backup job, you choose what you want to back up (source) and a destination where it is to be stored. Depending on the backup software, you may have several different destinations to select from. Examples include iSCSI storage area networks (SANs), network-attached storage (NAS), tape library units (TLUs), or even cloud-based storage, such as Amazon S3. These are just some examples; there are many different media options for storing backups. Each backup media option uses a specific media type, and each media type has unique advantages and disadvantages. Here are the three media types commonly used for backups:

Disk-to-Tape   Disk-to-tape backups have evolved quite a bit throughout the years. Today, *Linear Tape-Open (LTO)* technology has become the successor for backups. LTO can provide 6 TB of raw capacity per tape, with plans for 48 TB per tape in the near future. Tapes are portable enough to rotate off-site for safekeeping. However, they require time to record the data, resulting in lengthy overall backup time. Restore requires time to tension the tape, locate the data, and restore the data, making the RTO a lengthy process.

Disk-to-Disk   Disk-to-disk backups have become a standard in data centers as well because of the proximity of the data and the short RTO. This type of media is usually based on site and then it is used to create an off-site copy. It can record the data faster than traditional tape, thus shortening overall backup time. It also does not require tensioning and seeking for the data, like a tape requires.

The capacity of a disk, however, is much smaller than a tape because the drives remain in the backup unit. Data deduplication can provide a nominal 10:1 compression ratio, depending on the data. This means that 10 TB of data can be compressed on 1 TB of disk storage. So, a 10 TB storage unit could potentially back up 100 TB of data. Again, this depends on the types of files you are backing up. The more similar the data, the better the compression ratio.

Disk-to-Cloud   Disk-to-cloud is another popular and emerging backup technology. It is often used with disk-to-disk backups to provide an off-site storage location for end-of-week backups or monthly backups. The two disadvantages of a disk-to-cloud backup are the ongoing cost and the lengthy RTO. Anytime you want to restore data, you must download the data from the cloud. Depending on your Internet connection speeds, this could require some time. The advantage is that expensive backup equipment does not need to be purchased along with the ongoing purchase of tapes.

Media Rotation

Administrators will adopt a rotation schedule for long-term archiving of data. The most popular backup rotation is *grandfather, father, son (GFS)*. The GFS rotation defines how tapes are rotated on a *first-in, first-out (FIFO)* basis. One of the daily backups will become the weekly backup on a FIFO basis. And lastly, one of the weekly backups will become the month-end backup. Policies should be created such as retaining 6 daily backups, 4 weekly backups, and 12 monthly backups. As you progress further away from the first six days, the RPO jumps to a weekly basis, then to a monthly basis. The benefit is that you can retain data over a longer period of time with the same number of tapes.

Backups are created for one of two main reasons: accidental deletion and disaster. Therefore, it makes sense that a disaster that could destroy your data center could also destroy the backup media. For this reason, media should be rotated off site from the on site presence of the original media.

The *3-2-1 backup rule* method is a common method for maintaining both on-site and off-site backups. The 3-2-1 method works like this: Three instances of the data should exist at all times. The original copy of the files and a backup of the files should be on site, and the third copy of the data should be off site in the event of tragedy at the site. Here's an example: You create a business proposal on your computer (first instance), and nightly your files are backed up (second instance). You now have two instances local to your immediate site (on site) in the event of an accidental deletion. A second backup job then backs the file up to the cloud. This provides a third instance of the file, which is off site.

There are a number of ways you can achieve this method of disaster recovery. For instance, you create the file, Volume Shadow Copy snapshots the drive on the hour, and a nightly backup copies the file to the cloud for off-site storage.

Backup Methods

There are several options for creating file-based backup jobs. Each backup method has advantages and disadvantages, depending on the media you are using and the amount of time in your backup window. The following are several of the backup methods you will find primarily with file-based backups:

Full   A full backup is just that: a full backup of the entire dataset. A full backup requires the longest backup window of all the methods, because it is the slowest. Therefore, full backups are generally performed on weekends, when you have a lengthy window. All files are backed up, regardless of the state of the archive bit. The archive bit is an attribute of each file; when a file is created or modified, the archive bit is turned on. When a full backup is performed, all the archive bits are reset on the files in the dataset. A full backup is not sustainable through the week because it backs up all the files, regardless of whether they have been modified.

Incremental   An incremental backup is used to speed up backups through the week when backup windows are short. An incremental backup backs up all files with the archive bit set. After the files are backed up, the archive bit is reset. Only the files that were created and modified from the last full or prior incremental backup are backed up, so backups are small. If you need to restore from an incremental backup, however, you will need to restore the full backup as well as all of the incremental backup files up to the RPO required. This type of restore creates a longer RTO because of the multiple backups that are required.

Differential   A differential backup is also used to speed up backups through the week. It will back up all the files with the archive bit set as well, but it will not reset the archive bit after it has done so. A differential backup creates a gradually larger backup until a full backup is completed and the archive bits are reset again. This type of backup has a shorter RTO than incremental backups, because only the full and the last differential backups are needed to restore to the RPO required.

Copy   A copy backup is used when you want to make an exact copy of the server. This backup method is identical to a full backup, with the exception that it does not reset archive bits. This backup method is often used when you want to make a copy of a server before a major upgrade. This backup method allows you to create a backup without affecting an ongoing nightly backup.

Synthetic   A *synthetic backup* is a full backup without the overhead of performing a full backup on the entire dataset. A synthetic backup is performed by the backup software. The software takes the latest full backups and applies the differential backups or incremental backups up to the desired date the job runs. For example, if you create a full backup once a month but want weekly full backups, a synthetic full backup can be created by taking the last full backup and applying the changes up to the current date. The synthetic full backup now serves as a full backup in the event a restore is required, thus lowering the RTO.

Backup Testing

Over the years, we've seen fellow administrators rely on their backups—up to the point when they try to restore them. It's a very different story when they fail during a critical moment. Fortunately, this only happens to you once, and then you adopt testing strategies. You should not consider data on a backup to be safe until you have proven that it has been restored successfully. There are so many things that can go wrong with a restore, the most common being media failure.

We recommend that you perform a restore of your backup at least once a month. This will allow you to verify that you actually have data that is restorable in the event of an emergency. Many backup products actually restores the data and compares allow you to schedule a test restore. The test restore it to what is on the backup media. When it's done testing the restore, it deletes the restored data and notifies you of any discrepancies.

Battery Backup/UPS

An uninterruptable power supply (UPS) is a battery backup system that allows for power conditioning during power sags, power surges, and power outages. A UPS should be used only until a power generator can start supplying a steady source of power. For workstations and server installations where backup generators are not available, the UPS allows enough time for systems to shut down gracefully.

UPSs are most often used incorrectly as a source of power generation during a power outage. The problem with this scenario is that there is a finite amount of power in the battery system. It may allow you some time to stay running, but if the power is out for too long, the UPS will shut down when its batteries are depleted.

UPS systems should be used to supply power while a power generator is starting up. This protects the equipment during the power sag that a generator creates during its startup after a power outage has triggered it.

There are several types of UPS systems. The main types are as follows:

Standby UPS   This is the most common UPS that you find under a desk protecting a personal computer. It operates by transferring the load from the AC line to the battery-supplied inverter. Capacitors in the unit help to keep the power sag to a minimum. These units work well, but they are not generally found in server rooms.

Line-Interactive UPS   This is commonly used for small server rooms and racks of networking equipment. It operates by supplying power from the AC line to the inverter. When a power failure occurs, the line signals the inverter to draw power from the batteries. This might seem similar to a standby UPS, but the difference is that the load is not shifted. In a standby UPS, the load must shift from AC to a completely different circuit (the inverter), whereas on a line-interactive UPS, the inverter is always wired to the load, but only during the power outage is the inverter running on batteries. This shift in power allows for a much smoother transition of power.

Online UPS   An online UPS is the standard for data centers. It operates by supplying AC power to a rectifier/charging circuit, which maintains a charge for the batteries. The batteries then supply the inverter with a constant DC power source. The inverter converts the DC power source back into an AC power circuit again, which supplies the load. The benefit of an online UPS is that the power is constantly supplied from the batteries. When there is a power loss, the unit maintains a constant supply of power to the load. The other benefit is that the online UPS always supplies a perfect AC signal.

Power Generators

Although power generators are not an objective on the 220-1102 exam, for completeness, we want to discuss them in contrast to UPSs. Power generators supply a constant source of power during a power outage. Power generators consist of three major components: fuel, an engine, and a generator. The engine burns the fuel to turn the generator and create power. The three common sources of fuel are natural gas, gasoline, and diesel. Diesel fuel generators are the most common type of generator supplying datacenters around the world. However, natural gas generators are common for small businesses and home installation.

As mentioned in the previous section, generators require a startup period before they can supply a constant source of electricity. In addition to the startup period, there is also a switchover lag. When a power outage occurs, the transfer switch moves the load from the street power to the generator circuit. UPSs help to bridge both the lag and sag in electricity supply during the switchover and startup periods.

Surge Protection

The power specification in North America is around 120 volts 60 Hz alternating current (AC). Normally, your voltage will be plus or minus 10 volts from 120 volts. Most equipment is rated for this variance in electricity. A power surge, however, can be upward of 500 volts for a split second, which is where damage to your equipment occurs.

A power surge can happen for a number of reasons. Two common reasons are lightning strikes and power company grid switches. A lightning strike is probably the most common reason for power surges during a storm. When the lightning hits near an electrical line, it will induce a higher voltage, which causes the surge. After a storm is over, you are still not safe from power surges. When the electrical company transfers a load back on with the power grid switches, a brief surge can sometimes be seen.

Luckily, you can protect yourself from power surges with surge protection. Surge protection can be implemented two different ways: point-of-use and service entrance surge protection. Surge protectors, UPSs, and power conditioners are all point-of-use devices, with surge protectors being the most common and obvious point-of-use device used for protection. Surge protectors look like common power strips but have protection circuits built in that can suppress up to 600 joules of energy. Many of them have coaxial protection for cable modems and telephone jacks, as shown in Figure 22.15. Some surge protectors even have RJ-45 network jacks, to protect your network equipment.

FIGURE 22.15   A common surge protector

Service entrance surge protection, also called a *transient voltage surge suppressor (TVSS)*, is normally installed by your electric company. It is commonly installed between the electrical meter and the circuit breaker box to protect you from any surges from the power grid. Most of these devices can handle over 1,000 joules of surge. These devices often come with a type of insurance from the electric company. In the event you suffer a power surge and your electronics are damaged in the process, you can submit a claim for reimbursement of the damaged equipment. Every electric company is different, so you should check before you contract these services. Figure 22.16 shows an example of a large, industrial service entrance surge protection unit.

FIGURE 22.16   An industrial service entrance surge protection unit

 A single joule is equal to the energy required to produce 1 watt of electricity continuously for 1 second. Ohm's law states that a watt is equal to voltage multiplied by amperage. During a power surge, voltage can exceed 700 joules.

Account Recovery Options

Disaster can strike in several different ways and is not limited to data loss or power problems. A critical admin or user account can be inadvertently deleted or you may simply forget the password. Fortunately, there are several different options, depending on the type of account involved.

Online Accounts

Starting with Windows 8, the push to use Microsoft accounts as your primary login has been emphasized by Microsoft. When you set up Windows for the first time, the default is to use a Microsoft online account. A Microsoft account allows you to download content and applications from the Microsoft Store. It also allows you to recover your account by using Microsoft services. When you sign up for a Microsoft account, you're asked for backup email accounts and even your cell phone number for text messages. All these alternate methods of contact make it easier to recover your account if you lose your password.

Local Accounts

If you are using a local account to log into the operating system, your options will be slightly limited. Fortunately, starting with Windows 10 version 1803, there is a built-in option to recover a password for a local account. During the setup of the administrator account, the operating system will ask you three security questions. If you forget the password, you simply need to answer the security questions you provided during setup to reset the password, as shown in Figure 22.17.

FIGURE 22.17   Windows 10 security questions

If the local account is deleted or the password is forgotten and you are not running Windows 10 version 1803 or later, then your only option is to perform a System Restore on the operating system to restore the affected account. Unfortunately, if the user account is completely deleted, a System Restore will not bring back the user files. It will, however, restore the local user account, after which a traditional restore from it can be performed.

Domain Accounts

You have several options with domain accounts versus local accounts. The first and most obvious option is that with domain accounts you have other privileged accounts. These other privileged accounts can reset passwords if they are forgotten or locked out after too many unsuccessful attempts.

If an account is deleted, you have several options as well, but they require that you've taken preventive measures before the account is deleted. The first option for account recovery with domains is the use of the *Active Directory Recycle Bin*. The Recycle Bin feature first appeared in Windows Server 2008 R2, so you must be running this version of Windows Server or later. A second requirement is having the Recycle Bin enabled, since it is not enabled by default. Once the Recycle Bin is enabled, if an Active Directory user account is deleted, it will show up in the Deleted Objects container. All you need to do is right-click the object and choose Restore.

Another way to restore Active Directory objects is from backup. Almost all Windows backup utilities have a provision for the backup of Active Directory. Even the Windows Backup utility allows for the backup of Active Directory by selecting the backup of the *System State* data on the domain controller. In the event that an object is deleted, most backup products allow you to restore the individual user account with a few clicks.

If you are using the Windows Backup utility, you must perform an authoritative restore, which is a little more complicated than a few clicks. The following is an overview of the steps to perform an authoritative restore with a backup program that supports only the restore of System State, such as the Windows Backup utility:

1. Stop the Active Directory Domain service by using the command **net stop ntds**.
2. Restore the latest System State backup.
3. Use the `ntdsutil` utility to update the object you need to restore.
4. Reboot the server.

Demonstrating Professionalism

As a professional technician, you need to possess a certain level of technical competence, or you'll quickly find yourself looking for work. Technical ability alone isn't enough, though; there are many people out there with skills similar to yours. One thing that can set you apart is acting like a true professional and building a solid reputation. As the noted investor Warren Buffett said, "It takes 20 years to build a reputation and 5 minutes to ruin it. If you think about that, you'll do things differently."

You could probably break down professionalism 100 different ways. For the A+ 220-1102 exam, and for the purposes of this chapter, we're going to break it down into two critical parts: communication and behavior.

Good communication includes listening to what the user or manager or developer is telling you and making certain that you understand completely. Approximately half of all communication should be listening. That a user or customer may not fully understand the terminology or concepts doesn't mean they don't have a real problem that needs to be addressed. Therefore, you must be skilled not only at listening but also at translating.

Professional behavior encompasses politeness, guidance, punctuality, and accountability. Always treat the customer with the same respect and empathy that you would expect if the situation were reversed. Likewise, guide the customer through the problem and the explanation. Tell them what has caused the problem they are currently experiencing and the best solution for preventing it from recurring in the future.

Professional Appearance

Demonstrating professionalism begins with your appearance and attire. You should always dress for the respect and professionalism that you deserve. It's an easy element of being professional, but it is often an overlooked element.

If you dress down, then you will be judged as being less professional than your intellect or position deserves. The customer might not communicate with you the way you'd expect, because the customer will make assumptions about your intellect or position based on your appearance. The opposite can also happen if you overdress. The customer might not give you the same respect that a technician of your caliber might expect. You could be viewed as overqualified for the customer's needs or non-technical.

These judgments shouldn't happen from the customer's perspective, but they often do because of the impression that appearance makes. Therefore, you should always attempt to match the required attire of the environment you are working in. For example, a technician on a construction site should have the expected attire, such as safety equipment and rugged clothes. Showing up in a suit is not what the customer would expect. Conversely, if you showed up at an office environment wearing jeans and a t-shirt you'd be looked at as being unprofessional.

Luckily for IT professionals there are two norms of appearance and attire that are expected, depending on the environment and workplace.

Formal   Business formal, also known as business professional, typically requires that male employees be dressed in a suit and tie. The male attire will consist of a long-sleeve dress shirt, tie, dark or striped pants, a suit jacket, and dress shoes. Female employees should be dressed in a business suit or business skirt. Women's clothes can be lighter in color than men's clothes, and long sleeves are preferable. Women should wear nylons and either heeled shoes or dress shoes.

Business Casual   Business casual is often interpreted as casual and therefore many professional organizations have not embraced it. The standard definition is dress pants or khakis, collared shirt, blazer, and professional-looking shoes. For male employees a tie is not required and the color palette can be lighter for both pants and blazer. Female employees can wear a collared or noncollared blouse, dress or skirt (typically below the knee), along with heels, dress shoes, dress boots, or flats.

The dress attire of the organization will differ slightly from the preceding definitions based on season, organization type, and even the day of the week. It is popular now for organizations to have a casual Friday that differs in definition based on the norm of business formal or business casual the rest of the week. Therefore, it is always best to check with your supervisor or coworkers about what is appropriate and what is not.

Communicating with Customers

The act of diagnosis starts with the art of customer relations. Go to the customer with an attitude of trust. Believe what the customer is saying. At the same time, retain an attitude of hidden skepticism; *don't* believe that the customer has told you everything. This attitude of hidden skepticism is not the same as distrust. Just remember that what you hear isn't always the whole story; customers may inadvertently forget to provide some crucial details.

One of the best ways to become proficient in communicating with customers is to put yourself in the shoes of the novice user. None of us are experts in every field, so think of an area where you are weak—auto repair or home repair, for example—and imagine how you would want a professional in that area to communicate with you.

For example, a customer may complain that their CD-ROM drive doesn't work. What they fail to mention is that it has never worked and that they installed it. On examining the machine, you realize that they mounted it with screws that are too long, preventing the tray from ejecting properly.

Here are a few suggestions for making your communication with the customer easier:

Use proper language.   End users are likely to be less computer literate than you—that's why you are there to fix the problem. Therefore, they might not know computer acronyms, slang, or jargon. In fact, the excessive use of computer terms might make them feel stupid (and make the situation uncomfortable) or make you seem aloof. It's always best to start off with basic terms, such as "Where does it plug into?" If the user answers, "Oh, it's an eSATA SSD," then you know you have the freedom to use more technical terms. Users with computer knowledge will often let you know. Users with little knowledge may be afraid to tell you that they don't understand something because they don't want to look dumb.

Have the customer reproduce the error.   The most important part of this step is to have the customer show you what the problem is. The best method we've seen of doing this is to ask, "Show me what 'not working' looks like." That way, you see the conditions and methods under which the problem occurs. The problem may be a simple matter of doing an operation incorrectly or performing the operation in the wrong order. During this step, you have the opportunity to observe how the problem occurs, so pay attention.

Identify recent changes.   The user can give you vital information. The most important question is, "What changed?" Problems don't usually come out of nowhere. Was a new piece of hardware or software added? Did the user drop some equipment? Was there a power outage or a storm? These are the types of questions that you can ask a user when trying to find out what is different. If nothing changed, at least outwardly, then what was going on at the time of the failure? Can the problem be reproduced? Is there a work-around? The point here is to raise as many questions as you need to ask in order to pinpoint the source of the trouble.

Use the collected information.   Once the problem or problems have been clearly identified, your next step is to isolate possible causes. If the problem cannot be clearly identified, then further tests will be necessary. A common technique for hardware and software problems alike is to strip the system down to bare-bones basics. In a hardware situation, this could mean removing all interface cards except those absolutely required for the system to operate. In a software situation, this may mean disabling elements within Device Manager.

Generally, then you can gradually rebuild the system toward the point where the trouble started. When you reintroduce a component and the problem reappears, you know that component is the one causing the problem.

Customer satisfaction goes a long way toward generating repeat business. If you can *meet* the customer's expectations, you will most likely hear from them again when another problem arises. However, if you can *exceed* the customer's expectations, you can almost guarantee that they will call you the next time a problem arises.

 Real World Scenario

Communication Is Key

Marriages disintegrate when couples do not communicate effectively—or so many experts proclaim. Communication is ranked as one of the most important skills needed to make a marriage work. The same can be said for business partnerships. It is important to make certain that you are listening to your customers, whether they are truly customers in the traditional sense of the word or internal users that you support. You also need to listen carefully to managers and vendors and make sure that you understand them before beginning a project.

Similarly, you need to make certain that the parties in question understand what you are saying to them. It isn't acceptable to resort to the "But I told you…" excuse when customers or partners aren't pleased with the results. Making certain that they understand what you are telling them is as important as making certain that you understand what they are telling you.

Customer satisfaction is important in all communications media—whether you are on site, providing phone support, or communicating through email or other correspondence. If you are on site, follow these rules:

- When you arrive, immediately look for the person (user, manager, administrator, and so on) who is affected by the problem. Make sure that the user knows you are there and assure that person that you will do all you can. Project a positive attitude and confidence that you can resolve their problem.

- Listen intently to what your customer is saying and avoid interrupting them. Make it obvious that you are listening and respecting what they are telling you.

- If there is a problem with understanding the client, go to whatever lengths you need to in order to remedy the situation. Look for verbal and nonverbal cues that can help you isolate the problem. Taking notes is also helpful. Make sure to say something to the user like, "I'm listening, and I am going to write down a few notes just to make sure I remember everything."

- Share the customer's sense of urgency. What may seem like a small problem to you can appear to your customer as if the whole world is collapsing around them.

- Be honest and fair with the customer and try to establish a personal rapport. Explain what the problem is, what you believe the cause is, and what can be done in the future to prevent the problem from recurring.

- Handle complaints as professionally as possible. Accept responsibility for errors that may have occurred on your part and never try to pass the blame elsewhere. Avoid arguing with a customer; it serves no purpose. Resolve the customer's anger with as little conflict as possible. Remember, the goal is to keep the customer, not to win an argument.

- When you finish a job, notify the user that you have finished. Make every attempt to find the user and inform them of the resolution. If you cannot find the customer, leave a note explaining the resolution.

  You should also leave a means by which the customer can contact you if they have any questions about the resolution or a related problem. In most cases, you should leave your business number and, if applicable, your cell phone number, in case the customer needs to contact you after hours.

You should also notify both your manager and the user's manager that the job has been completed.

If you are providing phone support, keep the following guidelines in mind:

- Always answer the telephone in a professional manner, announcing the name of the company and yourself.

- Using the customer's name can help build rapport. Using it in every sentence can sound condescending, but using it once in a while can make you seem more personable.

- Make a concentrated effort to ascertain the customer's technical level and communicate at that level, not above or below it.

- The most important skill that you can have is the ability to listen. You have to rely on the customer to describe the problem accurately. They cannot do that if you are second-guessing or jumping to conclusions before the whole story is told. Ask broad questions to begin, and then narrow them down to help isolate the problem.

It is your job to help extract the description of the problem from the user. For example, you might ask the following questions:

- Is the printer plugged in?
- Is it online?
- Are there any lights flashing on it?

Complaints should be handled in the same manner in which they would be handled if you were on site. Make your best effort to resolve the problem and not argue. Again, your primary goal is to keep the customer.

Close the incident only when the customer is satisfied that the solution is the correct one and the problem has gone away.

End the phone call in a courteous manner. Thanking the customer for the opportunity to serve them is often the best way.

Talking to the user is an important first step in the troubleshooting process. Your first contact with a computer that has a problem is usually through the customer, either directly or by way of a work order that contains the user's complaint. Often, the complaint is something straightforward, such as, "There's smoke coming from the back of my monitor." At other times, the problem is complex, and the customer does not mention everything that has been going wrong. Regardless of the situation, always approach it calmly and professionally, and remember that you get only one chance to make a good first impression.

 **Real World Scenario**

Communication Is Everywhere

Almost every profession stresses the importance of good communication, and the IT industry is no different. Jamie Walters, founder and chief vision and strategy officer for Ivy Sea, Inc., and Sarah Fenson, Ivy Sea's guide to client services, wrote an article for `Inc.com` on steps to smooth conversations (`www.inc.com/articles/2000/08/20000.html`) that included the following advice:

- Don't take things personally. If someone acts inappropriately toward you, just react in a calm manner. They are likely responding that way because of outside factors.

- Admit when you don't know the answer to something. It's okay to defer to somebody else or tell the user or customer that you'll have to look into their complaint and will get back with them as soon as possible.

- It is better to validate someone's feeling or respond to the information that they have given to you than to react to them. For instance, if somebody complains that a help ticket has not been handled in a timely manner, tell them that you understand how they feel and will look into it, instead of reacting in a defensive manner.

- Don't let your personal opinions or feelings get in the way of the real complaint. Try to put yourself in the user's or customer's shoes.

- Be sympathetic. If you need a user to leave their laptop with you overnight, tell them that you realize it's frustrating and apologize.

- Try to provide a solution from which you both can benefit. Look for commonalities between you and the client, and work to find a solution that is agreeable to both of you.

- Try to be as informative as possible when discussing a solution to their problem. Most people are uncomfortable with change, so explaining the benefits of a particular solution might help ease this discomfort.

- Try to keep a positive attitude and be optimistic.

- Always work on your listening skills!

Using Appropriate Behavior

Critical to appropriate behavior is to treat the customer, or user, the way you would want to be treated. Much has been made of the Golden Rule—treating others the way you would have them treat you. Six key elements to this, from a business perspective, are punctuality, accountability, flexibility, confidentiality, respect, and privacy. The following sections discuss these elements in detail.

Punctuality

Punctuality is important and should be a part of your planning process. If you tell the customer that you will be there at 10:30 a.m., you need to make every attempt to be there at that time. If you arrive late, you have given them false hope that the problem will be solved by a set time. That can lead to anger because it can appear that you are not taking the problem seriously. Punctuality continues to be important throughout the service call and does not end with your arrival. If you need to leave to get parts and return, tell the customer when you will be back, and be there at that time. If for some reason you cannot return at the expected time, alert the customer and tell them when you can return.

Along those same lines, if a user asks how much longer the server will be down and you respond that it will up in five minutes only to have it down for five more hours, the result can be resentment and possibly anger. When estimating downtime, always allow for more time than you think you will need, just in case other problems occur. If you greatly underestimate the time, always inform the affected parties and give them a new time estimate.

To use an analogy that will put it in perspective: if you take your car to get an oil change and the counter clerk tells you it will be "about 15 minutes," the last thing you want is to be still sitting there four hours later. If you ever feel that you won't be able to meet the timeline you proposed, communicate that as quickly as possible. It's better to overcommunicate than to have users wondering where you are.

Exercise 22.1 is a simple drill that you can modify as needed. Its purpose is to illustrate the importance of punctuality.

EXERCISE 22.1

Understanding Punctuality

1. Consider this scenario: You call someone important in your life—your spouse, a parent, an in-law, or a close friend—and tell them that you have something very important that you need to discuss. You give that person no other details but ask them to meet you in exactly one hour at a location familiar to both of you.

2. Now imagine that you waited two hours before showing up.

3. What would be that person's reaction? How would that person feel about having to wait for you? What kind of an impact would it have on the person's mood and behavior?

This is an interaction with someone who matters in your life. Imagine how it would affect a customer who does not know you. Punctuality can go a long way toward keeping dialogue pleasant between two parties.

Accountability

Accountability is a trait that every technician should possess. When problems occur, you need to be accountable for them and not attempt to pass the buck to someone else. For example, suppose you are called to a site to put a larger hard drive into a server. While performing this operation, you inadvertently scrape your feet across the carpeted floor, build up energy, and zap the memory in the server. Some technicians would pretend the electrostatic discharge (ESD) never happened, put the new hard drive in, and then act completely baffled by the fact that problems unrelated to the hard drive are occurring. An accountable technician would explain to the customer exactly what happened and suggest ways of proceeding from that point—addressing and solving the problem as quickly and efficiently as possible.

Accountability also means that you do what you say you're going to do, ensure that expectations are set and met, and communicate the status with the customer. Here are some examples of ways to be accountable:

- Offer different repair or replacement options, if they're available.

- Provide proper documentation on the services that you provided.

- Follow up with the customer at a later date to ensure satisfaction.

The last one is the most overlooked, yet it can be the most important. Some technicians fix a problem and then develop an "I hope that worked and I never hear from them again" attitude. Calling your customer back (or dropping by their desk) to ensure that everything is still working right is an amazing way to build credibility and rapport quickly.

Flexibility

Flexibility is another trait that's as important as the others for a service technician. You should respond to service calls promptly and close them (solve them) as quickly as you can, but you must also be flexible. If a customer cannot have you on site until the afternoon, you must make your best effort to work them into your schedule around the time most convenient for them. Likewise, if you are called to a site to solve a problem and the customer brings another problem to your attention while you are there, you should make every attempt to address that problem as well. Under no circumstances should you give a customer the cold shoulder or not respond to additional problems because they were not on an initial incident report.

 You should always follow the express guidelines of the company you work for as they relate to flexibility, empowerment, and other issues.

It's also important that you remain flexible in dealing with challenging or difficult situations. When someone's computer has failed, they likely aren't going to be in a good mood, which can make them a "difficult customer" to deal with. In situations like these, keep in mind the following principles:

Avoid arguing or being defensive.   Arguing with the customer—about anything—is only going to make the situation worse. The customer may be mad and may be yelling at you, but don't argue back, act defensive, or take their comments personally. Try to defuse the situation by calmly reminding them that you're there to help and you want to understand what's going on so you can do that. They may need to vent for a bit, so let them to do that. Just focus on doing what you need to do to resolve the problem.

Don't minimize their problems.   Although the customer's problem might seem trivial to you, it isn't to them. Treat the problem as seriously as they're treating it. Keep in mind that facial expressions and body language are also important. If someone tells you their problem and you look at them like they're delusional, they're probably going to pick up on that, which can make the situation worse.

Avoid being judgmental.   Don't blame or criticize. As previously mentioned, focus on what needs to happen to fix the problem. Accusing the user of causing the problem does not build rapport. Even seemingly innocent statements such as "What did you do to the computer?" can be considered judgmental and put the customer on the offensive. Stick with more neutral language, such as, "Can you help me understand what happened?"

Focus on your communication skills.   If you have a difficult customer, treat it as an opportunity to see how good a communicator you really are. (Maybe your next job will be a foreign ambassador.) Ask nonconfrontational, open-ended questions. "When was the last time it worked?" is more helpful than "Did it work yesterday?" or "Did you break it this morning?" These can help you narrow down the scope of the problem.

Another good tactic here is to restate the issue or question to verify that you understand. Starting with "I understand that the problem is. . ." and then repeating what the customer said can show empathy and proves that you were listening. If you have it wrong, it's also a good opportunity to let your customer correct you so that you're on track to solve the right problem.

Confidentiality

The goal of confidentiality is to prevent or minimize unauthorized access to files and folders and disclosure of data and information. In many instances, laws and regulations require confidentiality for specific information. For example, Social Security records, payroll and employee records, medical records, and corporate information are high-value assets. This information could create liability issues or embarrassment if it fell into the wrong hands.

Over the last few years, there have been a number of cases in which bank account and credit card numbers were published on the Internet. The loss of confidence by consumers due to these types of breaches of confidentiality can far exceed the actual monetary losses from the misuse of this information.

Confidentiality entails ensuring that data expected to remain private is seen only by those who should see it. Confidentiality may be implemented through authentication and access controls.

As a computer professional, you are expected to uphold a high level of confidentiality. Should a user approach you with a sensitive issue—telling you their password, asking for assistance obtaining access to medical forms, and so on—it is your obligation as a part of your job to make certain that information goes no further.

Confidential materials on workspaces and printers should always be protected.

As part of confidentiality, don't ever disclose work-related experiences via social media. You might have had a terrible day and really want to say something like, "Wow, the people at XYZ company sure are insufferable morons," but just don't do it. It's not professional, and it could expose you to legal action.

Respect

Much of the discussion in this chapter is focused on respecting the customer as an individual. However, you must also respect the tangibles that are important to the customer. While you may look at a monitor that they are using as an outdated piece of equipment that should be scrapped, the business owners may see it as a gift from their children when they first started their business.

Treat the customer's property as if it had value, and you will win their respect. Their property includes the system you are working on (laptop/desktop computer, monitor, peripherals, and the like) as well as other items associated with their business. Avoid using the customer's equipment, such as telephones or printers, unless it is associated with the problem you've been summoned to fix.

Another way to show respect is to focus on the task at hand and avoid distractions. For example, you should avoid the following:

- Personal calls

- Texting or social media sites

- Talking to coworkers while interacting with customers

- Personal interruptions

As for texting or talking to coworkers, there may be times when it's appropriate for you to do so based on the situation. The key is to find the right time to do it and, if appropriate, tell the customer what you are doing. For example, after gathering information, you might say something like, "Do you mind if I give my coworker Jen a quick call? The other day she told me about a situation she had that sounded exactly like this, and I want to see if her fix worked well." But then make the call quick and business-focused.

The Customer Respect Group (www.customerrespect.com) measures the behavior of corporations and the respect they give to customers through their websites. Items such as privacy, responsiveness, attitude, simplicity, transparency, and business principles are combined to create a Customer Respect Index (CRI) ranking. The items they rank in the online world are just as important in the offline world and mirror those presented here.

Respecting the customer is not rocket science. All you need to do—for this exam and in the real world—is think of how you would want someone to treat you. Exercise 22.2 explores this topic further. This exercise, like Exercise 22.1, can be modified to fit your purpose or constraints. Its goal is to illustrate the positive power of the unexpected.

EXERCISE 22.2

Surprise Someone

1. Pick a random, toll-free number used for business solicitation and call it.

2. Chat with the operator for a few moments about the company's product or service, and then ask to speak to the supervisor.

3. When the supervisor comes on, commend the operator you were talking to for the job that they have done.

It is likely the operator became confused when you asked to speak to the supervisor; this almost always occurs only in a negative situation. How did the operator handle the request? Did it change the tone of the communication that was taking place? Did they fulfill your request even though they feared they could lose from it? Did the supervisor respond by expecting negative comments? How was the positive information you offered accepted?

Ideally, this illustrated the importance of staying professional and keeping the channel of communication open even in a tough situation. You should be able to adapt this to the workplace when a customer asks to speak to your superior or has another request that is difficult for you to fulfill.

One last area to consider that directly relates to this topic is that of ethics. *Ethics* is the application of morality to situations. While there are different schools of thought, one of the most popular areas of study is known as *normative ethics*, which focuses on what is normal or practical (right versus wrong and so on). Regardless of religion, culture, and other influences, there are generally accepted beliefs that some things are wrong (stealing, murder, and the like) and some things are right (for example, the Golden Rule). You should always attempt to be ethical in everything you do, because it reflects not only on your character but also on your employer.

Privacy

Although there is some overlap between confidentiality and privacy, privacy is an area of computing that is becoming considerably more regulated. As a computing professional, you must stay current with applicable laws because you're often one of the primary agents expected to ensure compliance.

Although the laws provide a minimal level of privacy, you should go out of your way to respect the privacy of your users beyond what the law establishes. If you discover information about a user that you should not be privy to, you should not share it with anyone, and you should alert the customer that their data is accessible and encourage them—if applicable—to remedy the situation. This includes information that you see on their computer, on their desk, on printers, or anywhere else in their facility.

🌐 Real World Scenario

A Little Goes a Long Way

The following examples of respecting and disrespecting the customer come from one of the authors' own experiences:

"My wife and I were in an unfamiliar part of Chicago without ready access to a vehicle when we started to get hungry. I am a meat-and-potatoes man, and I rarely take a chance on anything else. There were no restaurants of that type around, however, and we wound up at an Asian grill. Expecting not to like the buffet, we ordered a side of lettuce wraps and then two buffets and drinks. As it turned out, I liked the buffet a great deal, and I went back through the line many times. We also liked the drinks and got several of those.

"Everything was great, except the waiter forgot to bring the lettuce wraps. I dismissed it and made a mental note to inform the waiter when he brought the bill and have him deduct them from our tab. Instead, the manager brought the bill over when we were finished eating, and he had scribbled on it 'no charge.' When I asked him why, he apologized that no one brought the wraps and said he hoped we would come back another time. I was beside myself with disbelief and thanked him profusely, and since then I have told many people about that restaurant, describing it as the best place in Chicago I know of to eat.

"In a very different situation, while driving home one night, the 'low tire pressure' dashboard light came on. Upon inspection, I could hear the right-rear tire hissing. I drove to a tire store and explained the situation. I had used this same tire store over the past 14 years for tires, oil changes, exhaust, maintenance, and a number of other things on the vehicles I've owned. The manager came out and said that they found a nail in the tire. They removed the nail, patched the tire, and charged me $13. I was delighted, expecting it to cost much more, and so I paid the bill and went on my way.

"The next morning, I woke up to find the right-rear tire completely flat. I canceled the morning's appointment, filled the tire with an air compressor, and drove back to the tire store. The manager came out and told me that they found another nail in that tire; they were going to eat the $13 on this one, but it had better not happen again. I could not believe the insinuation—that I was driving about looking for nails to hit with that one tire just so I could spend my morning taking them for $13! Instead of offering the possibility that they had overlooked a nail the previous night, apologizing for the inconvenience, or anything of that sort, he shifted the responsibility to me. Needless to say, I have not been back since, and all of my repair business is now done elsewhere."

These two examples illustrate two different approaches to treating the customer. In the first example, the customer is well respected and treated better than expected. In the second example, the customer is disrespected and is treated as an inconvenience. Given the lifetime value of customers, it is always better to respect them—and retain them—than to dismiss them offhandedly.

Putting It All in Perspective

Whether you are dealing with customers in person or on the phone, there are rules to which you should adhere. These were implied and discussed in the previous sections, but you must understand them and remember them for the exam.

- Use standard language and avoid using jargon, abbreviations, and acronyms. Every field has its own language, and outsiders feel lost when they start hearing it. Put yourself in the position of someone not in the field and explain what is going on by using words they understand.

- Maintain a positive attitude and tone of voice, and project confidence. The customer is counting on you to fix their problem. The last thing they want is for you to sound defeated when you hear about the problem.

- Listen to your customers and take notes. Allow them to complete their statements and avoid interrupting them. People like to know that they are being heard, and as simple an act as it is, this can make all of the difference in making them feel at ease with your work.

  Everyone has been in a situation where they have not been able to explain their problem fully without being interrupted or ignored. It is not enjoyable in a social setting, and it is intolerable in a business setting.

- Be culturally sensitive. Some people may have a language barrier that makes it difficult to explain their problem. (Think about how much computer language you learned in your high school language courses.) Others may have different habits or practices in their workplace. Be respectful of their world. In some cases, using the appropriate professional titles is a sign of respect, and not using them is an insult.

- Be on time. If you're going to be late, be sure to contact your customer. Not doing so indicates that you think their problem isn't important.

- Avoid distraction and/or interruptions when talking with customers. You need to make them feel that their problem is important and that it has your full attention. Distractions can include personal calls, texting or social media, talking to co-workers, and other personal interruptions.

- Exercise patience with difficult customers and situations.

- Avoid arguing with customers and/or becoming defensive.

- Do not minimize a customer's problem. While it may be a situation you see every day, it is a crisis to them.

- Avoid being judgmental and/or insulting or calling the customer names.

- Clarify the customer's statements and ask pertinent questions. The questions you ask should help to guide you toward isolating the problem and identifying possible solutions. Don't be afraid to nod, ask questions, and repeat to the customer what you think they are saying to make sure that you understand it correctly.

- Don't vent about customers on social media.

Set and meet—or exceed—expectations and communicate timelines and status. Customers want to know what is going on. They want to know that you understand the problem and can deal with it. Being honest and direct is almost always appreciated.

Deal appropriately with confidential materials. Don't look at files or printouts that you have no business looking at. Make sure the customer's confidential materials stay that way.

Summary

In this chapter, we covered ticketing systems and how they are implemented for an organization. We also covered the various documentation types that you will encounter as a technician throughout your career. Some of the documentation is created from external regulations. This, in turn, creates policies, which dictate processes and procedures. You'll create some of the documentation as you are troubleshooting a problem and some of the documentation after fixing a problem. We also covered documentation often used with the change management process.

Next, we looked at disaster prevention and recovery. The two main areas are data loss and equipment failure due to power issues. Data loss can be prevented with data backups and other user-facing strategies, such as Volume Shadow Copy. Power problems can be prevented with the appropriate use of uninterruptable power supplies and surge protection equipment.

Finally, we moved on to professionalism and communication. You should treat your customers as you would want to be treated. Your actions and behavior should let them know that you respect them and their business.

Exam Essentials

Understand the elements of a ticketing system.   You should have a clear understanding of the importance of clear communications in the support process, as well as the important elements in a ticket, such as user information, device information, category of problem, severity of the problem, and most important, the description of the problem.

Know the various types of network diagrams.   Network documentation is used for both troubleshooting and documentation purposes. You should know the difference between physical diagrams and logical diagrams. Also, be familiar with the various symbols you will see in these diagrams.

Know the common documentation in a network.   Incident documentation is created when a computer, network, or security incident has happened. You should be familiar with various elements of this documentation. The acceptable use policy (AUP) is a soft policy that protects an organization's resources from employee abuse. The password policy is also a soft policy that describes best practices for password creation and expectations of the end user.

Know the elements of change management documentation. Change management is adopted by organizations to standardize the methods and procedures for any changes in the organization. Change management documentation is an integral part of this process. It is used to document a change so that it does not impede the organization's operations.

Understand how to prevent disasters and recover from data loss. Data loss is the most common disaster an organization can suffer from on a day-to-day basis. You should understand how to prevent data loss with the implementation of data backups and other prevention methods. You should also understand how to protect an organization from power-related problems using uninterruptable power supplies and surge protection.

Know proper communication techniques. Listen to your customers. Let them tell you what they understand the problem to be, and then interpret the problem and see if you can get them to agree to what you are hearing them say. Treat your customers with respect, whether end users or colleagues, and take their issues and problems seriously. Use professionalism when working with customers, such as minimizing distractions, speaking in plain English, being punctual, and following up.

Review Questions

The answers to the chapter review questions can be found in Appendix A.

1. You just finished repairing a network connection, and in the process you traced several network connections. Which type of documentation should you create so that another technician does not need to repeat the task of tracing connections?

   A. Logical diagram

   B. Knowledge base article

   C. Change management document

   D. Physical diagram

2. You are executing the primary plan in the change management documentation and realize that you cannot proceed. Which section details the original configuration?

   A. Purpose

   B. Risk analysis

   C. Rollback

   D. Plan for change

3. Which section of the change management documentation contains whom the change will affect?

   A. Business processes

   B. Scope of change

   C. User acceptance

   D. Plan for change

4. You just had an outage of Internet connectivity. Which document should you complete so that stakeholders understand the reason for the outage?

   A. Change management documentation

   B. Knowledge base article

   C. Acceptable use policy

   D. Incident documentation

5. Which regulation is enforced by the Securities and Exchange Commission (SEC) to regulate financial records and sensitive financial information?

   A. SOX

   B. FERPA

   C. HIPAA

   D. GLBA

6. You are currently troubleshooting a network issue. Which type of diagram allows you to view the flow of information from a high-level overview? (Choose the best answer.)

    A. Logical diagram

    B. Physical diagram

    C. Symbol diagram

    D. Knowledge base article

7. End users are abusing the email system by selling personal items. Which policy would detail the proper use of the email system for business purposes?

    A. MDM

    B. Password policy

    C. AUP

    D. Incident management

8. Which backup media is the fastest from which to recover?

    A. Disk-to-tape

    B. Disk-to-disk

    C. Disk-to-flash

    D. Disk-to-cloud

9. You need to upgrade a server and want to make a backup of the data before you begin. Which backup method should you choose so that your normal backups are not affected?

    A. Full

    B. Copy

    C. Incremental

    D. Differential

10. Which type of power protection is used between the electricity coming into the premises and the power meter, to protect from surges in electricity?

    A. Surge protector strip

    B. Uninterruptable power supply

    C. Service entrance surge protection

    D. Generator

11. You promised a customer that you would be out to service their problem before the end of the day but have been tied up at another site. As it now becomes apparent that you will not be able to make it, what should you do? (Choose the best answer.)

    A. Arrive first thing in the morning.

    B. Wait until after hours and then leave a message that you were there.

    C. Call the customer and inform them of the situation.

    D. Email the customer to let them know that you will be late.

12. A user reports that a workstation has two significant problems that do not seem related. How should you approach these problems?

   A. Look for what the two problems would have in common.

   B. Assume that a virus is involved.

   C. Deal with each issue separately.

   D. Order a new machine.

13. A customer is trying to explain a problem with their system. Unfortunately, the customer has such a thick accent that you are unable to understand their problem. What should you do? (Choose the best answer.)

   A. Just start working on the system and look for obvious errors.

   B. Call your supervisor.

   C. Ask that another technician be sent in your place.

   D. Apologize and find another user or manager who can help you translate.

14. You have been trying to troubleshoot a user's system all day when it suddenly becomes clear that the data is irretrievably lost. When you inform the customer, they become so angry that they shove you against a wall. What should you do?

   A. Shove the user back, only a little harder than they shoved you.

   B. Shove the user back, only a little easier than they shoved you.

   C. Try to calm the user down.

   D. Yell for everyone in the area to come quickly.

15. A customer tells you that a technician from your company spent three hours on the phone making personal calls. What should you do with this information?

   A. Nothing.

   B. Inform your manager.

   C. Talk to the technician personally.

   D. Ask the customer to prove it.

16. You arrive at the site of a failed server to find the vice president nervously pacing and worrying about lost data. What should you do?

   A. Offer a joke to lighten things up.

   B. Downplay the situation and tell him that customers lose data every day.

   C. Keep your head down and keep looking at manuals to let him know that you are serious.

   D. Inform him that you've dealt with similar situations and will let him know what needs to be done as soon as possible.

17. You are temporarily filling in on phone support when a caller tells you that they are sick and tired of being bounced from one hold queue to another. They want their problem fixed, and they want it fixed now. What should you do?

A. Inform them up front that you are only filling in temporarily and won't be of much help.

B. Transfer them to another technician who handles phone calls more often.

C. Try to solve their problem without putting them on hold or transferring them elsewhere.

D. Suggest that they call back at another time when you are not there.

18. At the end of the day, you finish a job only to find that the user you were doing it for had to leave. What should you do? (Choose two.)

A. Clean up and leave no evidence that you were there.

B. Leave a note for the user detailing what was done and how to contact you.

C. Notify the user's manager and your own manager that you have finished.

D. Put the system back to its original state.

19. A user on the phone does not seem to be able to explain their problem to you without using profanity. That profanity is making you unable to understand their problem. What should you do? (Choose the best answer.)

A. Ask the user to refrain from the offensive language.

B. Overlook the profanity.

C. Hang up.

D. Show them that you know just as many expletives as they do.

20. Which of the following is not a benefit of implementing asset tags for inventory management?

A. Tracking of the equipment

B. Scheduling the depreciation of the equipment

C. Identifying assets

D. Providing ownership of the equipment

Performance-Based Question

You will encounter performance-based questions on the A+ exams. The questions on the exam require you to perform a specific task, and you will be graded on whether or not you were able to complete the task. The following requires you to think creatively in order to measure how well you understand this chapter's topics. You may or may not see similar questions on the actual A+ exams. To see how your answers compare to the authors', refer to Appendix B.

A user has called in and explained they accidentally overwrote a file and need to retrieve the freshest copy of the file. Luckily, you have Volume Shadow Copy configured on the share where the file was overwritten. What are the steps to recover the file?

Appendix A

Answers to the Review Questions

Chapter 1: Motherboards, Processors, and Memory

1. A. The spine of the computer is the system board, otherwise known as the motherboard. All other computer components plug into the motherboard. On the motherboard, you will find the CPU, underlying circuitry, expansion slots, video components, RAM slots, and various other chips.

2. C. DDR4 SDRAM is manufactured on a 288-pin DIMM, as is DDR5 (although the two are keyed differently and are not compatible). DIMMs with 224 pins and 296 pins do not exist. DIMMs with 240 pins are used for DDR2 and DDR3 SDRAM.

3. B. Remember the 8:1 rule. Modules greater than but not including SDR SDRAM are named with a number eight times larger than the number used to name the chips on the module. The initials *PC* are used to describe the module; the initials *DDR* are used for the chips; and a single-digit number after PC and DDR is used to represent the level of DDR. The lack of a single-digit number represents DDR as long as the number that is present is greater than 133 (such as PC1600). Otherwise, you're dealing with SDR (such as PC133). This means that PC3-16000 modules are DDR3 modules and are populated with chips named DDR3 and a number that is one-eighth of the module's numeric code: 2000.

4. D. The ITX motherboard family consists of smaller boards that fit in standard or miniature cases and use less power than their larger counterparts. ATX are "standard" sized motherboards in today's world. AT is a legacy form factor that was bigger than ATX. There are no DTX motherboards.

5. C. The Core i5-10600K is a Comet Lake–series processor, which uses the LGA 1200 socket. LGA 1150 sockets are for older i7s, and the LGA 1366 socket is for even older ones than that. The LGA 1700 socket is for 12th-generation Intel Core processors.

6. B. Thermal paste is used to attach heat sinks and fans to processors. A heat sink usually gets attached to the processor using thermal paste, and then the fan is attached to the heat sink. Superglue would make it adhere, but it does not transfer heat properly—it would likely melt and cause a mess and processor failure.

7. B. Overclocking is when someone sets the speed of the processor to run faster than it was rated for. While overclocking can make a computer faster, it can also cause the processor to overheat, and it voids the warranty. Hyper-threading allows for a processor core to handle multiple processes simultaneously. Virtualization is when you create multiple virtual machines on a computer. Multicore means that the processor has more than one core—it's not a configurable option.

8. A. Liquid cooling systems require a reservoir of liquid and a pump to circulate the liquid. It's possible that the system could malfunction, causing a mess inside the computer. Thermal paste is used to adhere a heat sink to a processor. Heat sinks and fans do not use pumps.

9. C. ARM processors generate less heat than do x64/x86 CISC processors and are therefore better options for mobile devices. LGA is a type of CPU socket.

10. B. Soft power is the feature whereby the front power button acts as a relay to initiate various system power changes, depending on the duration that the button is held. Programmable power, relay power, and hot power are not valid power options.

11. B, F. DIMMs used in desktop motherboard applications have one of four possible pin counts. SDR SDRAM is implemented on 168-pin modules. DDR SDRAM is implemented on 184-pin modules. DDR2 and DDR3 are implemented on 240-pin modules with different keying, and DDR4 and DDR5 DIMMs have 288 pins but different keying. Older dual-channel DIMM modules have 232 pins. Modules with 200 and 204 pins are used in the SODIMM line, and there are no modules with 180 pins.

12. C, D. For virtualization to work, both the CPU and BIOS need to support it. The operating system does as well. Virtualization support may need to be manually enabled in the BIOS. RAM does not need to support virtualization, and neither does the motherboard (except for the BIOS).

13. D. Most motherboards have a jumper or similar momentary closure mechanism that will allow you to clear the CMOS memory of any user settings and cause the BIOS to use factory defaults, including no user or supervisor passwords.

14. A. The easiest solution that works to cool your CPU is to connect the four-pin connector into the three-pin header. The missing pin allows you to control the speed of the fan. Without it, the fan will run at top speed, which is fine, albeit a little noisier. There is no four-pin to three-pin power adapter. The heat sink alone should not be relied upon for proper cooling of modern CPUs, and an extra chassis fan isn't designed to specifically help cool the CPU.

15. C. The PCIe 1.1 specification provided 250 Mbps of throughput per lane per direction. With the 2.x versions of PCIe, this rate was doubled to 500 Mbps. As a result, each v2.0 lane is capable of a combined 1 Gbps. An x16 slot consists of 16 lanes, for a total bidirectional throughput of 16 Gbps.

16. C. The reset button causes the computer to return to nearly the same point it is in when you power it on, but without the need for power cycling. Using Restart in the Start menu does not reboot as deeply as the reset button. Hibernation is a power state that completely removes power after saving the contents of RAM to the hard drive; pressing the power button is required to resume the session in the same manner as starting the computer after a complete shutdown. The power button cannot be used as a method of restarting the system.

17. B. None of the options are required, but a UPS is by far the most helpful among the answers in that loss of power during this procedure can range from annoying to devastating.

18. A. The only viable option listed is to install two new 32 GB DDR4 RAM modules. Check the motherboard documentation first to make sure the system will support that much memory, though. DDR4 does not come in modules larger than 64 GB. DDR5 is not compatible with DDR4 motherboards.

19. C. Laptop motherboards are usually custom-built for the specific case. A replacement board should be obtained that is the exact same size as the one that failed.

20. B. PCIe is the newest and fastest slot for video cards. AGP and PCI are legacy technologies. SATA is for hard drives.

Chapter 2: Expansion Cards, Storage Devices, and Power Supplies

1. **D.** Although technically PCI could be used for graphics adapters, PCIe supports high-speed, 3D graphic video cards. PCIe offers better performance than older graphics adapters. USB can stream video, but it is not used for attachment of internal graphics adapters. NVMe is an SSD communications interface.

2. **A.** A conventional hard disk drive system consists of the hard disk and its often-integrated controller as well as a host adapter to gain access to the rest of the computer system. The drive interface is a common component of the controller and host adapter.

3. **B.** A network interface card (NIC) is used as a communications device. It enables the computer to talk to other computers on a network. It does not provide multimedia, input/output (such as a USB port does), or storage capabilities.

4. **D.** To protect against a power supply failure, use a redundant power supply, which is basically two PSUs in one unit. More wattage will not help if the power supply fails. There are no voltage output selectors on PSUs. There are voltage input switches on some but that wouldn't help in this case. A modular power supply has removable and attachable cables to support a variety of peripherals.

5. **B.** The fastest SSD communications interface is NVMe. SATA 10,000 rpm and 15,000 rpm refer to conventional hard drive spin rates, and conventional hard drives will always be slower than SSDs.

6. **B.** Blu-ray discs have a single-sided, single-layer capacity of 25 GB. A double-sided, single-layer DVD can store about 9.4 GB, and a double-sided, double-layer DVD can store about 17.1 GB.

7. **A.** Hot-swappable devices can be removed while the power to the system is still on. Warm-swappable devices need to be stopped in the operating system before being removed. The term has nothing to do with the heat level of the device.

8. **C.** Power supplies and AC adapters use standard wall outlets for an input of AC voltage, which they convert to the DC voltages required by the components to which they supply power.

9. **A, C, D, E, F.** A PC's power supply produces +3.3VDC, +5VDC, –5VDC, +12VDC, and –12VDC from a 110VAC input.

10. **D.** PC power supplies accept alternating current (AC) as input and produce direct current (DC) for the internal components. Europe requires that the voltage selector switch be set at the higher setting. SATA drives most often use a specific power connector that is not compatible with the Molex connector used by PATA drives. ATX motherboards can have a 20- or 24-pin single power connector but an adapter is not always required.

11. C. Today's hard drives, regardless of their rpm, have standard internal power connections. The other options are valid concerns when installing an internal drive.

12. A. Memory cards such as SD cards were designed for devices such as digital cameras. Optical discs are larger and used mostly with laptops and larger systems. Flash drives are USB. Some cameras may have a USB port, but that is external storage and not internal storage. mSATA is a laptop expansion card technology.

13. A. PCIe video cards may be bridged together, enabling two cards to function as one system. Sound cards and I/O expansion cards such as USB and eSATA cards do not have bridging capabilities.

14. E. For a video card, the best standard currently available is PCIe, and the widest channel width is x16. There are no PCI x16 or PCI x128 slots, nor is there a PCIe x128 slot. AGP is an older video expansion standard that is now obsolete.

15. B. Personal computers do not have permanently installed power supplies. Like other electrical and electronic components, power supplies can and do fail on a regular basis. Permanently mounting a power supply to a chassis would be a disservice to the consumer. You should consider the cumulative power needs of your installed components, and you might have to obtain adapters and splitters if you do not have enough or you have the wrong types of connectors coming from the power supply.

16. C. The smallest of the options is microSD, at 15 mm × 11 mm. Perhaps "micro" gives it away, but that also makes it easy to remember. SD cards are 32 mm × 24 mm. CompactFlash cards are the largest, at 36 mm × 43 mm. MiniSD cards measure 21.5 mm × 20 mm, and xD cards are 20 mm × 25 mm.

17. C. M.2 and NVMe are both relatively new SSD options, and both are incredibly fast. NVMe is slightly faster, though. SATA is limited to 600 Mbps transfer speeds, whereas PCIe is not. An NVMe PCIe card can sustain data read rates of about 3,500 Mbps.

18. D. RAID 5 arrays require a minimum of three hard drives to implement. If one drive fails, the data is fine and the system can still function, albeit slowly. If more than one drive fails, the system will be inoperable. RAID 5 provides both fault tolerance and a performance improvement.

19. C, D. Most likely, the new card will be detected and function properly once the computer is booted up. However, the driver will need to be installed. Odds are the new card will be a different model than the integrated card, which will require a new driver. On some systems, you will need to go into the BIOS and disable the integrated adapter. Bridging happens between two PCIe video adapters, not an integrated video chipset.

20. A. Power supplies are rated in watts. When you purchase a power supply, you should make sure the devices inside the computer do not require more wattage than the chosen power supply can offer. The voltage is fairly standard among power supplies, and it has nothing to do with the devices connected to the power supply. Amperage and resistance are not selling points for power supplies. Another thing that could vary is the number of power connectors—make sure the new power supply has enough to support all installed peripherals.

Chapter 3: Peripherals, Cables, and Connectors

1. B, E. Analog monitors require an analog signal. VGA is an analog video standard and will work. DVI-A is also analog. (DVI-I would work as well.) HDMI, DVI-D, and DisplayPort are all digital standards.

2. A. USB 2.0 has a maximum speed of 480 Mbps. USB 3.0 is 5 Gbps, USB 3.1 is 10 Gbps, USB 3.2 is 20 Gbps, and USB4 is up to 40 Gbps.

3. C. A yellow USB port is an "always on" charging port. It could be either USB 2 or USB 3. USB-C connectors are oval in shape vs. the older rectangular USB connectors.

4. D. As you lower the resolution, the maximum refresh rate allowed tends to increase. The refresh rate is most often expressed in cycles per second (Hz), not millions of cycles per second (MHz). You must usually select the refresh rate that you want from the display settings dialog boxes, not through the monitor's built-in menu system, although the monitor can often tell you the refresh rate that you're using. Finally, both the monitor and adapter must agree on the refresh rate you select. If either device does not support a particular refresh rate, such a rate cannot be used.

5. C. DB-9 connectors are most often used with serial cables and are not associated with hard drives. USB-C, eSATA, and SCSI are examples of connectors used with hard drives.

6. A. For smaller electronic devices such as cameras, micro-USB and mini-USB connectors are common. Thunderbolt is primarily used for video. Molex is a power connector. Lightning is the Apple proprietary connector.

7. B, D. HDMI cables transmit digital video and audio signals. They can be used to connect to projectors or monitors. HDMI cables can have standard HDMI connectors, mini-HDMI connectors, or micro-HDMI connectors.

8. A. Intel and Apple collaborated on Thunderbolt to add PCIe to VESA's DisplayPort and to make the resulting interface smaller and less expensive to connect. HDMI, DVI, and VGA are not equivalent to DisplayPort with PCIe added in.

9. B, C. USB4 is based on the Thunderbolt 3 specifications, and both natively use USB-C connectors.

10. C. Such a connection should not be made. DVI-I cables act like universal cables; they can connect two DVI-A interfaces or two DVI-D interfaces with adapters. Natively, they are used to connect two DVI-I interfaces, both of which are configured as either analog or digital. They are unable to convert the analog signal to a digital one, however. Analog and digital DVI interfaces are too disparate to interconnect.

11. D. A Molex connector is a power connector for IDE (PATA) storage devices. This includes hard drives and optical drives.

12. D. Thunderbolt 3 uses the oval-shaped USB-C connector. Thunderbolt 2 used a proprietary connector that was more of a square. Micro-USB and mini-USB connectors look more like trapezoids.

13. A, C, E. USB cables and eSATA cables can transmit power and data. You will find Lightning, USB-C, and micro-USB connectors on the ends of USB cables. A Molex connector is power-only. A DB-9 is for serial cables and is data-only.

14. D. The eSATA standards limit throughput to 6 Gbps, which is much slower than USB4 and Thunderbolt 3, both of which can get to 40 Gbps. Standard eSATA cables do not provide power, although there are versions of eSATA that do include power. The connectors are larger than USB-C connectors.

15. B. Peripherals most often use USB today, but they can also use D-sub connectors (rarely), and audio devices such as microphones and speakers use 1/8" jacks. Molex connectors are power connectors for PATA hard drives and optical drives.

16. C. A projector uses a standard video cable. In this case, HDMI is the most likely choice. eSATA is for hard drives, and DB-9 is a slow serial cable. It's possible that the projector has a USB interface, but the best selection is HDMI.

17. B. Starting with the iPhone 5, Apple products use the proprietary Lightning connector for charging and connecting peripherals. Thunderbolt connectors are on MacBooks for peripherals. iPhones do not have built-in mini- or micro-USB connectors.

18. B. Classic serial ports and serial cables have the slowest data transmission speeds of any cable discussed in this chapter.

19. C. Full Speed USB is 12 Mbps. High Speed is 480 Mbps. SuperSpeed runs at 5 Gbps and SuperSpeed+ at 10 Gbps.

20. B. VGA signals are analog, uncompressed, component signals that carry all of the video information for all three components of the original RGB signal. VGA signals are not digital, composite, or compressed.

Chapter 4: Printers and Multifunction Devices

The answers to the chapter review questions can be found in Appendix A.

1. A. Because the toner on the drum has a slight negative charge (−100VDC), it requires a positive charge to transfer it to the paper; +600VDC is the voltage used in an EP process laser printer.

2. C, D. A page printer is a type of computer printer that prints a page at a time. Common types of page printers are the inkjet printer and the laser printer.

3. D. The rate of transfer and the ability to recognize new devices automatically are two of the major advantages that currently make USB the most popular type of printer interface. However, it is the network printer interface that allows the printer to communicate with networks, servers, and workstations.

4. D. Dot-matrix printers are impact printers and therefore are the best for multipart forms. Daisy-wheel printers can be used with multipart forms as well.

5. A. The exposing step uses a laser to discharge selected areas of the photosensitive drum, thus forming an image on the drum.

6. C. 3D printers use filament or resin to create objects. Printers that have an extruder use filament, which is often plastic but can contain metals, too. 3D printers do not use dye. There is no extrusion powder.

7. A. Audit logs will track print jobs and the users who printed them. User authentication is where a user is required to log into the printer. This can be done via badging—or swiping an employee badge on a badge reader on the printer—or by manually entering credentials. Secured prints is when a print job is held until a user authenticates at the printer and tells it to start printing.

8. B. In an inkjet printer, the ink cartridge is the actual print head. This is where the ink is expelled to form letters or graphics. Toner cartridges are used by laser printers to store toner. A daisy wheel is the device that impacts the letters on the paper in a daisy-wheel printer. Paper trays are the storage bins in laser printers and inkjet printers that allow the pickup rollers to feed the paper into the printer.

9. D. The correct sequence in the EP imaging process is processing, charging, exposing, developing, transferring, fusing, and cleaning.

10. C, E. Two ways for users to authenticate are to use user authentication (which requires typing in the username and password) or badging, which requires the MFD to have a badge-scanning feature. Secured print will save print jobs until they are ready to be released. SMB is a file- and print-sharing protocol used by MFDs to send scanned documents to a shared network folder. There are no printer authentication logs, but audit logs may be used to see who has used the MFD.

11. A, B, D. An electrophotographic (EP) laser printer toner cartridge includes the toner, print drum, and cleaning blade. The laser is usually contained within the printer, not within the toner cartridge.

12. A. After a laser has created an image of the page, the developing roller uses a magnet and electrostatic charges to attract toner to itself and then transfers the toner to the areas on the drum that have been exposed to the laser. The toner is melted during the fusing stage. The laser creates an image of the page on the drum in the exposing stage. An electrostatic charge is applied to the paper to attract toner in the transferring stage, which happens immediately after the developing stage.

13. A, C, D. Printers can communicate via parallel, serial, USB, wireless, and network connections. SATA is a bus interface that connects host bus adapters to storage devices such as hard drives and optical drives.

14. C. If a printer is using out-of-date or incorrect printer drivers, the printer may produce pages of garbled text. The solution is to ensure that the most recent printer drivers are downloaded from the manufacturer's website.

15. B. The daisy-wheel printer gets its name because it contains a wheel with raised letters and symbols on each "petal."

16. A. The high-voltage power supply (HVPS) is the part of the laser printer that supplies the voltages for charging and transferring corona assemblies.

17. C. The transfer corona assembly gets the toner from the photosensitive drum onto the paper. For some printers, this is a transfer corona wire; for other printers, it is a transfer corona roller.

18. D. Developing happens after exposing. The correct order is processing, charging, exposing, developing, transferring, fusing, and cleaning.

19. B. The fuser assembly presses and melts the toner into the paper. The transfer corona transfers the toner from the drum to the paper. The printer controller circuitry converts signals from the PC into signals for the various printer assemblies. The paper transport assembly controls the movement of the paper through the printer.

20. A. Firmware upgrades for laser printers are downloaded for free from the manufacturer's website. A technician does not need to install a new chip, because firmware is upgraded via software. It's unlikely that the manufacturer will send you the upgrade on a DVD; it will refer you to its website to download it.

Chapter 5: Networking Fundamentals

The answers to the chapter review questions can be found in Appendix A.

1. D. Companies that want to ensure the safety and integrity of their data should use fiber-optic cable because it is not affected by electromagnetic or radio-frequency interference. Even though some copper cables have shielding, they are not immune to EMI or RFI. This eliminates twisted pair and coaxial. CSMA/CD is an access method, not a cable type.

2. C. Coaxial cable can use BNC connectors and F type connectors. RJ-11 and RJ-45 are twisted pair connectors. SC is a fiber-optic connector.

3. C. A crossover cable will flip pins 1 and 3 on each end. Therefore, this end needs to have the white/orange wire as pin 1. The correct order for this cable should be white/orange, orange, white/green, blue, white/blue, green, white/brown, brown.

4. B. Carrier Sense Multiple Access with Collision Detection (CSMA/CD) specifies that the NIC pause before transmitting a packet to ensure that the line is not being used. If no activity is detected, then it transmits the packet. If activity is detected, it waits until it is clear. In the case of two NICs transmitting at the same time (a collision), both NICs pause to detect and then retransmit the data. CSMA/CA listens to the line as well but tries to avoid collisions. T568A/

T568B are twisted pair wiring standards. Demand priority is a media access method, but we didn't discuss it at all in the chapter as it's not related to the A+ exam. It's used with a standard called 100BaseVG.

5. A. Cat 5 was the first UTP standard ratified for 100 Mbps transmissions. Before that, Cat 3 was popular but only supported 10 Mbps. Cat 5e, Cat 6, and Cat 6a all support at least 1 Gbps and came after Cat 5.

6. D. A hub or a switch is at the center of a star topology. A NIC is a network card, which each computer must have to be on the network. Bridges and routers are higher-level connectivity devices that connect network segments or separate networks together.

7. C. Fiber-optic cable can span distances of several kilometers because it has much lower attenuation, crosstalk, and interference as compared to copper cables.

8. A. Routers are designed to route (transfer) packets across networks. They are able to do this routing, determining the best path to take, based on the internal routing tables that they maintain.

9. D. A managed switch can create virtual LANs (VLANs) using its management software. A firewall is a hardware or software solution that serves as your network's security guard. Patch panels and unmanaged switches cannot create VLANs.

10. A. Bluetooth networks are often called wireless personal area networks (WPANs).

11. C. Fiber-optic Internet connections use an optical network terminal (ONT) to terminate the fiber and translate it into a digital connection over copper cable inside your home. A cable modem and DSL modem connect copper to copper. Power over Ethernet (PoE) is not relevant in this situation.

12. A. For areas where a cable must be fire retardant, such as in a drop ceiling, you must run plenum-grade cable. Plenum refers to the coating on the sleeve of the cable, not the copper or fiber within the cable itself. PVC is the other type of coating typically found on network cables, but it produces poisonous gas when burned.

13. D. The local connector (LC) is a mini form factor (MFF) fiber-optic connector developed by Lucent Technologies. If it helps, think of LC as "Little Connector."

14. A. If you need to make a connection that is 5 kilometers long, then you are limited to fiber-optic cable, specifically single-mode fiber (SMF). Two common SMF standards are 10GBaseER and 10GBaseEW. (Think of the E as *extended*.) A T designation in an Ethernet standard refers to twisted pair. SR and LR are fiber standards that do not stretch for 5 kilometers.

15. B, C. Storage area networks (SANs) have many advantages, including block-level data storage, which is more efficient. They also reduce network loads, provide faster data access, and are easily expandable. They do not inherently provide more storage space (although they are easy to expand) or do automated data backups (although they are easier to set up).

16. C. Ethernet over Power can transmit network signals over power lines within a closed circuit, such as a house. It's the best choice. PoE devices provide power to devices that have only an Ethernet connection available. A router is for connecting network segments together.

17. B. The job of a firewall is to block unwanted network traffic. Firewalls do this by using a list of rules called an access control list (ACL). Routers connect networks to each other, and switches are central connectivity points for networks. A network attached storage (NAS) device is like a dedicated file server.

18. A. The two RG standards used for cable television are RG-6 and RG-59. Of the two, RG-6 is better because it can run longer distances and can handle digital signals. RG-59 is for analog signals only. RG-8 is thicknet coax, and RG-58 is thinnet coax.

19. D. A switch is a Layer 2 device; therefore, it works with hardware (MAC) addresses. Hubs and patch panels work at Layer 1 and deal with bits, and routers work at Layer 3 and work with logical IP addresses.

20. B. Multimode fiber (MMF) can transmit up to 550 meters, depending on the Ethernet specification. Other standards using MMF can transmit only up to 300 meters. If you need to transmit up to 40 kilometers, you will have to use single-mode fiber (SMF).

Chapter 6: Introduction to TCP/IP

The answers to the chapter review questions can be found in Appendix A.

1. B. A Dynamic Host Configuration Protocol (DHCP) server provides IP configuration information to hosts when they join the network. A Domain Name System (DNS) server resolves hostnames to IP addresses. Network Address Translation (NAT) translates private IP addresses into public IP addresses. There is no IP configuration server (other than a DHCP server).

2. B. Lightweight Directory Access Protocol (LDAP) is designed to access information stored in an information directory typically known as an LDAP directory or LDAP database. This typically includes employee data and network configuration data. FTP is designed to transfer files. RDP is a remote desktop protocol, and CIFS is used to share files and printers.

3. A. HTTP uses port 80. HTTPS uses port 443, Telnet uses port 23, and POP3 uses port 110.

4. D. An IPv6 interface is not limited in the number of addresses that can be assigned, although there could be limitations based on practicality.

5. A, B, C. An IPv6 address contains 128 bits, written in eight 16-bit fields represented by four hexadecimal digits. Option A contains all eight fields expressed in full. Option B is an IPv4 address expressed in IPv6 form. Option C is the same address as option A, but written in accepted shorthand. Option D is not valid because the double colons (::) can be used only once within an address.

6. A. DNS servers resolve hostnames to IP addresses. On the Internet, a DNS server needs to have a public IP address. The address 10.25.11.33 is in a private address space, so that address would not be valid for a DNS server on the Internet.

7. D. The address assigned to the computer is an APIPA address. Microsoft client computers (and others) will configure themselves with an address in this range if they are unable to reach a DHCP server.

8. C. Simple Mail Transfer Protocol (SMTP) is responsible for sending email. IMAP4 and POP3 both receive email. SNMP is a network management protocol.

9. D. Remote Desktop Protocol (RDP) works on port 3389. DNS works on port 53, IMAP4 works on port 143, and LDAP works on port 389.

10. D. DKIM authenticates messages from email servers using private-public encrypted key pairs. SPF authenticates via IP addresses. DMARC is a TXT record that allows an administrator to specify how they want rejected emails to be handled. VLAN is a virtual LAN and is not a TXT record type.

11. A, D. TCP is a connection-oriented protocol that establishes virtual circuits and acknowledges delivery of packets. Because of these features, it has higher overhead than UDP and is a little slower.

12. B. The HTTP protocol is inherently unsecure, but the HTTPS protocol is secure. (SSH and TLS are secure as well, but they are not protocols used to connect to websites.)

13. A. The router is your doorway out into other networks, and it is known in TCP/IP terms as the default gateway. Without this configuration option, you would not be able to get to external networks. The subnet mask tells a host which network it's on. The DNS server resolves hostnames to IP addresses, and a DHCP server provides IP configuration information to hosts.

14. A, B. The only mandatory IPv4 configuration items are an IP address and a subnet mask. If you are not connecting to another network, you do not need a default gateway. DNS servers resolve hostnames to IP addresses, but they are not mandatory.

15. D. IMAP4 and POP3 are the two protocols that are used for email retrieval. Of the two, only IMAP4 provides security features. SMTP sends email. SNMP is a network management protocol.

16. D. A virtual private network (VPN) is a secure point-to-point connection made over a public network. NAT translates private IP addresses to public IP addresses. APIPA is an automatic IP address assignment if a client computer can't reach a DHCP server. VLANs are virtual local area networks configured through switches.

17. A. Simple Network Management Protocol (SNMP) is used for networking device administration and management. It uses ports 161 and 162. Simple Mail Transfer Protocol (SMTP) is for sending email and uses port 25.

18. E. IPv6 does not have broadcasts. IPv6 does have multicasts, which are a bit like targeted broadcasts. FF00:: is the first part of a multicast address.

19. A. DNS is typically known as a name resolver on the Internet, but it will work on private networks as well. DNS resolves hostnames to IP addresses. DHCP automatically configures clients with IP address information. FTP is for file downloads. APIPA is a process used to assign clients a private IP address automatically when they can't reach the DHCP server.

20. C. The Address Resolution Protocol (ARP) resolves IP addresses to hardware (MAC) addresses. RARP does the reverse—it resolves MAC addresses to IP addresses. DNS resolves hostnames to IP addresses. DHCP automatically configures TCP/IP clients.

Chapter 7: Wireless and SOHO Networks

The answers to the chapter review questions can be found in Appendix A.

1. **B, D.** Both 802.11b and 802.11g operate in the 2.4 GHz range and use similar transmission standards. Some legacy devices are listed as 802.11b/g, meaning they will work with either system. Alternatively, 802.11a and 802.11ac operate in the 5 GHz range.

2. **C.** A service-set identifier (SSID) is the unique name given to the wireless network. All hardware that is to participate on the network must be configured to use the same SSID. Essentially, it is the network name. When you are using Windows to connect to a wireless network, all available wireless networks are listed by their SSID.

3. **A, C.** The two technologies that 802.11ac employs to achieve high throughput are channel bonding and MIMO. Channel bonding is the combination of multiple smaller channels into one large channel for greater bandwidth. MIMO is enhanced over 802.11n to allow for multiple inputs and outputs. 802.11ac also uses beamforming, but that helps the range, not the throughput.

4. **C.** WEP was the original encryption standard developed for Wi-Fi networks, but it is easily hacked. WPA is an upgrade, but WPA2 is more secure and incorporates the entire 802.11i standard. WPA3 is of course the safest, but it's not one of the options. SAFER+ is used to encrypt Bluetooth communications.

5. **C.** Wi-Fi 6 is faster than Wi-Fi 5, and the network range is similar. More users should be able to access each access point, not fewer. Devices may have lower power usage in Wi-Fi 6 due to a new sleep feature.

6. **A, B.** You should always change the default administrator name and password as well as the default SSID when installing a new wireless router. Enabling encryption is also a good idea, but WPA, WPA2, and WPA3 are better options than WEP. The channel has nothing to do with security.

7. **D.** Of the options listed, fiber provides the best speed. DSL and cable provide similar speeds but can't match fiber. Satellite is the slowest of the options listed.

8. **D.** Network Address Translation (NAT) allows users to have a private IP address and still access the Internet with a public IP address. NAT is installed on a router and translates the private IP address into a public address for the user to access the Internet. DHCP assigns IP configuration information to clients. DNS resolves hostnames to IP addresses. DSL is a type of broadband Internet access.

9. **C.** There are 14 communication channels in the 2.4 GHz range, but only the first 11 are configurable. The three nonoverlapping channels are 1, 6, and 11.

10. **A, C, D.** Three standards listed—802.11ac (1,300 Mbps), 802.11g (54 Mbps), and 802.11n (600 Mbps)—give users the required throughput. 802.11ax would do so as well, although it's not an option.

11. B. To join the network, client computers need to find the SSID, ensure that the security settings are correct (to match the router), and enter the security passphrase. As an administrator, you should have configured this passphrase to be different from the router's administrator password.

12. B. Radio frequency identification (RFID) can operate in three frequency bands: 125 kHz to 134 kHz, 13.56 MHz, or 856 MHz to 960 MHz. Bluetooth is 2.4 GHz, NFC is 13.56 MHz, and LTE is between 600 MHz and 6 GHz.

13. B. The feature of Wi-Fi 6 that reduces channel interference is Basic Service Set (BSS) coloring, which adds a field to the wireless frame that distinguishes it from others. Orthogonal Frequency Division Multiple Access (OFDMA) is a modulation technique that improves speed because it allows transmission to multiple clients at once. MU-MIMO also increases speed because in Wi-Fi 6 it works for uplink connections as well as downlink ones. Dynamic Frequency Selection (DFS) was introduced with 802.11n, and it detects radar interference and adjusts frequencies accordingly.

14. B. WEP could use a 64-bit or 128-bit security key, but it was a static key. TKIP introduced a dynamic per-packet key. AES and CCMP came after TKIP.

15. D. The good news is that 802.11g is backward compatible with 802.11b. The bad news is, if you run in a mixed environment, all devices that communicate with the WAP (or router) will be forced to slow down to accommodate the older technology.

16. D. MAC filtering is a security option that can specify that only computers with specific MAC (hardware) addresses can access the network. Port forwarding is a feature of firewalls. WPS is an easy setup mechanism for wireless networks. SSID is the wireless network name.

17. B. The set of rules for access on a firewall is called an access control list (ACL). An SLA is an agreement on service level for QoS. NAT translates private IP addresses into public ones. APIPA assigns an IP address to a client that can't reach the DHCP server.

18. C. If your router is using AES, the clients need to use WPA2. TKIP is a protocol utilized by WPA. WEP is the weakest of the encryption options.

19. A, C. Bluetooth also operates in the 2.4 GHz range, and long-range fixed wireless can if it uses unlicensed frequencies. Satellite uses satellite waves; 5G cellular mmWave is between 24 GHz and 86 GHz, and NFC uses 13.56 MHz.

20. D. The gateway, also known as a default gateway, is the address to the router to take a client to the next network (or Internet). Gateways can be configured with a static assignment or dynamically through a DHCP server. APIPA will automatically configure a client with IP address information if it's set to get its configuration from a DHCP server but none is available. APIPA-configured clients can't get on the Internet.

Chapter 8: Network Services, Virtualization, and Cloud Computing

The answers to the chapter review questions can be found in Appendix A.

1. B. For secure transactions, the web server will be using HTTPS, which uses port 443. If the website works from an internal workstation, then the server is fine. It's most likely that the firewall is blocking inbound traffic on port 443. Port 23 is Telnet.

2. C. It sounds like the manager wants a unified threat management (UTM) device. They are designed to be one-stop network protection devices. Spam gateways help with spam email but not with other malware. A load balancer spreads work around to multiple servers. A proxy server fulfills requests for clients.

3. C. If the data on the server does not need to be accessed via the Internet, then the server should be in the most secure place possible, which is inside the firewall(s) in the secure network.

4. A. Platform as a service (PaaS) is probably the right level of service for the developer team. It provides infrastructure, like IaaS, and also supplies needed programming elements. Infrastructure as a service doesn't provide runtime environments; think of it as hardware. Software as a service provides apps and is too high a service for what's needed here. There is no current DaaS on the exam objectives.

5. A, C. Print servers should make printers available to clients and accept print jobs. They also process print jobs and manage print priorities. Finally, they provide client computers with the right print drivers when the clients attempt to install the printer. They do not turn printers off on demand or provide notification that a job has printed.

6. A. The ability to expand services quickly means rapid elasticity. High availability guarantees uptime for services. All cloud services use resource pooling. Metered utilization is how many suppliers track usage and charge accordingly.

7. A. A proxy server can be configured to block access to websites that contain potentially dangerous or inflammatory material. Web servers host web pages, some of which may have objectionable content. DHCP servers provide clients with IP addresses, and DNS servers resolve hostnames to IP addresses.

8. D. A hybrid cloud provides the best of public and private clouds. You get the scalability and cost effectiveness of a public cloud but also the security that you need for important files on the private portion of the cloud.

9. B. Every DHCP server needs to have a scope, which is the range of addresses available to clients, as well as other options that it can give to client computers. A DHCP server can optionally provide clients with the address of a DNS server. There is no DHCP range. A DHCP relay agent is a system configured on a subnet with no DHCP server that relays DHCP requests to the DHCP server.

10. C. When multiple organizations with similar objectives want to combine efforts in a cloud, the best choice is generally a community cloud. This allows for the flexibility and scalability normally found in a public cloud, but it also limits the number of users to a smaller, trusted group.

11. A. DNS server records are contained in the zone file, which must be configured by administrators. A hosts file is an alternative to using DNS (but that does not work well when scaling to the Internet). A scope is created on DHCP servers. There is no DNS proxy.

12. B, C, D. Cloud solutions are great for enhancing scalability and reliability while generally lowering costs. Security could be an issue with cloud computing, depending on your organization's needs, because the resources aren't locally controlled and managed.

13. D. Simple Mail Transfer Protocol (SMTP) is used to transfer (send) email between servers. POP3 and IMAP4 are used to download (receive) email. SNMP is Simple Network Management Protocol and not related to email.

14. B. Each virtual machine will use its own virtual NIC, so you need three virtual NICs. The virtual NICs will communicate with one virtual switch managed by the hypervisor. The virtual switch will communicate with one physical NIC on the host system.

15. D. A load balancer can spread the work around to multiple servers. It accepts the inbound request and then sends it to the most appropriate web server. DNS resolves hostnames to IP addresses. DHCP provides IP configuration information. A proxy makes requests (usually outbound) on behalf of clients.

16. B. There needs to be enough RAM to support both OSs, so the answer is 6 GB. More is better, though!

17. A, B, C. Legacy systems are ones that use older hardware, software, or network protocols that are not commonly used today. A system with only 1 GB of RAM might be woefully underpowered, but that in and of itself does not make it a legacy system.

18. D. Each instance of the OS you are running requires its own security software.

19. B. A sandbox is a temporary operating system environment, kind of like a "lite" version of a virtual machine. It's ideal for testing software such as this. An AAA server is for authentication, authorization, and accounting of security. SCADA is a legacy hardware and/or software environment used to control industrial systems. Application virtualization is used for legacy apps or cross-platform virtualization.

20. A. A Type 2 hypervisor sits on top of an existing OS, meaning that OSs installed in VMs will compete for resources with the host OS. The amount of resources available to a guest OS can be configured. Virtual OSs can get on the physical network if configured properly.

Chapter 9: Laptop and Mobile Device Hardware

The answers to the chapter review questions can be found in Appendix A.

1. D. Laptop service manuals can be obtained from the manufacturer's website. It's very rare that paper service manuals are shipped with the laptop. Pressing F1 while in Windows will open Windows Help, and pressing F2 on many laptops during the system boot will take you into the BIOS/UEFI.

2. B. The inverter, which transforms AC power into DC power for an LCD backlight, is found in the display. It's not underneath the keyboard, next to the heat sink and fan, or near the processor, which are all located in the bottom half of the laptop.

3. A, B. The components of an LCD screen are the inverter, screen, and backlight. LCD display units also have a Wi-Fi antenna (not the card), webcam, and microphone. There is no backdrop component.

4. A. The touchpad sits below the keyboard, where the user's palms may rest when they are typing. That contact may cause the mouse cursor to appear to jump on the screen. Disabling the touchpad should prevent this from happening.

5. B. A DC adapter converts the DC output from a car or airplane accessory power plug into the DC voltages required by your laptop. An AC adapter is used with standard wall electrical outlets. There is no battery converter. Airplane mode shuts off all wireless communications.

6. C. DDR4 SODIMMs have 260 pins. DDR2 SODIMMs have 200 pins, DDR3 SODIMMs have 204 pins, and DDR5 has 262. No SODIMMs currently have 288 pins, but DDR4 DIMMs do.

7. C. If the touchscreen is not responding properly, the first step is to recalibrate it. If it continues to have problems, the screen may be defective and might need to be replaced. Degaussing is a process used on old CRT monitors and is not relevant to touchscreens.

8. C, D. Two wireless connectivity options are NFC and Bluetooth; hotspot (not mentioned) is the third. USB, Lightning, and serial are wired connectivity methods.

9. C. Sometimes the only way to ensure that equipment doesn't walk away is to lock it down physically. Laptops come equipped with holes for cable locks that can be used to secure them to a desk or other workstation. GPS tracking might help after the device is stolen, but it's best to prevent that in the first place. A docking station does not prevent physical theft, nor does a screensaver with a password.

10. C. The laptop power supply converts AC power into DC power for the laptop's internal circuitry. The display backlight, if used, needs AC power. The inverter's job is to convert (invert) the DC power into AC power for the backlight.

11. D. To migrate data from one hard drive to another, you can manually copy the data or use a migration app. There is no NFC disk transfer utility.

12. C. The user needs a digitizer, which takes input from the device, such as drawn images, and converts them into electronic images on the computer. The user could also use a touchscreen for the same purpose. An inverter changes DC power into AC power for a display backlight. There is no capturer laptop device. A touchpad is a pointing device that allows a user to control the mouse cursor.

13. A. Laptops use SODIMMs (or possibly MicroDIMMs), which are much smaller than the standard DIMMs used in desktops. DDR2 and DDR3 SODIMMs are 67.6 millimeters wide, whereas DDR4 SODIMMs are 69.6 millimeters wide. It's likely that the technician has DDR4 SODIMMs and the motherboard supports DDR3 SODIMMs.

14. A. A docking station made specifically for its associated brand and model of laptop can host desktop components permanently, regardless of whether the laptop is attached to the docking station. When the laptop's portability is not required, but instead use of the desktop components is the priority, attaching the laptop to the docking station makes such components available to the laptop without separately attaching each component.

15. D. The processor can reduce how fast it's working, which is called throttling, to help conserve battery life. CPUs do not perform underclocking, cooling, or disengaging.

16. B. Think of wattage as a "bucket" of power that the attached device can draw from. A bigger bucket simply holds more power but does not force the power on the device. Less wattage is not advised, however. Voltage can be thought of as the pressure behind the power to the device. Anything but the proper voltage is dangerous for the device. When you replace a laptop's AC adapter, you should match the voltage ratings of the original adapter. This also means that you should use an adapter with a fixed voltage if that matches the characteristics of the original; otherwise, obtain one that automatically switches voltages at the levels needed.

17. C. Battery calibration for Li-ion batteries allows the powered device to drain the battery's power before recharging. Battery exercising is the initial charging and discharging of nickel-based batteries so that they will function as expected. You should never short a battery's terminals, and replacement is a last resort, used when any battery has reached the end of its life.

18. D. Laptop hard drives commonly have a 2.5" form factor, and smaller drives, such as M.2, are becoming more popular. The most common form factor for desktop hard drives is 3.5". Laptop hard drives use the same drive technologies as their desktop counterparts, such as serial and parallel ATA. Like desktop hard drives, laptop hard drives are available in both solid-state and conventional varieties. Unlike desktop hard drives, laptop hard drives do not have separate power connectors.

19. B. A USB Bluetooth adapter should do the trick. There are Mini PCIe Bluetooth adapters, but installing one is trickier than inserting a USB device. There aren't really any Wi-Fi–compatible headsets on the market—headsets are exactly what Bluetooth was designed for. Replacing the laptop is a much more expensive proposition.

20. C. A docking station is a device that a laptop can be plugged into that replicates common laptop ports, and may also have full-sized bays for PC desktop expansion cards and storage devices, such as hard drives and optical drives. A port replicator will replicate laptop ports but does not usually have expansion bays. There is no specific laptop base accessory or a Mini PCIe dock. (Mini PCIe is an internal laptop technology.)

Chapter 10: Mobile Connectivity and Application Support

The answers to the chapter review questions can be found in Appendix A.

1. **D.** Whenever you have a reliable Wi-Fi signal available, which you do not pay for "as you go," you should feel free to disable your cellular access to data networking. The wireless network is often faster and does not cost you anything to use. If data networking works better when you leave the cellular network available as a fallback, you can choose to disable it only for certain large downloads or disable it completely until the download is complete. Phone calls will continue to be sent over the cellular network. This does not imply that your data is not using an available Wi-Fi connection. Therefore, unless you are particularly sensitive to the situation or know that data is going out over your cell access, you might not need to disable the cellular data-networking feature.

2. **C.** The range of Bluetooth connections is considered short compared to Wi-Fi connections. Bluetooth is a fully standardized protocol that supports file transfers using FTP. Rebooting, or even restarting, paired devices is not a requirement for Bluetooth connection.

3. **A.** SMTP sends mail to the server on TCP port 25. POP3 uses port 110. IMAP4 uses port 143. POP3 uses port 995 securely over SSL or TLS.

4. **B.** SMTP with TLS uses port 587 by default. With SSL, SMTP uses port 465. IMAP4 with SSL/TLS uses port 993, while POP3 with SSL/TLS uses port 995.

5. **B.** Four commercial email providers to be familiar with are iCloud, Google/Inbox, Exchange Online, and Yahoo Mail. Hotmail used to be a commercial email provider, but it no longer exists; it's now part of Outlook.com.

6. **C.** In iOS (at least through iOS 15.3.1), Location Services are under Settings ➤ Privacy. There are no Location Services, Communications, or GPS sections directly in Settings.

7. **C.** Each mobile phone has a separate processor that manages wireless communications, also known as radio communications or baseband communications. There is a baseband OS that manages this, and it works with the primary OS on the phone. A SIM OS is for managing data transfers between the phone and the SIM chip. There is no wireless OS.

8. **A.** Mobile application management (MAM) is a service that allows administrators to control corporate software on mobile devices, including updating and wiping apps. Mobile device management (MDM) controls which devices are on the network and can wipe entire devices. Location services does not manage software. Synchronization can back up apps and data but does not help with updates or deleting apps.

9. **A.** Microsoft 365 is able to sync desktop settings between multiple Windows-based computers. ActiveSync is for syncing mobile devices with an Exchange email server. Mobile application management (MAM) and mobile device management (MDM) are for managing apps and network access for mobile devices.

10. C. The next step is to enter the PIN code. The steps, in order, are as follows: enable Bluetooth, enable pairing, find a device for pairing, enter the appropriate PIN code, and test connectivity.

11. B, D, F. Contacts, calendar, and apps are commonly synchronized, along with pictures, music, videos, email, bookmarks, documents, location data, social media data, e-books, and passwords.

12. B. GPS is generally more accurate than cellular when determining location. MAM and MDM are mobile device management concepts, not location services.

13. B. Mail access uses standard secure or unsecure TCP ports, not UDP ports. Exchange access to such mail services is not unheard of, but it is exceedingly rare. Mobile devices tend to have email clients built in.

14. A, B, C. On an Android phone, airplane mode disables all radio communications, including cellular, Wi-Fi, and Bluetooth (and NFC as well). It does not affect the opening of any other apps or the lock screen. In recent versions of iOS, Bluetooth is not affected by airplane mode.

15. A, C, D. Three common connection types for synchronization to a desktop (or laptop) are cellular, Wi-Fi, and USB. Bluetooth is not used for desktop synchronization. Tethering is when a laptop or other device is granted cellular network access by connecting to a mobile device, such as a smartphone.

16. C. The devices verify each other's identity via mutual authentication. Pairing is done for the initial connection. MAM is mobile application management. Synchronization is used between a mobile device and a desktop/laptop or the cloud.

17. A. The preferred roaming list (PRL) is the list of cell towers a mobile device should connect to while roaming. It is not a description of the user and network, a carrier code, or the configuration settings of the network.

18. B. Mobile device management (MDM) is a type of service that allows network administrators to specify which mobile devices can join the network. It also gives administrators the ability to remotely lock and completely wipe mobile devices. Mobile application management (MAM) lets an administrator control the corporate apps on a mobile device. Two-factor authentication is a security concept. Location services can help find a mobile device, but not remotely wipe it.

19. C, D. Apple devices natively sync with iCloud and iTunes. Android devices sync with Google Drive. SharePoint is a Microsoft service that can be used to share files.

20. B. When roaming, the mobile device uses the preferred roaming list (PRL) to connect to the proper cell phone tower. The product release instruction (PRI) contains settings for configuration items on the device that are specific to the network that it's on. Baseband refers to all wireless communications. The international mobile equipment identity (IMEI) is a 15-digit serial number that is unique to each phone and is not relevant to this issue.

Chapter 11: Troubleshooting Methodology and Resolving Core Hardware Problems

The answers to the chapter review questions can be found in Appendix A.

1. D. According to the best practice methodology, you should always consider corporate policies, procedures, and impacts before implementing changes. The user's budget, company reputation, and upgrade feasibility are not mentioned in the best practice methodology to resolve problems.

2. D. This system is producing a beep code and not completing the POST process. Different BIOS manufacturers use different beep codes. Look up this beep code on the manufacturer's website before replacing any hardware.

3. A, E. The two sub-steps to identify the problem are: gather information from the user and identify user changes to the computer, and inquire regarding environmental or infrastructure changes. Conducting internal or external research is part of establishing a theory of probable cause. Referring to the vendor's instructions for guidance is part of establishing a plan of action to resolve the problem. Determining the next steps to resolve the problem is part of testing the theory to determine the cause.

4. B. Capacitors store energy and are located on the motherboard and inside the power supply. Since the capacitors are exposed, it likely means the technician is seeing the problem on the motherboard. CPUs and RAM do not have capacitors.

5. B. The second step in the best practice methodology is to establish a theory of probable cause (question the obvious). While it makes sense to question the obvious at all times during troubleshooting, it officially falls under this step in the best practice methodology.

6. C. The fifth step in the best practice methodology is to verify full system functionality and, if applicable, implement preventive measures. This step occurs after a plan of action to resolve the problem has been established and before findings, actions, and outcomes have been documented.

7. B, D. Intermittent shutdowns are hard to troubleshoot but are most likely hardware related. When troubleshooting, always make one change at a time to try to resolve the issue. Replacing the RAM or the CPU to see if it resolves the problem could be a good next step, but replacing three components at once is too many changes unless you have specific reason to believe it is all three. Reinstalling Windows is probably overkill as well. Narrow down the issue before implementing sweeping solutions such as that.

8. C. When troubleshooting, always question the obvious. In this case, the system beeps once, which is usually a signal from the BIOS that POST completed successfully and air is coming from the system fan. All of that appears to be normal. Check to see that the monitor is connected properly to the desktop computer and that it's receiving power.

9. B. The fourth step in the best practice methodology is to establish a plan of action to resolve the problem and implement the solution, which was done already. The next step is to verify

full system functionality and, if applicable, implement preventive measures. The final step is to document findings, actions, and outcomes. Reviewing system and application logs is part of identifying the problem, which is the first step.

10. A, B. When the system is powered off, BIOS settings on a motherboard are maintained by the CMOS battery. If the battery fails, the system will likely forget the BIOS time and date settings and the boot order configuration. Replacing the CMOS battery will resolve the issue.

11. C, D. Continuous reboots are most likely caused by the motherboard or CPU failing. It's possible it's the RAM, but less likely. The power supply is the least likely cause of the problem in this scenario.

12. A. After verifying full system functionality and implementing preventive measures as needed, the final step in the best practice methodology is to document findings, actions, and outcomes.

13. A, C. If the wall outlet is functioning and the power cable is connected properly (always check the obvious), then the most likely culprits are the power supply or the power cord. The motherboard, CPU, and RAM are unlikely to cause a complete power failure in a computer.

14. C. The processor runs the hottest of all computer components and is the most likely to overheat. Motherboards and RAM don't generate a lot of heat. Power supplies most often have fans to help dissipate heat, and they don't run as hot as CPUs.

15. A. Only components with moving parts can make ticking or clicking noises. (Bombs can too, but hopefully you recognized that as a fake answer!) This question assumes that the hard drive is an HDD and not an SSD, but none of the other components would make a ticking noise.

16. C. The second step in the best practice methodology is to establish a theory of probable cause (question the obvious). As part of that, if necessary, conduct external or internal research based on symptoms.

17. A, B, C. Only components with moving parts can make ticking, clicking, or squealing noises. It's probably a fan of some sort (such as the CPU fan or power supply fan), or it could be a conventional hard drive. SSDs, CPUs, and RAM do not have moving parts and therefore could not be causing this problem.

18. A. Smoke and foul odors such as burning smells are not normal for computers! The most likely component causing the problem is the power supply. With the system off, open the computer case (not the power supply case!) to examine the inside for possible physical damage.

19. C. When Windows-based systems crash, as can happen due to a memory, CPU, or motherboard problem, they will most likely display a Blue Screen of Death (BSOD). The good news is that the BSOD can often provide useful information, such as an error code, to help troubleshoot the problem. There is no stop sign proprietary crash screen, and the pinwheel is used in macOS. A black screen may indicate a system crash but is not proprietary to one operating system.

20. A. The second step in the best practice methodology to resolve problems is to establish a theory of probable cause, which has been done here. The next step is to test the theory to determine the cause. After that, establish a plan of action to resolve the problem, verify full system functionality, and document findings.

Chapter 12: Hardware and Network Troubleshooting

The answers to the chapter review questions can be found in Appendix A.

1. **A, B.** Two helpful things to try are toggling the video output function key (usually something like Fn+F8) and plugging an external monitor into the laptop. Removing the display is possible but not necessary yet. Powering the system off and back on isn't likely to correct the problem.

2. **C.** Printing preferences sets configuration options such as color versus black and white, paper size, and page orientation. The print spooler is where print jobs are held for printing. The print queue is the list of print jobs waiting to be printed. There is no paper selection switch on printers (at least not that we've seen).

3. **A.** With a swollen battery, the best solution is to replace the device. If you are experienced with mobile device batteries, you may be able to replace the battery, but be careful! You should not charge a swollen battery or freeze the system. A battery calibration utility will do no good.

4. **C.** Distance matters in wireless networks. Being too far away from an access point will result in a weaker signal, which can cause intermittent signal drops and poor performance. Moving closer to the wireless access point (WAP) or wireless router can help, as can installing additional WAPs or wireless routers. The IP address from the DHCP server won't matter, and since they reported no error message, there is not likely to be an IP address conflict. Unless there are other issues, replacing the NIC seems to be overkill.

5. **B.** The `ipconfig` command is perhaps the most-used utility in troubleshooting and network configuration. The `ipconfig /renew` command sends a query to the DHCP server asking it to resend and renew all DHCP information. For a more detailed look at the `ipconfig` command, type **`ipconfig /?`** at the command prompt. The `ifconfig` command is used with Linux and macOS clients. There are no `/refresh` or `/start` switches for these commands.

6. **B.** If print jobs are seemingly getting "stuck" in the printer queue, you should stop and restart the print spooler service. There is no Printer Troubleshooting utility. Deleting and reinstalling the printer and/or Windows is not necessary.

7. **C, D.** Perpetually dim or flickering screens are most likely caused by a failing backlight or inverter, which supplies power to the backlight. LCD devices are not subject to interference from fans. An incorrect video driver will not cause a flickering image.

8. **B.** The manufacturer's website is the first place you should go for information on your products, including troubleshooting information. Many years ago, manufacturers would provide paper manuals with their products, but that's almost unheard of today, unless you download a PDF version from the website. Server logs can show error codes, but they won't tell you how to fix anything.

9. A. The most likely cause is a groove or a scratch in the EP drum. Toner is collecting in that groove or scratch, and then it is being deposited onto the page. A broken drum-cleaning blade would result in unreadable images (too much toner). Low toner would cause faded images, and a bad transfer corona wire would cause blank images.

10. B. It has to be a problem with the LCD display. If it were the video card, the display would appear warped and fuzzy on the external monitor as well. While many motherboards contain video circuitry, this answer is not specific enough. If the video driver were corrupted, you would have the same problem on all displays.

11. A. If an ink cartridge is faulty or develops a hole, it can release excessive amounts of ink, which leads to smearing. A corrupt print driver would result in printing garbage. Inkjet printers do not have a fuser. Excessive humidity may cause smearing, but it wouldn't cause the disbursement of too much ink.

12. B. A loopback plug is used to test the ability of a network adapter to send and receive. The plug gets plugged into the NIC, and then a loopback test is performed using troubleshooting software. A toner probe is used to trace a cable. Multimeters test for electrical issues. Cable testers are for verifying that a cable works properly.

13. C, D. Seeing images from previous print jobs is a phenomenon called ghosting (or ghost images). It's most likely due to a bad erasure lamp or a broken cleaning blade. If the transfer corona wire were faulty, there would likely be blank pages. An overheating printer will not necessarily leave residue behind.

14. D. A toner probe is used to trace a cable from one location to another. A loopback plug is for testing the ability of a network adapter to send and receive. Punch-down tools are used to connect the wires of a cable to a wiring rack, such as a 110-block. Cable testers are for verifying that a cable works properly.

15. B. If the hard drive is not recognized, the BIOS/UEFI is the place to check. Most systems do not come with built-in S.M.A.R.T. diagnostics software, even if the hard drive is capable of gathering S.M.A.R.T. data. And if there were one, it would give you potential errors on a working drive. Windows Device Manager is inaccessible without the drive being recognized. There is no boot sector manager, although this issue could be related to the boot sector.

16. C. The only components that make noise are the ones that have moving parts, such as fans and conventional hard disk drives. In most cases, a rhythmic ticking sound will be something that's generated by a conventional hard disk drive (HDD).

17. C. If there is a consistent blank space, it likely means that a pin is not firing properly and that the print head needs to be replaced. If the print ribbon is old, you would have consistently faded printing. If the ribbon is not advancing properly, you would get light and dark printing. If the wrong driver was installed, you would get garbage.

18. A. A crimper is used to make network cables. Punch-down tools are used to connect the wires of a cable to a wiring rack, such as a 110-block. Cable testers are for verifying that a cable works properly (and may be handy after you complete the cable). A loopback plug is for testing the ability of a network adapter to send and receive.

19. D. The first step should be to try to reboot the device. In most cases with a frozen smartphone, holding the power button down for about 10 seconds will force it to power off. If that doesn't work, then you can move to trying to reset the phone by holding down the power button and the sleep/wake button for 10 seconds. There is no need to restore the device to factory settings (yet) or replace the battery.

20. C. A RAID 0 array is also known as disk striping. RAID 0 actually decreases your fault tolerance versus one hard drive because there are more points of failure. You need to replace the drive, and hopefully you had it backed up so that you can restore the data.

Chapter 13: Operating System Basics

The answers to the chapter review questions can be found in Appendix A.

1. B, C. You can open a command prompt by typing cmd or command in the Start menu. The command prompt utility will pop up in the search results. Run is not a command; it is a dialog box. Open is not a command; it is an operating system action.

2. D. A driver is specifically written to instruct the operating system to communicate with a piece of hardware. Source code is the original code the software is written in. An application is a program written to perform a specific purpose to interact with the user. The kernel is the core of the operating system.

3. C. You can increase the size of the taskbar by placing the cursor over the top of the taskbar and dragging it up. This assumes the taskbar is not locked.

4. A. If you wanted to install a program on a virtual machine, the preferred method would be to mount an ISO image of the application. USB and optical discs are not common installation methods for virtual machines. Although ZIP files could be used, a ZIP file is only a compression method and not a delivery method.

5. B, C. The Windows File Explorer program can be used to copy and move files. Windows File Explorer can also be used to change file attributes. Windows File Explorer cannot be used to browse the Internet or to create backup jobs.

6. D. The maximum allowable length for a filename is 255 characters.

7. B. The shell is a program that runs on top of the OS and allows user interaction with the operating system. The taskbar is an element of the Desktop. The Desktop does not allow for commands to be executed. Source is not related to the graphical interface.

8. B. Typing the program name in the Start box allows you to launch the program. The shutdown command will shut down the operating system. Run is not a command; it is a dialog box. The cmd command starts the command-prompt application.

9. D. When a program is multithreaded, it is written to allow for multiple requests into the processor at one time. Multiuser mode, dystopia, and preemption are not correct answers.

10. B. The Recycle Bin is a temporary spot that files are deleted to but from where they can be retrieved if deleted mistakenly. The My Computer icon is another, older way to start the File Explorer. Control Panel and the Settings app are used to customize the operating system.

11. D. In Windows 10/11, when you click the Start button, a power icon is displayed on the lower left or lower right in Windows 11. From the power icon, you can sleep, reboot, or shut down the operating system. There is no command named turnoff. Turning the power switch off and unplugging the machine are not graceful ways to power off the operating system. Pressing Ctrl+Alt+Del alone will not power down the computer.

12. D. The minimum amount of memory required for the installation of the 32-bit Windows 10 operating system is 1 GB.

13. C. The minimum amount of free hard drive space required for Windows 10 64-bit is 32 GB.

14. C. The minimum amount of memory required for the 64-bit installation of the Windows 10 is 2 GB.

15. C. A quick method of accessing Help is to press the F1 key. The Windows key on the keyboard launches the Start menu or Start screen. The F12 key and the Alt key perform various tasks, depending on the application.

16. A. The Start screen was introduced with Windows 8 and replaced the Start menu by providing a full-screen Start menu. Gadgets and the Sidebar were introduced in Windows Vista. The system tray is what the notification area is now called in the current operating system.

17. C. The notification area is the area on the rightmost portion of the taskbar. It is used to display the date and time and running background applications. The Quick Launch and Start menus are located on the leftmost portion of the taskbar. Shutdown options are found inside the Start menu in Windows 10.

18. A. Clicking the Settings gear in the Start menu will open the Settings app. From there, the System category will allow you to change the Display Properties. Clicking the System icon under Control Panel allows you to change system settings. Pressing Ctrl+Alt+Esc launches the Task Manager. Pressing Ctrl+Alt+Tab launches the Task View in Windows 10/11.

19. B. The File Explorer allows you to navigate the file/folder structure in Windows. The Start menu allows you to launch applications. KDE and GNOME are Linux desktop shells.

20. C. The minimum processor speed required for the 64-bit installation of Windows 10 is 1 GHz.

Chapter 14: Windows Configuration

The answers to the chapter review questions can be found in Appendix A.

1. B. Task Scheduler will allow you to start a program based on a condition met, such as the computer starting up. The Programs and Features applet is not an MMC snap-in. The Disk Management MMC snap-in allows you to manage the disks attached to the computer. The Group Policy Editor lets you edit the local Group Policy.

2. D. The CDFS filesystem is used for CD media. NTFS is the native filesystem for Windows. FAT32 is a filesystem that was popular with Windows 9*x* operating systems and is also commonly used for USB flash drives for compatibility between platforms. EFS is a technology that encrypts files.

3. C. The `shutdown` utility can be used to schedule a remote shutdown—for example, `shutdown /t 60 /m \\computer`. The `taskmgr` utility is used to view tasks, `kill` is used to kill processes, and `netstat` is used to view network statistics and activity.

4. D. The System event log would contain an entry when the operating system reboots. The Application log is used to log applications installed on the system. The boot log is not a valid log. The Security log contains log information pertaining to the security of objects and files.

5. D. The exFAT filesystem is a Microsoft proprietary filesystem created for large flash drives. GPT is a partition table type, NFS is a network filesystem used with Linux/UNIX, and ext3 is a filesystem used with Linux.

6. D. The Update and Security section allows you to access the Backup screen, where you can configure backups for the operating system. The System section allows you to configure a multitude of options for Windows itself. The Devices section lets you configure devices, and the Apps section allows you to uninstall and configure applications.

7. C. The Apple File System (APFS) is a proprietary filesystem created for SSD support; it can be found on macOS Sierra 10.12.4, iOS 10.3, and tvOS 10.2 and later operating systems. Hierarchical File System (HFS) is a proprietary filesystem that was developed by Apple for the Mac OS back in 1985, ext4 (Fourth Extended File System) is used with Android and other Linux-based operating systems, and exFAT is a Microsoft proprietary filesystem created for large flash drives.

8. A. The System Control Panel applet is used to change the operating system computer name and change its membership from a workgroup to a domain, or domain to workgroup. The User Accounts applet is used to make changes to your user account or others on the operating system. The Internet Options applet is used to set options for Internet Explorer. The Programs and Features applet is used to uninstall and repair installed programs, as well as manage Windows features.

9. D. When a program is not responding to any commands, the process must be terminated via the Task Manager. You can end the process by opening the Task Manager, right-clicking the application, and selecting End Task. Viewing the performance will not make the process respond. Adding more memory is not possible without shutting down the computer. Pressing Ctrl+Alt+Delete without any further action will not reboot the computer.

10. B. The command `eventvwr.msc` will start the Event Viewer snap-in. The command `eventviewer.exe` is not a valid command. The command `lusrmgr.msc` will start the Local Users and Group snap-in. The command `devmgmt.msc` will start the Device Manager snap-in.

11. C. The iSCSI Initiator utility can be found in Control Panel, in Administrative Tools. The Storage Spaces applet is used to configure storage spaces of already connected storage. The Disk Management snap-in is used to configure disks already connected to the operating system. Device Manager is used to configure hardware attached to the computer.

12. A. Hardware resources are configured in the Device Manager console. Files and folders and applications are configured in the operating system GUI. Memory is configured in System Properties.

13. C. The mechanical hard drive should be periodically defragmented to arrange concurrent blocks of storage of files so that the hard drive arm does not need to move much when reading and writing files. Solid-state drives (SSDs) do not suffer poor performance from fragmentation, because they have no moving parts. Freeing up space and emptying the Recycle Bin are good ideas but do not contribute to the hard drive's performance. Trim is a feature used with SSD drives, where the operating system notifies the SSD device that data blocks have been freed up.

14. C. The Indexing Options applet allows you to configure custom extensions so that metadata can be searched. The Internet Options applet is used to configure Internet Explorer. The File Explorer Options applet is used to view and configure the File Explorer. The Ease of Access Center applet is used to configure options related to user disabilities to make the operating system easier to use.

15. A. The operating system must boot from an active primary partition if MBR style partitioning is used. Extended partitions are used to contain logical partitions. There is no such thing as a dynamic partition.

16. B. The HKEY_LOCAL_MACHINE Registry hive contains information about the computer's hardware. It is also known as HKLM. HKEY_CURRENT_MACHINE and HKEY_MACHINE are not valid Registry hives. HKEY_RESOURCES was used with Windows 9x operating systems but is no longer used.

17. C. GUID Partition Tables (GPT) allocates a 64-bit logical block addressing entry to partition tables to accommodate larger drives. GPT has rapidly replaced the MBR-style partition tables. LILO and GRUB are boot managers for Linux. NFS is a network filesystem used with Linux/UNIX operating systems.

18. A. Disk Defragmenter will rearrange blocks of files on a hard drive to create contiguous files and space. Windows File Explorer is used to navigate the filesystem. Scandisk is not a command. Windows Backup allows for file backups.

19. A. The hibernate power mode will write the contents of the RAM to the disk so that the computer can enter a low power state. The standby power mode will turn off the monitor and lower power consumption by the computer. The sleep and suspend power mode will lower power consumption, but it will not write the contents of the RAM to the disk.

20. C. The Dynamic Disk partition style allows up to 2,000 volumes to be created on a physical disk. GUID Partition Tables (GPT) allow up to 128 volumes to be created on a physical disk. The Master Boot Record (MBR) and Basic Disk partitioning scheme are one and the same and allow up to 26 partitions to be created on a physical disk.

Chapter 15: Windows Administration

The answers to the chapter review questions can be found in Appendix A.

1. A. You will be prompted after you agree to the end-user license agreement (EULA) with upgrade or custom. A custom installation is a clean installation when it comes to Windows. An upgrade is just that—an upgrade of the operating system—and is not a clean installation. A repair installation is a reinstallation of system files and retains the user data files. Refresh is a term used with Windows 8.1; it will retain user data files and only refresh the operating system files.

2. A. The Generalize pass is where the operating system detects hardware and installs the appropriate drivers. The Out-Of-Box Experience (OOBE) is the pass that is responsible for configuring and creating the user environment during the setup process. The Specialization pass is where the operating system is configured during setup. The WinPE pass starts the procedure of installing the operating system.

3. D. The WinRE partition is where the Windows Recovery Environment is located. The BCD is a term used with the boot configuration data to direct the operating system how to boot. The system partition contains the kernel of the operating system. The EFI system partition (ESP) contains the boot configuration data (BCD) that is used to boot the rest of the operating system on a UEFI system.

4. A. The Windows Deployment Service (WDS) is a server role that is used to create a Windows image for mass deployment. The Microsoft Assessment and Planning (MAP) toolkit is used to create reports on system hardware for image deployment. The User State Migration Toolkit (USMT) is used in corporate environments to migrate user data. The sysprep utility is used to prepare an operating system for imaging.

5. D. The `robocopy` command copies all data and includes NTFS permission to remain intact. The `xcopy` and `copy` commands copy files from a source folder to a destination folder but do not copy NTFS permissions. The `chkdsk` command is used to check the integrity of the NTFS filesystem.

6. B. The General Availability branch installs updates as they are released to the general public. The Semi-Annual Channel is no longer a channel supported by Windows 10/11. The Long-Term Servicing Channel never installs new features during the life of the version of Windows. The Insider Program allows for the installation of brand-new features before they are publicly released.

7. A. Windows 10 Home only allows for the General Availability branch releases. Windows 10 Pro allows for the use of the Insider Program branch releases. Windows 10 Education allows for the use of the Insider Program branch releases. Windows 10 Enterprise allows for the use of the Insider Program branch releases.

8. C. The date code of the edition is yymm, so 1703 is March of 2017. The 63rd day of 2015 and the 145th day of 2015 are incorrect answers, because the build number is the number of builds of Windows 10. The build number does translate to a version of Windows, but that information is in the date code and does not need to be looked up.

9. C. The pathping command measures the packet loss at each router as the packet travels to the destination address; it combines the ping and tracert commands. The ping command returns a single destination's response time. The nslookup command is used to resolve DNS addresses. The tracert command allows you to see how a packet travels to its destination.

10. B. The msinfo32.exe tool allows for the remote reporting of a computer's hardware. regedit.exe is used to edit the Registry. msconfig.exe is used to change the startup of services and change the boot process. dxdiag.exe is used to diagnose DirectX problems.

11. C. The chkdsk command is used to check a volume for corruption, as well as attempt to repair the corruption. The diskpart command allows you to create, modify, and view volumes on a disk. The format command allows you to format a filesystem on a volume. The sfc command is used to fix corrupted files but not volume corruption.

12. C. Users will not be able to change the wallpaper or personalize the operating system until it is active. Applications will still launch fine. Windows Updates will continue to function to keep Windows up to date. Browsing the Internet will not be affected.

13. B. The Out-Of-Box Experience (OOBE) is the pass that is responsible for configuring and creating the user environment during the setup process. The Generalization pass is where the operating system detects hardware. The Specialization pass is where the operating system is configured during setup. The WinPE pass starts the process of installing the operating system.

14. A. When installing Windows, you can control telemetry data in the Privacy Settings dialog box. The Cortana options allow you to control how Cortana is used. Disk partitioning is configured during the initial installation in order to direct Windows where to install. Account creation is performed to create the first user on the operating system.

15. D. You will need to upgrade to Windows 7 Home Basic first, since Windows 10 does not have a direct upgrade path from Windows Vista. Upgrading to Windows 10 Home can be achieved after upgrading to Windows 7 Home Basic. Upgrading to Windows 10 Pro or Windows 10 Enterprise directly cannot be achieved, even after upgrading to Windows 7 Home Basic. However, you can upgrade editions once you have upgraded to Windows 10.

16. D. There is no way to directly convert a 32-bit installation of Windows to 64-bit Windows without performing a clean installation. Upgrading directly to Windows 10 Pro 64-bit is not possible. Upgrading to Windows 10 Pro 32-bit is possible, but you cannot upgrade to a 64-bit edition. Upgrading to Windows 8.1 64-bit is not possible.

17. A. The Boot Configuration Data is stored in the EFI System Partition on an EFI installation of Windows. The WinRE partition is used for the Windows Recovery Environment. Secure Boot is a feature of an EFI installation and does not contain its own partition. The C:\WINDOWS folder is where the installation of Windows exists.

18. A. The netstat command can be used to view ports in use by the operating system and network applications communicating with the network. The ipconfig command allows you to see the current IP address and DNS information for the operating system. The pathping allows you to view packet loss along the path to a destination IP address. The nslookup command is used to resolve DNS records.

19. C. The Wireless Wide Area Network (WWAN) connection is a cellular connection and is configured on the Cellular screen in the Settings app. A wired connection is configured on the Ethernet screen in the Settings app. A wireless connection is configured on the Wi-Fi screen in the Settings app. A virtual private network (VPN) connection is configured on the VPN screen in the Settings app.

20. C. The maximum number of connections that can simultaneously be made to a Windows workstation is 20. All other answers are incorrect.

Chapter 16: Working with macOS and Linux

The answers to the chapter review questions can be found in Appendix A.

1. C. The command `ls -la` will list all the files in a long format. The command `ls -a |` `ls-l` will not work. `ls -s; ls -a` will show two listings: one with the size and the other with all the files. The `ls -a\ls -l` command will show two listings—one with all the files and the other in a long format—but it will not show all the files in a long format.

2. B. Mission Control is a quick way on macOS to view what is currently running. Keychain is a tool that saves credentials so that the user does not need to be prompted. The Finder is the macOS equivalent to Windows File Explorer. Force Quit is a function of the macOS for killing a process.

3. A. Time Machine is the Apple application that can be used to create backups on a regular basis. The Finder is the macOS equivalent to Windows File Explorer. VSS is a Windows technology that is used to create snapshots of a volume. Keychain is a tool that saves credentials so that the user does not need to be prompted.

4. B. The `nano` command is used to edit files. The `ps` command lists processes running. The `rm` command removes files or directories. The `ls` command lists files and folders in the filesystem.

5. C. The `ip` command can be used to edit an Ethernet connection's configuration settings. The `dd` command is used to duplicate disks. The `apt-get` command is used with the APT package management system for downloading packages. The `pwd` command shows the current working directory.

6. B. Keychain is a tool that saves credentials so that the user does not need to be prompted. Spotlight is a utility in macOS that allows a search of the operating system and Internet for search terms. The Dock is the macOS application menu that is located on the bottom of the screen. Gestures allow you to use more than one finger on the trackpad to perform different functions.

7. A. The shell is the interpreter in Linux between the operating system and the user. The translator is a wrong answer. Login is something you perform to access the shell. The graphical user interface (GUI) does not interpret commands and therefore is not considered an interpreter.

8. D. Working copies are backups that are kept on site at the computer center for immediate recovery purposes. An on-path attack is an attack where an eavesdropper listens between two people or devices. Cloud copies are backups that are sent to cloud storage and cannot be immediately recovered. Journal copies is a wrong answer.

9. C. The apt utility can be used to download and apply patches to a Linux installation. The update command is not a utility. Shell/terminal is an interface for interacting with the operating system with the command line. The patch command is not a utility.

10. C. The chown command is used to change ownership of a file. The cd command changes the working directory. The chmod command changes permissions on files. The pwd command displays the current working directory.

11. A. The fsck Linux utility is used to check and repair disks. The chkdsk utility is a Windows utility used to check and repair disks. The du utility is used to show the current disk usage. dumgr is not a utility and is a wrong answer.

12. B. By pressing the Home button twice on an iPad, you can Force Quit an application that will not stop running. The kill utility can be used only at the command line of Linux/macOS. The Task Manager is a Windows utility. Close Quit is not a feature and therefore a wrong answer.

13. C. Bash is the most common command-line shell used with Linux. Tcl/Tk is a shell used with Linux, but it is very uncommon. Terminal is a utility used to access the command-line shell. SSH, or Secure Shell, is a secure protocol used to access the shell over a network.

14. D. The Dock is the area at the bottom of the macOS screen that is used to launch applications. The footer is not a valid answer. Mission Control is a macOS feature that allows you to see all the applications running. The Taskbar is a Windows Desktop element that is used to track running applications and quickly launch them.

15. C. The Command+spacebar key combination will bring up the Spotlight utility. Control+Shift, Option+Tab, and Alt+Home are wrong answers.

16. A. The sudo command can be used to run a single command as another user. The su command allows you to change user logins at the command line. The passwd command changes the user's password. The ifconfig command allows you to view and modify the wired network interface.

17. C. The ps command will display a snapshot of the current running processes on a Linux operating system. The ls command will display a listing of files from the working directory. The cat command will display the contents of a file. The su command allows you to change user logins at the command line.

18. B. The command cd .. will take you one level back from the current working directory. The command cd . will do nothing, because the period signifies the current working directory. The command cd ... is not a valid command. The command cd ~ will change directories to the home directory of the user.

19. B. The effective permissions are read and write. From left to right, the permissions are rwx for the user, rw- for the group, and r-- for everyone else. Since the user is only a member of the group applied to the file, they will have read and write permissions.

20. C. The -p option on the mkdir command allows subfolders to be created as well as the target folder. All other answers are incorrect.

Chapter 17: Security Concepts

The answers to the chapter review questions can be found in Appendix A.

1. A. Fences are intended to delay or deter entrance into a facility. Access control vestibules are used for mid-layer access control to prevent tailgating. Multifactor authentication is used for mid- and inner-layer access control. Strong passwords are used for mid- and inner-layer access control.

2. B. A magnetometer, also known as a metal detector, can detect weapons on a person entering a facility. Biometrics are used to authenticate someone based on their face, retina, fingerprint, or some other method that biologically verifies their identity. A motion sensor is used to detect motion. A badge reader is used to scan security ID badges.

3. A. Social engineering uses the inherent trust in the human species, as opposed to technology, to gain access to your environment. IDSs are network-based systems that detect intrusions. Perimeter security describes physical security. Biometrics describes an authentication method based on human physical traits.

4. C. A fingerprint scanner, or any device that identifies a person by a physical trait, is considered a biometric security control. Access control is the system that controls access for users. Physical barriers are structures that limit physical access. Softening refers to weakening of security.

5. A. Although the end result of any of these attacks may be denying authorized users access to network resources, a denial-of-service (DoS) attack is specifically intended to prevent access to network resources by overwhelming or flooding a service or network. Worms reproduce and move throughout the network to infect other systems. Trojans are programs that enter a system or network under the guise of another program. Social engineering is a process in which an attacker attempts to acquire information about your network and system by social means, such as talking to people in the organization.

6. B. A distributed denial-of-service (DDoS) attack uses multiple computer systems to attack a server or host in the network. A denial-of-service (DoS) is a one-on-one attack to disrupt service. Worms reproduce and move throughout the network to infect other systems and therefore do not attack one victim. Rootkits are software programs that have the ability to hide themselves from the operating system.

7. D. Tokens are rotating numerical keys that you must physically have with you to gain access to the operating system or applications. Biometrics relies on a physical characteristic of the user to verify identity. Biometric devices typically use either a hand pattern or a retinal scan to accomplish this. Smartcards contain a private certificate key and are protected with a password. Geofencing uses your GPS coordinates to ensure that the authentication happens when you are in a defined geographic area.

8. A. An on-path attack intercepts data and then sends the information to the server as if nothing were wrong while collecting the information. Zero-day attacks are attacks in which a developer has not properly patched a hole yet and is unaware of the hole. A denial-of-service (DoS) attack is used to disrupt legitimate requests from being answered. A smurf attack is a type of distributed denial-of-service (DDoS).

9. A. A spoofing attack is an attempt by someone or something to masquerade as someone else (IP address) and is often used to disrupt access. Social engineering is a process in which an attacker attempts to acquire information about your network and system by social means, such as talking to people in the organization. Worms reproduce and move throughout the network to infect other systems. Password attacks are used in an attempt to guess passwords.

10. A. A worm is different from a virus in that it can reproduce itself, is self-contained, and doesn't need a host application to be transported. A smurf attack is a type of distributed denial-of-service (DDoS). A phishing attack is an attempt to gain a user's credentials to a network resource. Trojan horses are programs that enter a system or network under the guise of another program.

11. D. The reflective attack is using a broadcast ping (ICMP) on a network. The return address of the ping may be that of a valid system in your network. The Transmission Control Protocol (TCP) is not typically used with a reflective attack. The Internet Protocol (IP) is a suite of protocols and solely used with a reflective attack. The User Datagram Protocol (UDP) is not described in this reflective attack.

12. C. A SQL injection attack is a method of passing a SQL query with a web request by using an escape code sequence. An insider threat is a threat from within your organization, such as a disgruntled employee. An evil twin attack involves a rogue access point with the same SSID as your organization. Tailgating is the act of walking behind someone who has swiped to get into an area so the attacker can gain entry.

13. B. A key fob is an example of authentication for something you have. A password is something you know. A fingerprint is something you are. A place is a geographical place in which you are.

14. B. End-user education is the best way to protect your users from the threat of phishing via email. Antivirus software is used to prevent viruses, not phishing attempts. SecureDNS can be useful in protecting your users, but not from phishing emails. The principle of least privilege assigns only the permissions that users need to do their work, and no more.

15. C. Spear phishing is a type of social engineering, where someone is trying to con your organization into revealing account and password information by pretending to be a high-level person. A spoofing attack is an attempt by someone or something to masquerade as someone else, with the intent of disrupting access. A replay attack is a form of on-path attack, where packets are replayed at a critical time. Trojan horses are programs that enter a system or network under the guise of another program.

16. A. Some viruses won't damage a system in an attempt to spread into all the other systems in a network. These viruses use that system as the carrier of the virus. A password attack would not prompt your antivirus software to notify you. Your antivirus software could be malfunctioning, but it would not suggest the same virus is infecting you over and over again. A denial-of-service (DoS) attack would not prompt your antivirus to notify you.

17. B. A symptom of many viruses is unusual activity on the system disk. The virus spreading to other files on your system causes this. A disk failure will not create high disk activity. A spear phishing attack is a social engineering attack and will not create high disk activity; neither denial-of-service attacks nor TCP/IP hijacking attacks will create high disk activity.

18. A. A brute-force attack is a type of password attack in which a password is guessed over and over until the right password is guessed. A backdoor attack is an embedded account that allows unauthorized access through an unpatched coding hole. A worm is different from a virus in that it can reproduce itself, is self-contained, and doesn't need a host application to be transported. A TCP/IP hijacking is an attack that attempts to redirect the TCP/IP conversation to the threat agent.

19. A. The thesis of your presentation should outline the need of a firewall to isolate the external network from the internal network. Firewalls will not scan packets for viruses. Firewalls will not prevent password attacks or harden physical security.

20. C. A login script is used by Active Directory during login to map drives and printers. A home folder is a private network location in which the user can store their personal files. Organizational units (OUs) are used to group computers and users so that Group Policy can be applied. The MMC is used to manage various aspects of Active Directory and the local operating system.

Chapter 18: Securing Operating Systems

The answers to the chapter review questions can be found in Appendix A.

1. C. A bring your own device (BYOD) policy defines the minimum specifications for an employee's device used for work-related access. The mobile device management (MDM) software would usually police these specifications, but it would not define them. The acceptable use policy (AUP) is a code of conduct when dealing with organization resources. The nondisclosure agreement (NDA) is an agreement used when dealing with intellectual property.

2. D. Synchronizing a mobile device with a computer system allows you to mirror personal data between the devices, regardless of which one contains the most current data. Calibration refers to matching the device's and user's perceptions of where the user is touching the screen. Remote wipes allow you to remove personal data from a lost or stolen device. Pairing is what must be done in Bluetooth for two Bluetooth devices to connect and communicate.

3. A. The Guest account should be disabled on the operating system, unless there is good reason to leave the account enabled. Print Operators is a group found on Windows servers. Power Users is a group found on both Windows workstations and servers. Userone is obviously a user account. Unless the user has left the organization, there should be no reason to disable the account.

4. C. Locator apps can find the phone and then display a message that can be read even while the phone is locked. Locator apps also often give the user the option to make the phone blare a noise to aid in finding the device. Failed login restrictions will wipe a device if a specific number of wrong passwords are entered. Antivirus apps make sure that your phone does not get a virus, but they offer no way to message or locate the device. Remotely wiping a mobile device is a feature of locator apps, but it is not itself an app that displays messages and produces noises.

5. C. A screensaver should automatically start after a short period of idle time, and that screensaver should require a password before the user can begin the session again. The system should neither shut down nor restart, since work could still be open. For the same reason, the system should not log out the user.

6. B. Android apps have an `.apk` (Android Package Kit) extension. Apps are developed with a software development kit (SDK), but `.sdk` is not a valid extension. Apple iOS apps use an `.ipa` (iOS App Store Package) extension. Only the Windows desktop operating system can execute `.exe` files.

7. C. The goal of single sign-on (SSO) is to allow a username/password combination. Once the combination is entered, claims are used to access additional resources. Tokens are given to the operating system after a user successfully logs in; they allow a user to access rights on the operating system. Kerberos is used (along with Active Directory) to authenticate a user on the Windows operating system. Multifactor authentication is the use of two or more factors to authenticate a user.

8. B. The Windows Credential Manager is a password manager that is built into the operating system of Windows. Edge and Internet Explorer 11 work in conjunction with the Credential Manager, but they are not password managers. Active Directory is used to authenticate domain users, but it does not manage passwords for end users.

9. A. The advantage to assigning the IP addresses statically is that you can make certain which host is associated with which IP address, and then use filtering to limit network access to only those hosts. Disabling DNS will limit all hosts on a network from getting to the Internet and will not limit network access. A default subnet mask will not limit network access and will cause other problems. An empty default gateway will not limit network access.

10. C. Wi-Fi Protected Access 2 (WPA2) offers the Advanced Encryption Standard (AES) for encrypting wireless communications. Wired Equivalent Privacy (WEP) offers weak 64- or 128-bit encryption. Wi-Fi Protected Access (WPA) uses the RC4 encryption algorithm. Temporal Key Integrity Protocol (TKIP) is a part of the WPA encryption protocol.

11. B. An extension is a type of add-on that will extend the functionality of the web browser in a way it was never originally designed. A pop-up blocker changes the way a web page is rendered. A plug-in changes the way a web page is rendered. An ad blocker also changes the way a web page is rendered.

12. A. When an employee is offboarded, their user account is deleted or disabled. A user account is not created, nor is its password reset, during the offboarding process. A user account normally is created during the onboarding process.

13. B. By default, a Google account is required on Android devices; it is used to synchronize data and app purchases to the cloud. The device does not require email to be set up, but the account can be used for the setup. The account is not used for desktop backups. The device does not require registration.

14. A. Fingerprint locks are the most secure of all the lock methods, since fingerprints are hard to duplicate. Face locks have a high number of false positives, which can be used to gain access to the phone. Passcode locks can be cracked or shoulder surfed. Swipe locks are not really locks; they just allow the screen to be opened with a swipe.

15. A. The Encrypted File System (EFS) is a functionality of the Windows NTFS filesystem. EFS can encrypt individual files and folders. BitLocker is a full-device encryption technology. NTFS is a filesystem that supports encryption and security, among other functionality. Bit-Locker to Go is used for full-device encryption of removable drives.

16. B. Because the user is in both groups and the Sales group has full share permissions and the Sales group has modify NTFS permissions, the most restrictive of the two is Modify, so that will be the effective permission for the user. All of the other answers are incorrect.

17. A. The permissions will be the same as before the move, since you are just moving the files and not creating a new entity. The permissions will not be inherited from the parent folder. The permissions will not be configured the same as the root folder. The permissions will not be blank.

18. B. The user will have only the Modify permission when logged in locally to the computer, since the filesystem is not shared with the appropriate permissions. The user will not have the Modify permission when connecting from the network. The user will still have the Modify permission when logged in locally, because of the NTFS permissions. The user will not have read-only permissions when connecting from the network.

19. C. The file attributes are most likely set to Read-only, and thus you are not permitted to delete the file. The Modify permission would not hinder the file from being deleted. The share permissions would not have any bearing on the problem, since the local filesystem is being accessed. The file attributes being set to System would not restrict a file from being deleted.

20. D. Mobile device management (MDM) software enables you to enforce profile security requirements on mobile devices. The acceptable use policy (AUP) is a code of ethics your users should follow when dealing with organizational resources. A nondisclosure agreement (NDA) is an agreement between an employee and the organization to protect intellectual property. A bring your own device (BYOD) policy explains how devices should be secured but provides no enforcement.

Chapter 19: Troubleshooting Operating Systems and Security

The answers to the chapter review questions can be found in Appendix A.

1. D. Windows Update is responsible for downloading and installing Windows service packs, patches, and security updates. Device Manager is used to view devices installed on the operating system. The Microsoft Management Console is a console that allows snap-ins to be added for management. Download Manager is a component of Internet Explorer.

2. B. Enable Safe Boot with the `msconfig` utility allows you to boot with basic drivers and minimal startup of nonessential services. Enable Debugging is used by kernel developers. Disable Driver Signature Enforcement is used to allow an unsigned driver to load during boot. Enable Low-Resolution Video will boot the operating system into a VGA mode.

3. B. The /REBUILDBCD option can be used with the bootrec tool to rebuild the boot configuration data (BCD). The /FIXBOOT option writes a new boot sector to the system partition. The /SCANOS option scans all other partitions that are found to have Windows installations. The /FIXMBR writes a new master boot record (MBR) to the partition.

4. B. The most important first step is to identify and verify the malware symptoms. You should quarantine the infected system once you have verified it is infected. Remediating the infected system happens after you disable System Restore. Education of the end user is the last step to malware removal.

5. A. The Profile tab of the Advanced Systems Properties dialog box allows you to view the total size of a local or remote profile. Regedit and the Windows Recovery Environment will not aid in troubleshooting a slow-loading profile. Windows Preinstallation Environment is the mini-Windows version used for installation of Windows.

6. D. winresume.exe is used to load Windows from a suspended state. The Boot Configuration Data (BCD) is used to direct Windows to boot the proper installation. ntoskrnl .exe is the Windows kernel. winload.exe is used for the normal booting of the Windows operating system.

7. A. The System Restore option should be used first to restore the operating system to an earlier point before the problem. This will restore the device back to a previous state before the installation of the drivers. System Restore will not affect user data files. Reset This PC will reset the PC back to factory default before the tax application was installed. Reimaging the laptop will erase all programs and data files. Manually reinstalling Windows 10 will erase all programs and data files.

8. A. When you have UEFI firmware, you must have the disk set up with a GUID Partition Table (GPT) partitioning type. The standard master boot record (MBR) partitioning type can be used with BIOS. Power-on self-test (POST) is a routine the BIOS or firmware performs to test hardware before boot. The Boot Sector is contained on both MBR and GPT partitioning types.

9. B. Pop-up blockers are used to prevent pop-ups and pop-unders from appearing. Antimalware utilities will remove and prevent malware. Phishing sites are used to collect users' credentials by tricking users. Antivirus software is used to protect the operating system from viruses.

10. C. Antivirus definitions should be updated daily, because new viruses are identified by the minute. Updating antivirus definitions weekly or monthly will open you up to the possibility of infection.

11. A. Resource Monitor can be used to identify slow and sluggish performance, as well as identify the source of the problem. The msconfig.exe tool can be used to enable or disable services on startup and launch tools, but it cannot be used to diagnose performance issues. The Device Manager MMC can be used to view and modify devices, but it will not help diagnose performance problems. Reliability Monitor will display the reliability of the operating system, but it will not help diagnose problems with performance.

12. B. Windows Update Troubleshooter can assist in diagnosing problems with Windows Update. The ntbtlog.txt file is used to diagnose problems with bootup. Windows

Recovery Environment is used to solve problems with Windows and is not typically used for problems with Windows Updates. Safe mode is a boot mode that loads minimal drivers and services.

13. A. Microsoft Defender Security is considered antimalware and antivirus protection for the Windows operating system. Mobile device management (MDM) software is used to manage mobile devices. Windows Action Center is a notification center for action to be taken in the operating system. VirusTotal is a third-party site that analyzes virus signatures, but it does not protect you from them.

14. B. The System File Checker (SFC) allows you to manually scan for modified operating system files and repair them. `regedit` is used to modify the Registry. `bootrec` is used to repair the boot records on an operating system installation. User Account Control (UAC) is used to control access to administrative credentials.

15. A. Establishing security policies and procedures will help eliminate security problems and guide employees on what to do if they arise. Optimizing drives will defragment drives and has no effect on security. Preventing booting into safe mode will only hinder diagnostics. Preventing booting into Windows Recovery Environment will also hinder diagnostics.

16. D. The device most likely has too many background applications open that are using RAM. That the device is not charged to capacity would not affect RAM. A digitizer not functioning properly would resemble inaccurate touchscreen responses. If the device were in Do Not Disturb (DND) mode, the speakers would not work.

17. B. If auto-reconnect is configured on an SSID, the device could be susceptible to an evil twin attack, in which the device connects to any device with the same SSID. The device will not reconnect to any SSID but only to the SSID configured as auto-reconnect. Battery life will remain unaffected with auto-reconnect. Exceeding limits can be avoided with auto-reconnect, because the wireless network is used for data usage.

18. B. Event Viewer will allow you to see more detailed information on why programs have crashed. The Event Viewer logs may not give the exact reason, but they will aid in understanding the root cause. Device Manager is used to view and manage devices connected to the operating system. The Windows Recovery Environment is used to repair the Windows operating system. The `msconfig.exe` tool is used to modify startup programs and launch other diagnostic tools.

19. C. The reason that the operating system would write out large amounts of RAM to the page file is that the system is running low on physical RAM and is attempting to free up physical RAM. The CPU might run high when paging occurs, but it will not trigger excessive paging. Although it is normal for the operating system to write out RAM to the page file, it is not normal for large amounts to be written out. The page file is not faster than conventional RAM.

20. B. Degraded battery life can be expected from an overheating mobile device if the problem persists for a long time. Higher RAM usage will not occur with overheating, but it could be a cause of overheating. Inaccurate touchscreen responses are not a symptom or a consequence of overheating. The inability to decrypt emails depends on having the proper certificate installed.

Chapter 20: Scripting and Remote Access

The answers to the chapter review questions can be found in Appendix A.

1. C. Scripting languages are interpreted languages that run on top of a runtime environment. Programming languages, not scripting languages, require a compiler. Scripting languages are not strongly typed; programming languages are strongly typed. Scripting languages have bad memory management because of loosely typed variables.

2. A. Scripting languages are considered high-level languages because they do not directly access hardware and use an intermediary called the interpreter. Mid-level languages are Java and C/C++, not scripting languages. There is no such thing as an intermediate-level language. Low-level languages are machine language and assembly language, which are not scripting languages.

3. C. Floating-point variables allow for precision math, also known as decimal math. Boolean variables allow for true or false values. Integer variables allow for whole numbers values. String variables allow for text values.

4. C. A program variable is the least significant and not inherited. A system variable is defined for the entire system and is the most significant because it is inherited by all users and programs. A user variable is significant as well, since all applications inherit the variable. A string variable is not inherited, but it is not an environment variable.

5. B. The statement `$xvar = 2` is a PowerShell statement that will load the variable `xvar` with a value of 2. The statement `xvar = 2` is Bash syntax. The statement `xvar = 2;` is JavaScript syntax. The statement `set /a xvar=2` is Windows batch script syntax.

6. D. A `for` loop has a defined beginning and end, and steps from the beginning to the end. A `do while` loop is a type of `while` loop and has only a defined end. A `while` loop has only a defined end. An `if` statement is branch logic, not a loop.

7. C. The `.bat` extension is used with the Windows batch scripting language. The `.vbs` extension is used with VBScript language. The `.js` extension is used with the JavaScript scripting language. The `.py` extension is used with the Python scripting language.

8. B. The VBScript language allows for the use of the Component Object Model (COM). The PowerShell scripting language allows for the use of the .NET Framework. Windows batch scripts use existing applications. JavaScript is primarily web browser–based and does not allow for the use of external objects.

9. D. The `.py` extension is used with the Python scripting language. The `.vbs` extension is used with the VBScript language. The `.js` extension is used with the JavaScript scripting language. The `.bat` extension is used with the Windows batch scripting language.

10. A. The PowerShell scripting language allows for the use of the .NET Framework and is commonly used with Microsoft Azure and Microsoft 365. The VBScript language allows for the use of the Component Object Model (COM) and is not used for cloud services. Windows batch script uses existing applications and is not used for cloud services. JavaScript is primarily web browser–based, does not allow for the use of external objects, and is not used for cloud services.

11. D. JavaScript is primarily web browser–based and allows for interactive content. The Power-Shell scripting language is used to manage the operating system. The Bash scripting language is primarily used with Linux and UNIX systems. Windows batch scripts use existing applications and are used to manage the operating system.

12. B. The `.sh` extension is used with the Bash scripting language. The `.vbs` extension is used with the VBScript language. The `.bat` extension is used with the Windows batch scripting language. The `.py` extension is used with the Python scripting language.

13. C. Before a script can be executed, you must use the `chmod` command to grant execute permissions. The `chown` command changes ownership. There is no such thing as an execute attribute. Adding `.sh` to the end of the script doesn't serve any purpose.

14. C. The statement `mvar = 8;` is JavaScript syntax to load a variable of `mvar` with a value of 8. The statement `$mvar = 8` is PowerShell syntax. The statement `mvar = 8` is Bash syntax. The statement `set /a mvar=8` is Windows batch script syntax.

15. D. PowerShell is the only scripting language that has a preinstalled Integrated Scripting Environment (ISE), called the PowerShell ISE. The VBScript language requires the installation of Microsoft Visual Studio Code. The Bash scripting language requires a text editor or other package to be installed. The Python scripting language requires a third-party integrated development environment (IDE), also known as an ISE.

16. A. The line `//comment` is used to comment JavaScript code. The line `'comment` is used to comment VBScript code. The line `REM comment` is used to comment Windows batch script code. The line `# comment` is used to comment Bash script code and PowerShell code.

17. A. The `.js` extension is used with the JavaScript scripting language. The `.sh` extension is used with the Bash scripting language. The `.bat` extension is used with the Windows batch scripting language. The `.py` extension is used with the Python scripting language.

18. B. Remote Desktop Protocol (RDP) allows for local drives to be available to the remote machine when an RDP session is initiated. Virtual Network Computing (VNC), Secure Shell (SSH), and Telnet are not capable of redirecting drives.

19. B. The SSH protocol operates on TCP port 22. The Remote Desktop Protocol operates on TCP port 3389. The Telnet service operates on TCP port 23. HTTPS operates on TCP port 443.

20. B. The built-in Microsoft Remote Access (MSRA) tool is used for screen sharing between a trusted helper and a user. The Remote Desktop Protocol (RDP) is a protocol used to allow an administrator to connect remotely to a Windows server or workstation, but it does not support screen sharing. Both Secure Shell (SSH) and Telnet are protocols used for text-based console access for administrating Linux/UNIX and network operating system environments.

Chapter 21: Safety and Environmental Concerns

The answers to the chapter review questions can be found in Appendix A.

1. C. A three-pronged grabber should be used to retrieve the screw from the computer. Using a magnetic-tipped screwdriver is not advisable, because many components are sensitive to magnets. Using a magnetic grabber is not advisable, because many components are sensitive to magnets. Shaking the computer until it falls out can be dangerous and make the screw harder to get out.

2. C. A high-voltage probe can dissipate the high voltage stored in a CRT. An antistatic wrist strap should not be worn near a high-voltage potential such as a CRT monitor. A screwdriver can dangerously arc the voltage and is not the proper way to discharge the unit. A power cord supplies power to a CRT monitor.

3. B. The material safety data sheet (MSDS) will have the necessary information about the cleanup procedures. The Occupational Safety and Health Administration (OSHA) is an organization that oversees safety in the workplace. The product label may or may not have this information. A cathode-ray tube (CRT) is a type of monitor that uses a glass tube.

4. D. You can download the MSDS by visiting the printer cartridge manufacturer's website. The store is not required to furnish an MSDS at the time of purchase. The manufacturer is not required to furnish an MSDS with the packaging of the product. You are legally allowed to have an MSDS for products, as per OSHA. You should have them on hand in case of an emergency.

5. A, C. An accident should always be reported so that if there is a hazardous condition, it can be fixed. Report hazardous conditions, such a spill on the floor, to the employer before they are a problem. A near-accident does not need to be reported unless it is caused by a hazardous condition, like spills. Rain forecasted for a workday is not a hazardous condition.

6. B. You can feel an ESD shock of 3,000 volts or more. 300 volts is too low for a human to feel. A minimum of 30,000 volts can be felt by a human. 300,000 volts can be felt by humans and could be painful.

7. A, B. Using an antistatic wrist strap allows you to ground yourself to dissipate a static charge. Using antistatic bags allows for a uniform charge around a component. Spraying disinfectant spray will only kill germs, not reduce static. Shuffling your feet will build a charge of static.

8. B, D. Providing properly maintained tools and equipment is a requirement for an OSHA-compliant workplace. Displaying an OSHA poster in a prominent location is also a requirement for an OSHA-compliant workplace. Attending yearly OSHA safe work environment seminars is not a requirement. Having an OSHA employee stationed within 5 miles of the facility is also not a requirement.

9. A. You should ensure that the company has the proper licenses to install 20 additional copies to be compliant with licensing. Microsoft Office is not an open source licensed product. Using the personal license key from an existing system violates the license agreement. Following normal installation procedures will not ensure compliance of licensing.

10. C, D. You should use a cart to move heavy objects. You should also ensure that no safety hazards are in your path. Lifting by bending over at the waist can hurt your back. Carrying CRT monitors with the glass facing outward is not safe, as the weight will be farthest from your body.

11. C. Alkaline batteries should be taken to a recycling center. Throwing batteries in the trash is not environmentally responsible. Incinerating batteries is not advisable, since they can explode and will create pollution. Flushing batteries down the toilet is not an acceptable disposal method.

12. B, D. The first step is to confiscate and preserve the prohibited materials on the drive. The next step is to report the prohibited materials through the proper channels. Destroying the prohibited material will not remedy the situation. Confronting the user about the material is not suggested, as they could become hostile.

13. A. You should research information on the Payment Card Industry Data Security Standard (PCI DSS). The General Data Protection Regulation (GDPR) is used for protecting EU citizens. Protected health information (PHI) is any data that defines a patient or an ailment of a patient. Personally identifiable information (PII) is any information that can be used to identify a person.

14. A. Wood and paper fires can be put out by a Class A fire extinguisher. Class B fire extinguishers are used for flammable liquids. Class C fire extinguishers are used for electrical files. Class D fire extinguishers are used for flammable metals.

15. B, C. Phillips and Torx are two common types of screwdriver. Neither circular nor helix is a type of screwdriver.

16. A, B. Good safety plans protect the interests of the workers and also help to keep company costs down. Periodic workplace inspections and a training program are good components to implement. Employees cannot be punished in any way for reporting safety violations. Third-party audits of safety programs are not necessary but can complement periodic inspections and safety and health training programs.

17. A. A good rule of thumb when it comes to magnetic-tipped screwdrivers is to avoid using them inside a computer case. Magnetic tools can damage data on disks that use a magnetic storage scheme. Magnetic-tipped screwdrivers should not be used inside a computer even if they are kept away from the processor and the RAM. Regardless of whether they are powered or not, magnetic-tipped screwdrivers should not be used inside computers.

18. B, C. Material safety data sheets (MSDSs) contain handling and storage instructions as well as personal protection instructions. MSDSs do not contain freezing point specifications or salinity levels.

19. B, D. To maintain a safe work environment, all employees must follow certain protocols. These include using protective gear and equipment and following all health and safety rules. Accidents must be reported to the employer, not OSHA (unless action is not properly taken by the employer). There are no rules requiring safety training, although it is a good idea to have these sessions and for employees to attend them.

20.   B. Nickel-metal hydride (NiMH) batteries are not considered environmental hazards. Alkaline batteries used to contain mercury, which is an environmental hazard, so they are assumed to be environmental hazards. Nickel-cadmium (NiCd) batteries and button cell batteries are considered environmental hazards.

Chapter 22: Documentation and Professionalism

The answers to the chapter review questions can be found in Appendix A.

1.   D. A physical network diagram details all connections so that the next technician does not need to trace connections. A logical network diagram shows the flow of information. A knowledge base article documents a symptom and solution for a problem but not the connections. A change management document is used to evaluate a potential change to a network.

2.   C. The rollback section contains the original configuration that can be used to revert the changes. The purpose section contains the reason for the proposed change. The risk analysis section explains the risks involved with the proposed changes. The plan for change section contains the primary change configuration and the alternate change configuration.

3.   B. The scope of change section details whom the change will affect. The business processes section details the current business processes the change will affect. The user acceptance section details how the changes were tested and accepted by the users. The plan for change contains the primary and alternate plans for the proposed change.

4.   D. Incident documentation should be completed so that key stakeholders can understand the reason for the outage. Change management documentation is used for proposed changes to the network. Knowledge base articles are used to document symptoms and solutions. An acceptable use policy (AUP) is used to protect an organization's resources from user abuse.

5.   A. The Sarbanes–Oxley Act (SOX) is enforced by the Securities and Exchange Commission (SEC) and regulates sensitive financial information and financial records. The Family Educational Rights and Privacy Act (FERPA) affects education providers and organizations that process student records. The Health Insurance Portability and Accountability Act (HIPAA) affects health-care providers and providers that process health records. The Gramm–Leach–Bliley Act (GLBA) affects providers of financial services and safeguards customer information.

6.   A. A logical diagram is a high-level overview of a system so that you can see the flow of information. A physical diagram shows specifics, and although it can be used to trace the flow of information, it is not used as a high-level overview. A symbol diagram is not a type of diagram. A knowledge base article details a solution for symptoms and is not used to view the flow of information.

7.   C. The acceptable use policy (AUP) details the acceptable use of the email system for business purposes. Mobile device management (MDM) is software that allows you to manage mobile devices in the workplace. A password policy details the appropriate handling and management of passwords. Incident management is how a network or security incident is handled.

8. B. Disk-to-disk is the fastest recovery method and backup method as well, because you are backing up from a disk to another disk attached via the network. Disk-to-tape is slower because you must re-tension the tape and then locate the data on the tape to recover it. Disk-to-flash is not a backup method, because of the price of flash. Disk-to-cloud is the slowest recovery method because you must recover from the cloud over a network connection.

9. B. You should use the copy backup method, since it will perform a full backup of the files without resetting the archive bits. A full backup makes a full backup and resets all the archive bits affecting the normal backups. An incremental backup copies only the files that have changed since the last backup and leaves the archive bits unchanged. A differential backup backs up only the files that have changed since the last backup and then resets all the archive bits.

10. C. A service entrance surge protection is used between the power meter and the main breakers, to protect from electrical surges. A surge protector strip is found under desks to protect from electrical surges. An uninterruptable power supply (UPS) is used as a backup power source until power is restored or conditioned properly. A generator is used during power outages to sustain power.

11. C. Calling the customer and informing them of the situation is the best action that can be performed, since you are having direct communications. Arriving first thing in the morning should be done, but communications is the first action. Waiting until after hours and then leaving a message is not an appropriate action. Sending an email letting the customer know that you will be late is lying, since you will not make it to their site.

12. C. If the problems do not appear to be related, then deal with them separately. Looking for commonalities between the problems would just waste valuable time. No assumptions should be made, such as that a virus is causing the problem, unless there is proof. Ordering a new machine is disruptive to the customer, unless the problem dictates that this action be performed.

13. D. If you do not understand the customer, you should apologize, treat the customer with respect, and seek a manager to help translate. Ignoring the customer and starting to work on the system is not an appropriate response. Calling your supervisor will not solve the problem, since your supervisor will have the same issue. Asking that another technician be sent in your place is being insensitive to the customer and "passing the buck."

14. C. You should avoid confrontations with the user by attempting to calm them down. You should *never* shove the user back. Yelling for everyone in the area to come quickly will escalate the situation, which is the opposite of what you want to do.

15. B. You should take appropriate action and inform your manager, as well as notify the customer that you've done so. Doing nothing is not an appropriate response to this situation. Talking to the technician personally will create a confrontation and should be avoided. Asking the customer to prove it is an inappropriate action to this problem.

16. D. You should assure the vice president that you are optimistic and skilled to deal with these problems. Offering a joke is an inappropriate action. Downplaying the situation does not show respect to the customer's problem. Keeping your head down and ignoring the customer does not display appropriate communications.

17. C. You should try to solve the customer's problem without further escalating the frustration by putting them on hold or transferring them. Informing them that you won't be able to help is only going to anger the caller, further validating their frustration. Transferring them to another technician is not the appropriate action, because it will add to their frustration. Suggesting that they call back will create more frustration and is poor customer service.

18. B, C. Leaving a note for the user detailing what was done and how to contact you displays appropriate communications. Notifying the user's manager and your own manager that the problem is resolved is also appropriate communications. Cleaning up and leaving no evidence that you were there is an inappropriate action, as it is deceiving to the user. Putting the system back to its original state is an inappropriate action because it does not solve the problem.

19. A. While the user's profanity is likely linked to frustration, it hinders the communication and should be eliminated. You should ask the user to refrain from the offensive language. There may be circumstances where it is necessary to overlook the profanity, if your request is likely to make the already upset customer even angrier, as long as you can understand what is being said. Hanging up is not an appropriate action and will further the user's frustration. Firing back with profanity is not an appropriate response, as it will escalate the situation further.

20. B. Scheduling of the depreciation of the equipment is performed in accounting software. Tracking of the equipment is a benefit to an asset tag. Identifying assets is a direct benefit of asset tags. An asset tag provides proof of ownership.

Appendix B

Answers to Performance-Based Questions

Chapter 1: Motherboards, Processors, and Memory

Answer to Performance-Based Question 1

Here is how to remove a DIMM and replace it with another one:

1. Pull the tabs on either end of the DIMM away from the DIMM.
2. Pull the loose DIMM straight out of the slot and away from the motherboard.
3. Ensure that the locking tabs are completely opened and out of the way of the slot.
4. Align the new module's notch with the tab or tabs in the slot.
5. Insert the new DIMM straight down into the slot.
6. Apply firm and even pressure downward until the locking tabs automatically snap into place.
7. Nudge the tabs inward toward the module to make sure that they are tight.

Answer to Performance-Based Question 2

The components are labeled in the following illustration.

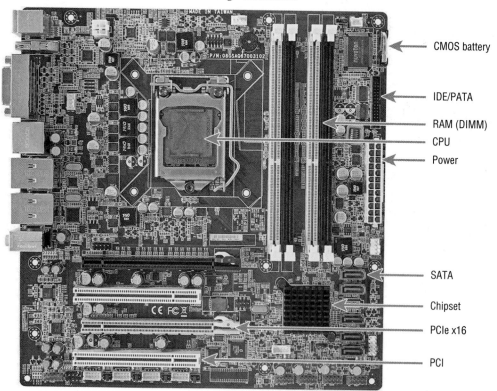

Chapter 2: Expansion Cards, Storage Devices, and Power Supplies

Answer to Performance-Based Question

Here are the steps to remove a power supply from a computer chassis:

1. Remove the power source from the system.
2. Ground yourself and the computer to the same source of ground.
3. Remove the cover from the system.
4. Locate the power supply.
5. Follow all wiring harnesses from the power supply to their termini, disconnecting each one.
6. Remove any obstructions that appear as if they might hinder removal of the power supply.
7. Locate and remove the machine screws on the outside of the case that are used to secure the power supply.
8. Pull the power supply out of the case.

Chapter 3: Peripherals, Cables, and Connectors

Answer to Performance-Based Question

The answers to the Chapter 3 performance-based question are as follows:

- A: VGA
- B: USB
- C: Audio (or 1/8")
- D: HDMI
- E: eSATA
- F: DisplayPort
- G: USB-C
- H: Mini-DisplayPort or Thunderbolt 2

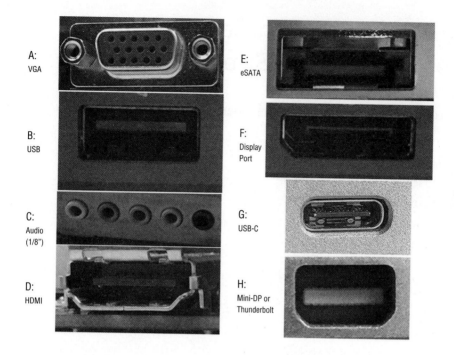

A:
VGA

B:
USB

C:
Audio
(1/8")

D:
HDMI

E:
eSATA

F:
Display
Port

G:
USB-C

H:
Mini-DP or
Thunderbolt

Chapter 4: Printers and Multifunction Devices

Answer to Performance-Based Question

Here are some example steps to take to clean an inkjet printer. The process for starting the cleaning cycle on inkjet printers can vary, and some printers have both quick and deep-clean cycles. Always check your documentation for steps specific to your printer.

1. Power on the printer, and open the top cover to expose the area containing the print cartridges.

2. Initiate a self-cleaning cycle.

3. When the print head moves from its resting place, pull the AC power plug.

4. Locate the sponge pads on which to apply the cleaning solution.

5. Using the supplied syringe, apply the cleaning solution to the sponge pads until they are saturated.

6. Plug the printer back into the wall outlet and turn it on. The print head will park themselves.

7. Turn off the printer. Let the solution sit for at least three hours.

8. Power the printer back on and run three printer cleaning cycles. Print a nozzle check pattern (or a test page) after each cleaning cycle to monitor the cleaning progress.

Chapter 5: Networking Fundamentals

Answer to Performance-Based Question

Possible answers for examples of physical network topologies could include bus, ring, star, mesh, and hybrid. The simplest topology, and the one that uses the least amount of cable, is a bus. It consists of a single cable that runs to every workstation, as shown in the following illustration.

MARGIN ICON

Lucent connector (LC)

Subscriber connector (SC)

F type

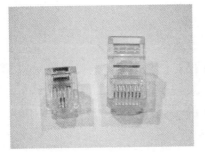
RJ-11, RJ-45

Straight tip (ST)

Chapter 6: Introduction to TCP/IP

Performance-Based Answer

Here is the correct matching of protocols and services to their ports:

Protocol (service)	Port(s)
FTP	20, 21
SSH	22
Telnet	23
SMTP	25
DNS	53
DHCP	67, 68
TFTP	69
HTTP	80
POP3	110
NetBIOS/NetBT	137, 139
IMAP	143
SNMP	161, 162
LDAP	389
HTTPS	443
SMB/CIFS	445
RDP	3389

Chapter 7: Wireless and SOHO Networks

Answer to Performance-Based Question

Here are the steps to install a PCIe network card for a Windows 10 desktop:

1. Power off the PC.
2. Remove the case and the metal or plastic blank covering the expansion slot opening.

3. Insert the new expansion card into the open slot.

4. Secure the expansion card with the screw provided.

5. Put the case back on the computer and power it up.

    Windows Plug and Play (PnP) should recognize the NIC and install the driver automatically. It may also ask you to provide a copy of the necessary driver if it does not recognize the type of NIC that you have installed.

    If Windows does not start the installation routine immediately, you can add it manually.

6. Click Start ➤ Settings (it looks like a gear) ➤ Devices ➤ Bluetooth & Other Devices, and then click the plus sign next to Add Bluetooth Or Other Device.

    That will bring up the Add A Device window.

7. Click Everything Else.

8. When Windows finds the NIC, choose it and continue the installation.

    After installing a NIC, you must hook the card to the network using the appropriate cable (if you're using wired connections).

9. Attach a patch cable to the connector on the NIC and to a port in the wall (or connectivity device), thus connecting your PC to the rest of the network.

Chapter 8: Network Services, Virtualization, and Cloud Computing

Performance-Based Answer

To enable Microsoft Hyper-V, perform the following steps:

1. Check for minimum system requirements

    - Windows 10 Enterprise, Pro, or Education
    - 64-bit processor with Second Level Address Translation (SLAT)
    - CPU support for VM Monitor Mode Extension (VT-c on Intel CPUs)
    - 4 GB of RAM or more

2. If requirements are met, then right-click the Windows (Start) button.

3. Click Apps And Features.

4. Click Programs And Features.

5. Click Turn Windows Features On Or Off.

6. Select the Hyper-V check box, and click OK.

7. After installation, restart your computer.

Chapter 9: Laptop and Mobile Device Hardware

Performance-Based Answer

Here is how to replace the hard drive in the example laptop computer:

1. Turn off the computer.
2. Remove the bottom of the case.
3. Remove the screw holding the M.2 drive in place.
4. Slide the hard drive straight out of the M.2 connector.
5. Insert the new drive into the connector at the same angle the old drive was at when it was unscrewed.
6. Press the drive down and secure it with a screw.
7. Put the bottom of the case back on.

Chapter 10: Mobile Connectivity and Application Support

Performance-Based Answer

Here are the steps to connect an iPhone to a Wi-Fi network:

1. Tap the Settings app on the Home screen.
2. Select Wi-Fi from the Settings menu.
3. Swipe the Wi-Fi switch to the right to turn it on if it is off. You can also tap switches to toggle them to the opposite state.
4. In the Choose A Network list, tap the name of the wireless network you want to join.

Chapter 11: Troubleshooting Methodology and Resolving Core Hardware Problems

Performance-Based Answer

The correct order for the best practice methodology is shown here. Getting the sub-steps in the exact order isn't critical, but getting the major steps in order and the right sub-steps under the correct major step is.

1. Identify the problem.
    a. Gather information from the user, identify user changes, and, if applicable, perform backups before making changes.
    b. Inquire regarding environmental or infrastructure changes.
2. Establish a theory of probable cause (question the obvious).
    a. If necessary, conduct external or internal research based on symptoms.
3. Test the theory to determine the cause.
    a. Once the theory is confirmed, determine the next steps to resolve the problem.
    b. If the theory is not confirmed, reestablish a new theory or escalate.
4. Establish a plan of action to resolve the problem and implement the solution.
    a. Refer to the vendor's instructions for guidance.
5. Verify full system functionality and, if applicable, implement preventive measures.
6. Document the findings, actions, and outcomes.

Chapter 12: Hardware and Network Troubleshooting

Performance-Based Answer

1. Open the Services app. One way is to click Start and type **Services**, and then click Services under Best Match.
2. Find the Print Spooler service.
3. Stop the spooler service. There are several ways that you can do this:
    Right-click the service and choose Stop.

Click the Stop square above the list of services.

Use the More Actions menu on the right.

4. Restart the spooler by right-clicking the service and choosing Start, or by clicking the Start arrow above the list of services.

5. Close the Services app.

Chapter 13: Operating System Basics

Performance-Based Answer

In order to accommodate the future requirement of BranchCache, your organization will need to purchase a volume license agreement with Microsoft. The BranchCache feature is only available in Windows 10 Enterprise. Windows 8.1 Pro is a retail operating system that can be upgraded to Windows 10 Enterprise. However, the upgrade will require a different 25-digit product key and activation of the Windows 10 Enterprise operating system.

Chapter 14: Windows Configuration

Performance-Based Answer

To check to see which background processes are running and the resources they are using, open Task Manager. Do so by pressing Ctrl+Alt+Delete and selecting Task Manager. You can also press Ctrl+Shift+Esc.

Once in Task Manager, click the Processes tab, as shown in Figure 14.85. If all the processes are not shown, then expand the More Details chevron in the lower left, if it is not already expanded. Click the CPU column header to sort by CPU usage. If a process is taking up a considerable amount of CPU time, you can highlight it and click End Process to shut it down. You can also sort by memory used and shut down processes that look to be using excessive amounts of memory. Note that shutting down critical processes may cause Windows to lock up or otherwise not work properly, so be careful what you choose to terminate. Note also that right-clicking one of the processes offers the End Process Tree option—a useful option when the process being killed is associated with others.

FIGURE 14.85   Windows Task Manager

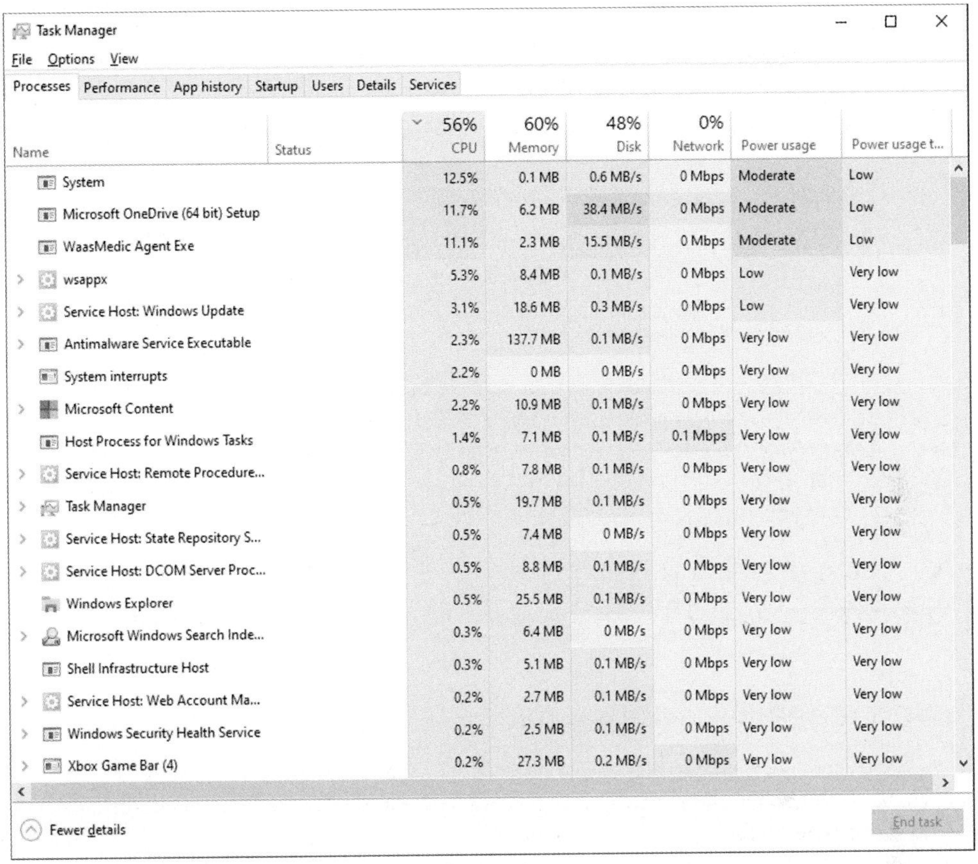

Chapter 15: Windows Administration

Performance-Based Answer

Assuming you are on the version of Windows 11, the process is as follows:

1. Click the Start menu.
2. Click the Settings gear.
3. Click Accounts.
4. Click Access Work Or School.
5. Click Connect.

6. When the Set Up A Work Or School Account dialog box appears, click Join This Device To A Local Active Directory Domain as the alternate action, as shown in Figure 15.55.

FIGURE 15.55 The Set Up A Work Or School Account dialog box

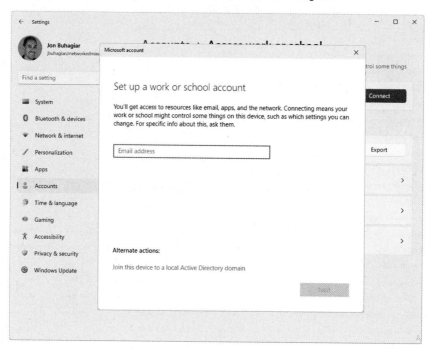

7. Enter the domain name in the dialog box, as shown in Figure 15.56.

FIGURE 15.56 Domain dialog box

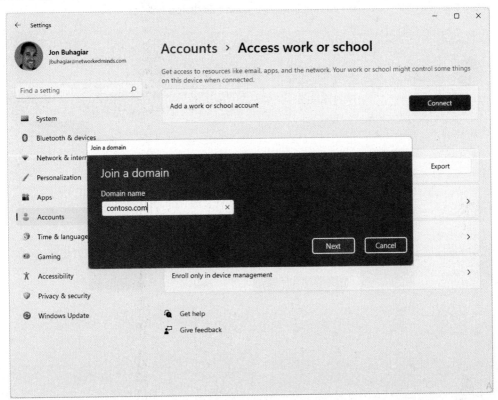

8. Enter the user account on the domain that has rights to join workstations, as shown in Figure 15.57.

FIGURE 15.57 Domain administrative credentials dialog box

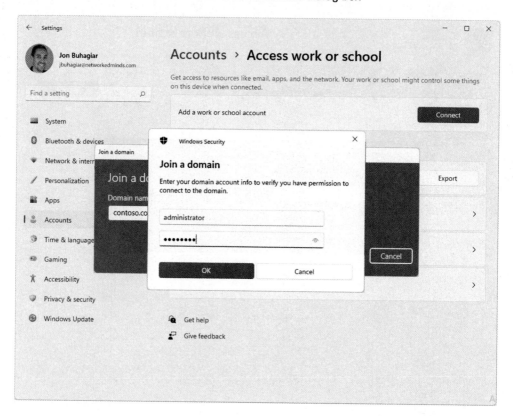

9. Enter the domain user and their respective security level on this PC, as shown in Figure 15.58. Or you can click Skip, and the user will automatically have the same rights as the domain.

10. Click the Restart Now option and reboot.

FIGURE 15.58   Local administrative rights dialog box

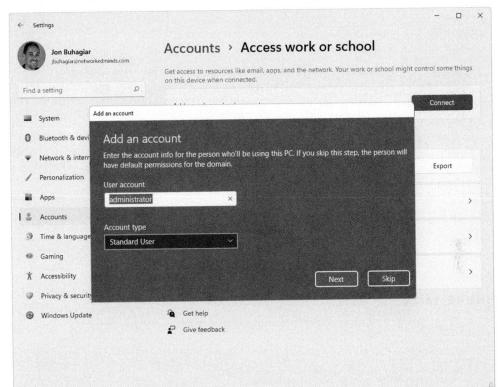

Chapter 16: Working with macOS and Linux

Performance-Based Answer

The listing you see when typing these commands will differ based on such factors as the system, the directory, your permissions, and the files/subdirectories present, but in all cases, there will be entries present with the –a option that do not appear in the display without it. Among those listings that now appear are a single period (representing the present directory) and a double period (representing the parent directory), as shown in Figure 16.25.

If there are any files or directories starting with a period, they will now appear where they did not before. The easiest way to "hide" a file or directory in Linux is to start the name of it with a period; thus, it will not show up in a listing unless the –a option is used. An example of this is shown in Figure 16.26.

FIGURE 16.25 An example of hidden files in various directories

```
root@sparkle: ~
root@sparkle:~#
root@sparkle:~# cd /
root@sparkle:/# ls -F
bin/   dev/  home/          lib/    lost+found/  mnt/  proc/  run/   srv/  tmp/  var/
boot/  etc/  initrd.img@    lib64/  media/       opt/  root/  sbin/  sys/  usr/  vmlinuz@
root@sparkle:/# ls -aF
./   bin/   dev/  home/          lib/    lost+found/  mnt/  proc/  run/   srv/  tmp/  var/
../  boot/  etc/  initrd.img@    lib64/  media/       opt/  root/  sbin/  sys/  usr/  vmlinuz@
root@sparkle:/# cd ~
root@sparkle:~# ls -l
total 0
-rw-r--r-- 1 root root 0 Sep 14 11:59 setting_xml
root@sparkle:~# ls -al
total 32
drwx------  3 root root 4096 Sep 14 12:05 .
drwxr-xr-x 22 root root 4096 Jan  9  2015 ..
-rw-------  1 root root 1050 Sep  9 19:04 .bash_history
-rw-r--r--  1 root root 3106 Feb 19  2014 .bashrc
drwx------  2 root root 4096 Jan  9  2015 .cache
-rw-------  1 root root  327 Apr 26  2015 .mysql_history
-rw-r--r--  1 root root  140 Feb 19  2014 .profile
-rw-r--r--  1 root root    0 Sep 14 11:59 setting_xml
-rw-------  1 root root  106 Apr 26  2015 .Xauthority
root@sparkle:~#
```

FIGURE 16.26 An example of hiding files in Linux

```
root@sparkle: ~
root@sparkle:~#
root@sparkle:~# ls -l
total 0
-rw-r--r-- 1 root root 0 Sep 14 11:59 setting_xml
root@sparkle:~# mv setting_xml .setting_xml
root@sparkle:~# ls -l
total 0
root@sparkle:~# ls -al
total 32
drwx------  3 root root 4096 Sep 14 12:07 .
drwxr-xr-x 22 root root 4096 Jan  9  2015 ..
-rw-------  1 root root 1050 Sep  9 19:04 .bash_history
-rw-r--r--  1 root root 3106 Feb 19  2014 .bashrc
drwx------  2 root root 4096 Jan  9  2015 .cache
-rw-------  1 root root  327 Apr 26  2015 .mysql_history
-rw-r--r--  1 root root  140 Feb 19  2014 .profile
-rw-r--r--  1 root root    0 Sep 14 11:59 .setting_xml
-rw-------  1 root root  106 Apr 26  2015 .Xauthority
root@sparkle:~#
```

Chapter 17: Security Concepts

Performance-Based Answer

A simple 8-character alphanumeric password contains 0–9 for a total of 10 characters, 26 uppercase and 26 lowercase characters. This gives you a total of 52 letters and 10 numbers, for a total of 62 combinations per character: 62 to the power of 8, or $62 \times 62 \times 62 \times 62 \times 62 \times 62 \times 62 \times 62 = 218{,}340{,}105{,}584{,}896$ combinations. A 25-character alphanumeric password with symbols contains 95 combinations per character; 95 to the power of 25 is 2.77×10^{54} combinations. If you are using a calculator, you might see 2.7738957e+49 as a result. Although the exact math is not significant, the deep understanding of combinations and complexity is the underlying lesson.

Chapter 18: Securing Operating Systems

Performance-Based Answer

The following explains how you would achieve the goal:

1. Create three folders on the local filesystem of the server: Sales, Marketing, and R&D.
2. Set NTFS permissions on all folders for Everyone and the Modify permission.
3. Set the Sales folder to have the following share permissions:
    - Sales: Change
    - Marketing: Read
4. Set the Marketing folder to have the following share permissions:
    - Marketing: Change
    - Sales: Read
5. Set the R&D folder to have the following share permissions:
    - R&D: Change
    - Marketing: Read

Chapter 19: Troubleshooting Operating Systems and Security

Performance-Based Answer

1. Investigate and verify malware symptoms.
2. Quarantine the infected systems.
3. Disable System Restore in Windows.
4. Remediate infected systems.
   a. Update antimalware software.
   b. Scan the removal techniques, such as booting into safe mode and using the Windows Preinstallation Environment.
5. Schedule scans and run updates.
6. Enable System Restore and create a restore point in Windows.
7. Educate the end user.

Chapter 20: Scripting and Remote Access

Performance-Based Answer

To write a PowerShell script to find other scripts in a user profile directory and all its subdirectories, you need the $home environment variable. There are a number of ways of writing this script to achieve the solution. The following is just one of the possibilities, using the parameters found on the Microsoft website:

```
Get-ChildItem -Path $home\* -Include *.ps1 -Recurse
```

> PowerShell cmdlets and their associated parameters are well documented on Microsoft's website. For more information about the Get-ChildItem cmdlet, visit:
>
> https://docs.microsoft.com/en-us/powershell/module/microsoft.powershell.management/get-childitem?view=powershell-6
>
> To learn about other PowerShell cmdlets, visit:
>
> https://docs.microsoft.com/en-us/powershell/scripting/overview?view=powershell-6

Chapter 21: Safety and Environmental Concerns

Performance-Based Answer

Here are some steps to take to look for trip hazards and eliminate them:

- Walk around the server room and count how many cables are lying on the floor.
- Walk around the client areas and see how many cables are lying on the floor or are exposed underneath cubicles.
- Devise a plan to secure the cables and prevent them from being hazards. For example, purchase and install floor guards, use *cable ties*, or install conduits, as necessary, to secure all loose cables.

Chapter 22: Documentation and Professionalism

Performance-Based Answer

1. Browse to the folder containing the overwritten file.
2. Right-click the file and select Properties.
3. Select the Previous Versions tab.
4. Find the latest version of the file and click the Restore button, as shown in Figure 22.18.
5. On the confirmation box, select Restore again, as shown in Figure 22.19.

FIGURE 22.18   The previous version of a file

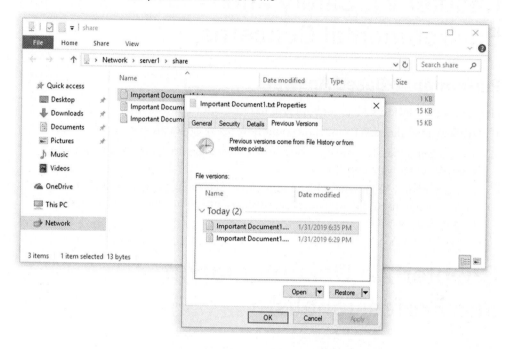

FIGURE 22.19   Confirming a restore from a previous version

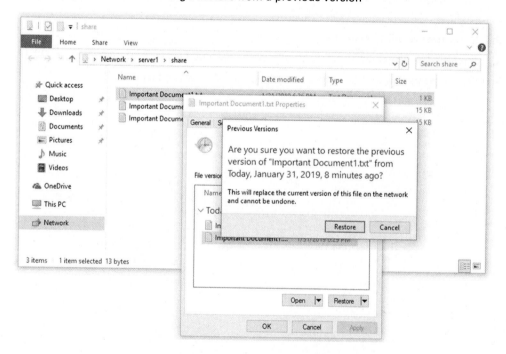

Index

C

M

O

W

X–Y–Z

Online Test Bank

Register to gain one year of FREE access after activation to the online interactive test bank to help you study for your CompTIA A+ certification exams—included with your purchase of this book! All of the chapter review questions and the practice tests in this book are included in the online test bank so you can practice in a timed and graded setting.

Register and Access the Online Test Bank

To register your book and get access to the online test bank, follow these steps:

1. Go to www.wiley.com/go/sybextestprep.
2. Select your book from the list.
3. Complete the required registration information, including answering the security verification to prove book ownership. You will be emailed a pin code.
4. Follow the directions in the email or go to www.wiley.com/go/sybextestprep.
5. Find your book on that page and click the "Register or Login" link with it. Then enter the pin code you received and click the "Activate PIN" button.
6. On the Create an Account or Login page, enter your username and password, and click Login or, if you don't have an account already, create a new account.
7. At this point, you should be in the test bank site with your new test bank listed at the top of the page. If you do not see it there, please refresh the page or log out and log back in.